A History
of
Ethnology

Franz Boas
1858–1942

A History of Ethnology

FRED W. VOGET
Southern Illinois University
at Edwardsville

HOLT, RINEHART AND WINSTON New York Chicago San Francisco
Atlanta Dallas Montreal
Toronto London Sydney

Library of Congress Cataloging in Publication Data
Voget, Fred W

    A history of ethnology.
    Bibliography: p. 806
    Includes index.
    1. Ethnology—History.   I. Title.
GN17.V63   301.2'09   75-6576

ISBN: 0-03-079665-2

Acknowledgments

For permission to reprint excerpts from copyrighted materials, the author is indebted to the following:

American Anthropologist. Barth, F., "On the Study of Social Change," 69(6), 1967; Fortes, M., "The Structure of Unilineal Descent Groups," 53, 1953; Geertz, C., "Form and Variation in Balinese Village Structure," 61(6), 1959; Kluckhohn, C., "Culture and Administrative Problems," 45, 1943; Steward, J. H., "Cultural Causality and Law: A Trial Formulation of the Development of Early Civilization," 51(1), 1949; Taylor, W., "A Study of Archeology," Memoir 69, 1948; Thompson, L., "Relations of Men, Animals and Plants in an Island Community (Fiji)," 51, 1949. All by permission of the American Anthropological Association.

Basic Books, Inc., New York. Lévi-Strauss, C., *Structural Anthropology*, 1963. Translated from the French by C. Jacobson and B. Schoepf. © 1963 by Basic Books, Inc., Publishers, New York.

Clarendon Press, Oxford. Fortes, M., and E. Evans-Pritchard, *African Political Systems*, 1940; Plato, *The Republic.* Translated by F. M. Cornford, 1941. By permission of the Clarendon Press.

Columbia University Press, New York. Kardiner, A., *The Individual and His Society*, 1939. By permission of the publisher.

Cornell University Press, Ithaca, N.Y. Selosoemardjan, *Social Changes in Jogjakarta*, © 1962 by Cornell University.

Ethnology. Rappaport, R. A., "Ritual Regulation of Environmental Relations Among New Guinea People," 6:17–30, 1967.

Eyre and Spottiswoode, London. Lévi-Strauss, C., *The Elementary Structures of Kinship*, R. Needham, ed., 1949.

Fortes, M., *Social Structure, Studies Presented to Radcliffe-Brown.* Oxford: Clarendon Press, 1949.

Harper & Row, Publishers, New York. Wright, R., *Black Power*, 1954.

Holt, Rinehart and Winston, New York. Hobhouse, L. T., *Morals in Evolution: A Study in Comparative Ethics*, 1925.

Humanities Press, Atlantic Highlands, N.J. Malinowski, B., *Crime and Custom in Savage Society*, 1926.

International Publishers, New York. Marx, K., and F. Engels, *Selected Works*, 1968.

Intext Publishers Group, New York. Nash, M., *Primitive and Peasant Economic Systems*, 1966.

Journal of Anthropological Research. Spindler, G., and W. Goldschmidt, "Experimental Design in the Study of Culture Change," 8, 1952; Voget, F. W., "Anthropology in an Age of Enlightenment," 24, 1968. Reprinted from the *Southwestern Journal of Anthropology* by permission of the editors.

Macmillan Publishing Co., Inc., New York. Durkheim, E., *Elementary Forms of Religious Life*, 1947; Murdock, G. P., *Social Structure*, 1949; "Sociology and Anthropology," in J. Gillin, ed., *For a Science of Social Man*, 1954.

Methuen and Co., Ltd., London. Schmidt, W., *The Origin and Growth of Religion Facts and Theories*, 1931. Translated from the original German by H. J. Rose.

New York Academy of Sciences. Gorer, J., "Themes in Japanese Culture," *Transactions of the New York Academy of Sciences* 5:106–124, 1943.

Prentice-Hall, Inc., Englewood Cliffs, N.J. Linton, R., *The Study of Man: An Introduction*, 1936. © 1936, renewed 1964. Reprinted by permission of Prentice-Hall, Inc.

Princeton University Press, Princeton, N.J. Ibn Khaldūn, *The Muqaddimah: An Introduction to History*, F. Rosenthal, trans. Bollingen Series XLIII. Copyright © 1958 and © 1967 by Bollingen Foundation. Reprinted by permission of Princeton University Press.

Random House, Inc., New York. Darwin, C., *The Origin of the Species*, 1936; Herodotus, *The Persian Wars*. Translated by G. Rawlinson, 1942; Lewis, O., *The Children of Sanchez*, Copyright © 1961 Random House, Inc.

Routledge and Kegan Paul, Ltd., London. Mair, L., *An African People in the Twentieth Century*, 1965; Malinowski, B., *The Sexual Life of Savages in North-Western Melanesia*. Copyright © 1929, 1957 by the estate of Bronislaw Malinowski.

Sheridan House, Yonkers, N.Y. Schapera, L., *Married Life in an African Tribe*, 1941.

Tavistock Publications, Ltd., London. Lévi-Strauss, C., *The Elementary Structures of Kinship*, 1949.

University of California Press, Berkeley. Erikson, E. H., *Observations on the Yurok: Childhood and World Image*, 1943; Kroeber, A. L., *Cultural and Natural Areas of Native North America*, 1939; Sapir, E. *Selected Writings of Edward Sapir in Language, Culture and Personality*, D. Mandelbaum, ed., 1949.

University of Chicago Press, Chicago. Jensen, A. E., *Myth and Cult Among Primitive Peoples*, 1963; Kroeber, A. L., *The Nature of Culture*, 1952; La Barre, W., *The Human Animal*, 1954.

University of Minnesota Press, Minneapolis. Erasmus, C. J., *Man Takes Control: Cultural Development and American Aid*. Copyright © 1961 by the University of Minnesota.

University of Pennsylvania Press, Philadelphia. Hallowell, A. I., *Culture and Experience*, 1967.

University of Washington, Seattle. Polanyi, K., and A. Rotstein, *Dahomey and the Slave Trade*, 1966.

William Morrow, New York. Mead, M., *Sex and Temperament in Three Primitive Societies*, 1935 (1950); *Male and Female: A Study of the Sexes in a Changing World*, 1949 (1952). Abridged by permission of William Morrow and Co., Inc. Copyright © 1949, 1967 by Margaret Mead.

Yale University Press, New Haven, Conn. Sumner, W. G., and A. G. Keller, *The Science of Society*, Vol. 1, 1927. By permission of the publisher.

Wenner-Gren Foundation for Anthropological Research, New York. S. Tax, "Integration of Anthropology," W. L. Thomas, Jr., ed., *Yearbook of Anthropology, 1955*.

For permission to reproduce copyrighted tables and figures, the author is indebted to the following:

American Anthropologist. Rouse, I., "On the Correlation of Phases of Culture," 57(4): 713–722, 1955.

The Bettmann Archive, 136 East 57th St., New York. Cover photo of Herodotus.

Cambridge University Press, New York. Sayce, R., *Primitive Arts and Crafts: An Introduction to the Study of Material Culture*, 1963.

Granger Collection, 1841 Broadway, New York. Cover photo of Charles Darwin.

Heyman, K., 64 East 55 St., New York. Cover photo of Margaret Mead in Bali.

A. Lesser. Cover and frontis photo of F. Boas.

Macmillan Publishing Company, Inc., New York. Boas, F., *Race, Language and Culture*, 1940; Westermarck, E., *The Origin and Development of Moral Ideas*, 1924.

Southwestern Journal of Anthropology. Spindler, G., and W. Goldschmidt, "Experimental Design in the Study of Culture Change," 8:68–83, 1952; White, L., "History, Evolutionism and Functionalism: Three Types of Interpretation of Culture," 1:221–248, 1945. Reprinted from the *Southwestern Journal of Anthropology* by permission of the editors.

Spiegel, B., 136 South Fairmount, Pittsburgh. Cover photo of G. P. Murdock.

University of Chicago Press, Chicago. Berreman, G. D., "Is Anthropology Alive? Social

Responsibility in Social Anthropology," *Current Anthropology* 9:391–396, 1968; Ribeiro, D., "The Culture-Historical Configurations of the American Peoples," *Current Anthropology* 11:403–435, 1970; Murphy, R., and J. Steward, "Tappers and Trappers: Parallel Process in Acculturation," *Journal of Economic Development and Culture Change* 4:348–349, 1956; Willey, G., and P. Phillips, *Method and Theory in American Anthropology*, 1958.

University of Minnesota Press. DuBois, C., *The People of Alor: A Socio-Psychological Study of an East Indian Island*, 1961. Copyright © 1944 by the University of Minnesota, University of Minnesota Press, Minneapolis.

University of North Carolina Press, Chapel Hill. Malinowski, B., *A Scientific Theory of Culture and Other Essays*, 1960.

Wenner-Gren Foundation for Anthropological Research, New York. G. P. Murdock, ed., *Social Structure in Southeast Asia*, 1960.

Dedicated to

Kay
Antoinette
Janie
Colleen

Preface

This book traces the intellectual history of cultural anthropology, with special emphasis on ethnology. It is impossible to master entirely a field as diverse and comprehensive as anthropology, but I have tried to describe and interpret the major intellectual strands and cultural-historical conditions which influenced development of the field and which guide its present course. The work has been written especially for students, but it is hoped that the presentation will be equally useful to professionals.

The study was approached with four perspectives in mind. First, anthropology is considered an institutional development of Western civilization, inspired in particular by the rise of science but also adaptively sensitive to the vast intellectual, economic, social, and political changes that have overtaken the West since the eighteenth century. Second, the development of anthropology is seen as cumulative and the result of historical and evolutionary processes normally affecting any institution. Third, like other disciplines, anthropology linked its destiny to a special subject matter (reality problem). Its uniqueness as a discipline correlates with application of an increasingly diverse and intensive methodology to effect a controlled collection of facts and permit analytic generalizations about the order, interrelations, and processes of this subject matter. The historical-evolutionary growth of anthropology led to a selection of the early history of mankind as its proper subject matter, and hence to a focus on the history, society, and culture of non-Western or preindustrial peoples. Fourth, in its quest for knowledge of the order, interrelations, and processes of its subject matter, anthropology, as other disciplines, confronts broad metaphysical and epistemological issues which must be accommodated if advances in controlled observation, analysis, and generalization are to be achieved. Such metaphysical and epistemological issues are found in efforts to determine the basic unit of investigation—whether culture trait, pattern, institution, or elemental social units. They are also reflected in attempts to locate basic order and process in the subjective perceptions and understandings of individuals, or in external forms which can be observed and measured as behavioral elements or as products of behavior. The persistent contrast of emic and etic approaches, and their respective association with an empirical idealism versus an inductive scientific empiricism, illustrate the critical nature of these perspectives in focusing research objectives and methods. Conceptual distinctions regarding "history" and "evolution," "mechanical" and "statistical" models, "ideal" and "real" patterns, and "unconscious" and "conscious" processes drew attention to fundamental metaphysical and epistemological issues posed by contrasting "internal" and "external" forces or "structure" and "variation." The persistent nature of these problems is reflected in recurrent confrontations as to whether the anthropological character is at base descriptive and historical or comparative and scientific. The marked trend toward specialization has not settled these issues; but as each specialization is forced to deal with such metaphysical and epistemological problems, a new basis has arisen for convergences in theory, concepts, and practice.

Discussion of the origins and development of cultural anthropology is organized into four parts. In the first, Greco-Roman, Renaissance, and Arabic (notably Ibn Khaldūn) intellectual traditions are reviewed to determine to what extent anthropological interests were generated and to assess their probable effects on development of a generalized social science base from which anthropology and sociology could differentiate. Part II describes the formation of a general social science during the eighteenth century and its differentiation from traditional history. This differentiation was accomplished by defining a new theoretical base, a new methodology, a different subject matter and factual content and formulating generalizations about the civilizing process derived from social facts. The idea of human advancement toward a perfected social state so pervaded the perspective of social philosophers from 1725 to 1890 that it may be treated as a unitary period—Developmentalism. Two phases need to be distinguished, however: (1) from 1725 to 1840 and (2) from 1840 to 1890. A humanistic view of human progress dominated the first phase, while the theory of biological evolution predominated during the second. It was during the evolutionistic phase that breakthroughs in geology, paleontology, prehistory, and anthropometry stimulated definition of a special anthropological science focused on the early history of man, society, and culture.

Part III describes the rise of Structuralism (1890–1940). Structuralist emphasis on system, function, and integration generated efforts to develop a general theory of society and culture and to link these domains to anthropology. The scientific nature of the discipline was strengthened by a program of controlled collection of data in the field. Inclusion of anthropological courses in the curricula of universities meant that for the first time professionals could be trained and equipped with both general and specialized theories. A differential emphasis on the social and cultural gave rise to social and cultural anthropology. Theoretical and methodological differences, reinforced by a degree of national insularity, provided further differential emphases within Structuralism— namely, culture historicism (American, German, British), social Structuralism (French and British), and biocultural functionalism (Malinowski).

Part IV focuses on the differentiation of specializations which began during the 1930s and accompanied the decline in Structuralism. The differentiations represented by economic, political, urban, psychological, juridical, and cognitive anthropology are of special importance, since for the first time emergent specializations pursued separate historical paths. Their strongest intellectual linkages are not within anthropology but with traditional disciplines, such as economics, political science, and psychology. At the same time these specialized developments established a basis for a more integrated perspective and methodology by which anthropology can realize its goal as the science of the preindustrial world and also make its special contribution to an integrated social science.

Others besides myself contributed to the completion of this book. I am especially indebted to the Canada Council for the grant which permitted initiation of this study and to the University of Toronto which made time available for research. The library of the University of California at Santa Barbara was helpful in providing facilities and extending full library privileges.

I am grateful to my wife who shared with me the heavy task of editing, and to Roger Pearson for his helpful suggestions and studied review of the manuscript in its early stages. Thanks are also due my colleagues at Southern Illinois University, Charlotte Frisbie and Ernest Schusky, as well as Wendell Ostwalt and Joseph Greenberg for reading and commenting on parts of the manuscript. Above all, the friendly counsel, constructive criticism, challenging queries, and encouragement of George and Louise Spindler were indispensable. To my colleague Sidney Denny I am indebted for discussions which kept me abreast of developments in archeology. At Holt, Rinehart and Winston I am grateful to David Boynton for his letters and calls, which seemed perfectly timed to pick up the sagging spirit, and to Françoise Bartlett for her skill and competence in readying the manuscript for final printing. Thanks are also due Ann Van Horn for assisting with the typing and retyping of the manuscript.

Edwardsville, Ill.   —F.W.V.
March 1975

Contents

A History
of
Ethnology

PART I

Cultural-Historical Antecedents for the Development of Anthropology

This section outlines historical and cultural developments in the West leading to a base upon which a generalized social science could be raised, and from which anthropology and sociology later could differentiate. Greco-Roman, Renaissance, and Arabic contributions are reviewed and evaluated to determine how far the origins of anthropology can be traced back to any or all of these sources. It is concluded that the beginnings of a generalized social science in the West properly belongs to the eighteenth century, for it is only then that the marks of a new scientific discipline can be detected in full. The Arabic scholar Ibn Khaldūn independently formulated a new discipline—what appropriately might be called historical sociology. However, his superb beginning did not bear fruit in the West because he was unknown until after the call for a science of mankind had been issued under aegis of the idea of progress. One impression that comes out of a review of these ancient materials is the importance of the practical art of government in stimulating an objective view of human institutions and their functions. The development of social science, and of anthropology, apparently owes much to a merging of a practical desire to comprehend and manipulate the political process with a consideration of the fate of states in history. By broadening the study of particular state societies to include the historical-social development of mankind as a whole, the foundations for social science and for anthropology were laid.

To aid in assessment of the contributions of the ancients, four criteria are introduced to weigh the presence or absence of anthropology or a general social science discipline. In applying these criteria, it will become evident that the operation is complicated by two kinds of influences: (1) direct and historic transmission and (2) indirect or general stimulation—and their opposites.

1

Prelude to Anthropology

INTRODUCTION: FOUR REQUISITES FOR SCIENTIFIC SPECIALIZATIONS

Anthropology is a product of scientific developments in the Western world. How far back, then, must its origins be sought as one follows the complicated channels of influence that have shaped Western civilization? Can a beginning be found in the Renaissance? the Middle Ages? Greece and Rome? Or must a start be made in the ancient East where the very foundations of civilization in the West were laid?

No search for the "origins" of any discipline can be made without a set of criteria which can define its presence. Here four criteria are useful:

1. The exponents of a discipline usually express a strong sense of difference by contrasting their special *subject matter* with that of others.
2. A *special theory of reality* and of "causal" explanation is claimed, even though these may not be made fully explicit.
3. A claim is made to a *distinctive methodology*.
4. A *special set of factual materials* is assembled that contrasts with those usually employed in related disciplines.

Once a likely source for a beginning has been located, it is reasonable that a line of continuous influence can be traced. What happens when the cultural stream gradually seeks out new channels and the old is left high and dry? This occurred as Christianity overtook the declining Greco-Roman tradition. Here a cultural discontinuity exists with relation to a humanistic and scientific posture first achieved by Greeks and Romans and not renewed until the Renaissance. Periods marking discontinuities seem at best to contribute a generalized influence from which special historic continuities may lead out at a future time. Insistence on a principle of lineal continuity helps prevent the assignment to past individuals of a special place in later developments simply because they may have explored an interest which the contemporary discipline now stresses. It is far better to assess such individuals in their proper historical and cultural context.

In reviewing the course of developments leading to a special science of man, Greco-Roman and Renaissance scholars stand forth as primary contenders for the honor of initiating the discipline. However, measured against the above criteria, Greco-Roman and Renaissance accomplishments are demonstrably insufficient to accord them a first place as "founders of anthropology." The founding civilizations of Egypt and Mesopotamia, as the Middle Ages, were too involved in theological explanations, and their courses too antithetical to a universal study of man, to warrant serious consideration even though their contributions to the development of Western civilization were profound.

WHY THE ANCIENT WORLD DID NOT PRODUCE ANTHROPOLOGISTS

Three Disadvantages: Metaphysics, Ethnocentrism, and Utopian Orientations

There are three basic reasons why cultural anthropology did not emerge from the historic, philosophic, and natural science curiosity of the ancient world. First, the ancients were inclined to view man's nature and destiny in a theological or metaphysical context. Second, ethnocentrism so bounded the outlook of Greco-Roman scholars that they measured the life-style of other peoples in relation to the framework of their own national interests. Third, the classical focus on man underscored a personal and ethical basis for life in society. An ethical orientation, as a theological one, accents relations and virtues that ought, or must, govern men in society. It is possible to study man in the context of an ideal society and culture, but the utopian emphasis restrains a comprehensive interest in man and his works. Man emerges as a universal type, an Everyman, and a universal curiosity in all things human is sacrificed to the definition of Everyman's nature, the design for utopia, and the way it is to be attained. Because of a basic utopian orientation, Greco-Roman thought with regard to society and custom turned in the direction of social philosophy. As for Greek and Roman historians, their vision was directed to political-military accounts of the rise and fall of nations and the careers of those who participated in these events. A vital interest in describing and comparing the life ways of peoples thus escaped the Greeks and Romans. Nevertheless, the Greeks and Romans did achieve a wider perspective of man and the universe, and it is to this world view and rephrasing of problems to which it led that we must look for possible contributions to a later anthropology. We must look for *general* rather than specific influences from the works of Aristotle (384–322 B.C.), Herodotus (ca. 485–325 B.C.), Hippocrates (460–ca. 359 B.C.), Plato (ca. 427–ca. 347 B.C.), Pliny the Elder (A.D. 23–79), Polybius (ca. 205–ca. 123 B.C.), Pausanias (fl. A.D. 2d cent.), Strabo (ca. 60 B.C.–ca. A.D. 21), Tacitus (ca. A.D. 55–120), Thucydides (ca. 460–ca. 400 B.C.), and others (see below).

GRECO-ROMAN HISTORY, GEOGRAPHY, AND HUMANISM

Herodotus and the Persian Wars

After the sixth century the tone of Greek thinking is quite different from that of the Egyptians and Mesopotamians. In place of sacred texts, political decrees exalting rulers, practical words of wisdom, economic contracts, and divinely sanctioned laws, the Greeks produced descriptions of human institutions and customs and made a determined effort to arrive at a naturalistic interpretation of man as a member of society. Greeks also began to write detailed histories of their wars, starting with the struggle against Persia.

Before Hecataeus (fl. 6th–5th cent.) and Herodotus Greek history leaned on the legendary sagas of heroes connected with the migrations of their ancestors and the siege of Troy. The repulse of Persia was another of these grand historic moments. Herodotus determined that he would record this magnificent event "to the end that time may not obliterate the great and marvelous deeds of the Hellenes and the Barbarians; and especially that the causes for which they waged war with one another may not be forgotten." His "causes" intermingled straightforward descriptions of historic relations and personal decisions with a divinely ordered predestination or fate.

Herodotus came from Halicarnassus in Ionia where the ancient civilizations of Egypt and Mesopotamia intermingled and confronted Greeks in a number of cities along the coast. Living in an area of some cultural diversity may have made Herodotus perceptive of differences in custom and turned him into an acute observer and recorder of a wide range of custom and belief. Too, he had the example of Hecataeus, who had written about Egypt and, perhaps out of provincial antipathy, expressed the opinion that the Greeks had an odd assortment of customs. Herodotus (1942) spruced up his history with a traveler's description of the dress of peoples in the ancient East, their armaments, religious ceremonies and beliefs, food taboos, burial practices, and temple structures. He also recorded dialectical differences, the location of peoples and their cities, productivity of the land, types of boats, practice of blood brotherhood, organization of tribute, and the succession of monarchs.

There is a broad range to Herodotus' interests, and his curiosity is ever tempered with a critical evaluation of what he observes. That contrasts of custom can be "stranger than fiction" Herodotus points out in a superb passage in which he compares Egyptian ways with those of the rest of the world.

Concerning Egypt itself I shall extend my remarks to a great length, because there is no country that possesses so many wonders, nor any that has such a number of works which defy description. Not only is the climate different from that of the rest of the world, and the rivers unlike any other rivers, but the people also, in most of their manners and customs, exactly reverse the common practice of mankind. The women attend the markets and trade, while the men sit at home at the loom; and here, while the rest of the world works the woof up the warp, the Egyptians work it down; the women likewise carry burdens upon their shoulders, while the men carry them upon their heads. Women stand up to urinate, men sit down. They eat their food out of doors in the streets, but relieve themselves in their houses, giving as a reason that what is unseemly, but necessary, ought to be done in secret, but what has nothing unseemly about it, should be done openly. A woman cannot serve the priestly office, either for god or goddess, but men are priests to both; sons need not support their parents unless they choose, but daughters must, whether they choose or no.

In other countries the priests have long hair, in Egypt their heads are shaven; elsewhere it is customary, in mourning, for near relations to cut their hair close; the Egyptians, who wear no hair at any other time, when they lose a relative, let their beards and the hair of their heads grow long. All other men pass their lives separate from animals, the Egyptians have animals always living with them; others make barley and wheat their food, it is a disgrace to do so in Egypt, where the grain they live on is spelt, which some call zea. Dough they knead with their feet, but they mix mud, and even take up dung with their hands. They are the only people in the world—they at least, and such as have learnt the practice from them—who use circumcision. Their men wear two garments apiece, their women one. They put on the rings and fasten the ropes to sails inside, others put them outside. When they write or calculate, instead of going, like the Greeks, from left to right, they move their hand from right to left; and they insist, notwithstanding that it is they who go to the right, and the Greeks who go to the left. They have two quite different kinds of writing, one of which is called sacred, the other common. (Herodotus 1942:133–135)

It is this lively sensitivity to contrast that turned Herodotus into a perceptive observer and a narrator who holds the interest of his reader. He noted how Persians revealed their status by the manner of their greeting. Equals would kiss on the lips, an inferior received a kiss on the cheek, and the lowly prostrated themselves before their superiors (Herodotus 1942:75). We also learn that the Persians "have no images of the gods, no temples nor altars, and consider the use of them a sign of folly" (Herodotus 1942:73). Yet, at a sacrifice, which is without fire, libation, music, and food offering, a Magus must be present. The Magi impressed Herodotus as a very peculiar race, differing entirely from the Egyptian priests, and indeed from all other men whatsoever. The Egyptian priests make it a point of religion not to kill any live animals except those which they offer in sacrifice. The Magi, on the contrary, kill animals of all kinds with their own hands, excepting dogs and men. They even seem to take a delight in the employment, and kill, as readily as they do other animals, ants and snakes, and such like flying or creeping things. However, since this has always been their custom, let them keep it. (Herodotus 1942:77–78)

Custom, History, War, and Politics

In his narrative history of the Persian War Herodotus seems to use vignettes of life as it was lived to kindle the interest and imagination of his reader and to furnish a background against which decisions and actions could be measured. He is always careful to filter hearsay from his own inquiries, and offers his own interpretations with a considered logic. It is Herodotus' live and let live attitude regarding alien custom that endears him to ethnologists of a later date, who find his accounts relatively free of bias, widely ranging, and at times detailed. For this reason he has been cited as a likely forerunner, if not the "father," of ethnography. It is unfortunate indeed that Herodotus had no apprentice to continue and strengthen the interest in custom for its own sake. However, political-military history enlivened with straightforward descriptions of strange places and curious customs does not add up to ethnography. With the onset of the Peloponnesian War, the processes of Greek history turned provincial, and historians like Thucydides (1934) now wrote of local politics and wars. Romans likewise became engrossed in local affairs as social, economic, political, and military changes generated political rivalries and civil war. Caesar's description of his Gallic conquests was designed to enlarge his political influence rather than to enlighten the public with regard to Gallic customs. Moreover, from the pragmatic viewpoint of conqueror and administrator, the geography, populations, dialects, settlements, roads, armaments, military tactics, leadership, and special natural resources summarized the important facts about any foreign land. As Greeks and Romans were caught up in an extended network of foreign contacts and launched themselves on careers of conquest, the momentum of change generated within their social and cultural systems prevented them from coming to grips with anything more than the pragmatic details of military-administrative relations and internal struggles for power. In consequence, politics, or the ordered governing of men, held greater relevance for the Greco-Roman experience than the investigation of custom and cultural diversity. Considering the major thrust of Greco-Roman cultural developments, it is understandable why the masterful braiding of custom into the political-military narrative accomplished by Herodotus made no lasting impact on the political-historical tradition of Greece and Rome. Two other domains within the Greco-Roman tradition stimulated a modest ethnographic impulse, notably geography and the moral essay.

Handbooks of Lands and Peoples

Geographers and naturalists (Hippocrates, Pliny, Pausanias, Strabo) compiled handbooks and encyclopedias of the world as it came to be known to the Greeks and Romans, and they usually included some brief descriptions of customs. Pausanias (1959–1961) described cities and monuments along every step of his journey through Greece, providing a mine of information for later historians and archeologists. Pliny (1938–1963) wondered how nature determined the habits of individuals and how the "temperate heat of the sun" made Indians "hardy" and free of aches and pains. Hippocrates (1962(1):66–137) described national character and customs in the light of extremes and means in climate and their significance for the grandeur of peoples. However, in their geographic and natural science descriptions, curiosity very often got the better of the critical acumen of the Greeks and Romans. They accepted all manner of tales about more distant peoples, and very often, as in the instance of Pliny, peoples were introduced because they had no tongues, lips, noses, or speech—or because they possessed such strange customs that "they will appear portentious and incredible to man."

Tacitus and the Didactic Ethnographic Essay

Within the Greco-Roman tradition Tacitus (1942) alone composed an essay on manners and customs which was more than a casual handling of the subject. The celebrated account of the Germans was composed in A.D. 98, and Tacitus seems to have written his essay to get Romans of his day to look more closely at their own way of life and to become fully aware of its defects by confronting them with a primitive contrast.

As a physical type Tacitus concluded that the Germans were "aboriginal and not mixed at all." Their "fierce blue eyes, red hair, [and] huge frames" made them fit "only for a sudden exertion," for while "their climate and their soil" might harden them to cold and hunger, they were not able to withstand heat or thirst.

Marriage among the Germans involved an exchange of goods between the kin of the groom and of the wife. The groom's kin presented "oxen, a caparisoned steed, a shield, a lance, and a sword," while the wife's kin offered the husband a "gift of arms." But what engaged Tacitus' interest here was the strictness of the marriage code—"indeed no part of their manners is more praiseworthy." Except for those of noble birth, the usual rule was to have but one wife. An adulteress, naked and with hair cut off, would be whipped through the village while her kin looked on. The Germans would not countenance abortion. Tacitus stressed the way personal morality was cultivated by family and marriage customs. Unlike the

Romans of his day, "No one in Germany laughs at vice, nor do they call it the fashion to corrupt and to be corrupted."

Tacitus was also impressed with the intermingling of the high- and the lowborn. They shared a common life "amid the same flocks and lie on the ground till the freeborn are distinguished by age and recognized by merit." Marriage was delayed until youth and maiden had attained their proper growth. The aged were respected and honored. Kin relationships meant something, and uncles would care for their sister's children as much as for their own. However, inheritance followed from father to sons and daughters, and only in the absence of direct descendants would inheritance pass to a man's brothers and to his uncles on either side. Both a father and his kin determined a son's friends and enemies, and these relationships were accepted as obligations; but Tacitus noted that homicidal feuding was not common and could be "expiated by . . . cattle and sheep . . . accepted by the entire family."

Germans settled disputes and established friendly relations through hospitality and exchange of gifts. Gifts were given unselfishly without any expectation of return, but the reciprocal offer of a gift, especially horses and weapons, was well received. Germans were immoderate when it came to drinking and fighting and were quite daring. But when it came to issues of war and peace, they reasoned with deliberation and never took counsel when under the effects of liquors. In council, too, they invested the youth with spear and shield, and here they rendered judgments regarding homicide and elected magistrates to administer laws.

Tacitus especially admired the way in which the Germans demanded honor and daring from leader and follower alike. Those of noble birth had to prove themselves in apprenticeship under a war leader. Leaders set the heroic example for their followers, and those who abandoned their leader to the enemy were disgraced. Loyalty of leader and follower was strengthened and maintained by the reward of a horse or spear taken from the enemy. The brave also were praised and singled out for an assignment of lands according to their rank.

Despite their worthy customs and many virtues, Tacitus found the Germans lacking in moderation, a serious defect. The men, obsessed by the warrior's role, mostly caroused and slept when not fighting. Brave though they might be, they still were the slaves of drink and of sloth, and so "will be overcome by their own vices as easily as by the arms of an enemy."

Tacitus as "Ethnographer." Tacitus' remarkable discourse on German character and custom is a landmark of Roman "ethnography." He spent some time in Germany (ca. A.D. 89), probably in an official capacity; but whether he was commissioned to gather information for policy decisions is unknown. Certainly there was no Roman "ethnographic" tradition to account for his sympathetic and admiring account of the Germans. However, like most historians of the day, Tacitus ascribes the greatness of peoples to their excellent customs and character. The timing of the essay "Concerning the Geography, the Manners and Customs, and the Tribes of Germany" may be a clue to its purpose, as it was written during the brutal political purge carried out by Domitian. Moreover, Tacitus, in writing histories of the Caesars from Augustus to Domitian, must have observed the decline in individual freedom and security in Roman society and the concomitant rise in imperial corruption and tyranny. Tacitus lets the reader draw his own conclusions about German freedom, character, and morality in contrast with manifest Roman servility, insecurity, duplicity, and depravity. His final note is a reminder that weakness in character presages a fall.

Aside from any personal admiration for the Germans, Tacitus was constrained to present them in a sympathetic and favorable light in order to get his point across, since such is the nature of a didactic essay. For this reason Tacitus' "ethnographic" contribution seems to appear spontaneously. Such, too, is the history of the didactic essay—it is born out of special historical circumstances and fades as those circumstances change. As in the case of Herodotus, Tacitus' ethnographic venture carried no lasting effect on Roman scholarship, and he himself did not continue the interest.

The Golden Mean, Climate, and National Greatness

In the light of a universal science of man, Greco-Roman history, geography, and natural science exhibit a narrow and even pseudohumanistic orientation, frequently grounded by limited political-military interests or a search for exotica. In attributing national virtues and temperaments to climate, Greeks and Romans agreed that their intermediate location between extremes of hot and cold had made them the best of all peoples. In the words of Vitruvius (fl. A.D. 1st. cent.; 1926:173–174), who wrote a history of architecture,

> Such being nature's arrangements of the universe, and all these nations being allotted temperaments which are lacking in due moderation, the truly perfect territory, situated under the middle of the heaven, and having on each side the entire extent of the world and its countries, is that which is occupied by the Roman people. In fact the races of Italy are the most perfectly constituted in both respects—in bodily form and in mental activity to correspond to their valour. Exactly as the planet Jupiter is itself temperate, its course lying midway between Mars, which is very hot, and Saturn, which is very cold, so Italy, lying between the north and the south, is a combination of what is found on each side, and her preeminence is well regulated and indisputable. And so by her wisdom she breaks the courageous onsets of the barbarians, and by her strength of hand thwarts the devices of the southerners. Hence, it was the divine intelligence that set the city of the Roman people in a peerless and temperate country, in order that it might acquire the right to command the whole world.

A potential for greatness and leadership thus followed the climatic curve. With regard to the superiority of one temperate group over another, with Roman over Greek, the advantage lay in the balance of their political institution, as Polybius argued in explaining the rise of Roman superiority. Theorists of a climatic cause for natural superiorities listed conquest as the measure of excellence, and coupled with this national pride. National character and the quality of institutions were measured by success, and consequently it was difficult for Greeks and Romans to develop a relativistic position toward the study of custom without regard to value absolutes and pragmatic results.

GRECO-ROMAN SOCIAL AND POLITICAL PHILOSOPHY AND THE NATURAL ORDER

Principles of Order and of Process in Nature and Society

If the beginnings of anthropology cannot be found in Greco-Roman curiosity and attention to foreign lands and peoples, perhaps their proper contribution can be found in their efforts to understand man as a product of a natural order. Greco-Roman interpretations of man and the universe, based on the twin concepts of a natural order and of natural law, were magnificent achievements. In this the Greeks had the historic advantage, and the Romans followed their lead. Initial attention to the substance of the universe produced the "atomic" theory of Democritus (fl. 5th cent. B.C.) and the "doctrine of ideas" of Socrates (ca. 469–399 B.C.) and Plato. Parmenides (fl. 5th cent. B.C.) and Heracleitus (fl. 500 B.C.) looked at reality within the context of stability and change. The former asserted that the universe and its components are essentially one and never change their essential relationships, the latter holding that all things are in a constant state of change. From a confrontation with the nature of the universe, Greek philosophers moved on to the nature of man and his destiny as a member of society.

The heart of Greco-Roman social theory was basically organismic with a consequent stress on structural-functional connections. This structural-functional position can be expressed in a number of propositions:

1. The universe is an ordered system composed of parts arranged according to a natural hierarchy of function and regulated by laws expressing the essential design of the system. It follows that
   a. The whole is determinative of ultimate purpose and therefore is greater than any of its parts,
   b. As the whole possesses a total design, so the parts possess a design or purpose according to their rank in the system, and
   c. The functioning of the system is dependent on the respective actions of the parts.
2. The proper functioning of any system represents a state, which may be called harmony or equilibrium, in which all units fulfill their respective actions to fullest capacity.
   a. The natural hierarchy of a system must be maintained or disharmony will prevail.

3. Change in any system is largely a movement toward harmonious relationships, with each unit working advantageously to capacity, or to its opposite, with units producing less and decay following. From this it follows that
   a. Change is an alternation or cycling of an advance to harmony (fulfillment or growth), or a regression from harmony (nonfulfillment or decay)
   b. Change is largely a matter of internal effects, and largely rearrangements of parts and their activities.

Within the context of these principles and corollaries Greco-Roman social and political philosophy stand out both in magnificence and in limitations. The concept of purpose geared in an inner design which drove units to actualization led naturally to consideration of conditions that seem ideal for self-realization. The problem for the individual was to discover how to maximize his natural endowment and find his natural place in an organized society. For the group the problem was to discover the conditions which provoked and supported national greatness. This self-centered and ethnocentric bias in Greco-Roman social philosophy was a distinct liability, since they saw the "manners" and "customs" of others only in terms of their worth for personal and national character, and especially in relation to themselves. Their concern for ideal conditions limited their work to a kind of logical deduction which did not generate an interest in wide-ranging observations and comparisons. The idea of an inner design moving naturally to a purposive fulfillment concentrated attention on internal relations and processes and conveyed a metaphysical bias to their social theory. The core of these principles stands clear in the discussion which follows.

NATURAL RANKING AND THE ORGANIZATION OF SOCIETY

Aristotle and the Principle of Natural Dominance

The social and political philosophy of Greeks and Romans required the political order to conform to the natural order. In Aristotle's (1943:252) view, the "state is a creation of nature, and man . . . is by nature a political animal." As everything in nature followed natural processes, so there is a natural history to the state. It begins with male-female relations in the family and master-slave relations in the wider household. The principle of dominance in nature is paralleled in human relations. The natural dominance of male over female, of master over slave, and of the older over the younger is fundamental to the social order. Households dominated by females were unlikely historical antecedents, for such would violate the natural order and lead to the corruption of the superior by the inferior. By unifying several households under the eldest male, a village was formed, and as colonies formed naturally by separation from parent villages, the eldest male in the colonies ruled as king. The state thus arose out of a unity of villages "large enough to be nearly or quite self-sufficing," and "though originating in the bare needs of life" it continued "its existence for the sake of a good life" (Aristotle 1943:251). In this way man's nature forced its design upon the social order. Indeed, social life was man's necessity, for under law and justice by which society is organized, men achieve excellence and virtue. If a man "have not virtue, he is the most unholy and the most savage of animals, and the most full of lust and gluttony" (Aristotle 1943:253). Men in state societies therefore joined together for the common purpose of justice, and Aristotle considered the man who "first founded the state ... the greatest of benefactors" (Aristotle 1943:253). If there had been a natural history for the state, Aristotle (1943:252) questioned it with the metaphysical argument that "since the whole is of necessity prior to the part," the state is "by nature clearly prior to the family and to the individual."

Human Nature and the Proper Ordering of Society: Plato

Socratic-Platonic theory about the human "soul" and its relation to the ordering of society presents another stress on a natural inner design. Reason, virtue, and passion are attributes of soul, with reason exercising a natural control in the interests of harmony. Since reason dominates other soul aspects, and since its natural distribution in nature is uneven, individual men are not equipped equally for the attainment of a personal harmony regulated by reason. The natural order thus is a rank order, and for that reason Plato, as Aristotle, argued for the inclusion of superior-inferior relations in the ordering of society.

In his *Republic* Plato presented a utopian model in which each attribute of the soul carried out a special function in the structure of society. Man's nature thus provided a blueprint for society. The attainment of a moral order that rested on justice could be solved by allowing each person to carry out those functional activities in society for which he had been designed by nature. Those heavily endowed with appetite could be producers, while those endowed with moral virtue and courage could administer and guard society from foreign danger. Maintaining the harmony of the society would be entrusted to men with souls balanced by reason. There could be no disharmony or injustice in a *natural* social order, for the ideal conditions permitting each individual to realize his proper excellence according to natural endowment would be present. Since most historic societies violated the natural order, injustice was present, and conditions making for degeneracy were more prevalent than those conducive to growth.

The maintenance of a society ordered according to nature's principles obviously must conform to the laws governing that nature. For his utopian Republic Plato promulgated the "natural laws" regulating society in special trainings and restrictions that would keep all entities in their proper places and at a top level of performance. For the person as for society, it will be the business of reason to rule with wisdom and forethought on behalf of the entire soul; while the spirited element ought to act as its subordinate and ally. The two will be brought into accord . . . by that combination of mental and bodily training which will tune up one string of the instrument and relax the other, nourishing the reasoning part on the study of noble literature and allaying the other's wildness by harmony and rhythm. When both have been thus nurtured and trained to know their own true functions, they must be set in command over the appetites, which form the greatest part of each man's soul and are by nature insatiably covetous. They must keep watch lest this part, by fattening on the pleasures that are called bodily, should grow so powerful that it will no longer keep to its own work, but will try to enslave the others and usurp a dominion to which it has no right, thus turning the whole of life upside down. At the same time those two will be the best of guardians for the entire soul and for the body against all enemies from without: the one will take counsel while the other will do battle. . . . (Plato 1958:140)

In the context of a natural order governed by natural laws, the customs of men and laws regulating their societies could be measured according to their congruence with the natural requirements of man and society. Did customs contribute to individual excellence and to the common purpose? Did law reflect the deliberate wisdom of cultivated intelligence directed to the common good? The law, Plato (1958:234) observed,

is not concerned to make any one class specially happy, but to ensure the welfare of the commonwealth as a whole. By persuasion or constraint it will unite the citizens in harmony, making them share whatever benefits each class can contribute to the common good; and its purpose in forming men of that spirit was not that each should be left to go his own way, but that they should be instrumental in binding the community into one.

Harmony, the Mean, and Governance

Emphasis on the mutual interrelation of different entities contributing their respective excellences to the total structure conveyed an organismic tone to the Socratic-Platonic and Aristotelean approaches to man in society. Control was most significant in producing harmony within the structure of human nature, so the exercise of control in human society was more significant than any other social activity. Thus, for both Plato and Aristotle the supreme focus of knowledge rested with politics or the governance of men. The issues engaged were never far from some conception of the "good" expressed as harmony or balance. For Aristotle (1964:171–176) the best rule would come from those whose wealth and share in the well-being of the state were moderate rather than those whose wealth gave them a greater or lesser share in the well-being of the state. The harmonious balance of the mean represented the absolute in excellence in Aristotle's view and provided the finest opportunities for the exercise of reason and the practice of ethics. Maintenance of natural harmony rested on the proposition that all parts serve by performing their proper functions. The cycling of political orders proposed by Greek theories followed a course of gradual corruption of the natural order as parts of lesser significance extended their influence upward into the control system. Out of such imbalances came conflict and decay. A complete democracy, then, would be the worst form of government, since it defied the natural order and placed those with least reason at the summit. Chaos could result, for rule would emanate not from reason but from passion.

The Mean and Comparisons: Polybius on Roman Superiority

Greeks and Romans used comparison to uncover the greatness of persons and of nations, and here they always applied the principle of the mean. In the case of Polybius (ca. 205–123 B.C.), for example, we find a political hostage analyzing why and how the Roman people had come to rule the world of their day. He credited harmony or balance for Roman success. The Romans had a balanced constitution that united kingship, aristocracy, and democracy.

> The three kinds of government that I spoke of above all shared in the control of the Roman state. And such fairness and propriety in all respects was shown in the use of these three elements for drawing up the constitution and in its subsequent administration that it was impossible even for a native to pronounce with certainty whether the whole system was aristocratic, democratic, or monarchical. This was indeed only natural. For if one fixed one's eyes on the power of the consuls, the constitution seemed completely monarchical and royal; if on that of the senate it seemed again to be aristocratic; and when one looked at the power of the masses, it seemed clearly to be a democracy. (Polybius 1960(3):295–297)

Besides this balanced allocation of power among the different segments of the population, Polybius found that the Romans held other advantages. The "Italians," he wrote, "in general naturally excel Phoenicians and Africans in bodily strength and personal courage . . ." (Polybius 1960(3):387). This they achieved through superior "institutions . . . [which] do much to foster a spirit of bravery in the young men." By ceremony and reward young men were excited to be "ready to endure everything in order to gain a reputation in their country for valour" (Polybius 1960(3):387–389). However, it was in religion that Polybius uncovered the most important condition for Roman solidarity and success, for fear of divine punishment and their participation in public ceremonies overcame the fickleness of the multitude, with its "lawless desires, unreasoning anger, and violent passion" (Polybius 1960(3):395). Thus, in Polybius' view, Roman superiority rested on four conditions:

1. Conformity owing to fear of divine retribution and to participation in public ceremony,
2. Inspirational instruction through the examples of heroes, thereby reinforcing excellence in customs,

3. Traditional cultivation of virtues, especially courage and strength,
4. A balanced distribution of authority and responsibility among the citizenry.

The Human Archetype and Ethnocentrism

A didactic interest in the customs, religion, and political organization of others is an advance over a narrow ethnocentrism. However, in endeavoring to learn lessons from the successes of others, the Greeks and Romans concentrated on the ideal, a line of vision that eliminated a comparative study of mankind. Ethnocentrism was an inadvertent but inevitable product of this point of view, reinforcing pride in national accomplishment and directing attention to weaknesses which had brought others down. In this context the best that could be achieved was a study in contrasts—moral essays like that of Tacitus, who pointed to violation of the authoritative principle of the mean as a step along the road to disaster. At its worst, this approach produced an arrogance well expressed by Pliny (1952:593): "The one race of outstanding eminence in virtue among all the races in the whole world is undoubtedly the Roman." Wherever the Greeks and Romans did approach a universal perspective on man, it was stroked with a metaphysical brush. The utopian focus in their social theory led Greco-Romans to posit a universal archetype of man, an Everyman, whose nature could be translated into an ideal social order. Or, as in the instance of Cicero (106–43 B.C.), a universal brotherhood of man was raised on a common sharing of some of the divine attributes. The primary purpose of man's nature, as God's, was to manifest the "virtues of right reason, whose operation is to urge us to good actions, and restrain us from evil." Law, the finest expression of right reason, had not been contrived by men of genius, but established by the "mind of God, enjoining or forbidding each separate thing in accordance with reason." The "whole human race" shared right reason, and indeed the "entire universe may be looked upon as forming one vast commonwealth of gods and men." The human world in its ordering was a replica of the divine world, and as individual gods held different ranks and powers, so the distribution of virtues and goods was uneven for mankind. Just as the "supreme law" is found in the "Divine Mind," so "it exists in the mind of the sage, so far as it can be perfected in man" (Cicero 1911:406–435). Greco-Roman universalism obviously had its limitations, and expectably there was no call to study social groups and their customs comparatively in order to discover what all men had in common and how they differed.

THE GRECO-ROMAN ACHIEVEMENT IN HISTORICAL PERSPECTIVE

Continuity of the Greco-Roman Intellectual Stimulus

The influence of the Greeks and Romans in the later development of anthropology should not be written of entirely because they did not produce a study of man that hewed close to the universal and comparative interests of anthropology when it did emerge. There are always indirect influences, and we know that no intellectual tradition has been more continuous and persistent in the Western world than the Greco-Roman. Not even the Christians who struggled against the "pagan" ideologies of Greece and Rome were impervious to this influence. Under the stimulus of Greco-Roman philosophy Christian theology developed a special intellectual sophistication just as the Church in its formal organization drew heavily on the Roman political model.

The intervention of the Christian tradition and its persistent development in strength during long centuries when the Germanic peoples were being acculturated sharpened the impact of the Greco-Roman intellectual contributions as they came to light. The Middle Ages and the Renaissance were two of these historic moments of rediscovery, and it is important that each made use of a different achievement of the ancient world. Aristotelean logic stimulated the burst of intellectual creativity of churchmen in the Middle Ages, while Greco-Roman humanism, science, history, geography, and literature spurred Renaissance developments.

Historians no longer consider the Renaissance a sudden enlightenment aroused by novel contact with the intellectual streams of the ancient world. The burst of creativity manifest in the Renaissance along humanistic, artistic, and scientific fronts had been brewing for some time during the late Middle Ages. Nevertheless, the time was ripe for what the Greeks and Romans had to offer, and this was considerable. Aristotle offered a perceptive discrimination of deduction and induction as techniques for reaching solid knowledge. There was a mature and straightforward history in Thucydides and an imaginative interest in different lands and peoples in the descriptions of Herodotus and Strabo. The magnificence of nations was attributed to virtuous customs, character, temperate climate, and a balanced political order. Man was viewed in a social context, and the necessity for an organized polity was underlined. In social philosophy the ideal features for the organization of society were accented, but at the same time evaluations of monarchy, aristocracy, oligarchy, tyranny, moderate democracy, and "extreme democracy" were offered together with causes that accounted for a succession of types of government. Cumulative functional imbalances in political systems held a central place in Greco-Roman interpretation.

Lucretius, following the materialistic philosophy of Epicurus and Democritus, formulated a poetic interpretation of processes applicable to nature and to man that accorded no place to the gods in directing the universe and human history. Primal atoms combined to form the universe, ascending in ever more complex combination to the shapes of animals and of men. Man himself arrived at his successes gradually, winning his way through ingenious inventions, and misguided apprehensions, from a tooth and claw life to a world of cities and temples. All would ultimately dissolve into the primal material as nature's law required. In their turn Sophists excited the mind with the challenge of skepticism and stress on the relativity of all things. Above all, the lessons of the golden mean and of harmony stood clear as principles to be widely applied. The notions that all things are part and parcel of a master plan proceeding under the close regulation of "natural laws" directed imaginative thought to structures and functions.

Some Difficulties in Assessing Greco-Roman Influence on Later Intellectual Developments

The tracing of influence through broad orientations offers peculiar difficulties when scholars of another time assemble their own materials. How shall we interpret Greco-Roman influence on the mathematical and telescopic observations submitted for the heliocentric hypothesis by Copernicus and Galileo? This same hypothesis had been advanced in the ancient world by Aristarchus of Samos (310–230 B.C.), but the geocentric hypothesis popularized by Ptolemy (A.D. 127–151) prevailed and was held under Christian belief. The new heliocentric proofs gave astronomy in the Western world a new platform, and there was no reason to refer further to the Greeks and Romans on this point except out of historic interest. In this way science disengages itself from the past and moves forward under its own steam. The rapidity of advance in the sciences is never the same, and in individual cases much depends on what the person is looking for. Charles Darwin paid special tribute to Aristotle for his wide-ranging and searching inquiries in biology. "Linnaeus and Cuvier," wrote Darwin, "have been my two gods, though in different ways, but they were schoolboys compared to old Aristotle." Yet by his own account it was not Aristotle who inspired the notion of "natural selection," but Malthus (1965), who stressed the grim struggle of life in the face of plague, hunger, and war.

Decline of Greco-Roman Scientific Authority

Anyone who had absorbed Greco-Roman philosophy and science would have a rich platform on which to build imaginative, perceptive, and sophisticated interpretations of man and his works. Ambitious men of the Renaissance, spurred by Greco-Roman humanism, aspired to the vision of a whole man, sensitive in thought, aesthetic appreciation, and dynamic in action.

As a prelude to the shaping of the modern world the Renaissance claims close attention in a search for the sources of anthropology (see below). As for the Greco-Roman lodestone, it must be recognized that the inspirational force of the ancient world decreased as the West moved toward a technological society. Initial denial of Greco-Roman competence came in the sixteenth century as fresh scientific discoveries stirred intellectual confidence in men like Galileo (1564–1642), Boyle (1627–1691), Newton (1642–1727), Descartes (1596–1650), and Francis Bacon (1561–1626). In "A Full and True Account of the Battle Fought Last Friday between the Ancient and the Modern Books in St. James's Library" Jonathan Swift (1704) lampooned the struggle over the right to speak for knowledge and truth and ridiculed the narrow scientific and mathematical base of the moderns. However, as new knowledge about the earth and the universe was uncovered under the guidelines of empirical science, the specifics of Greco-Roman knowledge became dated or functionally obsolete; and the effects of their influence became more indirect and restricted to broad orientations. In the nineteenth century the struggle over the right to adjudicate knowledge and truth brought theologian and scientist into conflict. But in the seventeenth century those devoted to uncovering nature's secrets looked upon emergent science as God's new tool for revelation. The new plan for revelation was eulogized in rhymed couplet by Alexander Pope,

> Nature and Nature's laws lay hid in night,
> God said, Let Newton be! and all was light.

Another difficulty in tracing influences through broad orientations comes with convergent discoveries. A case in point are the French economists known as Physiocrates, who analyzed the "political economy" of France according to a structural-functional model based on an organismic analogy. What brought about this independent invention parallel to the Greco-Roman structural-functional position was the opening up of a whole new scientific endeavor as a consequence of the special political, economic, and social developments in Europe. The Physiocrates added a novel reference point to eighteenth-century economic theory, and Adam Smith (1723–1790) absorbed some fundamental ideas from Quesnai (1694–1774) and associates before completing his *Wealth of Nations* (Smith 1937). Smith's analysis is noteworthy for its dynamic structural-functionalism, and his challenge was the new face of industrialization. He stressed the fruits of a division of labor in crafts, defined national wealth as an annual product of labor, and insisted that nations expand their wealth naturally by a competitive diversification of labor to achieve more efficient production. The ancient world offered no economic analysis to serve as a model for these new political economists.

The eighteenth century revealed another record of the diminishing influence of the ancient world. Greeks and Romans became subjects for study and for comparison. One may suspect Montesquieu (1689–1775; 1900) of ingeniously applying the Greco-Roman formula (national character, the mean, temperate climate, virtuous customs, rule by law) to prove that Western Europe, especially France, were so favored with natural conditions that they could not miss national greatness provided the right kind of political order were established. Gibbon (1737–1794) compiled a vast assemblage of fact that charted Roman history step by step in its rise and fall. Their best and their worst is revealed in matter-of-fact prose. Gibbon (1776–1788) mourned passage of the Greco-Roman tradition largely because an intellectual light was extinguished by a wave of religious superstition. In this he echoed those who saw the Church as a barrier to the intellectual progress of man. For Adam Smith (1937) the Greeks and Romans had little to offer other than the facts of their economic life, to be analyzed and compared with other economies. The use of Greeks and Romans as subjects for study by the eighteenth-century scholars further reduced the influence of the ancient world—a diminution that had begun in the Renaissance and which accelerated with each new scientific discovery and technological invention. The ancient world now was seen as a segment in the cultural stream that had produced the contemporary world.

RENAISSANCE ANTECEDENTS TO THE SCIENCE OF MAN

Advantages and Disadvantages for a Renaissance Science of Mankind

A number of special developments in the course of Western civilization conspired to make the Renaissance a prophetic moment in the rise of a science of man. First, there was the stimulus conveyed by a renewal of contacts with Greco-Roman humanism and science. Second, the Renaissance witnessed the rise of a scientific orientation and the accomplishment of scientific proofs that gave scholars a sense of importance and of confidence in their own discoveries. Third, voyages of discovery followed by conquest and settlement brought a vast new world to light, unknown to the ancients and not even alluded to in Christian tradition. At the same time there were a number of conditions present during the Renaissance that militated against an objective investigation of mankind. There was, first, the hard strength of the Christian tradition, which narrowed interpretation and problem definition to Christian history. Second, the rise of national states fostered a special concern with a national past, a national literature, and a national character. Third, the Greco-Roman tradition was an insufficient model, for no objective and comparative orientation to mankind had been achieved. Of these disadvantages, the weight of Christian theology was largely responsible for the failure of Renaissance scholars to escort a wholly new discipline into the scientific community. Within the context of Christian dogma, the best they achieved was an extension of biblical history into a universal history of mankind. Under Greco-

Roman stimulus the best products were geographic encyclopedias that sketchily described lands, peoples, and customs with a dash of history added. Italian concern for their national past gave focus to Roman life and history and also stirred a new interest in literature, language, and custom. Each of these strands converged in some ways on custom, but only the Christian "ethnohistorians" focused directly on customs and their scriptural connections.

To achieve a universal science of man something more than a combination of Greco-Roman ethical humanism and Christianity would have to be attempted. Instances of reactions to both the Greco-Roman and Christian traditions occurred during the Renaissance, but the influences of these cultural heritages were seldom shed entirely. Only in political theory and in science do we find a relative independence. The Florentine political theorist Machiavelli (1469–1527; 1935) defies both traditions with a worldly, cynical, and pragmatic posture that accents a "scientific" approach to politics. He admonishes princes to make war their primary aim "for that is the only art that is necessary to one who commands, and it is of such virtue that it not only maintains those who are born princes but often enables men of private fortune to attain to that rank" (Machiavelli 1935:65).

More often Renaissance scholars adjusted Christian tradition with a dash of humanism. Giovanni Pico, Count of Mirandola (1463–1494; 1948), immersed himself in the humanistic literature of the Greeks, Romans, Persians, and Arabs and argued for a new perspective on man. Pico was persuaded that the "most reverend fathers," who dwelled on Adam's sin and the corruption of mankind that followed, underrated man's place in God's design. Truly man had been created to appreciate God's handiwork: "To contemplate the reason of such a great work, to live its beauty, to wonder at its vastness." But the real miracle of man lay in the exercise of reason by which man could determine his own nature and fate—this was God's unique gift to man. Man could "by the determination of ... mind ... be reborn into those higher creatures, which are divine," or he could simply "degenerate into those lower creatures, which are brutes. . . ."

Using a universal humanistic platform Pico arrived at a conception of humanity which stressed the dignity of man in place of the corruption accented in Christian theology. But though man deserved to be studied and to be praised for his accomplishments, the basis for such study rested in God's design for His human creation. A similar orientation was found in natural scientists. Both Boyle and Newton viewed science as God's contemporary instrument for revealing Himself and his world to men. Scientists would surpass the revealed truths of the Patristic Fathers, for it was God's purpose that they should advance in knowledge. The view that God wished man to cultivate his mind through knowledge and to advance to new meanings through the medium of science contributed to the later formulation of the idea of progress. However, the political-religious strife which erupted during the Renaissance sharpened distinctions between orthodoxy and heterodoxy, and Church hierarchies were alerted to a suspicion that the disarming candor of a scientific search for truth under the banner of God often cloaked heterodox inclinations. The Protestant movement may have fractured Catholic unity, but an important effect was to underline the religious foundations of communities and states. Pico was refused permission to debate his 900 theses about man, Galileo was forced to recant his heliocentric position, while in Geneva Servetus was burned at the stake under the direction of Calvin.

Basic Premises and Interpretations of Renaissance Christian "Ethnohistory"

When approaching the study of man within the biblical context, Renaissance scholars were led to begin with three premises. First, the sacred creation represented a graduated chain rising from the lowest to the highest beings. Second, the course of sacred history began with a state of moral perfection, spoiled by Adam's sin, and to which subsequent generations have added their own measure of corruption. Man's historic course is to degenerate until God's righteous intervention will end the process of corruption. Third, human history began in the Holy Land and it is from there descendants of the original pair have dispersed during the times of Cain and of Noah.

In tracing all peoples back to Adam and Eve Christian "ethnohistorians" stressed the unity and genealogical continuity of mankind. Those who fell into corruption, as Cain and his descendants, were "black sheep," but they still were Adam's line. To prove their case Christian ethnohistorians described and compared customs, especially those of North American Indians, with those recorded for the ancient world and the Holy Land. In the customs of whose who had wandered far from their homeland, losing bits and pieces of the holy teaching along the way, one could expect to find only "vestiges" of the original revelations and of ancient custom. Yet, at the very least, the vestiges of custom would prove connection, and also might suggest when the migrants had started out—whether at the flight of Cain or during the dispersal in Noah's time.

Probably the most studious effort to extend Christian history to all peoples belongs to the Jesuit Father Lafitau (1671–1746), who set out to disprove the contentions of "atheists" that the Indians had no religion. From his researches he would prove that North American Indians preserved traces of Greek customs and religion practiced during the days of Homer, and there also were vestiges pointing to the time of Moses. What Lafitau (1774, Preface) now urged was a "science of custom" to reveal the Christian unity of mankind and to place people in the sweep of scriptural history.

Given the theological design, the course and product of such a history was not difficult to predict. Without scriptural reference, and unknown to the ancients, the Indians emerged as likely descendants of the "lost" tribes of Israel—or migrants from the sacred homeland, once or twice removed. There was much argument, according to Acosta (n.d.(1):67–68), in the latter part of the sixteenth century,

> that there are great signes ... amongst the common sort of the Indians, to breed a beleefe that they are descended from the Iewes; for, commonly you shall see them fearefull, submisse, ceremonious, and subtill in lying. And, moreover, they say their habites are like vnto those the Iewes vsed; for they weare a short coat or waste-coat, and a cloake imbroidered all about; they goe bare-footed, or with soles tied with latchets over the foot, which they call ljatas. And they say, that it appears by their Histories, as also by their ancient pictures, which represent them in this fashion, that this attire was the ancient habite of the Hebrewes, and that these two kinds of garments, which the Indians onely vse, were vsed by Samson, which the Scripture calleth *Tunicam et Syndonem*; beeing the same which the Indians terme waste-coat and cloake.

However, Acosta cited the lack of notable practices commonly associated with the Jews (for example, circumcision, writing, ceremonial masses) as supportive of a contrary and more acceptable argument. The absence of references to the origins of the Indians was due to the fact that they were migrants long removed from the homeland. Acosta did not think that shipwrecks, organized military expeditions, and sea exploration could account for the presence of Indians in the New World.

> But in the ende I resolve vpon this point, that the true and principall cause to people the Indies, was, that the lands and limits thereof are ioyned and continued in some extremities of the world, or at the least were very neere. And I beleeve it is not many thousand yeeres past since men first inhabited this new world and West Indies, and that the first men that entred were rather savage men and hunters, then bredde vp in civill and well governed Common-weales; and that they came to this new world, having lost their owne land, or being in too great numbers, they were forced of necessitie to seeke some other habitations; the which having found, they beganne by little and little to plant, having no other law, but some instinct of nature, and that very darke, and some customes remayning of their first Countries. And although they came from Countries well governed, yet is it not incredible to thinke that they had forgotten all through the tract of time and want of vse, seeing that in Spaine and Italie we find companies of men, which have nothing but the shape and countenance onely, whereby we may coniecture in what sort this new world grew so barbarous and vncivill. (Acosta n.d.(1): 69–70)

By tying Indians and other "savages" to scriptural history, Renaissance ethnohistorians also made them a part of the corrupting process premised by Christian dogma. Here, too, lay the explanation for the diversity in manners and customs. As members of lines that had strayed farthest from holy soil and broken contact with the mainstream of divine revelation and history, savages certainly could not be held to be less corrupt than the civilized peoples of the West who had stayed in midstream. The common view during the Renaissance, according to Hodgen (1964:362), was strongly antisavage. In the "deforming fantasies of Solinas, Mela, Isidore, Mandeville, and their ilk they [savages] were introduced to the European public not as nature's noblemen . . . living in romantic communion with rustic surroundings, but as half-human, hairy wild men degraded by 'dayly tumultes, fears doubts, sispitions, and barbarous cruelties' " (Hodgen 1964:362).

The attempt to give savages a place on the ladder of creation simply reinforced the prejudicial evaluations that flowed equally from attempts to bring savages into scriptural history through a comparison of customs. Under the hand of Sir William Petty (1623–1687) savages were assigned a place intermediate to ape and true civilized man. In searching out the degrees of graduated distinctions leading to true men, one could detect a series of "missing links" stretching upward from the least to the highest—"gradations of improuvements which man hath made from the lowest and simplest condition that mankind was ever in, unto the highest that anie man or Company of men hath attained" (Petty 1677, cited by Hodgen 1964:450). Here Petty stood at the bottom of the ladder and raised his vision along the ascending scale of being, and even suggested that man had advanced himself. However, the path upward was not accented in the popular view so much as the descent. What struck John Ovington when he made the acquaintance of the Hottentots was their appearance as " 'the very Reverse of Human Kind, Cousin Germans to the Helachors [East Indian outcasts] only meaner and more filthy; so that if there is any medium between a Rational animal and a Beast, the Hotantot lays fairest claim to the Species' " (cited by Hodgen 1964:422). In Christian theory all men have been corrupted by Adam's sin, but some had degenerated more than others—notably the savage.

SAVAGE AND CUSTOM IN THE PERSPECTIVE OF RENAISSANCE HUMANISM, POLITICAL THEORY, AND GEOGRAPHY

Savage Noble Simplicity versus Civilized Hypocrisy

The other important current in Renaissance thought, Greco-Roman humanism and science, promoted a view of savage societies that emphasized the natural quality of life in a state of nature. Where people lived without the artificial constraints of organized society, they were not inclined to be hypocrites. In 1511 Peter Martyr (Arber 1885, Decade I, Book 3:78) depicted the inhabitants of Cuba as exemplifying that golden age to which so many writers had referred with deep nostalgia. Martyr was stirred by the lack of formal controls among the Arawaks. Without laws or punitive enforcement people lived together and got along without fencing their garden plots. They lived simply and quietly in answer to their needs, free of the division of resources into "Myne and Thyne (the seedes of all myscheefe)."

Montaigne (1946) extolled the simple naturalness of Indian life in Brazil, for above all it was free of the hideous cruelties perpetrated so frequently in Europe in the holy name of religion. The untutored directness of the Brazilian Indians was refreshing, and though they warred incessantly, their warfare was "entirely noble and generous," seeking only personal glory—not the lands of others. As for eating their captives, could it be worse than what happened to the victims of religion in Europe?

> I think there is more barbarity in eating a live than a dead man, and in tearing on the rack and torturing the body of a man still full of feeling, in roasting him piecemeal and giving him to be bitten and mangled by dogs and swine (as we have not only read, but seen within fresh memory, not between old enemies, but between neighbours and fellow citizens, and what is worse, under the cloak of piety and religion), than in roasting and eating him after he is dead. (Montaigne 1946:176–181)

Savagery and Political Theory

Political strife between monarchs and the emergent middle classes during the Renaissance focused on savagery as an apolitical state and drew it into the humanistic, legal, political, and scriptural arguments regarding political society. Men in their natural state lived without visible laws, and this condition underlined the necessity for individual men to band together under the protection of organized government. The imagined state of nature was sufficient for the political-legal argument, and neither Hobbes (1958) nor Locke (1947) spent much time on descriptions of life in "savage" societies available to them. Thus it happened that political theorists issued no call for a study of men in the alleged "state of nature." It was sufficient that early men were viewed as roaming the forests in solitude, separated from others by the weight of personal fear, conflict, and insecurity. To overcome these personal disadvantages a cooperative arrangement under the guarantee of civil law had to come into being, with each person surrendering the extreme liberties enjoyed in the "state of nature." Whether persons retained residual title to their "natural rights" would prove a matter for debate. However, it was agreed that man had improved his lot in historic development by establishing civil society and that organized society provided the best medium for the fullest exercise of human endowment.

Exploration, Conquest, and the Description of Lands and Peoples

Political theory may not have stimulated an interest in the peoples and customs of other lands, but travel to the Far East and voyages of discovery stirred Renaissance scholars to new efforts in geography and in mapping. The model of Greco-Roman geography and natural science supplied a descriptive format that included attention to the physical characteristics of a people, history, features of the land, special resources, population, settlements, social rankings, political authority, national character, ways of making war, and an assortment of customs with stress on marriage and religion. The administrative and resource development demands of the European states also found such data useful in furthering their competitive interests during the sixteenth and seventeenth centuries.

Johan Boemus (1520) and Sebastian Muenster (1544) were two outstanding collectors of customs and other bits of knowledge about foreign lands and the character of peoples (Hodgen 1964). However, neither Boemus' *Fardle of Facions* nor Muenster's *Cosmographie* marked a step forward in the study of custom. Both brought together in one piece what the Greeks and Romans had written about the Mediterranean world and peoples contacted as far as India, North Africa, and Celtic and Germanic Europe, but hardly extended themselves in the direction of the New World. Such collections proved convenient, as Boemus observed, and they also might instruct people on " 'what orders and institutions' were 'fittest to be ordayned' in their own lands for the establishment of perfect peace" (cited by Hodgen 1964:131–132); but they were not suitable models for an anthropological ethnography. Like the Greco-Roman naturalists, Boemus and Muenster uncritically accepted any report of monstrous peoples— whether one-eyed, tailed, or dog-headed. Their descriptions of national characters were merely popular stereotypes, often distorted and vindictive. When it came to a systematic collection of social and cultural evidences, natural scientists were of little help, for their interests directed attention to the lie of the land and to resources.

The encyclopedias of Boemus and Muenster are insignificant when compared to the descriptions of foreign lands and peoples supplied by explorers, missionaries, and conquerors. During the sixteenth century Richard Eden (d. 1626), Richard Hakluyt (d. 1616), and Samuel Purchas (d. 1626) facilitated the spread of knowledge about these new lands by assembling travel and discovery accounts. The Spanish provided descriptive narratives of their conquests (Bernal Diaz del Castillo 1908–1916) and "natural histories" of the "Indies" (Acosta n.d.; Oviedo y Valdés 1885). In reporting of their activities, missionaries included substantial accounts of the area and its peoples with description of customs and religious practices (for example, *The Jesuit Relations*, Thwaites 1896–1901; Diego de Landa's *Report on Yucatan* 1565). Without Sahagun's general history of conditions in New Spain, description and interpretation of Aztec life and ceremony would be very sketchy indeed.

EMERGENT NATIONALISM AND ANTHROPOLOGICAL INTERESTS

Italian Unity and the Roman Heritage

A final source for Renaissance interest in customs stemmed from rediscovery of past grandeur. Italians held an advantage over other Europeans, as they were surrounded by monuments of ancient Rome and Greece. For Italians of the fifteenth century links with Rome held special interest as they sought to forge a vision of a renovated Italian state free of warring dukedoms and the tyranny of foreign monarchs. In the sixteenth century Machiavelli concluded his political discourse with an appeal to Lorenzo the Magnificent to free Italy from that "barbarous domination [which] stinks in the nostrils of everyone."

The first to study Roman monuments was Ciriaco de' Pizzicolli (1391–1452). As a man of commerce he traveled and resided in the eastern Mediterranean countries and spent part of his time in diligent copying of inscriptions carved on the surviving monuments. According to Rowe (1965 (67):10), Pizzicolli was "inspired by the idea that archaeological monuments could provide more direct testimony of antiquity than the literary tradition." Unfortunately, all but a fragment of his work was lost by fire. Equally striking was the achievement of Flavio Biondo (1392–1463), who in a number of works (*Rome Restored* 1471; *Rome Triumphant* 1473; *Italy Illustrated* 1474; *History from the Decline of the Roman Empire* 1483) described the historical continuity between ancient Rome and the Italy of his day. His attention was focused largely on Roman religion, government, war, and the family, with attendant marriage customs and laws. Biondo used ancient literary sources and followed their leads in tracing Egyptian influences on later Roman religion. At the same time he utilized the inscriptions of monuments to supplement the literary materials. Biondo wished to accord the Romans their rightful position as founders of all that was magnificent in the literature, customs, and virtues of the European peoples. He described Roman culture (*cultas*) in order that later Italians would never forget the dignity and glory of their past. With such intentions Biondo was more inclined to admire than to deprecate Roman life, and to compare Roman customs with practices of his time.

The historical orientation achieved by Italians during the Renaissance thus was rooted in their Roman foundations. They called up the past in the service of the present. In the view of Leonardo Bruni Aretino (1369–1444) Italians should understand the origins and development of their own history, for there was written the "achievement of Peoples and of Kings." More than this,

> the careful study of the past enlarges our foresight in contemporary affairs and affords to citizens and to monarchs lessons of incitement or warning in the ordering of public policy." (Cited by Woodward 1897:132–133; see Olschki 1954:203–217 regarding Petrarch's intent and influence.)

Italian concern for their Roman past provided a lesson in objective scholarship, which, according to Rowe (1965(67):12–14), was passed on to the Spanish. As an Italian scholar at the court of Ferdinand and Isabella, Peter Martyr became especially excited about the discovery of the Americas and prodded those who had been there to give him the fruits of their observations. These were incorporated in a work on the New World written between 1493 and 1526. Martyr also, according to Rowe (1965(67):12–14), inspired Gonzalo Hernandez de Oviedo y Valdés to compile his *General and Natural History of the Indies* (1526), which Eden had translated into English by 1555.

Renaissance Assessment

If the four criteria set forth at the opening of this chapter are applied to the Renaissance, it is evident that scholars did not attain a science of man. First, there was a general failure to call for a special discipline that would be distinct from established studies and would be especially relevant to man. The best that can be allotted to the Renaissance, as Rowe (1965 (67):14) admits, is the achievement of a perspective on alien customs relatively free of distortions engendered by "ethnocentric prejudice." Now travelers and missionaries were much better observers and had a greater interest in recording customs when afoot in foreign lands. But travel narratives and descriptions of peoples and their customs by missionaries do not make a science even though their substance may be useful.

As to the second criterion, a special theory of reality and of causal explanation, Renaissance scholars moved beyond Christian dogma when stressing "natural laws" or processes. In this they were stimulated both by Greco-Roman example and by the implications of their own scientific discoveries. Scientists even challenged theology as "queen of the sciences," but their intent did not go beyond the theological purpose—to reveal the immutable perfection of God's design for the universe and for man. However, this position bore an important fruit, for accent on the advancement of human knowledge led to the idea of progress as a uniquely human manifestation, made possible by that special human faculty, intellect. Various writers, including Bodin (1966), disputed the idea that the course of human history began with a "golden age" or a "paradise" and that subsequent events were a record of degeneration.

No claim for a distinctive methodology, the third criterion, can be made for Renaissance scholars in their concern for man-oriented studies. Christian ethnohistorians compared likenesses in ceremonial customs, ritual objects, dress, and even language forms to show affiliation with scriptural peoples. According to the dogma of degeneration, connection might be found in shreds and patches drawn from any part of the life of peoples in distant lands. Comparisons of this order hardly introduced a new method, and criteria for similarity were so relaxed that controlled comparison and analysis in a scientific way were bypassed. It is to the credit of Italian historians that they initiated a critical scrutiny of documents to test validity and also introduced the use of inscriptions on Roman monuments as documentary materials. Pizzicolli and Biondo pointed the way to archeology, but national history provided the background for their work—not the founding of archeology.

In like fashion Italian interest in the continuity of Latin and vernacular Italian, and the use of language as a literary medium, pointed the way to language studies. Leonardo Bruni's controversial hypothesis that Latin always had served as a special literary instrument prompted Flavio Biondo to undertake a study to prove that the literary and spoken language of Rome were cut from the same cloth. Lorenzo Valla (1406–1457) was stimulated to write a manual on literary style for Latin, and Elio Antonio de Lebrija (1444–1522) compiled a dictionary and grammar of his Spanish mother tongue. Here was a new interest in language, but no vision of a science of linguistics directly relevant to a study of man.

As for the fourth criterion, assembly of a set of factual materials not usually employed in other disciplines, it must be granted that Renaissance Christian historians did just that. The collection of customs and artifacts according to their similarities with Greco-Roman and Judaic traditions was quite different from the effort of those who wrote of customs for encyclopedias or from those whose curiosity for customs was aroused by travel in strange lands. The assembly of novel facts and the universalizing of human history to encompass Indians, Asiatics, Africans, Europeans and the ancient world can be taken as evidence for the development of a new science of man by Christian ethnohistorians. However, by focusing on scripture, Christian ethnohistorians switched the study of man onto a siding.

It is apparent that Renaissance scholars were at the threshold of a new science of man. Their main contributions were found in the new perspective on man and their interests in collecting hitherto unused materials (customs, artifacts, religious ceremony, and inscriptions on monuments) in writing a Christian history of mankind.

The soil stirred by Renaissance scholars, and the seeds they scattered, were cultivated and harvested by those who later, under the banner of progress, attempted a "natural history of the species." It is to the eighteenth century that we turn for the first clear definition of a science of man directly relevant to the later development in the West of anthropology as a discipline. However, before turning to eighteenth-century origins, consideration must be given to the possibility of Arabic contributions. Like civilization in the West, Arabic culture drew upon the ancient Mesopotamian, Egyptian, and Greco-Roman traditions. Its scholars, inspired by the Greco-Roman philosophy, geography, history, and science, ranged over a wide field of learning, including the writing of histories. One such history, the "universal history" of Ibn Khaldūn, composed between 1377 and 1381, was hailed by Toynbee (1935–1961(3):122) as a "philosophy of history which is undoubtedly the greatest work of its kind that has ever yet been created by any mind in any time or place." Sorokin, Zimmerman, and Galpin (1930(1):54) estimated Khaldūn's work as marking him the founder of sociology, and at the very least, the founder of rural-urban sociology.

THE MORAL-HISTORICAL SOCIOLOGY OF IBN KHALDŪN (1332–1406)

Islam and Arabic Culture

Arabic peoples began to shape political history in the Middle East and in North Africa a little more than a hundred years after the official fall of

Rome (A.D. 476). The catalyst for expansive Arabic energies was a new faith promulgated by Muhammad around A.D. 610 when the prophet of Allah was about forty years of age. Within a hundred years after Muhammad died in A.D. 632, bold and courageous leaders had conquered a vast stretch of land, reaching from Persia through North Africa into Spain. The whole of this imperial domain ostensibly fell under the rule of Muhammad's successors or caliphs. The lure of booty and control of trade and the labor of captive populations provided special impetus to the Arabic conquests, but difficulties over the distribution of trade and wealth, fortified by political-religious factionalism, divided the empire before lines of communication, administrative experience, and a firm national tradition could be formulated. Nonetheless, adherence to Islam inspired among the followers of Muhammad the image of a community of the faithful, sharing a common destiny, a special cultural heritage, and rights of citizenship which infidels could not have.

In the administrative and trade cities of Byzantium (not wholly conquered until overrun by the Ottoman Turks), Persia, Egypt, and Spain, where the nomadic conquerors established themselves, Arabs confronted new forms of art, literature, science, bureaucracy, and kingship. Under the combined stimulus of these cultural traditions, which drew most of their philosophic and scientific substance from the Greco-Roman heritage, the Arabs set out on a new intellectual adventure and soon made their own contributions to mathematics, geography, astronomy, physics, chemistry, medicine, agriculture, art, literature, geography, and history. From the eighth to the twelfth centuries Arabic accomplishments surpassed those of the West, and it was through the hands of Arabs that knowledge of Greco-Roman philosophy, history, and science was conveyed to medieval scholars in Europe. Even today the commentary of Averroës (d. A.D. 1198) on Aristotle is considered the best.

The Ebbtide of Arabic Fortunes: The Challenge of Growth and Decay

At the time of Khaldūn's birth the political decay of Arab conquest had been going on for several centuries. It was not just a succession of kingdoms that was involved, but the breakup of the Arabic culture region by the intrusion of Turks and Mongols. Moreover, from 1100 Christians in the north of Spain had advanced steadily against Moorish emirates until only Granada remained, and that too fell in 1492. The general context of Arabic withdrawal and decay was crucial for Khaldūn as he sought to combine, according to family tradition, an administrative career with scholarly pursuits. Khaldūn's family established themselves in Seville at the time of the Moorish conquest, then fled on the eve of Ferdinand III's capture of the city.

Arabs became engrossed in histories, but when Khaldūn set himself the task of writing a universal history, he determined to understand the processes of history. History, in his view, was nothing more nor less than a "record of human society," and he hoped to understand those constant "transformations that society undergoes by its very nature" (Khaldūn 1950:26–27).

Khaldūn (1950:30) premised his study of change in human society on the assumption that change was the law of the universe "laid down by God for his worshippers." Laws of process applied to human society suggested the idea of a science, which, "like all other sciences, whether based on authority or on reasoning, appears to be independent and has its own subject, viz. human society, and its own problems, viz. the social phenomena and the transformations that succeed each other in the nature of society" (Khaldūn 1950:36). The transformation of lands, peoples, and societies proceeded so gradually that changes passed unnoticed, but in time the original was hardly recognizable. Rulers were crucial to change in human society, for everyone imitated his betters. By intermingling their ways with those of their predecessors and by adopting customs from those whom they had conquered, rulers set the tone for change. As rulers were central to the development of the state, they were also critical for the breakup of that state. In historical events Khaldūn (1950:102) discerned the inevitable working of laws that carried a group into prominence and also those predictable processes which sapped their strength and cast them down. The fate of society and state thus were intermingled, since the "real force which operates on society is solidarity and power, which persists through [successive] rulers." When solidarity and power alter and fade, serious changes in the social order appear and fragmentation must follow.

Structural-Functional Premises of Khaldūn's Analysis of Social Processes

Khaldūn's insistence that all things, including society, are organized to act purposefully according to the laws of their natures echoed Aristotle and stressed the shaping and modification of form by internal processes. Out of this typical Greco-Roman formula Khaldūn developed a structural-functional model as follows:

1. Reality is an ordered hierarchy of parts, structurally and functionally integrated so that alteration in one part will spread its effect to other parts.
2. An internal mechanism of control is necessary to the proper functioning of the parts.
3. Change is inevitable and takes the primary form of growth and decay, and these processes are a function of the degree to which the control mechanism maintains its cohesiveness. The individual as he matured and withered into senility supplied the model for the growth-decay cycle to which all societies were bound.
   a. For human society, cohesive control varies according to the extent to which the social body becomes differentiated and heterogeneous as the control mechanism allows through its own adulturation and insulation.

4. The most appropriate context for action is that area between two extremes, or the mean.

In demonstrating the operation of these principles and processes in Arabic society, Khaldūn drew upon ethnic characteristics (Arabic peoples versus Jews, Persians, Byzantine Christians, and Franks) and differences between countrymen and townsmen. He discussed trade, crafts, wealth, and taxation in relation to the economy of the state and related population size to productivity and wealth. None of the above, however, was central to the origins of the state; for this was rooted in a group feeling or national consciousness. However, the course of growth and decline of states did involve these factors as they were integrated by model-actions set by the ruler which affected group cohesiveness. In the ordering of human society, human nature provided two important constants: the impulse to dominate and the urge to plunder others of their wealth.

Origins of Society and the State

The heart of Khaldūn's concern for the historic processes of Arabic civilization is found in his theories about organized rule and society. He began with the Aristotelean assumption that men are social by nature, and, must cooperate to obtain food and defend themselves against others. However, the internal necessity of providing an orderly protection of life evoked the exercise of powerful constraints over others. Sovereignty, then, was indispensable to man's existence and suitable to his nature. If aggressiveness and lust for power were basic to human nature, so too must be submissiveness. Habit training apparently could strengthen and perhaps challenge the tendencies of human nature as a kind of secondary nature. Those who are conquered become accustomed to a docile demeanor before their rulers and wait for command. Younger generations of the ruling class become softened by luxurious living as the "old habits acquired in their free life are shed, and forgotten the nomadic ways which had secured for them dominion . . . firmness of character, predatoriness and the capacity of going out and roaming in the wilderness" (Khaldūn 1950:125). Likewise the manners of tradesmen were "inferior to rulers, and far removed from manliness and uprightness," since they were habituated to flattery, litigation, evasiveness, and disputation in their pursuit of profit (Khaldūn 1950:69).

Power, Solidarity, and Civilized Society

Power wielded by a ruler alone could not overcome the natural urges to dominate and to plunder a neighbor, nor induce that second nature of habit which strengthens social character and gives people a first place among others. To this must be added what Khaldūn referred to as *asabiyah*, which some have translated as *esprit de corps* and social solidarity. Those with blood ties possessed *asabiyah* because they presented a united front against those who would do harm to any one of them. The social solidarity found in tribal kinship had a primitive and natural quality that was difficult to duplicate in other relationships. Ties between noblemen and allies or clients were "almost as powerful as those of blood," and intermarriages within a city could produce a manner of solidarity among factions (Khaldūn 1950:104). For the most part, however, the tribal solidarity founded on blood lines was weakened in the village as genealogies became confused and tribal names were cast aside, merging the individual with the village or city rather than a group of kin.

Apparently Khaldūn accepted conquest and the transformation of nomads into townsmen as inevitable in the process of creating Arabic civilization and society. Hence his concern in contrasting nomad and townsmen and charting the effects of this transformation. The townsman came off second best in the comparative contrast; and, in pointing to the deterioration of nomadic manners, habits, and solidarity, Khaldūn alerted rulers to important variables that must be considered in governance. He also brought out the crucial role rulers played in creating and in sustaining the unity of the group according to their place in the historical-social cycle.

Movement from nomadic tribal fields to settled towns profoundly affected the nature of solidarity and shifted its centrum. The natural solidarity of the tribe permitted chiefs and elders to control aggression within the group without compulsion. In the city, as tribal filiation vanished, tribal solidarity also disappeared, to be replaced with a new solidarity, that of sovereignty. Sovereignty required compulsion exercised by a ruler, but rulers need followers, and in the relation between king and follower a new kind of social solidarity sprang up.

> Kingship is the natural end to which social solidarity leads, and this transformation is not a matter of choice but a necessary consequence of the natural order and disposition of things.... For no laws, religions, or institutions can be effective unless a cohesive group enforce and impose them and without solidarity they cannot be established. Social solidarity is, therefore, indispensable if a nation is to play the role which God has chosen for it. (Khaldūn 1950:137)

In the state-society, as it moved from one condition to another, the demands for social solidarity varied or called for the ruler to relate himself to different segments of society. Once conquest was achieved and kingly sovereignty established, the ruler at first might dispense with solidarity. The immediate impact of conqueror upon conquered can be mediated by harsh coercion to induce a habit of ready obedience to the ruler. After obedience is instilled, the ruler has no need of a vast armed force, and he can proceed to develop a special clientage, drawing upon freemen within the royal household or attaching hired mercenaries to his person. Administrative needs in turn expand to produce a bureaucracy, and during this middle time of the dynasty, solidarity links ruler and civilian servants through the collection of taxes and services. However, when decline sets in, rulers must cultivate again relations with the military arm.

In charting the inevitable fate of the state Khaldūn concentrated on the nature of *asabiyah* in the successive transformations of society. Relations between ruler and follower were the measure for this critical component, and Khaldūn cited the growing estrangement of ruler from followers as primary. This estrangement was accompanied by a secularization of purpose, so that the ultimate ends to which the religious consciousness of Islam pointed, were subverted to practical and private ends. The effects of this creeping estrangement and secularization of purpose could be seen in the rise of corruption and the increase in coercive measures by hired mercenaries in order to maintain power and a life of luxury. The state would fall to revolts at the periphery or a revolution at the center.

The decline of a state usually occupied no more than three generations of forty years, as conquerors shed their courageous, energetic, and physical virtues and cultivated submission to the ruler in pursuing a life of corruption and luxury. As a nomadic chief was transformed into an absolute monarch, he was insulated by mercenaries and alienated from former followers. *Asabiyah* in turn vanished. Now the state must use coercion and extend taxation to satisfy the ever-increasing demands for luxurious living. As taxes become exorbitant, merchants and tradesmen are drained of their incentive for work and wealth declines. The relation between taxes, work incentives, and income was clear. Prosperity "leads to a further increase in economic activity which leads to a rise in incomes and increasing luxury, the new wants so created will lead to the creation of new industries and services, with consequent increases in income and prosperity . . ." (Khaldūn 1950:93). A healthy economy also evokes more procreative energy and population increases, but when a city or ruler uses a disproportionate amount of wealth according to the size of the population, then the economy declines and opposite changes follow. Finally, in their degradation the erstwhile conquerors fall victim to those vicissitudes of spirit that had overtaken those whom they had subdued.

[23] A nation that has been defeated and come under the rule of another nation will quickly perish.

The reason for this may possibly lie in the apathy that comes over people when they lose control of their own affairs and, through enslavement, become the instrument of others and dependent upon them. Hope diminishes and weakens. Now, propagation and an increase in civilization (population) take place only as the result of strong hope and of the energy that hope creates in the animal powers (of man). When hope and the things it stimulates are gone through apathy, and when group feeling has disappeared under the impact of defeat, civilization decreases and business and other activities stop. With their strength dwindling under the impact of defeat, people become unable to defend themselves. They become the victims of anyone who tries to dominate them, and a prey to anyone who has the appetite. It makes no difference whether they have already reached the limit of their royal authority or not.

Here, we possibly learn another secret, namely, that man is a natural leader by virtue of the fact that he has been made a representative (of God on earth). When a leader is deprived of his leadership and prevented from exercising all his powers, he becomes apathetic, even down to such matters as food and drink. This is in the human character. A similar observation may be made with regard to beasts of prey. They do not cohabit when they are in human captivity. The group that has lost control of its own affairs thus continues to weaken and to disintegrate until it perishes. Duration belongs to God alone. (Khaldūn 1958(1):300–301)

So it had been with the Persians and usually with the Negroes whose submission to slavery disclosed their deficient character.

So strong was the impression of inevitable process as Khaldūn read it in the history of Arabic states that he held well-intentioned rulers incapable of arresting the process. Efforts at reform were only temporary restraints, for the "same disorders . . . reappear" until "God decrees the total extinction of the state . . ." (Khaldūn 1950:126–127).

Religion and Politics

Khaldūn is not reputed to have been a man of religion, yet his course of Arabic empire was a lesson in morality and in the consequences of losing sight of God. He noted the nomad as too untutored and too much given to plunder to be capable of building the administrative machinery of empire and of establishing a rule of law. "They become fit for ruling only when religion has transformed their character, driving out these [defects] and leading them to restrain themselves and to prevent other people from encroaching on each other's rights . . ." (Khaldūn 1950:59)." In the image of the Caliphate the followers of Muhammad raised their eyes to the kingdom of God and their true purpose, rule by divine law.

> Divine laws, then, seek to prescribe the conduct of men in all their affairs, their worship and their dealings, even in those relating to the state, which is natural to human society. The state, therefore, is patterned on religion, in order that the whole should come under the supervision of the lawgiver. (Khaldūn 1950:135)

But the Caliphate was subverted by the pride and greed of men. It had been transformed into a monarchy that rested neither on *asabiyah* nor divine law. The path to secularization in actuality was a path to destruction, for "men have not been created solely for this world, which is full of vanity and evil and whose end is death and annihilation" (Khaldūn 1950:135). Once it lost its religious purpose—the *asabiyah* of Arabic empire—the end of Arabic civilization was dissolution and subjugation by others imbued with holy purpose. In short, things of the flesh corrupt, and the corrupted passeth away.

Placed in the context of worldliness it is possible to see why the city— the repository for flattery, deception, greed, power seeking, submissiveness, and lust for luxurious comfort—became the symbol of corruption for Khaldūn. In contrast, the free and spirited nomad, despite rude ways, demonstrated a natural and primitive superiority in character. To the city, of necessity, belonged the arts, science, and cultivation of the mind. Nonetheless, the city with all its civilization represented not a beginning but a decay. Wrote Khaldūn:

> We will even go so far as to state that the character of men formed under the influence of sedentary life and luxury is in itself the personification of evil. A man is not a man unless he is able to procure by his own efforts that which will be useful to him and is able to reject that which would be harmful; it is for this purpose that he has received such a perfectly organized body. The resident of the city is incapable of providing his prime needs. Slothfulness contracted from living in ease hinders him in this attempt; or it may even be the pride resulting from an education acquired in the midst of well-being and luxury.... When a man has lost the force of acting according to his good qualities and his piety, he has lost the character of a man and falls to the level of the beasts.... It is thus evident that civilization marks the point of arrest in the development of a people or of an empire. (Cited by Sorokin, Zimmerman, and Galpin 1930(1):64)

Like Rousseau, though his path was different, Khaldūn concluded that civilization had not brought progress, because its culture violated the natural character of man and stimulated the unbridled lusts of human weakness. What does it profit a man if he conquer the whole world and lose his soul? This is the theme of Khaldūn, and he read this loss of soul in the petty traffic of craftsmen and traders as well as in the mansions of merchants and the palaces of kings.

Did Khaldūn Found a Science of Society?

Measured by the four criteria useful in detecting the presence of a discipline, Khaldūn (1958(1):77) must be credited with seeking to ground an "independent science ... [with] its own peculiar object—that is, human civilization and social organization." For Khaldūn civilization was the establishment of an orderly and regulated society in which men were freed of concern for their ultimate needs—food and security of person. Khaldūn saw himself as attempting a new synthesis of all evidences relating to man and his destiny. In substance his universal history was limited largely to the Arabic world, but it was universal in the sense that the spotlight was on man and his fate as a social being.

Admittedly, none of the ancients, perhaps excepting the poet Lucretius, had set for himself the task of charting the human destiny and analyzing the processes affecting that destiny. But poetic philosophy is one thing; the assemblage of historical facts for comparison and analysis is quite a different operation. St. Augustine, the great Christian apologist of the fifth century, had developed a philosophy of history in which man was linked to a universal and divine process. For St. Augustine the divine historical process was in the struggle between two antithetical "cities"—the city of God and the ungodly city of flesh and corruption. Khaldūn also contrasted antithetical forces of good and of evil and described the inevitable end of those alienated by their lust from the supreme ruler of the universe. The tragedy of the Caliphs, who were intended to rule under Allah's divine law, was their alienation from divine purpose and protection. Khaldūn, as administrative adviser, was interested in charting the basic contrast between the primitive nomadic community and the corrupted city community. In the Western world the nearest thing to a universal history came at its earliest in 1725 from the pen of Vico (1948:93), who counseled that the world of nations had been made by men and its processes therefore must be read in the nature of man, especially the processes of the human mind. More so than others of his day, Khaldūn succeeded in defining man and society as proper subjects for investigation, and well in advance of anyone in the West.

With regard to the nature of reality and how it operates, all aspects of Khaldūn's structural-functional posture could be extracted easily from Greek sources. The description of chainlike effects that followed an action appears to have been a time-worn instrument to advise Arabic rulers. However, the way in which Khaldūn applied the concept of *asabiyah* as central to the growth and decline of human society, and his tracing of the importance of group cohesion in the process of urbanization, mark him as a singular contributor to the description and explanation of social processes. The ultimate structure of the world, he admits, must be sought in the divine plan; but this is hidden from man, and hence he must study himself and his society if he is to come to any understanding about God and his purpose. As Khaldūn (1958(1):83) noted, when contrasting his purpose with other scholars, "We, on the other hand, were inspired by God. He led us to a science whose truth we ruthlessly set forth."

Khaldūn cannot be credited with innovations in methodology, although his attention to verified fact made his descriptions and analysis superior to those of his predecessors and contemporaries. When Khaldūn dealt with the west of Arabic Africa with which he was most familiar, he tended to achieve this standard of superiority. However, his presentation of historic events and causes in the eastern areas have been challenged, and grave doubts have been cast on the Yemenite genealogy which Khaldūn set forth for his family. Nonetheless, Khaldūn set a scholarly tone that well could be emulated. He certainly winnowed fact from fancy much better than Vico did some three centuries later. His analysis of institutions and their processes did not suffer from the intrusion of metaphysical or theological principles, despite the repetitious allusions to God as the "friend of believers" and as giving "His Kingdom (royal authority) to whomever He wants to give it" (Khaldūn 1958(1):377, 378). For the first time since Greek historians like Thucydides and Polybius there is the impression of a scholarly analysis of institutions and processes *qua* institutions. Khaldūn is less successful when applying the principle of the mean to climate, geography, and ethnic character, for he was too inclined to follow the bias of Greco-Roman interpretation.

With his goal of presenting a unified view of man in society and of the structural transformations of society, Khaldūn assembled an array of fact that was more synthetic than what had been brought together before. The factual evidences upon which Khaldūn drew included a wide range of variables—human psychology, sexual energy, population, land, climate, race, group character, economy, religion, and political organization. With regard to the information relevant to history or "human social organization" he reports:

> It deals with such conditions affecting the nature of civilization as, for instance, savagery and sociability, group feelings, and the different ways by which one group of human beings achieves superiority over another. It deals with royal authority and the dynasties that result (in this manner) and with the various ranks that exist within them. (It further deals) with the different kinds of gainful occupations and ways of making a living, with the sciences and crafts that human beings pursue as part of their activities and efforts, and with all the other institutions that originate in civilization through its very nature. (Khaldūn 1958(1):71)

The list of conditions can be taken as social facts, and when Khaldūn later tells us that the truth or falsity of reported fact can be measured by conformity to the intrinsic conditions of human society, he seems to be citing the need for special kinds of facts.

In reviewing Khaldūn's accomplishments one can conclude that he set the stage for a new and dynamic study of human society—what might be called historical sociology. The emphasis, owing to Khaldūn's own experience, was weighted toward political process, but nonetheless it was a magnificent new beginning. It is likely that this emphasis on political conditions and processes may have limited Khaldūn's influence on Arabic historical scholarship until, as Rosenthal (Khaldūn 1958(1):lxvi–lxvii) observed, the Ottoman Turks appeared, "who, like the Romans, were mainly concerned with politics and therefore concentrated their intellectual interests upon history." Upon the West Ibn Khaldūn had no effect until the beginning of the nineteenth century, when European scholars began to translate limited portions of the *Muqaddimah* or *Prolegomena*, the first volume of the universal history. Thus, by the time Khaldūn became known to the West, the development of social theory was well underway, inspired by the idea of progress.

SUMMARY

A conception of man, society, and culture which could be considered a direct antecedent for a general social science or of anthropology in particular was not developed by the social philosophers and historians of the ancient world. Greco-Roman social philosophers failed to lay out the subject matter of such a field with its special kinds of facts, theory, and methodology. Captivated by a geographic interpretation of national character, they were inclined to see the distinctive nature of social orders and cultural achievements as products of national temperaments shaped by climatic forces. In applying the principle of the mean, peoples who occupied lands at the extremes of cold and hot invariably exhibited character and achievement inferior to Greeks and Romans who lived under the climatic mean.

However, Greco-Roman philosophers and historians did introduce a special concern for social, cultural, and historical analysis into the mainstream of intellectual development in the West. This was a result of their examination of factors affecting national ascendancy and decline and their concern with moral relationships that ideally should exist in society. Moreover, Greco-Roman philosophers, natural scientists, geographers, and historians developed a structural-functional model. This model was highly useful in exploring and organizing phenomena as to their hierarchical organization, processual relationships, and purposive activities. The structural-functional model, with its emphasis on harmony and the mean, was a constant stimulus to later scholars who sought to develop theories of society and to explain the nature of national character, politics, and historic achievement.

Greco-Roman interest in the manifest destinies of historic peoples limited their vision with regard to a science of mankind. In consequence, their attention to customs and to social and political systems was confined to an assessment of their importance in relation to national grandeur or weakness. The introduction of ethnographic description into their accounts was distinctly secondary and commonly linked to didactic considerations, or to the pragmatics of military, political, and commercial purposes.

The Greco-Roman theoretical perspective, which united climate, human nature, national character, and structural-functional principles of organization, had a profound impact on Renaissance intellectuals. However, the ideas of Renaissance scholars were challenged by the discovery, conquest, and settlement of the New World, which introduced them to peoples who had not been present at the creation and who apparently had no connection with the ancient world or with Christian history. Practical considerations regarding the the Christianizing and administration of these strange peoples heightened a curiosity to learn about their character, dress, customs, language, economics, social organization, and religious beliefs and practices. The urge to give these alien peoples a place in the Christian creation and history led to comparison of their customs, tools, musical instruments, dress, beliefs, and ceremonies with those of the ancient world, particularly with the Hebrews. In this way a vision of a universal Christian history took on the character of a comparative Christian ethnology. However, the biblical orientation severely limited the scholarly effort, since, of necessity, all peoples had to be drawn into the dispersion of peoples from the Holy Land. Thus, in 1775, a trader to the Cherokee Indians, James Adair (1930), devoted nearly one half of his work to a consideration of similarities between Cherokee customs and ceremonies and those of the Hebrews.

Despite generating a basis for studying preindustrial peoples and their customs, Christian ethnology failed to provide a comparative study of mankind which was scientific and free of preconceived ideas.

Greco-Roman science and philosophy also proved an important source from which Arabic scholars drew inspiration for their own special contributions. The rapid spread of Arabic conquests prompted social and political histories which embodied explanations of national ascendancy and decline. Conquest led to the incorporation of peoples with different traditions and laws and elicited special concerns with regard to governance. It was during the rapid decline of Arabic fortunes in the fourteenth century that Ibn Khaldūn developed a general theory which explained the growth and decline of national states through a combination of factors which accented social relationships. By focusing on the social relationships within the community, and especially between leaders and followers, Khaldūn added a social dimension to his historical analysis. Khaldūn's call for a science of society, coupled with his considered use of social facts to explain other social facts, stamped him as a singular forerunner of social science. However, his influence on the development of social science in the West was minimal, since Khaldūn's work did not become known until late in the eighteenth century. By this time forces internal to the development of Western civilization already had prompted efforts to establish a general science of mankind based on a progressive evolution from savagery to civilization.

PART II

Developmentalism; Social Science and Anthropology (ca. 1725-1890)

The period between 1725 and 1890 was characterized by an overriding interest in tracing the history of mankind according to natural law. The development of ideas and social institutions from earliest times to the present was the primary objective. Two phases can be distinguished: (1) from 1725 to 1840 and (2) from 1840 to 1890.

During the first phase, philosopher scientists succeeded in separating the study of man, society, and civilization from history and thereby formulated a general social science. To reach the objective of a natural or scientific history of mankind necessitated discriminating the new science from traditional history. This was accomplished by defining a new theoretical base, a new methodology, a different subject matter and factual content, and generalizations derived from the new kinds of facts. The perspective and guidelines developed during this first phase provided the basic framework for the Developmentalist period, despite new emphases on biological processes which followed promulgation of the theory of evolution.

The idea of progress provided the intellectual stimulus for the view that human society began with a stage of savagery, advanced to barbarism, and then achieved the final threshold of civilized development. Through the exercise of reason in accordance with laws governing mental processes, human beings gradually accumulated a greater store of knowledge and utilized this organized experience to advance their social life and to realize the true human potential. Seventeenth- and eighteenth-century scientific achievements in astronomy, mathematics, biology, and chemistry gave exponents of a natural science of mankind a confident expectation that laws of similar exactitude regulated the human process. At the time, however, the projection of a progressive and continuous advancement according to laws regulating mental growth and the accumulation of knowledge outran the natural science view of the natural ordered process. In the eighteenth century a mechanical structural-functional view of nature and of nature's processes predominated. The universe was a unique mechanism which changed outwardly, but superficially. Basic structure and process never really altered, and hence there could be no grand transformations of structure or of advancement from lower to higher orders. Geologist-paleontologist Sir Charles Lyell expressed this view in his *Principles of Geology* (1877) when supporting the theory that natural processes, rather than cataclysms, accounted for the sedimentary and volcanic nature of earth's strata. The succession of life forms observable in the strata also could be accounted for by oscillations in natural processes rather than by continuous transformation.

In his *Positive Philosophy* (1893), Auguste Comte drew up the ultimate synthesis of the progressivist intellectual contribution to general social science. His call for a distinctive science of sociology was based in part on the fact that sociology went beyond natural science in its dynamic view of progressive modification. Comte's work thus marked the transition to the next phase.

The second phase (1840–1890) corresponds with the transition in the natural sciences from a static equilibrium model to a dynamic model. Its culmination came with the introduction of thermodynamic and Darwinian evolutionary theory. The coordination of natural science and social science models of reality led social scientists to rely once again on natural science as the authority for legitimate interpretations of processes which formed and changed societies. Thermodynamic and evolutionary theory thus were applied to man, society, and culture.

The transition to a thermodynamic and evolutionary perspective in the natural sciences was accompanied by a continuous differentiation and specialization of disciplines. Some of these new specializations produced new materials directly relevant to man as a biological, intellective, and social being.

The idea that man had lived in association with extinct animals sparked a search for Adam's ancestors. At the same time, prehistorians began to demonstrate that there was a continuity between the ages of stone, bronze, and iron. Comparative linguistics indicated that it was possible to relate languages historically by analyzing their etymologies and phonology. Comparative mythology disclosed the similarities in the fundamental ideas and identifications of natural forces by distant peoples which could be traced either to common human mental processes or to historic contact. Anthropometry promised a way to connect the different races historically and genetically by a small number of metrical indexes. What these manifold developments regarding man required was a catalytic agent to draw their diverse purposes together. This catalyst was evolutionary theory. Vigorous calls for a general anthropological discipline which would concentrate on the early history of man appeared in the 1860s. However, it was not until 1870 and later that the distinctive character of anthropology began to manifest itself in the unification of physical anthropology, prehistory, and ethnology in professional organizations. With this organized action anthropology split from the main stem of social science and began a growth of its own.

The historic differentiation of anthropology as the science of early man, society, and culture left sociology to pursue the investigation of complex societies, particularly those of the West. However, it was not until sociologists and anthropologists began their respective fieldwork that ambiguities between the two disciplines gave way to substantive distinctions with regard to objectives, kinds of facts collected, and methodology.

The new evolutionary anthropology continued the prior emphasis on the developmental history of ideas and institutions. At the same time, it incorporated a biological orientation that gave a prominent place to genetic processes and natural selection in the formation of racial, ethnic, and individual superiorities. Biological and psychological processes were welded into a unified theory of development in which the advance to civilization was coordinate with a differential advance in body and in mind.

Evolutionary anthropologists, focusing on the early history of mankind, assembled a considerable body of factual detail on the customs, beliefs, marriage practices, ritual, and political organization of primitive societies. They also produced a conceptual inventory for classifying and comparing customs and ideas. The ultimate goal of such comparison was a chart of forms and ideas setting out the intellectual history of man in a logical progression, and which described the evolutionary development of society and culture in three stages—savagery, barbarism, and civilization.

The Developmentalist epoch corresponded in time with the emergence and expansion of industrialization in the West. Its decline came when the expansion of empires halted because there were no new lands and peoples to conquer. The great thrust toward national-state unions was completed. The industrial world looked for new and efficient ways to produce, manage, market, and finance large-scale operations. Europe, as well as the United States, ended a frontier type of expansion and entered a period of consolidation. Interestingly, this shift in objectives in the wider society corresponded with the shift in objectives within the developing science of anthropology.

2

Developmentalism: Foundations for a Study of Man

PROGRESS AS REVELATION AND AS NATURAL LAW

The notion that man had advanced his knowledge and was capable of definite advancement was set in motion before 1725 by scientific achievements in astronomy, mathematics, chemistry, and microscopy. In the works of Copernicus, Newton, Galileo, Descartes, Boyle, Hooke, and Leeuwenhoek, the genius of the human mind reached out to the future. Formulation of a specific theory of human progress, however, was delayed until the eighteenth century, when, according to Bury (1920), Abbé de Saint Pierre published on the perfection of government (1733) and then on the continuous improvement of human knowledge and intellect (1737).

As the idea of progress moved into a central position in the intellectual thought of the eighteenth century, three basic points of view emerged. First, there was the position of seventeenth-century scientists that science was God's own instrument for the revelation of truths. In the eyes of Newton and Boyle, science promoted piety while adding to the theological discoveries passed down from the hands of "commentators . . . preachers, and the ancient fathers themselves" (Boyle, cited by Tuveson 1964:114). Lord Clarendon in an essay, "Of the Reverence Due to Antiquity" (1670), echoed Boyle's sentiments:

> We may indeed well wonder at their gross Ignorance in all things belonging to Astronomy, in which many of the Fathers knew no more than they [Greco-Roman astronomers] and so could not understand many places in the Scriptures. . . . We do not flatter ourselves, if we do believe that we have as much knowledge in Religion as they had, and we have much to answer if we have not more. (Cited by Tuveson 1964:109)

The new scientific view accorded reason a signal place in man's capacity to know God through His Works. It was God's design that man should enlighten himself through the exercise of his reason.

If a rational investigation of nature revealed divine laws and brought man closer to God, why could not human history, rationally studied, promote piety and knowledge of God? For Giambattista Vico (1668–1744; 1948:383) his new science of human history would be a "rational civil theology of divine providence." The task of the *New Science* (Vico 1948: 90–91) would be to demonstrate the historical fact of providence itself. Such a history would reveal the grand design through which providence worked out the destiny of this earthly world—a design which men little understood and which often contradicted human ends. The regularities of human mental processes provided the foundation for the science. History was man's own product, generated in the "modifications of our own human mind. And history cannot be more certain than when he who creates the things also describes them. Thus our Science proceeds exactly as does geometry, which, while it constructs out its elements or contemplates the world of quantity, itself creates it . . ." (Vico 1948:331).

By merging providence and an orderly process in the universe Vico pointed to a scientific explanation of human events which kept divine intervention in the background. The Bishop of Carlisle, Edmund Law (1745), also accommodated science and religion when he set out to reconcile progress and revealed religion to those who now found revelation incompatible with their conception of deity as a first cause (Law 1774:Preface). His discourse was "part of a larger design, tending to show that arts and sciences, natural and revealed religion, have upon the whole been progressive, from the creation of the world to the present time." The Bishop wished to prove that religion and the sciences were not at odds during this progression. There had never been any degeneration of mankind, for God had established different orders of intellectual beings and imparted new knowledge through revelations as men were ready (Law 1774:6, 15). This upward movement in religion was tied to an improvement and a growth in the complexity of society and of human reason. It was not always clear, however, whether Bishop Carlisle saw religion leading the way to human advancement or whether religion accommodated itself to the advances in human knowledge.

Progress and revelation need not be contradictory. There could be progress in theological matters as well as in the arts and sciences. As Tuveson (1964:201) ably demonstrated, Christian metaphysics was no bar to acceptance of the idea of progress during the eighteenth century, for "the metaphysical, almost sacred character of the dogma of unilinear progress was connected with a faith in progressive redemption effected through temporal history."

The idea that God in his benevolence watched over and guided man's enlightenment could be translated into a closely related second attitude. This held that God was only a first cause. Having designed a mechanical universe governed by law, He stood aloof, leaving it to run itself. However, the products of man's reasoned efforts to understand would be no different from what would flow from a view of deity as providence. In unraveling the design of the universe, as Montesquieu (1949(1):1) noted, man discovered the laws governing animals, men, and deity—all traceable to God as creator and preserver. To admit God's hand behind nature's design would not be difficult, for there was something about nature, as Hume (1854(4):420) observed, that indicated an intelligent maker. Hume was convinced that no reasonable person could seriously doubt the primary role of God and religion in life.

The very regularity of a universe governed by natural law impressed most eighteenth-century intellectuals as good reason for believing the design had a maker. Hence, they preferred to count themselves deists.

The third point of view stressed materialistic processes and denied any place to a creator. Here French Encyclopedists led the way as they criticized Church dogma as repressive of man's full intellectual development. Man's richest asset was reason. Subject to natural law, reason provided the surest guide to the human destiny. Science, the gift of reason, had been secured only as reason was liberated from fetters religion forged out of superstition. According to Isaak Iselin (1723–1782), man's progress might follow a providential plan, but the great lights who had brought salvation to mankind were the scientists of England, France, and Germany and not the saints and apostles (Clark 1955:189–191).

In attempting to separate natural processes from divine intervention, French materialists directed their attention to human nature. Perfection of life in society could be reached through perfection of reason and morality by following the model of nature. An ethic inspired by nature, as Baron D'Holbach (1723–1789) counseled, was far superior to any drawn out of religious prejudice. Nature counseled man to love himself, to reproduce, and to extend his happiness by forming peaceful communities where citizens united to heal each other and where human character could be formed in pursuit of an active, courageous, and useful life guided by reason (D'Holbach 1853:280–281). Religion subverted both society and human character by rendering man a slave to God and to superstition, by introducing fratricidal strife, and by urging man to be useful to himself without any real concern for others. Religion destroyed the natural liberties of man and sustained political tyranny. By following nature mankind could build a much better morality, common to all.

> True morality should be the same for all the inhabitants of the globe. The savage man and the civilised; the white man, the red man, the black man; Indian and European, Chinaman and Frenchman, Negro and Lapp have the same nature. The differences between them are only modifications of the common nature produced by climate, government, education, opinions, and the various causes which operate on them. Men differ only in the ideas they form of happiness and the means which they have imagined to obtain it. (D'Holbach 1770, cited by Bury 1920:166–167)

As for God and the soul, they simply did not exist. They had no part in what happened to human beings.

Actually, it made little difference for explanation whether one took a stand as a crass materialist or as a providential naturalist. Natural processes accounted for human progress under either view. Herder (1774–1803), who defended God's design against the materialists, underscored the fact that "In natural philosophy we never reckon upon miracles; we observe laws, which we perceive everywhere equally effectual, undeviating, and regular. And shall man, with his powers, changes, and passions, burst these chains of nature?" (cited by Slotkin 1965:286).

Both providential naturalists and materialists looked to John Locke (1947) for their interpretation of mental processes. Locke set out to disprove the presence of "innate principles [or] ... primary notions ... stamped upon the mind of man" by showing that all human knowledge was a product of experience derived from the interplay of sensory perception and the reflective operation of the mind.

Through Locke's sensory psychology every man began life as a *tabula rasa* and proceeded to a mature organization of experience. From this new empirical base man could be proved the master inventor of society and all its associated products—technical, legal, moral, religious, and artistic. Without surrendering his Catholic faith, Condillac (1746) introduced Locke's empirical sensationalism to the French. With regard to language, for example, Condillac described a beginning in the cries and gestures with which man was endowed by nature to express his feelings. Through the interplay of judgment and self-interest, mediated by self-other comparison and pleasure-pain considerations, Condillac even found a natural source for morality. With increasing faith in the use of reason to comprehend experience, the role of divine revelation in seeking truth faded. Only a few progressivists, such as Monboddo (1795(4):157–164), linked the advancement of civilization to intermediaries sent from God, who, as god kings of Egypt, China, and Peru, revealed the inventions of civilization to their people.

The Original Human Estate: Corruption or Ignorance?

A singular stumbling block to the progressive view of human history centered in the biblical view of man and his relation to God. Man, in Christian doctrine, began his earthly career with an act of arrogant disobedience, thereby corrupting his relation to God and committing all his descendants to a step-by-step descent into a fulsome degradation. Consequently, the newly discovered savages represented not an initial step along a ladder of progress but a last step into the dungeon of corruption.

How were exponents of a new-won faith in human reason to combat the theological dogma? Some, like the Encyclopedists and those of a materialist persuasion, attacked the established Church as a perversion of a true and natural doctrine. Others, like De Brosses (1760) and Goguet (1775), accommodated degradation and progression by holding that man indeed had been reduced to a state of savagery as a result of acts which led to the Deluge and the dispersion. From that degraded estate man had moved forward to civilization by virtue of reason. One could, of course, ignore the Christian theory of degradation by segregating theological and scientific purpose and method. However, it was difficult to ignore the efforts of churchmen to invest the scientific interpretation of man with the stench of heterodoxy. The new geological, paleontological, biological, and archeological discoveries that strengthened support for the theory of human progress provoked counterinterpretation by churchmen. Archbishop Richard Whately (1861) spearheaded a theological attack, which prompted Tylor to devote a full chapter to refutation of the degradation theory. Tylor (1874(1):36) wrote in some irritation that he was tired of hearing the pulpit derogate the ethnological theory that man had risen from a low original condition as delusive fantasy. For Tylor all evidence contradicted the degradation theory. Archeology, history, and ethnography disclosed a gradual cumulation of skill and knowledge that never was wholly lost even though individual empires fell into rubble. Civilization was the fruit of man's reason, and to be human meant to be guided forward by the light of reason (Tylor 1874(1):63–69).

Parallels in Christian Doctrine and Developmentalist Theory

The sharp conflicts between Christian exegetes and Developmentalists in point of fact masked some rather striking parallels in their respective positions. Carl Becker (1932:31, 129) called attention to similarities in the theological and progressivist positions when chiding eighteenth-century Philosophes for demolishing the Heavenly City of St. Augustine and then substituting their own faith, the religion of humanity.

First, it is evident that both Christian and Developmentalist believed that human history moved according to a universal plan. In the instance of Christian dogma, the hand behind the human drama was God's. In the case of progress, man was nature's handiwork, with God sitting in the wings or excluded entirely. For both, too, the importance of any historical event would rest with the way in which it clued the human design. Christian historians used events to write a divine history, while Developmentalists gathered data to describe a universal advancement in reason and morality.

Second, both Christian and Developmentalist were utopian. According to the former, God would arrest human corruption with a timely entrance on stage and introduce the millennium. According to the latter, natural processes would carry mankind forward to realization of an inner humanity—to a free society populated by a free citizenry; to a state where man responded to the elegances of taste; to a world organized by the voluntary cooperation of men governed by right attitudes, thoughts, and intentions.

Third, Christians and Developmentalists were fascinated by contemplation of fulfillment of the design. Christians looked forward with awesome exultation to the closing out of human rule, and a progressivist dreamed of human excellence realized. Priestley (1771:4–5) could not suppress a happy exuberance at the thought of that future paradise which must arrive. Progress followed inevitably from the natural course of human affairs and expressed the true nature of man.

Fourth, the metaphysics of both Christianity and Developmentalism linked events by a chain of causes, divine or natural, that led inexorably and irreversibly to a single and uniform end. Christians and progressivists, as well as later evolutionists, were committed to a nonreversible, unilinear, and developmental process. The directions, of course, were different. Christian exegetes saw man beginning at the summit and sliding to the bottom, at which time God would intervene to save man from his own corrupt nature. Developmentalists, on the other hand, saw man as beginning at the bottom and toiling up the slope, faltering at times, but regaining his balance and pulling himself forward by hewing to the prescriptions of natural law.

Fifth, both Christian and Developmentalist applied absolute standards in their evaluative judgments. As evil concentrated the antithesis of the Christian ideal, so unnatural acts contradicted the natural and forestalled the path to progress.

Sixth, the human drama constituted a war between conflicting forces, but with the outcome foreordained. The corrupting forces of evil would be overcome just as the natural would triumph over the corruption of the artificial or unnatural. Even Marxists committed capitalist and proletarian to an inevitable conflict which followed the direction of natural law (dialectical materialism). There never was any doubt in scientific Marxism that good would triumph over evil.

Here the coincidences between fundamental Christianity and Developmentalist doctrine come to an end; for explanations made the difference. Key processes in biblical history turned on divine intervention, whereas Developmentalists underscored the materialistic processes by which the human mind operated. Without divine revelation and intervention, change in Christian society would be impossible because men were unable to rise above their corrupted natures. Under the doctrine of advancement, men moved forward through the natural operations of the mind, cumulating knowledge and ethical experience to be applied to ever wider sectors of human life and affairs.

PROGRESS AND FORMULATION OF A SCIENCE OF MAN

History, Natural Law, and a Natural History of Mankind

The enthusiastic optimism regarding man and his destiny which captivated social philosophers during the Age of Enlightenment seems to have been generated by two primary ideas. First, nature was very much like a machine, governed by principles of organization and processes that were purposeful; and second, in science man had uncovered the key for unlocking nature's secrets. Man was a part of nature, and in the book of nature man must read his own history, past, present, and future. It is this idealization of nature and nature's laws that led Rousseau to contemptuously reject the distorted image of man so commonly revealed in traditional histories. In prophetic tone, he declared,

> O man, of whatever country you are, and whatever your opinions may be, take heed; behold your history, such as I have thought to read it, not in books written by your fellow-creatures, who are liars, but in nature, which never lies. All that comes from her will be true; nor will you meet with anything false, unless I have involuntarily put in something of my own. The times of which I am going to speak are far distant, but how much you have changed from what you really are in that time. (Rousseau 1962(1):142)

Appealing to natural law, Rousseau argued that social distinctions were artificial historic inventions that contravened nature's design. Unnatural arrangements forged under the name of civilization had corrupted and continued to corrupt man's intrinsic nature.

The certitude of natural processes also was used by Condorcet (1795) to defend his sketch of the progress of the human mind and to forecast future developments.

> If man can, with almost complete assurance, predict phenomena when he knows their laws, and if, even when he does not, he can still, with great expectation of success, forecast the future on the basis of his experience of the past, why, then, should it be regarded as a fantastic undertaking to sketch, with some pretence to truth, the future destiny of man on the basis of his history? The sole foundation for belief in the natural sciences is this idea, that the general laws directing the phenomena of the universe, known or unknown, are necessary and constant. Why should this principle be any less true for the development of the intellectual and moral faculties of man than for the other operations of nature? (Condorcet 1955:173)

There was a place, then, for a new kind of history, a natural or scientific history of mankind. Such a natural history held a number of advantages over traditional history. First, the new scientific history was concerned with the invariant determinism of natural law, and hence could achieve a level of prediction denied to historians confined to the accidents of wars, migrations, and revolutions of nations. Second, the natural history would be comprehensive, expressing that singular unity of mankind and the continuity of human development. As Kames (1779(1):1) put it, only a history of the progress of the human species from its savage stage to its highest civilization could convey a proper sense of unity and of destiny. This unity was visible not only in the shared capacities and potentials of mankind as a species but in common aims and directions discoverable in the continuity of human development. Both the savage and the philosopher, Ferguson (1789) noted, were imbued alike with a desire to progress. Each had made different advances, but the results were comparable.

> The latest efforts of human invention are but a continuation of certain devices which were practiced in the earliest ages of the world, and in the rudest stage of mankind. What the savage projects, or observes, in the forest, are the steps which led nations, more advanced, from the architecture of the cottage to that of the palace, and conducted the human mind from the perceptions of sense to the general conclusion of science. (Ferguson 1789:122–123)

The savage represented a rude and simple beginning, and not the end of a process of degeneration. The progressivist format accorded the savage a secure place in history and introduced him to the Western world as the model of one's own cultural ancestors and essential contributors to the human adventure. As Ferguson (1789:6–7) noted, "The Romans might have found an image of their own ancestors in the representations they have given of ours. . . . It is in their present [savage] condition, that we are to behold, as in a mirror, the features of our own progenitors."

The equivalence of contemporary and ancient savagery could be justified by the parallel between the social ontogeny of the individual and the social phylogeny of the species. Kames suggested (1779(2):468–469) that the individual progresses from infancy to maturity somewhat as every nation progresses from a savage state to a maturity in arts and sciences.

A third advantage of the new natural history of the species lay in the fact that it would be a people's history. Unlike historians, who dealt with the individual careers of rulers, the natural historians were concerned with social or group affairs. Hence, the emphasis was on institutions, ideas, and customs—what later would be referred to as social and cultural facts.

The institutional and ideological focus projected for the new science meant that natural historians must write up their materials differently from the format found in traditional histories. Monboddo (1795(4):401) made this quite clear after completing his account of the history of religion.

> I have also given the history of Arts and Sciences, and likewise of Government, which, together with religion, comprehend what I call the History of Man, at least in the state of civil society: For, as intelligence is of the essence of man, and that which distinguishes him from other animals on this earth, I consider his history to be that of the operations of his intellectual faculty, which are all guided and directed by . . . the . . . arts and sciences, government, and religion; as it is by these that his character, sentiments, manners, customs, and institutions, are produced.

In turn Ferguson (1789) wrote on the general characteristics of human nature, the history of "rude nations," and the history of "policy and arts." He included discussions on the state of nature, self-preservation, principle of union among mankind, war, intellectual powers, moral sentiments, and happiness. Like most intellectuals in the eighteenth century, Ferguson had a special interest in the history and purpose of political organization, and in this connection he discussed the influence of climate and situation, population and wealth, effects attending advances in civil and commercial arts, nature of civil liberty, and lastly the causes of corruption and decline. In his project for a history of mankind, Meiners (1785:1–10) called for statements on the history of the earth; the oldest residence of mankind and how men had distributed themselves over the earth; the physical, intellectual, and character potential of the different peoples; degrees of refinement in subsistence, drink, dwellings, clothing, ornament, and table customs; the education of children; the treatment of wives; forms of government and laws; manners; beliefs regarding prosperity and decency, pride and shame; and, finally, the opinions and knowledge of all peoples, especially the "unenlightened and half-civilized."

The fourth and final advantage that natural history held over history lay in the sense of purpose and of self-direction which it brought to the human drama. After reviewing the rise and fall of the Roman Empire, the historian Edward Gibbon (1776–1788) declared that human history was nothing more than a tabulation of the crimes, foolishness, and misfortunes of mankind. Progressivists held greater expectations for man. A natural history of the human species would help to promote the future happiness of man. By studying the exciting character of man, Ferguson (1789:4) hoped he might discover the laws governing man's animal and intellectual natures. Practical suggestions then could be derived and applied to the purposes of human life. The new science of man thus would be more than a simple record; it would produce substance that could advance man to the ultimate realization of the human self. The immediate purpose was to apply a scientific method to human history in order to trace a natural growth which began in savagery, passed through the intermediate stage of barbarism, and then moved up to civilization. However, the ultimate goal was to draw the guidelines by which civilized men could avoid the painful turns and the tardy pace that had dogged savage and barbaric steps because of errors at odds with nature's laws. So it happened that the wide spectrum of the human situation opened before eighteenth-century philosopher-scientists, and they were forced to confront the nature of man, society, tradition, how things change, and how nations may lose their sense of direction because of artificial laws and extravagances. The idea of progress drew scholars into ultimate human purposes. They were attracted by the notion that the processes of civilization finally would produce a type of community and a mode of life congenial to human nature and the best that could be achieved according to the potential of that nature.

Like ancient Greeks and Romans, progressivist natural historians were utopian in orientation. However, in the eighteenth century the utopian ideal had the advantage of a scientific validation unavailable to the ancients. Roman history itself had become universalized, linked to a continuum, and given a common direction according to the determination of natural law. Progressivist historians also went beyond Greek and Roman social philosophers in that they defined the domain of a separate science. They made group phenomena the substantive domain of fact for their discipline. Conceptualization of a theory of social and cultural progress likewise led eighteenth-century natural historians to the formulation of a special method —the so-called comparative method.

BASIC ASSUMPTIONS AND METHOD FOR A NATURAL HISTORY OF MANKIND

Uniform and Continuous Processes and the Psychic Unity of Mankind

The laws by which scientists hope to express their findings necessarily coordinate with the assumption that regularity and recurrence are a part of the phenomena under investigation. The image of the physical sciences in the eighteenth century, sparked by the achievements in astronomy, chemistry, and mathematics, emphasized the production of uniform effects through the operation of continuous and uniform processes. This was the lesson to be drawn also from James Hutton's (1785) description of the incremental effects of water dropping to the earth's surface—processes now at work in altering the earth were the same as those acting in the past, both in type and in degree.

The commitment to a natural history of mankind necessarily meant a commitment to a principle of uniform and continuous processes. Without such an assumption it would be impossible to account for the continuous production and linkage of past and present events which the doctrine of progress required. The location of these uniform processes lay not outside but within man himself. Though exhibiting physical variety in different climates and habitats, and even demonstrating differences in character, all men in nature appeared basically alike. When comparing the rude character, customs, ways, and accomplishments of American tribes with the more "polished" nations, Robertson (1822(1):218–219) was quite convinced that

> a human being as he comes originally from the hand of nature, is everywhere the same. At the first appearance in the state of infancy, whether it be among the rudest savages, or in the most civilized nations, we can discern no quality which marks any distinction or superiority. The capacity of improvement seems to be the same, and the talents he may afterwards acquire, as well as the virtues he may be rendered capable of exercising, depend in a great measure upon the state of society in which he is placed. To this state his mind naturally accommodates itself, and from it receives discipline and culture. . . . It is only by attending to this great principle that we can discover what is the character of man in every different period of his progress.

Robertson's linkage of the concept of uniform processes, the human faculty, and the psychic unity of mankind was supported by the judgment of those who would study man as a social being capable of perfecting his character and society. Perfectibility was intrinsic to man's nature, as man's penchant for intellectualizing and moralizing his world disclosed. Progressivists hoped to arrange the triumphant march of mankind in a logical chain of ideas and institutions that coordinated an advance from simplicity to complexity. The equality of races meant that each was capable of moving ahead independently. However, owing to the principle of uniform processes, the logic of development would be the same or parallel. The logic for the exclusion of history or historic variants from a natural history of mankind is apparent, since the principle of uniform processes, which dealt with structural change described by the stages of savagery, barbarism, and civilization, overrode historic variation.

Man's rational and moral nature led progressivist social historians to take man out of nature while subjecting him to natural law. The "human faculty" lifted man above the raw forces of nature and accorded him a special environment, society. This was tantamount to ordering reality into two levels—notably, the social or psychosocial and the organic, to which a third, the inorganic, could be added. Man was supraorganic, a distinct grade of being, and his basic nature, reproduced with each passing generation, had never changed or evolved in coordination with body changes. There would be no advantage, then, in taking man out of his natural social setting—"like a wild man . . . caught in the woods"—with the intention of locating his original nature (Ferguson 1789:6–9). It would be equally pointless to come at man's original nature by describing a supposed advance from a "state of animal sensibility, to the attainment of reason, to the use of language, and to the habit of society." Man had always been a separate and distinct race and superior to animals. Pleasure-pain, self-preservation, reproduction, affiliation with kind, and pugnacity could be found in both man and animals. However, man was not characterized by a rigid governance of instinct found in animals. Man was a generalized being and a rational being besides, unfettered by instinct. Thus the terms "propensity," "inclination," and "disposition" better described the variable quality of human nature. Smith (1937:13) observed that barter was common to mankind and a natural propensity of man which probably stemmed from the human faculties of reason and speech. Whether a "given" of original human nature or not, Smith reported that no animal other than man exchanged products by barter and trade, and the disposition was one that could be cultivated.

Whatever its source, man's capacity for society was vital to realization of his essential qualities. Reason distinguished man from other animals, and by reason man was led to separate the admired from the despised and right from wrong. In the basic moral relations linking man to man, one found incontrovertible proof of man's uniqueness (Herder 1952(2):85–104; Ferguson 1789:16–17). In Ferguson's (1789:25) judgment one had to begin, as had Montesquieu, with the fact that everywhere man is born in society and never leaves it. Indeed, man needs the company of other men to call forth moral sentiments and to stimulate inventiveness (Kames 1761). Outside society every man was nothing but an "imperfect animal who cannot answer the purpose for which he is in this world . . . intended by God and nature" (Monboddo 1795(4):96–97). Even Rousseau, who delighted in idealizing the natural at the expense of the artificialities and corruptions of civilized society, never considered the natural state of man to be a life of individual isolation (Lovejoy 1923).

Coordinate Biological and Psychosocial Gradation?

Taxonomy and the Great Chain of Being. Looking out upon the universe of nature, eighteenth-century philosopher-scientists were impressed with the fact that everything had its place in the hierarchy of difference and of perfectibility. The universe expressed a grand design in which each part, great or small, illustrated and fulfilled a part of that design. Man had a place in that grand design, and the efforts of progressivist social historians to assign man a social and cultural domain can be viewed as an attempt to locate man in the natural order of things.

Developments within the natural sciences at the time both supported and questioned the integrity of the psychosocial level which natural historians accorded to man. The emergent biological evolutionary theory fostered by Buffon and Lamarck challenged the fixity of species and raised the possibility of evolving biological and psychosocial gradations. A more immediate and direct influence for splitting mankind into a graded series and for emphasizing distinctions of a biological and psychosocial nature can be traced to the taxonomic energies of eighteenth-century natural scientists. These taxonomic attempts were not wholly free of Christian views of the creation and the metaphysical conception of a great chain of being linking higher forms with lower ones through a descending scale of spirituality. Linnaeus (1735) dedicated himself to formulating a scheme of classification that would systematize the diversity of God's creation, plant, animal, and man.

Classifications in kind or in grade are not easily made because of fine distinctions that constantly challenge the judgment of the taxonomist. Ambiguities faced in a graded chain of being were cleverly drawn into focus in *The Lay Monastery* (cited by Lovejoy 1942:234–235).

> 'Tis easy to distinguish . . . kinds, till you come to the highest one, and the lowest of that next above; and then the difference is so nice that the limits and Boundaries of their Species seem left unsettled by Nature to perplex the curious, and to humble the proud philosopher. The Ape or the Monkey that bears the greatest similitude to Man, is the next Order of Animals below him. Nor is the Disagreement between the basest Individuals of our species and the Ape or Monkey so great, but that, were the latter endow'd with the Faculty of Speech, they might perhaps as justly claim the Rank and Dignity of the human Race, as the savage *Hotentot* or the stupid native of Nova Zembla [Novaya Zemlya, Samoyed] . . . . The most perfect of this order of Beings, the Orang-Outang, as he is called by the natives of Angola, that is the Wild Man, or the Man of the Woods, has the Honour of Bearing the greatest Resemblance to Human Nature. Tho' all that Species have some Agreement with us in our Features, many instances being found of Men of

Monkey Races; yet this has the greatest likeness, not only in his Countenance, but in the structure of his Body, his Ability to Walk upright, as well as on all fours, his Organs of Speech, his ready Apprehension, and his gentle and tender Passions, which are not found in any of the Ape Kind, and in various other respects.

A surgeon and member of the Royal Society, Edward Tyson (1699), had examined and dissected one of these "wild men." "Our Pygmie [actually a chimpanzee]," he concluded, "is no man nor yet a common ape, but a sort of animal between both" (cited by Cunningham 1908(38):15). The pygmy, in point of grade, represented the link between animal and man, just as man, "part a Brute, part an Angel," bridged the "Visible and the Invisible World next about us" (cited by Greene 1959:176–178).

Confronting the classification of man, Linnaeus boldly assigned man and ape to the order Anthropomorpha, under the class Quadrupeds. Writing to J. Gmelin in 1747, he observed that he could find no generic difference between man and ape, and he challenged his critics to produce evidence to the contrary (cited by Greene 1959:184). He ended on the note, "But, if I had called man an ape, or vice-versa, I should have fallen under the ban of all the ecclesiastics. It may be that as a naturalist I ought to have done so." At first Linnaeus (1735) distinguished four varieties of man within the species *Homo sapiens* (European, American, Asiatic, African). By 1758, however, there were two species of *Homo*, notably *sapiens* and *troglodytes*, the latter of which included Tyson's *Homo sylvestris Orang Outang*.

A classificationist imbued with the doctrine of a creation in grade would be inclined to consider each of these graduated forms as fixed in species. Such was Linnaeus' view, and such was the position of Monboddo (1795 (4):25–34) when attempting to erect a series of grades stretching from brute to man. He began with a "wild boy" found in the woods near Hanover, Germany, who crawled on all fours and could utter only a few cries. Next came the brutish "wild man" or Ourang-Outang. Monboddo described the Ourang-Outang as possessing "a sense of what is decent and becoming, which is peculiar to man . . . a sense of humour . . . the feeling of humanity in strong degree; and a sense of justice." "Wild men" also had made progress in the arts of life, building huts and using sticks in attack and defense. Their use of fire and burial of their dead, though in error, convinced Monboddo that the "Ourang-Outang is not only a man, with respect to his body, but also in mind, the principal part of man and all other animals." Though incapable of speech at present, Monboddo anticipated that "wild men" would learn to speak as soon as Europeans and Africans settled nearby and instructed them in the art. A "wild girl" taken up in Labrador and shipwrecked on the coast of France represented a higher stage because of a fully erect posture, full use of the hands, and possession of special arts, notably swimming, language, and music. She and her people also were more advanced since they no longer lived by collecting nature's fruits and vegetables but by hunting and fishing. Monboddo (1795(4):38) used this point to underscore the fact that man was largely a product of the arts. Indeed, man was "so much a creature of art, that without art he has not the perfect use of his own body."

The last statement is the key to Monboddo's attempt to coordinate a graded scale of body use and body gradations with a graduated sequence of the arts. He held that man was highly variable within his species, as befitted his place at the top of the organic scale; hence the inclination to accept the Ourang-Outang or "wild man" as a variety of the human species, or a species of man, as had the illustrious taxonomist Linnaeus. It is not surprising, then, that Monboddo, in constructing a developmental sequence in grade, based on a progressive coordination of body, mind, and arts, denied that any qualitative mental gap separated his second grade, the "wild man," from civilized man. The potential was there, hidden from view, simply because the "wild man" had yet to be induced to cultivate his mind and the arts.

> There is no *natural* difference between our minds and theirs [the "brutes"] and the superiority we have over them is *adventitious.* . . . Allowing that . . . we can go farther than the brute with any culture can go . . . this is saying no more than that . . . we have by Nature greater capabilities than them. . . . I deny that there is any other difference betwixt us and them. (Cited by Lovejoy 1933(30):289)

In the above statement Monboddo seemingly asserted a common affinity between man and the higher apes with regard to their mental qualifications. In effect, he anticipated Darwin. However, it should not be forgotten that Monboddo was defending inclusion of the "wild man" (chimpanzee) in the human species at a time when the proper taxonomy of the chimpanzee and higher apes was ambiguous. Moreover, the fixity of his graded series allowed no room for a coordinated physical, mental, and social alteration—although, as noted, he anticipated that his "wild man" would improve his culture when Europeans instructed him in language and domestic arts. The idea of an intraspecies transformation would not come until 1813, when Prichard (1855) suggested an evolution that began with the Negro race and culminated with the white. Prichard used geographic and social circumstances to account for changes in physical constitution in coordination with the advance to civilization.

Man—A Superorganic and Unitary Species: Eighteenth-Century Naturalists

The issue of racial differences leads naturally to a consideration of the possibility of separate or unitary origins and histories for human types. It also implicates the structural fixity and variability of forms.

Christianity supported a unitary creation since all men were descendants of the primal pair. However, in 1655 Isaac de la Peyrère, in a work entitled

Praeadamitae, stirred the problem of multiple versus single origins by arguing that Adam and his descendants had not sired all the races and peoples of the world. More than this, Adam was not the first man. The ancestors of Chaldeans, Egyptians, Chinese, and Mexicans had preceded him. In scientific dress, the issue of a single or multiple creation would be translated into a debate over monogenesis versus polygenesis. Kames (1778(1):10–12) supported the polygenetic position by arguing that human varieties were created for their special environments and hence were not altered and shaped by climate. He pointed out that in the Arctic men, birds, beasts, and fish were endowed with a layer of fat which serves to protect them from the cold. Neither food, climate, nor accidental causes appeared capable of accounting for the differences among human types. Moreover, when scanning unmixed peoples in islands distant from a continent, one could not help being struck by the variability of their basic character. Some were bold, mischievous, and intractable—such as the Negroes adjacent to New Guinea—whereas others turned out to be simple and peaceful. Yet Kames also held that there were universal features in human nature that were invariable and unchanging, despite time and place. Failure to arrive at a working relationship between the general and the particular with regard to human types led Kames into ambiguities comparable to those faced in discriminating general social history from particulate history.

With regard to multiple and single origins, the weight of natural science judgment at the time inclined to monogenesis. Man was a unitary species, and variation was a product of modification of an archetypal form induced by the influences of geographic environments and modes of life. Leaving aside the troglodytic species distinguished by Linnaeus, the known human races were grouped under one species, *Homo sapiens.* Buffon (1812) likewise held to the theory of degeneration from a primal type:

> there was originally but one individual species of man, which after being multiplied and diffused over the whole surface of the earth, underwent diverse changes, from the influence of the climate, from the difference of food, and of the mode of living, from epidemical distempers, as also from the intermixture, varied *ad infinitum* of individuals more or less resembling each other; . . . at first, these alterations were less considerable, and confined to individuals . . . afterwards, from continued action of the above causes becoming more general, more sensible, and more fixed, they formed varieties in the species; . . . these varieties have been, and are still perpetuated from generation to generation, in the same manner as certain deformities, and certain maladies, pass from parents to their children. . . . (Cited by Greene 1959:224)

Blumenbach (1775), in turn, explained human variation by the theory of degeneration. Unlike Linnaeus, Blumenbach was struck by the fact that man, in contrast with animals, possessed reason, speech, upright posture, true hands, and was uniquely lacking in instinct (Blumenbach 1865:82–86). Hence, he assigned man to the Bimanus Order and the manlike apes to the Quadrumana. Moreover, Blumenbach denied the possibility of some kind of intraspecies evolution. There was no rudimentary ancestral wild species to which individual man, like cattle escaping into the forest, might revert. On the contrary, man was the most perfect of all domestic animals. Furthermore, no original wild species of man existed, for there were no conditions in nature, climate, or mode of life that could maintain such a wild original (Blumenbach 1865:240).

Man was, indeed, a very special kind of social animal.

Exploration of man's relations to the rest of the world through the instrument of taxonomy provided new evidence for considering his kinship with the animal world. Combined with the idea of a graded series of created types, taxonomy aroused some to project a natural continuum in grade of physical, mental, moral, and social development. However, at all points, human reason and man's social capabilities expressed in language, morality, government, religion, and the technical and fine arts described such a wide gap that man and animal were better viewed as qualitatively different and designed for separate ends. Animals followed an organic path, man a supraorganic destiny. The most important criteria for uniting men in a single species were not physical but mental, moral, and social. Such was Herder's conclusion when conceding that Tyson's anatomical comparisons of man and the Ourang-Outang revealed similarities, both inside and out, including the "shape of the brain . . . the broad breast, flat shoulders, a similar face, a skull of like form; heart, lungs, liver, spleen, stomach, intestines . . ." (Herder 1952(2):87–89). It was not so much the gross anatomical comparisons that counted as relations and functions. In man the size of brain in relation to weight exceeded that of animals, and man's upright bearing was central to the very purpose of his genus and of his unique character (Herder 1952:86–93). After making physical comparisons based on skin color, type of hair, shape of head, configuration of face and orbits, and noting correspondences in the foramen magnum of Negro crania and of other races, Prichard (1855(1):113–119) concluded that the Negro did not fall outside the human species. However, the high variability of physical type according to climate, and especially mode of life, suggested to Prichard that the structural homologies that would reveal the unity of mankind in no uncertain terms would not be physical. In mind, morality, and religious beliefs, Prichard (1855(2):713–714) found that the simplest and the most civilized peoples were so similar that they must be considered members of a single human family.

Clearly, eighteenth-century taxonomists issued no mandate for a consideration of biological processes in accounting for differences in civilizational achievement. On the contrary, whether one pursued the search for man's intrinsic nature from a physical or a social viewpoint, the pathways converged on the distinctive human faculty. Reason separated man from animal, and reason united mankind in a single species. Though physical environment induced body variations, at no point could such variations be considered sufficient to describe a separate species—and, apparently, never would. Man was a relatively fixed species, varying within a narrow range, but never changing his essential nature. Man's superior mental and moral faculties, in contrast with animals, indicated that his natural environment was society and not the physical world. The natural history of the human species therefore was not inscribed in a common physical growth shaped by constant environmental forces. Rather, the key to the history of mankind must be sought in social institutions which, following the logic of the human mind, could be arranged in sequences exhibiting a flow from the rude to the refined and from the simple to the complex. The uniformity and constancy of the human faculty, together with the moral imperative to improve, insured that this development everywhere would follow a similar course.

Theory and Method of Natural Historians: The "Comparative Method"

With a natural history of mankind as their objective, progressivists of the eighteenth century committed their science to a synthesizing role. Facts from many different peoples were collected and compared for similarities and differences to construct chapters in the history of human progress. As gleaners and sifters of facts, they combed the reports and reminiscences of navigators, explorers, missionaries, traders, captives, military officers, and administrators; but they would not be inspired to enter foreign lands to observe and record for themselves. Sifting the hearsay and the fabulous thus would be one mark of the outstanding scholar. More often than not, as Robertson (1822(1):157) observed, the reporting of the customs and character of strange peoples fell to adventurers, who, under the spell of prejudices, were unable to contemplate the variety of mankind objectively and in a discerning way. Consensus in the reporting of facts constituted a firm criterion of reliability, to which one applied the measure of reasonable expectation. At all costs the new science of man should not be cluttered with speculations like those indulged in by theorists on the "state of nature" and the beginnings of society in a social compact. The "natural historian," Ferguson (1789:3–13) cautioned, "thinks himself obliged to collect facts, not to offer conjectures."

Establishing the authenticity of data drawn from the narratives of explorers and travelers was but one aspect of the task confronting natural historians if they were to distinguish themselves from traditional historians. The other task was to establish the validity of facts deriving from group rather than individual choice and action. Progressivists were group oriented and concerned themselves with behavioral uniformities prescribed in habits, customs, manners, laws, modes of life, as well as national characters entrenched by habitat, climate, and mode of life. Millar (1806:5–8) cited the chance probability that special persons might leave their mark on a community and its organization, but he doubted the power of individual interposition in which historians placed their trust. Rather, outstanding personalities, educated in the ways of their countrymen and "Under the influence of all the prejudices derived from ancient usuage[sic], . . . he will commonly be disposed to prefer the system already established. . . ." Hence, gradualism predominated, for though the individual could vary, he could not easily transcend the tradition of his group. In accenting the group nature of their materials, natural historians pinpointed what later would be referred to as social, cultural, and ethnographic facts.

Establishment of the ethnographic fact as an authentic substantive unit provided progressivists with a descriptive and measurable form useful in discriminating themselves from historians. Method could be used in the same way. Seeking to clothe themselves in the garment of science, progressivists were alive to the need for induction from empirical facts. Their method ideally combined deduction and induction. Yet their inductive operation fell short because they were committed to a metaphysical concept —progress—which they had secured with the ironclad guarantee of natural law.

A primary classification and comparison of ethnographic bits and pieces according to their similarities would be the beginning. The next task was to arrange them in a sequential order that implied the derivation of a succeeding form from a prior form. At this point the historian of progress applied the principle that the rude, the simple, and the irrational always preceded the refined, the complex, and the rational. Moreover, the constancy of mental processes in the face of similar challenges permitted the reading of the savage mind by the technique of analogical introspection. Man reasoned largely with the aid of analogy, and hence analogies provided the surest access to the motives, feelings, and ideas of savage and civilized alike. "Every man," observed Kames (1778(3):214), "is conscious of a self-motive power in himself, [and] from the uniformity of nature, we infer the same power in every one of our species." Progressivists were so confident that analogical reasoning constituted a uniform intellective process among mankind that they unhesitatingly set out to probe the very origins of beliefs and customs. An empirical associational psychology stemming from Locke (1947) supplied the theoretical base. Every mental phenomenon began with physical sensations. Sensory perceptions at first gave rise to concrete or representational ideas, which were gradually refined to higher levels of abstraction or generality as human mental experience grew and the exercise of faculties sharpened the mind's operations. Sensory ideas were first steps in the organization of knowledge.

The technique of analogical introspection, in combination with the principle of simplicity-complexity, was indispensable to the kind of history natural historians intended to write. The tool of analogical introspection liberated them from reliance on the kinds of documentary materials to which historians were anchored. Though undocumented in a historical sense, the thought and activities of savage men could be given documentation through the natural laws which governed human mental processes. Equivalent situations must produce equivalent habits and thoughts. "What," queried Ferguson (1789:6–7), "should distinguish a German or a Briton, in the habits of his mind or his body, in his manners or apprehensions, from an American [Indian], who, like him, with his bow and his dart, is left to traverse the forests; and in a like severe or variable climate is obliged to subsist by the chace [sic]?" Contemporary savages thus were stand-ins for the savage past of mankind.

The strategy developed by natural historians was much simplified owing to their assumptions. An investigator would conduct a preliminary survey of world societies and selectively assemble links in a logical chain of development. As Kames (1761:22–23) observed when investigating the evolution of law:

> In tracing the [natural] history of law through dark ages unprovided with records, or so slenderly provided as not to afford any regular historical chain, we must endeavour, the best way we can, to supply the broken links, by hints from poets and historians, by collateral facts, and by cautious conjecture drawn from the nature of the government, of the people, and of the times. If we use all the light that is afforded, and if the conjectural facts correspond with the few facts that are distinctly vouched, and join all in one regular chain, nothing further can be expected from human endeavors. The evidence is compleat [sic] so far at least as to afford conviction, if it be the best of the kind. This apology is necessary with regard to the subject under consideration. In tracing the history of criminal law, we must not hope that all the steps and changes can be drawn from the archives of any one nation. In fact, many steps were taken, and many changes made, before archives were kept, and even before writing was a common art. We must be satisfied with collecting the facts and circumstances as they may be gathered from the laws of different countries; and if these put together make a regular system of causes and effects, we may rationally conclude that the progress has been the same among all nations, in the capital circumstances at least. . . .

Here Kames laid out a scientific strategy that later would be christened the comparative method and which would be followed by all who set out to describe a general history of mankind.

Progress and the Functional Ordering of Society

The utopian orientation of eighteenth-century progressivists inevitably involved them in a systemic-functional analysis reminiscent of all those who in an imaginative way projected their hopes for a perfected man in a perfect society. There was an important difference, however, between the usual utopian functionalist description and what excited the enlightened hopefuls of that pregnant century. The idea of progress applied to human history ushered in a new and dynamic image of an inevitable human destiny. Man, as generic man, was fated to march from one stage of accomplishment to another even though individual nations might falter and slip into such an abyss of corruption that they would forever after run with the laggards. Indeed, both Goguet (1775) and Herder (1952) in their histories described the shift of inventive and creative character from the nations of the ancient East to the West. What made nations great and how they maintained their greatness and ability to lead absorbed the attention of pro-gressivists in their private nationalistic moods. At such times they could not refrain from admonishing their compatriots to avoid personal corruption found in the pursuit of unbridled power and wealth. Personal corruption, they warned, was the prelude to national decay.

The projection of any ideal order of society involves the social philosopher in a theory of man and society. Progressivists followed the Greco-Roman lead in stressing the primacy of human nature in the ordering of society. That is, society should be shaped to accord with human nature, rather than the reverse. In the arrangement of their parts societies should be designed to function harmoniously, that is, in a state of equilibrium. This meant that each part fulfilled itself through its proper functions. Not all parts would carry out the same functions, and hence a natural order of importance prevailed among the parts of any social system. Moreover, the natural ranking of relationships must not be disturbed, or the system would become corrupted and disharmony inevitably followed. The harmonious balance desirable in the operation of social systems echoed the principle of the mean favored by Greco-Roman philosophers when judging private behavior. The better social systems would be so arranged that parts would fall into a natural or functional balance, curbing tendencies for any one part to overweight another and thereby heighten the friction of the system. The tendency in all systems would be to maintain a harmonious equilibrium among the parts, and, as deviations led to disturbances, or a marked state of disequilibrium, the natural inclination would be a move to restore the state of harmony.

SUBSTANTIVE CONTRIBUTIONS OF PROGRESSIVIST SOCIAL SCIENCE

The assumptions concerning the nature of reality which progressivists were forced to make in projecting a natural history of mankind pointed their contributions in two directions. First, there was the dynamic movement through time of man's intellectual, moral, social, and political refinement. This would be cast in three stages—savagery, barbarism, and civilization. Second, in projecting a natural society attuned to man's nature and potentials, progressivists were led to theorize on processual arrangements that kept man and society in motion along the path of progress.

The first orientation led progressivists to assemble factual substance to prove the rise of civilization. Here the beginnings of society and the continuities of social institutions held considerable importance, and for origins the evidences supplied by "rude peoples" were vital. The original state of savagery, however, was only part of the picture, and progressivists turned to accounts of early Greeks, Scythians, ancient Germans, Norsemen, and to New World Aztecs and Inca to obtain information on the stage of barbarism. Greece, Rome, and China supplied the evidences for civilization, with Europe the model of modern civilization. In no case, however, did progressivists fill in the details of the three stages. Rather, their works tended to be sketches, and they had special difficulties in formulating the characteristics of barbarism. The contrasts of rude and polished societies were more clearly drawn.

The second orientation focused attention on the nature of social relationships and the moral basis for society. Attention was drawn to social and political arrangements that promoted individual creativity and integrated individual skills and talents in the interests of society as a whole. Like utopianists generally, progressivists considered the human person to be the elemental and sole basis for society. Society existed for man, not man for society. Since individuality, and the freedoms essential to individuality, seemed linked to property, eighteenth-century social scientists clued their descriptions of the rise of civilization to the economic, legal, and political institutions.

The contributions of progressivists to a general social science thus fall into two categories: (1) the origins and continuities of institutions and (2) a theory of society and of social progress. Both, however, were commonly united in the progressivist discourse.

Origins and Continuities: Economic Stages

Progressivists generally considered that the rise of civilization was closely tied to the rise of the technical arts. The production of surplus foods was essential to social differentiation and craft specialization, as well as the release of time that could be devoted to an advancement of knowledge. In his economic history man began as a collector and hunter. He next entered a pastoral stage and then proceeded to the domestication of plants. Presently, as in Europe, man had advanced to a commercial stage. Movement from one stage to the next was largely prompted by necessity as population growth favored by a new economic invention in time outran production. Starvation was so prevalent that people turned to cannibalism, and this practice, underscoring the extremity of their need, forced them to invent the pastoral or agricultural economies.

Certain institutional arrangements could be coordinated with each stage. Property, for example, was a product of agriculture, and, according to Ferguson (1789:125), signalized the transition from savagery to barbarism. A patriarchal family was characteristic of pastoral societies, while the communal ownership of land and resources found in hunting, and mixed hunting-cultivating societies such as the Iroquois, did not encourage an emphasis on paternity (Ferguson 1789:126–127). In their rude savage state men appeared undomesticated, as it were, to civil laws and government. Within the technical arts, one also could trace a series of refinements. For example, men began as workers in stone and next proceeded to the working of the softer, malleable ores—copper, silver, and gold. The use of iron of necessity came later since it was not so visible in its natural state as copper or gold, and, more important, it was more resistant to forging (Goquet 1775).

The Origins of Language and Thought

Any problem in origins and development may be approached along three major axes. First, the general origin of an element can be sought in a universal of human experience, and its subsequent evolution can be traced through a succession of universal contexts. Second, the origin of an element can be seated in functional-need requirements. Third, the specific origin of an element can be located in time and space, and its subsequent historical development and transmission in space can be plotted. In approaching the problem of language origins, progressivists largely operated with a combination of one and two, without, however, wholly neglecting historic origins and relations.

The problem of a generic origin of language inevitably engaged the problem of language as a gift from God. Locke's sensory psychology served as a base for speculating on a natural origin for language, and for accenting a fundamental distinction between man and animals. Between 1749 and 1755 Rousseau completed his "Essay on the Origin of Languages," pointing to the conventionalizations of language as distinct from the natural cries and gestures common to man and animals. Animals seemed well enough endowed for communication but had failed to make use of it. In Rousseau's (1969) judgment, human beings, in relating to each other, uttered their first words. Language was thus a social phenomenon and drew upon expressions of love, hate, compassion, and anger. This passionate base for language expression led Rousseau, and others of his day, to see early language as an outpouring of feeling in figurative or metaphorical form. Metaphorical words thus preceded words to which a literal meaning came to be attached by linguistic convention or contract. This passionate and figurative quality of early language evoked the idea that grammar was secondary to cadence and to the beauty of sounds. Early men thus were stimulated through feeling to construct metaphor and imagery commonly associated with the poet.

Condillac (1930), like Rousseau, emphasized a human impulse to communicate with others. Language began with a passionate action to which reasoned reflection later attached meaning. The earliest communication involved the whole body in a dramatic action that called attention to some personal deprivation or prior experience of fear or affection. A viewer extracted cues from the dramatic performance by following a natural tendency to decompose action into its parts. Language origins thus were like charades, with repetition gradually fixing cues and meanings. The course of language thus flowed from the general to the specific, and from signs to symbols.

Herder (1772) rejected tactility and vision in favor of the auditory experience as the best source for sound-idea conventionalization. For Herder nature was vibrantly alive with sounds, and in naming these sounds in imitation man collected his first vocabulary. In repeating the baa-baa of "that which bleats" men came to discriminate sheep. The lilting cadences of nature's sounds thus found their way into early languages, contributing a songlike quality. In romantic mood Herder could find the best of ancient Greek poetry in samples traceable to the time when language was sung.

With regard to historic origins, biblical teaching traced all languages back to Hebrew. Herder did not follow this course, but he did consider Hebrew a peculiarly primitive or original language (Sapir 1907(5):112). Monboddo (1795(4):127–149), on the other hand, traced all the important arts, including language, to an Egyptian source, from which they had diffused first to Jews and Indians and much later to the Greeks. It was the resemblance between Sanskrit and Greek that led him to conclude that both Greek and Latin had obtained their language and other arts from Egypt (Slotkin 1965:239).

Monboddo's conjecture about the link between Sanskrit and Greek was soon put on more solid ground by Sir William Jones. In 1786 Jones addressed the Royal Asiatick Society as follows:

> The *Sanscrit* language, whatever be its antiquity, is of a wonderful structure; more perfect than the *Greek*, more copious than the *Latin*, and more exquisitely refined than either, yet bearing to both of them a stronger affinity, both in the roots of verbs and in the forms of grammar, than could possibly have been produced by accident; so strong indeed, that no philologer could examine them all three, without believing them to have sprung from some common source, which, perhaps, no longer exists: there is a similar reason, though not quite so forcible, for supposing that both the *Gothick* and the *Celtick*, though blended with a very different idiom, had the same origin with the *Sanscrit*; and the old *Persian* might be added to the same family. . . . (Cited by Salus 1969:172)

The pioneering work of Jones in historical linguistics is especially important in that it illustrates how an historic variation (linguistic specialization) taking place outside a system (theory of social progress) can add a dynamic component that will contribute to the transformation of the system. Jones had studied oriental languages at first, but for financial reasons transferred his energies to law. Having been appointed judge of the supreme court of judicature at Calcutta in 1783, he was led to study Sanskrit in order to get at Hindu legal authorities in the original. He not only aroused interest in oriental studies by founding the Bengal Asiatic Society (1784) but set to work publishing institutes of Hindu and Mohammedan law, Hindu poetry, and selections from the Vedas.

The historic turn which Jones gave to the study of language supplied Rask (1818), Bopp (1816), and Grimm (1822–1837) with the stimulus for their historical-comparative grammars of Icelandic, Greek, Latin, German, and Sanskrit. The historical connections uncovered by grammatical and phonological comparisons of languages separated in space raised the hope that language would prove the perfect instrument for tracing the racial history of man. However, a focus on the relations between language and thought was not wholly lost in these comparisons of form elements. Wilhelm von Humboldt steadied the philosophic roots for language study in a work on the language of the Kawis of Java. In his introduction von Humboldt pointed up the variety of human language and noted how language served as the "formative organ of thought" (cited by Salus 1969:190). Indeed, language was nothing less than the external form of thought. "Seen from its other side, language is the organ of inner existence; in fact it is inner existence as it gradually attains first to self-consciousness and then to utterance" (cited by Salus 1969:179). Drawing upon the notion of an inner drive toward actualization, von Humboldt saw language as the vehicle through which human nature, driven by its intrinsic spiritual energies, could attain a more comprehensive world view, sharpen thinking processes, and extend communication with others. Language thus constituted the ultimate instrument for humanizing man, and its true substance would not be found in the formal rules of grammar, but in the "totality of sense impressions and spontaneous spiritual movements which precede, by the help of language, the formation of concepts" (cited by Salus 1969:187). Here, as well as in the sound system, one intuitively sensed the uniqueness of a language, and likewise experienced frustration in trying to describe and convey its inner form by means of traditional concepts. Every language, in externalizing its inner form, had undergone a continuous transformation. Historically speaking, there were no primordial or original languages available for study.

Emphasis on an inner form that impelled a coordinate external manifestation was not a new idea, but the argument from design gave wide currency to the idea during the eighteenth century. Progress was an inevitable emergent of man's nature, true enough. However, few were inclined to borrow Herder's "creative" force or Blumenbach's *nisus formativus* (formative impulse) to account for cultural advances or biological shapes. Reason and ethical disposition were sufficient to guarantee a desire for improvement. Yet the statements of progressivists consistently implicated them in a teleological position. Wishing to avoid a vitalistic teleology in accounting for the general similarities of languages and their individual peculiarities, von Humboldt noted that once the external form has become structured, it develops a thrust of its own.

Progressivist Views on the Origin and Development of Religion

Providence and Enlightenment. For the deeply religious, providence, or the benevolent direction of God, accounted for human works and the human destiny. The world as God's school for men was an interpretation of long standing. Herder used it when contesting the enlightened in their accusations of religious bigotry and their contempt for the Middle Ages because of gross superstition. For Monboddo, all the great inventions and moral truths known to man were God given. The Egyptians had provided the initial impulse for civilizing the ancient world and India. Egyptian prog- ress in the arts and sciences proclaimed them to be a people of genius, and from their material and governmental advances they moved to the discov- ery of "beings of power and of wisdom infinitely superior to man..." (Monboddo 1795(4):157). Throughout their history the Egyptians had been aided by god-kings or demons. Such intermediate beings, standing between men and gods, existed out of God's wisdom and goodness and apparently carried out tasks in accordance with the divine plan (Monboddo 1795(4): 159). God had sent god-kings or guardian angels to the Chinese and to the Inca of Peru. The demigod "Manco Capuc," the first Inca, introduced the arts, including cultivation, to the ancient Peruvians. Thus, in the mythology of culture heroes, Monboddo discovered spiritual beings who had taken flesh at the bidding of God and dwelt among men the better to instruct them.

Lafitau (1774(1):7–17) also accorded a first place to the Egyptians. However, he saw them as the first, after the Deluge, to invent and transmit a corrupted version of the true religion practiced by the original parents of mankind, Adam and Eve. In his search for stages in the corruption of reli- gion, Lafitau pointed to the Hurons and Iroquois as representative of an early stage by virtue of their linkage with the Hellenes and Pelasgians of the Eastern Mediterranean. Government, mode of life, and character equally disclosed the ancient connection, and the presence of the tortoise as a religious symbol and bearer of the earth, according to Huron and Iroquois creation legends, established a common Hellenic and Pelasgian descent beyond question.

Science and Natural Religion. Enlightened progressivists of the eight- eenth century were not averse to admitting that a creative intelligence had created the world and established its natural order. However, their experi- ence of this intrinsic truth was an intellectual rather than an emotional one encased in the ritual and dogma of formal religion. Science provided the instrument for their search for truth, and they turned their backs on the revealed truths of the conventional church. "Natural religion is the worship which reason, left to itself, and to its own light, apprehends that it should render to the Supreme Being, author and conserver of all beings who make up the sensible world—by loving, adoring, and by not abusing its creatures" (French *Encyclopedia* 1967(14):78–79). Natural religion of necessity em- bodied the "moral or ethical because it directly concern[ed] the customs and obligations of men to each other, considered as creatures of the Su- preme Being." Under such definition, the course of worship led from rude intimations of the supreme intelligence to an orderly and comprehensive realization of God's nature and purpose. God revealed Himself through His works, but the medium was man's own sensory-reflective apparatus rather than semidivine messengers. That man would discover God through the majestic creation of nature seemed a self-evident proposition—something which physical scientists had been saying, beginning with the discoveries of Kepler, Copernicus, and Newton. Much in the spirit of the times, Goguet (1775(1):342) wrote that "the contemplation of the admirable order and beauty of the universe must convince every reasonable and thinking creature of the existence of one Supreme Being, the first cause and sovereign disposer of all things."

Nature, then, provided mankind, from savage to civilized, with a model of God. But the impressions of early times, now available through savage custom, were poorly registered and signals of fundamental truths but dimly perceived. If the reports of many travelers were correct, certain peoples were without any religion. There were tribes in America, wrote Robertson (cited by Avebury 1870:124),

> which have no idea whatever of a Supreme Being, and no rites of religious worship. Inattentive to that magnificent spectacle of beauty and order presented to their view, unaccustomed to reflect either upon what they themselves are, or to enquire who is the author of their existence, men, in their savage state, pass their days like the animals round them, without knowledge or veneration of any superior power. Some rude tribes have not in their language any name for the Deity, nor have the most accurate observers been able to discover any practices or institution which seemed to imply that they had recognized his authority, or were solicitous to obtain his favour.

In the French *Encyclopedia* (1967(14):729) savages by definition were "barbarous peoples who live without laws, regulated society, or religion, and who do not have any fixed habitation." Others, like Kames (1778(2):244–245), held that "Savages, even of the lowest class, have an impression of invisible powers, though they cannot form any distinct notion of them." The sensory impressions of pristine men might be "too faint for the exercise of devotion," but Kames (cited by Schneider 1967:255–256) was convinced of the universality of religious belief and would not accept testimony to the contrary from "illiterate voyagers."

The tendency of savages to respond to external sense more easily than to internal sense could not be taken as a denial of what they apprehended through the latter. Everywhere, argued Kames, men even in the presence of stones to which they paid devotion, were worshipping some invisible power and not stones as simple physical objects.

A zero point of no religion was not in contradiction to the progressivist position. One could begin with an unformalized state and chart the upward movement. However, such a view trod dangerously upon that hypothetical presocial natural state for which progressivists criticized political theorists. The problem of savages without religion survived long into the nineteenth century until Tylor (1874(1):424) supplied a minimum definition, a simple belief in spiritual beings.

Duality of the World and the Animation of Nature. Eighteenth-century interpretations of religious origins stressed the view that savage men were sensitive only to external sensations. However, the unfolding of a rational understanding of deity must follow man's awareness of his inner consciousness. Religion, in progressivist views, began with nature deities—the sun, stars, forest, mountains, and all that press heavily upon the senses and excite fear or wonder and perhaps love. Whether religion began with astral or animal deities, or with great men raised to the stature of deities, as Euhemerus had argued in ancient times, was already the subject of debate. In considering the effects of climate on religion, an English surgeon, Falconer (1781:130–135), observed that people in hot climates were more sensitive to the impressions of their environment than peoples in milder climates. Hence, they tended to be image worshippers, devoted to sun, moon, and fire gods, and also to female deities because of their deference to women. Falconer was not above using his climatic interpretations to fulfill his religious prejudices. He rationalized that the truest ideas of religion and science were found in temperate climates, and it was also here that the purest form of Christianity flourished.

However, progressivists were not inclined to give priority to climate when searching religious origins. Usually climate aided in explaining the character of religious practices. For example, in the judgment of Monboddo (1795(4):171–172) early religion was sensual, and as in Egypt, made use of processions, music, sacrifices, and oracles because men were more responsive to feeling rather than to intellectual stimulation. Some tangible object was required for savage men to focus upon (Kames 1778(2):444–445).

Stress on rudimentary perceptions and feeling states led progressivists to the view that savage men in their religious development first became aware of the inanimate world. Later their attention was drawn to the animate. It followed that heavenly deities were antecedent to animal deities. This conclusion was supported by the appearance in 1760 of de Brosses's *Du Culte des Dieux fétiches* in which he described the worship of stone figures and other material objects.

Progressivist preoccupation with outlining a basis for religion in sensory experience and with charting a logical course to the idea of deity tended to divert them from a considered treatment of the role of religion in society. The breakthrough in this regard was achieved by Comte (1893) as the progressivist phase of Developmentalism drew to a close. In Comte's view human history could be divided into three great epochs: the theological, philosophical, and scientific. The character of society is determined by the kind of knowledge system. Fetishism made up the basis of the theological philosophy, and Comte (1893(2):545–548) argued that it all began with animation of the inanimate. Man derived his ideas of movement and of purpose from observation that animals were purposefully active. He then applied this idea to inanimate forms of nature. The primitive assignment of passion and will to the most inert forms of nature led almost spontaneously to the assignment of deities to the inanimate and to the animate. When star worship had been achieved, in Comte's view, fetishism was on the threshold of polytheism, and organized religion under a priesthood was not far distant.

Social Origins and Continuities. When studying society, kinds of social relations were the primary concern of progressivists—the treatment of wife and children, the nature of paternal and political authority, the linkage of person to property, and the freedom with which individuals acted. What *should* exist according to the best in human nature was of as much concern to the progressivist as what in actuality did exist. Science was ever tempered by a humanistic anxiety for man and his values, and therefore progressivists found little contentment in simply grubbing for facts.

The family consisting of man, wife, and children occupied a central place in progressivist theory on social origins. Most would agree with Goguet (1775(1):21; cf. Ferguson 1789:27–30) "that the mutual inclination of the two sexes towards each other, is the principle which continues and perpetuates society"; but they could not accept the notion, derived from classical sources, that humans in their original state (or prepolitical state) conducted sex as a promiscuous rape. The economic necessities of life were against an early stage of promiscuity, for, as Robertson (1822(1):175; cf. Herder 1952(2):233; Ferguson 1789:125–127) countered:

> A general state of promiscuous intercourse between the sexes never existed but in the imagination of poets. In the infancy of society, when men, destitute of arts and industry, lead a hard precarious life, the rearing of their progeny demands the attention and efforts of both parents; and if their union had not been formed and continued with this view, the race could not have been preserved. Accordingly, in America, even among the rudest tribes, a regular union between husband and wife was universal, and the rights of marriage were understood and recognized.

Again, devotion to a martial life led the ancients to turn aside from the subtle allure of woman and to treat the weaker sex very much as domestic slaves (Millar 1806:32–34). Certainly one could expect the natural dominance of the male, expressed protectively, to mark the original family with the sign of paternalism (Millar 1806:140–142).

In constructing a natural history of the family Millar (1806:140–142) inferred a tendancy for sons to establish their families near a father, and in this way an "original society is gradually enlarged." Fear alone did not attach son to sire. By sharing their wisdom and experience fathers elicited "habitual attitudes filled with admiration, fear, and respect." Then, with the "invention of taming and pasturing cattle" (Millar 1806:59–60), distinctions in rank other than age and sex arose; for now property could be used to separate the wealthy from the poor. Wealth and rank strengthened the paternal hand and a "patriarchal family" became the characteristic unit of the nomadic stage of economic and social development. Wealth conferred a new sense of dignity, and men added wives through purchase and insisted on chastity from brides. However, the polygamous arrangement so stirred jealous passion, hatred, and strife that the head was forced to extend the severity of his controls in order to maintain order. Thus, the patriarch was a product of a chain of events which began with an economic change but which reached its more characteristic form only as authority expanded to meet a destruction threatened by the sexual competition of its members. A patriarchal type of family could come into being and thrive only under conditions where children could be forced into a dependent relation. Economic arrangements found in hunting, fishing, agricultural, and pastoral societies supplied the condition so essential to paternal authority. Under a commercial economy, however, sons were no longer dependent upon the father. In seeking a trade they left home, an action which diminished parental authority and led the way to greater individual freedom.

Theoretically, all important social institutions, including organized political authority, could be traced back to the family since it was *the natural* and *original* social institution. Indeed, families had initiated the move to larger aggregates as they cooperated to achieve common interests. Convinced that by his nature man was a fighter, progressivists generally looked to war as inciting defensive alignments among families, gradually expanding to the level of states and empires. Herder (1952(2):240) alone countered that man's natural state was peace, not war. The cooperative unions men formed grew out of the hard necessities of winning a living and because of an inner conviction directing them to advance humanity. "Nature educates families [tribes?]," wrote Herder, "[and therefore] the most natural state . . . is a Folk, with a national character." To expand a state through conquests that intermingled natural folk arrangements would raise an artificial empire and defeat the very purpose of union among mankind.

In more typical progressivist fashion Millar (1806:145–225; cf. Ferguson 1789:92–202; Kames 1778(2):221–230; also, Vico 1948) began the course of government with a council of elders headed by a chief admired for his superior character, skill in war, and wealth. This primitive form of democracy was found among American Indians (who possessed the "rudest form of government") as well as among Tartars, Chinese, Spartans, Jews, and ancient Romans. At this stage people were organized in villages and "tribes" composed of families subject to the jurisdiction of elders cast in the father-image. Villages exercised a high degree of independence, and a tribal chieftain's authority was spread unevenly across the villages according to his personal influence. Only as disputes arose between families were chief and council inclined to intervene as mediators. However, it was not the mediation of disputes but war which elevated military leaders to a position where they controlled jurisdictional and legislative powers. It happened frequently that "admiration of a military leader in rude countries . . . proceeded so far as to produce a belief of his being sprung from a heavenly original, and to render him the object of that adoration which is due to the Supreme Being" (Millar 1806:165). Thus, the Natchez, Huron, Inca, Loango, and even the Greeks considered their rulers descended from the sun god.

Wars for conquest produced a landed gentry who ruled a group of kindred and slaves. At this stage of development people were familiar with cultivation. Under a farming economy population increased at such a rate that people were forced to migrate in larger bodies, as instanced by the Germanic tribes, or to establish colonies duplicating the parent-village. Migrations and wars provoked an intermingling of peoples, and societies took on a more heterogeneous tone. Out of the urgencies of war military leaders would host different groups, establish alliances, and intermarry. In time these military liaisons developed into confederate councils, to be invested later with authority over all and provided with an executive, the elected great chief or king. When this happened, the feudal order arrived, exemplified so well in the many kingdoms found in Africa and Asia, and among the ancient Gauls and Germans, the Greek city states, and early Rome. Permanent councils or parliaments next grew out of the feudal councils called to determine military operations, to divide booty, and to rectify abuses by establishing regulations. By capturing military and judicial control kings centralized the loose feudal system and set themselves up as monarchs.

In Millar's sketch of the natural course to monarchy—the characteristic political organization of his day—war obviously provided the springboard for leadership and the lever for centralization of power. So long as the "martial ardor" was cultivated, Millar considered the individual protected against outright "oppression." Unfortunately, improvement in the arts and luxuries subverted the "minds of men" as they were persuaded that "lucrative employments" and a life of ease were preferable. The absolutism of monarchs grew as people were enchanted by the comforts and diversions of industry. Unable to depend on his subjects for defense of the land, the king would be forced to hire mercenaries and to rely on a professional army (compare Khaldūn).

PROGRESS, UTOPIA, AND FUNCTIONALISM

Despite their faith in the inevitable advance of human society according to natural law, progressivists could not suppress a pessimistic anxiety when reviewing the history of particular nations. History was filled with opportunities missed and fallen idols because nations ignored the clues to nature's design.

When progressivists confronted the issue of processes directing the course to a civilized humanity, they could undertake nothing less than a theory of society and culture. They would need to call upon the full repertory of their theory, ranging human nature, the proper organization of society, who should hold power, how change should be introduced, and related matters. Moreover, the idea of human progress quite obviously housed the notion of a model type of individual living in a model society and operating with model thoughts and values. It is at this point that the utopian functionalism of the progressivists makes its appearance. Utopian models, as any systems, are conceived with parts neatly interrelated in order that the individual units can fulfill their roles and contribute their part to the functioning system under the best conditions possible.

Principles of Organization and Processes of Civilization

Progressivists insisted that the civilized human order hopefully to be achieved through natural advance must expand the quality of the basic human nature. The end was attainable largely because man was a moral, reflective, and relatively flexible being. Progressivist concern with the moral basis of society was expressed in two principal ways. First, they endeavored to explain how men were equipped by their natures to appreciate moral and value-laden judgments, and in the second instance they argued that societies and nations were "moral persons." In this concern with ethics progressivists underlined the simple fact that neither society nor progress would be possible unless men regulated selfish needs by just principles.

Progressivist concern with the moral foundations of society is openly expressed in their treatises. Adam Smith (1892:3–4) preceded his theory of economic society by a work entitled *The Theory of the Moral Sentiments.* Here he traced the ethics of social living to a human capacity to sympathize imaginatively with others during moments of joy and anguish (pleasure and pain). Circumstances would encourage ideas of the proper and improper according to the emotional distance separating the sympathy of actor and spectator. However, nature ever seeks a "concord" in human sympathy, and it is on this sentimental foundation that common agreements as to the improper and proper can be established (Smith 1892:14–15). Standards of propriety naturally incline human beings to rewards and punishments ("merit and demerit") and to insist that proprieties take on the quality of duties, thereby promoting "self-command" and sensitizing the individual to "the shame of self-condemnation" in ways unknown to those who might follow a practical and selfish principle of utility (Smith 1892:277). Beyond lay the vision of "universal benevolence" which Smith (1892:345) reposed in the Christian deity. For Ferguson (1789:19), too, there was a special affection, "love," which carried the "attention of mind beyond itself" and freed men from the narrow limitations of selfish needs and animal appetites. Men did not oscillate between primitive pleasure and pain, for reason prompted the establishment of principles of rightness and wrongness beginning with a sensitive admiration or condemnation of action. Why could not "everyman in his senses," queried Ferguson (1789:20), grant that a "good understanding, a resolute and generous mind" were as much a part of human nature as "stomach or . . . palate, and much more than . . . [man's] estate or . . . dress?"

An urgent concern for the reign of moral principles in both internal and external affairs can be detected in the press to establish international law and to free humanity from the selfish brutality of war. "Nations or states," wrote Vattel (1916(3):3),

> are political bodies, societies of men who have united together and combined their forces, in order to procure their mutual welfare and security.
>
> Such a society has its own affairs and interests; it deliberates and takes resolutions in common, and it thus becomes a moral person having an understanding and a will peculiar to itself, and susceptible at once of obligations and of rights.

Society also was a natural product, and "the end of the natural society established among men in general is that they should mutually assist one another to advance their own perfection and that of their condition; and Nations, too, since they may be regarded as so many free persons living together in a state of nature, are bound mutually to advance this society" (Vattel 1916(3):6). In his *Perpetual Peace*, Kant (1939) moved for a federation of states to take the lead in promoting peace, in preventing the enslavement of peoples, and in ending the capricious exchange of populations by governments acting as if people were a royal inheritance. The best and surest path to peace lay in the establishment of a "republican" form of government.

There can be little doubt that the humanistic and moral tone distilled from the idea of progress muted national tempers and promoted a spirit of international cooperation—at least among the scholars. No area of European life provided a better illustration of national jealousy than trade and manufacture policies. The "immorality" of the mercantilist economic philosophy was clear to Adam Smith (1937:460–461), for, under the banner of a favorable balance of trade, each state was impelled to struggle selfishly for affluence and power while "beggaring all their neighbours." Smith had a vision of societies cooperating competitively to advance the economic level of all and, in the process, to raise the standard of living for the laboring class.

PARADIGM FOR PROGRESS

A host of postulates and corollaries can be derived from the twin principles that human nature must provide the foundation for society and that society must be so organized that it will advance humanity by eliciting the best in morality and in intellectuality of which man is capable. To organize the postulates and corollaries of any group of thinkers is at best a difficult and hazardous task, and in this instance there is no neat packaging. However, progressivists have provided clues as to where they placed their emphases, and a paradigm can be hazarded in which relevant assumptions are collected in one piece, including eighteenth-century preferences.

Bearing in mind that progressivist theory at all times kept an alert eye on the person, it is to be expected that parallels with Greek social philosophers can be detected, for these ancients also placed man at the center of their social planning. In anticipation of convergence, we note that progressivists and Greeks both developed a structural-functionalist position and that their utopian functionalism contrasts with later scientific functionalism, since the latter stresses the needs of the system as central to social stability rather than the needs of the individual.

Private Initiative, Competition, and Property

The progressivist focus on the individual is clearly revealed in the assumption that the basic needs of society are best served by giving a relatively free rein to private initiative. Fulfillment of private needs and interests conveyed a twofold advantage: (1) the ongoing processes of society would be taken care of, and (2) individuals distributed themselves usefully in the total order according to their special excellences. One must begin with the core needs and wants shared by humans, for these give the basis for individual response, which is ever sensitive to the polar extremes of pleasure and pain, but not under their domination. In eliciting private response a moderate challenge or need stimulus is better than a weak or a harsh one. Like the Greeks, progressivists believed in the mean and found their best support in the character and achievements of those favored by a moderate climate and resources. A free competition would assure individuals that they must work diligently and with initiative to fulfill their needs; and it could be further expected that individuals would advance the skill of their performance. Competition pointed individuals to self-improvement. Without a competitive arena human faculties would degenerate and end in shoddy and flabby performances.

If progressivists were asked to arrange human needs in a rank order of importance they would undoubtedly place personal survival, liberty, and property in first, second, and third place. In their competitive relations men would admire the efficient excellences of top performers and would strive to emulate them, for nothing attracted the attention of mankind so much as the secure advancement of life, liberty, and the pursuit of wealth. These outstanding performers also would be guided by a concern for the rightness of an action, and so they would serve as models for the solid virtues of character. In theory, the human desire to emulate provided the base for a majority increase in excellence and goodness.

Law and the State

The progressivist assumption that the individual can realize his potential best in situations where regulation is minimal led to special reflections on law, authority, variability, innovation, and the preferred size of the human community. There was indeed a natural community where the prime social virtues could be promoted advantageously; but in history societies more often than not exhibited "artificial" qualities that barred human progress. As social units increased to the size of empires, throwing peoples of quite different character together in a common destiny, the amount of organized force required to sustain the state would of necessity increase. Any unnatural increase in administrative regulation would inhibit variability and innovation, and progress must be slowed. In place of a citizenry loyally devoted to a common welfare and regulating their lives by shared ethical conventions and laws, a privileged class would rule a heterogeneous state through artificial decrees designed to entrench their power. Such a situation disturbed the natural balance of power and privilege on which nature's communities should be raised. To construct society according to artificial specifications is a design to frustrate human progress. Indeed, in the midst of artificial privilege, the lower classes would have no virtuous models to follow; and as they pursued the coveted wealth and positions of influence, they would end with an impoverished character. Mass corruption could only lead to a fall. Progress required communities of moderate size where the social virtues could be solidly entrenched in a uniform citizenry, for only in such a limited state would it be possible for individuals to participate to the fullest level of their potentialities and to contribute loyally to the sustenance and advancement of society.

THE PARADIGM ILLUSTRATED

Human Nature and the Natural Society

A society constructed according to function requires the interrelation of units each of which contributes something of value to the total process. None understood this better than Adam Smith (1937) as he pursued implications of the division of labor. Efficient production was governed by a division of labor, and the logic of division of labor argued for a cooperating community where men in free competition were encouraged "to apply . . . [themselves] to a particular occupation, and to cultivate and bring to perfection whatever talent or genius . . . [they might] possess for that particular species of differences" (Smith 1937:14–15; cf. Ferguson 1792(1):2). Assuredly men were moved by "self-love," but the "study of his own advantage naturally, or rather necessarily leads him to prefer that employment which is most advantageous to the society" (Smith 1937:14, 421). The advantage to society accrued from the functional interweaving of human skills into a system of production (Smith 1937:15–16). Smith was so certain that the uninhibited flow of natural talent would produce a functionally efficient and dynamically expanding production that he could not refrain from any opportunity to attack trade laws that restrained the flow of goods. Indeed,

> The natural effort of every individual to better his own condition when suffered to exert itself with freedom and security, is so powerful a principle, that it is alone, and without any assistance, not only capable of carrying on

the society to wealth and prosperity, but of surmounting a hundred impertinent obstructions with which the folly of human laws too often incumbers its operations; though the effect of these obstructions is always more or less either to encroach upon its freedom, or to diminish its security. (Smith 1937: 508; see Montesquieu 1900(1):book 1, pp. 3–5)

What held at the individual level held also at the level of groups, and Smith's theory envisioned a free competition among nations that would stimulate each national group to improve its talents and resources, and advance the common needs and purposes of humanity.

Functional Diversity and Human Diversity

A functional diversification in tasks added complexity to a society and provided new means for cultivating untapped human talents. At the level of organized states, as Ferguson noted (1789:36; also 194, 213ff., 273–277), the "necessity of public defense, has given rise to many departments of state and the intellectual talents of men have found their busiest scene in wielding their national forces." Different modes of life accommodated to diverse environments or to a unique historic situation likewise promoted new skills and character traits exhibited in "temper," "disposition," and "intellectual faculties." A "commercial life," according to Falconer (1781: 415–417), improved the faculties of "memory" and "methodic arrangement." The enlargement of "ideas" accompanying commerce broadened vision and helped to eliminate "the most pernicious prejudices." However, there were disadvantages to a commercial mode of life, and those Falconer found were common to the Enlightenment. Practical sciences and law thrived at the expense of the "polite and rather ornamental branches"— literature, history, "taste," and art. Among commercial peoples a preference for defensive fortifications testified to a softening of the aggressive spirit. "Glory," "honour," and "love of liberty" were bypassed for a life that was frugal and industrious, with riches serving as the prime measure for happiness. Commerce also heightened individual pursuit of private interest, often at the expense of the public good. Riches corrupted morals, and the "want of generosity and private benevolence" underscored the shallow quality of friendship (Falconer 1781:410–412). Yet, under a commercial existence, individuals became "more just and honest in their private transactions," pursued sobriety, eschewed violence, and cultivated "courteous and agreeable" manners (Falconer 1781: 413–414).

Wants, Invention, Competition, and Corruption

Satisfaction of human needs and wants supplied the motive power and gave direction to human activity. Need was the mother of invention. Goguet (1775(1):279–283) attached one need to another on a chain of continuity leading from a barter in necessities to a commerce in luxuries. Without the "agitation" generated by wants "there would be little to be desired, and less to be dreaded: our mental faculties would for ever lie dormant; and we should for ever remain ignorant that we have such faculties," wrote Kames (1778(2):204–207; cf. Ferguson 1789:94). Struggle winnowed the chaff of human character and strengthened the social "virtues" just as the love of parent for child thrived best when "it [met] . . . with greatest difficulties" (Ferguson 1789:29). Kames (1778(2):204–207) was willing to argue that "agitation . . . [was so] requisite to the mind as well as the body" that society could not improve if a perfect order were instituted and people were "scrupulous [in their] adherence to the rules of morality." By organizing themselves in such free competition that individuals responded to their natural inclinations for profit, reputation, and privilege, the ancient Greeks had achieved extraordinary success as exporters of ideas and a civilization which others sought to emulate (Ferguson 1789:270–271). In contrast, the evil products of luxurious wealth could be traced to the relaxing of tensions ("desires") essential to purposeful activity, for the lure of "lucrative employments" swept individuals into a life of ease that would "enervate the minds of men" (Millar 1806:222; see Ferguson 1789, parts V and VI; Falconer 1781:410–411, 514–518; Kames 1778(2):223; Herder 1952(2): 239–240).

Worse still, luxury so corrupted leadership and entrenched inequities that people had no worthy model to emulate. At best the public could *imitate* those in power and influence, and eighteenth-century progressivists were in general agreement that those holding the reins of political, social, and economic control in Europe in their time held little hope for the progress of mankind. Smith (1892:87–89; see Ferguson, cited by Lehmann 1930:126–127) cautioned the poor man against beggaring his character by placing "his glory in being thought rich." In attaining this "envied situation" he would be forced to adopt fashionable "vices and follies," "abandon the paths of virtue," engage in "fraud and falsehood," and finally wind up "disappointed in the [anticipated] happiness [and] . . . honour" of his position, since his "exalted station [would appear] . . . both in his own eyes and in those of other people, polluted and defiled by the baseness of the means through which he rose to it." Eighteenth-century progressivists could not agree with Rousseau (Bury 1920:179–182) that "civilization" was a mistake, but they could not agree more with the old thesis that luxurious wealth and unrestrained power corrupts.

Property, Individuality, and Progress

Progressivists inveighed against corruption inspired by a love of luxury and boundless privilege, but at the same time they looked to property as providing a unique stimulus to human advancement. The natural desire for private property had released individuality, maintained a flexible disposition in human character, and stimulated innovative alertness (Ferguson 1789:59ff., 125–127, 307–309). According to Kames (1761:80–81; see Ferguson 1789:148; Hume, cited by J. H. Stewart 1963:115–120), countless social blessings could be traced to the institution of property:

> Industry in a great measure, depends on property; and a much greater blessing depends on it, which is the gratification of the most dignified natural affections. What place would there be for generosity, benevolence, or charity, if the goods of fortune were common to all? These noble principles, being destitute of objects and exercise, would for ever lie dormant; and what would man be without them? Truly a very groveling creature; distinguishable indeed from the brutes, but scarce elevated above them. Gratitude and compassion might have some slight exercise; but how much greater is the figure they make in the present state of things? The springs and principles of man are adjusted with admirable wisdom to his external circumstances; and these in conjunction form one regular constitution, harmonious in all its parts.

The Key to Human Variability and Progress

Viewed in the context of sensory stimulation, eighteenth-century progressivists held that intensity of response varied according to the strength and duration of the stimulus, and that a moderate stimulus best suited the human constitution in its physical, moral, and intellectual organization. Moderate stimuli permitted greater flexibility in response and evoked a natural variability—conditions essential to the differentiation of human talent and the promotion of innovations that broadened the character base of human society. The natural world obviously provided extremes in the sparse offerings of the soil and in the heat and cold of tropical and arctic climates. But the fact that human character and culture matured in temperate regions revealed nature's preference for the middle range, as ancient Greeks and, more recently, Montesquieu argued (see also Herder 1952(2): 168–191; Ferguson 1789:171; Falconer 1781:1–24; Robertson 1822(1):189; Kames 1779(1):283–286).

The central impact of climate derived from extremes that affected the "nervous, sanguineous, and glandular systems" (Falconer 1781:3; see Montesquieu 1900(1):12, 221, 228; Hippocrates 1962:116–135; Vitruvius 1926:170–174). Heat excited the nervous system generally and especially the "cutaneous nerves," thereby increasing the vividness of sensations and prompting more impulsive responses. Under extreme cold, sensory penetration was weak, owing to the retraction of "cutaneous papillae" (Falconer 1781:4–5). Under heat, excessive perspiring drained strength from the body and increased a flow of bile that led to an "aversion to motion" in body and mind. Heat in excess thus provoked indolence and joined it to an "acrimonious temper" (Falconer 1781:4, 12–13). Moderate climates activated a "middle degree of sensibility between heat and cold" and peoples were neither so excitable as southerners nor as long suffering as northerners. It is in moderate climates that "love . . . appears to the greatest perfection" as does friendship and "moderation of conduct." True, people in moderate climates tend to be impatient and so may be "fickle of disposition," but they possess "more courage of the active kinds, and are more enterprising, and able to take advantage of their success" (Falconer 1781:18–22).

The interrelations of climate, character, and authority commonly accepted by progressivists in the eighteenth century are briefly summarized by Robertson (1822(1):189) thus:

> cold or temperate countries appear to be the favourite seat of freedom and independence. There the mind, like the body, is firm and vigorous. There men, conscious of their own dignity, and capable of the greatest efforts in asserting it, aspire to independence, and their stubborn spirits stoop with reluctance to the yoke of servitude. In warmer climates, by whose influence the whole frame is so much enervated, that present pleasure is the supreme felicity and mere repose is enjoyment, men acquiesce almost without a struggle, in the dominion of a superior.

In sparse and harsh environment, one might find compensations inasmuch as people would be encouraged to be "sober, industrious, vigorous; and consequently courageous, as far as courage depends on bodily strength" (Kames 1779(1):284). Certainly a fertile soil was no happy gift, for the "disadvantages ... are more than sufficient to counterbalance its advantages: the inhabitants are rendered indolent, weak, and cowardly ... soft and effeminate, and consequently an easy prey to every invader" (Kames 1779(1):285). Surely a soil is "more widely accommodated to man" if he is continually challenged but not defeated.

"Natural" and "Artificial" States

When applying their principles of the mean, of harmonious function, and of the "natural" to the state, eighteenth-century progressivists were led to reject the imperial order. There was a natural design for human communities varying according to circumstances and character. "The history of the human species as a whole," wrote Kant (cited by Walsh 1951: 126), "may be regarded as the realization of a secret plan of Nature for bringing into existence a political constitution perfect both from the internal point of view, and, so far as regards this purpose, from the external point of view also: such a constitution being the sole condition under which Nature can fully develop all the capacities she has implanted in humanity." In empires one witnessed the unnatural aggregation of peoples and the unnatural subordination of different orders in society, which arrangement could only be sustained through despotism.

In backward glance the republican governments of both Greece and Rome impressed many progressivists as the nearest thing to a natural community achieved by man. Here one found communities that exhibited few inequities, demonstrated integrity in moral principles, stimulated gentility, provoked intellectual growth, fostered the humanistic arts, and evoked a sense of unity impossible in large empires. Ferguson (1789:92) deplored the fact that in the Europe of his day republics comparable in size to those of ancient Greece were "choaked [sic] by the neighbourhood of more powerful states," dwarfed like "shrubs, under the shade of a taller wood," and thereby deprived of their natural function as "nurser[ies] of excellent men."

Property, Law, Individuality, and the State

Property, law, and individuality provided three interrelated conditions governing the rise of political society, and indeed required that a political order should be established. The impact of property on the organization of society, law, and individual liberty had increased as mankind advanced from a simple hunting to a complex commercial economy. "Nations which depend upon hunting," observed Robertson (1822(1):185), "are, in a great measure, strangers to the idea of property," for, having no investment in the care of forest game there was no basis for a private claim. Continuing his summary of the characteristics of hunting societies, Robertson (1822 (1):186–188) found that

> People in this state retain a high sense of equality and independence. Wherever the idea of property is not established, there can be no distinction among men, but what arises from personal qualities. . . . Every circumstance indicates that all the members of the community are on a level [in having the same dress, food, possessions]. . . . All are freemen, all feel themselves to be such and assert with firmness the rights which belong to that condition. This sentiment of independence is imprinted so deeply in their nature, that no change of condition can eradicate it, and bend their minds to servitude. . . .
>
> Among peoples in this state, government can assume little authority and the sense of civil subordination must remain very imperfect. . . . They are conscious of their own connection with the companions in conjunction with whom they act, and they follow and reverance such as excel in conduct and valour. . . . All their resolutions are voluntary, and flow from impulse of their minds. . . . The right of revenge is left in private hands. . . . They do not aim at maintaining interiour order and police by public regulations, or the exertions of any permanent authority, but labour to preserve such union among the members of their tribe, that they may watch the motions of their enemies, and act against them with concert and vigor.

This generalized statement of features common to savage hunters and their societies can be duplicated easily in the judgments of other eighteenth-century progressivists. One cannot help but be struck by the consensus which prevailed: that man in the savage state maintained a stubborn liberty in personal action, that inequalities based on property hardly existed, that food resources tended to be shared, that leaders arose and were admired according to their excellences, that enacted laws were quite lacking, that public authority was not concentrated in the hands of one or a few but dispersed among individuals and families, and finally that governance was achieved largely through persuasion, example, and custom (see Falconer

1781:301–311; Ferguson 1789:123–146; Kames 1778(2):93–95; Millar 1806:168–170).

The achievement of a pastoral economy invited private ownership of stock, but only as people attained the agricultural state did ownership in usufruct give way by degrees to disposal of land by private testament. With the advent of the commercial age property stood forth as the "mainspring or mover" of laws (Falconer 1781:426). There could be no disagreement with Kames (1761:79–81) that property was "one of the great objects of law."

In laws enacted to govern the protection of life and private possessions eighteenth-century progressivists found a special instrument to regulate society and to assure the freedom of action and justice needed by individuals to improve themselves. As individuals *en masse* improved, humanity advanced. In only one form of government could Montesquieu (1900(1): 13–26) find that signal virtue, "love of equality," which promoted the public welfare. This was the democratic or republican. Such a government was suited to public-spirited citizens, and Montesquieu was optimistic in the use of law to educate men in their social virtues. By its very definition a republic lacked the coercive force of monarchies, and therefore the "nearer a government approached a republic, the more the manner of judging" became fixed by laws (Montesquieu 1900(1):75). "In order to love equality and frugality, in a republic," he assures us, "these virtues must have been previously established by law" (Montesquieu 1900(1):42). Law could also be used to maintain a proper challenge for the individual. In a commercial economy, "the estates of individuals in proportion to the increase of commerce, should set every poor citizen in such mediocrity as to be obliged to take some pains either in preserving or in acquiring a fortune" (Montesquieu 1900(1):46).

Law could be used to keep the orders of society in proper balance. "The pretensions of any particular order," wrote Ferguson (1789:194–195), "if not checked by some collateral power, would terminate in tyranny. . . ." Frequently enough, war had provided the urgent condition for subordinating individuals to political leadership in the interest of concentrating a unified strength, but "Nations . . . have been fortunate in the tenor, and in the execution of their laws, in proportion as they have admitted every order of the people, by representation or otherwise, to an actual share of the legislature" (Ferguson 1789:252). The mutual adjustment of differences by law was the surest guarantee of justice and the best guide to maintaining equality of the parts as the perfection of rule by law in both Rome and England demonstrated. Kames (1779(2):107) praised the governments of Mexico and Peru because of their balanced qualities. In the instance of Mexico monarchical power was checked by a hereditary council of nobles, whereas in Peru a strict "agrarian law" barred the

> inequality of rank and riches, as lead to luxury and dissolution of manners: a commonwealth is naturally the result of such a constitution: but in Peru it was prevented by a theocratical government under a family sent from heaven

to make them happy. This wild opinion supported by ignorance and superstition, proved an effectual bar against tyranny in the monarch; a most exemplary conduct on his part being necessary for supporting the opinion of his divinity. Upon the whole, comprehending king and subjects, there perhaps never existed more virtue in any other government, whether monarchical or republican.

The laws that progressivists would use in the interests of society, of course, would reflect nature's design. They would preserve a hierarchy of interrelated parts in a competitive balance, moving ahead in dynamic harmony, and always expanding and improving the usefulness of the parts and the organization of the whole. This is all neatly summarized by Dugald Stewart (1892:liv) when commenting on Adam Smith's economic theory:

> the great and leading object of his speculations is, to illustrate the provisions made by nature in the principles of the human mind, and in the circumstances of man's external situation, for a gradual and progressive augmentation in the means of national wealth; and to demonstrate that the most effectual plan for advancing a people to greatness, is to maintain that order of things which nature has pointed out; by allowing every man, as long as he observes the rules of justice, to pursue his own interests in his own way, and to bring both his industry and his capital into the freest competition with those of his fellow-citizens. Every system of policy which endeavours, either by extraordinary encouragements to draw towards a particular species of industry a greater share of the capital of the society than what would naturally go to it, or, by extraordinary restraints, to force from a particular species of industry some share of the capital which would otherwise be employed in it, is, in reality, subversive of the great purpose which it means to promote.

PROGRESS AND UTOPIAN AND SCIENTIFIC FUNCTIONALISM

Looking backward we may consider eighteenth-century progressivists to be wayward anthropologists at best, since their enthusiasm for what lay ahead turned their thoughts away from the beginnings of civilization and directed their attention to its most complex and perfected state. Once they had made their theoretical position clear, progressivists often were inclined to chart the advances of Western civilization from Greco-Roman times to the present, or to read some lesson for the future out of the rise and decline of the Roman Empire, or to sketch the emergence of nation-state out of barbarism. Yet, owing to their emphasis on a developmental continuity, "savages" and "barbarians" were credited with special contributions to a human destiny. Without the catalytic enthusiasm which inspired progressivists with the idea that writing a "scientific" history of mankind was both possible and necessary, it is difficult to see how people could have been aroused to take and sustain a sympathetic and objective interest in primitive society, belief, and custom.

The humanistic vision of a social millennium held by progressivists offers some striking parallels with Christian Millenarism when the apocalypticism of the latter is excluded. However, the "psychological materialism" to which progressivists turned in subjecting mankind to "natural law" provided a base for "scientific" interpretation and eliminated the need to explain the rise of human society and civilization as a product of divine intervention. Yet both Christian and progressivist, as we have seen, shared the idea that men everywhere participated in a common destiny and that the path to this end was purposive, "unilinear," and "irreversible" (see Tuveson 1964 and Hodgen 1964).

Like later evolutionists, progressivists preferred to focus their attention on the dynamics of change; but, at the same time, they could not take their eyes from the vision of a model society. It is at this point that progressivists (and evolutionists) assume the dress of a "functionalist." In both instances, however, the functionalist posture was tempered by the primary focus on change. Faith in the inevitabilities of "natural selection" actually disposed nineteenth-century evolutionists to compromise their utopian functionalism although Spencer (1900(3):609–611) argued that the repressions, injustices, cruelties, and bitter warring witnessed in militant societies would pass with establishment of the "industrial" type of society among mankind at large. There is an important difference, however, between progressivists and evolutionists that must be noted. The former are more concerned with *how* to arrange a social and "cultural" mileu that would be congenial to human nature, would add to the humanizing of mankind, and would provide conditions requisite for awakening the common human impulse to move up to something better. Considerable emphasis is placed on a planned cultivation of proper attitudes, industrious habits, morality, intellectuality, aesthetic taste, and human attributes expressing generosity, sympathy, and compassion. Progressivists are at their best when describing the way in which private interest, the general welfare, rule by law, authority, and heroic leadership must be harmonized if variability and innovation were to stimulate human advancements. For their part evolutionists were inclined to leave the planning to nature. In the "give and take" of natural living the organism either would alter adaptively to requirements of external conditions or perish. Consequently the attributes essential to human progress would be winnowed in the harsh struggle, as only the "fittest would survive."

At first glance progressivists may look like better "functionalists" than those committed to evolution. However, it is the latter, with their stress on the conflicts of groups and the roles performed by groups in a social setting organized according to a dominance-subordination principle, that provided the seed bed for the study of *social processes* and the emergence of *scientific functionalism*. As stress on the interrelations of groups moved into the forefront of scientific interest, there occurred a corresponding shift from a concern for the individual and his needs to the needs of the social system.

Beyond their respective emphases—whether the individual or the social system is used as a starting point—utopian and scientific functionalism turn out to be very much alike in conceptual interest and in vocabulary. Parts are arranged in a system, and the system functions best in a state of harmony or equilibrium. Parts are arranged in a rank order and must not get out of place or the system will move into a state of disharmony ("corruption") or disequilibrium. The better systems are so arranged that parts fall into a natural or functional balance, curbing tendencies for any one part to overweight another and thereby heighten the friction of the system. The tendency in all systems is to maintain a harmonious equilibrium among the parts, and, as deviations lead to disturbances or a marked state of disequilibrium, the natural inclination is to a move to restore equilibrium or harmony.

The problem of unit conformity in the interests of efficient operation of the whole again reflects basic differences in emphasis. Utopian functionalists are inclined to see systemic efficiency as possible only as the individual realizes an inner potential, with harmony a product of a mutual accommodation of private and group interests, rights, and duties. On the other hand, scientific functionalists tend to view the individual as molded or conditioned according to the need expectations of the system.

EIGHTEENTH-CENTURY FOUNDING FATHERS OF SOCIAL SCIENCE

The Measure of Progressivist Social Science: Four Criteria

If we return to our four criteria (see Chapter 1) by which the presence of a discipline can be measured, it is clear that progressivists must be credited with laying the foundations for a general study of mankind. It is out of this generalized social science base that anthropology and sociology differentiated soon after the midpoint of the nineteenth century.

With regard to subject matter, progressivist concern for a psychological and social history of mankind contrasted with the narrow national and "great man" interests of historians. Progressivist concerns centered in the origins and development of institutions—family, state, social classes, religion, technical arts, language, and the fine arts. Their focus was on man as a social being. Here their interests proved to be twofold. First, they sought to chart the human adventure from savagery to civilization. They expected to record the gradual liberation of man's human faculty from the irrational beliefs, practices, and social arrangements which in the past had restricted the directive influence of reason and forestalled fulfillment of the human destiny. Second, they undertook the task of describing the social arrangements and processes governing social relations by which the humanization of man could be accelerated. Such interests did not exclude the description of physical differences ranging the human species. However, progressivists were not oriented to a research of racial distinctions. It was enough that minkind belonged to one species, shared common appetites, needs, and satisfactions, but above all possessed a common human faculty which impelled all men to intellectualize and order experience. As generalists, natural historians left the specialized research and collection of facts to others. From these specializations, as in the case of language, they extracted data relevant to thought processes discernible in savage, barbaric, and civilized languages and described the ideological continuities which these revealed. Their developmental interests defined goals distinct from those found in traditional histories and allowed the takeover of a distinct and separate area of investigation. The proof of this new substantive domain lay in the institutional format of the natural histories. Finally, progressivists contrasted the scientific character of their natural hisory with the accidental or nonpredictive character of traditional history.

The "comparative method" utilized by progressivists to trace the logical growth of ideas and institutions was a significant departure from the traditional method of history. Lacking written documentation, progressivists constructed conjectural linkages between antecedents and consequences, relying on the principles of analogic reasoning, uniformities in cause and effect, and developmental continuity (simplicity to complexity).

Finally, progressivists made use of facts usually ignored by historians. The facts necessary for a natural history of mankind were group or social facts, although progressivists did not so designate them. However, their intent is clear in the use of customs, beliefs, and institutions in contradistinction to the military and political exploits of monarchs and their followers to which historians commonly turned. In determining the features characteristic of the states of savagery, barbarism, and civilization, social facts emerged as the natural descriptive units. Thus, Ferguson (1789:154–159) enumerated the following characteristics of barbarism: piratical type of warfare; military leaders preeminent, governing at first through the influence of heroic example but later through organized loyalty as found in feudal arrangements; individual ranking by military exploits but no special classes; social bonds depending primarily on mutual attachment and courage which men develop and admire as a consequence of the war experience; social communities to which persons are attached usually are small territorial units with chieftains of cantons uniting on occasion to fight a common threat; quasi-hereditary succession; property hereditary in families.

In light of the four criteria, there can be little doubt that eighteenth-century progressivists laid the foundations for a new discipline—a generalized social science. The fact that their general outline for a natural history of mankind was expanded and refined during the nineteenth century, and served as a model for an anthropological science of culture, testifies to the remarkable breakthrough achieved by progressivist social philosopher-scientists and historians.

One caveat can be raised in the assignment of a preeminent place to eighteenth-century progressivists as forerunners of anthropology. By leaving the collection of specialized facts to others, progressivists in effect elevated themselves to the rank of social and cultural theorists. In consequence, they did not have any direct connection with developments that would lead into prehistory, physical anthropology, linguistics, and other anthropological specialties. Yet it was the convergence of these specializations that generated the differentiation of anthropology from the general social science base. Here one can detect the interplay between structure and variation. Progressivists provided the general structure, which, through its continuity, guided future developments and provided the dynamic context for selectively integrating the results of such specialization. At the same time, historic variations (emergence of prehistory, human paleontology, and so on) pursuing courses relatively independent of each other and of the generalized structure stimulated change through functional differentiation. The convergence of interest on the early history and condition of mankind forged by prehistory, human paleontology, linguistics and ethnology forced the differentiation of anthropology from the social science trunk. This illustrates a simple but vital datum. Historic and evolutionary processes had been at work in the emergence of the anthropological scientific institutions, just as in the case of any institution (see Chapter 3).

Eighteenth-Century Founders of Social Science

Historic points at which differentiations take place of necessity are rooted in a generalized base. Such a situation multiplies problems in any effort to pinpoint a true innovator and to follow a line of descendants. Such is the case for eighteenth-century founders of social science. The idea of progress cast such a wide net that contributions to the emergence of a general social science must be widely credited. Some who antedated the rise of progressivism also must be accorded special credit. For example, Vico (1948) developed an original argument for a scientific history of man and society and attempted to illustrate the natural course and cycling of human society following the social histories of Greece and Rome. In 1724 Lafitau attempted to show how the comparison of customs and the vestiges of customs could be used to show the unity of mankind, as Christian theology taught, and to trace the migrations of mankind. At the same time, Lafitau's missionary experiences allowed him to describe firsthand the customs of Indians, and he must be credited with the first description of the Iroquois kinship system. Smith (1892), Condillac (1746), Rousseau (1782), Herder (1772), and Monboddo (1773) speculated on the origins of language, stressed the importance of language as an instrument for thinking, and noted its vital necessity for life in society. Kames (1761) traced the evolution of law and formulated the basis for the comparative method. Hume in 1757 wrote an essay on the natural history of religion, and de Brosses (1760) described West African fetishism as an original basis for religion, at the same time drawing attention to Egyptian and West African parallels. Turgot (1750) traced the development of knowledge through three stages, anticipating the theological, metaphysical, and scientific stages upon which Comte (1893) later grounded his description of the progress of human society. Meiners (1785) surveyed the peoples of the world, compiling information in accordance with an outline he considered essential for a study of peoples and their life ways (*Völkerkunde*). Ferguson (1789), Millar (1806), Dunbar (1780), Kames (1778), and Robertson (1822) described the nature of society in its savage, barbaric, and civilized stages, including the forces making for stratification and the state.

In review, the Scottish moral philosophers and historians appear to hold a special place in the foundations of social science. They illustrate an example of the clustering of genius that marks moments of transition and of efflorescence. Their number included David Hume (1711–1776), Adam Ferguson (1723–1816), Adam Smith (1723–1790), William Robertson (1721–1793), James Millar (1735–1801), Henry Hume (Lord Kames, 1696–1782), and James Burnett (Lord Monboddo, 1714–1799). The Scottish social historians formed a tight company, maintaining relatively close interpersonal relations and an attentive exchange of ideas. Perhaps by virtue of this mutual stimulation, they were able to surpass others in the breadth of their ethnographic and sociological interests and in formulation of an explicit and systematic project for a natural history of the species. It is not difficult to find theoretical and methodological parallels between these eighteenth-century beginners and later nineteenth-century reformulators of a science of man (Voget 1967). Both Bryson (1945) and Lehmann (1930) have discussed the importance of the Scottish social historians for anthropology and sociology and have discussed or urged their acceptance as founders (see also Schneider 1967).

3

Progressivist
Epilogue: 1800-1840

PURE AND APPLIED SOCIAL SCIENCE

By the time the Napoleonic Wars engulfed Europe, the initial work of drawing up a plan for a natural history of mankind had been completed. Like any science, this early definition of social science had two orientations, a pure and an applied. Pure science seeks to detail things as they are and as they happen, and as a result strives for objective descriptions of events, processes, and causes without special regard to ultimate values or pragmatic applications. An intermingling of the pure and applied can be seen in the emergence of sociology under St. Simon and Comte. Caught up in the political and military turbulence of the passing of the *ancien régime*, both urged an application of science to human affairs. In his *Positive Philosophy* Comte hailed sociology as the queen of the sciences, since its proper use would permit transition from one social stage to another without bloodshed and turmoil. While he traced a general course of development from early times, Comte did not advocate a study of contemporary primitive societies. Rather, he narrowed the focus to Western societies, the bearers of the civilizing thrust. This distinction between pure and applied aspects is important in understanding basic differences between sociology and anthropology today, including the narrowed range of interest of sociology as compared with anthropology. A humanistic orientation likewise embraces total human experience in time and space. This value orientation has turned up consistently to temper, and sometimes confound, anthropological scientific aspirations.

The distinction between pure and applied science is not only informative but also proves of signal importance in the differentiation of anthropology from the general social science trunk. To follow the path to this differentiation, it is necessary to go outside the progressivist format and note two special developments: (1) individual quests for knowledge in natural science disciplines whose findings could be brought to bear on the human experience and (2) advance in specializations that later would be incorporated into a science of anthropology. Discussion will be confined largely to the period between 1800 and 1840, since the latter date marks the phasing out of the progressivist impulse and the transition to a theoretical structure anchored to biological evolution.

UNIFORMITARIANISM AND CATASTROPHISM: GEOLOGY AND PALEONTOLOGY

Developments in geology and paleontology which appeared at the end of the eighteenth century played an important role in shattering the bonds of Christian dogma, as well as in generating an effort to explain the earth and man as products of continuous and uniform processes natural to earth and to man. Acceptance of the idea of continuous uniform processes overturned the theological view that change is a product of interventions, and hence is intrinsically discontinuous. There was also the implication that the antiquity of the earth and of man extends far beyond the usual theological estimates of four to six thousand years.

During the eighteenth century geologists were busily studying the exposed strata of mountainous areas and arranging them into classes according to their special characteristics and relative ages. Theological time, anchored to the critical moment of the Deluge, supplied the rationale for the ordering of strata. Rock formations without evidences of life (for example, gneisses and schists) were assigned to the time of the creation, and hence constituted the Primitive class. Those exhibiting fossiliferous forms were assigned to the Secondary or Tertiary, with the former usually attributed to the time of the Deluge. In contradiction to these discontinuous interventions by deity, James Hutton in 1785 introduced the Royal Society of Edinburgh to the view that the earth had undergone changes in the past through actions of wind, rain, frost, tide, deposition, subterranean pressure, and the uplifting of underwater depositions to form land just as it was continuously undergoing change at present. Hutton stressed the continuous action of uniform processes and effects—the principle of uniformitarianism.

Hutton did not suggest that these continuous alterations of the earth's surface were directional. Like Newton's machine, the earth was simply in continuous motion according to its operational principles. "The result, therefore, of our present inquiry is that we find no vestige of a beginning, no prospect of an end" (Hutton 1788:304, cited by Berry 1968:22). The earth simply alternated between land building and land erosion. From this one could conclude that both earth and man were on a treadmill.

Hutton's model of a self-sustaining earth machine provided no comfort for either Christian theologue or purpose-minded philosopher-scientist. Confirmation of Hutton's static equilibrium model arose through a combination of geological and paleontological stratification. England took the lead, capitalizing on the pragmatic charting of strata in connection with coal mining and canal construction. In the identification of strata within a local area, the presence of fossiliferous materials proved useful. However, the full significance of this correlation of life and land forms was not realized until the local sequences were merged into a broader regional perspective. This was accomplished by a surveyor-engineer, William "Strata" Smith. Topographic mapping is a prime art of the surveyor, but Smith ingeniously contrived a geologic map for use in his survey of a canal route to Somerset. Later he was assigned to different parts of Britain and worked on completion of a geologic map of Britain and Wales. The significance of Smith's correlation of strata with the aid of fossil aggregates and his proficiency in arranging fossil collections in a stratigraphic sequence amazed his friends (members of an agricultural society, Bath). This astounding demonstration opened up new possibilities for utilizing stratigraphy to chart a succession of life forms. Interest was aroused, public subscriptions were taken, and with the aid of Sir Joseph Banks, *The Geological Map of England and Wales* was published in 1815 (Berry 1968:53–57).

In France, the Abbé Giraud-Soulavie (1780–1784) likewise charted the differences of three superimposed limestone strata according to their shell life. Above the limestones he observed a slate and shale formation, and then alluvium, both containing recent life. Many of the shells of the uppermost limestone stratum exhibited recent forms. Giraud-Soulavie believed that he had a basis for building a succession of life forms, and hence for constructing a history of the earth (Berry 1968:51–52).

The charting of stratigraphic life succession in France was carried on by Cuvier (1834–1836), culminating in his theory of catastrophism. Cuvier relied on Bonnet's theory of preformation to help explain why there was no gradual modification of life forms by natural processes (Ley 1968:224–225). Moreover, the geological-paleontological successions were not notable exhibits of gradual modifications, but rather they evidenced sharp discontinuities. It was common, as in the Paris Basin examined by Cuvier and Brongniart (1808), for freshwater deposits to be overlaid by marine formations, and for alternations of these to occur. There were empirical grounds, then, for considering the succession of life forms a product of a geologic-biologic saltation. In Cuvier's view, the organism prefigured in the egg was modified partially by the catastrophe which had overtaken the organisms living at the time. Through such partial modifications, Cuvier hoped to explain the structural differences seen in related classes found in any stratigraphic sequence. Cuvier's theory presumed that not all creatures were overwhelmed by the catastrophe, but that some survived in refuge areas. Curiously, the geological catastrophism proposed by Cuvier to explain structural differences in life successions at a later time was restated within the biological context, as mutation, by Hugo de Vries.

The idea of a general flooding of the earth's surface had wide currency among geologists of the day, but not all correlated such a diluvial epoch with the Noachian Flood. In Germany, Werner's experience with the sedimentary formations of Saxony convinced him that periodic floodings, both general and local, alone could account for their layered aggregates. However, Cuvier's theory elicited scientific and theological attention, since it admitted a succession of life forms and yet did not challenge biblical teaching. There were two great diluvial epochs, according to Cuvier. The first was a great flooding of the present land surface when ocean waters rushed from their basins, exposing present-day ocean areas as dry land. This was the time when mammoths and other extinct forms perished. Following this, man and modern species were created within a six-day period, and the present sea bed was their homeland. Next came the great deluge described by Noah, with the waters gradually receding from the land to refill the original ocean bed (Page 1969:261). With such a theory it was obvious that human remains never would be found in association with extinct forms of life. Moreover, in estimating the last flooding of the earth at no more than 5,000–6,000 years before, Cuvier brought the natural history of the earth and its inhabitants into accord with theological time.

Cuvier's theory of catastrophism, formulated in 1812, was a compromise with theological interpretation and stirred contentious disputation over the presence or absence of diluvial man. In England, the geologist William Buckland (1823) consistently refused to admit the association of antediluvial animals with human bones and artifacts he had uncovered in his cave researches. Biblical scholars could accept the growth of the earth in a succession of interventions, and they could accept the stratigraphic sequence from mussel to extinct animals to man as a progressive renovation of the earth in preparation for the appearance of its prime actor, man. In the words of John Sumner (cited by Page 1969:262),

> We are bound to admit, that only one general destruction or revolution of the globe has taken place since the period of that creation which Moses records, and of which Adam and Eve were the first inhabitants.... *But we are not called upon to deny the possible existence of previous worlds, from the wreck of which our globe was organized, and the ruins of which are now furnishing matter to our curiosity.*

The number of these previous worlds and their catastrophic successions could and would be increased according to necessity in explaining the different classes of animal and plant life as they appeared in time, experienced their moment of life, and then disappeared in a great convulsion—to be succeeded by a new creation. According to Bourdier (1969:60), Alcide d'Orbigny in 1849 held that there were twenty-nine successive creations. The more creations added, the more difficulty geologists and paleontologists had in determining whether an intermediate species should be assigned to X creation species or to Y.

Inadvertently, as the number of successive creations multiplied, paleontologists holding to the doctrine of the fixity of species slipped into an evolutionary way of thinking. Bourdier (1969:60) commented, "One would not suspect after reading Marcel de Serres' paleontological work, *Du Perfectionnement gradual des êtres organisés* (1851–1862), that the author believed in the fixity of species." However, the position and the dilemma were not new. The doctrine of the great chain of being had allowed eighteenth-century divines and some scientists to hold the idea of a progression in grade without giving up the notion of fixed species and separate creations.

CATASTROPHISM VERSUS TRANSMUTATION OF SPECIES

Catastrophism was linked to the idea that species had been fixed in their characteristics for all time by their structural design. A theoretical position that accepted the fixity of species need not rest on biblical faith, although Cuvier based his paleontological reconstructions on the principle that "God had created each species, and even each being, to play a definite role in nature . . ." (Bourdier 1969:40). Since animals were equipped structurally and organically to thrive in a special environment, there was little reason to think they would be versatile enough to modify themselves in the face of drastic changes in environment. Rather, in Cuvier's judgment, organisms were so functionally specialized that, like fish out of water, they could not survive outside their environments. Such an approach was not conducive to the notion of a dynamic progression or purposefulness. Indeed, Cuvier was equally contemptuous of scientific theories and metaphysical speculations that projected an evolutionary movement or a graded chain of being leading to man. Rather, he preferred facts, and especially those which testified to the functional fit between organic structure and environment. For the organic world Cuvier appears to have arrived at a structural-functional position not unlike that assumed by Hutton with regard to the earth. There were organic successions, but the integral operations linking each organism to its special environment were time-bound in the sense that the life history of forms ended with extinction owing to sudden environmental change—and no dynamic linked one form to another.

Meanwhile, two of Cuvier's erstwhile colleagues, Lamarck and Geoffroy Saint-Hilaire, were relentlessly pursuing a theoretical course that emphasized the gradual modification of structure as organisms adapted to gradual changes in environment. Lamarck (1914) concluded his *Philosophie Zoologique* with a genealogical tree of the vertebrates, extending their history into the unnamed millennia of antediluvian times. Lamarck (1801) espoused the view that life began with simple forms and gradually became more complex when mature organisms, in accommodating to differing environments, strengthened certain organs and parts through habitual use, while other organs atrophied through disuse. In time the changes induced by habitual use became entrenched, and these adaptive modifications then were passed on to descendants as structural modifications. Such a view was in accord with eighteenth-century ideas concerning the easy modification of external structure by differences in environment, climate, altitude, and mode of life. However, such alterations remained variants of a basic archetype that did not change. In opposition to this theory of endless variation without change, Lamarck proposed that changes induced by use-disuse could penetrate the structural heartland of an organism and bring about a modification in species, given sufficient time. Conceivably, then, the successive modifications could be linked in a grand continuum from a radically different original to the present species. Lamarck's colleague and staunch ally, Geoffroy Saint-Hilaire, was equally excited about the possibility of mutations due to sudden changes in the environment. Where environmental effects were concerned, it appeared to Geoffroy that the embryo, and not the mature adult, represented the critical stage for modification. If the right accident overtook the embryo of a reptile in the course of its development, for example, the reptile could be transformed into a bird. How could this take place? Assume that

> the pulmonary sac of a reptile in the early stages of development should undergo a constriction at its midpoint, in such a way as to separate all the blood vessels in the thorax from the bottom of the pulmonary sac in the abdomen, there would result a circumstance favoring the development of the entire structure of a bird ... the air ... forced back by the muscles of the abdomen ... [and] compressed ... [would contain] more oxygen in a smaller volume. (Geoffroy 1829, cited by Bourdier 1969:51)

This would result in the "production of warmer, redder, more fluid blood, more energetic muscular action, and the transformation of tegmentary tufts into feathers" (Bourdier 1969:51).

The key to the requirement for a more effective respiratory system, as found in birds and mammals, would be found in environmental changes. If the amount of oxygen in the atmosphere were to be reduced, perhaps locked up in greater quantities in calcareous rocks, then the imagined constriction of the reptilian embryo would become an environmental reality and stimulate extension of the respiratory system for survival purposes.

Both career and circumstances seemed to propel Geoffroy into the role of challenger to Cuvier's influence over the scientific community. After a brief period of collaboration in 1795, the two became protagonists of opposite positions. Geoffroy not only accepted the idea of progressive change through structural modification but compounded the affront by acceptance of the idea that ontogeny recapitulates phylogeny. The latter had been put forward by Professor Kielmeyer of Tübingen in 1796, and in the 1820s the theory of recapitulation was firmed up by the French biologists Etienne Serres and Giron de Buzareingues according to Bourdier (1969). Moreover, Geoffroy's experiments with chicken eggs, in the hope of modifying embryonic development, were designed to overturn the idea of germinal preformation with which Cuvier bolstered his theory of species fixity. On top of this, Geoffroy theorized that sudden changes in environment could produce rapid structural adaptations in the evolutionary mode.

The public confrontation between Cuvier and Geoffroy took place early in 1830. In retrospect, the clash between the protagonists of the fixity and the transmutation of species theories came at a time of a transition from one ideology to another. Considerable advances had been made in paleontology, biology, and geology that urged acceptance of the idea that structural modifications in both the earth and in life forms had occurred, and that these structural successions exhibited a continuity and directionality. Furthermore, the processes that had produced past changes were of the same order and degree as those presently observed at work in the world. Lamarck had been dead less than a year, and this added to the timeliness of the exchange.

Cuvier's tactics largely aborted the grand debate, and the politics of the July Revolution gave further reason for ending the intellectual conflict. Cuvier's reputation was sufficient to hold the line against all forms of progressionism. He called for facts, and went back to the Collège de France to reiterate the uselessness of theory for scientific interpretation. Seemingly the Cuvier-Geoffroy debate left intact the eighteenth-century position which asserted that the world varies but does not change in character. Curiously, in 1830 Lyell stated an identical position for geology while arguing that the earth's surface had been shaped and altered by relatively constant and uniform processes (see below). However, the facts that would contradict the "father of paleontology" soon would be painstakingly extracted from the limestone caves of England, France, and Germany. The task of transforming the homeostatic model of the world favored by eighteenth-century natural scientists and exponents of natural theology thus fell to the nineteenth century.

TRIUMPH OF GRADUALISM AND UNIFORM PROCESSES IN GEOLOGY: LYELL

Winning scientific acceptance for Hutton's theory of gradual and uniform processes was largely the work of Charles Lyell. *The Principles of Geology* was published in three volumes between 1830 and 1833, and was "an attempt to explain the former changes of the earth's surface by reference to causes now in operation." Lyell's interest in geology had been aroused by the Horatio-like exponent of biblical catastrophism, the Reverend William Buckland of Oxford University. A vibrant lecturer who illustrated his points with a rich collection of fossils, Buckland excited his students to scholarly collection by inviting participation in geological walking tours. Buckland was in close touch with William Smith, and consequently his students were introduced to a combination of mineralogy and paleontology in the identification of strata.

The 1820s were a time of great discovery and excitement in the development of the geological and paleontological sciences. The challenges posed by the origin of marl and the discovery in England of fossil crocodiles and iguanas so captured Lyell's interest as to draw him irresistibly from his legal career. Matters began to come to a head in 1826 after Lyell completed a preliminary review of the state of geology. At this time he formed the conviction that fossils entombed in strata gave no indication of destruction through grand convulsions of the earth. To the contrary, they lived out their lives, and their remains were deposited quietly and naturally in ocean and freshwater sediments. The earth was never in a state of repose, as catastrophists claimed, but was constantly and inexorably producing, and then annihilating what it had produced. So far as the earth was concerned, the combined and continuous action of aqueous and igneous processes could account for the geology. Igneous action accounted for the rise and fall of local shorelines and the gigantic upward thrust that turned marine sediments into mountains. Erosion and deposition could account for the continuities and discontinuities visible in the geological record.

Early in 1827 Lyell determined to write a book that would introduce needed reforms into his geological science. He faced the audacious task of convincing geologists that the very discontinuities they used to support their theory of universal and convulsive change were produced on a day-to-day basis by rain, wind, frost, sleet, snow, ice, temperature oscillations, and liquid thrusts from below. Geological time would have to be substituted for theological time. To turn geology around in the way Lyell contemplated would require a weighty synthesis. It would mean a compilation of meticulous records detailing the nature of strata, their origins, historic placement, and estimates of their antiquity. The coordination of local geologies was essential to determine the extent to which identical strata prevailed over wide areas or were restricted to narrow regions. Lyell had to reassess important geological sites which were cited as evidence to support catastrophic change.

The continental tour began in 1828 with a visit to the Auvergne region where Scrope had detailed the lava flows and proved the volcanic origin of basalt. Viewing river valleys carved through the basalt flows, Lyell marvelled at this astonishing proof of the moving force of water carried out over thousands, perhaps millions, of years. He also delighted in uncovering evidences Buckland had missed on his visit. Such evidence would make it hard for Buckland to maneuver and wriggle out of the logical admission that the topographic features of the Auvergne valleys had been produced by uniform natural forces and not by a deluge. In Sicily he ascended Mt. Etna, sketching its flows and noting how the volcano appeared to be resting on stratified limestone of recent Tertiary age. Observing the presence of recent marine life in beds beneath the stratified limestone, Lyell dismissed an earlier inference that stratified limestone always must be old (Rudwick 1969:296). The suggestion of a pre-Etna vulcanism that cut through the limestone on which Etna rested, in conjunction with the more than seventy volcanic cones and their individual lava flows, argued for a great span of time. Moreover, some of the lava flows already had been shaped into gorges by existing rivers. What amazed Lyell in his Sicilian tour was the way in which sea and lava beds were interspersed without evidence of grand convulsions. Near Aizzini a stratum twenty feet in thickness was filled with oyster shells that could have graced any restaurant table—yet this oyster bed rested on a lava bed and in turn was capped by a basaltic flow. He also observed a bed of coral, standing erect as in life, intruded within a series of alternate volcanic and sedimentary layers (Wilson 1972:251). All of this suggested a rise and fall of the land surface attributable to vulcanism. Equally startling was the discovery that Sicily was younger, geologically speaking, than its fauna and flora. These ancient Mediterranean plants and animals thus must have migrated to Sicily after it emerged out of the Mediterranean waters and when a connection with the mainland existed (Wilson 1972:255).

With perceptions that brought new insights and reassessments of geologic sites, and with reasoned explanations of facts, Lyell presented the case for gradualism and uniform processes. His work marked the beginning of modern geology. Henceforth it no longer would be possible to argue that geological forces in ancient times were greater in magnitude than in contemporary times. Nor could it be maintained that the whole earth had experienced a universal geologic event. Geologic events were localized and regional at best. Moreover, the time for these geologic events must be extended with great generosity. Archbishop Usher's theological estimate of the creation of the world at 4,000 years before Christ now was meaningless. Henceforth, men must turn to geological time to measure the antiquity of the earth and its inhabitants. By example and with text, Lyell reminded his readers of the necessity to observe and to describe what is before one, since knowledge of what is happening presently can be used to understand the past. Unfortunately for the science of the earth, geologists had filled out the past with imaginative speculation instead of prompting students to pursue "laborious enquiries into the natural history of the organic world, and the complicated effects of the igneous and aqueous causes now in operation . . ." (Lyell 1877(1):318). Geology now had come of age because the world could be treated as an object and was open to study as a complex of natural processes. Such was the singular achievement of Lyell.

In substantiating gradualism and uniform processes Lyell confined himself studiously to descriptions of what things were in fact, and how they had happened. The model he sketched for the earth was like that of Hutton. The earth was engaged in an endless cycling of land building, erosion, and deposition. There were successions of strata, but they were timeless in that they did not lead anywhere. Organic remains within strata proved useful in determining the relative age of stratified beds. With the aid of Deshayes, the famous French conchologist, he divided the Tertiary into three grand divisions according to the relative proportion of recent and living mollusca observable within the strata (Wilson 1972:259–260). In this way the Eocene, Miocene, and Pliocene were distinguished as successive epochs of the Cenozoic.

A descriptive classification of successive strata and organic life is one thing. Acceptance of a series as representing a directional progress was something else. It is interesting that while Lyell unseated Cuvier's catastrophism, he aligned himself intellectually with Cuvier and Linnaeus in denying that changes in organic life exhibited by the geological succession were progressive. He constantly cautioned that nature was not concerned with preserving a perfectly continuous record, and discordances in a series were expectable and inevitable. Indeed, the fact that plants and animals were engaged in a kind of struggle for existence meant that some species would multiply and others would face extermination. Extinction would compound the problem of transmutation of species, as argued by Lamarck. In 1830, the evidence that would convince Lyell of a continuum of modification leading from simple to complex organisms was not at hand. By 1863, however, he was convinced that Darwin's theory of variation and natural selection offered the most comprehensive explanation of the facts.

> Variation and natural selection would . . . afford a key to a multitude of geological facts otherwise wholly unaccounted for, as, for example, why there is generally an intimate connection between the living animals and plants of each great division of the globe and the extinct fauna and flora of the post-tertiary or tertiary formations of the same region; as, for example, in North America, where we not only find among the living mollusca peculiar forms foreign to Europe . . . but meet also with extinct species of those same genera in the tertiary fauna of the same part of the world. In like manner, among the mammalia we find in Australia not only living kangaroos and wombats, but fossil individuals of extinct species of the same genera. So also there are recent and fossil sloths, armadilloes, and other edentata in South America, and living and extinct species of elephant, rhinoceros, tiger, and bear in the great Europeo-Asiatic continent. The theory of the origin of new species by variation will also explain why a species which has once died out never reappears, and why the fossil fauna and flora recede farther and farther from the living type in proportion as we trace it back to remoter ages. It would also account for the fact, that when we have to intercalate a new set of fossiliferous strata between two groups previously known, the newly discovered fossils serve to fill up gaps between specific or generic types previously familiar to us, supplying often the missing links of the chain, which, if transmutation is accepted, must once have been continuous. (Lyell 1863:414–415)

The association of geology and paleontology was prophetic of another shift in the view of man and his world. Copernicus and Newton had reduced man's earth to the position of a satellite of the sun. Man no longer stood on a fixed point in the center of things and looked out in awe and wonderment at the firmament. With the triumph of Hutton's and Lyell's gradualism, the world was drawn farther from a unique place in a creator's design. Earth now was an object to be studied, and not a marvel of divine engineering. The close affiliation of geology and paleontology meant that man, like star and earth, would become an object of scientific study. In theological context man's world and man himself would be stripped of all mystery. However, man now would be in a position to see himself more clearly through a prism of objectivity, and in exploring his manifold character, move toward a new consciousness of self.

GEOLOGY, PALEONTOLOGY, AND PREHISTORY

The discovery of fantastic extinct life forms accompanied a tremendous interest in the history of the earth and inspired a search of caves in hope of finding associations of ancient men and long-gone monsters. La Peyrère argued for pre-Adamite men; now the search was on for diluvial men, and by implication antediluvial men. Certainly if bones of ancient men were found in the flood silts of the Deluge, then it was logical that they antedated the biblical catastrophe. In 1797 John Frere wrote a simple factual statement linking man-made flint weapons with a huge thighbone and jawbone of an unknown animal. The flint pieces were found at a depth of twelve feet in stratified gravelly soil in such numbers that Frere believed they must have been manufactured on the spot. This Suffolk county site was an open and not a cave site. It was excavated to furnish clay for bricks; and before Frere gave his attention to the stone tools, basketfuls of these flint pieces were used to fill the ruts of a nearby road. Buckland (1823) himself took to the caves, but following his meticulous observations concluded that the associated human and extinct animal remains were of different age and products of different floods. In Buckland's judgment, the skeleton found in Paviland Cave could be explained as that of a female camp follower of the Romans.

At about the same time, Father MacEnery explored Kent's Hole cavern near Torquay in Devonshire and discovered mammoth, cave bear, and rhinoceros in apparent association with flint tools that bore the mark of great antiquity. MacEnery and Buckland published a joint memoir on Kent's Hole, but the two were at opposite poles in interpreting the antiquity of the finds. Out of deference to Buckland, and with faltering commitment in the face of Buckland's arguments, MacEnery deferred publication of his views (Gruber 1965:379). The fact that the tools and the extinct animals were recovered from a red loam underlying a covering of stalagmite suggested to MacEnery an undisturbed association of very ancient men and animals.

On the Continent a similar search of caves was underway. In Blue Cavern in southern France, Tournal and Christol thought they had evidence associating human bones with extinct mammals. However, their case was not altogether convincing because of the intermingling of materials of great diversity and apparently of different age. In some cases pottery was found below the bones of extinct mammalia (Lyell 1863:60). In a tour of European caves Lyell (1863:62) became convinced that the association of extinct animal and human remains could not be accepted automatically and must be carefully researched. At times Buckland's argument regarding a mixture of remains of different ages was correct. However, in the case of Dr. Schmerling's (1833–1834) arduous and persevering excavation of limestone caves near Liège, there seemed tempting grounds for accepting the association of human remains, tools, and extinct mammals along with existing species such as the beaver, weasel, hare, field mouse, fox, and wolf.

The caves had difficult access, and frequently Schmerling and his workmen had to let themselves down by rope ladders and crawl through narrow passages before entering the limestone chamber. There they usually found the bones of humans and animals scattered in disarticulated array, sometimes partially articulated, in a mixture of stalagmite and mud lying beneath a limestone crust. In one cavern, Engis, the skulls of three humans were recovered along with the remains of rhinoceros and horses. However, only one of the skulls was saved for study. Similarities in the dispersion and intermingling of the human remains, flint knives, and animal teeth and bones led Schmerling to the conclusion that all were of the same antiquity. Here was evidence of diluvial man and his stone tools. The appearance, color, and chemical condition of the human and animal remains supported a common association.

For the time being Lyell kept an open mind and did not commit himself for or against the Liège finds. There were difficulties in interpretation, since naturalists assumed the elephant remains to be those of a tropical animal and were hard put to explain their presence in nontropical Europe. Schmerling muddied the problem by accepting this view, which necessitated deriving the elephant bones from a great distance. Knowledge of the glaciations that covered portions of Europe, and of warm interglacial periods, was just around the corner. The Ice Ages would resolve the ambiguities posed by the apparent association of "tropical" animals like the mammoth with subarctic reindeer. For the time being, however, the line against acceptance of antediluvial and diluvial man held firm, and it was another twenty years before that intellectual line was broken. The timing of that breakthrough coincided with acceptance of the idea of organic evolution. In the meantime, Lyell did not lend his reputation in support of a theory of species transmutation or of a progressive string of creations leading on to man. Lyell's reality model expressed a general view of eighteenth-century natural scientists, as well as one voiced by Hutton, that the earth operated as a timeless machine. It was in perpetual motion, varying, but always tied to a structured cycle.

ANTIQUARIES, MUSEUMS, AND PREHISTORIC CHRONOLOGY

The start of scientific specializations frequently can be traced to the pursuit of hobbies by amateurs. This was the case for geology and paleontology in the seventeenth and eighteenth centuries. Amateur interests and a desire to collect art objects likewise played an important part in the emergence of archeology as a scientific discipline. During the eighteenth century educated travelers discovered the antiquities of the ancient world, including the Near East, setting off a collecting fad that duplicated the avid search for Greco-Roman mementos that accompanied the Renaissance in Italy. Local antiquarians were busy in Britain during the fifteenth and sixteenth centuries also, and in 1533 John Leland was appointed king's antiquary with the task of listing historic monuments (Daniel 1950:18). In time these often romantic interests of local antiquarians precipitated more scholarly efforts to excavate chambers commonly assumed to be the work of druids. The most comprehensive of these prescientific investigations of county antiquities was produced by Colt Hoare in his *History of Ancient Wiltshire* (1812–1821). Hoare excavated a large number of barrows (ca. 379) and attempted to distinguish the relative age of interments and to categorize the barrows into long and round types (Daniel 1950:30–31). National pride played its part in arousing interest in a national past that antedated Roman times. As European states achieved national unifications and embarked on modernization, they cultivated the link between land and ancestor in a romanticized literature, drama, and music. The desire to preserve national monuments and to draw unity and purpose from times long past inevitably drew prehistory within its orbit. Academies dedicated to Celtic, British, and Germanic antiquities sprang up, and governments assisted with the establishment of museums to collect and display the objects that symbolized the nation's past (for example, the Royal Society of French Antiquaries in 1814; the Danish National Museum in 1807).

The Danish effort to collect national antiquities produced the first breakthrough in sorting the chronology of tools and ceremonial objects of the prehistoric past. At the time students of antiquities confronted a chronological issue similar to that faced by those seeking to uncover the association of man with extinct animal forms. The geologist-paleontologist had to hurdle the pre- and post-Deluge chronology. National prehistorians had to get beyond a pre- and post-Roman dichotomy and set up local chronologies that were not anchored to Roman datum points. This was especially the case in northern Europe where Roman influences had not been carried directly by conquest but had infiltrated through secondary diffusions. Such was the case in Denmark.

The Danish effort at museum display relied heavily on classification to sort the ancient handiwork and to assemble tools and ceremonial objects that were alike. In 1813 a Danish historian, Videl-Simonsen, pointed out that prehistoric artifacts, taking account of their substance, could be arranged in a stone, copper, and iron sequence. This was the same chronological ordering proposed by Goguet in 1758 and by the Roman poet Lucretius. In 1837, the curator of the Danish National Museum, Thomsen, formally outlined a stone, bronze, and iron sequence for northern antiquities. As one walked from one case to another the assembly of pieces by their formal similarities and substance was convincing. Those who had been excavating the barrow burial chambers could observe Thomsen's evidence that such was the work of people who possessed some metal objects, usually gold and bronze, but never iron. Antiquaries thus were provided with a fixed point in a chronological sequence. Thomsen also noted that all of Europe, including the Romans, probably had participated in a Bronze Age culture. Certainly by the time the Romans pushed northward into Germany they had been in possession of iron for some time. Ornamentation also seemed to correlate with the different stages. Stone Age peoples pecked or incised bands or flamelike designs reminiscent of the work of primitive peoples. Bronze Age designs exhibited a narrow range of curvilinear motifs based on circles within circles and connected circular whorls. In contrast, Iron Age designs were representational, portraying conventionalized serpentine forms. As Christian influence began to penetrate, the heathenish forms were replaced by dragons and other fantastic animal forms.

IMPERIALISM AND SCIENTIFIC EXPEDITIONS

Imperialistic aims favored the collection of scientific data in the field. On his Egyptian expedition Napoleon carried scientists to survey natural resources, collect specimens, and delve into antiquities. Napoleon's campaign uncovered the famed Rosetta Stone that provided French, Swedish, and English philologists with a key to translation of Egyptian hieroglyphics. In 1800, shortly after the Egyptian episode, a Captain Nicholas Baudin proposed a scientific exploration and survey of New Holland (Australia). A newly founded Société des Observateurs de l'Homme (1799), originally organized to push forward a comparative study of man in "all the different scenes of his life," supplied a rather sophisticated outline for making observations on the native peoples (Stocking 1964(55):135). Joseph Degérando (1969) in typical progressivist mode laid out the steps by which an observer could penetrate savage life and thought, proceeding from simple sensations to abstract ideas without being trapped into attributing to "savages" the logic of Western science. Degérando stressed the need for making systematic and objective records to include the relations of the sexes in domestic society, the moral education of infants, and a description of the society in its political, civil, economic, and moral-religious aspects. Knowledge of the native tongue was a necessary first step to proper observation and communication, but in the meantime one could uncover information on the physical characteristics of the people with regard to their strength of body, physical dexterity, health, and lifespan.

The French expedition to New Holland (1800–1804) seems to have been the first attempt to make a scientific collection of information about a primitive people. The fact that it carried scientifically trained personnel distinguished the French expedition from the descriptive reports of travelers, explorers, and missionaries. Owing to various accidents, the collections of the expedition were dispersed or otherwise lost, but some observations on the physical, intellectual, and moral characteristics of Australian and adjacent peoples were published along with dynamometer tests of Tasmanians, Malays, and Europeans. Peron, the "ethnologist" of the expedition, discovered that he could construct a strength scale ranging from the "degraded" and weak Tasmanians to the strong and civilized Europeans.

An earlier scientific venture (1768–1771) by the Royal Society of England under the command of James Cook produced descriptions of Tahitian and Maori life and custom by Sir Joseph Banks (1734–1820). In this instance the expedition was directed to Tahiti to observe the transit of Venus, and but for the personal inclinations of Banks, no detailed account of how the Tahitians lived would have been made. Banks hoped to collect plants on this tour of the world, and the entourage of the *Endeavor* was weighted with botanists. Ethnographic information was incidental, and Banks was at his best when describing the making of tapa cloth or the use of natural products in the crafting of tools.

SCHEDULES AND NOTES AND QUERIES

The move to establish a list of questions to guide observation of primitive peoples did not surface again until 1839. That year J. C. Prichard delivered a paper before the British Association for the Advancement of Science (BAAS) in which he pointed to the danger of a rapid extinction of native peoples. The British association responded by underwriting a committee of three (Prichard, surgeon and "physical anthropologist"; Richard Owen, surgeon-anatomist; Thomas Hodgkin, surgeon and prime figure in founding the Aborigines Protection Society of London, 1837) to draw up a schedule of questions to systematize observations and guide those in contact with native races. The original schedule of 1843 drawn up by this committee served as the base for subsequent *Notes and Queries on Anthropology*, published by the BAAS (Penniman 1965:53).

COMPARATIVE ANATOMY AND COLLECTION OF CRANIA: BLUMENBACH

During the time when ethnological and anthropological societies were forming (ca. 1840–1865), most of those who led in sponsoring a systematic assembly of material data gathered in the field were trained in anatomy and displayed a lively interest in race. In the eighteenth century there was a similar concern by anatomists for material evidence that would permit measurement of the critical differences separating man from the apes and the races of man. In 1795 the best collection of anthropologia was made by Johann F. Blumenbach (1752–1840), physiologist, comparative anatomist, and the reputed father of physical anthropology. At that time Blumenbach had assembled eighty-two skulls, samples of hair, and firsthand portraits of representatives of the different human varieties. Largely from cranial comparison, he determined that human beings belonged to a single species, though racially separated into Mongolian, American, Caucasian, Malay, and Ethiopian varieties (*On the Natural Variety of Mankind* 1865). Blumenbach's enthusiasm for scientific observation and collection inspired a number of famous naturalist explorers, including Alexander von Humboldt (1769–1859), who in 1799 financed his own expedition to South America at his own expense. The collection of botanical, zoological, and mineralogical materials were important objectives of the expedition, and after a five-year traverse von Humboldt (1814–1829) returned with a harvest far surpassing any previous effort. He also brought skulls from the New World for his old teacher, but von Humboldt's interests were neither anthropological nor ethnographical even though he provided brief descriptions of the mode of life of Indians living close to nature (for example, the Chaima of British Guiana).

RACE, LINGUISTICS, AND ETHNOLOGICAL SOCIETIES

Paleontology and geology, coupled with the vision of a transmutation of the species inspired by Lamarck, increasingly focused attention on the probable antiquity of man and the possibility of reconstructing his physical history. This was rendered more feasible by the historical linkages between Sanskrit and European languages which structural and lexical comparisons made by philologists had brought to light. Through the decoding of Egyptian hieroglyphics, the secrets of that ancient people were on the verge of being revealed. Advances in prehistory were bringing order out of the chaos of pre-Roman remains. Ancient Celts, Teutons, and Goths were taking their place in a broader prehistoric context. As the nineteenth century dawned, Europe was stirring to visions of national histories and destinies which aroused a romantic interest in ethnos and ethnic culture. All of these developments forged a linkage between folk, language, and culture which later evolutionists would translate into race, language, and culture. The European conscience was also being challenged by the moral issue of slavery and the need to protect aborigines from the rapacious activities of those who enslaved them and otherwise violated their human rights. Denmark took the lead on the slavery issue and by 1807 renounced its lucrative traffic in human cargo. However, Pope Pius II condemned the slave trade as early as 1462, and subsequent pontiffs added their condemnation just about every hundred years.

The works of Lawrence (*Lectures on the Comparative Anatomy, Physiology, Zoology, and the Natural History of Man* 1819), Prichard (*Researches into the Physical History of Man* 1813), and Desmoulins (*Histoire naturelle des races humaines* 1826) demonstrate that a comparative interest in the racial history of man was well entrenched by the second decade of the nineteenth century. At this time data of all kinds were sparse, and such works customarily included linguistic and cultural, as well as anatomical, evidence to establish the logic of comparisons and conclusions.

Use of linguistic and other cultural materials as evidence useful in the discrimination of physical differences and similarities was acceptable, since the eighteenth century view of man as a fixed but highly plastic species prevailed. Usually differences in climate were used to explain the standard deviation of human types, but Prichard (1855(1):99–100) turned to mode of life as the primary factor in physical differentiation. His view was that there were

in mankind three principal varieties in the form of the head and other physical characters, which are most prevalent respectively in the savage or hunting tribes, in the nomadic or wandering pastoral races, and in the civilised and intellectually cultivated divisions of the human family. Among the rudest tribes of man, hunters and savage inhabitants of forests, dependent for their supply of food on the accidental produce of the soil, or on the chase, among whom are the most degraded of the African nations and the Australian savages, a form of the head is prevalent which is most aptly distinguished by the term prognathous, indicating a prolongation or extension forward of the jaws; and with this characteristic other traits are connected. A second shape of the head . . . belongs principally to the nomadic races, who wander with their herds and flocks over vast plains, and to the tribes who creep along the shores of the Icy Sea, and live partly by fishing and in part on the flesh of their reindeer. These nations have broad and lozenge-formed faces, and what I have termed pyramidal skulls. The Esquimau, the Laplanders, Samoiedes, and Kamchatkans, belong to this department, as well as the Tartar nations, meaning the Mongolians, Tungusians, and nomadic races of Turks. In South Africa, the Hottentots, formerly a nomadic people, who wandered about with herds of cattle over the extensive plains of Kafirland, resembling in their manner of life the Tungusians and the Mongoles, have also broad-faced pyramidal skulls, and in many particulars of their organization resemble the Northern Asiatics. Other tribes in South Africa approximate to the same character, as do many of the native races of the New World.

The most civilised races, those who live by agriculture and the arts of cultivated life, all the most intellectually improved nations of Europe and Asia, have a shape of the head which . . . [is] oval, or elliptical.

Prichard (1855(1):100–101) noted that when the mode of life changed, there was a transition from one head shape to another. He pointed to the Turks now long civilized who had become "completely transformed into the likeness of Europeans." What Prichard (1855(1):1, 9–10; (2):714) intended, however, was not a transformation from one species to another, for he considered all mankind to be of one species or tribe. The different races were permanent varieties and constituted deviations from an original type. Prichard based his physical comparisons on skin color, type of hair, shape of head, configuration of face and orbits, and positioning of the foramen magnum. From such comparisons he concluded that the Negro race did not fall outside the human species (Prichard 1855(1):113–119). Finding that physical type varied according to climate and especially to mode of life, Prichard turned to language as the stable measure for establishing the physical linkage of people. What brought out the essential unity of mankind were not the variable physical features but what men shared by virtue of their psychic nature.

> We contemplate among all the diversified tribes who are endowed with reason and speech, the same internal feelings, appetences, aversions; the same inward convictions, the same sentiments of subjection to invisible powers, and more or less fully developed, of accountableness or responsibility to unseen avengers of wrong and agents of retributive justice, from whose tribunal men cannot even by death escape. We find everywhere the same susceptibility, ... of opening the eyes of the mind to the more clear and luminous views which Christianity unfolds, of becoming molded to the institutions of religion and of civilised life; in a word, the same inward and mental nature is to [be] recognised in all the races of men. When we compare this fact with the observations ... as to the specific instincts and separate and psychical endowments of all the distinct tribes of sentient beings in the universe, we are entitled to draw confidently the conclusion that all human races are of one species and one family. (Prichard 1855(2):713–714)

Holding such views, and accepting the idea of modification by transmission of acquired habits to offspring, Prichard suggested a kind of intraspecies evolution. In his view the human race had started out black and evolved to white. The same, of course, held for the change from the rudimentary state to the civilized life.

The cumulative effects of the new view of man and his relations to the physical world evoked an increasing interest in man as a physical being and in the differences in type exhibited by the races of man. Nationalism added a special emphasis to the physical aspect by stressing the superiority of one nation over another by force of arms. Scientific growth at the same time prepared the ground for the convocation of forums where information about man and his works could be exchanged. To some extent humanitarian impulses expressed as a need to protect the aborigines facilitated such developments. However, the founders of ethnological societies in Paris (1839), London (1841), and New York (1842) had much more than this on their minds. The Ethnological Society of Paris, for example, wished to uncover "the principal elements which serve to distinguish the human races" (cited by Tax 1955:316; translated). Such elements would include not only physical features but intellectual, moral, language, and historic traditions as well. They were concerned that none of these elements had been studied together and in sufficient depth to permit a sound base for a science of ethnology. The ethnological umbrella obviously would give shelter to every kind of scientific and humanistic interest. However, the primary goal lay in tracing historic relations by comparison of human physiques, languages, and customs. The Swedish archeologist Nilsson (1868:4) hastened to add that archeology should have a place in this new ethnological science.

> by the combined exertions of the many, a new field for human knowledge can be opened through this science, and that if ever we shall succeed in obtaining an exact knowledge of the origin and dissemination of the various nations, it must be by ... the help of comparative ethnology. I cannot coincide in the opinion ... that all endeavours in this direction are as yet premature; the first attempt must always be unsatisfactory, but it induces fresh

research, directs our attention to new objects, and leads ultimately, by its very imperfections, to more profound and more complete results.

Nilsson expressed a growing perception on the part of those impelled to set up a study of the historic interrelations of races, languages, and cultures —that it would require the cooperation of specialists from many different fields.

PHASING OUT OF EIGHTEENTH-CENTURY THOUGHT

The 1830s, in retrospect, were rather critical in that these years marked the transition from eighteenth-century thought to the emergent intellectual emphases of the nineteenth century. Curiously enough, it seemed to mark that moment when the intrinsic character of eighteenth-century natural science reached its finest expression. The model of the world as a perfected mechanism, visibly changing yet never altering in basic structure, was reaffirmed in Lyell's geology. True, gradualism and uniformitarianism triumphed over biblical and scientific catastrophism, but the world of nature and of man oscillated between successive periods of expansion and contraction as one force prevailed over another in an endless cycle. The same model explained the unity of the human species, fixed by an archetype from which varieties deviated without actually becoming distinct species. Man, richly endowed with moral and intellectual faculties, maintained a vast distance from the organic forces which guided the destinies of animal and plant life.

In the area of social science, Auguste Comte (1798–1851) synthesized the general thrust of progressivist thinking and elevated sociology to first rank among the sciences. An objective study of man's social life revealed the natural laws by which his nature and his social life had moved forward in the past, and such a science would guide him into a perfected future. Comte accepted the basic separation of man from the organic world and insisted that the human species had never evolved. Human advance was simply the perfection of a natural potential, and the moral and intellectual faculties were central to this advance. In character with the Age of Enlightenment, Comte described human progress as a succession of knowledge systems. From a rude fetishistic base, early men systematized their explanations of things in theology, then moved to a rationalization of first principles in a metaphysical system, and finally grasped the intellectual achievement of science, at least in the West.

According to natural law, the future belonged to civilization, and therefore Comte did not recommend paying much attention to peoples in the savage state. The important things were to know what natural laws governed social advancement and to utilize them in order that the march into the future could be controlled without the violence and warfare that had accompanied the French Revolution and the Napoleonic era. The future of man must be entrusted to science, for the day of a planned society had arrived. The fate of mankind should not be entrusted to tyrannical despots and upstart militarists.

The central issue of the human process, as Comte saw it, was its dynamics. Hence he opted for a study of social change or social dynamics rather than a study of social structures and their operations or social statics. The statical view he admitted to be the basis for sociology as a science, but the dynamical was more interesting, more involved in ultimate philosophical concerns, and distinguished from biology by the "master-thought of continuous progress, or rather of the gradual development of humanity" (Comte 1893(2):229). The primary objective of science was to discover the laws which regulated societal continuity and the course of human advancement.

The sociology envisioned by Comte would treat the facts of social life as natural scientists approached the material world, that is, as objects. This implied that sociologists would avoid value judgments about the worth of one practice against another. However, a dynamic advance to civilization, whether under the aegis of science or not, inevitably would provide the absolutes against which all human behavior must be measured. Comte had been influenced by the enthusiasm for social reform which had accompanied the French Revolution, and soon after his association with the social reformer St. Simon, he in 1822 drew up "A Plan on the Scientific Operations Necessary for Reorganizing Society." He went on to publish his *Positive Philosophy* (1830–1842, 6 volumes), and between 1851 and 1854 the *Positive Polity* (4 volumes), both based on previous statements. The chaos of the Revolution whimsically erased personal fortunes and lives, and the Napoleonic era simply added to the chaos, subverted the revolutionary drive for reform, and paved the way for a conservative Restoration. All this vividly impressed Comte, who became dedicated to his own maxim: "Progress is the development of order." His science of society projected programmed progress with order and a perfected commonwealth grounded in scientific principles. In 1849, as revolution shook European capitals and Marx issued the *Communist Manifesto*, Comte's newly formed Positive Society countered with its own declaration of faith.

Positivism is a scientific doctrine which aims at continuous increase of the material, intellectual, and moral well-being of all human societies, and in particular of the societies or nations of Europe. It seeks to effect this object by special modes of instruction and education. Positivism has three divisions:

1. Philosophy of the Sciences, summed up in the conclusion that mankind must rely solely on its own exertions for the amelioration of its lot. The sciences co-ordinated in this philosophy are: mathematics, . . . astronomy, physics, chemistry, . . . biology, sociology . . . and ethics. . . .

2. Scientific religion and ethics. Positive religion has nothing to do with any supernatural or extra-terrestrial being; it is the Religion of Humanity. The moral code of Positivism may be summed up thus: physical, intellectual, and moral amelioration with the view of becoming more and more fit for the service of others. . . .

3. Positive politics, aiming at the suppression of war and the formation of the Commonwealth of European States. . . .

In this transformation of society Positivism repudiates all violent procedure. It acts by demonstration and persuasion, not by compulsion. Its device is: Love the Principle; Order the Basis; Progress the End. Morally its formula is: Love for Others. (Cited by Chambliss 1954:400)

The reformative function which Comte intermingled with his social science assured the presence of a strong humanistic thread in any future social science, at the same time introducing a quality of ambiguity into the scientific posture of social science. However, its presence certified that social science existed for the purpose of aiding mankind. Though muted at times and subject to benign neglect, this goal would never be surrendered by social scientists. This is especially the case for sociology and anthropology, whose origins are traceable to this common social science branch.

The phasing out of progressivism and its humanistic bias around 1840 marked the beginning of the new biological emphasis that evolutionary theory would bring in its wake. The humanistic and progressivist impulse remained, however, despite the hard line toward life and living things which natural selection conveyed. More important in the phasing out of progressivism was the alteration of course brought about by efforts to uncover the antiquity and history of man. This new-found interest, which required the cooperation of manifold disciplines, established a basis for developing an integrated discipline dedicated to the study of man's early development and led to the splitting of anthropology from the main social science stem around 1860.

SUMMARY

The years between 1800 and 1840 witnessed the culmination of eighteenth-century natural and social science. Auguste Comte consolidated the progressivist impulse to develop a science of society by making sociology central to future human development and focusing the study on Western societies. At the same time developments in geology, paleontology, prehistory, and philology prepared the ground for the emergence of anthropology.

Scientific breakthroughs in geology, paleontology, and prehistory opened the door to interpretations which accented natural processes rather than catastrophic interventions by the creator. Publication of Sir Charles Lyell's *Principles of Geology* (1830–1833) offered substantial proof that the earth was constantly undergoing modification and renovation through the action of subterranean forces, uplift and subsidence of land masses, erosion, and sedimentation. Moreover, the same forces had been at work continuously throughout the past. Building upon newly won principles of stratigraphy and of paleontological successions, Lyell also consolidated known stratigraphic sequences into a Cenozoic Era and provided a time chart by which fossil forms could be ordered temporally within this period of earth history. Although Lyell won acceptance for James Hutton's ideas that the earth was a product of natural processes, he did not conclude that the stratigraphic and paleontological successions represented a directional evolution. To the contrary, he maintained the position of natural scientists of the Enlightenment who saw the earth as a mechanical system. Like the heavenly bodies, the earth cycled through an orbit of physiographic change according to its properties, but never altered its basic structure and relationships. In consequence, the full weight of acceptance of natural processes with regard to the earth did not bear on the issue of structural modification and succession of life forms. The vision of an evolution of life from simple to complex forms, which Lamarck consolidated, proved unacceptable to current views as to the fixity or unchangeable quality of species structures. Like the earth, a species developed different shapes as its members migrated into different environments; but these modifications never changed the basic archetypal structure. The paleontological record indeed turned up extinct forms of large mammals unknown to man. However, contemporary animals, though different, frequently were related, as in the instance of mammoths and elephants. To believers in the fixity of species types, like Cuvier, the presence of these curious animal relics in alluvial strata, or in caves, was due to a radical or catastrophic change in life conditions. Old forms had been wiped out over vast regions by floods, as was obvious from the alluvial deposits. Then, as the waters receded, variants of the archetype which had occupied refuge areas reentered the area. The succession of forms revealed in the successive strata thus represented no structural transformation, but a succession of variants of an archetypal form. The notion of structural evolution thus was an illusion.

Holding the line against species evolution coincided with the view of constancy of earth processes which stemmed from the perspective of natural science in the eighteenth century. Acceptance of strange kinds of mammals associated with "flood" depositions suggested the possibility of recovering the human remains (so-called diluvial man) in association with these extinct animals. However, the strength of the biblical tradition, which gave man but a short time in history (ca. 6,000 years), militated against efforts to extend his history through association with extinct forms. Evidence of an apparent association of human remains with extinct animals in caves (for example, Schmerling in the 1830s near Liège) was turned aside. The human remains were considered to be of different historic times and were intermingled at the time of the flood.

The consolidation of eighteenth-century natural science views regarding the structure of the earth, of life forms, and of processes governing their changes came during the 1830s. This consolidation illustrates how transitional phases are ambiguous, since evidential proof of a theoretical model confirmed a perspective while at the same time its research generated facts which the model could not reconcile. Certainly the new geological and paleontological evidence sustained an imaginative view of evolutionary change. It also stimulated a continuing search for further data of earth history and the history of life forms, including man before the dawn of documented history. At the same time, Danish prehistorians ordered a segment of human history into three stages: stone, bronze, and iron. Philologists likewise enlarged opportunities to extend human history by demonstrating that the languages of Europe were connected structurally in grammar, phonology, and in word forms with Sanskrit. Through the science of language, the ancient civilizations of Egypt and of Babylonia now could be reached through translation of the hieroglyphic and cuneiform writing. There was every reason for advancing a broad study of the history of mankind rather than limiting investigation to the Western world as Comte counseled. The formation of ethnological societies in Paris, London, and New York between 1839 and 1842 focused this emergent ethnological interest in human history rather than the history of the West. However, new developments in prehistory, paleontology, and physical anthropology, coincident with the rise of biological evolution, would be necessary to focus an anthropological discipline devoted to the early history of man.

4

Differentiation of Anthropology as the Science of Preindustrial Man

INTRODUCTION

Scholars seeking to reaffirm their interest in a general science of mankind faced the same kinds of problems which confronted progressivists in the eighteenth century. They had to form themselves into a company of scholars distinguished from other intellectuals by subject matter and by the goals they wished to reach through investigation of their special subject matter. They had to develop a general theory and methodology which accorded them a measure of difference from related disciplines. Finally, this theory and methodology had to be applied to special facts which, in their gradual accumulation, would constitute a body of knowledge distinctive from that of other disciplines.

Between 1840 and 1870 there was ample ground for the establishment of a new discipline focused on the physical and cultural history of mankind (see Figure 4-1). A broad outline of the world and its inhabitants had been reached; and while interior Africa remained to be breached, European expansion and circumnavigations of the world in the eighteenth century had widened knowledge of India, Asia, and the Oceanic Islands. Second, the Comtean synthesis limited the new science of sociology largely to the West and its future development. Third, and most important, new evidences coming in from prehistory, geology, paleontology, craniometry, philology, and mythology indicated a need for a human discipline that would incorporate these data and give them meaning in a comparative and general theory of human development. Fourth, an emergent evolutionary theory suggested a new basis for grounding human development, both biological and cultural, in the processes of natural laws.

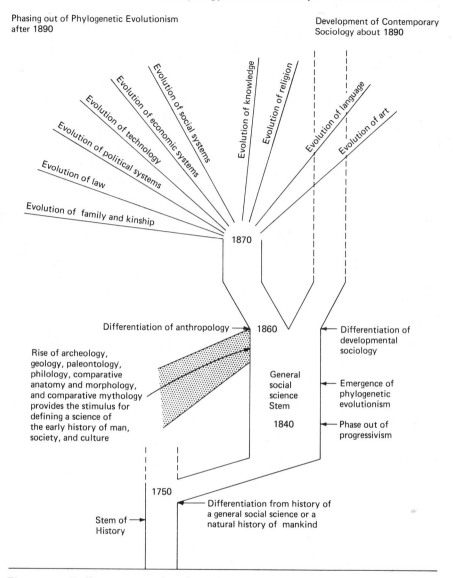

Phasing out of Phylogenetic Evolutionism after 1890

Development of Contemporary Sociology about 1890

Evolution of knowledge

Evolution of religion

Evolution of social systems

Evolution of economic systems

Evolution of technology

Evolution of political systems

Evolution of law

Evolution of family and kinship

Evolution of language

Evolution of art

1870

Differentiation of anthropology → 1860

Differentiation of developmental sociology

Rise of archeology, geology, paleontology, philology, comparative anatomy and morphology, and comparative mythology provides the stimulus for defining a science of the early history of man, society, and culture

General social science Stem

1840

Emergence of phylogenetic evolutionism

Phase out of progressivism

1750

Differentiation from history of a general social science or a natural history of mankind

Stem of → History

Figure 4-1. Differentiation of anthropology from a general science of mankind, about 1860, and elaboration of specializations integrated by evolutionary theory.

Two courses were open to those reaching for a new definition of a science of man. The first was to define the discipline as a kind of holding company for everything concerning man as a physical, psychological, and cultural being. Under such a view the anthropological science would serve as the integrative discipline for all sciences dealing with man. Such a definition clashed with established disciplines and contradicted the role of philosophy, which had assumed the task of synthesizing knowledge of all kinds including the nature of man and his destiny. The second course would narrow the scope of the discipline through its subject matter, as was usual in the case of economics, government, law, and the like. As for anthropology, there was some logic for limiting the discipline to a consideration of man's biological and cultural development before historic times. As primitive contemporaries of an evolutionary and ancestral past, pre-industrial societies fell within the anthropological domain and must be researched to disclose the stages of evolutionary development.

In perspective it is apparent that the formation of ethnological societies, beginning with Paris in 1839, signaled the formation of a company of savants separate from other professions, and who, by virtue of their common interests, could be described as ethnologists. Like historians, they were interested in historical relationships. However, the units of investigation for ethnologists were not nations or individuals, but races. Their goal of tracing historical relationships among races, and of comparing them in intelligence, morals, language customs, and other cultural features was sufficient to set them off from traditional historians, despite overlaps. The description of mythologies, languages, customs, and social organization associated with racial types provided a special set of factual materials for comparing the historical relations of the racial groups. However, the rise of prehistory, anthropometry, and knowledge of human evolution transformed such historical and comparative investigation through imposition of a dynamic evolutionary model. The idea of evolution provided the unifying theory for the emergent anthropological discipline and the rationale for its unique comparative method as well. The factual substance that anthropologists would study related to the early history of mankind. Such factual material would be correlated with race only as one spoke of lower and higher races in an evolutionary sense. Between 1840 and 1870 a consolidation of prehistoric and fossil evidence refocused the earlier emphasis on social and cultural advancement. This served to promote anthropology as a composite discipline uniting both the physical and cultural development of mankind as an evolutionary process.

ESTABLISHING THE ANTIQUITY OF MAN AND CULTURE

Biological and cultural evidences were equally useful in demonstrating human association with extinct mammoths and reindeer that lived during the alleged diluvial period. This period of flood, inspired by the Noachian Deluge, was reinterpreted in geological terms by Lyell as the Post-Pliocene. It was not so much a time of deluges as of glacial advances and retreats which precipitated local glacial moraines and the deposition of alluvium in beds that sometimes attained a thickness of thirty feet or more. In 1839 Lyell (1863:6) introduced the term "Pleistocene" to describe the nature of molluscan fossils in what he had called the New or Pliocene. Such terminology was not to last, as Edward Forbes in 1846 used "Pleistocene" to refer to the glacial epochs of Lyell's Post-Pliocene, and it is this usage which has continued.

The work of geologists in establishing a sequence of glacial and inter-glacial periods was an essential preparation for the dating of fossil and cultural remains. By 1860 two glacial periods and their interglacial periods had been determined both in the Alps and the European plains. Compacted beds of lignite between glacial gravels at Dürnten near Zurich indicated a warmer climate; cones of scotch and spruce firs as well as the leaves of oaks and yews were interspersed with forms of extinct elephant, bear, and rhinoceros. All this was similar to that found in Norfolk, England, where the lignite or Forest Bed of Cromer displayed a similar flora and fauna and again was capped with an overlying assortment of boulders, gravel, and earth, which testified to the presence of a succeeding glacial period (Lyell 1877(1):194–195).

By 1860, the collaboration of geologist, paleontologist, and archeologist accumulated evidence for acceptance of the antiquity of man and his works. The validity of the physical and cultural associations was paramount, since prior claims had been discounted on the grounds of shoddy techniques that permitted the possible intermingling of materials of different ages. Brixham Cave in England and the glacial gravels of the Somme River near Abbeville were critical in that the former provided evidence carefully extracted from cave deposits, while the Somme River finds were taken from the face of exposed glacial gravels. The recovery in 1856 of the Neanderthal fossil type from a cave near Düsseldorf, Germany, aroused once more the idea that the distant ancestors of present-day men were more primitive in de-velopment and that a concerted search would bring these ancestors to light.

Rise of Archeology

The rise of archeology owed much to its association with proof of the antiquity of human culture. To authenticate the association between human and cultural remains and extinct mammals of admitted antiquity, there must be no evidence of prior disturbance. This was the problem at Kent's Hole, in South England, which first promised to produce the evidence re-quired to sustain the thesis of man's antiquity. Repeated diggings had so disturbed Kent's Hole that it appeared best to look elsewhere. West of Torquay, not too distant from Kent's Hole, a new bone cave came to light when a rock-quarrying operation revealed a number of fissures leading into caverns. Such was Brixham Cave, an ideal site for proof, if any, that man and mammoth had walked the South England downs together (see Lyell 1863; Gruber 1965). A distinguished committee of geologists was formed, consisting of Falconer, Ramsey, Prestwich, Lyell, Godwin-Austen, and Pengelly. The excavation, supervised by Pengelly, turned up three impor-tant strata:

1. A stalagmite containing bones of reindeer and cave bear, varying from one to fifteen inches in thickness.
2. A reddish loam with many bones of mammoth, cave bear, rhinoc-eros, cave lion, reindeer, horse, and wild ox, not to mention rodents; usually from twelve to fifteen inches in thickness.

3. A gravel composed of many water-rounded pebbles, exceeding twenty feet in depth but without any trace of fossil remains.

Brixham Cave gave up no evidence of human occupation except for the stone knives, chips, and cores recognizable by any stone knapsman. The tools were not clustered as if deliberately deposited, but were scattered throughout the red loam. The fact that the tools were apparently deposited by water action at the same time as the bones of extinct mammals—and the whole later sealed by the stalagmitic formation—was considered sufficient proof for accepting the association of the tools and the animals as undisturbed, and hence of a common age.

Lyell commented on the sudden change of opinion in England that made acceptance of the association of extinct mammalia and man a distinct probability. This was due in large part to the theory of evolution put forward by Wallace and Darwin in 1858. The finds at Brixham Cave thus added substance to the idea of human evolution.

Contacts which British geologist-paleontologists maintained with their Continental colleagues facilitated interchange and prepared the way for acceptance of further evidence of the association of stone tools with extinct mammals of the Pleistocene. Hugh Falconer visited the Somme while on a geological trip to Sicily to investigate cave excavations and was convinced that Boucher de Perthes's claims for the antiquity of stone axes gathered near Abbeville were worth investigating. This led Prestwich and Evans to the Somme, and Prestwich drew the different finds associating stone tools with extinct fauna into perspective with a paper, "On the Occurrence of Flint Implements, Associated with the Remains of Animals of Extinct Species in Beds of a Late Geological Period at Amiens and Abbeville and in England at Hoxne" (Daniel 1950:60). John Frere's earlier report of large numbers of flint tools and chips found at Hoxne, as well as Kent's Hole, Brixham Cave, and the Somme gravels and sands now could be seen as independent pieces of evidence all pointing conclusively to the association of manufactured stone tools with the remains of extinct mammals. Prestwich was not prepared to push man's antiquity into the remote past, and favored an interpretation that viewed the extinction of the ancient mammals as not too distant from the present. Such extinction had come suddenly with a flooding of the land. Lyell (1863:143) likewise made several trips to the Somme Valley, and, as in the case of evidence from St. Acheul, had no doubts about the association of flint hatchets and knives with fossil quadrupeds. This conclusion was made even though the relative age of the upper and lower gravels in which tools were found was a matter of debate.

In France the case for the association of diluvial man with extinct mammals was largely the work of Boucher de Perthes. In 1805 Boucher went cave hunting in the south of France when visiting the brother-in-law of Cuvier. However, this interest in man's ancestors was diverted by a preoccupation with political economy and attendance at Napoleon's court where Boucher turned out a mélange of literary pieces and at times traveled around Europe on special missions. With the end of the Napoleonic era he took a post at Abbeville, where he served as collector of customs. Like many of his day he was excited by the intellectual ferment which ranged over political economy, earth history, fossils, and evolution. At one point he was inspired to write a five-volume defense of the theory of species transmutation put forward by Lamarck and Saint-Hilaire (Wendt 1956: 203). By the time de Perthes picked up the trail of diluvial man in the quarries of Moulin-Quignon near Abbeville, he was a well-known, if not always believable, literary figure.

De Perthes began his argument for man in the diluvial age even before he had solid evidence. Once he had the evidence in hand, he went on to theorize on the presence of antediluvian man. To counter scientific critics he formed the Société d'Emulation in Abbeville, and as president addressed a captive audience on the merits of his theory. By 1838 he provided members of the society with their first view of diluvial axes. In 1839 he carried his finds to Brongniart, who had worked on the dating of the Paris Basin with Cuvier; but Brongniart was unconvinced that these crude pieces of stone proved that man had been an associate of antediluvial pachyderms. He and Cuvier had decided that matter some time ago. Had Boucher been more discriminating in his selection of stone pieces that demonstrated artificial working, he might have made a better case. However, he included all manner of pieces that suggested possible use, which, on closer inspection, proved to be formed by natural forces.

The antediluvial dating of man to which Boucher remained addicted to the bitter end was inspired by Edouard Lartet's find in 1837 of an anthropoid ape that appeared to be ancestral to present-day gibbons. Cuvier's view was that monkeys and men were both latecomers, since none had been found in association with the large mammalian fossils. Lartet's discovery of *Pliopithecus* immediately suggested the possibility of fossil types of men during the mid-Tertiary. The notion was kept alive by Lartet's description in 1856 of *Dryopithecus*, again found in the South of France and of Tertiary age. *Dryopithecus* was held to resemble man more than any monkey known at that time. Its discovery aroused a stormy discussion, but in 1890 Gaudry, with a better-preserved jaw in hand, was able to show that *Dryopithecus fontani* was less developed than the higher apes (Boule and Vallois 1957:82–83).

Boucher de Perthes first set forth his theory of human antiquity in *De la Création: essai sur l'origine et la progression des êtres* (1838–1841, 5 volumes). By 1847 he saw Picardy as the setting for Tertiary hunters who were Adam's ancestors. Picardy, in fact, was the cradle of civilization, and the Gallic race its creators (Wendt 1956:205). Boucher's tenacity and literary flair for publicity which drew upon feelings of national pride kept the issue before the public and forced members of the National Academy to reply. The Academy maintained a hostile and skeptical attitude toward anything that undermined Cuvier's teaching and genius. Locally, however, Boucher made one important conversion. Dr. Rigollot of Amiens, long a skeptic of Boucher's claims, came to Abbeville for an inspection and tour. On returning to Amiens he searched the local flint gravels corresponding to the Abbevillean formations and in a few years collected several hundred hand axes. He immediately published his findings with the conclusion that the stone tools and animal remains were of the same age, and that the human makers of these tools must therefore have lived at that time (Lyell 1863:95–96). Four years later British geologists concurred with this conclusion. However, they never convinced Boucher that his finds came from the Quaternary. In 1863, at the age of seventy-five, Boucher, still in pursuit of the bones of Tertiary Man, reported the recovery of a fossilized human jaw from the quarry at Abbeville. The debate over this find was long and heated, but in the end the British view prevailed that the jaw was a hoax perpetrated by the workmen. However, the episode drew attention to the fact that in all their searches for evidences of early man, the bones of these ancient tool makers had eluded them, or like the Neanderthal discovery, had been dismissed as pathological.

The issue of Tertiary man did not end with Boucher de Perthes's passing in 1868. Actually, in 1867, at the International Congress of Prehistoric Archaeology and Anthropology in Paris, bones and flints ranging in age as far back as the Oligocene were exhibited as evidence of Tertiary Man. Incisions and scratches on bones were considered to be the handiwork of ancient men until disproved as the probable action of natural forces, including the teeth of animals which had gnawed and broken the bones. In France, Gabriel de Mortillet (1900) used flints from the Upper Miocene near Aurillac (Cantal) to establish an eolithic period. Eoliths were not deliberately shaped, but their natural form suggested use as a tool (de Mortillet 1900:96). The British geologist Prestwich in 1889 likewise described flints from Kent which he considered were crudely worked by man (Penniman 1965:175). British interest in an eolithic industry was continued by Reid Moir (1919), who in 1910 called attention to rostrocarinate or eagle-beaked flints from the Pliocene in the vicinity of Ipswich. Present dating of *Australopithecus* hominids and their pebble tools in the Upper Pliocene has made Boucher de Perthes's dream of a Tertiary man come true.

Developing a Paleolithic Chronology

By 1860 archeology was well on the road to being established as a discipline with specializations in the Bronze Age, Iron Age, Stone Age, and the ancient civilizations of the Near East. Funding from both government and private sources appeared. At this critical moment, when the antiquity of man was being accepted on geological and paleontological grounds, Henry Christy, British financier and friend of Lyell, funded Lartet's continuing search for the remains of Paleolithic man. It was largely through the researches of Lartet and Christy in the Vézère Valley that men of the Upper Paleolithic became a living reality, and the chronology of this period began to become clear. The sites of Les Eyzies, Laugerie Haute, La Madeleine, Le Moustier, and Cro-Magnon now took their place in the annals of prehistoric man. The Vézère caves and shelters introduced the scientist and public to a new cultural world. Ancient hunters not only left their tools and bones but also a message of their life in polychrome paintings that portrayed the bison, mammoth, reindeer, ibex, rhinoceros, and horse by which they survived and against whom they fought.

As early as 1858 Lartet began to refute the catastrophic theory of geological and paleontological change which French savants still preferred. The geological and paleontological successions which could be read in the earth's strata suggested to Lartet that man's history likewise was continuous. He (Lartet and Christy 1866–1875) then proposed a sequence of paleontological epochs to describe the stages through which primitive man in Europe had passed: (1) Age of the Great Cave Bear, (2) Age of the Elephant and Rhinoceros, (3) Age of the Reindeer, and (4) Age of the Aurochs. Both Lartet and Christy were anxious to distinguish their Reindeer Age from the earlier time when diluvial men wielded hand axes like those found at Abbeville and St. Acheul as well as from the polished stonework of the time of the Aurochs and the pre-Neolithic Danish kitchen-middens.

The Lartet-Christy chronology implied that the Paleolithic consisted of an older and a later phase. Lord Avebury in 1865 distinguished the Paleolithic as the age of chipped stone in contrast with the age of polished stone, or Neolithic. The Danish kitchen-middens suggested an intermediate phase between the Upper Paleolithic and the Neolithic.

Gabriel de Mortillet renovated the paleontological chronology of Lartet and Christy by substituting a nomenclature of type stations or sites where distinctive tool assemblages could be found. In his view the only proper chronology was archeological, based on the products of human industry. This nomenclatural practice became widely accepted and still prevails in describing prehistoric successions. De Mortillet's original sequence included a series of epochs beginning with Le Moustier, next Le Solutré, L'Aurignac, and La Madeleine. Later (1872) he substituted the Chellean, Mousterian, Solutrean, and Magdalenian. At that time he was unclear as to the proper placement of Aurignacian and dropped it. He also added the eolithic Thenaisian (after Thenay in France) and a Neolithic phase, Robenhausien.

De Mortillet's Paleolithic sequence, minus the eolithic Thenaisian, provided the basic framework within which a stone-industry chronology for the Pleistocene ultimately was developed. With the discovery of Azilian (1879), Tardenoisian (1879), Maglemosian (1903), and other cultures that appeared intermediate between the Upper Paleolithic and the Neolithic, the necessity to define a transitional phase became more evident. The term "Mesolithic" came into general use following the suggestion of de Morgan (1909). It now was possible to connect a cultural continuity in the West leading from the Paleolithic to a Mesolithic, then Neolithic, and finally to the Bronze and Iron ages. The latter, through Egypt and Mesopotamia, was linked directly to the rise of Western civilization through ancient Greece and Rome.

In Search of Paleolithic Man

In 1860 there was nothing in the record of the physical history of man to match the continuity of cultural history opening before the archeologist. Indeed, both nature and men seemed in a conspiracy to forestall the recovery and objective analysis of finds of fossil man. The alleged Red Lady of Paviland dug up by Buckland in 1823 had been quietly disposed of by identifying her as a camp follower of the nearby Roman fort. The Engis skull uncovered by Schmerling in 1835 was forgotten, as well as a curious skull fond at Gibraltar in 1848. Lartet's efforts to trace the seventeen skeletons found by a farmer at Aurignac in 1852 had been frustrated. Sighting a rabbit entering a hole, the farmer rummaged about and pulled out a human bone. Intrigued, he removed various debris, disclosing a large stone that all but covered the entrance to a small chamber. Within he found skeletons along with pieces of worked bone and flint. The mayor of Aurignac promptly reburied these skeletons with Christian ceremony, and when Lartet heard of the find eight years later, no trace of the skeletons could be found. The best he could conclude from the disturbed materials was that the remains probably were pre-Neolithic (Daniel 1950:93; Lord Avebury 1913:314–317).

Edouard Lartet did not live to see the remains of Upper Paleolithic man for whom he had searched so diligently in the rock shelters of the Pyrénées and in the caves of the Vézère Valley. However, his son Louis, in 1868, excavated the rock shelter at Cro-Magnon, where railway workmen had uncovered five skeletons. The skeletal remains lay at the back of the shelter and included the now famed Old Man of Cro-Magnon, three young males, a female, and the remains of an unborn child. A deep gash on the woman's skull indicated a severe wound from which it appeared she was recovering. Then disaster had befallen all, and they were buried together. Under anthropometric analysis the Cro-Magnon group emerged as a distinct race. They tended to be tall (6 feet, average), long headed, and big brained (about 1,600 cubic centimeters). They were soon noted to be somewhat variable as similar remains turned up at Mentone, Laugerie-Basse, Solutré, La Madaleine, and at Obercassel and Brünn. It now was evident that the Cro-Magnon race were the builders of Upper Paleolithic culture and the master craftsmen and ceremonialists who had perfected the superb cave art of the span stretching from the Aurignacian to the Magdalenian. The alleged Red Lady of Paviland now could be placed in the Aurignacian according to the associated tools. Moreover, these Cro-Magnons appeared not to be extinct but to have survived in West European populations. Their type was found among the Guanches of the Canary Islands (Boule and Vallois 1957:301).

The Cro-Magnon race may not have been the first Paleolithic fossil type to be found, but it was the first to be given recognition. It demonstrated no significant difference from modern man, and hence was a superior type. Before full recognition was accorded Upper Paleolithic man, however, two significant finds of another type were made, in 1848 at Gibraltar and in 1856 in the Neander Valley in Germany. The latter discovery proved the more sensational and critical. The story of Neanderthal man began in 1857 with the announcement by Professor Schaafhausen of Bonn and Dr. Fuhlrott of the recovery of an extraordinary skull, together with fragments of ribs, pelvis, humerus, and femur. The skeleton had been exposed near the entrance to the cave by workmen during quarrying operations (Hrdlička 1930(83):148–150). The local natural science teacher, Dr. Fuhlrott, became aware of the bones when informed that he could pick up some old cave bear bones (Wendt 1956:216–217). It was several weeks, however, before Dr. Fuhlrott realized that the bone fragments belonged not to a bear but to a form of man. However, the huge brow ridges, the elongated skull with a pronounced constriction in the temporal area, and the curvature of the thigh bone indicated that this was no ordinary type of man. From his inspection Schaafhausen (in Heizer 1962:117–118) concluded that (1) the general conformation of the skull was not to be found in any known race; (2) it probably belonged to one of the wild races reported from Europe by Latin writers, and encountered by ancient German immigrants; (3) the human being represented by these skeletal fragments had lived at the same time as extinct diluvial animals; and (4) the fossil status of the bones was uncertain because of the circumstances associated with their recovery.

The ambiguities surrounding the discovery of the skeleton were compounded by the striking contrast which it presented to modern man. Virchow for one did not accept the view that man in earlier times was of necessity more primitive in physical features. The large supraorbital torus and low frontal area, in conjunction with the low cranial capacity of little more than 1,000 cubic centimeters (subsequently raised to 1,230), suggested something pathological, meaning that some circumstance external to heredity had induced variation from the norm. Disease had attacked the legs, leading to a curvature characteristic of rickets. To cap it all, the individual in question suffered from arthritis. However, Broca supported Schaafhausen's view that there was nothing pathological about the skull and other bones, and that the scientists were in the presence of an ancient type of human being.

The Neanderthal find is significant in that for the first time it focused the issue of whether a more primitive type of man existed. An admission would open the door to acceptance of the idea that man had evolved. The Neanderthal skull, as Huxley (1896) observed, demonstrated a type that exhibited characteristics which were more simian than any form then known. However, he saw no reason for looking upon Neanderthal as intermediate between ape and man, or any clear reason for separating the type from the genus *Homo*. Other finds at La Naulette, Belgium (1866), and at the Spy Cave (1886) near Namur sustained interest in the Neanderthal form. In 1864 Busk, who had come into possession of the Gibraltar skull found in 1848, compared it to Neanderthal. However, it was not until Dr. Eugene Dubois (1891; see Hrdlička 1930(83):32–36) announced the recovery of teeth, a femur, and a skull cap of the Java Ape Man (*Pithecanthropus erectus*) that the idea of a primitive apelike beginning for man could be accepted on the basis of fossil evidence and Neanderthal could be accorded a place in that evolutionary development. By the time of Dubois' discovery, the world had thirty years to debate and accept Darwin's theory of evolution.

The *Pithecanthropus* remains were no accidental discovery. Dr. Dubois had requested assignment to Indonesia in hope of finding traces of man's evolutionary development. He arrived in Java in 1889 and immediately began his search along the Bengawan or Solo River where Pliocene and Pleistocene formations were exposed. Near Trinil in 1891 he found a very rich fossiliferous stratum and in September and October of that year recovered a molar tooth and a skull cap a meter away (see the reprint of a portion of his 1891 report in Hrdlička 1930(83):29–32). In the following year, in the same bed, but fifteen meters away from the skull cap, he turned up a left femur and a second molar.

In his initial report Dubois was of the opinion that *Anthropopithecus troglodytes*, as he first termed the manlike ape, was a new genus of Pleistocene chimpanzee. By 1892 he was ready to state that "it seems ... quite possible that man has evolved from this old-Pleistocene [lower Pleistocene] Anthropopithecus erectus" (cited by Hrdlička 1930(83):36). In his 1894 memoir Dubois introduced the nomenclature *Pithecanthropus erectus*, which remained standard until this type, along with *Sinanthropus pekinensis*, were reassigned to the taxon *Homo erectus*. Dubois considered the skull cap, femur, and teeth to be from a single female individual. The femur gave a height of 5 feet, 7 inches and indicated a semierect posture. The height seemed too great for a female of the species, and hence there were grounds for doubting that it belonged to the skull cap. The configuration of the brain, taken from an endocranial cast, demonstrated remarkable human characteristics. Cranial capacity, estimated at 900 cubic centimeters, was 300 cubic centimeters above the best recorded for the gorilla and not far below the minimum of some modern crania. After considered review Dubois formed the judgment that *Pithecanthropus* must represent "the precursor of man" (cited by Hrdlička 1930(83):40). However, in his final report of 1924, Dubois shifted his position again and took *Pithecanthropus* off the main line of development of man.

The ambiguities exemplified by Dubois' own interpretations were echoed in the pro and con positions assumed by paleontologists. However, as Hrdlička (1930(83):55) observed in his critical summary of the evidence, the exact placement was not important. Nor did it make much difference whether the individual finds were from one being or from several. The general implication was clear: *Pithecanthropus* represented "a form some-where between the status of all the known apes and all except perhaps the earliest man" (Hrdlička 1930(83):55). In the context of later finds, subsequent interpretation accorded *Pithecanthropus* the distinction of being the first man type (*Homo erectus*), from which *sapiens* subsequently evolved.

The *Pithecanthropus* find not only pushed the probable ancestry of man back to the early Pleistocene but also permitted vision of an evolutionary series of fossil forms. *Pithecanthropus* appeared as distant and intermediate to Neanderthal as Neanderthal appeared in relation to Cro-Magnon. A coordination of the evolution of culture and of the human species now was possible, stretching back through the corridors of time and linked to the successive glacial epochs and a succession of animal forms. To achieve this had required the combined forces of geologists, paleontologists, prehistorians, and comparative anatomists practicing as physical anthropologists.

RISE OF PHYSICAL ANTHROPOLOGY

In the eighteenth century Peter Camper initiated the first anthro-pometric description of a facial angle, originally designed to help artists discriminate racial characteristics. Blumenbach contributed further to crani-ometry with his collection of skulls and descriptive analysis of the Caucasian, Mongolian, Ethiopian, American, and Malayan varieties of mankind. Besides the general contour of the skull, Blumenbach relied on skin color, hair, and body build. In Blumenbach's view the Caucasian was the arche-type from which all others derived. The Ethiopian and Mongols represented the extremes in this degenerative process, while the American Indian stood in between in relation to the Mongol, and the Malayan was midway in relation to the Ethiopian (Cunningham 1908(38):26). Prichard (1855)

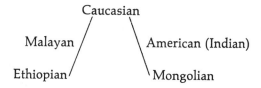

paid full attention to the items used by Blumenbach, but insisted that no single feature such as facial angle or globular contour could be used to describe the shape of the head, and recorded observations to give a more precise description. However, he resorted to the general roundness or nar-rowness of the head to focus differences between Mongols and Negroes and Caucasians.

Anders Retzius in 1842 devised the cranial index to distinguish brachy-cephalic and dolichocephalic types. He attempted to prove that most West European peoples were dolichocephalic, while East Europeans were predominantly brachycephalic. To give greater precision to his craniometric distinction, Retzius also made use of a facial angle. In a world survey of races from the evidence of cranial materials, Retzius (1856) distinguished orthognathic European dolichocephals (for example, Norwegians, Burgundians, Franks, Germans, Celts, Welsh, and ancient Greeks) from orthognathic brachycephals such as the Laplanders, Finlanders, Slovaks, Russians, Albanians, Basques, and modern Greeks. In Asia the dolichocephalic races were divided into the orthognathic (Hindus, Arian Persians, Arabs, and Jews) and the prognathic (Tungusians and Chinese). Asiatic brachycephals were all prognathic (for example, Mongolians, Manchu Tartars, Samoyeds, and Yakuts). In Australia the Austral Negroes were all prognathic dolichocephals, while Malays, Polynesians, and Papuans were prognathic brachycephals. With regard to the Americas, Retzius' cranial survey indicated that dolichocephaly predominated in the eastern portions of North and South America, while brachycephaly followed the west coast down to Tierra del Fuego.

Retzius' survey was made possible by museum and private collections of skulls. He drew heavily on Dr. Samuel Morton's (1839) *Crania Americana* for the American survey and received four American Indian skulls from this avid student of craniometry. However, Retzius was not above supporting his contention that the ancient Greeks were dolichocephalic by noting that their statues of Apollo and Venus exemplified the dolichocephalic type which classic Greeks apparently idealized.

The significance of Retzius' craniometry lay in the development of a simple mathematical formula to state cranial relationships (breadth/length $\times 100$ = cranial index). Anthropometry developed rapidly, and in 1848 at Frankfort-am-Main physical anthropologists established the Frankfort Plane as the basic orientation for measuring the skull and determined on a number of points of measurement.

Anthropometry was indispensable in describing fossil and historic skeletal materials and in time was extended to the description of living races. The cranial index gained rapid acceptance and favor as the best and most definitive measure of racial differences. J. Aitken Meigs, in his contribution to Nott and Gliddon's (1857) *The Indigenous Races of the Earth*, maintained that "cranial characters constitute an enduring, natural, and therefore strictly reliable basis upon which to establish a true classification of the races of men" (cited by Count 1950:90–91). It also was his contention that the cranial forms of the human family represented a natural and regular series of gradations. The climatic extremes of hot and cold favored a dull uniformity of plant, animal, and human types, and hence the lower forms of man were found in the arctic and in the tropics. It followed that the highest forms of mankind would be found in the richly diverse temperate zone. Waitz (1863), however, was highly skeptical of the inference of racial affinities from the skull alone. Toward the end of the century Topinard (1892) and Virchow (1896) attacked the uncritical reliance upon the cranial index or at best a limited number of features to distinguish races.

Topinard accused anthropologists of confusing peoples with races and mistakenly taking traits derived from anthropometric measurements as types. In fact, anthropometric traits were not linked definitively to any one people. Although historians viewed the French as composed of Iberians, Celts, and Gauls, who could say that these were races? Certainly the traits taken to distinguish the Iberians—small, brown, dolichocephalic—were useless in differentiating them from Berbers, Sicilians, and southern Greeks. Nationalities combined many different hereditary groups, and Topinard felt that physical anthropologists should leave the study of nationalities to the ethnographer and confine their researches to descent lines in imitation of those who bred stock. Virchow also noted the welter of confusion as to the term "race" and the way in which nationalistic fanatics seized upon special features to distinguish, for example, so-called Aryans from non-Aryans. Once it had been determined that dolichocephaly and a light skin were characteristics of the Aryan race, linguistic relatives like the Armenians were excluded because of their dark eyes and hair and brachycephaly. As for skin coloring, it varied according to the density and location of pigment particles (now referred to as melanin) common to mankind. Eyes were not colored blue. They simply looked blue if the pigment shone through from deeper layers. A brown coloring of the eyes was due to the presence of pigment particles in the outer portions of the iris. All of this meant that anthropologists should not construe variations in skin color as representing fixed traits which identified particular races in a qualitative and definitive way. The coloring of skin and of eyes, rather, depended on variations in the nature of pigmentation common to mankind and hence represented quantitative rather than qualitative differences.

Topinard and Virchow addressed themselves to those who sought to intermingle physical and cultural history and to make race the determinant of national greatness. According to Klemm (1843–1851), there were two kinds of races, the active and the passive. Consistently the European races, especially the Teutonic, were the creators and bearers of civilization. Comte de Gobineau (1915) interpreted the social transformation of Europe as a decline accompanying the mongrelization of the Nordic race. Nationalism was linked to militaristic processes tied to the unification of nation states and the dominance of inferior neighbors and colonial peoples. Chamberlain (1899) identified these basic forces as ones which made the nineteenth century an epoch of racial clash and national creativity. In Chamberlain's view, the future of Europe was in the hands of the Western Aryans or Germans who possessed the creativity and orderliness essential to the future advancement of European society and culture.

Previous to the development of anthropometry impressionistic and insightful description served to convey the distinctions observable among the varieties of mankind. With anthropometric techniques, physical differences could be described with precise statements of fact and of relationship. Even before Darwin and Wallace, anthropometry focused the importance of an assemblage of physical features in distinguishing human types and facilitated acceptance of the theory of evolution as a basis for the graded differences among the races of mankind. In its application to skeletal materials of fossil and historic populations, anthropometry also helped to develop a scientific and popular consensus that the study of man as an object was justified and necessary. In its own way, physical anthropology-as-anthropometry contributed a special impulse to the demand for a special study of man that would include the physical as well as the psychological and cultural history of mankind. The capstone to this redefinition of man's place in the world and in nature, however, was supplied by the rapid and wide acceptance of the theory of evolution. When this occurred, the drive to define an anthropological science uniting prehistory, physical anthropology, and ethnology was not only logical but compelling and inescapable, since no other science of this order existed.

MAN JOINS THE ANIMALS: TRIUMPH OF BIOLOGICAL EVOLUTION

Closing the Anatomical Gap

The supraorganic distinction progressivists asserted for man during the eighteenth century continued to dominate Developmentalist philosophy until Darwin, Wallace, and Huxley offered substantial proof that man himself was an extraordinary product of biological processes that accounted for all of earth's varied life forms—past, present, and future. Arguments for reassigning man's place in nature would have to include evidence not only of comparative anatomy but also that bearing on mind and character. The argument could be made that man and animal were anatomically comparable, but man's reason set him apart and above the animal world.

The attack on man's distinctive placement outside the mainstream of biological forces followed three channels. First the totality of nature was used to show a common genealogy, leading from simple to complex forms. The implication for man was obvious. If the whole of organic life revealed identical tendencies to alter in form through the twin processes of differentiation and selection, why should man stand apart? Second, comparative anatomical evidence was marshaled to prove that structural similarities linked man closely to some animals and more distantly to others. Third, evidence was brought forward to show that the mental, emotional, and even moral qualities of man were foreshadowed in animals, and that the manifest differences here, as with bone and soft parts, were not structural but rather a matter of degree. Differences in size and proportion were quantitative and did not alter qualitatively the essential structural-functional operations of the organs, including the brain.

In drawing *The Origin of Species* (1859) to a close, Darwin pointed to the genealogical linkage and interdependence of life forms. This linkage and interdependence could be seen in any tangled bank, clothed with many plants of many kinds, with birds singing on the bushes, with various insects flitting about, and with worms crawling through the damp earth, so different from each other, ... [yet] dependent upon each other in so complex a manner, ... [and] all ... produced by laws acting around us. These laws, taken in the largest sense, being Growth with Reproduction; Inheritance ... ; Variability from the indirect and direct action of the conditions of life, and from use and disuse: a Ratio of Increase so high as to lead to a Struggle for Life, and ... to Natural Selection, entailing Divergence of Character and the Extinction of less-improved forms. Thus, from the war of nature, from famine and death, the most exalted object which we are capable of conceiving, namely the production of the higher animals, directly follows. There is grandeur in this view of life, with ... powers, ... originally breathed by the Creator into a few forms or into one; ... whilst this planet has gone cycling on according to the fixed law of gravity, from so simple a beginning endless forms most beautiful and most wonderful have been, and are being evolved. (Darwin 1936:373–374)

By 1871 (*The Descent of Man*) Darwin assembled the necessary anatomical, embryological, and atavistic comparisons to substantiate a bold assertion of man's lowly origins, and to join his genealogy to the rest of the world. Man's genetic history must be linked to that of his nearest relations, the four-handed monkeys and higher apes.

We thus learn that man is descended from a hairy, tailed quadruped, probably arboreal in its habits, and an inhabitant of the Old World. This creature, if its whole structure had been examined by a naturalist, would have been classed amongst the Quadrumana, as surely as the still more ancient progenitor of the Old and New World monkeys. The Quadrumana and all the higher mammals are probably derived from an ancient marsupial animal, and this through a long series of diversified forms, from some amphibian-like creature, and this again from some fish-like animal. In the dim obscurity of the past we can see that the early progenitor of all the Vertebrata must have been an aquatic animal provided with branchiae, with the two sexes united in the same individual, and with the most important organs of the body ... imperfectly or not at all developed. This animal seems to have been more like the larvae of the existing marine ascidians than any other known form. (Darwin 1936:911)

With this genealogical tree Darwin traced man's ancestry to an ultimate origin in miniscule organisms at the very beginning of time!

Thomas Huxley (1825–1895), Darwin's apostle in popularizing the theory of natural selection, supplied the comparative evidence to disprove the contention that the human brain was structurally unique. In 1857 at the Linnaean Society of London he had been aroused by the presentation of anatomical evidence that claimed features of the human brain stamped man as unique, separate, and superior to all other animals. From his own meticulous comparison Huxley (1899:125, 145) concluded that Blumenbach was wrong in assigning man to a separate bimanous order and that Linnaeus had been right in stressing man's affinities with the primates, along with apes and lemurs. The comparative anatomy of the primate brain, except for recognizable differences in size and proportions, could be readily detected in man as well as in the chimpanzee and gorilla.

Closing the Mental Gap

Evaluations of man's place in nature and of similarities in his mental operations as compared to other animals can be detected in the eighteenth century. Linnaeus (cited by Blumenbach 1865:163–164) was inclined to brush aside the great mental gap which allegedly separated ape and man. "It is wonderful," wrote Linnaeus, "how little the most foolish ape differs from the wisest man." Monboddo (cited by Lovejoy 1933:289) also narrowed the gap between man and animals by denying any difference between the mind of man and the "wild man" (the chimpanzee) of Africa.

In treating man's evolutionary genealogy, Darwin (1936:446) knew that he must demonstrate that there were no real differences between the mental operations of men and the higher mammals. The graded differences existing between man and animals also held for complex emotional states. Man's best friend, the dog, was a prime witness for similarities in the emotional responses of men and animals. "The love of a dog for his master is notorious," wrote Darwin (1936:449), and it was equally easy to recognize expressions of jealousy, response to approbation, pride, shame, modesty, magnanimity, and fear. Like man, animals paused, deliberated, and resolved problems (Darwin 1936:450–453). It was Darwin's judgment that some distinction would have to be made in degree between savages and civilized men, just as differences in degree separated man from the higher mammals.

Viewing man in the fantastic vista of evolution, Darwin cautioned those who saw man as transcending his organic base. One must not underplay the importance of body by overstressing the power of the human mind and man's superior social habits (Darwin 1936:432). Present-day man had lost the instincts possessed by his early ancestors, but the mutual love and sympathy which men shared struck Darwin (1936:480) as instinctual and traceable to his early physical history. Whether sympathetic feelings for one's fellows were instinctual or acquired as a habit, Darwin (1936:480–481) argued that the primitive generalized social impulse was there, and with improved intellectual faculties man responded to this social impulse by using his reason and experience. However, the exercise of reason in the operation of the social instincts was not unique to man. Granting that a descent in scale to the lower forms of social animals revealed an increasing role for instincts, Darwin (1936:481) found their behavior impelled in part by mutual love, sympathy, and reason. From his considered analogies Darwin (1936:456, 920) concluded that

> man and the higher animals, especially the Primates, have some few instincts in common. All have the same senses, intuitions, and sensations,—similar passions, affections, and emotions, even the more complex ones, such as jealousy,

suspicion, emulation, gratitude, and magnanimity; they practise deceit and are revengeful; they are sometimes susceptible to ridicule, and even have a sense of humour; they feel wonder and curiosity; they possess the same faculties of imitation, attention, deliberation, choice, memory, imagination, the association of ideas, and reason, though in very different degrees. The individuals of the same species graduate in intellect from absolute imbecility to high excellence. They are also liable to insanity, though far less often than in the case of man. . . .

Man may be excused for feeling some pride at having risen, though not through his own exertions, to the very summit of the organic scale; and the fact of his having thus risen, instead of having been aboriginally placed there, may give him hope for a still higher destiny in the distant future . . . We must, however, acknowledge, that man with all his noble qualities, with sympathy which feels for the most debased, with benevolence which extends not only to other men but to the humblest living creature, with his god-like intellection which has penetrated into the movements and constitution of the solar system—with all these exalted powers—Man still bears in his bodily frame the indelible stamp of his lowly origin.

Huxley and Primate Brain Morphology. The Darwinian thesis envisioned a gradient linking simpler to more complex organisms. Within an order of genus organisms also could be arranged along a simple-complex continuum. However, in such a comparative continuum, despite variations in size and proportion, a fundamental structure persisted for any organ observed. So it was with man and the primates. Structural differences that distinguished man and the higher apes, Huxley (1899) affirmed, were of secondary importance. Moreover, differences between man and gorilla, for example, were no greater than those separating the gorilla from chimpanzees, orangutans, and others within the order (Huxley 1899:143–144). What held for bony structure also held for anatomy, including the brain. If attention were directed to convolutions, for instance,

the brains of the apes exhibit every stage of progress from the almost smooth brain of the Marmoset to the Orang and the Chimpanzee, which fall but little below Man. And it is most remarkable that, as soon as all the principal sulci appear, the pattern according to which they are arranged is identical with that of the corresponding sulci of man. The surface of the brain of a monkey exhibits a sort of skeleton map of man's, and in the manlike apes the details become more and more filled in, until it is only in minor characters, such as the greater excavation of the anterior lobes, the constant presence of fissures usually absent in man, and the different disposition and proportions of some convolutions, that the Chimpanzee's or the Orang's brain can be structurally distinguished from Man's. (Huxley 1899:139)

The implication was twofold: (1) the brain of all primates was shaped to a common structure and man's brain in this regard differed only in size and proportions; (2) the organic similarity implied psychical similarity in the functioning of primate brains, taking due note of degrees of difference. It was Huxley's (1899:152) judgment that no absolute structural line of demarcation, wider than that between the animals which immediately succeed us in the scale, can be drawn between the animal world and ourselves; and I may add the expression of my belief that the attempt to draw a psychical distinction is equally futile, and that even the highest faculties of feeling and of intellect begin to germinate in lower forms of life.

Curiously, as he reviewed his argument, Huxley (1899:155–156) was moved to conclude on a note that exalted man and stressed the behavioral differences between man and animal.

Our reverence for the nobility of manhood will not be lessened by the knowledge that Man is, in substance and in structure, one with the brutes; for, he alone possesses the marvellous endowment of intelligible and rational speech, whereby, in the secular period of his existence, he has slowly accumulated and organised the experience which is almost wholly lost with the cessation of every individual life in other animals; so that, now, he stands raised upon it as on a mountain top far above the level of his humble fellows, and transfigured from his grosser nature by reflecting, here and there, a ray from the infinite source of truth.

In assembling comparative and developmental evidences that would put man irrevocably in nature, Darwin, Wallace, and Huxley moved to eliminate metaphysical distinctions that took man out of the natural world and assigned him a special destiny subject to laws applicable to man alone. Now under natural selection man was subordinate to the same primitive processes that operated against and through all living organisms. Human beings, as animals, had to adapt, or perish through failure to reproduce. All organisms were locked in dynamic relations to their environments. Somehow, in adjusting, newly established responses fed messages to the vital internal structure, provoking alterations in structure that made the species more adaptable. At times the apparent natural tendency to vary produced a change that strengthened the correspondence between organic structure and environment. But all organisms were in the grip of a fierce competition for existence. The keynote of the natural world was "survival of the fittest."

THE RISE OF ANTHROPOLOGICAL SOCIETIES AND THE SCIENCE OF MAN

The evolutionary perspective provided a perfect intellectual catalyst for the emphasis on the physical and prehistoric development of man and culture. The idea that all living forms were united in a common descent with modification opened up panoramic vistas with regard to the physical history of man. Scientists now could intensify their search of Quaternary caves and glacial sands and gravels in the sure expectation that they would turn up man's ancestors. More than ever, it seemed imperative to create a new science that would unite the investigation of the physical, linguistic, psychological, and cultural history of mankind. Birth of the new discipline rested on a new confidence conveyed by methodological breakthroughs in geology, paleontology, prehistory, and anthropometry. Science now possessed the means for controlling the collection, ordering, and analysis of the varied materials which such a discipline required. The "considerable revolution in natural history" predicted in 1876 by Darwin (1936:371) was extended rapidly to man, turning him into an object of scientific study just as any other particle of nature. The strength of this impulse to found a new science of man can be read in the rapid rise of anthropological societies, beginning in Paris (1859), then London (1863), Berlin (1869), Vienna (1870), Stockholm (1873), and Washington (1879).

Anthropological societies developed in response to the need to study the origins and development of man as a biological species and to extend the science of ethnology beyond racial history, character, and customs. The time was at hand for "Anthropology [to become] ... the Science of Mankind," in the words of James Hunt (cited by Tax 1955:319) when promulgating the intentions of the new London Anthropological Society. Henceforth, their purpose would be directed to "everything that will throw light on the physical or psychological history of Man. It will be essentially our object to trace the primitive history of Man. But in doing this we require the aid of the geologist, archaeologist, anatomist, physiologist, psychologist, and philologist" (cited by Tax 1955:319).

After listing this impressive series of physical sciences Hunt noted how imperfect the new field was; for, considering the present state of the science, the task of mastering all these subjects was formidable indeed. The obstacles faced in integrating so many different disciplines in a unified investigation of the history of mankind made Hunt doubt whether the time was truly ripe.

In Paris a year earlier, Paul Broca, an accomplished anatomist, paleontologist, and student of the human brain, was more confident that the time for anthropology was at hand.

> In this incomparable half century, which has seen so many discoveries, which has explained so many enigmas, which has transmitted to us precious documents, as to the past of humanity; the study of human races has become enriched with an enormous mass of facts. . . . These isolated researches in the various branches of man, have, no doubt, been fruitful. Many particular questions have been better fathomed by being treated exclusively, and the number of demonstrated facts was considerably increased thereby; but this was not sufficient for the formation of a fascicle of methodically connected branches, which alone in the present day can constitute a science. The various branches of anthropology were already in existence, but anthropology itself, towards which they were to converge, did not exist, and to give it organization and life, more was required than individual efforts. . . .
>
> To describe and classify the actual races, to point out their analogies and differences, to study their aptitudes and manners, to determine their filiation by blood and language, is no doubt to run over much ground in the field of anthropology; but there remain higher and more general questions. All the

human races, in spite of their diversity, form a great whole, a great harmonic group, and it is *important* to examine the group in its *ensemble*, to determine its position in the series of beings, its relations with other groups of nature, its common characters, whether in the anatomical and physiological, or in the intellectual order. It is not less necessary to study the laws which preside in maintaining or changing these characters. . . . Finally, in a more elevated sphere, and without venturing to attain the regions which conceal the problem of origin (a fascinating and, perhaps, insoluble problem), our science eagerly searches for the first traces of man's appearance on earth, it studies the most ancient remains of his industry, and gradually descending from incalculably remote epochs toward the historical period, it follows humanity in its slow evolution, in the successive stages of its progress, in its inventions, in its struggles with the organic world, and its conquests over nature. (Cited by Tax 1955:317–318)

The fields which converged to form anthropology were listed by Broca as zoology, anatomy, physiology, philology, and paleontology, along with archaeology and geology. "Henceforth," he continued, "general anthropology and ethnology form but one science,—the most noble of all sciences, since it has for its object humanity, considered not only in itself but in its relations to the rest of nature" (cited by Tax 1955:317–318). At last, realization of the eighteenth-century vision of a universal science of mankind was possible.

To the biologist Huxley (1896:210), anthropology would be "the great science which unravels the complexities of human structure; traces out the relations of man to other animals; studies all that is especially human in the mode in which man's complex functions are performed; and searches after the conditions which have determined his presence in the world." The anthropologist would be a researcher with many parts, seeking to consolidate the human stage. As zoologist he described the anatomical and physiological peculiarities of mankind. As ethnologist, following Blumenbach, he traced the past and present modifications of distinctive racial features. In studying language he became a philologist, concerned with language—that vital measure of man's humanity—or he might turn to manners and customs in order to discover the origin of similarities and differences among nations. If desirable, he could use history proper, or, failing history, archaeology, which used the record of man's works to document the history of that long epoch before man reached his present condition. Beyond archaeology lay palaeontology, which had unearthed the remains of truly ancient populations which had been sealed in river beds and caves since the beginning of society and tradition (Huxley 1896:211).

The new biologically anchored general anthropology to which Broca and others pointed obviously would be a synthetic science, but not a mere compilation of the findings of anatomists, physiologists, psychologists, geographers, and historians of civilization. Anthropology, according to Theodore Waitz (1863:1–10), needed to take up its own empirical ground. No science attempted to treat mankind in the full range of physical, psychological, and historical diversity and development. Therefore, anthropology should assume the task of determining the importance of physical and historical processes in the development of mankind. Such a focus would place anthropology on the high road to becoming "the science of man in general; or, ... the science of the nature of man." Taking mankind at that historic moment before social living had begun, anthropology would record the steps by which a community type of life was initiated and a mature development of human qualities was elicited. Anthropology embraced all peoples in a broad effort to bring out their biological similarities and differences, including the influences of special circumstances and climate on their modes of life and characters. Above all, anthropologists would concentrate on peoples without a written history, plotting the natural history of society and the culture stages through which mankind had passed to civilization.

Waitz echoed a consensus that the anthropological purpose could be only achieved by joining a comparative study of the anatomical, physiological, and psychological characteristics of mankind with a like comparison of their social and cultural circumstances. Where the emphasis should be placed was another matter. There was a growing concern for race and culture as a special focus of anthropology, sparked by inflammatory debates over the inferiority of passive races engendered by antislavery movements and a renewed concern for national greatness (see, for example, de Gobineau 1915; Nott and Gliddon 1855). However, publication of *The Origin of Species* gave added support to the biological emphasis in accounting for different levels of cultural achievement and the rise of civilization. As early as 1857 Spencer (1910(1):53; 1880:295–296) had written, "The civilized European departs more widely from the vertebrate archetype than does the savage," for the European was more differentiated, with "a more complex or heterogeneous nervous system." By 1881 Letourneau considered the testing of the major black, yellow, and white races with regard to their intellectual, moral, and general civilizational capabilities to be the primary task of ethnographic sociology.

FORMAL LINKAGE OF PHYSICAL ANTHROPOLOGY, PREHISTORY, AND ETHNOLOGY

The search for a unified science of man intensified with acceptance of biological evolution and the implied monogenetic origin of mankind. A formal consolidation of physical anthropology, ethnology, and archeology in special societies newly organized or renovated to exchange information and promote publication in the interests of a general anthropology quickly followed. The International Congress of Anthropology and Prehistoric Archaeology met for the first time in 1866 at Neuchatel in Switzerland, site of Neolithic lake dwellings. In Berlin, the ethnologist Adolf Bastian and the pathologist and anthropometrist Rudolf Virchow teamed to found a Society for Anthropology, Ethnology and Prehistory (1869).

Aside from forging new linkages among ethnology, prehistory, and physical anthropology, formation of the general anthropological societies responded to a broadened public and scientific interest. The new societies were directed toward a national following superseding the earlier city-based associations, as the British society formed in 1871, entitled, The Anthropological (later Royal) Institute of Great Britain and Ireland.

The formation of new anthropological societies signaled a trend toward a distinction of professionals and the enhancement of professional status. Ethnology was accepted into the British scientific community in 1851 when the British Association for the Advancement of Science set up a special ethnological section. In the United States in 1882 anthropology was admitted to the American Association for the Advancement of Science under Section H. National anthropological societies conferred an even more distinctive professional status and allowed establishment of an independent base for commanding resources for research and publication. The strain toward professional organization was accompanied by efforts to introduce and expand the training of anthropologists within universities. With formalization of professional training in degree programs, the gap between laymen and professionals widened, forcing the former to channel their interests through local antiquarian and historical societies. As events in the United States moved toward the organization of a national anthropological association (1902), Boas, with his no-nonsense approach to science, argued strongly for a strictly professional society (Stocking 1960). However, Boas' protest over inclusion of amateurs was circumvented by others led by McGee, who proceeded to the legal incorporation of The American Anthropologic[al] Association and then called for an organizational meeting to draw up the constitutional by-laws.

PROGRESS AND THE SCIENCE OF CULTURE: E. B. TYLOR

The rising tide of biological evolution did not wholly smother the humanistic-progressivist image of a science that charted the successive achievements of the human mind in its progress to civilized society. Biologically oriented scholars themselves found the notion of a chain of ideas indispensable for tracing the origins and development of law, morals, religion, esthetics, and the technical arts.

When Tylor (1871) published *Primitive Culture*, he was but extending earlier research in which he relied on the processes of the human mind to give clues to the history of human institutions without the aid of historic documentation. *Primitive Culture* represented Tylor's considered effort to make what he called ethnography into a science of culture.

Culture or civilization, taken in its wide ethnographic sense, is that complex whole which includes knowledge, belief, art, morals, law, custom, and any other capabilities and habits acquired by man as a member of society. The condition of culture among the various societies of mankind, in so far as it is capable of being investigated on general principles, is a subject apt for the study of laws of human thought and action. On the one hand, the uniformity which so largely pervades civilization may be ascribed, in great measure, to the uniform action of uniform causes; while on the other hand its various grades may be regarded as stages of development or evolution, each the outcome of previous history, and about to do its proper part in shaping the history of the future. (Tylor 1874(1):1)

When taking up these two major processes for investigation, a key problem would be

the relation of the mental condition of savages to that of civilized men, [and here] it is an excellent guide and safeguard to keep before our minds the theory of development in the material arts. Throughout all the manifestations of the Human intellect, facts will be found to fall into their places on the same general lines of evolution. . . . The study of savage and civilized life alike avail us to trace in the early history of the human intellect not gifts of transcendental wisdom, but rude shrewd sense in taking up the facts of common life and shaping from them schemes of primitive philosophy. (Tylor 1874(1):1)

The formation of knowledge systems—what Tylor called philosophies—taken in their successive stages proclaimed the progress of mankind and disproved the theory of degeneration.

In Tylor's (1874(1):5) view, the science of culture was not identical with history. It was much narrower. He had no mind to write about specific tribes or nations, but of their general conditions with regard to knowledge, religion, art, and custom. Moreover, much of the investigation, as in the relation of savagery to barbarism, lay outside the documented record of history. The science of culture, therefore, belonged properly to anthropology, and to ethnography in particular.

Since Tylor was interested in successive stages, his use of the term "culture" or "civilization," represented a state of cultivation or refinement for a level of advancement. These stages of culture he described as Savagery, Barbarism, and Civilization. Such usage for culture or civilization did not break new ground, and later anthropologists in their eager search to pin down the scientific beginnings for their concept of culture have misread Tylor's meaning (see Kroeber and Kluckhohn 1963 and Stocking 1963). Nonetheless, Tylor was the first to encapsulate neatly what a definition of culture should comprehend. He apparently was stimulated to a clearer definition by Gustave Klemm (1854–1855), who used the term to include "customs, information, and skills, domestic and public life in peace and war, religion, science, and art . . . manifest in the branch of a tree if deliberately shaped, . . . the cremation of a deceased father's corpse, . . . and the transmission of past experience to the new generation" (cited by Lowie 1937:12).

There are echoes from the eighteenth century in Tylor's approach to the science of culture or civilization. He was an optimistic humanist, with faith in man's capacity to improve his lot through reason. He was not an exponent of progress by violent elimination of the inferior. In *Primitive Culture*, dedicated to the evolution of civilization, he felt an apology might be due readers for neglecting Darwin and Spencer, but his study was arranged on lines which did not find the works of these eminent philosophers especially relevant. Indeed, for his purposes, it appeared

> both possible and desirable to eliminate considerations of hereditary varieties or races of man, and to treat mankind as homogeneous in nature, though placed in different grades of civilization. The details of the enquiry will, I think, prove that stages of culture may be compared without taking into account how far tribes who use the same implement, follow the same custom, or believe the same myth, may differ in their bodily configuration and the colour of their skin and hair. (Tylor 1874:(1):7)

There were others like Tylor who muted conflict as a central process in the making of civilized man—Comte, Hobhouse, Morgan, and Waitz. However, considering the importance of biological evolution as an integrative principle, it was inevitable that the foundations of humanistic progressivism should be breached and eroded. By 1881 Tylor (1937(1):46, 91) was ready to grant that savages held their primitive condition because their absolute cranial-mental capacity was inferior to that of civilized men. In *Ancient Society*, Morgan (1877:507) made a similar pronouncement. However, the biological argument never was central to the thesis of either Morgan or Tylor, for it contradicted their use of a common psychic unity, operating without regard to climate or race, to produce similarities in technology, social organization, morality, religion, and the arts.

REDEFINING SOCIAL SCIENCE: SOCIOLOGY AND ANTHROPOLOGY

The rise of biological evolution led to a reshaping of general social science and provided a sound basis for using the model of the natural sciences for the science of mankind. The alignment of the "study of man" with the natural sciences challenged the humanistic orientation which had generated the idea of a general social science. Humanism, however, remained an integral part of the orientation of those who were determined to establish a science of mankind. The history of anthropology and of sociology is marked by ambiguities traceable to the alternating ascendancy of a rigid scientific or an humanistic inspiration. Humanists, as eighteenth-century progressivists illustrated, viewed the human process as subject to natural laws, but at the same time man was not subject to the organic processes governing the lives and destinies of animals. The point was made by Comte (cited by Lévy-Bruhl 1903:234) when he asserted that "there are laws ... for the development of the human species as for the falling of a stone." However, Comte (1893(2):229) did not accept the model of the physical and biological sciences because they did not admit the notion of progressive development. Hence, sociology was independent of biological theory and method. On the other hand, Spencer geared most of his social theory to the natural sciences and the biological model, seeing society as an organism both in its day-to-day operations and in the trajectory of its evolutionary history.

While anthropology was shaping itself around disciplines which focused the early history of man as a biological and social being, efforts were underway to establish the science of sociology. During much of the second half of the nineteenth century, however, the lines between sociology and anthropology were not sharply drawn because of their common acceptance of evolutionary process as intrinsic to an understanding of man, society, and culture. The prehistorian Gabriel de Mortillet (cited by Daniel 1950: 120) strikingly summarized this common concern with three thoughts at the end of his popular guide to the Paris Exposition of 1867:

LAW OF PROGRESS OF HUMANITY.
LAW OF PARALLEL DEVELOPMENT.
HIGH ANTIQUITY OF MAN. [translated]

Efforts to place sociology and anthropology among the sciences necessarily involved justification of their existence in terms of subject matter. The anthropological trend focused on the early history of mankind and the simpler preindustrial peoples as stand-ins for a precivilized age. The sociological effort was directed toward the separation of the social as a distinct level of reality which sociologists would study exclusively. With his definition of culture, Tylor posed the same issue for anthropologists—that their proper subject matter was culture. Attention to early attempts to define sociology therefore is vital to understanding similar efforts to discriminate anthropology and its proper domain of investigation.

Sociology, or the Science of Society

Both Comte (1893) and Spencer (1857) first composed studied arguments for a science of sociology and tied it to an order of reality that existed separately and above the biological. For Comte, as for Spencer, the three orders of reality—the inorganic, organic, and superorganic—were interrelated or overlapped at certain points. Nevertheless, each of these orders of reality possessed its own special structurings and functions, and operated according to special laws governing its intrinsic form.

The idea that reality processes are divided into a number of levels raises important problems for causal explanation. First, each level can be viewed as conceptually distinct and operating causally independently of the other levels. Second, a higher level can be seen as an emergent phenomenon of a lower level. Third, the several levels can be considered to be interrelated and capable of mutually stimulating modifications in other levels.

In their efforts to define a subject matter for sociology, both Comte and Spencer were led to construct the social as superorganic. This meant that the social constituted an autonomous and self-contained causal system which could not be explained by the organic or inorganic. Indeed, in the history of the sciences, development of the physical and biological sciences was a necessary prelude to the emergence of social science. This was logical, since the social was far more complex than either the inorganic or the organic. Hence, the science of sociology represented the culmination of scientific progress and surpassed all other sciences in its significance for mankind (Comte, cited by Lévy-Bruhl 1903:233; Spencer 1874).

Having achieved a separate and autonomous dimension for sociological investigation, Comte and Spencer attempted to give it a proper orientation. Two paths could be followed. One path would lead to the study of structural processes by which a society was ordered and sustained; the other would seek to understand the process of structural change as the society was modified through time. In the words of Spencer (1862:196), "Social Philosophy [science] may be aptly divided (as political economy has been) into *statics* and *dynamics*; the first treating of the equilibrium of a perfect society, the second of the forces by which society is advanced towards perfection."

The proper orientation of sociology, in the judgment of both Comte and Spencer, must be dynamical, for the objective of science was to understand change. Explanation of continuities in development represented the ultimate challenge for the natural sciences as for the science of sociology. Though historical in direction, the new science of society would not be history as normally written. According to Spencer (cited by Youmans 1874:iv),

> That which constitutes history, properly so called, is in great part omitted from works on this subject [social evolution]. . . . As in past ages the king was every thing and the people nothing, so, in past histories, the doings of the king fill the entire picture, to which the national life forms but an obscure background. . . . *The thing it really concerns us to know is, the natural history of society.* [Italics supplied]

What Spencer wanted was nothing less than an accurate description of the social institutions of peoples: how they conducted their daily lives; their technical, educational, and esthetic accomplishments; customs regulating intercourse among classes, morality, laws, habits, and deeds. He then continued,

> These facts, given with as much brevity as consists with clearness and accuracy, should be so grouped and arranged that they may be comprehended in their *ensemble*, and contemplated as mutually-dependent parts of one great whole. The aim should be so to present them that men may readily trace the *consensus* subsisting among them, with the view of learning what social phenomena coexist with others. And then the corresponding delineations of succeeding ages should be so managed as to show how each belief, institution, custom and arrangement, was modified, and how the consensus of preceding structures and functions was developed into the consensus of succeeding ones.

Such alone is the kind of information, respecting past times, which can be of service to the citizen for the regulation of his conduct. The only history that is of practical value is, what may be called Descriptive Sociology. And the highest office which the historian can discharge is that of so narrating the lives of nations as to furnish materials for a Comparative Sociology, and for the subsequent determination of the ultimate laws to which social phenomena conform. (Cited by Youmans 1874:iv)

The facts which sociologists Comte and Spencer sought mirrored group life. They would study group actions and products and leave study of the individual to others. The important thing to remember about society was the fact that it was composed of families—not individuals (Comte 1893(2): 289). Through a natural process of differentiation in structures and their functions, societies moved forward, drawing individuals into ever more complex relations that required specialized skills and sophisticated moral and intellectual decisions (Comte 1893(2):218–232; Spencer 1910(1):8–62). Hence, social science must seek out the laws regulating social continuities and human developments (Comte 1893(2):230).

For Comte and Spencer the state held a special interest, since in the political domain individuals were integrated in a most differentiated and complex set of social relations. They argued that social scientists had a special contribution to make to the future organization of society, since their studies would reveal not only the proper order governing functional-structural operations in industrial society but also—and more important—the proper direction change should take in conformity with the natural laws of social evolution. It was clear to Comte (1893(2):229) that social dynamics must take precedence over social statics. Admittedly, a statical view of society was the proper one for the study of sociology, but the dynamic orientation was more interesting and scientific. For Spencer (1900 (1):435–443) the science of sociology should first describe the ways by which family, political, and ecclesiastical structures evolved by differentiating and integrating as society grew in numbers and in complexity. To this must be added the evolution of regulative (law) and operative (economic) structures, including language, knowledge, morals, and esthetics. The goal would be to illuminate the "origin and development of those ideas which are leading agents in social evolution." By comparing societies of different kinds according to their levels of development, sociologists could plot the gradual differentiation of society. Once the successive forms had been determined, study could be directed to structural and functional interrelations and the systemic relations of parts (Spencer 1900(1):442).

The view of two kinds of sociology, static and dynamic, owed much to a model derived from biology. As Spencer (1880–1896(2):449–462) argued, the closest parallel to the principles by which social components were arranged could be found among living organisms. The way societies grew in size through aggregation of smaller societies and through differentiation, produced novel activities that led to more complex integrations paralleling the growth of organisms. The close affinity of the biological and the social was reflected in Comte's and Spencer's acceptance of an overlapping of animal and human characteristics. One could, they said, discern rudimentary expressions of sociality, morality, and even intelligence in higher animals. However, in man such characteristics were the distinctive attributes of his social advancement.

The view of reality as a structure of levels, relatively independent in their processual operations, carried the risk of dividing the unity of context in which action might take place. The social belonged to man and the social was superorganic and autonomous. Comte and Spencer thus seemingly removed man from the biological context through which they apparently hoped to advance a more comprehensive view of the human reality process. The relation of the biological and the social or cultural proved an enduring problem, with these two variables often being segregated and set in contrastive opposition. Comte did remove man from the biological evolutionary context by insisting that no biological modification of the human species had occurred. The social was man's environment, and there the potential of human virtues was cultivated and fulfilled. In turn, Spencer sought a merger of biological and social processes by applying the Lamarckian principle to the inheritance of socially acquired intellectual and moral skills. He added the process of natural selection in order to produce biologically and socially superior men who advanced society and civilization through their newly acquired adaptive capabilities.

The Science of Man: Anthropology or Sociology?

The rapid differentiation of the natural sciences, in conjunction with the accumulation of new evidences on the physical and cultural antiquity of man, induced three different emphases in efforts to fixate the core of a new science of man—(1) anthropological or physical, (2) cultural, and (3) social. Their significance is twofold. First, there is the effort of proponents to win acceptance of their definitions and orientations for a general science of man. Second, the anthropological, cultural, and social emerge as variables for the later specialized differentiation of physical anthropology, cultural anthropology, social anthropology, and sociology. The cultural and social also served as bases for distinguishing American and German anthropology from British and French anthropology. The German and American culture tradition began in the eighteenth century when the Germans and French evidenced a preference for the terms "culture" and "civilization," respectively. Tylor drew these two usages together in 1871 and provided the base for scientific renovation of the culture concept by American anthropologists early in the twentieth century. British social anthropologists drew upon the social tradition initiated by Spencer, but their immediate inspiration came from French sociologists, who traced their intellectual origins through Comte to Rousseau and Montesquieu.

Regarding method and purpose, it made little difference during the Developmentalist period whether the new science was called sociology, social science, or anthropology. The years between 1850 and 1890 were like a period of transition during which sociology and anthropology drifted into a clearer definition of their respective goals, subject matter, and methods. The trend in anthropology, it is true, was toward a special concern for the early history of man. But as late as 1911 Tylor (1911(2):108) joined sociology and the science of culture in a common concern "with the origin and development of arts and sciences, opinions, beliefs, customs, laws and institutions generally among mankind within historic time; while beyond the historical limit the study is continued by inferences from relics of early ages and remote districts, to interpret which is the task of pre-historic archaeology and geology." In a 1908 lecture Sir James Frazer (1913:160–161) assigned to anthropology, using the term in its widest sense, the task of discovering the general laws which in the past regulated human history and which would continue to direct human development in the future. Such an aim made the science of man very much like the study pursued by philosophers of history and akin to a newer study, sociology. Holding a chair of social anthropology at Cambridge, Frazer determined to clarify the limits of this new subject. Sociology, he thought, should be viewed as the most general science of society. Social anthropology would be a part of sociology, restricted to the "origin, or rather the rudimentary phases, the infancy and childhood, of human society."

By limiting social anthropology to a study of savage life, Frazer echoed the ideas of Waitz and of Tylor in placing the anthropological emphasis on the early history and institutions of mankind. Contemporary primitives offered the most immediate source for anthropological materials. Study of these simpler peoples and the antecedents to complex civilized developments thus came to be a major focus for anthropology, providing it with a recognizable substance and assuring it an independent place in the scientific division of labor. Sociologists gradually restricted their interests in a panoramic history of mankind and turned to the study of human groups in complex societies, especially European. This was the emphasis which Comte gave to the science of society as he outlined it in his *Positive Philosophy*.

The assignment of social anthropology to a place within a broad sociological discipline muted competition between social anthropologists and sociologists in the traditional sense, especially in Britain and France. A similar *modus vivendi* was reached in the United States when the concept of culture received wide acceptance and was formally linked to anthropology. Nonetheless, ambiguities in the relational limits of the social and the cultural produced differences over the scope of their disciplines and competition over the relevance of the two disciplines in formulating general laws. In 1895, Lester Ward, a sociologist, contended that anthropology, comprehensive though it was in its coverage of the human race, still remained a descriptive science, that is, it was more concerned with material facts than laws or principles. Sociology, on the contrary, was a generalizing science, devoted to the study of human associations and the way social relations contributed to the "general differentiation of the faculties and refinement of the mental and moral organization of the race." Anthropology, in Ward's definition, was a handmaiden to sociology. Sumner and Keller (1927(3):2165–2170) offered a like comparison, observing that if the "science of society contrast[ed] with history much as a science with an art," anthropology and sociology were related much as labor to management. Needless to say, Sumner and Keller relied heavily on anthropological materials to illustrate their ideas about social evolution, and objectively it is hard to say whether they are sociologists or anthropologists.

The procedural distinctions by which early sociologists sought to separate and to relate anthropology and sociology did not hold in the historic development of the disciplines. Both anthropology and sociology, following the model of science, combined description and generalization. The pragmatic distinction between these two disciplines came when their respective exponents began fieldwork. At such time, anthropologists and sociologists distinguished themselves and their disciplines not by what they said but by what they did. Anthropologists entered the field to record the life ways of Trobrianders, Zulus, and Zunis, while sociologists compiled information on urban life in the West from census data, interviews, and questionnaires. The necessity for gathering firsthand facts about the beliefs, customs, ceremonial, art, technology, and social organization of preindustrial peoples made an enduring impact on anthropology and emphasized a continuing collection of new data. Compared with sociology, this anthropological operation delayed development of an elegant formal theory and method and accented the role of the anthropologist as a participant-observer and a naturalist-collector of social and cultural data.

NINETEENTH-CENTURY FOUNDERS

A Potpourri of Founding Fathers

Nineteenth-century founders of anthropology present a professional profile similar to eighteenth-century founders of a general social science. All combined a public or professional career with their anthropological avocation. They included anatomists, bankers, classicists, economists, geographers, geologists, lawyers, literary critics, missionaries, and the medically trained.

The differentiation of anthropology from the generalized social science base necessarily added a special focus to contributions designed to establish and extend the foundations of the new discipline. Three kinds of founders emerged according to their special contributions:

1. Formulators of the general theoretical base used to develop an integrated approach to the study of man.

2. Those who labored to define the nature, subject matter, and methodology of the new discipline.
3. Pioneers in opening up specialized subject matter within the discipline.

Evolution: Theoretical Base for the Study of Man

Looking to summative principles which provide the most general interdisciplinary influences, Charles Darwin (1809–1882) must be accorded a prominent place in shaping the study of man not only in its biological dimension but also with regard to social institutions and social processes. *The Origin of Species by Means of Natural Selection* (1859) was devoted not to man but to biological processes viewed through the life experiences of fish, animals, birds, worms, insects, and plants. Yet Darwin prophetically concluded that extensions of these biological discoveries would be made to the study of human psychology and human origins. *The Descent of Man and Selection in Relation to Sex* (1871) reviewed man as a physical, emotional, social, intellectual, moral, and aesthetic being—but always against the comparative backdrop of his favorite nonhuman subjects. Moths, birds, and mammals were constantly cited by Darwin to demonstrate that man, though different in many striking ways, still was their partner in an organic universe. Differences in degree, and not in kind, related the mental processes of man to the higher animals (Darwin 1936: 494). Human sexual dimorphism exhibited in the tendencies of males to possess a more rugged body build with stronger musculature, greater size, and pugnacity, in comparison with females, bore witness to man's "inheritance from his half-human male ancestors" (Darwin 1936:872).

Darwin stimulated a new interest in the biological foundations and phylogenetic inheritance of human behavior. The theory of biological evolution also provided the base for uniting physical, psychological, and social processes. In the theory of natural selection students of society likewise found the primary process by which institutions and societies grew adaptively or perished.

Pioneers in Establishing the Nature of the Social and a Science of Society

Sociologists August Comte (1798–1857) and Herbert Spencer (1820–1903) pioneered in developing a theoretical base for an evolutionary science of society. In the process each drew attention to the social as a distinct order of reality which sociologists could study as their very own subject matter. However, in practice both turned to intellectual processes to account for social change and advancement.

Comte early became associated with vigorous attempts to reform society which accompanied the French Revolution. His *Positive Philosophy*

(1830–1842, 6 volumes) and *Positive Polity* (51–54, 4 volumes) were dedicated to the thesis that change in society could come without violence, and the instrument for the advancement of society was the science of society.

Spencer early manifested an interest in natural science, biology, and mechanics and for ten years served as a railway engineer before taking up writing on public issues and science. By 1850 he had assembled a number of essays (*Social Statics*) outlining his position on evolutionary processes and their relation to stability and change in physical matter, organic life, human psychology, and society. From this base he went on to publish, with the aid of public subscription, *The Principles of Psychology* (1855, 2 volumes), *First Principles* (1862), and *The Principles of Biology* (1864–1867, 2 volumes). *The Principles of Sociology* (1876–1896, 3 volumes) served as the crown to his design. To answer the challenge which the doctrine of survival of the fittest posed for the moral advancement of mankind, he added *The Principles of Ethics* (1879–1893, 2 volumes). He defined ethical behavior in evolutionary terms as a functional adaptation of means to ends. Mankind realized a more perfected ethics as adaptive arrangements relating the individual to his material and social environment improved; and, equally, as group needs were adapted to the requirements of individuals, to the demands of the physical environment, and to other societies.

None at the time equalled Comte and Spencer in the grandeur of their design for bringing the physical, biological, and social orders under the direction of a comprehensive unitary principle and for demonstrating that the purposeful impulse of this integrative principle must find its finest perfection in a science of society. Comte and Spencer differed, however, on three important counts. First, Comte's placement toward the end of the progressivist impulse prevented him from sharing with Spencer an expanded base for unifying the biological and the social. Comte always maintained in good progressivist fashion that the human species was an unchanging entity, while Spencer, following the principle of natural selection, brought dynamic quality to man as a physical-psychological being, and interrelated this processually with the material and social environment. Spencer's assumptions concerning the alteration of human physique and intellect through acquired characteristics proved erroneous, but at the time he presented a highly plausible and scientific interpretation and achieved a more unified explanation of important variables than Comte. Second, Comte programmed a planned society by rational, scientific man, whereas Spencer, relying on the natural impulse of nature, argued that man should let nature take the reins. Like Adam Smith, Spencer considered efforts to legislate the human process usually produced artificial restraints that violated the natural order. As a process, adaptation was more of an expedient than a planned operation. A succession of adaptive modifications that gradually improved functional relations with regard to environmental challenges might produce directionality, but the effect was not by the organism's own design. Third, Comte's eager desire to frame a new society deterred him from a lengthy excursion into the primitive past, while Spencer drew heavily on primitive custom to substantiate evolutionary continuity. Comte appears more sociological in his concern with the rise of society in the West while Spencer speaks more directly to the diversified anthropological interests of his day.

Conceptualizing Culture and the Science of Culture

To Edward B. Tylor (1832–1917), son of a brass manufacturer, belongs the distinction of holding anthropology to a cultural rather than a biological or sociological centrum. Tylor was forced to travel to improve his health, and in Cuba he met Henry Christy who collaborated later with Edouard Lartet in the recovery of "Reindeer Age" art in the Périgord. In 1856 Christy and Tylor set out together for Mexico, and out of this tour Tylor produced *Anahuac, or Mexico and the Mexicans* (1861). By 1865 he had assembled a wide range of essays that served as a prelude to his most important work, *Primitive Culture, Researches into the Development of Mythology, Philosophy, Religion, Language, Art, and Custom* (1871, 2 volumes). Writing very much in the humanistic vein of progressivism, Tylor cited the ethnographic task to be the charting of mental advancement by a rational analysis of human cultural products. For Tylor, culture, as Stocking (1963) observed, represented a level of refinement or a cultivation of a skill, and it was his intention to chart human advancement in a series of stages. Tylor's logical and erudite presentation of the theoretical and methodological bases for studying human progress, in conjunction with a happy talent for conceptualization, immediately placed him in the front rank of anthropologists. Overnight, he became the foremost of British anthropologists. Tylor's elevation was easily warranted, for

> The extent of his reading, his critical acumen, his accuracy, his power of exposition, his open mind, and his scientific caution make this book no passing essay, but a possession for ever. He laid the firm foundation of a structure to which, with accruing information, others may make additions; he himself has made and is making additions; but his science passed, thanks to him, out of the pioneering stage, at a single step. He stood on a level with Bastian; their names are, in the pre-historic history of man, what the name of Darwin is in regard to the evolution of animal life. (Lang 1907:5–6)

Tylor (1874(1):13) accented culture as a group product and defended ethnography's concern for the customs, social habits, beliefs, and knowledge of particular peoples on the principle that collective social action was an additive product of many individual actions. There must then be no great inconsistency between individual and group motivation and purpose, and passage from one to the other should offer no methodological barriers. Maintaining a sensitive methodological pace, Tylor (1889) subjected materials on marriage and descent practices to statistical controls for probable association to see if ethnographic data could satisfy the rigorous canons of natural science. Perceptively, Tylor used his tabulations and correlations to test hypotheses dealing with the origins of exogamy and the couvade. This methodological tack was not used again for nearly sixty years until Murdock (1947) tested five hypotheses accounting for bifurcate-merging kinship terminology. Finally, it was Tylor's persuasive authority that helped turn anthropology into a science of early man, thus providing for the time a distinction in the substance of sociology and anthropology.

The well-traveled Adolf Bastian (1826–1905) has been referred to as the "father of ethnography," even though Morgan's Iroquois ethnography appeared nearly ten years before publication of *Der Mensch in der Geschichte* (1860, 3 volumes). Bastian, however, continued to produce ethnographic sketches (*Die Völker des östlichen Asien* 1866–1871, 6 volumes; *Die Culturländer des alten Amerika* 1878–1889, 3 volumes). In *Der Völkergedanke im Aufbau einer Wissenschaft vom Menschen und seine Begründung auf ethnologische Sammlungen* (1881) and *Zur Lehre von den geographischen Provinzen* (1886) he presented his theories about folk ideas and their variation according to geographic conditions. He deferred formal treatment of his theory of elemental ideas—the generalized psychic platform from which historic folk expressions derived—until publication of *Ethnische Elementargedanken in der Lehre vom Menschen* (1895). In positing elemental ideas with historic-cultural folk variants, Bastian brought structure and variation into a meaningful conceptualization of reality. It was a model he shared with many, including the American culture-historicist Franz Boas. However, in seeking the basic source for cultural variations in environment Bastian limited the importance of historic contact in the growth of culture. Lowie (1937:36) credits Bastian with starting applied anthropology; but his idea that the laws of culture growth should be uncovered and put to use in reforming the artificialities and in eliminating the survivals that violated natural law and restrained human development was widely shared at the time.

Innovators in the Biological Basis for Social Institutions

Once evolutionism had become entrenched, a number of investigators, including Westermarck, Crawley, and Schurtz, extended the implications of evolutionary inheritance along separate biopsychic lines.

Edward Westermarck (1862–1939), born and educated in Helsingfors, made his mark by assembling evidence linking the monogamous family as a primary human institution to instinctive impulses induced by the evolutionary process (*The History of Human Marriage* 1922, 3 volumes). This work earned him the reputation of destroying the theory of primitive promiscuity—a problem which has recently been renovated. He followed his marriage study with a two-volume work entitled *The Origin and Development of Moral Ideas* (1906–1908). Westermarck also used his travel-as-recreation wisely, producing descriptive works on the Arabs of Morocco, including *Ritual and Belief in Morocco* (1926, 2 volumes) and

Marriage Ceremonies in Morocco (1914). From 1907 to 1930 he held the position of professor of sociology at the University of London.

In *The Mystic Rose* (1960) the classicist and headmaster Alfred Crawley (1869–1924) contended that the universality of ritual transmissions and taboos regulating the relations of the sexes before and after marriage required a constant functional relationship that only a biological base could supply. The appearance, similarity, and persistence of sexual taboos were anchored to fundamental human responses, notably survival fears. Ancient physiological-psychological responses generated in the face of dangerous social and environmental circumstances tended to persist in the human experience as unconscious regulators of behavior. Like Spencer, Freud, and Jung, Crawley accented a phylogenetic inheritance of social behavior. However, in wedding these physiological responses to elementary ideas produced in the primary experiential context, Crawley reached a level of specificity in the interpretation of customs and institutions that Freud would not attain until publication of *Totem and Taboo* (1913). The conceptualization of elemental physiological ideas led Crawley to the conclusion that neatly interrelated and consistent ideas which ostensibly explain customs in all probability are secondary rationalizations. Crawley's work signaled that the turn to biological explanations would underline not human rationality but unconscious irrationality and feeling states.

Heinrich Schurtz (1863–1903), who bridged geography, economics, and ethnology, first assembled comparative evidence demonstrating that the biology of age and sex provided the initial basis for social differentiation in primitive society and regulated the evolution of society. The *Alterklassen und Männerbünde* (1902) followed a prehistory of civilization (*Urgeschichte der Kultur* 1900) and earlier works dealing with African trade, the origins of money, and costume. Prior to Schurtz, J. J. Bachofen linked the drive to civilization to the opposition of male and female principles. However, in *Das Mutterrecht* (1861) Bachofen drew his examples largely from classical sources which dominated his studies in law, legal history, and the influence of the Near East on the Greco-Roman world. Nearly seventy years later, under new biological emphasis stimulated by ethological studies, Lionel Tiger (1970) echoed Schurtz's argument that the social bonds linking males provided the substantive relations for the formation of society.

Innovators in the Interpretation of Religion

In both the eighteenth and nineteenth centuries a common interest in the intellectual development of man focused special attention on religion as a knowledge system. Sociologist Comte's "law of the three stages" charted a succession of knowledge systems—theological, metaphysical, and scientific. Each of these knowledge systems embodied a philosophy of life which penetrated the life and thought of an age and left an indelible mark on their culture. In the Western experience, formal religion restricted the freedom and creativity of the mind, and scientist and theologian competed for men's minds. However, science inevitably must triumph. In *Psyche's Task: A Discourse Concerning the Influence of Superstition on the Growth of Institutions*, the evolutionary anthropologist Frazer (1913:154–155) was critical of the role of religion in the development of society. Superstition, or religion, was credited with five contributions:

1. Superstition aided measurably in the establishment and maintenance of civil order by strengthening respect for government, and especially monarchy.
2. Superstition taught respect for private property.
3. Superstition helped to establish a secure social order by emphasizing respect for marriage and adherence to a strict sexual code.
4. Superstition advanced human security by strengthening respect for life.
5. Superstition benefited society "by furnishing the ignorant, the weak, and the foolish with a motive . . . for good conduct. . . ."

Despite these social advantages, superstition was offensive to the human mind and must be judged a common criminal under sentence of death. For Marx, the materialist, and for Frazer, who studiously avoided materialist interpretations, religion and superstition were one and the same—an "opiate of the masses" which had outlived its usefulness.

Following the logic of Developmentalism, religion apparently could hold no secure place in the future of an enlightened mankind. For Spencer (1900–1901(3):133) the diffusion of knowledge accompanying the rise of the voluntary industrial society correlated with a loss in "sacerdotal authority and power." The farther one traveled into the past, the greater the authority of superstition. As a kind of self-fulfilling prophecy, eighteenth- and nineteenth-century Developmentalists anticipated human progress and the inevitable conquest of the less adaptive religious philosophy by the natural and rational scientific system.

Basic Theorists of Religious Origins. In the origins of religion Tylor (1874) and Spencer (1900–1901) early dominated the field with their animistic theories, a term renovated by Tylor. Animistic theory limited the distinction of the sacred and the secular to man's experiential awareness of his own duality, derived through the emotional and psychological context of death and dream phantasms. As a psychological theory, animism contradicted the theories of mythologists and linguists who traced the distinction of the natural and the supernatural to the sensory impact of natural phenomena—sun, moon, stars, lightning, fire. McLennan theorized that primeval totemism was a basis for the bonding of communal local groups with which organized society had begun. The Edinburgh lawyer presented his totemistic theory in two articles in 1869 and 1870, before either Tylor or Spencer had provided documentation for their animistic theories. Between 1890 and 1910 other challenges to animism appeared from three classically trained British scholars: James G. Frazer (1854–1941), Andrew Lang (1844–1912), and R. R. Marett (1866–1913).

Frazer's interest in anthropology was kindled by his reading of Tylor's *Primitive Culture*. His first anthropological writing was at the invitation of W. Robertson Smith to contribute articles on totemism and taboo to the ninth edition of the Encyclopaedia Britannica. Peasant customs and folklore excited Frazer's interest, since they exhibited mental operations readily discerned in savage magic and religion. Frazer began his long trek into what he later called mental anthropology (1931:241) with a decoding of the ritual slaying of a priest-king who in Roman legend circled with drawn sword a sacred oak dedicated to Diana the huntress. From this Roman beginning he followed the winding path of folklore to Asia, Africa, the Americas, the Pacific Islands, the Mediterranean, and north to the Vikings, in order to assemble the separate pieces of a primitive mental mosaic which explained the ritual slaying of the priest of Nemi. As it turned out, the plot for the ritual sacrifice was nothing less than a great fertility drama uniting sacred tree, king, and mistletoe.

In the course of his intellectual journey Frazer defined and classified the different modes of magical thought and concluded that magic had preceded religion, since magic represented a more rudimentary type of thinking and allowed for serious errors in attitude, observation, and judgment about the nature of the world. In poetic metaphor Frazer (1900(1):237–240) described the anguish of the transition from magic to religion. With magic men asserted their dominance over the world. In time, however, shrewder intellects perceived that the spells and incantations did not produce the effects desired. Men began a long retreat from their proud position of dominance and gradually accepted the fact that the rains fell, the seasons turned, and the moon completed her nightly journey because of beings superior to men. However, this

> deepening sense of religion, this more perfect submission to the divine will in all things, affects only those higher intelligences who have breadth of view enough to comprehend the vastness of the universe and the littleness of man. Small minds cannot grasp great ideas; to their narrow comprehension, their purblind vision, nothing seems really great and important but themselves. Such minds hardly rise into religion at all. They are, indeed, drilled by their betters into an outward conformity with its precepts and a verbal profession of its tenets; but at heart they cling to their old magical superstitions, which may be discountenanced and forbidden, but cannot be eradicated by religion, so long as they have their roots deep down in the mental framework and constitution of the great majority of mankind. (Frazer 1900(1):240)

Frazer's redundant metaphorical style easily made him the most widely read anthropologist of his time. Following Frazer through the ideological jungle as he uncovers the intellectual clues of ritualized homicide, turns the scientific search into a kind of detective mystery. Frazer's passages illustrate the typical Developmentalist reliance on a hypothetical but persuasive logic to link ideological stages which the undiscerning reader can readily accept. Finally, he brings out the idealization of the intellect, and the contempt commonly expressed for the untutored mind.

The erudition Frazer displayed in *The Golden Bough: A Study in Magic and Religion* (1900, 3 volumes) catapulted him to immediate fame. Continuing his studies in depth, he produced another major compilation, *Totemism and Exogamy* (1935, 4 volumes) while expanding *The Golden Bough* to a 12-volume set between 1907 and 1915. In 1918 he subjected the Bible to anthropological analysis in a work entitled, *Folklore in the Old Testament* (3 volumes). The materials Frazer extracted in the course of his researches were collected in the four volumes of *Anthologica Anthropologica* (1939).

Andrew Lang (1844–1912), a literary and journalistic figure, admired Tylor and used Tylor's theories of animism and survivals in his early works (*Custom and Myth* 1904; *Myth, Ritual, and Religion* 1887). In 1898, Lang produced *The Making of Religion*, in which he argued that animism did not provide the groundwork for religion, since some lowly peoples, notably the Australians, possessed the idea of a beneficent, moral, and all-powerful being. *Magic and Religion* (1901) and *Secret of the Totem* (1905) contributed nothing new to religious theory, but in *Social Origins* (1903), which included *Primal Law* by Lang's cousin, J. J. Atkinson, a patriarchal polygynous horde was put forward as the beginnings of human society. It was this incestuous patriarchal unit which Freud (1913) borrowed for the first Oedipal drama.

Robert R. Marett (1866–1943), who succeeded Tylor at Oxford, entered anthropology after winning a prize essay on ethical behavior among primitive peoples. Like Tylor and Frazer, Marett became famous overnight, but his was no heavy volume produced after years of research. His short essay, "Pre-animistic Religion," was presented to the British Association for the Advancement of Science in 1899 at the request of a friend, who engaged Marett to liven up the meeting. In 1900 the essay was expanded into a collection, *Threshold of Religion*. Marett challenged the animistic and other intellectualistic theories of religion with a kind of physiological-psychological explanation. Religion was based on a kind of emotional thrill that included awe and wonder, leading primitive man to attribute a mystical power or life to all of nature's works. Throughout his life Marett produced slim volumes of collected essays about religion, ethics, and psychology that achieved a modest popularity (*Anthropology* 1912; *Psychology and Folklore* 1920; *Faith, Hope and Charity in Primitive Religion* 1932; *Sacraments of Simple Folk* 1933; *Head, Heart and Hands in Human Evolution* 1935).

Innovators in Religion and Social Process. To find special innovators in religion and social process one must go back to J. J. Bachofen (1861) and to Numa Denis Fustel de Coulanges (1830–1889), professor of history at Strasbourg and at the Sorbonne. Both Bachofen and Fustel began with the assumption that in ancient times religious institutions were the core of society. In *The Ancient City: A Study on the Religion, Laws, and Institutions of Greece and Rome* (1956:13) Fustel developed the thesis that a

> primitive religion constituted the Greek and Roman family, established marriage and paternal authority, fixed the order of relationship, and consecrated the right of property, and the right of inheritance. This same religion, after having enlarged and extended the family, formed a still larger association, the city, and reigned in that as it had reigned in the family. From it came all the institutions, as well as all the private laws of the ancients. It was from this that the city received all its principles, its rules, its usages, and its magistracies. But, in the course of time, this ancient religion became modified or effaced, and private law and political institutions were modified with it. Then came a series of revolutions, and social changes regularly followed the development of knowledge.

Both Bachofen and Fustel developed their theses in the context of Greco-Roman culture history. W. Robertson Smith (1846–1894), who specialized in Hebrew and applied historical criticism to the Bible in imitation of trends then current in Germany, extended the thesis of the sacred community to the Arabic world. His efforts at biblical criticism ultimately cost him his professorship in Hebrew studies at the University of Aberdeen; after which he served as editor for the Encyclopaedia Britannica. His early works on the Old Testament and the historic importance of the prophets were followed by two important works on Semitic social organization and religion, *Kinship and Marriage in Early Arabia* (1885) and *The Religion of the Semites* (1889).

W. R. Smith's anthropological interests were kindled by contact with J. F. McLennan, who had theorized about the bonding effect of religion in the form of animal worship in early society. In an article on sacrifice (Encyclopaedia Britannica, ninth ed.) editor Smith presented evidence to show that sacrifice originated as a sacred communion to maintain the mystical protective bonds linking a fraternity of kinsmen with a localized totemic spirit and to strengthen the fraternal blood bond. The article outlined a theoretical analysis that Smith carried forward in later works, in each case emphasizing the psychological and ethical relations linking a group with spirits of their environment and underscoring the social functions of religion.

The sudden preoccupation of the academic world in research and debate over the social evolutionary significance of totemism originated with McLennan. However, it was Smith's determined effort to apply it to the Semitic world that supplied the substantive support for the thesis, tenuous though some of the surviving evidence appeared. In a kind of editorial laying on of hands, Smith inspired Frazer to begin his researches in totemism. However, Frazer (1935) did not continue Smith's social origins thesis but reverted to an individualized psychological context by assigning the origins of totemism to the mental delusions of pregnant women during an age when mankind was totally ignorant of physiological paternity. Individual totemism thus had preceded group totemism, and only later picked up its social and religious attributes when totems became hereditary.

The late publication of *Totemism and Exogamy* allowed Frazer (1935 (4):101–102) to criticize the sociological-functional interpretations of Durkheim. Durkheim made totemism too much of an abstract and mystical religion, thereby violating, in Frazer's judgment, the canons of primitive thought and inverting the evolutionary flow of ideas from simple concrete modes to the more abstract. However, the theory that human society began as a primitive sacra-communal community held interpretation on a quasi-sociological course. The theory of cult worship as a necessary force for social cohesion in early society attracted the support of a diverse assemblage of scholars: the folklorist Laurence Gomme (1853–1916), *Folklore as an Historical Science* 1908; Frank B. Jevons (1859–1936), professor of philosophy at Durham University, *An Introduction to the History of Religion* 1927; Wilhelm Wundt (1832–1920), a pioneer in experimental psychology, *Elements of Folk Psychology* 1928; Walter Bagehot (1826–1877), political economist and essayist, *Physics and Politics* 1875; a German pedagog, director of an Oberrealschule and one-time member of the Austrian Parliament, Julius Lippert (1839–1909), *Kulturgeschichte der Menschheit in ihrem organischen Aufbau* 1886–1887; and a political economist and Episcopalian clergyman, William Graham Sumner (1840–1910), and his faithful student and co-author, A. G. Keller (1874–1956), *The Science of Society* 1927, 4 volumes).

In approaching the evolution of ethics, both Leonard T. Hobhouse (1864–1929, *Morals in Evolution* 1925, 2 volumes, and Edward Westermarck (1862–1939, *The Origin and Development of Moral Ideas* 1906–1908, 2 volumes) became heavily engaged in an evaluation of religion as a source and force for moral behavior, as had Comte (1893), Waitz (1863), Tylor (1874), and Spencer (1897). Analyzing religion and ethics in order to assess their contributions to social history was but a step away from the investigation of religion as social process, to which structural-functionalists would soon dedicate themselves.

Innovators in the Nature of Society and of Law

Four lawyers, J. J. Bachofen (1815–1887), J. F. McLennan (1827–1881), Lewis H. Morgan (1818–1881), and Sir Henry Maine (1822–1888), set the stage for research and debate over the origins and evolution of social institutions, more especially, family, kin groups, kin terms of address, and laws of marriage. Reference has already been made to Bachofen's (1861) effort to unite maleness and femaleness with different orders of social, religious, and political institutions. J. F. McLennan was attracted to a comparative study of marriage ceremonies when writing an article on law for the eighth edition of the Encyclopaedia Britannica in 1857. *Primitive Marriage: An Inquiry into the Origin of the Form of Capture in Marriage*

Ceremonies (1865) was the result of an interest provoked by symbolic abduction found in Spartan and Roman marriage custom. Food imbalances, female infanticide, population imbalances, and bride capture were all involved in the formation of exogamy (out-marriage), a term which McLennan coined at the time, together with its opposite, endogamy. His other major contribution lay in the suggestion that early social aggregates were given formal shape by a ritual bond, probably through the medium of animal worship, or totemism (1869 and 1870). In a posthumous work edited by his son, McLennan (1885) castigated Maine's notion that the original social unit of mankind was the patriarchal family.

Lewis Morgan contributed a signal breakthrough when he discovered similarities in kinship terminology and went on to theorize that the terms existed in their variant forms by virtue of differing social relationships associated with special family types and marriage rules. These materials were presented in *Systems of Consanguinity and Affinity of the Human Family* (1871). *In Ancient Society* (1877) Morgan summarized his ideas concerning the evolution of technology, family and kinship, and property inheritance. The primitive communism and democracy depicted in the latter work inspired Marx to extend his thesis to early man, since primitive egalitarianism documented that capitalistic society violated all that was natural to man. Capitalist Morgan is a curious companion for Marxist dialectic even though he did end *Ancient Society* on the note that man could not live for property alone. Morgan scored another first in *Houses and House-Life of the American Aborigines* (1881), attempting to show how family and house architecture are related. He also pioneered in the ethnographic tradition of field work, beginning with *League of the Ho-De-No-Sau-Nee or Iroquois* (1851).

Sir Henry Maine, classically trained at Cambridge, continued his historical interest in the ancient world after admittance to the bar in 1850. *Ancient Law* (1861) brought instant fame to Maine and led to the offer of a post in India. As legal counsel to the governing council he extended his interest in comparative jurisprudence to include Hindu law and the Germanic and Celtic foundations of feudal law (*Lectures on the Early History of Institutions* 1875 and *Dissertations on Early Law and Custom Chiefly Selected from Lectures Delivered at Oxford* 1883).

Maine accepted the beginnings of law in sacred proscriptions and traced the gradual secularization and individualization of law. Using changes in law as evidence, Maine traced the gradual breakdown of an early sacred kin-based society and the rise of a territorial-based society. His Hindu materials provided Maine with patriarchal family arrangements and he posited a male-centered base for the beginnings of society. His patriarchal theory opened controversy over the primacy of maternal and paternal organization and stimulated a closer look at the influence of economy, residence, and the exercise of legal rights over property and persons in the formation of family types and descent rules (see, for example,

C. N. Starcke (1858–1926), *The Primitive Family in Its Origin and Development* 1889 and C. S. Wake (1835–1910), *The Development of Marriage and Kinship* 1967).

Maine's contribution to comparative law lay in a focus on the exercise of legal rights as intrinsic to social relations. The same orientation was applied to Anglo-Saxon, Frankish, Celtic, and Slavic law and society by a number of scholars who looked to Maine for their inspiration: Maxime Kovalevsky (1851–1916), *Sketch of the Origins and Evolution of the Family and of Property* 1890 and *Modern Customs and Ancient Laws of Russia* 1891; F. W. Maitland (1850–1906) and F. Pollock (1845–1937), *The History of English Law Before the Time of Edward I* 1899, 2 volumes, Rudolf Huebner (1864–1945), *Historical Sources of the Frankish Period* 1891–1893, 2 volumes; Frederick Seebohm (1833–1912), *The English Village Community* 1833 and *The Tribal System in Wales* 1895; Paul G. Vinogradoff (1854–1925), *The Growth of the Manor* 1905 and *Outlines of Historical Jurisprudence* 1920, 2 volumes). In a more psychological-evolutionary vein, A. H. Post (1839–1895) launched a natural science of law with the aid of comparative ethnology (1880–1881 and 1894–1895, 2 volumes) while a Dutch professor of sociology, Sebald Steinmetz (1862–1940), described the evolutionary course of punishment as a sequence of psychological attitudes (1928, 2 volumes).

Innovators in Anthroposocial and Social Selection

Under stimulus of biological evolution, social theory began to move to an accommodation of the organic, the psychological, and the sociocultural within a process of conflict and selection. Herbert Spencer arrived at a primary synthesis of body, mind, and social processes linked to the biological processes of acquired characteristics and natural selection. This model provided the stimulus for most evolutionary theorists. However, even before Darwin and Spencer, Comte Joseph de Gobineau (1816–1882) had wedded national grandeur with race and class and deplored the decline of Nordic creativity as an consequence of miscegenation (*The Inequality of Human Races* 1853–1855, 4 volumes). In North America Josiah Nott (1804–1873) and George Gliddon (1809–1857) pressed differences in race and culture into the service of a polygenetic theory that upheld inequalities and justified a different role for inferior and superior races in the civilization process (*Types of Mankind; or, Ethnological Researches, Based upon the Ancient Monuments, Paintings, Sculptures, and Crania of Races, . . .* 1855). Gustave Klemm (1802–1867) also used the old division into active and passive races to explain the bustling energy and creativeness of one race as against another (*Allgemeine Kultur-geschichte der Menschheit* 1843–1851, 7 volumes).

After Darwin, stress on the need to explore the biological foundations for individual and group behavior intensified. Research by Francis Galton (1822–1911) and Havelock Ellis (1859–1939) in England concentrated on the interrelations of genius, family lines, professional achievement, and social class (Galton 1962, *Hereditary Genius: An Inquiry into Its Laws and Consequences*; Ellis 1926, *A Study of British Genius*). In Germany, Otto Ammon (1842–1916) developed a theory of natural social selection that brought superior dolichocephals to the throbbing city environment (*Anthropologische Untersuchungen der Wehrpflichtigen in Baden* 1890). Conflict and natural selection served both Ludwig Gumplowicz (1838–1909, *Der Rassenkampf* 1883) and Gustav Ratzenhofer (1842–1904, *Wesen und Zweck der Politik, als Theil der Sociologie und Grundlage der Staatswissenschaften* 1893, 3 volumes) as primary instruments in the formation of the state. This theme had been sketched earlier by Spencer (1900–1901) and by Bagehot (1875).

Concentration on social contacts through migration, trade, and conquest shifted attention from emphasis on a brute struggle governed by organic processes to a war between those with inferior and superior institutions. This new look paved the way for the emergence of the *social* as a causative agent for other social events, a point of view stated categorically by Gumplowicz in his *Outlines of Sociology* (1963). In the United States, Lester Ward (1841–1913) used Ratzenhofer's theory of conflict, but stressed man's capacity to transform his environment by intelligent action (*Dynamic Sociology* 1883). Social evolution was considered the unique province of mankind, but Ward developed a purposiveness that the pragmatists, Sumner and Keller (*The Science of Society* 1927, 4 volumes), did not share. In a revision of his 1915 lectures (*Societal Evolution* 1931) Keller admitted that he had overplayed human rationality in his original statement. Social selection (Social Darwinism), though distinct from natural selection, nonetheless shared its automatic and undesigned processes. "The elimination or persistence of the mores is determined by the action of men in masses through conflict between societies or between the groups, or classes, within a society" (Keller 1931:141).

Keller did little more than echo the position of his strong-willed mentor W. G. Sumner, who in his 1906 publication, *Folkways*, outlined the later *Science of Society* that Keller would edit. Beginning with the assumption that men act first to satisfy basic needs, and only later bring deliberation into their activities, Sumner sketched how the trial-and-error actions of individuals developed a consensus and turned into folkways. When folkways were invested with heavy sanctions because of group welfare, they took on the character of mores. Four basic "needs," probably inherited from man's beast ancestors, supplied the take-off for all human behavior: "hunger, sex passion, vanity, and fear (of ghosts and spirits)" (Sumner 1960:33). Sumner relied heavily on Spencer and Lippert and accepted the idea that instincts could be acquired in association with the mores. Mores constrained and guided human behavior in its mass expression and changed without conscious direction on the part of men. Yet Sumner (1960:114) counseled resistance to foolish customs, and was inspired by the idea that a science of society which could bring intelligence and science into the administration of society would be a signal achievement and beneficial for mankind.

Innovators in a Sociopsychological Phylogeny of Human Behavior

The theory of acquired instincts embraced by Spencer was flexible enough to permit stress on the importance of the *social* context in conditioning individuals to respond in special psychophysiological ways. Such a position countered interpretations which traced basic human behaviors to an evolutionary inheritance. Derivation of psychological-physiological reflexes from a social context, and their phylogenetic persistence, was advocated by Spencer. This course was in step with the emergence of the social as an explanatory tool as it took clearer shape in the 1880s. Certain basics of man's animal ancestry need not be rejected, but the humanizing effects could not be a simple elaboration of the animal platform. Carveth Read (*The Origin of Man* 1925) thought that the humanizing experience began with man in a hunting pack, an idea voiced earlier by Charles Morris (1833–1922) (*Man and His Ancestors* 1900). As the first of all predators, men in packs would be subject to adaptive processes, and in time natural selection and heredity would produce a human character "more like a dog or a wolf than . . . like any other animal" (Read 1925:32). Provocation for the primeval Oedipal crime, to which Freud (1918), in a phylogenetic mode, traced contemporary Oedipal anguish, obviously required a special social context—a family or horde tyrannized by a patriarch who preempted sex relations with all women of the group. Robert Briffault (1876–1942) provided the summative epilogue for social phylogeny in *The Mothers. A Study of the Origins of Sentiments and Institutions* (1927, 3 volumes). Briffault maintained that only a social matrix could provide the substance for mental evolution. He criticized those who considered the human family merely an extension of an animal model unerringly provided by natural selection. For Briffault the human family was a social and economic arrangement which could never have been initiated and sustained by organic sentiments like sex and maternal love.

Innovators in Technology and Economics

Innovations in technology and economics followed three major channels: (1) the distribution of tools and the modification of tool types as an evolutionary process, (2) stages in economic development and their cultural correlates, and (3) classification and distribution of specialized economies.

Developments in archeology after 1830 supplied special impetus to the description and distribution of tool types and their arrangements in evolutionary-industrial sequences. The Danes were the first to set up a comparative tool typology. The relation between archeological concern for artifacts and an ethnological concern for material culture in the nineteenth century can be illustrated in the work of Gustav Klemm (1802–1867), who surveyed tools and weapons, fire, foods, beverages, and narcotics (*Allgemeine Kulturwissenschaft. Die materiellen grundlagen menschlicher Cultur* 1854–1855, 2 volumes). Klemm was curator of Japanese vases in Dresden and secretary of the archeological society of Saxony, and published a manual of Germanic archeology in 1835. His thesis that nature had provided the models for primitive technology was not unusual, but he did advance analysis at the time by presenting comparative illustrations. He also pointed to certain of the simplest hunters (Botocudos, Bushmen) to illustrate the zero point in tool development and noted how the inventory of hunters differed noticeably from that of agriculturalists.

Colonel (later General) Lane Fox Pitt-Rivers (1827–1900) came to the study of technology through a pragmatic interest in the improvement of British army rifles. Between 1867 and 1875 Pitt-Rivers gave a number of lectures on primitive warfare, navigation, and the evolution of culture, later edited by J. L. Myres under the title, *The Evolution of Culture and Other Essays* (1906). Pitt-Rivers' tools and weapons, arranged in a graduated sequence from the simple to the complex, made impressive viewing and reflected, in his judgment, the ideological progress of man. Tylor's interest in technology was stimulated by the growth of archeology and by knowledge of Klemm's work. In his *Researches into the Early History of Mankind* (1964) Tylor devoted a chapter to the "Stone Age" and awakened a lively interest in the distribution of fire-making devices, cooking practices, and pottery. He coined the terms "fire-drill" and "stone-boiling," currently in use. In this early work Tylor (1964:236–237) traced the implications of similarity in forms widely space to the logical conclusion that here was proof of the transmission of culture. However, he welcomed the additional proof of linguistic affiliation and geographic continuities to establish a firm connection. The presence of any form or custom in any place was grist for the ethnological mill, posing a question to which three solutions were available; "independent invention, inheritance from ancestors in a distant region, [and] transmission from one race to another."

The relation of technology to the advancement of culture was generally well appreciated by nineteenth-century Developmentalists, but they were not inclined to give economics precedence over ideas. The economic stages usually began with hunters and fishers, proceeded to a pastoral life, next to cultivation, and finally to industrialism. A serious challenge to this sequence did not arise until the geographer Eduard Hahn (1856–1928) published *Die Haustiere und ihre Beziehungen zur Wirtschaft des Menschen* (1896). Hahn interpreted pastoralism as historically derived from the pressing of cultivators into marginal areas by superior peoples—an idea earlier suggested by Meiners (1785). Hahn continued his interest in the relations of pastoralists and cultivators and in the origins of agriculture (*Das Alter der wirtschaftlichen Kultur der Menschheit* 1905; *Die Entstehung der Pflugkultur* 1904; *Von der Hacke zum Pflug* 1919). He distinguished hoe cultivation as marking the beginning of male association with plant cultivation found in agriculture, and perceptively observed how different economies involved differences in a division of labor according to sex. Lewis H. Morgan (1877) gave special consideration to the problem of correlating economic stages with other dimensions of culture, but a more serious effort did not appear until 1915 when Hobhouse, Wheeler, and Ginsberg catalogued and compared technology and social advancement in 643 societies (*The Material Culture and Social Institutions of the Simpler Peoples* 1965).

In the New World, unlike the Old World, the metaphysics of religion had no place in the study of economic origins. Otis T. Mason (1838–1908), curator of anthropology at the U. S. National Museum, studied invention from the standpoint of man's increasing control over kinetic energy. Necessity supplied the spur, but it was disciplined thinking and experiment that produced inventions (*The Origins of Invention: A Study of Industry among Primitive Peoples* 1895). Domestication arose not out of fearful sacrifice to the gods, but out of man's impulse to tame wild animals and bend them to his uses. In *Woman's Share in Primitive Culture* (1894) Mason traced all important industrial, social, and religious developments to women, since early division of labor associated her with domestic arts (for example, basketry making, pottery making) and with the earth, first as a collector of roots and then as cultivator. From his museum post Mason stimulated studies in material culture with comparative surveys of American Indian basketry (1884, 1902), skin dressing techniques (1889), bows and arrows (1893), transportation (1894), harpoons (1900), and traps (1901).

William J. McGee (1858–1912) anticipated the idea of an ecological community embracing animals, plants, insects, man, and environment in two articles dealing with the arid Southwest ("The Beginnings of Agriculture" 1895, and "The Beginning of Zooculture" 1897). McGee stressed the solidarity of life that accompanied the cooperative interrelations of plants and animals in Papagueria. Vital energies were directed not against their own kind or aliens but against the physical environment. A strong sense of individuality flowed from the cooperative relationships and resultant solidarity (McGee 1895(8):368–369). The Papago Indians also formed a cooperative relationship with both carnivores and herbivores, even the coyote, whom man spared as the scavenger. In turn, the animals

> reciprocate[d] by forming a semi-conscious cordon of protectors about the camp or village; and in these and other ways a partial cultivation of plants and domestication of animals is brought about collectively, and man enters into and dominates the solidarity of desert life. (McGee 1895(8):374).

Holding that "necessity is the mother of progress" and that "strength lies in union; and progress in combination leads to solidarity," McGee (1895 (8):374–375) held that agriculture was a product of desert artisans. For his ecological observations, McGee drew upon twenty years experience with the U.S. Geological Survey and with the Bureau of American Ethnology under J. W. Powell.

Innovators in Historical Materialism: Marx and Engels

The Communist social philosophers Karl Marx (1818–1883) and Friedrich Engels (1820–1895) supplied the materialistic interpretation for the evolutionary development of society which Developmentalists, because of their idealistic position, could not formulate. The position of Marx and Engels was similar to that of Rousseau, who described the malign inequities that had accompanied the growth of civilization. Similar inequities in industrial society aroused Marx and Engels, and like Rousseau, they pinpointed economic imbalances as the source of human inequalities. Rousseau attacked property in land, and Marx and Engels castigated the industrial owners of production who erected a new type of class society and protected it with laws of their own making. The contrast between a natural and an artificial order was as important to Marx and Engels as to Rousseau, and to Developmentalists generally. Reaching into the past for documentation of violations of the natural order perpetrated in industrial society, Marx and Engels (Engels 1942) drew upon Morgan's theory of primitive communism. They used his data and interpretation to chart the erosion of the primitive democratic gentile-based society as civilization advanced and established itself on a foundation of social, economic, legal, and political inequalities. Defining civilization as marking that stage in societal development when the "division of labor, the exchange between individuals arising from it, and the commodity production which combines them both, come to their full growth and revolutionizes the whole of previous society," Engels (1942:158–159, 161) concluded that civilization was based on the exploitation of one class by another and that the entire development was a constant contradiction. Added efficiencies in production simply widened the distance between the exploiters and the exploited. The state, which owed its origin to the "need to keep class antagonisms in check" was used by the "economically . . . [and] politically ruling class" as a weapon for exploitation of the oppressed class (Engels 1942:156–157). In its capitalistic industrial mode civilization compounded its built-in evils and under a "cloak of love and charity . . . introduce[d] a conventional hypocrisy which was unknown to earlier forms of society and even to the first stages of civilization" (Engels 1942:162). A *natural* developmental process (dialectical materialism), however, directed the human destiny and Engels ended his work on *The Origin of the Family, Private Property and the State in the Light of the Researches of Lewis H. Morgan* (1884) on a prophetic note drawn from Morgan himself. Society would reform itself, and in its new state the *"liberty, equality and fraternity* of the ancient gentes" (Engels 1942:163) would be restored.

As exponents of economic determinism Marx and Engels contradicted the usual Developmentalist interpretation. However, in projecting an amelioration of the human condition and an ultimate realization of human nature through a natural and inevitable process, they shared the basic posture of Developmentalists. Their immediate impact on Developmentalist ideologues was virtually nil. Tylor (1873, cited by Opler 1968:1–8) did seek to counter theoretical politicians who counseled the introduction of communism and socialism into the modern world. "Socialism in its most pure and absolute form" could be found up through barbarism. However, the system was unable to meet the needs of modern commercial exchange, individualism, and private property, and therefore communism was discarded as mankind moved on to civilization. Thus, to advocate a communal-based economy would be tantamount to sponsoring an inefficient and developmentally outmoded system of society.

To hail Marx as the "Darwin of the social sciences" as Harris (1968: 217–249) advocates, following Engel's judgment that Marx had uncovered the primary law of evolution in human history, seems a premature assessment. The interrelations governing cause and effect in human situations are far more complex and Marx's explanation of cultural differences and similarities is still being tested, as other theoretical positions, in the light of available data. Nonetheless, Marx and Engels must be accorded a place among those who, during the nineteenth century, opened up new territory in the analysis of societal evolution based on conflict and social adaptation.

SUMMARY

Research interests in prehistory, paleontology, and geology initiated during the first decades of the nineteenth century gathered momentum between 1840 and 1860 and eventuated in the branching of anthropology from the main stem of social science. There was a growing acceptance of the idea of biological evolution which Darwin synthesized in the *Origin of Species* (1859); and this supplied a final impetus for the formation of a general anthropological discipline which would concentrate on the early history of mankind. Evolutionary theory provided the interpretation of processes which permitted an integrated view of man's development as a physical and social being.

The consolidation of a comprehensive view of man as an evolutionary product required an extension of processes through a time span far beyond that which biblical time permitted. A new view of time—geological time—was a necessary prerequisite for acceptance of the principle of uniform processes as an explanation for a gradual transformation of life forms, and of the human species through cumulative change. It was also necessary to confirm the apparent association of human remains with extinct animal forms of considerable antiquity. Skeletal remains were the best kind of evidence, but in their absence tools shaped by intelligent hands could serve. In the perspective of evolution, that earlier forms would not be replicas of present-day human types might be anticipated. They would exhibit archaic features which suggested a more primitive type.

By 1860 evidence for the association of human artifacts with extinct animals dating back many thousands of years beyond biblical time was assembled. British geologists teamed to extract this documentary proof from Brixham Cave in the South of England. This confirmation of their reasoned surmise led to an inspection of evidence which had been offered earlier but had either been rejected or shelved. Boucher de Perthes's associations of handworked stone tools with diluvial and antediluvial human and animal life obtained from a quarry near Abbeville in France were now inspected by British geologists and judged to be authentic, even though they disagreed with Boucher over the age of the remains. The recovery of anthropoid ape remains by Edouard Lartet in the South of France as early as 1837 stirred a search for "fossil" types of man. Actually, in 1848, there was at hand a "fossil" skull from Gibraltar which could have been used to support the evolution of man. However, acceptance of man's development from earlier primitive forms was not fully acceptable until the Pithecanthropus finds of Dr. Eugene Dubois in Java in 1891. By this time the Cenozoic time-life chart had been completed and the dating of remains could be readily correlated in a relative chronology. The Pithecanthropus type undoubtedly was older and less developed cranially than the Neanderthal, whose discovery in 1856 had aroused such controversy over whether the specimen represented an archaic man form or a case of pathological disorder. *Sapiens* types were uncovered in 1868 at Cro-Magnon in France and associated with artifacts which contrasted with the crude stone axes of earlier times. The biological succession from Pithecanthropus, to possibly Neanderthal, and then to the *sapiens* Cro-Magnon "race" was paralleled by a chronology in tool industries leading from a lower to an upper Paleolithic, and then through a Mesolithic to the Neolithic. The development of a basic lower to upper Paleolithic sequence which included Chellean, Mousterian, Solutrean, and Magdalenian was projected by Gabriel de Mortillet by 1872. Archeological discoveries thus reached far back into time and documented a progressive advance in the application of skill to the shaping of tools and a progressive diversification of tool types according to functional needs. Archeological discoveries not only matched the human paleontological finds in suggesting a graduated development, but at certain points confirmed the association of tools with the remains of ancient populations, as in the case of upper Paleolithic sites in the Vézère Valley in France. Moreover, the imaginative extension of an eolithic industry into the Tertiary matched the view which projected man's biological ancestry into this same period of geologic time.

Comparative anatomy supported the emergent evolutionary perspective through comparison of anatomical resemblances between man and the higher apes as well as fossil forms as they came to light. Anatomical resemblances between man and the higher apes had been explored by Sir William Petty back in the seventeenth century. These resemblances were confirmed by comparative anatomy in the nineteenth century. However, the major stumbling block to acceptance of man as a product of organic processes rested in the assumption that man's brain was a special and distinct organ. Man's supreme faculty, reason, was a distinct correlate of the structure of the brain. Animals, it was argued, were hampered by the structures of their brain, and hence were governed by instinct. In 1863 Huxley compared primate brain structures and concluded that the differences between man and his primate congeners were a matter of degree rather than of qualitative difference. Animals could reason, but at a rude level of competence.

The convergence of influences stemming from geology, paleontology, comparative anatomy, and prehistory pointed to the necessity for a discipline which would integrate the study of man before the dawn of written history. Scholars who shared this interest in the early history of man, both as a physical, psychological, social, and cultural being, now united in special anthropological societies which included prehistory, physical anthropology, and ethnology (ca. 1860 and later). At the same time various efforts were made to define the proper subject matter of the new discipline, which must address itself to both the physical and societal development of mankind. In an effort to focus the direction of anthropology, E. B. Tylor in 1871 determined that the primary aim of the discipline should be the investigation of the processes underlying the development of culture or civilization.

The professionals who were drawn to anthropology came from all walks of life. In response to their interests, anthropology began to take shape as a multifaceted physical, psychological, linguistic, social, cultural, archeological, and paleontological (human) discipline. The varied interests of these anthropologists by avocation led them to explore the evolutionary development of art, language, family and social organization, religion, types of economies, political organization, law, and morality. Their focus on savage peoples, as they called them, led to the use of special concepts to describe the nature of savage society and custom. A special anthropological inventory of concepts was developed to identify their social, psychological, cultural, prehistoric, and paleontological materials. This facilitated the identity of the discipline and discriminated its subject matter from other fields. By 1880 the field was assured of a place among the other sciences, and during the next two decades anthropology was gradually accepted as a part of university education.

The founding of anthropology as a distinctive discipline in the period following 1860 was the work of individuals who, by definition, were not anthropologists. Influences stemming from individuals of diverse background and interest makes it difficult to attribute its founding to any outstanding individual. Founders can best be viewed in accordance with three kinds of contributions: (1) formulators of the general theoretical base used to develop an integrated approach to the study of man; (2) those who labored to define the specific nature, subject matter, and methodology of the new discipline; and (3) pioneers in opening up specialized subject matters.

5

Problems
and Issues of
Developmentalist
Social Science and
Anthropology

INTRODUCTION

Every science in its developmental course is unified by a most general theory of the nature of its subject matter and the processes by which this subject matter is structured and modified. Any general theory rests on certain basic assumptions which shape the nature of problems to be solved and determine the methods to be employed in the resolution of these problems. The general theory of Developmentalism shared by progressivists and evolutionists drew eighteenth-century founders of a general social science and nineteenth-century founders of anthropology into consideration of common problems and the use of a particular methodology and techniques. The differentiation of prehistory, human paleontology, and physical anthropology simply fed special evidences into the Developmentalist perspective. This broadened the base for the study of mankind and focused on the early history of man as a logical basis for the new anthropological discipline.

This chapter focuses on similarities between eighteenth-century progressivists and nineteenth-century evolutionists resulting from a common Developmentalist posture, and differences which stemmed from the nineteenth-century emphasis on biological processes. The evolutionist position not only engendered special problems regarding process but also led to redefinitions of problems. For example, the biological emphasis led evolutionists to challenge the psychic equality of primitive men in relation to civilized men, and to be highly skeptical of the savages' will to progress. New evidences likewise stimulated new perspectives with regard to the nature of primitive society and religion.

THE SCIENCE OF MAN: EIGHTEENTH- AND NINETEENTH-CENTURY PARALLELS

In retrospect there are a number of important similarities between the eighteenth- and nineteenth-century efforts to define a new science of man. First, both reflected the urgent need to develop a discipline that would chart man's progress as a rational and moral being. Second, there was a common effort to ground the new discipline in natural processes that would give scientific control. Third, in both centuries there was an urgent need to discriminate the natural history of man from history proper. Fourth, the common assumption that inevitable and constant processes of nature accounted for human progress led to the idea that, by revealing these processes, science could benefit mankind. That is, the study of the past could not be simply a capricious interest of antiquarians. Fifth, in developing stages in the evolution of human society and culture, both made use of a special "comparative method." The comparative method was designed to arrange ideas, institutions, and customs on a graded scale running from the rude to the refined, the illogical to the logical, and from the simple to the complex.

THE SCIENCE OF MAN: EIGHTEENTH- AND NINETEENTH-CENTURY CONTRASTS

Two developments seem to have provided the base for contrasts between the eighteenth and nineteenth centuries in the search for a science of man—the rapid differentiation of the natural sciences and the uncovering of evidences that lengthened the perspective of human history and related man to basic earth processes.

With differentiation of the natural sciences, the vision of a science securely anchored to the general processes of nature appeared near realization. Repercussions of the astounding advances in the natural sciences were distributed along three lines. First, use of nature as the model of reality was strengthened. Second, the natural sciences appeared to be the only proper model for a science of man. Third, interpretations of materialistic processes uncovered by the natural sciences could be transferred to the human reality.

New discoveries about the materialistic processes of nature widened the base for interpreting the human process by summative principles drawn from physics and biology. New discoveries in thermodynamics were used by Spencer to anchor his equilibrium-disequilibrium theory of reality process as evolutionary change, integration and disintegration. In 1847 Helmholtz formulated the first law of thermodynamics—that the total energy within a system is a constant, and though it may be redistributed, it is never destroyed. This famous law of the "conservation of energy" emphasized energy systems as functioning in a state of equilibrium. William Thomson (Lord Kelvin) promulgated the second law of thermodynamics in 1851. Here the total energy in the universe was a constant; however available energy for useful purposes did not maintain an equilibrium state but diminished at a proportional rate. After 1851 the instability of energy systems came to be accented, for only states of disequilibrium accounted for the freeing of energy and its transfer from one system to another. Inspired by the "persistence of force" (conservation of energy) and the redistribution of energy, Spencer (1862) conceived a universal history in which matter, organisms, and human societies progressed from an unstable homogeneous state to a more differentiated state of equilibration. The state of equilibrium inevitably was followed by a loss of motion, when external forces acting upon the system excited the parts and shattered the integrative bonds holding them together. Following this model, social systems would reach an equilibrium climax and then disintegrate, to be followed by new differentiations and integrations. To the physicist Ludwig Boltzmann it appeared that free energy in unstable systems presented a key to the whole of organic life and to the very development of civilization, since advances in complexity were due to increasing control over the available energy. Organisms and societies must compete for this free energy if they were to survive and to advance.

In stressing a struggle to control energy, Boltzmann touched upon a second summative principle of the nineteenth century. Eighteenth-century progressivists viewed competitive emulation as important in stimulating mankind to advance, both at the individual and group levels. The principle of natural selection translated competition into a war of survival. However, even before Darwin, the emergent social and national consciousness of Europe which accompanied the rise of the national-industrial state encouraged the view that conflict was intrinsic to the resolution of human issues, advancement, and national superiority. The interpretation of history advocated by Karl Marx in 1848 in the *Communist Manifesto* stressed the necessity of overcoming an opposite if human progress were to continue. The violent conflict of classes for control of the forces of production had propelled human society from a feudalistic to a capitalistic state. The final struggle would witness the overthrow of capitalistic bourgeoisie by proletarian workers who would then organize production for the good of the many.

The newly found importance of biological processes generated an interest in male and female qualities and their relevance for society. J. J. Bachofen (1931), a metaphysically oriented classicist, based the human advance on a triumph of the male principles of activity and reason over the female principles of passivity and feeling. The matriarchal type of society with its dark concern for subterranean forces gave way to the progressive patriarchal society, regulated by higher law and morality and also freed in spirit from the natural materialism associated with the gynocratic stage of culture. In Bachofen's view, the advancement of mankind meant overcoming a less desirable vital principle by a higher principle. Races, too, might be subject to grand integrative principles that paralleled the opposition of maleness and femaleness in the distinction of active and passive races.

A prime advantage which nineteenth-century students of man held over eighteenth-century progressivists was an appreciation of the fact that man must be viewed processually in relation to other life forms and earth's environment. Darwin's evolutionary theory underscored the graduated nearness of man to other species and traced the species history of man to processes no different from those that accounted for the transformation of other life forms. For the first time the unity of man in both his physical and cultural dimensions stood forth clearly and pointed the new science to uncovering relations between these two variables. Henceforth it would be necessary to study man with regard to his biological history and the importance of physiology for human behavior. The science of man would have to include the vast panorama of man's gradual ascent from a lowly biological, social, and cultural condition to the enriched estate of civilization created by supermen.

ACCOMMODATING BIOLOGICAL PROCESS AND SOCIAL PROGRESS

Darwin's caution that one must never forget the indelible marks of animality which man carried in his body, mind, and emotion made a profound impression on Developmentalist thinking and stimulated their efforts to unify the biological, psychological, and sociocultural processes. The leading theorist in this regard was the sociologist Herbert Spencer, whose ideas gained wide acceptance. The key to growth and survival was the advance in human capacities to overcome the challenges of nature and to accommodate to the functional requirements of social living. Such adaptability was assured by a coordinate increase in biological, psychological, and social adaptability. By emphasizing a hereditary transmission of acquired biological, psychological, and social characteristics, Spencer implied that the social was an emergent of the biological and psychological processes. The superorganic and autonomous quality of the social as a distinct level of reality thus was cast into doubt. Appreciation of this difficulty and the growing suspicion of Lamarckian-acquired characteristics led certain sociologists to drop the biopsychic emphasis of Spencer. By restricting themselves to the social domain, and by applying the idea of adaptive or functional selection to the social, the theoretical posture of Social Darwinism was generated.

Spencer focused on mental processes and ideas as central to an increase in the adaptive capabilities of man as a technical, social, intellectual, and moral being. The less evolved races, resting at the nadir of civilization, naturally would share more primitive processes with animals than the civilized. In the long march to civilization, the animal in man appeared a heritage to be jettisoned rather than a base for future development. If man in his evolutionary advance increased the distance between himself and organic processes, a time must arrive when the social prevailed over biological and psychological processes. From a primitive biopsychic and social process, mankind could be imagined as graduating to an intermediate psychosocial stage, and in civilization moving on to a social-psychological stage. In the last stage the social truly represented a superorganic level.

Julius Lippert, who followed Spencer's biopsychic evolutionary lead, illustrated the tendency to emancipate civilized man from processes linked to nature, and to see him as a different order of social and psychological man. In Lippert's view, savages or nature peoples represented a lower biological and cultural stage in evolution because they did not possess that special human or spiritual factor called the regard for life. This human factor arose in the course of cultural evolution and transformed the human process from a lower to a higher order of development. Cultural evolution proceeded from the instinctual to the rational, and as natural selection advanced the intellectual powers of the higher races, the lower races, as in the case of animals, faced extinction. Lippert thus consigned man's lowly origins and primitive processes to his early history, where, in developmental perspective, they properly belonged.

Biology and Historical-Evolutionary Processes: Comte, Bastian, Waitz, and Wundt

The humanistic nonbiological evolutionary position maintained by progressivists in the eighteenth century was not entirely muted by the rise of biological evolutionism. This perspective was sustained not only by sociologists like Comte but by ethnographers Bastian and Tylor, and by the folk psychologist Wundt. At issue was the role of reason as a distinctive mark of man's nature in comparison with animals. Cultivation of the human intellect in the social and cultural milieu could account for the advance to civilization. Hence, Tylor (1874), following the path of human logic, felt that the evolution of civilization owed little to biological processes. For Bastian, man's uniqueness was no product of a transformation of species and races—that uniqueness, like a seed, had always been there, ready to sprout with the right ground. Bastian saw men of all races as very much alike, inclined to begin their historic-cultural paths with primary or elemental ideas. Local habitats might produce regional variants (folk ideas), but the limitations of these geographic provinces would be overcome through historic contact, resulting in ever larger civilized mental communities.

Wilhelm Wundt laid the foundations for modern experimental psychology in Leipzig in 1879 and researched the physiological bases of psychology. However, as folk psychologist Wundt (1900–1920) dedicated ten volumes to the study of human psychology as a social phenomenon expressed in art, myth, religion, and language. Wundt (1897:296–297) saw development as a historical continuity in which individuals and groups were drawn successively into ever larger, more complex, and meaningful networks of mental communication. The end result would be formation of a world mental community, characterized by recognition of a common humanity despite diversity of race, language, and culture. Mental communities formed by animals differed from their human counterparts on two counts. Animal life revolved around physical existence and survival needs of the individual animal, and hence did not constitute integrated mental communities. Survival instincts dominated the animal world and restricted social and mental growth. Wundt accented the sociopsychological uniqueness of the human experience, and his emphasis on the ultimate importance of mental communication made him a forerunner of later symbolic interactionalism.

Theodore Waitz's (1863) survey of the physical and psychological characteristics of the so-called nature peoples appeared during the period of critical response to Darwin's evolutionary thesis. Waitz (1863(1):239) believed that a classification of mankind based on physical features was wholly unreliable. In language he hoped to find the carrier of unconscious thought processes and the instrument for probing the deeper relations among peoples. Human types in various stages of cultural development revealed a unity in social and cultural features which physical features masked. All men apparently shared the following: (1) reason or perfectibility; (2) speech and the use of signs; (3) a unique social life which included attachment to locality, country, family, ethical ideas, and private property; and (4) the practice of worship. Men possessed a common psychic unity which bore no relation to cranial capacity (Waitz 1863(1): 264–266). Moreover, if the physical differences separating the different races of men were no greater than what could be found within a particular race, Waitz (1863(1):264–266) held that the variability was insufficient to establish differences at the species level. What held for body also held for mind. "The great difference in civilization amongst peoples of the same stock, testifies that the degree of civilization does not chiefly depend on organization or mental endowment" (Waitz 1863(1):327). He further concluded that in moral endowment the white race was not superior to other races. Civilized man clearly exhibited a rude primitive nature whenever he was freed from social restraints.

Biological and Sociopsychological Phylogenesis: The Spencerian Synthesis

The most comprehensive synthesis of biological, social, and psychological processes influencing human development achieved during the nineteenth century was produced by Herbert Spencer. New discoveries in science, notably physics and in biology, gave Spencer a considerable advantage over Comte, but his real advantage was in drawing man into the mainstream of processes that natural scientists had proved to be operative in inorganic and organic matter. His evolutionary view of human nature attracted favorable comment from Darwin (1936:373), who noted, "Psychology will be securely based on the foundation already well laid by Mr. Herbert Spencer, that of the necessary acquirement of each mental power and capacity by gradation."

As early as 1852 Spencer argued for a Developmentalist position and grounded his evolutionary superstructure on two key propositions: (1) that the tendency for life forms is to differentiate according to circumstances from a simple homogeneous base to a more complex and heterogeneous state; and (2) that past experiences which modify body, mind, and emotions are transmitted from one generation to another.

In an 1857 essay on "Progress: Its Law and Cause," Spencer (1910(1): 35) turned to Karl Ernst von Baer's embryological evolutionary discoveries for scientific proof of his first proposition.

> Abundant proof has been given that the law of organic development formulated by von Baer, is the law of all development. The advance from the simple to the complex, through a process of successive differentiations, is seen alike in the earliest changes of the Universe to which we can reason our way back, and in the earliest changes which we can inductively establish; it is seen in the geologic and climatic evolution of the earth; it is seen in the unfolding of every single organism on its surface, and in the multiplication of kinds of organisms; it is seen in the evolution of Humanity, whether contemplated in the civilized individual, or in the aggregate of races; it is seen in the evolution of Society in respect alike of its political, its religious, and its economical organization; and it is seen in the evolution of all those endless concrete and abstract products of human activity which constitute the environment of our daily life. From the remotest past which Science can fathom, up to the novelties of yesterday, that in which progress essentially consists, is the transformation of the homogeneous into the heterogeneous.

The universal cause which produced the universal differentiative effect rested on the law that "Every active force produces more than one change —every cause produces more than one effect" (Spencer 1910(1):37). This second proposition had been outlined in 1855 and developed exhaustively in the second edition of *Principles of Psychology* (1870–1872). Spencer (1910(1):253–255) elaborated his evolutionary brand of associationism when criticizing the psychologist Alexander Bain for failing to treat human emotion and will in a developmental context. In Spencer's view, no adequate conception of the emotions and of their significance for human behavior was possible until it was understood how emotions were modified, fixated, and transmitted from one generation to the next. He then went on to point out that

> All are familiar with the truth that, in the individual, each feeling may be strengthened by performing those actions which it prompts; and to say that the feeling is *strengthened*, is to say that it is in part *made* by these actions. ... We know that emotional characteristics, in common with all others, are hereditary; and the differences between civilized nations descended from the same stock, show us the cumulative results of small modifications heredi-

tarily transmitted. And when we see that between savage and civilized races which diverged from one another in the remote past, and have for a hundred generations followed modes of life becoming ever more unlike, there exist still greater emotional contrasts; may we not infer that the more or less distinct emotions which characterize civilized races, are the organized results of certain daily-repeated combinations of mental states which social life involves? Must we not say that habits not only modify emotions in the individual, and not only beget tendencies to like habits and accompanying emotions in descendants, but that when the conditions of the race make the habits persistent, this progressive modification may go on to the extent of producing emotions so far distinct as to seem new? And if so, we may suspect that such new emotions, and by implication all emotions analytically considered, consist of aggregated and consolidated groups of those simpler feelings which habitually occur together in experience. When, in the circumstances of any race, some one kind of action or set of actions, sensation or set of sensations, is usually followed, or accompanied, by various other sets of actions or sensations, and so entails a large mass of pleasurable or painful states of consciousness; these, by frequent repetition, become so connected together that the initial action or sensation brings the ideas of all the rest crowding into consciousness, producing, in some degree, the pleasures or pains that have before been felt in reality. And when this relation, besides being frequently repeated in the individual, occurs in successive generations, all the many nervous actions involved tend to grow organically connected. They become incipiently reflex; and, on the occurrence of the appropriate stimulus, the whole nervous apparatus which in past generations was brought into activity by this stimulus, becomes nascently excited. *Even while yet there have been no individual experiences, a vague feeling of pleasure or pain is produced; constituting what we may call the body of the emotion.* And when the experiences of past generations come to be repeated in the individual, the emotion gains both strength and definiteness; and is accompanied by the appropriate specific ideas. (Spencer 1910(1):253–255; italics supplied)

By joining physiological and psychological processes in a developmental mode, Spencer achieved two purposes. First, he established a continuity between past experience and present potential; and second, he drew body and mind processes into an interrelated context. The earliest evolutionary experiences were so imprinted on the biopsychic structure that effects were never wholly lost. Any evolutionist could see that these experiences which had recurred constantly over tens of thousands of years would produce organic changes. The process was no different than what could be observed in other animals. For example, birds on isolated islands contacted by Western voyagers gradually developed an instinctive dread that could be detected in the flight behavior of the young. In humans, the child in arms rejected the unfamiliar face and broke into a cry of fear. Such behavior was organic in part and was traceable to the instinctive dread of strangers and enemies that was a part of man's social experience in the distant past, and which was transmitted as a racial heredity (Spencer 1900(3):436). Upon this organic base, common both to animal and man, the social bond linking kin and nonkin was raised. From this elemental datum Spencer concluded that the earliest human group was a communal aggregate of kindred who clung together for protection against those who were not kin (Spencer 1900(3):436–437). The blood tie thus was the basis for the first social groups.

Spencer found support for his theoretical position in the intellectual tidal wave set in motion by Darwin. Regarding use-inheritance, Darwin spoke especially to this point in the second edition of his controversial work:

> I . . . take this opportunity of remarking that my critics frequently assume that I attribute all changes of corporeal structure and mental power exclusively to the natural selection of such variations as are often called spontaneous; whereas, even in the first edition of the "Origin of Species," I distinctly stated that great weight must be attributed to the inherited effects of use and disuse, with respect both to the body and mind. (Cited by Spencer 1910(1):420)

Stress on a competitive struggle which led to advances in functional organization was important to Spencer's early interpretations, and Darwin's principle of natural selection provided strong support for this position. Civilized societies, however, were not the products of infallible perspicacity. The path to civilization was paved with countless mistakes and failures. Trial and error prevailed, and it would be a misreading of evolution to consider that it implied a directional tendency toward improvement. Rather, one must conclude that

> There is no uniform ascent from lower to higher, but only an occasional production of a form which, in virtue of greater fitness for more complex conditions, becomes capable of a longer life of a more varied kind. And while such higher type begins to dominate over lower types and to spread at their expense, the lower types survive in habitats or modes of life that are not usurped, or are thrust into inferior habitats or modes of life in which they retrogress.
>
> What thus holds with organic types must hold also with types of societies. (Spencer 1900(3):610)

Yet Spencer (1900(3):610) projected an image of a federation of the most advanced nations that would eliminate wars and "put an end to the rebarbarization which is continually undoing civilization." This idealized product of evolution constituted a structural adaptation in which faculties and outer necessities would be neatly balanced in a stable configuration (integration). In this, Spencer was not far from the eighteenth-century aspirations of Kant (1939) in his essay on *Perpetual Peace*.

Despite its apparent plausibility, the Spencerian synthesis contained an important contradiction stemming from the theory of acquired characteristics. In evolutionary perspective mankind increased the distance separating the human from the animal species. Having attained a more generalized and adaptive base, man moved up to a biosocial inheritance and freed himself from the primitive organic inheritance governing animals. In his more primitive mode, man exhibited a subjection to organic process; but in his civilized state, the acquisition of social instincts in conjunction with the widened intellectual gap raised man to his own level of superorganic process. The ambiguity of man subject to organic processes, yet pulling clear of the organic world, at best represented a compromise with biological evolution. In actuality Spencer's superorganicism drew him close to the traditional progressivist position which maintained that man was species distinct from animals and therefore must be assigned a different order of natural law.

An End to Locke's Tabula Rasa

Evolutionists joined progressivists in selecting intellect and morality as primary attributes essential to human success. In any society, evolutionist Letourneau (1881:559) observed, "intellectual activity . . . is the prime mover in all great progress, industrial, moral or social." Both progressivists and evolutionists agreed, too, that external conditions accounted for the physical, intellectual, moral, and social differences exhibited by man throughout the world. However, evolutionists parted company with progressivists when they accepted the transfer of environmentally induced characteristics into a phylogenetic inheritance of quality difference. What progressivists considered variable secondary features, easily altered by a change of habit or opportunity, now became fixed parts of an evolving race. The Lockeian premise, that savage could be changed into civilized gentleman through cultivation, seemingly was overturned by the evolutionary thesis. No one began life as a blank slate, for each was imprinted with the experiential template of his ancestors. Rejection of Locke's notion of the unformed blank mind which took shape during the life experiences of the individual was a necessary corollary of the theory of phylogenetic inheritance (see, for example, Freud 1939; Jung 1916; Briffault 1927).

HUMAN BIOLOGY, RACE, AND CULTURE

Darwin on Intraspecies Evolution and Difference

The theory of evolution implied a monogenetic origin for all who could be classified as men. Darwin's (1936:910–911) studied conclusions set the tone:

> But since he attained to the rank of manhood, he has diverged into distinct races, or as they may be more fitly called, sub-species. Some of these, such as the Negro and European, are so distinct that, if specimens had been brought to a naturalist without any further information, they would undoubtedly have been considered by him as good and true species. Nevertheless all the races agree in so many unimportant details of structure and in so many mental peculiarities that these can be accounted for only by inheritance from a common progenitor; and a progenitor thus characterized would probably deserve to rank as man.

According to evolutionary theory, differentiation from a common ancestor meant that races at the moment of divergence shared a fundamental biological and psychological potential. This equal potential remained constant provided no intraspecies evolution in grade subsequently occurred. The inclination at the time was to hold that intraspecies evolution had markedly increased the biological, psychological, emotional, and social distance between the races. In evolutionary perspective, the psychic unity of mankind could better be assigned to that distant time when the apelike ancestors had attained manhood. Once more Darwin (1936:445–446) provided substance for an evolutionary ranking of races by noting that differences in intellect and morality between the "highest men of the highest races and the lowest savages, are connected by the finest gradations." Though differences between the highest and the lowest, in Darwin's judgment, were not slight, it still was conceivable that development from the lowest to the highest was possible.

Language was especially crucial for mental development and enlargement of the brain. At first a kind of half-art and half-instinct, the continuous use of language gradually modified the brain, which then became an inherited effect. In turn the inherited adaptation influenced an improvement in language (Darwin 1936:912). The continuous interstimulation of language and organ so exercised the various mental faculties that their development and enlargement forced a like enlargement of the brain (see contemporary exchange over language origins among Washburn and Lancaster and Carini 1971). Such mutual give and take between speech and organ gradually evoked the "higher intellectual powers of man, such as those of ratiocination, abstraction, self-consciousness" (Darwin 1936:436, 912). Darwin (1936:436–437) also noted that races could be ranked according to size of head. Earlier peoples usually had smaller heads, and the contemporary European outranked American Indians, Asiatics, and Australians in cranial capacity—and Darwin observed that major changes making for difference in head size occurred in the frontal portion of the skull where the higher intellectual faculties were seated.

In the persistent competition between tribes and between races, selection worked to eliminate the weaker. Darwin noted how the uncivilized races succumbed to new diseases and failed to maintain their fertility. "When civilised nations come into contact with barbarians the struggle is short, except where a deadly climate gives its aid to the native race," and Darwin (1936:543) went on to conclude that the "grade of their civilisation seems to be a most important element in the success of competing nations." If lowly races were structurally incapable of adapting to changes which brought considerable diversity into their nearly uniform conditions, race crossing might save them from extinction. At any rate, Darwin (1936:549) argued that

> The immunity of civilised races and domesticated animals is probably due to their having been subjected to a greater extent, and therefore having grown somewhat more accustomed, to diversified or varying conditions, than the

majority of wild animals [and wild races]; and to their having formerly immi-grated or been carried from country to country, and to different families or sub-races having intercrossed. It appears that a cross with civilised races at once gives to an aboriginal race an immunity from the evil consequences of changed conditions. Thus the crossed offspring from the Tahitians and En-glish, when settled in Pitcairn Island, increased so rapidly that the Island was soon overstocked; and in June 1856 they were removed to Norfolk Island.

Evolution, Energy, and Extinction: Spencer

In a natural competition for survival, the transformation of energy into vital (organic-physical), mental, and social power was crucial. This was an early observation of Spencer (1880:180–189, 208–209), and he concluded that the only way to reach a greater fund of these energies was through functional differentiation and social individuation. Western civilized peo-ples concentrated a magnitude of vital, mental, and social power vastly superior to savage peoples because they possessed a diversified economy, large populations, and a more complex nervous system (Spencer 1897: 261). The evolutionary process had no place for the maladaptive, for these natural forces were impervious to moral considerations. Nature played no favorites, and just as the savage had displaced lower creatures, so he, in turn, inevitably must give way to his superior (Spencer 1880:238). In the evolutionary prognosis this was just, for the record of conquest revealed that the weaker, the antisocial, and the less adaptive succumbed to the superior (Spencer 1880:239). Those who survived the merciless discipline of nature (Spencer 1880:241) rode the crest of the wave, superior in body, mind, morality—and in mode of life. There was little hope, then, for bring-ing the savage up to standard by exposing him to the cultivated tastes and education of civilized men, as progressivists recommended. Rather, savage peoples were dead weight, for, as Letourneau (1881:5) so aptly phrased the evolutionary view, over some races there "hangs an organic maledic-tion, the weight of which can only be reduced by millenary efforts, and by a struggle for improvement constantly going on during geological cycles."

Savagery, Custom, Conformity, and Extinction: Bagehot

When the political philosopher Walter Bagehot in 1872 applied natural selection and inheritance to political society, he found savage races wasted away before the civilized because they had interfered with the natural orig-inality and adaptability which nature sought to produce through individual variation. Saddled with superstitious customs and prone to persecute indi-viduals for nonconformity, savage peoples dug their own graves by com-pelling uniformity, and the consequence was inflexibility in physical makeup, morality, and mode of life. They were bound to fall to the ad-vanced races because they were biologically slow to change, ill equipped to resist new diseases, sparse in numbers, weak in capacity to multiply, mentally inert, and socially and militarily unsystematized. They simply fell under the dead weight of very bad institutions, for "the best institutions have a natural military advantage over bad institutions" and win out in the competitive selection by trial (Bagehot 1875:215).

Savages and the Will to Progress: Unconscious and Conscious Processes

Waitz and Tylor defended the idea of a progressive advancement of mankind against evolutionary ideas of retrogression, nonpurposive advancement, and the physical and psychological inferiority of the less advanced races. Their views indicated that some outstanding scholars were greatly influenced by the humanistic tradition traceable to the Age of Enlightenment. They responded negatively to Spencer's judgment that most savages were the degraded descendants of civilized ancestors. Reason or perfectibility still stood as the hallmark of humanity in contrast with animality. However, Waitz (1863(1):269, 290–291) found men in their natural state shared a fondness for indolence which precluded a desire for improvement or intellectual progress. Increasingly the savage emerged encrusted with the cake of custom, a description popularized by the political theorist Walter Bagehot (1875:27, 104–105). Savage devotion to custom also impressed Tylor (1937(2):159–160).

> The savage by no means goes through life with the intention of gathering more knowledge and framing better laws than his fathers. On the contrary, his tendency is to consider his ancestors as having handed down to him the perfection of wisdom, which it would be impiety to make the least alteration in. Hence among the lower races there is obstinate resistance to the most desirable reforms, and progress can only force its way with a slowness and difficulty which we of this century can hardly imagine.

Admittedly savage life was so precarious that a hesitancy in trying new things was not always unreasonable. Change among savages was so tardy that progress must be more a product of unconscious than of conscious processes.

The idea that improvements and reforms leading to civilization were not due to conscious planning but must be credited to the unconscious processes of the human mind was conceded in the eighteenth century by Ferguson (1789:186–187), Kames (1761:15–20), and Robertson (1822(1):170–173). In the nineteenth century, however, savage and civilized were gradually drawn apart by the assignment of largely unconscious processes to the former, and of conscious cognition to the latter. As a mental operation, the rise to civilization now appeared as a trend from the unconscious to the conscious, paralleling the evolutionary emphasis on the release of civilized man from instinct or reflex behavior.

Race Mixture and the Rise of Civilization

If civilization were a product of acquired biological, moral, and intellectual characteristics, the quickest way to improve the inferior races would be through race crossing. In Quatrefages' (1879:284) view, increased communication favored a mixture of races which induced a genetic sharing of inclinations, wants, and interests. This newly established solidarity of blood and mind laid the foundations for greater social and cultural achievements. Quatrefages (1879:284) did not expect racial differences and inequities to be wholly eliminated by race mixture.

> As long as there are poles and an equator, continents and islands, or mountains and plains, races will exist distinguished by characters of every kind, and superior or inferior in a physical, intellectual, and moral point of view. In spite of crossings, varieties and inequalities will continue. But as a whole, mankind will be perfected; ... and the civilizations of the future, without causing ... the past to be forgotten, will outstrip them in some as yet unknown direction, just as ours have outstripped those of our predecessors.

Rather than weakening the creativity of pure races, as polygenists argued, race mixture added to the civilizing potential. For all its alleged superiority, the white race had never produced a civilization of its own. The barbaric Germans and half-pastoral Aryans attained the refinements of civilization only after crossing with local populations. Fertility, enhanced beauty, strong physique, and creativity were the consequences of mixture.

In America, sociologist Lester Ward's (1841–1913) theory of creative synthesis and the principle of *synergy* represented a culmination of the necessity for peoples and cultures to intermingle if progress were to occur.

> Just as in biology the world was never satisfied with the law of organic evolution worked out by Goethe and Lamarck until the principle of natural selection was discovered which explained the workings of that law, so in sociology it was not enough to formulate the law of social evolution, ... and the next step has been taken in bringing to light the sociological homologue of natural selection which explains the progress of social evolution. That principle is not the same as natural selection, but it serves the same purpose. It also resembles the latter in growing out of the life-struggle and in being a consequence of it; but, instead of consisting in the hereditary selection of the successful elements of that struggle, it consists in the ultimate union of the opposing elements and their combination and assimilation. Successively higher and higher social structures are thus created by a process of natural synthesis, and society evolves from stage to stage. The struggling groups infuse into each other the most vigorous qualities of each, cross all the hereditary strains, double their social efficiency at each cross, and place each new product on a higher plane of existence. It is the cross-fertilization of cultures. (Cited by Bristol 1915:225–226)

The emergent historical-geographic orientation adumbrated by Bastian and developed by Friedrich Ratzel (1844–1904) likewise contested the thesis that racial inheritance conditioned the level of civilization which people attained. In Bastian's view the intermingling of peoples through migration, and the contact of cultures at the margins of geographic-cultural regions, brought an exchange of folk ideas which stimulated new and more advanced developments. History furnished proof of cultural continuities that reached back to prehistoric times, and it could be concluded that "civilized peoples . . . are but the highest product out of an infinite number of mixtures" (Bastian, cited by Penniman 1965:113). Selective breeding for race purity in the interests of civilized creativity thus was sheer nonsense.

In Ratzel's view the idea of natural races did not involve anthropological or physiological distinctions in relation to civilized peoples. The alleged natural races were simply nations poor in culture. Every race possessed its natural and civilized peoples. The Caucasoid Ainu, which the Mongolic Japanese considered a natural race, permitted but one conclusion:

> Race as such has nothing to do with the possession of civilization. It would be silly to deny that in our own times the highest civilization has been in the hands of the Caucasian, or white, races; but, on the other hand, it is an equally important fact that for thousands of years in all civilizing movements there has been a dominant tendency to raise all races to the level of their burdens and duties, and therewith to make real earnest of the great conception of humanity—a conception which has been proclaimed as a specially distinguishing attribute of the modern world. . . . But let us only look outside the border of the brief and narrow course of events which we arrogantly call the history of the world, and we shall have to recognize that members of every race have borne their part in the history which lies beyond, the history of primeval and prehistoric times. (Ratzel 1896–1898(1):20)

Bastian and Ratzel were in agreement on another point—that interchange of ideas and culture elements had played an important part in the development of successive stages of civilization. The humanistic thread and emphasis on contact processes embodied in the historical-geographic posture of Bastian and Ratzel furnished the platform upon which American and German culture-theorists would build their scientific ethnology.

SAVAGE NATURE AND CHARACTER

Savage Nature: Progressivist Views

A common acceptance by progressivists and evolutionists of the uncultivated state of savage peoples led them to compile parallel and monotonous lists of features of savage character. What Kames (1778(2):93, 131, 165) had to say in the eighteenth century is echoed in the nineteenth. Savages, Kames observed, possessed a "violent propensity to intemperance," "indolence," "unconcern about futurity," a miserable deficiency in "invention and perceiving relations," gross ignorance of "causes and effects," and little sense of "propriety, dignity, and grace." The savage exhibited a "moral sense," but it was "not sufficiently vigorous to give him compunction."

Basing his description of man's nature in rude nations before establishment of private property, Ferguson (1789:123–146) drew a more favorable picture of savage character. From the reports of Lafitau, Charlevoix, and Colden he learned that rude peoples were fond of war, responsive to individual merit, tenaciously egalitarian, friendly and fond of company, eloquent, discerning, and unflinchingly courageous. Ferguson obviously sketched savage man in the image of Indians in New England, particularly the Iroquois. He also noted an impulsiveness without regard to consequences, as when they gambled until they were left with nothing but their nakedness. Spontaneous affection, not duty, ruled their acts of generosity and kindness. To act they must be stirred by some immediate passion, but such passions were quickly satisfied, and therefore they cared little for wealth or commerce. Danger and honor drew a quick and enthusiastic response, but they had little vision beyond their immediate experience in hunting and in war. Submitting themselves to the vagaries of each season, they made no plans for the future. Though sometimes anxious or uneasy, savages did not experience "ingenuous shame, compassion, remorse or a command [restraint] of appetite." Whether sober, aroused by feeling, or debauched, custom did not hold the savage responsible for acts of violence; and, in consequence, they never were forced into acts of repentance. Their superstitious practices betrayed an anxious weakness and absurdity. Stoic in hardship and fatigue, rude nations resisted domination and rules which limited freedom or stifled action that sprang from the "simple dictates of the heart." Therefore, to consort with civilized men could only be temporary, for savages loved personal freedom too dearly to conform to the rigid rules of civilized society.

The historian Robertson was equally impressed by the savage's love of freedom. This devotion to independence Robertson attributed to the fact that hunters possessed but limited ideas about property. Continuing, he noted that

> People in this state retain a high sense of equality and independence. Wherever the idea of property is not established, there can be no distinction among men, but what arises from personal qualities. . . . Every circumstance indicated that all the members of the community are on a level [same dress, food, possessions]. . . . All are freemen, all feel themselves to be such and assert with firmness the rights which belong to that condition. This sentiment of independence is imprinted so deeply in their nature, that no change of condition can eradicate it, and bend their minds to servitude. (Robertson 1822(1):185–186)

Pursuing the impact of mode of life on character implied in the progressivist position, Monboddo (1794(4):55–59) distinguished two types of character among nations in the first stage of civil society after men had learned to speak and had established families. At the beginning, men, as gleaners of the natural fruits of the earth, displayed kind, hospitable, friendly, noble, generous, and humane attributes. When taking to the hunting of animals, however, man turned himself into a predator "more cruel and ferocious . . . more cunning and deceitful than he would otherwise be; for it is by cunning and surprise that he seizes his prey."

In the nineteenth century Tylor (1874(1):28–31) in a progressivist mode defended the inherent superiorities of civilization against philosophic critics and also against those who saw a noble simplicity and generosity in savage nature. Tylor admitted that with the development of values emphasizing life and property, virtues such as courage, honesty, and generosity declined in importance. He even found slavery under savage and barbarous races preferable to that practiced in European colonies. Moreover, in accounts of savage life, deeds characterized by morality and social responsibility were common. The savage in contact with a civilized invader often was stripped of his rude virtues without gaining anything in return. However, savagery was no paradise, as evidenced by the malignant ferocity of Caribs in their torture and eating of prisoners.

The logic of progress obviously was not compatible with the image of savage gentlemen. A noble savage, as reasoned, gentle, generous, and with the disciplined control of feelings characteristic of the civilized gentleman simply did not exist. Passion, not reason, ruled archaic character.

> So when we read descriptions of the hospitality, the gentleness, the bravery, the deep religious feeling of the North American Indians, we admit their claims to our sincere admiration; but we must not forget that they were hospitable literally to a fault, that their gentleness would pass with a flash of anger into frenzy, that their bravery was stained with cruel and treacherous malignity, that their religion expressed itself in absurd belief and useless ceremony. The ideal savage of the 18th century might be held up as a living reproof to vicious and frivolous London; but in sober fact, a Londoner who should attempt to lead the atrocious life which the real savage may lead with impunity and even respect, would be a criminal only allowed to follow his savage models during his short intervals out of gaol. Savage moral standards are real enough, but they are far looser and weaker than ours. We may, I think, apply the often-repeated comparison of savages to children as fairly to their moral as to their intellectual condition. The better savage social life seems in but unstable equilibrium, liable to be easily upset by a touch of distress, temptation, or violence. . . . Altogether, it may be admitted that some rude tribes lead a life to be envied by some barbarous races, and even by the outcasts of higher nations. But that any known savage tribe would not be improved by judicious civilization, is a proposition which no moralist would dare to make; . . . the evidence goes far to justify the view that on the whole the civilised man is not only wiser and more capable than the savage, but also better and happier, and that the barbarian stands between. (Tylor 1874 (1):30–31)

The psychology of uncultivated peoples that Waitz (1859) extracted from his comparative treatment of savage custom and character conformed to usual progressivist views. The motivations of uncultivated nations were three:

> physical well-being, chiefly directed to the gratification of the appetites, sexual enjoyment, and indolence, . . . social enjoyment, . . . and, thirdly, habit, the power of which influences all actions, and to a great extent perpetuated physical and moral misery. (Waitz 1863(1):293–294)

Superficially the varied modes of life of the uncultivated peoples gave the appearance of difference; but with regard to their inner life, they were very much alike.

> The individual character among uncivilized nations is not so decided as among the cultivated. Want of self-control, improvidence, intemperance, indolence combined with perseverance in the pursuit after actual necessaries, and ornamentation of the person, are general characters. . . .
>   Gluttony, drunkenness, and sexual excesses, are the most generally spread vices. Next to licentious festivities, savage passion is displayed in the chase. When there is abundance of game, the hunter exhibits, like a soldier in battle, the greatest rage; he finds delight in killing and destroying the game indiscriminately and uselessly. Hence hunting tribes require a great space, and are frequently in want, as they do not economize their provisions. (Waitz 1863(1):293–294)

Savage morality exhibited what one might anticipate from their uncultivated state: "great abnormalities . . . not merely in individual actions but in the fixed habits of life. There is no doubt that cannibalism, infanticide, and similar deeds, have been and are still practised without any consciousness of their criminality" (Waitz 1863(1):296).

Despite obvious physical differences and wide distances separating untutored peoples in their locations, similarities in religious beliefs, views of nature, and the inner core of their mental lives were so compelling that all must be members of the same species (Waitz 1863(1):303–305).

Savage Nature: Evolutionist Views

Like the progressivist, the evolutionist sketched the savage as a polar extreme to more evolved civilized man. Lippert (1931:36) pronounced impulsiveness and spontaneous reactions to the "impressions of the moment . . . [without] premeditation and deliberation" to be fundamental traits of savage character. Expectably, primitive men were carefree, improvident, brutal, callous, indolent, without a desire for property, and unwholesomely free of a sense of cleanliness—which Lippert (1931:37–42) considered essential to civilized man and civilized living. The evolutionary political theorist Bagehot (1875:113) produced a like catalog of savage and pre-savage characteristics:

> prehistoric [pre-savage] men . . . were "savages without the fixed habits of of savages"; . . . like savages, they had strong passions and weak reason; . . . they preferred short spasms of greedy pleasure to mild and equable enjoy-

ment; . . . they could not postpone the present to the future; . . . their ingrained sense of morality was, to say the best of it, rudimentary and defective.

With little concern for human life savages eagerly killed all old people, parents included, because they could not be bothered with their care (Bagehot 1875:115–116). As for the truth, they would just as soon lie and their "ideas of marriage . . . [were] so vague and light that the idea [of] communal marriage' (in which all the women of the tribe are common to all the men, and them only), has been invented to denote it" (Bagehot 1875:115–116).

For Spencer (1900(1):41–93) the savage's essential qualities were rooted in his level of biological development and the mode of life he was able to raise on his limited biological foundations. Comparisons with civilized men revealed savages to be shorter in stature, less powerful physically, less energetic but earlier in maturation, larger in jaw and teeth, better able to withstand pain and discomfort, and stronger in recuperative powers. The basic disadvantage of savage man was his less-evolved condition, which limited the higher intellectual functions. Early maturation was symptomatic of biological underdevelopment, for the insufficient growth time arrested physiological and neurological development. Consequently, the savage's nervous system operated largely by reflex action, and his mental life was dominated by immediate response to sensorimotor action and feelings directly connected to these. Hence, variable emotionality was demonstrated by savage man in his impulsive acts, oscillating between excitatory or constrained states, a quick turn from laughter to tears, from fondness to anger, and a dogged dedication to revenge. Savage man also exhibited a basic egoism in his indolence, a childish gaiety without thought of future, an intolerance of restraint, an exceeding vanity, and a fear of public disapproval and ridicule. The parental instinct, which man shared with animals, was discerned in savage fondness for children, but this savage parental love often was qualified by brutal killings of children for harmless mistakes, and by infanticide.

Savage hospitality and generosity reflected altruism, but the treatment of women illustrated to Spencer the limitations of savage feelings. Regarding intellect, savages were unable to rise above immediate sensation and found it hard to deal with generalities or future events. Abstract ideas like uniformity, cause, and truth were beyond savage capacity, and even imagination was restricted to reminiscence. The vagueness or imprecise quality of primitive ideas underlined the narrow attention span and lack of critical acumen, creating serious difficulties in construction of a logical chain of related events. More amoral than moral or immoral, the savage was organized neurologically to be a conservator of habit. He thus was less adaptable than civilized man, since accelerated maturity caused earlier fixation of his simpler nervous system and restricted variability. For savage man to be anything more than he was required the destruction of his present mode of life; only through the reorganization of his social experience could primitive man advance to the use of higher intellectual faculties.

The convergences of progressivists and evolutionists in their estimates of savage nature are so parallel that it is no wonder that later critics of Developmentalism lumped them together as evolutionists. In the long perspective of development, primitive men could not help but come out second best. Yet primitive men had initiated social life, and the continuity in human development could be traced back to their original ideas. Primitive conceptualizations and mental processes were like a golden ore awaiting extraction from the matrices of savage custom and institution.

Savage Evolutionary Inferiority and the Childhood of Man

From the evolutionary perspective, the elevation of mankind was not a simple matter of education, as progressivists optimistically argued. The uneven evolution of the races made the difference. After differentiating from a common platform, the races followed their own paths along the high road to civilization. Though separate, their paths were parallel as each, subject to the law of natural selection, passed from one adaptive stage to another. In this biopsychological and moral run to civilization, the white race led the pack. The savage was inferior in all respects—body, mind, and morality—for the

> theory of the evolution of civilisation postulates the evolution of man, mentally and morally as well as physically. At the moment when the anthropoid became entitled to be properly denominated man his intellectual capacity was not that of a Shakspeare, [sic] a Newton, a Darwin, or even of an average Englishman of the twentieth century. He was only endowed with potentialities which, after an unknown series of generations . . . issued in that supreme result. The savage . . . is . . . undeveloped. His intellectual faculties are chiefly employed in winning material subsistence, in gratifying his passions, in fighting with his fellow-man and with wild beasts. . . . Many of them, therefore, are dormant, like a bud before it has unfolded. . . . Credulous as a child he is put off from the solution of a merely speculative question by a tale that chimes with his previous ideas, though it may transcend his actual experience. Hence, many a deduction, many an induction, to us plain and obvious has been retarded, or never reached at all: he is still a savage. (Hartland 1909–1910(45):255–256)

In analogy, the savage was a child and savagery the childhood of man. "These primitive men are children, with the intelligence of a child," but as Elie Reclus (1891:xii) observed, one could expect savages, despite their artlessness, to generate "sudden illuminations, inspirations of genius, heroic conceptions, inventive faculties" after the fashion of children. Letourneau (1881:77, 249) found so many reminders of the thought ways of children in the conscient life of primitives that he recommended study of the dreams of children as the best way to uncover the mental condition of primitive man (Letourneau 1881:274). In religion, according to Spencer (1900(1): 834–835, Appendix B) one found feelings common to all undeveloped minds. Savage, civilized child, and uncultured adult in civilized society were all dreadfully frightened of ghosts.

The savage-child metaphor sometimes used by progressivists in both the eighteenth and nineteenth centuries became, in the hands of evolutionists, a biological fact of life. Savages also emerged as nature men chained to primitive animal instincts that kept body alive and exercised no restraints over desire. In a pre-Freudian mode Lippert (1931:11–12) sketched uncivilized man torn between untamed natural instincts and reason. Lippert's score for the human drama was little more than a variant of Spencer's, where social civilized man triumphed over antisocial (instinctual, organic-driven) savage man. The savage as natural man was no metaphor to evolutionists; it was a biological fact of life.

EVOLUTIONARY DISTANCE IN CIVILIZED SOCIETY: PEASANTS, PROFESSIONALS, AND THE MASSES

It was tempting to apply the idea of biopsychic distinctions to the class arrangements of complex societies. The mentally uncultivated in civilized societies supplied a counterpart to the childlike untutored savage. Peasants maintained many survivals of savage practices, and Frazer (1935:Preface), Lang (1908), and Tylor (1874(1):6–7) counseled the use of peasant beliefs as a point of departure in the search for primitive mentality.

In his study of hereditary genius Galton (1962) supplied a more relevant scientific base for those viewing social classes in a natural biological hierarchy. He found that any historic genius produced a clustering of outstanding personages in collateral and lineal relations; but three successive dilutions of a bloodline, as in the instance of judgeships he observed, apparently exhausted the vigor of the line (Galton 1962:123–124). Galton's treatment of classes was hardly sociological, but he did raise the specter of degeneracy of the race and of decline in civilization as the complexity of civilization outraced physical constitution. The English pyramid of ability was explored in 1904 by Havelock Ellis (1926:78). Artisans and laborers, who comprised nearly three quarters of the population, made a very poor showing in their proportion of great men. Using portraits from the National Gallery, Ellis (1926:295–296) worked out a pigmentation index that revealed outstanding political reformers and agitators, men of science, sailors, soldiers, royal family, created peers and their sons to be fair. Divines, men of low birth, explorers, and theatrical people tended to be dark. Ellis considered that he had independently confirmed Beddoe's (1885) index of nigrescence and professional status. Nothing but race, therefore, could explain the predisposition and intellectual flair of an individual for a chosen profession.

The scientific finds of evolution developed no support for the image of the common man—not even in America. The struggle for survival which prevailed in nature and in society was designed to produce supermen and not average men—hence the tendency was for evolutionists to focus on genius and on the elite. The masses, as social evolutionist Sumner noted, were natural-born followers rather than leaders.

> The masses are not large classes at the base of a social pyramid; they are the core of the society. They are conservative. They accept life as they find it, and live on by tradition and habit . . . the great mass of any society lives a purely instinctive life just like animals. (Sumner 1960:55)

The historical classes were the innovators and the pace setters imitated by the masses. The masses also were persuaded to accept the leadership of the upper classes, for a hierarchical organization of society was essential to improvement. "Masses of men who are in a substantial equality with each other never can be anything but hopeless savages" (Sumner 1960:57).

EVOLUTIONISTIC EROSION OF PROGRESSIVISM

Tylor's Conversion to Biopsychic Evolution

In an intellectual climate saturated with biosocial evolutionism, the humanistic spirit attached to the idea of progress would scarcely come through unscathed. In 1871 Tylor (1874(1):Preface) offered an apology for writing *Primitive Culture* without special reference to the "theory of development or evolution . . . [expounded by] Mr. Darwin and Mr. Herbert Spencer, whose influence on the whole course of modern thought on such subjects should not be left without formal recognition." The omission stemmed from a simple fact: Tylor's theory of the evolution of culture rested on a progressive substitution of ideas rather than on a struggle for survival. He did make occasional use of the word "evolution" and acknowledged that the "institutions which can best hold their own in the world gradually supersede the less fit ones, and that this incessant conflict determines the general resultant course of culture " (Tylor 1874(1):68–69). He attributed the progressive and uniform improvement of human institutions to the human mind rather than race. Tylor referred to the lower races and to savages in the same spirit as eighteenth-century progressivists, defining a rude state of cultivation rather than a biopsychic condition. In savage religion, behind the apparent follies and superstitions, he detected principles which were essentially rational even though their application reflected a condition of gross ignorance (Tylor 1874(1):23).

The situation for Tylor had altered considerably by the time he wrote the first basic text for anthropology in 1881. Now he had made biopsychic evolutionism central to his understanding of race differences and of the march to civilization. Mind power now was a function of the size and complexity of the brain. This conclusion was drawn from a comparison of gradations within the primates. The connection between race and civilization was further demonstrated by the fact that the "brain of the European is somewhat more complex in its convolutions than the brain of a Negro or Hottentot." Admittedly this conclusion rested on imperfect evidence, but it did suggest a relationship between neurological complexity and intellectual power among races which had attained a level of civilization (Tylor 1937(1):46). The frontal lobes of Australian and African in comparison with the European were less full, and the faces of these less-civilized peoples consequently took on a more apelike profile (Tylor 1937(1):47–48). Climate could not be called upon to account entirely for what must be an inbred temperament and mental capacity; for within the same tropical climate the Indian was dull and sullen, while the black overflowed with exuberant feeling and gaiety (Tylor 1937(1):57). Tylor (1937(1):58) also echoed Spencer's observation that Europeans who taught children of the lower races agreed that savages held their own with whites up to about twelve years, but then began to slip behind children of the ruling race. This observation corresponded with what anatomy had to say about the relative brain development of Australian, African, and European and also with what the history of civilization recorded. Savages and barbarians maintained a life much like that of the ancestors of the British and other civilized peoples, but they were incapable of going beyond that level of culture. It took progressive races of superior intelligence to push on to civilization. Tylor reminded his European readers that, though now dominant, their race had no monopoly on intellectual prowess. The history of civilization disclosed that brown Egyptians were leaders in that early dawn and that dark whites (Assyrians, Phoenicians, Persians, Greeks, and so on) had moved it ahead. The yellow Chinese, whose hair and general features betrayed their Tatar affinities, had reached a civilized state more than four thousand years ago. Yet Tylor (1937(1):91) concluded that it was reasonable to see the white race as superior to other races since it was the last to be formed. Confined to the temperate zone because of an inability to tolerate extremes, the white race likewise was more dependent on the apparatus of culture for comfort and survival. Gifted with a special talent for knowledge and for governance, the race seemed destined to rule the world.

Tylor's conversion to evolutionism took place during the decade between 1870 and 1880. His progressivist position stands clear in 1871 (1874(1):6–7):

> Surveyed in a broad view, the character and habit of mankind at once display that similarity and consistency of phenomena which led the Italian proverb-maker to declare that 'all the world is one country.' ... *To general likeness in human nature on the one hand, and to general likeness in the circumstances of life on the other, this similarity and consistency may no doubt be traced,* and they may be studied with especial fitness in comparing races near the same grade of civilization.... Even when it comes to comparing barbarous hordes with civilized nations, the consideration thrusts itself upon our minds,

how far item after item of the life of the lower races passes into analogous proceedings of the higher, in forms not too far changed to be recognized, and sometimes hardly changed at all. Look at the modern European peasant using his hatchet and his hoe, see his food boiling or roasting over the log-fire, observe the exact place which beer holds in his calculation of happiness, hear his tale of the ghost in the nearest haunted house, and of the farmer's niece who was bewitched with knots in her inside till she fell into fits and died. If we choose out in this way things which have altered little in a long course of centuries, we may draw a picture where there shall be scarce a hand's breadth difference between an English ploughman and a negro of Central Africa. These pages will be so crowded with evidence of such correspondences among mankind, that there is no need to dwell upon its details here, *but it may be used at once to override a problem which would complicate the argument, namely, the question of race. For the present purpose it appears both possible and desirable to eliminate considerations of hereditary varieties or races of man, and to treat mankind as homogeneous in nature, though placed in different grades of civilization.* [Italics supplied]

Morgan's Course to Biopsychic Evolution

Unlike Tylor, Morgan was early involved with problems of race and heredity, and civilization. First, he was more than a sympathetic witness to the demoralization of the Iroquois as the advancing frontier engulfed them. Incorporation of the Iroquois "into the great brotherhood of American nations as equal citizens" (cited by Resek 1960:31) appealed to Morgan as a proper alternative to the policy of removal. Integration was feasible because education was at hand, and Indians responded to it. Morgan inspired the Grand Order of the Iroquois, of which he was the moving spirit, to sponsor Ely Parker, Parker's sister, and a friend at Aurora Academy, New York. In 1843 Morgan held no dissent with the Christian creation described in Genesis, nor with the idea that man was a single species with a career marked by cultivation without species transformation. He did tilt with the theological argument of savage degeneracy and offered in contrast the agricultural and educational progress then being made by the Iroquois. Second, Morgan addressed himself to the polygenist-monogenist controversy, because of its implications for human origins, theology, and race slavery. By 1850, Morgan's attitudes toward Negro slavery apparently were colored by polygenist race arguments. However, he made his own interpretation, arguing that slavery was bad because it failed to prevent reproduction of blacks—a race which he considered "too thin . . . intellectually to be fit to propagate (cited by Resek 1960:63, note 21). By 1857, Morgan rejected polygenism in a paper critical of Louis Agassiz, observing that the use of many pairs and creations to account for racial differences was absurd (cited by Resek 1960:63, note 21).

Many of Morgan's ideas linking heredity to culture seem to have formed during writing of the famous *Systems of Consanguinity and*

Affinity of the Human Family (1871). At the very start Morgan (cited by Resek 1960:6) voiced the conviction that, in the use of singular terms of relationship, he would be able to determine biological affinities between peoples separated by continental distances. Following the same logic, he was convinced that clothing, family types, and other items of culture were perpetuated in the "streams of blood through indefinite periods of time"(!). In his opinion neither linguistic nor ethnological (racial) studies had proved the unity of the race. Morgan (cited by Resek 1960:note, 207) noted the malign effects engendered by European-Indian intermixture. The animal passion conveyed by the European could not be controlled by the half-breeds who drifted into indiscriminate licentiousness as the quantity of white blood increased.

In *Ancient Society* (1877) Morgan returned to the theme of the unity of mankind and human progress. Through his researches into the development of human institutions he hoped to show that the steps in advancement everywhere corresponded to "the natural logic of the human mind and the necessary limitations of its powers" and certified the unitary origin of mankind (Morgan 1963:17–18). He paid tribute to savage progenitors who first won the battle for existence and ensured progress by stabilizing subsistence and developing speech. By means of these early inventions man spread over the world. However, in his pristine state, the lower status of savagery, there was little difference between man and the animals whom he fought (Morgan 1963:507). The

> inferiority of savage man in the mental and moral scale, undeveloped, inexperienced, and held down by his low animal appetites and passions, though reluctantly recognized, is, nevertheless, substantially demonstrated by the remains of ancient art in flint stone and bone implements, by his cave life in certain areas, and by his osteological remains. It is still further illustrated by the present conditions of tribes of savages in a low state of development, left in isolated sections of the earth as monuments of the past. (Morgan 1963:41)

Diet had much to do with enlarging the brains and mental powers of peoples. The meat and milk used by pastoral Aryans and Semites gave them an advantage over village-dwelling Hindus; and Morgan (1963:25) held that the latter in consequence were even inferior in size of brain to Indians in the lower status of barbarism. Great institutional advances like the gens reorganized society and created stocks which were physically and mentally vigorous. Intermixtures between progressive tribes increased size of skull and brain and added new capabilities to both stocks. Now, contrary to his previous view, a mixed stock was an improvement on the originals, and this superiority expressed itself in an increase in numbers and improved mental capacities. Morgan's views on race and culture obviously moved with intellectual climate, following a course from a progressivist view of the unity of the races to polygenism, and then to monogenism with racial distinctions based on intraspecies evolution.

NEW LIGHT ON HEREDITY: CHALLENGE TO PHYLOGENETIC INHERITANCE

Evolutionism began to lose its favored position in the 1890s, owing to new biological and historical-cultural evidences that cast doubt on the linkage of race, psychology, and culture. In the 1880s August Weismann opened a hard and sustained drive against the theory of inheritance of acquired characteristics. In Weismann's view, a germinal plasm was central to heredity and could not be altered by environment. Under experimental conditions he had clipped the tails of mice at the moment of birth, and over twenty generations not one mouse turned up without a tail. By 1884–1885 Weismann and others identified the cell nucleus as the centrum for inheritance, and in 1900 the experiments of Carl Correns, Hugo de Vries, and Otto von Tschermak reproduced the findings of Gregor Mendel's controlled crossing of peas. Within ten years Thomas Hunt Morgan formulated the gene theory based on his magnificently detailed observations of generations of fruit flies.

DECLINE OF BIOSOCIAL EVOLUTIONISM: SEPARATION OF ORGANIC AND SOCIAL PROCESSES

Sensitive to the meaning of new developments in biology, Huxley (1899), loyal defender of Darwin's survival of the fittest, finally urged that organic evolution be separated from social evolution. The biological and the social represented processes that were intrinsically different. Reviewing English history since the Tudors, he had found no conclusive evidence that Englishmen had been modified in physique and in mental capabilities by the evolutionary process (Huxley 1896:38). Huxley was willing to accept a Hobbesian description of war outside the family as the usual primitive condition, but he did not consider survival of the toughest and shrewdest as a victory in perfection. Following the primitive organic process, the "strongest, the most self-assertive, tend to tread down the weaker ... [but] social progress means a checking of the cosmic process at every step and the substitution for it of the ethical process; the end of which is not the survival of those who may happen to be the fittest ... but of those who are ethically the best" (Huxley 1896:81). Thus man, at least, was raised above the raw base of nature and insulated behind his institutions. Heredity maintained a basic physiological continuum and served as a platform for common human behavior, but it could not be imprinted by social experience and habits.

Some ten years earlier, Major John W. Powell, the geologically trained director of the Bureau of American Ethnology, voiced a similar view. Man's destiny was not tied to the primitive organic, for he had freed himself from the struggle for existence against plants and animals through technical inventions. Through social institutions, man would free himself from a deadly struggle of man against man (Powell 1888a(1):310–311). "Animal evolution arises out of the struggle for existence; human evolution arises out of the endeavor to secure happiness: it is a conscious effort for improvement in condition." Powell described nature as tricking man by misleading him through his natural impressions into false beliefs about the flatness of the earth, the sun traveling around the earth, and superstitions about ghosts.

Toward the end of the nineteenth century Spencerian evolutionism began to crack under the combined assaults of new biological evidence, geographical historicism, and humanistic counterthrusts. These developments brought renewed efforts to discriminate the social (and later cultural) from the biological. Future developments diverged along three lines: (1) social evolutionists transferred the struggle for existence to the realm of institutions and avoided the linkage of race-psychology-civilization; (2) social phylogenists insisted on the inheritance of sociopsychological experiences independent of the primitive organic processes to which natural selection administered; and (3) sociologists and culture historians asserted that social and cultural processes should be studied in their respective contexts without regard to organic processes and psychological processes coordinate with a general human nature.

By 1900 it was evident that the linkage of race, psychology, and culture would no longer carry the main thrust of social and cultural investigation. However, the task of expunging psychological explanation and an evolutionary design from anthropology continued over several decades as lingering exponents of bioevolutionary interpretations of social and cultural processes provoked lively counterthrusts.

DEVELOPMENT AND PURPOSE

When development is charted in successive stages it is exceedingly difficult to avoid the implication of purposive change and ultimate cause. Developmentalists consistently viewed the natural history of man as divisible into major structural turns that followed in tandem: (1) savagery, barbarism, civilization; (2) theological, metaphysical, positivistic knowledge systems (Comte); and (3) communal organization of blood kin, militaristic society, industrial society (Spencer); and (4) primitive communism, feudalism, capitalism, socialistic communism (Marx). For Developmentalists, ideas were the touchstones of change, and they commonly strung them together in a linear-causal chain.

Purposive change poses three issues holding special implications for the way in which reality is held to be structured. First, does human progress follow a straight or uniform line of development that is irreversible? Second, is the process of advancement dependent upon some immanent principle or intrinsic organization that predestines man and generates his wish for fulfillment? Third, is directionality the result of a succession of accommodations between intrinsic and extrinsic forces? This latter view was the special contribution of the theory of evolution, which stressed a line of successful adaptations. Directionality of the adaptive process flowed through a line of reproducers, the fit who survived natural selection. Adaptive change through natural selection was not unlike the Marxian dialectic, which emphasized the generation of tensions between two opposing classes, owing to maladaptive distributions within the political economy. Feudalism, capitalism, and socialism represented successive adaptive improvements produced through dialectical selection.

Progress, Purpose, and Unilinear Change: Eighteenth- and Nineteenth-Century Continuities

Eighteenth-century progressivists advanced a purposive and unilinear interpretation of human history. Progress was an inevitable emergent of man's nature based on his ethical and intellectual faculties. Surveying the history of the human species, the prior efforts of savages and barbarians were linked in a continuity that ultimately gave rise to civilization.

A similar stress on linear continuity with the past is found in Morgan (1963:59) over one hundred years later:

> Out of a few germs of thought, conceived in the early ages, have been evolved all the principal institutions of mankind. Beginning their growth in the period of savagery, fermenting through the period of barbarism, they have continued their advancement through the period of civilization. The evolution of these germs of thought has been guided by a natural logic which formed an essential attribute of the brain itself. So unerringly has this principle performed its function in all conditions of experience, and in all periods of time, that its results are uniform, coherent and traceable in their courses.

Morgan's statement testified to the coherence and stability of the progressivist position, for he relied on the natural logic of the human mind to account for the inevitable improvement that could be read in the rise of civilization. His germs of thought were similar to the original ideas with which progressivists generally began the natural history of specific institutions. In his turn Tylor (1874(1):15) looked to mechanical inventions for apt examples of the gradual and continuous modifications which cumulatively and successively advanced civilization. The clumsy wheellock of flint and steel gave way to the flint-lock, and this to the percussion lock, just as savages in making fire had developed the bow drill from the hand drill. In the development of culture there was a gradual "movement along a measured line from grade to grade of actual savagery, barbarism, and civilization" (Tylor 1874(1):32).

Evolution and Purposive Unilinear Change: Spencer on Differentiation and Retrogression

The biological-evolutionary model followed by Spencer suggested that progress was neither purposive nor inevitable. At the individual level the life of any organism described a path to mature flowering and decline. In the broad spectrum of biological evolution there were numerous extinctions, and in remote areas one found instances of arrested development. Applied to physical types, the evolutionary process did not produce a lineal succession. The finding for the evolution of civilization would be no different. Indeed, the intrinsic process of evolution was

> not linear but divergent and re-divergent. Each differentiated product gives origin to a new set of differentiated products. While spreading over the Earth mankind have found environments of various characters, and in each case the social life previously led, has been partly determined by the influences of the new environment; so that the multiplying groups have tended ever to acquire differences, now major and now minor; there have arisen genera and species of societies. (Spencer 1900(3):331)

Moreover, since the contest for survival among animals operated equally for men, it was quite probable that there were many abortive attempts in the evolution of society. Rare were occasions when some new combination of elements stimulated a social advance. However, when a new social type did appear, it possessed a drive to expand, and in extending itself, less-evolved societies were forced into unfavorable habitats where they were consigned to a process of decline and ultimate decay (Spencer 1900(1): 96–97).

Spencer argued that adaptation was intrinsic to the evolutionary process. Adaptive changes were induced by the cooperative and coordinate action of inner and outer factors, and this ruled out any intrinsic tendency to advance to a higher form (Spencer 1900(1):95). The moving equilibrium of a system, delicately adjusted to the opposition of internal and external forces, could trend either to a static equilibrium or to dissolution. As the integrative process tightened relations among the parts, the moving equilibrium would slow down and ultimately come to a point of rest, or stasis. Even if prompted to alter, owing to some change in external conditions, a return to equilibrium would forestall either evolutionary differentiation or recession, that is, the withering of functional differentiations then operative (Spencer 1900(1):95–96; 1880:450). A structural-environmental equilibrium induced a standoff that could not generate energy for change, or a loss of energy.

There were ample illustrations of decline in the histories of empires. The examples of Egypt, Babylonia, Assyria, Phoenicia, Persia, Israel, Greece, Rome, Peru, Mexico, Cambodia, and Central America clearly demonstrated the disappearance of richly evolved societies, which gradually dwindled into barbarous hordes or experienced a protracted period of decay. It was clear that

> causes like those which produced these retrogressions, have been at work during the whole period of human existence. Always there have been cosmical and terrestrial changes going on, which, bettering some habitats, have made others worse; always there have been over-populations, spreadings of tribes, conflicts with other tribes, and escape of the defeated into localities

unfit for such advanced social life as they had reached; always, where evolution has been uninterfered with externally, there have been those decays and dissolutions which complete the cycles of social changes. And the implication is that remnants of inferior races, taking refuge in inclement, barren, or otherwise unfit regions, have retrograded.

Probably, then, most of the tribes known as lowest, exhibit some social phenomena which are due, not to causes now operating, but to causes that operated during past social states higher than the present. (Spencer 1900(1): 97–98; 1880:450–65)

Direct evidence for retrogression was found among contemporary Australians, whose complex social relationships and ceremonials appeared to be a survival of a more developed social and political system. To cap his argument that contemporary savages were not the noble ancestors of civilized man, but rather retrograded elements unable to make it in a higher civilization, Spencer denied them the human virtue of self-improvement. Contrary to the progressivist argument, he found uncivilized tribes so unwilling to respond positively to altered circumstances that they would rather die out than adapt (Spencer 1900(1):577).

Geology and the Model of Successive Culture Strata

At the very time that Spencer, using a biological model, was challenging the inevitable linearity of change and progress, Morgan (1877) and Tylor (1874(1):58–62) were drawing analogies from geology, paleontology, and archeology to project a uniform progression of intellectual-cultural strata stretching from savagery to civilization.

Like the successive geological formations, the tribes of mankind may be arranged, according to their relative conditions into successive strata. When thus arranged, they reveal with some degree of certainty the entire range of human progress from savagery to civilization. A thorough study of each successive stratum will develop whatever is special in its culture and characteristics, and yield a definite conception of the whole, in their differences and in their relations. When this has been accomplished, the successive stages of human progress will be definitely understood. Time has been an important factor in the formation of these strata; and it must be measured out to each ethnical period in no stinted measure. Each period anterior to civilization represents many thousands of years. (Morgan 1877:499–500)

As for decline, history illustrates that civilization is not always pressing forward and that motion in itself cannot be taken for progress (Tylor 1937 (1):14). However, a decline in civilization did not contradict the general theory that the beginnings of civilization were to be found in the lowly condition of savages. Even though certain tribes may evidence a decline from a state of civilization, one still had to account for the rise of the parent civilization.

On the whole it appears that wherever there are found elaborate arts, abstruse knowledge, complex institutions, these are results of gradual development from an earlier, simpler, and ruder state of life. No stage of civilization comes into existence spontaneously, but grows or is developed out of the stage before it. This is the great principle which every scholar must lay firm hold of, if he intends to understand either the world he lives in or the history of the past. (Tylor 1937(1):15–16)

The move from savagery to civilization, therefore, could be nothing less than progress, and to this theme Tylor returned when concluding his *Anthropology: An Introduction to the Study of Man and Civilization* (1881):

> But we civilized moderns have just that wider knowledge which the rude ancients wanted. In a word, mankind is passing from the *age of unconscious to that of conscious progress.* . . . The knowledge of man's course of life, from the remote past to the present, will not only help us to forecast the future, but may guide us in our duty of leaving the world better than we found it. (Tylor 1937(2):160; italics supplied)

The Conversion of Evolution into Unilinear Progress

By attributing the directionality of evolutionary change to natural selection, the improved line of functionally adapted forms could not be held a product of ultimate cause or design. This was Spencer's view. However, by joining physical, intellectual, moral, and social evolution to a theory of acquired characteristics, and by stressing the logic of the human mind in selecting the appropriate adaptive answer, Spencer unwittingly came out on the side of purpose and of unilinear development.

> The law which is conformed to by the evolving human being, and which is consequently conformed to by the evolving human intelligence, is of necessity conformed to by all the products of that intelligence. Showing itself in structures, and by implication in the functions of these structures, this law cannot but show itself in the concrete manifestations of these functions. Just as language, considered as an objective product, bears the impress of this subjective process; so, too, does that system of ideas concerning the nature of things, which the mind gradually elaborates. (Spencer 1900(1):434)

Such was the law which had led men from an indefinite ghost-theory to clearer and progressively improved conceptions of spiritual beings, with attributes precisely spelled out in developed mythologies (Spencer 1900(1): 434). The same unilinear progression from simple to complex and from generalized to individuated was outlined in the rise of fetish theory out of ghost theory:

> Evidence has been given that sundry low types of men have either no ideas of revival after death, or vague and wavering ideas: the conception of a ghost is undeveloped. If . . . the worship of the fetich is the worship of an indwelling ghost, or a supernatural being derived from the ghost; it follows that the fetich-theory, being dependent on the ghost-theory, must succeed it in order of time. Absent where there is no ghost-theory, fetishism will arise after the

ghost-theory has arisen. That it does this, proofs are abundant. (Spencer 1900(1):322)

The differentiation of political organization from simple homogeneous units to compound, double compound, and triple compound types clearly described a unilinear flow, for Spencer (1900(1):551–555) insisted that such "stages of compounding and re-compounding have to be passed through in succession."

A unilinearity in the flow of ideas can also be traced in Spencer's differentiative network owing to developmental convergence. At certain points the differentiative variants were drawn together by formulation of critical concepts, and the course of these summative ideas described a linear path (see Figure 5.1). For example, with regard to religion, death induced a generalized and primitive sentiment that intermingled fear with love. Out of this came the idea that the dead must be placated, commonly manifest in burial, treatment of the body, and offerings. In burial one found a spontaneous attempt to keep the deceased in familiar quarters; hence burial in caves, huts, and groves. The idea of the altar was derived from the offering of food and drink to the dead at the burial site. The grave itself, or the scaffold on which a body might be raised, could serve equally as models for the altar. Placation of the dead by primitive men originally involved the idea of physically revivifying the deceased. Failing in this regard, they next interpreted death as a long-suspended animation and added hair, blood, and sacrificial victims as offerings. Next the idea of reanimation was entertained. This provoked efforts to preserve the body through artificial drying and to hold the bones and other relics of the dead as loci for the ghost of the deceased. At this point primitive men intellectually were prepared for the idea of a special house or temple for the dead, the roots of which could be found in the original practice of burial in a dwelling. Addition of the altar and an image where the ghost of the deceased could be readily located provided a context for fetishism. When the fetish was transformed into a locus of deity, to which the devotee gave fealty, the worship of idols as the representations of deity prevailed. Thus, the sequence of sentiments and ideas flowing from an original practice of placating the dead led to convergences in thought that eventuated in offerings, dwelling burial, altar, temple, fetish, and deity.

When evolutionists ignored differentiation and kept their eyes on the structural change of species or genus, they readily accepted the fact that natural selection meant improvement by survival of the better adapted. They also could accept the idea that developments of a parallel kind would occur in distant parts of the world as human beings, following the laws of their very nature, responded with similar adaptive responses. For Lippert (1931) the evolution of culture meant the unfolding and application of a creative humanizing instinct embracing not only adaptive survival but also fulfillment of life through intellectual and moral progress. Cultural evolution meant progress, and therefore the notion that savages had fallen from

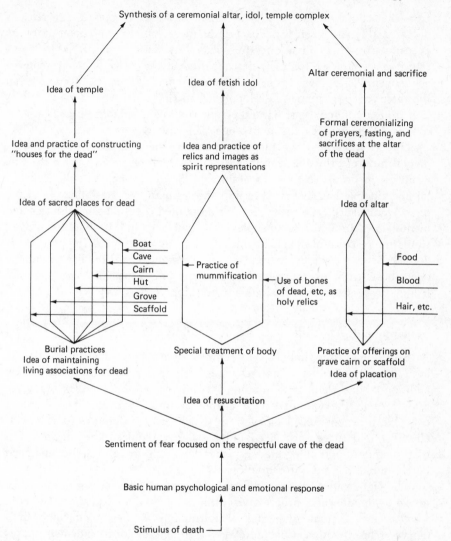

Figure 5-1. Sketch of the course to a ceremonial altar, idol, temple complex, according to Herbert Spencer. The diagram illustrates the processes of divergence and convergence involved. Spencer emphasized divergence and redivergence in order to avoid the charge of a unilineal evolutionary sequence and to bring the ideological-social process into line with the differentiative process described for biological evolution. However, the convergence of forms drawn together by the force of integrating ideas involved Spencer inevitably in an ideological unilineal progression.

an elevated moral and intellectual state had to be rejected (Lippert 1931: 3–4). Those who lagged in progress were the retarded, the passive races. Passive peoples consistently failed before the challenge of new and diverse experiences. They meekly endured their situations rather than migrating from one climatic zone to another when striking changes in the seasons occurred (Lippert 1931:43). The fate of races actually was determined by ancestral responses to nature, for what they dared against nature set a traditional character for their descendants. In the struggle to overcome a challenge, progress was born; and it was Lippert's (1931:127) opinion that the forces shaping human development had shifted in the course of evolution from a dominance of natural conditions to a dominance by social conditions. In the process, instinctive behavior gave way to ideas.

Lippert integrated the human experiment in civilization by a fundamental natural principle identified as *Lebensfürsorge*, or a regard for life. Manifest in primitive times as a simple reflex phenomenon, this humanitarian principle had increased in influence as man became rationally aware of its significance. The regard for life accounted for the basic impulses and mental laws to which all peoples were subject, and it induced a basic similarity in cultural developments in all times and places (Lippert 1931: 2–3). Wherever peoples met, those with a greater regard for life triumphed over those with less humane feelings, and this especially was the case if they possessed some social advantage (Lippert 1931:44).

Development: An Additive or a Differentiative Process?

The trend from simplicity to complexity presented Developmentalists with three alternatives. First, change might move forward through the addition of one element to another, inciting a new and complex organization through the cumulation of elemental units. Second, change might begin with a generalized block from which units differentiated functionally. To hold these specialized units together required the forging of a more complex and integrated organization. A third alternative included both cumulation and differentiation.

The significance of these different processual alternatives does not lie in the distinction of a progressivist from an evolutionist posture, for both were aware of cumulation and differentiation. Rather, their importance derives from theoretical debate over the origins of ideas and institutions, according to a preference for either of the first two alternatives.

Social Complexity: Cumulative and Differentiative Processes. Progressivists in the eighteenth century generally stressed the individual family as the primal unit upon which more complex social and political groupings had been raised. Tylor agreed (1937(2):131–134) and noted that from the beginning of time mankind had been organized in families or households united by ties which stressed marriage rules, obligations of parents and children, and affection for each other. The "natural way in which a tribe is formed is from a family or group, which in time increases and divides into many households, still recognizing one another as kindred" (Tylor 1937(2):131–134). Human society thus grew in size and complexity by the replication and aggregation of units.

On the other hand, Spencer (1900(1):643–653), following the natural logic of his position, began social life with an undifferentiated state of promiscuity and rapine. The small defensive units that emerged out of this unorganized homogeneous situation included relatively stable family arrangements that were polyandrous, polygynous, and monogamous. The marital practices of the Veddas of Ceylon attested to the presence of monogamy in those primeval times. Out of this primitive differentation Spencer traced a further evolution in which polygyny became linked to the militant society and monogamy to industrial society. The triumph of monogamy was assured, since societies so organized enjoyed a fertility advantage expressed in a differential in mortality rates. The greater attention to human life made possible by the monogamous family paid off in a greater rate of population increase. The aggregation of families into more stable units and the development of a more integrated political organization added a further advantage (Spencer 1900(1):682–683).

Morgan's (1963:396–515) model for the development of the family likewise was differentiative. Beginning with a territorial unit, the horde, in which resources and wives were held in common, the monogamian family had gradually differentiated by a series of unconscious moral reforms that forced individuals first to seek marriage partners outside the family and then the clan. The record of this moral-social progress was read in the new types of social organization and kinship terminology associated with each stage; and Morgan (1963:455) held that monogamy was made possible by a positive growth in the moral and mental potential of the human species.

The notion that human social life began with a primeval promiscuity that gradually evolved into more stable spouse and parental relations obviously rested on impulses basic to mankind. But if one assumed as Crawley (1960(2):32, 259) that men were naturally impelled by an egoistic impulse, there could be no original primitive communism in sex, property, or in social organization. On the contrary, the tendency of change in society, beginning with primitive animals, would lead from individualism to socialism, from private possession to shared possession.

Cumulation and Differentiation in Technology. A succession of improving inventions illustrates the growth in technology by addition. In the domain of transportation, imagine the savage astride a log, swishing the water with his hand. Later he propels a dugout or balsa with a paddle shaped in imitation of arm and hand. At a later time sails are added to assist the oarsmen of larger ships, but it is a long time before oars are eliminated as a basic means of propulsion. Steam power was added to sail power in the nineteenth century, and Tylor (1937(2):22–24) noted how the screw propeller was on the point of supplanting the paddle wheel. A technical differentiation of tools was equally easy to document. According to Pitt-Rivers (1906), tools usually began their evolution as undifferentiated multipurpose implements. From this generalized form, through minute gradations answering specialized needs, a number of new forms were differentiated according to function. Thus, in the instance of the Australian boomerang, it had "passe[d] by minute gradations into at least three other classes of weapons in common use by the same people, and may therefore be regarded as a branch variety of an original normal type of implement used by the most primitive races as a general tool or weapon" (Pitt-Rivers 1906:131). That general tool was a simple stick, which had differentiated into lances, throwing sticks, shields, bird clubs, and boomerangs—each order with its own minute gradations (see Figure 8-1). Pitt-Rivers' functional differentiation of tools from a generalized ancestral form seemed to describe a technological adaptive radiation to which biological evolutionists pointed when describing the differentiation of forms at the level of class, such as the mammalia.

Cumulative and Differentiative Processes in the Origins of Language. Applied to language, the logic of associational psychology suggested an incremental development through the attachment of secondary associations to primary sensory ideas. Exclamations and imitative monosyllabic forms preceded polysyllabic verbs, nouns, and the formation of phrases and sentences. One could begin with an opposite view, that men in a rude stage of development expressed themselves in an undammed stream of feeling and at first were incapable of discriminating the specifics of their sensory experience. According to the linguist Otto Jespersen (1928:420), civilization had moderated the primitive tendency to passionate expression. Savage men, overwhelmed by feeling, sang out what they felt and were not inclined to put ideas together in an analytical string. In time, however, meaning was attached to the original sequences of syllables, and there followed a progressive tendency to analyze and reduce larger units into lesser elements. The trend in language formation thus was from "original polysyllabism towards monosyllabism" in conformity with the law that development proceeded from the whole to the particular (Jespersen 1928: 428–429).

The view that linguistic development began in a diffuse state, owing to savage passion and inexperience in perceptual discrimination, reached back into the eighteenth century and was central to Monboddo's holophrastic hypothesis (Penniman 1965:151). In the eighteenth century Adam Smith (1892:505–538) argued the contrary view—that primitive man began with simple word-object associations and gradually added word-ideas to discriminate qualities and relationships. Languages at first had grown by the addition of specific elements designating each quality or relation; but in time, as the base for abstract operations improved, languages were simplified through application of a limited number of principles. English well exemplified the trend toward analytic simplicity.

THE SEARCH FOR PRIMAL ORIGINS

Developmentalists needed a zero point from which to plot the ascent from savagery to civilization, and hence they were committed to the problem of origins. In sounding for origins, they had to cope with two contrastive conditions, ever present and always in a relation of mutual influence—what Spencer contrasted as internal and external factors, and progressivists generally distinguished as human nature and circumstances. The task was complicated by the fact that man's nature in his civilized state was not identical to that of man in his primitive state. However, his problem was solved by operating as if the differences between primitive and civilized man were largely matters of degree. It was possible to introspect the savage mind and to point out how it was swayed by feeling states or faulty perceptual chains of association that rendered it a fallacious instrument at best. To introspect the past, Developmentalists had to assume that the savage, as the civilized, responded to sensations that registered differentially according to the strength, duration, and contextual associations of stimuli; and further, that savage men proceeded to organize these impressions conceptually and to arrange them in causal sequences. This was the bedrock of commonality relating savage and civilized that Developmentalists were forced to acknowledge.

Pathways to the Past

There were six major principles available to Developmentalists in their search for zero points. Some they rejected as too speculative and others as not wholly useful to their purpose.

The principle of historic continuity was rejected for theoretical reasons and because what they sought lay beyond the reach of recorded time. Therefore they could not restrict themselves to the undoubted facts of history advocated by Herder (1952) in the eighteenth century and reargued by Maine (1887) when working with Hindu materials. Prehistory supplied a few leads, but the evidences of archeologists were little used. In the eighteenth century archeological data were absent, and in the nineteenth Developmentalists found other means more congenial to their purposes.

A second principle, hypothecation, could be used to construct a model of a pristine state or condition. The solitary state of nature conjured by social contract theorists illustrated the use of a hypothetical construct. The male and female dyad, proposed by Condillac (1746) as the original social unit whence language as a rational means of communication took its start, exemplified the use of a hypothetical model. Empirically oriented Developmentalists considered their original states as grounded in fact, but their logical constructs hardly avoided the speculative qualities of the state of nature construct which they criticized.

A third principle, ultraprimitivity, was acceptable but never systematically exploited. In the nineteenth century the Indians of Tierra del Fuego supplanted the eighteenth-century preference for Hottentots as representing the nadir of cultural beginnings. However, none exploited the alleged zero point of Hottentot and Fuegian culture as the base from which civilization had taken its start. Lord Avebury's (1913:430) casual remarks in the seventh edition of *Prehistoric Times* are quite typical: the "van Diemaner

[Tasmanians] and South American are to the antiquary what the opossum and the sloth are to the geologist." The most celebrated case in the use of a people as the elementary base for institutional developments would be by the social structuralist, Durkheim (1926). Use of contemporary tribes as types for take-off was one thing; their use as historic beginnings was quite another matter. Developmentalists, and sociologist Durkheim, had no intention of pinpointing a contemporary native group as the source for historic developments in the rest of the world.

A fourth principle, analogy, supplied Developmentalists with a rationale for drawing parallels between nature and man, especially those graduated continuities in which they were vitally interested. In maturational analogy, savages were like children, barbarians approached immature youths, and the civilized shouldered the mature responsibilities of adults. Through comparison of similarities in culture forms among widely separated peoples, Developmentalists constructed the successive cultural inventories that allowed assignment of peoples to the stages of savagery, barbarism, and civilization. Clued to the simplicity-complexity continuum, the principle of analogy allowed anachronistic behaviors or survivals to be treated as one-time practices. According to the doctrine of survivals popularized by Tylor (1874), one could extract the savage background of civilized practices by following a chain of survivals back to the original primitive base.

Uniform response, a fifth principle, permitted the use of universal experiences as common sources for origins. Universal experiences narrowed the range of alternatives available as probable sources for religion, art, language, family, and other institutions. Uniform responses guaranteed parallel origins in common sensory-ideations, which were evoked almost spontaneously by striking natural phenomena as well as disease, death, birth, dreams, and other critical human experiences. Both Bastian's elementary ideas and Morgan's primary germs of thought were predicated on the arousal of a common set of ideas in response to common circumstances. Resting on the assumption of a universal human nature, the principle of uniform response permitted Developmentalists, sympathetically, to introspect the customs of distant and alien peoples, and to extract the logic behind them without resorting to the doctrine of innate ideas. The causal linkage of stimulus and response imparted a materialistic determinism to Developmentalist interpretation, but both progressivists and evolutionists left little doubt that their main concern was for the ideological product and its subsequent influence on the course of human affairs.

A sixth and final principle, phylogenesis, was a favorite device of evolutionists. By plugging into an earlier evolutionary phase they hoped to uncover the source for attitudes, ideas, and customs present among savages and even civilized men. Darwin's (1936:878–880) hypothetical account of the origins of language furnishes an excellent example. Articulate speech, especially in the manifestation of rhythm and cadence in oratory, owed much to musical powers developed out of the courtship practices of man's half-human ancestors when "excited not only by love, but by the strong passions of jealousy, rivalry, and triumph." During times of passionate arousal, musical tones and rhythm appeared spontaneously; and Darwin, in good evolutionist fashion, suggested that the arousal of vague feelings and ideas by music, and the rhythmic expressions found in oratory, were like mental reversions to emotional responses and ideas entrenched in experiences of the distant past.

SUMMARY

Developmentalism illustrates how basic assumptions about the nature of things (reality) may prevail over long periods of time and produce uniformities with regard to subject matter, goals, methods of investigation, kinds of facts collected, analyses, explanations, and conclusions. This was true of humanistic progressivists and biological evolutionists despite differences in emphasis and explanation introduced by the theory of natural selection.

First, the axiomatic assumption of a progressive advance from the simple to the complex led to the goal of charting a sequence of ideas and institutions linked in a continuum of development. Human development was divided into three stages: savagery, barbarism, and civilization. The idea of a progressive advance conveyed a utopian quality to progressivist and evolutionist views. A study of man should produce materials which could be applied to advance human development toward a goal of a perfected mind, morality, and society. The linkage of human history in a common developmental process from the savage to the civilized state, and the goal of collecting data that would facilitate attainment of a perfected society, added up to a new science far different in emphasis from traditional history. Emphasis on improving the human situation focused attention on the social and the dynamics of social processes. However, the idea of human advancement limited the study of social processes to an evolutionary continuum, and Developmentalists were not inclined to explore the kinds of problems and systemic processes open to a structural-functional orientation.

Second, the task of charting a natural history of mankind focused the attention of progressivists and evolutionists on conventionalized ideas and institutions which contrasted factually with the biographical and related materials with which historians commonly documented their descriptions. Both assembled social and cultural facts. However, advances in geology, paleontology, prehistory, comparative anatomy, comparative linguistics, and comparative mythology reinforced the tendency to seek proofs of evolution in the past. In consequence, evolutionists pioneered in the gathering of facts about primitive societies and in orienting the anthropological discipline in the early history of mankind.

Third, progressivists and evolutionists grounded their discipline on natural processes and were tempted to model their procedures after the natural sciences. Differences in explanations by progressivists and evolutionists stemmed from advances in the physical and biological sciences. Thus, Spencer adopted nineteenth-century thermodynamic theory to explain equilibrium changes of systems and their general evolution. Though agreeing with progressivists that the human mind was the key factor in change, evolutionists introduced a biological process to account for the adaptive modifications which permitted the human mind to carry out more complex operations. Evolutionists, in applying the principle of natural selection, widened the gap between savage and civilized man, since the latter represented a more complex adaptation. This biological emphasis aroused a host of new issues centered in race differences and the effects of miscegenation.

Fourth, the goal of charting the advance from simplicity to complexity led progressivists and evolutionists to a common methodology. Both compared ideas and institutions from all parts of the world and at all levels of complexity in order to obtain a graduated series which described a logical sequence in development from the rude to the refined. Ideas were abstracted from observable forms, and progressivists and evolutionists used analogical reasoning to introspect primitive thought.

Fifth, the division of human history into three stages: savagery, barbarism, and civilization led Developmentalists to formulate the features of each stage by means of contrastive distinctions based on the simplicity-complexity continuum. Hence, they arrived at similar views regarding savage and civilized character and habits. Savages by definition exhibited a lack of control over emotions, a sensitivity to primitive bodily needs, illogicality in thought processes, indolence, immorality or amorality, selfish egoism, rude ideas of justice, and a custom-bound conservatism toward new ideas. To fill out the elemental features of the barbarian and savage stages, progressivists and evolutionists treated symbolic notions ("survivals") as historic usages which truly existed in previous times. At times they attempted to locate the most primitive of all peoples in order to establish an elementary idea from which subsequent developments took place. However, in their search for origins they usually relied on universal experiences which mankind faced in relation to nature, others, and self in order to derive the sensory responses and associations which finally gave rise to an idea (for example, parenthood).

Sixth, progressivists and evolutionists equally faced the issue of a unilinear or teleological kind of change. Faith in the logic of the human mind implied that all peoples found their way to similar ideas and advanced along parallel lines to the civilized state. The principle of natural selection avoided the teleological issue by transferring the directionality of change to external conditions which narrowed the range of available response. The organism either changed adaptively to fit the changing environment or it perished as a type. Spencer also argued that evolution was not unilinear but divergent and redivergent. However, his reliance on summative ideas which integrated future changes conveyed unilinearity to his model. Progressivists and evolutionists also confronted the problem as to whether the evolutionary process began with elemental units which were gradually added together to form a complex whole, or whether evolution began with separation from a generalized unit of parts performing different functions, which then were organized into a more complex system.

6

Religion, Morality, and Society

ETHNOLOGY AND COMPARATIVE RELIGION, MYTHOLOGY, AND PHILOLOGY

In their pursuit of origins and continuities in human thought Developmentalists relied heavily on religion, mythology, and language. By the middle of the nineteenth century comparative religion, comparative mythology, and comparative philology were well entrenched as separate specializations. Each pursued a course relatively independent of the major thrust to formulate a synthetic science of man. These specializations were largely confined to investigation of Indo-European connections, and with regard to mythology Tylor (1874(1):284) cited the contribution which ethnology could make to the widening and deepening of interpretation.

> To the human intellect in its early childlike state may be assigned the origin and first development of myth . . . [;] learned critics . . . have almost habitually failed to appreciate its childlike ideas, conventionalized in poetry or disguised as chronicle. Yet the more we compare the mythic fancies of different nations, in order to discern the common thoughts which underlie their resemblances, the more ready we shall be to admit that in our childhood we dwelt at the very gates of the realm of myth. In mythology, the child is . . . father of the man. Thus, when in surveying the quaint fancies and wild legends of the lower tribes, we find the mythology of the world at once in its most distinct and most rudimentary form, we may here again claim the savage as a representative of the childhood of the human race. Here Ethnology and Comparative Mythology go hand in hand, and the development of Myth forms a consistent part of the development of Culture. If savage races, as the

nearest modern representatives of primaeval culture, show in the most distinct and unchanged state the rudimentary mythic conceptions thence to be traced onward in the course of civilization, then it is reasonable for students to begin ... at the beginning. Savage mythology may be taken as a basis, and then the myths of more civilized races may be displayed as compositions sprung from like origin, though more advanced in art.

During the nineteenth century comparative philology achieved striking successes and was well along the road to fulfilling Friedrich von Schlegel's prophecy that comparative grammar would unlock the genealogical relationships of language much as comparative anatomy was doing in natural history. In 1817 Rasmus Rask, through a comparative grammatical analysis, demonstrated connections between Greek, Persian, German, and Sanskrit. Jakob Grimm's (1819–1837) comparison of Germanic languages elicited similarities underlying conventionalized sound shifts within dialects.

Etymological analysis suggested a promising way to ferret out historical relations and the psychological roots of mythologies and religions. In 1835 Jakob Grimm used etymology to track Teutonic gods and sprites hidden in German folklore. Nearly forty years later Max Müller (1873: 144–216) recommended the use of etymology to bare the origins of religions. Müller was convinced that the three great language centers—Turanian, Aryan, and Semitic—also were religious centers. With etymological comparisons, students of comparative religion could construct a basic sacred vocabulary that would reveal the religious interests, beliefs, deities, objects of devotion and of sacrifice common to a language family before separation had taken place. Müller emphasized that the researcher, if he were to recapture the thoughts of the ancients, must avoid thinking like a modern. Like Tylor, Müller (1873:44) held that the student of mythology must eliminate the irrational and irreverent secondary additions and read the "childish fables ... in their original child-like sense."

Despite their plausibility, the historic and psychological leads offered by philology in the search for mythic and religious origins were not taken up by Developmentalists. Developmentalists generally were not schooled in grammatical analysis and they possessed their own methods. The doctrine of analogy, as Tylor (1874(1):296–297) so aptly labeled it, served the ethnological mythologist as a primary instrument to discover and illustrate primitive meaning. He admitted that the doctrine of analogy did not meet the canons of exact science, but that men of former times actually experienced or believed what moderns took to be nothing more than metaphor provided good grounds for the use of analogical explanation. Through the medium of analogy, the ethnologist could introspect the "far deeper consciousness ... [by which] the circumstance of nature was worked out in endless imaginative detail in ancient days and among uncultured races" (Tylor 1874(1):297). Uniformity in human sensations and ideas engendered through reflection thus provided Developmentalists with their own secure pathway to the past.

ORIGIN AND DEVELOPMENT OF RELIGION

Basic Problems

In seeking the origins and development of religion, Developmentalists faced a number of interrelated problems. How did mankind arrive at the idea that the world was material and spiritual? What universal experience(s) prompted the notion of duality? What stages could be charted in the progressive unfolding of religious ideas? What relation do religious belief and practice bear to cause-and-effect interpretation? What part has religion played in the intellectual and moral advancement of mankind?

Providence and Enlightenment

For the deeply religious, especially in the eighteenth century, providence, or the benevolent direction of God, accounted for human works and the human destiny. To see the world as God's school for men was an interpretation of long standing, and Herder (1952) used it to counter accusations by intellectuals of religious bigotry and gross superstition. For Monboddo (1779–1799), all the great inventions and moral truths known to man were God-given, revealed to mankind by heaven-sent culture heroes. The importance of the idea of providence lay not in the simple reaffirmation of God's guardianship over his creatures but in the accommodation it permitted between sacred truths and new scientific facts.

Science and Natural Religion

Enlightened progressivists of the eighteenth century were not averse to admitting that a creative intelligence had created the world and established its natural order. However, what they strained for was an intellectual experience of this intrinsic truth. Science was the instrument for this search, and hence they rejected the revealed truths of the conventional church. The goal of a scientific religion was a natural or intellectualized religion rather than a revealed faith. Science, by uncovering the secrets of nature and nature's laws, would reveal God as the creator of beauty, truth, and order.

Religious Origins and the Problem of Duality

The Animation of Nature. Eighteenth-century interpretations of religious origins stressed a view that savage men were sensitive only to external sensations. The unfolding of a rational understanding of deity followed man's awareness of his inner consciousness. Religion, then, must begin with nature deities—the sun, stars, forest, mountains, and all that pressed heavily upon the senses and excited fear or wonderment, and perhaps love. Whether religion began with astral or animal deities, or great men raised to the stature of deities, as Euhemerus argued in ancient times, were issues for debate. Early men were constructed to respond more to feeling sensations than to intellect; and hence they required visible objects and processions, music, and sacrifices to arouse and fix their attention. The animation of the inanimate had produced an early worship of stone figures and other material objects.

The Duality of Man and of World: Spencer and Tylor. Early explanations of how savage men came to view the world as dual skirted the central issue of the progression of experience by which this idea was achieved and the notion of spiritual beings was conceived. Some thirty years after Comte, Spencer (1910) and Tylor (1874) filled the gap with detailed explanations on how duality emerged from the psychological experience.

Spencer (1910(1):note, pp. 310–312) briefly sketched his ideas when commenting on McLennan's discussion of animal worship or totemism. Religion had not begun, as McLennan implied, with devotions to animal spirits, but with a simple belief in the spirits of dead ancestors. A number of experiences could provide the savage with a vague idea of his own duality. The shadow cast by the sun, echoes, and reflections of faces and figures in pools of water were likely sources. However, dreams provided the most realistic and striking experiences by which early men would be driven to recognize that they possessed a second self.

Hampered by the imperfect distinctions of their languages, savages were unable to state the precise differences between what was seen and what was dreamed. Hence, the two experiences were considered alike. Confirmation of another vagrant self also came from loss of consciousness and other derangements which occurred from time to time. When death occurred, savages were inclined naturally to see this as a departure of the other self. However, the idea of a destruction of self was beyond savage comprehension, and they expected the departed self to return at any time.

When amplifying his interpretations in the *Principles of Sociology*, Spencer (1900(1):110–143) underscored man's inner experience of a double self as central to comprehension of the fact that the world held two complementary states of being, the animate and the inanimate. Savages perceived changes in the shape of substances and noted how living things (for example, insects during their life cycles) took on different forms. The passage of wind followed by calm suggested an alternation or succession of states. However, only when man, through dream experience, verified for himself that he had a double existence of the order of other things was he able to finalize his thinking. Now he possessed a germinal principle for ordering his random observations. Ancestor worship grounded in fear of the ghost might be the roots of religion, but behind ancestor worship lurked the psychic experience which had produced the idea of duality. This was the primal association or germ of thought which Spencer underscored in his theory; and on this base primitive man erected his ideas of cause and effect, and of the nature of the universe.

When Tylor (1874(1):428–429) searched for the primary experience behind religion, he also located it in primitive reflections on the nature of body experiences such as waking, sleeping, dreaming, dying, trance, and disease.

> Looking at these two groups of phenomena [death and dreams], the *ancient savage philosophers probably made their first step by the obvious inference that every man has two things belonging to him, namely a life and a phantom.* These two are evidently in close connexion with the body, the life as enabling it to feel and think and act, the phantom as being its image or second self; both, also, are perceived to be things separable from the body, the life as able to go away and leave it insensible or dead, the phantom as appearing to people at a distance from it. The second step would seem also easy for savages to make, seeing how extremely difficult civilized men have found it to unmake. It is merely to combine the life and the phantom. As both belong to the body, why should they not also belong to one another, and be manifestations of one and the same soul? Let them then be considered as united, and the result is that well-known conception which may be described as an apparitional-soul, a ghost-soul. This, at any rate, corresponds with the actual conception of the personal soul or spirit among the lower races, which may be defined as follows: It is a thin, unsubstantial human image, in its nature a sort of vapour, film, or shadow; the *cause of life and thought* in the individual it animates; independently possessing the personal consciousness and volition of its corporeal owner, past or present; capable of leaving the body far behind, to flash swiftly from place to place; most impalpable and invisible, yet also *manifesting physical power*, and especially appearing to men waking or asleep as a phantasm separate from the body of which it bears the likeness; continuing to exist and appear to men after the death of that body; able to enter into, possess, and act in the bodies of other men, of animals, and even of things. . . . *They are doctrines answering in the most forcible way to the plain evidence of men's senses, as interpreted by a fairly consistent and rational primitive philosophy.* (Italics supplied)

Once men had grasped through dreams and visions the notion that souls were ethereal images of bodies they could project duality upon the world (Tylor 1874(1):450). The stage was set for beliefs and practices that were recognizably religious. In essentials the "conception of the human soul . . . [was] continuous . . . from the philosophy of the savage thinker to that of the modern professor of theology . . . [uniting] in an unbroken line of mental connexion, the savage fetish-worshipper and the civilized Christian" (Tylor 1874(1):501–502). For Tylor (1874(1):424) a belief in spiritual beings was sufficient for a definition of religion.

The Spencerian and Tylorian theories, in rooting religious origins in an inner awareness, represented a natural fruit of the psychological materialism embraced by eighteenth-century progressivists. One could, as Kames (cited by Schneider 1967:255–270), insist that man's awareness of deity and the duality of the universe was dependent upon a built-in sense of deity. But such a faculty still depended on a reasoned discrimination of unorganized sensation before the notion of multiple deities could be originated. Whatever the sensory-intellective course by which men became aware of spiritual beings, once conceived, men used the model of their own social experience as the model for divine governance. In the instance of the high gods found under polytheism Tylor (1874(2):248) observed,

> Among nation after nation it is still clear how, *man being the type of deity, human society and gover[n]ment became the model on which divine society and government were shaped.* As chiefs and kings are among men, so are the great gods among the lesser spirits. They differ from the souls and minor spiritual beings ... , but the difference is rather of rank than of nature. They are personal spirits, reigning over personal spirits. Above the disembodied souls and manes, the local genii of rocks and fountains and trees, the host of good and evil demons, and the rest of the spiritual commonality, stand these mightier deities, whose influence is less confined to local or individual interest, and who, as it pleases them, can act directly within their vast domain, or control and operate through the lower beings of their kind, their servants, agents, or mediators. The great gods of Polytheism, whose dominion thus stretches far and wide over the world, are not, any more than the lower spirits, creations of a civilized theology. (Italics supplied)

Primitive "High Gods" without Animism: Lang

The logic of the extension from a ghost-soul to spirit detailed by Spencer and Tylor was clear enough. Development from a rude spirit or ancestor worship to higher polytheistic divinities which culminated in a supreme ethical being again presented no logical difficulties. However, in 1898 Andrew Lang, classicist and student of Tylor, challenged the animistic theory with a variant of the degeneracy theory. Alerted to the presence of supreme beings among the southeastern tribes of Australia, Lang argued that gods of the order of Daramalun and Mangan-ngaur had not derived from death or dream experiences. These all-powerful sky gods existed before death—in a world that, according to the native Australians described by Howitt and Fison, knew not death. When death did enter the world, it followed from a blunder, a ritual error, or by decision of the god himself. Moreover, these supreme beings were closely associated with the moral instruction of youth in initiation ceremonies, where the natives projected an idealized self-image that aspired to omnipotence, omniscience, and morality. Finding that the lowest savages, including the Andamanese, held views of an external and benevolent high god, Lang concluded that the original primitive conception had been subverted by a polytheistic animism derived from death and dream experiences. Hence, "Our conception of God descends not from ghosts, but from the Supreme Beings of non-ancestor worshipping peoples" (Lang 1898:191).

From Magical Powers to Spiritual Beings: Frazer

In 1890 Frazer published a voluminous compilation of primitive thought and custom to support his argument that magic and religion described two different world views and that an age of magic had preceded religion (*The*

Golden Bough: A Study in Magic and Religion). Frazer began his tortuous path to the beginnings of human thought and world view in the Roman grove of Nemi, sacred to Diana, patroness of wild and domestic animals. Here a priest king kept vigil beside a tree with drawn sword to prevent intruders from breaking a bough, thereby earning the right to battle him for the sacred office. Frazer considered Roman legends associating Diana and her companions with Nemi to be nothing more than later inventions—they were secondary and unhistorical interpretations. To find a solution to the curious practice at Nemi the issue must be cast in a wider context. Here the comparative method would be indispensable.

> The strange rule of this priesthood has no parallel in classical antiquity.... To find an explanation we must go farther afield. No one will probably deny that such a custom savours of a barbarous age, and, surviving into imperial times, stands out in striking isolation from the polished Italian society of the day, like a primaeval rock rising from a smooth-shaven lawn. It is the rudeness and barbarity of the custom which allows us a hope of explaining it. For recent researches into the early history of man have revealed the essential similarity with which, under many superficial differences, the human mind has elaborated its first crude philosophy of life. Accordingly, if we can shew that a barbarous custom, like that of the priesthood of Nemi, has existed elsewhere; if we can detect the motives which led to its institution; if we can prove that these motives have operated widely, perhaps universally, in human society, producing in varied circumstances a variety of institutions *specifically different but generically alike*; if we can shew, lastly, that these very motives, with some of their derivative institutions, were actually at work in classical antiquity; then we may fairly infer that at a remoter age the same motives gave birth to the priesthood of Nemi. Such an inference, in default of direct evidence as to how the priesthood did actually arise, can never amount to demonstration. But it will be more or less probable according to the degree of completeness with which it fulfils the conditions I have indicated. (Frazer 1900(1):10)

Frazer's subject led him back to the very beginnings of man's efforts to understand and control the world. In the beginning, there was magic, and the medicine man represented the first professional. At a later time, the functions of the magician—control of weather, health, and fertility—were joined to chiefship and then to kingship. The prototype for the priest king of Nemi could be located in divine kings who were slain as their physical powers diminished. The Shilluk of the Upper Nile provided Frazer with a contemporary example of primitive logic essential to understanding the ritual slaying of the Roman woodland priest.

> On the whole the theory and practice of the divine kings of the Shilluk correspond very nearly to the theory and practice of the prests of Nemi, the Kings of the Wood, if my view of the latter is correct. In both we see a series of divine kings on whose life the fertility of men, of cattle, and of vegetation is believed to depend, and who are put to death, whether in single combat or otherwise, in order that their divine spirit may be transmitted to their suc-

cessors in full vigour, uncontaminated by the weakness and decay of sickness or old age, because any such degeneration on the part of the king would, in the opinion of his worshippers, entail a corresponding degeneration on mankind, on cattle, and on the crops.... (Frazer 1925–1930(3):28)

Beginning with a survival, Frazer followed the intellectual spoor, with the aid of formal analogies, back to the thought of the magician. The characteristic weakness of primitive thought was well illustrated in the logic of magic. Primitive thinkers uniformly operated with a "mistaken deduction from the association of ideas. Men mistook the order of their ideas for the order of nature, and hence imagined that the control which they have, or seem to have, over their thoughts, permitted them to exercise a corresponding control over things" (Frazer 1900(1):420).

Under Frazer's analysis (1922:54–55), magic was nothing but a fallacious application of the most elementary of mental processes based on an association of ideas clued to similarity and spatial and temporal contiguity. The idea of conscious personal beings, which men acknowledged to be superior to themselves, obviously was more complex than magical ideas and required more intelligence and reflection. Therefore, Frazer (1900(1): 420) concluded,

> if magic be deduced immediately from elementary processes of reasoning, and be, in fact, an error into which the mind falls almost spontaneously,... it becomes probable that magic arose before religion in the evolution of our race, and that man essayed to bend nature to his wishes by the sheer force of spells and enchantments before he strove to coax and mollify a coy, capricious or irascible deity by the soft insinuation of prayer and sacrifice.

Yet as a form of thought, magic, very much like science, assumed a regular succession of events. Magical spells introduced an element of determinism comparable to the immutable laws of nature (Frazer 1922:48–49).

The magician was not wrong in assuming regularities in nature, but erred in the way he formulated the laws governing a succession of events. Religious thought destroyed magical thought by introducing the attribute of indeterminacy into cause-effect relations. Acknowledgment of supernatural beings superior to man, who must be propitiated because of their control over nature, shattered the autistic dominance of primitive man. Frazer pictured man-the-magician retreating grudgingly step by step from the heights to which he had elevated himself, as experience gradually eroded his primitive egotism and drove home the hard fact that an intelligence superior to his own existed and controlled the world.

Frazer (1922:55) supported his argument for the precedence of magic in the development of human knowledge by pointing out that magic ran rampant in the most primitive societies known, and more particularly the Australian aborigines.

> But if in the most backward state of human society [Australian] now known to us we find magic thus conspicuously present and religion conspicuously absent, may we not reasonably conjecture that the civilized races of the

world have also at some period of their history passed through a similar intellectual phase, that they attempted to force the great powers of nature to do their pleasure before they thought of courting their favour by offerings and prayer—in short that, just as on the material side of human culture there has everywhere been an Age of Stone, so on the intellectual side there has everywhere been an "Age of Magic?"

The principle of ultraprimitivity thus clinched the argument for the precedence of a magical philosophy over religious philosophy.

Animatism and Supernaturalism: Marett

Lang's undying high gods and Frazer's age of magic challenged animism as the earliest intellectual adventure of man in interpreting the natural world and its causal relations. In 1900 R. R. Marett (1909:1–32) reintroduced the time-worn theory of animation and urged that it be accorded first place in the philosophies of mankind. Marett cautiously protected himself against the charge that animatism was a preanimistic religion, but his discussion left little doubt that animatism constituted the earliest phase of religion. He argued that the rudimentary religious feelings of primitive men did not spring from nature's terrifying motions and noises, nor from an intellectualizing of dream experience, but from awe and wonder when in the presence of the uncanny or extraordinary. "A solitary pillar of rock, a crumpled volcanic boulder, a meteorite, a pebble resembling a pig, a yam, or an arrowhead, a piece of shining quartz, these and such as these are . . . invested by his imagination with the vague but dreadful attributes of Powers" (Marett 1909:19). The thunderous booming of the bull roarer must have aroused a feeling of awe in its inventors, who would naturally animatize it with life and power. To Marett, Lang's Australian high gods were nothing more than personalized bull roarers dressed out in mythologic heroics and genealogies.

Personalization of the inanimate gave rise to gods or the supernatural, and experiences associated with dreams were not required to account for the idea of spirit, or the duality of the world. Marett (1909:4) considered the animistic explanation of religious origins too intellectualized, since it ignored the most characteristic element of religion, its emotional foundation. A primitive awareness of the presence of the mysterious, or what might be called supernaturalism, seemed a logical, and probably a chronological, antecedent to animism. Supernaturalism, and what some were compelled to discriminate as religion, or what some contrasted as magic and religion, actually were joined in a common philosophic mode based on awe of the mysterious. If the similarities of human impulses, when coping with the natural environment, were to be comprehended, the definition of religion must not be restrictive. Wherever one could detect a "reverence . . . towards supernatural powers and obedience to their mandates," genuine religion must be present (Marett 1909:19). For man, the religious experience must be detected not where thought began but where it broke down into feeling (Marett 1909:32).

The impersonal power, *mana*, described by Rev. Codrington (1891), supplied Marett with the objective support which his theory of animatism required. The magician, using the naive tendency of elementary thought to personify whatever manifested an independent existence, furnished the emotional, logical, and instrumental ingredients for generating the beginnings of religion. Religion and magic did not follow two separate intellectual courses, with the former presenting a reversal of trends found in the latter, as Frazer argued. On the contrary, the evidence demonstrated a natural and unconscious transformation of charm symbols into idols, with prayers added at the point of personification (Marett 1909:79). Marett (1909:32) saw magic, animism, and idealist philosophy united by a common impulse to grasp the spiritual unity of the universe.

Final Status of the Duality Problem and Origins of Religion

Developmentalist theories of duality and religious origins can be divided into two theories of long standing. First, there were theories that insisted on the primacy of man's sensory awareness of the natural world, with distinction of the animate-inanimate providing the basis for duality. Second, were theories that developed comprehension of duality out of a special internal human experience, notably dreams and visions. Though Tylor apparently accepted the animate-inanimate distinction as sufficient to produce an idea of duality, he seated its origin in death, a specifically human and universal experience. To account for something like spirit, the common substance of religion, a dream experience in the appearance of a phantom was necessary. Likewise, Spencer rejected the idea that nature in its daily and seasonal alternations could provide a sufficient base for the idea of spirit and religion. With Lang, Frazer, and Marett the naturalistic origin was argued and given precedence over the human subjective experience in point of chronological development. Here the matter came to rest, for the psychological theories of Developmentalists could carry them no farther into the mists of the past. The only alternative to the precedence of the animatistic or the animistic interpretations would be acceptance of the two as coeval—as present in primitive thought from the very beginning—a suggestion made by Marett.

For greater understanding, new sources for the origins of religion must be found. The social constituted one of two untapped segments of human experience, and here the subsequent study of religious origins and meanings struck a novel and unworked ore (see Chapter 13). Psychological reactions to physiological processes and their importance for social action provided a second untapped resource for understanding the mainsprings of religion (Crawley 1960; Freud 1918).

Stages in the Development of Religion

Unilinear Stages and Religious Prejudice. Acceptance of the idea of an advance from the simple to the complex led Developmentalists into certain general agreements irrespective of whether they grounded religion in a personalizing of the inanimate or in a belief in spirits. Vague and unorganized beliefs in supernatural beings or spirits were succeeded by a belief in powerful deities who reigned over natural domains or special functions essential to human life (for example, childbirth, disease, fertility, war). The malevolent spirits of savagery gave way to the lusty anthropomorphized spirits of barbarism; in turn, the humanized gods of the barbarians yielded, under the mature logic of civilization, to the image of a beneficent creator. The visible connection between deity and moral injunctions in civilization was hardly hinted in the stage of savagery. If progress meant a triumph of reason over unreason, then the organized religion of the priesthood must give way to organized intellect, that is, to natural religion and science. For example, Kames (1779(2):337–469) began the course to true theology with malevolent deities. The end product of rational thought would be a "Supreme Being, boundless in every perfection," who existed alone and ruled the world. At such time benevolent polytheistic spirits and the malevolent satanic band both would be banished from human thought. Klemm (1843–1851(1):22–23, 210–214) began religion with a fraud. To insure survival, old women and impotent men foisted a shamanism of malevolent spirits on the primitive community. This was usual among hunters, fishers, and herders. Cultivation made men so dependent on their crops that they appeased the malevolent spirits with offerings. In this situation the family head naturally became the first priest; and as society grew, a priesthood assumed control, continuing the original deception with a mythologic theology and temple ceremonies. This was the situation among non-creative or passive races. The imperialistic strain in active races, such as the Persians, Arabs, Greeks, Romans, and especially the Germans, broke the back of the priesthood. Once free to follow their restless nationalistic energies, active races searched out unknown places, investigated all manner of things, and struggled for empires in distant lands. Under the rational analysis of Developmentalists, religion invariably appeared as a knowledge system and social order which had outlived its usefulness.

From Theology to Science: Comte

Comte held religion to be the initial stage in the intellectual development of man (theological-metaphysical-positivist systems). The theological stage in turn divided into three connected phases: fetishism, polytheism, and monotheism. Under fetishism, the root of theological philosophy, every substance or phenomenon that caught the attention of early men was deified. Fetish gods were fixated in concrete objects, and there was little opportunity then for a priesthood to develop or for religion to quicken a feeling of national unity. Hence, fetish gods remained individual, at best family deities, though Comte admitted that tribal and even national fetishes might be found occasionally. Beginning with inanimate things in nature immediate to his experience, the fetishist advanced to a worship of animals whose striking characteristics arrested his attention. Soothsayers or conjurers practicing astrolatry served as the prototype for the first priesthood. Conjurers evolved into priests as the stars and sun generated a more compelling and pervasive awareness of deity. The priest emerged as a necessary intermediary for a more generalized and superior god.

Polytheism ushered in the second phase of the theological stage, and during this time the idea of a religious spirit received its fullest development. The proliferation of spirits confronted mankind with such a demanding crowd of heterogeneous and unruly divinities that men came to believe that their fate was foreordained and in the hands of the gods. Because there was no escape from the overwhelming numbers of spirits, men were inspired to bring some order into their lives by devising rules to subordinate the willful deities. From this point they advanced to the notion of invariable natural laws (Comte 1893(2):175–176). Comte traced an intellectual path from theological predestination to monotheism and then to science.

In the early stage of polytheism governments were run by priests, but as chiefs, kings, and emperors succeeded in concentrating spiritual and temporal power in their own hands, gods and priests were used to sanction wars and conquests. Differences in the geographic environments of Greeks and Roman induced differences in their views of the spiritual world. The diversity of the Greek peninsula kept Greeks apart, and they were unable to establish the militarized family organization to which Roman conquest was anchored. Forestalled from grand conquests, the Greeks diverted their cerebral energy into cultivation of the intellect. However, Comte (1893(2):201) admitted that the "Germs of this intellectual and moral development were derived from theocratic societies by means of colonization."

Theocracy, war, and empire were not the only accomplishments of the polytheistic phase. Industry advanced through the introduction of slavery, and under the Greeks a true scientific spirit emerged in the cultivation of mathematical ideas. "The Polytheistic priesthood was the first social corporation which could obtain sufficient leisure and dignity to devote itself to the study of science, art, and industry" (Comte 1893(2):184). Worship now took on a public character, and in ceremonies, myths and heroic sagas, the polytheistic age imaginatively dramatized the critical relations linking gods and men. Imagination was exalted over reason, and this conveyed an individualistic spirit which perpetuated the individualized quality of fetishism (Comte 1893(2):179). By joining mind and heart, polytheism united education, intellect, and morality as never before, and in its varied functions widened the horizon of individuals and promoted a greater sense of the social.

Beyond polytheism lay monotheism, to which both Greek philosophy and Roman conquests contributed. The intrinsic quality of monotheism was the projection of a universal and unified organization. The trend toward monotheism received its first stimulus from Greek efforts to analyze and formulate the logical ordering of society. Roman conquests suggested to discerning polytheists the need for a universal morality by which one and all could be united (Comte 1893(2):209–210). Historically the Jews may have set the stage for monotheism and universal morality, but if the Jews had not taken the initiative some other nation would have done so. For Comte, the determinism of social circumstances projected a future that waited neither upon the genius of great men nor upon the appearance of historic nations.

The achievement of monotheism was possible only in the West because there the necessary antecedent developments had taken place. The actual achievement belonged to Catholicism, which attained the idea of a supreme being by discarding the Greek ideal of rule by reason. Catholicism also united military and national morality under a universal ideal of peace which accented supremacy over the state. This historic reversal of control over morality made its effects felt at all levels—personal, domestic, and public. All phases of life—philosophy, science, art, and industry—altered to accord with the new intellectual and moral order. It transcended the narrow and savage patriotism of the ancient world and substituted the ideal of humanity or universal brotherhood (Comte 1893(2):243). Yet Catholicism was but a way station to the positive or scientific regime, and monotheistic Catholicism always was precariously balanced between the pulls of naturalistic and moral philosophy. Out of the internal dissensions that drove these two into opposition, there arose a metaphysical spirit which preceded the change to positivism (Comte 1893(2):249–250). Protestantism spurred the dissolution of the Catholic order by using political power to force acceptance of a more pluralistic and emancipated view of doctrinal matters. However, in Comte's view, the decline that led to positivism began as early as the fourteenth century.

From Ghost-Souls to Monotheism: Tylor and Spencer

After mid-century Tylor (1874) and Spencer (1900) dominated the study of religion with their theories of its origin and development. Beginning with the idea of a soul derived out of reflections on the experience of death, according to Tylor, men proceeded through the medium of dreams to the idea of a ghost-soul and then to the idea of spirits (see discussion on duality, pp. 209–211). Once past the doctrine of souls, and in possession of the doctrine of spirits, the rude philosophers of old expanded their ideas into what amounted to a philosophy of nature and of the universe. Primitive natural religion, as Tylor (1874(2):108) called it, viewed the world as impelled by the willful actions of spiritual beings. This idea was based on reasonable inference about cause and effect, with spirits nothing more than personified causes. In the minds of lower races, nature was alive and pervaded with spiritual beings (Tylor 1874(2):185).

This ancient spiritism seemed naturally to divide itself into two special manifestations. One expression led directly to manes worship. The other, following the "theory of Embodiment" (Tylor 1874(2):123ff.), divided itself into fetishism and demoniacal possession. The idea of demon possession pursued a course from disease possession to oracle possession, while fetishism branched into stock-and-stone worship, animal worship, and nature spirits, both local and general. Stock-and-stone worship led into idolatry as anthropomorphic features were attached to stones and to rude posts (Tylor 1874(2):168). Animals might be worshipped because they incarnated a deity or because they represented a class of creatures over which a god presided (Tylor 1874(2):231–232). In another context, Tylor (1874(2):234–235) considered cases in which an ancestral soul was incarnated and worshipped in an animal as links between ancestor worship and animal worship. However, this was not the sole pathway to the worship of animals, for families, clans, and tribes among the lower races were reported to venerate special animal species. In Tylor's (1874(2):237) view, "direct worship of the animal for itself, indirect worship of it as a fetish acted through by a deity, and veneration for it as a totem or representative of a tribe-ancestor, . . . account in no small measure for the phenomena of Zoolatry among the lower races, due allowance being also made for the effects of myth and symbolism.

Worship of local nature spirits associated with mountains, streams, and valleys reflected an advance in primitive ideas about nature spirits and indicated a higher level of culture (Tylor 1874(2):204–205). In this respect classic Greeks were similar to North American Indians, West Africans, and Siberians (Tylor 1874(2):206). Out of this nature worship the Greeks, as history recorded,

> evolved the germs of the new philosophy. Led by minuter insight and stricter reason, thoughtful Greeks began the piecemeal super-session of the archaic scheme, and set in movement the transformation of animistic into physical science. (Tylor 1874(2):207)

Local nature spirits at times became species deities, but this did not mean that they would be transformed by a process of abstract thinking into higher nature deities. In his survey Tylor found spirits associated with all kinds of water phenomena but none that stood out as an original and elemental water deity. Generally speaking, the lower races found generalization of the manifold forms of water into a single deity a difficult intellectual task (Tylor 1874(2):274).

Among islanders who had attained a higher stage of barbarism, two conceptions prevailed—a personalization of the sea and an anthropomorphized god of the sea. The two conceptions represented "two stages . . . of one idea—the view of the natural object as itself an animated being, and the separation of its animating fetish soul as a distinct spiritual deity"

(Tylor 1874(2):276). With this statement, Tylor admitted that nature deities, as the prior worship of stocks and stones, originated in a kind of personalization, as Marett argued. A personalized god concept was followed by the idea of an in-dwelling god. Nonetheless, nature deities seemed to be derived from functions central to nature's workings—earth, fire, water, air, and the like. Here, too, there was a continuity between the savage past and the barbaric present, as in the case of the Aryan thunder god, who was simply a poetic elaboration based on ideas found among peoples in the savage state. Too, in Greek religion, Tylor (1874(2):273) found transitions, as in the generalized mother-earth deity, Gaia, who become transformed into the anthropomorphic earth mother Demeter.

Polytheism, rather than monotheism, characterized the beliefs of savages and barbarians. However, their ideas foreshadowed monotheism in that they held the view of a supreme deity who ruled over all other gods (Tylor 1874(2):332). These primary gods of polytheism might be primeval ancestors, but more often they symbolized some great principle of nature which worshippers emphasized. Tylor noted that the polytheistic divine society mirrored the stratified social orders of human societies. At bottom one faced the common crowd of human souls and other spirits, with great nature deities like an aristocracy and the supreme ruler of the gods comparable to a king (Tylor 1874(2):335).

The continuity between primitive and cultured animism among the civilized could be discerned in the way both grappled with the problem of the ultimate order of the world. Both civilized and primitive reached out for a first cause and attained this perspective by gradually uniting many spirits in one god. A supreme deity ultimately became a first cause by fusing the functions and attributes of the great polytheistic gods into one personality. This god personality entered actively into human affairs, for it is he "who holds up the heavens, shines in the sun, smites his foes in the thunder, and stands first in the human pedigree as the divine ancestor" (Tylor 1874(2): 335–336). In other cases, however, the supreme being was conceived by savages and barbarians as an "unshaped divine entity looming vast, shadowy, and calm beyond and over the material world, too benevolent or too exalted to need human worship, too huge, too remote, too indifferent, too supine, too merely existent, to concern himself with the petty race of men" (Tylor 1874(2):336).

Confronted with findings that suggested instances of a high god among primitive peoples, Tylor de-emphasized their importance as supporting the degeneration theory. In attempting to prove that the theory of degeneration contradicted the facts, he produced the most considered, detailed, and influential of anthropological investigations of religion of his day—and one that today still commands respect. The preferred course to monotheism followed by Tylor led from the idea of the soul⟶ghost soul⟶spirits ⟶ fetishism⟶functional nature spirits⟶functional nature gods ⟶a supreme nature god. Throughout this movement toward monotheism, man provided the model: first, in his inner awareness of his other self; and second, in the hierarchy of society, from which, as a centralized authority made itself felt, the notion of high gods and finally a single high god was born. To clarify the animistic continuity he took pains to define fetishism as spirit embodiment and not simply a personalizing or animatizing of the inanimate. Tylor never clearly admitted that a personalizing of the object or of a natural phenomenon was distinct from the idea of a spirit permanently attached or intrusive. Though logically distinct, the two ideas were found so intermixed in primitive thought that effective discrimination was impractical. Therefore, he preferred to treat both ideas as emanating from the idea of the human soul (Tylor 1874(2):153–154). At the same time he distinguished each as a logical step in the conceptualization of deity —the simpler personalization pertaining to fetishism and the more spiritual relating to polytheism. Take fire, for instance,

> The real and absolute worship of fire falls into two great divisions, the first belonging rather to fetishism, the second to polytheism proper, and the two apparently representing an earlier and later stage of theological ideas. The first is the rude barbarian's adoration of the actual flame which he watches writhing, roaring, devouring like a live animal; the second belongs to an advanced generation, that any individual fire is a manifestation of one general elemental being, the Fire-God. (Tylor 1874(2):277)

Spencer began the course to religion with a fundamental datum of savage nature, shared with the rest of the animal world. Men in the savage state, like animals, tended to subordinate themselves in awesome fear before the strange and evident power of things, whether animal or person. At least the title of god was applied without discrimination to any person or object which struck the viewer as strange and incomprehensible (Spencer 1880–1896(1, Part 1):396). The tendency to propitiate the living whose reputations inspired awe and respect, laid the basis for deity. As Spencer (1880–1896(1, Part 1):398) argued, "if the ghost in general is feared, still more feared will be the ghost of a man distinguished during life." The path to ancestor worship thus began with offerings to superior human beings. Chiefs, medicine men, strangers, and conquerors supplied the sources for deification of the living. However, the real beginnings of religion derived from dream experiences in which the ghost of the recent dead appeared to those left behind.

Dreams were the source for the primitive idea that each person is two personalities. This second self at first was only a physical copy of the body self, and at this stage in primitive thought could not be turned into a mental self or something more ethereal. Gradually this etherealization occurred by observation that the apparitions of dreams were not real but ethereal reproductions (Spencer 1880–1896(1, Part 1):143).

Primitive men first interpreted death as a long-suspended animation (Spencer 1900(1):157). This idea came from observation of people who fainted or suffered apoplexy. Death, as a concept, emerged by gradually postponing reanimation of the dead from months to years, and finally, until the end of time. Observations of the shadow and the breath alerted the developing intelligence of savages to the fact that the double was not physical like the body. Developments with regard to death also fostered spiritualization of the second self (Spencer 1880–1896(1, Part 1):182–183).

A cringing fear of the superior person was easily transferred to the dead. Owing to their limited ideas of death, primitive men easily accepted the notion of feeding the corpse, and the idea that food offerings should be left for departed souls. Here, in the funeral rites, "propitiation of the dead ... develops into ... worship in general" (Spencer 1880–1896(1, Part 1): 326).

Once the deceased was translated into a spirit deity, a differentiation into animal, nature, plant, and idol gods followed. Ghost-souls were able to reside in everything, and when the worship of plants, animals, sun, moon, mountains, and storm is analyzed all lead back to a human personality (Spencer 1880–1896(1, Part 1):430). Idol worship differentiated out of images or relics associated with the dead, leading to fetishism, which Spencer considered largely witchcraft. Both idolatry and fetishism, as well as plant worship, turned out to be aberrant since they did not contribute to the major evolutionary flow of deity formation (Spencer 1880–1896 (1, Part 1):326–328, 367). Conceptually the pathways to idol, nature, animal, and plant deities were divergent, and for the last three, usually diverged in three ways. In animal worship, for example, the ancestors might affiliate with animals thusly: (1) as men during their lifetimes take on the disguise of animals, according to primitive belief, the dead may do likewise; (2) burial in caves brought the deceased into association with birds, bats, and other cave creatures; (3) during his lifetime an individual may be given an animal nickname, and over time the nickname is confused with the animal itself (Spencer 1880–1896(1, Part 1):329–330, 336, 347). Spencer's preference for the third explanation, the transformation of personal nicknames into a worship of bears and lions through a process of semantic confusion, aligned his interpretation with that of philologists (for example, Max Müller); but he carefully disengaged himself from their specific interpretations. The association of the animal deity with a deified human source through a chain of illogical associations was wholly consistent with Spencer's view of the obtuse logic so characteristic of primitive man; and consequently, he preferred this interpretation when accounting for nature deities. Honorific titles alluding to the sun, mountain, moon, stars, and sea led to a confusion of spirit with sun or mountain, and a sun god or a storm mountain god would be born (Spencer 1880–1896(1, Part 1):376; 393–394). As a class, all deities emerged through the use of proper names which gradually became more precise in denotation.

The whole trend in deity formation followed the law of evolution. Progress toward integration is first shown in a simple increase in mass. For example, the lower tribes held such ambiguous ideas about the spiritual nature of the dead that they were unable to discriminate supernatural beings by category and class. Later, ghosts were distinguished, accumulating in numbers once the idea that they continued to exist forever was added. The multiplication of spirits in mass led to their sorting into classes. This process of sorting meant that the homogeneous mass of spirits now were transformed into heterogeneous classes. This trend toward heterogeneity signaled a more complex evolutionary stage.

When societies were organized into social ranks, a similar process organized the gods. The spiritual hierarchy distributed powers and deities alike, from great gods to the partially deified ancestors (Spencer 1880–1896(1, Part 1):433). A process of functional differentiation continued to create ever-higher gods. The conceptualization of these gods revealed an increasing precision in the definition of their features and functions, confirming an evolution from the indefinite unorganized homogeneous to the more definite, organized, heterogeneous state (Spencer 1880–1896(1, Part 1):434). The primitive Semitic conception of deity was no exception to the course pursued by primitive men generally according to the law of evolution. Cultivated people held no innate ideas of deity. A more civilized view of deity was possible only when sufficient knowledge had accumulated, when greater mental acuity was possible, and when loftier feelings arose with an advanced stage of civilization (Spencer 1880–1896(1, Part 1):421).

RELIGION AS A MORAL AND SOCIAL FORCE: RENOVATING OLD PROBLEMS

The stages of religion sketched by Developmentalists measured important turns in the continuity of ideas men had invented when coping with the hard realities of nature and in following the speculative leads of curiosity. The Developmentalist focus on a succession of ideas did not lend itself to a detailed investigation of the interrelations and functions of institutions in a particular society. Owing to their consideration of religion as *the* primitive philosophy, Developmentalists explored the meaning of religion in the life and society of man in his primitive state. As the integrative perspective of primitive man, religion was found to combine "philosophy, science, historic tradition, poetry" (Ratzel, 1896(1):39).

During the last quarter of the nineteenth century reaction to the amoral nature of the principle of natural selection generated a new concern for the role of religion in society. The doctrine of survival of the fittest raised questions for those who looked to civilization as a humanizing process. Natural selection meant that the weak were predestined to be ravaged and overcome by the strong, and this contradicted the vision of civilized society regulated by law, morality, and justice. To avoid the ethical dilemma posed by natural selection, Huxley, the biologist and prime popularizer of survival of the fittest, was led to deny that the social process of man was identical to the biological. Indeed, in its ethical drive, the social was counterselective to the biological—the weak were protected, and rightly so.

The new social evolutionism generated by revolt against the stark implications of evolutionary theory once more drew a line between man and organic processes. Thus, the welding of the biological to the social, which Spencer and his corps of assistants labored to achieve, was in process of eroding almost as soon as completed. Lippert (1931:19–24), for example, distinguished natural and social instincts and maintained that the social were not based on or derived from the animal instincts. In 1931 when Keller published *Societal Evolution*, he pointed to the development of civilization as a product of a special evolutionary process which supervened upon organic processes. Such human evolution at first might be "little more than a variation on the process of nature . . . [but] as it develops, it takes on a characteristic [social] mode of its own . . . specifically distinguishable from natural selection" (Keller 1931:252).

By viewing man as outracing biological processes and evolving his own special social environment, Keller and other social evolutionists secured the independence and causal autonomy of a social reality. Separation of biological and social processes also laid new foundations for the opposition of nurture and nature.

The intellectual current, which placed man's destiny beyond the reach of primitive organic processes, contributed a special interest in religion as a social force. As the first intellectual adventure of man, religion was credited with supplying ideas of causation, instilling a sense of right and wrong, stimulating imagination in the production of mythologic literature and poetry, inspiring the creative symbolism of art, and shaping social and political organization.

The new look at religion is reflected in Frazer's (1922:48–49) comparison of the magical interpretation of cause with the scientific. It turned up in the search for religious motives behind inventions, which especially fascinated Germans at the time. Thus, Wundt (1928:292–293) traced the origin of the wheel to a sun amulet—first used in the form of fiery sun wheel rolled down a slope to symbolize the sun god's movements in the heavens, then on a chariot to draw the gods in ceremonious procession. In time, the idea of the wheel was applied to spinning and transportation. Rings, bracelets, and fillets were all worn at first as amulets to protect the individual from dangers that followed a breach of custom. Dress began, according to Wundt, not with the idea of protection against inclement weather or for reasons of modesty but rather with the idea of binding a wife to faithfulness by magically girdling her with a loin cord. This marital rite was an analogical transfer of a magical rite whereby disease was transferred by binding the ailing limb and then wrapping the cord around a tree.

The domestication of animals, according to Hahn (1896:135), originated in the persistent demands of gods for sacrifices. To insure a supply of animals for sacrifice, they were put into corrals. The requirement to feed the gods also led to the art of milking. In Hahn's view the sacred incentive led to the idea of milking animals, since undomesticated varieties were so sparse in their supply that there was no practical incentive. Through a fantastic chain of ideas Hahn built up an ancient fertility complex. The waxing and waning of the moon suggested fruitful growth and decay, and this idea was connected to female menstrual and pregnancy cycles. From this association a goddess emerged with moon horns, and from the horns a connection with cattle was made. Then came the logic of offering cattle and their products to the moon goddess. In time cereals, the plough with oxen, and the wheeled cart were all joined in a fertility goddess configuration. Expectably, Hahn (1896:97) saw the "plow . . . [as] the holy instrument to open up the womb of the universal mother to bring forth fertility." For Hahn, religious motives furnished the incentive for all important inventions. Practical applications always followed a sacred use.

The observation that the trend in human knowledge moved from the sacred to the profane was quite compatible with the historic rise of science. To search religion for origins thus was quite logical. However, the determination with which some nineteenth-century Developmentalists sought to root minute details of human life in religion betrayed an uncritical and even romantic search for a final cause. At the same time, the enthusiastic search for relations among morality, intellect, religion, knowledge, and society renewed fundamental issues earlier engaged by eighteenth-century progressivists. The lure of wealth and the emulation of the easy living of a decadent aristocracy was anachronistic to the emergent industrial society of the eighteenth century and threatened to corrupt individual and national character and jeopardize human progress. The enlightened philosophers sought to instill a proper moral idealism among those moving up from the lower classes. Both progressivists and evolutionists debated as to whether morality or reason should be accorded first place in human nature and in the progress of mankind. The popular social philosopher Benjamin Kidd (1920:199) restated Kames's (1779(2):132) position when he observed that social development in the Western world was not the product of reason but of an altruistic feeling which had been built into civilized living.

The debate as to whether churchmen or scientists should be the adjudicators of truth continued throughout the Developmentalist period. Darwin's evolutionary theory refueled this long-standing controversy and placed churchmen in the position of defending so-called superstition against truth very much as Voltaire had drawn the issue during the Enlightenment. From the evolutionary base Nietzsche attacked the Christian ethic as an unnatural protection of the weak.

Whether out of controversy or theoretical considerations, religion continued to hold a high priority in the thought of eighteenth- and-nineteenth century Developmentalists. While Marx was attacking religion as a strategem to deceive and control the masses, Bachofen (1861:xiii) was extolling "Religion . . . [as] the only efficient lever of all civilization."

Ethics, Religion, and Society

The Secularization of Morality: Eighteenth-Century Views. Progressivists in the eighteenth century insisted that the natural advance to a civilized order must be coordinated with an expansion in the quality of human character. This goal was attainable because man, by nature, was a moral, reflective, and relatively flexible being. Progressivists expressed their concern with the moral basis of society in two principal ways. First, they endeavored to explain how men were equipped to appreciate moral and value-laden judgments, and second, they argued that, like the individuals composing them, societies and nations were moral entities. In their concern with ethics, progressivists underlined the fact that neither society nor universal progress were possible unless men regulated selfish needs and adjusted their relations by the principle of justice.

The progressivist contribution to an assessment of the role of religion in the formation of a moral community was more a testing of naturalistic, reasoned alternatives than a considered analysis of the empirical facts of religion and morality in savage, barbarian, and civilized societies. The corresponding debate in the nineteenth century, though distorted by the logical artifacts of evolutionary theory, traversed a surer ground of ethnological fact. Developmentalists in both centuries, however, were agreed that relations linking men in society defined the proper domain of morality —and not the relations linking a worshipful believer to a god.

The Secularization of Ethics and Social Advancement: Nineteenth-Century Views. Reason appeared the keystone of any naturalistic interpretation of ethics, and, in joining intellect and morality in a common progress, nineteenth-century Developmentalists followed the well-worn lead of the eighteenth century. Hobhouse (1925:622) observed how the "phases of Ethical development will show a rough parallelism with that of Thought in general . . . since the two movements are in constant interaction." Both mind and ethics began as undirected, hesitant actions and gradually achieved purpose and self-direction. The challenge of contradictions advanced morality through a process of accommodation. Society provided the setting for advancement of mind and morality; and in social evolution, ethical and religious development moved forward in unison. Hobhouse (1925:632) was quick to point out that a growth in social complexity did not correlate necessarily with ethical progress. It appeared, however, that social, ethical, and religious advancements were coordinated in some degree and fell naturally into four stages:

> Among many simpler societies we see (1) the fundamental institutions of the family and government still very incomplete. We trace (2) the growing consolidation of the little community on the basis of kinship, then (3) the extension and improved organization of society on the principle of Authority and (4) finally, the advance towards a harmony between liberty and authority in the state. In the first two stages we have the morality of custom gradually passing into that of impartial law. In the third we have the reign of law and in its higher phases the ethics of the world-religions. The fourth is associated with humanitarian ideas. . . . (Hobhouse 1925:632)

Hobhouse theorized that the advance to humanity was purposive and ultimately arrived at a union of social and ethical behaviors. This happy fusion was dependent upon a correlative mental growth. The human mind must reach the same control over its own growth that it possessed over nature. Two challenges stood in the way: first, physical survival; and second, cultivation of a healthy mind. Once these two conditions were met, the intellect was released to attack the prerequisites for social living in a rational and ethical way. Cultivation of that infant science, sociology, was necessary since social progress was possible only as the mind exercised an increasing dominion over the conditions essential to life. Each age built on its predecessor and extended itself toward the goal of a consciously evolving idea of humanity (Hobhouse 1925:633–637).

Religion contributed to the ethical advance; but, in Hobhouse's naturalistic view, religion diverted man from his true ethical self on two counts. First, man in theological perspective was assumed to be intrinsically evil, and second, his ethical energies were misdirected "to the greater glory of God . . . [rather than] to the maintenance of human life" (Hobhouse 1925: 542). This meant that neither the moralistic theologies of Buddhism nor of Christian monotheism were psychologically geared to elicit a true ethic from man. Rather the important impulse for mankind came from the ethical idealism which extended the best of man's nature by directing him to serve his fellowmen. Chinese culture had operated on this social philosophy for well over two thousand years, and the solid foundation of this philosophy was grasped in ancient Greece. Hobhouse's humanistic ethic was founded on the assumption that

> Human nature . . . is neither intrinsically good nor intrinsically bad. It needs no supernatural grace to lift it out of the slough of original sin, . . . It has originally a natural capacity to be influenced by training and teaching, and if favourably situated where the winds blow upon it from healthy and salubrious climes, it flourishes and grows up into wisdom and moral goodness. . . . (Hobhouse 1925:558)

The Greek contribution to ethics lay in teaching that moral obligation and self-fulfillment were two sides of the coin. Moreover, Greeks applied their ideas of ethical conduct to all mankind, and hence set the foundations for a universal ethic. In the Greek view these ethical ideals transcended state law as well as social custom and individual behavior (Hobhouse 1925: 567), and modern philosophers now saw that the ideal of a universal ethic must be placed in a rational, humanistic, scientific, and developmental context.

The vague and hesitant traces of morality Hobhouse detected in early times were highlighted by Tylor (1874(2):360–361) when sketching the progressive advance in religion and ethics. "So far as savage religion can stand as representing natural religion," he wrote, "the popular idea that the moral government of the universe is an essential tenet of natural religion simply falls to the ground." Historically, too, it was evident that religion and ethics were not intrinsically joined. The effective juncture of religion and ethics came later in human development.

> Looking at religion from a political point of view, as a practical influence on human society, it is clear that among its greatest powers has been its divine sanction of ethical laws, its theological enforcement of morality, its teaching of moral government of the universe. . . . But such alliance belongs almost wholly to religions above the savage level . . . [;] the introduction of the moral element separates the religions of the world, united as they are throughout by one animistic principle, into two great classes, those lower systems whose best result is to supply a crude childlike natural philosophy, and those higher faiths which implant on this the law of righteousness and of holiness, the inspiration of duty and of love. (Tylor 1874(2):360–361)

Tylor noted how in its earlier stage prayer was used for personal advantage and revealed no strong ethical tone. Later, however, worshippers not only entreated the god for prosperity but asked for his help in overcoming the evil of personal behavior. By adding the element of personal virtue, religion became the instrument of morality (Tylor 1874(2):364).

Waitz (1863(1):368) assessed savage religions very much as Tylor. The original form of religion was but a raw polytheism wherein primitive man responded to threats to his survival and personal welfare. Malevolent spirits haunted primitive man, who became so engrossed in accommodating to their demands that he neglected his own basic interests. Waitz (1863(1): 370) considered savage religion so filled with the "most senseless actions, the coarsest immorality . . . and purely utilitarian" objectives that it could not help but impede progress. Religion attained the level of a civilizing force only when emulation became a spiritual force by making inspirational heroes into gods (Waitz 1863(1):373–374).

The primitive mystical posture based on awe of nature to which Marett (1909) looked for the beginnings of religion did not connect morality directly with rudimentary religious practice. The awesome qualities of nature generated a sense of immanent mystic powers that operated automatically. True, mana acted positively in man's behalf, and tabu brought punishment for derelictions. Nevertheless, mana and tabu were morally neutral. "Presented in its double character of *tabu* and *mana* the supernatural is not moral or immoral, but simply unmoral" (Marett 1909:131). Frazer (1922: 54) agreed that magical practice also was amoral, even when a propitiation or conciliation of spiritual beings acknowledged man's inferiority. After reviewing primitive sources of morality, Westermarck (1924(1):233–234) granted that a system of taboos and curses which operated mechanically with a mysterious energy offered little opportunity for moral involvement. Nevertheless, Westermarck (1924(2):696) concluded that, because of the possible use of magical powers against the person, magic exerted a stronger influence on the moral conduct of uncivilized races than belief in the intervention of gods to punish moral wrongs. Westermarck argued that religion alone could not account for moral behavior. Moral emotions were retributive and directed against those who willingly brought pleasure or pain to others; and though curses, ordeals, and taboos might operate in a mechanical way, they were grounded on a primitive process of retribution upon which a more enlightened morality could be raised (Westermarck 1924(1): 314–315, 326).

To some degree, the ethical advance of mankind could be charted through the character of the gods men worshipped. In primitive times morality was obscured by ritual and the giving of gifts to appease malevolent supernaturals without regard to the ethics of their demands. Even in ancient Babylonia, the gods, though guardians of morality, appeared more interested in the ritual sacrifices and devotions by which worshipper was bound to god. Nevertheless, the gods served men as allies and protectors in their struggles against dreaded demons.

> But they helped only those who piously observed the prescribed rites, who recited the conventional prayers and offered them sacrifices; on such persons they bestowed a happy old age and a numerous posterity. On the other hand, he who did not fear his god would be cut down like a reed; and by neglecting the slightest ceremonial detail the king excited the anger of the deities against himself and his subjects. During the whole of their lives the Chaldeans were haunted by the dread of offending their gods, and they continually implored pardon for their sins. But the sinner became conscious of his guilt only as a conclusion drawn from the fact that he was suffering from some misfortune, which he interpreted as a punishment sent by an offended god. It mattered little what had called forth the wrath of the god or whether the deity was acting in accordance with just ideas; and in none of the penitential psalms known to us is there any indication that the notion of sin comprised offences against fellow men. (Westermarck 1924(2):702)

Westermarck assigned ritual duties a first place in the religion of early societies, and even of early civilizations, echoing the consensus of Bachofen, Fustel, and W. R. Smith. The clear impact of religion came with the emergence of monotheism and the guarding of a universal morality by a benevolent creator god. But even with monotheism, morality was limited by ritual obligations and the egoistic concerns of the worshipper. The Christian sacrifice of self to god was indeed a magnificent achievement, but it fell short ethically in not embracing humanity as a whole (Hobhouse 1925: 514–526). To achieve the ideal of a universal moral community, the expansive inspiration of an altruistic sentiment was needed (Westermarck 1924(2):746). The future of moral development lay not with religion but with secular society. Secularization of the ethical process, according to Hobhouse, did not mean that new instincts or impulses would arise or that old instincts would disappear. Rather, in the long perspective of mental evolution the

> Spiritual consciousness deepens, and the ethical order is purged of inconsistencies and extended in scope. The deity, who is at first much less than a man, becomes progressively human and then, in the true sense of the word, superhuman. Blind adherence to custom is modified by an intelligent perception of the welfare of society, and moral obligation is set upon a rational

basis. These changes re-act upon the actual contents of the moral law itself, what is just and good in custom being sifted out from what is indifferent or bad, and the purified moral code re-acts in turn on the legislation by which more advanced societies re-model their structure. The psychological equipment of human beings on the one side and the actual needs of social life on the other are the underlying factors determining rules of conduct from the lowest stage upwards, but it is only at the highest grade of reflection that their operation enters fully into consciousness ... The true meaning of ethical obligations—their bearing on human purposes, their function in social life—only emerges by slow degrees. (Hobhouse 1925:30)

Morality and Biological Evolution: Spencer and Westermarck

In Spencer's (1897(1):560) biological perspective, moral evolution would show a more "appreciable progress, when there have died out the fatuous legislators who are continually impeding it." Unlike Hobhouse, Spencer had little use for legislation as an instrument in the moral progress of man. Moral and biological evolution moved forward together, and the only way to produce individuals who would be fit for life in society was to remold human nature (Spencer 1897(1):560). Protective laws simply impeded the selective elimination of asocial man by the process of natural selection.

In the evolutionist context, a physiological base would be a proper source for the beginnings of moral conduct, and Spencer (1897(1):21–46) turned to pleasure-pain discrimination for the roots of moral judgments. However, the restraints and incentives which operated in the political, social, and religious institutions of early societies to curb human aggression and greed did not involve morality in the fullest sense of the word. Political religious, and social restraints were required if stable communities were to exist. Only those living in stable communities would possess the intellectual and moral depth to experience a sense of moral revulsion toward criminal acts (Spencer 1897(1):122). The creation of a feeling of moral revulsion was highly significant in that a new dimension was added to the human inheritance and social adaptation. It evolved gradually from specific sentiments (for example, temperance, providence, kindness, justice, truthfulness, and duty) to a generalized or abstract conception, applicable to every act and every person (Spencer 1897(1):124). The ultimate end of this ethical evolution led from egoistic competition to an altruism which gratified egoistic satisfactions as well as the altruistic expectations of others (Spencer 1897(1):256). Full realization of man's best human nature came only when private conduct was prompted by natural impulse and the private activities of all achieved a state of dynamic equilibrium (Spencer 1897(1):560–561). One must not push nature's remoulding too rapidly, nor become engrossed in exaggerated self-criticism. A balanced perspective was essential to ensure a healthy mind (Spencer 1897(1):561).

When confronting the ethical problem, Spencer mellowed and advocated elimination of the aggressive militancy which made survival of the fittest a natural reality. He even ridiculed those who labeled the uncivilized as savage in contrast with the civilized. The thieving and murderous Homeric Greeks, the ruthless Romans, and Christian persecutors of heretics, witches, and political offenders belied the charge that only the uncivilized were ferociously inhuman. The actions of Australian settlers, the beachcombers, and the labor kidnappers of the Pacific testified to the barbarous conduct of Europeans with regard to the native races (Spencer 1897 (1):395–396).

In tying moral development to evolution, Spencer rested his case on a continuity that began with pre-ethical ("pro-ethics") elements and ended with a rational ethic. An incipient altruism was equally present at the start with primitive egoism. "Self-sacrifice . . . [was] no less primordial than self-preservation" (Spencer 1897(1):203). Westermarck (1924) agreed except that moral beginnings were traced to a specific tendency of humans and animals to hit out at those who inflict injury and to respond favorably to those who brought pleasure, or to retain whatever brought pleasure (Westermarck 1924(1):73–94; see Figure 6-1). Moral disapproval and approval had their sources in the pain and pleasure of human and animal biology, and both could be accounted for by natural selection (Westermarck 1924 (1):94–95). True, retribution generated by a kindly desire to reciprocate pleasure for pleasure was more prevalent in humans, but it could be found in all gregarious animals which gave evidence of social affection (Westermarck 1924(1):93–94). Retributive disapproval went from a nonmoral resentment to moral indignation, and this sentiment was expressed in punishment and in religious and legal sanctions. Social affections were extended by a sympathetic altruism originating in the maternal and paternal instincts and created a feeling of community and ultimately of a brotherhood of man (Westermarck 1924(1):42–43; (2):190–191, 227–228). The course of mental evolution led to higher levels of moral development. In the instance of retaliatory anger, mental development translated a vengeful feeling into a desire to forgive, and in time to forgive became an obligation (Westermarck 1924(1):73).

The social context was indispensable, since it was here that moral judgments found their more impartial and general applications. "Society is

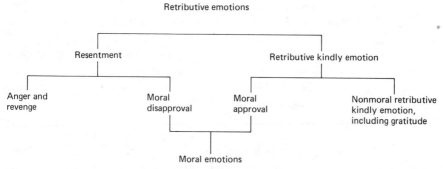

Figure 6-1. Origin of moral emotions, according to Westermarck (1924(1):21).

the birthplace of the moral consciousness; . . . the first moral judgments expressed, not the private emotions of isolated individuals, but emotions which were felt by the society at large; . . . tribal custom was the earliest rule of duty (Westermarck 1924(1):117–118).

To custom one must look for the earliest expression of moral indignation, since the breach of custom aroused public indignation, the basic antecedent to moral judgment (Westermarck 1924(1):119).

Convergence in Humanistic and Evolutionary Views of Moral Development

Despite their humanistic or evolutionary postures, Hobhouse, Westermarck, and Spencer came to similar conclusions about the development of morality and its future course in civilized society. Human character, shared in primitive basics with animals, was extended morally through participation in a social community. Custom stabilized the moral commitments of early communities, and the rule of custom certified the subordination of individuals to the public good. Ethics began as a directive of the public will, but the natural course of events led to a moral will centered in the individual conscience. Ethical idealism depended more on the application of reason to moral judgments than on a particular set of social institutions, even though the latter were necessary for all intellectual and moral development. As Westermarck (1924(2):744) observed,

> All higher emotions are determined by cognitions—sensations or ideas; they therefore vary according as the cognitions vary, and the nature of a cognition may very largely depend upon reflection or insight. . . . The change of cognitions, or ideas, has thus produced a change of emotions.

The cutting edge of reason thus assisted the advance to higher moral sentiments and promoted the gradual secularization of morality. Like Maine (1877:16), Hobhouse, Spencer, and Westermarck saw mental progress as the cause for the separation of religion from law and of law from morality. Where humanists and biological evolutionists differed was the extent to which moral progress could be linked with biopsychic progress. An incremental inheritance of psychic and emotional experience through natural selection explained historic and evolutionary differences in moral refinement for Spencer and Westermarck. Hobhouse (1925:635–636) was less certain that natural selection improved human nature. "Ethical progress," in Hobhouse's (1925:635–636) judgment, "[was] essentially a progress in ethical conceptions, acting through [social] tradition."

In summary, the primary lessons which Developmentalists drew from their considered investigations of the rise of ethics as a social force in society hinged on four facts. First, all agreed that the intrinsic quality of social relations were moral relations. Second, the unity of morality and conduct initiated and developed by religion was imperfect. God's providential instruction for man was insufficient because it fostered a private relation between self and God, despite universalistic claims made by the church. The true school for men was society, not the church. Third, the future task of man was to translate the meaning of the social experience into a rational ethic that would embrace and define relationships among all men. Fourth, the intrinsic nature of this socializing experience, in drawing out the essential humanity of man, must come in the private sector. That is, though existing in a social context, the foundational process of a humane morality lay in the formation of a private conscience. No confidence was placed in institutions, such as law and government, to create the moral basis for the social community.

In their concern for the moral basis of society, Developmentalists voiced an ideal sought by those who viewed society as man's special environment. They linked the future development of society to the creation of a humanistic and rational social ethic. Perhaps society in the West, and in the rest of the world, may have entered this phase of moral evolution during and after World War II.

RELIGION AND THE ORGANIZATION OF SOCIETY

Religious Foundations of Matriarchal Society: Bachofen

In *Das Mutterrecht* (1861) Bachofen sketched human history not in the opposition of empires but in the opposition of cultures integrated by different principles. A classicist, he contrasted the languid Oriental culture with the fresh exuberance of the West—symbolized by the Hellenic victory over the Persians. The Hellenic-Persian conflict, however, was part of a great cultural-historic drama in which a superior principle won out over an inferior principle. The struggle between East and West in actuality represented the victory of reason over feeling, of nonmaterial over material values, and of maleness over femaleness.

Suggestive references concerning the importance of women among the ancient Lycians, Locrians, Egyptians, and Cantabrians led Bachofen to conclude that a matriarchal society had preceded the known patriarchal communities of the ancient world. Gradually Bachofen pieced together a matriarchal mosaic that included the following features: fertility, earth mother goddess, night, moon, left hand, sexual promiscuity, relative absence of aggression and warfare, passivity, collective ownership of children by women, descent and rank traced through females, dominance of female goddesses conceived as life givers, preoccupation with death and mourning ceremonies, and a materialistic ethic. The seeming precedence of this matriarchal constellation before the patriarchal led Bachofen to identify maleness and femaleness as the basic principles in historic and evolutionary opposition. In listing matriarchal features, Bachofen obviously strained to find elements coordinate with a common stereotype of woman's character.

Rules of descent and family organization offered visible evidence for discriminating the matriarchal from the succeeding patriarchal system.

Bachofen focused on the collective promiscuity and the common sharing of children by women under the matriarchy and used survivals to describe the gradual restriction of collective sexuality until it existed only in symbolic form. The primary force behind change from a collectivity to a monogamic family was religion, and Bachofen used modifications in religious prostitution to show how it had become a means of symbolic expiation for deviation from the ancient matriarchal promiscuity. In its symbolic form, however, religious prostitution itself became the guarantor of chastity and of the patriarchal family.

Societies were organized in two different modes, according to Bachofen, notably the religious and the civil. Of the two, the religious was the more important since it supplied the integrative principles by which an organization came into being. Ideas connected with worship came first, and the civil forms of life were their result and expression" (Bachofen 1861:xv).

The virtue of Bachofen's work lay not in the substance of his romantic and prejudiced conclusions but in his effort to portray matriarchy and patriarchy as separate culture types. At the same time, Bachofen brought into focus an old issue, namely, the probability of a matriarchal-patriarchal succession. By appealing to the uniformity of human nature and the human mind, Bachofen generalized the apparent historical succession in the ancient world and generated a problem area that would occupy first place in ethnological research and scholarly debate for nearly three quarters of a century.

Religious Rites and the Rights of Citizenship: Fustel de Coulanges

The Ancient City (1864) of Fustel de Coulanges took up the theme that rights of citizenship in the ancient world were contingent on religious rights. Like Herder, Fustel stressed the historic uniqueness of Greek and Roman life and noted that their rules and customs never again would be reordered into a working system. The past was irrevocably gone, for human intelligence moved on and changed institutions and laws (Fustel de Coulanges 1956:12).

Fustel identified a patrilineal kin group, the gens, as the original form of Greek and Roman society and of the whole Aryan race. This family, as he mistakenly called the gens, was characterized by special rules of descent, inheritance, marriage, and adoption. However, the basic unity of the gens was a product of a common worship of domestic ancestors and the domestic hearth. Death evoked a religious sentiment which led naturally to the idea of the supernatural and to family worship, and Fustel concluded that a "religion of the dead appeared to be the oldest that has existed amongst this race of men" (Fustel de Coulanges 1956:24–25).

Early cities operated very much as if they were extended kin groups or families established with sacred rites centered in worship of the founder (Fustel de Coulanges 1956:134–146). Citizens alone could worship, and their private rights and privileges were linked to participation in sacred ceremony. The rise of philosophy in Greece prepared the way for liberation of the human conscience from submission to immutable tradition, but it was the work of Christianity to universalize freedom of conscience and attach it firmly to the idea of individual liberty (Fustel de Coulanges 1956: 354–395). In overturning the domestic penates and their sacred fires, Christianity also irrevocably altered the ancient constitution of the family. The father as a sacrosanct patriarchal leader faded, and with Christianity came the conjugal family based on the moral equality of husband, wife, and child.

The sacra-civil character of the ancient city set the stage for social and political conflicts, since those excluded from the *sacra* struggled to achieve full citizenship. In Rome the history of the landless and unenfranchised plebs was simply a contest for religious rights that would confer civil equality. At the very start of this conflict the heads of gentes had overthrown the kings because they tried to undermine patrician religious and economic status through alliance with the plebs. Once the plebs attained their religio-civil rights, government altered profoundly. The center of activity shifted from the performance of scheduled religious ceremonies to the maintenance of order within and security without. "What had before been of secondary importance was now of the first. Politics took precedence of religion, and the government of men became a human affair" (Fustel de Coulanges 1956:319).

The role of the plebs thus had been to secularize the social process. As secularization proceeded, an aristocracy of wealth supplanted the hereditary and sacerdotal estate. A more democratic spirit thrived, but the democratic advance was subverted as men warred in pursuit of their special interests. Later Greek and Roman history recorded how rich and poor wasted their energies in civil wars and opened the field to tyrants.

What Fustel had written was a religious parallel to the materialistic class struggle expounded by Marx, but without the projected happy ending. In making religion central to social and political events marking the rise and fall of the Roman Republic, Fustel also called attention to a complex of features delineating an ancient culture type. His historical analysis of the ancient city added substance to the theory of change from the sacred to the secular. In his work can be detected the growth of another ideological currency—that ancient communities in actuality were societies of communicants.

The Primitive Totemic Horde: McLennan

The idea that religious bonds supplied the integrative sinew of early societies soon turned up in the analysis of primitive communities. J. F. McLennan (1865) had already developed his theory of primitive marriage and society when he suddenly realized that animal worship, or totemism, was absolutely necessary to the origins of exogamy. He addressed himself to this problem in articles on "The Worship of Animals and Plants" (1869 and 1870) and postulated a universal totemic stage. He reasoned that the idea of kinship was not a simple one, certainly not innate to humans, and therefore it must have developed gradually.

At the start of human society it was unlikely that groups, assembled for protection from hostile forces, would generate any sentiment of kinship. If, however, members of these groups speculated on their relationships, it might be logical for them to conclude that they all came from a common ancestor; and being savages, they might connect this ancestor with either a plant or an animal. These local aggregates or stocks, as McLennan called them, held no further ideas about descent until the notion of consanguinity was derived from the obvious relation of child to mother. A child now would take his mother's totem and relate himself to all others with the same totem (McLennan 1896:47–48). A maternal descent group thus came into being, united by a religious regard for the totem and obligated by the blood feud. Supported by the religious bond and the revenge obligation, McLennan was confident that when the maternal descent groups separated as bands from the original stock, they still retained an affiliation with the ancestral stock. Religious sentiment added strength to the kinship bonds; it also proscribed capture of wives from one's own stock or affiliated bands. To forcibly seize a wife within one's own local group would be "more than an act of war; it would be felt to be an outrage or a crime; more than that, it would be felt to be a sin—a violation of the religious obligation which the blood feud imposed; for it could not well be accomplished without the shedding of kindred blood" (McLennan 1896:60–61). When the full disapproval of the stock was directed against a band violating the sacralized kinship and blood feud, the sanction against in-capture of brides was intensified to a point of horror by the rise in public sentiment. This resulted in a rule that a man must capture a woman from an alien group. All that remained to explain the origins of exogamy was to transform this limitation of the right to seize women within the state into a restriction of marriage rights. This arose when the idea of marriage was transformed by the idea of wife as a manly possession or slave. Marriage was now identified with a wife owned and guarded by her captors, and the negative sanction against in-marriage was fortified with a religious feeling of sin. This then could be transferred into a positive sanction for out-marriage or exogamy.

McLennan's reasoning is tortuous. Yet his efforts underline how Developmentalists' assumed that ideas set the course of change as old meanings were translated into new contexts and new ideas were generated out of altered circumstances. Primitive organic forces might provide an initial stimulus, but in time ideas took control. In McLennan's theory, the primitive struggle for survival never mastered the food problem, and female infanticide was introduced to overcome the population excess. Female infanticide then led to a shortage of females, and this provoked bride capture. Nonetheless, primitive social organization based on kinship and exogamy was born not out of the hard-core problems of survival but rather out of reflection on ancestry, sin, wife, and marriage. However erroneous the chain of logic McLennan used to explain exogamy, he must be credited with scientific coinage of the terms "endogamy" and "exogamy" and also with engaging the attention of scholars on the relation between totemism as a cult worship and exogamy as a marriage rule.

Cult as Social Tradition: W. R. Smith

Bachofen and Fustel drew heavily on classical resources to document the significance of religion in the formation of social groups and their subsequent histories. McLennan turned the relation of cult worship to the organization of early society into a broader anthropological perspective. However, the most detailed and documented analysis of the relation of cult and society was made by a friend of McLennan, W. Robertson Smith, professor of Arabic at Cambridge University. *The Religion of the Semites* (1889) culminated a number of Hebraic and Arabic studies and was preceded by *Kinship and Marriage in Early Arabia* (1885). In the earlier work Smith considered that he had confirmed McLennan's general theory about totemism, female kinship, bride capture, and the institution of exogamy. In the later work he addressed himself to Hebrew religion, tracing its various stages and comparing the races to which the Hebrews were related by natural descent and with which they had constant historic contact. Smith thus extended the seemingly inexhaustible resources and stimulus of classical scholarship one step farther into the past. However, he relied on the Roman gens, with its annual common sacrifices, to supply an analogy to what he found among the Semites.

Beyond the historic record of Semitic ritual lay the misty darkness of the primitive past. In order to explain the beginnings of traditional Semitic practices, Smith had to go back to the fundamental characteristics of primitive thought where men reasoned by analogy and did not easily discriminate thought from objective reality. More often, they responded to an inner awareness or a self-consciousness when interpreting experience. Thus, in reaching the distinction of body and soul, primitive thinkers relied on an inner consciousness, brought to a vivid awareness by psychic experiences, especially dreams. Smith (1957:87) held that

> the unbounded use of analogy characteristic of pre-scientific thought extends this conception to all parts of nature which becomes to the savage mind full of spiritual forces, more or less detached in their movements and action from the material objects to which they are supposed properly to belong.

To this stage of thought belonged ideas about the descent of men from gods, transformations of men into animals, and frequent visitations by the gods.

The initial impulse for the sacred developed from dread of natural forces which generated an anxious desire to emancipate the "society of men from the dread of certain natural agencies, by the establishment of the conception of a physical alliance and affinity between the two parts" (Smith 1957:125). Primitive men attempted to ingratiate themselves with the natural forces they feared by merging with them. Early society was characterized by totemic affiliations similar to the Arabic tribes which often took names from animals. Their members were considered sons of the wolf, or little wolves, for example, and also worshippers of the animal eponym. In drawing religion out of everyday life situations, Smith (1957: 134–135) rejected the explanation that the extraordinary in nature, such as volcanoes and the stars, generated the notion of some living force or agent to the primitive mind. Their ideas of supernatural beings were the products of immediate and concrete experience, localized in springs, bushes, and trees.

Ancient religion possessed two prime characteristics which Smith considered to have originated in totemism. First, ancient religion at base was a community affair, and second, religious occasions involved the bringing of a sacrafice to the god. Behind the idea of sacrifice was the primitive notion that, by taking flesh together, worshippers would be bonded into a mystic union and united with their god (Smith 1957:313). The fact that a private slaying of the totemic animal was forbidden—though Smith had only indirect evidence for his Semites—strengthened the idea that in the Semitic past the killing of a kin animal was a community affair and the occasion for communion. It was widely held by primitives that by eating flesh or by drinking blood a person absorbed the very nature or life of the flesh and blood. When animals lost their original sacrosanct quality by no longer being considered kin, animal sacrifice gave way to human sacrifice, where again kinship might be affirmed through adoption or selection of the most perfect of human victims from special families (Smith 1957: 361–365).

In the beginning, then, the religious and the political community were joined. This religious community did not rest on the family, as among the later Romans, but upon a wider set of kinsmen, the totemic clan. By taking holy flesh together, kinsmen renewed their mystic unity and blood feud obligations. As long as a man carried out these traditional acts in common with others, he had no need to fear that a god would find him derelict in some way.

Ritual dominated early religions and not belief, even though myths later were coined to explain ritual. The myths were there to excite the worshipper and not to evoke dogma, as the variant mythological explanations well illustrated. Religion in primitive times was a "part of the organized social life into which a man was born, and to which he conformed through life in the same unconscious way in which men fall into any habitual practice of the society in which they live" (Smith 1957:22). Thus, primitive religion was a sacralized social tradition rather than a theology wherein individuals strove for personal atonement.

Totemism, Age Classes, and Secret Societies: Schurtz and Webster

Heinrich Schurtz and Hutton Webster extended contemporary interest in the relation of primitive sociology and religion with the first surveys of age classes and secret societies. More metaphysical in spirit than Hutton, Schurtz drew social organization into a universal process where oppositions were constantly at work dividing and reuniting people in social groups. The consolidation of contrast through division was the more fundamental social process, but ambivalence characterized all social relations—within and between the sexes, within and across generations. Sex and age offered fundamental contrasts to which society in its organization had responded from earliest times. The male sex added a special social principle that transcended the family and kin principle emanating from women. The generational separation of society into the age classes of boys, youths, and married men was accompanied by ceremonies designed to ready youth for war, hunt, and marriage. Religious ceremony, prompted by nature's accent on puberty, supplied a ritualization of status as young men were tested through ordeal (for example, circumcision and knocking out of teeth) and introduced to ancestors governing war and the hunt. Out of the contrastive consolidation of young men versus married men came the young men's house with free love privileges for the unmarried. Various differentiations flowed out of the generalized young men's house, leading in one direction to craft and dancing groups and in the other, through the medium of war, to a cult of ancestors and secret societies (Schurtz 1902:203–210). Secret societies involving worship of the dead or of animals (totemism) represented a degeneration rather than a necessary product of social development. They usually were correlated with the rise of family heads who strengthened their control with priestcraft, ultimately establishing a monopoly over cult ceremonial.

The natural kin organization, based on family and clan, contrasted and conflicted with the integration of males into classes according to the most fundamental and ancient of biosocial oppositions, sex and age. Through family and clan the elders countered the weight of the young men's society, which could exercise political influence only in war (Schurtz 1902:319–325). For Schurtz and Bachofen, the great design of culture history was found in the triumph of maleness over femaleness. "One can conclude," wrote Schurtz (1902:39), "that the whole history of culture is to burst the narrow and clumsy natural associations [built upon the womanly principle of blood relationship] in order to construct a freer, progressive and better adapted group." This was the sympathetic, voluntary, interest-centered group so characteristic of male relationships and fraternal associations.

In Schurtz's theory the cult group associated with family and clan grew in strength as the social significance of age classes declined. Webster (1968: 136–137) placed clan initiations before the historic development of tribal initiations and saw the secret societies as correlated with the decline of totemic clan organization, not its rise.

That tribal solidarity of which initiatory ceremonies are the recognition is not a primitive development. Tribal initiation ceremonies presuppose the tribe. Yet their beginnings must be sought in a stage of development of human society more remote than that of the tribe; in a word, in the primitive totemic clan itself. Initiation into the tribe must have been preceeded by some form of initiation into the clan. When in process of time various clans unite to form tribal aggregates, ceremonies of initiation as well as the dramatic and magical rites of the separate clans are transferred to the newly formed tribe. Where the puberty institutions still retain their primitive vigor, as among the Australians and New Guinea tribes, the original clan ceremonies are clearly seen underlying the existing tribal rites. Where, from the puberty institutions, secret societies of more or less limited membership have arisen, as in Melanesia and Africa, we shall find in these organizations fewer traces of the antecedent clan structure. Disintegration of the clans has there been largely accomplished. In the fraternities of the North American Indians, on the other hand, the clan structure underlying the organizations is still, in a number of instances, plainly perceptible. The rise of secret societies in their developed form appears, in fact, to be invariably associated with the decline of the totemic clans.

Totemism and Ethnological Theory

Totemism, Primitive Social Bonds, and Political Evolution. Smith's sacra-civil interpretation of early society, extracted from his Semitic researches, inspired considerable speculation over the place of totemism and of cult worship generally in the history of human society. Following Smith, Jevons (1890), Lippert (1886–1887), and Wundt (1912) traced the early evolution of society in a replacement of a natural blood bond by an artificial or sacra-social bond. As *the* primeval cult, totemism was viewed as the primary instrument in the forging of true social bonds. Cult totemism tightened relations within maternal descent lines and stimulated the formation of a cult-kin group from which individual families later differentiated.

In explaining the origin of totemism, the idea that it represented a sacramental affiliation to counter a primitive dread of nature received wide acceptance. Jevons (1927:96–110) saw totemism as a base for the elimination of the original hostility existing between man and animal and which also induced the religious sentiment of love. United under a benevolent totem god, the early community reacted to breaches of totemic injunctions by stoning the offenders. This act of condemnation actually expressed an ethical judgment and at the same time organized the community as a political force. In time, this incipient merger of ethics and authority was united in the figure of the war leader. Totemism thus was a prelude to the state. According to Lippert (1931:483), the establishment of cult worship was important in two ways: (1) it produced a unified social group dedicated to a common purpose—worship of the cult spirit; and, (2) it united people by an artificial social principle in place of the natural blood relationship of maternal descent. Indeed, a cult union was the *sine qua non* for the exercise of political authority.

> In early times ... there was never a state without a state cult. The last of the great states of antiquity fell in the struggle for this principle, upon which it was built. In the tragedy of its fall, however, its principle conquered. Christianity and Islam sought once more to realize the old ideal of the coextensiveness of cult and government on the new basis of a universal idea of God. From the new idea of the unity of God, in conjunction with the old conception of the necessary unity of cult union and political organization, flowed the claim of both to world dominion. (Lippert 1931:604)

Totemism as an Evolutionary Stage or Culture Type. The view that totemism played a significant role in the formation of early society clearly implied that it may have constituted an important stage in the evolution of civilization. More than others of his day Wundt (1928) labored to unite the economic, social, political, religious, and artistic components of totemic culture. The totemic age was the formative period in human society, lying midway between the unorganized horde society of early times and the age of heroes and gods of ancient civilizations (for example, Babylonians, Egyptians, Hindus). Wundt divided the totemic era into three stages illustrated by contemporary Australians, Malayo-Polynesians, and Africans. In its pristine form totemism organized a tribe behind the worship of an animal ancestor. Taboos against eating the totemic ancestor evoked the idea of the sacred, which then was applied to plants and everything in nature. Totemic groups were the first to practice exogamy, and men's associations developed out of totemic ritual. In time, individual totems were differentiated on the principle of sex. These individual guardians were useful for those who led the totemic tribe in war. Indeed, war as a human phenomenon was the special contribution of totemism. The individualization of totems likewise fostered the possession of personal property and the exchange of goods. Through ritual, totemism deepened the relations of human societies to the land and to animals and stimulated the beginnings of cultivation (hoe cultivation), animal herding, and breeding. Animal tales, celestial mythologies, and representative art also belonged to the totemic age. African totemism, however, signaled the end of an epoch; the rise of despotic states, polygyny, slavery, animistic fetishism, and ancestor worship in conjunction with the family testified to the breakup of totemic culture and the dawn of a new age (Wundt 1928:235).

Totemistic Epilogue. *Totemism and Exogamy.* In a first ethnographic venture in 1891, Durkheim jumped into the thick of the totemic controversy, offering a complex theory that drew upon a number of current emphases. At the outset Durkheim accepted the totemic clan as the primitive exogamic unit. Originally the "totem ... was transmitted exclusively by the uterine line; and ... the clan, as a result, was composed only of matrilineal descendants" (Durkheim 1963:45). The exogamic prohibition was ideologically the same as religious taboos found in all primitive religions and developed religions (Durkheim 1963:70). Behind the negative prohibition of taboo was the notion of turning aside the malign effects of magical contagion. Taboos became attached to sacred persons or things wherein dwelled a god whose powers were so dreadful that no ordinary mortal could contact it without harmful effects (Durkheim 1963:70). The totem obviously was inhabited by a god. All who shared a totemic ancestry were enjoined by a supreme taboo—not to spill the divine blood nor to use the totemic god for food (Durkheim 1963:83–87). Durkheim traced the notion of the penetrating and blighting power of blood to the fact that the god, in giving birth to his progeny, in fact fragmented his own vital force—that is, the divine blood.

> Thus the totemic being is immanent to the clan; it is incarnate in each individual, and it is in the blood that it resides. . . . As a result, there is god in each individual organism (for he is complete in each), and it is in the blood that this god resides; from which it follows that the blood is a divine thing. When it runs out, the god is spilling over. (Durkheim 1963:89)

Woman was the singular vehicle through which the divine totemic blood was diffused, and by which the group was made one (Durkheim 1963:90). Through the menstrual cycle woman proved to be the "theater of . . . bloody demonstrations" evoking a "more or less conscious anxiety, a certain religious fear," that made her "taboo for the other members of the clan" (Durkheim 1963:85). Menstrual blood tripped anxiety over contact with the divine totemic blood and laid the emotional base for rejecting women of the totemic group. The logic for outmarriage or exogamy was an unconscious awareness of a spiritual affinity that was dangerous if not controlled.

For someone who only two years before had enunciated the principle that "every time that a social phenomenon is directly explained by a psychological phenomenon, we may be sure that the explanation is false," Durkheim (1938:110) offered a curious, Leviticized, and psychological interpretation of totemism.

In 1899 Tylor produced an essay designed to bring a more realistic perspective to totemistic studies and to the place totemism held in the development of society and religion. Tylor queried the facts right down the line. There was no conclusive evidence that totem gods were a necessary antecedent to higher gods. Evidence for the totemic sacrament was so sparse that discussion was highly speculative (Tylor 1899:145). How clan members came to be related to a species of animals or plants was explained readily, Tylor thought, by his general theory of animism. The idea that animals were possessed by the disembodied souls of ancestors served to unite animals and men in kinship through lineal descendants that included both men and sharks (Tylor 1899:147). Totemism and exogamy were not always joined in human society, and may have had a separate origin and existence. However, Tylor did not deny the frequent association of the two and admitted that this fact pointed to totems as exerting considerable influence and force at the level of the clans, drawing them into alliances within a tribal organization.

Within eleven years Tylor's short critique was overshadowed by the four-volume work of Sir J. G. Frazer, an intellectual intimate and close friend of W. Robertson Smith. Smith invited Frazer to write articles on taboo and totemism for the 9th edition of the Encyclopaedia Britannica (1887), and Frazer's notes were used by the former in his study of religion among the Semites. The format Frazer laid down in the initial article on totemism was followed scrupulously in all his other publications, including *Totemism and Exogamy, a Treatise on Certain Early Forms of Superstition and Society* (1935).

None who read Frazer could come away without admiration for the impressive range of his knowledge and his assiduous pursuit of a subject. Using an overwhelming mass of descriptive notes as his base, Frazer threaded them together with theoretical speculations, embellished with classical references, and artistically adorned with literary color and metaphor. At the time, both scientists and the public at large found Frazer's erudition and style most persuasive.

Ever ready to shift his ground as new evidence surfaced, Frazer altered his interpretation of totemism when Baldwin Spencer and John Gillen published on the central Australian tribes. Like others of his time, Frazer made the Australian natives central to his description and theorizing. The initial essay distinguished clan, sex, and individual totems and avoided speculation about origins, save for a brief summary of Spencer's and Lord Avebury's ideas about animal ancestors and nicknames. In his third and "final" explanation of totemism Frazer (1935(4):64) traced its origins to the "sick fancies of pregnant women ... a creation of the feminine rather than of the masculine mind." In the absence of any notion of physiological paternity—a necessary and indisputable condition of early life—primitive men and women readily accepted the idea (still current in Frazer's time among animal and poultry breeders as well as among many housewives and husbands) that what is eaten and seen during pregnancy establishes such a special connection between the external object and the fetus that an indelible imprint is made. These dietary and sensory markings might not be permanent, but they raised the idea that the form bore some relation to a mother's heavy diet of fruits or special meats, and that the child's personality characteristics also reflected the choice of dietary animals (Frazer 1935(4):64–71). This absolutely primitive totemic base was found among the Banks Islanders, who believed that "their mothers were impregnated by the entrance into their wombs of spirit animals or spirit fruits, and that they themselves are nothing but the particular animal or plant which effected a lodgment in their mother and in due time was born into the world with a superficial and deceptive resemblance to a human being" (Frazer 1935(4):60–61). They refused to eat animals or plants from which they descended since such an act would be a "kind of cannibalism; they would in a manner be eating themselves" (Frazer 1935(4):59–60).

Frazer found his first psychological clue to totemism among the most primitive of all peoples, the Australian aborigines. It was logical to find the basis for totemism among those known to have the most elemental beliefs and customs. Oddly enough the more advanced Banks Islanders provided the missing link to totemism in its simplest form, antedating even the Australians. To test his theory Frazer relied on one or more examples of what his hypothesis reasonably called for, including a congruence between the explanatory capabilities of the theory and the manifold features of totemism. Frazer listed these requirements as follows:

1. The respectful abstention from injuring and eating the totem.
2. The periodic eating of the totem in order to identify and strengthen the self by "assimilating from time to time its flesh and blood or vegetable tissues."
3. The sharing of special qualities and powers by individuals with the same totem.
4. Descent from a totem as woman "sometimes [was] said to have given birth to these animals or plants" by entrance into her body.
5. The wide variety of totems in accordance with the unrestricted pregnancy fancies of women.
6. The confusion of ancestors with totems, since primitive men have difficulty in distinguishing "even in thought between their outward human appearance and their inward bestial or vegetable nature; they think of them vaguely both as man and as animals or plants (Frazer 1935(4):60–61).

Frazer subscribed to the Developmentalist assumption that uniform processes of the human mind accounted for the occurrence of similarities on a world-wide scale. This held for totemism. He was not convinced, however, that totemism had played an important part in the social and religious advancement and so rejected the thesis inspired by W. R. Smith.

> In estimating the part played by totemism in history I have throughout essayed ... to reduce within reasonable limits the extravagant pretensions which have sometimes been put forward on behalf of the institution, as if it had been a factor of primary importance in the religious and economic development of mankind. As a matter of fact the influence which it is supposed to have exercised on economic progress appears to be little more than a shadowy conjecture; and though its influence on religion has been real, it has been greatly exaggerated. By comparison with some other factors, such as the worship of nature and the worship of the dead, the importance of totemism in religious evolution is altogether subordinate. Its main interest for us lies in the glimpse which it affords into the working of the childlike mind of the savage; it is as it were a window opened up into a distant past. (Frazer 1935(4):Preface, xiii–xiv)

In this estimate Frazer edged close to Tylor's position and also underlined the fact that totemism and exogamy were not connected intrinsically. They had different origins and functions and their combination among certain tribes was an historic accident (Frazer 1935(4):xii).

Totemism, Psychology, and History: Goldenweiser. Frazer's monumental treatise on totemism and exogamy climaxed the efforts of Developmentalists to solve the vexing problems of primitive belief and practice with the aid of associational psychology. The rise of historicism and functionalism provoked counterarguments to the involved logic, basic assumptions, and methods of Developmentalism. In a studied analysis Goldenweiser (1933:319) first demonstrated that no classic totemistic complex existed, for its features varied in time and place. He then reduced totemism psychologically to nothing more than a "specific socialization of emotional values" (Goldenweiser 1933:319). Finally, he used the Northwest Coast Indians to show that the psychological process in totemism was a product of complex historic relationships. The complexity of the historic process could be inferred from the variant features of the totemic complex when surveying individual tribes, and also in the variability of social organization and mythology. To explain totemism or any cultural feature according to generalized psychological processes would be foolhardy. Goldenweiser concluded: "I do not hesitate to predict that further research in Australia will show that the interactions of cultural elements within each group are as intricate as are those between tribe and tribe. The conditions would then be analogous to those of the North-West" (Goldenweiser 1933:332).

Totemic Ritual and Social Solidarity: Radcliffe-Brown. In turn, functionalists pressed for an understanding of the socio-psychological processes by which human groups had become affiliated with some part of nature. The pioneer of functional social anthropology, Radcliffe-Brown (1965), traced the origins of totemism to a ritualization of sentiment in the hunting of animals for food. Out of this generalized totemism, specific moiety or clan totemism might develop through segmentation. Through the totemic relation "the clan recognises its unity and its individuality ... a special example of the universal process by which solidarity is created and maintained by uniting a number of individuals in a collective relation to the same sacred object or objects" (Radcliffe-Brown 1965b:128). The import of totemism was not limited to the clan, however. Beyond and through its clan segments a totemic society established ritual relations with the whole of nature. Through personification of species as ancestors or culture heroes, they reached a philosophic conception in which nature was considered to be a society of persons in the image of human society. Using the model of their own social and moral order, totemic societies projected a social and moral order for nature.

Radcliffe-Brown touched on old issues when he aligned totemism with the early history of hunting and gathering societies. By stressing the role of totemism in giving peoples a comprehensive view of the universe as a moral and social order, he took a position comparable to those who previously emphasized the sacred and moral character of early society. Small wonder, then, that he turned back to W. R. Smith, for ritual as the focus of primitive religion. In Fustel's *The Ancient City* he also found a "valuable contribution to the theory of the social function of religion" (Radcliffe-Brown 1965h:155–156, 161).

Return to Psychological Interpretation: Lévi-Strauss. Drawing upon the psychological orientation and methodology of structural linguistics, Lévi-Strauss (1963b:129–147) recently proposed a psychological interpretation of the totemistic phenomena. Reviewing explanations of totemism, Lévi-Strauss found that Radcliffe-Brown had stumbled upon a central feature of human thought when wrestling with the problem of Australian totemic classification. This universal feature of human mentality was simply the principle of the association of opposites. Intent on reaching a sociological explanation, Radcliffe-Brown was unable to fully appreciate or to bring out a fundamental psychological process—and one previously used by Rousseau and Bergson to account for totemism. To reinforce his advocacy of psychological explanations based on universal thought processes, Lévi-Strauss recommended that modern structuralism should set to work and refurbish associationist psychology. Associationists had in fact outlined the nature of elemental logic or the "lowest common denominator of all thought" (Lévi-Strauss 1963b:129–130). Their only mistake had been to attribute this basic logic of the human mind to an external sensory operation rather than to its proper inner configuration, or Gestalt. Gestalt was not Lévi-Strauss's term, and Gestalt psychologists did not appear in his bibliography, but his intent was obvious. Lévi-Strauss seemingly followed the simple logical process of configurating things in contrastive oppositions, for his interpretation centered on the contrast of intrinsic organization and extrinsic form.

It is interesting that both Radcliffe-Brown and Lévi-Strauss followed the intellectual spoor of nineteenth-century Developmentalism for clues to resolve the totemic problem. Their paths obviously were different, but their choices underscored the long-standing reality problem faced by anthropologists as well as other social scientists. In the theories of Smith and Jevons, Lévi-Strauss could have found explanations utilizing the principle of a union of opposites. Schurtz and Spencer, on the other hand, accented the processual segregation of contrastive types, as did Radcliffe-Brown.

SUMMARY

The rise of science challenged religion as the primary arbiter of truth. The idea of progress implied that knowledge, as other institutions, was a product of natural and cumulative growth. The idea of progressive revelation could accommodate religion in a developmental view. However, the apotheosis of reason during the Enlightenment provided an interpretation of man expanding his knowledge of God and the universe through extension of his capacity to critically analyze what he observed, especially in nature. Natural religion thus was opposed to revealed religion. The continuing advancement of knowledge, especially the observation of facts which contradicted religious teaching, reinforced a developmental view that religion was inadequate as a knowledge system and would be superseded by science. This was the meaning of Comte's sequence of knowledge systems and their coordinate social system—theological, metaphysical, and positivistic.

The eighteenth-century intellectual view encouraged an attitude which viewed religion as an institution which developed historically, as other institutions. However, it was not until advances in biology, human paleontology, geology, and prehistory added factual certainty to the developmental thesis that religion became an object of scientific investigation. Evolutionists continued the rationalistic lead initiated by eighteenth-century progressivists and renovated basic problems, such as the origins of a dualistic view of man and the universe, the transformation of spirit into deity, the relation of ethics to religion, and the importance of the religious institution in the development of society.

Developmentalist theories of duality and the origins of religion focused on man's sensory experience in relation to self-other awareness. The animistic theory of Tylor and Spencer derived from man's response to universal human experiences, such as death and dreams. Tylor viewed man positively as groping his way gradually to greater understanding as he developed the ideas of a double, ghost-soul, spirit, and deity. Spencer, on the other hand, saw primitive man negatively—his ideas of ghost, spirit, and deity illustrated lack of reason. Toward the end of the century Lang challenged the animistic interpretation with the theory that primitive man had developed supreme beings by apotheosizing great men because of their qualities of leadership and moral virtue. Marett rejected the institutionalization of Tylor's animism and theorized that a feeling of awe and wonder were inspired by the striking qualities of natural objects which led men to personalize them. This personalizing of natural phenomena and of objects made by man represented a stage in the development of religion that antedated animism. Marett's theory renovated an animatistic view of long standing just as Lang's ideas about the deification of great men coincided with those of Euhemerus. Frazer considered that man's experience with the supernatural began before an animistic religion was invented. Man first attempted to bend the world to his needs with the aid of magical formulas, and only when he failed did he realize that superior beings existed and must be propitiated.

In the evolution of religion there was considerable agreement that a general spirit worship preceded the rise of polytheistic nature gods and that monotheism represented a final intellectual step. However, religion was ineffectual in the modern world largely because it was incapable of organizing the ethical forces which modern society required. In place of an ethic based on a private relation between self and God, man in society needed to have the meaning of the social experience translated into a rational ethic that would embrace and define relationships among all men. Ethics must be secularized and made relevant to social needs in the same way that science was secularizing knowledge and making it relevant to human welfare.

In developmental perspective, religion belonged to the past. However, looking backward it was apparent that religion provided the integrative fiber of early societies before the commercial and industrial era. The rights exercised by citizens in the ancient world, as Fustel de Coulanges observed, were dependent on access to religious rites. According to Bachofen, the earliest society was matriarchal, and the whole social, legal, and political system was based on a religion in which the values and feelings as well as female symbols of fertility and of social relationships were accented.

Without the integrative bond of animal worship (totemism) McLennan found it hard to explain how early men were able to bring stability and continuity in their little bands expressly formed to insure protection and food for survival. Early society thus took on a sacred quality which W. R. Smith located in a sacrificial communion of the totem animal. The work of McLennan and of Smith called attention to totemism as a primitive religious phenomenon associated with social groups. An intensive exploration of totemism followed, with Jevons, Lippert, and Wundt theorizing that totemism supplanted the natural blood bond of early society with social relationships upon which complex societies could be formed. In Jevons' view, totemic worship even inspired the religious sentiment of love by eliminating the original hostility between men and animals. Lippert considered totemism a necessary antecedent to the development of a state organization, since it united people in cult worship under a political authority. Frazer, on the other hand, denied the historic and social significance of totemism and derived it from the hallucinations and other psychological associations of women at the time of pregnancy.

The social significance of cult totemism highlighted by Developmentalists in emphasizing the integrative function appealed to social structuralists like Durkheim and Radcliffe-Brown. Durkheim saw totemic members as mystically sharing a part of the divine totemic god. He explained the proscription of spilling the divine totemic blood by associating primitive anxiety over menstruation with descent from the totemic ancestor. Woman was the medium for transmitting the fundamental social relationship of the totemic clan, and the unconscious transfer of anxiety over menstruation united the taboo against killing the totem and the taboo against marrying a totemic member in a common complex. The maternal clan thus was the basic totemic and exogamic unit of primitive society. Totemism shaped primitive society by bringing to it a special philosophy which symbolized the unconscious affiliations felt by its members, and through ceremonial and ritual taboos made totemic affiliates consciously aware of the social bonds by which they were united.

Radcliffe-Brown derived totemism from a sentiment engendered by the dependence of hunters on animals for food. Totemism ritualized the primitive sentiment and in its association with clans increased the solidarity of primitive society. Personification of totemic animals as ancestors was a projection of man's own social and moral order onto the natural order.

The critical analysis of totemism made by culture historicist Goldenweiser led to the conclusion that there was no complex of features universally associated with totemism. Totemic complexes varied from area to area according to the circumstances of historical developments. His view that totemism psychologically was nothing more than a "specific socialization of emotional values" brought his explanation into line with Radcliffe-Brown's.

Anthropological explanations of totemic origins have oscillated between appeals to social and psychological processes. Recently Lévi-Strauss suggested that the social and ceremonial oppositions found in totemism are explainable by mental processes traceable in structural*functional operations of the human brain.

The prevalence of totemism in hunting and collecting and gardening societies explains the attention accorded the phenomenon in anthropological literature. Investigation of totemism was most intense from 1870 to 1930. By virtue of the complex interweaving of totemic ceremonial into their social and political life, native Australians emerged as central to discussion of the social, psychological, and evolutionary meaning of totemism.

7

Social Origins
and Continuities

●

PROBLEMS AND TRENDS IN NINETEENTH-CENTURY THEORIES

Developmentalists in the nineteenth century began the natural history of human society with a presavage state, traces of which could be found in symbolisms carried by the customs and institutions of contemporary savages. Although holding that the earliest social units were little more than aggregates of individuals banded together for survival, they held no brief for an original state of individual isolation. Like eighteenth-century progressivists, later evolutionists picked up the trail of man in his natural social state. There were, however, a number of unresolved issues. Did social development begin with elemental family units which gradually aggregated into larger communities? Or had social evolution begun with a primeval local group or horde, out of which lineages and then elemental families differentiated? Was the original condition of mankind one of peace or war?

Evolutionary concern for the dynamics of change might be expected to direct attention to adaptive processes accommodating internal and external forces. However, evolutionists found their real causes in ideas which were generated when men confronted a challenge or reflected on their circumstances. Social change was largely a continuity in social and legal understandings—ideas of paternity, kinship, ownership, incest, exogamy, marriage, mother-right, and father-right. The scientific problem consisted in determining the conditions by which socially relevant ideas had been evoked and developed. In their orientation to social origins and continuities, evolutionists renovated old problems; however, at the same time they broke new ground with a vast assemblage of facts and the coining of concepts that are still used in ethnology. Legally trained minds found the investigation of sociolegal ideas and norms operating in primitive societies a congenial endeavor. The three competing theories of social origins of that day were formulated by lawyers—McLennan, Maine, and Morgan.

The assumptions that simplicity and uniformity prevailed in early times largely shaped nineteenth-century conceptions of social origins. The human mind, conceptually speaking, was unorganized and subject to impulse. The struggle to get food was harsh and physical aggression was ever present. Necessity drove men into cooperation for protection and food; consequently, the earliest social units were local groups sharing land and women without any firm ideas of kinship. When the idea of kinship arose, it followed the natural association of mother and child. The idea of paternity appeared only when a wife and children could be legally possessed through purchase. Property and ideas associated with ownership stimulated new social arrangements, eroding an ancient maternal order and installing a paternal system. In shattering the primitive social communism, with its subjection of the individual to group demands, the idea of property opened the path to individual rights and freedoms. Custom, with its divine sanctions, gave way to a secular law drawn to the specifications of private interests. As a guarantor of private right and liberty, the state was as central to nineteenth-century evolutionists as to eighteenth-century progressivists. An enlightened and moral citizenry constituted the backbone of the perfected state, and as law moved from the divine to the secular, knowledge and morality also took on a more secular tone. During change, the relations of institutions were vital in determining the extent and rapidity of alteration. Although different institutions never changed at the same rate or in the same degree, a sufficient natural balance was maintained during change to produce a correlation in advancements in economy, society, law, knowledge, and morality.

ACQUIRED INSTINCTS AND HUMAN SOCIALITY IN EVOLUTIONARY PERSPECTIVE

The acceptance of man's affinity with the animal world directed attention to the physiological background of human nature and raised the problem of the source of human sociality. Was man a social being because of a biological given, or had the attribute been cultivated? Darwin (1936:498–499) was hesitant to leave the origin of the social instincts to the purposeless process of natural selection. Sympathy, fidelity, and courage, to which Darwin added Bagehot's obedience, were social qualities shared with animals; but in man habit and response to praise or blame had added measurably to man's social qualities. Darwin considered the pleasure experienced in social contacts to be a kind of extension, in all probability, of parental or filial sentiments which developed as a result of the prolonged childhood to which humans were subject. This social instinct owed its extension and entrenchment partially to habit but largely to natural selection. However, it was an advance in reasoning capabilities and in foresight that suggested to men the importance of sympathy and benevolence for survival. In aiding others, men formed ideas of reciprocity and of mutual aid and condemned those who ignored the morality intrinsic to social living. Indeed, the necessities of social life demanded that natural selection evoke the moral faculty. "Ultimately," observed Darwin (1936:500), "our moral sense or conscience becomes a highly complex sentiment—originating in social instincts, largely guided by the approbation of our fellow-men, ruled by reason, self-interest, and in later times by deep religious feelings, and confirmed by instruction and habit." At the private level the impact of moral advance would hardly be discerned,

> yet an increase in the number of well-endowed men and advancement in the standard of morality will certainly give an immense advantage to one tribe over another. A tribe including many members who, from possessing in a high degree the spirit of patriotism, fidelity, obedience, courage, and sympathy, were always ready to aid one another, and to sacrifice themselves for the common good, would be victorious over most other tribes; and this would be natural selection. At all times throughout the world tribes have supplanted other tribes; and as morality is one important element in their success, the standard of morality and the number of well-endowed men will thus everywhere tend to rise and increase. (Darwin 1936:500)

Adaptation to altered circumstances lies at the heart of the evolutionary process. Species, and even species varieties, may differ in the rate and degree of adaptation. In Darwin's view, man outstripped his nearest animal relatives and developed a singular capacity for social life by expanding the social context into a complex web of relations which involved feeling states, reason, and moral judgment. At the dawn of time it was expectable that primitive men would lack the social capacities of civilized men. In Spencer's judgment, the different varieties of mankind were not alike in their social capabilities. In the case of primitive man, it was not just that he was improvident—he lived " 'as if there were no other person in the world but himself' " (Spencer 1880–1896(1, Part 1):62). To this supreme egoism, savages added an impatience with all restraint, and hence they lacked a vital requirement of social living. The pressure of population, forcing individuals to cluster, induced primitive men to be more sociable and to realize the necessity for increasing the social quality of life in order to contain the anarchic strain of selfish egoism. To Spencer, primitive men were virtually destitute of social sentiments. Their loose aggregates were anchored precariously to appetite, approbation, and personal survival. Above all, the primitive incapacity for social living was evident in the lack of the altruistic sentiment, which accommodates personal ends to the needs of others. Primitive men also demonstrated a singular incapacity to comprehend abstract principles, such as equity and duty, which must govern public and private social relations (Spencer 1880–1896(1, Part 1): 73–74).

The fact that natural selection advanced the humanizing instincts obviously affected what man, according to his evolutionary state, shared with animals. According to Spencer's (1880–1896(1, Part 1):59–60) evolutionary views,

> the civilized man, passing through phases representing phases passed through by the race, will, early in life, betray this impulsiveness which the early race had. The saying that the savage has the mind of a child with the passions of a man (or, rather, has adult passions which act in a childish manner) possesses a deeper meaning than appears. There is a relationship between the two natures such that, allowing for differences in kind and degree in the emotions, we may regard the co-ordination of them in the child as analogous to the co-ordination in the primitive man.

In the individual ontogeny of civilized man, the instinctual past was lived through, but shed in manhood like the skin of a snake. Pitt-Rivers (1906:5) observed that the contrast between primitive and civilized man was not unlike the contrast between wild and domestic species. Animals under domestication lost the instincts acquired in their wild state, and so it was with man. There was more passion and less reason in the behavior of primitive. Moreover, savages were prone to draw faulty conclusions about things and relationships, whereas the civilized had perfected the logic of thought processes. Hence, Frazer (1935(4):41) warned against

> rationalistic theories which explain the customs of uncivilised peoples on the assumption that primitive man thinks and acts precisely in the way in which we should think and act if we were placed in his circumstance. No doubt it is hard for us to put ourselves at the point of view of the savage, to strip ourselves, not merely of the opinions imprinted on us by education, but also of the innate tendencies which we have inherited from many generations of civilised ancestors, and having thus divested ourselves of what has become a part of our nature to consider what we should do under conditions of life very different from those by which from infancy we have been surrounded. None of us can ever do this perfectly. . . .

The evolutionary orientation did not provide easy agreement on what man may or may not have shared with animals once the point of social take-off had been reached. Lippert (1931:23) held mother love to be the sole original social instinct possessed by man, and derived all social instincts from an intellectual faculty, foresight. Mankind did not even share a monogamous instinct with animals, which apparently accounted for the social grouping of some of the higher animals. It seemed wise to separate human instincts into primary or animal instincts anchored to body needs, and secondary, or acquired, social instincts. After all, Lippert noted, body and mind were distinctive operations. Pitt-Rivers (1906:56) described three primary instincts for man: "Alimentiveness, for the sustenance of life; amativeness, for the propagation of species; and combativeness, for the protection of species, and the propagation by natural selection of the most energetic breeds."

Evolutionist efforts to unite the biological and the social inevitably forced them into ambiguities in their quest for the sources of social behavior. Mind and will constantly got in the way of a thoroughgoing instinctual social evolutionism. In 1891 Westermarck (1924(2):370–373) attributed the origins of exogamy to an acquired instinct. The daily and intimate contacts of childhood generated an aversion which excluded close associates as sex objects. Frazer (1935(4):98) criticized Westermarck's explanation because it was rooted

> too exclusively [in] physical and biological causes without taking into account the factors of intelligence, deliberation, and will. It is too much under the influence of Darwin, or rather it has extended Darwin's methods to subjects which only partially admit of such treatment. . . . They would write the history of man without taking into account the things that make him a man and discriminate him from the lower animals.

Westermarck's intention was to show that the development of the instinctual aversion for brother or sister and for mother and father was a purposive, yet unconscious, product of natural selection. Since Darwin had demonstrated that inbreeding was injurious to the species, Westermarck (1924(2):370–373) concluded that natural selection worked to build a sentiment in man which forestalled injurious unions. Such a sentiment accrued naturally as inbreeding populations decayed and perished in the presence of the physically superior out-marrying populations. Westermarck did not know whether the sentiment was inherited from prehuman ancestors or whether it arose with the appearance of true man. It seemed to him that the sentiment must have appeared at a stage when the elementary family was strengthened by close sentimental bonds and children remained with parents until puberty.

Crawley's (1960) emphasis on the universality and constancy of physiological functions in organizing human behavior illustrated again the biological and psychological orientation that accompanied evolutionism. A changeless physiology supplied a constant factor uniting primitive and civilized thought, and Crawley (1960(1):4–5) stressed the subconscious persistence of primitive ideas among the civilized, despite outward changes due to education and environment. The prime characteristic of primitive thought was a concern for physiological functions associated with the instinct of self-preservation. An animal-based will to live drove every human being to insulate himself from whatever threatened his life (Crawley 1960(1):38–39). This was demonstrated by the universal primitive compulsion to protect survival functions by investing them with a sacred potential or quality. Nutrition, excretion, and sex formed a triad upon which primitive thought was reared. Taboos designed to insulate the person from harmful contacts and closures were the ideological counterparts of subconscious impulses associated with self-preservation. Hence the prohibitions against eating with strangers, the ritualization of food preparation and eating, including fasting, food avoidances, separation of the sexes, and special contacts to strengthen the individual. Mutilations, such as filing teeth, knocking out of teeth, circumcision, and perforation of the hymen, were all due to an apparant fear of closure, the idea being that by sacrificing a part the remainder will be preserved (Crawley 1960(1):169–172). From the start, then, primitive thought and society were organized by religious ceremony and regulations that protected the life, health, strength, and general well-being of the individual and of the community. This primitive concern for the primary functions followed man right into the stage of civilized living, constituting a part of the subconscious evolutionary heritage and ready to be awakened and channeled into religious activity as needed. Origins must begin with the elementary ideas arising from the basic functional processes and which must be universally present and relatively uniform in their effects (Crawley 1960(1):110).

Despite the use of biological processes to explain differences in race and culture, evolutionists had too much concern for the selective humanizing of mankind to abandon human behavior solely to biological devices. Mind, rather than physiology, provided the important constant for man as a social being. The task of subordinating human activity to instinctual impulses or dispositions fell to psychologists. In the instance of the psychologist McDougall (1914:26), instinct combined mental and physiological processes; but the driving force of instinct consisted of an inherited "compound system of sensori-motor arcs" not under the control of psychic processes. McDougall considered that all human activity, habituated or intellectualized, began with the driving force of instinct.

> The instinctive impulses determine the ends of all activities and supply the driving power by which all mental activities are sustained; and all the complex intellectual apparatus of the most highly developed mind is but a means towards these ends, is but the instrument by which these impulses seek their satisfactions, while pleasure and pain do but serve to guide them in their choice of the means.
>
> Take away these instinctive dispositions with their powerful impulses, and the organism would become incapable of activity of any kind; it would lie inert and motionless like a wonderful clockwork whose mainspring had been removed or a steam-engine whose fires had been drawn. These impulses are the mental forces that maintain and shape all the life of individuals and societies, and in them we are confronted with the central mystery of life and mind and will. (McDougall 1914:44)

The instincts which McDougall discriminated included flight, repulsion, curiosity, pugnacity, self-abasement, self-assertion, the parental, reproduction, gregariousness, acquisition, and construction. Each of these instincts had its own specific excitant. Under Watson's (1913) behaviorism, McDougall's mind and will dissolved in the physiological processes of stimulus-response and of Pavlov's conditioned reflexes.

WAR AND PEACE IN EARLY SOCIETY

In the perspective of evolutionism, the primeval state of man was war. At times evolutionary descriptions of early society recalled Hobbes's (1651) dictum that man in his precivil state lived in "continual fear and danger of violent death; and the life of man [was] solitary, poor, nasty, brutish, and short."

Following the law of survival, men in primeval society looked after themselves and ignored the rights of others. Taking note of the importance of natural selection, Maine (1887:226) wrote that

> Each fierce little community . . . [could be seen in perpetual] war with its neighbour, tribe with tribe, village with village. The never-ceasing attacks of the strong on the weak end in the manner expressed by the monotonous formula which so often recurs in the pages of Thucydides, "they put the men to the sword, the women and children they sold into slavery."

McLennan (1886:73) concurred: "Lay out the map of the world, and wherever you find populations unrestrained by the strong hand of government, there you will find perpetual feud, tribe against tribe, and family against family."

The step from war as a primitive condition of mankind to war as the social analog to biological natural selection was congenial to the evolutionist position. The political theorist Bagehot (1875:123–124) considered war a primary instrument for the adaptive modification of group heredity and the rise of civilization. Organized strength was the key to population increase and survival. Survival required disciplined obedience, intelligence, and morality. These conditions were met only in those societies that were organized militarily and instilled male values in the home. In making war the central condition of human progress, Bagehot followed the principle of survival of the fittest to its logical conclusion. Spencer avoided this step and pointed to the ultimate triumph of a countersurvival principle, altruism. However, for Bagehot war was the universal and necessary condition of man, and one which would not lessen with civilization. The biological struggle for survival must continue inexorably to eliminate the unfit. Whether one concentrated on the contacts of races or of cultures, Pitt-Rivers (1927:1–2) pointed out in the twilight of scientific evolutionism, natural selection was the key process.

> In whatever direction we turn throughout the world we may observe the same phenomenon: the clash and struggle for supremacy between races, between cultures and between warring groups—social, cultural, economic or occupational—banded together in defence of their interests. If we look deeper we discover that this competition is not merely for supremacy, but is a struggle for survival.

The healthy competition that progressivists of earlier days considered essential to the development of human character and society now was translated into a bitter survival struggle of individual and group dominance. An anxious, uncontrollable egoism ruled man's character, and it was hard to argue that serious differences separated civilized man from his primitive ancestors in this regard.

Those who found man's existence something more than a callous struggle for survival turned to the family as the elementary cooperative and peace-abiding unit of human society. In Tylor's view, there was no time when men struggled egoistically against all others; for the family exhibited that basic and orderly arrangement upon which society everywhere was founded. According to Wundt (1928:111), families in ancient times were relatively isolated, and except for the occasional slaying, people lived in peace. The search for food played an important part in keeping family groups apart, thereby minimizing opportunities for conflict. According to Westermarck (1924(2):195), primeval family groups in all probability followed the diet of the manlike apes and gathered in large numbers only during a fruit harvest. Even after man took to the use of fish and flesh foods, he still must have existed in some isolation. Noting that friendly tribes were known to prohibit the killing of their neighbors, Westermarck (1924(1):333–334) cautioned against assuming that savage tribes lived either in isolation or were continually fighting with their neighbors. War was a later condition of mankind, usually generated by population growth, economic pressures, and migrations.

THE PRIMITIVE HORDE, POLYANDRY, AND PATERNITY: McLENNAN'S THESIS

McLennan presented a complex argument for the rise of exogamy out of bride capture. This practice was prompted by the cruel custom of infanticide, which was initiated to save food for males in an economy disrupted by constant war and aggression. The local horde, or stock, as McLennan called it, was the original social unit of mankind. It practiced a communal sharing of food, protection, and sexual resources, but gradually was translated into a maternal descent group by the idea of a kin blood bond perceived and reasoned out of the mother-child relationship. As yet there was no fatherhood, for marriage in a civilized sense was not practiced. Wrote McLennan (1865:163), "As we go back, we find more and more in men the traits of gregarious animals; slighter and slighter indications of operative intellect. As among other gregarious animals, the unions of the sexes were probably in the earliest times, loose, transitory, and in some degree promiscuous."

Once motherhood emerged with the notion of female descent, brothers and sisters were distinguished and collected with their maternal kin through common residence, as among the Nairs of Malabar. Here a rude type of polyandry was found, since women remained with their descent groups and held husbands who were not related. In the next step along the road to paternity a woman was detached from her kin by establishing a separate residence with the husbands. The children still were affiliated with the wife's kin with heirship rights to kin property, since the husbands were not related and hence were not in a legal position to appropriate the children. Such would be the situation under nonfraternal polyandry. Subsequently a group of brothers married a single woman and brought her to their kin. The community of blood among the husbands then would permit them to take possession of the children. With this act they disqualified the children as heirs of their mother's kin (McLennan 1865:190–193). The fraternal polyandry of the Tibetans illustrated a trend toward a kind of *paterfamilias* in that the eldest brother managed the family, including his junior brothers. The idea of fatherhood emerged as putative fathers made gifts to their putative children, and economic considerations were added to discourage reversion of children and property to the maternal line. The succession of a younger brother to the position of household head under a levirate arrangement, which enjoined him to procreate children for the deceased, also fostered paternalistic trends, since all children now were considered to have a father. Considerations of property and heirship thus aroused the idea of fatherhood; and as paternity and wealth were combined, the social force necessary to produce a system of kinship through males was at hand (McLennan 1865:244). The economic interests of this emergent patriarchal system led to the treatment of women as property, especially when purchased as brides.

The practices of exogamy and endogamy held opposite effects for the make-up of local populations. Exogamy increased the heterogeneity of the group while endogamy moved toward homogeneity. McLennan envisioned social groups based on bloodlines as cycling between trends toward heterogeneity. For example, the ancient maternal organization, which male kinship succeeded, moved to a condition of mixed population through bride capture and formal exogamy. However, as warrior groups out of pride indulged in endogamous marriages, a trend toward heterogeneity and homogeneity set in. In time the limited supply of available nonkin spouses was exhausted and the group was forced into wife capture in order to fulfill the exogamic injunction. The same history followed male kinship. Here McLennan (1865:249–262) had in mind Hindu *gotrams* operating exogamously within endogamous castes and also the case of Bedouins and Hebrews who exercised endogamous preference.

McLennan viewed the family as a product of the decay of the kin group, and not its antecedent. He thus opposed Maine's idea that political units had gradually developed as kin multiplied around the patriarchal family, successively arranging themselves into gens and tribes. On the contrary, bloodline groups arose as the local stocks split. With the emergence of agnatic lines, political ties among these localized blood kin strengthened. However, the agnatic process was heavily involved in a new idea of property ownership—private possession. The ancient idea of communal property under maternal descent lines naturally was destroyed by succession of the agnatic kin; but in the process the kin group or gens also was seeded with decay. What emerged in time was a patriarchal type of family, which, like the Roman, served as the fundamental intermarrying and property-holding unit. With the fading of kin groups based on the blood tie, exogamy and endogamy could no longer be sustained (McLennan 1865:266–286). Throughout this process of social differentiation the control of property proved vital to heirship, and it was equally important for the emergence of monogamy. War contributed materially to the idea of monogamous possession as powerful chiefs sought to keep their wives to themselves (McLennan 1865:244–245).

FROM PROMISCUITY TO MONOGAMY: MORGAN'S THESIS

"In treating the subject of the growth of the idea of government," wrote Morgan (1964:49), "the organization into gentes on the basis of kin naturally suggests itself as the archaic framework of ancient society; but there is a still older and more archaic organization, that into classes on the basis of sex." To Morgan (1964:49–50) the Australian marriage classes described by the Reverend Fison were of great importance, since they represented an ancient and extraordinary stage in the social history of the human race, because here one discerned the germinal principle of the gens.

The Australian materials held an even greater theoretical meaning for Morgan since they confirmed inferences about early society set forth in his *Systems of Consanguinity and Affinity of the Human Family* (1871). In that work he used kinship terminologies to infer corresponding kinds of family organization; but it was the latter, in his view, which gave rise to the former. The imaginative linkage of family types and kinship types, drawing on the assembly and analysis of 139 tribal systems, produced a new turn in the study of social organization. In the words of Lowie (1937: 62), "Morgan's unique distinction lies in literally creating the study of kinship systems as a branch of comparative sociology." There were none, with the exception of Lafitau (1724), who had been persuaded to pay more than passing attention to classifications of kin, and Morgan apparently wrote in ignorance of the Jesuit missionary. Morgan hoped to unfold the genealogical history of mankind by tracing descent through resemblances in their fundamental institutions—more notably the systems of consanguinity and affinity. This hope received added fuel in 1859 when Morgan received a list of Tamil kin terms and noted that they were similar to systems found among certain American Indians. Morgan was convinced that he now held solid evidence that the American Indians originated in Asia (White, in Morgan 1964:xvi). In his kin terms Morgan was convinced, too, that he had a more stable and reliable instrument than language for tracing ethnic relations. Sharing a common view that symbolic forms (survivals) were perfect witnesses for the real thing, Morgan used his classificatory categories as pathways to the distant past. Thus, if peoples held that the children of brothers and sisters were sons and daughters of one and all, this could only be a relic of the time when brothers in fact did marry sisters, real and collateral. It was this tendency to classify consanguine or lineal and collateral relations in categories that led Morgan to discriminate classificatory and descriptive terminological systems. In place of merging lineals and collaterals, descriptive systems used primary terms of relationship or their combinations to give precise denotations to relationships—for example, a brother's son or father's brother's son (Morgan 1964:333–334). The descriptive system was a recent product of human social progress and was associated with monogamous marriage, especially with the Aryan, Semitic, and Uralian language families.

In the Australian record Morgan found what he considered direct evidence for the earliest human family type, the consanguine. This earliest of units was composed of males drawn together for the joint purposes of a common subsistence and protection of their wives. Morgan (1964:508) seemed to think that the original state of society required cooperative action because of the internecine warring that went on. For example, among the Kamilaroi situated along the Darling River north of Sydney, Australia, the sexes were organized into marriage classes (four male and four female); and Morgan (1964:50) also inferred that an "inchoate organization into gentes on the basis of kin " also was present. Descent through females suggested an archaic gens, and the antiquity of the marriage classes was clued to the practice of group marriage. According to their marriage class system, one quarter of Kamilaroi males would be united with one quarter of the females. The Kamilaroi marriage system was but once removed from promiscuity, the original condition of mankind (Morgan 1964:53). The *punalua* marriage system of the Hawaiians was like the Australian variant, and Morgan (1877:59–60) went on to observe:

> Wherever the middle or lower stratum of savagery is uncovered, marriage of entire groups under usages defining the groups, have been discovered either in absolute form, or such traces as to leave little doubt that such marriages were normal throughout this period of man's history. It is immaterial whether the group, theoretically, was large or small, the necessities of their condition would set a practical limit to the size of the group living together under this custom. If then a community of husbands and wives is found to have been a law of the savage state, and, therefore, the essential condition of society in savagery, *the inference would be conclusive that our own savage ancestors shared in this common experience of the human race.*
>
> In such usages and customs an explanation of the low condition of savages is found. If men in savagery had not been left behind, in isolated portions of the earth, to testify concerning the early condition of mankind in general, it would have been impossible to form any definite conception of what it must have been. An important inference at once arises, namely, *that the institutions of mankind have sprung up in a progressive connected series, each of which represents the result of unconscious reformatory movements to extricate society from existing evils.* The wear of ages is upon these institutions, for the proper understanding of which they must be studied in this light. *It cannot be assumed that the Australian savages are now at the bottom of the scale, for their arts and institutions, humble as they are, show the contrary; neither is there any ground for assuming their degradation from a higher condition, because the facts of human experience afford no sound basis for such an hypothesis. Cases of physical and mental deterioration in tribes and nations may be admitted, for reasons which are known, but they*

never interrupted the general progress of mankind. All the facts of human knowledge and experience tend to show that the human race, as a whole, have steadily progressed from a lower to a higher condition. *The arts by which savages maintain their lives are remarkably persistent. They are never lost until superseded by others higher in degree. By the practice of these arts, and by the experience gained through social organizations, mankind have advanced under a necessary law of development, although their progress may have been substantially imperceptible for centuries.* It was the same with races as with individuals, although tribes and nations have perished through the disruption of their ethnic life. (Italics supplied)

In the Australian case Morgan detected an unconscious reformatory tendency for social progress in breaking down the partially promiscuous marriage classes by marriage rules of the more advanced gens organization. The change for the better revealed operation of the principle of natural selection (Morgan 1877:425). With the perspective of a lawyer, Morgan viewed individuals and groups as possessing special rights sanctioned by custom and law, and it was resistance to abandonment of rights in hand that maintained tradition. Indeed, the marriage regulations of the Kamilaroi exerted such a restrictive hand on their development that Morgan (1877:59) considered they must remain in that cultural state for thousands of years. Here Morgan perceptively observed the integral connection between social rules and laws, and the social order, and saw change as possible only when the rules were modified.

The consanguine family represented an advance over promiscuity in that parent-child marriages were forbidden. At the same time, the countenancing of brother-sister marriage on a group basis, deduced from the Malayan terms of address in which cousins were merged with brothers and sisters, indicated a long way to go. Morgan (1877:408) was convinced that the classificatory implications of the Malayan system of consanguinity allowed the inference that a consanguine family was in existence at the time the system was formed. When real brothers and sisters were forbidden to marry but putative brothers and sisters (collaterals) could do so, the Punaluan family, as found among the Hawaiians, arose.

A change in family type precipitated changes in social organization and in the system of consanguinity. The important trend lay in the development of the gens, which brought more restrictions with regard to marriage partners. "As intermarriage in the gens was prohibited, it withdrew its members from the evils of consanguine marriages, and thus tended to increase the vigor of the stock" (Morgan 1877:69). The sequential changes produced two new systems of consanguinity and affinity, the Asiatic Turanian (patrilineal with gens) and the American Ganowanian (matrilineal with gens). Actually but minor differences separated the two systems, for both were designed to register extensions of a prohibition of the marriage of collaterals (first cousins in this case) who were classified as brothers and sisters. Both the Turanian and Ganowanian systems were engrafted, as it were, on the prior Malayan and naturally carried over some of its features. That changes in the systems of consanguinity followed modifications in the family was disclosed by the fact that the Punaluan family had not yet changed to the Turanian system, while the Australians had (Morgan 1877:433–442).

The process of change to the Turanian and Ganowanian orders was long and gradual. A drying up of a consanguineal pool of wives was especially critical. Morgan (1877:458) pointed to the structure and principles of gens organization as a primary factor in creating a "prejudice against the marriage of consanguinei, [especially] as the advantages of marriages between unrelated persons were gradually discovered through the practice of marrying out of the gens." Lacking a sufficient pool of consanguines, a gens negotiated for brides and acquired wives by purchase and capture. However, purchase and capture were not conducive to sharing, and a rather unstable type of paired marriage arose, the Syndyasmian. The Syndyasmian union of single male and female spouses carried no severe sanctions and, for stability, relied largely on the persuasiveness of the gentile kin. In an evolutionary sense Morgan found no signal impact of the Syndyasmian marriage on the systems of consanguinity and affinity. In a further qualification, Morgan was willing to admit differences in the evolutionary appearance of family types among historic peoples. Some Punaluan families might appear quite by accident during the time when the consanguine type prevailed. Morgan (1877:462) added that "some tribes attained to a particular form earlier than other tribes more advanced; for example, the Iroquois had the syndyasmian family while in the Lower Status of barbarism, but the Britons, who were in the Middle Status, still had the punaluan."

The Monogamian family appeared in the later period of barbarism. The germ of monogamy was present in the lower Syndyasmian family where single males and females were paired (Morgan 1877:471). Monogamy accompanied the emergence of paternal power as the gens was transformed from a female to a male descent group. The source for this great transformation was property, which aroused the idea of transmitting an inheritance to children, and this awakened and stabilized paternal power. The massing of wealth in quantity and in variety (houses, lands, flocks, herds, commodities), stimulated a collection of agnates around the patriarch, as exemplified in the Hebrew and Roman family types. It was largely through the medium of the soil that the family became identified as a distinct property-making organization, holding its own slaves and servants. Before that time, Morgan (1877:543–544) observed,

> flocks and herds would naturally fall under the joint ownership of persons united in a group, on a basis of kin, for subsistence. Agnatic inheritance would be apt to assert itself in this condition of things. But when lands had become the subject of property, and allotments to individuals had resulted in individual ownership, the third great rule of inheritance, which gave the property to the children of the deceased owners, was certain to supervene upon agnatic inheritance.

The effect of property upon civilization indeed was enormous. But though property stimulated man to new heights—establishing moral possession over spouse, promoting a Monogamian family, translating the systems of consanguinity from classification to description (Aryan, Semitic, and Uralian varieties), provoking complex social and political organization, and assuring individual rights through inheritance—man's final purpose could not be found in property. The rise of civilization owed much to the Semitic and Aryan families. Indeed, the Aryan family clearly demonstrated its superiority over other peoples and its central place in the civilizing process by gradually extending its control and influence throughout the world (Morgan 1877:553). Still the advance to civilization struck Morgan as a chain of fortuitous circumstances. The fortuity, however, was there by design. Morgan (1877:554) considered the "labours . . . trials and . . . successes [of mankind's evolutionary history] were a part of the plan of the Supreme Intelligence to develop a barbarian out of a savage, and a civilized man out of this barbarian."

PRIMITIVE PROMISCUITY: PRO AND CON

Exogamic Rules and Sexual Reform

In advancing the idea of primitive promiscuity Morgan recycled an ancient and timeworn idea, and one generally rejected by eighteenth-century progressivists. Primitive promiscuity was acceptable to McLennan (1865) but not essential to his argument. Bachofen (1861) argued for an original promiscuity supported by religious sanctions. He considered the custom of temple prostitution a symbolic act of ritual expiation to atone for formal marriage, which violated the ancient sacralized promiscuity. A zero point of promiscuity, of course, was quite logical in the context of a primitive economic communism. An original promiscuity also was congenial to those, who, like Bagehot (1875) and Lippert (1931), stressed the uncontrolled egoism of savage man and his lack of regard for life. Those who looked upon rules of exogamy as steps in moral reform also found savage promiscuity to be a logical beginning. Frazer (1935(1):351–357) cited traditional native explanations of exogamy as a basis for accepting a primeval promiscuity and the tendency for moral reform. He noted that in their myths the Australian Dieri recounted that their exogamic rules were deliberately introduced to eradicate the evil of promiscuity. In the process of reform Frazer was willing to find primitive analogs to historic lawgivers. Some man of "keener mind and stronger character" persuaded his fellows to accept his social invention as meritorious. Emphasizing that differences in degree rather than kind separated savage from civilized brother, Frazer (1935(1):282) anticipated that primitive deliberations and legislations had occurred that were not unlike historic councils and parliaments. "Among savage customs," wrote Frazer (1935(1):282), "there are few or none that bear the impress of thought and purpose stamped upon them so clearly as the complex yet regular marriage system of the Australian aborigines." The formal licenses and sexual hospitality accorded categories of kin in Australian practice also were viewed as relics of a time when sexual communism prevailed (Frazer 1935(1):313). Finally, there was the challenge of the classificatory kinship systems raised by Morgan. Both Frazer (1935(1):307) and Rivers (1907:323) were in agreement that the nearly universal distribution of the classificatory system indicated that its origin rested on a near-universal stage of social development characterized by group marriage.

Sexual Jealousy and Promiscuity: Darwin

Curiously, counterarguments to primitive promiscuity developed in strength as the rise of evolution prompted a more considered examination of animal habits in trying to find analogs to human sociality. Darwin (1936:893–894) in *The Descent of Man*, while admitting that the "licentiousness of many savages is no doubt astonishing," called for more evidence before accepting an original state of promiscuity as fact. Even though marriage probably did develop gradually, Darwin could not believe that the prehuman ancestors of man were promiscuous in an absolute sense. A strong feeling of sexual jealousy ran throughout the whole animal kingdom, and this, in conjunction with the sexual behavior of animals closest to man anatomically, precluded an unrestrained promiscuity. Man's quadrumanous congeners demonstrated both monogamous and polygamous family arrangements, and the fighting which erupted at the time of pairing not only supported his theory of sexual selection but also rendered it improbable that promiscuous intercourse was a fact of life in the natural state (Darwin 1936:895).

> Therefore, looking far enough back in the stream of time, and judging from the social habits of man as he now exists, the most probable view is that he aboriginally lived in small communities, each with a single wife, or if powerful with several, whom he jealously guarded against all other men. Or he may not have been a social animal, and yet have lived with several wives, like the gorilla.... (Darwin 1936:896)

THE PRIMAL PATRIARCHAL HORDE AND SEXUAL POSSESSIVENESS: ATKINSON AND LANG

Taking their cue from Darwin, Lang and Atkinson (1908) held that a patriarchal sexual group was characteristic of early society. When a patriarch allowed an elder son, perhaps on the plea of a mother, to remain with the group—provided he obtained a mate from outside—exogamy began. A polygynous family raised on sexual jealousy provided Freud (1918) with a primordial setting for a primeval Oedipal situation which would be re-enacted in the sexual ontogeny of all descendants. This was a theme reminiscent of the wrath of God incurred by the sin of Adam. The theme was also found in Greek tragedy where Furies were unleashed to avenge the misconduct of an ancestor. Hose and McDougall (1912(2):197–198, note 1) saw a patriarchal sexual group advancing morally when young men from abroad appeared with price in hand and tempted the patriarch to sell a bride. In exchange for wealth, the patriarch was forced to regulate his own sexual appetites and to refrain from taking daughters as wives. The instinct of jealousy provided a basis for the beginnings of exogamy, but pecuniary motives were necessary to formalize the practice in an expanded family community.

Social Sentiments and Promiscuity: Wake

The review of human marriage which Wake (1835–1910) published in 1889 also challenged the original presence of promiscuity and communism. Wake tilted at the evidence cited and cast doubt on the priority of maternal descent over the paternal. For his disproof, Wake (1889:1–3) relied on secondary social instincts to exert restraints over the instincts of sex and self-preservation shared by man and animal. A fraternal instinct or a feeling of kindred countered the sexual instinct with a strong feeling that alliances should not occur between those closely related. Custom simply formalized this instinctive feeling in rules of exogamy. An original promiscuity thus was impossible, although Wake was willing to admit that group marriage did exist in Australia and in Hawaii. He objected to Morgan's theory of the reformatory extension of a prohibition against intermarriage to include tribal brothers and sisters not closely related. It was more logical to see the prohibition as the result of powerful revulsion against blood intermarriage which uncultured peoples universally experienced. Wake (1889:269) also called upon a parental instinct, evident in the social rights exercised over a woman and her children by father or kindred to throw up a powerful barrier to promiscuity. With such arguments Wake (1889:129) attempted to turn back Morgan's family sequence from consanguine to Punaluan —derived inferentially from the classificatory systems—as pure hypothesis.

In charting the developmental history of the family, Wake (1889:131–134, 226–227) was willing to begin with the Australian type of group marriage and the simple Punalua of the Hawaiians, where several brothers in one instance shared wives in common, or several sisters shared husbands. By reducing the male or female spouses to one, under the above arrangements, polygyny or polyandry resulted. Polyandry, Wake noted, was most often found where peoples were impoverished, and polygyny was a correlate of affluence. Both were found predominantly among peoples who traced their descent in the male line. Wake (1889:227–228) distinguished simple and advanced types according to whether the spouses were real brothers and sisters or related in no way. By reducing the multiple spouses of polyandry and polygyny to one each, *monandry*, or individual marriage, resulted. This might arise out of a group marriage situation or equally out of polyandry or polygyny. But monandry could not be monogamy until it was strengthened by a sacralizing and moralizing of the husband-wife relation—an apparent accomplishment of the Aryan nations (Wake 1889:434–475). The trend to monogamy produced the descriptive system of relationship. This had the effect of accenting descent through both male and female lines alike. Descriptive systems, monogamy, and bilateral descent thus were associated, as Morgan had found. For Morgan, the rich attainment of monogamy was due to the certainty it conveyed to parentage. Wake (1889:473–475), in recalling theological preferences for virginity over the married state, hazarded the idea that intellectual and moral objections to marriage might lead to acceptance of the view that a virginal existence was proper for those intellectually and morally ahead of their fellows!

Wake also raised doubts about the precedence of maternal over paternal descent. Kinship (descent) discriminated a narrower range of relations than was potentially available; for a "man may be related generally through his father to one class of individuals, and through his mother to another class" (Wake 1889:267). The parental instinct led peoples to apply the principle of a general relationship to the child, thereby connecting him to both father and mother, rather than the narrower kinship principle of descent through males or females (compare Fortes' concept of filiation). Therefore, something more than the idea of paternity or maternity must be involved in kinship. The answer, Wake (1889:269) claimed, could be found in the conditions governing the marital relations of parents. What appeared important was not the husband-wife relation but whether a natural right to the children was surrendered. In the absence of a marriage contract specifying surrender by a woman's kin of their rights over the children, they normally could claim the children. With the bride price as an incentive, a woman would be inclined to separate herself from her family; and in residing with her husband he would exercise legal control over the offspring (Wake 1889:325). Wake glimpsed the importance of residence as influencing a group toward female or male kinship, but did not consider residence sufficient to effect the change (see Smith 1903:61–63). For example, females might reside with the kin of their husbands, but the totemic affiliation early associated with female kinship would continue to exercise a restraining influence as to rights over the children by the husband's kin.

Natural Selection and Promiscuity: Westermarck

Although devoted to the evolutionist position, Westermarck (1922(1): 103–336) assembled voluminous evidence to contradict the notion that primitive promiscuity stemmed from an unorganized biological and psychological base. The whole thrust of natural selection lent itself to the preservation and improvement of life; and, since inbreeding was harmful, organisms were biologically and psychically organized through gradual adaptation to avoid what was injurious to the species. In man, the process leading to incest regulations (exogamy) drew heavily upon the psychic quality of human nature, and it was here that Westermarck (1922(2):218–219) located the incest-control processes. At the same time he stressed a "deep biological foundation . . . suggested by a multitude of facts relating both to animals and plants." The jealousy of animals alluded to by Darwin also applied to men, and the apparent seasonal expression of the sexual impulse recorded in the statistics of births likewise was used to discount the idea that a continuous sexual excitation promoted promiscuity (Westermarck 1922(1):78–102). The psychic expression of the biological impulse to preserve and improve the species became an instinctual aversion to sexual relations with near relations and associates during the time when the sexual instinct was unfolding. What kept males attached to females following sexual relations was an instinct. An instinct, Westermarck concluded, also must be operating to account for the interest which a father showed in the care of his offspring. As Westermarck (1922(1):70) saw it, a paternal feeling was as prevalent among savages as among civilized. Various habits, customary rules, and institutions were raised upon these maternal and paternal instincts, and if a man abandoned a woman whose children he had sired, the act would arouse moral resentment among the people. Westermarck (1922(1):71) traced conceptions of personal rights and duties to this public moral resentment.

Monogamy thus must be considered the natural state of man, from earliest to civilized times. For one thing, monogamy alone was universal. Monogamy was present even where polygyny, polyandry, and group marriage were practiced (Westermarck 1922(3):104). Polygyny thrived on new economic and status opportunities accompanying a more affluent life. Westermarck considered the reversion to monogamy in the highest grades of culture due to more refined views on moral relations uniting the sexes, and a general desire for smaller families during the rise of industrialism. Genuine group marriage seemed to exist in association with polyandry and also arose out of a combination of polygyny with polyandry; but in no instance could it be proved that groups of real brothers were married to a number of real sisters (Westermarck, 1922(3):328–338). However, the widespread occurrence of a family organization among primitive peoples suggested to Westermarck (1922(1):69) that the "family may have been an inheritance from the parent species out of which the Anthropoids and the Hominides—the *Pithecanthropus, Homo primigenius,* and *Homo sapiens*— gradually developed." The lowest savages, as well as the most civilized races, were organized in families. The father as protector and supporter of the human family had his counterpart among the manlike apes (Westermarck 1922(1):37). With the father serving as family head and protector in early families, Westermarck (1922(1):45–46) judged that the idea of a primitive matriarchy, in which the father had no rights or duties, would be hard to sustain.

ANCIENT LAW AND THE PATRIARCHAL FAMILY: MAINE

Both Wake and Westermarck concluded that the important social unit of early society was a paternal monogamous family. Moreover, the paternal family was the primary unit in the evolution of society. More than thirty years before, Maine's (1861) researches on Hindu family law led him to propose the patriarchal family as the cell with which Aryan and Semitic social history had begun. By coincidence *Ancient Law* appeared in the same year that Bachofen published *Das Mutterrecht* and theorized that a matriarchal period preceded the male-dominated Greek, Roman, and Semitic societies. Like Aristotle, Maine pointed to a natural hierarchy where males were dominant over women and children, and the strong, with appropriate customary or legal restraints, ruled the weak. The patriarchal family was founded on two basic facts of nature: (1) the implicit obedience which was given to a male parent and (2) sexual jealousy, the mightiest of all passions, and one which men shared with animals (Maine 1887: 133–136; 1883:205). Indeed, Maine (1883:205) was willing to make sexual jealousy the "force binding together and propelling the ancient social order." Males were the core of that social order and dominated it to the virtual exclusion of females, who were incapable legally of passing on descent or the right to property. Women were included in the descent group through the exercise of guardianship and nothing more. By adopting strangers and slaves, the family expanded in size, with all subject to the rule of a petty monarch, the patriarch. At ritual sacrifices the consanguine bond would be reconsecrated, the pledge and witness of the perpetuity of family brotherhood (Maine 1883:131, 191–193).

In looking backward to those ancient times Maine (1887:183–184) imagined the land occupied by numerous small despotic kingdoms, each separate from the other and ruled by a patriarchal monarch. However, the patriarch was no unrestrained tyrant, and could not be called *Paterfamilias* in the Roman meaning of the term:

> though the Patriarch ... had rights thus extensive, it is impossible to doubt that he lay under an equal amplitude of obligations. If he governed the family, it was for its behoof. If he was lord of its possessions, he held them as trustee for his children and kindred. He had no privilege or position distinct from that conferred on him by his relation to the petty commonwealth which he governed. The Family, in fact, was a Corporation; and he was its representative or ... its Public officer. He enjoyed rights and stood under duties ... as much those of the collective body as his own. (Maine 1883:183–184)

The position of the patriarch exemplified the common principle by which primitive society and even the ancient civilized world was organized. The individual did not exist as a discrete person but only as a member of a group (Maine 1883:183). The individuality of any person was swallowed up in family, gens, social class, and society at large. Whether real or fictional, the blood relationship constituted the fulcrum of early society—not the individual. Yet,

The movement of progressive societies [of which the Aryan and Semitic were most prominent] has been uniform in one respect. Through all its course it has been distinguished by the gradual dissolution of family dependency, and the growth of individual obligation in its place. The individual is steadily substituted for the Family, as the unit of which civil laws take account. (Maine 1883:168)

In other words, the trend had been from kin reciprocities to contract, from obligations binding upon the individual because of his group membership to a social order in which rights and duties were freely entered by individual agreements. The choice of the starting social unit differed from McLennan and Morgan, but Maine agreed that primitive society was organized for group welfare and not designed to serve the individual in pursuit of his private interests. The emancipation of the individual was a product of civilization.

The notion that the patriarchal family united a group of male kin (agnates) subject to a powerful father figure naturally countered the matriarchal theory as well as the idea expressed by McLennan and Spencer, that the first social units were territorial aggregates formed for survival by unrelated individuals without any conception of kinship. Maine (1883:183) opened new grounds for controversy by observing that the simpler societies exhibited the beginnings of a universal patriarchal succession. In counterarguments to McLennan and Spencer, he continually emphasized sexual jealousy and the power of the strong man as basic to the formation of kin groups and of political organization generally (Maine 1883:204–216). Maine defended his Aryan ancestors against the challenge of promiscuity with evolutionary arguments. He noted that the paramount successes of the Aryans implied that they were a powerful race. They must have been monogamous and fecund, since the two were associated. Female descent actually represented an aberration and depended upon special conditions. Moreover, if there was a stage antecedent to paternal rule and kinship, it must have been composed of both male and female groups united over a number of generations. Inevitably, however, agnation would reappear with "paternity . . . in association with Power and Protection" (Maine 1883:287–288). Maine underscored the fact that the basis for agnation was a father's authority, and not the marriage of a father- and mother-to-be. The *potestas* determined the beginnings and the end of kinship, for when a father emancipated his son he lost all rights of agnation.

Maine's contribution lay not in countering the matriarchal theory with priority of the patriarchal but in his attempt to bring out the corporate nature of the kin group. The kin corporation was succeeded by a territorial unit, and in the process kinship obligations gave way to individual contract. Beginning with a patriarchal family uniting the male descendants of an ancestor, there was a transition in the Hindu joint family inasmuch as kinship still reigned but members were occupied as much at trades and crafts as in working the land (Maine 1875:78–79). House communities found among the southern Slavs represented a next step. They still retained many of the features of the joint family, but were more closely tied to the land as an enterprise. From Maine's (1875:80–81) viewpoint,

> House communities seem ... to be simply the Joint Family of the Hindoos, allowed to expand itself without hindrance and settled for ages on the land. All the chief characteristics of the Hindoo institution are here—the common home and common table, which are always in theory the centre of Hindoo family life; the collective enjoyment of property and its administration by an elected manager. Nevertheless, many instructive changes have begun which show how such a group modified itself in time. The community is a community of kinsmen; but, though the common ancestry is probably to a great extent real, the tradition has become weak enough to admit of considerable artificiality being introduced into the association, as it is found at any given moment, through the absorption of strangers from outside. Meantime, the land tends to become the true basis of the group; it is recognized as of pre-eminent importance to its vitality, and it remains common property, while private ownership is allowed to show itself in moveables and cattle. In the true Village-Community [which next develops] the common dwelling and common table which belong alike to the Joint Family and to the House-Community, are no longer to be found. The village itself is an assemblage of houses, contained indeed within narrow limits, but composed of separate dwellings, each jealously guarded from the intrusion of a neighbour. The village lands are no longer the collective property of the community; the arable lands have been partially divided; only the waste remains in common.

The present-day Indian village community had all but lost its sense of common blood and descent and it was now the land which held the men together. Maine (1875:82) forecast that the effect of English law on Indian social and legal arrangements would lead to the eventual dissolution of the village community and correlated rights and obligations with regard to land and inheritance.

Land and other forms of property were at the center of change from a kin-based to a territorial social order. The press to separate common lands was observed in the history of the joint family; but the rise of chieftaincies on the mainsprings of war hastened the trend to private possession. The development of a feudal aristocracy out of the *comitatus*, or companions of the king, followed a gift of land for services rendered; and also as chieftains put out their surplus stock to underlings, who received some for themselves while obligating themselves to pay rent for pasture (Maine 1875:130–167). Such had been the Aryan experience, which Maine reconstructed by looking, at times, through the window of Irish history. Cattle, that oldest form of capital, effected great social changes and laid the foundations for feudal society.

CUSTOM, LAW, SOCIETY, AND ETHNOLOGICAL CONCEPTS

The pathway to understanding the natural history of the human family was as divergent and ramifying as the rise of other social institutions projected by evolutionists. In considering the origins of the family, nine-teenth-century Developmentalists examined the following: relations of the sexes; the emergence of ideas of maternity and paternity; the nature and obligations of kin groups; interrelations of religion and the social order; moral impact of the family; relations of family to economy; continuity linking family, kin and state; relative contributions of males and females to the social order and to civilization generally. In the process they began to conceptualize special types of organization, relations, and obligations binding the individual to society. The terms they introduced assumed the quality of an anthropological currency: matriarchy, patriarchy, gens, clan, agnates, cognates, phratry, exogamy, endogamy, kinship, consanguinity, lineal and collateral relations, classificatory and descriptive systems of re-lationship, marriage classes, polygamy, polyandry, polygyny, joint family, levirate, sororate, *patria potestas*, promiscuity, group marriage, marriage classes, age classes, cross cousin, kindred, lineage, bride purchase, bride service, blood feud, wergild, totemism, taboo, mana, and some others that have since faded in use, along with sept and stirps. Many of these terms derived from the investigation of customary rights and duties legally shared by members of families and kin groups found among the Hindus, Semites, Greeks, Romans, and the Celtic and Germanic tribes. The list is vivid testimony to the contribution which the legally trained made to the for-mal analysis of social relations and the formation of ethnological concepts.

CUSTOM AND SOCIAL CONTROL OF SAVAGE EGOISM

Probing legal relations within family and kin led naturally to a con-sideration of law and custom and their place in the social history of man-kind. In the developmental view primitive and civilized society stood at opposite poles, with the one regulated by custom, the other by law. The importance of custom in primitive society grew out of the fact that even at best savage societies were, as Tylor (1874(1):31) put it, "in but unstable equilibrium, liable to be easily upset by a touch of distress, temptation, or violence." Personal control over impulse being less subject to intelligence and moral restraints, primitive societies could not escape the unstable and inharmonious condition. McLennan's hypothesis that hunger led to the killing of newborn females, thereby drastically upsetting the balance of the sexes and necessitating raids to capture women, and Morgan's hypo-thetical state of consanguine marriage, illustrated the idea that life in sav-age society was more a state of capricious turmoil than a comfortable and steady condition.

Since savage man was ruled by passion, Developmentalists considered that whatever tempered primitive man's egoism and kept it under control must be beneficial to the civilizing process. For human society to develop, in Waitz's (1863(1):360) view, the masses must be disciplined to an habit-ual obedience and self-control. A disciplined community enjoyed a greater protection of life and property, and people developed objectives which aroused common interests and united them against external powers. Waitz (1863(1):358) was so struck with descriptions of savage indolence that he recommended a pure despotism to force the savage to learn the habit of industry and moral restraint. In the absence of a polity based on a rigid, definite, concise law, Bagehot (1875:27–30) held that the soft fiber of early man had to be shaped into conformity. To gain the obedience and uniformity essential to advancement early societies created a veritable "cake of custom" sanctioned by religion and intermingled with political authority. It mattered not, in Bagehot's (1875:24) view what manner of order existed, for "any form of polity is more efficient than none." It was not simply that custom dissolved primitive egoism with its constraints, but that it was essential that it do so in order that man could be put into the civilized mold (Bagehot 1875:27). It would be a mistake to assume, wrote Lord Avebury (1912:363–364), that the savage enjoys more personal freedom than what could be found in civilized communities. On the contrary, "The savage is nowhere free. All over the world his daily life is regulated by a complicated and often most inconvenient set of customs (as forcible as laws), of quaint prohibitions and privileges; the prohibitions as a general rule applying to the women, and the privileges to the men." Savage conservatism was for tradition and in Tylor's (1874(1):156) view accounted for the absence in rude tribes of police to maintain order. Custom, according to Sumner and Keller (1927(1):29–30), constituted the focus of social investigation.

> Primitive peoples are ruled by custom . . . [and] all of society's forms and institutions are found, when reduced to lowest evolutionary terms, in custom. It is the germ of them all. Nothing in the societal realm is more original, underived, and elemental. The study of custom is, for a science of society, what the study of the cell is for biology.

Uniformity and conservatism belonged to the past, variation and progress to the future. An intelligent balance between the restraint of custom and the gratification of impulse was assured through cultivation of self-discipline. Individuality meant character, and the progressive release of human character called for the triumph of reason and morality over instinct through self-discipline.

CUSTOM: PRECEDENT TO CODIFIED LAW

Maine (1887) first gave impulse to the idea that the early law codes were nothing more than customs put into writing, but that custom was not the basis for the first legal decisions. Maine shared the common view of nineteenth-century Developmentalists that religion suffused early society and sanctioned authority and regulations. Hence, he began his history of law with patriarchs and kings deciding disputes by direct inspiration. This followed because intervention by a personal agent was the only way mankind in a primitive condition could be moved to act (Maine 1887:4). Law did not begin with custom but with divine commands, and this was then formalized in the idea of a deity dictating a code of law, as illustrated by the Hindu laws of Manu. As the sacred nature of monarchical power waned an aristocracy succeeded to power. The aristocracy then exercised a virtual monopoly over the legal process by retaining the vital knowledge of the laws and of the principles by which judicial decisions were made. This truly was the epoch of customary law, when a segment of a society guarded an unwritten law. In the East, religious aristocracies dominated, whereas in the West a military and civil order wrested power from the sacred kings and priests. Quite likely aristocratic abuse of legal prerogatives compelled the codifying of law, especially after the invention of writing. These early codes were a mixture of religious, civil, and moral ordinances, which later legal development would separate (Maine 1887:16).

Maine's contribution lay in his analysis of the relation of law to the distribution of authority, rights, and duties within a social system. In historic review the patriarchal family, at least in Aryan history, was the wellspring for primary definitions of legal relations. Upon this point the testimony of Roman and Hindu family law was firm, and Maine (1861:129) stressed the impressive persistence of the influence of this ancient law into modern times.

> Older probably than the State, the Tribe, and the House, it left traces of itself on private law long after the House and the Tribe had been forgotten, and long after consanguinity had ceased to be associated with the composition of States. It will be found to have stamped itself on all the great departments of jurisprudence, and may be detected, I think, as the true source of many of their most important and most durable characteristics. At the outset, the peculiarities of law in its most ancient state lead us irresistibly to the conclusion that it took precisely the same view of the family group which is taken of individual men by the systems of rights and duties now prevalent throughout Europe.

Maine saw society as a corporation of individuals bound by rights and duties conferred by birth. Law accommodated the differences of individuals and strengthened social bonds of the society. However, rule by law did not mean that individuals held equal rights in society. The equities and inequities of society were underwritten by law that extended or excluded possession over persons and over things. "Our studies in the Law of Persons," wrote Maine (1887:261), "seemed to show us the [patriarchal] Family expanding into the agnatic group of kinsmen, then the Agnatic groups dissolving into separate households; lastly, the household supplanted by the individual; and it is now suggested that each step in the change corresponds to an analogous alteration in the nature of Ownership." Consanguinity or kinship (Maine 1875:64–65) was the original basis for citizenship, and only as societies shifted their economies to cultivation did settled territory become important to the social and legal process. When this happened, a new conception of citizenship based on location rather than ties of kinship developed, especially as the conquests of military leaders redistributed and feudalized the land and as individuals were accorded personal rights in real estate (Maine 1861:70–115).

Those who followed Maine's lead in the study of customary law among the ancient European tribes invariably uncovered a primitive communal family unit of the patriarchal variety as the center of early social organization. "The most profound difference between modern and ancient organization," observed Vinogradoff (1920, cited by Krader 1966:57), "consists in the fact that modern society starts from individuals and adjusts itself primarily to the claims of the individual, whereas ancient society starts from groups and subordinates individual interests to the claims of these groups" (compare Pollock 1883; Seebohm 1902; Huebner 1918; Vinogradoff 1920; also McLennan 1865:15–16; Spencer 1900(2):261–262; Sumner 1960:55–57; Westermarck 1924(1):158–170 for derivation of law from custom). German students of law (for example, J. Kohler 1918 and A. H. Post 1894), though casting their researches in a broad developmental mode rather than the narrower Aryan field, came to similar conclusions about the subordination of the individual in primitive society to both custom and the group. The psychological basis for types and degrees of punishment for violations of custom engaged their attention, with Steinmetz (1928) tracing the development of punishment from a blind and indiscriminate revenge to a reasoned social punishment leveled at the criminal. However, as Westermarck (1924(1):30–42) perceptively noted, the alleged indiscriminate nature of primitive retaliation should be placed in the context of collective responsibility so often expressed in the blood feud. Even this circumstance did not prevent the meting out of vengeance first upon the culprit, and failing this, his next of kin.

SOCIAL EQUILIBRIUM AND STATE CONTROL

The Practical Need for Governance

In the eighteenth century progressivists rested their case for the improvement of human society on an enlightened self-interest made aware of its responsibilities by the social experience of the marketplace. At the same time they acknowledged the importance and necessity of government to accommodate the antagonistic demands of private and group interest. The state could and should regulate and distribute justice.

In the evolutionary context of nineteenth-century thought, the state took on greater significance. There were three reasons commonly cited by evolutionists for according the state a dynamic role in the advancement of society: (1) the organic interdependencies of society, (2) the antipathies of private and social interests, and (3) the need to unify masses of people in a functionally differentiated hierarchy to assure evolutionary momentum.

Organic Functions and Governance: Comte and Spencer

A functional view of society stressed subordination of private interest to the social good. The operations maintaining society came first. This was the point made by Comte (1893(2):115–123) when noting how individuals in their different employments performed organic functions for society; therefore, they had to be subordinated to the whole. Expanding on the organic analogy in studied detail, Spencer (1880–1896(1, Part 2):455) compared societies and organisms as to growth, increase in structures, progressive structural differentiations and integrations, and reciprocal interdependencies. But Spencer, whose brusque independence led him to reject financial assistance to aid in his education, was not deterred from his individualistic liberalism by the logic of the organic-functional prerequisites of society. After all, society was a super-organic phenomenon. An organism might be a concrete whole, but individual units were diffused throughout society which were capable of experiencing happiness and misery much in the same way. Shared individuality of the human experience was directly related to the objectives of society and the state. In Spencer's (1880–1896(1, Part 1):461–462) view, organic though society might be in its basic ordering, "there is no social sensorium, [and therefore] the welfare of the aggregate, considered apart from that of the units, is not an end to be sought. The society exists for the benefit of its members; not its members for the benefit of society."

Any society was bound together by cooperation, exhibited first by individuals spontaneously cooperating to fulfill personal needs and goals and, secondly, by individuals consciously working together in the service of public ends (Spencer 1895(2):245–246). The former was voluntary, the latter involuntary. The former created economic social arrangements, the latter political organization. Both held advantages and disadvantages. In the early stages of human development, before mankind acquired the appropriate character for social living in a voluntary cooperation, unity was commanded and supported by a credulous acceptance of control by a deified chief (Spencer 1895(2):272). However, in many races there were physical, moral, and intellectual deficiencies that forestalled their reaching a stage of political evolution sufficient to sustain momentum. Evolution demanded more than a rudimentary division of labor by which small social groups were united. "Neither the required complex combinations of individuals," wrote Spencer (1895(2):250), "nor the elaborate mechanical appliances which facilitate manufacture, can arise in the absence of a large community, generating a great demand." In such an industrial society Spencer looked for conditions that made voluntary cooperation possible.

In the perspective of development, Spencer, like Waitz, admitted that early men required controls to insure progress. In a sense, individuals existed for society, since the evolutionary-bound institutions transcended all private ends. However, looking at the resources which societies at any one time could generate, Spencer (1895(2):262) saw that administrative instrumentalities were antagonistic to social growth, since they absorbed nutrients essential to continuous social growth. If government proliferated and absorbed the major part of social nutrients, evolutionary progress would grind to a halt. A dynamic balance therefore must be maintained between public and private needs; and Spencer opted for an open society in place of a stable society based on hereditary privilege and succession. A principle of hereditary succession carried a degree of social rigidity that kept the best fitted from filling important posts, whereas a succession by efficiency encouraged social flexibility and evolutionary growth (Spencer 1895(2):263–264). In earlier times private interests sapped growth by working against the welfare of the whole. "The evidence obliges us to admit," Spencer (1895(2):361) concluded, "that subjection to despots has been instrumental in advancing civilization."

Survival, War, and the State: Sumner and Keller

Sumner and Keller (1927(1):404–406) agreed with Spencer on the virtues of an industrial type of society. However, unlike Spencer, they did not distrust the functions of government. At all times government must be there to coordinate activities vital to group survival. With such a posture, the thesis that the person was a servitor of group needs proved inevitable. Sumner and Keller (1927(1):459–460) boldly affirmed that

> The basic function of government has been the securing of coördination; of peace and order within the range of its authority. It is readily enough seen that such coördination constitutes an advantage in the struggle for existence; the society possessing it is better adjusted to its life-conditions than the one that has it not. To secure the coördination it is not sufficient, however, to rely upon the natural impulses of group-members, for there is too much variation in them and too many antagonisms between them; the vision of the constituent individuals and groups must be surmounted by a super-vision over them all. Coöperation is too strongly tinged by the element of antagonism to pursue its course in the absence of a coördinating agency. While individuals can see their own interests, ... they do not readily appreciate those of others, much less the interests of society as a whole. These will be taken care of in the end by rude and violent selection; but any device which can effect such selection without the need of flying to extremities and fighting it out constitutes an adjustment with high survival-value. It is expedient ... that a society shall be a peace-group. Here is the prime reason for government.

The basic ingredient of government was exercise of power, and just as the stronger male seized power in the family, so the strong ever seized authority and turned it into an efficient instrument for survival, gradually refined through selection and rendered more reasonable through reflection. Government had another natural right drawn from the evolutionary process;

with increase in specialization, there was a coordinate demand for administration.

War, as a general state of mankind, offered a direct correlate to the process of natural selection and added justification to the necessity for strong government. In the opinion of Sumner and Keller (1927(1):401), war had

> dissolved whatever primitive equality there was, and introduced social inequality, discipline, and organization. ... Now this very recognition of inequality is an adjustment to the facts of life; it allows the fitter to get their desserts and stimulates individual initiative.
>
> If there had been no war, it is quite probable that exogamy and the father-family would not have developed so widely; and war, as a phase of contact with others, was at least more favorable to the development of culture than was utter isolation. ... War and conquest, if they do not actually make the state, create more complex states and more comprehensive societies, and the larger combinations render possible enterprises of greater scope. Conflict stabilized the societal forms and so is the source of political power. It has fostered deliberation concerning group interests involved and fathered deliberative assemblies. ...

War, according to sociologist Gumplowicz (1963:125–126), laid the foundations for "every political organization, and hence every developing civilization, begins at the moment when one horde permanently subjugates another."

War and Social Principles of Organization: Schurtz

The theory that masculine social orders replaced primitive female-based societies strengthened the idea that war played an important role in the advance of human societies. War was a masculine activity, and Schurtz (1902), who considered the social impulses of males to be the basis for true association, described the beginnings of the state in age classes organized for defense. War was the source of political power. In primitive times the mother-clan served its evolutionary purpose by joining groups in an exogamic social arrangement that improved the race through proper breeding. Female-oriented exogamic societies also provided opportunities for the power and enterprise of men to be realized in a warrior band. However, peace, in favoring family life, chained man to wife and children and subordinated him to the conservative restraints of the alien female principle. Family and clan thus stood in the way of groups based upon free association—the unique products of man's social endowment. Conquest produced new social classes and professional associations and ultimately those larger unions essential to formation of the state. Primary groups based on the female principle of blood relationship belonged to the infancy of society, while secondary groups based on the masculine principle of voluntary organization belonged to civilization.

Man at War with Self and Society: Freud

Psychoanalyst Freud transferred the war of community against community to the arena of human personality. The half-civilized *id* was constantly at war with *ego* (rational process) and *superego* (censoring process). The spread of a compulsive conscience (superego) over the rational domain was like a conquest of empire. This personality analog is curious but expectable, considering the heavy infusion of evolutionary biologism which Freud carried in his personality theory. It took Freud until 1930 (*Civilization and Its Discontents*) to formalize in print the theme of man against society—or rather, how man brought the warring ground of his personality, fixated by the antagonism of the life and death instincts, into the middle ground of society. To speak of human aggression, man was "*Homo homini lupus*; who has the courage," queried Freud (1958:61), "to dispute it in the face of all the evidence in his own life and in history?" Man's primitive hostility proved a constant menace to civilized society and threatened to destroy it. Cooperation based on a reasoned appreciation of common interests could not prevail over the violent passion of instinct-directed behavior. Therefore, according to Freud (1958:61–62),

> Culture has to call up every possible reinforcement in order to erect barriers against the aggressive instincts of men and hold their manifestations in check by reaction-formations in men's minds. Hence its system of methods by which mankind is to be driven to identifications and aim-inhibited love-relationships; hence the restrictions on sexual life; and hence, too, its ideal command to love one's neighbour as oneself, which is really justified by the fact that nothing is so completely at variance with original human nature as this. With all its striving, this endeavour of culture's has so far not achieved very much.

Like the individual, civilization developed a cultural superego to persuade the ego to exercise firm control over the impulsive id. And like the individual superego, the cultural counterpart was equally unrealistic. "The command is impossible to fulfill . . . [but] Civilization pays no heed to all this; it merely prates that the harder it is to obey the more laudable the obedience" (Freud 1958:102). The product of this unforgiving demand was either rebellion, neurosis, or unhappiness, and in his therapy Freud waged war against the superego in order to force a moderation of its imperious demands. There was a balance here that needed to be maintained, and it was up to a rational ego to achieve it. In final analysis, Freud's (1939) paradigm described man as compulsively subordinate to the overweaning power of an unsympathetic society and to the impenetrable dark stream of a symbolic struggle against the authoritarian control of a primeval polygymous and incestuous patriarch. At the same time Freud was prophetic in voicing anxious concern for individual integrity beset by the tyrannical demands of society. In effect, Freud's war against the imperious demands of the superego was a war against society and culture.

THE STATE IN RETROSPECT

The State in the Evolution of Civilized Society

For eighteenth-century progressivists and nineteenth-century evolution-ists, the state remained the primary instrument for organizing human re-sources in the attainment of civilization. Hard controls by the state were justified in the progressivist context by the necessity to discipline the per-verse modification of human nature by hot or cold climates; while in the evolutionist perspective it was essential to contain the egoistic impulses of partially socialized men. In raising the political voice of the proletariat, Marx advocated a necessary and tyrannous control—the dictatorship of the proletariat—as a prelude to voluntary associations cooperating for the total good. Despite their hard pragmatism, social evolutionists Sumner and Keller (1927(1):406), like Spencer, held the vision of an industrial society operating as a "constitutional or jural state, [a] democracy [with] delegated powers, liberty, free competition, private judgment, personal responsibility, enactment, [and] equal rights before the law."

Any accent on the role of organized authority must tip the balance against private interest and upgrade the importance of the group *vis-à-vis* the individual. As Hofstadter (1964:104) observed, it made little difference whether one took his stand on the battleground of evolutionary survival or held, as Kropotkin (1902), that mutual aid was more characteristic of organic and social processes. "They all endorsed solidarism; they saw the group (the species, family, tribe, class, or nation) as the unit of survival, and minimized or overlooked entirely the individual aspect of competi-tion." Yet the problem of the individual remained. The vision of increasing individuation held by Spencer, as well as the idea that the state advanced to a more democratic and voluntary type of association, testified to the optimism of evolutionary thought. Society was the central instrument, but it worked for the individual and guaranteed his individuality. In lyrical progressivist but at times cynical mode, Hobhouse (1925:352–353) sketched the emergence of private concerns in the development of civilized society.

> The poet tells us that with the advance of civilization the individual withers, but the truer romance of historical prose tells a different story. In early soci-ety the individual is nothing apart from his community. The sphere of pri-vate property is very small. . . . Land, . . . is communally owned and there is little incentive to individual industry. On the other hand, if there is no wealth, there is also no pauperism. Inequality grows as society advances, and in this advance, on its economic side, private ownership and free contract play the principal part. . . .
>
> At a still higher stage these restrictions fall away. Men stand fully free to enter into occupations of all kinds, to acquire wealth in all forms, and to dispose of and . . . bequeath it at their will. No divisions of class or even of nationality interfere with their movements or prevent them from entering into relations with other men in which they may find advantage. But these

general statements have to be taken with one limiting condition. The liberties that men enjoy are secured only by the social order maintained by the state, and the state in its turn has to demand that every right must be defined in terms of the common good, and neither private property nor free contract can escape this general law. Thus the modern world rests in a fuller sense than previous civilizations on the free individual, but the individual owes his freedom to state law, and the obverse side of the rights which he enjoys is the social duty which he owes.... If the individual is one pole, society ... is the opposite pole of the modern ethical system.

Finally, customs admitting the acquisition and holding of property have ... the necessity for dealing with those who have and can acquire none.... In primitive society there is an easy communism among the kinsfolk, often—but by no means always—much consideration for children, the aged and the helpless, and lavish hospitality for the stranger if the host chooses to receive him. In the more advanced societies the duties of the governing classes are strongly insisted on by religion and social ethics. Those whom the decay of primitive communal institutions has left helpless and who have fallen outside the regular lines of the social structure are recommended to the charity of their superiors.... At a higher stage, again, the method of arbitrary doles to a dependent class gives way to the conception of a reciprocal obligation between the state and its citizens, and contented acquiescence in perpetual poor relief to the systematic attempt to get at the roots at once of poverty and pauperism by organic reform in the economic structure of society.

The central place Hobhouse accorded property in the development of individuality echoed a consensus that reached back into the eighteenth century—barring followers of Rousseau and Marx. War provided the initial base for wealth and class divisions, just as war nurtured the rise of authority in the persons of chiefs and kings. The rise of the state brought a reorganization of society on a territorial basis and rendered kin-organized societies obsolescent.

In thoughtful consideration of the meaning of Iroquois governance for human political development, Morgan (1964:107) discovered in the council of chiefs a form germinal to the modern parliament, congress, and legislature. These children of the forest had passed from a spontaneous miniature monarchy (chief and followers) to a tribal and then a kind of national aristocracy, which Morgan (1954(1):137–138) considered "more perfect, systematic and liberal than those of antiquity ... [and indeed] it would be difficult to find a fairer specimen of the government of the few" in the security offered against misgovernment. In their political development, the Iroquois demonstrated the common tendency of institutions to move in the direction of democracy as races advanced themselves in the scale of civilization. In *Ancient Society* Morgan (1877:119–120) described the three-stage political development of kin-based organizations as a prelude to the emergence of the territorial state.

The growth of the idea of government commenced with the organization into gentes in savagery.... The first stage was the government of a tribe by a council of chiefs elected by the gentes. It may be called a government of *one power*; namely, *the council*. It prevailed generally among tribes in the Lower Status of barbarism. The second stage was a government co-ordinated between a council of chiefs, and a general military commander; one representing the civil, and the other the military functions. This second form began to manifest itself in the Lower Status of barbarism, after confederacies were formed, and it became definite in the Middle Status. The office of general, or principal military commander, was the germ of that of a chief executive magistrate, the king, the emperor, and the president. It may be called a government of *two powers*, namely, *the council of chiefs*, and *the general*. The third stage was the government of a people or nation by a council of chiefs, an assembly of the people, and a general military commander. It appeared among the tribes who had attained to the Upper Status of barbarism; such, for example, as the Homeric Greeks, and the Italian tribes of the period of Romulus. A large increase in the number of people united in a nation, their establishment in walled cities, and the creation of wealth in lands and in flocks and herds, brought in the assembly of the people as an instrument of government. The council of chiefs ... found it necessary ... to submit the most important public measures to an assembly of the people for acceptance or rejection; whence the popular assembly. This assembly did not originate measures. It was its function to adopt or reject, and its action was final. From its first appearance it became a permanent power in the government. The council no longer passed important public measures, but became a pre-considering council, with power to originate and mature public acts, to which the assembly alone could give validity. It may be called a government of three powers; namely, *the pre-considering council, the assembly of the people*, and *the general*. This remained until the institution of political society, when, for example, among the Athenians, the council of chiefs became the senate, and the assembly of the people the ecclesia or popular assembly. The same organizations have come down to modern times in the two houses of parliament, of congress, and of legislatures. In like manner the office of a general military commander ... , was the germ of the office of the modern chief executive magistrate.

The invention of cultivation revolutionized society by stimulating the growth and concentration of populations. Wars over desirable lands intensified and drove people to protect themselves behind fortified walls. New ways of waging war brought individual rewards, and the additive effect of all these changes was the destruction of the gentile-type society and the creation of political society (Morgan 1877:541–542). Monarchy, the zenith of the warring state, was but a way station to the "democratical, which ... [is] the last, the noblest, and the most intellectual" of all political institutions (Morgan 1954(1):122).

In actuality, there were few differences between the position of eighteenth- and nineteenth-century Developmentalists regarding the rise of the state and its significance for human development. War was a prime creator of political power, and property broadened individual privileges and rights. The future would see the state as less coercive and a guarantor of private rights to a citizenry keenly aware of its social responsibilities. Those who excoriated property as the cursed instrument of class oppression were invited by Tylor (1873, cited by Opler 1968:3–5) to look at the evolutionary role of primitive communism before advocating a natural state socialism.

> When several families dwell together in more or less close approach to the union of a single family, cultivating jointly their plot of ground and living on the produce, their way of life is not the mere communism which has just been spoken of, but reaches the closer intimacy of actual socialism. The savage family is the original germ of the socialistic community, and it is interesting to notice that among races of low culture, as in the two Americas, socialistic communities are found in operation, formed by the amalgamation of several families who may even inhabit a single dwelling, a sort of savage phalanstery. Arriving at this level, socialism continues into barbaric ages as a somewhat important institution. . . . Thus there arose among savage tribes, and continued to our own day among people at a middle level of civilization, socialism in its most pure and absolute form.
>
> It is a matter of wonder to me that the theoretical politicians who have advocated the introduction of communism and socialism into the modern world, should . . . shut their eyes to the ethnology of these institutions. Communism in land, and socialism in life, are simply two results of the attempt to extend the primitive household system to the whole village or tribe, endeavouring . . . to live as a single family. The place of the two systems in history is . . . experimental fact. . . . But when it came to pressure of population and necessity of industrial and social progress, the [socialistic] plan showed its worse side. The individual was . . . secured from . . . destitution, but . . . he could not rise. The use of money . . . accustomed men to fair payments, but the communal system of equal division was . . . unfair between the better and worse labourers. Lastly, . . . the most doggedly conservative and obstructive . . . had the power of resisting improvements on ancient custom. No wonder . . . ancient communism failed to compete commercially with individualism . . . and has . . . been discarded in the civilized world. Perhaps, in modern times, co-operative schemes may be so contrived as practically to meet the difficulties against which the ancient schemes were now helpless, while retaining the noble qualities of the old united society. But the arguments of modern doctrinaires for communism and socialism, on the abstract principles, seldom go much beyond an attempt to throw society back into the very institutions long ago tried and found wanting.

War, Biological Superiority, Individuality, and Nation State

Evolutionary extremists countered the democratic proprietarian utopia of rational Developmentalism with the biological doctrine of supermen. In this view the physically, intellectually, and morally powerful would rule the inferior. For Nietzsche (1844–1900) the only morality was selfish egoism backed by power. "It is necessary," Nietzsche wrote (1910(1):298), "for higher men to declare war upon all the masses!" There was no point in uniting mediocre people so they should become masters. Protection of mediocrity meant a pampering and softening. Whoever sought to give the mediocre, or women, a greater role in society simply prepared the way for

a universal suffrage of inferiors. The problems facing mankind had nothing to do with the amount of freedom individuals and groups had. The
real question was

> the degree of power which the one or the other should exercise over his
> neighbour or over all; and more especially with the question to what extent
> a sacrifice of freedom, or even enslavement, may afford the basis for the
> cultivation of a *superior* type. In plain words; *how could one sacrifice the
> development of mankind* in order to assist a higher species than man to come
> into being. (Nietzsche 1910(1):298)

Nietzsche's call for the sacrifice of inferior men in the interest of
evolving supermen was little more than a metaphysical translation of the
thesis that race was the proving ground for the inheritance of superiorities.
Logically enough, the problem of physical and cultural diversity produced
two opposing interpretations: (1) mankind had a single origin (monogenesis), and the varieties produced by time and external conditions remained
equal in endowment, despite differences in cultural achievement; and (2)
each race was differently endowed at the start to fill a special environmental, cultural, and historical niche; or that subspecies had evolved at different rates, and consequently some races were superior to others. Nationalistic
and imperialistic impulses during the nineteenth century had a compelling
affinity for interpretations that anchored superior achievement to biological superiority. The critical economic, social, and political problems of
Europeans during their industrial transformation—marked by the rise and
fall of nation states and social classes—seemed easily explained by a superior, or ineffectual, endowment rather than by opportunity. De Gobineau
(1853–1855) thus voiced his anguish for a class elite ruined by miscegenation. Nott and Gliddon (1857) extolled the creative imperialism of whites
over blacks, while von Treitschke and Chamberlain focused on race and
national destiny. According to Chamberlain (1912(1):256–257) the nineteenth century had become a "century of races" as a "necessary and direct
consequence of science and scientific thinking." Scientific comparisons of
anatomy, language, and religion demolished the alleged unity of the human
race. Nature taught that there were no equalities and never would be.
Nature also informed man that the fate of the individual was linked to a
racial destiny. Nourished by the nobility of his race, the individual elevated
his aspirations and achievements—and what race accomplished for the individual, the nation accomplished for the race. As a political structure the
nation state created conditions which fostered the most characteristic activities of the race and of the individual. The law of all individual life thus
reposed in the nation, for a "firm national union . . . signifies common memory, common hope, common intellectual nourishment; it fixes firmly the
existing bond of blood and impels us to make it ever closer" (Chamberlain
1912(1):297).

In the view of von Treitschke individual and state were bonded by
mutual obligations and rights. However, the individual must subordinate

his interests and life to the state, since his destiny was locked up in the state.

> The greatness of the State lies precisely in its power of uniting the past with the present and the future; . . . no individual has the right to regard the State as the servant of his own aims but is bound by moral duty and physical necessity to subordinate himself to it, while the State lies under the obligation to concern itself with the life of its citizens by extending to them its help and protection. (von Treitschke 1916(1):65)

War created the state, and war would be the companion of human history so long as a multiplicity of states existed. War moved nations forward to civilization and tested their right to be leaders of the civilized. According to von Treitschke (1916(1):67), "The grandeur of war lies in the utter annihilation of puny man in the great conception of the State, and it brings out the full magnificence of the sacrifice of fellow-countrymen for one another . . . [while] foster[ing] the political idealism which the materialist rejects." The state was not a necessary evil; it was the state which furthered the innate capacity of man to organize politically.

In the evolutionary perspective of the nineteenth century, there was a compelling sense that the emergence of science and the modern state marked the crossing of a threshold. "The government of human societies is now a science," proclaimed evolutionist Letourneau (1881:593), ". . . and the object is progressive amelioration of our kind from a threefold point of view: physical, moral, and intellectual."

As the nineteenth century ended nationalism tied the individual to a group and accented the social solidarity which theorists found so congenial to the evolutionary context. The bitter struggle between bourgeoisie and proletariat projected by Marx also accented the submersion of the individual destiny in an emergent consciousness of group solidarity and destiny. Now, however, class became the fulcrum for social evolution and the determiner of a changing human nature which responded to the historic character of social relations (Venable 1966:121).

Epilogue for the Evolution of Civilized Society and the State

The theoretical turn which anthropology took at the end of the nineteenth century witnessed the leveling of serious charges against the evolutionist position and their findings with regard to race, psychology, and the civilized state. However, the idea that structure and the processes of structure predominated over the units composing it left its mark on the flow of later thought. There was continuity between accent on the group as containing the evolutionary destiny of the individual and the interpretation that the mass processes of society and culture, separate and autonomous in their own rights, molded and ruled the individual. Society, as in progressivist thought, still was the making of man; but in the new conception, society did not draw out the individual with moderate competitions. On the contrary, the structuralist theory of the new anthropology saw individuals surrounded by an iron curtain of social demands to which they must conform—or at least the vast majority in their inertia do so.

A new social and cultural anthropology hovered in the wings as the old century bowed out to a twentieth century vibrant with the buildup of a new industrialism and the desire to raise science to the point where its technical proficiency, so evident in harnessing nature, could be translated into social science skills. Relations of men in society loomed as the most immediate and relevant problems in a world revolutionizing its technology and maintaining but a perilous peace. The time for a clear and studied analysis of societies—how they were structured and maintained by group processes—was at hand. Developmentalism proved the handmaiden for the new structural anthropology in two ways: (1) it initiated investigation of broad issues that could not be avoided if the human reality problem was to be understood; and (2) the theory of development was a point of challenge and reaction which stimulated new avenues of investigation and a redefinition of goals and problems.

SUMMARY

In dealing with the origins and continuities of society nineteenth-century evolutionists had to determine mankind's original condition and then trace the influence of factors which directed human society to the civilized political state. They agreed that ideas of paternity, kinship, ownership, incest, exogamy, marriage, mother right and father right, and other social concepts were important inventions that opened new lines of social development. However, the human capacity to formulate and to extend these seminal ideas was a function of the level of biopsychic evolution. In the continuum from savagery to civilization, the savage demonstrated that his capabilities for social living were rudimentary and tied to elemental ideas related to survival instincts and to descent based on childbirth. These natural or primitive ideas were superseded in the course of evolution by an acquired social instinct which elicited more varied and complex associations based on interest rather than physiological needs. Natural selection was indispensable to the adaptive addition of a true social instinct to the biopsychic inventory of mankind.

The limited social capabilities of primitive men were visible in the small bands formed for defense and personal survival through economic cooperation and sharing. Beyond this they were able to establish social units based on female descent, to extend their capacities for survival by exogamic rules which favored population increase, and to advance a regard for life by limited applications of moral values. However, in the primitive state the natural inclination was to gratify personal wants and needs; hence the necessity to contain primitive egoism with a "cake of custom." The need for the heavy restraints of custom underlined the maladaptability of primitive physiology and explained the innate conservatism of peoples at the level of savagery.

The view that mankind evolved new social instincts directed attention to a contrast of relationships based on a primitive natural sociality with a complex and "artificial" sociality. In part this explains the vital interest in totemism as introducing a new kind of social principle into primitive society, which, as Lippert observed, allowed development of the ancient city-state.

While theorists like Bachofen, McLennan, W. Smith, Wundt, and Fustel de Coulanges explored the significance of religion in integrating early society, Schurtz, Spencer, and sociologists Gumplowicz, Sumner, and Keller directed attention to the transformation of society by the war activities and fraternities of males. Schurtz, like Bachofen, described the transformation of an original female social order by application of true social principles based on masculine interest groups. Age classes linked to war constituted the first step toward true sociality and the formation of complex associations (classes, professions) essential to a state society. Without war and conquest human society would have remained at a primitive level of organization.

The theoretical controversies over social evolution stemmed largely from differences regarding the original state of mankind and the presence or absence of particular social sentiments selectively operating to influence the nature of social arrangements. Regarding the original state, Morgan began with a promiscuous communal horde; while Wake held that the presence of a social instinct which tabooed sex relations between parent and child and brother and sister forestalled sexual communism. Taking the view that the evolutionary process induced adaptations which aided human survival, Westermarck concluded that the biological family was central to the evolutionary process. A theory of primitive promiscuity was contradicted by natural selection. The controversy between McLennan and Maine regarding the priority of the matriarchal or the patriarchal family derived from emphasis on different processes working to produce descent. McLennan tied original notions of descent to inferences from childbirth, whereas Maine linked descent to the natural dominance of the male and his control over family and inheritance.

In the perspective of evolution mankind advanced from a primitive collectivity rooted in physiological reflexes to a society organized on voluntarism and interest. The course of development suggested a gradual release of the individual from social constraints. This growth in individual rights and in individuality could be traced through the medium of property (Maine) or through natural selection acting on man's biology and social institutions (Spencer). However, some sociologists and political theorists (for example, Gumplowicz, Ratzenhofer, Chamberlain, Nietzsche, von Treitschke) saw the evolutionary process as submerging individual identity and personal destiny in a group destiny. Nation and state emerged as the basic evolutionary unit, a counterpart of the biological species which served as the natural evolutionary unit for survival. Since war was the supreme instrument of biological and social selection and called for individual sacrifice in the welfare of the group, such theorists viewed war as a process which was natural, inevitable, and indispensable to future biological and social advance. Similar emphases on the group and on an evolutionary-conflict process were incorporated into the communist theory of Marx and Engels.

The rise of Structuralism continued the stress on group processes and subjection of the individual to the needs of society. Freud described the human process as an Oedipal tragedy in which the individual warred against himself, others, and society because of his incapacity to accommodate the urgent impulse satisfactions to the seemingly whimsical requirements of social living. Rather than improving man's capacity to live with himself and others, social evolution, through its linkage with biopsychic processes, steadily exacerbated the human situation and forced men into ever greater maladaptive behaviors.

8

Technological Origins and Continuities and Assessment of Developmentalism

TECHNOLOGY AND PROGRESS

With an eye on the revolutionary character of ideas, Developmentalists expectably made no special contributions to the study of savage, barbaric, or civilized economies. There never was any doubt about the importance of the material arts in providing a leisure base for more refined developments and social advancement. Men chained to the service of bodily needs had no time for creative speculation and cultivation of the fine arts. This observation, ably expressed by Robertson (1822(1):170), was early appreciated by eighteenth-century progressivists.

> What, among polished nations, is called speculative reasoning or research, is altogether unknown in the rude state of society, and never becomes the occupation or amusement of the human faculties, until you . . . have secured, with certainty, the means of subsistence, as well as the possession of leisure and tranquility. The thoughts and attention of a savage are confined within the small circle of objects, immediately conducive to his preservation or enjoyment. . . . Like a mere animal, what is before his eyes interests and affects him; what is out of sight, or at a distance, makes little impression.

While recognizing that economic and technological necessities were related to the quality of human life, Developmentalists did not make human progress dependent on economic processes. Economic and technological necessities might limit property concepts and place restrictions on the complexity of the social and political order. However, subsistence needs were not static and diminished as man advanced the comforts and organization of his life, at which time his mind was increasingly freed for creative speculations. Economic processes, like the primitive organic needs which they served, were more to be transcended than accorded a central place in the march to civilization.

To Developmentalists, technology was useful in that it gave visible confirmation of man's gradual extension of his control over nature. When in the nineteenth century Tylor (1874(1):68) sagely advised that development in the material arts provided an excellent guide for charting the rise from a savage mental state to that of civilized man, he simply echoed a common view of Developmentalists generally. The study of technology was always approached with the idea that the tool was the expression of an idea. Refinements in tools linked a succession of ideas, exhibiting a graduated keenness in perception and logical functional specialization. Thus, for Spencer (1900(1):89–90) primitive technology confirmed his argument that primitive men lacked constructive imagination.

> This lack naturally goes along with a life of simple perception, of imitativeness, of concrete ideas, and of incapacity for abstract ideas.
>
> The collection of implements and weapons arranged by General Pitt-Rivers, to show their relationships to a common original, suggests that primitive men are not to be credited with such inventiveness as even their simple appliances seem to indicate. These have arisen by small modifications; and the natural selection of such modifications has led unobtrusively to various kinds of appliances, without any distinct devising of them.

Material inventions, though useful guides, were no more important indicators of mental processes than other arts, and were less amenable to ideological analysis than language, religion, and mythology. The proper orientation, as Goguet (1775(1):Preface) directed, would be to describe the "whole mass of knowledge of all kinds among each people, in each age," for the "history of laws, arts, and sciences, is . . . the history of the human mind." What this meant in point of method Bury (1920:154) makes clear when summarizing Turgot's position and that of progressivists in the eighteenth century generally. In assessing man's relations to his environment,

> the psychical or moral causes are the first elements to consider, and it is a fault of method to try to evaluate physical causes till we have exhausted the moral, and are certain that the phenomena cannot be explained by these alone. In other words, the study of the development of societies must be based on psychology; and for Turgot, as for all his progressive contemporaries, psychology meant the philosophy of Locke.

Cause thus began with sensations, often involving pleasure or pain, which produced perceptions of differences and became, in the words of Ferguson (1789:40) "a faculty of . . . mind; and the inferences of thought are sometimes not to be distinguished from the perceptions of sense."

SUBSISTENCE STAGES: EIGHTEENTH-CENTURY
PROGRESSIVISTS

Progressivists and evolutionists generally were not particularly concerned with defining the characteristic features of economic stages or types of economies. Usually they were satisfied with a correlation of the state of savagery with hunting societies, barbarism with pastoral and agricultural societies, and civilization with commercial or industrial societies. Monboddo (1779–1799(4):55–59) began economic growth with the gathering of fruits and roots, followed by hunting. Kames (1778(1):87–88) did not think that fishing antedated hunting, for, "Water is not our element; and savages probably did not attempt to draw food from the sea or from rivers, till land-animals turned scarce."

In the perspective of subsistence stages, a population increase produced scarcities, and out of necessity a new and improved subsistence was invented. Primitive man, bound by habit, was inclined to settle into an economic niche, whether as hunter, gatherer, or pastoralist, and Developmentalists considered a crisis essential to move him in other directions. In Kames's description, the hunter, pressed by food scarcities, might take another look at the "fawn, a kid, or a lamb, taken alive and tamed for amusement" and perceive that he could keep them in flocks and herds. The idea thus was father to the act. As men multiplied in response to a more plentiful supply of food, conflicts and migrations likewise increased, especially when food became harder to get.

> Necessity, the mother of invention, suggested agriculture. When corn growing spontaneously was rendered scarce by consumption, it was an obvious thought to propagate it by art: nature was the guide, which carries on its work of propagation, with seeds that drop from a plant in their maturity, and spring up new plants. As the land was possessed in common, the seed was sown in common; and the product was stored in a common repository, to be parcelled out among individuals in want, as the common stock of animals had been formerly. (Kames 1778(1):93)

In the Americas, there was no shepherd state, not because they lacked cattle amenable to domestication but because people never experienced a rapid population growth and a consequent critical shortage of food (Kames 1778(2):87). Without the critical press of necessity, there was no stimulus to invention. Inventions were pragmatic problem-solving devices and not responses to play and ingenuity.

Meiners (1785:84–85), using historical sources, viewed the Asiatic and European pastoralists of his day as remnants of an expansion that at one time had included all of Europe. But now pastoralists survived only at the margins where they were driven by the more industrious agricultural peoples, and where no other economic life was possible. Such were the Lapps, the Tungus, Chukchi, Kirgis, Turkomans, and Arabs. The withdrawal of

Arab pastoralists from Egypt and West Africa left only the pastoral Hottentots and Caffirs.

Meiners' historic orientation allowed for the peaking and decline of broad economic developments analogous to the rise and fall of states and of peoples. While he distinguished savage, barbaric, semicultivated, and cultivated peoples, he maintained that these did not represent universal stages in advancement. Many people could have—and did—drop back into the deep pit of savagery. Nonetheless, Meiners considered pastoralists as typical barbarians, and more advanced culturally than rude hunters and fisherfolk.

THE IDEA OF PROPERTY: THE PULSE OF PROGRESS

To eighteenth-century progressivists the nature of social relations, property, and authority was far more arresting and significant than the characteristics of savage, barbarian, and civilized economies. "It must appear very evident," wrote Ferguson (1789:125), "that property is a matter of progress." Basic to property was a definition of possessory rights based on individual industry. Industrious habits were acquired slowly, and Ferguson considered industriousness a principal measure of the advancement of the mechanical and commercial arts. Thus the idea of possession and the application of this idea to the desire to work for possessions created the distinctions found in the ascending stages of human society. Cause must not be sought in the material arts, for these came into being and prospered only with desires generated by ideas. Where peoples hunted, fished, or mixed hunting with cultivation, property was confined to personal items, such as the weapons, utensils, and furs which an individual could carry on his person. Therefore, pastoralism must have come later than hunting and fishing, since pastoralism recognized property as hereditary in families. Moreover, the war leader, in creating a band of followers, began the transformation of society into monarchy with class distinctions (Ferguson 1789:153–154). Kames (1761:91) credited the invention of herding with bringing mankind into a second level of social life. Possession still supplied the basis of a property right, but the care lavished on domestic animals strengthened the possessory bond. Hunters, according to Condorcet, got to keeping about their huts the more docile of the animals they hunted as insurance against a time of want. As these animals multiplied and produced milk, hunters probably were weaned from the chase and so entered the second or pastoral stage. The significance of pastoralism, as in any subsistence advance, was its quickening of mental capabilities. "A more sedentary and less strenuous form of life afforded man leisure and this in turn favored the development of the human mind. When men were certain of their sustenance and were no longer anxious about their elementary needs, they looked for new sensations in the means of satisfying them" (Condorcet 1955:19–20).

Observing that his stock thrived better on certain plants, man, who gathered nature's free cereals for his own diet, now conceived the idea that he should protect these food cereals by giving them special care. Cultivation began near home as men, observant of nature's best gardens, carefully separated weeds from choice plants. Thus one idea with its set of observations led to another. The invention of taming and pasturing cattle, according to Millar (1806:59–63), increased wealth, produced the patriarchal family, separated people by rank, and induced possessory tendencies such as female chastity, which was a prerequisite for courtship and marriage. The pastoral state constituted the first important improvement in savage life.

ECONOMIC AND IDEOLOGICAL STAGES: MORGAN

Developmentalists in the nineteenth century hardly improved on what their eighteenth-century counterparts had to say about savagery, barbarism, and civilization as economic stages. Prichard's (1855) effort to tie the variant modes of subsistence to head shapes constituted no economic breakthrough, since he simply underscored the progressivist view that radical physical changes usually accompanied any alteration of circumstances.

In *Ancient Society*, Morgan (1877) offered the most extended formulation (three chapters) of economic and technological correlations with the stages of savagery, barbarism, and the beginnings of civilization. It was entirely probable, according to Morgan (1877:9) that

> the successive arts of subsistence which arose at long intervals will ultimately, from the great influence they must have exercised upon the condition of mankind, afford the most satisfactory bases for these divisions.... Even though accepted as provisional, these periods will be found convenient and useful. Each ... will be found to cover a distinct culture, and to represent a particular mode of life.

If mankind had not succeeded in expanding the subsistence base and had not gained absolute control over food production, progress would have come to a halt. At that time progress depended on increased population and the formation of a multiplicity of populous nations (Morgan 1877:19). Although subsistence was critical, Morgan's (1877:4) sketch of human progress was drawn more especially from domestic institutions which expressed the growth of basic ideas and feelings.

Morgan (1877:3–18) correlated a special status or culture with each of his three periods, dividing savagery and barbarism into older, middle, and later stages. Civilization was assigned an ancient and a modern aspect. Pastoralism followed a fruit and root gathering, fishing, and hunting sequence in the Old World. Morgan (1877:23) cited the linguistic fact that "there are common terms for [domestic] ... animals in the several dialects of the Aryan language, and no common term for the cereals or cultivated plants" to prove that the discovery and cultivation of cereals by the Aryan family followed the domestication of animals. Like Kames a century before, Morgan was aware that pastoralism had not developed in the New World, the llama excepted. However, unlike Kames, he assigned this absence to a lack of animals which could be domesticated. In the New World, plant cultivation (maize) actually began earlier (lower status of barbarism) than had the domestication of animals (middle status of barbarism) in the Old World.

Much like Condorcet, Morgan (1877:23) argued that tillage of open alluvial land came before the enclosed garden (*hortos*), and finally field (*ager*) cultivation. Whether root or cereal cultivation came first was undetermined for lack of evidence, but he thought that horticulture stemmed more from the necessities of animal husbandry than from critical food needs. Domestication of animals in the Old World and of plants in the New World freed mankind from the scourge of cannibalism which was practiced universally during the savage stage of gathering, fishing, and hunting. Captives were the primary target of savage cannibalism, but in time of famine even friends and kin were eaten (Morgan 1877:24). Considering cannibalism a universal practice stemming from population pressures on savage economy, Morgan echoed a common eighteenth-century interpretation.

Man, in Morgan's view, did not march in measured step in advancing civilization but rather leaped from one ledge to the next. These saltations were a product of grand inventions that accelerated change and then were spent. Morgan referred to the "essentially geometric . . . ratio . . . of human progress." One could imagine even the most advanced of the human races grinding to a halt and languishing "until some great invention or discovery, such as the domestication of animals or the smelting of iron ore, gave a new and powerful impulse forward" (Morgan 1877:39–40).

In responding to the challenges of life, men at first poured their creative energies into technology and advancements which facilitated an enlargement of their institutions. The production of inventions and discoveries and the growth of institutions coincided with the growth and expansion of the human mind. This led to a gradual enlargement of the brain itself, particularly in the cerebral portion (Morgan 1877:37).

Uneven technological and institutional developments demonstrated that the extension of intellect had not been uniform. Aryans and Semites had quickly shown that they were leaders in human progress. As early as the middle period of barbarism, the Aryan and Semitic families gave indication that they were in the main line of progress, and with the dawn of civilization the Aryan dominated the civilizing process (Morgan 1877: 40).

In final analysis, Morgan's attitude toward technological invention and progress was close to that of eighteenth-century progressivists who considered the securing of material comforts essential to leisure and the release of human creativity. Nine tenths of *Ancient Society* was devoted to plotting the "Growth of the Idea of Government," "Growth of the Idea of the Family," and "Growth of the Idea of Property." There was no studied attempt to connect family, social institutions, and property to economic determinants. Yet interrelations exist among the social institutions, and Morgan labored to prove that family types and special systems of consanguinity and affinity were all interrelated and connected with economy. More than other nineteenth-century Developmentalists, Morgan must be credited with an effort to capture the interrelatedness of institutions in evolution. He kept the problem in the foreground with a detailed inventory of features associated with savagery, barbarism, and civilization and made repeated references to correlated developments. Like eighteenth-century counterparts, Morgan was more successful in teasing out interrelations when describing how economic transitions sparked new ideas about property. Thus,

> When field agriculture had demonstrated that the whole surface of the earth could be made the subject of property owned by individuals in severality, and it was found that the head of the family became the natural center of accumulation, the new property career of mankind was inaugurated. It was fully done before the close of the later Period of Barbarism. A little reflection must convince any one of the powerful influence property would now begin to exercise upon the human mind, and of the great awakening of new elements of character it was calculated to produce. Evidence appears, from many sources, that the feeble impulse aroused in the savage mind had now become a tremendous passion in the splendid barbarism of the heroic age. Neither archaic nor later usages could maintain themselves in such an advanced condition. The time had now arrived when monogamy, having assured the paternity of children, would assert and maintain their exclusive right to inherit the property of their deceased father. (Morgan 1877:544)

Monogamy, prefigured in the kin-structured Syndyasmian family, was secured by development of an exclusive property right, which had derived from cultivation and the resulting intensification of man's attachment of a person to his use-holding. Nonetheless, Morgan (1877:552) repeatedly elucidates, as in the prophetic mood below, that ideas are really the inspiration for change and for the goals of civilized society.

> The human mind stands bewildered in the presence of its own creation [property]. The time will come, nevertheless, when human intelligence will rise to the mastery over property, and define the relations of the state to the property it protects, as well as the obligations and the limits of the rights of its owners. . . . The dissolution of society bids fair to become the termination of a career of which property is the end and aim, because such a career contains the elements of self-destruction. Democracy in government, brotherhood in society, equality in rights and privileges, and universal education, foreshadow the next higher plane of society to which the experience, intelligence, and knowledge are steadily tending. It will be a revival, in a higher form, of the liberty, equality, and fraternity of the ancient gentes.

Morgan's assignment of Polynesians to the middle status of savagery alongside the technologically primitive Australians underscores his reliance on the social and ideological to supply the proper measures for developmental classification. The logic of the assignment, as Rivers (1907:311) observed, flows from Morgan's conclusion that the presence of a "Malayan ... system of relationships revealed a corresponding primitive state of the evolution of the human family." Since Polynesians possessed the primitive Malayan system, the remainder of their culture must have been equally primitive.

CONTINUITIES IN TOOLS AND WEAPONS: GRADATIONS IN INVENTIVE IDEAS

An infusion of new substance and ideas drawn from an emergent historical geography gave the study of primitive economics a new theoretical stimulus. In the meantime, Developmentalist theory inspired a few investigators to arrange tools and weapons in graded forms which correlated with a corresponding arrangement of conceptual gradations. Form stabilized and conserved the idea base, and therefore, in the judgment of Colonel Lane-Fox (Pitt-Rivers 1906:29),

> The task before me is to follow by means of ... [forms] the succession of ideas by which the mind of men has developed, from the simple to the complex, and from the homogeneous to the heterogeneous; to work out step by step, by the use of such symbols as the arts afford, that law of contiguity by which the mind has passed from simple cohesion of states of consciousness to the association of ideas, and so on to broader generalizations.

Since 1851 Pitt-Rivers had been collecting firearms and related weaponry to determine the sequence of ideas behind their graded improvements. It was his view that nature suggested to primitive man those generalized forms from which more specialized types gradually were differentiated. A straight stick was the general source for the radiating gradations that led to teardrop throwing clubs, oval shields, mushroom-headed clubs, semicircular and S-shaped boomerangs, knobbed and curved boomerangs (waddy), war picks, and the recurved war pick (leangle), as well as barbed and unbarbed lances (see Figure 8.1). By observing crustacea and animals with scaled armor, men modeled protective clothing of jointed plates or scales (Pitt-Rivers 1906:74–75). The first slicing instruments were made of flint flakes arranged in wood according to the dental pattern of the animal which suggested the idea in the mind of the primitive craftsman. Although Pitt-Rivers extolled the prehistorian as a kind of cultural paleontologist and one who could fill out the innumerable links of technological development, he preferred his own method of grading tools in logical steps, occasionally turning to primitive survivals for assistance.

The correlation of form with idea in a graded continuum also served the German Klemm (1854–1855) in his encyclopedic survey of tools, weapons, fire-making devices, foods, beverages, and narcotics. In estimating the

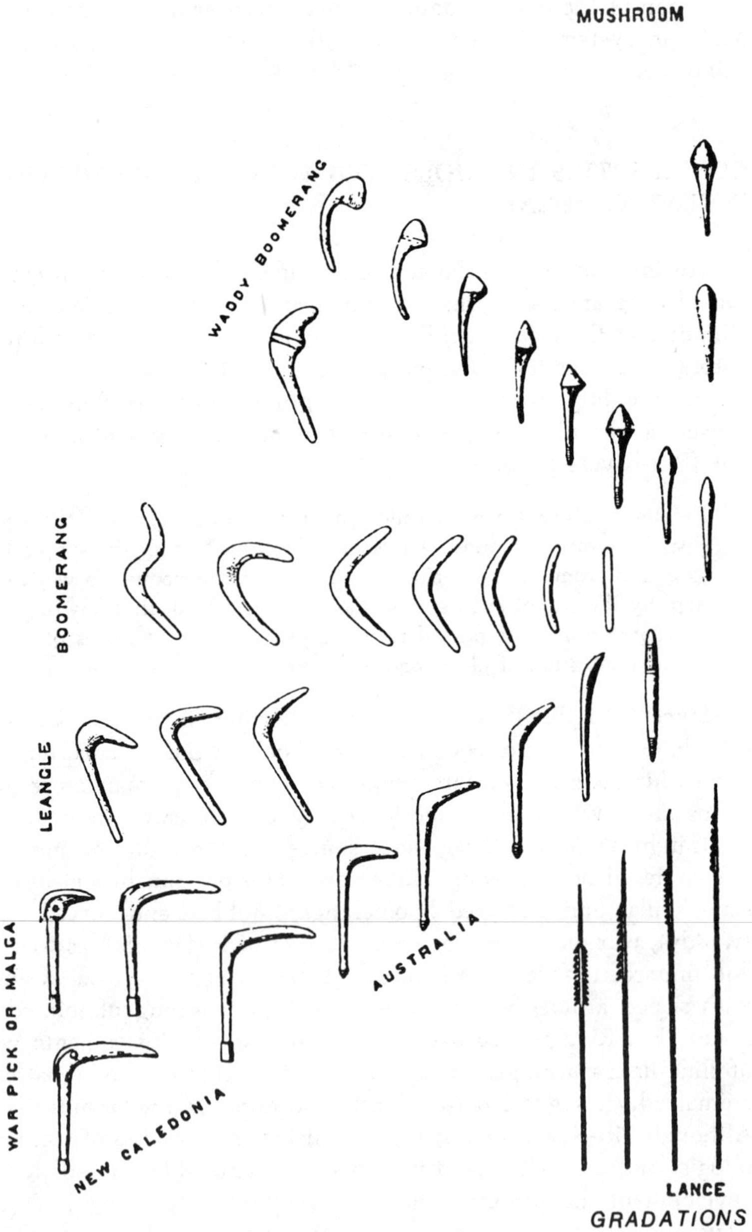

Figure 8-1. Evolution of hand-thrown weapons and shields, beginning with a generalized form and evolving by gradations into specific forms (after Pitt-Rivers, reproduced from Sayce 1963:74–75).

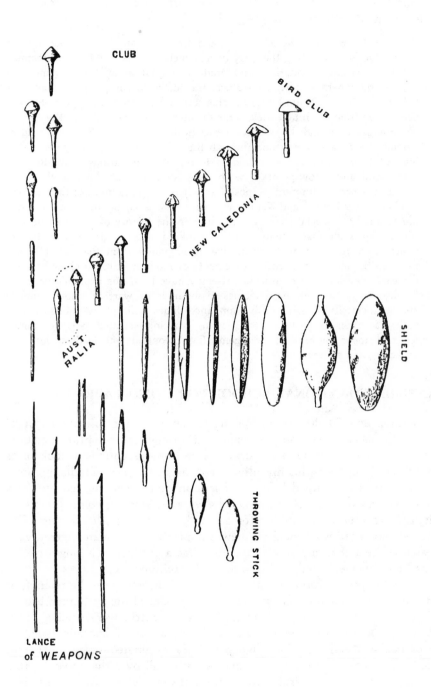

CLUB

BIRD CLUB

NEW CALEDONIA

SHIELD

AUST
RALIA

THROWING STICK

LANCE
of *WEAPONS*

importance of Klemm's and Lane-Fox's (Pitt-Rivers) contributions to technological research, Tylor (1874(1):64–65) praised them for contradicting Nilsson's instinct hypothesis:

> It seems to me that Dr. Klemm . . . and Colonel Lane-Fox . . . take a more instructive line in tracing the early development of arts, not to blind instinct, but to a selection, imitation, and gradual adaptation and improvement of objects and operations which Nature, the instructor of primeval man, sets before him. Thus Klemm traces the stages by which progress appears to have been made from the rough stick to the finished spear or club, from the natural sharp-edged or rounded stone to the artistically fashioned celt, spear-head or hammer. Fox traces connexion through the various types of weapons, pointing out how a form once arrived at is repeated in various sizes, like the spear-head and arrow-point; how in rude conditions of the arts the same instrument serves different purposes, as where the Fuegians use their arrowheads also for knives, and Kafirs carve with their assagais, till separate forms are adopted for special purposes; and how in the history of the striking, cutting and piercing instruments used by mankind, a continuity may be traced, which indicates a gradual progressive development from the rudest beginnings to the most advanced improvements of modern skill. To show how far the early development of warlike arts may have been due to man's imitative faculty, he points out the analogies in methods of warfare among animals and men, classifying as defensive appliances hides, solid plates, jointed plates, scales; as offensive weapons, the piercing, striking, serrated, poisoned kinds, &c; and under the head of stratagems, flight, concealment, leaders, outposts, war-cries, and so forth.

NATURE: VOCATIONAL SCHOOL FOR HOMO FABER

Klemm and Pitt-Rivers, in looking to nature as the primary technical school for savage man, simply reaffirmed an eighteenth-century position. There was another lesson to be drawn from these gradations in tool forms and ideas. Man began his inventive career as an imitator. Gradually, however, his needs, enlarged by more discriminant perceptions, led him to a point where existing tools and weapons were the starting points for inventions. Here was the beginning for a new kind of man, *Homo faber*. The graded modifications brought a new perspective to human ingenuity; it was now clear that any single invention was a product of a long series of small improvements rather than a flash of intuition.

The analysis of form-idea also contributed insights into the relation of invention to accident. Accident could have produced the first crude bronze alloy when tin and copper held in a natural matrix were smelted. Pitt-Rivers (1906:159) saw the utility of analyzing alloys to determine whether a particular metal may have independently originated or whether uniformities suggested that it may have "diffused all over the universe from a common source." In turning to weapons of the Western world, technologists used historical materials to call attention to the role of contact in change.

DEVELOPMENTALISM AND MARX'S ECONOMIC DETERMINISM

The correlation of form and idea in a graduated scale of technological improvements carried out by Klemm and Pitt-Rivers was designed to show how the human mind had progressed from a simple to a complex comprehension of material, tool, and functional specialization. Prehistoric tools collected by archeologists by midcentury confirmed the advance from chipped to polished stone tools, followed by the use of bronze, and then iron. The stone, bronze, iron sequence was established by 1840, and by 1865 Lord Avebury (1913:2) distinguished the chipped and polished stone sequence with the terms "Paleolithic" and "Neolithic." However, the main interests of Developmentalists lay not with technology but with the ideas by which the continuity to civilized institutions could be traced—the monogamic family, law and justice, state and property, language and knowledge.

With their primary concerns located in the ideological background of the social institutions, Developmentalists were unsuitably prepared for economic determinism. The Marxist interpretation not only assigned primitive economic forces precedence over the directional inspiration of ideas but also flouted natural law. To advance mankind—whether by the polish of education according to the progressivists, or the polish of biological superiority according to the evolutionists—functions must be distributed and arranged in a natural hierarchy in accordance with nature's model. In many ways the Developmentalist concept of society, and of social progress, echoed views set forth by Plato. In his *Republic*, those endowed with reason, justice, morality, and conscience stood at the top of a natural hierarchy and set standards for those below who were largely engrossed with sensual satisfactions. Marx and Engels proposed an inversion of the natural order and dared to place the ignorant, uncultivated proletariat—and, in the evolutionist view, an organically inferior man—at the top. Nothing more at variance with nature's purposes could be imagined. The determinism, purpose, social improvement, and accent on class conflict with which Marx and Engels clothed their social philosophy converged on points of theoretical importance with that of Developmentalists. Thus, Marx would abolish private property, the central institution to which Developmentalists credited the best virtues of human character—industry, thrift, independence, and morality. The security of person and individual freedom which Developmentalists charted in the progress of civilization also was anchored to private property. In consequence, the Marxist thesis hardly provoked a counterargument.

The sweep of development described by Marx and Engels was directed principally to economic and social change in the Western world. Consequently, their interest in primitive economy and society was casual. As Harris (1968:227) observed, "Marx's treatment of pre-feudal society is highly schematic, superficial, and disorganized." Shortly before his death Marx did move to supply a stronger ethnographic platform, drawing upon

Morgan's *Ancient Society* (1877). In 1884 Engels completed the assignment with a work entitled, *The Origin of the Family, Private Property, and the State*. In touching upon family, property, and the state, Engels obviously brought dialectical materialism into a more direct confrontation with the primary concerns of Developmentalism. But why the heady idealization of Morgan, the American lawyer? According to Engels (1902:9), who viewed his work as a testamentary assignment,

> It was no less a man than Karl Marx who had reserved to himself the priv-ilege of displaying the results of Morgan's investigations in connection with his own materialistic conception of history—which I might call ours within certain limits. He wished thus to elucidate the full meaning of this conception. For in America, Morgan had, in a manner, discovered anew the materialistic conception of history, originated by Marx forty years ago. In comparing barbarism and civilization, he had arrived, in the main, at the same results as Marx.

Marx and Engels greatly overstated the case for economic determinism in Morgan's position. In a narrow sense, Morgan's interpretation of the role of subsistence and technological change in providing a seedbed for ideas that reached into family, property, and political reorganizations could be viewed as economic and materialistic. But then, progressivists in the eighteenth century had been alert to the importance of the material arts in providing a leisure platform for intellectual development; they, too, had described the close relation among the patriarchal family, a militarized state, and the transition to a pastoral economy. Like Morgan, they were interested in tracing continuities in ideas leading to civilization, and here they placed their emphasis. When Morgan is placed, as he must be, in the context of the Developmentalist position, the misreading by Marx and Engels is apparent, and Opler (1964) is more on target than contemporary anthropologists (for example, White 1949; Leacock 1964) who seek to find in Morgan an American Marx. In upending the social philosophy of the Age of Reason by explaining "ideology and social organization as adap-tive responses to techno-economic conditions," as Harris (1968:233, 240) phrased it, Marx and Engels likewise turned the whole Developmentalist position upside down, including Tylor, Morgan, and Spencer. However, both Developmentalist Marx and his Developmentalist opponents shared a basic emphasis on ideas in organizing outlooks and in communicating a basis for action.

MORALS AND MATERIALISM: EPILOGUE TO DEVELOPMENTALISM

The cautious approach to materialistic interpretations characteristic of the Developmentalist tradition continued into the twentieth century with publication of *The Material Culture and Social Institutions of the Simpler*

Peoples (1915) by Hobhouse, Wheeler, and Ginsberg. L. T. Hobhouse was not at all satisfied with the pragmatic ethics of natural selection, and in 1906 (*Morals in Evolution*) he sketched the evolutionary interrelations of ethics, religion, and politics. He put his research on a firm basis by surveying world societies and comparing their institutions, moral ideas, and political systems to see to what extent societies, according to the clustering of their attributes, were arranged on a developmental continuum. According to Ginsberg (1965:xiii), their goal was to sketch a "general theory of social development . . . by determin[ing] in what ways advances in knowledge and its applications are related to changes in other domains of human achievement and in what conditions a rational control of future developments may be attainable." They determined that material culture, which measured man's control over nature, was their best guide. While apologizing for using material culture as a prime measure, they considered it a useful instrument in coordinating levels of intellectual development. They simply wished to know whether advances in technical knowledge were correlated with advances in morality, justice, religion, and the basic organization of society.

Over 150 years earlier Rousseau (Cole 1950) delivered a judgment to the scientific academy at Dijon that men in civilized society had allowed the comforts accompanying technological advances to subvert their natural humanity, and in so doing pitted man against man in an immoral struggle for wealth and power. The phrasing and treatment of the problem by Rousseau and by Hobhouse and his associates was different, but a concern with moral and intellectual advance bridged the centuries and helps explain why Marx's dialectical materialism could not reach Developmentalism at this time. In the instance of Hobhouse, use of material culture as a measure of continuities and correlates turned out to be a matter of strategy, much as in the case of Morgan and as in the counsel of Tylor. Developmentalists backed into materialistic interpretations for which, generally speaking, they had no deep conviction.

A survey of some 643 unit groups distributed through hunting, pastoral, and agricultural groups brought Hobhouse, Wheeler, and Ginsberg (1965:253) to the conclusion that the "degree of correlation between social institutions and economic development . . . varies very greatly from case to case." In a general way, a rough index of the intellectual and organizational potential of societies could be correlated with their economic development (Hobhouse, Wheeler, and Ginsberg 1965:254). However, the level of economic development bore no direct relation to ideas and practices affecting justice, morality, and the status of women. An authoritarian family under paternal control was correlated with pastoralism. With economic advance, government became more complex and the administration of justice became a public matter. Economic causes made special contributions to the

> development of organized warfare and the substitution of the enslavement of prisoners for their slaughter, liberation, or adoption. With the decline of

infanticide, the better security for food, and the extension of order, we may infer a growing population, in some cases a desire for territorial extension, in others a demand for slave labour. The mere extension of regular industry makes for social differentiation, since the effects of energy and thrift become cumulative. Hence we have a partial rise of a nobility and the more extensive development of a servile or semi-servile class. Hence, also, the communal tenure of land gives way, and while in some cases it blends with individual occupation or ownership, in others it passes more or less effectively into the hands of a chief or a nobility. On all sides social and economic differentiation replace the comparative equality of the hunting peoples. The extension of order is also, upon the whole, an extension of subordination. (Hobhouse, Wheeler, and Ginsberg 1965:254)

The study of Hobhouse, Wheeler, and Ginsberg was especially important in that it attempted to put general ideas regarding social evolution to a numerical test. Like Tylor (1889), they had to cope with the comparability of their categories and units, and were forced to settle for something less than scientific quality control. For example, their use of thirty-one local groups in Australia allowed insufficient weight to the probability that historical contacts might have produced enough similarities in institutional forms that tribes could not be compared as self-standing units. However, Hobhouse and associates included discussions of their problem in establishing equivalent units, and though their statistical practices did not go beyond numerical rankings and percentages, they added a tone of methodological rigor to comparative studies. *The Material Culture and Social Institutions of the Simpler Peoples* still stands as an ambitious landmark and epilogue to Developmentalism. None later was inspired to imitate it, even though, according to Ginsberg (1965:xiii–xiv), scholars have at their disposal an "enormous increase in ethnographic material, [added] statistical sophistication, and technical aids."

SUMMARY

Developmentalists generally agreed that the comforts and refinements of any level of social development were underpinned by the state of the economy. Production of surplus foods not only won the battle against insecurity but also released leisure time for creative thinking and the arts. Although the quality of life was related to economic necessities, human progress was not determined by economic forces. Marx and Engels were notable exceptions to this general view.

Technology was useful in demonstrating man's gradual ascendancy over nature. However, technology, as other institutions, responded to human needs according to shifting circumstances and was advanced by inventive ideas. Necessity was the mother of invention. Without the pressures of population outstripping food production, the great subsistence inventions (pastoralism and agriculture) would not have taken place. Progress was a matter of challenge and response.

Material inventions were no more important indicators of mental processes than other arts, and were less amenable to ideological analysis than language, religion, and mythology. Savagery, barbarism, and civilization generally were correlated with hunting, pastoral and agricultural, and commercial-industrial societies. However, Morgan alone endeavored to detail the economic, institutional, and ideological correlates of each stage.

Developmentalists considered property the central institution in the advance to the civilized state. Property elicited industry and thrift so essential to civilized character. Property also served as the instrument for accommodating individual rights and responsibilities according to law, thereby establishing a moral basis governing social relationships and guaranteeing personal safety in a stable society. The pursuit of property also provided incentives which broadened individuality, and through social stratification, released numbers of the population to carry forward a refinement of the intellectual and creative arts. Property began to exert a social force with the appearance of pastoralism, and this civilizing influence increased with the transition to agriculture and to the commercial-industrial economy.

Marx and Engels, as well as Morgan, challenged the Developmentalist assessment of the contributions which property made to the advancement of human welfare. Morgan admitted that property had advanced human morality, law, and industry, but in the process basic values regulating human relations were lost. These values could be found in force in the ancient tribal societies where resources were shared and mutual love, respect, and obligation regulated social relationships on the basis of kinship. Property appeared like a Frankenstein which its creator no longer controlled. In Morgan's (1877:552) judgment,

> A mere property career is not the final destiny of mankind, if progress is to be the law of the future as it has been of the past. . . . Democracy in government, brotherhood in society, equality in rights and privileges, and universal education, foreshadow the next higher plane of society to which experience, intelligence and knowledge are steadily tending. It will be a revival, in a higher form, of the liberty, equality and fraternity of the ancient gentes.

From the viewpoint of Marx and Engels civilized industrial society, with its class-controlled economy and political order, deprived the vast majority of their right to be human. The rights of class and of property were given precedence over human values. The industrial society based on private ownership of production was an artificial construct which carried the seeds of its own destruction. Through an inevitable class war the ownership of production would be returned to the people, and only then would mankind reach a social condition which permitted attainment of the full potential to be human.

ASSESSMENT OF DEVELOPMENTALISM

Foundations of Social Science, Anthropology, and Sociology

Eighteenth-century progressivists must be credited with outlining the base upon which a social science could be erected. To accomplish this task, progressivists first defined an area of investigation that could be discriminated from history—the natural history of the species. Second, they developed a body of theory to account for human improvement based on the assumption that uniform causes produce uniform effects. In this eighteenth-century view, man was subject to natural laws, but his flexible nature was so regulated by mental and moral processes that he was not subject to the rude organic processes that limited animal development. Third, they invoked a special comparative method, by which institutions, ideas, and customs drawn from diverse peoples could be arranged on a continuum that would demonstrate advancement in logicality, morality, and social complexity. Thus, in the stages of savagery, barbarism, and civilization they sought to capture the scale of progress running from the simple to the complex, from the less to the more logical, and from the amoral to the moral. Fourth, they claimed a new kind of fact—a group fact—expressed in custom, social ideas, artifacts, groups, and institutions. The assembly of these group facts to prove their thesis of human progress initiated the accumulation of a distinct body of evidence for their science.

Nineteenth-century Developmentalists broadened and deepened the eighteenth-century effort by anchoring social processes to laws governing the organization and processes of matter and organisms which physicists, geologists, and biologists promulgated between 1830 and 1860. Fresh discoveries in archeology, human paleontology, earth history, and biological evolution aroused an enthusiastic interest in the origin and development of man as a physical, psychological, social, and cultural being. On the basis of these new materials, the general social science goal pursued by ethnological interests was refocused on the early history of mankind; and this special subject matter was claimed for a new anthropological and ethnological science. Comte and Spencer sought to define a general social science based on a conceptualization of the social as the proper subject matter for sociology. This effort intermingled historically with attempts to separate and differentiate an anthropological discipline concerned with uniting man's biological, social, and cultural development. Tylor took the view that the anthropological or ethnographic science should focus on the study of culture, which he viewed as a composite of features man learned as a member of a society. Distinction of the social and cultural at this time formalized differences implicit in the writings of previous social theorists in their use of the terms "social," "culture," and "civilization." These conceptualizations were prophetic for future developments in that sociologists took up the social as their subject matter and ethnologists seized upon culture as their unique domain. The conceptualization of the social and cultural also provided the basis for the differentiation of social and cultural anthropology.

The differentiation of anthropology and sociology raised on conceptual ambiguities of the social and cultural, produced a rivalry over which was the science of mankind. Both self-styled sociologists and anthropological ethnologists at first were inspired to reconstruct the general history of mankind. This was especially the case with regard to sociologist Spencer and certain of his followers. Comte, however, emphasized that sociology should concentrate on man's future rather than on his past—the same emphasis which Marx and Engels brought. The ambiguous relationship between emergent sociology and anthropology continued until both developed their true interests and character through fieldwork; hence, the old saying that sociology is what sociologists do and anthropology is what anthropologists do.

Fortified with the evolutionary theory of natural selection, nineteenth-century Developmentalists extended the anthropological horizon by including biological processes as intrinsic to comprehension of psychological and social processes. Out of this new-found relation came a determination to see the human process as a unitary one. However, the side effects of this initial holistic orientation were unfortunate. Weighted though it was in terms of biological processes, it implicated the discipline in a Lamarckian phylogenetic inheritance which was nationalistic, racist, and had dubious ideas about the unconscious transmission of effects of ancestral social and psychological experiences.

The special place anthropology gained among the sciences was not due to any methodological breakthrough reached by nineteenth-century Developmentalists. The comparative method they used was a practice of long standing. The same held for the doctrine of survivals, which simply refined and justified prior use of symbols and symbolic behavior as doorways to the past. Rather, their contributions stemmed from the enthusiastic dedication and inexhaustible energy marshaled to produce the proof of human origins and development. The cumulative effects of their efforts signaled that a new discipline was at hand:

1. Establishment of an impressive body of social facts drawn from the customs, institutions, ideas, and to a lesser extent, from the technology of primitive peoples. Materials relating to the physical history of mankind and the prehistoric development of culture added a whole new dimension of factual evidences which correlated human beginnings and continuities with the history of the earth. Such information confirmed, extended, and refocused the ethnologic purpose on a distinctive set of factual evidence related to the origin and early history of mankind.
2. Formulation of a useful set of concepts that could serve as a scientific currency in the classification of group facts.
3. Formulation of a recognizable and exclusive body of hypotheses as-

sociated with the nature, beginnings, and development of social institutions.

4. Formulation of special associations, journals, and museums for the distribution of information, storage, and exchange of ideas relevant to mankind—especially in man's early estate.

Added together, they spelled anthropology: anthropological facts, anthropological concepts, anthropological theories, and anthropological societies. While not exclusive to anthropology, the comparative method became the trademark of evolutionary anthropology. Nineteenth-century Developmentalists must be given credit for holding the vision of a unified anthropology, with specializations reaching out to other sciences. Physical anthropology, however, provided the entrée for acceptance by the natural sciences (for example, the British and American Association for the Advancement of Science).

To raise the natural history of mankind to the point where it was admitted into the convention of sciences and accepted as a course of study in the universities was no small accomplishment. The worth of Developmentalist hypotheses, especially those which traced the origins of human institutions to a particular idea, is another matter. To satisfy the canons of science, Developmentalists usually assembled a modest number of supporting illustrations, not always carefully screened for clear resemblances, and resorted to universal experiences in order to eliminate the possibility of variability in the determining conditions. One difficulty of universal correlates is that there may be more than one universal experience to choose from, and hence a number of hypotheses compete for acceptance. Universal features as correlates of universal processes of the human mind, to which Developmentalists called attention, also were used by Freud and presently by Lévi-Strauss.

In the instance of religion, the proliferation of psychological universal hypotheses was fantastic, with some forty-two being catalogued by Van Gennep (1920) regarding totemism. Presuppositions about the dominating role of religion and magic in primitive thought betrayed a narrow and unyielding prejudice that conveyed some curious origins, as in Wundt's (1928:241–243) explanation of the kiss. Admitting that sex set the standard for beauty and its enhancement through ornament was not lost on the opposite sex, Wundt nonetheless denied any original connection between the kiss and courtship. The source for the kiss must be sought in the ritual exchange of the breath soul during initiation, as in the instance of the Australian native priest who pressed his teeth against those of the novice to loosen one for removal. The exchange of the breath soul was intended to influence procreation, and nose kissing was a variant induced by lip plugs or other devices that interfered with mouth kissing. With psychological explanations of this order, there was little to substantiate them and little opportunity for building new hypotheses that could be operationalized.

The principle of analogical reasoning which Developmentalists favored when introspecting their way into the savage mind presented obvious difficulties. Formal resemblances are not always what they seem, and the ideological routes taken may be diverse, even though similar conclusions may be arrived at. The mere presence of opposing psychological explanations for institutional origins pointed up a methodological ambiguity. Speculative hypotheses were hard to avoid; yet it is probable that some of these scientific guesses were not wide of the mark—but which ones? Some interpretations based upon common human experience were plausible—for example, the animistic and animatistic origins of the sacred. It is also true that analogical introspection is indispensable to those who make inferences regarding motive from observed behavior.

A revival of interest in evolutionary problems during the 1930s renovated the issue of social origins and again focused explanation on the fundamental operations of the human mind. Lévi-Strauss (1963a) viewed totemism as a product of a human tendency to think in terms of linked opposites. Lévi-Strauss recommended that the older associationist psychology be renovated and stiffened with the precise operations available in symbolic logic, apparently to reach a more objective assessment of Developmentalist hypotheses. Presently the origins of incest and exogamy have been re-engaged, and new investigations of primate behavior once more have induced opposing biopsychic and psychosocial explanations. After the manner of Westermarck, Kortmulder (1968) implied that avoidance of sex relations between parent and offspring and between siblings existed as an evolutionary adaptation. On the other hand, Livingstone took the position that tendencies toward exogamic practices could not take place until a cognitive-linguistic threshold had been reached. However, Livingstone (1969(71):48) conceded that primate carnivores who were gregarious and hunted cooperatively in gangs would have found a fairly large endogamous band congenial to their mode of life. If this were the case, early hominids possessed such pongid social organization, and the "ideas of Bachofen, McLennan, and Morgan on primitive promiscuity are not as ridiculous as we have been taught" (Livingstone 1969(71):48).

How far this modern reassessment of Developmentalist hypotheses may go depends on the extent to which control over unknowns reduces the limits of speculation that now follow contemporary interpretations of origins, just as the problem haunted nineteenth-century explanations. Alert to the need for extending the precise controls achieved by the natural sciences through mathematics, Tylor in 1889 published results obtained when the principle of chance or probable association was applied to a number of social practices. Working with 350 different societies, he attempted to show that such data could be classified, tabulated, and handled mathematically to uncover features which had a tendency to cluster together on a better-than-chance basis. There were adhesions, as he called the correlations, between avoidance of a wife's relations and matrilocal residence, teknonymy and matrilocal residence, and exogamy and the classificatory relationship. Exceedingly cautious in the interpretative implications of his results, Tylor called attention to how imperfect the anthropological records were; for one faced contradictory descriptions at times, or no statement at all bearing on the item required. At the same time, he pointed to a future often enunciated by Bastian—"that in statistical investigation the future of anthropology lies" (Tylor 1889:268–269). Systematic application alone could elicit the principles by which social development had taken place.

Having defined their scientific role as systematizers, one should hardly fault Developmentalists for failing to initiate fieldwork. Yet in Morgan's Iroquois researches, in the collecting expeditions inspired by Bastian, and in the naturalist-initiated expedition to Torres Straits led by Haddon, the beginnings of field investigation are found. In the meantime, the image of first hand description was carried by naturalists, traders, captives, and missionaries. By the end of the nineteenth century, the bibliography of such accounts was enormous, and many were priceless because they described native life before European contacts introduced striking modifications. The timing of certain missionary offerings, as in the instances of Rev. Lorimer Fison (ca. 1872) and Bishop R. H. Codrington (1891), supplied Developmentalists with exciting new materials relevant to their interest in the origins of social organization and religion.

Preconceptions stemming from the theory of development precluded the critical objectivity essential for a proper evaluation of alien peoples and cultures. Realistic descriptions of savage character usually were passed over in favor of a savage portrait congenial to theoretical expectations. In comparison with the civilized, savages standing at the threshold of human development were expected to be illogical, impulsive, improvident, cruel, immoral, and dominated by superstitious fears. The overall effect of Developmentalist theory was a widening of the gap between savage and civilized. Under evolution, the differences in degree implicit in the progressivist view were transformed into qualitative differences. Whether the evolutionist thought in terms of transformations within a single human species or between different species races, the alleged gap between savage and civilized minds became a distinction of two qualitatively separate minds. The most ambitious effort to prove that primitive mental operations at base were qualitatively different from those of civilized men came from Lévy-Bruhl, who, in theory, made no claims as an evolutionist and stressed the significance of the social context for thought processes. The template of primitive prelogical mentality portrayed by Lévi-Bruhl was etched with features common to the Developmentalist design, despite an accent on collective representations. In final analysis, Developmentalists, owing to preconceptions flowing from their problem orientation, were unable to assess critically the descriptive substance offered by explorers, traders, and missionaries. Consequently, their views served to entrench popular prejudice by stamping it with a scientific label.

Evolutionism and Process

Evolutionary emphasis on adaptive necessities prepared the ground for attention to structure and functional interaction characteristic of the next stage in ethnological theory. Such a structural-functional focus was known to both Comte and Spencer, but their developmental preferences prevented their study of static structure and process. However, in their search for the dynamics of continuous development, evolutionists added some understanding of process by calling attention to the unconscious nature of change. Use of the organic analogy, and perceptive awareness of the interdependent and competitive relations of groups, helped to create the idea that there were social analogs to the bioecological configurations observed among plants and animals.

The emergence of the concept of the unconscious under evolutionism was of singular importance in that it influenced theories of process and supported a structural view of the reality problem. Obviously, unconscious processes were not immediately visible, and their recording and measurement present special difficulties for social and cultural investigation. Yet, this covert dimension of human behavior represented in theory the locus for the real or the core of human behavior. In biological analogy, the unconscious stood in relation to the conscious very much like the way in which genotype stood to phenotype. Ultimate reality thus resided in an inner structure to which the observable activities of human beings, and their ideas, gave clues but not answers. Here, in a new guise, old questions reappeared—the relation of history to evolution and of variation to structure. Finally, the emergence of the unconscious constituted a profound alteration in estimating the essence of human nature. The view of man as a rational being, to which social science under the impulse of the idea of progress had been dedicated, now was rejected. Man emerged less a product of his own hands than a victim of dark and hidden forces, a mannequin shaped by the pressures of circumstances. Such being the case, there was a place for a rational science that would help make the unknown known.

While Developmentalism did not succeed in achieving a full distinction of the social and cultural as the special province of the sociological and anthropological disciplines, it did prepare the ground for this distinctive association. During the first two decades of the twentieth century, a strong tendency to establish the autonomy and causal precedence of the social over the biological gathered momentum within the phylogenetic perspective emphasized by Spencer. This meant the substitution of a sociopsychological phylogeny for the biopsychic phylogeny espoused by evolutionists. The epilogue for this sociopsychological phylogenetic point of view was written by Robert Briffault in a summative work of three volumes entitled *The Mothers* (1927).

Human consciousness has in fact, come to dwell almost exclusively in the sphere of socially inherited concepts, sentiments, and values. Not only has

> conceptual thought, owing to its far greater efficiency and distinctiveness, superceded more primitive, instinctive, impulsive modes of reaction, but it is with social relations and intercourse that human behavior is chiefly concerned. (Briffault 1927(1):69)

No individual began life free of the human social-psychological inheritance. The private psyche was no *tabula rasa* at birth. The individual during his lifetime did not construct a human social psyche out of sensory and reflective experience as humanistic progressivists, following Locke, argued. On the contrary,

> no apparently whimsical curiosity of savage social ethnology or folklore is without the counterpart in twentieth-century civilization. . . . In the same manner as the reactions of primitive protozoa and primordial marine creatures survive in the modes of activity of our physiological organism, so every idea, every custom, that has at one time become firmly established in human society, whether its origin dates back ten or ten thousand years, is perpetuated in traditional heredity; no item of that inheritance is ever lost or abolished. The social constitution may be changed, the primitive idea may become adapted to functions the very opposite of those in relation to which it originated; yet in no instance is it wiped away from the human mind. The record of social evolution is hence far more complete than the geological and palaeontological record of the past; its fossils are not odd fragments that owe their preservation to a lucky chance; they survive for ever and ever in the continuity of social and psychological tradition. (Briffault 1927(1):80–81)

More important, however, was the accent on social process expressed in social conflict and social selection, the natural consequence of the application of the principle of natural selection to society. The important focus now was societies in contact, social institutions, or social groups. The give and take and overcoming of one society by another, or the superseding of one social institution by another more functionally adaptive one, focused attention on a process that was social and interactional. Subsequent developments, as anthropology made the turn to Structuralism, built on the new-found emphasis on social and cultural processes, interaction, and function which began to overtake Developmentalism as its time drew to a close. Finally, as the theoretical establishment of the day, Developmentalism aided the birth of a new theoretical order by serving as a whipping boy for structural interactionists seeking to lay new foundations for a scientific anthropology. Many of the problems engaged by functionalists and historicists were designed to overturn Developmentalism and to fixate its historical place in the steps leading to the new anthropology.

PART III

Structuralism (ca. 1890-1940)

Three Kinds of Structuralism: Cultural-Historical, Social, and Biocultural

The approximately fifty years covered by Structuralism witnessed the entrenchment of both sociology and anthropology as disciplines with distinctive subject matters, factual content, theories, methods, and professional organizations. In anthropology the differential emphasis on the social and cultural gave rise to a social and a cultural anthropology.

Social anthropology drew upon the pioneer work of Emile Durkheim for its substantive theory and method. The structure of social units and their maintenance processes, as well as the way institutionalized activities and symbols promoted a collective impulse and a sense of group identification, were central to the social anthropological approach to the study of primitive society, and of society in general. The interrelations of individuals as holders of status and social categories were described and analyzed in order to bring out the functional (or dysfunctional) contribution which their activities conveyed to the total social system. The model of an organism was freely applied, with a consequent emphasis on structure, equilibrium-disequilibrium, and the physiology of social processes (interaction). Historical and evolutionary problems were not of great moment to social structuralists, and, in their view, posed serious methodological difficulties. As a concept, culture played a secondary role in the social interactionist context, and the range of its definition came to be quite restricted. Indeed, the course of social anthropology under British guidance during the first fifty years appeared so aberrant to the American anthropologist Murdock (1951(53): 463–473), that he held them to be sociologists rather than anthropologists. Their most serious mistake was lack of concern for the full range of cultural phenomena. Social anthropologists were to prone to confine themselves to kinship and related matters such as marriage, property, and government.

At the time that Radcliffe-Brown was firming up the theory of social Structuralism, Malinowski proclaimed his functionalism (biocultural Structuralism). In place of social structure, Malinowski began his analysis of society and culture with human nature. Culture was an instrument designed in its various institutions to fulfill human needs relating to survival, reproduction, health, comfort, and the like. Both social and biocultural Structuralism emphasized functional interrelationships. However, the former gave rise to a theory of society, while the latter contributed a theory of culture (see Chapter 13).

Culture historicism carried the third intellectual current associated with Structuralism. As in social and biocultural Structuralism there was an emphasis on process as a relation between units. However, under culture historicism the relationship was between objects and activities—customs, artifacts, patterned modes of thinking, values, and stylistic expressions of language, art, and literature. The objective of culture historians was to explain how individual tribes, and tribes clustered in geographic regions, built up their cultures by adding and combining culture traits borrowed from their neighbors, or from more distant areas and times.

Historicists divided themselves into three camps or schools which bore a curious relation to national origins: (1) American historicists, (2) German-Austrian *Kulturkreislehrer*, and (3) British migrationists. All emphasized the use of empirical criteria to measure the formal resemblances of elements widely distributed or clustered in space for determining the historic movement and cumulative growth of culture elements and of whole cultures. Of the three, American historicists contributed the theoretical thrust which led to recognition of culture as an autonomous and substantive level of fact and explanation. More

than others they wrestled with a proper scientific concept of culture, explored its ramifications, and endeavored to associate culture with the science of ethnology.

The Shared Meanings of Structuralists

Despite their variable interests and methodological emphases, anthropological Structuralists converged on a common ground of problems and objectives. The main features shared by Structuralists of any persuasion run as follows:

1. Negative reaction to Developmentalist theory, problem definitions, and methodological procedures. This reactive tone rendered structuralists part-captives of Developmentalism in that many problems were taken up to refute errors of the past. At the same time an advancement in perception followed the intellectual challenge of Developmentalism, and occasionally some worthy substance was drawn from the Developmentalist effort.

2. Establishment of the social and/or cultural as substantive areas of investigation and of causal explanation, and their exclusive association with social anthropology and ethnology.

3. Conceptualization of reality as a series of ranked orders with the social and/or cultural at the top. Owing to their ranked causal orders, Structuralists were anxious that the social and cultural should not be explained by the psychological or the biological orders.

4. A necessity to view social and cultural facts in a structured context in order to uncover social or cultural laws. Some individual ir-

resolution as to the structured necessity of the social and cultural occurred, especially with Boas and certain of his students. Difficulties in effective data control prompted skepticism regarding social and cultural determinism.

5. An emphatic preoccupation with form, order, and systemic operations. This is reflected in the conceptual vocabulary: social structure, culture pattern, culture area, social solidarity, cultural integration, social system, configuration, equilibrium-disequilibrium, and organization in contrast with disorganization. At the individual level, the problem of order centered in the processes of habituation and unconscious conditioning. The conditioned nature of culture patterns prevented a conscious grasp of pattern, configuration, and basic premises regulating choice of ends and means. Individual attitudes were averaged into a social consensus or normative behavior, or individuals were used to illustrate typical behavior according to the culture pattern.

In straining to understand the orderly arrangement of society and culture, Structuralists commonly gave substance to averages, norms, and patterns. The problem of reification, and the significance which it held for theory and method, was bypassed in the description of empirical data—the social and cultural facts of tools, clans, family groups, customs, marriage rules, and ceremonial. Linguistics supplied the working model for the concept of pattern developed by Americanists, with Boas, and later Sapir, especially using linguistic data to illuminate and fixate the reality of culture patterns (See Aberle 1957; Sapir 1949c.)

6. A strong attraction for inductive natural science. Structuralists accented the necessity to develop hypotheses that were testable and supported by controls which began with field collection of facts and ended with data analysis. Thus fieldwork became entrenched.

7. Abandonment of value judgments, except as stress on function, called for judgment in favor of solidarity as an ultimate social value. Sapir's (1949b) "Culture, Genuine and Spurious" was a notable exception in that he contrasted cultures according to the richness of involvement and experience contributed to the individual personality. Nevertheless, Structuralists used value contrasts to bring out the distinctive qualities which separated one social order, or cultural system, from another. As cultural historicism ebbed during the thirties, American ethnologists explored the role of values in cultural integration and in selective acceptance and rejection of cultural features in contact situations.

8. Cultural historicists, social Structuralists, and biocultural functionalists generally eschewed any interest in the ultimate origins of beliefs, customs, and institutions. Their objective was to describe and to analyze the relations of social and cultural things. Historicists necessarily were interested in the historic origin of culture elements and made determined efforts to assign features to their cultural origins. With social Structuralists and biocultural functionalists, the problem of origins dissolved in the final purpose or function of an activity.

9. Denial of the immediate importance of evolutionary-type problems for social and cultural research. Structuralists could hardly deny the reality of a temporal succession of social and cultural types or structures. However, their inductive perspective led to the conclusion that evolutionary sequences must be arrived at through a controlled comparison of individual cases. The critical posture and practice of Structuralists inhibited evolutionary studies, and the reintroduction of an evolutionary perspective in American ethnology occurred when anthropology was entering a dynamic period of specialized differentiation during the thirties.

10. A final concordance among Structuralists can be found in the assumption that individual psychological and traditional explanations of social and cultural features were not the true explanations. Rather, when informants offered motivations, or pointed to a popular explanation of custom (for example, respect as the basis for avoidance behavior), it was assumed that this was an *ex post facto* rationalization. This followed from the fact that both individual and group behavior were governed by implicit premises and rules which the subject intuitively apprehended but did not comprehend. The scientific role was to discover the real world behind the externals, to find out what lay behind the secondary rationalizations.

Social anthropologists, cultural historicists, and biocultural functionalists generally maintained a theoretical distance from fellow-Structuralists. However, all suffered serious challenges to their structural determinism as the thirties drew to a close.

Structuralism: Founders and Followers

With Structuralism the problem of founders entered a new phase owing to new differentiations within anthropology and the establishment of anthropological programs at the university level (see Figure 1). With university programs, anthropology broke out of the narrow confines of the museum and constructed a training base relevant to professional careers.

Periods of transition, as the change from Developmentalism to Structuralism, encourage a focus of personal energy and an unusual concentration of creativity. Historic figures emerge, ranging widely over the field, yet striving to organize a general theory. Such was the case with regard to the founders of culture historicism (North America, Franz Boas 1858–1942; Germany, Friedrich Ratzel 1844–1904; Fritz Graebner 1877–1934; Wilhelm Schmidt 1868–1954; England, G. Elliot Smith 1871–1937), social anthropology (France, Emile Durkheim 1858–1917; Marcel Mauss 1872–1950; England, A. R. Radcliffe-Brown 1881–1955), and biocultural functionalism (Bronislaw Malinowski 1884–1942). Historical founders were never equally enamored of theory, nor equally endowed with a talent for systematic presentation. Boas, for example, reportedly had a marked distaste for theory. He preferred to talk about method; but in demonstrating how problems should properly be defined and researched, and in his constant public reminders of the goals and methods

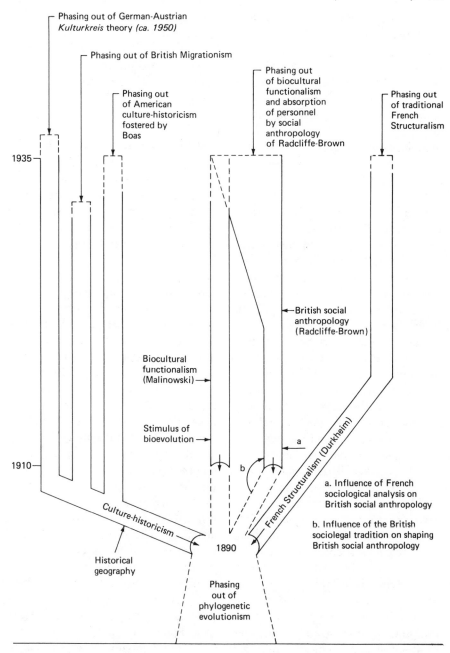

Figure 1. Differentiation of anthropology between 1890 and 1940. The reactive nature of the new intellectual developments to Developmentalist theory is indicated thusly:←─)

of ethnology, Boas conveyed and reinforced a theoretical orientation that was absorbed by those he guided and instructed. As he observed in 1936, "When I thought that these *historical* methods were firmly established I began to stress, about 1910, the problems of cultural dynamics, of integration of culture and of the interaction between individual and society" (Boas 1940o: 311).

It is interesting that historic founders of the different theoretical orientations manifest in Structuralism were successful largely because of a conversion of students to a sensitive regard for their points of view. This was true for Boas, Radcliffe-Brown, Malinowski, and Durkheim and Mauss. Between 1918 and 1937 Radcliffe-Brown traveled to South Africa, Australia, and the United States, persuading audiences with the clear logic of his theoretical position, and remaining long enough to inspire a team of researchers to put his theory into practice. Like Boas, Malinowski attracted students with challenging problems that fieldwork alone could solve. Graebner, the systematizer of *Kulturkreis* theory and method, did not build a coterie of devoted students, but his collegial convert Pater Schmidt established a company of *Kulturkreis* theorists in Vienna. The extreme position taken by Smith in tracing all ancient civilizations back to Egypt militated against a scientific following.

Theoretical differentiations within Structuralism (for example, culture-historical "schools"; comparative sociology or social anthropology; functionalism) came early in the century. Each achieved its classic formulation during the second decade. The thirties brought a crystallization of difference, as in the instance of cultural and social anthropology. This distinction within anthropology paralleled the separation of anthropology and sociology which was firmly established in the United States in about 1920. Culture theorists in the United States produced further differentiations as they extended their investigations to culture and personality and the value orientations of cultures.

After 1940 exploration of structure, with its emphasis on social and cultural determinism, faced increasing challenges. Following Kroeber (1963) one might speculate that Structuralism, as a culture pattern, may have exhausted its potentialities for creative elaboration and faced involutional processes. Other developments eroded the foundations of Structuralism. The differentiation of subfields after 1935 emphasized an intensive researching of focused problems, resulting in an increased sensitivity to significant variations in the face of structure. The introduction of psychoanalytic theory undermined the habituative conditioning on which structural theory relied for the consistencies and coherencies of system processes. Finally, reason emerged as a signal component of human nature, and man now was viewed as a more flexible agent vis-à-vis culture. At any rate, the enculturated individual was no longer considered a passive imprint of the culture process. What held for the cultural held for the social.

9

Diffusion and Culture History

INTRODUCTION

Culture historicism reintroduced the importance of individual histories into the general problem of culture growth. It constituted a reaction to the evolutionary design, which ignored individual histories in favor of a general history and relied on universal psychological processes to account for identities in the trajectory of cultural development. Introduction of historical variation into the anthropological perspective marked a step forward, since it opened the way for a more comprehensive view of the reality process. Unfortunately, the dichotomy between structural and variational processes continued as culture historicists rejected the investigation of sequential change. They did not deny the probability of evolutionary stages, but dismissed such investigation in favor of controls they thought were available in their historical method.

Formulation of the culture concept and its association with ethnology was the work of culture historicists (see Chapter 10). They saw culture as a special domain operating according to its own laws, and which could not be derived from individual psychological processes. Nor could culture in its workings be explained by such psychological processes.

Efforts of geographers to map cultural features on a world-wide basis, and to determine cultural boundaries based on distributions, supplied the immediate stimulus for the historical interest in ethnology. This historical focus emerged almost simultaneously in the United States and on the Continent. Major European contributors to the historical orientation appeared early in the century in Scandinavia, Britain, Germany, and Austria. Theoretical emphases growing out of the limitations of their respective experiences lent a distinctive quality to the historicism of each of these countries. However, American and Scandinavian diffusionists were sufficiently alike to be contrasted with both British migrationists and German-Austrian *Kulturkreislehrer*.

American culture historians, influenced by Franz Boas, dealt with a narrow domain of analysis in the interests of firming control over their data. They viewed relatively homogeneous natural and cultural regions as interactional universes in which culture traits and complexes were connected historically. Continental historians, especially *Kulturkreis* theorists and British migrationists, strove for broad regional, continental, and world-wide culture histories.

The basic challenges of culture historians centered in how to transform the flat distributions in space into dynamic processes of cultural interchange through time. They were forced to cope with uniformities and differences in rates of transmission, and to determine whether tools, ideas, and social organization differed in their diffusion rates. Uniform rates in transmission raised the possibility that the more widely distributed the trait, the older it must be. Age was a function of space measured from an inferred point of origin; the oldest features could be expected at the margins of the interactional universe. A studied analysis of elements with regard to form, substance, meaning, use, and other special attributes was used to establish similarities, identities, and complexities from which a probability of contact could be inferred and the historic direction of spread could be plotted. Continuous distributions could be reliably interpreted as evidence of contact, but even where no continuous distribution was present, an inference of contact might be made if form and related attributes were quite similar. The case for contact would be incontrovertible if the forms compared were complex enough to warrant the inference that human ingenuity could not be expected to produce such a form independently. The more features two societies shared, the more reliable the inference of a past historical relationship, despite separation in space.

In their common task of translating spatial distributions into historic relationships, culture historians developed similarities in conceptual inventories and explanatory principles. Their works could always be counted on to include lists of culture traits with pluses and minuses indicating a presence or absence within a tribe or region. This practice led Malinowski to jeer at their laundry list approach to culture in contrast with his functional integrative approach. Yet out of both American and German culture historicism came efforts to see individual cultures as systems and life-styles integrated by value principles.

The undated materials with which culture historians worked did not permit firm methodological controls, in spite of meticulous concern for trait identities and distributional exactness. Hence, their specific historical interpretations attained only a plausible level of probability. The cultural geography produced through their mapping of trait clusterings did constitute an important contribution and confirmed the importance of contact on the growth of cultures.

While culture-historical investigation added fresh insights to processes of culture change, by-products emanating from the focus on an interactive process were more significant. From cultural exchange, culture historicists in the United States moved to consideration of the interrelations between individuals and culture. Interest in how individuals absorbed culture patterns opened new avenues of research in social organization, culture and personality, and in the retention or transformation of habits, meanings, and attitudes under the press of persistent culture contact and exchange.

The following discussion first concentrates on the influence of Boas in establishing the historical method in American anthropology. The contributions of Scandinavian, British, and German-Austrian diffusionists are described in that order. An assessment at the end lists the basic contributions of culture historicism to the development of ethnology.

AMERICAN CULTURE HISTORICISTS

Franz Boas and the Historical Method

The central figure in the emergence of American cultural anthropology was Franz Boas (1858–1942). It was typical of Boas that he attacked prior ethnological efforts through the transparent fallacies of their methods. In this vein he viewed the different fields of anthropology (ethnology, linguistics, physical anthropology, archeology) as methods for dealing with the complexities of cultural phenomena rather than specializations. Boas' ideas had been simmering for ten years when in 1896 he urged renunciation of the "barren . . . comparative method . . . [and its] vain endeavor to construct a uniform systematic history of the evolution of culture" (Boas 1940c:280). To correct evolutionary fallacies Boas substituted the historical method of controlled investigation of the dynamics of culture growth.

From the outset Boas worked tirelessly and systematically to destroy evolutionary anthropology and to turn the discipline toward the inductive precision found in the natural sciences. Boas had been trained in physics, mathematics, and geography; and when he viewed the field of ethnology, he saw a multiverse of unsolved problems. In 1896 he reminded his anthropological audience that "The solid work is still all before us" (Boas 1940c:280). In part Boas was inspired to challenge the Developmentalist position by his own field experiences, first among the Eskimo (1883–1884) and later among Northwest Coast Indians. Between 1886 and 1931 Boas visited the Northwest Coast thirteen times, accumulating a total of twenty-nine months in the field (Rohner 1966, in Helm 152–153).

The Range of Boas' Contributions to American Anthropology. The historical and antievolutionary posture Boas brought to American ethnology was not an imaginative innovation of his own. He was part of a new intellectual wave. With German *Kulturkreis* theorists he shared a common stimulus emanating from the historical impulse conveyed to German geography by Friedrich Ratzel, and from Bastian's notions of the historic build-up of cultural-geographical provinces. Estimates of Boas' influence on American anthropology frequently overlook or underplay the historic-evolutionary trends transforming the intellectual base of anthropology at the time (see Stocking 1960; Gruber 1967).

If Boas were no singular innovator, to what then can his extraordinary impact on American anthropology be traced? First, he fired the first shot in the New World against Developmentalism and worked tirelessly to reorient the field and to gain acceptance of the new historical method. In firing his salvo, Boas spoke from strength by virtue of his own fieldwork. He had been there, and so could testify against the fanciful fact and interpretation of armchair anthropologists. Second, despite his open aversion for theory, Boas was forced to present a theoretical rationale for changing to the historical method and pointed out how the anthropological problem must be rephrased. His theoretical score might never be presented as a system, and indeed was left unfinished, but Boas constantly studded his discourses with methodological statements that revealed how he thought anthropologists should reorient their aims. Third, through his researches Boas contributed substance to physical anthropology, linguistics, and ethnography. Fourth, through his organizational activities Boas extended the participation of anthropology in the scientific community and strengthened its professional image. Fifth, in attracting a versatile community of students, Boas assured a measure of continuity to his ideas. However, he did not saddle his followers with the intellectual lockstep that commonly accompanies exposure and conditioning to a theoretical system. The very ambiguities of Boas' theory, plus his basic insistence on precision in problem definition and method, militated against the formation of a "school."

Theoretical Assumptions of Boasian Historicism. Boas made a number of basic assumptions which guided his approach to the phenomenon of man and dictated his theoretical and methodological contributions to anthropology. The heart of his position can be found in the postulate that the human process is structured, retaining an inner core that remains relatively stable in the face of altered conditions. Outer form coordinates with inner structure, but outer forms change with circumstances. In many ways Boas' approach to cultural processes paralleled the genetic model, where an inner structure or genotype accounted for phenotypic features but varied according to environmental conditions.

Boas located this internal structure in unconscious processes fundamental to human psychology. He shared Bastian's view that a limited number of basic psychological processes accounted for a limited number of basic ideas shared by all men. However, he never committed himself explicitly to the doctrine of elementary ideas, and was more inclined to first check out the role of limited possibilities in the production of similarities in form. From his linguistic data, Boas noted the different ways people perceived and categorized things in nature, and concluded that the internal psychological structure common to mankind carried general tendencies but gave no specific directives. That is, people classified things, and this could be taken as a common human propensity, but what and how they classified showed considerable variability.

The apparent failure of an internal psychological base to account for specific manifestations of cultural phenomena raised serious epistemological and methodological issues. If an internal process were assumed to be structurally coded to produce specific effects, and these effects in fact turned out to be variable, any thought of an internal determination must be abandoned. In the eighteenth century "faculty" psychologists employed the tactic of adding an internal faculty for each counterpart discerned in human behavior. The roster of structural features grew in length, but ostensibly permitted correlation of the specifics of an internal organization with external forms. The determinism of an internal psychological structure also could be salvaged by connecting uniform tendencies in response to universal situations. Such was the tactic of Developmentalists when they endeavored to explain the origins of religion in universal experiences—for example, a fear response to the awesome qualities of sun, moon, thunder, or the dead. The trouble here lay with the inability of investigators to agree on *the* universal experience. Hence, theories of religion and of totemism proliferated and explained nothing. Later, psychoanalytic theorists attempted to introduce controls regulating variation in response by correlating responses with a limited number of universal experiences.

Boas rejected such methodological tactics. At the same time he drew conclusions about the structuring and variability of psychological processes and their causal relations to behavior. Since each historical people evidenced differences in how they organized their world and made their choices, the traditional modes of thought they shared provided a constant in the relation between psychology and culture form. However, the variability observable in the social psychology of peoples suggested that their common thoughtways had been shaped by special circumstances. For Boas these special circumstances were environmental relations and historic contacts with other social traditions. It followed that every culture, and the traditional psychology of those practicing the culture, was largely the result of interplay between environmental and historical-cultural stimuli and general psychological processes (Figure 9-1). Every culture at heart was a local phenomenon, and here Boas seemed to follow Bastian's lead in conceiving the psychological core of a culture (the *Völkergedanken*) to be the product of a technical, social, and ideological working relation with the local environment. Regarding culture forms, the only way to get back to the nuclear culture would be through elimination of everything that had been incorporated through contact. From that point one could use the remaining nucleus of culture forms to penetrate the traditional psychology of the group. The solution to the structural characteristics of a culture thus must

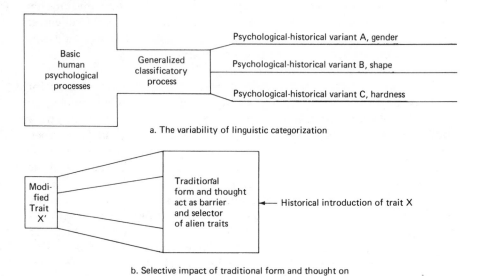

a. The variability of linguistic categorization

b. Selective impact of traditional form and thought on historic innovations

Figure 9-1. Two views of structure, following Boas.

Boas at first was convinced that certain general "laws" of culture growth could be uncovered. Central to his understanding of culture processes, however, were psychological processes associated with human nature. The variable manifestations of these elemental psychological processes in historic traditions constituted the problem to be explained. In time Boas seems to have concluded that the lack of product specificity in the historic manifestations must mean that the general mental processes could not be depended upon to produce "laws." Hence, his later statement that the "general laws" which anthropologists would be able to formulate must be "vague and, we might almost say, so self-evident that they ... [will be] of little help to a real understanding" (Boas 1940l:258). What this amounted to was a general rejection of the idea that specific determinants or narrow limitations of variability operated in the human reality. Hence, his conclusion that basic understandings could come only through a tracing of historic relationships.

His concept of structure can be illustrated with the principles people use in classification. In certain languages gender may be central to classification, in others, the hardness or shape of an object may take precedence. What this suggests is nothing more than a generalized human potential for classification, with limited possibilities and other factors reducing variability in certain cases.

On the other hand, cultures possessed traditionalized forms and associated conventionalizations of meaning that conveyed structure to culture. It was to this structuring of culture that Boas and other culture historicists appealed when following the course of innovations. Logically they also concluded that environmental factors must affect the acceptance, rejection, and modification of alien elements.

begin with control over the history of its form inventory. Hence, Boas' call for the historical method as the method of ethnology.

> The historical inquiry must be considered the critical test that science must require before admitting facts as evidence. By its means the comparability of the collected material must be tested, and uniformity of processes must be demanded as proof of comparability. Furthermore, when historical connection between two phenomena can be proved, they must not be admitted as independent evidence. (Boas 1940c:279)

The historical method alone provided the controls needed by the ethnologist to get inside the native mind so that he might comprehend how the culture had grown. In the individual histories of forms, ethnologists could track down important clues to which native psychology was attuned when rejecting, incorporating, or selectively modifying alien traits. However, the problem was sorely complicated, for "All cultural forms appear in a constant state of flux and subject to fundamental modifications" (Boas 1940i:284). Forms were deceptive in that they often looked alike when their meanings differed from one society to another and hence possessed different psychological histories. Such forms could not be compared because they were not homologous. It was clear that the psychological qualities shared by mankind were too imprecise to produce general laws governing the workings of social life and how it developed. One had to begin with individual societies and unwind the complicated histories of their culture elements before any sound idea could be reached about what their cultures were like at base. Accounting for form variability was a first order of business, since only after such an accounting could one get inside the psychological processes which connected individual forms, united them into larger wholes, imbued them with meanings, and brought stability and continuity to the culture as a structure.

However, Boas was too involved in his meticulous historical analyses to find much time for probing the structural foundations and organizational principles of a culture. Boas worked with nothing but facts. He approached fieldwork as a naturalist, eager and determined to describe things as they were to make sure the data were not distorted to prove a theoretical point of view. At the time there was no room for the larger view. Developmentalists had filled the air with their alleged scientific theories and proofs, and it was time for spadework. Fieldwork must produce a documentary of facts which others could use with confidence.

Many of Boas' research problems seem to have been sparked by his opposition to Developmentalism. He was determined to overturn individual psychological explanations by substituting a group or sociopsychological process, which he assumed to be ultimate. In language, myth, and art Boas found contrasts of style in form and in thought that contradicted evolutionist dogma. Tubular Alaskan needle cases proved how, even in a tradition of geometric decoration, the imaginative interplay between Eskimo craftsman-artist and material gave rise to representational forms (Boas 1940g).

Evolutionist theory of a primitive psychological process which began with representation and ended with geometric conventions and abstract symbols thus was reversed. Yet, in citing the imaginative interplay between material and artist, Boas used common human psychological capabilities against the psychological explanations of evolutionists. He was convinced that no general interpretation based on human psychology could account for all forms that appear alike. He also vindicated his view that the history of any individual element or art form is complicated, and that valid psychological explanation could only be reached by respecting the importance of the historical context. In folklore Boas (1908:21) found an admirable foil for the historical method, since "nothing seems to travel as readily as fanciful tales." For thirty years he labored to produce a compilation of folklore elements throughout the Northwest Coast so that he could analyze meticulously the psychological processes by which mythic components had been altered or reinterpreted in the course of their historic wanderings from tribe to tribe (Boas 1916).

Much of Boas' theory of culture history, and the way he looked at the integration of culture, derived from his close pursuit of mythological elements throughout the Northwest Coast. The fact that mythic elements were disengaged from narratives and plots and widely diffused convinced him that culture seldom, if ever, diffused as a unified whole. He therefore opposed the *Kulturkreislehrer*, who assembled disparate elements into culture complexes and treated them as if they had diffused *en bloc*. Analysis of myth repeatedly offered confirmation to his notion that any cultural tradition is a complicated product of intricate historical and psychological processes rooted in the social life of a people. The loose connection between any culture element, its function, and meaning also reinforced Boas' suspicion that cultures were not rigidly coherent and tightly bonded entities. In 1930 Boas (1940k:268) observed that analytic descriptions of the dynamics of the interrelations of different parts of cultures was sorely needed. But for Boas (1940k:268) such analysis was significant primarily in that it provided information on the "reaction of the individual to the culture in which he lives and of his influence upon society." Reaction of the individual to culture could clear up many aspects of change and variation in culture. Attention to individual reactions did not mean that Boas embraced the abreactive symbolisms developed by Freudian theory, since Freudian interpretation rested on individual psychology and ignored variability introduced through the historic process (Boas 1940i:288–289).

Boas' view of cultures as assemblages of disparate elements derived from a multiplicity of sources did not encourage him to accept the view that cultures were bound together by overriding principles. One must expect and always would find contradictory elements. The complex historical interrelations of culture forms and their reciprocating causal connections likewise doomed efforts to account for cultural forms by a single cause (Boas (1940l:256). As for laws derived from structural processes, he was convinced that the phenomena of anthropology were "so individualized, so exposed to outer accident that no set of laws could explain them" (Boas 1940l:257). With variability so prominent in the phenomena of culture, there was no place for determinism of any kind, whether internally within the culture or external to it, as asserted by such geographic determinists as Semple (1911). In like fashion, Boas was skeptical of Structuralists who overemphasized the unity of culture and gave every act and idea, great or small, a function. With regard to the simple unity claimed for primitive cultures, Boas (1940h:447) countered with the query, "Have we not reason to expect that here as well as in more complicated cultures, sex, generation, age, individuality, and social organization will give rise to the most manifold contradictions?"

Boas approached physical anthropology, a fourth instrument for promoting scientific anthropology, with the same conviction and design that guided his researches in myth, language, and art. The complexity and variability of physical process and variation in form must be comprehended with searching thoroughness. Hence, he attacked the genetic process not at the level of race but in descent lines and their subdivisions ("fraternities," as he called them). Physical measurement of nearly 18,000 immigrants in New York provided Boas (1910, 1928) with data that confounded anthropometrists who treated their indexes as constant ratios based on fixed traits. In the New World urban setting, round-headed East European Jews became more long-headed, while South Italians, long-headed to begin with, became more round-headed. Two ethnic groups with different head shapes thus converged in the special urban environment of New York. Changes in the bodily shape of children confirmed the trends found in adults, with native-born children registering a greater increase in stature and in size of head than foreign-born. Although Boas drew on his data to emphasize the plasticity of human types, he realized that genetic organization had not changed. Nonetheless, the study called attention to the dynamic relation linking body type and environment. He cautioned against ready acceptance of external form as a mirror image of genetic type, since every local type contained elements that were not genetic but due to environmental influences (Boas 1936:525).

As to genetic structure and process, Boas conceded that the predominance of heredity over environment assured the permanence of human types. However, the problem of physical variability had to be dealt with first, since variability was not entirely a matter of biology, but a result of unknown influences on the more permanent characteristics. Thus, like the ethnologist, the physical anthropologist must work with secondary features, through which, hopefully, he might get through to the structural core. Plotting human types according to their geographic distribution therefore must be the first order of business, with close attention given to variations stemming from mixture, the fixing of types through inbreeding in isolation, and differentiations that followed natural tendencies of succeeding generations to vary from the parental stem. Subtle physiological changes induced by nutrition and mode of life also could not be ignored, because man, as other domesticated species, was not impervious to such influences. Faced with such historic complexities in anatomical variation, it was futile to search for pure races, or an original race from which a rigid genealogical descent could be charted. Similar difficulties prevented hope of finding the *Ursprache* from which other languages descended. Impressed by the complexity of phenomena and the apparent ambiguity between internal structure and external form, Boas was suspicious of any application of the newly discovered Mendelian laws of inheritance to elucidate the genetic process.

Boas' Contribution to the Concept of Culture. When Boas first addressed himself to the phenomenon of man, he confronted a systematic interpretation that unified three different orders: race, psychology, and culture. In denying the validity of evolutionary reconstructions, Boas attacked the individual psychological explanations used by Developmentalists charting origins and advances from savagery to civilization. In place of postulated psychological relations between an archetypal human individual and nature, to which Developmentalists subscribed, Boas stressed the historical exchange and transmission of observable culture elements. The shift in focus was distinctive. It meant that Boas agreed with Developmentalists that the anthropological goal must be clued to the history of human society, but he disagreed on the processual relationships to be stressed. For Boas the important relation was between cultural objects and traditional meanings. For Developmentalists, the critical relation was between the human psyche and nature.

Culture elements did not exist in a vacuum. Their interrelations and integrations were sustained by traditional meanings and thought processes. In the case of a star design applied to moccasins by the Arapaho, Sioux, and Shoshone (Figure 9-2) its very complexity suggested a single origin, yet the meaning for each of the tribes was different.

> The design is interpreted by the Arapaho as the morning star, the bar on the instep, as the horizon; the short lines, as the twinkling of the star. To the mind of the Sioux the design conveys the ideas of feathers, when applied to a woman's moccasin; when found on a man's moccasin, it symbolized the sacred shield suspended from tent-poles. The identical design was explained by the Shoshone as signifying the sun (the center) and its rays; but also the thunderbird, the cross-arms of the cross evidently being the wings; the part nearest the toe, the tail, and the upper part, the neck with two strongly conventionalized heads attached. If these are the ideas conveyed by this design to the makers, it is clear that they must have developed after the invention or introduction of the design; that the design is primary, the idea secondary, and that the idea has nothing to do with the historical development of the design itself. (Boas 1940f:555)

The history of forms thus could be traced independently of associated ideas, but it was typical that Boas' interest in process led him to test the relation between form and idea in the historical context and to draw from such examples more general observations. For example:

the history of the artistic development of a people, and the style that they have developed at any given time, predetermine the method by which they express their ideas in decorative art; and . . . the type of ideas that a people is accustomed to express by means of decorative art predetermines the explanation that will be given to a new design. It would therefore seem that there are certain typical associations between ideas and forms which become established, and which are used for artistic expression. The idea which a design expresses at the present time is not necessarily a clue to its history. It seems probable that idea and style exist independently, and influence each other constantly. (Boas 1940f:562)

Figure 9-2. Moccasin design and the problem of meaning (Boas 1940f:554).

The fact that this design was common to the Arapaho, Sioux, and Shoshone, but held different meanings for each tribe, was cited by Boas as proof that form may have a history distinct from meaning. This fact is also relevant for the independence of form and meaning within a society. It affords grounds for arguing that what sustains certain social practices is not a sharing of common meanings but a contractual consensus in which separate interests may be served by a mutual instrument.

Attention to the interrelations of style and meaning obviously focused a relation between object and idea quite different from the Developmentalist effort to establish a relation between mental processes and natural phenomena. With style one confronted an historical tradition, and Boas iterated and reiterated that explanation must be traveled back to social tradition and actional context. The psychology (mental associations) of style harbored not an individual psychology but a social psychology. Like Durkheim and other social Structuralists, Boas concluded that the individual was a product of social psychology and must be understood through the medium of the social. "Folk psychology," he wrote in 1904 (Boas 1904(20): 513–524), "deals with those psychic actions which take place in each individual as a social unit, and the psychology of the individual must be interpreted by the data of a social psychology, because each individual can think, feel and act only as a member of the social group to which he belongs."

Boas transmitted this awareness of the social learning process to his students, and it was they who translated his use of social tradition into the concept of culture. For a long time Boas avoided use of the term "culture," probably because of valuative connotations in nineteenth-century usage, and German usage in particular. For Boas the issue of use of the term was resolved only when Radcliffe-Brown distinguished between the cultural and the social early in the 1930s. However, social psychology, like the generalized psychological explanations of Developmentalists, could not be penetrated by the method of analogic reasoning of those seeking to plot evolutionary developments in ideas and institutions. Historical analysis must come first, or, as Boas (1940c:279) observed, "The [social] psychological problem is contained in the results of the historical inquiry." In short, the primary causal explanation must be sought in the cultural-historical nexus, and, such being the case, only an antecedent cultural-historical fact could explain a subsequent cultural-historical fact.

Variation, Fact, Fieldwork, and the Historical Method. Through the historical method Boas hoped to achieve the critical and exhaustive analysis essential to scientific control over the variability of cultural phenomena. There was no substitute for facts, and field collection alone supplied the needed details about the interrelations of forms, ideas, psychological processes, and their antecedent-subsequent relationships. Above all, then, the anthropologist must be a fieldworker, devoted to scientific objectivity. The ethnographer must be free of prejudices and preconceptions that could trap him into distorting facts and forcing them into artificial or ethnographic categories. For this reason Boas looked to the naturalist collector as a model for fieldwork. A properly trained anthropologist must interpret the world of the native through the eyes of the native. With regard to language, for example, the description of grammar should be carried out "as though an intelligent Indian was going to develop the forms of his own thoughts by an analysis of his own form of speech" (Boas 1911–1938(1): 81). Interviewing should not be tightly structured. It was better to present an informant with a problem and leave him free to develop a narrative which followed his own interests. The language of discourse should be the language of the informant. Language mastery was essential if the investigator were to achieve quality control over his data. In the absence of the language skill, texts dictated by the informant in his language could be recorded phonetically. Such a textual record then served as a permanent document for continuing analysis of native thought processes.

Idiosyncrasies of individual style and interpretation led Boas to recommend the collection of similar materials from several informants. However, he made no considered effort to quantify his data by increasing the number of informants to increase reliability. Usually Boas, owing to his preoccupation with historic analysis, sought control by expanding the list of elements and their distribution in space. This historic emphasis tended to focus attention on problematic relations other than the determination of culture patterns or literary styles. Boas' discussion of Kwakiutl metaphor and his summary of the stylistic features of primitive literature indicated that he was alert to these issues. However, he was very much inclined to turn a stylistic comparison into a record of the presence or absence of literary form—for example, riddles, moralizing fables, epic poetry—to show that primitive literature had a history and was not a natural and spontaneous product of common human mental processes.

The analytic rigor of Boas' approach to any problem obviously was modeled upon natural science. First, he underscored the fact that all classifications are relative, and the scientist must realize this when he conceptualizes his findings. The error of forcing the logic of one's own categories of thought on the primitive must be carefully avoided. Second, classification is no substitute for process—for what actually happens. This was the error of evolutionism. The remedy for this mistake is the collection of data in such detail that variations in forms, and the causes for these variations, are brought to the surface. Third, only homologies can pass muster for scientific comparison. In short, functional analogies will not do. Ethnologists constantly were faced with similarities in form, but to be accepted as equivalents, the histories of the forms must be proved to be identical and not convergent. Here the historical method was indispensable in that it alone permitted the researcher to determine that the psychological histories of the cultural forms were alike. If similar psychological processes produced forms that were alike, one could reasonably conclude that a cause-effect relation existed. Fourth, coincidence must not be taken for a causal connection. Boas' classic target here was the alleged relation among race, language, and culture. With well-known historic illustrations, supplemented by examples out of his own fieldwork, Boas showed that race, language, and culture varied independently of each other. Hence, to explain language and culture as an effect of racial psychology was utterly untenable in a scientific way and simply compounded popular error. In his anthropometric correlations, too, Boas cautioned that no causal connection was established by the mathematical formula. Despite his considered use of statistics in studies of human growth, Boas, in seeking the dynamics of human types, pursued the problem through application of the historical method to family lines. Interestingly, he avoided application of statistical techniques to cultural phenomena. Everything hinged on the need to determine processual relations, the heart of the researcher's problem. Hence, one could not be content with formal classification and the analysis of structure. Fifth, valid interpretation is possible only when derived from a relevant context. To seek the source for religious behavior in a contemplation of nature is suspect because a more likely source for ideas commonly held by a group are the feelings and imaginative play accompanying social experience. Sixth, Boas held that data must be quantified if comparison were to yield general laws.

It may seem curious that Boas did not add measurably to the conceptual inventory of anthropology. However, he was more interested in assuring that the classificatory process was reputable rather than in developing a set of concepts. Concepts, like systematic theory, had a way of getting in the researcher's way by fixating the range of his vision. General orientations were preferable, at least in this early stage of ethnological development. A proper definition of problems was appropriate to the ethnological purpose, for discourse could focus on methods to resolve the problems. Boas had no desire to shackle his successors with a theoretical formulation that would lessen their chances to formulate problems which would bring process to surface.

This self-same preoccupation with problem and method prevented Boas from leaving a legacy of laws regarding the dynamics of culture growth. Boas' laws were methodological rules. In explicating the nature of cultural phenomena posed by distributions and variations in meaning, he used his works as cautionary tales to warn the naive researcher not to overstep the bounds of reasonable interpretation. In point of fact, the historical method could not produce hard and fast rules. At certain points, as in the insistence on "continuity of distribution as one of the essential conditions for proving historical connection" Boas (1940c:277) could meet his own scientific canons. However, the best he could offer with regard to discontinuous distributions was a caution against assuming the former presence of connecting links. Basic controls could be reached by limiting oneself to a small geographic territory and refraining from cultural comparisons outside the limits of the area under study. This Boas did by confining himself to the Northwest Coast. Yet his analysis of mythological elements here revealed the presence of elements from all over the continent, with the Northwest Coast sharing more features with contiguous areas. Moreover, there was evidence that mythic plots and elements found in western Europe had diffused to Indonesia, Japan, Siberia, and even to the coastal area of North America down to the Columbia River (Boas 1940d:433–434). Such distributions emphasized the complex histories of any tribal mythology. However, every mythology demonstrated a localized or areal quality, and here the researcher was on surer ground. In the case of the Northwest Coast, for example, crest legends associated with clans among the northern tribes suggested a probable source for crest legends among the Kwakiutl who did not possess clans. Actually, there were two kinds of crest legends: the first told how the ancestor of the social unit came down from heaven, or sprang out of the earth or the ocean; the second described the encounters of the ancestor with spirits as he became more powerful. From internal evidence Boas concluded that the guardian-spirit crest legends were the more recent, and the development of the association between guardian-spirit quest and crest legend was a function of social organization. In the acceptance of mythological elements, Boas held that any myth was more easily introduced into a social organization if the prestige of a social unit within that organization were enhanced.

The wide distribution of certain tales and elements throughout the Americas raised the issue of the purposes of myths and the creativity involved. Much creativity centered around the assembly of plots and elements into a narrative, and therefore Boas concluded that myth was not the work of a primitive philosopher and was not designed as an explanation of nature. On the contrary, the folk tale was a product of the primitive artist, and the explanatory element was secondary, usually injected by the artist to create an effect. From the trickster cycle in the Plains, it appeared that no single tribe was more creative than any other. One thing was notable, however; wherever folk tales could be given meaning in the context of social organization, ritual, or other socially meaningful aspects of life, the number of tales proliferated. Moreover,

> The more important the tale becomes on account of its association with the privileges and rituals of certain sections of the tribe, and the greater the emotional and social values of the customs with which it is associated, the more have the keepers of the ritual brooded over it in all its aspects; and with this we find a systematic development of both tale and ritual. (Boas 1940h:482)

Limitations of Boas' Perspective and of the Historical Method. There is no doubt that in applying the historical method to mythology, art, language, and body types, Boas generated a whole new domain of problem definition, and equally important, a new perspective on the reality problem. By conceiving structure as a generalized process which could be made to vary in its effects according to circumstances, he supplied fresh justification for including variation and the historical process in the goal of anthropological research. Controlled case studies were used to extract processual parallels which could be translated into a general process effecting structural or evolutionary change. However, because of his overriding methodological concern and ceaseless drive to discredit evolutionary theory, Boas missed a golden opportunity to present a more unified view of reality. In consequence, the problem of structural change was thrust so far into the background that White (1949a), in reintroducing the evolutionary orientation, reasserted a structural determinism that already was on its way out.

As for the touted historical method, its controls proved too ambiguous. One could admit with Boas (1940b:438) that if a complex of elements were found in the same combination in two different regions, their sameness or identities must be due to diffusion. Again, the more complex a form, the less likelihood for independent invention. But the problem of simplicity-complexity requires some criteria that allow replication of consensus. Quantification of features provides a reasonable basis for judging complexity, but what about simplicity? Simplicity implies the idea that the probability of independent origin is increased. This Boas was willing to admit, and cited the case of a legendary "pigeon drop" found among the

Ainu, in Andersen's fairly tales, and in Shakespeare's Falstaff. In each case a cunning miscreant spreads the story of a treasure to which he possesses the key, and institutes a search. To reach the treasure requires a risk of life, and the sly rascal induces a blind man to take his place on promise of receiving sight. The blind man perishes in the river and the rascal takes his property. The internal consistencies of these respective narratives led Boas (1940b:439) to accept the probability of the independent origin of similar ideas. Cases of independent invention required more corroborative evidence. Ideas of the origin of death, however, did not require stringent corroborative evidence because they arose spontaneously out of a desire to see the dead alive once again and a wish for life without death. To support his contention about the omnipresence of death ideas, Boas (1940h:490) pointed to their universality.

> The behavior of man in all societies proves ... this statement. Thus the im-
> aginative processes are set in motion which construct a deathless world, and
> from this initial point develop the stories of the introduction of death in
> accordance with the literary types of transformation stories. The mere occur-
> rence of stories of the origin of death—in one place due to the miscarriage of
> a message conveyed by an animal, in others by a bet or a quarrel between
> two beings—is not a proof of common origin. This proof requires identity of
> the stories. We can even understand how, under these conditions, stories
> of similar literary type may become almost identical in form without having
> a common origin. Where the line is to be drawn between these two types of
> development cannot be definitely decided. In extreme cases it will be possible
> to determine this with a high degree of probability; but a wide range of
> material will always remain, in which no decision can be made.

Boas obviously had no illusions concerning the limitations of the historical method. Through example he set the tone for reasonable inference
where ambiguity prevailed. Others employed the historical method with
less rigorous criteria, and, as with the *Kulturkreislehrer*, endeavored to
reconstruct the prehistory of the whole world through spatial distributions.
For the daring, the very discontinuities which Boas cautioned must be used
sparingly would signal an original continuity of ancient traits. Continuous
distributions in such a case suggested more recent trait diffusion rather
than antiquity!

There is a quality of irony in Boas' persistent jousting against speculative interpretation. On the one hand, he proclaimed the need for his historical method to counter the general psychological interpretations favored
by evolutionists. However, once world-wide diffusionist histories made
their appearance, he was forced to fall back on general psychological tendencies in order to controvert historical world-wide diffusions which assumed that by nature men were dull-witted and incapable of independent
inventions. Boas' first opponents were those who interpreted the universality of nature symbols (for example, sun, moon) as evidence of a chain
of contact. At this point Boas turned to Bastian's concept of elementary
ideas to refute the uncritical use of the criterion of universality as a sign

of diffusion. To the contrary, he contended that a universal presence indicated a general response, or elementary idea. Indeed, in the relation between elementary and folk ideas as drawn by Bastian, Boas (1940d:435) found the model for his view of things as well as the logical necessity for the historical method.

> The forms which these [elementary] ideas take among primitive people of different parts of the world, the "Völker-Gedanken," are due partly to the geographical environment and partly to the peculiar culture of the people, and to a large extent to their history. In order to understand the growth of psychical life, the historical growth of customs must be investigated most closely, and the only method by which the history can be investigated is by means of a detailed comparison of the tribe with its neighbors.

However, Boas' methodological concern, in conjunction with his concentration on manageable historical problems, did not permit any systematic attack on the problem of a general human nature and universal ideas. The structured processes of human nature would be focused on once again by the French ethnologist Lévi-Strauss (1963) and made central to his linguistic structural theory. In explicating his theoretical position, Lévi-Strauss pointed to Boas as the first to clearly elucidate the heart of the structural problem and the relation of variation to structure. The great French linguist Ferdinand de Saussure made a similar distinction eight years later between structure and variation with his concepts of *la langue* and *le parole* (Lévi-Strauss 1963ae:209). De Saussure's insistence that languages were composed of arbitrary and conventional features also opened the way for the study of language as a sociopsychological process. Like Boas when viewing the modification of form and meaning in the dynamics of culture growth, de Saussure opened the door to the dynamics of language growth.

Boas and Fieldwork. Boas' ethnographic contributions were designed with two ends in view: the field investigation must produce a substance that would throw light on the sociopsychological nexus of form and meaning, and the product must serve as an historical scientific document. The former explains his special researches in art, myth, and language, while the latter helps us to understand the terse, even laconic, translations of the linguistic texts. In the light of his ever-present need to instruct, one may guess that Boas viewed his field products as models which others should follow and improve upon. Though fieldwork was already underway in North America and had become a part of the operations of the Bureau of American Ethnology under Powell, none contributed as much to the entrenchment of fieldwork in anthropology as Boas. His eagerness to enlist support in collection led him to encourage a young girl from the Bella Bella mission to take down folk tales according to his instructions (Rohner and Rohner 1969:48). He also impressed James Teit, a Scotsman married to an Indian woman, into writing extensively about the interior tribes of British Columbia. George Hunt, a mixed-blood Tlingit reared among the Kwakiutl, was persuaded to compile data on that tribe. His most direct influence, of course, was conveyed to his students, whose fieldwork reveals an orientation toward the production of cultural protocols to which others could turn in secure confidence that they were handling a reliable, if not wholly accurate, document.

The validity of field protocols would be measured in final analysis by the degree to which they captured the view of the native. Hence the emphasis on description as it came from the lips of the informant. The ethnographic goal was a description of aboriginal tribal culture joined to an analysis of prehistoric influences shaping its content. It is not surprising then that some of Boas' students pioneered in the use of historic documents, including travel and exploration accounts, to reconstruct a precontact culture. Both Kroeber's (1925) survey of the California Indians and Spier's (1935) derivation of postcontact prophetic movements in the interior plateau of the Pacific Northwest from an indigenous prophet complex relied heavily on historical records. In the southeast Swanton (1946) carried out a remarkable salvage operation based on historic records. In every case, ethnographic interviews with tribal descendants were used to extend or confirm the reliability of the historic documents.

The guiding hand of Boas can be seen in the differentiation of interest in the fieldwork of his earlier and later students. According to Boas (1940o: 311), the shift in research goals followed according to plan: "When I thought that these *historical* methods were firmly established I began to stress, about 1910, the problems of cultural dynamics, of integration of culture and of the interaction between individual and society." Ruth Benedict illustrates these shifting emphases. Her dissertation on *The Concept of the Guardian Spirit in North America* (1923) traced tribal-geographic variation both with regard to style and individual features, while her later work, *Patterns of Culture* (1934), explored the relation between the individual and culture. Sapir (1916) early addressed himself to the contribution which linguistics could make to cultural-historical investigation. He then moved to a consideration of culture as a communication system, and to the relation of the individual personality to the cultural model of personality (Sapir 1949e). Coming later in Boas' career, Mead (1928) investigated the processes of cultural learning among the Samoans. At the same time she subjected a psychological theory, adolescence as a biological and psychological time of troubles, to the test of culture, and concluded that, as culture varies, so does adolescence. Following Benedict, who had picked up Boas' suggestion that individual differences in response to culture could be related to differences in temperament, Mead (1935) went on to psychologize culture through the medium of temperament. Goldenweiser's (1910, reprinted in 1933) famed analytic study of totemism served in a sense as the prototype for Benedict's comparative and analytic treatment of the guardian spirit concept. Goldenweiser concluded that no standardized totemistic complex existed, and that the individual variants derived from a most general emotional and psychological relation to nature. Benedict's findings for the guardian spirit quest were identical. This view, with the inference that the nature of areal variants of the totemistic and guardian spirit complexes could be illuminated only through historical analysis, obviously corresponded with Boas' conception of the relation between structure and variation.

The concept of style, or pattern, as concentrating the intrinsic quality of form and differences in form was one of the most important ideas Boas conveyed to his students, but there was no common agreement on the meaning of style for the analysis of culture (see Kroeber 1956(58):158). In the context of myth and of language, Boas discovered style in the geographic clustering of elements and narrative and in the clustering of grammatical form. Kroeber made elucidation of the reality of style or pattern in culture his life work. In effect, the culture pattern served Kroeber as the primary unit for investigating culture, and he tested its presence in women's fashions (1919, 1940), in art styles, and in the clustering of genius associated with periods of cultural creativity (1944). Kroeber sought the reality of pattern within the continuum of a changing culture tradition (for example, Western civilization). Herskovits (1934, 1941) viewed the manifestation of pattern in the persistence of West African culture in Negro life ways in the New World. In the context of the historic contact continuum, Herskovits was faced with the problem of factoring Africanisms and Americanisms from a composite milieu whose forms had been subject to complex modifications and reinterpretations of meaning. From this base Herskovits (1936) pioneered, along with Redfield and Linton, the formulation of the study of culture contact, and in 1938 produced the first systematic survey of acculturative situations and processes.

As to Boas' fieldwork, the strength and weakness of his effort rests with his commitment to the historical method and his focus on sociopsychological processes. His research on the Northwest Coast was designed to uncover historic lines of communication within a relatively homogeneous interactive universe, and consequently he conducted what amounted to a survey of the area. The Jesup North Pacific Expedition (1897–1900), for which he was largely responsible, simply extended the range of the search for channels of cultural communication and historic influence. The survey approach produced a wealth of textual materials from the Kwakiutl, Bella Coola, Tsimshian, Chinook, Tillamook, Kathlamet, and Kutenai; but it did not result in a considered analysis of any one tribal culture or an effort to cover the institutional range of Northwest Coast culture. Boas was not among the Indians as a participant observer. The details of their daily lives lived out in potlatches, to which Boas was witness, were far less important than their psychic life as it had become fixed in language, art, myth, and religion (Rohner and Rohner 1969:xxix). Though Boas gave small potlatches himself to create good will, he fretted at the delays in his fieldwork occasioned by the social get togethers of the Kwakiutl. If the meaning of contemporary Kwakiutl life escaped Boas, owing to his primary concern for historic-psychic process, it is no surprise that he ignored the investigation of psychological processes accompanying changes in Kwakiutl culture at the time of his field visits.

In spite of the ambiguities and omissions of Boas' fieldwork, the five-foot shelf of his Northwest Coast researches to which Murdock alluded is impressive. The Northwest Coast also provided the major substance for understanding the nature of language and accounted for Boas' concentration on grammar as intrinsic to linguistic structure and the key to historic relationships (Boas 1911–1938). In the domain of physical anthropology, Boas (1940:103–130; 1928) broke new ground in the study of human growth and in the expressive variability of body form due to changes in environment. His work on the growth of children suggested a coordinate relation between physiological and mental maturity and pointed to the effect of inadequate diet in slowing growth during the maturation cycle. In stating his conclusions concerning the relation of nature and nurture, Boas never opted fully for either. However, he granted that the predominance of heredity in the organic rhythm produced mental differences between individuals and similar patterns of maturation among siblings. He cautioned that there were differences in behavior which could not be accounted for solely on the basis of anatomy, and vice versa.

Boas' Contributions to the Professionalization of Anthropology. Boas' professional activity spanned a critical period in the emergence of anthropology in the New World and afforded opportunities to influence not only the directions which the field should take but also its professionalization. His early association with F. W. Putnam paved the way for acceptance of anthropology as a member of the American Association for the Advancement of Science (Section H). In 1899 an anthropological club Boas founded in New York merged with the American Ethnological Society and brought new vigor to the organization. When, at the turn of the century, a movement developed for establishment of a national anthropological association, Boas (Stocking 1960) argued for an organization exclusively for professionals. Though he failed to get the exclusion of amateurs into the charter (1902), Boas read correctly the strain toward professionalizing the social sciences which was then taking place (Stocking 1960(62):14). By 1917 only two important officers of the association were without Ph.D.'s granted after 1900 (Stocking 1960(62):13). Boas was present at the founding of the American Folklore Society in 1888, and his editorship from 1908 to 1924 accounted for over half the memoir volumes published to that time. Soon after editing the *Handbook of American Indian Languages*, Boas in 1917 took the initiative in founding the *International Journal of American Linguistics*, often supporting it with funds out of pocket and serving as editor until his death. In addition to serving as president of the American Anthropological Association in 1907 and 1908 and the American Association for the Advancement of Science in 1931, Boas matched the vigor and dedication of his substantive researches with a professional participation that helped advance the organizational means for realizing a scientific anthropology.

Did Boas Create a Culture-Historical "School"? Those trained by Boas sometimes have been referred to as an American historical school such as the *Kulturkreislehrer* and British migrationists. However, the Boasian trainees lacked the classic features by which a school is recognized. They did share intellectual association with a founder, but Boas' students did not endlessly replicate similarities in theory, method, content, and conclusions modeled after the patriarch. If the charge has any validity at all, it must be applied to the earlier period in Boas' career when he strove to inculcate the historical method. In the dissertations of his students, one detects a predominant concern with historical problems—whether defined in terms of trait distribution or in a reduction of alleged formal and psychological similarities in culture complexes to their variant historical-cultural psychologies. In short, historicists drew out the analogies of alleged homologies and redefined the analogies as historical-causal rather than functional-causal derivatives.

Training in the methods of historical analysis conveyed by Boas to his students surfaces in the way they utilized his linguistic approach to fieldwork and devoted a considerable measure of their research time to mythology (for example, Kroeber, Sapir, Lowie, Herskovits, Benedict, Reichard, and Jacobs). However, once his students passed through the methodological experience, Boas was relatively tolerant of their research aims, provided they did not openly violate sacred scientific canons or disregard his most cherished teachings. Some did remain closer to the Boasian model than others, more notably Lowie, Spier, and Herskovits. The former, for example, constantly propagandized the validity of the historical method by writing works on *Primitive Society* (1920) and *Primitive Religion* (1924) that dealt the *coup-de-grâce* to evolutionary doctrine. In rejecting the seemingly speculative history flowing from his historical analytic treatment of the sun dance of the Plains Indians, Spier drew closer to Boas' position.

Others of Boas' students became deviationists, methodologically speaking, if not downright heterodox. In Boas' view, Kroeber (1935; Boas 1940o) was too inclined to work with blocks of culture (pattern) and to engage in historical construction without the exhaustive spatial analysis required as a prelude to generalization. In turning to psychoanalytic doctrine, Sapir and Mead were evident apostates. Since Boas wrote the Introduction to Benedict's (1934) psychocultural treatment of the Zuni, Kwakiutl, and Dobu, to what extent he considered her work heterodox is unclear. Acceptance of sociopsychological process as the ultimate basis for the cultural process would indicate that he favored cultural-psychological investigation that threw light on the relation of the individual to culture. His introductory statements concentrate on sociopsychological process and ignore the historical selection of contrary types of temperament in accounting for cultural differences. It was this emphasis on sociopsychological process that led to the further differentiation of anthropology under Boas and prevented the crystallization of a monolithic research design to be replicated over and over again in the work of followers (for evaluations of Boas by former students, see Kroeber *et al.* 1943; Goldschmidt 1959a; Herskovits 1953).

Beyond the core of his own students Boas confronted exponents of historical interpretation quite different from his own. Wissler (1917, 1923), who produced interpretations that united the histories of continents and the world (Figure 9-3) countered Boas' view of a loose integration of cul-

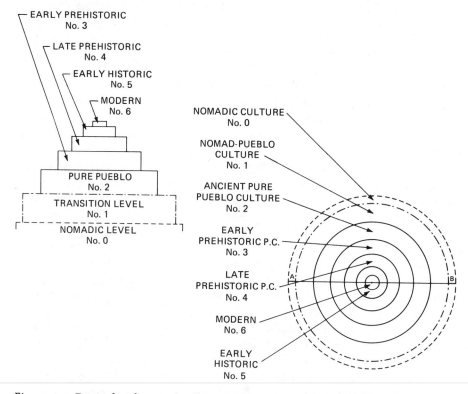

Figure 9-3. Principle of age-area illustrated by concentric distribution of pottery types in the Southwest, according to Wissler (1923:60, after Nelson).

Wissler drew upon the work of the archeologist N. C. Nelson to support his contention that "natural diffusion" usually proceeded at a uniform rate and that the most widely distributed traits must be the oldest. Nelson's surface collection of pottery revealed that the widely distributed types could be correlated with earlier stages in Pueblo culture development.

Considering that prehistoric culture processes were conformant with an age-area principle, Wissler applied this explanation with confidence to the distribution of ethnographic features to produce a relative chronology or history. The analysis also attempted to locate "centers" where cultural innovations tended to cluster, and from which new traits diffused to adjacent peoples. The age-area principle was widely accepted by culture historians and proved central to their historic reconstructions.

ture elements with functionally integrated trait complexes which diffused as wholes. He also borrowed Tylor's term "adhesion" to describe the temporal association of traits without the tie of functional necessity. Roland Dixon (1923, 1928) wrote a racial history of man based on the spatial distribution of head shapes, and then compounded the error by suggesting that differences in race and nationality accounted for the inventive productivity exhibited by different cultures. To cap it all, Paul Radin (1933), who took some of his training under Boas—but drew more inspiration from the historian James H. Robinson—openly attacked the historical method for eliminating the human element in history. In Radin's view culture historians were victims of a pseudoscientific methodology. A proper study of history must endeavor to control internal and external conditions affecting the culture of a people at the time they are observed. The "primary task [of the culture historian]," Radin (1933:32) asserted, "is to describe a specific culture as he finds it, without any reference to what has preceded or what is to follow." Radin (1923) elaborated his historic functionalism through his Winnebago Indian researches. He described changes affecting their lives at the time and paid close attention to individuals who had modified the content of Winnebago culture, for example, John Rave, who had introduced peyote. Radin's (1920) approach stressed differences in cultural life-styles, and this led him to pioneer in the collection of autobiographic narratives.

The variability of cultural-historical emphasis and of culture theory both within and without the Boas camp effectively forestalled the formation of a static research design in North American ethnology. Wissler (1923) casually referred to the evolution of culture. Radin (1927, 1937), although denying evolution in art design or ideas, traced an evolutionary path from magician to priest, and set up three stages in the development of the idea of offerings. Common problems in the historic interpretation of spatial distributions inevitably produced commonalities as to how culture historicists shaped their problems and the principles they applied in their analyses. Their major differences appeared in the magnitude of their ambitions and in the rigor with which they applied their analytic principles. However, ethnological efforts to write history out of spatial distributions quietly eroded in the United States during the late twenties, to be supplanted by the study of culture contact, or acculturation, during the thirties.

EUROPEAN CULTURE HISTORICISTS

Scandinavian Diffusionists

In speaking of the place of ethnology in Sweden, K. G. Izikowitz (1959 (61):669–671) described a situation common to much of Europe, with the exception of England and France. In Sweden, ethnology gained a foothold only through association with museums and with a sister discipline, geography. Consequently, opportunities in ethnology were decidedly scarce, and the linkages with museums and geography turned the ethnological course toward studies of material culture and culture history.

On two counts American culture historicists found Danish and Swedish ethnological investigations especially congenial to their tastes. First, their field research filled gaps in American Indian ethnography and distributions; second, their historic reconstructions were governed by a meticulous concern for facts and inductive inference. In a series of expeditions, Danish ethnographers and archeologists (Kaj Birket-Smith, Knud Rasmussen, and Therkel Mathiassen) worked their way west from Greenland, describing in fresh abundance the material technology, linguistics, social customs, and religious beliefs of the Eskimo. In so doing they also reopened the challenge of the origins of Eskimo culture. The issue was laid out originally by E. Rink (1875), who derived the Eskimo from a subarctic inland base. Later the geographer-ethnologist Gudmund Hatt (1914, 1916), using clothing and transportation distributions, determined that the circumpolar area held two types of cultural adaptation, coastal and inland, the coastal being the older. In 1917, another geographer-ethnologist, H. P. Steensby, paying closer attention to hunting adaptations, argued for an Eskimo move from inland to coast. He pointed to Coronation Gulf as the locus for the classical adaptation and the center for the dispersion of a Palae-Eskimo ice-hunting which still relied on inland caribou hunting for summer subsistence. In the West, around Bering Strait, the Palae-Eskimo culture was modified through contacts with Asiatic seafarers and fishermen. The ethnologist of the Danish Thule expeditions, Birket-Smith (1924, 1929), seconded Steensby's interpretation of Eskimo coastal culture as a derivative of an ancient inland adaptation and pointed to the Caribou Eskimo as the prototype. Taking note of the circumpolar distribution of an inland and a coastal culture recorded by Hatt, Birket-Smith hazarded that the inland or ice-hunting stage ultimately derived from the Epipaleolithic of the Old World. On the other hand, Mathiassen (1924, 1930), on the basis of archeological evidence, argued that Eskimo living along the Siberian coast were the first to develop a technology adapted to life on the coast, and that the spread of this classical Eskimo culture to the east occurred in relatively recent times. In this view, the inland adaptation exemplified by the Caribou Eskimo represented an erosion of classic Thule culture rather than the simple base from which it was developed.

The Eskimo case illustrated how easily controversy could be generated, and an impasse reached, in historical reconstructions based on trait distributions. The Eskimo case also made clear that the writing of prehistory must be left to the archeologist.

In the Swedish ethnologist Baron Erland Nordenskiöld (1877–1932), American culture historicists found an intellect congenial to their expectations of what a cultural-historical researcher should be. Nordenskiöld traveled widely in South America, filling out ethnographic gaps, concentrating on those hazardous and little-known areas of central South America, the Chaco and the Amazon. He made reasonable inferences from charts that plotted the presence or absence of features and endeavored to sketch lines of intercultural diffusion. When he finished, Nordenskiöld agreed with the North Americanists that American Indian cultural development was largely indigenous.

Beginning in 1919 with a comparative treatment of Chaco tribes, especially the Choroti and Ashluslay, Nordenskiöld advanced systematically to a general culture history of the material goods of South American Indians. As the data reasonably suggested, he related change to migrations, environmental adaptations, and the diffusion of inventions. In larger perspective he attempted to uncover older from more recent traits and the relative age and source of indigenous inventions, and he assessed what could be traced to trans-Pacific and European contacts. When Nordenskiöld completed the ninth volume of his *Comparative Ethnographic Studies* in 1931, he credited American Indians with a significant roster of inventions and suggested the nature and probable lines of contact between the Americas, the Pacific Islands, and Asia. "Cultural influence from Oceania . . . must in the main date from some exceedingly remote past," wrote Nordenskiöld (1919–1931(9):75), "before the banana, sugarcane, fowls, and domesticated pigs were known in Oceania." When dealing with technical similarities that suggested Asiatic origins for certain items discontinuously present in Central and/or South America, Nordenskiöld perceptively pointed out that none of the traits had a wide or homogeneous distribution in the New World. Further, their presumptive sources of origin were equally discontinuous and heterogeneous—Egypt for the T-shaped axe; the Chinese for duck hunting with calabashes, the coolie yoke, and double rafts of inflated skins (Western China); Indonesia for ikat and batik techniques in dyeing, and the like. For Nordenskiöld (1919–1931(9):47–49), such distributions and scattered points of origin meant only one thing—the basic independence of developments in civilization in the New World. To Friederici's (1926) argument that the coconut palm along the Pacific side of the Isthmus of Panama indicated a pre-Columbian Malayo-Polynesian presence, Nordenskiöld (1919–1931(9):26) quietly countered with the observation that "the Indians have nevertheless not become acquainted with a single one of the appliances that are used in Oceania for the utilization of the coco-nut palm." Moreover, the basic food plants of the New World (maize, manioc, potato, and sweet potato) argued for independence, and both Friederici (1907) and Laufer (1938) proved conclusively that the sweet potato spread westward from America, and that this diffusion was a post-Columbian phenomenon. What Nordenskiöld's meticulous distributions and comparisons revealed was a sporadic intrusion of alien elements, none of which was essential to the groundwork and elaboration of New World civilizations from Peru to Mexico.

The basic soundness of Nordenskiöld's conclusions about the inventiveness of American Indians in South America stands unchallenged. Nevertheless, the problem of indigenous developments has remained a tantalizing issue because archeologists have not uncovered the gradual advancements that expectably should precede the rise of civilization in nuclear America. The oldest cultures seem too advanced, and in 1951 Heine-Geldern and Eckholm reopened the problem of Asiatic influence. They pointed to apparent Hindu and Buddhist forms and motifs in the art and architecture of Middle America between the second and twelfth centuries, which seemingly had diffused by way of Cambodia and the Hinduized kingdoms of Java and Sumatra. In China Heine-Geldern (1959) also discovered the source for South American metallurgy and the tiger motif of Chavin culture (ca. 750 B.C.). In 1965, Meggers, Evans, and Estrada (*The Early Formative Period of Coastal Ecuador, the Valdivia and Machalilla Phases*) suggested that the pottery and carved stone figures which appeared on the Guayas coast of Ecuador some 5,000 years ago without apparent local antecedents could be traced to Early and Middle Jomon of Japan (Kyushu Island). In their view, similarities in technique, form, and design were so marked that a trans-Pacific origin for Valdivia Phase pottery offered the most reasonable explanation (Meggers, Evans, and Estrada 1965:158). They speculated that a boat load of Early Middle Jomon fishermen may have made the long journey of 8,320 nautical miles with the movement of the North Pacific currents, coasting down the Mexican shore to a natural ending on the Guayas Coast. The Jomon Nipponese presumably found coastal dwellers like themselves, who ate shellfish, hunted and gathered, and practiced incipient agriculture. However, Meggers, Evans and Estrada (1965: 167–168) were forced to admit that, if the Valdivians were stimulated by these accident-prone voyagers, they soon produced pottery that surpassed their Japanese mentors. Moreover, the Valdivians apparently were highly imaginative and innovative in that they possessed four features affecting pottery design and shape unknown to Jomon, namely pseudocorrugation, braid impression, fine-line incision, and tapered rims. There were also differences in decorative techniques (finger-grooving, combing, and incising) that pointed to a local evolution in technical style.

Lured by the possibility of intercultural contacts directed by ocean currents, a Norwegian romantic, Thor Heyerdahl (1953), launched a Peruvian-style raft to prove that a natural drift to the Polynesian islands from the American coast was possible and could account for the presence there of American Indian physical and cultural features. But when the speculative interpretation of the American Indian presence in Central and Eastern Polynesia had been sifted, it was apparent that cultural developments there were as indigenous as those in South America. Undaunted, Heyerdahl in 1969 set forth from Africa on an Egyptian-type balsa boat, dubbed Ra, and managed to sail and drift with wind and current to the South American coast, thereby demonstrating the possibility of the transmission of influences from the ancient Near Eastern civilizations to Indian cultures in the New World.

That ocean currents may have facilitated intercontinental contacts now must be accepted as a distinct possibility. Indeed, during the nineteenth century an occasional Chinese junk was carried across the Pacific following the North Pacific current reaching the coast of California. However, Nordenskiöld's arguments in defense of the autonomous origin of American Indian civilization were not overturned by the early pottery culture of Ecuador. The great diversity in sources for cultural features, the variable time span with which individual forms were associated, and the marginal importance of the alleged importations for cultural developments in the New World still presented a formidable barrier to acceptance of an Asiatic stimulus to the rise of nuclear America.

British Migrationists: Smith, Perry, and Rivers

The Old World is filled with a history of migrations that sometimes spread cultured peoples into backward terrain and often spilled barbarians at the doorstep of the civilized. Trade was a frequent accompaniment of migration, certainly after the discovery of metallurgy. Thus, some time before 2000 B.C. Bell-Beaker peoples moved northward from settlements along the central Portuguese coast into Brittany and southern England, and then into north-central Europe. Wherever they went, they exploited local copper and gold and transformed stone-working peoples into knowledgeable miners and metal workers. Their lead men must have been traders and prospectors, replicating the historic experience of their own ancestors who were stimulated by metal-hungry migrants from out of the eastern Mediterranean around the middle of the third millenium B.C. (Piggott 1965:73–77, 100–102). Some 2,500 years after the Bell-Beaker migrations, Germanic tribes from western Asia moved into Europe, skirting and intruding upon the Roman domain, testing its defenses for booty, tribute, and land. Out of these barbarian migrations Vandals, Goths, Franks, Jutes, Angles, Saxons, Alemanni, and Frisians emerged and took their places in history. In the thirteenth century Jenghis Khan and his Mongols would sweep into eastern Germany before retiring to form their khanates in Russia. In that same century Marco Polo traversed the long caravan route that followed the rim of the Tarim Basin into central China and ended his journey in the ancient Imperial Capitol of China at the court of Kublai Khan, grandson of Jenghis Khan.

The lessons from Old World history were clear. Migration, trade, and conquest played a signal role in carrying inventions and arts from east to west and from south to north. Through colonization and exploitation of metal resources, backward areas were brought within the province of civilization, and in turn served as the transmitters of civilization to the simpler peoples surrounding them. This lesson of European history was not lost on the zoologist and comparative anatomist Grafton Elliot Smith (1871–1937). To Smith the growth of civilization was like the addition of one link after another to a chain, or series of chains, that stretched not only westward but eastward from Egypt to India to China and out through the Pacific islands to the higher centers of civilization in the New World. Migration, trade, and conquest were the central agents of the diffusion of culture, but the real impulse behind this restless quest for civilization was religion.

Smith built his reputation on studies of cranial morphology and the Egyptian practice of mummification, and while at the Government Medical School in Cairo he X-rayed royal mummies. Along with F. Wood Jones, Smith examined hundreds of Egyptian skeletons, extending over a span of 4,000 years, which had been unearthed in a survey of lands to be submerged with construction of the Aswan dam. Shortly after writing a history of mummification in Egypt Smith began to project that ancient civilization as the hearth of all civilizations. Egypt possessed the conditions essential for all the great inventions—cultivation, technical arts, calendar, and mummification. The latter was critical in providing the central impulse for integrating the skill and productivity of men and giving them a momentum that carried them far beyond the necessities of bare subsistence. "It is no exaggeration," Smith (1933:216) wrote, "to claim that the arts and crafts, the social and political organization and the innermost beliefs and the symbolism of the whole world were largely shaped by the practice of embalming." Around this funereal requirement bricklayers, stone masons, metal workers, carpenters, and priests developed their arts to satisfy a royal need. Once invented in Egypt, the idea of embalming and its practical techniques were conveyed through trade and colonization to adjacent lands, with some expectable loss of special features along the way. However, the essentials made their way eastward through India to Cambodia, on to Polynesia, and ultimately to the New World, where a distant outpost was aroused to civilize itself after an Egyptian original, several times removed.

Once introduced to great inventions, as Smith saw it, a people moved on to civilization. This was so because any invention generated new needs that challenged human ingenuity to come up with derivative inventions. For example, irrigation demanded the mastery of new mathematical skills in measurement. In this way a civilization grew locally. More important for world history, any civilization, to satisfy its own needs, used trade to thrust its inventions upon others. Egyptian needs required that they seek timber, ores, and precious wares from ancient Syria and Mesopotamia. Wherever the core complex of mummification of the god king made its way, local arts and crafts took on a civilized organization. However, Egyptian influences were not the only ones to find their way across the Pacific to the New World. Greco-Roman armor and helmet styles transmitted to India were dispersed eastward during Gupta times to China and Southeast Asia, together with Hindu traits. The Gupta cultural wave spilled into Oceania and rolled across the Pacific to Central America. From China the Central Americans received the dragon design and Buddhist influences. The crested helmets of Polynesia and of Mayaland betrayed the Greco-Roman military trace. Hindu influences could be detected in elephant designs, in a Mayan rain god associated with thunder and a serpent (Indra), and in the Aztec game of patolli, the counterpart to Hindu parcheesi (Smith 1924, 1929).

In Smith's eyes, a great chain of transmission linked all the civilizations of the world, ultimately traceable to a civilizing complex put together for the first time in the land of the pharaohs.

An English headmaster, W. J. Perry, was Smith's staunchest ally on the effort to link all the great civilizations to a common civilizing impulse generated in Egypt. *The Children of the Sun, A Study in the Early History of Civilization* (1923) was dedicated to Grafton Elliot Smith. Glancing over the ruins of the mighty civilized states hidden in the "fever-haunted jungles of India, Cambodia, Java, Guatemala . . . [and] the islands of Micronesia," Perry (1927:1) pondered not only the stimulus for their growth, but the causes that had doomed them to decay. In the human longing to find the elixir of life, early associated with precious metals, gold, and jewels in particular, Perry discovered the stimulus for the spread of the basic Egyptian civilization inventory.

Both Smith and Perry pointed to the integrative role of religion in organizing the civilizing process. As these ancient sacred civilizations began to form and to flourish, they came increasingly under self-generative processes, and it was to these, ironically, that their similar declines could be traced. Internal conflicts arose, bringing secular warriors to power, and as the energies of people were wasted on war and violence, the archaic model disintegrated. However, surrounding each of these ancient centers of civilization, one presently found primitive peoples whose customs disclosed that they were directly or indirectly the residue of those glorious days. For Perry, as for Smith, the path to civilization began with the sacred and skidded downward with the rise of the secular. In their prime these civilizing hearths reached out to peoples near and far, and as the great centers of civilization declined, the quality of life for those they touched likewise declined. Most primitives thus must be the degenerate heirs of a once-civilized estate.

The transition to cultural-historical investigation in British ethnology owed much to W. H. R. Rivers (1864–1922). Like Smith, Rivers began in medicine but later concentrated in neurophysiology and psychology. Participation in the Cambridge University expedition to Torres Straits under A. C. Haddon brought Rivers into contact with native peoples and customs and kindled his anthropological interests. In 1906 he published a substantial ethnography on the Todas of southern India, analyzing their customs as psychoevolutionary products in the tradition of Developmentalism. However, the new historic current in American ethnology, and especially the work of Graebner and Schmidt (see p.348), reinforced an emergent dissatisfaction with psychological interpretations of culture. From his own fieldwork it was apparent to Rivers that cultural uniformities existed despite diversities in geography. The answer to these uniformities in trait distributions must lie in something other than psychology and geography. In

Melanesia, Rivers began to see cultural historical processes at work which could account for both the diversity and uniformity of trait distributions (Rivers, 1914a, 1926). The matrilineal and patrilineal culture strata he detected traced the migrations of peoples, and before long Rivers found that Oceanic megaliths and sun worship were associated with Egypt. Further, they owed their presence in Melanesia to immigrants whose ideas, including mummification, could also be traced to Egypt, as Smith and Perry reasoned.

Neither Smith, Perry, nor Rivers was able to build a steady set of followers for his culture historical interpretation. Indeed, Rivers (1910) soon turned his efforts to the study of social organization where he proposed the genealogical method to achieve scientific control of kinship materials. From this fresh concentration on social relations Rivers (1914b, 1924) revitalized the study of kinship and kinship terminology by pointing to the correspondence between a kin term and role assignment. Rivers also continued his psychological interest. He kept pace with psychoanalytic developments and sought to construct a theory of the unconscious based on the conflict of instinct, censorship, and reason (1920, *Instinct and the Unconscious*).

Early in his career C. Daryll Forde worked in close association with Smith and published *Ancient Mariners* (1927) to support the theory of Egyptian origins. By 1930, however, Forde was defecting from the Smith-Perry camp owing to contact with the archeologist V. Gordon Childe and American culture historicists. In *The Threshold of the Pacific* (1925) Charles Fox reconstructed the culture history of San Cristoval (Solomon Islands) out of a series of waves of immigrants. A wave of Atawa people, who practiced a sun cult, mummification, and other features associated with archaic civilization, overran peoples possessing an earth-cult philosophy and earth burial. Here, in distant Oceania, the great drama of the succession of earth by solar deities would be repeated, just as in ancient Egypt, if Fox's historical reconstruction based on Smith and Perry could be believed!

Decline of Diffusionism in England. *Integrating change processes: Invention, diffusion, and evolution.* By 1930 diffusion studies entered a decline in England that paralleled similar trends in the United States. Interest in the transmission of cultural features was not surrendered entirely, but more attention was given to the way in which discoveries and inventions had occurred and the course which improving inventions had taken. This shift toward a more considered investigation of culture processes can be viewed as intellectual staging for the study of contemporary culture-contact processes and change. The transition to change-oriented studies took shape in England and the United States in the mid-thirties. In this connection it is of interest that those who led in acculturative research were either engrossed in a structural-functional orientation (Malinowski) or in the process of being exposed to structural theory (Linton, Redfield, Thurnwald) or engaged in studying processes of change in a contact context (Herskovits). Field experience drew attention to the vast changes taking place in native societies as a consequence of European contact and proved a vital experience for those who initiated the study of culture contact.

The shift to the study of culture process first concentrated on technology in hope of eliciting general laws. The biological analogy for culture processes was pressed into service by Harrison (1930), but the classification of inventions as mutations and the like did not add much to the understanding of process.

Sayce's *Primitive Arts and Crafts* (1933) represented a most considered effort to examine physical environment and historic contexts for clues to explain the processes of discovery and invention. Like Harrison, he used the biological model, holding that technical change developed an evolutionary directionality, and that in invention one could detect processes akin to mutation and hybridization. Traits also degenerated or disappeared through loss of original meaning and by competition from alternatives, or by change of function (Sayce 1963:131–132). However, in any advance in the development of material culture, as in organic evolution, progress was detected in the production of more functional forms and a more complex integration of technology. Technological progress required the challenge of contacts not available to remote areas. Here, in technical refuge areas, one reasonably could expect Paleolithic survivals of tools and techniques (Sayce 1963:134) long superseded in civilized areas. Indeed, Sayce noted that even within a civilized area one could observe survivals of this kind, for example, the caschrom found in the Hebrides and in Scandinavia and the breast plough used until recently in Wales. In Wales one still found wooden dishes, spoons, and plates made by local craftsmen that bore strong resemblances to pieces unearthed at Glastonbury Lake Village, and in some cases to examples from the Neolithic lake villages of central Europe (Sayce 1963:135). Neither modern crockery nor cheap metal substitutes had succeeded in driving out these traditional wooden shapes.

Sayce produced in *Primitive Arts and Crafts* a considered sampling of change situations and explanations, with an emphasis on the complexity rather than the simplicity of causal relations. He turned to the American culture historians Dixon and Wissler to support the diffusion of a complex of traits bound together in what the former called a logical complex; but at the same time Sayce noted that single traits may also travel separately, as Boas argued. Geographic and cultural conditions that facilitated or inhibited diffusion were so variable and effectual in altering the speed of transmission that there was no secure reliance on the age and area theory. The number and kinds of variables involved in diffusion were too complex for rule of thumb principles. The manner and ease with which a trait diffused was subject to geographical, cultural, ideological, commercial, and political factors (Sayce 1963:191). Many developments in regions might be due to the introduction of traits by immigrants from higher cultures, but food plants taken over by Europeans from American Indians (for example, maize, cocoa, tomatoes, rubber, tobacco, quinine, and ipecacuanha) should alert the researcher to possibilities of reverse transmission (Sayce 1963: 180–181). Granting the indigenous quality of American Indian culture growth in accordance with Nordenskiöld's analysis of material culture, Sayce reintroduced the possibility that winds and ocean currents brought Asiatics to the American coast. Some Asiatic culture traits could have entered the Americas in this way (Sayce 1963:267–270).

One is always on surer ground when historic checks are at hand, and this applies especially to evolutionary changes. A typological series can not be expected to correspond to the actual development, in linear fashion, from an ancient to a modern form. "Evolution is such a complicated process," wrote Sayce (1963:114–115), "involving . . . local developments, cross-mutations, convergence, borrowings and suggestions from different directions and at different times, that a linear, genealogical scheme is generally very difficult to establish." The best a typological series can do is foreshadow general trends. Thus, in the case of the lyre and of the harp, the simple bow was the start, with later attachment of some kind of resonating unit and additional strings.

Though Sayce had nothing fresh to say about methodology, he sensed that the explanatory problem of culture growth involved both historic and evolutionary processes. An epilogue to diffusional history was written by Margaret Hodgen (1950(52):461), who dedicated herself to demonstrating that documented distributions reveal far more about change processes than the undated distributions of ethnologists. Hodgen concluded that a unified study of man required a merging of historical and nonhistorical methodologies. Unless the anthropologist professionalized himself as an historian, and the historian acquired an anthropological perspective, the barriers separating the two disciplines would remain. The domain of dated distributions would not be cultivated, and valuable knowledge about culture change would be passed by.

The goal of unifying history and anthropology in the common cause of sorting out processes of culture growth through documented data has yet to be realized. An increasing sensitivity to the importance of situational context in producing shifts in direction has led more anthropologists to base their research on historic documents, especially when they must reach into a past beyond the limits of their ethnographic materials. However, an historical anthropology of the order projected by Hodgen would harness only a small portion of the potential of the discipline. Only those ethnographic data which relate to the introduction and dissemination of culture traits within a datable time span would be acceptable. Moreover, the dated materials and distributions of prehistorians are not considered in the study envisioned by Hodgen.

German-Austrian Kulturkreis Theoreticians. *The geography of history: Friedrich Ratzel (1844–1904).* In his conception of the civilizing process, Adolf Bastian began with elementary ideas common to mankind. Elementary ideas became historically significant in geographically localized folk ideas. However, ideas became significant for the civilizing process only as they were freed from limitations imposed by the survival adaptations which engrossed local *Völkergedanken*. The key to civilization hence lay in the intermingling of peoples and their ideas. In good humanist fashion, Bastian characterized the growth of civilization as a function of a mental community that absorbed and integrated more and more people within its folds. Despite his attention to the regionalizing of culture in geographic provinces, Bastian did not supply the impulse for German-Austrian culture-historical studies. This was the work of geographers, and more especially Friedrich Ratzel.

From their studies of men in relation to the earth geographers drew striking conformities between technology, mode of life, and habitat. They pointed this out by noting the spatial range of special kinds of artifacts, art styles, languages, social and political organization, and races. Where contrasting environments came together, peoples with different modes of life also confronted each other, and out of these intersections came cultural and racial interchanges.

The geographic impetus to historical-cultural studies during the latter part of the nineteenth century owed much to the fact that for the first time a cultural geography of the whole world could be presented. True, many areas still were sparsely covered, such as the interior of Africa but recently opened by exploration. Despite their incompleteness, the mapping of cultural boundaries and intersections of races and languages prompted speculation about the contact of peoples, which cultural items were indigenous and which intrusive, and how and by what routes elements and inventions had been transmitted. Geographic distributions promised some important lessons in history as well as explanations that challenged racial theories of civilization.

Ratzel's influence on the development of historical ethnology flowed from the world perspective which he brought to his geographic studies and the cultural contrasts he drew from geographic distributions. The use of iron, Ratzel (1896–1898(1):6–7) observed with some inaccuracy, was a diagnostic trait of great importance.

> The boundary between countries which do and do not use iron corresponds with those of other important regions of ethnographic distribution. Where there is no iron, cattle-breeding, the staple of which is oxen, buffaloes, sheep, goats, horses, camels, and elephants, is also unknown; pigs and poultry also are seldom bred in lands without iron. . . . In America, Oceania, and Australia [where iron is lacking] we have a much older stage of development: group marriage, exogamy, mother-right, and clan division; in Europe, Africa, and Asia, the patriarchal system of the family, monogamy, states in the modern sense. Thus among mankind also east and west stand over against each other. America is the extreme east of the human race, and thus we may expect to find there older stages of development than in Africa and Europe, the extreme west.

The very generality of Ratzel's contrastive summary produced inaccuracies. However, the weight of his description conveyed a sense of men restlessly spreading their inventions by land and sea as their cultural capabilities permitted, with the civilizing process largely a product of interchanges fostered by technical advances in economy and population increases.

> If the history of the world shows a spread . . . of civilization throughout the earth, the natural numerical preponderance existing among civilized folk is an important factor therein. The people who increase the more quickly pour out their surplus upon the others, and thus the influence of the higher culture, which itself was the cause or condition of the more rapid multiplication, gets spontaneously the upper hand. Thus the spread of civilization appears as a self-accelerating outgrowth over the world of civilizing races, ever striving more completely to effect that unity of the human race which forms at once its aim and task, its desire and hope. (Ratzel 1896–1898(1):13)

In the scope of their expansions, the great civilizations affected simpler peoples; in order to understand the natural races attention must be paid to the nature of their contacts with each other, and with civilized peoples (Ratzel 1896–1898(1):82). Geography had a way of creating fringe lands, and people remote from the great streams of traffic inevitably suffered a cultural impoverishment (Ratzel 1896–1898(1):83). The presence of traits at the extremes of an arc of distribution suggested that here one would find older features, often modified and stripped of their original uses. There was the possibility, then, of discovering chronological relations and of even determining culture strata.

The clustering of culture features led Ratzel, as Bastian, to differentiate ethnographic provinces. To add precision to his comparisons, as Leser (1964:417) reports, Ratzel used the criteria of form and quantity and employed geographic concepts like refuge area, marginal zone, and wedge to reach a relative chronology.

Leo Frobenius and the Malayo-Nigritian Kulturkreis. Credit for coining the term *Kulturkreis* belongs to one of Ratzel's students, Leo Frobenius (1897). In 1898, following Ratzel's observation that African culture was more richly developed along the east coast, and that the marginal Atlantic coastal zone housed ancient elements, Frobenius searched the East Indies for the stimulus of African culture origins, paying special attention to cultivated plants and art. To account for these cultural similarities, Frobenius constructed a Malayo-Nigritian culture tradition, or *Kulturkreis*—a relatively bounded interactional region where similar culture features existed by virtue of historic contact. Recently, G. P. Murdock (1959:204–270) rekindled the possibility of early contacts between Indonesia and Africa which may have brought new food plants into the West of Africa. According to Murdock, Maanyan speakers out of south central Borneo contacted Madagascar, and from there transmitted yams, taro, and bananas to the East African coast, anciently known as Azania. From that point, a network of trade carried these food plants westward across the Subsaharan grasslands to the Niger coast. The introduction of these Indonesian plants is conjectured to be a few centuries before or after A.D. Unlike Frobenius, however, Murdock did not attempt to set up a traditional culture that diffused *en bloc*, but dealt with individual elements or limited complexes (for example, the Malaysian complex of yams, taro, bananas, and sugarcane) whose components normally traveled together.

Frobenius soon surrendered his interest in historic reconstruction for the problem of the integration of culture. Oswald Spengler, through his concept of destiny ideas, seems to have provided Frobenius with the philosophic base for approaching the integration of cultures, or culture morphology. Adolf Jensen, successor to Frobenius, continued the search for the ultimate integrates of primitive culture and determined that the primitive world view was the key. The most expressive vehicles of the primitive world view were religion, myth, and cult. Behind the self-realizing process of creativity and change affecting both primitive and civilized man, Jensen, like Redfield, found a determinative orientation toward the world. As this world view changed, creativity and culture likewise changed.

Formulation of the Cultural-Historical Method: Fritz Graebner (1877–1934). The field of culture-historical reconstruction from which Frobenius turned was soon cultivated by Fritz Graebner, who was trained as an historian. Once accepted for a position in the Berlin Museum of Ethnology, Graebner's cataloguing of specimens for Von Luschan soon brought familiarity with primitive technology and art, especially in Melanesia. At the museum Graebner came to know B. Ankermann, and at the 1904 meeting of the Berlin Anthropological Society, the two produced papers which were the beginnings of the German-Austrian culture-historical school (Ankermann 1905, "Kulturkreise und Kulturschichten in Afrika"; Graebner 1905, "Kulturkreise und Kulturschichten in Ozeanien"). In 1906, W. Foy invited Graebner to continue his cultural historical interests with the newly established Rautenstrausch-Joest Museum in Cologne.

Graebner's analysis of Oceanian *Kreise* disclosed two culture traditions associated with Negroid peoples. He identified the two *Kreise* as a West and an East Papuan tradition. The fact that East Papuan elements were found in an east-west traverse of the Australian continent indicated an intrusion of the former into a segment of the West Papuan *Kreis*. To the north and south of this intrusive band one also could find the unmixed remains of the West Papuan culture. From the distributional configuration, Graebner concluded the West Papuan culture had been pushed back into the more remote areas of the Australian continent, and therefore must be the older of the two *Kreise*. This inference appeared probable, since the presence on the east coast of a purer manifestation of East Papuan elements suggested that the penetration had been from east to west. The determination of the relative chronology of *Kreise* allowed Graebner to designate a sequence of culture strata (*Kulturschichten*). Beneath both the East and West Papuan traditions he thought he could detect an older Negroid stratum represented by the Tasmanians.

The Melanesian bow culture represented a culture stratum that preceded the seafaring Polynesian cultures. The former tradition featured skin drums, decorated bamboo combs, spoons of mussel and coconut, pile dwellings with gabled and projecting roofs, porches or platforms and benches confined to one side of a house, a wide use of matting that included a woman's raincap and fiber apron, and a social organization based on descent groups and moieties. This land-based bow culture Graebner (1909) later traced throughout most of the world—westward to India and Africa and northward to Siberia and thence the Americas.

In 1911 Graebner produced a statement of the analytic controls which must be pressed into service if the validity of *Kulturkreis* formulations were to be assured. He modeled his *Methode der Ethnologie* after Bernheim's *Lehrbuch*, a manual of the historical method and of the philosophy of history, and consequently held that ethnology was properly a branch of historical science. Problems of source material came first, and Graebner recommended the use of stylistic features to authenticate the time and provenience of an observer's record. Careful analysis of form and ornament would disclose patterned relations expressive of a unique psychology that identified a traditional folk art in comparison with other folk arts.

Graebner identified the culture-historical problem as a use of the clues of culture elements to reconstruct and reunite the features which at one time formed an historic unit and shared a collective history. Single features would not do, although they often provided clues for reconstructions that could be fitted to other elements. Quantification of any kind increased the plausibility of an identification of a *Kreis*. For example, if a moon myth included a reciprocal refusal of food, and in another group a refusal of food were associated with a refusal of shelter, one could justifiably assume the presence of a moon myth in both groups. Both the refusal of food and of shelter were integral components of the myth. Close comparison of form resemblances was basic. The greater the number of similarities one found in conjunction with the relative complexity of form, the greater the probability of a prior association in a culture tradition even though distribution might be discontinuous. One could start with a regional complex of forms that suggested homogeneity, then look for supportive evidence in language and physical type.

The association of a culture tradition with specific peoples distinguished by physical, mental, and linguistic characteristics was basic to Graebner's effort to locate the original homeland of a *Kreis*. He may have been led to this combination of race, language, and culture by the ethnic and linguistic clustering found in Oceania and by differences in race and culture exhibited by inland and coastal groups. Moreover, the settlement of Oceania was suggestive of intrepid voyagers discovering new lands and bringing an advanced mode of life to natives whose ancestors had migrated to the area in distant times. The nature of Oceanic geography, ethnics, and culture readily suggested that different cultures were brought by migrants and that the contact of old and new had produced cultural blends. Referring to Ratzel's lead, Graebner (in Calverton 1931:421) reported that he had verified the importance of the "meeting and interaction of various cultural phenomena" in the production of mixed forms. As to fundamental processes of cultural change, Graebner's insistence that migrants carrying a unified culture inventory accounted for the spread of culture aligned him with British migrationists. The Americanist claim that single elements were dispersed throughout the world by a simple passage from the hands of one group to another was culture-historical nonsense, according to Graebner (1911:116).

Museum-bound, and retiring in personality, Graebner did not inspire a student following. Moreover, within three years of his succession as director of the museum at Cologne, a stroke seriously curtailed his activities. Publication of the *Method of Ethnology* in 1911, however, converted the Jesuit Wilhelm Schmidt (1868–1954), who proved to be the most creative and industrious of *Kulturkreis* advocates. In this endeavor Schmidt was fortunate in enlisting the Jesuit Wilhelm Koppers as enthusiastic student and later collaborator.

Following leads supplied by Ratzel, and more particularly by Graebner, Schmidt ambitiously determined to chart the emergence of ancient cultural traditions and their spatial ranges. The goal was nothing less than a world history, or prehistory, since the focus was largely on primitive cultures.

> It must be the ultimate goal of our comparisons to establish . . . the distribution of the several cultures over the whole earth; and then, by comparing them reciprocally, to find which is the oldest in the whole history of cultural development, and also the absolute sequence in which the others follow it . . . [and] in what region it arose. (Schmidt 1931:234–235)

Schmidt's search for the oldest culture stratum was highly colored by the twin convictions that the pygmies represented an archaic physical and cultural condition of mankind and that ancient primitives had a conception of a high god, later obscured by magical and animistic conceptions. Here, in a new key, was the theological dogma of degeneration; but Andrew Lang, with his conception of Australian high gods, provided the stimulus for Schmidt's ethnological researches. Between 1912 and 1955, Schmidt prepared twelve volumes to show that early hunters and gatherers, now found in marginal and refuge areas, possessed the idea of a creator god, and more important, a supreme being who was a guardian of morality. Schmidt was able to complete his work because he inspired both Wilhelm Koppers and Martin Gusinde to take up fieldwork among the Alacaluf, Yaghan, and Ona at the margin of South America. Both Koppers (1924) and Gusinde (1931–1939) uncovered the moral high god, and also described the technology, property rights, social organization, and the position of women expectable in the primitive culture stage. Paul Schebesta (1929, 1938–1950) in turn followed the tropical spoor of pygmies in Malaysia and in the African Congo. Pygmies also were found to have a notion of a moralistic high god, and, in apparent substantiation of Schmidt's thesis, their technology and social organization were unique enough to warrant inclusion of pygmy culture as a distinctive variant of the primitive culture stage. In other words, pygmies did not live with culture hand-me-downs borrowed from their more advanced neighbors, as scholars commonly believed.

The human history described by Schmidt developed through four primary successions. First came the food-gathering primitive cultures, followed by the primary cultures of cultivators and pastoral nomads; then secondary cultures, noted for nonexogamous patriliny and matriliny and picture writing; and finally the tertiary cultures, or ancient civilizations of Asia, Europe, and the Americas (Schmidt 1931:350–351). A number of *Kreis* variants were recognized under each of the evolutionary successions. The secondary and tertiary cultures were products of culture mixing, a trend that increased with each evolutionary step.

Locating the original homelands of the *Kreise* was a special problem of the historical method. Assuming that the human race originated in Asia, Schmidt (1931:234–235) concluded that in every continent,

> the oldest movement of population made its ways to the farthest district, or at least was thrust there by the following waves of migration; while ... the most recent strata of peoples in those parts of the world are those who are nearest the entry. Apart from this, however, remnants of older populations can maintain themselves more easily in out-of-the-way districts, such as mountainous tracts difficult of approach, primeval forests, deserts, and other inhospitable regions; also on distant islands.

In reconstituting the inventory of the ancient cultures, Schmidt relied on comparison. To discriminate centers, he utilized the criteria of quality, quantity, continuity in spatial distribution, and degree of relationship. The latter criterion anticipated an increase in the number of culture resemblances as one approached the heart of an area. With regard to the primitive cultures, Schmidt (1931:223) observed that some homelands

> could be established with some certainty. All the American Primitive cultures, the South American (Fuegians, Gez-Tapuya) and the North American (north central Californians, the Algonkins) once formed an old culture together with the Arctic culture (Samoyedes, Koryakes, Ainu, Ancient-Eskimo), whose habitat was somewhere in (North) Eastern Asia. To the southwest, the Pygmy culture joined it and was the first to separate from there and split up into an African and a (South) Asiatic group. On the Southeast, the preparatory stages of the later Southeastern Australian Primitive culture joined, which migrated from there over the present Indonesia and New Guinea to Australia.

Schmidt justified the writing of world prehistory by ethnologists rather than by archeologists on the grounds that both faced common methodological problems in erecting cultural chronologies. The ethnologist lacked the controls available to a prehistorian working with the natural stratification of a site. However, this advantage vanished when the prehistorian compared different sites and attempted to relate cultural strata sequentially. At this point, since sites differed in sequential stratification as well as in artifact content, the archeologist, in Schmidt's (1939:301–302) judgment, was forced to rely on space-form distributions in order to show the boundaries and contacts of cultures. In short, the archeologist manipulated his data in the same way as the historical ethnologist. So the ethnologist actually held an advantage with his conceptualizations of "contact and overlay phenomena . . . intrusions, penetrations, encirclings and other results of migrations" (Schmidt 1939:301–302).

However, the historical reconstructions of prehistorians and of ethnologists seldom correspond. This was the case with Otto Menghin's (*Die Weltgeschichte der Steinzeit* 1931) effort to draw up prehistoric *Kulturkreise* and correlate them with ethnological *Kreise*, even though he followed the general ethnological plan of determining primary cultures and then deriving secondary cultures through intermingling. The fate of *Kulturkreise* reconstruction ultimately depended on its capacity to produce sufficient convergences with the findings of archeology in order to justify confidence in the method. As with other attempts at writing history through ethnographic distributions, the confidence was never forthcoming. Officially, the end to *Kulturkreislehre* came in 1959, when, according to Heine-Geldern (1964(5):414), "Koppers himself, who had long since abandoned the Kulturkreis theory, wrote its obituary, tracing its history and pointing out its merits and its failure."

CULTURE HISTORICISM: AN ASSESSMENT

No one today takes the reconstructions of culture historicists seriously as history. Their histories failed for the same reason that evolutionary history failed. In the absence of clear documentation, culture historicists substituted formal analysis and classification for process. To infuse life into the barren space of distribution, they constructed a simple model of diffusion and made some rather liberal assumptions. Their basic model held that all cultural developments emanated from a heartland and moved outward like ripples in a pool. Such a model presupposed a uniform rate of diffusion for all traits, regardless of kind, and posed no barrier to transmission other than mountain ranges and large bodies of water. The oldest traits thus were found at the margins of a diffusion circle, and the widest circle was the oldest of all. Discontinuous distributions suggested eruptions of more recent traditions, or overlays of the older stratum.

If the reconstructions of culture historians held little value, what then were their accomplishments? Was all their effort water over the dam? Not entirely. A list of their credits would include the following:

1. Entrenchment of fieldwork as intrinsic to the accumulation of a valid and reliable factual base.

2. Development of the concept of culture and a conceptual inventory for description and analysis. Terms like "culture trait," "culture complex," and "culture area" were used to describe the integration of culture elements into larger wholes. The attention accorded form and function in the comparison of traits was extended by Linton (1936) and Barnett (1940, 1942)

to include meaning, use, and principle in their search to find how culture altered. In its association with ethnology, the culture concept provided a substantive rationale for the independent existence of the discipline. Ethnologists studied culture as psychologists studied mental processes. By studying culture processes the causal nexi of culture were brought to surface and no attention need be paid to variables lying outside culture—at least so it was argued. Finally, the rise of the culture concept shattered the combination of race, psychology, and culture forged with the rise of evolution.

3. In their mapping of trait distributions and their clusterings, culture historicists contributed a geography of culture that is useful to this day. Culture areas suggest a network of interrelations within a relatively bounded space that has produced a striking degree of uniformity in traits and patterns. Culture areas thus imply that participating tribal societies shared a common history, though the time at which any society entered the field must be determined individually. The mapping of culture traits was not only a useful classificatory device but it was also serviceable in drawing inferences about lines of communication linking continents. Form could be utilized to determine these lines of communication, as Kroeber (1923:211–214) demonstrated when tracing the diffusion of tobacco to the Eskimo. The form of the Eskimo pipe indicated that the diffusion route led from the New to the Old World, across European Russia to Siberia, and thence via the Bering Strait to the Eskimo!

4. Culture-historical analysis produced some important insights into culture processes, especially as these related to culture and environment, the role of complex centers in the dissemination of culture, and processes involved in the invention, acceptance, modification, and rejection of alien forms.

The mapping of culture-environment correspondences precedes any determination of culture-environment relations. This advantage was conveyed by the Swedish geographical ethnologists Hatt (1914) and Steensby (1916). Hatt discriminated cultural features associated with circumpolar inland and coastal adaptations, while Steensby focused on the role of ice seal hunting and inland caribou hunting in the Eskimo adaptation. Technico-economic adaptations in food production set the stage for Wissler's determination of culture areas in the Americas, and the spread of culture was viewed in the perspective of its adaptation to a particular environment. Noting that tundra, mesa, and jungle constituted three great diffusion zones, Wissler (1923:230–231) observed that the mesa had been the homeland of all the great civilizations.

> Here is where the great agricultural trait-complexes were built up as well as the metal-complexes. The domestication complexes—ox, horse, camel, sheep, goat, etc.—belong here also. Just why the centers of origin for these trait-complexes lie in this zone it may be unprofitable to consider; but once they did arise and became adjusted to the local environments, their diffusion would follow the *mesa*.

In his review of culture-environment correlates, Kroeber (1939) found that cultures reached a climax where resources were readily available.

The diffusion of culture varied according to whether transmission was relatively unorganized, as was usual among simpler peoples, or organized, as was common among the civilized. According to Wissler (1923), organized diffusion was usually preceded by colonization, missionary zeal, and conquest, and technical items and techniques were more handily diffused than ideas and rituals. It was also characteristic of trait complexes to diffuse and extend themselves in space, and the organized diffusion of militarism accelerated this trend (Wissler 1923:178). The notion that culture centers served as points of elaboration, innovation, and dissemination coincided with what was known to have occurred in the ancient urbanized hearths of the Near East, India, China, and nuclear America. Certainly, once a new trait started up a pattern evolved, maturing through a process of elaboration and then disintegration (Wissler 1923:198).

In the reception of alien traits, compatibility with culture and with environment loomed impressive. For a new idea to survive, Wissler (1923: 184) hazarded that it should be closely related to some part of an existing complex. The same held for the acceptance of inventions generated within a culture.

The preoccupation of culture historicists with their several problems focused their respective contributions. *Kulturkreis* historians were so busy formulating their culture circles that they found no time for the study of culture processes. Their special contribution was concentrated in methodological procedures that could be counted on in the determination of historical relationships and the sequencing of culture strata. On the other hand, British migrationists and American culture historians engaged broader issues, including process, with a corresponding drop in concern for the methodology of form comparison. The former, in accounting for modifications of the Egyptian complex, turned to the limitations of environment, accumulated knowledge, and human error in replicating experience. Americanists directed their attention to the culture-environment relationship, but also investigated sociopsychological processes comprehended in the meanings and functions of culture forms. More so than others, American culture historicists engaged culture and culture process as a special phenomenon. Their concern for process, in conjunction with the rise of structural-functional analyses of cultures, helped culture theorists in the Old and New Worlds to pioneer in acculturation studies where the processes of change could be directly observed.

In initiating acculturation as a field of study, British and American anthropologists may have possessed an advantage because of the custodial rule exercised by their governments over peoples whose cultures were highly contrastive with industrial culture. However, rule over alien peoples was not the sole determinant, for French social anthropologists were slow to take up acculturative investigation despite a colonial empire. Moreover, in Richard Thurnwald, the Germans, who had lost their colonies in World

War I, had a functionally minded ethnologist who studied on-the-spot change in East Africa.

SUMMARY

Culture historicism represents one line of the focus on structural necessities, functions, and integrative processes which characterized the rise of Structuralism from 1890 to 1940. Developments in historical geography, stemming largely from Friedrich Ratzel, supplied the stimulus for translating cultural geography into history. The ethnological historian set out to reconstruct the history of world cultures before documented history, and in the process hoped to elucidate the dynamics of culture growth. In the absence of historic documents, ethnologists made inferences from spatial distributions as to the relative age of features, probable centers of origin, and the directions of diffusion. To establish criteria that would demonstrate contact, ethnologists compared forms as to their resmblances, functions, and meanings, and supplemented these measures with the principles of simplicity, complexity, quantity, and quality. The principles of simplicity and complexity were useful in determining whether an artifact or belief, owing to its very simplicity, could be developed independently by any number of peoples. The complexity of things precluded independent invention. The more features (quantity) shared by two widely spaced peoples, the greater the presumption of prior connection; and this inference was strengthened if supported by some qualitative features (for example, treatment of narrative). Quantity and quality were useful in establishing a basis for prior contact despite discontinuity in distribution. Rates of diffusion were important to inferences as to the relative age of features, but historicists had no way of controlling this variable and generally assumed that the more widespread the element the older it was.

Culture historians divided into three basic "schools": American diffusionists, German-Austrian *Kulturkreislehrer*, and British migrationists. This national manifestation reflected a variability in the perceptual experience of researchers traceable to the nature of the materials with which they worked. Americanists had no evidence available at the time which suggested that culture features had spread in the New World by migrants possessing different cultures. German *Kulturkreislehrer*, working in Africa, but more especially in Melanesia, confronted coastal and upland peoples who differed in race, language, and level of culture. Such evidence suggested that migrants were responsible for cultural differences and that some migrants had entered the region earlier than others. The European experience was filled with culture migrants and trading colonies which facilitated transmission of whole blocs of culture rather than a diffusion of single elements, or of limited complexes, as argued by Americanists. Grafton Smith's chance experience with Egyptian mummification led to the view of history diffusing from a single civilized center, Egypt. *Kultur-*

kreis theory, on the other hand, made use of a number of regional centers linked to an evolution of economies and social organizations.

Each of the culture-historical "schools" was stimulated in its development by historical figures. When the historical impulse eroded, it was not entirely due to the passing away of these founders. New facts and theoretical inputs from other disciplines, as well as the modernization of pre-industrial societies, altered the factual base of ethnography and directed investigation into new channels. The wide range of interests of Franz Boas turned American anthropology in the direction of historical reconstruction and also laid the groundwork for future investigation of the relation between language and cognition and of enculturation to personality. The German-Austrian theorists, Graebner and Schmidt, limited themselves to historical interpretations and problems of method. British migrationists, Smith and Perry, likewise limited themselves to the accumulation of evidence indicating that all great civilizations, including Mexico, Yucatan, and the North-central Andes, exhibited the stimulus of the Egyptian god-king culture.

The historical orientation drew attention to the variability of culture growth according to accidents of contact, and hence opposed an evolutionary perspective which relied on general psychological tendencies to produce uniformities in cultural developments. Concern for variation and the particulars of individual histories ultimately gave way in American ethnology to considerations of cultural integration and the systemic qualities and functions of cultures. Attention to value orientations and world views also crossed the interests of German culture morphologists (Frobenius). The interest in cultural integration led to a greater consideration of how cultures were structured, how they functioned through their structural relationships, and how structural continuities were maintained. Such concerns reinforced a structural determinism already associated with the view that cultural behaviors were imprinted by habit-conditioning and hence individual behavior was determined by unconscious cultural forces.

Culture historians developed the concept of culture and made the investigation of culture the special domain of ethnology. However, their methodological controls proved insufficient to justify acceptance of their historical reconstructions. Nevertheless, their mapping of culture traits brought to light the wide distribution of traits and complexes and verified their contention that culture contact was a vital factor in culture growth. A clustering of features permitted the mapping of culture areas throughout the world. At the same time culture historians undertook fieldwork in order to assure a valid and reliable factual base for their inferences of culture history. Through their analysis of culture elements according to form, function, and meaning they also advanced the study of sociopsychological processes involved in the acceptance and rejection of alien elements. Their attention to the patterning of culture served as a base for the study of cultural integration.

10

Establishing the Autonomy of Culture

INTRODUCTION

Conceptualization of the cultural as distinct from the social was of singular importance for anthropology. For the first time anthropologists could claim they possessed a substantive domain uniquely their own, and could rationalize the existence of anthropology as a distinctive discipline. Culture became the central concept for culture historicists and for Malinowski's biocultural functionalism. Social Structuralists, on the other hand, took the social as their basic construct. The differential emphasis on the cultural versus the social produced a schism in anthropology in that cultural anthropologists and social anthropologists considered that their problem interests were distinctive. French and British social anthropologists viewed themselves essentially as sociologists, with a special concentration on primitive society. Cultural anthropologists, particularly in the United States, saw themselves as part of a unified anthropological discipline comprised of two major divisions—physical and cultural anthropology, with the study of social organization included in the latter.

In the rest of Europe, various anthropological specializations developed historically as special affiliates of the natural sciences or of the humanities. Frequently historical ethnology was joined with geographic studies and based in a museum. This fragmentation and narrow specialization prevented the development of a unified conception of an anthropological discipline on the part of continental students.

Establishment of the concepts of the cultural and the social was accomplished by continuing the hierarchical view of reality found in the nineteenth century. Behind this hierarchical arrangement was the idea that the different sciences investigated domains that were conceptually and causally distinctive. Such a differentiation of disciplines in the search of separate truths was not only necessary but pragmatic. As Lowie (1929:5–6) observed with regard to culture and ethnology,

> Culture is, indeed, the sole and exclusive subject-matter of ethnology, as consciousness is the subject-matter of psychology, life of biology, electricity of a branch of physics. Culture shares with these other fundamental concepts the peculiarity that it can be properly understood only by an enlarged familiarity with the facts it summarizes . . . ; but as every analysis and explanation of particular conscious states adds to our knowledge of what consciousness is, so every explanation of particular cultural phenomena adds to our insight into the nature of culture. . . .
>
> For purely practical reasons, connected with . . . specialization, ethnology has in practice concerned itself with the cruder cultures of peoples without a knowledge of writing. But this division is an illogical and artificial one. As the biologist can study life as manifested in the human organism as well as in the amoeba, so the ethnologist might examine and describe the usages of modern America as well as those of the Hopi Indians.

When phenomena are ordered in layers, it is sometimes tempting to explain a higher level by a lower. To do so, however, is to commit the error of reductionism; and in establishing the reality of culture, theorists found themselves combating efforts to reduce culture to a product of psychological and biological responses common to mankind. Once over this hurdle, culture theorists explored and elaborated the concept, especially with regard to its integrative functions. Social anthropologists, on the other hand, moved to a more restricted definition of culture as they sought to distinguish the domain of the social.

Discussion of the concept of culture begins with the development of the idea of culture as an object and process, occupying a separate level within a ranked system of causal variables. Discussion of the culture concept leads naturally into consideration of methodological relativism and culture as a distinctive causal process. The findings of anthropologists regarding the nature of culture as they explored its parameters is discussed next. Basic assumptions commonly held by culture historians and later by culture theorists about the nature of culture and the deterministic role played by culture in ordering social structure and behavioral patterning follow. The chapter concludes with a summary and commentary on the use of the culture concept by culture historians.

RISE OF CULTURAL OBJECTIVITY

To be useful as a scientific concept, culture had to be stripped of the valuative emphasis common to Developmentalist usage during the eighteenth and nineteenth centuries. The capacity to treat culture-as-object was the work of culture historicists as they arranged museum specimens and compared the distribution of artifacts in space. Liberation of the concept of culture from its use in describing a state of cultivation or civilization can be attributed to three sources: (1) the classification of artifacts and modes of life; (2) methodological relativity in the allocation of cause, that is, citing culture as causing culture; and (3) philosophic relativity, that is, the recognition of the validity of different styles of life.

The word "culture" in its original Latin usage apparently described a process of cultivation or nurture. As Kroeber and Kluckhohn (1963:283) observe, "The application of culture to human societies and history was late—apparently post 1750—and for some reason was characteristic of the German language and at first confined to it." Gustave Klemm (1843–1851) pointed out that primitive men created culture when they fashioned a branch in the shape of a club. The French in their turn had preferred the term "civilization" in describing the sophisticated and refined quality of peoples and nations. In 1871, Tylor (1874(1):1) equated both culture and civilization. Culture or civilization described the habits and capabilities men acquired by virtue of their participation in a society. Tylor urged the scientific study of man's advancement in culture correlated with the stages of savagery, barbarism, and civilization. So the matter stood until culture historians began to describe the artifacts of peoples, to compare the technical and ideological inventory of one people with another, and to map the extension of cultures in time and space.

Papers by W. H. Holmes (1915) and Clark Wissler (1915) illustrate how the practical work of museum classification and arrangement advanced a vocabulary that employed the term "culture." Both Holmes and Wissler tackled the problem of making an inventory of tools, weapons, dress, foods, and other items that could be compared by tribe and region. Holmes spoke of material culture and the geographical limitations of culture units. He also referred to the study of culture and culture relationships and noted how cultures overlap and blend along the borders of regions and along lines of ready communication. Holmes also distinguished more advanced cultures while noting that his descriptions of the different archeological areas simply listed features which facilitated comparison in order to define the cultures represented. When Holmes (1915:59) wrote of the gradual fading of the "typical culture of the agricultural mound-building peoples of the Mississippi valley" as one approached the Rocky Mountains, his usage was quite modern. Similar terminology by Wissler reveals a wide acceptance of the term in ethnological practice at the time; for example, a tribe's material culture, ceremonial culture, culture areas, culture traits, culture centers, trait complexes, and Plains, Pueblo, and Plateau cultures. Wissler likewise commented on the environmental factor in culture and distinguished a type unit or type culture which shared no appreciable traits characteristic of other centers.

In both the New and Old World, museum classification of artifacts according to geography was largely responsible for the view of culture as an aggregate of objects. In his *Methode der Ethnologie*, Fritz Graebner speaks of cultural facts, cultural forms, cultural complexes, traits, and culture categories and refers to the transmission of culture and earlier and later stratums of culture. In "Kulturkreise und Kulturschichten in Ozeanien," Graebner (1905) distinguished a number of different cultures—for example, the land-based Melanesian culture and the seafaring Polynesian culture. Each culture tradition was distinguishable by a basic inventory of features. For example, the seafaring Polynesian culture exhibited the following: outrigger with a three-sided sail or derived forms, fishhooks, nets, weirs, triton horn, fire-plow, and coconut shredder. The Polynesian axe and tapa manufacture were significant indexes of the culture, but like the fire-plow and coconut shredder, were distributed more widely than the limits of Polynesian culture itself. As for social organization, Polynesian culture featured a developed chieftainship, rank, and tapu. All of these traits could be found in Micronesia, and traces also could be picked up in Melanesia. Owing to the irregular distribution of Polynesian-type elements of social organization, Graebner concluded that their presence in Micronesia and Melanesia must be due to later Polynesian influence. He also noted that Polynesian features of social organization shared a pattern of distribution similar to that of tattooing, circumcision, and kava drinking.

The use of culture as a descriptive qualifier of traits and complexes, in conjunction with the conceptualization of cultures differentiated by special inventories, facilitated the conceptualization of culture-as-object. Culture was located in tools, processes of manufacture, ideas, customs, elements of social organization, rituals, and other conventionalized components. The human environment could be brought under the scrutiny of science and studied as dispassionately as a cell under a microscope. The spread of culture elements across geographic lines suggested that culture had its own cause independent of geographic influences. It is not surprising then to find Foy in his introduction to Graebner's (1911:v) *Methode der Ethnologie* took ethnology to be a "history of culture." He noted that "as a branch of historical science our discipline can only deal with cultural manifestations when determining the conditions of its causal operations and must exclude therefrom all historical-philosophical and folk-psychological points of view." Foy's statement anticipated Lowie's (1917) association of culture with ethnology by six years. Both German and American culture historians converged, in that they were rigidly empirical. They avoided the speculation usually found in philosophies of history and in the notion of ethnic psychology tied to race and soil. In the United States the concept of culture at first shared honors with the social tradition and social heritage. The concept of culture became thoroughly entrenched during the twenties only as ethnologists began to view cultures as independent modes of life to which individuals were enculturated.

DEFENSE AGAINST REDUCTIONISM:
KROEBER AND THE SUPERORGANIC

The first American culture theorist to address himself to the autonomy and causality of culture was Kroeber. In retrospect Kroeber viewed his "Eighteen Professions" (1915) and "The Superorganic" (1917) as a protest against those who linked race and civilization in cavalier fashion and filled the popular mind with fallacies. The 1915 professions of faith in large part were a prerun of the thesis developed in "The Superorganic." From a selection of Kroeber's (1915(17):283–288) "credo" we learn that

1. The aim of history is to know the relations of social facts to the whole of civilization. . . .
2. The material studied by history is not man, but his works. . . .
3. Civilization, though carried by men and existing through them, is an entity in itself, and of another order from life. . . .
4. A certain mental constitution of man must be assumed by the historian, but may not be used by him as a resolution of social phenomena. . . .
6. The personal or individual has no historical value save as illustration. . . .
7. Geography, or physical environment, is material made use of by civilization, not a factor shaping or explaining civilization. . . .
8. Heredity cannot be allowed to have acted any part in history. . . .
11. Selection and other factors of organic evolution cannot be admitted as affecting civilization. . . .
13. There are no social species or standard cultural types or stages. . . .
15. There are no laws in history similar to the laws of physico-chemical action. . . .
16. History deals with conditions *sine qua non*, not with causes. . . .
17. The causality of history is teleological. . . .
18. In fine, the determination and methods of biological, psychological, or natural science do not exist for history, just as the results and the manner of operation of history are disregarded by consistent biological practice. . . .

Item 3 above is critical, since it asserted the essential autonomy of the social and prepared the way for Kroeber's own conceptualization of the superorganic. That is, the social did not constitute a "link in a chain, not a step in a path, but a leap to another plane" (Kroeber 1952b:49). Like steam generated out of water, the social represented a new state with its own properties.

Kroeber conceived reality in the form of a Jacob's ladder, beginning with the inorganic at the bottom, the organic a step above, next the psychological or biopsychic, and finally the social and cultural. Each, though connecting with the next in rank, constituted a separate and distinct area of investigation with its own special facts and causal explanations. There was no point to reducing the explanation of one level to a lower in the hope of finding a better or real explanation. A lower level provided a generalized process for the more specific processes and events of the next higher rank, and this was insufficient for causal explanation.

Laws of a lower level set the frame within which phenomena of a higher level operate. They do not per se produce those phenomena. The lower-level laws will explain the constants, universals and uniformities of phenomena on an upper level. They will explain or describe those properties which an upper level shares with a lower—that an organic body has mass or conductivity, for instance. They fail to explain or even describe those properties that are specific of a level, distinctive of it—as how an organic body repeats itself in its off-spring.

In short, it appears that the total work of science must be done on a series of levels which the experience of science gradually discovers. To reduce every-thing in the universe to a monistic set of principles, mechanical or otherwise, may be a legitimate philosophy—or may not be; it is certainly not an adequate operational method of science. It involves using the hard-won earnings of phys-ics for verbal extensions into biology or sociology, and thereby short-circuit-ing genuine problem solution in those very domains. Apparently true progress is made when every science is autonomous in its procedures, while also real-izing its relation of dependence on the subjacent ones and of support to the independent overlying ones. It is investigation on autonomous levels that is a precondition of most extensions of our understanding of the world. After enough such extensions have been made, it is valid reductionism that grad-ually integrates and consolidates them. Premature reductionism is just verbal forcing. (Kroeber 1952e:121)

Kroeber's statement on the superorganic marked the beginning of structural determinism in American culture theory. Use of the term "social" in these early articles, Kroeber confessed, was a mistake; he now preferred the term "culture" to cover the same ground, with the social one ranked below the cultural. Later Kroeber (1948b(50):413) reasserted his determin-ist position, though admitting that in actual life he acted "as if . . . [he] enjoyed freedom of will."

The cultural determinism to which the concept of the cultural super-organic pointed immediately brought a challenge from Goldenweiser (1917) and Sapir (1917). In Goldenweiser's (1917(19):449) judgment, the bio-graphical individual was unique in that he transcended the biological, psy-chological, and civilizational matrix. The same objection to the elimination of the influence which individuals exerted on history was raised by Sapir. Yet Sapir (1917(19):441) admitted that individuals were so shaped by social traditions that even the contributions of original minds appeared the result of culture. Neither Sapir nor Goldenweiser conceded that the social and the psychic were separated by the vast chasm delineated by Kroeber. How-ever, both agreed with Kroeber that the cultural and the social could not be reduced in explanation to the psychological or the sociopsychological.

The position of Goldenweiser and Sapir accented a fundamental am-biguity about culture and the individual that dogged Americanists in their exploration of the culture concept. Yet the flexibility of ambiguity aided Americanists in preserving a focus on the individual and in returning con-sistently to the individual-culture relation in the manifold contexts of social life and personality. In the meantime a structural orientation to culture grew imperceptibly, with the tendency to trace the diversity of human behavior regardless of time and place to different culture traditions. The rise of this structural posture coincided with the rise of behavioristic and stimulus-response psychology.

As for Kroeber, he utilized the concept of pattern to demonstrate the reality of structure and the relative independence of structural process. Pattern served Kroeber as his primary unit, since it produced regularities in the form of style and system. Moreover, by comparing one pattern against another, contrast and interdependencies elicited fresh understanding (Kroeber 1948b(50):411). Kroeber selected two domains that were worlds apart in order to prove the presence of an independent pattern process. In women's fashions one could hardly expect to find any patterning to the shifts that took place, but Richardson and Kroeber's (1940) study revealed that over a period of three centuries, women's dress and dress proportions had fluctuated in a rhythmic manner. Again, in *Configurations of Culture Growth* (1944), Kroeber argued that the clustering of genius that created an art style could be explained only by the presence of pattern.

Once he had completed his reality model, with culture at the top of the ranks, Kroeber (1948b(50):411) found that those who sought "to derive specific cultural effects [forms and patterns] from specific psychic or social causes" had failed conspicuously. Addition of the phrase "social causes" was significant, for it denied the derivation of culture from a social matrix that could produce a social psychology. Kroeber had to meet the argument of social anthropologists who derived social sentiments from group activities and saw culture as an instrument for symbolizing collective sentiments. He reaffirmed the task of anthropology as essentially historical and rejected the organic structural-functional model of Durkheim and his followers. In linguistics there was a far better model for culture. Under linguistic analysis phonetic and grammatic forms were treated impersonally, "with a minimum of reference to its carriers and their psychology (Kroeber 1948b(50):411–412). The relations of linguistic forms were paramount and not the physical motions of larynx and air flow by which they were produced. Language, like the culture of which it was a part, was something more than specific events.

The linguistic model served Kroeber time and again as a primary support for his theoretical position regarding the determinism exerted by culture patterns on everything they touched. Even before he came to a clear distinction of the social and cultural, Kroeber (1909) used linguistic patterns of thought—a cultural phenomenon—to refute the determinism of social institutions implied by Morgan's use of kinship terminologies to reconstruct the evolution of social organization. In analyzing kinship terminologies, Kroeber observed that they operated with a limited number of idea categories. These included generation, relative age, lineal or collateral relationship, sex of speaker, sex of relative, sex of connecting relative, blood or marriage relations, and the present state of the individual through whom a relationship is traced (for example, living, deceased, married, divorced). Kroeber (1952a:181) concluded that "terms of relationship reflect psychology, not sociology." By psychology in this case Kroeber meant that kin terms were nothing more than logical categories employed by people to classify near and distant relatives, including kin by marriage. Such classifications, even where they involved the extension of a sibling term to a mother's sister's child, did not mean that ego would treat him as own brother or sister. The usage was simply a social convention and did not involve a definition of equivalent social rights and obligations. No one could maintain that the Western classification of cousins was anything more than a handy way of describing relationships without any semblance of obligatory reciprocities.

At the time, Kroeber was interested in countering the claims of Developmentalists that kin terms defined a living social relationship, or did so at one time. On this assumption, Developmentalists had built rather complicated social histories, in which the classification of all male first cousins, for example, as brothers was taken to mean that they were the offspring of a common set of mothers married to a group of fathers. The position taken by Kroeber was also used against social Structuralists like Radcliffe-Brown, who insisted that kin terms reflected vital social relationships.

Culture, as language, thus was vindicated as the context in which a social phenomenon was made intelligible; and in retrospect Kroeber (1952: 172) did not see any reason to seriously alter his position. The early article on the language of kinship smothered claims for social determinism and upheld his own ideas of historical-cultural determinism as they matured.

METHODOLOGICAL RELATIVISM AND THE STUDY OF CULTURE AS PROCESS

The problem of culture as the proper context by which human behavior can be explained obviously is connected to the issue of levels of reality to which Kroeber, like Comte and Spencer before him, addressed himself. Boas had no mind for metaphysics; yet between 1890 and 1910 he undoubtedly did more than any anthropologist to promote the idea that anyone investigating other cultures must assume the posture of a methodological relativist. Methodological relativism, in one instance, meant that any culture form, to be understood, must be placed in its appropriate culture context. Second, methodological relativism alerted the investigator to the fact that his own cultural experience was a constant threat to his ability to view the other culture without bias and without attempting to force it into a mold of his own cultural inventory of forms, ideas, values, and intrinsic relationships. The proper exercise of these two operations would guarantee the objectivity in recording and analyzing to which the scientist aspired. The step from a methodological to a philosophical relativism was short and easy.

Boas defended primitive peoples from the derogatory stereotypes by which they commonly were sketched. True to his scientific orientation, he saw culture not as a state of sophisticated omniscience but rather as an attitude and a way of thinking that got in the way of understanding. "The data of ethnology prove that not only our knowledge, but also our emotions are the result of the form of our social life and of the history of the people to whom we belong. If we desire to understand the development of human culture, we must try to free ourselves of these shackles (Boas 1940a: 636).

Culture thus was a methodological problem in which the behavior of Europeans appeared as mystifying to the native as the latter appeared incomprehensible in the logic of his action to the European.

> To the mind of primitive man, only his own associations can be rational. Ours must appear to him just as heterogeneous as his to us, because the bond between the phenomena of the world, as it appears after the elimination of their emotional associations, which is being established with increasing knowledge, does not exist for *him*, while we can no longer feel the subjective associations that govern his mind. (Boas 1904(17):253)

The impersonal materialism of the science-oriented West was worlds apart from the subjective bond uniting man and nature which was emphasized in primitive societies. Nonetheless, each possessed its own brand of logic.

The implications of Boas' methodological relativism were twofold. First, the understanding of any culture form must be traced back to its proper culture context. Second, the scientific goal must strain to establish a perspective that is not culture bound, that is, reflecting the inevitable bias of the observer's culture. Culture emerged as the important referent, and Boas closed the gap between primitive and civilized by pointing to the emotional base of action, and noting that the civilized were as much slaves of custom as primitives, and equally prone to secondary explanations or rationalizations (Boas 1938:204–225). As Stocking (1966(68):878) observed, "Almost unnoticed, the idea of cultures, which once connoted all that freed man from the blind weight of tradition, was now identified with that very burden, and that burden was seen as functional to the continuing daily existence of individuals in any culture."

PHILOSOPHIC HUMANISM AND
THE RELATIVE VALUE OF CULTURES

A humanistic impulse within anthropology must be credited with transforming the pragmatic classification of culture into a sensitive awareness of the meaning of culture in the human experience. Developmentalists had tried to chart the meaning of the cultural experience in their vision of a perfected human society. The humanistic experience of twentieth-century anthropologists was different. Suddenly they became aware of the fact that cultural diversity was a human phenomenon—something to be cherished and protected. Cultures now emerged as life-styles of special worth because they were a part of the human experiment.

Sapir (1924) signaled the trend toward a new appreciation of the meaning of culture with his discourse on genuine and spurious cultures. Complexity was no valid measure of the good life. Simple cultures might be organized with far more sensitivity for human personality than the depersonalized and despiritualized life of the industrial culture of the West. Benedict (1930, 1932) continued the thrust toward new understanding with a distinction of personality types associated with American Indian cultures in the Southwest and in the Plains. Each culture was seen as a unique historic product, and for that reason difficult to compare. The culture of any people was their cup of life, and therefore worthy not only of study but of preservation. Lessons drawn from the study of other cultures allowed a greater penetration into the meaning of one's own culture. Benedict (1934) applied her findings by urging a greater tolerance for individual life-styles within standardized American culture. She realized the impact the humanities had made on her own perceptions of the integrative relation between personality and culture. In her presidential address to the American Anthropological Association, Benedict (1948(50):587) urged that anthropologists not neglect the humanistic tradition.

> No one is more convinced than I am that anthropology has profited by being born within the scientific tradition. The humanist tradition did not construct hypotheses about man's cultural life which it then proceeded to test by cross-cultural study; such procedure belongs in the scientific tradition. My conviction is simply that today the scientific and humanist traditions are not opposites nor mutually exclusive. They are supplementary, and modern anthropology handicaps itself in method and insight by neglecting the work of the great humanists.

The path of humanism led directly to the problem of value, and of ultimate values. None was more inspired to elicit the humanistic experience in the field situation than Robert Redfield. In the Mexican community of Tepoztlán and in the secluded villages of Yucatan, Redfield (1930, 1941) discovered an integrated moral universe that contrasted sharply with the heterogeneity of urban secular living. Through value premises, preeminently the covert, one could grasp the fundamental axes shaping one culture as against another.

Whether the holistic perspective of anthropology could have been achieved without the humanistic impulse is a moot question. Structural-functional theory, especially Malinowski's biocultural functionalism, contributed in some measure to the appreciation of value and style in the integration of cultures. However, as Bidney (1953:695–696) observed, the position of Malinowski and of Radcliffe-Brown emphasized survival as the ultimate value, both for the individual and society. The aesthetic and covert premise approach of American culture theorists thus was more amenable to a sensitive regard for cultural life-styles. This holistic posture kept alive an interpretative approach to fieldwork in which, at times, the investigator saw himself as communicating the ultimate values of peoples and factoring what is generically human, much as a poet communicates intuited truths about man and his life.

The rise of holism strengthened the view of cultures as unique entities—as something greater than their trait inventories. A philosophic cultural relativity emerged in support of Boas' methodological relativism. Cultural relativity accented the positive worth of different culture style and rejected or dodged the issue of absolute values. The problem of universal values must be faced ultimately, as Bidney (1967:400–432) observed, or anthropology would miss an important opportunity to contribute to the quality of human life. A rush to radicalize anthropology and to involve it in a value credo erupted toward the end of the sixties. In his own fieldwork Redfield found it most difficult to split his personality as scientist and as civilized humanist. The philosophic position of cultural relativity was insufficient for mankind. For Redfield (1953:163) anthropologists had a "responsibility to look at the culture of other peoples in the light of civilized ethical judgment." In reaffirming that there is a pathway to civilization that extends man's humanity, Redfield echoed a basic assumption of Developmentalists, and it perhaps is no coincidence that his restatement came at a time when evolutionary problems again were being taken up with vigor in cultural anthropology.

CHANGING PERSPECTIVES ON CULTURE

The centrality of the culture concept makes it a good indicator of the progress of the anthropological discipline. This progress can be plotted more advantageously through American culture theorists than through their continental counterparts for two reasons: first, Americanists in adapting the concept were not encumbered with a philosophic tradition linking culture to refinement or the genius of a people; second, Americanists explored the concept far more than others.

There has always been a vigorous link between the culture concept and psychological processes. Behind any custom lurk the psychological processes by which it is inculcated and maintained. Progressivists were the first to stress the link between a learning process and the cultivation of mind, morality, and the arts. Evolutionists merged the cultivation of mind with a biosocial inheritance in which the habit learning of primitives alledgedly was suffused with more reflex responses than in the case of more highly evolved civilized peoples.

To make scientific the concept of culture and accord it the autonomy which they thought it deserved, culture theorists attacked the linkage of race, psychology, and culture forged by evolutionists. Now the stress was on nurture or learned behavior, and the biological and psychological bases for acting were treated as constants for all men. Goldenweiser (1922:14) said it in an apt phrase, "Man is one, civilizations are many." Like their progressivist antecedents, culture historicists affirmed that psychic unity reigned among the races and peoples of the world. Kroeber (1952d:75), who influenced early usage of the concept, pointed to the anthropological experience as conveying a singular awareness of the reality of culture in contrast with the experience of historians.

> The rarity of recorded events in primitive life has helped to force anthropologists into recognition of the forms or patterns of culture, and from this into the clear recognition of culture as such. In short, more perhaps than any one other group, they discovered culture. To be sure, this was long after intelligent historians had known the fact; but these took it for granted and tended to deal with culture indirectly or implicitly, whereas anthropologists became explicit and culture-conscious.

There are four interrelated facies to every concept, which must be discussed in order to elicit the penetration and ramifications of the concept. First there is the matter of etymology, the lexical source from which the term is derived. Second, there is a referential usage of both a general and particulate nature. Third, there is a methodological usage in description and explanation. Fourth, concepts hold implications for what is to be described and explained—the reality problem. The concept of culture is no exception.

Etymology

Due to the rich endeavors of Kroeber and Kluckhohn (1963) it is clear that, in its early application to mankind, the appeal of the concept of culture lay in the intrinsic meaning of the Latin root—to bring to maturity and domesticity through careful control of growth. Bee culture, horticulture, and agriculture accent the ancient usage. Early distinctions of technical and spiritual arts led to some association of the former with culture and the latter with civilization. However, as early as 1782 Johann Adelung focused culture on the transition from a more "sensual and animal condition to the more closely knit interrelations of social life" (Kroeber and Kluckhohn 1963:37). The trend in usage was to associate culture as a process of enrichment of life or a sophisticated state of cultivation.

General and Specific Usage

General and specific usage intermingled ambiguously during the time that anthropological theory was directed by the principle of development. States of culture or cultivation were distinguished. Savage culture, as a rudimentary state, along with the intermediate barbarism, was contrasted with the polished or civilized culture of European man. Savage societies were seen as stateless aggregates ruled by feelings that only custom could check, while cultured societies were orderly and governed by the reasoned logic of law. Savage nature folk were anchored to the primary concern of subsistence, and hence their arts were small. The civilized enriched their lives with intellectual, philosophic, moral, and artistic endeavors since they were freed from the burden of scratching for a living. The distinction of nature and civilized peoples thus found a parallel in the distinction of material and intellectual culture.

With the press for political unity in Europe during the nineteenth century, the quest for national greatness and historic identity merged with culture as ethnic tradition. The extremes of cultural nationalism spanned an emotional and intellectual narcissism which fostered a natural affinity for ideas of racial superiority manifest in a capacity to excel in cultural achievements. The nationalistic prism, when turned upon culture, simply reemphasized culture as a cultivation of intellect, character, order, and the general quality of life. Thus, in any dichotomy of culture into the material (technical) and the nonmaterial (intellectual and social), the latter served as the focus of vital energies by which men advanced their capabilities and enriched their lives. The same distinction, though in a critical mode, surfaced in the United States in Sapir's (1924) defense of the simpler cultures because of their cultivation of human values which in civilized society were smothered by rampant materialism.

Methodological Distinctions and Explanation

Any generic construct, such as culture or society, is useful as a means of orientating thought. However, to be useful, the concept must be explored in two modes: (1) the systematic or totalistic and (2) the particulate. The problem of system and integration of culture is discussed in Chapter 11 and therefore is touched upon but briefly here. A particulate analysis seeks to uncover the components by which one culture can be compared with another. Efforts to formulate the components of culture for purposes of comparison and measurement can be grouped into three clusters:

1. Conceptual discrimination of units according to problem analysis and comparison.
2. Distinction of generic segments of cultures.
3. Distinction of specific analytic components.

Conceptual Discrimination of Forms for Problem Analysis and Comparison. Traits and complexes utilized by culture historians when presenting comparative distributions were generated by a reasoned approach to the need for mapping culture elements. The association of a number of features frequently exhibited inner connections that logically compelled their discrimination—for example, bow and arrow, horse complex, totemistic complex. Traits and complexes offered a useful convention in description. Any discrimination of a form for comparative purposes must involve conventionalized features that easily distinguish one form from another, as in the University of California culture element surveys stimulated by Kroeber and the categories developed by Murdock and associates for the Human Relations Area Files.

Generic Segments of Cultures. The early culture historians felt no compulsion to discriminate the cultural from the social. Common usage in America treated social organization as an aspect, albeit an important one, of culture. In proposing the universal culture pattern for cultures generally, Wissler (1923:75) noted that the "facts of culture may be comprehended under nine heads . . . ; viz., Speech, Material Traits, Art, Mythology [and Scientific Knowledge], Religion, Social Systems, Property, Government, and War." The universal culture pattern described an institutional arrangement, which Wissler (1923:75) admitted that a reader could elaborate were he to put his "constructive imagination" to work.

The lure of commonalities in cultures, and their sources are intriguing questions to which a general theory of culture must address itself. Murdock (1945) and Kluckhohn (1953) sought to answer the question of uniformities in culture by returning culture to variables associated with human nature and the requirements of social living. Murdock's partial list of seventy-six items included age-grading, athletic sports, cosmology, courtship, dancing, divination, division of labor, education, ethics, family, folklore, food taboos, gestures, government, greetings, hospitality, hygiene, incest taboos, kin groups, language, law, magic, marriage, medicine, modesty concerning natural functions, mourning, music, mythology, obstetrics, penal sanctions, population policy, property rights, propitiation of supernatural beings, puberty customs, residence rules, sexual restrictions, soul concepts, status differentiation, tool making, trade, and weather control. Malinowski (1944) raised a general theory of culture by correlating biopsychic needs with the commonalities of cultural institutions. He contended, moreover, that any institution conformed to a basic organization that began with a legitimating charter, which defined a personnel governed by a normative code and utilizing specific technical devices to reach goals that ultimately satisfied the functional needs of individuals. However, in trying to formulate universal institutional types, Malinowski (1944:62–65) intermingled biological and social principles to account for institutions such as the family, age and sex grouping, secret societies and clubs, and social estates and castes. Malinowski, of course, was no culture historian, and he is cited presently to show convergences in the strain to develop a general theory of culture with coordinate blocks of culture.

The basic distinction of units larger than institutions (that is, material and nonmaterial or intellectual culture) achieved during the nineteenth century was hardly improved upon during the first three decades of the twentieth century. In 1950 Kroeber (1952f:152–166) delivered a paper in which he discriminated reality culture (technical), social culture, and value culture, with pure science being included in the latter. Kroeber considered the distinction of these orders of culture valid and important owing to differences in their processes. Reality culture was largely diffusional and accumulative, while value culture was ever recreative. The societal, in contrast, was "neither specifically accumulative nor specifically creative" (Kroeber 1952f:165). Refinements in classification beyond this point were not especially fruitful. "A step farther and we are back at the rough-and-ready, table-of-contents listing of Wissler's 'universal pattern,' which neither he nor anyone else has ever been able to do anything with as a tool" (Kroeber 1952f:166).

A behavioral orientation led Linton to distinguish ideal from real culture patterns. Ideal patterns represented the "consensus of opinion on the part of the society's members as to how people should behave in particular situations" (Linton 1945a:52). Real patterns, on the other hand, consisted of actual behavior, and "Such range of normal responses to a particular situation may be designated as a pattern within the real culture" (Linton 1945a:45). Linton used "real" and "ideal" to refer not only to the nature of specific culture patterns but also to real and ideal kinds of culture. A similar distinction contrasting ideal with behavioral patterns was made by Kluckhohn in 1941. A growing involvement in culture and personality relations led Linton to approach culture as a sociopsychological phenomenon. Cultures, like personalities, were considered to possess a core not readily available to observation. The hidden or covert thus came to be contrasted with the overt.

> I begin by taking the widest definition of culture as established . . . anthropological usage. A culture thus includes the implements and objects used by any society, the behavior of its members, and the habit patterns, knowledge, value system, and attitudes shared by these members. The concept thus includes phenomena of three distinct orders: material (tools and objects); kinesthetic (overt behavior); and psychological (habit patterns, etc.). I use the term overt culture to refer to phenomena of the first two categories, which are directly observable and recordable, in most cases by impersonal, mechanical means. Covert culture . . . refers to the phenomena of the psychological order as a whole, the existence of these phenomena being deducible only from their manifestations in phenomena of the first two orders. Thus, from the repetitive behavior of the individual in response to a particular repetitive stimulus, one deduces the existence within the individual of some condition which leads him to make the same response to the same stimulus, i.e., a habit. (Cited by Kluckhohn 1943(45):217–218)

A culture core modeled on the idea of a personality core suggested the primary distinction of overt and covert culture. A culture core, in Linton's (1936:358) view, consisted of "that mass of largely subconscious values, associations and conditioned emotional responses which provide the culture with its vitality and the individual with motivations for exercising and adhering to its patterns." The covert dimension referred to by Kluckhohn (1943(45):218) in explaining administrative failures with regard to American Indians consisted of "implicit or suppressed premises which tend to be characteristic of members of a certain group." Such unconscious assumptions were in the nature of cultural configurations, and the dominance of an integrating principle would designate the ethos of a society.

Efforts of anthropologists to deal with statistical averages and modes anchored to behavioral frequencies led to the distinction of culture as a methodological construct. The problem surfaced for Linton when coping with the relations between ideal and real culture patterns. Acknowledging difficulties in describing fully either the individual variations or the normal reactions of a society's members to particular situations, Linton (1945a: 45–46) saw the anthropologist making use of a conceptual strategem—the culture-construct pattern. Such a pattern was derived from the most popular response and thus would represent a statistical mode. The connection between real culture and construct culture would not be hard to comprehend if it were remembered that the construct expressed the limited variability of individual behaviors. Linton (1945a:46) asserted that such constructs allowed study of the structural qualities of cultures and the interrelations of patterns and also increased the level of predictability of behavior. This was possible, since the "mode of each [real] pattern is [so] closely correlated with the type of experience which individuals derive from their contacts with it ... that a culture construct can be used to summarize the social-cultural environment from which the members of any society derive the bulk of their experience" (Linton 1945a:49).

The very concept of pattern obviously involved abstraction of commonalities from a number of concrete instances. Kroeber and Kluckhohn (1963:305) determined that the anthropological concern for patterns must rule out actual behavior from culture. For one thing, there were some behaviors, presumably rooted in unconscious physiological processes, that could not be derived from culture. And, "Second, culture being basically a form or pattern or design or way, it is an abstraction from concrete human behavior, but is not itself behavior." Cultural data fell naturally into three classes: (1) the ideal behavior to which individuals were pointed, (2) the conceptions people had about the behavior actually followed by members of the group, and (3) the behavior as objectively determined through observation and other scientific apparatus. From these classes of data the "anthropologist abstracts his conceptual model of the culture" (Kroeber and Kluckhohn 1963:318).

The conception of culture as a logical construct reflected a growing emphasis on value premises as basic to systemic integration. The view of culture as a construct thus was associated with the psychologizing of culture. The important relations were not between concrete forms or observable actors and events but in the mental relations, or patterns, unifying forms, actors, and events. For this reason, apparently, Kroeber and Kluckhohn (1963:341) pointed to the ideal patterns as more important for eliciting the structure of a culture than the behavioral patterns:

> one need not take too seriously the criticism sometimes made of ethnographers that they do not sufficiently distinguish the ideal culture from the actual culture of a society: that they should specify what exists only ideally, at all points specify the numbers of their witnesses, the personalities of their informants, and so on. These rules of technical procedure are sound enough, *but they lose*

sight of the main issue, which is not validation of detail but sound conception of basic structure. This basic structure, and with it the significant functioning, are much more nearly given by the so-called ideal culture than by the actual one. This actual culture can indeed be so overdocumented that the values and patterns are buried. It might even be said . . . that . . . *the description of the ideal culture has more significance than the actual, if a choice has to be made.* If the picture of the ideal culture is materially unsound or concocted, it will automatically raise doubts. But if the picture of the actual culture makes no point or meaning, it may be hard to inject more meaning from the statistical or personalized data available. In short, the "ideal" version of a culture is what gives orientation to the "actual" version. (Italics supplied)

In the preceding statement, Kroeber and Kluckhohn reaffirmed the basic reality of culture as a structured set of relations which the scientist-as-anthropologist would discover. Culture awareness was not a part of the experience of those living it. Variation as a problem did not exist in the presence of this structural emphasis, since variation was visible only in a narrow range of difference exhibited in a patterning of events which derived from structural processes.

White (1954(56):467) moved to correct the view of culture as an abstraction by pointing out that any science must possess a subject matter consisting of a class of objectively observable things and events, not abstractions. True, culture rested on a mental base in that everything cultural had a value or meaning bestowed upon it that was not dependent upon the physical properties of the object nor of the activity (White 1949b: 25). Such a process in the assignment of meaning was peculiar to man. Things and events dependent upon symboling could be investigated within two contexts—with regard to somatic referents or in terms of their own interrelationships. The former context gave rise to psychological relationships whose study properly belonged to psychology. The latter described extrasomatic relationships—what was best designated as culture—and their study properly belonged to anthropology, or to *culturology* (White 1959a (61):231). The only way to rescue culture from the ambiguities which threatened its existence as a conceptual domain was to treat it as an object, dependent on symboling yet having an existence independent of body and mind. For scientific purposes, culture as thing and event could be described, measured, and subjected to analysis (Table 10–1). Moreover, such a view allowed a sharp distinction "between behavior—behaving organisms—and culture; between the science of psychology and the science of culture" (White 1959a(61):234).

In locating culture in a social symboling of things and relationships, White simply affirmed that the basic cultural process was sociopsychological. For White as for Kroeber (1948a:8), "Culture is the special and exclusive product of men, and is their distinctive quality in the cosmos." And the mind was all important in this distinction. This entrenchment of mind in culture constantly evoked parallels between language as a convention

TABLE 10-1. THE RELATION OF HISTORY, EVOLUTIONISM,
AND FUNCTIONALISM, ACCORDING TO WHITE (1945b(1):243)

Process	History *Temporal*	Evolution *Temporal-Formal*	Functionalism *Formal-Functional*
Cultural sciences	History of customs, institutions, ideas, art forms, etc.	Evolution of traits, institutions, philosophic systems; evolution of culture as a whole	Studies of social structure and function The "anatomy" and "physiology" of cultures or societies
Biological sciences	History of species, varieties, etc. Racial history of man Biography Case histories	Evolution of life, of species Growth of individuals	Studies of structure and function Anatomy Physiology Psychology
Physical sciences	History of solar system, of mountain systems, rivers, glaciers, etc.	Evolution of universe, stars, galaxies, molecules, etc. Radioactive substances	Studies of structure and function: of nontemporal, repetitive processes

White maintained that there were three processes operating in the human reality—the "historical, evolutionary, and formal-functional." As a matter of fact, according to its momentary interest, any science could interpret its data in terms of these three fundamental processes.

The historic process is concerned with "a chronological sequence of events, each unique in time and space." It is the very particularity of the events that militates against their recurrence with the same actors, and in the same sequence. The formal-functional process describes the tendency for similarities in forms or structure to arise because of functional necessity. The scientist here is interested in functional types without regard to time or place, and hence the particulars of historic events are of no consequence for this kind of analysis. As evolutionist, the scientist is concerned with sequencing the appearance of form types or structures. Whereas the formal-functional process is repetitive and reversible, this is not so for the temporal-formal evolutionary process.

The importance of these processes stands out in two ways. First, they represent different and exclusive data according to the problem goals of the scientist. Second, they represent different levels of integrative certainty in explanation. "From this [latter] point of view, the interpretation supplied by the evolutionist is more basic, more fundamental than the interpretation of the historian or functionalist." This was so because the "evolutionist grasps and interprets events in their wholeness and entirety, in terms of their space-time properties and relations, whereas the historian and functionalist each deals with one aspect only—the temporal or the formal." Every science, in seeking a precise and comprehensive perspective, had moved to the evolutionary position, and White called upon anthropologists to do likewise and thereby advance the maturity of their discipline.

White, in effect, argued that reality could not be understood in its wholeness but must be comprehended partially in one of three ways. That is, the relative exclusiveness of each of these processes meant that they could not be united into a single operation. However, the merits of each process and perspective were not the same. To be scientific one must select the operation that provided the most comprehensive interpretation, that is, the evolutionary.

for communication and culture as an organized system of thought processes. As language under the cybernetic model assumed the mode of a communications system, culture followed. Taking their cue from basic communication instrumentalities, designated as primary message systems, Hall (1961:174–175; with Trager) developed a map of culture that included the following institutionalized relations: interactional, organization, economic, sexual, territorial, instructional, recreational, protective, and exploitational.

The stimulus for a linguistic understanding of culture started with Boas in 1911. Sapir in 1929 formulated the position in strength, and his student Whorf carried it forward during the 1940s. The semiotic turn which the new ethnography or ethnoscience took owes much to the percolation of linguistic theory and method into ethnology. The fresh presence of formal (structural) analysis found in American linguistics accounts for the continuation of a Structuralist orientation in ethnology and the effort to see culture as a cognitive map.

Distinction of Specific Analytic Components. In the succession of American culture theorists, Linton (1936:272–273) was among the first to offer a set of concepts to discriminate the structural variation of culture patterns.

> First, there are those ideas, habits, and conditioned emotional responses which are common to all sane, adult members of the society. We will call these the Universals. . . .
>
> Second, we have those elements of culture which are shared by the members of certain socially recognized categories of individuals but which are not shared by the total population. We will call these the Specialties. . . .
>
> Third, there are in every culture a considerable number of traits which are shared by certain individuals but which are not common to all the members of the society or even to all the members of any one of the socially recognized categories. We will call these Alternatives.

Linton apparently was interested in the conditions affecting variation and the degree of individual participation. Alternatives were of two kinds: (1) variable responses to like situations and (2) different ways to achieve an end (Linton 1936:274). Universals, alternatives, and specialties were all conventionalizations, and hence, in their limited variability, defined the structure of culture. What was not conventionalized must be classed as individual peculiarities outside the bounds of culture. In the same vein, Kluckhohn (1941) set out compulsory, preferred, typical, alternative, and restricted patterns. The patterned participations to which Linton and Kluckhohn directed attention quite obviously were variations derived from formal specifications or ideal patterns. Neither was unduly concerned with modal variations generated by reactions to the ideal patterns or by circumstances external to a culture viewed as a structure. Their formal analysis of the structure of culture paralleled the formal analysis of social structure carried out by British social anthropologists. Indeed, the ideal patterns of American culture theorists bore a striking resemblance to Radcliffe-

Brown's (1965:10–11) institutions, which provided the normative prescriptions for regulating the interactions of any class of social relationships. Malinowski's definition of an institution as including a group or category of individuals operating under a set of premises, norms, and technical apparatus was flexible enough to be drawn within the same context of structural analysis.

The structural analysis of culture which took hold after 1930 focused on the quality of integration. Premises governing man's relation to the world, to other men, and to the nature of human purposes and destiny emerged as central influences in the integration of cultures. Redfield's (1941, 1953) world view, Kluckhohn's (1952) value orientations, and Benedict's (1959) unconscious canons of choice illustrated attempts to register the significance of value premises in programming behavioral unity among those sharing a common cultural-historical tradition and in differentiating the motives of peoples possessing different life-styles. Opler's (1945) themes described existential and normative principles regulating behavior. The former stated assumptions about the nature of the world, whereas the latter related to life in society. In Opler's view, themes should not be viewed as great summative principles, but as frequently expressing contradictions in relationships. Themes, in short, stressed a way of integration through complementarity, as observed in the ideas of struggle, rivalry and opposition, which described the relationship between the sexes in Jicarilla Apache society (Opler 1949(51):324).

> Thus, evil was introduced into the world as a result of infidelity and the dispute and hostility between the sexes that grew from it. In vulgar discourse the sexual act is referred to as "eating one's prey." Conception occurs only when the blood (semen) of the man accumulates and overpowers blood in the womb of the woman. Mates are used as pawns in the attempt to test or humiliate joking relatives. Contests in which members of one sex seek to influence and subdue emotionally members of the other sex (love magic) are common. Relations between the sexes at the time of ceremony have to be strictly supervised; otherwise the purpose of the rite may be defeated. A youth who has never had relations with a woman is at his prime; at first intercourse speed and vigor are lost which can never be regained. Contact of any kind with menstrual blood has the most deleterious effects upon males.

British social anthropologists also found that basic value premises were manifest in the principles that structured social relationships. Values expressed in the symbolism of ceremony exercised a profound role in the bonding of African polities, especially those governed under kingship. In the ritual of kingly office, one sensed the symbolic dramatization of the value base for rights, duties, and sentiments intrinsic to the political solidarity and continuity of the nation. Myth and traditional history thus validated the Mukama's position as head of Nyoro society and detailed why the Mukama and his close relatives were not kin of their subjects but their rulers. Rituals accented three aspects of kingship: (1) the divinity of the Mukama and the relation of his physical well-being to the land and people of Nyoro; (2) the ways by which kingly power must be acquired, sustained, and relinquished; and (3) the ways kingly authority could be delegated in ruling the land (Beattie 1960:26–29). Benedict (1959:43) supplied the rationale for both social and cultural integration when she asserted, "Cultures . . . are more than the sum of their traits."

However, cultures are not only functioning wholes but also are changing and are the products of change. The major thrust of the special distribution of culture traits and their temporal relations was to prove that cultures grew largely by accumulation of features introduced by contact, direct or indirect, with other cultures. The cloth of any culture, though making a whole garment, nonetheless was fabricated from pieces drawn from many different cultures and cultural traditions. Hence Lowie (1920: 441) referred to civilization as "that planless hodge-podge, that thing of shreds and patches." The point also was made by Linton (1936:325–328) when describing the complex derivations of the culture of the typical American.

The historical orientation predisposed the researcher to view cultures not so much as tightly configurated entities but as possessing features and patterns broadly distributed in time and space. This was illustrated by Kroeber, who had little time for Wissler's universal culture pattern, since it emphasized a general theory of culture without attention to the contact process. Thus, in distinguishing systemic, total, climaxes of whole-culture patterns, and style patterns, Kroeber ever maintained an historic perspective. Systemic patterns described a logical and functional clustering of features, as in the instance of "plow agriculture, monotheism, the alphabet, and, on a smaller scale, the *kula* ring of economic exchange among the Massim Melanesians." According to Kroeber (1948a:312–313),

> What distinguishes these systemic patterns of culture—or well-patterned systems, as they might also be called—is a specific interrelation of their component parts, a nexus that holds them together strongly, and tends to preserve the basic plan. This is in distinction to the great "loose" mass of material in every culture that is not bound together by any strong tie but adheres and again dissociates relatively freely. As a result of the persistence of these systemic patterns, their significance becomes most evident on a historical view.

Quite obviously systemic patterns like plow cultivation and the alphabet have diffused, and the elements of such patterns are logically connected without basic modification. What impressed Kroeber (1948a:313) about these systemic patterns was the "point-for-point correspondence of their parts, plus the fact that all variants of the pattern can be traced back to a single original form." Systemic patterns thus exhibited an historical growth and a persistence of form and content.

Total culture patterns related to whole cultures. They distinguished national variants within the tradition of European civilization and also European from Asiatic civilization. To grasp the character of a civilization required consummate skill in addition to knowledge, and Kroeber (1948a:

317) admitted that perhaps the most vivid and stimulating characterizations sprang out of intuitive understandings. When dealing with the wholeness of civilizations, one applied terms like "configuration," "spirit," or "genius." The climax of whole-culture patterns described the tendency of "Successful growth . . . to come intermittently, in pulses or irregular rhythms" (Kroeber 1948a:326). Stylistic patterns were important in understanding the growth of culture in that they represented an historically distinctive selection of methods or techniques. Elaboration followed such selection, ultimately running a course to exhaustion as the pattern variants played out (Kroeber 1948a:329–330). The clustering of genius in exposition of the style was basic to its growth. The fact that similar clusterings of inventors were discerned in technology led Kroeber (1948a:343) to conclude that the clustering of both artists and inventors revealed the causal input of the culture pattern even as the genius clusters added to the growth of that pattern.

Kroeber's pervasive historical-cultural orientation led him to place any cultural development in a configuration of relations broader than any single culture. As historical phenomena, patterns did not gain their ultimtae significance from their functional associations within a particular culture but from their relations to the development of culture within a region or on a broader front. The ultimate significance of patterns rested in their contributions to cultural development as measured by their persistence and extensions to other regions. As Lowie (1936(52):306) argued in defense of American historicism versus functionalism, "To wrest a fact from its tribal context is no more arbitrary than to wrest the tribe from its contacts with the rest of humanity."

In seeking the likenesses and modifications of forms and patterns, culture historicists and later students of acculturation found that culture elements could be factored into a useful set of meaningful attributes. Linton (1936:402) determined that "every element of culture has qualities of four distinct, although mutually interrelated kinds: i.e., it has *form, meaning, use,* and *function*." Trait complexes were centered in activities which fulfilled societal needs and hence were the primary units of analysis. The "*form* of a trait complex" described the "sum and arrangement of its component behavior patterns" (Linton 1936:403). Meaning referred to the "subjective and frequently unconscious" associations attached to the trait complex (Linton 1936:403). Use described the relation between the trait complex and things external to the social-cultural configuration, while function related elements within a configuration. For example, a medicine might be used to reduce fever, but its function would be found in the restoration of health. According to Linton (1936:404), "The function of a trait complex is the sum total of its contribution toward the perpetuation of the social-cultural configuration. This function is normally a composite which can be analyzed into a number of functions each of which is related to the satisfaction of a particular need." In considering the modification of trait complexes, Linton (1936:405) agreed with Boas that form is a predominant attribute and that the factors accounting for it largely are historical.

> In other words, the trait complex is presented to the society as a definite entity which is incorporated into the configuration by the attachment to it of use, meaning, and function. Although its form may be progressively modified during the process of incorporation, the initial form has a strong influence on the initial ascriptions of use, meaning, and function and through these on all subsequent ascriptions.

Finding that neither form, meaning, use, nor function constituted a tightly integrated whole, Linton (1936:410), like Boas, concluded that the relationships actually were rather tenuous and easily altered.

> Use and meaning are probably more closely related to each other than either one is to form, but even so their mutual adaptations are loose enough to permit of a wide range of variation. When we try to ascertain the relation of these three elements to function, the situation becomes vastly more complex. Function seems to derive least from form, somewhat more from use, but most from meaning. Any attempt to analyze these relationships in a particular case reveals still another disturbing factor. Many elements of culture have multiple uses, but nearly all of them have multiple meanings.

In his survey Linton observed that form often persisted when changes in meaning and in function occurred. Moreover, it was difficult to find a single trait complex that functioned in fulfillment of a specific need. Usually several trait complexes were involved. Function derived most of its significance from meaning. Meaning did not diffuse as readily as form or use, and the linkage of function to meaning meant that it was resistant to change (Linton 1936:409, 419). Finally, Linton questioned whether cultural features without meaning and function could exist. Mere presence was not enough. If elements had no meaning or function except in relation to the complex to which they belonged, then it was reasonable to conclude that such elements were without meaning and function for the society at large. Such features were like the idiosyncratic beliefs and practices of an individual and held no cultural significance.

Barnett (1940, 1942), when studying the rejection and acceptance of culture traits and complexes among Indians of Northwest California and the Northwest Coast, added the concept of *principle* to Linton's form, meaning, use, and function. Principle conveyed a dynamic quality to form both in organization and in operation.

> A principle is an operative system or plan and in itself has nothing intrinsically to do with human behavior, although the latter shapes itself about principles. It is advisable to distinguish at once between these operational principles which are action schemes, and still others which might be termed principles of construction. (Barnett 1942(44):15)

Though more easily comprehended in the operation of technical traits, principles were equally intrinsic to social features. The disjunction of native and alien form and principle often was critical in the way new traits were treated. Thus, the Tsimshian never bridged the differences between form and principle separating the native canoe and the rowboat. It wasn't that they did not possess the technology to construct plank boats with oars. Differences in construction and in propulsion (paddle versus oar) rendered the rowboat incompatible and dissuaded the Tsimshian from including it in the potlatch. This was all the more curious since they utilized other items drawn from American culture (for example, blankets). Later, after aboriginal craft production decayed, modern products were readily accepted as potlatch goods, including motors, motorboats, bathtubs, and the like. The same held for Christian and native names. Christian names became associated with patrilineal inheritance attached to modern boats and houses, while names transmitted matrilineally remained bound to surviving ceremonial rites and privileges. Two separate inheritance complexes operated within Tsimshian society, with matrilineal kin attempting to lay a traditional claim to those properties that have come to be associated with patrilineal descent (Barnett 1942(44):24).

The contact of different cultures actually presented innovative situations similar to the introduction of inventions. Four combinations were possible, according to Barnett (1942(44):23): "different forms utilizing different principles but serving the same function; different forms utilizing the same principle but serving different functions; different forms utilizing the same principle to serve the same function; and different forms utilizing different principles for different functions." The last provided no clear basis for a meeting of minds, but in a number of instances (for example, the use of thimbles as a substitute for deerhoof rattles), the Tsimshian were able to equate two dissimilar forms by equating principles and function.

DEFINITIONS OF CULTURE: CHANGING PERSPECTIVES

Tylor (1874) defined culture, or civilization, as the knowledge, morality, religion, custom, and habits men acquired by virtue of their membership in society. Between that time and 1903 Kroeber and Kluckhohn reported not a single scientific definition of culture. Then, between 1903 and 1916 six definitions appeared—two by sociologists, two by the chemist Ostwald, and two by the anthropologist Wissler (Kroeber and Kluckhohn 1963:292). After 1920, and until 1950, some 157 definitions were formulated, of which 100 appeared between 1940 and 1950, no doubt due to an acceleration in the number of anthropologists and publications. However, there was considerable interest in the concept of culture during the thirties and forties as cultural anthropologists explored its parameters and social anthropologists attempted a distinction of the social from the cultural.

To some extent, trends in definitions of culture reflect the special emphasis of the definer, but theoretical orientations in social science at the time were more predominant. Thus, the psychologically trained Wissler in

1916 viewed culture as an associational complex of ideas, whereas in 1929, when the idea of cultural life-styles began to emerge, he described culture as representing a mode of life. The trend toward psychologizing culture picked up considerable strength as culture patterns were analyzed within a learning context and cultures came to be viewed as more than the sum of their parts. The psychological view of culture also was aided by the model of language, which focused attention on the coding of human thought and action in symbols. As Sapir (1949:515–516) observed, one must look for culture in the interactions of individuals and subjectively in the meanings which each person unconsciously forged out of his interpersonal relations. For White (1949) the locus of culture must be found in man's unique capacity to manufacture symbols and to associate arbitrary meanings with objects. However, Sapir and White were poles apart in their approaches to the subjective reality of culture. Sapir approached culture from the selective meanings which integrated individual experience and focused on the individual as the carrier of culture. White stressed the superorganic quality of culture and saw the individual as a temporary symbolic moment in the evolutionary movement of a symbolic tradition.

By 1940 anthropologists were ready to produce definitions of culture that reflected the special attributes of cultures. That is, cultures were historical developments, systemic configurations, learned, shared, and transmitted from one generation to the next through formal or informal inculcation. According to Goldenweiser (1937:45–46),

> culture is historical or cumulative, . . . it is communicated through education deliberate and non-deliberate, . . . its content is encased in patterns (that is, standardized procedures or idea systems), . . . it is dogmatic as to its content and resentful of differences, . . . its contribution to the individual is absorbed largely unconsciously, leading to a subsequent development of emotional reinforcements, and . . . the raising of these into consciousness is less likely to lead to insight and objective analysis than to explanations *ad hoc*, either in the light of the established status quo, or of a moral reference more or less subjective, or of an artificial reasonableness or rationality which is read into it; also, finally, . . . culture in its application and initial absorption is local.

Murdock in 1940 (364–369) listed the attributes of culture as follows: learned; inculcated, socially engendered habits; ideational, that is, conceptualized or verbalized as ideal norms; gratifying with regard to basic biological and derived secondary needs; adaptive in the sense that any culture becomes sensitively adjusted to environmental conditions; and integrative, in that the elements of any culture tend to be interrelated and relatively consistent. Kluckhohn and Kelly (1945:98) saw any culture as an "historically derived system of explicit and implicit designs for living, which tends to be shared by all or specially designated members of a group." Cultures, according to Linton (1945a:32) exhibited a "configuration of learned behavior and results of behavior whose component elements are shared and transmitted by the members of a particular society." The character of cultures, in Redfield's (1941:133), view, consisted in their conventional understandings or meanings attached to acts and objects.

All of these definitions exhibited efforts to locate culture in idea patterns and accented the integrative or systemic nature of cultures. But it was increasingly apparent that the concepts of pattern and mode were once removed from the objective base, which meant that anthropologists dealt with a construct, or an abstraction from the reality base. Where then was the locus of culture—in the individual or in society? To Kluckhohn and Kelly (1945:93–94), the posing of the question in this fashion was fallacious.

> Remember that "culture" is an abstraction. Hence culture as a concrete, observable entity does not exist anywhere—unless you wish to say that it exists in the "minds" of the men who make the abstractions. . . . The objects and events from which we make our abstractions do have an observable existence. . . . Just as a map isn't the territory but an abstract representation of the territory so also a culture is an abstract description of trends toward uniformity in the words, acts, and artifacts of human groups. The data, then, from which we come to know culture are not derived from an abstraction such as "society" but from directly observable behavior and behavioral products. Note, however, that "culture" may be said to be "supra-individual" in at least two non-mystical, perfectly empirical senses:
> 1. Objects as well as individuals show the influence of culture.
> 2. The continuity of culture seldom depends upon the continued existence of any particular individual.

In their efforts to understand the nature of the cultural reality, anthropologists uncovered an old metaphysical dichotomy that had hounded medieval realists and idealists. Anthropological realists, according to Bidney (1967:24), viewed culture as an "attribute of human social behavior and usually define culture in terms of acquired habits, customs, and institutions." The important element of cultural realism was the view that culture had no life of its own but existed solely in the actions of those who lived it.

Idealists were more complicated, dividing themselves into subjective, objective, and conceptual types. Those who insisted that culture consisted of ideas conceived by individuals through social communication could be characterized as subjective idealists. Such were Sapir and Osgood (1951), who saw culture as "all ideas of the manufacture, behavior, and ideas of the aggregate of human beings which have been directly observed or communicated to one's mind and of which one is conscious" (cited by Bidney 1967:24). Linton, Kluckhohn, and Gillin were conceptual idealists in that they located culture in a pattern or construct abstracted from individual behavior. Objective idealists like Kroeber (also Sorokin, Spengler, and White) held culture to be a " 'superorganic' stream of ideas . . . hav[ing] a transcendent reality of their own, independent of the individuals or societies which happen to hear them" (Bidney 1967:25–26).

The immediate importance of the realism-idealism distinction never penetrated anthropological thinking in any depth. The pragmatics of anthropological operations prevented any diversion into metaphysics. As Bidney himself wrote, anthropological time could be devoted better to analysis of the two interpenetrating modalities of culture—the ideal and the real.

> Normative, impersonal, ideational culture has no existence unless it is practiced and influences men's behavior and thinking in social life. Practical, real, or actual culture—the actual behavior and thought of men in society—is not intelligible apart from the social ideals which men have created or discovered for themselves and endeavor to realize in their daily lives. It is the task of the empirical social scientist to determine to what extent there is agreement between theory and practice in any given culture and whether the culture is "genuine" or "spurious" in Sapir's sense . . . , that is, to what extent it allows for maximum participation on the part of its adherents. (Bidney 1967:30)

EFFORTS TO SEPARATE THE CULTURAL AND THE SOCIAL

During the thirties leading culture theorists in the United States found some utility in separating the social from the cultural. About this time the leading exponent of comparative sociology or social anthropology, Radcliffe-Brown, dropped his equation of culture and social life and turned to social structure and social system as the proper subject matter for this branch of anthropology. By 1952 Radcliffe-Brown (1965:5) had reduced culture and the cultural process to a segment of the social process, though willing to grant that culture as process referred to the "transmission of learnt ways of thinking, feeling and acting." Such transmission was a part of the social process or social reality and could be most readily distinguished as a class by the term "cultural tradition"—for example, the medical and engineering traditions. But cultural learning also implied the addition to one's life of new appreciations in art, knowledge, skill, ideas, beliefs, tastes, and sentiments acquired through contact with persons, books, or objects. Social structure, on the other hand, referred to the orderly arrangement of persons in a society or social groups. Radcliffe-Brown (1965:11) defined institutions as established norms of conduct or rules that specified and guided proper behavior for a type or class of social relationships and interactions.

In the United States, Ralph Linton took the lead in making the conceptual distinction between the social and the cultural. Linton (1936:262) distinguished the social system as a part of any culture—"that fraction of the whole which provides the members of a society with designs for group living." The social system embodied that portion of the culture which regulated reciprocities among individuals and between individual and society (Linton 1936:105). Now the guides to these reciprocal behaviors were "ideal patterns . . . carried in the minds of individuals . . . [that defined] what the behavior between individuals or classes of individuals should be" (Linton 1936:102–103). An aggregate of reciprocal ideal patterns defined the limits of a social system (Linton 1936:105). It is obvious that Radcliffe-Brown's institutions were the correlates of Linton's ideal patterns. When it came to positioning an individual in the social table of organization, both Linton and Radcliffe-Brown converged on the concepts of status and role, rights and obligations, reciprocities, and sanctions, both legal and social.

Linton made social structure a part of his vocabulary in 1945. He saw it as a derivative of culture in that the basic categorizations of people and how they were organized and assigned roles in the corporate operations were traceable to cultural definitions, and "primarily to the areas of culture organization or integration" (Linton 1945a:56–57). Linton (1945a: 61–62) found five basic structural patterns that accounted for most of the organization of any primary society (for example, band): (1) age and sex, (2) specialized occupations, (3) family groups, (4) association groups based on congeniality and/or common interest, and (5) ranking in prestige series with consequent differentials in importance and influence.

At the time Linton attempted a methodological distinction of social systems, and then of social structure, the discrimination of "social organization as a part of culture was of long standing." In *Primitive Society* Lowie (1920:1) began by noting that "Primitive society is in a sense coextensive with primitive civilization . . . or culture." However, in this work he limited himself to "those aspects of culture known as *social organization*, i.e., with the groups into which society is divided, the functions of these groups, their mutual relations, and the factors determining their growth."

The conceptual distinction between the cultural and social raised by Kroeber in his levels of reality followed Lowie in that groups in action were the locus of the social, whereas the rules regulating action constituted the cultural. This also was Kluckhohn's position (1945:631–633), since the interactive behavior of the social was traceable in part to biological and in part to cultural pressures. Status accordingly defined the social in that it prescribed how categories of individuals were interrelated, while role prescribed patterned ways of interacting and hence was cultural. Though distinct, the social and cultural were inseparable—that is, the sociocultural. This essentially was Malinowski's position when pointing to the institution as the basic unit of research and understanding. For Malinowski, as for culture theorists, culture, provided the basic charter for action, and by determining the nature and flow of social interactions, took precedence over the social. This was so because, as Kroeber and Kluckhohn (1963: 340–341) asserted,

> Values are important in that they provide foci for patterns of organization. *. . . In fact values provide the only basis for the fully intelligible comprehension of culture, because the actual organization of all cultures is primarily in terms of their values.* This becomes apparent as soon as one attempts to pre-

sent the picture of a culture without reference to its values. The account becomes an unstructured meaningless assemblage of items having relation to one
another only through coexistence in locality and moment—an assemblage that
might as profitably be arranged alphabetically as in any other order; a mere
laundry list.

In methodological perspective the cultural and the social could be
viewed as the difference between the qualitative and quantitative aspect
of social facts. According to Fortes (1949:57–58),

> The concept "structure" is, I think, most appropriately applied to those fea-
> tures of social events and organizations which are actually or ideally suscep-
> tible of quantitative description and analysis. The constant elements most
> usually recognized in any social event by ethnographers are its cultural com-
> ponents; its structural aspect, being variable, is often overlooked. It should be
> emphasized that I am not suggesting a division of the facts of social life into
> two classes; I am referring to the data of observation. "Culture" and "struc-
> ture" denote complementary ways of analysing the same facts. In the present
> stage of social anthropology all analysis of structure is necessarily hybrid, in-
> volving descriptions of culture as well as presentation of structure.

In Nadel's (1951:79–80) judgment,

> Society ... means the totality of social facts projected on to the dimension of
> relationships and groupings; culture, the same totality in the dimension of
> action. This is not merely playing with words. In recent anthropological liter-
> ature, in fact, the terms "society" and "culture" are accepted as referring to
> somewhat different things, or, more precisely, to different ways of looking at
> the same thing.

Continuing, Nadel pointed out how the term "sociocultural" was used to
include both the social and cultural. However, such usage did not add
greater precision. Nadel considered conventionalized behavior as the
proper focus of anthropological inquiry and defined culture as the integrated totality of standardized patterns. Status and role apparently
described the complementary relation of the social and cultural, and in
concentrating on behavioral patterns he logically joined Americanists in
the study of culture.

The clear separation of the social and cultural has not progressed
beyond these early attempts at conceptual and methodological distinction.
Some American anthropologists have abandoned culture as a conceptual
framework and focused on the social because it is easier to describe the
interaction of groups, large and small, than the contact and interchange
of culture elements. As Bennett (1954) observed, one can operate pragmatically in contact situations with groups and communicate readily with
other social scientists; but the idea of culture and of cultures in contact is
too difficult to understand, and consequently proves ineffectual in establishing a working conceptual relationship with fellow-social scientists.
Moreover, culture did not allow a ready focus on differences existing
among status groups and hence was more clumsy for purposes of descrip-

tion. Increasingly it became evident that the broad orientations implicit in the concepts of the social and of the cultural, useful as they are, must be factored into measurable entities if they are to prove their worth in the assignment of cause.

CULTURE HISTORY, ARCHEOLOGY, AND CULTURE

The cultural-historical and archeological approaches shared a basic orientation to the study of culture in that both were concerned with historical relations manifest in spatial ranges and in temporal sequences. Consequently, neither arrived at an integrative conception of cultures such as accompanied ethnological interest in the relation of personality to culture. As culture-historical studies gave way during the thirties to the investigation of the systemic nature of cultures, archeological theory also began to stress a more integrated and structural functional approach. Taylor's *A Study of Archeology* (1948) synthesized the emergent concern of archeologists with the study of culture and culture processes. In Taylor's (1948:7) judgment, archeologists were so engrossed in the comparison of forms and in the development of taxonomies that they had forgotten that their task was to describe the cultures of human groups. Culture at base was a fabric of ideas. It was formed of

> attitudes, meanings, sentiments, feelings, values, goals, purposes, interests, knowledge, beliefs, relationships, associations. These ideas . . . are objectified and made observable . . . in the form of behavior. . . . In turn, this behavior results in material objects . . . and non-material manifestations such as dance patterns, musical tones and rhythms, styles of graphic and fictile representation, etc. For example, there is present in an Indian's mind the idea of a dance. This is the trait of culture. This idea influences his body so that he behaves in a certain way. The result of this behavioral activity is the pattern of the dance. . . . Both the behavior itself and the resulting patterns are observable, but . . . fleeting. The culture idea is not observable but endures in the Indian's mind to be repeated again.
>
> Both behavior and the results of behavior, if they stem from ideas, pertain to culture. They are not culture, but they are "cultural." Thus we are dealing with three orders of phenomena, two of which pertain to culture and are thus cultural, but only one of which *is* culture. A stone axe, a song, a dance performance are not culture traits. They are objectifications of culture traits. The elements or traits of culture are unobservable and must be inferred from their objectifications, from behavior or the results of behavior. (Taylor 1948:101–102)

Taylor's insistence that culture must be the proper focus for archeology drew this subdiscipline effectively within the orbit of anthropology. Archeology then must contribute to a general theory of culture as well as to the source and development of particular cultures. If culture were largely a mental code for ordering a world of relationships, archeologists must strive for classifications that corresponded with the thought categories utilized by peoples of the past. To do so necessitated a controlled comparison that elicited the relations or inner coherence of features—what Kluckhohn called a configuration. This required comparison of a multitude of items in "cultural contexts and/or broad cultural complexes as "wholes" (Taylor 1948: 169). What the archeologist must seek were not comparisons based on the presence or absence of techniques but similarities and differences reflected in style. The goal of describing culture rather than types necessitated the utmost control in excavation and the saving of total materials from which a pattern could be derived. Taylor referred to this totalistic analysis as the conjunctive approach.

Developments in ethnology provided immediate inspiration for Taylor's clarification of the cultural goal of archeology. Nonetheless, prehistory could not escape a fundamental preoccupation with spatial and temporal relations. The focus thus lay not in specific cultures but in the impact of patterns for cultural developments in regions and in broader areas. In short, archeologists duplicated Kroeber's findings with regard to culture history. Willey and Phillips pointed to the archeological unit designated as phase rather than the lesser units of site or component as the proper unit of study (Figure 10-1). A phase possessed *"traits sufficiently characteristic to distinguish it from all other units similarly conceived, whether of the same or other cultures or civilizations, spatially limited to the order of magnitude of a locality or region and chronologically limited to a relatively brief interval of time"* (Willey and Phillips 1965:22). By definition, a phase (or focus) was confined to a subarea within a broader areal manifestation. Within any areal manifestation, sequential developments at certain points exhibited a distinctive set of features (for example, cult or art style) that in their distribution united several regions both culturally and temporally. The limited temporal range of the "horizon" contrasted with a "tradition" which reflected long-term developments traceable to persistent technologies or other features, including social organization, and which conveyed a sense of unity to the cultural development of an area. Bennett (1948) used the term "area co-tradition" to describe the interactional universe of cultures participating in the development of a cultural tradition within a broad area, as in the Andes of Peru.

None of these classificatory distinctions of archeologists corresponds to Kroeber's patterns, but some relation appears to hold between his systemic patterns and traditions and total culture patterns and area co-traditions. Kroeber's notion of climax was used in archeology in defining the maximum intensity and individuality of an archeological horizon or tradition as well as of whole cultures.

The heart of the archeological venture undoubtedly lies in the sequencing of prehistoric cultural developments. Willey and Phillips (1965:31) asserted that prehistorians must strive for cultural-historical syntheses. Such a synthesis could be local, regional, or areal or address itself to a more general developmental process. At this general level, form similarities

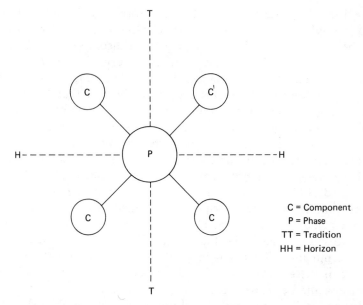

Figure 10-1. The interrelations of component, phase, horizon, and tradition (Willey and Phillips 1965:41).

The phase is centered as the primary archeological unit of classification and analysis. It is manifested at a number of components, and, indeed, is constructed out of component features. Phases can exhibit temporal depth in that they are products of a persistent tradition, and at certain points in time a horizon may provide an integrative style in association with other features. With horizon and tradition, space-time considerations take precedence over culture content, which finds emphasis in the conceptions of phase and component. Quite expectably, Willey and Phillips found that horizons and traditions on the one hand and phases and components on the other could vary independently of each other. Single phases could be manifest in more than one horizon, and the same could hold with regard to traditions. However, it would appear that such situations must be more characteristic of phases which abut or bridge two different ecocultural regions (FWV).

would be utilized to distinguish culture types without regard to specific historical relationships (Figure 10-2). This was McKern's (1939) approach with the Midwestern Taxonomic Method whereby relationships were established solely by formal resemblances which did not necessarily disclose temporal connections. Classification, nonetheless, can be useful in suggesting temporal relations conceived as stages of development. The zoological classification of man as a primate linked his past to the general trends of primate evolution, and directed attention to those early epochs of the Cenozoic when primates appeared and differentiated to give rise to Old World monkeys, the higher apes, and man's first ancestors. Developmentalists utilized a classification describing trends from the simple to the complex in building an evolutionary sequence for culture. The focus on classification and formal processes linking one stage to another lent credence to White's (1945) assertion that the formal-structural-evolutionary analysis exemplified the ultimate in the scientific analysis of culture.

Archeologists interested in raising a general theory of process based on structural necessities found a classification of forms and processes basic. Demand for a general theory arose, as Willey and Phillips (1965:62) noted with regard to New World prehistory, from the fact that the individual histories of regions never merged into a single stream of continuous development. To uncover general processes of development it was necessary to classify and compare formal structural resemblances much as Steward (1949) did when comparing the order of events and institutions shared by early civilizations in an apparent evolutionary course. As Willey and Phillips noted (1965:71), "Historical causality is important only in that it has to be eliminated from the equation." Nonetheless, like the products of McKern's Midwestern Taxonomic System, the possession of similarities by any two cultures could be the result of "historical contact, environmental determination, homotaxis in a truly evolutionary sense, or any two or all three of these" (1965:71). The significance of these factors in a particular case would be exposed only on closer analysis.

Willey and Phillips began their culture history of the New World with the immigrant big-game cultures which were distinguished by their specialized tool assemblages (Figure 10-3). They defined this culture type as Lithic. Archaic was used to describe the next stage of migratory hunting and gathering cultures that formed on the heels of the extinction of the large mammals, and the gradual approximation of environmental conditions, including plant and animal types, to present time. Diversification in the economic bases and in technologies occurred, leading on to more practiced ecocultural efficiencies (Caldwell 1958). The Formative stage was characterized by the presence of agriculture, or any other subsistence economy of comparable effectiveness, and by the successful integration of such an economy into well-established, sedentary village life. The time of

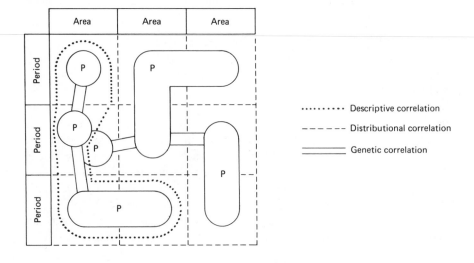

Descriptive correlation

Distributional correlation

Genetic correlation

Figure 10-2. Determining genetic cultural relations through the combination of descriptive and distributional correlations of phases. (Rouse 1955(57):720, and 719, modified)

In correlating phases of culture Rouse pointed to three procedures. First, one could proceed descriptively or typologically, as proposed by McKern in the Midwestern Taxonomic Method. This procedure would yield classificatory resemblances only and thus would not allow conclusions about the necessary spatial and temporal relations of two cultures. The distributional procedure would plot the actual occurrence of particular phases with regard to space and time. Rouse underlined the fact that the temporal-spatial succession of phases would not always mean that they were genetically related, that is, a later phase derived from an earlier. "In its pure form, therefore, the distributional approach establishes contemporaneity and contiguity, or lack thereof, and nothing else." Both of these operations, however, must precede establishment of "genetic" relations, since resemblances and contact must be present if one is to conclude that one phase developed out of an antecedent phase. In Rouse's view, horizons and traditions in themselves were insufficient to demonstrate the genetic development of phases. In the determination of genetic relations, one must be careful to control for resemblances which are not the product of contact and possibly are due to logical adaptations to a similar environment. Once this is accomplished one can determine which kind of genetic model fits the situation:

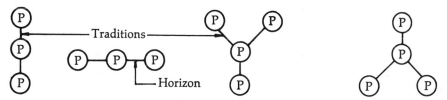

Determination of genetic relations, in Rouse's judgment, was often hazardous, and one must bring every available technique to bear. "It would seem prudent to make one's basic synthesis by means of descriptive or distributional correlation and then to point out the genetic relationships only in the instances where sufficient data are available and they indicate that this particular type of relationship has occurred" (Rouse 1955(57):714–720).

Rouse's procedure demonstrated that the archeologist, in good scientific measure, began first with classification in order to determine types according to similarities. He then proceeded to employ relevant criteria that would determine relationships based upon a preponderance of homologous (in this case "genetic" historic-evolutionary) characteristics.

plant-cultivation witnessed a homogenizing of the culture base in the diffusion of pottery making, weaving, stone carving, and a specialized ceremonial architecture. Some of these technologies could be found sporadically in archaic-type cultures, but with cultivation they formed an assemblage that prepared the ground for a culture takeoff. Henceforth, the criteria for distinguishing cultural developments would involve more than technologies. "They pertain to social and political organization, religion, aesthetics —to the whole of what Redfield has termed the 'moral order'" (Willey and

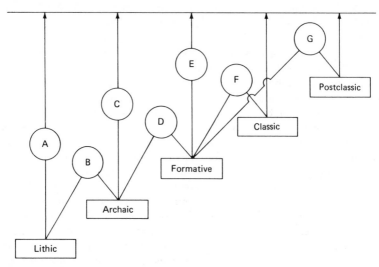

Figure 10-3. The developmental sequence of culture types in the New World, according to Willey and Phillips (1965:75).

Willey and Phillips maintained that their classification of developmental stages was not an "evolutionary scheme." By this they meant that they had not proposed a "unilinear or universal evolution" model. They preferred to consider their position akin to the multiunilinear evolution of Steward in that in other parts of the world "there are other quite unrelated lines of development." Nonetheless, they had to admit that the presence of a "theocratic irrigation state" in both Peru or Mesopotamia—if the stages of progression were parallel—would reflect an "inherent cultural causality."

The vertical figures A, C, and E represented "belated" cultures. That is, such cultures as types demonstrated "essential characteristics of a given stage long after the time generally considered to be appropriate to that stage." The intermediate figures represented "marginal" cultures. For example, "Culture B . . . is marginal Archaic in the sense that it has incorporated sufficient Archaic elements to take it out of the Lithic category but not enough to qualify fully as an Archaic stage culture." Many Plains Archaic cultures would qualify here. Culture D, which was marginal Formative, was well illustrated by "many of the Middle Woodland cultures of Eastern North America, which received significant elements of the Formative Adena-Hopewell culture without profound modification of their essentially Archaic pattern." It was possible for higher cultures to regress technologically and socially if they moved into an unfavorable area, or as "unfavorable" changes in climate occurred. Many New World Formative cultures exhibited such regression. Culture G demonstrated that special conditions of contact, as in the influence of Classic Inca on the Formative base in Northwest Argentina, could lead to a skipping of stages (Willey and Phillips 1965:72–76).

Phillips 1965:73). As a culture type and stage, the Classic was characterized by urbanism and a striking virtuosity in technologies and the arts. Certain cultures succeeded in integrating the various inventions of the formative stage into unified patterns. The Classic was a time of artistic climax and of regional stylization. Postclassic culture was marked by a disintegration of Classic regional styles, urbanization, and secularistic and militaristic trends (Willey and Phillips 1965:193). With militarism, migration and conquest seem to have spread entire art and architectural styles from one region to another. Whereas in Classic times ceremonial centers dominated the urban environment, now these were dwarfed by the city and fortifications that surrounded them.

The stages in development described by Willey and Phillips echoed those depicted by Steward as well as by Classic historians of the Near East, India, and the Far East. In every case the religious institution served as the primary integrator and stimulus for cultural elaboration. Secular interests associated with the rise of militarism severely undermined the religious integration. Like the Old World, the New moved to an era of cyclical conquest, suggesting a trend from the sacred to the secular.

The effort to type cultures produced controversy over classifications where cultures did not readily meet the expectations of primary criteria. Thus, the socially complex cultures of the Northwest Coast were classified by Willey and Phillips as Archaic on the basis of their technologies. Middle Woodland cultures were classified as Formative, despite a lack of agriculture. The fact that Adena, Poverty Point, and Hopewell possessed a complex ceremonial architecture suggestive of social stratification and an economic base suitable for stable settlements overrode the primary economic criterion in this instance.

In summary, common culture-historical interests had produced a convergence on culture patterns among American culture historicists and archeologists. As ethnological theory moved under the stimulus of culture and personality interests, and structural-functional theory to a configurative view of individual cultures, this theoretical orientation diffused to archeology. Nonetheless, the archeological focus remained centered on the relationship of culture patterns in their spatial and temporal linkages. It was as difficult for archeologists as for culture historians, to deal with individual cultures as integrated and functioning entities. To some degree, the perspective of integrated cultures was achieved when dealing with more complex protourban developments. In the protourban context the relationships of institutions, particularly religion, were seen as providing an initial stimulus toward urban life. As a systemic type, the secular militaristic-political combination was contrasted with the religious integration achieved under a priesthood.

Aside from a natural reference to traits, complexes, and centers, the terminological inventory of the archeologists seldom crossed that of the culture historicist. There were times when classification turned up the presence of identical features at a number of sites and this was taken to mean that the traits were historically connected and constituted a culture complex (see McKern 1940:19). Such a conclusion followed the practice of *Kulturkreislehre* and recalled the nonfunctional, but temporal, association of features which Wissler (1923) referred to as adhesions.

Like their ethnological counterparts, archeologists found themselves engrossed with a more general as well as a partitive theory of culture processes. That is, they engaged the problem of structure and variation. When dealing with the classification of cultures by types, archeologists described similarities that ostensibly grew out of the necessities of structural relationships, and hence presented a basis for evolutionary development. However, archeologists in the field were overwhelmed by the connections between regions and found it exceedingly difficult to come out in favor of the logical structural relations which the evolutionist position stressed. Hence, they were skeptical about natural evolutionary synthesis until all evidences for contact had been eliminated. This position echoed the historical posture of Boas with regard to evolutionary stages.

THE CONCEPT OF CULTURE AND THE REALITY PROBLEM

Basic understandings of the culture concept developed by American culture theorists can be summarized in two modes: (1) assumptions about the nature of the human reality and (2) assumptions about the nature of culture.

Assumptions About the Nature of the Human Reality

1. The human reality consists of a number of superimposed levels, each of which is conceptually distinct and causally autonomous.
   a. There are four levels of reality, ranked as follows: the cultural, social, psychological, and biological.
   b. The explanation of relationships and causes is not advanced by reducing one level to the explanatory context of the level below.
   c. The higher the reality level, the more integrative the role, and the more causally significant.
      1—As the capstone for the several levels, culture performs a signal integrative function and supplies a more comprehensive framework for explanation than any of the other orders.
2. Structure is the essence of the natural and of the human reality.
   a. Process is largely a part of structure or a derivative of structure.
      1—The unit parts of a structure receive their directionality from the structure, and operate according to the conventions of the structure.

Assumptions About the Nature of Culture

1. The essence of culture is found in its structure and in the continuity of structure.
   a. Culture is structured operationally in two modes: value premises and functional interdependencies.

1—Value premises provide the organizational principles and normative rules governing relationships and activities within the system. Like the rules of grammar for any language, value premises program structured relationships and activities designed to produce a conventionalized effect.

    a) Value premises bring the functioning parts of a system into a condition or state of congruence, thereby producing a stylistic integration.

    b) Value premises take precedence over functional interdependencies in the organization and operations of a culture.

        1) Basic value premises are entrenched as intuitive understandings and unconscious guides to action gradually acquired during the course of enculturation and reinforced by habit conditioning. They are difficult to verbalize and usually are not subject to open debate, and normally are nondebatable. Basic value premises belong to the realm of the implicit or covert.

        2) The covert premises, or unconscious canons of choice, are given overt form in normative specifications, or ideal patterns, which regulate the totality of relationships—notably to nature, things, time, space, other persons, and society as a whole.

2—Functional interdependencies describe the operational relationships of a system.

    a) Functional relations belong to the domain of rational accommodation and adaptation.

        1) Rational accommodations and adaptations describe a range of individual responses permitted or possible within limits defined by the ideal pattern. In short, empirical behaviors (Linton's real culture patterns) are programmed to meet ideal specifications.

3—The essential and fundamental modalities of individual behavior reside in the unconscious and conditioned acceptance of basic value premises. Individuals thus are prone to be creatures of habit, conforming to the emotionally loaded specifications of the ideal patterns. By extension, culture serves as the primary determinant in the organization and establishment of a person's relations to the rest of the world.

2. Culture structure provides for continuity in tradition.

    a. Culture changes directionally through elaboration of variations permissible within the pattern. Once these patterned variations are exhausted, the limits of creativity are reached and involution follows (Goldenweiser 1936; Kroeber 1963).

        1—The creative foci and historic periods of culture growth are characterized by pattern elaboration.

    b. Culture structure maintains continuity by restricting heterogeneity.

        1—Cultural forms introduced from alien cultures are rejected, accepted, and modified to the degree to which they are incompatible with the forms and meanings of the host culture.

3. Every culture is an historical development in that its content is derived from manifold sources and from different periods of time.

   a. Culture content in large part will be ordered by the underlying premises and basic orientations of the individual cultures.

   b. Participation of cultures in regional configurations induces shared similarities in form content and of basic premises by which primary institutions are interrelated and integrated.

   c. The participation of cultures in regional configurations induces the elaboration of specific patterns and the development of culture climax centers in which innovations tend to be generated and from which they are disseminated.

SUMMARY

Culture historians and their immediate successors, especially in the United States, must be credited with establishing culture as a popular and scientific concept. Under their tutelage the cultural assumed its place among the primary variables that organized the human context (for example, the biological and psychological). Moreover, they strained to assert the predominance of culture over all other variables, and they produced a theory of cultural determinism resting on two assumptions: (1) that culture existed as a distinct and autonomous level of reality and (2) that culture in its structuring organized all other relations relevant to human nature and to social action. To achieve this end, they resisted efforts to reduce a higher level of reality to the one next below. Hence, the constant vigilance to see that culture was not explained by processes of a common human psychology, that is, in an individual or behavioral mode. If culture existed psychologically, it must be social and not individual. Their insistence on the autonomy of culture and its self-determinism naturally led them to resist all other determinisms—for example, biological and environmental.

Culture-historical theorists began with the study of processes shaping the modification and growth of cultures. In time their interpretations of culture processes, implicitly anchored to culture structure, became more explicit. As structure emerged as a fundamental characteristic of culture, the linguistic model, with stress on grammatical rules and unconscious learnings, played an increasing part in the ethnological image of culture. Structural-functional theory added stimulus to the structural formulation of culture, but the value premises which American culture theorists, held to be intrinsic to the integration of cultures could be more easily affiliated with the rules of grammar than with functional necessities.

The unified interpretation which was ultimately produced under structural analysis programmed both personality and change processes as a derivative of structural prescriptions. As Kluckhohn (1949a) indicated in his popular title, culture was *The Mirror for Man*. While Boas sought to approach the problem of structure through the analysis of variation. Structuralists turned the emphasis around and saw variability as a function of structure (see, for example, F. Kluckhohn and Strodtbeck 1961).

The structural analysis of culture led to the discrimination of various factors that aided in describing the nature of culture (institutionalized patterns, technical, social, and value culture). However, no systematic effort followed to operationalize the variables and their factors in order to observe them in action and measure their effects. Casual use of the concept of culture in a generic way continued a state of ambiguity dramatized in the overlapping claims for the social and cultural.

Trends in anthropology subsequent to 1940 have accorded importance to variables which cultural Structuralists sought to hold at arm's length (for example, ecological relations and common human psychological processes). Whether principles immanent to a culture organize and produce an effect—or whether external circumstances condition and consistently compromise the products of that structure at certain points—are vital and lively issues for understanding the human reality.

Anthropologists have been inclined to concentrate on structure to the near exclusion of variation. Progress will not be made until anthropologists stop dichotomizing the reality problem by contrasting and separating structural and historical variational processes. Both processes are integral to understanding the order, contradictions, and processes of the human reality.

11

The Integration of Culture

INTRODUCTION

The concept of cultural integration assumes that any given culture is more than a planless hodgepodge of features and that there are functional interdependencies and value orientations which bring structure to a culture and regulate its systemic processes. In the course of its historical development any culture will reveal an elaboration of its organizational principles and a systematizing of its processes. Given time and advantage, a culture will shape a life-style suited to the total environment and characterized by a high degree of consistency, coherency, and congruity. The process of integration seems to fall into two organizational modes. First, there is a mechanical interconnection of parts whose proper functioning keeps the system in efficient balance. Second, there is the integrative process by which parts are drawn into congruence by the rationalizing of dominant values or principles, thereby producing a pattern or style.

Social Structuralism and biocultural functionalism uniformly stressed the mechanical interrelation of parts, and in this view the integration of the structure emerges as an attribute of frictionless operations. Balance or equilibrium, and the notion of a strain toward a homeostasis, are ideas commonly associated with mechanical models. Disequilibrium and disorganization contradict mechanical operations, and hence the impairment or withdrawal of a unit activity is the beginning of a chain of effects toward imbalance. Value principles can be applied to mechanical models, but usually such principles are derived from the purpose of the structure. For example, social Structuralists centered ultimate purpose in group unity, and hence an ultimate collective value symbolized that unity.

The view that cultures are integrated by unique value emphases or stylistic principles was pursued with some vigor by American and German culture theorists. Configurational or logico-meaningful integration has been approached in four ways. Those who stress a basic emotional stylization, such as Benedict and Mead, anchor culture types to the historical selection of different temperamental or psychological types. Closely allied are those of Freudian or modified-Freudian persuasion (for example, Kardiner), who pursue the integration of culture in the psychodynamics of personality frustration and conflict caused by cultural repressions connected with feeding, toilet training, sexual control, and adjustment to authority figures. A second category includes those who stress institutionalized patterns organized around primary interests and activities—what Linton called orientations. A third category includes those who emphasize the integrative role of values and world view (for example, Kluckhohn and Redfield). Finally, there are those who seek integrative process in epistemological assumptions underlying perception and the explanation of cause. The sociologist Pitirim Sorokin (1937–1941; also, 1941) and the philosopher F. S. C. Northrop (1949) are leading exponents of this approach to understanding the structuring of culture.

Lacking the literary works available to historians and philosophers of civilization, anthropologists have utilized magic, myth, and cult to uncover the epistemological assumptions found in primitive cultures. Developmentalists first explored this terrain through the archetypes of savagery, barbarism, and civilization. Recently, owing to renewed influence of linguistics and emphasis on perceptual and classificatory processes, fundamental integrates are again sought in mental processes. German culture morphology locates the integration of culture types in experiential ideas derived not from principles of logic but from poetically intuited truths. Accordingly, men use these intuitive truths to organize their life experience; and their search for self is largely a realization of the meaning of truths with which they have designed their cultures and experience. Back of cultural morphology lies the philosophic idealism of German romanticism.

The anthropological emphasis on the central importance of values for the integration of cultures correlated with a vigorous social criticism of Western industrial society and culture that began to take shape at the turn to the twentieth century. The rise in a concern for values also coincided with a decline in the capacity of Western civilization to continue its triumphant expansion. Oswald Spengler completed his analysis of Western civilization shortly before the outbreak of World War I and concluded that the West, as other civilizations, followed an organic path. The flowering of Western civilization had passed, and it now faced an epoch of decline and disintegration. Others were alarmed by the threat of the new industrialism to individuality as the dignity and worth of individuals appeared increasingly to be measured by functional utilities geared to the job. Was man to be the master or the slave of the machine?

In American anthropology Sapir (1924) opened the attack on the "crass materialism" of American culture by contrasting genuine and spurious cultures. Sapir argued that the complexities and the rationalization of work in Western industrial societies threatened the intellectual and moral development of the individual. Industrial man emerged as a fractionated and spiritless robot. The measure of a culture was not found in its size, complexity, or gross national product; rather, the true measure of a genuine culture lay in the human values and quality of life available to the individual.

The critique of American society ultimately penetrated the policies and practices of the Bureau of Indian Affairs and produced a reversal of assimilative programs tied to nineteenth-century theory regarding the evolution of civilization. According to civilization theory, the white man must accept the burden of enlightening those who continued to live out their lives in the dark shadows of savagery. As a critic of industrial society, John Collier discovered the humanistic values he cherished in the culture of the Pueblo Indians, notably the Hopi. As Commissioner of Indian Affairs, he sought to reconstitute shattered Indian communities by reawakening their humanistic value base. The simpler Indian societies, which appeared incongruous in the modern world, actually had a special message which, if understood and heeded, could save the modern from a self-destructive fate. It is interesting that the experiment in rebuilding or preserving traditional Indian communities coincided with the decline of Structuralist emphasis in social and cultural theory.

A suspicion that cultures were not tightly integrated wholes appeared shortly before World War II and grew in strength during the 1960s in the wake of accelerated postwar change. As traditional values and customs dissolved in the search for new life-styles, the idea that primary value orientations penetrated the whole fabric of a culture and shaped the texture of its design was increasingly unacceptable as a working hypothesis and a point of fact.

HISTORICISM AND CULTURAL INTEGRATION

The historical view of culture promulgated by Boas did not focus on the dominant profiles of cultures but viewed any culture as an inventory of borrowings from a wide range of sources. This was the initial position of Ruth Benedict when surveying the guardian spirit complex in North America, her doctoral dissertation under Boas. In *The Concept of the Guardian Spirit in North America*, Benedict (1923(29):84–85) concluded there was no organic connection between traits associated with the complex in the Plateau, Northwest Coast, Plains, Southwest, and other culture areas. The guardian spirit complex illustrated how culture elements became disengaged from larger wholes and diffused separately over broad areas, to be selectively incorporated by different tribes into their guardian spirit assemblage according to their respective interests and purposes.

There is then no observed correlation between the vision-guardian-spirit concept, and the other traits with which it is associated . . . and we have found no coalescence which we may regard as being other than fortuitous. . . . In one region it has associated itself with puberty ceremonials, in another with totemism, in a third with secret societies, in a fourth with inherited rank, in a fifth with black magic. Among the Blackfoot, it is their economic system into which the medicine bundles have so insinuated themselves that the whole manner of it is unintelligible without taking into account the monetary value of the vision. Among the Kwakiutl, their social life and organization, their caste system, their concept of wealth, would be equally impossible of comprehension without a knowledge of those groups of individuals sharing the same guardian spirit by supernatural revelation. It is in every case a matter of social patterning—of that which cultural recognition has singled out and standardized.

It is an ultimate fact of human nature that man builds up his culture out of disparate elements, combining and recombining them; and until we have abandoned the superstition that the result is an organism functionally interrelated, we shall be unable to see our cultural life objectively, or to control its manifestations.

The last paragraph is strong language for someone who later would pioneer in the psychocultural integration of tribal life-styles. Three years earlier Lowie (1920:440–441) set out similar views when arguing against the invariant sequences entrenched in social evolutionary theory.

The belief in social progress was a natural accompaniment of the belief in historical laws, especially when tinged with the evolutionary optimism of the 'seventies of the nineteenth century. If inherent necessity urges all societies along a fixed path, metaphysicians may still dispute whether the underlying force be divine or diabolic, but there can at least be no doubt as to which community is retarded and which accelerated in its movement toward the appointed goal. But no such necessity or design appears from the study of culture history. Cultures develop mainly through the borrowings due to chance contact. Our own civilization is even more largely than the rest a complex of borrowed traits. The singular order of events by which it has come into being provides no schedule for the itinerary of alien cultures. Hence the specious plea that a given people must pass through such or such a stage in *our* history before attaining this or that destination can no longer be sustained. . . . In prescribing for other peoples a social programme we must always act on subjective grounds; but at least we can act unfettered by the pusillanimous fear of transgressing a mock-law of social evolution.

Nor are the facts of culture history without bearing on the adjustment of our own future. To that planless hodge-podge, that thing of shreds and patches called civilization, its historian can no longer yield superstitious reverence. He will realize better than others the obstacles to infusing design into the amorphous product; but in thought at least he will not grovel before it in fatalistic acquiescence but dream of a rational scheme to supplant the chaotic jumble.

Lowie's description of civilization as a thing of shreds and patches was unfortunate, but it was not hard to draw out the web of historic strands that had contributed to Western civilization and to prove that no national culture, indeed no ethnic group, could long remain a cultural island. The importance of diffusion and its benefits in enriching the culture cannot be overemphasized, and Linton (1936:325) hazarded that 90 percent of the elements found in contemporary cultures—even the modern ones—had been borrowed. American culture, despite an acceleration of national inventiveness, was no exception.

> Our solid American citizen awakens in a bed built on a pattern which originated in the Near East but which was modified in Northern Europe before it was transmitted to America. He throws back covers made from cotton, domesticated in India, or linen, domesticated in the Near East, or wool from sheep, also domesticated in the Near East, or silk, the use of which was discovered in China. All of these materials have been spun and woven by processes invented in the Near East. He slips into his moccasins, invented by the Indians of the Eastern woodlands, and goes to the bathroom, whose fixtures are a mixture of European and American inventions, both of recent date. He takes off his pajamas, a garment invented in India, and washes with soap invented by the ancient Gauls. He then shaves, a masochistic rite which seems to have been derived from either Sumer or ancient Egypt.
>
> Returning to the bedroom, he removes his clothes from a chair of southern European type and proceeds to dress. He puts on garments whose form originally derived from the skin clothing of the nomads of the Asiatic steppes, puts on shoes made from skins tanned by a process invented in ancient Egypt and cut to a pattern derived from the classical civilizations of the Mediterranean, and ties around his neck a strip of bright-colored cloth which is a vestigial survival of the shoulder shawls worn by the seventeenth-century Croatians. Before going out for breakfast he glances through the window, made of glass invented in Egypt, and if it is raining puts on overshoes made of rubber discovered by the Central American Indians and takes an umbrella, invented in southeastern Asia. Upon his head he puts a hat made of felt, a material invented in the Asiatic steppes.
>
> On his way to breakfast he stops to buy a paper, paying for it with coins, an ancient Lydian invention. At the restaurant a whole new series of borrowed elements confronts him. His plate is made of a form of pottery invented in China. His knife is of steel, an alloy first made in southern India, his fork a medieval Italian invention, and his spoon a derivative of a Roman original. He begins breakfast with an orange, from the eastern Mediterranean, a cantaloupe from Persia, or perhaps a piece of African watermelon. With this he has coffee, an Abyssinian plant, with cream and sugar. Both the domestication of cows and the idea of milking them originated in the Near East, while sugar was first made in India. After his fruit and first coffee he goes on to waffles, cakes made by a Scandinavian technique from wheat domesticated in Asia Minor. Over these he pours maple syrup, invented by the Indians of the Eastern woodlands. As a side dish he may have the egg of a species of bird domesticated in Indo-China, of thin strips of the flesh of an animal domesticated in Eastern Asia which have been salted and smoked by a process developed in northern Europe.
>
> When our friend has finished eating he settles back to smoke, an American Indian habit, consuming a plant domesticated in Brazil in either a pipe, derived from the Indians of Virginia, or a cigarette, derived from Mexico. If

he is hardy enough he may even attempt a cigar, transmitted to us from the Antilles by way of Spain. While smoking he reads the news of the day, imprinted in characters invented by the ancient Semites upon a material invented in China by a process invented in Germany. As he absorbs the accounts of foreign troubles he will, if he is a good conservative citizen, thank a Hebrew deity in an Indo-European language that he is 100 per cent American. (Linton 1936:326–327)

INSTITUTIONALIZED INTERESTS AND CULTURAL INTEGRATION: LINTON AND HERSKOVITS

Taken at face value these extracts of American culture historians produced a description that made any culture look like a curious assemblage of traits whose connections were quite accidental. But this was not their studied view. Admittedly in the early period of American historicism, the study of cultures as systems was a secondary problem; but that cultures possessed a structure, as Boas insisted, was constantly implied when explaining the alterations made in alien traits to make them congenial and useful to the receiving culture. Linton in 1936 (443–444) described cultures as "includ[ing] a number of focal points of interest each of which provides orientation for a certain group of culture elements. However, most of these focal points themselves tend to show orientation with respect to a small number of major interests which thus dominate the whole configuration."

Thus, for the Comanche, the warrior's life dominated all other interests and elevated him above all other groups. On the other hand, Tanala rice growers in the hill country of Madagascar organized themselves in a joint family of patrilineal descent which submerged private interests in order to preserve the unity of the group (Linton 1936:444–463). How these dominant concerns came to be fixated must remain largely unknown. Linton (1936:463) hazarded the idea that the process would prove to be

highly complex and in large measure accidental. At the same time, these interests were of overwhelming importance to the culture configuration, molding the other elements within it to serve the ends which they indicated as desirable. Such interests remain an unexplained and unresolved element in all culture equations, and their presence foredooms to failure any purely mechanistic approach to the problems of culture and society.

By 1945 Herskovits (in Linton 1945b:164–165; see also Herskovits 1948: 542–553) was applying Linton's concept of a dominant culture interest or focus to explain variation and change.

Thus as we examine different cultures, we perceive that they differ not alone in their outer form, but also in the dominant concerns of their carriers. This factor is of the greatest importance in cultural change. For of the many aspects of culture by which men live it is those which . . . hold greatest sway that are the least prone to be taken for granted, that will be most discussed, and that will therefore be farthest removed from unthinking response. Looked at in structural terms, these aspects of culture will exhibit the most variable patterns. Or . . . a people's dominant concern may be thought of as the focus of their culture; that area of activity or belief where the greatest awareness of form exists, the most discussion of values is heard, the widest difference in structure is to be discerned.

TEMPERAMENT AND PSYCHOCULTURAL INTEGRATION: BENEDICT AND MEAD

When discussing the integrative foci of cultures, neither Linton nor Herskovits made direct reference to Ruth Benedict. Yet Benedict (1930) was among the first to rekindle an interest in the grand design of cultures with a paper on "Psychological Types in the Cultures of the Southwest." The reason for the omission was clear. Following Nietzsche's use of Dionysian and Apollonian to describe exaltation as against measure, Benedict rested her cultural typology on psychological types. Thus Benedict unwittingly reduced culture to psychology. According to Benedict, a great span of human potential and purpose is available; to achieve meaning and direction in their way of life individuals make a choice among options. Long-ago ancestors of present-day Zuni Indians drew the blueprint for contemporary culture by a preference for a temperament that held a middle ground and avoided the agitation of psychological and emotional excess (Benedict 1959:79). In contrast with this Apollonian style, the Dionysian thrilled to the exciting and patterned life with adventures in terror and danger (Benedict 1959:119). Of such temperament and culture were the Kwakiutl and peoples surrounding the Pueblos. Across the Pacific, near the southeastern tip of New Guinea, one might detect a third kind of temperament (paranoid), exemplified by the dour, hostile, treacherous, and suspicious Dobuan.

Once selection of a temperament type had been made, the historic course of development in culture winnowed out the contradictions until a body of custom wholly consistent and congruent with that temperamental preference was achieved. Such, at least, were the integrated cultures, which, like personalities, were more than the sum of their traits. Seemingly, in the analogy of a personality life history, cultures took on their distinctive characters as the integrating principle infiltrated and pervaded every component of life.

A culture, like an individual, is a more or less consistent pattern of thought and action. Within each culture there come into being characteristic purposes not necessarily shared by other types of society. In obedience to these purposes, each people further and further consolidates its experience, and in proportion to the urgency of these drives the heterogeneous items of behavior take more and more congruous shape. Taken up by a well-integrated culture, the most ill-assorted acts become characteristic of its peculiar goals, often by the most unlikely metamorphoses. The form that these acts take we can understand only by understanding first the emotional and intellectual mainsprings of that society. (Benedict 1959:46)

The subtle inversion of cultural causation in Benedict's treatment of Zuni, Kwakiutl, and Dobuan personality-culture relations received no special comment in Boas' introductory remarks to *Patterns of Culture* (1934). The "Papa Boas" family of scholars conformed to the popular observation that the later-born are treated with greater indulgence than the first-born. At least the young women who entered the family later, and who prevailed upon Boas to take up smoking, were given a lot more leeway than the young men who were first indoctrinated with the historical method. If the problem of origins were ignored, Benedict's treatment would conform to Boasian requirements. This meant adherence to cultural relativism based on methodological considerations, a view of the individual largely shaped by the cultural legacy, and a concern for sociopsychological problems which throw light on the dynamic processes of change. Moreover, Boas himself suggested that individual variability in the face of conventionalized learnings could be the result of temperamental difference.

Given Benedict's concern for temperament and behavior and a preference for unconscious cultural conditioning, it is clear why Mead (1959:202) describes her approach to culture as "personality writ large," rather than the reverse. In Benedict's view, and subsequently in Mead's as well, integrated cultures represented and expressed the exaggerated dominance of a special personality type. Such being the case, there was little room for other personality configurations expressive of other choices along the arc of temperament; hence, Benedict's concern with behavior which deviated from conventionalized patterns as a conflict of temperament. She appealed for tolerance of heterodox behavior that individuals were powerless to control because it was rooted in biology. The temperament-cultural definition of normality held implications for a general definition of normality. Normality was relative, varying from one cultural-temperament definition to another. The deviate of one culture might be accorded first place in another.

Margaret Mead (b. 1901), long associated with the American Museum of Natural History (1926–1969; curator of ethnology in 1964), obtained her Ph.D. under Boas in 1929 with fieldwork in Samoa. Her close association with Benedict led Mead to accept the arc-of-temperament cultural-selectivity approach to understanding how cultures were put together in terms of values. Mead (1950) soon attempted a test of sex-linked temperament—so commonly assumed in the masculine and feminine stereotypes of Western culture—against the realities of social temperaments conventionalized in primitive societies. What she uncovered in a comparison of temperamental preferences in three New Guinea societies—Arapesh, Mundugumor, and Tchambuli—was this singular fact:

We have now considered in detail the approved personalities [as tempera-
ments] of each sex among three primitive peoples. We found the Arapesh—
both men and women—displaying a personality that . . . we would call maternal
in its parental aspects, and feminine in its sexual aspects. We found men, as
well as women, trained to be cooperative, unaggressive, responsive to the
needs and demands of others. We found no idea that sex was a powerful
driving force either for men or for women. In marked contrast . . . we found
among the Mundugumor that both men and women developed as ruthless,
aggressive, positively sexed individuals, with the maternal cherishing aspects
of personality at a minimum. Both men and women approximated to a personality type that we in our culture would find only in an undisciplined and very
violent male. Neither the Arapesh nor the Mundugumor profit by a contrast
between the sexes; the Arapesh ideal is the mild, responsive man married to
the mild, responsive women; the Mundugumor ideal is the violent aggressive
man married to the violent aggressive woman. In the third tribe, the Tchambuli, we found a genuine reversal of the sex-attitudes of our own culture, with
the woman the dominant, impersonal, managing partner, the man the less
responsible and the emotionally dependent person. These three situations suggest, then, a very definite conclusion. *If those temperamental attitudes which
we have traditionally regarded as feminine—such as passivity, responsiveness,
and a willingness to cherish children—can so easily be set up as the masculine
pattern in one tribe, and in another be outlawed for the majority of women
as well as for the majority of men, we no longer have any basis for regarding
such aspects of behaviour as sex-linked. And this conclusion becomes even
stronger when we consider the actual reversal in Tchambuli of the position of
dominance of the two sexes, in spite of the existence of formal patrilineal
institutions. . . .*

We are forced to conclude that human nature is almost unbelievably malleable, responding accurately and contrastingly to contrasting cultural conditions. The differences between individuals within a culture are almost entirely
to be laid to differences in conditioning, especially during early childhood,
and the form of this conditioning is culturally determined. Standardized personality differences between the sexes are . . . cultural creations to which each
generation, male and female, is trained to conform. (Mead 1950:190–191;
italics supplied)

Mead (1937a(39):558–559) traced the origins for these culturally approved temperamental types back to an accidental, historical selection from
the wide range of physiological-derived traits that occurred naturally in
any population. In such view, women were just as often born with aggressive temperaments as men, and some men found alleged feminine features
temperamentally congenial to their personalities.

There appears to be about the same range of basic temperamental variation
among the Arapesh and among the Mundugumor, although the violent man
is a misfit in the first society and a leader in the second. If human nature were
completely homogeneous raw material, lacking specific drives and characterized by no important constitutional differences between individuals, then individuals who display personality traits so antithetical to the social pressure
should not reappear in societies of such differing emphases. If the variations

between individuals were to be set down to accidents in the genetic process, the same accidents should not be repeated with similar frequency in strikingly different cultures, with strongly contrasting methods of education.

But because this same relative distribution of individual differences does appear in culture after culture, in spite of the divergence between the cultures, it seems pertinent to offer a hypothesis to explain upon what basis the personalities of men and women have been differently standardized so often in the history of the human race. This hypothesis is an extension of that advanced by Ruth Benedict in her *Patterns of Culture*. Let us assume that there are definite temperamental differences between human beings which if not entirely hereditary at least are establishd on a hereditary base very soon after birth. . . . These differences . . . are the clues from which culture works, selecting one temperament, or a combination of related and congruent types, as desirable, and embodying this choice in every thread of the social fabric—in the care of the young child, the games the children play, the songs the people sing, the structure of political organization, the religious observance, the art and the philosophy. (Mead 1950:193)

The significance of this finding accented the waste of human talent caused by cultural definitions which limited the creative potential offered by natural temperamental variation. There was also loss due to frustration, suffering, and neurotic inversion, which necessarily pursued those innately disposed to be in conflict with the conventions of society (Mead 1950:198). Speaking not as a suffragette but as a social scientist, the logic of Mead's position appealed for the abolition of the social image of masculine and feminine and for a society open to all temperaments and the pecularities of behavior associated with them.

Historically our own culture has relied for the creation of rich and contrasting values upon many artificial distinctions, the most striking of which is sex. It will not be by the mere abolition of these distinctions that society will develop patterns in which individual gifts are given place instead of being forced into an ill-fitting mould. If we are to achieve a richer culture, rich in contrasting values, we must recognize the whole gamut of human potentialities, and so weave a less arbitrary social fabric, one in which each diverse human gift will bring a fitting place. (Mead 1950:217–218)

The Benedict-Mead thesis for the integration of culture had grown during the twenties in correspondence and in discussion with Edward Sapir. Benedict once described Sapir as impelled to prove that culture really didn't count. He constantly scanned literary works for affirmation of his conviction that individuals generally transcended their cultures (Mead 1959:201). To some degree the approach was similar to Radin's, who in *Primitive Man as Philosopher* (1957a:5) presumed that temperament and ability were found in the same distribution among primitive and civilized peoples. Personality temperaments provided Radin a base for cultural interpretation and for denial of the overwhelming constraints of custom. Radin observed that men in primitive societies cultivated and protected their individuality and did not subordinate themselves unthinkingly to custom or a collective purpose.

For Benedict, as for Mead and Radin, temperament remained the staunch citadel of individuality. This might well be true, but more problems were raised by introducing temperament into the cultural picture than were resolved. Acceptance by the Arapesh and the Mundugumor of a unisex definition might be clear enough, but why did Tchambuli males, if they had their share of aggressive temperaments, settle for a soft image while their women played a role usually considered masculine? On the one hand, as Benedict (1959:253–254) asserted, the biological background of temperament was impervious to cultural pressures. Yet the vast majority of the members of any society conformed to custom and gave in to institutionalized expectations no matter how idiosyncratic. Such conditioning in spite of diversity in temperaments, some of which were at odds with the normative pattern, proved the boundless plasticity of human nature. "Most people are shaped to the form of their culture because of the enormous malleability of their original endowment. They are plastic to the moulding force of the society into which they are born" (Benedict 1959:254).

From this it appeared that temperament didn't count for much in the individual-culture equation. Indeed, Benedict (1959:17) assured her readers, "The conditioned responses make up the greater part of our huge equipment of automatic behaviour." The relation of individuals to their culture was illustrated in the historic development of integration in any culture. Unconscious canons shaped choice and generalized an increase in homogeneity, consistency, and coherence throughout the institutional framework (Benedict 1959:48).

Patterns of Culture was not a smashing success among anthropologists. Though favorably reviewed by Kroeber (1935(37):689), he apparently sounded a consensus when he dismissed it as appealing to the layman but not a methodological work designed for the anthropologist. Benedict's offense centered in her approach to culture through psychological types. She had hoped to avoid the accusation of reducing culture to individual psychology by introducing historical processes to account for the selective integration of cultures. However, for undocumented tribal societies, the historic path to integration remained an assumption, never to be tested.

> The difficulty with naive interpretations of culture in terms of individual behaviour is not that these interpretations are those of psychology, but that they ignore history and the historical process of acceptance or rejection of traits. Any configurational interpretation of cultures also is an exposition in terms of individual psychology, but it depends upon history as well as upon psychology. It holds that Dionysian behaviour is stressed in the institutions of certain cultures because it is a permanent possibility in individual psychology, but that it is stressed in certain cultures and not in others because of historical events that have in one place fostered its development and in others have ruled it out. At different points in the interpretation of cultural forms, both history and psychology are necessary; one cannot make the one do the service of the other. (Benedict 1959:232–233)

Mead compounded the Benedict error by seeking to eliminate sexual temperament as a basis for culture patterns restricted to one sex. Yet the majority of cultures accented differences between males and females in the belief that there were masculine and feminine characteristics correlated with biological functions. Male roles called for mobility, aggression, protection, and arduous and controlled energy output. The excitement of life and its public laurels were open to men, whereas women trudged behind, serving their men and children without the rewards of public life and deprived of opportunities to cultivate innate talents.

Mead's attempt to minimize the importance of maleness and femaleness as a biological given brought a prompt and querulous response from those who rested their case on the obvious realities of sexual dimorphism. At the same time, the critics ignored implications of the common assumption that cultural conditioning overrode human physiology at every significant turn. In her Preface to her "most misunderstood book," Mead (1950) wished it clearly understood that she did not deny sex differences, but that sex differences, biologically speaking, could not account for the behavior expected of the sexes as defined in culture patterns. In Mead's perspective, the correlation between the biological bases of sexual dimorphism and cultural distinctions were out of phase. Cultural distinctions between males and females were artificial and should be modified to correlate the cultural with an equitable distribution of natural biological temperaments and individual talents.

Diverse sources provided Benedict with a stimulus to study the stylistic profiles of cultures. Gestalt psychology supplied the analogy of wholeness in the way mankind perceived the phenomenal world. Malinowski's functionalism stressed the interrelatedness and uniqueness of Trobriand Island culture. Students of art insisted that art styles must be studied as unique expressions of historically developed values and life orientations. The ancient civilizations continued to challenge scholarly penetration of the genius or ethos upon which a distinctive national character and destiny had been raised (for example, Dilthey, Nietzsche, and Spengler). Each intellectual strand in its own way contributed to a paramount concern with the nature of structure, the uniqueness of each society and culture, and the resultant standardization of the individual due to the pressures of the structure. The rise of Structuralism in the scientific and humanistic modes shaped Benedict's holistic perspective and her search for the intuitive truths by which men selectively regulated their aspirations and their life-styles.

VALUE PREMISES AND THE INTEGRATION OF CULTURE: REDFIELD, KLUCKHOHN, AND OPLER

By the mid-thirties the view that values held the key to a comparative understanding of culture was becoming entrenched. Redfield early took the lead in values analysis, but a more considered effort at controlled comparison of cultural values was initiated by Kluckhohn in the American Southwest. Opler entered the values field in 1945 to challenge the view that cultures were tightly integrated wholes. Values were important in giving direction to behavior; but cultures generally housed contradictory values, Opler argued, and consequently were not unified by a dominant and pervasive principle.

The Moral World of the Folk Society: Redfield

Redfield's (1930) description of Tepoztlán was the first ethnological study of the meaning of values in the life of a traditional Mexican village. Tepoztlán served as a general outline for Redfield's (1941, 1947, 1953) future research of a rural-urban continuum in Yucatan, as well as his later conceptualization of the folk society and its transmutation through the forces of urbanization.

A relatively isolated, self-sufficient, and ceremonious community, the folk society recalled that ancient sacred city described by Fustel de Coulanges in 1864. The folk placed group purposes over private interests. Membership in the community was based on kinship, and kinship designated the moral reciprocities which governed relations linking the individual to other individuals, to the community as a whole, and to the community of spirits ruling over man and the universe. Custom reigned, weighted with ritual and sacralized sanctions. Conformity to tradition in combination with the technical and social simplicity of the folk society limited the range of variation and thus conveyed a static quality to life. Moral order was dominant over technical order, and emphasis on moral reciprocities left no room for a stranger, anonymous and without kin or sacred obligations.

Embedded within the folk society construct one can detect three analytically distinct yet interrelated areas of conceptualization: social process, value process, and historic (evolutionary) process.

As social process, the folk society construct emphasized the uniformities deriving from the common social experience. Out of the intimacies of face-to-face interaction a strong attachment to other persons emerged. This social sentiment crystallized a hard and fast in-group or we-feeling against the out-group, or they. A strong attachment to other members of the group was correlated with strong feelings regarding their ends and means. Behavior hardened into social conventions that stressed a show of form that always governed social contacts. The jealous sense of togetherness restricted individuality and entrenched uniformity in a sacralized tradition. Following custom thus became an end in itself, and the folk were unable to project a goal of improvement in their affairs. The sense of interdependence and interrelatedness suffusing folk psychology manifested itself in a ramifying exchange of services. Even in the exchange of objects, personal relationships were predominant. Hence, things exchanged took on the quality of gifts, and the value of the exchange resided more in the social relationship than in a purchase value. Folk projected their personalized and familized values into all their relations—between individuals and between individuals and spirits located in nature. Here was an implicit world view, a sensed moral order, which bound man to man and man to spirit.

A personalized world view in conjunction with sacralized conventions restrained the folk from systematizing or expanding their knowledge to the point where one could speak of science or theology. Knowledge was largely a product of experience and found its finest expression in the wisdom of the elders. Age and sex were intrinsic to the conferral of status. Since interpersonal relations were charged with affect, the folk dramatized their needs spontaneously yet ceremoniously and rehearsed their desires and fears in magical acts involving spiritual personalities. Doing, feeling, thinking were so unitary among the folk that their social expectations were achieved not through legalized coercion but through a moral imperative which bound the individual by habituation.

As an historic process, the folk construct envisions the moral order and internal cohesion of a folk disrupted by technological and commercial changes normally associated with the development of the city. City living is characterized by diminution in the social integration of the individual, by the shallow depth of the emotional life, and by the fragmentation of personality. The lesser degree of ego involvement holds potential for a more critical attitude and more individualized behavior. As the urbanite is separated from the solid moral integration characteristic of the countryman, his personality becomes less certain of its direction and of the moral basis of social life. Urban secularism and heterogeneity contrast sharply with folk sacredness and homogeneity. History, as evolution, begins with the folk, moves to the peasant, and terminates with the city society. A second aspect of the historic-evolutionary process, then, is the engulfment and pushing back of the folk in time and in space by urban communities and their peasant dependencies. This was the lesson of the study of the four Yucatecan communities, for it was in the isolated forest community of Tusik that one found visible persistences of a traditional culture that was both Mayan and sixteenth-century Spanish Christian. Inadvertently, Redfield produced evidence in support of the age-area hypothesis!

What Redfield had to say about the ritualization of customs and of objects revealed influence traceable to social Structuralism expounded by Durkheim and Radcliffe-Brown. Finally, in his placement of the folk society in a developmental sequence that led to a civilized state, Redfield reaffirmed the judgments of earlier Developmentalists. The basic trends were three:

1. From the sacred to the secular.
2. From the homogeneous to the heterogeneous.
3. From the ethically less advanced to the ethically advanced.

Speaking of ethical advancement, Redfield (1953:163–164) observed,

> The change is far from steady and the future course of the ethical judgment is not assured to us. But . . . on the whole the human race has come to develop a more decent and humane measure of goodness—there has been a transformation of ethical judgment which makes us look at noncivilized peoples, not as equals, but as people on a different level of human experience. . . . We do not expect the preliterate person to cultivate and protect individual freedom of thought as we expect civilized people to do. . . . We do not expect a people to have a moral norm that their material conditions of life make impossible. . . . We judge the conduct of primitive peoples—as of other people—by their success in acting in accordance with the ideals they have chosen.

Redfield, however, rejected relativism as the final answer to human ethics. There was an absolute human ethic toward which mankind cautiously directed its highest expression; and this evolutionary moment was found in the moral commitments of the civilized communities. In final analysis, Redfield reaffirmed the limited alternatives of the evolutionary prospectus: mankind had either advanced or fallen from a noble estate; the primitive was either ill-formed in experience or he was more noble in a life made natural to humans by its utter simplicity; civilizations either enhanced or raised artificial barriers to the full realization of human nature. Such contrasts are the constant phantoms of evolutionism.

Covert Value Orientations and the Integration of Culture: Kluckhohn

The theoretical interests of Clyde Kluckhohn (1905–1960) also converged on values as integral to the character of a people and their cultural design for living. An illness during his freshman year at Princeton forced him to exchange the classroom for the informal learning of the neighborly Navaho. Kluckhohn became enthralled with the experience and returned again and again in pursuit of his magnificent obsession, the understanding of the Southwest as an historic culture region where indigenous and intrusive traditions intermingled yet preserved their independence. Translation of this interest into a research design began in 1936, the year he received his Harvard doctorate, and culminated in the comparative study of values in five cultures in the Southwest (1949–1953)—Navaho, Zuni, Mormons, Spanish-Americans, and Texas Homesteaders. What Kluckhohn (1951:viii) observed in the Southwest was an apparent persistence of traditions despite conditions that should have facilitated change. "Why," he queried, "do different value systems continue to exist in five cultures all having to meet similar problems of adjustment and survival in the same ecological area, all having been exposed by actual contact and by stimulus diffusion to each others' value ideas and practices?" What he had in the Rimrock area was a readymade laboratory for studying in cross-cultural perspective the factors which held cultures to their traditional charters despite participation in a complex network of relationships.

The values project gave major consideration to processes and focused on three orders of problems: (1) how individuals acquired a personal value base centered in a normative value orientation; (2) group patterns and variations within the value base; and (3) the importance which value orientations held for contact with other ethnocultural groups and their influence on the direction of change. At one time thirty-seven different investigators were drawn into the project, and a short list of titles reveals the range of problems engaged:

Leighton, A. H. and D. C., 1949. "Gregorio, The Hand-Trembler: A Psychobiological Personality Study of a Navaho Indian." Vol. 40, No. 1, *Papers of the Peabody Museum of American Archaeology and Ethnology, Harvard University*, 40(1).

Roberts, John M., 1951. "Three Navaho Households: A Comparative Study in Small Group Culture." *Ibid*, 40(3).

Vogt, Evon Z., 1951. "Navaho Veterans: A Study of Changing Values." *Ibid*, 41(1).

Rapoport, Robert, 1954. "Changing Navaho Religious Values: A Study of Christian Missions to the Rimrock Navahos." *Ibid*, 41(2).

Landgraf, John L., 1954. "Land-Use in the Ramah Area of New Mexico: An Anthropological Approach to Areal Study." *Ibid*, 42(1).

Kaplan, Bert, 1954. "A Study of Rorschach Responses in Four Cultures." *Ibid*, 42(2).

Smith, Watson, and Roberts, John, 1954. "Zuni Law: A Field of Values." *Ibid*, 43(1).

Florence Kluckhohn (*Variations in Value Orientations*, 1961), with the assistance of the statistically trained Fred Strodtbeck, capped the values project with a test of her theoretical model of dominant-value profiles and variations. However, when Florence Kluckhohn stressed the significance of variation, she was not pointing to variations induced by historic accident but to variants natural to any system. Kluckhohn and Strodtbeck assumed, and attempted to prove, that variations in cultural phenomena followed rules and occurred systematically just as variations in the biological and physical domains. The approach thus was a Structuralist one. Variation was a part of any structured process, but it was defined and limited by structure. The presence of variations meant that societies were not integrated by monolithic value orientations but required a degree of controlled variability for a healthy existence (Kluckhohn and Strodtbeck 1961:43). Basic change processes nonetheless were located interior to the system as described by Spengler, Toynbee, and Sorokin, and all structural determinists. "All variant patterns, those permitted as well as those required, are seen as having the maintenance of the ongoing system as their primary function. But at the same time they contain the seeds of potential change which often spring into growth when nurtured by external influences" (Kluckhohn and Strodtbeck 1961:344)

What Clyde Kluckhohn brought to the values project, aside from its design, was a breadth of academic experience which impelled him to seek linkages with sister disciplines, notably psychology (psychiatry) and sociology. Shortly after World War II he collaborated in founding the Department and Laboratory of Social Relations (Harvard), designed to provide students with a richer appreciation of advantages to be found in a combination of anthropology, psychology, and sociology. His endeavors to establish meaningful connections with related fields, especially those throwing light on the relation of personality to culture, were accompanied by participation in psychoanalytically oriented seminars coordinated by Abram Kardiner of the New York Psychoanalytic Institute.

Kluckhohn's acceptance of unconscious processes as basic to enculturated behavior followed a common path. Taking his cue from Linton's reference to overt and covert culture, Kluckhohn (1943(45):218) located the essence of culture in a sociopsychological configuration of intuitive values and premises.

> A cultural configuration may be defined as a principle of the covert culture—either a way of doing a variety of things (a means) or an end (a culturally defined goal). Since configurations are part of the *covert* culture they are *unstated* premises. One is tempted to say that configurations are cultural principles of which there is characteristically no sustained and systematic awareness on the part of most members of a society. This statement, however . . . must mean "awareness with respect to customary or even habitual verbalization." The members of the society are, of course, aware in the sense that they make choices with the configurations as unconscious but determinative backgrounds.

In a later clarification, Kluckhohn (1952:395) defined values as a *"conception, explicit or implicit, distinctive of an individual or characteristic of a group, of the desirable which influences the selection from available modes, means, and ends of action."* As a concept, any value was a logical construct of the same order as the constructs, culture, and social structure.

To extend his comprehension of cultural integration, Kluckhohn developed the concept of value orientation. A value orientation constituted a value complex; that is, value orientations had an element of organization, enunciated a general value base, and included postulates about the nature of the world (Kluckhohn 1952:409). Kluckhohn's value orientations, as a complex of values and existential postulates which applied to broad segments of life, converged on the broad context of cultural meaning that Redfield and others had attempted to master through the concept of world view.

Throughout his approach to the integration of culture, Kluckhohn sought to relate fundamental structure to psychological processes operating within a value context. The structure of culture appeared to the observer like a stream of events whose form, organization, and order of appearance were regulated by the covert premises and intuitive categorizations shared by members of the society (Kluckhohn 1949b:358). Under Kluckhohn's (1949b:360) analysis, the world of the Navaho was ordered by eight fundamental propositions:

1. The universe is orderly; all events are caused and interrelated.
   a. Knowledge is power.
   b. The basic quest is for harmony.
   c. Harmony can be restored by orderly procedures.
   d. The price of disorder, in human terms, is illness.
2. The universe tends to be personalized.
   a. Causation is identifiable in personalized terms.
3. The universe is full of dangers.
4. Evil and good are complementary, and both are ever present.
5. Experience is conceived as a continuum differentiated only by sense data.
6. Morality is conceived in traditionalist and situational terms rather than in terms of abstract absolutes.
7. Human relations are premised upon familistic individualism.
8. Events, not actors or qualities, are primary.

The orderliness of the universe in the Navaho view was evident in the interrelatedness of things. Moreover, the gods themselves consented to be governed by the laws upon which the universe was constructed in those mythic times. For a spirit to intervene and reverse a course of events, or— as the *deus ex machina* of Greek drama—descend to rescue a hero in peril, was unthinkable. Men controlled the powers of gods through the formulas or rituals, and knowledge of ritual and songs thus meant a power to do. Without such knowledge a person was helpless and powerless against the forces at work in the world. By cultivating harmony in one's relations to gods and men and to the personalized world of nature, the eruption of forces normally held in check by the countervailing powers of the gods could be avoided. One never knew when the universe of forces might be askew, and Navaho recognized that the world could at any time become a dangerous place. There is some evil within both individual and god. Some divinities have no great interest in human needs but seem to exist, as First Woman and First Man, to bring harm. A complementarity of forces turned up in ceremony, poetry, and art where elements occurred in pairs or groups of four. There were recognizable symptoms of the presence of disharmony —a flood, an inner state of tension, constant troubles with relatives and friends, and illness. Through ritual, however, the individual overcame the imbalance that caused the problem, particularly illness. The Navaho view of the universe, others, and self was highly personalized and was demonstrated by concern for what was going on in particular situations and by their definition of moral acts as simply adherence to what tradition prescribed for a particular situation. Navaho morality, in Kluckhohn's view, was tied to public judgment of a specific act and not to conscience. The personalized quality of Navaho life was evidenced in the narrow range of their affiliations; however, personalization of their experience and their relationships did not turn a Navaho into an egoistic type of person. Within the family he found a measure of security and individuality. "One's first loyalty is neither to oneself nor to society in the abstract but rather, in attentuating degrees as one moves outward in the circle of kin, to one's biological and clan relatives" (Kluckhohn 1949b:367).

The Navaho might be less self-conscious than the American, but most of the cultural stream of events in both societies followed a path governed by premises seldom if ever verbalized. Like social Structuralists, Kluckhohn apparently considered verbalization and ceremonious dramatization a conscious rationalization of deeply rooted value premises. In any case, the thought and action feeding the patterned stream of cultural events were derived not from conscious but from unconscious or unverbalized premises (Kluckhohn and Leighton 1962:315).

When cultures met, the core of unstated premises exerted a paramount influence. Government programs for Indians foundered because they failed to understand or correctly interpret the unconscious system of meaning implicit in a particular culture. Unless one could effectively deal with the deep-seated emotional-rational commitments of a cultural design, efforts to program change would end in frustration and failure.

> Actually the tenacity of cultural structure, and especially of the covert structure, is one of the widest and most useful generalizations with which anthropology can provide the administrator. As Boas well says, "In comparison to changes of content of culture the configuration has often remarkable permanency." Sapir has made the same induction as to the conservation of organizational principles in language. (Kluckhohn 1943(45):219)

Kluckhohn seemingly validated the unconscious patterning of culture in his meticulous pursuit of the nonverbalized domains of Navaho life. Ranging the implicit conceptions of the world held by the Navaho, their intuitive value orientations, and the hidden logic of their language categories, Kluckhohn ultimately found his best evidence for his culture theory in the jealous anxieties of witchcraft. *Navaho Witchcraft* (Kluckhohn 1967) was written and revised principally between 1938 and 1942. The thesis was drawn according to psychoanalytic principles: the frustrations of objective reality engendered fears, which were distorted by the anxious imagination of individuals, thereby accelerating a sense of personal insecurity. These fears and insecurities seeped into all personal conflicts, arousing hostile feelings that could not be openly expressed because of the intimate nature and precarious state of Navaho economic life and the need for cooperation. Any hostility must be displaced, and not-to-be-contained aggression was projected onto the world of objects, natural phenomena, and persons. An unconscious suspicion and hostility, generalized in all directions, was fundamental to the Navaho outlook. This unconscious emotional and psychological configuration served as a creative catalyst for aesthetic ceremony that quieted personal insecurities, provided an emotional safety valve, and was an instrument for strengthening the solidarity of the basic survival groups. The witchcraft ideology thus was not a simple outlet for a generalized tension that accompanied the hardships and anxieties of Navaho life. Witchcraft was the specific instrument for releasing tensions stemming from a cultural configuration of suspicion and hostility and interpersonal conflicts characteristic of the social structure. With this conclusion Kluckhohn favored Radcliffe-Brown's social Structural interpretation over Malinowski's psychological interpretation.

Navaho held some rather curious and striking beliefs about witchcraft. Witches were reported to have killed their brothers and sisters, preyed like were-animals upon their siblings, and also killed their siblings as part of the initiation into the company of witches. Certain characteristics of Navaho socialization supplied the cues that explained these beliefs. For one thing, a tender maternal care ended for a child when a new baby arrived, bringing in its wake a sense of rejection and a hostile frustration with regard to the newborn. Older siblings, as custodians of younger children, were prime targets of hostile and ambivalent feelings by the younger. However, this frustration-aggression syndrome between siblings was covert because of the economic necessity of getting along and because open hostility violated a social ideal and brought severe punishment and disapproval from the group. Pointing out that family among the Navaho provided ample cause for both anxiety and aggression, Kluckhohn (1967:109–110) sprinkled his summation with references acknowledging his debt to psychoanalytic theory.

> The unconscious contents which manifest themselves in dreams and in witchcraft phantasies plainly evidence intro-family resentments. But a constant effort must be made to conceal them, and, as Horney says, ". . . the more a child covers up his grudge against his own famiy . . . the more he projects his anxiety to the outside world and thus becomes convinced that the 'world' in general is dangerous and frightening." The anxiety . . . in turn fosters malicious destructiveness, and thus the circle is complete. "Anxiety" and "aggression" are indeed intimately related. . . . So, following Reik, we may suggest that identification with witch-aggressors may be a special instance of identification for the purpose of mastering anxiety.
>
> To sum up: witchcraft is a major Navaho instrument for dealing with aggression and anxiety. It permits some anxiety and some malicious destructiveness to be expressed directly with a minimum of punishment to the aggressor. Still more anxiety and aggression is displaced through the witchcraft pattern assemblage into channels where they are relatively harmless or where, at least, there are available patterns for adjusting the individuals to the new problems created. Individual adjustment merges with group adaptation.

Through the medium of adaptation and adjustment Kluckhohn thus attempted to interrelate functional processes of both the individual and the group. He viewed accommodations at the personal level as feeding a greater or lesser degree of stability into group activities according to the success of personal adjustment. His functional analysis was bolstered with the concepts of "manifest" and "latent" modes derived from the sociologist Merton. Keeping this adaptive-adjustive structuring in mind, he observed how witchcraft tended to swell and subside according to the crisis quality of Navaho life as reflected in their historic experiences with Europeans and their reactions to the pressure to become acculturated. He concluded that the data on Navaho witchcraft indicated that in point of methodology the historical and structural explanations were complementary as well as vital to understanding the extraordinary data he had documented. A time-ignoring structural analysis would miss core problems in economy, social structure, and personality which accompanied contact.

> To understand recent structure we *must* know many of the central events in Navaho history since 1870. Very recent materials are utterly incomprehensible unless we are aware of the disintegration of the native social organization and of the stresses and strains in the economic environment that have resulted from the recent full dependence of Navaho economy upon that of the United States generally. (Kluckhohn 1967:128)

Kluckhohn early became aware of the problem of variation both with regard to personality variants and cultural alternatives. The former problem was taken up in an initial theoretical statement in which the various determinants of personality (biological, physical-environmental, social, cultural) were viewed in terms of a social-personal continuum (universal, communal, role, and idiosyncratic) in order to extract meaningful distinctions (Kluckhohn and Mowrer 1944(46):4). The authors wished to correct the tendency of some professionals to look upon personality as simply a subjective mirror of culture, thereby missing the importance of other factors. The Kluckhohn and Mowrer chart permitted recognition of biopsychic determinants at both the individual and racial level. Admittedly the data were not without ambiguities, but nonetheless Kluckhohn and Mowrer concluded that some of the personality traits which were rather unique to the members of a society derived from their distinctive biological inheritance. The *schema* of this article provided the outline for Kluckhohn's collaboration with the psychoanalyst Henry A. Murray in an anthology entitled, *Personality in Nature, Society and Culture* (1948).

In the absence of a systematic phrasing of the problem of structure and variation, Kluckhohn's statements on the relation of personality to any of the determinants, including culture, were as ambiguous as Sapir's. The generalized accounts of Navaho culture (1946) and of Navaho socialization and personality (1947) undertaken with Dorothea Leighton stressed uniformities traceable to pattern rather than differences induced by temperament or situational repressive syndromes. When Kluckhohn reviewed with Kroeber the concept of culture, the idea of the cultural configuration as an unconscious press for behavioral conformity was paramount. His premise that "A culture is an interdependent system based on linked premises and categories whose influence is greater, rather than less, because they are seldom put in words" (Kluckhohn 1949a:35) guided Kluckhohn on a Structuralist course in his approach to culture and personality.

Though a Structuralist at heart, Kluckhohn must be credited with bringing theoretical perspective and attention to the issue of variation. However, variation for Kluckhohn was usually a derivative of the structured cultural configuration. Thus, in the Foreword to Kaplan's monograph on cross-cultural Rorschach responses, he pointed out that a monolithic cultural determinism of personality could no longer be sustained.

> Members of the Values Project research team must carefully examine these materials as they bear upon the internalization of cultural values. They must give special attention to the wide variation in personality that Dr. Kaplan discovered in each of the four [Southwestern] cultures, for it seems plausible that there is a nearly concomitant variation in the values held and interpreted in personal ways by the component individuals. The very minutiae of responses to the Rorschach blots afford many clues as to the aesthetic canons dominant or present in the four cultures.
>
> With Dr. Kaplan's central conclusion in the personality field that culture influences but does not determine personality, only the extremists among anthropologists-sociologists and psychologists-psychiatrists would disagree. However, the richness of concrete documentation provided in this study takes this generalization beyond the status of an important but highly abstract conclusion. (Kluckhohn 1954:v)

When it came to individual differences in personality, the signal determinants were social and situational, rather than cultural.

> It would seem that culture is the factor of greatest importance in determining distinctive social stimulus value as between groups who possess contrasting life-ways and also, often, contrasting physical appearance. But it would also appear that social or situational factors are, along with genetic ones, of the utmost significance in creating those personal characteristics which distinguish one individual from another within a cultural group. (Kluckhohn 1962a:181)

While one usually found biological and cultural forces combining to guide social interaction, Kluckhohn reminded his readers that not all situations are dependent on culture, nor do culture patterns determine all social acts. This point Sapir (1949e) also made in his article on "Personality," published in the *Encyclopedia of the Social Sciences.*

Following Linton's (1936:272–274) distinction of universals, specialties, alternatives, and individual peculiarities, Kluckhohn (1941:103–130) discriminated a variety of culture patterns for the Navaho. Navaho culture was structured in part by a limited number of compulsory ideal patterns, the majority of patterns ranging from a preferred to typical, alternative, and restricted modes. Typical, preferred, and alternative patterns seemingly described the real culture distinguished by Linton, and their presence and significance would have to be established through frequency tabulations.

Contrast and Complementarity of Values and Cultural Integration: Opler's Themes

The approach of American cultural integrationists, including Kluckhohn, emphasized the pervasive influence of a predominant value or a value-ranked profile. In 1945 Opler challenged this view, observing that cultures held contradictory values which belied the tight order argued by integrationists. Frequently these contrastive values accented a relationship that was complementary rather than in opposition. Among the Hindus, the otherworldliness theme of separation of the spiritual from the temporal needs of the body was countered by the concept of responsible involvement during one's active life. Neither *anashakti* (self-detachment) nor *dharma* (active involvement) was the sole integrater of Hindu life. Both must be understood as points for unifying a consistent set of activities, but at the same time *anashakti* and *dharma* placed limitations on an extreme expression of the other. There was a kind of complementary reinforcement here—a balancing of opposites—that conveyed a degree of integration, but not the pervasive penetration expected from dominant values (Opler 1948).

Opler formulated the concept of "theme" as an analytic tool for understanding the nature of cultural integration. A theme would "denote a postulate or position, declared or implied, and usually controlling behavior or stimulating activity, which is tacitly approved or openly promoted in a society" (Opler 1945(51):198). Such postulates obviously could appear in two modes: existential, or statements about the nature of the world; and normative, or statements about the nature of human relations.

Themes were detected in formal or informal expressions, as in the assignment and timing of activities, prohibitions, and special references that affirmed a valued theme. For example, the Chiricahua Apache formalized the theme of a long life in the rite of walking the adolescent through a life trail of pollen footprints. A girl who failed to undergo the puberty ceremony would have a short life. The theme of male dominance and general superiority was expressed in deferential behavior by females toward men. Women walked behind their men, and the virile strength of men was reflected in the belief that the active turning and thumping of a fetus meant a male birth. Women could not use the sweat lodge nor impersonate the masked mountain spirits. When men played the hoop-and-pole game, women stayed clear. To take a good look at the game made a woman liable to punishment by supernaturals.

However, the theme of male dominance was limited by the practice of matrilocal residence. A man hunted for his parents-in-law as for his wife, but he had to hide from the former because of a strong avoidance custom. Women were not prevented from becoming shamans. Regardless of sex, supernaturals were available to anyone seeking a special knowledge and power to live by. The girl's puberty rite was an important ceremony for the whole tribe, and the restriction of use of the sweat lodge to men was of no great moment, since it played an inconsequential part in Chiricahua ceremony as a whole.

Differential emphasis of themes within the two related societies was useful in viewing differences accompanying contact. For example, the Chiricahua Apache were inclined toward an individual search for power to achieve life goals and a long life, whereas the Jicarilla emphasized ceremonies that assured longevity. Though more insulated from white contact than the Chiricahua, the Jicarilla nonetheless experienced considerable erosion of their ceremonial life and they adhered rigidly to ceremonial protocol. In one case they abandoned a drought-preventing ceremony rather than permit participation by youths who had been shorn of their long hair when attending school. Members of the dancing fraternity must have long hair to symbolize clouds and rain or risk bringing about a prolonged drought to the community. The Chiricahua, on the other hand, faced no problem in incorporating Jesus as another source of supernatural power.

In a later paper contrasting Jicarilla and Lipan Apache life ways, Opler (1959) attempted to show how such closely related groups could vary and differentiate their cultures by a differential treatment of thematic elements. He cited *"selective emphasis, extension, intensification, combination and placement"* as the important processes regulating variation in the expression of themes (Opler 1959(61):955). To handle his analysis, Opler turned to an activity model like that found in the traditional view of a culture complex. The event of death, for example, became organized around a complex of ideas, symbols, artifacts, and behavior (Opler 1959(61):962). These individual elements constituted the components of a larger assemblage—hence, the importance of their placement. Again, various components might be found commonly linked to a number of assemblages. Such a persistent cluster would be referred to as a nexus.

Lipan Apache, for example, avoided burial of kin by hiring outsiders for this fearsome task. Fear of the ghost of dead relatives was a common trait of Apaches, but the extreme avoidance practiced by the Lipan illustrated how this feature was differentially intensified.

The kinds of elements combined also revealed differences between Apache groups. The Apache custom of respect and obedience to affinal kin, and obligations and ritual purification performed at the death of a spouse, provided a striking example. Thus, Jicarilla sons-in-law not only must continue the usual respect and obedience accorded a deceased spouse's relatives but also had to obtain their permission before undergoing purification. Their refusal could block remarriage and full re-entry into the social life of the community. Lipan, on the other hand, separated affinal respect and obedience from ritual contamination and purification. Differential emphases and component combinations thus produced cultural differences despite a common sharing of a value theme centered in death ceremonial. The importance of these distinctions was found at the level of perception—in the way in which the individual was clued into the total environment.

> The Jicarilla and the Lipan may be close in culture and may be representatives of cultures which are not historically far removed from an ancestral way of life. In terms of trait list comparisons and major complexes, the cultures may still seem very similar indeed. Yet the animals they encounter, the birds they watch, the forces of nature that surround them, and even the dreams that occur to them at night have sufficiently diverse meanings for them that they

move in differently organized worlds of symbol, fancy, laughter, and fear. (Opler 1959(61):961)

Opler's efforts to reach a more controlled understanding of cultural similarities and differences through a meticulous analysis of themes signaled an intensification of a concern for the process of variation as well as integration. The new perspective regarding cultural integration also held important implications for the Structuralist approach to the integration of social structure. This discovery was made by a number of investigators, for example, Clifford Geertz (1959) when analyzing "Form and Variation in Balinese Social Structure." Usual approaches to social description and analysis which were identified by Geertz as the "lowest common denominator" and "representative unit" approaches constructed a synthetic average or typical structure. Neither of these tacks worked when applied to Balinese villages.

> The lowest common denominator approach obviously depends on the possibility of finding some fairly simple fundamental patterns—a territorial village, a clan and lineage system, a developed caste structure—which appear over and over again in various parts of the culture area in a broadly similar fashion. But in Bali, though certain patterns are common . . . the form . . . differs so widely that any synthetic picture must . . . have little substantial reality of any kind. One could easily enough construct a "Balinese village" with a "typical" temple setup, hamlet organization, kinship system, irrigation society, title distribution, and so on; but such a composite construct would utterly fail to express the two most fundamental characteristics of Balinese village organization, namely, that these patterns take widely differing forms from village to village, and that their relative importance within any particular village integration varies greatly. For similar reasons, the representative unit approach is also almost certain to be misleading. . . . If we are to discriminate what is really essential and characteristic in Balinese village organization we need to take a somewhat different tack and conceptualize that organization not in terms of invariance in overt structure throughout the whole island, or from place to place within it, but rather in terms of the range of overt structure which it is possible to generate out of a fixed set of elemental components. Form, in this view, is not a fundamental constancy amid distracting and adventitious variation, but rather a set of limits within which variation is contained. (Geertz 1959(61):1009–1010)

Here Geertz raised an old issue, the relation between structure and variation. Should structure be conceived as a stable core surrounded by satellite variations—an archetype, as it were, from which all differences were deviant? Or should structural points in a configuration be plotted at those individual extremes where individual variations ended? The latter view was the correct one in Geertz's judgment. Such a perspective accented a dynamic approach to process and structure and recalled Boas' emphasis on beginning with variation and working through to structure. Geertz's point about Balinese villages exhibiting distinctive characteristics despite sharing a common set of general elements obviously paralleled Opler's effort to understand the subtle divergences of Lipan and Jicarilla culture based on thematic emphases and combinations.

Structure in both these perceptive analyses could no longer be construed as a fixed type. In the eighteenth century physical anthropologists such as Blumenbach used a fixed type as the source from which other biological forms derived through secondary modification. Such modifications were described as degenerations, or deviations from a parental type. However, the approach was not confined to those who tried to define physical types but crept into the thinking of social Structuralists and cultural integrationists. Any time a mode or a mean or average was constructed, thought seemed to slip inadvertently into the notion of a type, from which all other points deviated in greater or lesser degree. Was either view correct, or were both, according to circumstances?

INTUITIVE TRUTHS AND CREATIVE SYNTHESIS: GERMAN CULTURE MORPHOLOGY

When Leo Frobenius joined Oswald Spengler in forming the Institut für Kulturmorphologie (later the Frobenius-Institut), the course was set for applying the German philosophic tradition of romantic idealism to the world of man as a whole. In this view, creative feeling and imagination, not the logic of cold reason, supplied the experiential symbols which guided men's lives. Culture could not be understood from its external components, the form elements, but must be grasped inwardly in the experience-interpreting ideas, or what Spengler came to call "destiny ideas." As art spoke the lnaguage of a world view, so it was with historic cultures.

Emphasis on world view and value ideas brought a broadly holistic approach to the study of individual cultures and a convergence with American culture theorists who turned to values as the staging for cultural integration. At the same time culture morphology became involved in historic-evolutionary issues relating the primitive world to the modern. In *Mythos und Kult bei Naturvölkern* Adolf Jensen (1963), foremost spokesman for culture morphology, outlined the world views of archaic hunters and archaic cultivators. Primary elements of the ancient world views found their way into every continent through migration and diffusion and succeeded each other as intellectual culture strata. Following the distributional principles and analysis of the culture-historical method, those in marginal areas can be expected, both in mode of life and in outlets, to preserve the world views of more archaic times. Regarding the problem of the relative age of religious phenomena, Jensen (1963:223–229), linked shamanism, owing to its psychophysical dualism, with archaic hunters rather than cultivators. Cultivators, on the other hand, held a view of life which was monistic in that man was unified in mind and body by a descent from God. From geographical distributions, Jensen also deduced that this archaic world view included the notion that the dead continued a bodyless existence in association with deity.

The totality of these historic-evolutionary strata provides the culture morphologist with substance from which to extract the general nature and mental processes of man. No fundamental distinctions separate man as primitive and man as civilized—only world views, dominating interests, compatible institutionalizations, and the not so important differences in technology. Generic man is the focal point of interest. In Jensen's view, the vital processes of the human experience are centered in an inner awareness and enrichment, the creation of idea symbols, and the projection of interior experiences into representational forms. Man is a creature moved intuitively to creative synthesis and inclined to stress the meaning of this creative moment of truth to the exclusion of all others.

> At any given creative period . . . only one aspect of reality . . . seizes man's imagination to such an extent that others are obliterated. One particular reality is abstracted from the total reality; the others are never actualized. This is by no means a sign of primitive mentality. . . . Abstraction from other realities is characteristic of all cognition, and archaic formulations are no less cognitive for having arisen from "seizure." We can neither accept the purposive explanation which primitive man is wont to offer for puberty rites, for example, nor can we call them products of a generically different mentality. . . . We must see them as formulations of a perceived reality. Procreation and death are not connected by *logic* only; the close bond between them is a fundamental aspect of life. It was revealed to man in a creative primal event and found formal expression in myth and cult. Puberty ceremonies make statements concerning the essence of male procreativity. They represent the recognition of an order in the human environment. . . . The relationship between a cult and reality must under no circumstances be confused with an explanatory purpose. Man's *Ergriffenheit* by "cosmic phenomena" and other realities, his representations of them in human transformations, his cognitive awareness of a world order and its enactment in the form of a human order, all this is no less purpose-free than the performance of a modern stage play. (Jensen 1963:55–56)

In seeking the primitive meaning of life, Jensen confronted the primitive substance in myth and cult. From these could be extracted the fundamental propositions of the primitive charater of life which frequently eluded the scientific investigator confronted with secondary psychological rationalizations by which later generations imputed purpose to their behavior. Like Boas and Malinowski, but not for the same reasons, Jensen concluded that the original meaning of rites was not accessible to the ethnologist through contemporary informants. Following Frobenius, Jensen saw the history of any world view and cult as passing from a primary creative phase to a secondary phase of application. The creative phase described the florescence of the world view and associated institutions, while the phase of application recorded a falling away, a degeneration of an exhausted imaginative impulse with completely altered significance and function (Jensen 1963:vii). Some of the primary creative forms and ideology still persisted as integrated parts of the cultural continuum, but their publicly stated purposes were hard to understand, anachronistic, and even absurd (Jensen 1963:vii–viii). "Survivals" of earlier culture strata, as Tylor pointed out, occur in every culture, and their apparent absence of meaning is because they occur out of their conceptual contexts (Jensen 1963:18).

Where then can the ethnologist find the raw material for his analysis of the primitive world views? There is no other source than myth and cult, where the central ideas of archaic times are enunciated and also communicated in the symbols of ceremony. Jensen's emphasis on the intuitive and holistic nature of the cognitive experiences of archaic men is reminiscent of Lévy-Bruhl's distinctions of the mystical prelogical mentality of the primitive. But Jensen rejected invidious comparisons of archaic man in his intellectual processes as an inferior antecedent to men of civilized logic. The two cognitions, as Lévy-Bruhl and others found, are incomparable. In romantic mood Jensen rejected the scientific mode and elevated the intuitive mode of archaic men to the superior position. Why? Out of this intuitive grasp of meaning and relationships creativity springs and new cultural forms appear (Jensen 1963:46, 320). Archaic man is thus very much a poet instinctively in search of great truths.

In the primitive world view, procreation and death dominated the imaginative experience, and these are the themes of cult activity. Formulation of the significance of these profound experiences must have been the work of creative personalities to whom the establishment of order or part-order in the universe is so commonly attributed in myth (Jensen 1963:67, 292). The primitive drama is the creative ordering of the world out of disorder, the forming of the world for man, as it were (Jensen, 1963:65). Jensen marveled that archaic men anticipated the transformation of an alien and unformed order into one suitable for men long before geology, paleontology, and archeology provided the scientific confirmation. However, the ancient mythic consciousness never grasped the idea of continuous progression and developmental stages. The mythic event was unique and in its magnificence served to sanction the present.

In the culture morphology of Jensen, culture types appear as a succession of integrative ideas and associated institutions, such as death and mourning, rooted in deeply felt perceptions about the nature of the world and its order and processes. These striking insights provided not only the basis for man's need to communicate but also the type of experience he sought and communicated in symbolic form. Societies were ordered so as to regenerate and communicate these life-enriching truths. Jensen pointed to primal psychological experiences involving man's relation to the natural world as the wellspring from which he drew inspiration and ideas for the organization of his social and cultural life. In effect, he turned the major proposition of social and cultural Structuralists around and, in so doing, he established a common meeting ground with the older psychological Developmentalists. However, he claimed no affinity with them.

Jensen's intuitive value and world view approach to cultural integration converged with trends in culture theory in the United States. Both American culture theorists and Jensen were interested in the value principles and implicit understandings which integrated cultural systems. However, unlike Americanists, he was not interested in particular historic cultures. Rather, his morphological approach emphasized a panoramic evolutionary sweep in which he contrasted the world view of archaic man with civilized man. There was possibly a unitary emphasis in the diverse approaches of culture morphology, social Structuralism, bioculturalism, culture integrationalism, and ethnopsychoanalysis in their approaches to the human situation. All agreed that a deep-seated emotional and psychological experience supplied the energy directives by which the social and cultural were organized and provided the substance of their symbolic and visual forms.

For culture morphology, the basic element of the primal human experience was an intuitive and imaginatively creative understanding of man's relation to the natural world. For social Structuralists, it was a matter of a socially engendered statement of solidarity. In Malinowski's bioculturalism, human institutions were rooted in survival needs and anxieties about the self which were experienced at great moments of crisis, such as death. American culture theorists stressed intuitive covert or implicit assumptions through which people looked at the world and organized their relations to others. Ethnopsychoanalysts described the basic structuring of personalities as a configuration of unconscious psychological and emotional constellations. The common emphasis on intuitive or unconscious conditionings meant that (1) men are unable to grasp the real basis for their actions or the inner need for this activity; (2) the inner experience is lived out in partial, if not complete, fulfillment through symbolic forms that have meanings only within the social context. Man is a social animal, and his unconscious strain toward self-realization depends upon the social community for fulfillment. In one sense the social experience may be seen as rationalizing the unconscious experience, or raising it to the level of the conscious. This was the preeminent function of ritual and ritualized symbols to which social Structuralists gave so much attention.

CULTURAL INTEGRATION AND PURPOSIVE CHANGE

Benedict's holistic approach to the phenomenon of culture obviously sharpened a trend already underway in anthropology and in related fields. In sociology, for example, Pitirim Sorokin (1937–1941) set forth the analysis of sociocultural systems and their dynamics of change, distinguishing a "mechanical" structural-functional and a "logico-meaningful" (stylistic) integration. In *A Study of History*, Toynbee (1934–1939) laid out the historic-evolutionary growth and disintegration of centralizing value patterns which fueled all great civilizations. The fate of civilizations depended on their capacity to maintain an inner fiber capable of generating the creative response necessary to overcome deadly challenges. Like an army that retreats to fight again, civilizations sometimes withdrew or retrenched, then extended themselves in a fresh engagement. Withdrawal and reengagement often occurred in the biographies of the great prophets. However, the interior structure, like any organic thing, ultimately broke down because of internal schisms and contradictions caused by rigidities of structure and consequent failure to adapt to altered circumstances. In their introversive defense of status quo, leaders lost their will to lead and lost contact with an internal proletariat disenchanted with the state of things. Events followed a deterministic inevitability initiated by a time of troubles, when social and political disorganization increased.

> This secession of the led from the leaders may be regarded as a loss of harmony between the parts which make up the whole *ensemble* of the society. In any whole consisting of parts a loss of harmony between the parts is paid for by the whole in a corresponding loss of self-determination. This loss of self-determination is the ultimate criterion of breakdown. (Toynbee 1947:279)

The stress on inner-structured self-direction voiced by both Sorokin and Toynbee in matters of cultural change can be picked up in a like emphasis on the pattern and unity of the individual personality by the psychoanalyst Alfred Adler. It was also present in the insistence of Gestalt psychologists on the unity of psychosensory experience as a function of the physiological ordering of processes in the brain. Both animals and men, for example, organized their experience in paired groups, and it was this organizing process intervening between stimulus and response which Behavioralists failed to appreciate in their simplistic particularistic interpretations (Köhler 1959:117–120).

In his *Configurations of Culture Growth* Kroeber (1944) reiterated the consensus that structural principles held the key to the destiny of cultures. Stylized patterns were limited in the range of possible variations, and when these were used up, creative genius had only imitation to sustain a declining performance. Something more than a concatenation of genetic accidents, Kroeber argued, accounted for the multiplication of genius that collaborated to make an age like that of Pericles or Augustus. This could be nothing less than the culture pattern, and the fact that the pulsative clustering of national genius was distributed irregularly throughout the historic course of Greek and Roman cultures added weight to this conclusion.

Kroeber anchored the stability of culture patterns to unconscious learnings, but the elaboration of pattern variation achieved by a creative genius required a conscious rationalization of pattern. Herskovits' view of culture focus and Linton's culture orientations converged on the process of pattern elaboration taken up by Kroeber in *Configurations of Culture Growth*. In the integration of culture patterns into a wider whole, however, ethos or the value system was crucial. Ethos defined the dominant values and ideals of a culture which determined how and when individuals would act. Without ethos, neither culture nor individual could develop a life-style (Kroeber 1948a:294).

> ... the ethos of Italian Renaissance culture was sensuous and passionate, but that of the northern-European Reformation, puritan and ascetic. Hindu civilization is not only otherworldly but mystical, rationalizing, and extravagant in its ethos; Chinese, this worldly, prosily moralistic, and matter-of-fact. The Japanese ethos differs from the Chinese in putting more emphasis on action, precision of form, and neatness.

Inner form, or ethos, contrasted with outer form, or eidos. Though he did not use a biological analogue, Kroeber's ethos corresponded to genotype and eidos to phenotype. As genotype held the stream of descendants to a basic reproductive continuity, so ethos determined the goals, values, and the direction of cultural activity and achievements. Ethos, in Kroeber's view, was like a charter which outlined the aspirations, procedures, type of creative achievement, and even destiny of the culture. Or, in another view, ethos was a kind of personality core, or psychological and emotional complex, which housed the guidance system of a culture.

Kroeber's view of pattern and structure conformed to Structuralist thinking generally in that an emotional and psychological complex constituted the foundation upon which structural form was constructed. This same foundational sentiment supported the continuities and directionality found in structured relations.

SUMMARY

The path taken by culture theorists to the broad issue of cultural integration began with an analytic focus on the geographic distribution and historical relations of culture elements or traits. They started with particulars and edged in the direction of systemic integration. Culture and personality investigation continued this systemic orientation in seeking to relate the constructs of modal personality and national character in a causal way to culturally structured experiences, or to see culture forms as derivatives of the personality organization.

American prehistorians followed the same route as culture historians to the broader issue of cultural systems. They first laboriously plotted the distribution and historic relations of artifact forms and assemblages at similar points in time and in chronological order. Through urban development in the New World they became sensitized to the rise of regional and interregional cultural traditions characteristic of nuclear America. Only then did prehistorians achieve the perspective of an extensive and complicated network of relationships exhibiting the character of an evolving cultural system. Regional variants unified by distinctive art styles and trait assemblages (horizons) were drawn into a joint development with other regions, owing to the influence of a general tradition generalized in historic depth as well as in space. The evolutionary growth of such interregional configurations (Bennett's area co-traditions) was comparable to a cultural tradition such as Western civilization, with its Greco-Roman, transitional, medieval, commercial, and industrial periods. Beyond this, prehistorians noted how religion shaped the integrative trends of these evolving co-traditions. Religion provided causes for why things happened, the substantive form of ceremony and of public architecture, the rhythmic control of economic activity and surplus use, and the basis for social and administrative distinctions. Later displacement of the religious-economic-political complex by a political-military-economic arrangement accented shifting emphases wihin systemic configurations. Steward (1949), in his discussion of integrative processes, focused on a core institutional complex anchored to the economy, since basic survival needs and comforts were ever uppermost in the minds of people and provided the basis for socioeconomic differentiation.

The shift from a religiously oriented complex to one accenting political-military considerations did not eliminate religion entirely from the institutionalized configuration. Political leaders in exercising a power right readily merged political power with religious sanctions, inasmuch as religious belief and practice continued to exert a general influence in the private and public life of the people. In these institutional trends and power shifts there was no significant correlation with a revolution in the knowledge system comparable to the use of science in the Western world and the challenge it posed to theology as the mediator of knowledge. Hence, neither enthnologists nor prehistorians were concerned with the directional influence of knowledge systems which Comte, Sorokin, and Northrop stressed in the epoch development of Western civilization. For anthropologists generally the knowledge system was incorporated in the broader spectrum of a world view, or of value orientations. Redfield was a partial exception, since in his Yucatecan study he described a trend from the sacred to the secular that reflected the dominance of pragmatic technical interpretations over the sacred. However, such a modification in the knowledge factor was not central to Redfield's explanation, which emphasized the general breakup of the sacral-moral outlook of the folk owing to contact with the secularized life of the city.

Exponents of the various approaches to cultural integration usually considered their emphases and methodology distinct from other approaches. However, it was impossible to launch any analysis without touching base with the substantive domains of other approaches (Voget 1964). For example, Benedict's psychocultural analysis of necessity established a coordinate relation with a primary institutionalized pattern through which primary personality types were developed. Culture theorists seemed to agree that folk societies were integrated by one or, at most, a few dominant value orientations. The primary institution for the Northwest Coast was the potlatch, for the Plains, warfare, and for the Southwest Pueblos, religion, and each correlated with a primary status personality. Social Structuralists likewise viewed the social order as unified by a dominant value which they described as collective solidarity.

The Structuralist orientation to cultural integration led American ethnologists to conclusions about the nature of structure that coincided with those of social Structuralists. At the heart of the human experience was a deep-seated emotional-valuational commitment. This psychological configuration anchored the institutional core and brought stability and continuity to its operations. At the same time, the influence of this configuration gradually permeated the culture and increased the degree of consistency, coherence, and balance. For social and cultural Structuralists unconscious processes and conditioned responses supplied the psychological backup. Psychoanalytic Structuralists likewise grounded their basic institutions and personality modalities in emotional-psychological constellations and unconscious conditionings.

American culture theorists had hardly attained their awareness of structural integration when theoretical shifts accompanying the differentiation of specializations breached their Structuralist model. Opler's description of contrastive and complementary thematic formulations signaled the beginning of a change in perspective. Yet the exploration of values and integrative processes significantly extended anthropological experience with regard to the structural organization and processes of society and culture. The formal order of structure, through which parts were linked according to their functions, was seen to be penetrated simultaneously by organizational principles of value.

The two modes of integration, functional and valuational, were vital to the operation of any system. Moreover, the structuring of forms and relations obviously must be considered a dynamic and intrinsic attribute of the human reality. The only serious criticism of cultural integrationists was their exaggeration of the extent of structural consistency and structural determinism.

12

The Psychoanalysis of Culture

INTRODUCTION

The rise of psychoanalysis brought new efforts to find the meaning of culture in psychological processes. The initial attempt was made by Freud himself in *Totem and Taboo* (1913), where he connected both primitive and contemporary neuroticism to a primeval Oedipal conflict event. In his last work, *Moses and Monotheism* (1939) Freud maintained a steady position, asserting that the transmission of unconscious psychic effects were part of the hereditary process from that primal day to the present.

On the Continent, the British psychologist W. H. R. Rivers (1920) invoked the Freudian concepts of repression and of the unconscious to explain the operation of instinct manifested in wartime neuroses observed in soldiers. C. G. Seligman and his wife Brenda also developed a keen interest in the application of psychiatric concepts to human behavior, especially in the interpretation of incest. In his association with Rivers and the Seligmans, Bronislaw Malinowski made himself thoroughly conversant with Freudian theory and accepted its basic tenets about the nature of psychological processes (for example, ambivalence) in the presence of conflict situations. However, finding himself in a mother-right society (Trobriands), Malinowski disputed the universality of the classic Oedipal situation. He noted that in the Trobriands incestuous desires of the male focused on sister rather than mother. Moreover, the thrust of Oedipal hostility was directed at the authoritarian mother's brother rather than the father (Malinowski 1927a, *The Father in Primitive Psychology* and 1927b, *Sex and Repression in Savage Society*). Since the social structuring of interpersonal relations channeled the generation of tensions, so culture, in Malinowski's view, must be substituted for the mass psyche linked to the past by a Lamarckian inheritance of acquired dispositions on which Freud relied to account for the patterned replication of psychosexual and psychosocial problems from generation to generation. Nonetheless, as Fortes (in Firth 1964:173) observed, Malinowski owed much to the Freudian psychology of interpersonal relations for his perceptive deductions and hypotheses regarding incest, family solidarity, and conflict control.

The penetration of Freudian theory into North American ethnology was equally spotty owing to the behavioristic orientation of culture historicists. Freud's theory, aside from the dubious racial phylogeny, was far too systematized for Boas. However, in the early twenties Edward Sapir warned his fellow-ethnologists to remember that their cultural-historical constructions neglected one of the most important datums about culture— that it was the individual alone who experienced culture and that individuals were the medium for transmitting culture from one generation to the next. The impulse to find a psychological typology for cultures, to which Sapir pointed, was communicated to Ruth Benedict and her close associate Margaret Mead. Translation of the cultural process into a personality psychodynamics was well underway during the thirties when the psychiatrist Abram Kardiner drew a core of American anthropologists into a psychoanalysis of cultures which included Cora DuBois, Ralph Linton, Ruth Benedict, and Clyde Kluckhohn. By the mid-forties, the psychoanalytic impulse tapered off when it became clear that the neo-Freudian model provided too narrow a base for understanding the diversity of any culture. Nonetheless, the entrance of psychoanalytic theory reinforced ahistorical trends and a consensus that human nature as a psychological variable must be included in any explanation of custom, culture change, and the transmission of tradition. The real contribution of psychoanalysis was not the substantiation of universal complexes and their symbolic correlates but the inclusion of negative conditioning as vital to the learning process and personality formation. This led to a merger of psychoanalytic theory and behavioristic stimulus-response psychology. In this marriage, psychoanalytic theory provided the hypotheses and behavioral psychology the mechanisms for explaining effects. When this was achieved during the late thirties, culture and personality investigators were primed for a wide-ranging exploration of social relationships, human relations, and the role of personal character in formulating and reformulating social relations and symbolic behaviors expressive of personality needs and conflicts. In effect, the psychoanalytic perspective reversed the culture-individual equation central to culture theory and derived culture from a personal psychological source.

Discussion of the psychoanalytic contributions to personality and culture relations in this chapter begins with a brief orientation to psychoanalytic theory. The presentation then is organized into four major areas. First, a brief historic sketch of the incorporation of psychoanalytic theory in the personality-culture equation introduces the important Columbia University seminars initiated by Abram Kardiner and the stimulus they brought to formulation of a model to be followed in personality and culture fieldwork. A discussion of efforts by John Dollard, Neal Miller, and others to unify behavioral and psychoanalytic theory follows. The second section details psychoanalytic attempts to explain the integration of culture as a product of infantile and early childhood conflicts and anxieties that find symbolic expression in the institutions of the society. Discussion of the role of anxiety in the social process is followed by psychoanalytic exploration of the conflictual ambiguities of culture-contact situations and the personality disturbances that stem from anxious irresolution and fear of the outside world. Third, efforts to test psychoanalytic hypotheses cross-culturally, notably the testing by Whiting and Child of probable relationships between the diagnosis and treatment of disease and positive and negative conditionings experienced during infancy and early childhood, are surveyed. Fourth, psychoanalytic perspective on the self in an evolutionary context is discussed, followed by an assessment of psychoanalytic contributions to a more inclusive grasp of the nature of culture processes and the interrelations of culture and personality.

FUNDAMENTALS OF PSYCHOANALYTIC THEORY

Though clinically centered, psychoanalytic theory dealt with the human personality on a universalistic plane. Man is described as the warring ground of three personality components—id, ego, and superego (Figure 12-1). The id was anchored to basic biological need impulses centered in survival and gratification. The superego represented internalized norms in the nature of commitments as to what was right as against what was wrong. The superego thus could be equated with a socialized conscience, and its censorship was directed largely against the partisan desires of the id. The ego, identified with rational operations, served as the balance wheel between the irrational demands of both id and superego. If ego failed to maintain its mediative role, there was danger that either the id or the superego would spread its influence and take over the dynamic field of personality interactions. In either case, the personality would be damaged; and if the war between id and superego finally forced ego to take flight, there would be nothing to rule the personality but the unconscious. Hence the psychoanalytic concern for building a strong ego in order that the individual could think his way through crises and maintain a flexible and steady performance as a rational, coping being.

Unfortunately, as Freud viewed the situation, damage to the human personality occurs so early in life that the growing child is incapable of coping with stressful occasions. Parents, with their own damaged personalities, are equally unprepared to sympathize and empathize with the child in crisis. Moreover, the whole problem of adjustment is complicated by

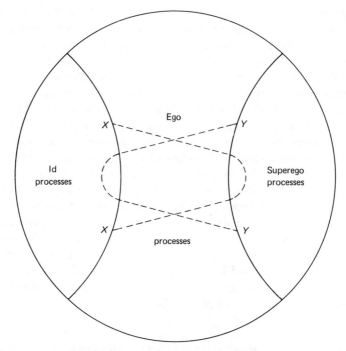

Figure 12-1. Freudian model of personality structure.

The stitching of a baseball admirably distinguishes the tripartite structure of personality conceived by Freudians. Rational ego processes mediate the biopsychic need impulses of the id and the socially induced restraints of the superego. Points x-x and y-y describe a hypothetical situation in which id and superego are in serious confrontation, preempting some of ego's ground and reducing rational effectiveness as the unconscious processes associated with id and superego take over. If in imagination one can conceive of a conquest of ego and superego terrain by expansion of x-x, id processes would come to dominate personal character, and egocentric tendencies might lead to psychopathology. If, to the contrary, superego processes should expand at the expense of ego and id, the personality could be overwhelmed by an overriding sense of guilt and fixated on symbolic acts of absolution.

The complexity of relations in the above diagram obviously are simplified. Id, ego, and superego are in constant interaction and cannot be conceived as bounded static entities. The life of personality begins with the domineering demands of the id and then moves on to an engagement with superego restraints, hopefully resulting in a rational accommodation of both demands in a realistic way. However, with their concept of fixation, Freudians portrayed personality as organized largely by reactive syndromes associated with biopsychic foci, notably the oral, anal, and genital areas. Hence, the ideal of man-the-rational-and-wise is a dream. Yet, when psychoanalysts speak in terms of a strong ego, or the necessity to strengthen the ego, they obviously are calling for a greater role for rational processes in the operations of personality.

The tripartite arrangement of personality conceived by Freud bears a striking resemblance to Plato's conception of man, where again reason was accorded first place as an arbiter.

unconscious processes that reach back into the phylogenetic psychology of man—to that original Oedipal moment described by Freud when those deprived of their sexual birthright seized the tyrannical patriarch of their band and slew him. Henceforth, the human unconscious bristled with towering father figures and tempting mother ideals that in dreams were so haunting or threatening that they must be destroyed, ravished, rejected, or accepted in humble submission. In waking life father and mother figures introduced the unconscious drama into daily interpersonal relations by springing the repressive trapdoors by which they were confined and raising anxieties with wish fulfillments that could not be. These complications presented a real danger that the unrealistic failures and solutions of childhood would become so fixated that they would dominate the individual in maturity. Because of fixations flowing from imperfections in adaptation to the universal biosocial contexts of nurturance (oral), bowel-bladder control (anal), sex (Oedipal), and aggression-submission (authority), adults reached a physiological-psychological maturity without attaining psychosocial maturity. As immature personalities they were destined to a lifetime of compulsively defensive and aggressive maneuvers both with themselves and with others.

The universal processes psychoanalysts attached to their archetypal man obviously required universal experiences that would produce uniformities in response. Hence the appeal to biologically rooted experiences associated with infancy and early childhood socialization. Uniformities in process meant uniformities in products, and this permitted development of a universal key to unlock the symbolic doors of unconscious intellection and impulse action for mankind as a whole. Owing to their clinical orientation and because they used the model of archetypal man, psychoanalysts tended to analyze an individual patient and then transfer these conclusions to the behavior of individuals at large, thereby confirming the universality of their conclusions. Variation in culture content thus was no bar to extracting the meaning of actions of similar form. However, immediate application of psychoanalytic theory by cultural anthropologists was slowed by Freud's insistence on a phylogenetic inheritance and acceptance of the idea that savage emotional and intellectual adjustment was fixated at the child level. Such ideas, along with the unconscious drama of life and death instincts emphasized by Freud, were dropped overboard when neo-Freudians addressed themselves to the psychoanalysis of cultures.

AMERICAN CULTURE HISTORICISM AND PERSONALITY DYNAMICS

Transformation of American culture theory progressed from a preoccupation with trait distributions and their historical relations into a search for the integrates of cultures and the influence of culture on personality. This shift in focus coincided with the rise of structural-functional theory. Outwardly it appeared that American culture historicists were no better equipped to move into the domains of cultural integration and of culture and personality than their Continental counterparts. However, Americanist concern with the processes of acceptance and rejection of culture traits linked their understandings to psychological processes—or rather to sociopsychological processes. This turned their attention, haltingly at first, to the process of enculturation and then to the typical enculturated individual. Their studious rejection of anything evolutionary led them to contradict the idea that sociopsychological processes found in the culture of primitive man were any different from those recognizable in more complex cultures. Americanists who followed the leadership of Boas focused on process and a narrow range of problem definition. This prevented them from directing their energies to the grand designs of cultural-historical reconstruction engaged by *Kulturkreislehre*. True, Frobenius, who first defined the *Kulturkreis*, turned his back on culture-historical research and focused on the inner structure or soul of cultures. However, Frobenius' acceptance of the organic model for the growth and decline of cultures meant that the problem definition would not include the process of enculturation experienced by typical individuals.

Boas influenced the psycho-enculturative trend in American culture theory by discussion of cultural-psychological processes. He communicated to his students the stimulus to examine the processes which fashioned the individual into the typical person of that culture. In his Foreword to Mead's (1928) *Coming of Age in Samoa*, Boas called attention to the habituative standardization induced by culture, but at the same time stressed that reactions of individuals to cultural standards should be a part of the ethnographic venture. One virtue of Mead's effort was that it came to grips with the problems and satisfactions of Samoan youth reaching for adulthood. For Boas another virtue in the work was that it denied the biopsychological determinism resident in psychoanalytic theory and affirmed the "suspicion long held by anthropologists, that much of what we ascribe to human nature is no more than a reaction to the restraints put upon us by our civilisation" (Boas 1928a).

Psychological analysis of culture followed by Americanists actually edged the study of culture to the brink of reductionism. There was a real danger that culture would be derived not out of historical process but out of common human personality predispositions. This was the direction taken by Benedict (1930) beginning with "Psychological Types in the Cultures of the Southwest" and by her colleague Mead. This theoretical turn in contradiction to "Papa" Boas is curious and illustrates the point made by Mead (1959:209) that Ruth Benedict never became a rubber stamp of her mentor's thinking. Indeed, Mead (1959:209–210) continues,

> her work represents a marked contrast to his. Boas had long ago rejected the "deep" intuitive plunges of German scholarship and philosophy; but in these same dubious sources Ruth Benedict now found inspiration. Under her master's somewhat jaundiced eye she turned to Nietzsche, Spengler and Dilthey,

whose ideas she somehow blended with the Boas tradition of intensive field work in a particular area. From this unexpected amalgam she managed to fashion her famous *Patterns of Culture.*

In 1934 Sapir (1949e:561) correctly drew the inference that psycho-analytic theory precluded any serious treatment of the relation of culture to personality. Stress on hereditary biopsychic foundations coupled with the idea of childhood fixation left personality formation largely a precul-tural phenomenon.

> The psychiatrist's concept of personality is to all intents and purposes the reactive system exhibited by the precultural child, a total configuration of reactive tendencies determined by heredity, and by prenatal and postnatal con-ditioning up to the point where cultural patterns are constantly modifying the child's behavior. The personality may be conceived of as a latent system of reaction patterns and tendencies to reaction patterns finished shortly after birth or well into the second or third year of the life of the individual....
> The genesis of personality is in all probability determined largely by the anatomical and physiological make up of the individual but cannot be entirely so explained. Conditioning factors, which may roughly be lumped together as the social psychological determinants of childhood, must be considered as at least as important in the development of personality as innate biological factors.

With this statement Sapir acknowledged the biological structure as a rock-bottom foundation for personality. However, this biological given was subject to cultural modifications, and the cultural input was of equal importance to the biological. If cultural conditioning were to have its profound influence on personality formation, the idea of fixation intrinsic to psychoanalytic theory must be challenged and eliminated. However, the concept of fixation need not be discarded entirely, provided it could be applied to later stages in the enculturation of the individual as he con-fronted the culturally defined discontinuities to which Benedict (1938) called attention. A developmental-maturational approach like that of Gesell and Ilg might prove useful in measuring the degree to which cultures were compatible or incompatible with normal biological and mental growth (Mead 1947).

However, the linguistic model from which Sapir drew his understand-ings of the enculturative process accorded little place to biopsychic and maturational determinants. Language acquisition demonstrated that indi-viduals gradually acquire their normative patternings and expectations by processes of which they have no real awareness. In "The Unconscious Patterning of Behavior in Society," Sapir (1949c:558–559) noted how "A healthy unconsciousness of the forms of socialized behavior to which we are subject is as necessary to society as is the mind's ignorance, or better unawareness of the workings of the viscera to the health of the body." Sapir deplored the way in which culture historicists analyzed culture traits and manipulated culture objects without dealing with the real problem—

notably, the relation of the individual to culture and the shaping of personality by culture. From Sapir's viewpoint, it was inevitable and necessary
that anthropologists should direct their attention to psychological characterizations of culture. To demonstrate the need for "The Emergence of the
Concept of Personality in Anthropology," Sapir (1949e) contrasted the
extroverted Eskimo and American Indian cultures with the introverted
Hindu.

FORMAL LINKAGE OF ANTHROPOLOGY AND PSYCHIATRY: THE COLUMBIA UNIVERSITY SEMINAR

By the mid-thirties intellectual forces clued to the study of cultures as
psychological systems developed into a theoretical trend. An increasing
number of definitions of culture appeared which stressed a life design,
configuration, symbolic conventions, and streams of ideas (see Kroeber
and Kluckhohn 1963:118–138). Attempts were made to unify the behavioral and psychiatric approaches into a more comprehensive theory of
learning (for example, Dollard and others 1939; Sears 1943). Actually the
pleasure-pain principle offered a common ground for Freudians and behaviorists to exchange ideas with regard to learning and personality formation.
The intellectual stirring of the thirties provided a favorable environment
for Abram Kardiner to draw cultural anthropologists of Columbia University and psychiatrists of the New York Psychoanalytic Institute into a
mutual exchange centered in personality and culture. In the seminar anthropologists furnished ethnographic descriptions for psychologcal analysis
(for example, Zuni—Benedict and Bunzel; Trobriand, Chukchee, and
Kwakiutl—DuBois; Tanala and Marquesa—Linton). It was soon apparent
that anthropologists normally did not gather situational data relevant to
the psychoanalyic approach to personality dynamics—hence the field study
of Alor by DuBois (1944), whose interest in personality psychodynamics
and culture had been aroused by Benedict, Mead, and Sapir.

In its publications the Seminar did not produce an amalgam of anthropological and psychoanalytic theory. For this Kardiner (1939) apologized,
but apparently he viewed the operation as a trial adaptation of psychoanalytic theory and method to the study of institutions. This was a serious
limitation, and he admitted that the psychoanalytic approach was better
at dealing with frustrations than with positive organization of personality
around satisfactions. The latter represented the heart of the anthropological approach at the time, in that the individual was viewed as a cultured
product of positive and negative reinforcement.

The historic importance of the Columbia Seminar was not just that it
constituted the first attempt to establish a bridge between anthropology
and psychiatry. It also illustrated the way in which common problems may
draw disciplines together despite theoretical differences. At the time Linton
(1939) expressed surprise at the psychological coherence of institutions

brought to light by psychoanalytic analysis, but he later reaffirmed his basic anthropological convictions in *The Cultural Background of Personality* (1945a). However, anthropological acceptance of the idea that an emotional component was responsible for the origin and stability of culture patterns provided a base for exploring the enculturated personality as an emotional organization. An increasing number of anthropologists suspected that neither the emotional basis for pattern retention nor personality formation could be explained solely by simple conditioning. Moreover, the commonalities of human nature to which psychoanalysis pointed re-introduced anthropologists to an issue of long standing in their discipline, but one which had become obscured by emphasis on cultural diversities. As Kluckhohn (1962b :350–351) observed when discussing Navaho dreams,

> I still believe that some of the cautions uttered by Boas and others on the possible extravagance of interpretations in terms of universal symbolism, completely or largely divorced from minute examination of cultural context, are sound. But the facts uncovered in my own field work and that of my collaborators have forced me to the conclusion that Freud and other psychoanalysts have depicted with astonishing correctness many central themes in motivational life that are universal. The styles of expression of these themes and much of the manifest content are culturally determined, but the underlying psychologic drama transcends cultural difference.

The entrance of cultural anthropology into a psychoanalytic exploration of personality and culture processes actually constituted an effort in the building of a general theory. It marked the translation of culture historicism into a structural-functional form, and the decline in culture and personality studies appears correlated with the decline in Structuralism.

PERSONALITY PSYCHODYNAMICS AND CULTURE: ABRAM KARDINER

In *The Individual and His Society* (1939) Kardiner relied heavily on Linton's data to illustrate his method and to test the utility of psychoanalytic social psychology. A redefinition of the extreme phylogenetic-ontogenetic approach laid out by Freud and continued by Roheim (1925, 1945) seemed necessary, since it excluded an effective view of the dynamic interrelations of personality and culture. Under the original Freudian view, cultures were personalities writ large, organized by anal, oral, phallic, anal sadistic, and similar drive emphases dominant in the individual personality. On the opposite extreme were those who saw culture as molding the person into its mirror image. Kardiner preferred a middle ground and set himself and his associates the task of testing the view

> that the individual stands midway between institutions which mold and direct his adaptation to the other world, and his biological needs, which press for

gratification. This viewpoint places a heavy emphasis on institutions and stresses the significant role they play in creating the adaptive systems of the individual. The institutions in this view can be identified and their effects on the individual traced. But the coordinates against which all these effects are charted are the basic biologically determined needs of man. (Kardiner 1939:17)

Yet when Kardiner approached the problem of ego formation, he proceeded under typical Freudian premises: (1) the predominant influence of early experience on character formation; (2) social norms as barriers to impulse gratification; (3) frustrative reactions prominent in the unconscious organization of the personality; and (4) the release of unconscious impulse in a symbolic behavior of some kind.

To give himself more specificity and methodological control, Kardiner defined a unit of socially organized experience which would generate "some disturbance in the individual or the group" (Kardiner 1939:7). Individuals sharing the same kinds of institutions developed a groundwork of experience organized as a "basic personality structure." Institutions were of two orders, primary and secondary. The former generated critical and inescapable problems of adaptation for the person, while the latter provided the institutionalized release mechanisms (Kardiner 1939:345). The relation between the primary and secondary institutions was direct and dynamic. Frustrations derived from the primary institutions aroused deep-seated hates, fears, and anxieties, which, in the presence of a reality need for repression, required ways of releasing such hatred or special rewards to make renunciation palatable (Kardiner 1939:41). At this point, wrote Kardiner (1939:133),

The concept of basic personality structure ... becomes an important tool in our research. It is qualified to act as a mirror of the institutions which helped to create it as well as the adaptive weapons of the individual once it is established. This concept obviates the hopeless task of dealing directly with biological forces within the individual, and confronts us with the finished products of the interaction of biological forces and external realities. Such end results are the only forms in which we ever get to know "instincts" or drives. Thus if we encounter in the folklore of a society a constellation like the Oedipus complex, instead of leaping from this phenomenon directly to some biologically determined drive, we can proceed to examine the conditions in the actual experience of the individual which contribute to the formation of such a constellation. As conditions vary, so will the basic personality structure. This latter concept lends itself, moreover, to empirical and comparative methods.

Kardiner's redefinition of the concept of institution was essential to establishment of institutionalized correlates for the universal contexts stressed in psychoanalysis. Thus, maternal nurturance, weaning, sexual discipline, and the association of clothing, sphincter control, and cleanliness all qualified as institutions (Kardiner 1939:22–23; see Figure 12-2).

In situations where repressive mechanisms did not dominate and where, in consequence, substitute gratifications usually were not found, individuals tended to be more direct, competitive, and conflictive in their approaches to problem situations. This could be seen in the goals of

Western society where success was of utmost importance because with it came the assurance of adequate self-esteem. And self-esteem was intrinsic to the appreciation of others.

> There are innumerable forms to which the idea of success can be attached. The "narcissistic" goals of prestige are identified in values of power to influence or exploit others, in the great fear of being the underdog, and in the powerful drive to be superior. Since, in democracies, subsistence values and prestige values are intimately bound together, the current goals are for the greater part directed into economic channels for the common man.
>
> The interference with prestige goals in our culture is therefore a potent source of intrasocial hostility, because the ideas by which these goals are connoted, the emotions that accompany them and the drives necessary to achieve them are not easily subject to repression. In fact, the reverse is true. They are not only not subject to repression, but, for a time at least, were commonly encouraged. In the absence of illusions which make it possible for some individuals to defer gratification of these goals, the social conflict about their achievement becomes all the sharper. (Kardiner 1939:76–77)

The illusion Kardiner had in mind was religion. In religious belief and ceremony he found a most expressive secondary institution. All the frustrations and conflicts generated in the primary institutions were projected

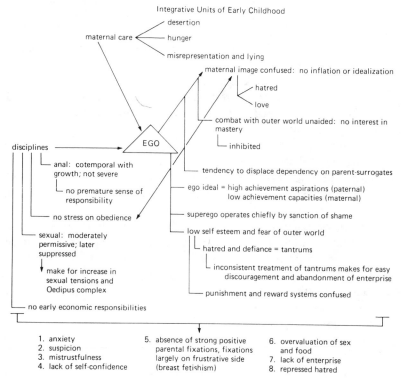

Figure 12-2. Chart by Kardiner designed to portray the dynamics of personal-social relationships and their psychological coordinates during early childhood of the Alorese. (From DuBois 1961(1):181)

and abreacted in symbolic figures of religious drama. The way Marxists, developmental rationalists, and psychoanalysts converged in their interpretation of the social function of religion is a curious and important historic and evolutionary datum.

Like Structuralists generally, Kardiner looked to intrinsic necessities for uniformities in process and in product. Social Structuralists commonly traced the logical consistencies of social institutions to social needs. On the other hand, Kardiner joined Malinowski in correlating basic uniformities of institutions with primary biological needs. Reactions to frustration were predictable in human nature, and one could predict that systematic and continuous interference with primary gratification would lead to institutionalized behaviors that symbolized or otherwise expressed the nature of the frustration. For the moment reasons for differential impulse restrictions in different societies could not be given. However, contrastive comparisons permitted the checking of uniformities in human response, and their respective effects could be traced in the cultures. In tracing institutional effects of impulse control, the age when restrictive discipline was instituted and gains or rewards were offered the individual for relinquishing gratification was important (Kardiner 1939:129). The reward component was vital, for without gain to the individual, an aggressive response could be predicted. Further, the society developed special institutions to reward aggressive behavior, such as war. An adequate reward-frustration ratio stabilized relations linking id, ego, and superego. Without sufficient rewards for impulse control, the superego lost its tonicity and the resultant personality instability carried violent and other perverse behaviors into society at large, thus affecting societal stability. With such pragmatics, psychoanalysis demonstrated its relevance for the disturbed social order as well as for the disturbed personality, indicating how the two were reciprocally interrelated.

The psychoanalytic focus on reaction formations drew a picture of cultural institutions that were largely repressive and were also surrogates for the release of impulse frustration. Since personality psychodynamics was central to the plan of investigation, the terminologies of anthropology and of sociology were used only in a limited way. Basic structurings and processes were handled much better with concepts like ego structure, reaction formation, instinctual frustration, inhibition, repression, suppression, masochistic syndrome, gratification, unconscious conflicts, release of tension, anxiety, Oedipus complex, oral mastery, narcissistic needs, oral sadistic stage, castration complex, father substitutes, ego's security system, sublimation, aggression, dependency, neurosis, transference, displacement, fixation, repetition compulsion, and projective systems.

Application of psychoanalysis to culture carried the hazard that culture patterns at base would be reduced to psychological illusions, as in the instance of religion. Moreover, restriction of the investigative field to reaction formations provoked by authority figures tended to limit the range of application. The psychoanalyst of culture found his best correlates of aggression, masochism, Oedipal yearnings, and the like, in dreams, folk-lore, and religious beliefs and practices. There was a tendency to follow the trail of the extreme and bizarre. When seeking a people to research psychoanalytically, DuBois (1961(1):Preface, ix) clued her choice to the presence of "gross pathologies ... since it seemed ... at the time that by the very grossness of its manifestations pathology could be more clearly understood than normality." At the same time, she considered the measure of the approach must be found in the degree to which a wide range of phenomena could be brought into a coherent relationship.

> If, for example, one can establish a coherent trend in methods of infant feed-ing, in sex attitudes, in attitudes toward food, economic activities, sacrifices and myths, in such a fashion that it has meaning on both cultural and psy-chological levels, then one will have achieved a functional synthesis of unusual importance for the comprehension of cultural processes. In determining how and to what degree social forms may be invested with emotion and how emo-tional investments may be transferred from one social form to another, we shall have made significant advances in understanding cultural change and stability. Only when we have some comprehension of the link between insti-tutions which the individuals bearing those institutions may make on an emo-tional level, shall we begin to grasp the repercussions involved in social alterations. (DuBois 1961(1):v)

The Alorese selected for testing Kardiner's modified Freudian theory were situated in Indonesia. DuBois supplemented her ethnographic obser-vations with dream materials, autobiographies, word associations, chil-dren's drawings, and the Porteus Maze and Rorschach tests. Independent analysis of the ethnographic, autobiographic, and projective test materials was introduced to reach some measure of control. The Alorese character structure as it emerged under these separate analyses disclosed a weak ego organization, preoccupaion with imagery and compensations regard-ing parental care, emotional constriction, fearful suspicion of the unknown, and inclinations to follow expediency. Both the Rorschach and autobio-graphic materials suggested considerable individual variability and posed a problem for generalization. Since the Rorschach test was programmed from European subjects, there were real doubts about its utility in un-covering Alorese character. However, the Rorschach expert Oberholzer, pointing to consistencies in an independent ranking of the subjects by the ethnographer and himself, concluded that the "principles of the test could be applied cross-culturally" (in DuBois 1961(2):589). Individual variation revealed by the autobiographies, in Kardiner's judgment, was not so great that such could not be considered variant reactions to the same situation (DuBois 1961(1):9). DuBois, while granting the general validity of Kardi-ner's basic personality construct, considered the limitation of personality structuring to childhood experiences too restrictive. The modal personality, as she described her construct, developed gradually during the life cycle of an individual (DuBois 1961(1):4). Individual personalities became standardized by constant exposure to standardized experiences, social relations, and value relations that were consistent and coherent throughout the maturational phases despite differences in resources available to child, youth, and adult.

The cultural exposure of Alorese from infancy to youth sketched by DuBois (1961(1):115) indicated that frustrations associated with food, sex, and wealth fostered unstable and mistrustful marriage relationships. The total effect of personal and conventionalized experience, where form and practice frequently clashed, forced the individual to withdraw and to rely upon himself, since others could not be trusted. The milieu in which Alorese experienced life thus

> should combine to make people isolated units, highly individualized and self-contained to the point of being encysted, without at the same time creating any basic self-assurance and independence born of self-confidence. The recognized patterns of teasing, deceit, lying, and chicanery may be considered both as contributing causes and as effects of such attitudes. All these factors should produce a modal personality whose independence rests upon frustrations, confusions, and surrendered goals. In some instances the inability to create human contacts may actually be phrased as a fear of them. As Mangma said after telling one of his dreams, "We die if people are fond of us." (DuBois 1961(1):115)

Alorese adults seemingly lived out the deprivations and frustrations of their childhood and youth in institutions characterized by hostility, suspicion, acrimonious dispute, unfulfilled threats of aggression, fulfillment of aggression, and deceit.

DIFFERENTIATIVE IMPACT OF PSYCHOANALYSIS: BEHAVIORISTIC PSYCHOANALYSIS

Incorporation of psychoanalytic theory, in effect, created an ethnological specialization that might be called ethnopsychoanalysis, conceivably a branch of ethnopsychology or culture and personality. Expectably, ethnologists steered clear of acceptance of precultural reaction formations as the basis for cultural institutions. In fact, one could turn the equation around and see the consequences of deprivation and frustration as a product of habit conditioning. By reconciling the syndromes discriminated by psychoanalysts with principles of learning espoused by behaviorists, a kind of behavioristic psychoanalysis was achieved. The first determined move in this direction came out of the Yale University Institute of Human Relations when Dollard and associates in 1939 translated the frustration-aggression and security-insecurity syndromes into the principles of stimulus-response learning, which accented drive excitation, reduction (need-arousal—response—reward-punishment), and habit reinforcement. "Past performances of the habit which have been followed by reward (drive reduction) increase the habit potential; those which have been followed by no reward or by punishment generally decrease the habit potential" (Whiting and Child 1962:21).

In 1942, Gorer issued a general statement of assumptions guiding behaviorist psychoanalysis. His postulates were drawn from social anthropology, psychoanalysis, and stimulus-response psychology, which, in his view, constituted an initial step in putting together a unified theory of social science.

(1) Human behavior is understandable: with sufficient evidence it is possible to explain any observed behavior, however incongruous isolated items may appear.

(2) Human behavior is predominantly learned. Although the human infant may be born with some instincts and is born with some basic drives whose satisfaction is necessary to its survival, it is the treatment which the infant undergoes from the other members of the society into which it is born, and its experiences of its environment, which are of preponderating importance in molding adult behavior. . . .

(3) In all societies the behavior of the component individuals of similar age, sex and status shows a relative uniformity in similar situations. This is equally true in unformulated and unverbalized situations.

(4) All societies have an ideal adult character (or characters, depending on sex and status) which is of major importance for the parents in selecting which items of their children's behavior to reward and which to punish.

(5) Habits are established by differential reward and punishment, chiefly meted out by other members of the society.

(6) The habits established early in the life of the individual influence all subsequent learning, and therefore the experiences of early childhood are of predominant importance.

(7) The chief learning in early childhood consists of the modifications of the innate drives of hunger, optimum-temperature seeking, pain-avoidance, sex and excretion, and of the (probably learned) drives of fear and anger (anxiety and aggression) which are demanded by the adult members of the society; consequently a knowledge of the types of modifications imposed, the means by which they are imposed, and the times at which they are imposed, is of major importance in understanding adult behavior.

(8) Since everywhere it is predominantly the parents who reward and punish their children, the attitudes of the child to his father and mother, and, to a lesser degree, toward his siblings, will become the prototypes of his attitudes toward all subsequently met people.

(9) Except in situations of the greatest physiological stress, adult behavior is motivated by learned (derived, secondary) drives or wishes superimposed upon the primary biological drives.

(10) Many of these wishes are unverbalized or unconscious, since the rewards and punishments which established the habits of which these wishes are the motives were undergone in early childhood, or because the verbalization of these wishes was very heavily punished; as a derivative from this hypothesis, people frequently cannot verbalize their motives, which have to be deduced from the observation of what satisfactions are actually obtained in a given situation.

(11) When these wishes, acquired through early training, are shared by a majority of the population, some social institutions will eventually be evolved to gratify them; and existing social institutions, and those that are borrowed from other societies, will be modified in congruence with these wishes, insofar as this is possible without impeding the gratification of the primary biological drives.

(12) In a homogeneous culture the patterns of superordination and subordination, of deference and arrogance, will show a certain consistency in all spheres from the family to the religious and political organizations; and consequently the patterns of behavior demanded in all these institutions will mutually reinforce each other. (Gorer 1948b:238–239)

Items 1–5 of the manifesto responded to the demands of behaviorism and social anthropology, while items 6–12 carried the core of the psychoanalytic orientation.

Armed with their battery of unified theory, behavioristic-psychoanalytic anthropologists challenged the wide spectrum of personality, society, and culture. Immediately they were caught up in wartime demands for psychological analyses of the enemy and produced thematic analyses of culture and personality that eventuated in the study of national character, especially the Soviet during the Cold War period. For the first time, anthropologists were drawn irresistibly into the study of complex cultures—but at a distance. Analyses of literature, art, drama, poetry, novels, films, child-training manuals, and social literature substituted for fieldwork. The thematic-values approach was easily translated into the wider problem of cultural integration. Like earlier culture theorists, behavioristic psychoanalysts used autobiography to portray typical covert processes which came from the cultural handling of the universals of childhood. Personality was examined in terms of the correlation of its covert organization with social process. The role of rationalization, sublimation, compensation, and repression in personality organization demonstrated the extent to which a society depended upon defense mechanisms in maintaining stable social relations. The clash of cultures and the subordination of peoples provided another window for viewing the twists and turns of defensive reactions as oppressive insecurity replaced the satisfactions of traditional expectations. Beyond the separate researches of individual peoples lay the task of formulating generalizations. This could be achieved only through cross-cultural comparisons generated out of psychoanalytic hypotheses. The end of such comparative research could be nothing other than human nature itself and its universal correlates in custom and traditional belief.

PRIMARY THEMES AND NATIONAL CHARACTER: GORER AND BENEDICT

Gorer initiated his study of culture and personality with a field investigation of the Lepcha (*Himalayan Village* 1938). There he analyzed the relation between child training and the passive, nonaggressive public behavior of the Lepcha. There was a larger problem, notably social evolutionary change. Why had not the Lepcha moved toward a feudalistic system as had their Nepalese and Bhutanese neighbors? The answer, in Gorer's judgment, rested in Lepcha suppression of overt competition and aggression.

World War II literally propelled anthropologists into psychocultural studies of national character. Within three months of Pearl Harbor, Gorer, at the request of the Committee on Intercultural Relations, prepared a memorandum on "Japanese Character Structure and Propaganda." In the harsh discipline of toilet training imposed upon the infant at the tender age of four to five months, Gorer found the roots of Japanese character structure. This, too, explained their paradoxical savagery in war and their cultivation of elegance in ceremonious eating and tea drinking. The imposition of controls on infantile neurological machinery before it had sufficiently matured forced the Japanese mother into a preoccupation with excretion and the use of harsh scolding to ward off, and punish, the soiling of garments and floor. Toilet training thus was charged with a heavy transfer of feeling that cut a deep pathway to the unconscious character organization of the child and produced institutionalized correlates in adult behavior. Mothers were inclined to overfeed their infants, and hence hunger anxiety was not present. In the absence of hunger anxiety, Japanese unconsciously diverted their attention from the enjoyment of eating to the aesthetic appreciation of foods, as manifested in the poetic naming of dishes and in the ritualization of preparation. The tea ceremony was the most marked. The lesser value Japanese placed on the gastric experience was more complicated, however. By a process of generalization, the shame associated with defecation became attached to eating and reinforced the low valence of food as a gastric delight. According to Gorer (1948b: 247), "the unpleasant effects surrounding defecation have moved forward to the eating of solid food, and . . . both aspects of the digestive process are treated almost identically."

Japanese concern for ceremonial purification of the body and their inability to discriminate sin from uncleanness was also derived from the drastic toilet training (Gorer 1948b:248). Their compulsion for neatness did not mark them as possessing the neurotic symptoms of overtrained European patients. Actually, unconscious hostilities lurked behind the compulsive ritualizations of Japanese life, and the primary function of ritual was to contain the hostility. Hence, the "striking contrast between the all-pervasive gentleness of Japanese life in Japan, which has charmed nearly every visitor, and the overwhelming brutality and sadism of the Japanese at war" (Gorer 1948b:250).

There were some themes in Japanese culture which Gorer did not directly trace to toilet training. Nonetheless, they were present in early childhood. For example, the contrast between the aggressive masculine order and the passive gratifying feminine order provided a basic orientation for all interpersonal relations, including those with foreigners. In

Japanese psychology, the feminine order, as boys learned during childhood, was a proper target for aggression. The same posture was employed during wartime against those whom the Japanese judged to be feminine.

> On December 7, 1941, this theory was put to the test; and the democracies still held their feminine role. Most convincing of all, they asked for mercy, declaring Manila an open city; and just as on such a plea the angry boy will destroy his mother's hair-do and break her pins, so in response did the Japanese destroy Manila with a special attention to buildings of religious or symbolic importance. (Gorer 1948b:252)

Gorer clearly demonstrated the drawbacks inherent in the psychoanalytic approach of deriving the multiples of character from a primary infantile fixation. Thus, *The American People* (1948a) were fixated by rejection of the father, and a concomitant Oedipal relation between mother and son presented a constant challenge to the American male's masculinity. The Russians (Gorer and Rickman 1950) in their personalities were constantly straining against the memory of infantile swaddling with its bothersome constraints. Through the window of swaddling, the political history of the Russians reflected their need to formulate a psychological restraint that was neither too tight nor too loose.

Benedict also was drawn into the wartime study of cultures and personalities with an assignment to analyze the Japanese. The title of her work, *The Chrysanthemum and the Sword* (1946), called attention to a contradictory duality in Japanese character which she correlated with discontinuities in childhood conditioning.

> The contradictions in Japanese male behavior which are so conspicuous to Westerners are made possible by the discontinuity of their upbringing, which leaves in their consciousness, even after all the "lacquering" they undergo, the deep imprint of a time when they were like little gods in their little world, when they were free to gratify even their aggressions, and when all satisfactions seemed possible. Because of this deeply implanted dualism, they can swing as adults from excesses of romantic love to utter submission to the family. They can indulge in pleasure and ease, no matter to what lengths they go in accepting extreme obligations. Their training in circumspection makes them in action an often timid people, but they are brave even to foolhardiness. They can prove themselves remarkably submissive in hierarchical situations and yet not be easily amenable to control from above. In spite of all their politeness, they can retain arrogance. They can accept fanatic discipline in the Army and yet be insubordinate. They can be passionately conservative and yet be attracted by new ways, as they have successively demonstrated in their adoption of Chinese customs and of Western learning.
>
> The dualism in their characters creates tensions to which different Japanese respond in different ways, though each is making his own solution of the same essential problem of reconciling spontaneity and acceptance he experienced

in early childhood with the restraints which promise security in later life. (Benedict 1946:290–291)

But if early childhood for the male was godlike in its permissiveness, especially with regard to woman, Benedict found a strain toward submission in the early toilet training of the infant. The inexorable training imposed on the Japanese baby was a preparation for his later acceptance of the more subtle compulsions of Japanese culture.

The lacquering of Japanese character to which Benedict alluded was a product of their conceptions of obligation and reciprocity. According to the metaphysics of Japanese obligation and reciprocity, the individual was the passive recipient of obligations (*On*) from emperor, parents, suzerain, teacher, and others according to the personal experiences of life. *On* reciprocities were divided into those that were never fulfilled (*Gimu* to emperor, parents, ancestors, and work) and those that must be returned with mathematical precision (*Giri* to suzerain, affinals and distant kin, and one's own name) (Benedict 1946:116).

The ambiguity inherent in Japanese cultivation of sensual pleasures and the unrelenting discipline regarding obligation dramatized the intrinsic discontinuity between early and late childhood experience. Early childhood was a period of carefree indulgence intermingled with the discipline of toilet training essential to later acceptance of constraints. Later childhood was a time of indoctrination of formal constraints. Japanese unconsciously yearned for the pleasures of childhood, but they were held in line by the ritualization of obligation in custom and the deep sense of shame attached to the breaking of custom. In their metaphysics Japanese applied disciplined meditation to break through the barriers of internalized social sanctions and their shame correlates. Through the discipline of Zen Buddhism, the observing self was obliterated in order to reach a state of instant and carefree intuitive knowledge (*muga*).

Benedict's analysis of Japanese culture and personality processes revealed a subtle shift on her part in the direction of the psychoanalytic position, even though she did not embellish her work with Freudian terminology. Her implication that infantile and early childhood experience left an indelible mark on Japanese character was countered by Sikkema (1947) in a study of Hawaiian Japanese, and in a special issue of *The Japanese Journal of Ethnology* (1949(14):no. 4) various scholars determined that Benedict's approach was methodologically unsound (see Bennett and Nagai 1953). Mead (1953:662) restated the position of national character studies and their basic assumptions, concluding that further developments must await multidiscipline field studies of complex nation-states guided by the theoretical findings of culture and personality research among the small communities of primitive societies. Mead implied that the study of national character from a distance through the medium of literature, cautionary tales and films, sometimes supplemented with questionnaires and limited interviewing of immigrants, was inadequate. There was no substitute for field investigation.

PSYCHOANALYSIS AND THE TYPOLOGY OF CULTURES: MEAD

In the perspective of psychoanalysis, culture housed projective systems that correlated with unconscious impulse reactions embedded in the universal experiences of early childhood. If an anal syndrome was central to personality, the culture must be integrated by affect emphases stemming from bowel training. In 1949 Mead renovated her earlier interpretations of South Seas cultures with psychoanalytic theory and used them to underscore unconscious conflicts of American culture and of cultures generally. Culture was important in shaping individual outlook and opportunity, but molding of the individual was the work of people following cultural conventions. Some people were more influential than others because their presence dominated the formative period of infancy and early childhood. "The relationships between men and women and parents and children are the crucial areas of human relationships. As these relationships are patterned, so are they conveyed to the infant at his mother's breast, who before he can toddle has absorbed a particular style of sex relations and learned to rule out other styles" (Mead 1952:13–14). Three biological needs—eating, elimination, and sex—supplied the staging for character formation. How each of these primary zones of erogenous experience was handled thematically within a culture determined the orientation of individuals to the world of objects, human beings, and the extent to which areas would become energized with affect. However, the variation to which these primary zones could be subjected was limited by the possibilities for structuring interaction. These interactional possibilities were three: symmetrical, complementary, and reciprocal. In the symmetrical relation, "the mother behaves as if the child were essentially similar to herself, and as if she were responding to behaviour of the same type as her own" (Mead 1952:64). Symmetrical relationships tended to generate considerable affect. Under the complementary relationship, mother and child performed different roles by virtue of their distinctive differences. If the dependency of the child is stressed, the mother may be viewed as giver and the child as receiver. The reciprocal relationship stressed mutual exchange. "In reciprocal phrasings of relationship, love, trust, tears, may become commodities, just as much as physical objects, but the interchange of physical objects remains the prototype" (Mead 1952:64–65). Variation in character was largely a function of the emphasis which cultures put on the interactional relationships, all of which were present in any culture.

The primary zones, interactional relationships, and quality of affect (dynamically assertive-giving versus passive receiving-retaining) supplied Mead with components by which cultures were typed. In the structuring of interaction, the oral tended to be complementary, the anal reciprocal, and the genital complementary. Under this typology the Arapesh emerged as oral-passive-complementary, the Iatmul oral-assertive-complementary with some symmetricality, and the Mundugumor oral-active-reciprocal. Predictably the Manus, whom Mead considered the model of South Seas capitalism, turned out to be anal-assertive-reciprocal, and expectably, possessing features also observable in the character of capitalistic Americans. With an emphasis on bowel training, according to Mead (1952:71–72), there is a corresponding shift from

> the complementary relationship to an emphasis upon the relationship between the child and that which he first takes in and then gives out. Person-thing relationships are learned here, reciprocal rather than simple complementary relationships are stressed. The later transfer to the genitals of attitudes focussed on elimination makes for prudery, haste, lack of pleasure and foreplay in intercourse. This character-type in which the most emphasized communication between parent and child has been an emphasis on control of elimination is one that occurs fairly frequently in our society. We find it writ large among the Manus tribe of the Admiralty Islands, a group of efficient puritans where women never swing their grass skirts—grass skirts after all are items in the endless exchange of goods that goes on—girls are never allowed to flirt, and all love, even the affection between brother and sister, is measured in goods. Here among these small Stone Age villages there was prostitution, and the owner of the war-captured prostitute made money. Here a woman never loosens her grass skirt even in the extremes of childbirth. Between husbands and wives sex is a hasty, covert, shameful matter; and otherwise it is adultery, heavily punished by vigilant, puritanical, ghostly guardians. Women's roles and men's roles are very slightly differentiated; both participate importantly in the religious system, both conduct economic affairs. If a man is stupid, his relatives seek for him a bright wife to compensate for his deficiencies. The sex act becomes a sort of shared excretion, and the attitudes that both sexes have learned during childhood come into play, not equally, for the female's sexual role is completely derogated, while the man is to a degree continuing an enjoined activity. But the general devaluation of sex and sex attraction is such that this difference in the images formed by males and females is less significant. A certain amount of sodomy among the young men is a natural concomitant of such a learning system.

Emphasis on the maternal suckling role served as the prototype for polarizing the sexes and their sexual roles. Complementary relations stressed contrast, and for Mead (1952:88) the act of suckling focused the most dynamic of complementary experiences. Suckling became the center of symbolic contrast between men and women, as well as of envy, overcompensation, and mimicry (Mead 1952:88). Among Samoans and Balinese, sexual distinctions were less sharply drawn because the child was treated as a whole and there was no focus on the suckling relationship. Sexual distinctions were made, but neither sex was denigrated nor envied.

Mead's Freudian reinterpretation of her seven South Seas societies expectably accented adjustment to bodily functions as the central experience in character formation. However, the body experience was filtered by cultural definitions regarding sexual distinctions and roles. The experiential sources for these sexual discriminations was vital to the understanding of basic similarities and distinctions in character which were raised upon the fundamental biology of sex. As one surveyed the world societies, it was apparent that the maternal-infant relationship was omnipresent. The maternal-infant relationship thus served as the prototype for relationships and feelings that found their way into national character, irrespective of differences that existed between families and social classes. It was even possible to find infantile contexts that revealed basic attitudes, quality of social relationships, and outlook expressed in adult behavior. In the film *Four Families,* Mead suggested that variations in national character could be detected in the way the mother handled the infant during the bath.

Mead never presented a studied classification of societies according to her components. However, by combining the different components (oral, anal, sexual; symmetrical, complementary, reciprocal relationships; assertive-passive effect) a classification of twenty-seven variants was possible.

THE ALIMENTARY METAPHYSICS OF THE YUROK INDIANS: ERIKSON

Whether addressing themselves clinically to individual character or to ethnic character, psychoanalysts strove for a total view comparable to the holistic approach anthropologists had attained in their pursuit of cultural integration. A character structure housed a world view just as cultures possessed a *Weltanschauung.* In psychoanalytic perspective, primary body openings and their functions furnished the initial vocabulary of social experience, and this orientation was projected outward to people and to the world at large.

> Incorporation and assimilation, retention and elimination, intrusion and inception, are some of the basic problems of organismc existence. Emotional and intellectual, as well as physical, self-preservation demand that one accept, keep, digest, and eliminate; give and receive; take and be taken in *fair ratio.* This ratio is the firm foundation for the later development of the infinite variability and specialization of human existence. (Erikson 1948:179)

The significance of Erik H. Erikson's (1943) study of the Yurok lay not in the oral, anal, and genital associations commonly illuminated in psychoanalytic interpretation but in his attempt to understand the metaphysical basis of Yurok culture. Behind the Yurok world view lurked a fear of closure derived from an oral syndrome which took the form of a one-way "tube configuration" (Erikson 1948:185). Fear of entering and leaving by the same entrance was intensified by their narrow valley riverine environment and the mystery of the spawning run of salmon.

Their ceremonial magic to control the salmon was designed to keep vital channels open and antagonistic fluids at a distance. Thus, men and boys spent much time in a sweat house with an oval entrance and a narrower second exit through which a man passed to demonstrate that he was ceremonially clean in body and eating habits. To purify himself fully a Yurok was required to swim the river. By sweating and swimming, men prepared themselves for fishing, thereby "denying . . . contact with women and . . . giving daily rebirth . . . through a tube-like womb" (Erikson 1948: 186).

In contrast with the sweat lodge, the home where women and young children passed their days was modeled after the female anatomy, with single entrance and exit. The Yurok home was a "dark, unclean, full of food and utensils, and crowded with babies . . . place from which a man emerged contaminated" (Erikson 1948:186). But for shamans, many of whom were women, and who cured diseases caused by intrusive objects ("pains"), the body metaphysics of the female anatomy was turned to advantage through the controlled swallowing and regurgitation of "pains."

> Long before F., the daughter and granddaughter of shamans, reached puberty, people had predicted that she probably would turn into a shaman because "she slept so much," that is, had a neurotic inclination to regress. During her premenarche, (i.e., her pre-menstrual period) her grandmother tested her by taking a "pain" out of her own mouth and trying to make F. swallow it. F. ran away from home. The following night, however, she had an anxiety dream in which an old woman threw a basket over her mouth in such a way that she swallowed its "yellow, black bloody nasty" content. She woke up in extreme anxiety but kept this dream to herself because she realized that people would force her to become a shaman if they knew that her grandmother's suggestion had invaded her dream life. At breakfast, however, she gave herself away by vomiting, whereupon the community made her confess and in great excitement prepared her novitiate. She now had to learn to transform this involuntary vomiting of stomach content into the ability to swallow and to throw up "pains" without throwing up food with it—a mastery over the oral-nutritional tube which gives F. the power to cure people. (Erikson 1948: 191–192)

By their curious blending of geographic features and the alimentary zone, the Yurok bypassed the classic anal syndrome with its linkage of object manipulation to sphincter control and feces. The alimentary focus of the Yurok was unique in uniting both the incorporative aspects of the mouth and the eliminative aspects of the anus. Though the Yurok experiences may have been more comprehensive than those fettered by the anal syndrome, they nonetheless exhibited similar characteristics: a compulsiveness, suspicion, and preoccupation with retention and giving through the manipulation of wealth objects. Erikson (1948:194) asserted that a concern for the "total inside of the body with its mixture of excreta . . . [might] be true for most primitives."

CULTURE VERSUS THE INDIVIDUAL: CONFLICT, TENSION, AND NEUROSIS

Incorporation of the psychoanalytic approach expanded ethnographic coverage with details of childhood at the expense of description of customs and institutions. This followed emphasis on how the learning experience was organized, and the principle of deducing unconscious patterning according to frustration-anxiety versus satisfaction-security ratios.

Through the window of psychoanalysis, the child in Western society emerged as a deprived, frustrated, immature, and tragic figure consigned to live out his deprivations in an adult world filled with hostility, unrequited love, and nonfulfillment. Such being the case, culture could no longer be considered a satisfaction-evoking and fulfilling instrument; rather, culture was a tension-creating and tension-fulfilling mechanism. The measure of any culture thus must be its mental health ratios. In Freud's (1930) judgment, the moralistic demands of Western civilization exacted too high a price in damaged and neurotic personalities. The end of social living, Fromm (1955:72–73) counseled, was the production of people who loved each other, who engaged in creative work, cultivated reason and objectivity, and experienced a sense of self which only mature productivity can bring. When society engendered mutual antagonisms and distrust and caused people to use others selfishly, and to find themselves exploited, then society robbed people of their sense of self and was a sick society. In the perspective of mental health, it was not the individual who must adjust to the needs of society, but society must bend to the needs of man.

Taking their departure from the individual and his needs, psychoanaysts thus pitted the individual against society and saw him as a defenseless victim of irrational society. Men were not in error; the traditions under which they lived were in error. The psychoanalytic philosopher portrayed human history as a tragic entrapment by false traditions which drove men endlessly to pursue worthless goals and illusions.

Psychoanalytic theory won acceptance among anthropologists, and society at large during an epoch time of troubles in the Western world. This was the time of the Great Depression and the national sociopolitical ferment that swept the West into World War II. The ailments of the grand society were much more visible than its cloistered virtues. Psychoanalysis was a generous contributor to the mounting criticism of Western civilization, demanding that human personality be released from the restraints by which it was artificially bound.

PSYCHOANALYTIC END TO THE MYTH OF THE NOBLE AND CAREFREE SAVAGE

As anthropologists turned the searchlight of psychoanalytic theory upon primitive cultures and sounded emotional depths with the aid of projective tests, they found primitive custom was no better instrument for developing character than the complex traditions of Western civilization. Actually, in *Totem and Taboo*, Freud maintained that early society, seemingly without a formalized moral-religious system, had foundered on the rock of Oedipal surges. There, the community of males rose up and slew the sexual tyrant. Man's unhappiness was traceable to unnatural restraints initiated in that ancient time on man's nature.

Searching beneath the mask of culture, anthropologists found that the basic unconscious processes brought to mind through psychoanalysis were rampant in primitive societies. This was so because, like Western civilization, the culture of primitive man was at variance with his needs, or it confused his nature with discontinuities and ambivalences. For example, the Kaska Indians, according to Honigmann (1949), were confounded by a major discontinuity in their emotional conditioning. During infancy, maternal warmth in a demand-feeding context gave the Kaska forest hunter a good start on the road to self-assertiveness so essential to mastery of the physical and social environment. However, an unconscious residue remained in an infantile identification of the mother as an ideal figure of great power and resourcefulness (Honigmann 1949:307). Consequently, this idealization of a mother-nurturant figure caused Kaska to give way in the face of stressful challenges. Psychoanalytically, in times of crisis, the Kaska were victimized by infantile regression.

The problem of Kaska adjustment was compounded by the withdrawal of parental attention and emotional warmth during the second or third year. "As a result of that shock, the child becomes afraid ever again to lose his identity in strong love relationships which might once more be destroyed at the individual's expense" (Honigmann 1949:308). The low valence of emotional life intensified a need for security, but for the Kaska, security could not be reached by cultivating relationships with others. Independence through noninvolvement alone provided the assurance people required, and Kaska moved through life with an air of self-detachment. Their suspicion of emotional ties was observed in the tendency to avoid cooperative ventures outside the family and in the early quarreling and divorce. The contradictions of self-assertion and passivity, and emotional independence and dependence, appeared as central conflicts for both Kaska males and females.

The fiber of Kaska personality was irrevocably marked with gratifications and deprivations traceable to parental figures. The withdrawal of maternal affection and succoring so traumatized the child that the image of mother as a transcendant giver of food and warmth were indelibly engraved on his unconscious. Unsure of himself, and emotionally isolated, the Kaska retreated to the comfort of his unconscious nurturant image, especially when confronting people with power and surpluses. Such apparently was the case for Kaska relations with whites and the Canadian government.

The fact that demandingness is most directly expressed toward the government and whites, suggests that these sources are unconsciously regarded as parental substitutes who have in abundance what the individual needs and so suggest themselves as suitable sources for restoring the balance of frustrated parent-child relations. The statement of Nitla referring to the traders as "Just the same as your daddy" is significant in this respect. The conception of authority, or bosses, as sources of protection also equates these concepts with the early parental ideal. (Honigmann 1949:309)

The Trukese of the western Pacific also incorporated a deeply rooted anxiety that linked food, security, and emotional relationships. However, unlike the Kaska mother, as soon as she regained her strength a Trukese mother was erratic in her attention to infantile food needs. By and large she loomed as a hostile and rejecting person, far less supportive than the father (Gladwin and Sarason 1953(20):234). Trukese projected their anxious oral frustrations into man-eating spirits and ghosts. Parents tended to be inconsistent, and their punishing-rejecting attitude prevented the child from internalizing the emotional base that allowed warm and intimate relationships with others. Rorschach protocols clearly revealed the low intensity of interpersonal relations (Gladwin and Sarason 1953(20):228). Without secure channels for establishing relations of emotional depth, Trukese, like the Kaska, were forced into a strategy of independence. To protect themselves in their relations with others Trukese curbed their feelings, suppressed overt aggression, and conformed. At the same time, however, they were fearful of being cut off from others. Sexual relations provided the arena for males and females to repair some of the damage to their egos; for each sex seemingly approached the experience with a sense of aggressive conquest.

Exploration of tension-producing relations in the simpler societies, as in complex societies, underlined a variety of sources for feelings of rejection and deprivation around which the unconscious integration of personality formed. Parent-child relations were central, and more often the mother-child tie was critical. In a clever experiment with dolls, David Levy (1939) exposed the sibling rivalry of Kekchi children in Guatemala and traced it to the mother's need to distribute her affection among a number of children. Experimenting with dolls among the Pilaga Indians of the Gran Chaco, the Henrys (1944) reported that children generally were quarrelsome and pugnacious. As a helpless infant each was cared for and protected, but parental neglect began as soon as the child could take care of himself. The rivalrous hostility of Pilaga siblings suggested displacement of Oedipal symptoms. Moral admonitions by parents were lacking, and the Pilaga child moved in a world of aggression and retaliation. U. S. society and Pilaga society exhibited comparable sibling rivalry. Their effects, however, were different in that the Pilaga child was not compelled to pass moral judgment on himself. All he had to fear was retaliation, whereas the American child had the added burden of remorse, loss of self-esteem, and guilt feelings.

In a Guatemalan village edging Lake Atitlan, ritual control of sibling rivalry was so direct that Paul (1950(52):206) considered the ritual to be the equivalent of a projective test.

> Pedranos believe that a child may destroy an infant sibling by "eating" its soul or spirit. To protect newborn babies from the appetite of such a child, parents occasionally resort to a well-patterned ritual which is supposed to "cure" the offender of his fratricidal craving. A ritual specialist, a midwife or shaman, grasps a chicken by the wings or legs, beating its body against the back of the culpable child until the fowl is dead. This is done privately and secretly and out of sight of the new infant which must not witness death. The sacrificial chicken is cooked in a savory broth and served exclusively to the older child who must finish the entire dish even if it takes three or four successive meals. While the chicken is being killed or when it is being eaten, the child is lectured on the meaning of the rite. The specialist or the mother warns, "Now that another little brother (or sister) is born you are not to eat him. The chicken will be your meal. Its meat is like the flesh of your little brother. You must take good care of him and never frighten him." If the child eats willingly it means that his predatory appetite is put at rest; reluctance would signify an unrepentant spirit.

Infant mortality was high at San Pedro La Laguna. Besides eating of the soul they recognized disease and death as naturally caused by epidemics and by supernatural punishment for failure to follow traditions sanctioned by their forefathers (Paul 1953:326). An older sibling feeding on the soul of a younger child was not an everyday occurrence; but if an infant or younger child were continuously ill, or were a succession of babies to die while an older thrived, the suspicion of soul eating immediately came to mind and called for the exorcistic rite. Fear of being eaten turned out to be a lively and imaginative theme in the mental culture of the Pedranos. Paul concluded that the sibling ritual symbolized the presence of social strains and that it also played a part in the way siblings perceived each other and their expectations from the relationship (Paul 1950(52):217).

On the other hand, sibling rivalry was no problem for the Rajputs of Khalapur, India (Minturn and Hitchcock 1963:343). The child could count on the continuing attention of adults, especially the mother, until five or six years of age. The bathing, dressing, and feeding services performed for children diminished as boys and girls around six years began to assume the adult dress of their respective sexes. There was no forcing of work responsibilities on either sex, and children directed their own energies so long as they stayed out of trouble. The child was neither aroused by a weaning trauma nor by a lavish bestowal or denial of affection. Moreover, there were plenty of mother-surrogates in the extended family, and children seldom made exclusive claims on parental love by virtue of being a first-born or only child. Rajput attitudes toward the child were continuously flexible, nondemanding, and generally protective. Males early learned that the proper targets for aggression were nonkin.

Generally speaking, the anthropological survey of childhood was not

reassuring with regard to the successes of primitive peoples in constructing cultures without human frustration and conflict. Whenever projective
tests, such as Rorschach and modifications of the Thematic Apperception
Test, were given, anxieties and aggressions, as well as their fantasy correlates, surfaced. This was clearly brought out in Lewis' (1951) reanalysis
of the Mexican village of Tepoztlán. Redfield's (1930) institutional analysis
portrayed the Tepoztecan as a simple, hard-working, traditionally conservative, and religiously moral person. Lewis, on the other hand, found
Tepoztecans to be emotionally constrained, filled with insecurity, hostility,
and suspicion and given to guarding interpersonal relations with formal
protocol. In coping with their own hostility, Tepoztecans conjured up fears
of direct bodily assault, but feared indirect assaults through sorcery most
of all.

PSYCHOANALYSIS AND SOCIAL PROCESSES

Psychoanalytic theory consistently emphasized the linkage between
individual perception of self and not-self and a successful internalizing of
norms. Acceptance of norms obviously was a vital social process essential
to the continuity of society. Behavioristic theory stressed a positive inculcation of value motivations and the elimination of nonsanctioned behavior
through punishment or lack of reward. If, psychoanalysts argued, reactions
to the social process produced covert anxieties and aggressions, then in all
probability the social process included measures to alleviate the anxiety
and curb aggression.

Among Canadian Ojibwa near Lake Winnipeg, A. I. Hallowell (1967a:
277–290) was struck by the presence of psychological characteristics
which the Jesuit missionary Le Jeune had reported for Montagnais-Naskapi
of Labrador early in the seventeenth century. Behind the overt facade
which encouraged getting along together, harmonious relations, laughter,
and self-control there lurked a dark and covert reservoir of aggression
which was channeled now into gossip and backbiting, now into sorcery
and magic. Seeking the aid of talented shamans, Montagnais and Ojibwa
committed symbolic homicides in secrecy as real to them as the physical
bludgeoning of the individual to death.

For the Ojibwa, anxiety provided the counter measure to aggression.
Hallowell (1967b:266–276) described how the linking of bad conduct with
a fear of disease assigned a special social function to anxiety about the
self. Not only did the individual suffer the consequences of his own antisocial conduct, he also was held accountable for diseases which felled his
children and other relatives. Freedom from disease was the social equivalent
of a moral life. Neither internalized feelings of guilt nor fear of censorship
by a god was important to Ojibwa conformity. Rather, conformity resulted
from anxiety over one's personal safety, signaled by critical disease which
was causally linked to secret aggression against one's peers. Public confes-

sion of the secret transgression alone brought relief. Evil was generated by the harboring of secret desires to hurt others.

> This explains why it is that when one person confesses a sexual transgression ... [the partner] will not become ill subsequently or have to confess. Once the transgression has been publicized, it is washed away or, as the Saulteaux phrase it, "bad contact will not follow you any more." (Hallowell 1967b:273)

An anxious striving for health (pǐmädazīwin) thus promoted conformity and maintained stable relations in small Ojibwa groups without the need for formalized authority and legal sanctions.

The wide prevalence of witchcraft in the simpler societies suggested an important function in relieving tensions and in maintaining social control. In a cross-cultural study growing out of fieldwork among the Oregon Paiute, Beatrice Whiting (1950) noted a probable correlation between the practice of sorcery and societies where formal institutional controls were weak. Fear of sorcery, however, did not prevent aggressive outbreaks in the Paiute family any more than among the Saulteaux, or for that matter among peoples possessing formal legal sanctions. According to John Whiting (1961:370), the presence of sorcery in small societies lacking formal controls was found in two combinations: (1) polygynous households with severe sex training, and (2) extended families with severe control of aggression. Kluckhohn (1967:114–117) noted the rise and fall of witchcraft accusations according to the stability or instability of Navaho culture history. During the period following their harsh confinement at Fort Sumner, some forty persons were accused of witchcraft by the Navaho leader Manuelito, presumably to quell further resistance to white domination (Kluckhohn 1967:112–113). From its private operation, Kluckhohn (1967:118) saw witchcraft as a defensive instrument for adjusting to personal deprivation through indirect release of aggression. Myths and rituals on the other hand served the public at large in resolving their frustrations when faced with persistent and difficult need demands. Similarly, Nadel (1946) determined that, among the Nuba Nyima, religion operated in the interests of the general welfare (rain-making, health, fertility) and interpreted the world as an orderly system, whereas shamanism addressed itself to the individual and his immediate problems.

Though ego-centered and reflecting irrational and antisocial tensions in personal relations, witchcraft nevertheless revealed some covert contributions to the wider social process. Its private successes indirectly supported social stability by diverting criticism from more systematic interpretations of life and the social order. Among the Wangala of Mysore, bad relations between persons were relieved by accusations that blamed not the person but an evil spirit that had taken possession of the individual and forced him to practice witchcraft (Epstein 1967). Whether under threat of retaliatory sorcery or under threat of accusation, the presence of witchcraft induced a measure of conformity. It is apparent from this that the anxiety on which psychoanalytic interpretation concentrated could be correlated with the concept of punishment employed in the behavioristic model. This fact may help explain why social structuralists were able to handle witch-craft with sociological explanations that made no use of psychoanalytic mechanisms preferred by American culture theorists.

ETHNOPSYCHOANALYTIC AUTOBIOGRAPHY AND MODAL PERSONAL-SOCIAL PROCESSES

It is interesting to speculate on the influence of national milieu on the theoretical posture and innovations of anthropologists. Living in a rela-tively open society, American anthropologists were ambivalent toward the determinacy of culture structure and tended to view cultures through the careers of typical individuals. European sociologists experienced a social life dominated by an orderly arrangement of statuses to which individuals must be clued in order to function in the system, and they clung tenaciously to formal analysis of the social order. Individuals were swallowed up in the demand rights of status duties and prerogatives. On the other hand, Amer-ican culture theorists pioneered in the ethnopsychoanalytic autobiography in hopes of illuminating covert images and processes shared by the typical individual. Even if atypical in some degree, as Dollard (1938(3):724) ob-served when presenting his analysis of a patient, the life history of a neu-rotic was useful in revealing two levels of processes, the societal and a personal-social. Dollard presented general criteria for a psychoanalytically oriented life history in 1935, and in 1940, in conjunction with Allison Davis, he used life histories of eight Negro adolescents to bring out psycho-logical correlates between personality and the cultural experience of lower-, middle-, and upper-class Negroes in the Deep South (see Kardiner and Ovesey 1951).

Son of Old Man Hat: A Navaho Autobiography (Walter Dyk, ed. 1938) was the first of the psychoanalytically inspired life histories to appear. It was followed by *Smoke From Their Fires* (Clellan Ford 1941) and *Sun Chief, the Autobiography of a Hopi Indian* (Leo Simmons, ed. 1942). In *Black Hamlet*, Sachs (1947) presented a psychoanalytic case history of an African witch doctor. From his experience with psychotherapy of a young Plains Indian, Devereux (1951) developed the thesis that despite heavy ero-sion of tribal cultures, the core of an areal basic personality traceable to the historic culture area pattern persisted in the unconscious and anchored contemporary Indians to their past.

A focus on feeding, toilet and sex training, dreams, and control of aggression presented materials not usually found in ethnographic personal documents. The intent, however, was not to concentrate on the individual or to elicit variation in personal character. Rather, the aim was to draw forth the covert modalities of personality which were traceable to the pressures of the cultural milieu. Psychoanalytic biography thus took its place alongside the ethnographic life history as one of many instruments for elucidating the linkage between culture and the individuals who live by it.

In anthropology the use of life-history documents was always a supplement to basic investigation. Consequently, anthropologists have not produced an extensive life-history literature, and their efforts in this vein usually follow new theoretical orientations.

ETHNOPSYCHOANALYSIS AND ACCULTURATION

The thesis that culture patterns change slowly due to unconscious conditioning received fresh confirmation as anthropologists turned their attention to ongoing culture-contact processes. Despite the cultural erosion and disruption of life accompanying European efforts to assimilate colonial subjects, native customs and value bases persisted in strength and even engendered reactive movements that reaffirmed identity with cherished tradition. Adaptation of European institutions to native needs, or intermediate accommodations, was more prevalent than outright acceptance of the dominant model. The causes for the slow pace of acculturative assimilation obviously were multiplex and included socioeconomic discrimination and personality disorganization that accompanied loss of meaningful self-identification and achievable goals. At the same time some differential in acculturation was observed in a spread of individuals along a conservative-assimilative continuum. There were ample reasons thus for assuming that covert processes were a vital domain of acculturative change and that psychoanalytic instruments were useful in extending basic understandings.

The first large-scale application of psychoanalytic techniques to the acculturative process was inspired and directed by Hallowell. Hallowell's (1946) initial fieldwork suggested that the Ojibwa shared certain character features with other northern woodlands tribes, which, if historic descriptions were correct, had persisted from the time of contact. Groups evidencing different levels of acculturation provided a logical test of character persistence. The eroded culture of the Wisconsin Ojibwa of Lac du Flambeau offered a striking contrast to Hallowell's Canadian Ojibwa. Nonetheless, Lac du Flambeau Rorschachs revealed such striking similarities in types of responses and percentages with those of the Canadian Ojibwa that Hallowell (1967d:351) concluded that Lac du Flambeau change was only on the surface.

> There is a persistent core of generic traits which can be identified as Ojibwa. Thus even the highly acculturated Indians at Flambeau are still Ojibwa in a psychological sense whatever their clothes, their houses, or their occupations, whether they speak English or not, and regardless of race mixture. While culturally speaking they appear like "whites" in many respects, there is no evidence at all of a fundamental psychological transformation. On the other

hand, the fact of psychological continuity must not be taken to imply that no modifications in the psychological structure of the Ojibwa have taken place.

The critical factor Hallowell detected in the acculturative process of the Lac du Flambeau was their tendency to lose their basic Ojibwa character without adequate replacement. The Ojibwa configuration simply dissolved, and there was little evidence of internal striving for some reintegration of personality. Given this situation the Lac du Flambeau had no other personality option than psychological regression.

> At Flambeau it is a striking fact that the protocols of adults are so much like those of the children. This means that these regressive trends in their personality structure make an optimum of mental health impossible under the conditions that now confront them. In this respect the Flambeau adults are the antithesis of the [less acculturated] Berens River Ojibwa, who are quite well adjusted on the whole. Thus the Flambeau Indian represents what is, in effect, a *regressive version* of the personality structure of the Northern Ojibwa. (Hallowell 1967c:366)

In Hallowell's judgment the crucial variable in the Ojibwa response to contact pressures lay in the value core, pĭmädazīwin, which integrated the traditional character by linking an anxious regard for health with control of aggression. When pĭmädazīwin became an empty word for the Flambeau, their aggressions and childhood deprivations surged to the surface and took command. Such was the meaning of the pervasive interpersonal conflicts, the ambivalence toward life goals, and careers that often plummeted into alcoholism.

Administration of the Thematic Apperception Test to the Lac du Flambeau confirmed Rorschach findings with regard to the Canadian Berens River Saulteaux. Continuity in Ojibwa character was detected in the introversive and emotionally constrained tenor of the children's responses and in the apprehensions regarding aggression in interpersonal relations. At the same time the TAT protocols revealed the Flambeau Ojibwa to be so damaged psychologically that they were incapable of establishing security in their interpersonal relations. Erosion of the aboriginal social system correlated with erosion of the personality system (Caudill 1949(51):423–426). In this disorganized social context, women made a better accommodation than men; yet it was apparent that the social vacuum deprived children of a necessary base for developing their personalities. What "life at Flambeau provides us with," wrote Caudill (1949(51):426), "[is] a painful example of the necessity of a well-functioning culture for adequate personality development."

Barnouw (1950) viewed the Wisconsin Chippewa historically, beginning with the trader and ending with Indian reserves ringed by white settlements. His objective was to demonstrate that the concept of basic personality type focused important variables and could be used to predict how people will react to similar pressures. Barnouw first went to the Court

Oreilles and Lac du Flambeau Ojibwa in 1944 to gather additional material in the form of life histories for the Linton-Kardiner seminars. Following Kardiner's lead, he hoped to prove that the "collective history of a society ... possesses the same sort of diagnostic value, with respect to 'basic personality type,' that a life history possesses with respect to an individual subject" (Barnouw 1950:7). In this position, Barnouw reiterated the signal importance of cultural-psychological structuring as a self-generating determinant in opposition to the pressure of external conditions; for example, in the use of economic factors by Hunt (1940) to account for *The Wars of the Iroquois.*

To point up the importance of personality organization for adaptation to the acculturative experience, Barnouw contrasted Dakota Indian responses to the trader and to government with that of the Ojibwa. The crucial condition separating the Dakota and the Wisconsin Ojibwa in their response apparently hinged upon their respective interpersonal experiences according to the nature of their social organizations. Dakota society exhibited a more organized and cooperative milieu, while the Ojibwa operated within an atomistic noncooperative social setting. The historic persistence of the basically leaderless and atomized Ojibwa social structure accounted for the persistence of the emotionally constrained, isolative, suspicious, covertly aggressive, yet emotionally dependent character of these northern hunters. With everyone following an egocentric path, social units were unstable; and the possibility for welding the small family units into larger cooperative bands or clans headed by chiefs was minimal.

The cooperative-noncooperative contrast of Dakota and Ojibwa culture and personality reflected differences in their respective hunting ecologies. This point had been made by Mead (1937a:464) in her survey of cooperative and individualized societies.

> The most conspicuous instance of correspondence between the natural environment and the culture emphases is to be found among the Ojibwa. Their highly individualistic way of life is completely congruent with the sparse distribution of game animals which makes it necessary for men to scatter widely for several months of the year. But it still remains a problem why the habits of the winter months should so completely dominate their whole outlook, rather than the habits of the summer months when they collect in villages. On the other hand, among the Dakota, it is the brief buffalo-hunting period in which everyone joins which is most congruent with the cooperative, socialized emphases of the culture.

Neither Mead nor Barnouw was willing to give first consideration to ecological accommodations in the forming of personality. Childhood experiences within the family accounted for the unique Ojibwa characteristics, according to Barnouw. Warm oral relations with the mother contrasted with fear of contact with menstruating women, whose touch might bring paralysis and even death. Fathers maintained an aloof posture with their sons, and Ojibwa depicted a heavily Oedipalized relation between the two. Moreover, Ojibwa controlled their children through fright techniques, and the psychological correlate to this was fear of the outside world. "To make these bogies the more vivid, parents sometimes drew a frightening face on a frying pan, or thrust a mask of bark into the wigwam to cow the youngsters" (Barnouw 1950:19). When the white man appeared as trader, he was readily associated with the nurturant image of a mother dispensing food and other necessities. At the same time, the white male was resented and generated a feeling of weakness and inferiority because he appeared to have extraordinary shamanic powers.

> Incidentally, this inflated conception of the powerful white man seems to echo the earlier inflation of the medicine man in Chippewa society. In aboriginal times the feared and respected shaman was a kind of omniscient father-figure, who was credited with the most extraordinary magical powers. It appears that for the half-acculturated Jim Mink, the white official plays a comparable role. (Barnouw 1950:60)

Even under the spell of liquor the Ojibwa hunter did not vent his aggression upon the trader, but submissively took whatever beating the latter might inflict. But with wife and children and other relatives it was a different story. In 1861 Peter Jones (cited by Barnouw 1950:60) wrote,

> I have seen such scenes of degradation as would sicken the soul of a good man; such as husbands beating their wives, and dragging them by the hair of the head; children screaming with fright, the older ones running off with guns, tomahawks, spears, knives, and other deadly weapons, which they concealed in the woods to prevent the commission of murder by their enraged parents; yet, notwithstanding this precaution, death was not unfrequently the result.

Continuity in the social structure insulated Ojibwa interpersonal relations from alterations accompanying intensive acculturation which had overtaken the Dakota. Consequently, the Ojibwa basic personality structure persisted, while the Dakota "gave evidence of important changes in personality structure that began when they were placed on reservations" (Barnouw 1950:76).

From ethnographic and projective test evidence a generic northern Indian personality appeared to persist with regard to acculturative pressures extending over several centuries. This was conformant to basic culture theory, which at the time emphasized the positive strength of covert patternings in maintaining direction despite changing circumstances. Material possessions, employments, and even social organization might change, but covert culture processes and their personality correlates persisted. However, agreement on personality continuities did not mean that there was agreement on causes. To account for the continuance of a generic northern personality, Hallowell (1967) linked it to core values, Barnouw (1950, 1961) to continuities in social structure, and Friedl (1956) to continuities in the structuring of expectations. Tendencies for traditional Ojibwa personality characteristics to persist were confirmed independently by Friedl (1956), Jenness (1935), and Landes (1937, 1938). Studies of the Kaska (Honigmann 1949, 1954), Menomini (G. Spindler 1955, L. Spindler 1962), and the Tuscarora (Wallace 1952) also supported the idea that generic features of personality did remain, despite apparent change. Rorschach and projective test materials formed part of the research design for the Kaska, Menomini, and Tuscarora studies.

The thesis of Ojibwa personality retention and social atomism was challenged by those who stressed the importance of historic change (James 1954;Hickerson 1967b). From ethnohistoric leads, Hickerson countered the conception of northern Indian atomism and personality with evidence suggesting that in former times corporate groups (unilinear or otherwise) were present among the Ojibwa, and that collective action was an important part of the aboriginal culture. The anxious, individualized qualities presently recorded for the Ojibwa were interpreted as a consequence of fur trade and other economic pressures. Speaking from the standpoint of method, Hickerson(1967b(8):337),like Boas and Lowie before him, asserted that he would use psychological or ideological explanations only after exhausting historical and ecological explanations which correlated the dynamics of processes operating on conditions both within and outside the area. James, on the other hand, related the personality traits of Court Oreilles Ojibwa to their depressed economic situation and their efforts to counter the denigrating effects of white prejudice.

PSYCHOANALYSIS AND ADMINISTRATION

Psychoanalysis has never been accorded a dominant voice in furnishing guidance for administrative policy. In the United States, psychoanalytic instruments were employed to supplement and confirm the findings of traditional ethnographic perception in the hope of easing administrative strain in decision-making. A New Deal for Indians was undertaken by the dynamic, humanistic Commissioner John Collier. As Collier drew the social sciences into problems of Indian administration in the United States, the British government also sponsored anthropological research of native peoples in the hope that knowledge and application could be used effectively on colonial problems which had accumulated in the conquest period.

In the United States Commissioner Collier was convinced that people generally, and administrators especially, needed to be made aware of the determinative role of the social milieu in maintaining and in creating the life potential of a people. Hence, an Indian Personality and Administration Research project was launched in 1941 with cooperation of the Committee on Human Development (University of Chicago). As the research design grew, it came to include five structurally interrelated variables: ecologic, somatic, sociologic, psychologic, and symbolic (Thompson 1950:12). While the research was intended to throw into relief the multiplex nature of Indian adjustments to an alien bureaucratic society, primary objectives concentrated on the ways personality characteristics and distinctive value orientations were implanted and reinforced during childhood. With such information it was anticipated that a more meaningful communication could be reached between Indians and white administrators, teachers, and missionaries.

Use of nonverbal devices (Goodenough Draw a Man and Arthur Point Performance Scale) conveyed hope for a more valid measure of intelligence, while the Stewart Emotional Response and the Bavelas Moral Ideology tests were administered to sound situations that evoked sadness or joy, approval or condemnation. Rorschach and Thematic Apperception tests revealed subtler features of personality and served to cross-check other findings. Summarizing the crisis facing the Hopi, Thompson (1950:179) stressed the ideological variable as crucial to maintenance of their eco-cultural structure. By disrupting the "logico-esthetic integration of the symbol system with the total environment" imbalances increased in number and in velocity, especially in Hopi communities where Mennonites undermined the traditional order of mutual aid and "intensity within tranquility."

The experiment of the United States Government in ethnopsychology produced studies of the Navaho (Kluckhohn and Leighton 1962; Leighton and Kluckhohn 1962), Hopi (Thompson and Joseph 1944; Thompson 1950), Zuni (Leighton and Adair 1966), Papago (Joseph, Spicer, and Chesky 1949), and Dakota (Macgregor 1946). It represented a unique effort to make use of social science in sensitizing public and administrator to the fact that *"human societies are ideological and spiritual in their most persisting and moving parts"* and that the future world order "must be pluralistic, not ... monolithic" (Collier, in Thompson 1950:xii). However, the first report was hardly off the press when the Collier era in American Indian administration came to an abrupt end, and the integrative research effort which the Commissioner had imaginatively inspired failed to turn the corner.

Research indicated continuing and intensified damage to Indian personalities and their quality of life. This was especially the case for the Pine Ridge Sioux (Macgregor 1946), whose depressed economic condition provided no opportunity for improvement. Through Rorschach and TAT protocols, Sioux children disclosed that they faced a hostile world which they could not overcome. Their psychic life appeared filled with an endless and anxious quest for identity. Their hope for a secure image was not in the future but in the past. The happier moments of Sioux childhood were identified with dreams of buffalo hunting and raiding for booty and prestige. Hopi also followed a life path toward personality disorganization and unrealistic adaptation as their insularity was penetrated and social and cultural conflict followed (Thompson and Joseph 1944).

BEHAVIORISTIC PSYCHOANALYSIS AND CROSS-CULTURAL CORRELATES

Psychoanalysis, insofar as it drew upon general psychological processes for its explanations, was open to a proliferation of psychological hypotheses. A multiplication of psychological hypotheses to explain totemism, exogamy, and religion were characteristic of Developmentalism and led to accusations that evolutionary theory was too speculative and nonscientific. In part, psychoanalysis controlled the proliferation of interpretations by concentrating on a limited number of experiential situations and insisting that specific situations produced specific syndromes (for example, Oedipus complex, castration complex, oral fixation, and so on).

Although psychoanalysis could not be faulted for theoretical ambiguities, it remained highly speculative owing to its failure to attain satisfactory methodological controls. Verification of alleged causal relations is difficult unless the instruments of observation elicit objective evidence and assure its replicability. Owing to its clinical orientation, the common tendency in psychoanalysis was to extrapolate from one to the many. Contradictory conclusions about the impact of situations on personality were not unusual, as Orlansky (1949) observed in his studied review of personality effects traceable to early versus late weaning. Projective instruments also were controversial, since interpretation admittedly was more an art than a controlled operation answerable to scientific precision. Moreover, the psychological effects presumed to be operative according to psychoanalytic theory were challenged by observations of behaviorists that suggested opposite effects, or at the least, the absence of covert residues. In his study of the Hopi child, Dennis (1940) found no malign residues traceable to restraint of infantile movements by use of a cradleboard. Hopi infants soon recovered their physiological mobility and probed their environment as willingly as unrestrained white infants (Dennis 1965:104). The limited effect of the cradleboard upon motor conditioning was well documented in a comparison of age when walking was attempted. Those subjected to the binding of the board walked as soon as those without this restraint, the average age in months being 14.5 (Dennis 1965:107). Thus, the life of the infant, as drawn by Dennis, was more or less alike regardless of cultural differences in binding or in feeding. He even found that Hopi children, traditionally confronted with a devaluing of competitive behavior, could be induced to compete for prizes—and in their competitiveness even exceeded white children.

The challenge of scientific precision could be met in part by a test of consistency. That is, if analytic inferences reached through the use of two different instruments of observation were congruent, there was good reason for trusting both instruments and the conclusions. This was the position of DuBois (1961) and Gladwin and Sarason (1953) when evaluating ethnographic and projective test observations of native personality organization and situations which probably elicited the characteristics identified. However, at the most general level, psychoanalytic theory required precise controls that only mathematical correlations drawn from broad cross-cultural comparisons could bring. This ambitious project was initiated by John Whiting and Irvin Child in their publication, *Child Training and Personality* (1953). In a New Guinea field experience, Whiting (1941) approached socialization of the Kwoma child in the context of behavioristic psychology, drawing inferences about positive or negative reinforcement with regard to dependency, avoidance behavior, submission, and aggression. The guidelines utilized by Whiting in 1941 were like those followed in the later collaboration with Child. Whiting and Child (1962:13) admitted that psychoanalytic theory was the major source for their hypotheses regarding personality development, however, their effort to translate psychoanalytic concepts into concepts derived from general behavior theory gave them a more unified body of theory. Their approach followed the lead of Dollard and Miller (1950), who were interested in uniting Freudian and behaviorist principles.

Whiting and Child selected five systems of behavior to test behavioral correlates cross-culturally. They obviously required universal behavioral situations, and consequently they turned to experiences common to infants everywhere—the oral, anal, sexual, dependency, and aggression response systems. Their ethnographic sample was drawn from the Human Relations Area Files of Yale University. The seventy-five tribal societies in their sample qualified according to adequacy of data available with respect to the five behavioral systems. Even so, the coverage was so uneven that a description running to several hundred pages might be juxtaposed to one page of similar substance.

Two vital issues confront any cross-cultural analysis. First, the functional discreteness of each unit of the sample must be assured, and second, there must be a guarantee of the equivalence of substance compared. The need to control units of a sample for discreteness arose from the assumption of invariant structural relations intrinsic to the logic of functional correlates. Consequently, the tribal sample had to be tested to ascertain whether historic contact had induced a number of shared similarities. At the time, Whiting and Child could not guarantee the functional quality of the tribal sample nor could they make up for deficiencies of the ethnographic substance. One thing was clear: they had to test for variation either on a presence-absence basis, or according to difference in degree. Considering their Freudianized hypotheses, the latter appeared the better approach, and three judges were utilized to rate seven degrees of difference in each of the five systems of behavior and to estimate psychological effects. Rating of cultural practices was projected on an indulgence–severity continuum; that of effect, along a satisfaction–anxiety continuum. Focus on satisfaction and anxiety probed the dynamics of motivation and also the way in which cultural practices might influence personality integration through the organization and energizing of affect. Initial satisfaction conveyed a positive affect to objects and relationships. A sense of initial satisfaction could be induced through indulgent treatment of infant and child before responsibility for actions and a tolerable conformity with adult behavior was enforced. The valence of the initial satisfaction variable for inducing a patterned impulse ("custom potential") was mediated by four factors, notably, "the duration of the initial period, the amount of freedom given the child to perform his initial habits, the amount of encouragement of these habits, and the amount of concurrent anxiety" (Whiting and Child 1962:50). The socialization anxiety variable was a product of blocked action and overt punishment designed to prevent the act. Four factors were relevant to socialization anxiety; namely, amount of time the child took in making the transition from indulgence to responsibility, symptoms of emotional distress, and severity and frequency of punishment (Whiting and Child 1962:53). The assessment of how each of these aspects was handled in a particular culture measured the potential of a behavioral system of responses and impulses to become entrenched as a custom through arousal of an anxiety drive in a typical child (Whiting and Child 1962:54).

In their broader intentions Whiting and Child hoped to uncover the psychological linkages binding the individual to culture. The dynamics of this relationship was anchored to child training. Personality organization derived from a common sum of childhood experiences was central to the integrative axes in cultures, since the anxious motives and acquired rewards of typical individuals were mirrored in the projective symbolism of cultures.

The relation of personality processes to the problem of cultural integration was evidenced in three interrelated modes. First, integration was measured by the equivalence of individual habit and custom. Second, integration resulted from the unification of a number of attributes, identified as practices, beliefs, values, sanctions, rules, motives, and satisfactions. To such a system Whiting and Child gave the term "custom complex" (Whiting and Child 1962:27). The third mode related to the ways in which personality variables influenced the integration of customs. As process, integration could be conceived as a product of psychological generalization. That is, a particular childhood practice might give rise to a custom complex that in turn would spread its influence to a related domain (for example, the integration of oral and anal syndromes).

A potential for impelling action was at the heart of any experience, for drive mobilized energy for action, whether physical or symbolic. Here one could rely on general learning theory for confirmation of the importance of reward and punishment in entrenching or eliminating habit and maintaining habit strength. In the absence of reward, habit strength ran down and finally evaporated. Theories of personality, however, emphasized structural continuities. Freudian personality theory was especially emphatic on this, since it clued structural continuity to early childhood. The process of fixation supplied Freudians with the rationale for maintaining the early formation of personality and its later continuity. Hence, measurement of fixative tendencies was critical in demonstrating the integrative stability of personality. In applying the reward-satisfaction–punishment-anxiety formula, Whiting and Child logically concluded that fixation was divided into two modes, positive and negative. The positive process was associated with reduction of anxiety states, whereas negative fixation thrived on heightened anxiety (Whiting and Child 1962:146).

In standardizing their measurement of the drive valence of each of the personality variables—oral, anal, sexual, dependency, and aggression—Whiting and Child determined that response to illness would be useful. The universality of illness guaranteed the presence of therapeutic practice and belief. Moreover, illness was a crisis situation and could be counted on to arouse anxiety. The habit capacity of satisfaction relaxes tension, and hence the measure of positive fixation could be taken from continued practice. For example, oral indulgence could be expected to associate a reduced tension with orality, and hence oral practices (for example, oral medication or sucking) would be prominent in treatment of illness. Negative fixation implied that some object or person was responsible for the acquired drive or anxiety, and hence explanations of disease were a credible measure of negative fixation. The raising of anxiety through severe toilet training produced theories of disease in which the patient's feces or other exuviae were used in ritual directed against his person. The association, directly or symbolically, of an orderly sequence with feces gave validity to the psychoanalytic hypothesis that severe toilet training, with its emphatic concern for a rightness of time, place, and manner of disposal served as the elementary model or prototype for compulsive ritualization and associated substance.

The correlations Whiting and Child derived from their comparisons of seventy-five societies produced no precise confirmations of relations affirmed by their psychoanalytic hypotheses. The evidence for positive conditioning or fixation during infancy was singularly lacking. Expectably, when situational continuity was plotted up the ladder of life, more effects of positive conditioning were demonstrated. Negative fixation, with its acquired anxiety drive, was more direct in its influence on orality and aggression. However, the relation between dependence socialization anxiety and dependence explanations of disease demonstrated only a modest confirmation. The arousal of anxieties in anal and sexual domains evoked little tendency to respond with anal and sexual explanations of disease. Since the research design was not set up methodologically to cope with cultural integration, this issue remained largely one of assumption and inference. Whatever induced conformity, of course, affected the problem of integration, and here their explorations of the origins of guilt are interesting and suggestive. A measure of guilt could be extracted from explanations of disease which held the patient responsible for his condition. In examining the timing of child training in weaning, modesty, heterosexual inhibition, and independence, Whiting and Child found that the pattern of correlations declined in self-accusatory explanations as the age of socialization increased. However, toilet training in no way conformed to this pattern. Since the societies initiated training in these domains on or before the sixth year, even in the case of heterosexual inhibition, Whiting and Child conjectured that early childhood was critical to the guilt-process. Identification, as Freud suggested, probably was crucial to the internalization of self-judgment.

Child Training and Personality represented the most ambitious attempt at the time to unify behaviorism and psychoanalytic theory. However, it failed to inspire others to expand the foundation, due perhaps to the lack of sharpness in the correlations. The limited options which were available to Whiting and Child for testing cross-cultural correlates of personality only underscored the many-sided deficiencies of ethnological substance bearing on this problem. More telling, however, was the realization that disease concepts, taboos, and mythological themes which filled projective systems were too limited in scope to support a dynamic and comprehensive perspective on culture-personality relations. The same limitation dogged the cross-cultural use of projective tests to recover the residues of childhood fixations. In the judgment of Kaplan (1961:238),

> A single Rorschach, TAT or both, even when augmented with life history materials and extensive observation studies such as in Vogt's (1949), must yield an incomplete account of the person. To the extent that the anthropologist or psychologist believes that personality is encapsulated in the microcosm of the test protocol, he is undoubtedly in error and in particularly serious error because he isn't likely to be aware of it. When the protocols are sparse and inexpressive . . . it is even more foolish to believe that one has the truth or some substantial portion of it. When the worker knows that his sample is seriously incomplete, as most psychologists do, but treats it as though it were not, he is equally in error.

Viewed in later perspective, the failure of Whiting and Child to produce firm correlations based on behavioral-psychoanalytic theorems confirmed the growing suspicion that unconscious conditionings were not all that determinative in mobilizing the organization and action of personality. Taken in conjunction with the variable modalities surfacing in Rorschach and TAT protocols, the Whiting and Child results pointed to the need for a perspective that accorded greater flexibility to the typical enculturated personality. In fact, the myth of a monolithic modal personality could no longer be maintained even for the simpler societies. The release of personality from the tight grip of the fixative experience tied to Freudian universals, and equally from the inertia of habituative conditioning, was seen in the emerging stress on the role of deliberation and choice in human action. This new orientation focused attention on the variability of relations linking the individual to culture and also on the differences among cultures with regard to such relations. The ground thus was prepared for Mead (1956) to argue that the Manus operated within their cultural milieu not as unconscious automatons but as strategists. Hence, they were predisposed to develop and accept innovative instruments, and to accelerate changes in their culture where they could perceive a personal gain.

There is no doubt that the waning of the psychoanalytic thrust in culture and personality investigation following World War II was coordinated with the emergence of a dynamic and more comprehensive perspective. Psychoanalytic personality theory left little room for cognitive process despite stress in the ideal on the development of a balanced ego. Culture-personality investigators proved it was necessary to consider sociopsychological processes manifest in organized personality configurations as important to the reality problem. However, the new perspective no longer admitted personality organization as the central variable for explaining culture and cultural differences, but rather placed it alongside a number of variables accountable for directionality in social action. Such an adjusted view is found in Spiro's (1961:490) reassessment of the place which culture and personality, as a specialization, should hold in the field of anthropology as a whole.

> I have suggested that, rather than persist as a distinctive subdiscipline within the total range of the anthropological sciences, culture-and-personality conceive of itself as part of that subdiscipline—social anthropology—which is concerned with the analysis of social and cultural systems. Thus the contributions of culture-and-personality theory can be combined with the important contributions of structural theory (notably those of British social anthropology) and of role theory (notably those of American sociology and social psychology) to advance our understanding of human society and culture. As a partner in this venture, culture-and-personality can make (indeed, has made) a unique contribution.

The clash which often occurred between gratification of needs and cultural conformity supplied the rationale for including the personality variable. As the stage for the interplay of need gratification and normative pressures, the understanding of personality dynamics was critical to the understanding of cultural processes linked to conformity, social control, and the functional operations of social systems (Spiro 1961:491). In Spiro's view, the necessity for including the personality variable hinged on the ultimate biopsychic givens of human nature.

PSYCHOANALYTIC THEORY AND EVOLUTION OF SELF

Psychoanalytic theory contributed vitally to anthropological understanding by refocusing the problem of man as an emergent self-conscious being. The issue was engaged by Developmentalists when charting the intellectual and moral advancement from savagery to civilization. On the wings of the fresh evolutionary impulse generated during the 1940s, Hallowell (1950(52):164; also 1959, 1960) pointed to the significance of the emergence of a *"generic* psychic structure in man" in the evolution of human personality and society. Obviously it was this generic psychic structure that differentiated man from his primate relatives and other animals. To ground man's human status on singular organic features (for example, foot, hand, or cortical additions to the brain) or on a tool-using capacity was a serious error. Such narrow definitions excluded the most critical of all variables—the human personality and the social milieu through which it developed. According to Hallowell (1950(52):163), the perspective must be panoramic and unitary, avoiding the pitfalls of false dichotomies, such as the mind-body problem.

In recent years the concept of personality structure, whose genesis lies in social interaction, offers the beginnings of a conceptual resolution of the old mind-body dichotomy, while at the same time, it relates the individual to his social setting. The assumption is that the individual functions as a psychobiological whole, as a total personality. Behavior has a structural basis, but this structuralization has arisen in experience and cannot, therefore, be reduced to an inherited organic structure. "Intelligence," "reason," or other mental traits then become specific functions of the personality structure. Thus, the distinctive psychological organization of the human being, whether described as mind or personality structure, is just as much a function of his membership in a social group as it is a function of his inherited organic equipment.

Hallowell (1950(52):165–70) attributed the unique personality of man to three primary characteristics. First, there was the unique capacity for guiding behavior through symbolization, manifest not only in reasoning but in "all other psychic functions—attention, perception, interest, memory, dreams, imagination, etc." Second, ego-centered processes served to bring organization to human personality, and this sensitive regard for self proved important in allowing man to evaluate his behavior in relation to others.

> The fact that every human social order operates as a moral order is, among other things, contingent upon man's becoming an object to himself. . . . As a result of self-objectification human societies become social orders of conscious selves, in contrast with the societies of other primates where the development of ego-centered processes as part of the psycho-biological structure of the individual do not become salient.

Third, man's emotional nature was structured by unconscious processes expressed through anxiety, guilt, and despondency. Anxiety, guilt, and depression signaled the degree of personal adjustment suffered in the antagonism between individual desires and social norms. Here the psychoanalytic concept of the superego was especially relevant, since it aided the investigator's understanding regarding the relation between the inner man and the social and cultural milieu.

In Hallowell's view human sociality and human psychic processes should not be considered of the same order as animals. There are continuities and some distinct resemblances in that animals learn and form conditioned habits, as does man. Moreover, the combining of a number of processes—symbolization, identification, conflict, repression—means that human learning and personality formation are far removed from the simple conditioning to which organisms generally are subject.

> Thus the transmission of culture, if realistically viewed, must be thought of not as the acquisition through a simple conditioning process, of habits or cultural traits as they appear in our descriptive ethnographic accounts, but as part of a very complicated and symbolically mediated learning process in which mechanisms like conflict and repression play their role in the total integrative structure that we call the human personality.

Traditional terms like the "psychic unity" of man, or "human nature" which have been somewhat emptied of their original meaning become genuinely significant again if we mean a primate whose level of adjustment implies such processes and mechanisms. (Hallowell 1950(52):171)

Spiro (1954), LaBarre (1954), and Henry (1959) likewise emphasized the point that a common human nature provided the background for universals to be found in all cultures. Spiro (1954(56):26) observed that without a universal human nature there would be no basis for a universal culture pattern and no foundation for a general science of mankind like anthropology. What supported and elicited culture was simply the dynamics of personality functioning. The needs, values, ego processes, and defense mechanisms intrinsic to the dynamic organization of human activity supplied the very basis for culture itself.

LaBarre (1954:xii, 209) also anchored his interpretation of man, society, and culture to elementary biopsychic components. Man could not be understood simply as a socialized person. The humanizing of man resulted from a long struggle to resolve fundamental conflicts of sexual dependency associated with his mammalian ancestry. The family was the critical institution where these fundamental conflicts were dramatized in the interpersonal relations of husband, wife, and child. Through the family the aggressive, promiscuous, nonaffectionate male was captivated by the gentle nurturance of infant, and through identification with mother and child was prepared for the creation of culture. The child was the center of the Oedipal drama, acting out his transfer of an infantile mother fixation to other objects of love and at the same time coming to terms with himself in a moral struggle with unconscious impulses which demanded that the father be eliminated. As the infantile love of mother found a more sublime outlet in the love of a mate, so the struggle of infantile lust against the father was transcended in a moral triumph that made society and culture possible.

> For there is no gainsaying it: all adaptive human institutions, *including morality* relate to man's oedipal nature. For lawgivers, judges, and kings are but larger social images of the father. All law that has any social substance is mere codifying of prior social convictions. It is the socially objective re-externalizing of morality which was internalized in childhood from the commands of the real father, and ultimately of the cultural fathers before him. The state is our struggle to find both paternal power and brotherly justice in the governing of men. Human character and morality is a peace-making between family-born conscience (superego) and animal organism (id). Religion is a yearning for rapport with the divine father, a seeking for a homeostasis of self and the organism with Superego and the Logos. Art is rebellion against the real, a stubborn defiance of the authority of reality, an unbending animal wilfulness in humans, a usurpation of creativity, a controlled psychopathy, a playful As-If schizophrenia that is only by courtesy of culture not psychotic. Poetry is a revolt against prose, an insistence that semantics be enlarged to contain recreant desire. Literature is the fantasies and the records of men who have struggled to resolve the moral, the social, and the erotic problems of men. Speculative philosophy (a branch of lyric poetry) tells us how greatly feeling men think projectively about the Universe, and persuasively invites to feel as they do. Painting and sculpture re-see the world, imposing on created and conceptualized forms the artist's wish for

the order and meaning he does not find in the world. Music, that abstractest art, is the pleasurable (since most largely self-chosen) apperception of that divine voice saying those things we most want to hear. All economic activity is the seeking of power over others and a means of demanding goods of them for the succorance of one's own. And Science itself is a disciplined, indefatigable, and largely masculine appetite to know the facts of life, despite the traditions and the untruths our cultural fathers have sometimes told us, and to find the true and only worthy father of man the high, implacable, invincible, inseductable and unbeseechable that-which-is, the real. (LaBarre 1954:220–221)

There was little of culture that LaBarre could not mold to the Oedipal procrustean bed with imaginative stretching and cutting. Within anthropology it marked an effort to produce an ultimate psychoanalytic synthesis, which, however, was soon dated.

Henry (1959) centered man's evolutionary development in the psychosomatic viability of human personality as it developed adaptive techniques to discharge stresses of the sociocultural environment. Those with hereditary predispositions for infertility or cancer, if unable to release the volume of their stress, reinforced the disease predisposition through a psychosomatic linkage. The social environment was man's own biome and the secret of evolutionary success lay in reducing somatic stress through sociopsychological safety valves. As Henry (1959(61):223) viewed personality and evolution,

> When these two processes genetic variability and impulse discharge became associated in man with his dependence on social life, the stage was set for the elimination from human society of all members unable to displace activity and feeling in socially tolerable ways. What social life did, then, was to put human displacement activity precisely in the center of biosocial adaptation, making it the veritable pivot of society as well as an important determinant of individual survival. We can see then that from the biological point of view, culture is the product of a patterned displacement and modification of response release guided by symbolic processes. Freud called this sublimation.

Evolution then could be plotted in the formula "E—Ss, e (Rs, Cda)," where evolution (E) was a function of stress (Ss) as it was mediated by experience (e) occurring within the context of genetic variability to stress (Rs) and capabilities for displacement (Cda) (Henry 1959(61):224).

SUMMARY

In retrospect, the penetration of psychoanalytic theory into American ethnology can be viewed as a logical extension of the latent psychologism in the historicists' approach to culture, as well as a reflection of the stimulus of structural-functional analysis which made an initial impact during the thirties. Sapir and Benedict took the lead in moving the individual into the forefront of culture analysis. However, it was not the individual as a particulate entity that engaged the attention of culture analysis, but the person as replicating the psychological patterning of the culture. The direct infusion of psychoanalytic theory through the Kardiner-Linton seminars did not alter the situation, as the concepts of basic personality structure and modal personality testify. Psychoanalytic explanations of functional linkages between psychobiological dynamics and nurturant and obedience figures actually were antithetical to cultural-historical explanations. This was so because invariant relations were substituted for the historical, and customs were derived from psychological and emotional precipitates accompanying interpersonal relations. The explanations of psychoanalysis once again turned the spotlight on the origins of culture, although Kardiner (1939:472) disclaimed any interest in the origin of the controls imposed on the child or of origins in general. What he was interested in were processual relations:

> In short, we abandon the quest for origins as an explanation of society, and substitute for it a study of the dynamic relationship between man and institutions. We can take as a base line some of these institutions, as specific family organizations and basic disciplines, and attempt to see what happens as we alter these conditions. This is as close as we can get to the conditions of "experiment" in sociology. (Kardiner 1939:108)

For those wary of psychological reductionism, Maitland's judgment that if ethnology were to amount to anything, it had to be historical, must have taken on new meaning. In fact, the psychoanalytic model, which emphasized feeling states derived from interpersonal relations as the source for conventionalized practice and symbolization, had more in common with social anthropology than behavioristically oriented culture historicism. Social Structuralists commonly grounded the social order and its ritualized conventions in sentiments derived out of social interaction whereas culture historicists linked the psychological bases for action to culture itself. Yet, in the broader context, Kardiner (1939:466–467) drew attention to culture as exerting a profound influence on personality formation, thereby contributing to social solidarity or its opposite.

> It is ... culture [that] molds the specific direction and activities of the personality. Culture can do this because the total personality is slow in formation. Not all of it is done by force; most of it is done by a kind of osmosis. This influence of culture, is of course, necessary for the preservation of the solidarity of the group. Though the immediate executive of a culture is the parent, or the protectors during the formative years, the disciplines to which the individual is subject are culturally determined. This leaves plenty of leeway for the individual. Society cannot prescribe the specific reaction to a given discipline; this is determined by the individual alone. In our society, for example, we prescribe sexual aims, but the reactions to these by the individual are legion.

The rise of ethnopsychoanalysis coincided with the rise of social Structuralism and Malinowski's biopsychic functionalism. Its explanatory model was quite congruent with the structural-functional-interactional construct upon which these two depended. In his biocultural formulation Malinowski was stimulated especially by the biopsychic orientation of psychoanalysis. However, ethnopsychoanalysis demonstrated a greater capacity for crossing traditional boundaries than either of these two theoretical positions. Thus, it was able to establish linkages with problems of maintenance and change in the social system, to relate personality to the securities and anxieties of economies, to connect personality integration to values and the integration of cultures, and to even draw personality into the perspective of psychobiological and sociocultural evolution. It also stimulated efforts to unify behavioral and psychoanalytic theory by applying the explanatory principles of the former to the hypothesized psychological relations of the latter. When Murdock (1949:Preface, xi–xvii) took inventory of the bodies of theory that assisted in the illumination of elements of social organization, psychoanalysis appeared in the company of functionalism (by way of Keller and Malinowski), historicism, and behavioristic psychology. While admitting the fertility of psychoanalytic theory in formulating hypotheses, its obscure methodology suggested that its theory would be "gradually incorporated into some more rigorous scientific system such as that of behavioristic psychology." In drawing together these various disciplines for the purpose of putting together a harmonious interdisciplinary science of human behavior, it is no surprise that the central figure to whom Murdock paid tribute was the educational psychologist Mark A. May, longtime director of the Institute of Human Relations, Yale University. In such a coordinated science, personality organization must take its place alongside other variables.

13

Social Structuralism and Biocultural Functionalism

INTRODUCTION

At the turn of the twentieth century, those who hoped to establish social anthropology as a distinctive discipline faced the same kind of task as those who sought to make anthropology the science of culture. Much would hinge on whether the social could be defined as an independent and causally autonomous dimension of reality. Once this was accomplished, other things would fall into an easy and respectable order. Social facts could be distinguished as the proper domain of the sociological anthropologist. The door would be open to development of a theory and method that would justify the collection, classification, and generalization of social facts and their interrelations. Considering the extraordinary successes achieved by natural science, it was not difficult to imagine that social anthropology could become a creative discipline by incorporating the model of natural science.

In backward glance, the Developmentalist outlook for sociology seemed incomplete. Their emphasis on a dynamic evolutionary sociology, to the neglect of a structural and processual sociology, failed to produce a measured analysis of social forms or social laws governing the system of relationships exhibited by functioning societies. The field of structural and processual relations which Developmentalists had neglected now was seized upon as the key to a general science and theory of society. This general theory was formulated gradually as the relations between social phenomena were described and analyzed in terms of themselves. Methodologically speaking, only social facts would be used to interpret other social facts.

These new social anthropologists had a number of good reasons for rejecting the Developmentalist model. The most serious error of these early students of society lay in dissolving the social in the processes of the human mind. In their psychological explanation of origins and stages in the advance to civilization, Developmentalists allowed the social aspect to slip through their fingers like sand.

Emile Durkheim and his associates of *L'Année sociologique* played a prominent role in developing structural-functional theory and method of social anthropology. The influence of French sociology on British social anthropology has yet to be researched in depth. However, Radcliffe-Brown (1958b:63) early cited Durkheim as a kindred soul, albeit somewhat tainted at times by ideas and terminology akin to Developmentalist anthropology. In his discourse on "The Present Position of Anthropological Studies," Radcliffe-Brown (1958b:85–86) equated his goals with those of the French sociologists:

> what is called sociology in France, or at any rate at the University of Paris, is the same study precisely as that which I have been describing as comparative sociology, and it is largely owing to the work of the French sociologists Durkheim, Huber, Mauss, Simiand, Halbwachs, Hertz, Granet and Maunier, to mention only some of them, that the subject is as far advanced as it is.

In the fifties, when reprints of classics became fashionable, British social anthropologists pioneered in the translation of Durkheim, Mauss, and their associates. The British intention was to publicize the inspiration French sociologists had brought with their "analytical notice . . . [of] 'transition,' 'polarity' (opposition), 'exchange,' 'solidarity,' 'total,' 'structure,' 'classification'" (Needham 1963, introduction, xlii; Durkheim and Mauss 1963).

DURKHEIM AND THE AUTONOMY OF THE SOCIAL

Emile Durkheim (1858–1917), considered to be the successor of Comte in French sociology, was born into a family oriented by tradition to the profession of rabbi and to a high level of intellectual sophistication. At the age of twenty-one, Durkheim was in Paris studying under Fustel de Coulanges who, through his Greco-Roman studies, reinforced for Durkheim the significance of the sacred in the bonding of ancient societies. In his doctoral dissertation, Durkheim (1960) credited Montesquieu and Rousseau with laying the foundations for social science. From the former he gleaned the essentials of a functional analysis of social regulations and laws. Travel and study in Germany brought Durkheim into contact with folk psychology and ethnological investigations on the evolution of culture. These two influences persisted in Durkheim's orientation toward sociological problems, despite his steady commitment to the study of social facts within a structural-functional context.

Durkheim's initial exploration of the significance of society for the individual's sense of self and fulfillment came in a study of suicide. There Durkheim (1951) attempted to correlate three patterns in suicide with three kinds of individual-social relationships. In certain societies extreme individualism occurred because a person could find no objective anchor in the community that gave meaning to life. An egocentric pursuit of meaning ended in egoistic suicide. The egoistic self-destruction that occurred within loosely integrated social systems contrasted with the altruistic sacrifice of self in service of the community. This type was characteristic of tightly integrated systems which encouraged the individual to aspire for more than could be realized in life. Finally, there was the anomic suicide, which thrived when crises disturbed the harmonious balance of the collective order, shattering traditional restraints. This occurred when a compelling passion to belong was complicated by desperate fears of rejection. Industrial societies with their built-in economic anxieties were peculiarly susceptible to suicide of the anomic variety.

In a work on the division of labor, Durkheim (1949) continued investigation of individual-social integration to show how a functional differentiation of tasks contributed to the emergence of human personality. As differentiation proceeded, the individual was drawn into more interdependent and moral-legal relations, creating an organic bond of solidarity linking the individual to society. The organic solidarity of complex societies contrasted with the mechanical bonding of the simpler societies. Individuals living in societies with little division of labor were like social atoms submerged in a collective conscience and will. Their freedom to act as individualized personalities was restricted by the collective unity of their lives. Both organic and mechanical solidarity operated in any social order, but organic solidarity increased with functional differentiation and was most characteristic of industrial societies.

There were echoes of Montesquieu in Durkheim's phrasing of the moral-legal problem. His view of human personality, growing in response to the fresh challenges that accompanied social diversification, echoed ideas expressed by progressivists, and especially of Adam Smith when analyzing the growth of economic systems through mutual differentiation and exchange. Durkheim repeated an earlier consensus when observing that social pressures exerted by tradition were a heavier weight on members of primitive societies than on members of complex societies.

Durkheim's formal presentation of the nature of the social and of sociological explanation was published in 1895 as *The Rules of Sociological Method*. At the outset he vowed to give sociology a new and scientific direction and to free it from its subsidiary role as a branch of philosophy. A first step lay in defining the social as an objective thing, obedient to laws of its own structure—and independent of both biology and psychology. The objective units of this social reality were social facts. Social facts encompassed *"every way of action, fixed or not, capable of exercising an external restraint; or again, every way of acting which is general through-*

out a given society, while at the same time existing in its own right independent of its individual manifestations." (Durkheim 1938:13) For Durkheim, gathering and explaining social facts had to be approached without
the bias of metaphysical preconceptions or speculations about the basics
of human nature. One could not begin with a blueprint of human nature
and then explain the social as a construction suited to the expression of
that nature. To the contrary, the social existed as a separate dimension of
reality. A social fact had to be explained in terms of the *"efficient cause
which produces it and the function it fulfills"*—that is, social facts and
social functions (Durkheim 1938:95). Since social facts existed outside the
individual and were not derived by adding together individual behaviors,
they could not be explained by individual consciousness whether in isolation or in a crowd. Indeed, asserted Durkheim (1938:104), "every time
that a social phenomenon is directly explained by a psychological phenomenon, we may be sure that the explanation is false." The ultimate in
the human reality thus was social and not psychological, for it was not
only supraindividual but also nonindividual.

> When the individual has been eliminated, society alone remains. We must,
> then, seek the explanation of social life in the nature of society itself. It is
> quite evident that, since it infinitely surpasses the individual in time as well
> as in space, it is in a position to impose upon him ways of acting and thinking
> which it has consecrated with its prestige. This pressure, which is the distinc-
> tive property of social facts, is the pressure which the totality exerts on the
> individual. (Durkheim 1938:102)

Social facts, in Durkheim's view, obviously derived from a social consciousness quite distinct from the individual psyche. A social fact was
rooted in collectively engendered sentiments and found expression in collective representations (ideas) and collective symbols. Any social fact
existed for a purpose, or function, and to understand it one had to see
what the social fact accomplished in establishing the social order. Again,
the social offered the rationale for function: *"The function of a social fact
ought always to be sought in its relation to some social end"* (Durkheim
1938:110–111).

Religion, Sociopsychological Sentiments, and Social Facts

To illustrate the supraindividual quality of social experience and of
social facts, Durkheim turned to religion, continuing his interest in totemism with new data supplied by Spencer and Gillen on the Australians. Here
he found, in what he considered the most primitive of peoples, the elemental social foundations of religion, and disproof of the origins of religion
in individual consciousness. To the sociologically oriented Durkheim, it
was inconceivable that a social phenomenon of the proportions of religion
could be rooted in the awesome perception of nature or in the fears springing from dreams and hallucinations which individuals might have (Durk-

heim 1947:68–70). Here was nothing but a shifting bed of sand that proliferated one psychological explanation after another.

In *The Elementary Forms of the Religious Life* (1913) Durkheim presented more than a theory of the origins of religion. In effect, he offered a general theory of social processes. At the same time he offered an explanation for the origins of totemism and joined those who held totemism to be the most elemental and original of all religious expressions (Durkheim 1947:89). Primitive society, in Durkheim's view, conformed to a sacra-civil type, and the evolutionary trend followed a course in which the individual was gradually emancipated from group demands. Durkheim began with the Australians because they were the best example of the totemic prototype, and because they were so well described in the literature. The problem of totemism as a universal stage in religion was secondary to his main purpose, which was to concentrate on the essential relations governing religious activity in order to learn better what religion was about. The wide-ranging comparisons found in the works of evolutionists such as Spencer and Frazer were not relevant to his typological analysis, since "One single fact may make a law appear, where a multitude of imprecise and vague observations would only produce confusion" (Durkheim 1947: 95).

Durkheim began with the assumption that behind every social institution one would find a collective feeling or sentiment. Although he did not pinpoint it as such, this collective sentiment was the social fact. A social sentiment cannot be raised privately by any individual, for it is only excited by individuals mutually stimulating each other. It is this social quality that makes the social fact, a thing in its own right. Once the collective sentiment has been induced, it is projected on to the external world in the form of collective representations (ideas) and given formal expression in symbolizations of one kind or another (see Figure 13-1).

The religious problem facing Durkheim divided itself into two parts. First, the collective sentiment had to be accounted for, and since any collective action was organized around some force or energy, this had to be an integral part of the collective experience. Certainly, as for religion,

> a god is not merely an authority upon whom we depend; it is a force upon which our strength relies. The man who has obeyed his god and who, for this reason, believes the god is with him, approaches the world with confidence and with the feeling of an increased energy. Likewise, social action does not confine itself to demanding sacrifices, privations and efforts from us. For the collective force is not entirely outside of us; it does not act upon us wholly from without; but rather, since society cannot exist except in and through individual consciousness, this force must also penetrate us and organize itself within us; it thus becomes an integral part of our being and by that very fact this is elevated and magnified. (Durkheim 1947:209)

Second, the formalization of this sentiment in idea, symbol, and ceremony had to be explained.

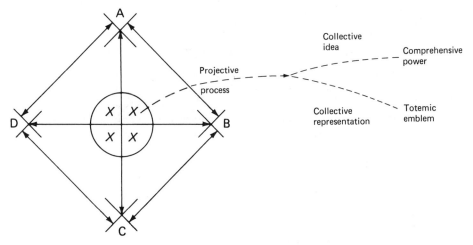

Figure 13-1. Generation of a social sentiment, social idea, and social emblem, after Durkheim.

A, B, C, and D represent persons interacting and sharing a common feeling X.

Durkheim maintained that only a social fact could explain another social fact. Social facts could not be generated from the individual psyche. A social fact required the interaction of individuals, who mutually stimulated each other, and, through suggestion, communicated a common excitation and sentiment to each other. The sharing of this socially engendered sentiment constituted a collective social fact. This primary social sentiment was entrenched in the unconscious experience. However, it was rationalized in the form of symbolic expressions (collective ideas and representations) that evoked the social sentiment, and hence reinforced it. The symbolic expressions, in point of fact, were projections of the social sentiment. It followed that the social sentiment was central to the ordering of the world and of society. A social fact thus was a collective bundle of sentiment, idea, and form.

The Sacred and Primary Social Sentiments

Durkheim considered a distinction of the sacred and the profane to be fundamental to the primitive world view. The process by which men had arrived at the conception of the sacred was profoundly important because it was the primary social-psychological experience upon which a sense of group unity and destiny was raised. The sacred intrinsically represented a transfiguration of the profane—the bringing of social meaning and purpose to the casual and unorganized gathering. The seasonal cycle of the Australians, which alternated a time of plenty with a time of scarcity, furnished a good beginning. During scarcity individual families fended for themselves, but when food was abundant, a clan or segment of the tribe gathered for a religious ceremony or a corrobboree. In a footnote Durkheim observed that the corrobboree differed from the religious ceremony by permitting women and the uninitiated to be present; at the same time both activities were very much alike and closely related in their collective functions. Continuing his argument, Durkheim pointed to differences in feelings aroused by economic as against corrobboree activity.

> These two phases are contrasted with each other in the sharpest way. In the first, economic activity is the preponderating one, and it is generally of a very mediocre intensity. Gathering the grains or herbs that are necessary for food, or hunting and fishing are not occupations to awaken very lively passions. The dispersed condition in which the society finds itself results in making its life uniform, languishing and dull. But when a corrobbori takes place, everything changes. Since the emotional and passional faculties of the primitive are only imperfectly placed under the control of his reason and will, he easily loses control of himself. Any event of some importance puts him quite outside himself Does he receive good news? There are at once transports of enthusiasm. In the contrary conditions, he is to be seen running here and there like a madman, giving himself up to all sorts of immoderate movements, crying, shrieking, rolling in the dust, throwing it in every direction, biting himself, brandishing his arms in a furious manner, etc. The very fact of the concentration acts as an exceptionally powerful stimulant. When they are once come together, a sort of electricity is formed by their collecting which quickly transports them to an extraordinary degree of exaltation. Every sentiment expressed finds a place without resistance in all the minds, which are very open to outside impressions; each re-echoes the others, and is re-echoed by the others. The initial impulse thus proceeds, growing as it goes, as an avalanche grows in its advance. And as such active passions so free from all control could not fail to burst out, on every side one sees nothing but violent gestures, cries, veritable howls, and deafening noises of every sort, which aid in intensifying still more the state of mind which they manifest. And since a collective sentiment cannot express itself collectively except on the condition of observing a certain order permitting co-operation and movements in unison, these gestures and cries naturally tend to become rhythmic and regular; hence come songs and dances. But in taking a more regular form, they lose nothing of their natural violence; a regulated tumult remains tumult. The human voice is not sufficient for the task; it is reinforced by means of artificial processes: boomerangs are beaten against each other; bull-roarers are whirled. It is probable that these instruments, the use of which is so general in the Australian religious ceremonies, are used primarily to express in a more adequate fashion the agitation felt. But while they express it, they also strengthen it. This effervescence often reaches such a point that it causes unheard-of actions. The passions released are of such an impetuosity that they can be restrained by nothing. They are so far removed from their ordinary conditions of life, and they are so thoroughly conscious of it, that they feel that they must set themselves outside of and above their ordinary morals. The sexes unite contrarily to the rules governing sexual relations. Men exchange wives with each other. Sometimes even incestuous unions, which in normal times are thought abominable and are severely punished, are now contracted openly and with impunity. If we add to all this that the ceremonies generally take place at night in a darkness pierced here and there by the light of fires, we can easily imagine what effect such

scenes ought to produce in the minds of those who participate. They produce such a violent super-excitation of the whole physical and mental life that it cannot be supported very long: the actor taking the principal part finally falls exhausted on the ground. (Durkheim 1947:215–216)

Durkheim based this hypothetic description of the arousal of a social sentiment on the fire ceremonies of the Warramunga reported by Spencer and Gillen. In the state of exaltation achieved through a reciprocating suggestion, possible only in a social context, the individual is made aware of a power that transcends the self. He feels himself transformed, and adds to this feeling with mask and decoration. The exultant power-filled self draws a sharp contrast with the mundane nature of daily life. Man lives in two worlds, as it were.

One is that where his daily life drags wearily along; but he cannot penetrate into the other without at once entering into relations with extra-ordinary powers that excite him to the point of frenzy. The first is the profane world, the second, that of sacred things.

So it is in the midst of these effervescent social environments and out of this effervescence itself that the religious idea seems to be born. The theory that this is really its origin is confirmed by the fact that in Australia the really religious activity is almost entirely confined to the moments when these assemblies are held. To be sure, there is no people among whom the great solemnities of the cult are not more or less periodic; but in the more advanced societies, there is not . . . a day when some prayer or offering is not addressed to the gods and some ritual act is not performed. But in Australia, on the contrary, apart from the celebrations of the clan and tribe, the time is nearly all filled with lay and profane occupations. Of course there are prohibitions that should be and are preserved even during these periods of temporal activity; it is never permissible to kill or eat freely of the totemic animal. . . . The religious life of the Australian passes through successive phases of complete lull and of super-excitation, and social life oscillates in the same rhythm. This puts clearly into evidence the bond uniting them to one another, but among the peoples called civilized, the relative continuity of the two blurs their relations. It might even be asked whether the violence of this contrast was not necessary to disengage the feeling of sacredness in its first form. By concentrating itself almost entirely in certain determined moments, the collective life has been able to attain its greatest intensity and efficacy, and consequently to give men a more active sentiment of the double existence they lead and of the double nature in which they participate. (Durkheim 1947:218–219)

The social sentiment thus is the catalyst for social action, and the collective representations and symbolizations are designed to evoke it again and again at each meeting.

The Symbolization of the Social Sentiment

Durkheim's next problem was to explain why the social sentiment among the Australians took the form of a clan totem. Since vibrant and deep sentiments expressive of group solidarity are difficult to grasp in the abstract, the natural tendency is to make use of a straightforward and simple symbol, for example, the flag. For Australians, Durkheim argued, totems are like clan flags, readily comprehended because animals were a part of the native's everyday experience. The totem is a natural surrogate for the clan, "for the clan is too complex a reality to be represented clearly in all its complex unity by such rudimentary intelligences" (Durkheim 1947:220). What might have been profane imitations of animals now are transformed and sacralized. Such are the churinga (soul embodiments), bull-roarers, body marks, and all other objects upon which the sentiment readily fixes itself, and through which it is continually sustained, recreated, and recharged (Durkheim 1947:221). Without knowing it, but rather sensing it, the Australian clan group deified itself as a mysterious vital force—a sacred force housed in a totemic god.

> Since religious force is nothing other than the collective and anonymous force of the clan, and since this can be represented in the mind only in the form of the totem, the totemic emblem is like the visible body of the god. Therefore, it is from it that those kindly or dreadful actions seem to emanate, which the cult seeks to provoke or prevent; consequently, it is to it that the cult is addressed. This is the explanation of why it holds the first place in the series of sacred things. (Durkheim 1947:221)

That the clan sentiment, as any social sentiment, was a manifestation of a collective experience and social consciousness and not a product of individualized sensory perceptions of particular objects in the environment was important for causal interpretation. A sociopsychological explanation was substituted for a psychological one. Moreover, the social sentiment was not hobbled to a specific external sensory experience but was free to fixate any and all objects. The historical diversity of sacred powers and why these might appear as physical or human powers, moral or amoral, could thus be explained (Durkheim 1947:223–225). The exuberant energy generated by the social sentiment ignored nothing, not even games or art. In retaining a religious character, important art forms and games betrayed their ultimate origins, according to Durkheim (1947:381).

Following Durkheim's premises, it was not difficult to second guess his derivation of the soul concept. It must be an individual fraction of whatever symbolizes the force uniting the group. Turning back to those early Australian times for the origin of the soul, it could be nothing else but a fragment of the totemic force that unites the clan as a body. In myth Australian ancestors were demigods, exhibiting animal or vegetable features, and it is their souls, uniting a human and animal quality, that replenish each human generation through reincarnation.

> Since no other souls than these exist, we reach the conclusion that . . . the soul is nothing other than the totemic principle incarnate in each individual. . . . We already know that this principle is immanent in each of the members of the clan. But in penetrating into these individuals, it must inevitably individualize

itself. Because the consciousnesses, of which it becomes thus an integral part, differ from each other, it differentiates itself according to their image; since each has its own physiognomy, it takes a distinct physiognomy in each. Of course it remains something outside of and foreign to the man, but the portion of it which each is believed to possess cannot fail to contract close affinities with the particular subject in which it resides; it becomes his to a certain extent. Thus it has two contradictory characteristics, but whose coexistence is one of the distinctive features of the notion of the soul. To-day, as formerly, the soul is what is best and most profound in ourselves, and the preeminent part of our being; yet it is also a passing guest which comes from the outside, which leads in us an existence distinct from that of the body, and which should one day regain its entire independence. In a word, just as society exists only in and through individuals, the totemic principle exists only in and through the individual consciousnesses whose association forms the clan. If they did not feel it in them it would not exist; it is they who put it into things. So it must of necessity be divided and distributed among them. Each of these fragments is a soul. (Durkheim 1947:248–249).

The prime social fact thus was the social sentiment, from which all other social facts derived, and the individual was a fragment of the ultimate social sentiment or fact. In his theory of origins Durkheim substituted a sociopsychological base for the individual psychological foundation used by Developmentalists in their explanations. The interpretation reaffirmed the priority of unconscious processes in the conventionalization of behavior. Moreover, in the projection from an inner sentiment to an outer reality, Durkheim offered an interpretation of group behavior structurally akin to that followed by Freud for individual behavior. Again in Freudian mode Durkheim saw sexual energy struggling to free itself from a sacralized familistic morality and winning some freedom through sublimation. A change in social organization—the beginning of clan exogamy—liberated human sensuality by separating sex from the family and the sacralized morality upon which it was founded. Religion and morality still continued to be associated with the family, and opposed to sensuality, but everything expressive of freedom was concentrated now in the sexual life, where it was converted into creative and imaginative energy. Thus, sexual energy was poured into art, poetry, and imaginative dreams, and women moved to the center of the aesthetic life (Durkheim 1963:109–110). In a strict sense, however, Durkheim's theory of social facts can be viewed as sociological, since the sentiment upon which all else is raised can be produced only through the interaction of individuals. No single individual could conjure up this collective sentiment.

What Durkheim hoped to prove through his methodological analysis was a correlation between social organization, sociopsychological sentiment, collective representations (ideas), and collective symbolizations. In this nexus, the social order stood center stage, for as Durkheim (1938:113) observed: "*The first origins of all social processes of any importance should be sought in the internal constitution of the social group.*" Hence the necessity for determining the social morphology of human societies and the principles which established and regulated the structure; for these same principles organized the outer world, reflecting as in a mirror the inner reality of the social. Like Boas, Durkheim turned to immanent social principles to explain man's ordering of the world of nature in opposition to those who pointed to nature as the model for man's understanding of the world, his values, and aesthetic choices.

For Durkheim any social type contained and expressed eternal truths concerning basic relationships, conceptualizations, and generalized extensions of the basic concepts and relationships. Therefore, a particular social type could serve as the homologue to all other cases of that social type. The task of a comparative sociology thus would be to identify the different kinds of social types. From this viewpoint, too, it was not illogical of Durkheim, when analyzing Australian totemism, to conclude that he had uncovered the prototype for religion everywhere. Thus Durkheim (1947:415–416) wrote,

> At the beginning of this work we announced that the religion whose study we were taking up contained within it the most characteristic elements of the religious life. The exactness of this proposition may now be verified. Howsoever simple the system . . . , we have found within it all the great ideas and the principal ritual attitudes which are at the basis of even the most advanced religions: the division of things into sacred and profane, the notions of the soul, of spirits, of mythical personalities, and of a national and even international divinity, a negative cult with ascetic practices which are its exaggerated form, rites of oblation and communion, imitative rites, commemorative rites and expiatory rites; nothing essential is lacking. We . . . hope that the results at which we have arrived are not peculiar to totemism alone, but can aid us in an understanding of what religion in general is.
>
> It may be objected that one single religion, whatever its field of extension may be, is too narrow a base for such an induction. We have not dreamed for a moment of ignoring the fact that an extended verification may add to the authority of a theory, but it is equally true that when a law has been proven by one well-made experiment, this proof is valid universally. If in one single case a scientist succeeded in finding out the secret of the life of even the most protoplasmic creature that can be imagined, the truths thus obtained would be applicable to all living beings, even the most advanced. Then if, in our studies of these humble societies, we have really succeeded in discovering some of the elements out of which the most fundamental religious notions are made up, there is no reason for not extending the most general results of our researches to other religions. In fact, it is inconceivable that the same effect may be due now to one cause, now to another, according to the circumstances, unless the two causes are at bottom only one. A single idea cannot express one reality here and another one there, unless the duality is only apparent. If among certain peoples the ideas of sacredness, the soul and God are to be explained sociologically, it should be presumed scientifically that, in principle, the same explanation is valid for all the peoples among whom these same ideas are found with the same essential characteristics. Therefore, . . . certain at least of our conclusions can be legitimately generalized.

What Durkheim proposed, in short, was a case study approach with a detailed analysis of social units. Such an in-depth procedure would uncover more valid meaning than could be achieved by superficial cross-cultural comparisons of items wrested from their contexts, the procedure used by exponents of the evolutionary comparative method. Here was the strength of any structural-functional analysis—that it viewed a unit in its ever-expanding relations within a configuration. Though the number of types compared might be expanded in a limited way, as Lévi-Strauss (in Gurvitch and Moore 1945:528) observed with regard to Marcel Mauss, the methodological course remained constant.

> He [Mauss] always considers a small number of cases, judiciously chosen as representing clearly defined types. He studies each type as a whole, always considering it as an integrative cultural complex; the kind of relation he aims at discovering is never between two or more elements arbitrarily isolated from the culture, but between all the components: this is what he calls *"faits sociaux totaux,"* a particularly happy formulation for the type of study called elsewhere—and later—functionalist.

EMERGENCE OF FRENCH COMPARATIVE SOCIOLOGY

Through the medium of the journal *L'Année sociologique,* founded in 1898, Durkheim proselyted for a social science that would emulate the controls of a natural science experiment. Durkheim and some of his early associates either fell in battle or died during World War I, and when work was resumed, Marcel Mauss, his nephew, shouldered the mantle of the master and mentor.

Mauss worked with Durkheim on his initial investigation of suicide. Collaborative work became the mark of *L'Année sociologique* publications during its formative years when one analytical experiment after another appeared to validate the sociological method. Thus, Hubert and Mauss in 1899 wrote an essay on the nature and function of sacrifice and followed this initial foray into religion with a social theory of magic (1904). In 1903 Durkheim and Mauss attempted to derive the principles of classification employed by primitive peoples in their ordering of spatial and natural phenomena from the ways people arranged themselves in social categories and in localized social units.

All of these studies tried to prove the centrality of the social order in the formation of collective sentiments, their formulation as collective ideas, and their expressive symbolization in ceremony and custom. As the social order varied, according to type, so would sentiment, idea and symbol. However, behind the apparent diversity of institutional forms of similar type there were common elements structuring them all. This idea led Mauss and his associates to make limited cross-cultural comparisons to reinforce the original findings and permit generalization of laws of social structure and process. For example, considering the seasonal variation of Eskimo society, Mauss, with Beuchat (1906), concluded that the alternation of summer and winter activities produced entirely different social arrangements with concomitant variation in economy, legal norms, and religious ceremonial. Moreover, the fundamental dichotomy in Eskimo society, mode of life, and intellectual culture furnished Mauss and Beuchat with a model applicable to alternations found in Indian societies of the Northwest Coast, and in pastoral and rural populations generally.

The institutional ramifications which Mauss traced throughout a social order stressed the logical extension of an idea in the ordering of a system. His concept of total social facts thus came to grips with the issue of integrative consistency and coherence and rested on the psychological process of generalization. Since ideas represented finalization of the inner socio-psychological reality, scientific understanding also was reached through ideas. With that conclusion Mauss began an investigation to probe the meaning of economic transactions, and especially gift exchange. Before writing his "Essai sur le don, forme et raison de l'échange dans les sociétés archaiques" (1925), Mauss had explored the origins of the idea of money, the obligatory expression of feelings in Australian funerary rites, and the obligation to offer gifts. In gift exchange in primitive societies, Mauss found an economic transaction quite different from the private contractual agreements of advanced societies. The logic of economic transactions in primitive societies was extracted from their obligatory exchanges of goods and services—including etiquette, songs, dances, and feasts. Obligatory exchanges linked social units,—families, clans, phratries, tribes—in mutual reciprocities. Such group exchanges, ranging over a wide variety of goods, were in no way utilitarian. Following Durkheim's emphasis on the sacred as the wellspring of primary social sentiments, Mauss suggested that the deep sense of obligation to return a gift was grounded in a collective sentiment associated with the sacred. A sacralized social sentiment of this kind might produce a collective representation not unlike the Maori idea of *hau*—the inner spirit which irresistibly draws an object back to its home.

Mauss's interpretation of primitive economic transactions as a form of social reciprocity challenged the archetypal economic man of Western economic theory. It also seemingly confirmed what Malinowski had earlier reported about the economics of the ceremonial Kula exchange among the island societies off the eastern coast of New Guinea. Here one found "A big, inter-tribal relationship, uniting with definite social bonds a vast area and great numbers of people, binding them with definite ties of reciprocal obligations, making them follow minute rules and observations in a concerted manner" (Malinowski 1961a:510). Malinowski noted that the Kula was partly commercial, partly ceremonial in nature. The exchange, like any ceremonial, was carried out for its own sake. The red shell necklaces and white armshell bands did not meet the usual specifications of a possessory good since possession by the rules was temporary. The valuables must be kept in circulation. The shell treasures did not serve as money because of the enforced exchange and limited possession.

Thus, for French sociologists primitive society was highly contrastive with modern industrial society. Durkheim (1926:5–6) made this clear in his preliminary distinction of the diversity and greater contradictions and individualities found in complex religions as compared with the elemental religious manifestations of simpler societies.

> Things are quite different in the lower societies. The slighter development of individuality, the small extension of the group, the homogeneity of external circumstances, all contribute to reducing the differences and variations to a minimum. The group has an intellectual and moral conformity of which we find but rare examples in the more advanced societies. Everything is common to all. Movements are stereotyped; everybody performs the same ones in the same circumstances, and this conformity of conduct only translates the conformity of thought. Every mind being drawn into the same eddy, the individual type nearly confounds itself with that of the race. And while all is uniform, all is simple as well. . . . Neither the popular imagination nor that of the priests has had either the time or the means of refining and transforming the original substance of the religious ideas and practices. . . . That which is accessory or secondary . . . has not yet come to hide the principal elements. . . . All is reduced to that which is indispensable, to . . . religion. But that which is indispensable is also that which is essential, . . . [and] which we must know before all else.

Primitive society contrasted with industrial society in a number of ways: principles of directional orientation and classification; type of economic exchange; specific sentiments, ideas, and mental processes. Yet primitive societies were indispensable to French sociological analysis because they were uncontaminated by historic accidents and cultural intermixings that set barriers to a structural-functional analysis. But to make them something more than social curiosities for a museum of man, primitive societies had to be linked to the advanced societies in a structural or evolutionary mode. Such, apparently, was the logic behind the entrance of Durkheim and associates into ethnology.

In turning to primitive societies, French sociologists thought they could use their data for sociological analysis in two vital ways. First, the simplicity of the primitive communities afforded a clearer path to comprehension of the pristine social realities that had produced primary collective sentiments and the integrative collective ideas. They were interested in elemental ideas derived out of elemental social situations, whereas Bastian had in mind elemental ideas which grew out of universal processes of the human mind. In sociological explanation an elemental idea was a projection of a collective social sentiment which had been generated by a basic set of interactions linking different social categories—for example, the primary categories of age and sex emphasized in Australian societies (Durkheim and Mauss 1963). Second, using this primordial context for binary categorization, the search could be extended to advanced societies.

The press to find the primeval social context is reminiscent of Freud's search for the appropriate social unit for his Oedipal trauma. Moreover, the variant arrangements of primitive societies were expected to yield intermediate social orders, together with their associated sentiments and ideas, that would chart a trend from an undifferentiated simplicity to a more differentiated and complex structuring and ideology. Social laws would be derived from universal and persistent structurings. From social universals, the functional prerequisites for social living, including the necessary legal and moral norms, could be determined. In anticipation of this problem Durkheim (1938:70) discussed the distinction of the normal and the pathological and pointed out the indisputable fact that any variation in the social type introduced variation into the domains of law and morality. This could be verified by simple comparison of societies and by noting historical changes in the laws and ethics of any society. Law and morality thus were relative, and the normal and abnormal could be measured only against their proper social orders. However, in the broad perspective of evolutionary continuity one found the total context within which any social institution and social type as a species must be compared. And the same held for law and morality.

> For example, in the matter of domestic organization the most rudimentary type that has ever existed will first be established, in order that the manner in which it grew progressively more complex may then be followed, step by step. This method, which may be called "genetic," would give at once the analysis and the synthesis of the phenomenon. For . . . it would show us the separate elements composing it, by the very fact that it would allow us to see the process of accretion or action. At the same time, . . . we should be in a much better position to determine the conditions on which depend their formation. *Consequently, one cannot explain a social fact of any complexity except by following its complete development through all social species.* Comparative sociology is not a particular branch of sociology; it is sociology itself, in so far as it ceases to be purely descriptive and aspires to account for facts. (Durkheim 1938: 138–139)

Mauss hardly deviated from Durkheim in his work and always included comparisons that traced stages in development. Classification by type supplied the clues to the arrangement by stages. Thus, the generalized total social exchanges involving family, clan, and tribe (with the potlatch of the Northwest Coast Indians and Melanesians forming a competitive subtype) was succeeded by the type of gift exchange common to Oceania. Credit and prestige arrangements found in Oceanic gift exchange pointed to the next stage—private contract. Appropriately, within this totalistic context, Mauss came to an absolutist position with regard to ethical judgment. To quote Leacock (1954(56):67):

> Mauss felt that modern European economics had become too impersonal, and advocated a return toward a type of society in which there was a greater

exchange of goods and services between individuals and groups. "The callous pursuit of individual goals is detrimental to the goals and peace of the group, to the rhythm of its work and its joys...." What is particularly interesting about this is that Mauss felt that he had derived these ethical conclusions from his analysis of gift-exchange, and that the discovery of such conclusions was a legitimate aim of sociology. However, this attitude did not last. By 1930, in "Les civilisations, éléments et formes," after suggesting that there was a growing trend toward the 'amalgamation of existing cultures, Mauss cautioned against applying value judgments to this trend, since it, as well as "progress," cannot be shown to lead necessarily to good or to happiness.

The new emphasis on methodological relativism followed Mauss's increasing acceptance of the idea that clues to understanding particular culture elements must be found in the matrix of the society in which they were nourished. The Durkheimian effort to formulate a series of social types, joined in an evolutionary continuum, was surrendered to a relativistic structural-functional analysis of a single society. This is why Lévi-Strauss (in Gurvitch and Moore 1945:534) praised Mauss for advancing French sociology, and sociology generally, with his illumination of the basic functionalist position. "From now on, the interest will be directed toward [functional] analysis, not synthesis." From then on, French sociology developed a field orientation, for detailed functional studies of single societies required a closely observed record. Such was the stimulus that took Alfred Métraux and Claude Lévi-Strauss to South America, M. Leenhardt to New Caledonia, and M. Graule to the African Dogon society, with Métraux especially combining a scholarly traverse of historic sources with ethnographic fieldwork. In commenting on the implication of a narrow craftlike interest that accompanied analytic functionalism, Lévi-Strauss (in Gurvitch and Moore 1945:536) envisioned a universal study that would unite principles of interpretation and methods drawn from all fields.

> They [sociologists] must, indeed, turn more and more toward concrete studies; but they cannot hope to be successful if they are not constantly helped and supported with a general, humanistic culture back of them. The philosophical ancestry of French sociology has played it some tricks in the past; it may well prove, in the end, to be its best asset.

Acceptance of this position was prophetic of Lévi-Strauss's future contribution to ethnology.

PSYCHOLOGICAL DEVIATIONISM IN FRENCH SOCIOLOGY: LÉVY-BRUHL AND VAN GENNEP

The theoretical understandings which Durkheimian sociologists asserted and attempted to validate through case analyses were derived from ethnographic material in hand. Their intent was to synthesize, and in this regard their scientific purpose was like that of Developmentalists. Lucien Lévy-

Bruhl (1857–1939) and Arnold van Gennep (1873–1957) also produced synthetic analyses of existing materials, but neither followed the theoretical lead of Durkheim. It was not that they were insensitive to, or antipathetic toward, the significance of the social for human behavior. Indeed, at the very beginning of *Les Fonctions mentales dans les sociétés inférieures*, Lévy-Bruhl (1910:1–2) paid tribute to the successes of the French sociologists.

> In order to comprehend the mechanism of institutions (especially in the lower societies) it is first necessary to rid ourselves of the prejudices which consist in believing that collective representations in general, and those of the lower societies in particular, obey psychological laws based on analysis of the individual subject. Collective representations have their own proper laws, which cannot be discovered—especially if it is a question of primitives—by study of the individual "white, adult and civilized." On the contrary, it is beyond doubt that the study of collective representations and their linkages in the lower societies will throw some light on the genesis of our logical categories and principles. Already M. Durkheim and his collaborators have given some examples of which can be achieved in following this way. Without a doubt it will lead to a new and scientific theory of knowledge, grounded on the comparative method.

Van Gennep (1960:3) in his turn acknowledged the importance of social solidarity by noting how "every change in a person's life involve[d] actions and reactions between sacred and profane . . . regulated and guarded so that society as a whole will suffer no discomfort or injury." Nevertheless, both Lévy-Bruhl and van Gennep succeeded in inverting the directionality of Durkheim's social-causal explanation and found themselves at odds with the sociologs. How and why did this inversion take place? The answer in large part derives from the fact that neither was particularly interested in finding the primary origins of phenomena but rather in understanding process in relation to structure. Lévy-Bruhl directed himself to the problem of knowledge systems and the mental processes followed when attributing cause to particular events. Van Gennep attempted to uncover the ideological base for the guarded transition from one status to another with which primitive peoples were preoccupied. Both followed the taxonomic trend set by Durkheimians but did not press the evolutionary implications. In fact, the contrasts they drew between primitive and civilized were so emphatic that one must conclude that a continuity in thought and social practice between primitive and modern either did not exist or the path was long and winding.

Lévy-Bruhl and Primitive Thought Processes

In his search for the logic of causation, Lévy-Bruhl soon arrived at a dichotomy of human knowledge systems. Primitive thinking about cause relied heavily on intuitive comprehension, and so he called it prelogical.

The civilized mind, on the other hand, could discern a series of events and causes. Such analysis conformed to principles governing reliable inference, and hence he referred to it as logical. The primitive mind impressed Lévy-Bruhl as so filled with the aura of mystical causation that the idea of chance or accident was beyond comprehension. In their pervasive search for some mystic agent they entertained a host of random possibilities or causal agents which precluded their connecting a particular event to its logical cause. The primitive mind, according to Lévy-Bruhl (1966:61), was short on inference and long on accepting as real what a close look would show to be unreal. Nonetheless, these intuitive apprehensions of reality were as real to the primitive as anything verified by the senses. Hence, the mind of the primitive was not dominated by a cognitive orientation. To the contrary, "It knows nothing of the joys and advantages of knowledge. Its collective representations are always largely emotional. The primitive's thought and his language are but slightly conceptual" (Lévy-Bruhl 1966:61).

The primitive mind in contrast with the sophisticated and analytic mind of the more complex societies was intuitively synthesizing. Primitive thinking paid no attention to space and time distinctions, but strained to apprehend an event all at once. Their synthetic effort introduced multiple agents as probabilities in the assignment of cause. This holistic approach to causal relations exhibited by primitives was termed by Lévy-Bruhl (1966:90) the law of participation. The sources for this law of participation must be sought in psychological experiences which could supply the basic intuitions upon which primitive knowledge was based. Whatever suggested the presence of the occult, especially dreams, omens, and visitations of ancestors, contributed substance for the primitive knowledge experience. To an ordinary sense experience, and to perceptions of relationships among things which excite the European, the primitive often appeared indifferent. However, "As soon as the agency of mystic powers is involved, these dormant minds awake. They are then no longer indifferent or apathetic; you find them alert, patient, and even ingenious and subtle" (Lévy-Bruhl 1966:97).

To appreciate the vital mental processes of primitives, one must grasp the fact that they depended on these mystic experiences for all manner of intelligence—to be forewarned or to be made secure in any venture. And "When these manifestations are not forthcoming of themselves, the primitive mind exercises its ingenuity to induce them; it invents methods of procuring them (such as dreams which are instigated, processes of divination, ordeals, and so on), and thus it arrives at various data which find a place in the scheme of primitive experience, and contribute, in no small degree, to making this puzzling to us" (Lévy-Bruhl 1966:98). If the sources of primitive ideas were actively sought in the experience of consciousness, then it followed that their organization of the world depended upon this psychic awareness. What held for the world of nature also held for their institutions—all mirrored the mystic law of participation. Thus, in observing how primitives related individual animals of a species, Lévy-Bruhl (1965:64) noted that the personification of the species spirit was like an elder brother to the younger brothers (individual animals). In Lévy-Bruhl's view man pictured his own relations to his species community in the same way in which he related plants and animals to their species communities. But though primitive man was aware of himself as a person vis-à-vis others, the primitive awareness of self was dominated by collective elements. Primitive man was no individualist or rebel. The mystical law of participation allowed no other conclusion—the individual intuitively felt himself to be a fragment of a greater whole, the social group.

Lévy-Bruhl traced all that was significant in man's intellectual and social experience to the particulate mental processes of individuals. Reducing the social to the psychological, and worse still, to the hallucinations of dreams, was bound to offend the rising French sociologists. In the *Elementary Forms of the Religious Life*, Durkheim (1947:444) answered such psychological reductionism with a counter assertion, denying that society was a chaotic melange of illogical and incoherent features. To the contrary, the collective consciousness exemplified the quintessence of the psychic life since it integrated the individualized consciousness into a superconsciousness—a kind of group mind. Since it was outside and above the individual, this collective consciousness cut through the extraneous variations and unerringly perceived the intrinsic and permanent in human affairs. Further, the collective consciousness recreated these truths in ideas so that all might grasp the eternal social verities and share in this powerful extension of consciousness.

Durkheim quite obviously was a bit mystical himself. He too saw the person as a fragment of a whole, with the individual consciousness participating in, and engulfed by the collective consciousness. But his sociological explanation was at odds with Lévy-Bruhl's psychological explanation. As for Lévy-Bruhl, he was content to leave mystical participation to the primitives and reserve the logic of rationality to the civilized. His search for the parameters of primitive thought processes, beginning in 1910 (trans. 1926, *How Natives Think*), maintained an enthusiastic pace for compilation and perceptive interpretation (*The Soul of the Primitive* 1927; *Primitive Mythology* 1922; *The Supernatural and Nature in Primitive Mentality* 1931; and *The Mystic Experience and Symbolization among Primitives* 1938).

To the logical mind of the philosopher scientist, however, the primitive mind remained something of a mystery, since it was structured by a different kind of relational experience. Lévy-Bruhl concluded that the European could not understand primitive mental processes through the medium of his own logical categories, a methodological point made by others, including Frazer and Boas.

Curiously, in his analytic construction of the primitive mind, Lévy-Bruhl independently arrived at conclusions comparable to those put forward by Developmentalists. First, primitive thought moved from the undifferentiated concrete to the differentiated abstract. Second, primitive thinking was not subject to critical procedures and hence was irrational and heavily infiltrated with feeling states. Third, individuality of thought had advanced as people were liberated from the dead weight of tradition. Fourth, even though the mental processes of primitive and civilized were different in a qualitative sense, the latter was an outgrowth of the former.

Van Gennep and Rites of Passage

Van Gennep in 1908 deviated from the basic assumptions and methodology of social Structuralism in two important observations. First, he stressed a biological datum, the maturation of the individual, as the model for rites that transported an individual from one status to another. Second, he was convinced that primitive peoples were sensitive to the periodic and alternating occurrences that framed their experience. These two universal perceptions—growth and periodicity—were symbolized in ceremony and formed the basis for relating the individual to society. Finding the world view of the semicivilized mind saturated with a sense of the sacred, as well as a necessity to bring individuals into contact with mystic figures and powers in the interests of public welfare, van Gennep drew upon religious ceremony for the substance of his analysis. A first task would be the classification of rituals to elicit basic patterning in the order of ceremonies.

Everywhere societies accented a succession of stages or transitions as one advanced from childhood to maturity or from one occupation to another (van Gennep 1960:3). The universal experience of approaching, entering, and moving through doorways—or passing by boundary markers —provided a model for rites of passage. The simple magical portal of African ceremony and the triumphal arch of Roman victory shared a common symbolic content and ordering of ceremony. In its logical fulfillment, a cycle of "rites of passage theoretically includes preliminal rites (rites of separation), liminal rites (rites of transition), and postliminal rites (rites of incorporation), [but] in specific instances," van Gennep (1960:11) admitted that these three types were not equally significant or elaborated in the same degree. Certainly in the instance of the arch of victory, the series was complete and the symbolism of crossing a threshold direct and clear. "The victor was first required to separate himself from the enemy world through a series of rites, in order to be able to return to the Roman world by passing through the arch. The rite of incorporation in this case was a sacrifice to Jupiter Capitoline and to the deities protecting the city" (van Gennep 1960:21).

In testing for the meaning of special ritual actions, van Gennep drew upon psychological classifications in vogue among the Developmentalists. Some rites thus were sympathetic or contagious, animistic or dynamistic (involving vital power, as *mana*), direct (magical spell or curse), or indirect (vow or prayer sets in motion a demon or a deity who intervenes). There also were positive or negative rites, commonly expressed in taboos. Though he erred in deriving his explanations from common human psychological processes particulate in the individual, van Gennep, like Durkheimian sociologists, looked for a typology that not only discriminated basic structures but also uncovered a hard core of processes linking the earlier primitive with advanced forms. Here, in processual constants and their correlated forms, one could detect the universals coordinate with social life.

> Two primary divisions are characteristic of all societies irrespective of time and place: the sexual separation between men and women, and the magico-religious separation between the profane and the sacred. However, some special groups—such as religious associations, totem clans, phratries, castes, and professional classes—appear in only a few societies. Within each society there is also the age group, the family, and the restricted politico-administrative and territorial unit (band, village, town). In addition to this complex world of the living, there is the world preceding life and the one which follows death.
>
> These are the constants of social life, to which have been added particular and temporary events such as pregnancy, illnesses, dangers, journeys, etc. And always the same purpose has resulted in the same form of activity. For groups, as well as for individuals, life itself means to separate and to be reunited, to change form and condition, to die and to be reborn. It is to act and to cease, to wait and rest, and then to begin acting again, but in a different way. And there are always new thresholds to cross . . . summer . . . night . . . birth . . . old age. (Van Gennep 1960:189–190)

CONVERGENCES IN PSYCHOLOGICAL AND SOCIAL EXPLANATION

What Lévy-Bruhl and van Gennep illustrate, together with Durkheim and associates, is the pervasive alternation and conflict between psychological and social or cultural explanations. By dichotomizing the human reality into the social and the psychological, with each a more or less self-contained system of explanations, a deterministic position that excluded or derived the opposite variable was inevitable. This was the social determinism which Durkheim and his followers asserted in their fierce defense of nurture against nature. Human nature, however, could not be dismissed summarily, and to Mauss's credit he attempted to accommodate human psychology and biology in his plan for descriptive sociology. He saw self-contained sociological, sociopsychological, and biopsychological approaches as contributing to the ultimate goal of sociological investigation, namely, the organic life cycle of individual societies (Lévi-Strauss 1945:535–536). The lesson was not lost on Mauss's pupil Lévi-Strauss, whose later psychological explanations of moieties and other binary classifications would have amazed his mentor. At the same time Mauss would be gratified at the way in which Lévi-Strauss (1963af:142–147) could find antecedents in French philosophy (Rousseau and Bergson) for those who, like Radcliffe-Brown, had uncovered the meaning of the totemic institution in a basic element of human thought, notably the unification of opposites. Lévi-Strauss observed that Radcliffe-Brown undoubtedly would have rejected the psychological interpretation he had extracted from the latter's argument; for Radcliffe-Brown was a staunch structural empiricist (Lévi-Strauss 1963af:

132). But in following Mauss's leads, Lévi-Strauss had discovered new methodological freedoms. According to the phenomena confronted, he would shift his explanation from one structural context to another— sociological, psychological, or biosociological. In *The Elementary Structures of Kinship* (1949) a sociological interpretation reigned, whereas in *Totemism Today* (1962) a psychological explanation was used. But throughout shifts in his interpretative base, Lévi-Strauss (1963b:130) remained the staunch supporter of Structuralism in maintaining that the real form is the internal structure of the human mind.

The dichotomy of the human reality into the social and the psychological carried another lesson, which Lévy-Bruhl realized toward the end of his life. Concentration on a large but still partial segment of the human reality produced an incomplete distorted explanation. At the same time there was the singular phenomenon of investigators beginning at opposite poles and arriving at understandings about primitive life and thought that were clearly similar. In Developmentalist theory the sacred quality of ancient society was considered a derivative of the supernaturally based knowledge system which governed primitive thought. French sociologists also concluded that primitive societies were organized as sacred communities by virtue of their symbolization of a collective sentiment. Developmentalist theory stressed the uniformity of primitive thought and a reign of custom which restricted individuality. French sociologists emphasized the homogeneous solidarity of the primitive community and found that collective ideas and customs induced a sociality that restrained variation.

What is the meaning of these convergences? How can investigators start from different explicit assumptions, yet reach like conclusions? Are the convergences a product of implicit assumptions unconsciously introduced into the methodological machinery? Or are the variables involved in the human reality so organized and interrelated that no matter what variable is elected as a point of theoretical emphasis one is led to similar conclusions about the fundamental nature of that reality? In the present instance it appeared that the way French sociologists defined their goal with relation to an assumed sequence of social types inclined them to make assumptions very much like those held by Developmentalists—for example, from simplicity to complexity. The fact that Durkheimians, as Developmentalists, concentrated their attention on the relevancy of ideas for conventionalized behavior and for social advancement also brought parallel conclusions. As long as ideas were central, it made no difference how they were born. Both were interested, though in a somewhat different way, in the social effects of ideas.

RADCLIFFE-BROWN AND BRITISH SOCIAL ANTHROPOLOGY

A. R. Radcliffe-Brown (1881–1955) followed Rivers into ethnology when the latter expanded his interest in primitive psychology to include cultural-historical reconstructions. When Radcliffe-Brown set out for the

Andaman Islands in 1906 as an Anthony Wilkin Student in Ethnology, he had the usual cultural-historical reconstruction in mind. However, by 1914 he rewrote his initial field study to accord with the functional leads of French sociologists. This about face stemmed from a growing suspicion that ethnological reconstructions produced at best a conjectural history, and one that could not be trusted to yield any really important results in understanding life or culture (Radcliffe-Brown 1948:Preface, vii). Aside from the untrustworthy nature of historic reconstructions of culture, there was disappointment in the failure of ethnologists to get at the meaning of myths and rituals in the mental life of those willing to tell them to an inquiring ethnographer. The ethnographer, more often than not, was forced to speculate about the meaning of mythic events, and to impute a significance drawn from his own mental experience (Radcliffe-Brown 1948: viii–ix). Radcliffe-Brown charged that ethnology must either develop methods to effectively grasp the meanings which peoples placed in their myths and rituals or it must abandon all hope of explaining and interpreting myth and ritual. To remedy this methodological deficiency, he proposed a functional approach. Meanings and functions were interrelated.

> The notion of function in ethnology rests on the conception of culture as an adaptive mechanism by which a certain number of human beings are enabled to live a social life as an ordered community in a given environment. Adaptation has two aspects, external and internal. The external aspect is seen in the relation of the society to the geographical environment. The internal aspect is seen in the controlled relations of individuals within the social unity. It is convenient to use the tern "social integration" to cover all the phenomena of internal adaptation. One of the fundamental problems of a science of culture or of human society is therefore the problem of the nature of social integration. This problem can only be approached by the study of a number of different cultures from this specific point of view, by an intensive investigation of each culture as an adaptive and integrative mechanism and a comparison, one with another, of as many variant types as possible.
>
> The discovery of the integrative function of an institution, usage, or belief is to be made through the observation of its effects, and these are obviously in the first place effects on individuals, or their life, their thoughts, their emotions. Not all such effects are significant, or at least equally so. Nor is it the immediate effects with which we are finally concerned, but with the more remote effects upon the social cohesion and continuity.
>
> Thus "meaning" and "function" are two different but related things. We cannot discuss the social function of mythology or ritual without an understanding of the meanings of particular myths and ritual actions. (Radcliffe-Brown 1948:ix–x)

What Radcliffe-Brown had to say in the Preface of his reinterpreted dissertation *The Andaman Islanders* was restated about a decade later in a presidential address before the South African Association for the Advancement of Science (Radcliffe-Brown 1958a:3–38). There he optimistically looked forward to a social anthropology which would uncover laws of social development comparable to those stated by natural scientists and psychologists, and thereby be of practical service to mankind. Obviously anthropology could not confine itself to simply restating or reconstructing the history of beliefs and customs but must discover their role in the social, moral, and psychological life of a people. An historically oriented anthropology, such as ethnology, was less important than a nomothetic or law-producing anthropology, such as social anthropology. To escape the accusation of prejudice, Radcliffe-Brown (1958a:28–29) turned to Kroeber's review of Lowie's *Primitive Society*. There Kroeber queried the results Lowie had achieved with his critical use of the historical method. In Kroeber's view there was little in historically oriented anthropology that was useful to other sciences, especially psychology, from which anthropology drew basic explanations of behavioral processes involved in custom and cultural change. Even more telling, observed Kroeber (1920(22):380), "*There are . . . no causal explanations. . . .* In essence, then, modern ethnology says that so and so happens, and may tell why it happened thus in that particular case. It does not tell, and *does not try to tell, why things happen in society as such*" (italics supplied).

Kroeber did not know whether this limitation was an artifact of the historical method, but he was convinced that ethnology had little to offer if it confined itself to historical analysis of the particulate and he studiously avoided coming to grips with broader issues and generalizations. People would demand to know what had brought about similarities and differences. One could condemn Morgan for his methodological errors and compliment Lowie for his critical method; but, nonetheless, Kroeber could not help but close the book with regret and disappointment that more ultimate issues had been neglected. Like the social functionalist Radcliffe-Brown, the historically oriented Kroeber dreamed of an anthropological contribution of substance—the laws of culture growth. Like Radcliffe-Brown, Kroeber sought to inspire his confreres to incorporate that dream into their investigations.

During the thirties and forties Radcliffe-Brown continued to formulate his ideas about the centrality of social anthropology as a "theoretical or nomothetic study of which the aim is to provide acceptable generalisations" (Radcliffe-Brown 1965:3). In presidential addresses, essays, and special lectures before scientific bodies, he insisted that social anthropology must be made part of a new discipline called comparative sociology (see, for example, "The Present Position of Anthropological Studies" 1931; "Meaning and Scope of Social Anthropology" 1944; "The Comparative Method in Social Anthropology," 1951; in 1958:42–95, 96–107, 108–129, respectively). He did not portray a widely based anthropological discipline which claimed a synthetic function for studies of man similar to the epistemological synthesis claimed by philosophy. True, one could see the "subject of anthropology . . . dividing itself into three subjects, distinguished either by differences of method or of subject-matter; Human Biology . . . Prehistoric Archaeology and Ethnology . . . and Comparative

Sociology" (Radcliffe-Brown 1958b:89). However, Radcliffe-Brown did not emphasize the interrelations of these specializations within an anthropological discipline. Rather, he pointed to the way physical anthropology, as a branch of human biology, must affiliate with the biological sciences, and how prehistoric archaeology and ethnology properly belonged with history. Comparative sociology divided its relations between psychology on one side and history and the social sciences on the other. Linguistics also was relevant to comparative sociology. Applied anthropology obviously must be an extension of social anthropology, drawing upon its social laws.

It was important to cultivate the most natural relations among specializations and disciplines, and Radcliffe-Brown could see no particular virtue in having social anthropologists involved with archaeology or historical ethnology. Anthropological teaching designed to help native administrators effectively carry out their jobs reflected what Radcliffe-Brown considered important to the training of the social anthropologist. Certainly he found no direct connection between social anthropology and the study of human races, nor between social anthropology and the dating and affinities of Paleolithic cultures. Yet,

> So long as ethnology continues to exist, it will provide a meeting-ground for archaeologists, physical anthropologists, students of linguistics, and social anthropologists. Such a meeting-ground has been provided for a century by the Royal Anthropological Institute and will continue to be provided in the future. Any attempt to impose a more rigid artificial unity will be likely to produce exactly the opposite of the result at which it aims. (Radcliffe-Brown 1958c:107)

Radcliffe-Brown obviously viewed anthropology as a loosely structured holding company for specializations linked only by their convergent interests in man. At the same time he admitted that anthropological data could be studied either historically or experimentally—that is, by the comparison of social structures and their operations. However, since the comparative method alone produced generalizations about conditions essential to the existence of social systems and regularities observable in social change, it was the only method for comparative sociology (Radcliffe-Brown 1958d: 128). Could the historical-processual and the structural-processual objectives be combined to reveal laws of social development to which Boas had pointed? This was possible, but in Radcliffe-Brown's (1958d:128–129) judgment this would be achieved only when the historical and sociological approaches were combined in an integrated research methodology. Did this mean, too, that the development of anthropology as a unified science was possible? To this query Radcliffe-Brown (1957) gave qualified affirmation. The practical orientations of most of the social sciences had differentiated and distributed the human reality like parcels of ground. Their separatistic tendencies maintained solid boundaries that restricted a more integrated theoretical social science. It was by reason of such vested interests that concern for a general and theoretical science of society had fallen to anthropology, as if by default, and by historic accident. "That is why it [theoretical social science] has had to take refuge in departments of anthropology as the only place left to it. Therefore, while a theoretical science of society is possible, I am not particularly optimistic as to the prospects of its immediate realization" (Radcliffe-Brown 1957:148).

Structure-Sentiment-Ritualization-Function: The Foundations of Society

For Radcliffe-Brown structure-sentiment-ritualization-function constituted the basic nexus for understanding primitive society and society generally. Structure represented the social framework by which and toward which all activities were directed. Function represented a correlated effect of these activities, which—both in their utilitarian and purposive modes—integrated the individual within the social matrix and made him an efficient contributor to processes through which social continuity was assured. Social sentiments linked to ritualized symbolic expressions and customs dramatized the logic of the structure and locked individuals into formal relationships and activities, thereby contributing to structure maintenance. In this socializing process the individual lost his awareness of any unique personal identity or interest by unconsciously identifying with group actions and purposes. The involved phraseology used to describe structural-functional linkages revealed how complicated tautologies interfere with any attempts to trace cause and effects back to a purposive design. It may be better to simply describe the relationships among things.

Radcliffe-Brown found the ultimate problem for sociological analysis to be determination of the social order, and how it was maintained by organizing the sentiments and actions of individuals behind it. His theoretical credo, admittedly, stemmed from Durkheim and followed the methodology of case studies in social morphology. However, Radcliffe-Brown (1965g:198–199) made his own special contributions to the study of social structure by analyzing the nature of social networks arising out of mutual interests and reciprocities. The declaration in *The Andaman Islanders* (1948:233–234) is prophetic of a position elaborated but not altered in its essentials.

Stated as briefly as possible the working hypothesis here adopted is as follows. (1) A society depends for its existence on the presence in the minds of its members of a certain system of sentiments by which the conduct of the individual is regulated in conformity with the needs of the society. (2) Every feature of the social system itself and every event or object that in any way affects the well-being or the cohesion of the society becomes an object of this system of sentiments. (3) In human society the sentiments in question are not innate but are developed in the individual by the action of the society upon him. (4) The ceremonial customs of a society are a means by which the sentiments in question are given collective expression on appropriate occasions. (5) The ceremonial (i.e., collective) expression of any sentiment serves both to maintain it at the requisite degree of intensity in the mind of the individual and to transmit it from one generation to another. Without such expression the sentiments involved could not exist.

Using the term "social function" to denote the effects of an institution (custom or belief) in so far as they concern the society and its solidarity or cohesion, the hypothesis ... may be more briefly resumed in the statement that the social function of the ceremonial customs of the Andaman Islanders is to maintain and to transmit from one generation to another the emotional dispositions on which the society (as it is constituted) depends for its existence.

From such a vantage point it is apparent that Radcliffe-Brown opposed all psychological interpretations of customs and was not inclined to interest himself in problems of individual variation or of change. The "study of social structure ... [as] social morphology and social physiology" proved far more attractive to Radcliffe-Brown (1965g:201) than investigation of how social structures may change or new structures originate. It was inevitable, then, that Radcliffe-Brown and Malinowski should clash over the interpretation of anxiety, for here psychological and sociological explanations once again were in conflict (see Homans 1941(43):164–172).

Malinowski (1954:29–32) had interpreted magic as ritualized activity designed by men to cope with the uncertainties of life. Arguing from his sociological base, Radcliffe-Brown (1965e:148–149) countered that, socially speaking, rites and ceremonies were intended to create a psychological mood or effect. Were it not for their traditional beliefs and ceremonies associated with turtle, dugong, and pork meat, Andamanese natives would not experience a feeling of insecurity or anxiety. At the same time, by following traditional practice the anxiety was relieved. For Malinowski magical rites were born out of the human effort to overcome anxiety; for Radcliffe-Brown anxiety was communicated to individuals in order that they might share the sentiment appropriate to continuance of a rite. What was needed, observed Radcliffe-Brown (1965h:157), was "a general theory of the social function of rites and ceremonies," and by implication, of institutions at large—like the one he propounded in 1908 when writing up his Andaman materials.

Stated in the simplest possible terms the theory is that an orderly social life amongst human beings depends upon the presence in the minds of the members of a society of certain sentiments, which control the behaviour of the individual in his relation to others. Rites can be seen to be the regulated symbolic expressions of certain sentiments. Rites can therefore be shown to have a specific social function when, and to the extent that, they have for their effect to regulate, maintain and transmit from one generation to another sentiments on which the constitution of the society depends. I ventured [at that time] to suggest a general formula that religion is everywhere an expression

in one form or another of a sense of dependence on a power outside ourselves, a power which we may speak of as a spiritual or moral power
(Radcliffe-Brown 1965h:157)

Boas (1963:205–215) called to mind another interesting aspect of anxiety and behavior when speaking of the problem of primary and secondary
rationalizations of customs. The traditionalizing of behavior lessens the
valence of associated feeling states, and the weight of feeling actually may
be transferred to situations where customs are not followed or are flag-
rantly violated. In such case the disturbance or displeasure would not
necessarily be coordinate with the traditionalized feeling, but with other
feelings such as anxiety and anger. In Boas' view this situation might pro-
voke a secondary rationalization of the custom, an important consideration
when dealing with the origins of social conventions. In Malinowski's interpretation, however, neglect of a rite could be expected to evoke the anxious
concern which had prompted it in the first place. According to Radcliffe-
Brown's interpretation, failure to perform the protective rite also aroused
an anxious state.

Radcliffe-Brown's concern for structure and the strain toward social
integration and a sense of solidarity led him to study formal social arrangements with little attention to the circumvention of rules and procedures
commonly found in the infrastructure or when conflict produced compromise. Recognizing that every social system has built-in mechanisms for
organizing and regulating antagonisms, he approached the study of society
from the standpoint of the organized weight of the social system upon the
individuals composing it. He gave his attention to legal, religious, and
moral sanctions that bound individuals to social rights and obligations and
gave him a position in the social order.

> The sanctions existing in a community constitute motives in the individual for
> the regulation of his conduct in conformity with usage. They are effective,
> first, through the desire of the individual to obtain the approbation and to
> avoid the disapprobation of his fellows, to win such rewards or to avoid such
> punishment as the community offers or threatens; and, second, through the
> fact that the individual learns to react to particular modes of behavior with
> judgments of approval and disapproval in the same way as do his fellows,
> and therefore measures his own behavior both in anticipation and in retro-
> spect by standards which conform more or less closely to those prevalent in
> the community to which he belongs. What is called conscience is thus in the
> widest sense the reflex in the individual of the sanctions of the society. (Rad-
> cliffe-Brown 1965c:205)

Social Structure and Organic Analogy

When it came to exploring the nature of social structure, Radcliffe-
Brown, like Spencer, found the analogy of society and organism a useful
device. "The concept of function . . . thus involves the notion of a *structure*
consisting of a *set of relations* amongst *unit entities*, the *continuity* of the

structure being maintained by a *life-process* made up of the *activities* of the constituent units" (Radcliffe-Brown 1945(37):396). Ideas about organic structure and function moved quickly to the idea of functional unity. At this point Radcliffe-Brown invoked the traditional Structuralist concepts of internal consistency and harmony. Perfect functional consistency or unity was never attained in any social system, and every system underwent changes brought about by functional inconsistencies, provoking conflicts which could be resolved only by modifying the system (Radcliffe-Brown 1965d:43).

Radcliffe-Brown pointed to a distinction of functional consistency and logical consistency as important to understanding the nature of social integration. Logical consistency was associated with coherence traceable to values and principles. Functional consistency was more important because it correlated with basic social adaptations. Indeed, the conditions or functional needs of human society were the key to the establishment of sociological laws and were considered their equivalent.

Functional consistency constituted a first law. Establishment of a formal structure with a set of relationships operating between individuals and groups was a second law or precondition. The unit parts in the network of relations were bound by rights and duties. Legal, religious, and moral sanctions were attached to these rights and duties to preserve the integrity of the structure and to assure basic and continuous operations. The conformity of societies to general functional prerequisites, or laws of social survival, underlined the adaptive quality of human society and a signal difference regarding the cycle of growth and decay found in the organic world. In Radcliffe-Brown's mirror of history, there were few societies which had passed away. On the contrary, human societies strained adaptively for a kind of harmony and social health and usually altered their structural operations and types without going under. There were some rare instances, Radcliffe-Brown admitted, where European contact with native societies had resulted in their extinction.

Radcliffe-Brown did not follow Spengler or Toynbee in describing the course of any civilization as a rise and fall comparable to the maturation and inevitable decay of organisms induced by the gradual exhaustion of inner and outer resources. Rather than looking for negative effects or contradictions within a system, Radcliffe-Brown preferred to illuminate the positive forces that assured social harmony, growth, and survival. Such was also the emphasis of Malinowski. Exploration of the structuring of culture and social order was designed to generate a theory of system process, and hence accented the positive and integrative processes of social life rather than seeds of destruction embedded in the system.

Conflicts of interest and contradictions naturally exist in any social order, but they can be and usually are accommodated by rules that minimize tensions. The seemingly inexplicable joking relationship, frequently found in kinship societies, was an example of the way social conflict could be stabilized by ritualization of aggression. Through an obligatory hostility

and disrespect, the joking relationship drew attention to a social discon-
formity intrinsic to the formal structure. At the same time, the joking
relaxed the tension accompanying the formal relationship with a friendly
demeanor and obligations of mutual assistance (Radcliffe-Brown 1965f:95).
Joking reciprocity thus took its place alongside three other modes of
alliance by which separatism was overcome: "(1) through intermarriage,
(2) by exchange of goods or services, (3) by blood-brotherhood or exchanges of names or sacra, and (4) by the joking relationship" (Radcliffe-
Brown 1965f:102). Yet, in opting for general functional prerequisites for
the maintenance of societies, Radcliffe-Brown implied that every social
system at its core was like every other social system. Functional needs, like
a primary guidance system, channeled the directionality of adaptation.
Social evolution did occur, and largely by a process of divergence which
Radcliffe-Brown considered the essence of evolutionary change (Radcliffe-
Brown 1962a:83).

Totemism and Universal Processes

When charting a sociological origin for totemism and its variable manifestations, Radcliffe-Brown made use of the process of evolutionary divergence. Any satisfactory theory of totemism, he argued, must conform
with a more general theory in explaining other things besides totemism
(Radcliffe-Brown 1965b:126). The ritual relationship between men in
hunting societies and animals mirrored in primitive mythologies, attitudes,
and activities was a datum of first importance. From this general relationship between men as a social collective (society) and natural species, one
could hypothesize that as society segments into groups such as clans, each
segment takes on a special relationship to one or more natural species
through a process of ritualization (Radcliffe-Brown 1965b:127). The trend
in totemic evolution moved from the general to the specific through a
process of differentiation. To fully comprehend totemism it must be viewed
as an expression of a universal process, found in religion, to represent the
universe as a moral or social order (Radcliffe-Brown 1965b:131). The
primitive personification of species as ancestors or culture heroes transformed nature into a community of persons, a social and moral order. The
differentiation of totemism thus was tied to the differentiation of society
into clans and lineages, and society provided the generic model for ordering the universe. Methodologically speaking, Radcliffe-Brown had substituted a sociological explanation for earlier attempts to explain this singular
primitive social and religious phenomenon psychologically.

Social Principles of Kinship

In carrying forward the Durkheimian search for social types among
primitive groups, Radcliffe-Brown (1924) became involved increasingly
with kinship. Kinship involved formal sets of relationships with clearly

defined rights and obligations, including supportive legal and moral sanctions. Kinship satisfied the basic criteria for recognizing structure. In his introduction to *African Systems of Kinship and Marriage* Radcliffe-Brown (1962a:1–85) summarized his theoretical position and findings regarding social classifications, nature of social relations, structure, function, sentiment, and social laws. Studies of African societies permitted a distinction of four ideal types described as father-right, mother-right, purely cognatic systems, and double lineage systems. Kinship systems exhibited variability when surveyed on a world-wide basis, but their variations clustered about a combination and application of a few general structural principles.

Assuming the primary unit of kinship structure to be the family, Radcliffe-Brown (1962a:5–25) observed how the principles of generation and sex and of the unity of the sibling group aided in the extension of social relations. Sensitively alert to the importance of keeping social tensions to a minimum, he noted how the freedom and equality linking alternate generations (grandparent-grandchild) countered tensions between proximal generations (parent-child), where a socially unequal relationship was common, and where subordinative and respectful behavior were required (Radcliffe-Brown 1962a:27–30). In the presence of the structural principle of lineage unity, however, the principle of generation would be overridden, as exhibited in the patrilineal Omaha system. The structural principle of lineage unity also turned up in the separation of a society into descent units that might function as corporate groups. The corporate nature of lineages or clans was recognized in unit ownership of land and ceremonies with collective rights frequently vested in a chief or council. When it came to explanation of the levirate and sororate marriage practices, Radcliffe-Brown (1962a:64) brought in the "principle of the unity of the sibling group, since brother replaces brother and sister replaces or supplements sister." However, preferential marriage with a wife's brother's daughter, usually associated with a patrilineal lineage structure, involved the lineage unity principle. Polygynous marriage customs thus might derive from distinct structural principles.

Behind Radcliffe-Brown's capacity to read new meaning into primitive custom and to provide new incentives to research lay his general theory, the lodestone to which all structural principles useful in specific interpretation must be related. In the instance of preferential marriage,

> The theory here proposed is simply a special application of the theory that the *raison d'être* of an institution or custom is to be found in its social function. The theory is, therefore, that the rules or customs relating to prohibited or preferred marriage have for their social function to preserve, maintain, or continue an existing kinship structure as a system of institutional relations. Where a marriage between relatives would threaten to disrupt or throw into disorder the established system it tends to be disapproved or forbidden, and the greater and more widespread the disturbance that would be caused by a marriage, the stronger tends to be the disapproval which it meets with. Inversely, preferen-

tial marriages are those which have for their effect to renew or reinforce the existing system. (Radcliffe-Brown 1962a:62)

With this statement Ralcliffe-Brown affirmed that the basic processes of any social order were sensitively tuned to preserving and increasing the integrity of the system. To find these sensitive processes one must first look to the ultimate design or function of the system as a whole, or any of its segments, which necessarily must be organized to serve this ultimate function.

The Structural Principles of Societies

Radcliffe-Brown drew a theoretical portrait of society unified by two different kinds of structural features. First there were those generic conditions or laws of existence to which all societies conformed—the laws of functional consistency, the differentiation of jural and moral rights, and obligations regulating social relationships and corporate continuity. Next came the structural principles by which individual societies achieved these conditional requirements. Some structural principles apparently were universal, as the formation of dyadic relationships, the unity of siblings, and generation. Others, like the lineage principle, were not universal. In the differential application of these principles one found the basis for stylistic distinctions in social integration and also the much-sought social types.

The effects of social functions permeated both subordinate and higher levels of organization, with the highest level supplying the basis and the principles by which the different levels were integrated. Function, finalized in the harmonious working of a near friction-free system, conveyed a teleological or final cause quality to the position of the social Structuralist. Moreover, the thrust of methodology was directed first to a comprehension of system manifest in its laws and morphology. Once laws and structure were determined, then one could relate the contribution of the parts to the system in accordance with its laws and structural principles. Radcliffe-Brown denied this, asserting that establishment of the social types was derived empirically. However, his stress on a general theory as a starting point for comprehending the particulars of the whole is reminiscent of Koffka's (1931(1):644–645) statement on the methodological posture of Gestalt psychology.

> Therefore, instead of starting with the elements and deriving the properties of the wholes from them, a reverse process is necessary, i.e., to try to understand the properties of parts from the properties of wholes. The chief content of Gestalt as a category is this view of the relation of parts and wholes involving the recognition of intrinsic real dynamic whole-properties.

The structural-comparative analysis proposed by Radcliffe-Brown was directed at the achievement of functional correlates, but immediate focus on the nature and integrative processes of social types restricted methodology to descriptive analysis. What the social Structuralist demonstrated in his studied analysis was the close fit or functional consistency of the system under review, and his inclination was to formulate models to show how prime social types were structured and how they operated. In such a situation one could describe relationships stemming from structural principles, but here causal explanations were as elusive as in the historical relations described by Lowie and criticized by Kroeber. As a unit activity in the service of the whole, function dissolved the need for causal determination and pointed to reciprocal effects, with final cause ultimately located in the totality of needs associated with social structure. Yet, the association of covariants to which Radcliffe-Brown pointed did imply a cause-effect nexus. Like Durkheim, he expected that as A varied (for example, presence of lineage principle), so aspects of B, social structure, would vary (for example, extension of sororal-type polygyny to lineage statuses, as in wife's brother's daughter preferential marriage). Such analysis was not historical, since the structural covariants came into being under appropriate conditions and in a sense were impervious to the historical process. An obvious move was to employ statistical techniques to establish structural-functional correlations. This, however, was not the direction Radcliffe-Brown would take, nor the one his followers took, although he did make statements of probable frequency. Thus marriage with a wife's sister would be found in more frequent association with patrilineal lineages where fathers exercised strong controls, since such a marriage strengthened the male-oriented marriage system (Radcliffe-Brown 1962a:65).

Initiative in establishing functional correlates through mathematical techniques came from American ethnologists well versed in the comparison of culture elements, and who were attuned to the use of statistics by psychologists and sociologists striving for added methodological controls. The lead was taken by G. P. Murdock, who tested five theories to account for a bifurcate merging-kinship terminology. In this statistical test involving 221 societies, Murdock (1947(49):62) entered Radcliffe-Brown's theory that bifurcate merging terminology and the levirate are products of the principle of the social equivalence of brothers. He found that its probability factor was quite low and therefore invalidated the principle. In contrast, Kroeber's theory that unilineal kin groups were associated with bifurcate merging terminology received a very respectable confirmation in a correlation of +.72.

There was another causal sequence, and one that Radcliffe-Brown considered the very root of all social phenomena. It began with an interactional relation, which induced a social sentiment, which then became formalized in a symbolic and ritualized activity of social relations. Among the Andaman Islanders, for example, food occupied a central place in ceremonies that accented transitions in status. Though food collected individually was privately owned, generous sharing of food was counted a social virtue. A young unmarried man must resign himself and his friends to accept the inferior parts of a pig he himself had killed, while the older men distributed and kept the choice parts for themselves (Radcliffe-Brown

1948:43). Hospitality and the exchange of presents, usually craft products, were encouraged, and this attitude was so pervasive both within and between local groups that a manner of communalism existed.

The primacy and symbolic value of food for the Andamanese apparently stemmed from the fact that it was obtained on a day-to-day basis. Consequently, food was tied to the emotional life of the society, as people oscillated between being happy or depressed according to its presence or absence (Radcliffe-Brown 1948:270). Basically a communal activity, since all must obtain it and share it, food getting generated the social feeling of esteem for the more successful and scorn for the lazy and careless. The arduous labor involved in obtaining food and the contentment which accompanied the eating of food contrasted with the anxious feelings aroused by its lack. Secure comfort or an anxious emptiness of stomach structured the basic social sentiments with positive and negative attributes. All Andaman sentiments pointed to food; hence, the cautious ritualization of important foods. It was natural that the young were ceremonialized into society through activities dramatizing the value of food.

> Since in the life of the Andamans by far the most important social activity is the getting of food, and it is in connection with food that the social sentiments are most frequently called into action, it is therefore appropriate that it should be through his relation to food that the child should be taught his relation to the society, and thus have those sentiments implanted in him or brought to the necessary degree of strength. (Radcliffe-Brown 1948:277)

For Radcliffe-Brown, and his sociological inspiration, Durkheim, an interactionally engendered sentiment constituted the heart of the social matter and carried the major thrust of institutional integration for any society. If the social sentiment provided the primary social fact, it appeared that more attention must be given to sociopsychological process. Immediately, however, concern for understanding the range of structural types and their organizing principles predominated. When this type of analysis was brought to its fullest maturation, dissatisfaction with formal analysis of the social system led to greater attention to contextual analysis. This provided fresh insights into the variability of the operation of social organization. The issue of variation, long ignored in the interests of structure, was again confronted.

BIOCULTURAL FUNCTIONALISM: BRONISLAW MALINOWSKI (1884–1942)

Malinowski grounded his theory of biocultural functionalism on the basic datum of man's biological and psychological needs. A native of Cracow, Poland, he died in New Haven, Connecticut, in 1942, shortly after appointment as professor of anthropology at Yale University. Malinowski took his Ph.D. in 1908 in physics and mathematics with high honors. Tubercular all his life, with an anxious concern for his health,

Malinowski was inspired to take up anthropology as a career during a period of recuperation when he read Frazer's *Golden Bough* to test his English. By 1910 he was in London, studying under C. G. Seligman and Edward Westermarck, at the same time cultivating Frazer, Haddon, Marett, and Rivers. Through the assistance of C. G. Seligman in 1914, Malinowski went to Melanesia as a Robert Mond Travelling Scholar. Among the Mailu, and particularly with the Trobriands, Malinowski began a career that marked him as an outstanding contributor to the image of the ethnographer as a scientist and a theoretical innovator in law, economics, and social organization. Malinowski's pragmatic concern for facts did not encourage an enthusiasm for systematic theorizing (Fortes 1964). Nonetheless, he considered himself the first of the functionalists. His works consistently began with remarks critical of former theories, for which his own were valid substitutes because they accorded with facts observed in the Trobriand field. So far as the ethnographer was concerned, he had

> the duty before him of drawing up all the rules and regularities of tribal life; all that is permanent and fixed; of giving an anatomy of their culture, of depicting the constitution of their society. But these . . . are embodied in the most elusive of all materials; the human being. But not even in human mind or memory are these laws to be found definitely formulated. The natives obey the forces and commands of the tribal code, but they do not comprehend them; exactly as they obey their instincts and their impulses, but could not lay down a single law of psychology. The regularities in native institutions are an automatic result of the interaction of the mental forces of tradition, and of the material conditions of environment. Exactly as a humble member of any modern institution, whether it be the state, or the church, or the army, is *of* it and *in* it, but has no vision of the resulting integral action of the whole, still less could furnish any account of its organisation, so it would be futile to attempt questioning a native in abstract sociological terms. The difference is that, in our society, every institution has its intelligent members, its historians, and its archives and documents, whereas in a native society there are none of these. After this is realised an expedient has to be found to overcome this difficulty. This expedient for an Ethnographer consists in collecting concrete data of evidence, and drawing the general inferences for himself. This seems obvious on the face of it, but was not found out or at least practised in Ethnography till field work was taken up by men of science. Moreover, in giving it practical effect, it is neither easy to devise the concrete applications of this method, nor to carry them out systematically and consistently. (Malinowski 1961a:11–12)

However, Malinowski's first publication, *The Family among the Australian Aborigines* (1963), was library research. It was a critical exercise to determine the nature of the individual family among Australian aborigines and particularly appropriate in that ethnological descriptions of native life and society had added substance to general conjectures about the history of marriage and the family (Malinowski 1963:292). After surveying methodological difficulties in evaluating the ethnological data and its reporters, Malinowski proceeded to demonstrate that the individual family, as an affectional, economic, socially, and legally sanctioned, reproductive, and need-fulfilling unit, was present in these aboriginal societies. Its presence was obscured by imperfect and casual observations that stressed the collective status and group role-playing of the natives, as well as by Western preconceptions about the moral-sexual nature of the marriage relationship.

> The careful survey of the facts has led . . . to the conclusion that in considering marriage, the importance of the sexual facts ought not to be exaggerated. In the majority of the tribes sexual facts do not seem to play any part in the formation of bonds of kinship. Ideas of consanguinity . . . are absent in these tribes, and herewith the sexual relations between husband and wife lose their chief influence upon the unity of the family. On the other hand, the sexual rights of the husband, although very well determined, are so often crossed by other customs that *exclusive* access to a woman must not be made a part of the sociological definition of marriage. The importance of the economic features of family life, and of the common affection for children, is much more in the foreground. (Malinowski 1963:299–300)

Malinowski drew heavily upon Westermarck's analysis of marriage and family as social institutions, pointing out that marriage was a product of the family, rather than family a derivative of marriage. Westermarck also insisted that economic factors played an important part in family life, especially in rearing children and in general mode of life. The library study of the Australian family was especially fruitful in that it gave Malinowski a methodological tool, the institution, through which to focus field investigation.

Institutions existed in human societies because they fulfilled human needs, sometimes biological but more often socially derived. Anything that satisfied a need had a function (Malinowski 1960:39). Hence, need-activity-purpose-function was intertwined in Malinowski's elaboration of the institutional theory on which he centered a general theory of culture. In simple and pragmatic comparisons between Trobriand and Western institutions, Malinowski observed how they constituted groups which were organized according to a set of traditional values and chartered for a specific purpose. The institutionalized personnel operated according to specific norms, which were fortified by social and legal sanctions. Finally the institutionalized group carried out mutually beneficial activities through the medium of instrumental resources allotted and designed for the activities (Malinowski 1960:36–66). The institution thus became the primary component for analysis, to which the specific culture elements—trait, custom, or idea—were related. The institutional context gave meaning and functional significance to individual features; hence no culture element could be understood out of its relevant institutional context. As an "organized system of purposeful activities," institutions universally followed the same structure (Figure 13-2).

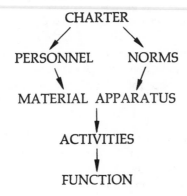

Figure 13-2. The attributes of an institution, according to Malinowski (1960:53).

Behind all institutional expressions were seven basic needs (metabolism, reproduction, bodily comforts, safety, movement, growth, and health). Basic needs forced human beings into a number of primary institutionalized activities: food getting, formation of groups based on kinship, satisfaction of body comforts, survival defenses, release of motor tensions and excess energy, training of individuals for institutional roles, and maintenance of health. The culturizing of these basic needs meant that a number of instrumental imperatives mediated each of these needs. There were four functional imperatives essential to social maintenance: technologizing of production (economics), conventionalization of behavior according to imperative norms (social control), transmitting of knowledge and skills (education), and organization of power to execute operations (political organization) (Malinowski 1960:125). Each category of instrumental imperative was realized through institutions, of which there were a limited number of types corresponding to seven principles of integration: reproduction, territorial, physiological, voluntary associations, occupational and professional, rank and status, and comprehensive, that is, wider extensions of community and tribal unity (Malinowski 1960:62–66).

Each of these principles of social integration would be found operative in all societies, but in different emphases, and gave rise to a different range of institutional arrangements. Thus, the reproductive principle of integration would be found operating in institutions such as the family, courtship, and the clan. The territorial principle covered institutions such as neighborhoods, villages, districts, tribes, and others where mutual interests grew out of proximity and there was opportunity for cooperation. Age and sex groupings revealed the physiological principle, while secret, mutual aid, and recreational institutions could be traced to the voluntary associations principle. Craft, professional, and administrative institutions disclosed the occupation and professional principle. The rank and status principle was involved in stratification by class, caste, race, and ethnicity. Finally, the comprehensive principle manifested itself in the integration of national and tribal institutions, including regionalized subgroupings and alienated minorities (Malinowski 1960:63–65).

Another vital sequence needed to be incorporated into any analysis of culture—the behavioral psychological process by which basic need drives and their goal satisfactions were translated into the instrumental activity of the institution. Here it is necessary to keep in mind the structural outline of institutions and their four functional imperatives when noting the relation betewen the cultural drive (D1) and the physiological drive (D2) as diagrammed by Malinowski (Figure 13-3).

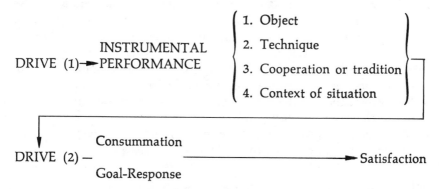

Figure 13-3. Response sequence and reinforcement, according to Malinowski (1960:137).

The problem was to relate the instrumental responses to the physiological need, thereby investing the instrumental response with the imperative of a drive. This meant that the instrumental response became an acquired drive and a substitute for the original physiological need, or so closely compounded that the two were difficult to distinguish. The equation of physiological and instrumental need was accomplished through psychological reinforcement of the physiological need. The effects of this were then generalized throughout the whole instrumental complex, including tools, techniques, rules governing cooperation, and awareness of the situational circumstances (Malinowski 1960:138).

In this way Malinowski invested culture with an emotional tone or sentiment, agreeing with Durkheim, Radcliffe-Brown, Boas, and Freud that human behavior in its collective and individual expression was deeply rooted in feeling. However, the path Malinowski took in drawing this conclusion was his own. He wished it understood, and indeed it was essential to his argument, that the generalization of the physiological imperative to the instrumental activity flowed into every part of that activity. For example, this physiological reinforcement stimulus permeated the whole domain of any institution—the charter, values, rules, type of personnel involved, technical apparatus, and the activities themselves. In modern industrial life, the job with its regulations, driving to work, money reward, and the comforts of home formed a complex whole permeated by physiological need imperatives that deepened the emotional valence of these instrumental activities.

The idea and analysis were good, but were they the whole story of socialized habit conditioning at the emotional level? The other side of the coin was the injection of socialized feeling by social conditioning. This Radcliffe-Brown and culture theorists used to account for the affect demonstrated by individuals in situations that symbolized a collective history and destiny, or a common devotion to an ethical principle. For Malinowski, culture was raised on human needs and served those needs. This was why culture existed in the first place. Social structuralists, on the other hand, viewed man as a social being once removed from his primary survival requirements. Survival needs were masked and transmuted into social needs. Hence, the analysis begins and centers in the functional needs of social life and not in the physiological and psychological needs of individuals. The issue raised by this dichotomy in approach has yet to be resolved, though present trends favor Malinowski's view that culture exists for man, and not man for society and culture.

The Institution: Locus for Field Research and Method

Fresh from his Australian success, Malinowski pressed to advantage the institutional approach in his fieldwork among the Trobriands. The individual family remained *the* central institution to Malinowski, and his argument for its presence in Australian societies contributed to final acceptance of the universality of this social unit. All of Malinowski's important ethnographic descriptions were centered on institutions—for example, 1954a, "Baloma; The Spirits of the Dead in the Trobriand Islands"; 1922, *Argonauts of the Western Pacific, An Account of Native Enterprise and Adventure in the Archipelagoes of Melanesian New Guinea* [Kula exchange]; 1926, *Crime and Custom in Savage Society*; 1927, *Sex and Repression in Savage Society*; 1929, *The Sexual Life of Savages in North-Western Melanesia. An Ethnographic Account of Courtship, Marriage and Family Life Among the Natives of the Trobriand Islands, British New Guinea*; 1935, *Coral Gardens and Their Magic. A Study of the Methods of Tilling the Soil and of Agricultural Rites in the Trobriand Islands* (2 volumes). His study of institutions also served Malinowski (1961b:65) when he addressed himself to the problem of culture change.

> all sociologically relevant impact and interaction is organized, that is, it occurs as between institutions. The real agencies of contact are organized bodies of human beings working for a definite purpose; handling appropriate apparatus of material culture; and subject to a charter of laws, rules, and principles. The chartered company of early days, the European colonial government, the missionary body or the industrial enterprise, a community of planters or settlers—these have been and are the effective influences of the Western world,

and each has to direct its impact primarily upon its indigenous counterpart: chieftainship, African religion, African systems of agriculture, hunting, fishing, or industry.

The range of Malinowski's study of Trobriand institutions largely documents the range of his contributions to ethnological theory in the areas of economics, law, magic and religion, family, and kinship (see Firth 1964). The significance of the institution as the primary integrater of field investigation also was communicated effectively to his early students who produced functional studies of primitive economics, law, marriage, and political organization—for example, R. Firth 1929, *Primitive Economics of the New Zealand Maori;* A. Richards 1932, *Hunger and Work in a Savage Tribe. A Functional Study of Nutrition Among the Southern Bantu;* L. Mair 1934, *An African People in the Twentieth Century;* I. Hogbin 1934, *Law and Order in Polynesia;* M. Hunter 1936, *Reaction to Conquest: Effects of Contact with Europeans on the Pondo of South Africa;* E. E. Evans-Pritchard 1937, *Witchcraft, Oracles and Magic Among the Azande;* I. Schapera 1941, *Married Life in an African Tribe.*

One methodological drawback to the institutional approach was that it produced descriptions bounded by the functions of the institutions. The difficulty was early perceived by Malinowski, who wrote Firth after his return from Tikopia urging that he proceed immediately to describe Tikopian culture in the round. He cautioned Firth not to make the mistake of writing it up piecemeal, as he had done ten years previous with his Trobriand materials (Firth 1964a:10).

The diversity and personal variants observable in Trobriand life convinced Malinowski of the necessity for ordering and classifying his social data while still in the field. Preliminary generalization of facts thereby could be checked against the organic whole of native social life (Malinowski 1954a:238–239). What was shared behaviorally by people offered an answer to the problem of diversity in private opinion and activity. In the instance of the spirits of the dead among the Trobriands, everyone, even those who were inarticulate about the *baloma* and how they felt about them, nevertheless behaved according to the traditional custom and social rules governing emotional reactions (Malinowski 1954a:242). Custom steadied private thought, and feeling toned and combined the two into a compelling social form.

Malinowski's model of an institution organized by a charter of beliefs, values, and norms steered him toward a theory of culture and of cultural learning rather than toward a theory of social structure and social processes. To find out how and why groups were organized and carried out specific functions, one must look to the charter. Yet, as with his criticism of Freudian Oedipal theory, Malinowski stressed the relevancy of social structure in the diversion of aggressive sexual feelings to persons outside the immediate family, for example, the mother's brother in matrilineal Trobriand society. It also appeared that a male child's sexual appetites were fixated on the sister rather than on the mother, for brother-sister relations carried a greater depth of horror and incest dread than parent-child relations (Malinowski 1926, 1929). But while Malinowski rejected a Freudian-type unconscious as the psychological anchor for custom, his bio-cultural theory of institutions made use of individually experienced need tensions as the source for cooperative social action. What Malinowski did, in effect, was to reverse the Freudian equation. Society was not the source for individual tensions and neuroticisms but the accommodator, the mollifier of individual psychological disturbances. The real source for these tension-producing experiences were the crises of death, puberty, disease, hunger, and other situations threatening to individual life (Malinowski 1954b:62–65). Malinowski interpreted the primitive's fear of death as probably an instinctual response shared by men and animals. Unable to face the idea of a final end to life and personality, mankind, in cooperative mourning and in basic religious ceremony, ritualized a poignant search for a life everlasting. The trauma of death aroused the basic instinct of self-preservation, and men instinctively mobilized their defenses against this threat to the solidarity of the group and the continuity of society, tradition, and culture. Religion functioned to counteract the stress of terror, panic, and demoralization and provided a powerful way to restore and reestablish the solidarity, morale, and morals of the group.

Like others before him, Malinowski (1954b:54) found primitive society a highly sacralized order. "Religion needs the community as a whole so that its members may worship in common its sacred things and its divinities, and society needs religion for the maintenance of moral law and order." Through worship society in its diverse institutionalizations is unified and made one—this was the prime function of religion in savage society. Thus, the ancestor cult was designed to draw family, sib, and tribe into a community of worshippers who strengthened the feelings of solidarity by participation in public ceremonies (Malinowski 1954b:65–66). In religion Malinowski (1939(44):954) discovered once more the importance of an institutional analysis in providing details of the social organization housed within the cultural milieu.

Unity of Individual and Group in Institutional Theory

If the analysis of culture were to contribute anything, it must, in Malinowski's judgment, find a methodological way to unite individual and group in the analytical context. This was the function of functionalism. The individual and society were at opposite ends of the equation, but were not separated. Individuals introduced the demands of a common human physiology and a personal concern for their own activities. Society, on the other hand, brought traditional beliefs, customs, norms, sanctions, and material apparatus which individuals must cope with and use in cooperation with their fellows (Malinowski 1939(44):954).

In each institution the individual obviously has to become cognizant of its charter; he has to learn how to wield the technical apparatus or that part of it with which his activities associate him; he has to develop the social attitudes and personal sentiments in which the bonds of organization consist.

Thus, in either of these analyses the twofold approach through the study of the individual with his innate tendencies and their cultural transformation, and the study of the group as the relationship and coordination of individuals, with reference to space, environment, and material equipment, is necessary.

Concern for the individual meant cooncern for drive, feeling, and cognitive awareness which belonged to each individual as his share of the evolutionary heritage of man and his ancestors. This was not a special concern for the individual vis-à-vis the cultural process, though Malinowski took note of individual variations and traced them back to inner tension states caused by insecurity. On the contrary, when Malinowski (1954b:57–59), in criticism of Durkheim, pointed out that primitive religion sprang up from purely individual sources, he meant that all individuals shared certain biopsychic crisis situations. Through the uniformity of their mental and emotional processes each person contributed a vital need impulse to religious institutions. These, by design, reduced the aroused anxious states by means of sacralized tradition; hence, the need for according individual psychology a place in explaining the function of any institution. It was this very individual psychology that limited the number of institutions and allowed a measure of social typing of behavior despite the infinite variation in belief, idea, and opinion. Thus, in the instance of magic,

> One thing is certain: magic is not born of an abstract conception of universal power, subsequently applied to concrete cases. It has undoubtedly arisen independently in a number of actual situations. Each type of magic, born of its own situation and of the emotional tension thereof, is due to the spontaneous flow of ideas and the spontaneous reaction of man. It is the uniformity of the mental process in each case which has led to certain universal features of magic and to the general conceptions which we find at the basis of man's magical thought and behavior. (Malinowski 1954b:78–79)

The linkage between biological needs and cultural instrumentalities forged a double bond that limited individual freedom and variation. Biological determinism was etched in the necessities for survival, and men found governance by traditional rules equally necessary. Persistent failure to cooperate socially or to accurately communicate meanings led to immediate destruction or gradual exhaustion and biological destruction (Malinowski 1960:121; see also 1931(4):621–645). Biological and cultural determinism were closer realities for primitive men largely because their technological efficiency was low; hence, the conservative tone of primitive life centered in the unifying forces of the religious institutions. Though Malinowski dissolved the needs of the archetypal individual in a biological and cultural determinism, he wavered between the determinism of culture in molding the individual to tribal standards and the individuality of those who successfully evaded the culture press. In fact, Malinowski had no deep theoretical interest in the problem of free will or of the individual versus culture. Like Radcliffe-Brown, he was fundamentally concerned with forces operating to produce the uniformity so essential to the maintenance of the social and cultural system. Nevertheless, his field observations revealed violations of norms, and he used individual cases to disprove the current interpretation of savages as slaves of custom. In fact, there was a clear difference at times between what natives said they did in conformity with their rules and what the ethnographer observed, even in the face of the most stringent rules forbidding the breach of custom, as in the case of incest.

> What I wish to make clear by confronting the gist of native statements with the results of direct observation, is that there is a serious discrepancy between the two. The statements contain the ideal of tribal morality; observation shows us how far real behavior conformed to it. The statements show us the polished surface of custom which is invariably presented to the inquisitive stranger; direct knowledge of native life reveals the underlying strata of human conduct, moulded it is true, by the rigid surface of custom, but still more deeply influenced by the smouldering fires of human nature. The smoothness and uniformity, which the mere verbal statements suggest as the only shape of human conduct, disappear with a better knowledge of cultural reality. (Malinowski 1929:505–506)

Law and the Normative Regulation of Society

Malinowski's involvement with operations of law grew out of his conception of norms as essential regulators of social life and the continuity of human society. He first engaged the issue in his study of the Australian family. It was clear that Australian social organization, as any social organization, was regulated by norms that applied to the whole of social life. However, the degree of strictness of application varied according to the type of social relationship. When norms were enforced by an organized body of sanctions, the social norms in effect had been translated into law (Malinowski 1963:11). Without an organized procedure for enforcement, the conventionalized behavior was seen as a moral rule or one of custom. By 1944 Malinowski distinguished law as social conventions regulating interpersonal relations. There was little temptation to break or stretch these regulators which were backed by public opinion and formulated by pragmatic considerations. Malinowski discriminated these customary regulators of conduct from rules concerned with order and maintenance. He thus hit upon a distinction comparable to Sumner's folkways and mores; positive and negative rewards were prominent in the laws of social order and maintenance. Finally, there was procedural law, or what Malinowski called "the mechanisms of law when breach occurs."

In pointing out the different degrees and kinds of sanctions for social behavior, Malinowski provided new insights into the nature of primitive law and custom. However, his approach made no clear parallels between civil and criminal law as he wished to avoid the imposition of Western concepts upon the law data of primitive societies. In Malinowski's view, the proper procedure was to use the distinctions that could be discriminated behaviorally and confirmed through discourse with informants capable of elucidating native concepts. Legal distinctions arrived at through usual ethnographic procedures could then be checked with illustrative biographies or case studies.

Concern with the functional-normative (normative system) prerequisites of society led Malinowski to emphasize that societies and their organizing institutions could not exist unless some positive human impulse supported the conventions. In essence, dread of punishment, so often stressed in learned treatises of savage law and custom, was not enough to ensure a viable social order. Such was his basic message in *Crime and Custom in Savage Society* (1926:67), where he let the Trobrianders speak for "a class of rules too practical to be backed up by religious sanctions, too burdensome to be left to mere goodwill, too personally vital to individuals to be enforced by any abstract agency." Here he located the real domain of law— the bonding of individuals in obligatory mutual reciprocities essential to their common welfare without intervention of dread-inspiring sanctions. The point was a needed corrective at the time, but hardly clarified the nature of law (see, for example, Schapera 1964:152–155; Hoebel 1954: 177–210). His separation of normative law from the sanction of religion contradicted his own repeated assertion about the central position of religion in primitive society—that religion to the functionalist was not a mere surface phenomenon but was deeply embedded in the moral and social life of a people. Indeed, the religious institution shaped the integration of human cultures.

The Kula Exchange and Primitive Economics

In the Kula exchange of Papuo-Melanesian voyagers east of New Guinea, Malinowski (1961a:510) uncovered another unusual ethnological fact. Here vast areas and great numbers of people were united by social ties and bound by mutual obligations into a unique intertribal exchange system. Moreover, strict protocol regulated the exchange. Considering the relative simplicity of culture in the area, the Kula exchange was a strikingly complex and sophisticated sociological mechanism.

What impressed Malinowski were certain differences in the attitudes of Trobrianders and Western man with regard to economic possession and use. The prime characteristic of the Kula was an exchange of shell and other valuables held in individual possession for a conventionalized period of time. To translate the native valuables into a kind of money exchange was not possible even though both were objects of consolidated wealth (Malinowski 1961a:511). Neither could the exchange be covered by a bartering or the giving of presents. Indeed, the Kula was unique in every respect—an engagement in a magico-economic-ceremonial rite of possession and exchange that emphasized sharing as the epitome of goodness

(Malinowski 1961a:97). An apparent common feature of human nature, a desire for possession of goods, was present. However, possession was so ceremonialized and restricted that the whole institution, regarding material, social apparatus, psychology, and purpose, was without parallel in the West or elsewhere. It documented for Malinowski the fact that man did not live by bread alone but was forever transmuting his bioeconomic values through his cultural institutions. Certainly the Kula exchange had no place for unrestrained pragmatic and acquisitive materialism, but concentrated its capital in establishing mutual and beneficial social relations and in enhancing social status.

Primitive economics, as primitive law, thus possessed unique qualities which made ready translations between the simple and complex societies a difficult, if not hazardous, adventure. In economics, as in law, Malinowski stimulated a new viewpoint in research. He provided a base for economists, who, like Karl Polanyi, distinguished primitive, archaic, and modern market economies and challenged any purely materialistic interpretation of human purpose and design. Such materialism, in Polanyi's view, was associated with the European economy as it evolved early in the nineteenth century into an interconnected system of markets organized and based on competition and profit. Historically society became a materialistic organism only at the time when a free market (laissez-faire) economy gripped the West (Polanyi 1966:xvi). The Kula exchange also influenced the French social anthropologist Mauss, then engaged in studying the reciprocities of primitive social and economic exchange, to distinguish the social matrix of primitive exchange from market-type exchange.

The Individual Family and Kinship Extensions

Malinowski's commitment to the family as the primal institution of human life led him to conclude that in primitive society other social units were extensions of that basic unit, and therefore at some points were grounded to deeply rooted feelings that stabilized familial relations.

> All the sociological divisions, local communities, clans, subclans, and classificatory kinship groups of the Trobrianders are rooted in the family. Only by studying the formation of the earliest bonds between parent and child, by following the gradual growth and development of these, and their ever-widening extension into bonds of local grouping and clanship, can we grasp the kinship system of the natives. (Malinowski 1929:514–515)

Since Trobriand society emphasized social descent based on maternal relations, it was logical to find the centrum for their kinship system in the terms *inagu* and *latuga*, "my mother" and "my child," respectively. Here one could locate a universal physiological-emotional bond upon which the individual family rested. Moving farther down the corridors of kinship, one could expect this sentiment and the social instruments supporting it, positive or negative, to gradually fade away. Thus, in the instance of brother and sister, their play and contact were severely restricted by negative feelings aroused by the term *luguta*, a reciprocal for brother and sister as a tabooed relationship.

> Round the word *luguta* a new order of ideas and moral rules begins to grow up at an early stage of the individual's life history. The child, accustomed to little or no interference with most of its whims or wishes, receives a real shock when suddenly it is roughly handled, seriously reprimanded and punished whenever it makes any friendly, affectionate, or even playful advances to the other small being constantly about in the same household [i.e., brother or sister]. Above all, the child experiences an emotional shock when it becomes aware of the expression of horror and anguish on the faces of its elders when they correct it. This emotional contagion, this perception of moral reactions in the social environment, is perhaps the most powerful factor in a native community by which norms and values are imposed on an individual's character.
>
> The circumstantial arrangements and set customs which preclude any possibility of intimate contact between brother and sister are also, of course, very important. Brother and sister are definitely forbidden to take part at the same time in any childish sexual games, or even in any form of play. And this is not only a rule laid down by elders, but it is also a convention rigorously observed by the children themselves.
>
> We know . . . that when a boy grows up and when there is a sister of his living in the parental house, he has to sleep in the bachelors' hut (*bukumatula*). In her love affairs, the girl must most rigorously avoid any possibility of being seen by the brother. When, on certain occasions, brother and sister have to appear in the same company—when they travel in the same canoe, for instance, or participate in a domestic meeting—a rigidity of behaviour and a sobriety in conversation falls upon all those present. No cheerful company, no festive entertainment, therefore, is allowed to include brother and sister, since their simultaneous presence would throw a blight on pleasure and would chill gaiety. (Malinowski 1929:520–521)

In a number of instances Malinowski indicated how the classificatory extension of primary terms involved a difference in affect. This was true for a mother's sister designated as mother and held in the instance of tabooed sex and other relations when the term *luguta* was extended to someone other than real sister.

> The same gradual extension, and corresponding change in emotional content, takes place with regard to other terms, and the word *luguta*, used to the mother's sister's daughter, conveys to the boy only an attenuated and diluted idea of sisterhood. The own sister remains a prototype of the new relation, and the taboo observed towards the own sister has also to be kept with regard to the secondary sister; but the distinction between the two taboos and the two relations is well marked. The real sister lives in the same house; for her the boy, as her future guardian, feels a direct responsibility; she remains the object on which the first and only serious prohibition has been brought home to him. The secondary sister lives in another house or even village; there are no duties or responsibilities towards her and the prohibition with regard to her is a weakened extension of the primary taboo. Thus the own sister and

the first maternal cousin appear in an entirely different light, not only as regards the degree, but as regards the fundamental quality of the relation. Incest with the first maternal cousin is regarded as wrong, but not horrible; as daring and dangerous, but not abominable. The early feeling for this distinction becomes, later on, crystallized in the doctrine of tribal law. The man knows and recognizes that *luguta* (1) is a person to whom he owes a great many duties, whom he has partly to support after her marriage, and with regard to whom he has to observe the supreme taboo. *Luguta* (2) has no specific claims on him, he is not her real guardian nor head of her household after marriage, and the sexual taboo does not operate with anything like the same stringency. (Malinowski 1929:526–527)

When following out the channel of incest feelings, Malinowski achieved reasonable success in charting the gradual diminution of emotional valence and obligation. However, he found it odd to call the father's sister's son "father" and demonstrated how language influenced customs and ideas (Malinowski 1929:531).

When Malinowski approached kinship terms, he saw their function as a primary ordering of the social environment by sociological symbols clued to interpersonal relations vital to individual needs. These individual needs centered in the child-parent relation, with extension of terms to wider kin on grounds of social equivalence (Malinowski 1960:156). Classificatory terminologies thus lacked the emotional punch generated in primary family relations and hence were only convenient linguistic devices for categorizing kin relations.

Kroeber (1909) came to similar conclusions about kinship terminology, but by a different route. Knowing that the Dakota used one term for father-in-law and for grandfather, Kroeber (1952a:179) found it absurd to infer that the relationships at one time were identical. To further assume from such terminology that a real social relationship was implied, notably marriage with a mother, simply compounded the error. There were only eight principles available for classification of kin: generation, lineality-collaterality, relative age, sex of the relative, sex of the speaker, sex of the connecting relative, consanguinity-affinity, and the life situation of the person through whom a relationship exists. It was logical to expect that some principles would receive greater emphasis than others in categorizing the hundreds of possible relationships. The pragmatics of the situation would lead to a lumping of people who shared certain social and biological characteristics. For example, the Sioux used the same root in their terms for a woman's male cousin and for her brother-in-law. But in this case,

> A woman's male cousin and her brother-in-law are alike in sex, are both of opposite sex from the speaker, are of the same generation as herself, and are both collateral, so that they are similar under four categories. In view of the comparative paucity of terms as compared with possible relationships, it is entirely natural that the same word, or the same stem, should at times be used to denote two relationships having as much in common as these two.

No one would assume that the colloquial habit in modern English of speaking of the brother-in-law as brother implies anything as to form of marriage, for logically the use of the term could only be an indication of sister marriage. It is easily conceivable that in the future development of English the more cumbersome of these two terms might come into complete disuse in daily life and the shorter take its place, without the least change in social or marital conditions. (Kroeber 1952a:179–180)

In Kroeber's view, insistence on the sociological reality of kinship terms confused Developmentalists investigating this domain of social relationships and raised unnecessary problems.

Both Malinowski and Kroeber placed a psychological interpretation of kinship terms in opposition to a sociological one. At this point, Malinowski seemingly failed to resolve the total context of social structure and began to lose his students to the structural perspective of Radcliffe-Brown and the French sociologists. In their field researches neither Firth (1936) nor Fortes (1945) confirmed the essential validity of Malinowski's approach to understanding kinship and clanship through the medium of the individual family. Speaking retrospectively as a social Structuralist, Fortes (1964:179) felt Malinowski had failed to discriminate the signal difference between the formal status infused with jural rights and obligations and the personal or psychological elements of kinship. This prejudiced his perception of the real significance of kinship terminology with relation to social structure. Under structural analysis, Fortes (1964:175; see also Leach, 1958) maintained, "These terminologies are not just metaphors and homonyms as Malinowski proclaimed. They are indicators of social relations and of modes of grouping and arranging persons which are present in the social structure of any people at the same time as family relations and which serve to bind the family into the total jural and political order."

Situational Context and Meaning

It was Malinowski's perception of nuances in meaning according to context, that led him to suspect the formal word as a conveyor of mixed meaning. For example, a Trobriand male behaved differently toward his own sister and a mother's sister's daughter even though both were classified as socially equivalent. The classificatory term covered two different meanings, or the formal definitions of the social relations were different. Meaning was not welded to a dictionary form, but shifted with the situational context. This was a lead extracted from P. Wegener and accounted for Malinowski's homonymic analyses which attempted to bring out the significance of native terms according to contextual usage. Here Malinowski once again made a perceptive contribution not to linguistic method but to the search for the nature of meaning (see "The Problem of Meaning in Primitive Language," in Ogden and Richards 1923:451–510). Applied rigidly, the contextual meaning of situation excluded the fixity of meaning with relation to any form, lexical or actional. The problem Malinowski concentrated on was variation within a structured domain. His focus on variation helps explain the studious avoidance by Malinowski of the label of Structuralist, as reported by J. R. Firth (1964:101) and Francis Hsu (1959). He began with parts and assembled a structure out of their relations and functions, rather than beginning at the opposite end with structure and organizing the parts to fit. Malinowski's biopsychic organization with its expressive impulses, his homonymic theory applied to kin terms and other native vocabulary, his insistence on the contextual significance of Kula economics, of the contextual nature of normative rules and custom, all expressed his rigid empiricism and concern for facts sensitive to the particulars of varying relationships according to situation. All meaning was coded to usage, purpose, or function in contexts and not in relation to a monolithic structure.

PARALLELS: MALINOWSKI AND BOAS

There is a curious parallel between Boas and Malinowski in that both concentrated on variation as the primary problem in the search for structural relations. At the same time, they entertained the position that social tradition or culture carried a special determination for variations within the structure or novelties intruding from outside. But the determinism of structure was not the immediate point of emphasis, as in the instance of social Structuralists. Rather, stress was on following the activities of parts and their accommodative variants in order to uncover general laws of process rather than the nature of structures and the principles on which they were founded (Malinowski 1939(44):943). Neither Boas nor Malinowski were systematic theoreticians, but both regarded themselves as bringing a revolutionary message to a discipline confused by a moribund theory. The same could be said of Durkheim and Radcliffe-Brown. Both Malinowski and Boas made extensive use of native texts in learning the language and uncovering the meaning of the word for the native; and both also bound lexical elements into their ethnographic descriptions. In their impact, both projected the image of the fieldworker *par excellence*, though Malinowski in the field context appears to have been more sensitively and emotionally involved in the life of his subjects and his own reactions to the field situation (see Rohner 1969, Malinowski 1967). Though their methodologies fell short of being comprehensive and certain in validation, their empirical image remained as a signal charge to those who advocated scientific controls in anthropology, and their techniques and insightful orientations have supplied a continuing stimulus for field research and data analysis. As Fortes (1964:174) observed with regard to Malinowski,

> No ethnographer with a "functionalist" training writing about kinship today will overlook the rivalry and conflict aspect of the relations between the legal possessor of parental authority and the filial generation, or the significance of reciprocity rules in kinship, or the educational (sc. "socialization") function of the family and its connection with incest prohibitions.

CONVERGENCES: MALINOWSKI AND RADCLIFFE-BROWN

Despite differences stemming from a beginning at opposites, Malinowski and Radcliffe-Brown shared a number of perceptive insights and demonstrated striking convergences in their discussions of the functional prerequisites of the social order. Malinowski's portrait of the institution with its charter, personnel, normative regulations, cultural apparatus, and purposive functions did not contradict Radcliffe-Brown's conception of the societal laws of existence detailed in functional consistency, differentiation of jural and moral rights and obligations, and maintenance of corporate continuity based on a common interest.

In focusing on a strain toward functional consistency and integration, both Malinowski and Radcliffe-Brown viewed society and culture as a whole, normally balanced by an accommodation of competing interests.

At first glance Radcliffe-Brown and Malinowski seemed to differ in their selection of a primary unit for investigation. Malinowski accented a group organized purposefully in an institution. Radcliffe-Brown emphasized social structure, an organized group or categories of individuals occupying separate statuses and carrying out roles in accordance with the institutionalized rights and obligations attached to these statuses. Such categories of institutionalized relationships were caught up in a larger network of institutions, such as factory, family, army, kinship, clan, monarchy. Organized groups of this order, regulated by institutionalized norms, were little different from Malinowski's institution. Moreover, Radcliffe-Brown's stress on the ritualization of value as the basis for group activity and social structure was not irrelevant to Malinowski's concept of the institutional charter (see Nadel 1956:108–110). In his theoretical articles Radcliffe-Brown (for example, "The Mother's Brother in South Africa" 1924 and "Religion and Society" 1945) very often concentrated on normative relations in order to elucidate social structure. Radcliffe-Brown used the conventionalized status obligations and rights governing roles to define the features of social structure. However, up to now no instrument has been devised to test the priority of either the customary behavior (role) or the coordinate feature (status) of social structure. Status and role appear inseparable and must be analyzed together (see Nadel 1951:141, 205–207).

With regard to the causal predominance of the social, cultural, or psychological, Radcliffe-Brown admitted that the method of structural analysis was not appropriate for problems of historic-causal origins. Only a controlled historic record could give insight into origins. However, given an operant system, it was possible to describe the structural features of the system and the interrelated activities of the parts. At this point one could introduce generic functional requirements and secondary principles governing particular structural alignments. This Radcliffe-Brown did, and it was these functional necessities and structural principles expressed in formal-legal relations linking one category of person to another that he cited as social determinants. Thus, in the instance of father right and mother right, the important difference was reported by Radcliffe-Brown (1962a) to be the type of marriage. Taking note of the strong bonds linking siblings, two extreme solutions to the opposing claims and loyalties arising between a woman's husband and her brothers and sisters were possible—either a matrilineal or a patrilineal social order. In the former, husband and kin did not abdicate rights to the children; it was a matter of brothers and sisters maintaining their solidarity on all fronts, including possession of the children. For their part the husband and his kin incurred no serious obligations. The patrilineal structure provided a stable system by establishing the jural machinery, including formal payment to the wife's kin, for a transfer of rights over the woman with regard to labor, sex, and children. In father-right systems, jural relations, emotional attachment, and respect were separated, for such was the special quality of legal rights upon which justice depends. But affection is not debarred either in matrilineal or patrilineal systems, and rather thrives in those relations where formal constraints are lacking. For example, in father-right systems, mother's brothers and sisters were expected to give her children loving attention and care. In turn, a sister's child was expected to show solicitude and fondness for maternal uncles and aunts. Social order thus had a way of reaching for social harmony through accommodation of justice and brotherhood, the twin factors upon which a harmonious social existence depended, as Aristotle pointed out centuries before (Radcliffe-Brown 1962a:77).

Malinowski likewise emphasized a balanced and harmonious solidarity as intrinsic to the social order. At times it was a product of proscriptions on behavior since free expression of certain behavior disrupted the social unit. This was the rationale behind incest prohibitions within the family. Sexual jealousy was too disruptive. Solidarity was achieved in the face of life crises by a ritualization of the crisis and by reaffirmation of unity through ceremonial participation. Release of feeling thus reemphasized the common feeling of unity and the security of belonging to a group.

Structural similarities in problem awareness maintained by Malinowski and Radcliffe-Brown in their analyses emphasized the common ground on which students of both could meet and accommodate. However, during the late thirties, the respective exponents of biocultural functionalism and of social Structuralism exchanged locations. Malinowski moved to the United States and to Yale, while Radcliffe-Brown left Chicago for Oxford. By that time Radcliffe-Brown was in a position to exert a strong influence on British social anthropology. He had rounded out his theoretical position with timely articles illustrating the new meaning which social Structuralism could bring to anthropological data, and he emerged as the prime authority on Australian social organization. The appeal of Radcliffe-Brown's studied arguments was in the way he set forth a reasonable association between a type of social structure and its underlying principles and relevant social practices (see Radcliffe-Brown 1913, 1930–1931). Proceeding first to a classification of types of social structures, as in kinship, he then endeavored to factor out the associated variants, and through comparison moved to the ideal of a comparative sociology. This Malinowski had not achieved, preferring to use his Trobriand model as the archetype for limited analogical comparison. What Radcliffe-Brown inspired, in contrast, according to Fortes (1953(55):30), was a regard for

> lineages and statuses from the point of view of the total social system and not from that of an hypothetical EGO, [thereby permitting appreciation of the fact that] . . . consanguinity and affinity, real or putative, are not sufficient in themselves to bring about these structural arrangements. We see that descent is fundamentally a jural concept as Radcliffe-Brown argued in one of his most important papers (1935) ["Patrilineal and Matrilineal Succession"]; we see its significance, as the connecting link between the external, that is political and legal, aspect of what we have called unilineal descent groups, and the internal or domestic aspect. It is in the latter context that kinship carries maximum weight, first, as the source of title to membership of the groups or to specific jural status, with all that this means in rights over and toward persons and property, and second as the basis of the social relations among the persons who are identified with one another in the corporate group. . . .

TRANSLATION OF BIOCULTURAL INTO SOCIAL STRUCTURALISM

When Radcliffe-Brown returned to England in 1937, he confronted a majority of ethnographic researchers ably trained by Malinowski. The core of those later labeled British social anthropologists were all trained as functionalists—for example, Raymond Firth, Audrey Richards, Monica (Hunter) Wilson, Godfrey Wilson, E. E. Evans-Pritchard, I. Schapera, Meyer Fortes, Lucy Mair, Hilda Kuper, and S. F. Nadel. Now well known on the British scene, Radcliffe-Brown supplied an immediate stimulus for a comparative analysis of social structures—the very thing which Malinowski, with his concentration on a general theory of culture rooted in human nature, had failed to provide. Under structural analysis the social person emerged as the counterpart and *alter ego* to the legal person in European law; that is, a social entity with rights and obligations under the security and threat of sanctions. In the African societies researched, kinship, law, political authority, and economy were seen as interrelated and intersupportive of a total social structure. The keystone of social structure was located in political power, whether centralized in bureaucratic monarchy or diffused and sometimes concentrated in the hands of lineage elders when corporate lineage rights were threatened. However, in native Africa, no social structure—and this held especially for the political order—was without "common ritual values, the *ideological superstructure* of political organization" (Fortes and Evans-Pritchard 1962:Introduction, 17; italics supplied). In themselves these symbolic expressions of relationships could not convey their inner meaning—certainly the meaning could not be extracted by looking to human nature and its biopsychic needs. The only datum which gave significance to these symbols was the social structure and the meaning of symbols made sense only when viewed through the prism of social function. Such was the case for monarchical African states where the ritual of kingship concentrated ritual symbols linked to the integrity of the society.

> Africans have no objective knowledge of the forces determining their social organization and actuating their social behaviour. Yet they would be unable to carry on their collective life if they could not think and feel about the interests which actuate them, the institutions by means of which they organize collective action, and the structure of the groups into which they are organized. Myths, dogmas, ritual beliefs and activities make his social system intellectually tangible and coherent to an African and enable him to think and feel about it. Furthermore, these sacred symbols, which reflect the social system, endow it with mystical values which evoke acceptance of the social order that goes far beyond the obedience exacted by the secular sanction of force. The social system is, as it were, removed to a mystical plane, where it figures as a system of sacred values beyond criticism or revision. Hence people will overthrow a bad king, but the kingship is never questioned; hence the wars or feuds between segments of a society like the Nuer or the Tallensi are kept within bounds by mystical sanctions.
>
> The African does not see beyond the symbols; it might well be held that if he understood their objective meaning, they would lose the power they have over him. This power lies in their symbolic content, and in their association with the nodal institutions of the social structure, such as the kingship. Not every kind of ritual or any sort of mystical ideas can express the values that hold a society together and focus the loyalty and devotion of its members on their rulers. If we study the mystical values bound up with the kingship in any of the societies of Group A [state or centralized], we find that they refer to fertility, health, prosperity, peace, justice—to everything, in short, which gives life and happiness to a people. The African sees these ritual observances as the supreme safeguard of the basic needs of his existence and of the basic relations that make up his social order—land, cattle, rain, bodily health, the family, the clan, the state. The mystical values reflect the general import of the basic elements of existence: the land as the source of the whole people's livelihood, physical health as something universally desired, the family as the fundamental procreative unit, and so forth. These are the common interests of the whole society, as the native sees them. These are the themes of taboos, observances and ceremonies in which, in societies of Group A, the whole people has a share through its representatives, and in societies of Group B [nonstate societies] all the segments participate, since they are matters of equal moment to all. (Fortes and Evans-Pritchard 1962:18)

In this statement Fortes and Evans-Pritchard drew out the intersupportive relations of values and myths and ritual—or culture—and the social order keyed to the supreme status-integrater, kingship. The centrality of culture admittedly disposed individuals to operate consensually and supportively within the social structure, but culture is not viewed as the source for structure. Rather, it was the rationalization of structure, clothing it with necessary sentiments and symbolic behaviors much as flesh covers the skeleton. The analogy might not be correct, since in the stress on social physiology social structure included not only skeletal parts but also the arrangement of organs and their activities in support of the total organism. However, from their descriptive analyses it was not always possible to discern where social Structuralists placed their emphases—on social structure or on the cultural rules governing status relations. Evans-Pritchard (1934(34):172) insisted that utilitarian economic considerations were insufficient to guarantee marriage stability among the Azande. His view that Azande family stability was largely a function of moral and legal norms underlined cultural learnings as the major support of structure. It was no different for African kingship. The relations of individuals and groups sharing mutual utilitarian interests were not as enduring as those forged by fixation on mystical symbols that expressed moral and legal values (Fortes and Evans-Pritchard 1962:23). Yet these bonds of sentiment and moral ritual commitment which brought life to the social order were derivatives of the social order, since they were designed to support it. When the social order changed, sentiments and mystical symbols changed. This happened when Europeans pragmatically applied their power to subvert the mystical bonds linking the African ruler with his people. A new administrative order was set up, enforcing obedience with overwhelming force. In effect, this helped to secularize the bonds linking the individual to his group affiliations, thereby upsetting the balance and causing collapse of the whole system. Perhaps with an eye to British monarchy, Fortes and Evans-Pritchard suggested that so long as kingship served as a moral and legal force uniting people as a political community, it would be maintained as the center of mystical values.

The Introduction to *African Political Systems* is of special interest, since it called attention to the explicit assumptions of British social anthropology under the influence of Radcliffe-Brown. Social structure was the preeminent focus of investigation, together with the supportive apparatus of sentiment, symbol, and moral-legal norms. Structural equilibrium was prominent in the theoretical orientation, achieved through ascending levels of structures by regulated accommodation of private and group interests. The prime function of political organization was adjudicating and muting conflict between opposing interest groups. The political institution achieved its function of promoting the ultimate social values of harmony and solidarity by permitting rather than excluding representative participation by varied sectors of the population. In the instance of African societies,

A relatively stable political system in Africa presents a balance between conflicting tendencies and between divergent interests. In Group A [state-type] it is a balance between different parts of the administrative organization. The forces that maintain the supremacy of the paramount ruler are opposed by the forces that act as a check on his powers. Institutions such as the regimental organization of the Zulu, the genealogical restriction of succession to kinship or chiefship, the appointment by the king of his kinsmen to regional chiefships, and the mystical sanctions of his office all reinforce the power of the central authority. But they are counterbalanced by other institutions, like the king's council, sacerdotal officials who have a decisive voice in the king's investiture, queen mothers' courts, and so forth, which work for the protec-

534 Structuralism (ca. 1890–1940)

tion of law and custom and the control of centralized power. . . . The balance between central authority and regional autonomy is a very important element in the political structure. If a king abuses his power, subordinate chiefs are liable to secede or to lead a revolt against him. . . . A king may try to buttress his authority by playing off rival subordinate chiefs against one another.

It would be a mistake to regard the scheme of constitutional checks and balances and the delegation of power and authority to regional chiefs as nothing more than an administrative device. A general principle of great importance is contained in these arrangements, which has the effect of giving every section and every major interest of the society direct or indirect representation in the conduct of government. (Fortes and Evans-Pritchard 1962:11–12)

The situation was different for segmentary lineage societies. Here one found a delicate balance between equivalent segments organized on territorial and lineage lines without a formal political organization. The segmentalized Nuer society was kept in a state of balance through the opposition of two patri-descent units aggregated in ascending levels to a point where allied descent groups were identified with a common name, territory, and dominant lineage in opposition to other Nuer tribal groups of the same order (Evans-Pritchard 1940). Without conflict there could be no political operation, and Evans-Pritchard viewed the internal balance of power, so characteristic of a segmentalized Nuer tribe, as a derivative of the chronic state of feud which existed. To regulate these oppositions the Nuer had recourse to a mediator backed by traditional and supernatural sanctions, the Leopard-skin Chief.

The theoretical statements of Fortes and Pritchard, drawn principally from Radcliffe-Brown, contain the hallmarks of social anthropology as it differentiated under British aegis beginning in the late thirties. Excellent sociological descriptions of African societies, principally in West, East, and South Africa, accenting kinship, political, moral-legal, and religious institutions, resulted, as well as a concern for alterations in native institutions induced by the European industrial-political presence. Except for S. F. Nadel (*The Foundations of Social Anthropology* 1951), who undertook the task of developing a synthetic statement of the aims and methods of social anthropology, social Structuralists were inclined to clue their hypotheses and causal explanations to presentations of their data in monographic books and special articles.

The novelty of these sociological studies lay in the challenging reversal of causal flow, substituting social explanations for traditional native and ethnological explanations that accounted for taboos and marriage prohibitions with an outpouring of psychological feeling. Incest and bride wealth came in for special attention as Evans-Pritchard (1951:43–44, 96) traced the presence of sentiments that supported incest definitions and marriage stability to the social structure.

Nuer say that marriage to persons standing in certain relationships is forbidden because it would be *rual*, incestuous. Speaking sociologically, I think we may reverse this statement and say that sexual relations with persons standing in these relationships are considered incestuous because it would be a breach of the marriage prohibitions to marry them. I would hold that the incest taboo can only be understood by reference to the marriage prohibitions, and that these prohibitions must be viewed in the light of their function in the Nuer kinship system and in their whole social structure.

As to the nature of bride wealth, he observed that payments did not convey stability to a marriage. Rather, the payments were made because people anticipated stability in the marriage. The interpretations coincided with Radcliffe-Brown's (1965e) as enunciated in his article on "Taboo," which challenged Malinowski's psychological theory of the functional relation between anxiety and magic. Radcliffe-Brown and Evans-Pritchard both argued that the sentiment was there simply because the needs of the social order demanded its presence and therefore ritually implanted it in the minds of all as a value sentiment.

British social anthropologists were also aware of the unstable balance which characterized certain social orders through divergent variations and contradictory oppositions. For example, divergent variations in marital arrangements and the high incidence of divorce might reflect not the weakness and instability of a particular social structure but its strength. High divorce rates could indicate tensile strength of the family and the kinship social structure to which it was related (Gluckman 1962b:190–193). The high incidence of matrilocality among the Nuer was possible because the emphasis on the patrilineal principle was not disputed and was even reinforced by the matrilocal contradiction (Evans-Pritchard 1951:28). Structures firmly rooted in their principles thus could tolerate more in the way of contradictory variation.

Economic materialism which emphasized pragmatic utilitarian aspects was rejected and criticized because social Structuralists were interested in dealing with ultimate values. The social order to them transcended the individual and his utilitarian needs and purposes.

The advance to more entrenched social structural-functional interpretation also brought a renewal of contact with French social Structuralists, largely through the medium of Lévi-Strauss. However, this French connection also brought a renewed confrontation with psychological interpretations of social organization such as those Lévi-Strauss interjected into his explanation of dual organization and related antinomies (see Homans and Schneider 1955 and Needham 1962 in their controversy). Except for Ashley-Montagu (1950), there was none who elaborated Malinowski's biopsychic cultural viewpoint.

SUMMARY

In historic review French Structuralism was the intellectual fountainhead for the immediate development of British social anthropology. Durkheim and associates supplied a basic format for introducing a truly sociological orientation into British anthropology at a time when it was breaking with Developmentalism and testing fresh approaches. The French contribution consisted, first of all, in establishing the social as a distinctive causal domain in which only social facts could explain other social facts. Second, Durkheim provided a paradigm for analyzing social facts and their relations. One began with a social sentiment aroused by mutual interpersonal stimulation and traced its conceptual expression in a collective idea which found symbolic expression in custom and ceremony. The comprehensive, proper analysis of any social fact must begin and end in the elucidation of its function with regard to the ultimate purpose of social living—namely, the formation of a unified community of socially conscious persons. The ultimate value of community life thus was a social awareness in depth and ceremonial dramatization of group solidarity.

However, British social anthropologists, largely through the efforts of Radcliffe-Brown, made their own contribution to social analysis. Drawing upon the powerful political-legal tradition embedded in the governing process of Britain, Radcliffe-Brown introduced a legalistic approach to the social order. The result was a conceptualization of social structure. He saw social structure as an arrangement of relationships between sets of legal rights and obligations, which, in their functions, stood in a complementary relation to each other (for example, king to subject). The formal arrangement of statuses and roles thus described the basic structure of any social unit, with the operations of the status network geared to the total design or function of the social system. Any social system, like any organism, was sensitive to the need for maintaining a high degree of consistency in order that operations would achieve and maintain a functional state of equilibrium. Structural arrangements rooted in basic social sentiments were relevant to equilibrium states, since any modification in activities that contradicted the structure was subject to adjustments and pressures seeking to reestablish the normative equilibrium.

At the level of general theory, social Structuralists attempted to lay down the functional prerequisites of social living, where general social laws were located. They could be uncovered through a studied analysis and comparison of different social types. Hence, British social anthropologists, as their French prototypes, were devoted to a comparative sociology and saw themselves as a branch of sociology with a substantive focus on non-Western and nonindustrialized societies.

Like American culture theorists, British social anthropologists were antipathetic to any evolutionary focus. Though not denying evolutionary sequences, such a problem orientation was not particularly helpful in understanding the physiology of social systems. Like Americanists, social anthropologists avoided and refuted explanations of any social phenomena in terms of individual psychological processes. Much of the theoretical interpretation of their ethnographic monographs centered in substituting sociological interpretations for psychological ones. Nonutilitarian values proved as important to British and French social anthropologists as to

American and German culture theorists when explaining the nature of social integration. If a value of social solidarity were ultimate, it obviously was not derived from utilitarian values operating in the economic domain. In the political institutions of organized states, British social Structuralists found the ultimate solidarity value symbolized in the ritual of induction and transmission surrounding the office which represented the group, sensitively administered to its welfare, and protected its unity and continuity. This contrasted with the earlier findings of Durkheim and his followers, who located the primary social sentiment and group unity in the religious institution and world view.

The hard line against psychological interpretations taken by social Structuralists both in France and in England prevailed over those who viewed man's social and cultural life as an extension of his biological and psychological organization. Hence, Lévy-Bruhl's efforts to relate primitive religion to its perceptual configurations were received with disfavor by French Structuralists. Van Gennep's attempt to tie primitive social institutions to a biopsychic rhythm likewise was not acceptable. Antipathy for psychological interpretations at the time similarly accounts for the demise of Malinowski's use of a biopsychic base to account for the kinds of institutions found in human societies. In some ways this driving out of psychological by sociostructural interpretation provided a kind of parallel in theoretical change to Gresham's law of strong currencies driving out the weak. At the same time, the contrastive interpretations of biopsychic and sociostructural analyses demonstrated once again that a structural-functional orientation could be reached through either posture. The ideas of harmony, balance, equilibrium, integration, and solidarity were as useful to Malinowski's bioculturalism as to Radcliffe-Brown's social Structuralism. Curiously, these respective positions reemphasized the fact that those who approached the study of society and culture from the standpoint of human needs were inclined to see society as the instrument of man; whereas those who accented social structure concentrated on the needs of the social system and viewed individuals as serving the purposes of the system. It is interesting to note that those who centered their analysis of social and cultural forms in man's biological and psychological characteristics developed a theory organized around conventionalized learnings, or culture. On the other hand, those who focused on the requirements of social life were inclined to formulate a theory of society. This was so in the case of Tylor, whose humanistic progressivist assumptions led him to see anthropology, or ethnography as he called it, as a science of culture. Such was also the case with Malinowski. As for Americanists, their continuing interest in the individual as a typical socialized person similarly induced them to take up a cultural rather than a sociological perspective.

In their individual histories social Structuralists and culture historians were equally involved in the problem of systemic integration. However, social Structuralists began with an exploration of the integrative principles of social systems and grandually moved to a meticulous examination of variability and its causes within social orders. Culture historians, on the other hand, began with particulate analyses of culture traits and gradually worked their way into an appreciation of cultures as integrated systems. Both, however, focused increasingly on the problem of variability in relation to structure shortly before World War II. This led American culture theorists to shift their attention to a study of cognitive processes which they saw as basic to the ways in which people looked out upon the world and organized their relations and activities. Traditional societies upon which social Structuralists based their descriptive analyses were drawn into the market and resource development operations of the industrial world. This upheaval brought about changes in family, clan, and nation, and social Structuralists were faced with the problem of dealing with psychological processes which accompanied them. They were also confronted by psychological explanations of social forms as French Structuralism, under Lévi-Strauss, incorporated a linguistic model into its reality perspective. French use of a linguistic model drew new lines of communication between American culture theory, which had long been influenced by linguistic analogues, and French Structuralism.

Presently British social anthropology, having exhausted the major thrust and implications of structural analysis, underwent a reevaluation of the reality problem. One of the interesting by-products of this transition was the effort of British social anthropologists to reaffirm their Structuralist position, and this apparently led to the translation of classic studies of French Structuralists. Breaches in the theoretical armor of Structuralism naturally appeared when the problem of variation was raised. Leach, for example, argued that continuities observable in the structured relations of marriage and the family were sometimes due to regularities in extra-structural contexts. Such arguments implied that structure could be—and often was—a product of historical circumstances. Developments of this order may be seen as a forecast of renewed contacts between culture theorists and social Structuralists that will produce a more comprehensive and systematic reality perspective.

PART IV

Differentiative Specialization (1940 to Present)

The period beginning with 1940 to the present is characterized by an energetic attempt to get at new facts through specialization. This has produced a number of subdisciplines within anthropology which are researching particular variables (for example, economic, social, political, psychological, ecological) now considered significant for understanding the processes of human behavior and its social, cultural, and environmental products. It is a time of theoretical transition during which the structural-functional paradigms are being modified by the incorporation of a new concern for evolutionary processes and the relation of variation to structure.

A process of differentiation and of specialization is essential to the growth of any discipline. The historical differentiation of economic, political, social, ethnopsychological, and other specializations raises once again the specter of fragmentation as each of the subdisciplines has moved toward closer theoretical and methodological relationships with its respective social science discipline. At the same time, fresh linkages with sister disciplines have resulted in the incorporation of a new fund of useful terms and techniques for observing and processing materials. The anthropological experience has been broadened by a growing appreciation of similiarities in theory and interpretation shared with related disciplines.

Widespread intellectual and sociopolitical changes following World War II brought important repercussions for anthropology. The exaltation of subjectivism increased pressure on the scientific objectives and character of the discipline. Demands for a revision of priorities to give first place to a social and political activism likewise generated schisms within the discipline.

The realignments which anthropology is undergoing at this time undoubtedly will have profound implications for future developments. The tendency to see the social and cultural as an environment within which individuals operate rather than as independent causal levels of reality is most significant. It forces anthropologists to rethink what is distinctive about their discipline, and reinforces the early conclusion that anthropology is distinguished not by investigation of the social and cultural *per se* but by

its primary concern with the preindustrial world and its transformations. During this time anthropologists have become convinced that unconscious processes are not the whole, nor the core, of human behavior. A renewed interest in cognitive behavior has stimulated a new perspective on the basis of which some enthusiasts proclaimed a new ethnography and ethnoscience rooted in linguistic theory and method. Man, as a subject of investigation, has emerged as a dynamic figure, partially determined by the limitations imposed by his environments (physical as well as social and cultural) and partially free in the determination and realization of human objectives.

The differentiation of important specializations, in conjunction with the theoretical perspective of man as a dynamic agent in a field of forces, suggests the increasing capability of anthropology to research the preindustrial world as it moves toward modernization. The addition of an active moral commitment to the scientific objective is an essential and timely aspect of this developing capability. It signals a progressive realization of the scientific and humanistic goals and principles which have guided anthropology since its inception.

14

Differentiation and Specialization within Social and Cultural Anthropology (1940 to Present)

DIFFERENTIATION, CONVERGENCE, AND INDIVIDUATIVE ELABORATION

The course of anthropological development reveals a working relationship between historic and evolutionary process. The historical branching of a discipline from a main stem and the development of specializations illustrate the differentiative process. A differentiative branching of a scholarly discipline is similar to the biological variation that turns into a species type under the selective grooming of natural selection and other evolutionary processes. Biological species emerge as variability is diminished through a process of genetic convergence, guided by natural selection. A kind of theoretical speciation attributable to processes paralleling biological speciation can be seen in anthropology. Application of a theoretical system to different investigative areas within a discipline results in an increase in theoretical and methodological integration. This is a process of individuative elaboration. As a process, individuative elaboration is analogous to the process of psychological generalization. The consistency and unity produced by individuative elaboration in theory and in method parallel trends toward consistency and coherence among institutionalized patterns which respond to the integrative directives of dominant values and principles. When this process of individuative elaboration penetrates the different domains of a discipline, theoretical convergence or consolidation is complete. At this time a fresh historical differentiation may get underway.

Historical differentiation appears to be a result of the cumulation of new experience which triggers a vigorous reaction to established problem definitions, methodology, and interpretation. The reactive thrust commands such attention that assessment of the influence of the cumulative process is very difficult. An impression that change in theoretical postures is more mutational than incremental may be conveyed. At times, however, the historical differentiation is quickly merged with the convergent evolutionary process. This happens when scholars formulate the outlines of a new position that radically contradicts established theory and method. At such time the tendency is to operate with logically derived postulates and corollaries, thereby producing an early synthesis which shortens the period of historic differentiation. Such, for example, was the case with Durkheim when developing his paradigm of a social fact. An inductive approach, on the other hand, usually moves forward without attempting an explicit systematizing of background assumptions and consequences. A comprehensive overview in the inductive context usually is gained through a process of incremental advance in theory, accelerated at times by an infusion of ideas or techniques borrowed from related disciplines, or from more sophisticated branches within a discipline. The gradual growth of culture theory in the United States is a case in point.

Looking backward, we can trace the beginnings of anthropology to a cumulative reaction to historical studies of the day. A general social science thus branched off from history. This differentiation in the eighteenth century was accompanied by a wide acceptance of the idea of progress, and on the basis of this integrative concept a general history of mankind was attempted. The later differentiation of anthropology from this main social science stem around 1860 was prompted by the historic growth of disciplines—such as geology and paleontology—which had much to offer in the search for man's ancestors. Once again a revolutionary idea, evolution, integrated the anthropological domain and defined its goals and the basis for explanation. The anthropological goal was clearly seen as revelation of the early history of mankind. Elaborative individuation followed as scholars traced the evolution of economics, social organization, political systems, law, religion, language, morals, and art. This individuative process was completed toward the turn of the century, when a new differentiation took place, again emphatically reactive to the established position. What prompted this historic differentiation was a growing interest in process as an interactional relation between social and cultural objects rather than between individuals and ideas.

This fresh differentiative impulse produced three historic variations—culture Historicism, social Structuralism, and Bioculturalism. A differential focus on the social or the cultural led to a dichotomy of social and cultural anthropology (see Figure 14-1). Social Structuralism quickly moved into a convergent process because of an immediate and direct commitment to general theory and a deductive methodology. Owing to its inductive posture, culture Historicism was unable to formulate a comprehensive theoretical statement until later. Secondary historical variations quickly appeared within social Structuralism and culture Historicism, while, guided by its

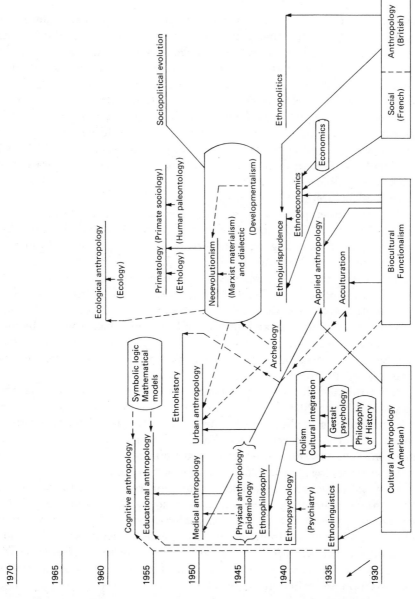

Figure 14-1. Differentiation of social and cultural anthropology after 1935.

The location of the differentiations in point of time is approximate. Theoretical ideas and fields which have contributed a special impetus to particular developments have been enclosed within solid lines. Primary lines of influence in differentiative specializations are indicated by straight lines; broken lines indicate secondary but important influences.

The present differentiation is more in the nature of an historic branching, rather than an elaboration, in that the theoretical and methodological focus of the several specializations tends to be located in the traditional discipline (for example, economics supplies the theoretical guidelines for economic anthropology) rather than in cultural anthropology.

founder Malinowski, bioculturalism maintained its integrity. Culture historians diverged into American diffusionists, British migrationists, and German-Austrian *Kulturkreislehrer*. At the same time, influences stemming from the world-view orientation of German philosophers of history stimulated a study of culture types and formulation of a general theory of culture. The focus of interest of this variation within the *Kulturkreis* development provided a cultural counterpart to the comparative social typology aimed at by social Structuralists. The social Structuralism initiated by French sociologues stimulated a renovation of an emergent British social anthropology. The latter soon developed its own character by drawing on the British political-legal tradition for its conceptualization and analysis of social structure.

Each of these primary historic differentiations—culture history, bioculturalism—social Structuralism—followed a course of individuative elaboration. Though pursuing separate intellectual paths, all were to meet on the common ground of Structuralism. In final analysis each proved profoundly committed to the reality of a structuring which lay behind the explicit forms of social and cultural behavior. Each, according to this basic orientation, looked for the positive forces by which society and culture were unified, maintained, and perpetuated through time. It would be up to the next generation of theorists to discover the contradictions and variations which all social and cultural systems seem to generate, tolerate, and generally shield from public view.

Since the mid-thirties anthropology has been undergoing a widespread historical differentiation of specializations unlike the individuative elaboration that follows application of a new and overriding theoretical orientation to a diverse subject matter. To the contrary, for the first time the emergent specializations of economic anthropology, political anthropology, urban anthropology, psychological anthropology, and anthropological linguistics, to name a few, seem to be pursuing separate historical courses. Their intellectual linkages outside anthropology are growing, since it is in economics, political science, and psychology that practitioners are found with the sophistication to define problems, extend theory, and apply novel techniques that have special relevance for these anthropological specialties. Ronald Cohen in 1968 ((9):18) summarized some of the reasons for this specialization and where it may lead:

> Twenty years ago the anthropologist was almost alone in his interest in the social, cultural, and psychological behavior of non-Western man; today he has been joined by many others. The anthropologist has to choose which particular aspect of the behavior of non-Western peoples he wishes to study. He is no longer the expert on everything. Besides this, the people themselves are changing, and the rapidly developing bureaucracies that review research (especially in Africa where I have worked) want to know rather explicitly what it is that the researcher is coming to ask questions about. Furthermore, change, urbanization, Western education, modern nationalism, and other forces are producing wide variations in attitudes and responses to questions.

Such situations, imposed by changing field conditions, must at the same time be informed by some theoretical schema. Where a theory comes from is irrelevant as long as it helps us to understand a particular problem. The rapid development and change of the non-Western world is forcing many of us, especially the younger anthropologists and graduate students, to look at fieldwork in terms of general social science theory, methodology, and techniques.

Cohen conveyed a twofold message. First, specialization is essential to contemporary problem definition and data control. Second, a general theory and method drawing upon the various social science disciplines appears necessary to the future development of anthropology. But what kind of anthropology? Would—or should—the separate specializations establish their primary linkages with traditional disciplines and in effect become subdivisions of such disciplines? This was largely the case in Continental developments, where ethnology, physical anthropology, and other specializations existed under the shadow of geography, biology, and linguistic science. Under this arrangement anthropology as a distinct discipline hardly existed, except, metaphorically speaking, in the minds and hearts of those who considered a general interest in mankind a sufficient magnet for attracting intellectual exchange. On the other hand, linkages between anthropological specialties and established disciplines could be viewed as opportunities for developing an integrated theory applicable to the study of peoples and cultures whose traditions had arisen and existed until recent times without direct influences from the West. From the very beginnings, such societies furnished the basic subject matter of anthropology and would continue to do so in the future. Their responses to the spread of industrial culture offered unparalleled opportunities to observe and to measure processes affecting structural continuities and variations.

During the postwar period anthropology moved into a time of critical decision when adjustments and reorientations loomed ever more imperative. The politics of world events invaded the scientific sanctuary and threatened to draw anthropologists into political alignments that could spell the end of their discipline as an objective instrument in the advancement of knowledge.

For the immediate future of anthropology, the state of the differentiative and convergent processes are vital. There are a number of clues that suggest that a rather comprehensive reorientation and synthesis are underway.

1. The social and cultural as self-contained and deterministic causal systems are now being abandoned.
2. There is a tendency to abandon the goal of prediction, or at least to place severe limitations on the capacity of structural analysis to provide precise coordinates between internal structure and external form.
3. It is now more generally accepted that causality is a complex process involving multiple variables rather than governed by any single overarching variable.

4. The necessity to unite historical and evolutionary processes is increasingly recognized.

5. The static quality of an equilibrium analysis of systemic processes has given way to a dynamic view of the reality process conveyed through a cybernetic-type model. Structural processes now are seen as constantly adjusting and adapting to signals that indicate changes in relationships and in resources both inside and outside the system.

6. There is a clear tendency to abandon the traditional emphasis on automatic conditionings and unconscious processes as ultimate to the reality process. Consequently, there is a fresh emphasis on the place of cognitive processes in the formation and operation of the social and cultural environment.

7. The individual is now seen as a strategist, maneuvering within and manipulating the social and cultural environment.

8. It is increasingly recognized that in certain cases structure is better seen as an emergent traceable along the boundaries of observable variations than considered as a closed system in which variation is limited and held in check by structural processes.

9. The tendency is to focus on situational variants in order to find out how structural processes vary dynamically according to circumstances.

10. There is a strong inclination to accept the idea that variability and contradiction are part of the integrative process. That is, social and cultural systems achieve a measure of integration by a dynamic interplay between opposing elements rather than by the generalization of a monolithic value throughout the system.

BASES FOR DIFFERENTIATION

A number of conditions, some internal to anthropology, others external, conspired to bring about the differentiation in specializations. With regard to internal factors, by the mid-thirties structural determinism reached a near peak of consolidation. The general format had been laid out and input now was limited to elaboration. As a dominant theoretical paradigm, Structuralism appeared on the edge of a new phase, pursuing a course parallel to that described by Kroeber (1963:763–764) for culture patterns of high value:

> This much is clear: the patterns which we adjudge as of higher quality are selective from among a number of potentialities. They cannot remain undifferentiated and attain quality. As they begin to select, early in their formation, they commit themselves to certain specializations, and exclude others. If this arouses conflict with other parts of the culture in which the pattern is forming, the selection and exclusion may be abandoned, the pattern as something well differentiated be renounced, and nothing of much cultural value eventuates. If, however, this does not happen, the other patterns of the culture rein-

force the growing one, or at least do not conflict with it, the pattern in question tends to develop cumulatively, in the direction in which it first differentiated, by a sort of momentum. Finally, either a conflict with the rest of its culture arises and puts an end to the pattern, or it explores and traverses the new opportunities lying in its selective path, until less and less of these remain, and at last one. The pattern can be said to have fulfilled itself when its opportunities or possibilities have been exhausted. Or more exactly, the value culmination comes at the moment when the full range of possibilities within the pattern is sensed; the decline, when there remain only minor areas of terrain to be occupied. After this, development may quietly subside, the results achieved being retained as institutions, but with repetitive instead of growth activity; and quality atrophies. Or again, energy still being vigorous in the field of culture in question, the limitations imposed on itself by the growing or culminating pattern are felt as restraints, and there is an effort to disrupt them. Such efforts may end in incoherent conflicts which sooner or later level out in undifferentiation.

During the thirties a degree of elaboration still lay ahead for social structuralism as law and politics were added to its theoretical core. On the other hand, culture history based on geographic distributions was in a profound state of decline. A differentiative thrust that would renew the advance was underway in the emergent interest of cultural anthropologists in culture and personality and acculturative change. Sapir (1949g:575–576) constantly criticized the Structuralist concern for a study of objects rather than of human beings and their behavioral variability.

What we have tried to advance is little more than a plea for the assistance of the psychiatrist in the study of certain problems which come up in an analysis of socialized behavior. In spite of all that has been claimed to the contrary, we cannot thoroughly understand the dynamics of culture, of society, of history, without sooner or later taking into account the actual interrelationship of human beings. We can postpone this psychiatric analysis indefinitely but we cannot theoretically eliminate it. With the modern growth of interest in the study of personality adjustment to one's fellow men, it is difficult to see how one's intellectual curiosity about the problems of human intercourse can be forever satisfied by schematic statements about society and its stock of cultural patterns. The very variations and uncertainties which the earlier anthropologists ignored seem to be the very aspects of human behavior that future students of society will have to look to with a special concern, for it is only through an analysis of variation that the reality and meaning of a norm can be established at all, and it is only through a minute and sympathetic study of individual behavior in the state in which normal human beings find themselves, namely in a state of society, that it will ultimately be possible to say things about society itself and culture that are more than fairly convenient abstractions. Surely, if the social scientist is interested in effective consistencies, in tendencies, and in values, he must not dodge the task of studying the effects produced by individuals of varying temperaments and backgrounds on each other. Anthropology, sociology, indeed social science in general is notoriously weak in the discovery of effective consistencies. This weakness, it seems, is not unrelated to a fatal fallacy with regard to the objective reality of social and cultural patterns defined impersonally.

External forces affecting the differentiation of anthropology came in two forms. First, differentiations occurring in related disciplines reached into anthropology and encouraged the borrowing of hypotheses and techniques. A psychiatric stimulus transformed the anthropological approach to personality; and, in countering traditional economic theory based on profit incentives, anthropologists became more precise in their descriptions of primitive economic behavior. Second, dynamic world forces operating through the economic depression, international conflict, rapid alterations in aboriginal cultures accompanying the spread of industrialization, and the emergent nationalism of colonial peoples drew attention to the role played by contact and conflict in bringing about structural and functional changes in societies. The time of troubles which the West had entered was not restricted to Europe and the Americas, but began to extend to remote portions of the globe through a vast interdependent network of political, economic, social, and ideological relations. There was much in these events that invited a rethinking of anthropological purpose, and the place of anthropology in the contemporary world (Gillin 1954; Maquet 1964; Bunzel and Parsons 1964; Diamond 1964). However, the cumulative effect of these changes did not begin to force a reorientation on anthropologists until after World War II.

Threat of fragmentation was an important side effect of differentiative specialization. By the sixties a growing lack of communication among specialists evoked efforts to reaffirm the integrity of anthropology as a discipline. The image of a unitary scientific discipline was projected by American anthropologists, while on the Continent the tradition of a humanistic federalism prevailed (Marshall 1967; Thompson 1961, 1967; Hultkrantz 1968). Fear that specialization might disintegrate the bonds uniting the discipline was not new. However, as Janowitz (1963) observed, the strength of anthropology was firmly rooted in a commonality of intellectual interests focused by the holistic approach to the study of man. The holistic perspective required prolonged and intensive observation in order to elicit intimate facts and provide awareness of life-style—a practice seldom employed by other social scientists. Hence, the uniqueness of anthropology in goals and type of research experience protected it from fragmentation. In its own way anthropology demonstrated the soundness of the holistic premise, that the whole is greater than a sum of its parts.

NATURE AND COURSE OF DIFFERENTIATIVE SPECIALIZATION

Acculturation, Urban Anthropology, Ethnopsychology, and Ethnolinguistics

It is always hazardous to set a specific date for emerging phenomena. However, the mid-thirties was the start of a feverish proliferation of new and specialized interests within social and cultural anthropology. In 1935 Redfield, Linton, and Herskovits drew up "A Memorandum for the Study of Acculturation" at a time when similar statements and culture contact studies appeared in Africa (Thurnwald and Thurnwald 1935; Hunter 1936). In the United States, The Society for Applied Anthropology was incorporated in 1941 to offer services of a consultant nature, and in particular to agencies of the federal government. Benedict's (1934) psycho-cultural approach to Hopi, Kwakiutl, and Dobuan personality developed into a full-bodied investigation of culture and personality by the Columbia Seminar initiated by Kardiner (1939). The leads of culture and personality theory were fed back into culture-contact situations (Thompson and Joseph 1944; Kluckhohn and Leighton 1962; Beaglehole and Beaglehole 1946; Ford 1941; Macgregor 1946). In emphasizing the distinctive perceptual and cognitive contexts of cultural definitions, Sapir and Whorf stimulated a new interest in ethnolinguistics and contributed to the rise of ethnoscience. Investigation of the steadying influences of world views and value orientations, explicit and implicit, on cultural stability and rate of change formalized an ethnophilosophic specialization (Redfield 1941, 1953; Kluckhohn 1949b; Hallowell 1967). The migration to urban centers by unskilled ethnic populations, especially after World War II, drew attention to the process of urbanization, and by 1950 urban anthropology and medical anthropology were initiated. At this point cultural anthropology divided into urban and rural (peasant) branches as had taken place in sociology.

Ethnohistory

In the United States the demand for documentary evidence which would substantiate tribal locations and land use in processing Indian land claims before the U.S. Claims Commission accelerated the emergence of ethnohistoric studies within anthropolgy. All of these land claims researches and legal presentations have been published and offer a rich and detailed history of tribal movements during the contact period (Horr 1973–1974). As archeologists worked their way forward into the proto-historic and historic periods, they found themselves researching documentary sources much as historians (Newell and Krieger 1949; Wedel 1959; Goggin 1968). Spanish documents provided the base for reconstructing Aztec and Inca cultures at the time of the conquest and during the colonial period. At a time when their living representatives preserved only a shredded patchwork of their ancient culture, Swanton (1942) drew on a wide variety of documentary sources to fill out the history and ethnology of southern Caddoan tribes. Ethnohistory thus served to draw prehistorians, ethnologists, and historians into a common enterprise.

Social, Economic, Juridical, and Political Specialization

Between 1925 and 1945 another set of interrelated specializations emerged in the form of social anthropology, anthropological jurisprudence, political anthropology, and economic anthropology. While social anthropology had been in the making since the time of Durkheim (ca. 1900), it did not become thoroughly entrenched until around 1925 when Radcliffe-Brown focused its definitive position and popularized its acceptance in the scientific community. Sparked by Malinowski's 1922 study of the Kula Ring and his institutional approach, Firth (1929) produced a study of New Zealand Maori economics. At the same time, Forde (1934), Thurnwald (1932), and Herskovits (1940) independently surveyed the economies of primitive peoples to determine their types and to see to what extent their economic processes were similar or different from commercial and industrialized market economies. Like Malinowski (1961a) and Mauss (1925), Firth, Thurnwald, and Herskovits distinguished the non-market economies of primitive peoples from the market economy of the Western world. They held that primitive economizing behavior was so embedded in a matrix of social and religious institutionalizations that nothing like a classic economic man was present. This point of view received support from the economic historian Polanyi (1944, 1947).

The idea that economic and political processes were interdependent was stated at the very start of the Industrial Revolution, a relation commonly expressed in the study of political economy. The Marxian formula refocused the relation in terms of social class and the exercise of political and economic control. The immediate stimulus to the differentiation of political anthropology stemmed, however, from the efforts of social Structuralists to arrive at a comparative typology. In the Preface to Fortes and Evans-Pritchard (1962), Radcliffe-Brown observed that the study of simpler societies as models from which a comparative analysis of political institutions could be made was an important and somewhat neglected branch of social anthropology. In elucidating the major principles of African political systems, Fortes and Evans-Pritchard underscored the multiplex relations among political, legal, social, economic, and religious institutions. The changing character of African life under colonial rule likewise focused attention on the state of native political institutions and their place within colonial administration (Lord Hailey 1957). Explicit racism, as in South Africa, complicated political relations between black and white, but it was clear that centralized rulers gradually were being shorn of their powers. At the same time, owing to retention of traditional ceremony associated with kingship, African rulers commonly found themselves a base for tribal conservatism in a situation moving rapidly toward political divisiveness and party-type loyalties. Tribes without strong rulers, on the other hand, watched the power of their leaders grow in the interests of colonial administration. In this respect the political experiences of African societies were similar to those of centralized states and tribes with a simple political leadership in the Americas.

A major stimulus for political anthropology came at the end of World War II. The restless press to end colonialism moved toward political independence in Africa, beginning with the Anglo-Egyptian Sudan in 1955, Ghana in 1957, and erupting with a host of republics, federations, and states in 1960. The precipitous transfer of political authority to African hands presented the political anthropologist with a wide range of dynamic variation concerning the formation, maintenance, and modernizing of states plagued with internal factionalism, party strife, and tribal conflicts over who should be dominant.

The differentiation of juridical anthropology owed much to Malinowski. His *Crime and Custom in Savage Society* (1926) described law in primitive society as a social process which bound individuals together in traditional obligations. In the absence of legal mechanisms, it was not supernatural sanctions or some collective sentiment, but rather the force of custom-as-law, grounded in a reciprocal give and take, which brought conformity. Social anthropology under Radcliffe-Brown also stressed the roles of law, religion, and morality in controlling human conduct. For Radcliffe-Brown (1965d:37) an individual's status at any moment in time was defined by the sum total of his rights and duties as prescribed by custom and law. Regarding political organization, he (Radcliffe-Brown 1962b) maintained that authority must be organized to exercise force in threat or in actuality if order were to be established and sustained within a territorial framework. The interrelation of law, status, morality, religion, property, and integrative social and political processes was clear. In 1938, I. Schapera, a student of Radcliffe-Brown, compiled a *Handbook of Tswana Law and Custom*.

Colonial governments also had a vital interest in native law, especially where native courts were maintained as an adjunct to administration under a policy of indirect rule. The existence of a traditional native law, as that in Indonesia, India, and much of Africa, was a necessary condition for such governmental policy. The need for familiarity with native legal precedent and procedure led to compilations of native law by the Dutch in the East Indies and the British in Africa and in India. For example, the anthropologically trained British administrator Rattray (1929) produced an exemplary study of *Ashanti Law and Constitution*, while C. K. Meek (1946, 1957) surveyed the development of law regarding land and custom in the colonies, with particular emphasis on Nigeria and the Cameroons.

Where indirect rule was not practiced, there was little concern for the study of native law and constitution. United States laws regulating Indians and their relations with government were largely embodied in treaties and special legislative acts. Useful compilations of Congressional legislation were attempted by Kappler (*Indian Affairs: Laws and Treaties* 1904) and by Cohen (*Federal Indian Law* 1942). During the thirties, a cultural anthropologist and a student of American legal institutions teamed to generate interest in aboriginal law (Llewellyn and Hoebel 1941). In the same year (1940) that Hoebel produced *The Political Organization and Law-Ways of the Comanche Indians,* Jane Richardson published *Law and Status among the Kiowa Indians.* Minutes of council affairs and legal records enabled Noon (1949) to chart the vicissitudes of Iroquois political-legal processes during acculturation, while Smith and Roberts (1954) extended the values orientation of the Rimrock Project to include Zuni law.

The Five Civilized Tribes are unique in that their situation in Indian territory after removal from their homelands allowed them to function as relatively independent nations until 1906 when Oklahoma was admitted to statehood. As early as 1852 the Cherokee began publication of their laws, constitution, and treaties, and the Choctaw, Chickasaw, and Muskogee soon followed with similar compilations.

In the United States the anthropological study of law generally languished, although the Wenner-Gren Foundation for Anthropological Research sponsored a symposium at Stanford University in 1964 (Nader 1965).

Renovation of Evolutionary Theory

The resurgence of evolutionary interests in anthropology introduced a perspective rather than a substantive domain for research. The same was true for the ecological approach and for ethnohistory as well. But while the evolutionary approach was characterized by a special way of defining problems and by a unique comparative methodology, it was nonetheless true that selective ordering of data assembled a special factual matter ordered according to a simplicity-complexity continuum.

Archeology always has been in a favorable position for uniting historic and evolutionary process. It was fitting, then, that in 1936 an archeologist, Childe (1951), generated a new interest in the evolution of culture by describing the great subsistence and technological revolutions which advanced man's social and mental life and added measurably to his capacity to survive. The strain toward urbanization in all the great centers of the Old and New World presented a constant challenge. Ethnologists like Smith and Perry argued for historic diffusion extending outward from an Egyptian hearth. In the content of New World civilization, however, there was much to suggest a separate origin. If this were the case, there was the possibility that cultural developments in different urbanized areas moved through structured stages in sensitive response to internal and external conditions. In 1949 Steward assembled comparative evidence to show that all the great civilizations shared similar developments of a structural order. Speaking to the "Era of Cyclical Conquests," he noted that it was a time

> of comparatively few culture changes, except those produced by warfare. It initiated a succession of empires and then local states or dark ages that alternated in a fairly stereotyped pattern until the Iron Age and Industrial Era brought cultural influences from other areas. In each center, large scale warfare, which probably originated from internal population pressures, from competition for resources, and from the pressures of outside nomads, was an instrument in creating true empires and starting dynasties. As the empires

grew, irrigation works were increased to the limits of water supply and population also increased. After reaching a peak, marked by a temporary florescence of culture, population pressure and abuse of the common people brought rebellion, which destroyed the empires and returned society to local states and a period of dark ages. Irrigation works were neglected and population decreased. New conquests initiated another cycle.

The cyclical phenomena are strikingly illustrated in China where, during 1500 years of the Era of Cyclical Conquests, each of the four major peaks of empires and dynasties coincided with a population peak. (Steward 1949(51):21)

Steward's cyclical conquests described a dynamic structural-functional-interactional model in which a number of factors (ecology, technology, social organization, military technology, administration, population growth, and cluster) contributed to an organized enlargement of the interactional field. Such was the nature of imperialistic expansion. After a point of maximum growth and equilibrium, disjunction in the interrelations of the factors increased until an uncontrollable state of conflict collapsed the interactional configuration.

Reintroduction of an evolutionary perspective into American ethnology was initiated by White in a series of attacks against the prevailing, but weakening, historicism of the day. In his theoretical thrust, White (1949a:8–11) pointed to the nature of facts and how their relations could be ordered, as follows: historical, geographical, structural-functional, and a combination of the historical and the structural-functional. White referred to these relational orders as temporal, spatial, formal, and temporal-formal, respectively. The basic problem for social science lay in uniting temporal and structural processes in an evolutionary model. "As social science matures," observed White (1949a:21), "the basic concept of science and philosophy, that reality is temporal-formal in character, will win its way on the cultural level as it has upon the biologic and inanimate levels." In 1945 White reaffirmed this position, seeing anthropology as the science of culture or culturology. Culture in the culturological sense constituted a suprapsychic structure which advanced according to its own laws. Energy, applied increasingly to technical operations, supplied the source for evolutionary advancement from raw human energy and simple social arrangements to the complexities of the industrial and atomic world.

The essence of the evolutionary process is the modification of structure in a sequence of time. Preoccupation with social structure, in conjunction with the conviction that laws governed social processes, made it a special target for evolutionary study. Disclaiming any nineteenth-century evolutionist purpose, Murdock (1949) noted that an evolution of social organization occurred because of the usual processes governing cultural change. As the Darwinian Centennial approached, acceptance of the view of J. S. Huxley regarding reality processes, whether biological or cultural, was well entrenched. "All reality is in a perfectly proper sense evolution, and its essential features are to be sought not in the analysis of static struc-

tures or reversible changes but through the study of the irrevocable pa-
terns of evolutionary transformation" (cited by Adams 1960(2):166).

The reawakening of interest in evolutionary and the coordinate ecological processes renovated and extended the biocultural perspective upon
which Malinowski grounded his theory of culture. Evolutionary and ecological perspectives called attention to the adaptive potential of body
evolution; for, as the hominid line advanced from proto-*Homo* to *Homo*,
and then to *Homo sapiens* and modern man, all evidence pointed to a
commensurate advance in a capacity to generate more complex and integrated technologies, ecological arrangements, social orders, knowledge systems, and ceremonials. In this long perspective the primate brain structure
had expanded in size and in neurological quality, thereby permitting the
complex symbolization intrinsic to life in human societies. Compared with
the limited communication systems of social insects, and even of man's
close primate relatives, the human potential for intellection appeared
infinite. However, the path to this quality brain was not solely the work
of biological evolution. The happy accident of man's hominid ancestors
choosing land instead of trees for their habitat prevented a narrow biofunctional adaptation. The challenge of savannah life initiated the process
of coordination between hand, eye, foot, and cerebrum characteristic of
man as a social and cultural being. By developing his own social and cultural environment man shifted his basic relations to trees, animals, and
waterways to strategems to extend his chances of survival and conven-
iences of life.

The lesson drawn from the evolution of man as a skill-possessing
being, as Oakley (1954) pointed out, was the coordination fostered among
hand, eye, and cerebral process. Tool making and tool use integrated a
variety of body movements, and this integrative operation advanced the
element of awareness and consciousness in human activities. In becoming
a tool maker man also became a strategist, for only by outwitting his
adversaries could he overcome the strength of mammoths and the challenges of air and water to catch birds and fish. Moreover, in the cooperative hunt he pooled his thoughts, learned through exchange, thought
aloud, and memorized the lessons of experience. All areas of the brain
case filled out by human evolution, in contrast with other primates, were
related to the integrative and associational functions of the brain. A strategist in his relations with animals, man became a strategist against himself.
Other men could be hunted as well as animals, and the possession of
superior technologies, skills, and organization became a requirement for
survival against men.

Despite the importance of man's social and cultural environment, in
his early history he was part of a primate evolution. A study of primate
communities suggested that their behavioral responses regarding dominance, dependency, sociality, sounds and gestures, affectional attachment,
mother-child relations, teaching-learning, and territoriality might provide

clues to the nature of early hominid behavior and social life. Some of these basics also might be intrinsic to the nature of contemporary man and suggest the background for relatively universal features in human behavior (for example, incest taboos, dominance). It was assumed, as Schultz (in Washburn 1961:86) observed, that early man, as well as monkeys and apes, probably varied greatly in size and form and in disposition and intelligence as well. Probing phyletic inheritances through relatively fixed action systems, ethologists extended this search to include issues of innate aggression and territoriality as well as inborn dispositions for a kind of protolearning, such as the imprinting discovered by Lorenz. In a study of his own coinage, proxemics, Hall (1959, 1966, 1968) outlined the subtle relations between an organic predisposition to maintain body distance and variability in the perception and use of space that could be traced to cultural learnings. This new search for biopsychic universals relied on the camera to record the situational context and social meaning of shame, anger, sexual attraction, embarrassment, smiling, aggression, and genital display. The persistent problems of incest and of exogamy also received ethological treatment. Kortmulder (1968(9):437–449; compare Wolf 1966 (68):883–898) observed that even geese avoided relations with a sibling or a parent when mating. Rhesus monkeys also were reported to demonstrate avoidance of sexual relations between mother and male offspring (Sade 1968).

Ethology, proxemics, and hominid evolution took on special meaning in the perspective of an emergent self-consciousness that grew into a sense of a personal and human destiny. Such an inner awareness could be generated only by the social experience. This was Hallowell's (1961:249–251) view when considering "The Protocultural Foundations of Human Adaptation."

> What occurred in the psychological dimension of hominid evolution was the development of a human personality structure in which the capacity for self-awareness, based on ego functions, became of central importance. The functioning of ego processes contributed new qualities to the psychological adjustment of individuals in the socialization process. Ego functions became integral factors in determining responses to the outer world in the interests of inner needs, particularly when delay or postponement of action is required. They became intimately connected with such cognitive processes as attention, perception, thinking, and judgment. Considered in evolutionary perspective, ego may be said to be the major "Psychological organ" that structurally differentiates the most highly evolved members of the Hominidae from infrahuman primates. At the same time, there is some evidence that suggests that rudimentary ego functions may be present in some of the higher apes, so it is possible that equivalent functions may have been present in the early hominids.

Hallowell observed that a primitive ego process does not require speech and culture, whereas self-awareness does. Self-awareness implies a process of socialization in which the individual responds to normative guidance and is clued to a world of symbols that he learns and manipulates.

Self-awareness thus was a necessary extension of the ego process if the hominid strain were to reach the level of cultural experience. Development of a capability to symbolize and to communicate the vital qualities of experience was essential for social and cultural experience to be aroused in human consciousness. This capacity to capture experience subjectively, and to recall and communicate this experience to others, separated the ego processes of man and his hominid ancestors from other primates. Without a capacity to think and communicate aloud through arbitrary symbols, organisms are confined experientially to the sensory cues of their immediate environment. Perception versus conception, and perceptual awareness versus self-awareness, made the difference between social animal and social man. The evolutionary design appeared as a purposive movement to an ever higher integration—the human personality.

The integrative process of inner awareness—of self distinguished from social evolution paralleled the integrative process regarding consciousness which Oakley attributed to the evolution of skill as a human attribute. The continuous differentiations, elaborations, and convergences evidenced by anthropology's own development could be viewed as a search for a scientific "personality," a reaching out for higher levels of conceptual comprehension and theoretical integration.

Interrelatedness and Complexity

There was a growing awareness that interrelations of persons in organized activities were more important to understanding the reality process than analyses limited to the demand rights and obligations of a status structure. This new perspective signaled an important change in outlook. In his introductory remarks assessing Vogt's study of Navaho veterans, Kluckhohn (1951:xii) observed:

> Perhaps the greatest increment to theory consists in the careful dissection of the intricate interdependence of personal, social, and cultural factors in the acceptance or rejection of aspects of a foreign culture. This examination would not have been possible within the framework of narrowly anthropological concepts.

Murdock (1954:28–29) spoke in the same vein when assessing the relations of anthropology, sociology, and psychology:

> In the first instance, the relations of both [anthropology and sociology] to psychology will require some revision. Each will have to become reconciled to the near certainty that the basic mechanisms of behavior will be established primarily by psychological research rather than by their own efforts. Concepts like the "processes of social interaction," "the processes of cultural change," and "the socialization process" must be recognized as nothing more than psychological processes, such as those of perception, learning, and personality development, operating under the special conditions created by human social life. There must be no more reification of "culture" or "social structure" as

causal forces, no more assumption of a specialized superindividual or super-organic level of phenomena characterized by a body of principles inaccessible to the psychologist.

Psychologists ... must desist from their efforts to explain social and cultural phenomena in terms of behavior mechanisms alone. All such attempts in the past have failed dismally, and they will fail equally in the future, for mechanisms, whether of learning or of personality, produce differential results depending upon the particular conditions of material environment, social organization, and culture prevailing in a given situation. It is the special province of the sociologist and the anthropologist to study such conditions and to determine what constellations thereof, in conjunction with behavioral mechanisms, produce this or that social or cultural manifestation. ... Both must recognize that each holds one indispensable key and lacks another, and that few, if any, of the rooms in the future mansion of human science can be unlocked without both.

To speak at the general level of the social, the cultural, and the psychological conveys little more than a perspective. However, Murdock's message was clear; one could no longer retreat behind a discipline's fence and fire causal-deterministic salvos into the other camp. Psychology was not the name of a discipline but of a generic variable, a host of processes, and the same applied to the social and cultural. If none of these variables constituted a self-contained causal system, then they must be in mutual contact. Hence, Murdock described the disciplines as cooperating methodologies, after the fashion of Boas, rather than as independent contributors of whom one was aware but largely ignored. To develop a psychological theory to suit the convenience of each discipline, as Gibson (1950, cited by Hallowell 1954:216) threatened, sounded curiously anachronistic. "If the social psychologist does not formulate a theory of learning, the cultural anthropologist will have to do so—and also the psychiatrist, the clinician, the educator, and the student of child development." There no longer was any basis for treating the human reality at one time as biological and at other times as social, psychological, cultural, geographical, historical, evolutionary, or functional. The day when the human reality could be cut to the scientific bias of a discipline—or theory —was drawing to a close.

Conceptual Complexity and Holism

Every science and specialization requires a set of analytic tools to describe and categorize its substance. Social Structuralists commonly referred to status, role, social sentiment, social norm, jural rights and obligations, institution, social function, and social principle. Culturalists put together an inventory that included culture traits, culture complexes, culture areas, culture patterns, ethos, value orientations, ideal and behavioral patterns, compulsory and alternative patterns, culture focus, and culture theme. In archeology, attempts to elicit the characteristics of artifactual assemblages led to definitions of horizon style, tradition, area co-tradition, phase, pattern, and component.

Conceptual inventories are not simple classificatory tools. They imply an interrelatedness of different elements or factors, which is probably the reason anthropologists have consistently maintained they must trace relations among and between sets of elements rather than between single elements. An institution, for example, in both Malinowski's and Radcliffe-Brown's conception, was a complex of features—charter, personnel, normative apparatus, material apparatus, and function. The same orientation lay behind Kroeber's and Kluckhohn's emphasis on pattern as the primary unit of observation. Durkheim's social fact likewise was a bundle of collective sentiment, idea, and form. Lévi-Strauss continued this configurative emphasis. When treating Pawnee mythology, Lévi-Strauss (1963ae:211) insisted that full understanding was possible only when myth was placed in a regional context of contrapuntal process. Moreover, the basic logical entities of myth were not found in the relations of isolated elements, but in their holistic relationships. Lévi-Strauss's focus on bundles of relations, as he called the basic unit of meaning and process, paralleled the growing emphasis on situational contexts. The goal of such analysis was a dynamic event sequence uniting both synchronic and diachronic time (Lévi-Strauss 1963ae:212). Kimball's (1955) event analysis and Lantis' (1960) vernacular culture approaches expressed anthropological concern for an actional package, as well as a desire to avoid becoming sidetracked in taxonomic problems or mathematical testing of probability linkages of single elements. The search for meaningful bundles or configurations expressed the true meaning of holism in anthropological perspective. Any configurated whole, however, must be dissected analytically to uncover its ingredients and the factors affecting process. In the instance of event analysis, Kimball (1955(57):1140) sketched the need to trace the interrelations of "time, space, activity, persons, and [environmental] conditions."

Context, Interaction, and Actional Systems

Anthropological concerns for the relevance of context in method and explanation stemmed largely from a corresponding focus on actional systems and their interactional networks. Traditional structural-functional analysis accented interaction in a superordinate-subordinate hierarchy of needs, operations, and values. The emergent perspective gradually abandoned definitions of relations among parts solely according to demand rights or organizing principles. The shift moved to model building in order to understand what actually went on. As Arensberg (1955(57):1145) observed,

it is clear that a model rather than a definition serves to represent the complex variables of a complex situation, thing, or process. A model serves better to put together empirical descriptions economically and surely and to handle summarily things of many dimensions, little-known organization, diverse functions and processes, intricate connections with other things. Definitions are too shallow and too full of verbal traps; summaries of propositions are too slow, piecemeal, and cumbersome.

The transfer of anthropological attention to models paralleled an empirical experience regarding variation in relation to structural processes. For example, there was a growing consensus that the fit between social personality and culture was far looser than had been assumed. Culture and society were not tightly integrated systems ordered by some primary value or function. If cultures were not tightly integrated, neither were personalities.

> Personality is not always "a whole"; that is, it is seldom perfectly integrated (completely unified). Since the course of life is punctuated by countless occasions when some choice must be made (between alternative, if not opposing needs, goals, goal-objects, concepts, tactics, or modes of expression) indecisions and conflicts are common and final resolutions of conflicts are rare. Consequently, the psychologist is well-advised to include some account of his subject's major dilemmas and conflicts during critical periods of his life. (Kluckhohn, Murray, and Schneider 1953:31)

When doubts were raised as to the imprinting of human behavior and personality by social and cultural learnings, emphasis on the role of habit conditioning and of unconscious processes also diminished. Habit conditioning and unconscious syndromes were present, but man was a reasoning being, even when offering *ex post facto* rationalizations for his behavior.

> Man's rationality is not a higher faculty added to, or imposed upon, his animal nature. On the contrary, it pervades his whole being and manifests itself in all that he does as well as in what he believes and thinks. Men may rationalize more often that they think objectively, but it is only because they are fundamentally rational beings that they are capable of rationalizing—or feel the need for it. Man is rational in all his acts and attitudes, however unreasonable these may be; he is rational also in his feelings and aspirations, in his unconscious desires and motivations as well as in his conscious purposes, and his rationality shows itself in the very symbolism of his dreams. Men could not act and feel as they do if they could not form concepts and make judgments, but neither could they make use of concepts and engage in the ideal activity of thinking if they had not developed their innate capacity for the "idealized" modes of behavior and feeling characteristic of human beings. (de Laguna 1949(51):380)

This view of man as a rational being accented the fact that those who were part of a culture were more aware of its patterns, functions, and inner meanings than had been recognized. Cultural awareness was apparent in organized efforts to change the hazards of life and to build a more satisfying culture. According to Wallace (1956), revitalization movements were produced by people who were aware of the general workings of their culture and especially those segments which aroused their dissatisfactions. A piecemeal manipulation of single elements could not renovate major segments of cultures, and thus the revitalization process involved the alteration and rebuilding of cultural systems as found in the prophetic messages of the historic reforms of society, morality, and culture.

In the case of the Manus, their culture promoted the idea of manipulating things and people as found in the industrial culture of the West. According to Mead (1961), they were ready to exchange their old lives for new ones when World War II expanded their contacts with Western culture with dramatic intensity. In the postwar period this wave of cultural influence ebbed with great suddenness, and with it the newly found affluence. The Manus responded to this sudden withdrawal with a mixed religious and pragmatic movement largely directed by a young prophet known as Paliau (Schwartz 1962). Paliau and associated prophets attempted to recapture the luxuries and excitements of the wartime life through a regimented magical imitation of the Westerner's ways, offices, churches, and other products. However, unless contact were renewed at its former level, the Manus had no way of developing the skills and experience that would establish firm relations with the industrial network. They could manipulate themselves imaginatively, live out a marginal existence punctuated with time abroad doing unskilled labor on plantations, or renovate their traditional ways.

The postwar period was alive with efforts to bring about broad social and cultural reorganization under the direction of nationalistic leaders. The goal of these Third World leaders was largely inspired by a desire to bring their countries into more equitable and autonomous participation in the modern world. At the same time, the widespread unrest provoked local and regional religious movements whose prophets frequently combined social, economic, and political aims with their religious messages. Such historic developments called attention to the role of outstanding individuals in formulating goals and in organizing popular action in the wake of social and cultural dislocations. The accelerated pace of change achieved by nationalistic leaders, both religious and political, during postwar periods presented serious challenges to the perspective of a slow-moving structural change (Barnett 1941–1942; Mead 1961; Spencer 1958; Worsley 1968).

Rethinking Social and Cultural Determinism

Actional contexts put increasing pressure on the continued use of the social and cultural as all-encompassing explanatory variables. In an article dealing with interdisciplinary research, Bennett (1954) pointed out that the broad use of the culture concept by anthropologists was not very useful in communicating with and working with members of related disciplines. Holding to an undifferentiated and diffuse variable such as culture left no common ground for a meeting of minds in the formulation of a common set of concepts relevant to the interactional networks of complex societies.

> . . . he [the cultural anthropologist] cannot afford to see all social scientific problems as problems of culture because he discovers that a whole range of problems require finer discriminations. If he studies social relationships in modern society and its institutions . . . he soon discovers that he cannot assume that his subjects are simple bearers of culture who are learning and interacting in the face-to-face group atmosphere. The more differentiated and impersonal structure of institutional systems of complex societies cannot be analyzed *initially* with the concept of culture pattern or learned behavior traits—other than in the most generalized and impressionistic manner. The anthropologist instead discovers a need for refined versions of certain familiar tools: studies must be made of the *roles* typical of a *system of social relationships*, the *values* and *norms* associated with these roles, the *expectations* of behavior brought to the situation by the individual actors, their *needs* and *motivations*, and, finally, the varying dimensions of the "situation" itself. Anthropologists are not unfamiliar with these analytical variables, but in the great body of cultural anthropological research, they often have been obscured by the emphasis on culture. (Bennett 1954(56):173–174)

Bennett had no intention of throwing the pilot concept of culture overboard. However, he insisted that analytic denotations of the culture construct had to be answered if the concept were to be usefully employed in a theory of social behavior (Bennett 1954(56):178, note 11).

There was another special quality of culture which commonly was overlooked, but which actional contexts brought into the open. Culture included specialized learnings readily discovered in social protocol, custom, and ceremony. However, in an actional context the sharing of the specifics of culture by participants was unequal and reflected different degrees of involvement in enculturating experiences traceable to personal and social factors. In many actional contexts individuals were united not so much by shared learnings as by common expectations as to how a particular cultural instrument served their respective interests. For example, conventionalized expectations of management and labor concerning a particular job permitted mutual action despite differences in motive, attitude, and satisfaction. Shared behavioral expectations, as Wallace (1961:41) observed, established a kind of implicit contract by which relationships were organized. Behavioral expectations, of course, shifted according to circumstances, and this brought modifications in the nature of contractual expectations and relationships. The important quality of contractual relationships was not the meeting of minds in shared meanings so much as in a sharing of complementary meanings, attitudes, and motives.

> Marital relationship, entry into an age grade, the giving of a feast—in all such contracts, the motives may be diverse, but the cognitive expectations are standardized. . . . From this standpoint, then, it is *culture* which is shared (in the

special sense of institutional contract) rather than personality, and culture may be conceived as an invention which makes possible the maximal organization of motivational diversity. This it is able to accomplish because of the human (not uniquely human, but pre-eminently so) cognitive capacity for the perception of systems of behavioral equivalence. (Wallace 1961:41)

Culture thus appeared as an instrumental framework for expectation and action, but not the determinant of action. Determinants of action were at the individual level, subject to pressures designed to produce actions that others would approve rather than prosecute. Implicit in all this was the idea that man was more an operator—a cultural strategist—than an enculturated automaton. The only restriction on a cultural strategist was a limitation of possibilities in which complementarity and group conventions were important considerations. Limited possibilities meant that preferred choices must be made among a number of available alternatives. Fresh contacts with economic theory and a closer look at primitive economic behavior added support for the view that men economized and rationalized their actions in constantly allocating resources that at some point approached scarcity. The principle of limited possibilities thus was a vital operation of the economizing process. A view of man as a strategist who estimated and manipulated his options likewise converged on game theory and was related to the systems theory of cybernetics.

The view of man as strategist obviously carried profound implications for a reality perspective and the kinds of models anthropologists should develop to elucidate how things operated. Anthropologists were directed to the problems of structure and variation, and of historic and evolutionary processes. Most important was a shift in the meaning of structure or pattern, and where basic processes were located. Everything in contemporary anthropological experience indicated that the closed process emphasized in the Structuralist position had to be modified to include accommodative and adaptive operations. In the perspective of resource allocation, the dynamics of structuring was found not in the replication of custom or of conventionalized role-playing but in the shifting alignment of variables in an interactional network to which individuals responded with appropriate action. Such was Barth's (1967b) argument when discussing the problems of social persistence, maintenance, and change through time. To avoid the static impasse in which anthropologists found themselves when coping with change under a narrow structural-functional orientation, Barth (1967b(69):661) recommended the following:

> (a) a greater attention to the empirical study of the events of change, and a need for concepts that facilitate this; (b) the necessity for specification of the nature of the continuity in a sequence of change, and the processual analyses that this entails; and (c) the importance of the study of institutionalization as an ongoing process.

Ordinarily, straight statistical studies of frequencies and rates of breaches of custom did not help because they told nothing about the direction or the imminence of change. What was needed, in Barth's (1967b(69):662–663) judgment, were

> concepts that enable us to depict the pattern itself as a statistical thing, as a set of frequencies of alternatives. If we, for example, look at social behavior as an allocation of time and resources, we can depict the pattern whereby people allocate their time and resources. Changes in the proportions of these allocations are observable, in the sense that they are measurable. New allocations are observable as concrete events that may have systematic effects and thus generate important change. And this view does not entail that we limit ourselves to the description of an economic sector of activities only; it can be applied to the whole field of social organization, to describe how people in fact manage to arrange their lives.
>
> Sharp's classic description of the introduction of the steel axe among the Yir Yoront of Australia (Sharp 1952) stands out as an illuminating case-study of social change precisely because it adopts this perspective. It provides an understanding of change by explaining the changing bases from which people make their allocations. We see how Yir Yoront women no longer need to offer as much submission to their husbands because they no longer need to go to them to obtain an axe; we understand why people no longer allocate time and resources to intertribal festivals because they are no longer dependent on them to obtain their tools.
>
> This way of isolating the underlying determinants of social forms, so as to see how changes in them generate changing social systems, implies a view of behavior and society that is rather different from what has frequently been adopted in anthropology. What we see as a social form is, concretely, a pattern of distribution of behavior by different persons and on different occasions. I would argue that it is not useful to assume that this empirical pattern is a sought-for condition, which all members of the community equally value and willfully maintain. Rather, it must be regarded as an epiphenomenon of a great variety of processes in combination, and our problem as social anthropologists is to show how it is generated. The determinants of the form must be of a variety of kinds. On the one hand, what persons wish to achieve, the multifarious ends they are pursuing, will channel their behavior. On the other hand, technical and ecologic restrictions doom some kinds of behavior to failure and reward others, while the presence of other actors imposes strategic constraints and opportunities that modify the allocations people can make and will benefit from making.

Barth's statement is of special interest, since it incorporates basic themes that can be connected with trends in the contemporary anthropological orientation. He concentrates on an event context as a dynamic and causally complex interactional universe. These event configurations are linked in an historical-evolutionary continuum in which the inputs of variables, and the kinds of variables present, alter the interactional network. This forces the researcher to analyze what is happening by concentrating on the dynamics of the interactional fields as they succeed each other. Man is placed in the center of the action. Pattern or structure emerges as an interactional relationship between human initiatives linked to the enculturative process and to special resource variables, including other human beings, which influence the choice of goals and the means used in reaching these goals. This position did not deny that particular events at times replicate and conform to a structured design. As Vogt (1965, 1969) described the case of the Zinacantecos, their sacracivil system was permeated by a principle of replication, and the same was true for the bureaucratic process. What this indicated, however, was the need to recognize different kinds and degrees of structuring. Furthermore, to effect control, the researcher must approach the problem of structured process through a study of particular contexts in order to make certain that structural processes are calling the tune. One must exclude the possibility that the relationship between structural process and the formal product is an artifact of special circumstances subject to limited possibilities. Structure thus is better defined in terms of the limits of variation rather than by formal prescriptions.

Reappraisal of Anthropological Goals

With the unwinding of society and culture as tightly coordinated and integrated structures, anthropological goals, and the precision hoped for, took on a more pragmatic tone. Speaking as an exponent of a new cognitive ethnography, Frake (1964a(66):132–133) indicated that the task of the anthropologist was not to predict behavior.

> The aims of ethnography . . . differ from those of stimulus-response psychology in at least two respects. First, it is not, I think, the ethnographer's task to predict behavior per se, but rather to state rules of culturally appropriate behavior (Frake 1964). In this respect the ethnographer is again akin to the linguist who does not attempt to predict what people will say but to state rules for constructing utterances which native speakers will judge as grammatically appropriate. The model of an ethnographic statement is not: "if a person is confronted with stimulus X, he will do Y," but: "if a person is in situation X, performance Y will be judged appropriate by native actors." The second difference is that the ethnographer seeks to discover, not prescribe, the significant stimuli in the subject's world. He attempts to describe each act in terms of the cultural situations which appropriately evoke it and each [cultural] situation in terms of the acts it appropriately evokes. (Compare Burling 1969; Hammer 1966; Wallace 1965)

Sounding much like Boas (1940l:257) some eighteen years earlier, social Structuralist Evans-Pritchard (1964:146) pointed to the arid failure of British social anthropology to achieve a thoroughgoing statement of sociological laws as it pursued the image of the natural sciences. "What general statements have been made are for the most part speculative, and are in any case too general to be of value. Often they are little more than guesses on a common-sense or *post-factum* level, and they sometimes degenerate into mere tautologies or even platitudes." He considered it unrealistic to expect social anthropology to continue to aim at establishing a set of sociological laws, when no one up to then had succeeded in bringing forward anything that remotely resembled a law of natural science (Evans-Pritchard 1964:152). Such being the case, Evans-Pritchard argued that anthropologists should declare for the historical camp. They should become social historians of culture patterns.

> The thesis I have put before you, that social anthropology is a kind of historiography, and therefore ultimately of philosophy or art, implies that it studies societies as moral systems and not as natural systems, that it is interested in design rather than in process, and that it therefore seeks patterns and not scientific laws, and interprets rather than explains. These are conceptual, and not merely verbal differences. The concepts of natural system and natural law, modelled on the constructs of the natural sciences, have dominated anthropology from its beginnings, and as we look back over the course of its growth I think we can see that they have been responsible for a false scholasticism which has led to one rigid and ambitious formulation after another. Regarded as a special kind of historiography . . . social anthropology is released from . . . philosophical dogmas and given the opportunity, though it may seem paradoxical to say so, to be really empirical and, in the true sense of the word, scientific. This, I presume, is what Maitland had in mind when he said that "by and by anthropology will have the choice between being history and being nothing." (Evans-Pritchard 1964:152)

As a culture historian Kroeber always maintained that the intentions and methods of anthropology were closer to history than to the "so-called social sciences." As the historian directed his efforts to descriptive integration, so the anthropologist tried to elicit the patterns of culture.

> The most important difference between history and anthropology lies not in the matter of dates but in the fact that anthropologists usually have few or no events—as distinct from patterns—given them in their data, whereas events are the accustomed primary material of historians. The abler historians weld the events into patterns or conceptual formulations; the less able cling to events and may end by believing that anything which does not deal with events happening to individuals at specifiable times cannot be historical. The rarity of recorded events in primitive life has helped to force anthropologists into recognition of the forms or patterns of culture, and from this into the clear recognition of culture as such. In short, more perhaps than any other group, they discovered culture. To be sure, this was long after intelligent historians had known the fact; but these took it for granted and tended to deal with culture indirectly or implicitly, whereas anthropologists became explicit and culture-conscious. (Kroeber 1952d:75)

The historical orientation of anthropology on which Kroeber and Evans-Pritchard insisted held important methodological implications. Anthropology was a humanistic craft rather than an integrated set of techniques rigorously applied to effect control over the observation, analysis, and generalization of particularizing processes regulating social behavior. The phenomenon of patterning intrinsic to the research focus of anthropology pointed the discipline to a broad canvas that led the mind imaginatively from the details of foreground to the subtle impressions of relationships and design conveyed by a perspective in depth. However, it was not always clear whether the history meant was historical or evolutionary or simply a pattern spotlighted at a point of time. It could be all of these or any one of them, according to circumstance. Both seemed interested in plotting a succession of patterns. Thus, Kroeber (1948a: 564–571) traced stages in the development of ceremonial in California Indian religions. Evans-Pritchard (1964:187) saw a distinction between the historian and the anthropologist in that the historian set out to describe the present in terms of antecedents and origins while the anthropologist did not. The anthropologist rather began with an integrated system of social relations, such as feudalism. By comparing feudal systems in their operations and how they changed through time, generalizations about the regularities of processes could be made. But to understand any structure in point of time, including its operations, continuities, and modifications, required an assessment of special events and situations that influenced relationships and induced structural reorganizations. This Evans-Pritchard tried to demonstrate in his work on *The Sanusi* of *Cyrenaica* (1949). In some way, as Evans-Pritchard (1964:187–188) saw it, historicity must be combined with structural-functional investigation: "I shall only say further that I believe an interpretation on functionalist lines (of the present in terms of the present) and on historical lines (of the present in terms of the past) must somehow be combined and that we have not yet learnt to combine them satisfactorily."

In 1949, when rethinking the history-anthropology connection, Lévi-Strauss (1963ab:18) aligned the disciplines as to subject, goal, and method. However, the disciplines differed in their substantive foci and explanations.

> We propose to show that the fundamental difference between the two disciplines is not one of subject, goal, or of method. They share the same subject, which is social life; the same goal, which is a better understanding of man; and, in fact, the same method, in which only the proportion of research techniques varies. They differ, principally, in their choice of complementary perspectives: History organizes its data in relation to conscious expressions of social life, while anthropology proceeds by examining its unconscious foundations.

The complementary function of history and anthropology was justified inasmuch as behind the explicit rationalizations offered in traditional explanations there were unconscious reasons to which Boas had referred earlier. Here in the depth of man's mental structure was the heartland of culture, and linguistics provided both the theoretical model and the model to reach that heartland.

> In anthropology as in linguistics . . . it is not comparison that supports generalization, but the other way around. If, as we believe to be the case, the unconscious activity of the mind consists in imposing forms upon content, and if these forms are fundamentally the same for all minds—ancient and

modern, primitive and civilized (as the study of the symbolic function, expressed in language, so strikingly indicates)—it is necessary and sufficient to grasp the unconscious structure underlying each institution and each custom, in order to obtain a principle of interpretation valid for other institutions and other customs, provided of course that the analysis is carried far enough. (Lévi-Strauss 1963ab:21)

What Lévi-Strauss said about the patterning of cultural forms through the unconscious organization of the human mind was not a complete throwback to the elemental ideas of Developmentalists, despite his recommendation for a return to a modified associational type of psychological theory. Emphasis on unconscious processes reaffirmed a place for the anthropologist and the social scientist generally, since the anthropologist was dredging and bringing to the surface the unconscious organization of behavior patterns which people themselves were unable to comprehend. The association of structure and unconscious process was of long standing in anthropology. At the same time Lévi-Strauss rescued an element of history in applying his dialectic process to a culture area. For example, the linguistically different Acoma, Zuni, and Hopi shared a complex of related mythic elements unified in the mytheme of an underworld existence and emergence to this world. Their explanations of these mythic elements and their symbolizations were not only different but in direct contrast. These antitheses bore a direct relationship to Acoma, Hopi, and Zuni organization. Hopi emphasis in the arrangement of figures and events was genealogical. The Zuni stressed a kind of periodic cycling, and the Acoma combined contrastive figures to produce a mythic event, as in the cooperation of powers from above and below (Lévi-Strauss 1963ad:74–75). But these contrapuntal patterns did not stop with myth—they could be found likewise in the organization of their respective kinship systems.

For the Acoma, Zuni, and Hopi, myth served as a kind of supergrammar for organizing the world. However, their respective mythic supergrammars had not developed separately but together through a process of contrastive opposition, or the dialectic process. Boas had noted that form apparently had a separate history from meaning, since the same form might hold different meanings in different tribes. Lévi-Strauss seemingly merged the history of form and meaning, since differences in meaning among different peoples were explained through the contrapuntal nature of the dialectic process. In the perspective of Lévi-Strauss's dialectic, one could imagine a cultural region evolving through a differential and antithetical elaboration of thematic scores within an aggregate of contiguous tribes, with broader antithetical syntheses occurring between subregions.

Had Lévi-Strauss stumbled upon a primary datum of the ego process? What is mine must be distinguished from what is thine. Invidious distinctions often involve complementary oppositions. The Westerner may be a successful materialist, but the culture of India promotes distinctiveness in the spiritual quality of life. Such ego contrasts resembled the complementary opposition between ingroup and outgroup accented by Sumner in 1906.

In some ways the contrast between Western materialism and Hindu spirituality was analogous to the linguistic contrast between classes of sounds, or phonemes. Differences expressed by the Hopi, Zuni, and Acoma treatments of the emergence mytheme resembled the oppositions found in the complementary distribution of allophones (sound variations of a particular phoneme). This linguistic model was used by Lévi-Strauss, in conjunction with the dialectic process to probe the meanings which adjacent peoples formed in accordance with the historical-psychological process of contrastive and/or distributional complementarity.

Lévi-Strauss's reduction of social and cultural processes to psychological processes commonly exhibited in the organization of phonemic and allophonic contrasts touched base with trends in American ethnology. However, Lévi-Strauss's embrace of the linguistic model came as American linguists were altering their position regarding the nature of linguistic structure and process. They were now skeptical of the idea that linguistic process was governed by unconscious processes; they began to see that language was an instrument of communication subject to manipulation and alteration by its users rather than an instrument for maintaining traditional throughtways. In this alteration Americanists transferred their interest from unconscious to conscious processes. Like Lévi-Strauss, they were equally interested in the universality of psychological processes, but they saw these universals as derived from an awareness accompanying a conscious manipulation of ideas and symbols, rather than from deep levels of unconsciousness. Such was the essence of ethnoscience. Deep-seated intuitive understandings also were present, as Chomsky (1959) argued in combating traditional habit conditioning models of programmed learning. However, the linguistic breakthrough to a new perspective accented cognitive rather than unconscious processes.

Structure and Variation Again: History, Evolution, and Mechanical and Statistical Models

A reappraisal of goals is necessary when there is an input of radically new information. The period following World War II witnessed the consolidation of fresh inputs in a re-engagement with the long-standing problems of structure and variation, and historical and evolutionary processes. In the United States, the issue was rekindled by White (1945a), who accused American culture historicists of being philosophically opposed to evolution and of failing to distinguish logically between general cultural evolution and the culture history of specific tribes. Lowie (1946), in reply, denied that culture historicists were unalterably opposed to the idea of cultural evolution—they simply insisted on the checking of general schemes with the facts of individual culture histories. Meanwhile Murdock

(1949) put forward a design for the evolution of kin-based social organization, and Redfield (1953) charted the transition from folk to urbanized peasant society. By the Darwin centennial, social and cultural evolution was well entrenched.

As anthropologists entered the sixties they were prepared to recognize the intrinsic relation between historic and evolutionary processes. Further, they increasingly called attention to the interdependence of variables in an interactional context. Thus, when ending his paper on "Behavioral Evolution and the Emergence of the Self," Hallowell (1959: 59–60) emphasized the importance of psychological evolution in making culture possible.

> The psychological dimension of evolution is as crucial as morphological evolution if we wish to understand the integral unity of culture, social structure and personality organization observed in *Homo sapiens*. The unified frame of reference envisaged by Darwin and others was sound. We must continue to work within it if we are ever thoroughly to understand man's place in nature.

On the other hand, there was good reason to consider that culture provided a milieu that had a profound and selective effect on biological processes. Without recognition of culture's role, according to Shapiro (1957:414), there was no way to account for the direction human evolution had followed. Moreover, the search for a dynamic interactional context was as vital to research in biological evolution as it was to work on cultural evolution. Such was the significance of the shift from typology to the nature and range of population units. A focus on populations necessitated the introduction of new variables, such as relations to land, ecology, genetic exchange, drift, and insulation into research on fossil hominids. This comprehensive approach, according to Mayr (1959:6), revolutionized the classification of fossil populations.

> On the basis of such considerations ... it appears possible, if not probable, that since the time of Australopithecus there has not been at any time more than a single biological species of hominid on the earth. It has been proposed to combine the numerous nominal species of fossil hominids into two polytypic species, *Homo erectus* for Pithecanthropus, Sinanthropus and their relatives, and *Homo sapiens* for the later hominids. All the known facts are consistent with this interpretation of the fossil evidence. Peking Man and Java Man will then have to be interpreted as two geographically and chronologically separated subspecies of *H. erectus*. Neanderthal would be a European subspecies of *Homo sapiens* (with nominate *sapiens* living somewhere in Asia or Africa prior to its invasion of western Europe).

To Mayr such classification implied that, in point of process, the advance to *sapiens* had not proceeded through formation of evolutionary species within the genus *Homo* but had involved transformations at the phyletic level.

The ferment generated in all domains of anthropology in the postwar period revealed a real effort by anthropologists to achieve a perspective and a model that would take them inside the dynamics of how things happen. By the 1960s a sense of breakthrough was imminent, expressed in talk about the new physical anthropology, the new linguistics, the new ethnography, and the new archeology. Lévi-Strauss's discrimination of mechanical and statistical models to illuminate the reality process was a part of this broad reengagement with fundamental problems. A mechanical model covered situations where a positive and consistent relation existed between a prescriptive rule and the product, or, as Lévi-Strauss (1963ac:283) put it, when the "elements . . . [of the model] are on the same scale as the phenomena." A statistical model applied to situations where there was no firm correspondence between the prescriptive regulations of the model and what actually occurs, or when the "elements of the model are on a different scale" from the phenomena (Lévi-Strauss 1963ac:283). Laws of marriage supplied a positive illustration. In exogamic marriage rules, there is a formal definition of groups from which an individual may or may not obtain a spouse. The rule is precise and determinate in prescribing who is excluded and who is included in a list of eligible mates. Hence, in societies possessing exogamic clans, a mechanical model accurately captures what goes on. If some cases of violation of the rule of exogamy are recorded, they are inconsequential, idiosyncratic events that can be comfortably ignored. However, in our own society, the exogamous rule works in a negative way, since its application to the nuclear family excludes a narrow range of persons as mates without prescribing a category of persons to be married. So it happens that family status, range of interpersonal relations, social mobility, and personality enter to complicate the search for regularities. To uncover regularities, frequencies must be charted and coordinate relations among a number of elements must be checked. Such a situation calls for a statistical model or construct.

In the context of the reality process (how things are ordered and operate), the distinction of mechanical and statistical models was not particularly new. Behind the two models were the old issues of structure and variation, and structural process and historical process. However, the special value of Lévi-Strauss's presentation lay in the way he outlined relations between these conceptual distinctions and history, evolution, structural functionalism, cybernetics, game theory, and probabilism. For example, speaking cybernetically, mechanical systems were characterized by a high degree of redundancy, while statistical systems, owing to their ambiguities, manifested a condition of entropy. Researching social orders in one instance called for application of a mechanical model, whereas less formalized relationships required methods associated with the statistical model. At other times the two models could be combined to achieve a proper explanation of what happened. This was the case when, as in cross-cousin marriage, society recommended such marriage but actual unions turned out to be infrequent. In explaining marital practices among the Yakö and Muria, Forde (1941) and Elwin (1947), according to Lévi-

Strauss (1963ac:284), realized the necessity to use a combined mechanical-statistical model. Three kinds of reality situations thus emerged: formal or mechanical; informal or statistical; and formal-informal, combining both structural and variational processes. In another perspective, the formal presented a high degree of stability and consistency, viewed both synchronically and diachronically. Owing to the emphasis on structured relations, the formal-mechanical model demonstrated evolutionary processes. The formal-informal, as a mixed order, exhibited the impact of both processes, thus uniting historical and evolutionary processes.

Any investigator must project some understanding of the characteristics of the phenomenon he is researching. This always has been the function of theory, and it appeared that model-building was simply a way of operationalizing theory. As Lévi-Strauss pointed out, structured entities were models in fact, exhibiting special form properties. The task of the Structuralist then would be to

> recognize and isolate levels of reality which have strategic value from his point of view, namely, which admit of representation as models, whatever their type. It often happens that the same data may be considered from different perspectives embodying equally strategic values, though the resulting models will be in some cases mechanical and in others statistical. This situation is well known in the exact and natural sciences; for instance, the theory of a small number of physical bodies belongs to classical mechanics, but if the number of bodies becomes greater, then one should rely on the laws of thermo-dynamics, that is, use a statistical model instead of a mechanical one, though the nature of the data remains the same in both cases. (Lévi-Strauss 1963ac: 284)

In this statement Lévi-Strauss pointed to a highly important attribute of the reality process. The application of a mechanical model to a situation involving a limited number of physical bodies, and a statistical model to situations where a greater number of factors were at play, described contexts that contrasted because of their simplicity or complexity. The terms "homogeneity" and "heterogeneity" frequently were used to describe differences in interactional situations and networks. Highly structured social and cultural systems possessed a high degree of consistency and homogeneity among their parts. Historically, prophetic religious and revolutionary political movements made use of periodic purges of their memberships to reach and sustain a high level of homogeneity in belief and practice. The spread of food plants useful to man usually followed zones that were compatible, or homogeneous to the adaptive ecology of the plants. The simplicity and homogeneity of rural society and culture contrasted with the complex heterogeneity of the urban world.

Though functionally interrelated at certain points, rural areas and urban centers defined two different kinds of structures and interactional universes. The bounding of any interactional field as a structured system required a determination of relationships with regard to spatial, temporal, and other attributes. Demographers commonly established the boundaries of interactional units at those points where striking discontinuities were apparent. It was Lévi-Strauss's judgment that issues with which socio-demographers grappled, and their techniques, were highly relevant for anthropology and furnished a basis for any and every kind of future anthropological research.

The plotting of elements in space to determine their relationships and to define the nature and extent of interactional fields was a primary goal of culture historicists. Significant discontinuities marked by a band of heterogeneous features separating two relatively homogeneous domains was employed to outline culture areas. Presently, students of anthropogeography were plotting genetic clines that allowed a proper definition of populations in accordance with a clustering of genetic features. The space and time disposition of social phenomena immediately evoked in Lévi-Strauss's (1963ac:290) mind a complex of processual relationships—historical, structural-functional, and evolutionary.

> Social time and space should also be characterized according to scale. There is in social studies a "macro-time" and a "micro-time"; the same distinction applies also to space. This explains why social structure may have to deal with prehistory, archaeology, and diffusion processes as well as with psychological topology, such as that initiated by Lewin or Moreno's sociometry. As a matter of fact, structures of the same type may exist on quite different time and space levels, and it is far from inconceivable that, for instance, a statistical model resulting from sociometric studies might be of greater help in building a similar model in the field of the history of cultures than an apparently more direct approach would permit.
>
> Therefore, historico-geographical concerns should not be excluded from the field of structural studies, as was generally implied by the widely accepted opposition between "diffusionism" and "functionalism." A functionalist may be far from a structuralist, as is clearly shown by the example of Malinowski. On the other hand, undertakings such as those of G. Dumezil, as well as A. L. Kroeber's personal case of a highly structure-minded scholar devoting most of his time to distribution studies, are proofs that even history can be approached in a structural way.

With this statement Lévi-Strauss perceptively acknowledged that American culture historicists at certain points transformed their descriptions of historical relations into descriptions of structured sequences, or evolutionary stages.

In retrospect, Lévi Strauss's (1963ac) summative statement on social structure carried a special impact because it touched base over a wide range of entrenched distinctions and focused on implicit trends in anthropology. His preference for a mechanical model featuring consistencies between premises and products simply reaffirmed a faith in and reliance on structural process as the proper base for scientific investigation. The mechanical model coordinated with Bateson's (1949) view of a "steady state." Correspondence between normative premises and products called up notions of universal (Linton 1936) and compulsory (Kluckhohn 1941) patterns. It was easy to transpose the mechanical and statistical models into the distinction of ideal and behavioral patterns. As Nutini (1965(67): 726) commented,

> (b) Following both Lévi-Strauss and Leach [1961] I maintain that mechanical models stand for or are constructed out of ideal behavior, and statistical models stand for or are constructed out of actual behavior, and they are the best type of models. But ideal behavior (or rather the ideal standards or rules that govern it) may lie in the "collective consciousness," hence the need to keep constantly in mind the conscious and unconscious character of social phenomena. (c) At the descriptive or observational level, I agree with Leach: by all means deal with statistical norms, as well as with "ideal paradigms." Indeed, we must deal with both, since they complement each other, but we must also keep in mind that they are not yet models, that is, supra-empirical constructs, according to the definition. *But at the experimentation level, we should whenever possible construct mechanical models, for they are superior heuristic devices.* (d) *In explaining a society or a part of a society in isolation, that is, at the experimental level, mechanical and statistical models complement each other, when they do not by themselves explain the phenomena in question.* In comparative situations, on the other hand, we must always compare mechanical models, for I do not think it possible to compare statistical models, or what people actually do. Even if we could, the models themselves would be of lesser heuristic value, and not as amenable to manipulation by the mathematical method, or by any other. [Italics supplied]

Mechanical models were better methodological devices for comparison since their structural consistencies aided the precise discrimination of homologues, the only basis for comparison. Statistical models, on the other hand, might betray the investigator into a comparison of functional analogies. Yet, the reality processes, as Nutini admitted, required the use of both mechanical and statistical models in arriving at trustworthy explanations. In effect, the reality process combined structural and variational processes.

Linguistic Analogy, Formal Analysis, and a Man and Culture Perspective

To American culturalists, the orderly arrangements of language held a special attraction as a model for exploring and explaining the cultural domain. The use of language was a learned proficiency. Rules of phonology and grammar were observed or social communication faltered. Moreover, violations of linguistic conventions could be checked against a formal body of rules that pointed the linguistic deviate to appropriate normative behavior. Individual transgressions of language form thus were limited as speakers were forced to take on a linguistic mantle by internalizing sound cues and syntax rules. Through habit, conventionalized speech was transformed into an automatic and unconscious operation. Language thus epitomized the model of culture as a structured or conventionalized habit system, in which individual variants were swamped by a consensus of usage. In language one found forms and processes that had a life of their own because they were supraindividual. Yet change did occur in language, as the formation of dialects illustrated. However, no dialect was purposefully conceived. The formation of transitional forms and dialects followed the cumulative drift, as it were, of "unconscious selection on the part of its speakers" (Sapir 1921:155).

The Sapir-Whorf hypothesis regarding the relation between language and thought stands as a signpost of a time when habit learning and unconscious and intuitive processes held the forefront of ethnological theory. In this hypothesis, as expressed by Sapir (cited by Hoijer 1954a(56):93–94):

> Language is not merely a more or less systematic inventory of the various items of experience which seem relevant to the individual, as is so often naïvely assumed, but is also a self-contained, creative symbolic organization, which not only refers to experience largely acquired without its help but actually defines experience for us by reason of its formal completeness and because of our unconscious projection of its implicit expectations into the field of experience. In this respect language is very much like a mathematical system, which, also, records experience in the truest sense of the word, only in its crudest beginnings, but, as time goes on, becomes elaborated into a self-contained conceptual system which previsages all possible experience in accordance with certain accepted formal limitations.... [Meanings are] not so much discovered in experience as imposed upon it, because of the tyrannical hold that linguistic form has upon our orientation in the world.

Stimulus impulses from cybernetics, game theory, and formal mathematical analysis gradually infiltrated and aided transformation of the anthropological view of culture process modeled on language process. Stress on learning as habit conditioning left no room for the play of intellect. The new trend emancipated individuals from the restrictive weight of unconscious sociopsychological processes, and individuals became operationalized as cognitive agents. Thus, the study of language shifted to a formal analysis of the cognitive operations involved in assembling a meaningful sound sequence and the rules by which such a sequence varied in form to generate different meanings (Chomsky 1957). By laying bare the formal properties of grammatical structures through a set of deductive theorems, the formal analyst undermined the rationale for exclusive reliance on unconscious processes in the formation and maintenance of structure.

Applied to kinship terminology, formal analysis sought to identify the semantic elements used to link or separate sets of kin. From this emerged a model or abacus with semantic counters placed at critical points for appropriate designation of kin. For example, in discriminating a child of a man's younger brother or a child of any other younger male blood relative of a man in his generation, a Lapp took seven different discriminant variables into account, according to Goodenough's (1967) analysis. In another perspective, a Lapp needed the information furnished by the discriminant variables if he were to make a correct designation of kin according to Lapp usage. In reducing a kinship terminology to its least common semantic denominators, it was not claimed that this was the way Lapps generally analyzed their kinship relations. However, Goodenough suggested that an experienced Lapp in time might grasp the total sense of design of his kinship system by ordering it into semantic variables that could be manipulated mentally according to context, much as the formal analyst had done.

Formal analysis was applied best to domains that were clearly bounded, and where classification was a paramount concern; hence its early application to kinship terminologies and native classifications of diseases, plants, and objects. Archeologists also found the technique of formal analysis useful in devising a code for segregating the social meaning of elements associated with artifacts and burial practices (Brown 1971). However, there was no guarantee that the social meanings of artifacts and ceremonial burial arrived at by the analyst through his logical procedure would correspond with the mental operations and meanings of his subjects, dead or alive, unsophisticated or sophisticated. Indeed, the fact that different mental models could be constructed to account for the same distribution of elements raised a basic methodological issue and challenged the aims of ethnological research (see, for example, Lounsbury 1964; Burling 1964). If the intention of the new ethnography were to understand "where people were at," or to probe the inner workings of the mind, then one must expect a positive correspondence between the mental operations of ethnographer and subjects (Frake 1964a).

The methodological issue conjured up the distinction between emic and etic perspectives as formulated by Pike (1966:153): "Descriptions or analyses from the etic standpoint are 'alien' in view, with criteria external to the system. Emic descriptions provide an internal view, with criteria chosen from within the system. They represent to us the view of one familiar with the system and who knows how to function within it himself." This echoed Boas' ideal of achieving a description of a grammar "as though an intelligent Indian was going to develop the forms of his own thoughts by an analysis of his own form of speech."

Emic or internal analysis, in Pike's view, maintained the natural integrity of a subjective system under investigation. An emic approach likewise questioned the validity of cross-cultural comparisons based on an etic categorization of forms according to the researcher's theoretical and conceptual bias. Yet formal analysis strained to state a general theory of mental processes. Lévi-Strauss universalized the process of dichotomized contrasts, and then operationalized the process historically in the dialectic. In a revised view of formal analysis, Burling (1970:53–55) conceded that the reduction rules developed by Lounsbury to account for the extension of kin terms from primary to secondary and tertiary relatives offered a promising explanation of this social phenomenon by a universal mental process. It was simply a matter of extending a core meaning to individuals who shared a special genealogical relationship to the core person. For example, in Burling's (1970:52) interpretation, "A term that can be applied to one's mother, to one's mother's sister, and even to one's mother's brother's daughter can now be reasonably said to have the central meaning of *mother*, and its other uses constitute extensions of this central meaning to kin-types related in specific ways to mother." Lounsbury apparently devised a new way to confirm that the classification of kin was produced by generalization of meaning. Such an explanation would vindicate Malinowski and those who drew upon the psychological process of generalization to explain kinship extensions.

The psychosemantic thrust of the new ethnography carried forward a trend in the psychologizing of culture that had already attained significance in ethnology. Concentration on the logic of classifications introduced an epistemological focus that drew the attention of cognitive anthropologists to all domains of classification. The comparative study of color classification by Berlin and Kay (1969) suggested that human beings make the same discrimination of primary colors regardless of cultural experience or definition. The general theory of knowledge to which cognitive anthropologists aspired now appeared attainable, since distinctions between primitive and civilized logic were no longer maintained. Their special innovation lay in the studious application of logical analysis to delimit the intrinsic and extended meanings of conceptual distinctions. In the wake of their elegant logic, man took on the image of a manipulator of ideas rather than of objects. The heart of culture thus must be sought in a network of symbolic communications, subject to procedural rules which regulated inclination and choice. The procedural rules constituted a system or cognitive model internalized by members of a society. It followed that the basis for choice or allocation of preference among a set of alternatives and exclusions was seated in the rules of the cognitive system. Cognitive systems constituted decision-making and procedural processes, and hence research needed to be directed to actional situations. Descriptive observation must be supported by a focused interview designed to elicit the basis for choice and to discern the differential importance of factors affecting the judgment. The broad intentions of ethnosemantics in ethnography were described by Kay (1970:29) "as a means of arriving at the cognitive system, or systems, employed by people as a device for classifying their environment, evaluating various states of that environment, predicting what the outcomes of the various behavioral possibilities open to them will have on that environment, and ultimately selecting a course of action." Kay (1970: 30) admitted that cognitive structures alone could not predict behavior, but when supplied with information essential to decision-making (for example, age, sex, wealth, social status), predictive accuracy was high.

The new epistemological anthropology touched base with other trends in anthropology and with research in psychology on "cognitive styles" (Cohen 1969; Cole 1971). A view of man as a rational allocator of meanings was congenial to the perspective of man as a pragmatic and logical allocator of resources in the interests of self, satisfactions, and maximization of ends and means. The emic orientation of getting inside a subject's logic coincided with a continuing emphasis on a valid basis for the collection of reliable data. Limiting research goals to a descriptive analysis of how groups operationalized their logical processes in a classification of phenomena within a unitary domain coincided with the situational holism currently being emphasized in anthropology.

However, this emic descriptive posture was antithetical to the particulate and noncontextual comparisons of those who, from an etic view, classified cultural phenomena according to the logic of their own principles of significance. This emic, descriptive, and noncomparative quality of epistemological anthropology continued an orientation associated with American descriptive linguistics from its beginnings under Boas. Once again, however, as in Boas' early history, there was an affirmative interest in the general laws of mental processes encased in the social conventions of language and custom. This shifted the focus of comparison, as is always the case with general theory, from a comparison of forms and substance to a comparison of processes. Yet, forms and processes could not be separated in description, analysis, and comparison. An internalized emic process is related to an external etic form as genotype is related to phenotype, and hence the two must be treated as a unit. Forms provide clues to processes, and in evolutionary sequences, forms can be used as indexes of changes in situation and mental process. Such was the practice of Berlin (1970: 8–16), when he suggested that the trend toward more refined and complex discriminations of color followed a mental pathway that was similar for all peoples. The simplest distinction began with white and black, to which red, green, yellow, and blue were added. However, if classifications were turned into a universal evolutionary trend in thought, one must make the same assumptions and follow the same comparative procedures as Developmentalists when they described the evolution of ideas, arts, and institutions. But if it were methodologically unsound to extrapolate process from classification, what alternatives remained? Three options seemed open. One was to follow Boas' lead and try to chart the historic process by which the classifications of individual peoples had been arrived at; or to observe the way present classifications were being adapted to changing circumstances; or, following an emicized structural-functional model, to study the operationalizing of the classification process within specific domains of activity. From comparison of classification processes found in different domains (for example, natural objects, tools, kinship terms), it was possible to step up to the level of a general theory of the classification process. Finished classifications, as Tyler (1969:6–11) noted, are of three kinds: taxonomies, paradigms, and trees. More often, however, the logical ordering of phenomena was only partial, and classificatory arrangements involved other bases for ordering. Mixed classifications then are frequent and create ambiguities which harass the precise taxonomist.

The epistemological development in anthropology opened up another exciting possibility. The separate social sciences, despite differences in substantive foci, indicated that their terminologies, though etymologically distinct, converged on important attributes of the reality process. An ethno-semantic analysis of terminology both within and across disciplines loomed as a most useful operation. Determination of a common fund of conceptual distinctions would constitute a real breakthrough at the general level of theory.

Mathematical Precision and Quantitative Measurement

Mathematical precision has always been an attractive lure for those seeking a scientific ethnology. Tylor (1889) applied statistical procedures in hope of proving to his natural science colleagues that ethnological materials also could be subjected to mathematical controls. In his review of the use of statistics in anthropology, Driver (1953) pointed out how Czekanowski (1911), in testing *Kulturkreis* theory, used statistical procedures to test the alleged historical association of traits which had no direct functional connections. In California, Kroeber sparked a drive to see to what extent correlation coefficients revealed the tendencies of tribes, villages, bands, and other culture-bearing groups to cluster geographically. From their cultural-geographical relations, Kroeber hoped to get evidence for reconstructing the individual histories of culture-bearing units and for describing the histories of broader cultural configurations. To shore up the data for statistical manipulation, trait lists numbering several thousand features were prepared and checked with informants from 254 groups in California, Mexico, the Great Basin, and the North Pacific Coast during the years 1934–1938 (Culture Element Distribution Series, University of California).

What Kroeber and associates attempted regionally, Murdock and associates engaged on a world-wide basis. Beginning with the Human Relations Files in the thirties, Murdock provided much of the inspiration to sample tribal societies in accordance with a standardized inventory of cultural materials. By 1949 he was able to draw upon a useful world sample of 250 tribes in his study of social organization. Continuing work on a world ethnographic sample, he (1957) coded thirty cultural traits for each of 565 tribes distributed unevenly over six major regions. Beginning in 1962 Murdock and associates of *Ethnology* began development of a world ethnographic atlas with a coding of over 1,100 societies. This number was reduced to 862 tribes arranged in 412 clusters (Murdock 1967). Murdock's summary carried 85 columns of trait categories, including mode of marriage, family organization, community organization, patrilineal kin groups and exogamy, kinship terminology for cousins, settlement pattern, mean size of local communities, high gods, postpartum sex taboos, type of animal husbandry, metal working, linguistic affiliation, class stratification, norms of premarital sex behavior, inheritance of movable property, and ground plan of dwelling.

The purpose to which Murdock held was production of an adequate world sample for statistical manipulation. In his view, the use of statistics was essential in that it added quantitative validation to functional relation-ships commonly postulated but which defied substantiation under a de-scriptive functional analysis. Much of the struggle to formulate a standard cross-cultural sample involved preservation of a random quality in the sample by excluding the possibility of historic contact. In the words of Murdock and White (1969(8):331–332):

> The establishment of such a sample has depended on three arduous but neces-sary preliminary research activities: (1) the analysis of more than 1,250 soci-eties (in the Ethnographic Atlas of this journal), a very high proportion of all those whose cultures have been adequately described, to identify those with the fullest ethnographic coverage and to make certain that no major cultural variant has been overlooked; (2) the classification of all the cultures assessed into "clusters" (Murdock 1967), i.e., groups of contiguous societies with cul-tures so similar, owing either to diffusion or to recent origin, that no world sample should include more than one of them; (3) the grouping of clusters, usually but not always adjacent, into "sampling provinces" (Murdock 1968) where linguistic and cultural evidence reveals similarities of a lesser order but still sufficient to raise the presumption of historical connections in violation of Galton's objections.

To arrive at the cross-cultural sample, Murdock and White finally abandoned the strategy of a random sample and set out to isolate his-torical units according to the clustering of similar features among con-tiguous tribes. Out of their cultural-historical sampling provinces, reduced to 186, they selected a most representative tribe for each cluster, and the work of the Cross-Cultural Cumulative Coding Center, established in 1968 at the University of Pittsburgh, is currently dedicated to the coding of selective data drawn from each of these sample societies.

The pathway to a useful sample had taken over forty years. Much time and a number of ingenious solutions were worked through in order to free the ethnological sample from the charge of contamination by historical contact among some of the units compared (Naroll 1961; Naroll and D'Andrade 1963; compare Greenbaum 1970). In final analysis, the prob-lem was solved in a workable way by accepting historical clusters as the basic units and then discriminating them somewhat arbitrarily by a dis-tance factor of some 200 miles (Murdock and White 1969).

Driver (1956; Driver and Massey 1957) likewise played a prominent role in plotting geographical distributions to see whether any tendencies toward clustering were due to functional interdependencies. Using cor-relational analysis, Driver and Massey (1957) attempted to determine the probable evolutionary sequence of institutional developments leading to patricentered, matricentered, and bicentered integrations. Functional cor-relations were low, and in a subsequent publication Driver (1970(26): 30–31) concluded:

> Although many cross-cultural researchers, including the present author (Driver 1956, 1966), have demonstrated significant relationships that conform to the expectations of comparative functional-causal theory, this has been accom-

plished for small samples of variables representing less than 10 percent of the entire range of a cultural inventory, as approximated in the *Outline of Cultural Materials*. When a broader range of inventory is compared, most "surface" correlations of raw trait categories fail to pass a conventional significance test and chaos is the dominant characteristic of the data. However, when "deeper" structure is unearthed by means of collapsing trait categories into variables and applying the factor type of multivariate analysis, a modest amount of order emerges. Such order transcends the chaos of an extreme shreds and patches view of culture, but it is very far indeed from attaining the control over cultural knowledge about which the rank and file in cultural anthropology are still writing in their verbalizations about functional-causal relations and patterning in culture.

The Place of Mathematics in Anthropology. Statistical correlations are no better than the data on which they are founded, and at times complex mathematical manipulation masks relations that the simpler mathematics of a frequency distribution would make clear (Chrétien 1966(7): 148–149, and Driver's reply, 1970(26):155–156). In a perceptive summary, Köbben (1967(8):3–19) reviewed the treacherous shoals to be navigated before reliability and validity could be built into mathematical analyses of social and cultural phenomena: bias in classifications, treatment of continuous relationships as dichotomous, differences in definitions, the probability of causal convergence and of multiplex causality. Similar difficulties attended the use of Guttman scalograms to derive historic and evolutionary developments (see, for example, Carneiro 1962, 1967, 1968; Goodenough 1963; Graves, Graves, and Kobrin 1969). As correlations gave no secure basis for imputing causal relations, so the Guttman scalogram failed to disclose what operated to produce the graduated series. However, both techniques were useful in the imaginative formation of new hypotheses—a not unusual conclusion with regard to techniques.

It became evident that the application of mathematical techniques to ethnographic data provided no panacea. Yet it was also clear that the ethnographic record must be quantified if it were to prove useful in controlled comparisons. Mathematical models grounded in a formal-structural analysis found a primary application in the domains of folklore, kinship, and folk taxonomies and did not rely on statistical procedures to reach results. Like Lévi-Strauss, Colby (1973(75):660) recommended that statistical techniques were useful as one instrument to elicit the patterning of mythic elements when attacking a large number of narratives. Statistical correlations, on the other hand, were important in the cross-cultural testing of postulated functional relations that provided a basis for general theoretical formulations.

Under statistical analysis, the tendency of cultural elements to cluster in apparent functional-causal relations was an important datum with regard to the structural process. It suggested that factors extrinsic to the hypothecated functional relationships were operative in the production of variants. Correlational analysis of Rorschach protocols likewise produced little support for the idea that culture processes were so structured and determinative in their effects that similar personality characteristics would be widely distributed among the population. Even cultures considered to be tightly integrated, and which could be expected to impress a high proportion of modal features on the character of its members failed to do so (Kaplan 1954). Findings of this order opened the door to a favorable consideration of factors extrinsic to structural processes in accounting for events. The findings of statistical analyses of social and cultural phenomena thus supported interest in the historical process, ecological relationships, and the role of cognition in a selection of ends and means for social action.

Ecology and Interactional Networks

An ecological orientation made its way into the ethnological consciousness during the postwar period. Steward (1955) began the process of formalizing the ecological perspective by calling attention to the fact that the potentials for cultural development were influenced greatly by their technical-ecological relations. As armies metaphorically crawl on their stomachs, so cultures advanced, or marked time in place, depending on how they were able to multiply relations with the environment. The multiplicity of environments militated against any unilinear theory of evolution. To the contrary, environmental differences forced differences in technicoecological adaptation, and perforce cultural evolution followed divergent or multilinear paths.

Adaptive responses to different environmental conditions were always important to anthropological thinking about variations in cultures. Developmentalists pointed to environments as inducing cultural variations. Kroeber's (1939) reexamination of cultural-environmental relations in North America corrected the position of culturalists who concentrated on culture processes to the exclusion of cultural-ecological relations. The ecological orientation, with its emphasis on the technical background of cultures, refocused attention on economic processes and socioeconomic organization as central to the functional and ideological integrity of cultures. The command over energy and its distributive use emerged as critical in the general evolution of culture (White 1943; Childe 1951).

An ecological perspective evoked the idea of a structured network of interrelations modeled on the biotic community. Any human group was viewed as operating in an ecosystem which included animal, plant, water, and other resources as well as climatic fluctuations and cooperative or competitive relations with other groups. The culture history of any group could be projected as a succession of cultural-ecological configurations which expanded or contracted according to circumstances. Such a perspective was congenial to established structural-functional theory. The addition of evolutionary process would give Structuralist theory the dynamism which it lacked. Goldschmidt (1959b:107) stated the relation between structural-functional and evolutionary theory thusly:

> This evolutionary theory is also a functional theory in the sense that it involves the basic functional thesis that (1) institutions are mechanisms of social interaction which serve the continued life of the society, and (2) all parts of the social system must form an integrated whole so that changes in one part require adjustments in others. In addition, the functional theory stresses the priority of some aspects of society over others. . . . Furthermore, certain areas of life activity lie closer to such external factors as environment or such internal ones as technical change and are therefore more vulnerable to their pressures.

The ecological perspective conveyed a broadly oriented and integrative approach to problems and reinforced the holistic posture in ethnology. There was stress upon an organic interrelatedness of parts, interactional impact (transaction), running adjustments to situational contexts (feedback), and a dynamic and delicate equilibrium or homeostasis. The interactional impact or transactional process was a new emphasis. Transaction underlined the fact that systems were never confined to simple replication of their parts and functions but were in constant contact with other systems that either restricted operations or opened up new opportunities. A transactional process implied that change was not random but directional. This adaptive directionality was manifest in a structured succession of living arrangements that strained to reach the optimal limits of living space and use of available resources (Thompson 1961). Biotic successions provided the analogue for ecocultural evolution.

Murphy and Steward's (1956) comparison of the ecocultural adaptations of Amazonian rubber tappers and Labrador Indian trappers described change in a succession of interactional configurations. Each successive field was discriminated according to differences in variables operating in an interactional network. Viewed as relatively bounded systems in contact with the commercial system of the West, the world of tappers and trappers was influenced by both internal and external factors. Production was determined in part by the expanding wants of the Indians and by their capacities to accommodate their living to the technicoecological requirements for processing rubber and furs. Both availability of resources locally and the stability or acceleration of demand were important factors in maintaining the interactional network and in inducing changes in patterns of settlement and social organization. Spicer (1961) and associates likewise underlined the importance of alterations in interactional configurations in the acculturation of selected American Indian tribes.

An acculturational model of successive interactional configurations was congruent with the concept of a succession of biotic communities. Such ideas also converged on Lesser's (1961) notion of social fields. In this perspective societies possessing distinctive technical and ecological systems were seen as establishing tentative linkages which widened their respective interactional domains. New opportunities for diversification and the interchange of organizational and ideological elements accompanied the gradual formation of a unitary interactional universe that embraced the various technicoecological systems. The pooling of resources of these different ecosystems greatly expanded a common potential for more complex developments and establishment of a common tradition that included technology, social organization, religion, and knowledge. Such appeared to be the case in the rise of civilization in the New World. According to Willey (1962(64): 9–10),

> in [their largely] . . . religious ideologies these early societies had developed a mechanism of intercommunication, a way of knitting together the smaller parts of the social universe of their day into a more unified whole. . . . In a way similar to that of the interchange of objects, plants, and techniques which had previously prepared the village agricultural threshold, the sharing of common ideologies led to the threshold of civilization by enlarging the effective social field. By this enlargement more individuals, more social segments, more local societies combined and coordinated their energies and efforts than at any time before. Regional differentiation in culture is an important precondition to cultural development insofar as differences contribute to the richness of the larger order, but without union the different parts remain isolated and in danger of stagnation.

Both Lesser and Willey implied that signal changes in structure resulted from an extension of interactional contacts by individual units and their increased participation in a wide-ranging interactional universe. This universe altered through functional differentiations and also progressively achieved an increasing degree of homogeneity. Consequently, there was an increasing degree of directionality and of integration. The empirical evidence of archeology, as of history, repeatedly testified to the importance of shifting patterns in the relations of societies and to the effects which functional differentiations and convergences produced. Recognition of the meaning of dynamic interchange led Taylor (1948) to outline for archeology an integrative or conjunctive approach in which relationships within a configurated universe were stressed in contradistinction to artifact inventories, form comparisons, and chronologies then prevalent in archeological reporting.

DIFFERENTIATION AND PHILOSOPHIC DIVERSITY

The differentiation of specializations in anthropology opened new channels of communication with other disciplines and with society at large. This not only stimulated importation of new theories and methodologies but also freshened concern for broader philosophic problems. A time of differentiation usually raises more controversy than agreement. Diversity and contradiction now are more a part of the anthropological character, as well as ambiguity with regard to self-image and purpose.

In the period immediately after World War II anthropologists experienced no immediate depression or melancholia over the state of their discipline or of the world generally. This may have been due to the rediscovery of consciousness as a meaningful component of human environment, and to the renewal of interest in social evolution.

In *Man Takes Control*, Erasmus (1961) reviewed the problem of cultural evolution and the role of aid programs in bringing developing peoples into greater articulation with the contemporary world. Noting the dangers of bureaucratic regulation for human values, Erasmus saw a desire for involvement and directionality as an essential component of man's nature, anchored to the need for response from others. Desire for social recognition and man's capacity to rationalize his activities marked the human pathway as one of progress.

> The concept of prestige or status as used to interpret culture in this book is not to be confused with the concept of economic man. Although I view self-interest as the underlying stimulus to action, the striving activity which results . . . is not directed merely toward the acquisition of useful goods. Nor have I invoked any self-regulating mechanism such as a competitive market system to keep self-interest working for the greater good of all. Here I contend that man's cognitive symbolizing ability, stimulated mainly by the desire for social recognition, accounts for the dynamic quality of progressive cultural development through the growth and spread of culture capital. As positive controls over the environment increase through specialization, social interdependence and reciprocity are extended to more people, and negative controls develop to regulate the delayed rewards of impersonal reciprocity. By this process, the cognitive component of cultural causality modifies the socially approved forms of behavior through which self-interest can seek expression. Whatever one wishes to view in this growth and expansion as a moral or ethical development must also be attributed to man's intelligence, the increasing probability of his knowledge, and a self-interest which is always socially mediated and sanctioned in some degree. (Erasmus 1961:309)

On concluding his survey of *The Primitive World and Its Transformations*, Redfield (1953) pointed with optimism to the enlargement of human wisdom, morality, and character that accompanied the human experiment. These advances had not been the work of gods but of men in communication with each other. Beginning in isolated communities, men in different societies were drawn gradually into a wider circle of contacts, and these new contacts always proved to be a fresh learning and moral experience.

> It is the contact and conflict of differing traditions that brings about the sudden alterations in society and, among other consequences, the change from a mythology that is retrospective to one that is prospective. Sometimes the mythology of the past contains within it the sleeping germ of a prospective mythology. The idea that Quetzalcoatl might some day return was . . . within the great culture myth of the Nahua peoples of ancient Mexico; the idea rose to current importance when Quetzalcoatl, in the person of the Spaniards, did apparently return. The Yucatecan Maya of the isolated villages told me that

an ancient race, pale-skinned builders of the great shrine cities, slept beneath the ground. When the American archaeologists arrived, the story was told me again, but now with the suggestion that the ancient race had arisen from its long sleep and—this was the forward turning of the ancient tale—would now guide the village Indians into a new world of progress and enlightenment.

In each of the nativistic movements among Indian or Oceanic peoples we find a prospective mythology. Mankind is on the move again, or is urged to be on the move, by leaders who now preach a new cult, a new and coming event. A ship will arrive with the spirits of the dead; the bison will return; the end of the world will come. In the course of these movements the people turn in some degree away from the leaders of the old and traditional ways of life to these preachers of new cults. "Mimesis is directed toward creative personalities who command a following because they are pioneers." (Redfield 1953: 125–126)

The omega of these philosophic trends in anthropology was an effort by the Jesuit Teilhard de Chardin (1961) to unite the cosmic process of cerebralization with divine reason. The whole process of evolution recorded a strain toward an increase in mental energy, and this was the special mark of man. Pointing to an ever-expanding conscious awareness brought about by the psychobiological intermingling of the world peoples, de Chardin (1961:251, 289–290) envisioned mankind as impelled to an ever-greater unity in mind-body—a "mega-synthesis."

We are faced with a harmonised collectivity of consciousness equivalent to a sort of super-consciousness. The idea is that of the earth not only becoming covered by myriads of grains of thought, but becoming enclosed in a single thinking envelope so as to form, functionally, no more than a single vast grain of thought on the sidereal scale, the plurality of individual reflections grouping themselves together and reinforcing one another in the act of a single unanimous reflection. . . .

To make room for thought in the world, I have needed to "interiorise" matter: to imagine an energetics of the mind; to conceive a noogenesis rising upstream against the flow of entropy; to provide evolution with a direction, a line of advance and critical points; and finally to make all things double back upon *someone*. In this arrangement of values I may have gone astray at many points. . . . My one hope is that I have made the reader feel both the reality, difficulty, and the urgency of the problem and, at the same time, the scale and the form which the solution cannot escape.

The only universe capable of containing the human person is an irreversibly "personalising" universe.

A reengagement with purposive development once again directed the attention of anthropologists to judgments about the values of cultures. Looking backward through the prism of advancement, anthropologists appeared to align themselves with the intellectual ideas of former Developmentalists, especially the humanists. An adjustment in the relativistic posture was imminent as anthropologists, in their involvements with foreign aid programs, were forced to rethink their purposes. The problem increased as governments moved ever deeper into power politics on a global scale.

Earlier, when anthropologists were invited by colonial governments and post-World War II trustees to participate professionally in the task of accommodating native ends and means to administration, they had approached involvement with the stipulation that it must have a value-free scientific purpose (Barnett 1956). Some twenty years later, acrimonious debate and cynical attacks on the objectivity of anthropological investigation resulted in a demand for a social and ethical commitment that would make anthropology relevant to a world where violence and oppression were practiced against the weak and the poor.

That neutrality in science is illusory is a point which has been made often and well. . . .

The rationale which supports this scientific unaccountability among moral men is the myth of a value-free social science, described by Gouldner (1964) as a Minotaur—a beast half man, half bull, confined to a labyrinth and sustained by human victims. This myth has been exposed to all but its most avid beneficiaries and the most credulous in its audience by events in this country since World War II, just as it was in Europe considerably earlier. Gouldner holds . . . that

> one of the main institutional forces facilitating the survival and spread of the value-free myth was its usefulness in maintaining both the cohesion and the autonomy of the modern university, in general, and the newer social science disciplines, in particular.

Perhaps more accurately, it maintains a whole segment of the profession— or at least the symbiotic relationship between that segment of the profession and the sources of its funds, namely corporate foundations and governmental agencies. It is in the labyrinths of those sources that the Minotaur is most welcome and most richly rewarded. Those whom the Minotaur has served have used it not primarily for what it produced, but for what they *made* of what it produced; and they have proved to be accomplished alchemists as they have turned the results of social science to their own ends. It was Alexander Leighton who said (1949:128) that "the administrator uses social science the way a drunk uses a lamppost, for support rather than for illumination." The uses and distortions of social scientific findings depend largely upon how amenable they are to such use and distortion, and *that* is where the social responsibility of the social scientist lies—to apply his knowledge and influence unstintingly in the attempt to insure their humane use. (Berreman 1968(9): 391–393; see also Gjessing 1968:397–402 and Gough 1968:403–407, and commentaries, 407–435)

This bitter and cynical indictment was prompted by the growing involvement of the U.S. government in overseas research for counterinsurgency purposes. The statement presented a choice of involvement, noninvolvement, or counterinvolvement and infused the decision with a sense of moral responsibility. However, the risk of taking sides, an action militantly argued by those who took an "antiimperialist" stand, was the polarization of the anthropological community and subversion of the scientific ideal of objective observation and analysis. Gough (1968(9):429) proposed to study the nature of the revolutionary process, both as a success and as a failure, in Third World countries such as Cuba, Algeria, Guatemala, Venezuela, Yemen, Cameroon, and Indonesia. As a "revolutionary socialist," she felt compelled "to aid revolution as best I can." Here was politically motivated research which carried counterinsurgency from the left just as the Camelot project, fostered by the CIA, served the Establishment by researching the nature of revolutionary movements in Latin America. In politicizing the scientific purpose, the obvious loser would be the discipline. The stage would be set for social science which weighted its facts in order to propagandize rather than to enlighten mankind with knowledge that was useful because it was secured by objective methods of collection, analysis, and generalization. A radicalizing of knowledge simply relativized truth and turned it into a warring ground of political faiths.

Yet it was equally obvious that anthropology, as other disciplines, existed in a historic-cultural context and could not entirely avoid the pressures of the crises and purposes of that context. This was the case from the very beginnings of anthropology in the eighteenth century. At that time progressivists marshaled evidence to show that empires were artificial and inefficient constructs that violated the natural liberties of men and interfered with natural creativity because of excessive restraints necessary to maintain them. This critical-intellectual role became a part of the scientific tradition of 19th-century anthropology. In exposing the fallacies of belief and the cultural hangovers of a savage past, anthropologists declared their role to be the advocate of human advancement, of reason, and of morality. However, acceptance of a biological-social evolutionism reinforced an intellectual and racial elitism despite anthropological concern with popular behavior as found in custom. The later upgrading of culture as the primary determinant of behavoral differences laid the foundation for acceptance of a relativistic position regarding the values of alien peoples and cultures. Cultural differences came to be viewed as natural to mankind and worthy of acceptance as different life-styles. Reviewing the pros and cons of anthropology and administration in the postwar period, Barnett (1956:187) noted the difficulties anthropologists and administrators faced in their definitions of goals and policies for the Trust Peoples and Territories:

> the tendency to veer from a neutral course has been the most difficult to master, although the temptation to formulate and recommend policy principles has not been less insidious. This is not surprising, for these are key elements in the experiment and . . . mark a departure from traditional thinking and teaching in anthropology. Understandably, most of the partisan leaning and pleading has been in favor of the Micronesians; and there have been instances of such consistent identification with a native group by an anthropologist that it has been . . . necessary, for headquarters to read certain field reports with a corrective constant. Rarely has the anthropologist identified himself with the administration.

The challenge now facing anthropologists is far more basic and filled with ramifications far more dangerous than any faced heretofore. It is not a matter of arguing for the validity of someone else's values. The challenge is addressed directly to the central values of science and the role of anthropologists as scientists. Shall anthropologists continue as scientific mediators of knowledge or transform themselves into scientifically trained leader-militants? New and ambivalent ambiguities dog the scientific image. The call for involvement, and the insistence upon relevance, chart a course where research may be evaluated more in terms of its practical utility than its acceptance as a contribution to knowledge. What losses and gains are to follow have yet to be seen as time and events unfold. One can only hope that the expanding challenges faced by anthropology will contribute vitality, strength, and dynamism to the continuous growth of the discipline and will aid in defining the place of anthropology in an integrated science of mankind.

SUMMARY

After 1935 anthropology entered a transitional period of specialized differentiation especially critical for the future of the discipline. The new developments in part were responses to processes internal to the theoretical and methodological growth of the discipline but more so to broad sociocultural changes overtaking the West and the nonindustrialized peoples researched by anthropologists. The Depression of the thirties and World War II accelerated change in world societies and introduced new materials which challenged the formal-structural analysis developed by anthropologists in their exploration of structure and systemic processes. These profound cultural-historical changes forced anthropologists to modify their perspectives regarding the nature and processes of the human reality, their methodology, kinds of factual material collected, views of causality, and the role of anthropology in a world of accelerating change.

A combination of industrialization and nationalism linked to "modernization" revolutionized the "traditional" societies after World War II. In place of relatively static equilibrium processes which bound individuals unconsciously to a collective tradition, anthropologists were introduced to collective action which accented a release from social tradition and a conscious shaping of society and culture to human needs. Such developments not only undermined the deterministic structural-functional model but also opened the way to explanations of the social and cultural by extrinsic forces, such as ecological and psychological processes common to mankind.

The necessity to modify the structural model reintroduced the problem of the relation between structural and variational processes. To achieve control over facts and processes, observation was narrowed to manageable contexts, and this meant greater attention to historic processes, the roles of historic figures, and the ways individuals maneuvered strategically within the system. It became increasingly evident that structural-evolutionary and variational-historic processes must be combined to achieve a comprehensive view of reality processes. Lévi-Strauss's mechanical and statistical models, as well as mixed mechanical and statistical models, pinpointed the issue. The trend toward unification of synchronic and diachronic processes was also facilitated by reintroducing an evolutionary perspective into American cultural anthropology by Leslie White and Julian Steward.

The process of differentiation within anthropology revealed that a social or cultural orientation affected the types of specializations. Social anthropologists concentrated on legal, political, and religious institutions, which, through ritualization of collective values, drew individuals together and gave them a sense of a common tradition. Cultural anthropologists, especially in the United States, explored acculturation processes, culture and personality, and cognitive processes and styles. In their investigations of social organization American anthropologists used an evolutionary perspective to describe the rise of complex social and political systems. From linguistics they borrowed a method of analysis to elicit the logic of classifications, especially kinship terminologies. Native responses to opportunities in the work world drew social and cultural anthropologists into studies of urbanization processes in the Americas, Africa, and Southeast Asia. Study of urbanization processes opened linkages with prehistorians engaged in plotting the rise of urbanized settings in association with regional and interregional cultural traditions.

Specialization generated new interests and broadened the factual base of social and cultural anthropology, intensifying intellectual exchange and the borrowing of theory and method from sister disciplines. This was especially so for cultural anthropology, which drew upon projective and other psychological tests and also pioneered in the use of statistical devices to order and analyze data. At the same time present techniques admittedly did not adequately control the ambiguities of the data, and hence the anthropological objective of prediction was abandoned for statements of probability.

The cumulative effects of such diverse and critical changes both within anthropology and in the world at large provoked attempts to reevaluate the status and role of anthropology at present and in future. Congruent with the emergent view of men using social, cultural, and natural resources to satisfy human needs, some anthropologists called for active participation in renovating inequitable socioeconomic systems and in shaping a future geared to human values. The urge to "modernize" social and cultural anthropology, in conjunction with a narrowing of opportunities for traditional research and job opportunities, stimulated anthropologists to expand their interests in the medical and educational areas to include interstitial subcultures (such as "drug," "alcohol," "commune") within the larger society. The anthropological method of participant observation was considered especially efficacious, since it elicited the life-styles of subcultural groups. The effect was to convey an increasingly pluralistic outlook to the anthropological perspective and to reiterate the holistic emphasis essential to the philosophy of cultural relativism which became entrenched in the thirties.

The course of anthropological development from 1940 to the present underlines the fact that it is an institutional product of the West and is sensitively tuned to changes in the broader sociocultural context. Expansion of the West into the far corners of the globe made possible the internationalizing of anthropology as the science of mankind. Without Western penetration and conquest ethnologists could not have developed their subject matter. Now ambiguities regarding goals and the divisiveness of the world at large are penetrating anthropology and eroding confidence in its scientific mission. Yet this scientific mission is essential to the humanistic goals projected by those who call for a renovation of anthropology. Without the inspiration of an objective pursuit of knowledge, anthropology and related disciplines will turn into a warring ground of political ideologies. The differentiation of specializations holds anthropology to its scientific course and steers it closer to realization of its mission as the science of non-Western peoples.

15

Differentiation of Social Anthropology and Theoretical Divergences

INTRODUCTION

Diffusion, structural differentiation, and synthesis—processes governing culture growth—were equally important in the development of social Structuralism. The diffusion of Durkheim's sociological analysis to England was largely the work of Radcliffe-Brown (see Chapter 13); however, Radcliffe-Brown also drew upon the British moral-legal-political tradition of Maine. The pragmatics of legal rights and obligations led him to expunge the mystical elements introduced by French sociologists to explain the symbolization of unconscious social sentiments and the solidarity of elementary societies. The theoretical orientation of Radcliffe-Brown actually was a combination or fusion of French sociological and British legal-political theory, infused with Spencer's organic view of society. At a later time Lévi-Strauss, through the pragmatics of alliance theory, likewise divorced French Structuralism from its preoccupation with sacred symbols and social solidarity.

The comparative social anthropology which Radcliffe-Brown forged from the above intellectual streams did not gain a firm foothold in anthropology as a subdiscipline until the 1930s. Even then there were ambiguities, since Radcliffe-Brown viewed social anthropology as a subdivision of a more general sociology. As social anthropology moved into its anthropological niche, French Structuralism maintained a separate course. This theoretical divergence between French and British social anthropology continued, since Lévi-Strauss's transformation of French Structuralism accented economic rights and exchange rather than jural rights and duties. Migrating to South Africa and then to the United States, Radcliffe-Brown inoculated students with his theoretical perspective. However, the structural theory Radcliffe-Brown diffused to the New World was more a grafting on the tree of culture than the planting of a sociological seedling. The behavioral and psychological orientation intrinsic to American culture theory stemmed from a focus on custom as learned social behavior. It was fortified by a pervasive linguistic tradition that concentrated on the psychological and learning background of culture forms. The American culture tradition thus produced a third divergence in the approach to social structure. In the United States, Murdock took a major step to a unified theory of behavior-as-custom by fixating psychological correlates through statistical frequencies and by developing a variety of social types based on the clustering of social elements. The year Murdock published *Social Structure* (1949), Lévi-Strauss's *The Elementary Structures of Kinship* also appeared; and within one year Radcliffe-Brown, in association with Forde, restated his position in *African Systems of Kinship and Marriage.*

Although offering differences in explanation, each of the three approaches to social structure was alike in that they explained the order of social relationships in laws derived from structural necessities. Their endeavors centered on the ancient fields of anthropological concern—incest, exogamy, descent, and affinity—so basic to understanding the nature of primitive society, and perhaps complex societies as well. Their mutual experiences included a defense of their respective positions and an exposure to new field materials from Southeast Asia and Oceania. These new materials challenged the structural foundations on which each of the approaches to social structure was raised.

Common problems often facilitate a turn to new connections; and challenges to the moral-legal-political theory of British social anthropologists in the fifties led them to renew their linkage to the conceptual perceptions of French Structuralism. Alliance theory provided the immediate provocation for review. In turn, Lévi-Strauss found the theory and method of French, Czechoslovak (Prague school), and American linguistics useful in analyzing the "universal" psychological tendency to incorporate binary oppositions in social and cultural terms.

The differentiation and divergence of social Structuralism occurred when the world societies entered a critical period of transformation during and after World War II. In the modern world, economic, political, and legal institutions supplied the social sinews for societies that depended not on kinship but on national territorial arrangements. Demands for fresh knowledge as to the interrelations of economic, political, legal, and stratification processes among the developing countries increased. In response, economic, political, and juridical anthropology differentiated and began to pursue specialized courses. The feedback which the differentiation of these subfields brought to the issues of incest, exogamy, and kinship was not so much a direct theoretical impact as it was a broadening and sensitizing of perspective. The most pervasive stimulus emanated from the ecological and economic orientation. Kinship was investigated as a possible arrangement for the exploitation and exchange of economic values (see Chapter 16). Lévi-Strauss's alliance theory was a case in point, but it was also evident in the sensitive appreciation of man-land ratios in the determination of group affiliations in Polynesian societies.

These postwar developments drastically modified the conception of societies as tightly structured entities organized functionally in accordance with moral, legal, and political necessities. Whatever utility this model had for African sociology, it had little significance for the sociology of Southeast Asia or Oceania. Societies were no longer seen as always manipulating individuals and binding them to uncompromising status assignments. The social and cultural emerged as an environment in which individuals applied adaptive strategies, just as in the technical world. From this perspective, the model of an actional system was projected as the proper focus for research.

The fresh perspectives accompanying the social exploration of Southeast Asian and Oceanic societies illustrate how the understanding of a discipline may accelerate through critical experiences. In science, the critical experience usually is found in the uncovering of new facts that do not fit traditional theory. Through their separate encounters, both British social anthropologists and American culture theorists almost simultaneously reexamined primitive societies in the light of their pragmatic operations, informal or latent organizations, and alliance perspectives. The new perspective outlined a general convergence in which the roles of ultimate social values and formal structuring were played down, and vital social operations were traced to flexible structures organized according to the dynamics of individual and group strategies. It is an interesting point that this anthropological discovery of the pragmatics of kith and kin in primitive societies came at a time when ultimate social values were being downgraded in the Western capitalistic nations and varied social behaviors became more prevalent.

The new-found emphasis on action and strategy obviously directed attention to specific social contexts. This once again brought the problems of the relation between structure and variation and of general and particulate theory into focus. Emic and etic distinctions in the approach to a controlled collection of data also surfaced, with a decided preference for the emic. Ostensibly in searching for operational determinants for native action a choice was made in favor of induction. The logic of native choice and mental processes now loomed as central to the whole emic operation. This meant analyzing the conceptual apparatus of the native in order to grasp the principles on which conceptual distinctions had been raised. Linguistic methods appeared appropriate, since linguists had successfully applied the controls of formal-logical analysis to establish valid phonemic and grammatical distinctions. The validity of these analytic distinctions rested on the facility of the linguist to grasp the structure of a language and its acceptable grammatical operations. However, unless the linguist's conclusions about language structure were tested against the awareness of informants regarding their own language structure, the method of formal analysis must be weighted toward the etic rather than emic procedures.

Application of linguistic methods to the study of kinship was a product of an American anthropological tradition which returned consistently to a linguistic model to elucidate culture as a mental phenomenon. The linguistic perspective stirred hopes of arriving at a body of mental processes shared by mankind. The possibility of relating fundamentals of cultures to the generic nature of mankind, and of writing a general theory of culture, surfaced once again. Enthusiasts hailed a new ethnography and set to work to unravel universal mental processes by focusing largely on the nature of classifications. By learning the principles guiding native classification, and the logic of their ordering of phenomena, ethnoscientists hoped to see into the operational procedures of the native mind. The new ethnography was not all that new but picked up old strands going back to Boas, Kroeber, and Malinowski; however, it did generate a new slice of anthropology—epistemological anthropology. As with other specializations, cognitive or epistemological anthropology brought into the open and formalized what frequently was treated incidentally or described in a general way.

Formal analysis of classifications is natural to the linguistic purpose and methodology. Through the technique of logical analysis of semantic elements it was hoped that the logic of social referents embedded in classificatory distinctions of kinship terminologies could be expressed. It was also anticipated that the logic of classification would provide a new and more meaningful basis for ordering data for cross-cultural purposes. When applied to kinship terminologies, the linguistic strategy was referred to as componential analysis. Componential analysis of kinship terminology produced principles by which conceptual distinctions were rationally ordered. However, such formal-logical analysis obviously bypassed the emic operation. In effect, componential analysis talked emically but behaved etically.

The formal-analytic innovation generated considerable appeal, since it could be applied to all manner of materials which were segregated into categories. It implied that human beings everywhere ordered their worlds of perception and discriminated contrastive elements by means of a classificatory logic. Two other perspectives accompanying the differentiative thrust of new specializations were also important in renovating the anthropological approach to social and cultural phenomena. The first renewed the objective of charting the evolutionary path of human society from the simple to the complex. The second drew upon economic and ecological perspectives and set out to correlate primitive social structures with their means of production.

INCEST, EXOGAMY, KINSHIP, AND DESCENT: THREE INTERPRETATIONS

For Developmentalist theorists, incest, exogamy, kinship, and descent were so closely interrelated and vital to the ordering of primitive society that they were accorded a central place in their explanations of the beginning and advancement of human society. Twentieth-century anthropologists considered them equally important for understanding the orderly processes of primitive societies. However, explanations varied as theoretical ground shifted, and Evans-Pritchard, Lévi-Strauss, and Murdock illustrate the respective emphases and contributions of British social anthropology, French Structuralism, and American culture theorists to these complex issues.

Social Structuralist Explanation: Evans-Pritchard on the Solidarity of the Nuer Lineage and Incest Rules

Explanations of social Structuralists emphasized the way a social practice contributed to the solidarity of the group and perpetuated the continuity of the social order. For example, as Radcliffe-Brown (1962a:72) wrote, incest not only created disruption in the family but shook the moral and religious foundations of the entire social order. Incest regulation thus was a social need if order and continuity were to prevail over anarchy and distintegration. Malinowski drew a similar conclusion with regard to incest control and the stability of the family.

In social Structural explanation, it made no difference whether a rule were phrased in the negative or in the positive. The ultimate function of negative and positive injunctions was the same—to assure group solidarity. Indeed, whatever was intrinsic to the social order inevitably became the focus for a positive or negative sanction that evoked the necessity to be bound by one's group. With regard to Nuer exogamy, Evans-Pritchard (1951:29–48) concluded that it was a functional adaptation in the interests of lineage solidarity. The central or core lineage was a group of paternal kin (agnates), but marriage prohibitions extended beyond lineal kin to close cognatic relatives. Other prohibited relations included close kin of a physiological father who held no legal rights over his offspring, near kin by adoption, close affines, and those considered related as fathers and daughters according to age-set regulations. The principle of agnation was extended to unify both agnates and cognates, and the age-set marriage prohibitions seemingly symbolized and affirmed the corporate character of the kin. According to Evans-Pritchard (1951:47–48),

> There is a tendency . . . for local communities to be groups of people, who, being all interrelated in one way or another, must marry into a different local community. This happens because the Nuer make any kind of cognatic relationship to several degrees a bar to marriage and, at least it seems to me, it is

a bar to marriage because of the fundamental agnatic principle running through Nuer society. In any Nuer residential group, of whatever size, there is . . . a great variety of personal ties of a kinship order bringing its members into a texture of relationships, but the warp of the texture is the agnatic lineage and to it everyone attaches himself locally. If a man is not a member of the lineage with which he lives, he makes himself a member of it by treating a maternal link as though it was a paternal one or through affinal relationship. The lineage is thus in its corporate character a composite structure of cognatic branches and attachments in which the value of agnation is the integrating principle. The solidarity of a group of persons living together, and thereby the lineage structure which contains them, is maintained by emphasizing cognation in the rules of exogamy.

It is useful to analyze Evans-Pritchard's statement since it supplies clues typical of social explanation employed by British social anthropologists. First, there is the emphasis on the ultimate design or purpose of the group, exemplified in the corporate solidarity of the patrilineage. Second, the value base, or principle of agnation, is viewed as the primary axis along which a more comprehensive social integration is achieved through extension. Third, the process of generalization is a sociological and not a psychological process. That is, the definition of the graded incestuous relations comes from application of the social principle of kinship distance rather than from unconscious generalization of sexual feelings invested in interpersonal relations within the family.

Emotional states are involved in both psychological and sociological explanations, and both make use of the principle of generalization. In the case of sociological explanation, the emotional component is organized and generalized along an axis of graded social relations (for example, family, lineage, clan). In psychological explanation, the primary axis is emotional, extending from a low to a high affect, or vice versa. This emotional axis, according to the degree of affect generated in a relationship, determines the emotional valence of the social relationship and the intimacy or formality which prevails. In both instances, the generalizing process reaches a boundary or limit. What determines the limit? Neither the psychological nor the sociological explanation offers a satisfactory answer. However, Evans-Pritchard pointed out that maternal linkages were constantly utilized by Nuer to build bonds with a set of patrilineally related males, and this was quite acceptable when the man did not reside where his own lineage mates were found. The agnatic principle in conjunction with the principle of exogamy accented the lineage and reinforced its existence, as well as the corporate meaning of lineage for its members. Abstract moral or psychological principles were not utilized by social Structuralists to explain the basis for native judgments or ways of acting. For the native, the important thing was a social rule which defined who or what fitted a special category and the type of behavior which should then be followed. Hence, in explaining marriage prohibitions, it was preferable to say that incest was a breach of a social rule governing marriage than to say that the sexual relationship of two people was incestuous, and therefore prohibited as a marital arrangement.

Like the culturalists, British social anthropologists found a constant advantage in turning a psychological or moral interpretation around. The anxiety one felt in breaching a rule was interpreted as a social product of a social regulation and was not an ephemeral product of an alleged human nature.

Elemental Psychic Processes, Reciprocity, and Incest: Lévi-Strauss

For Lévi-Strauss (1969), incest, exogamic rules, descent, and kinship rested on elementary psychic processes universal to mankind, and equally elementary interpersonal relations rooted in survival needs. From Durkheim and Mauss he derived the notion that the human reality was experienced in oppositions that made up parts of a whole (Lévi-Strauss 1969: 129). From this French sociological tradition he also derived the notion that the social reality with which men worked in both simple and complex societies rested on certain elemental and fundamental structures of the human mind (Lévi-Strauss 1969:75). Parallels in social structures thus would exceed in number and in significance similarities which derived from historic contacts. Localized and intraregional contact admittedly brought uniformities and variation to historic social organizations. However, for Lévi-Strauss the primary role of culture was to stabilize and continue the group's existence. This meant that structural necessities were far more important in explaining uniformities than accidental contacts. Social organizations possessed an indigenous structural core that was impervious to historic contact; therefore any variations induced by historic contact would be superficial. Structural form thus held the key to process.

Structural necessities allowed the analyst to dissect a social order both as to form and organizational principle, and Lévi-Strauss was convinced that such analysis would turn up elementary forms integral to the system as a whole. Beneath every social system one could find simple and fundamental social forms that were flexible and adaptive to the demands of the local environment, and which persisted despite evolutionary change (Lévi-Strauss 1969:155–156). It is the elementary relationships that structure the system, determine the range of variability in form, and direct adaptive modifications as circumstances require. There is a core structure, then, that imprints the social order, and it is up to the anthropologist to grasp the nature of this elemental unit in the formation of social systems. It is an interesting fact that while Durkheim anchored his thesis of *The Elementary Forms of the Religious Life* in Australian materials, so too Lévi-Strauss rested *The Elementary Structures of Kinship* on a considered analysis of Australian social organization.

Mauss supplied Lévi-Strauss with a base for viewing the integrative role of elementary social forms and elemental processes of the human mind. As Lévi-Strauss (1969:52) wrote, Mauss had sought to show that exchange in primitive societies consists not so much in economic transactions as in reciprocal gifts, that these reciprocal gifts have a far more important function in these societies than in our own, and that this primitive form of exchange is not merely nor essentially of an economic nature but is what he aptly calls "a total social fact", that is, an event which has a significance that is at once social and religious, magic and economic, utilitarian and sentimental, jural and moral.

Reciprocity constituted the bedrock upon which elemental social forms were raised.

Lévi-Strauss sought the roots of reciprocity, in experiences which had a collective impact. He found this collective consciousness in deprivation associated with the allocation of scarce resources. The social rationale for reciprocity was simply need to regulate competition regarding access to resources—thereby restricting monopoly and eliminating artificial inequities. Reciprocity was integral to social living, since it arose almost spontaneously from a need to overcome the emotional and social pressures accompanying a collective existence (Lévi-Strauss 1969:42). In primitive society, the total social fact of reciprocity was manifested ambiguously, yet clearly, in a practical and mystical exchange that encompassed all manner of things—food, crafted tools and ceremonial objects, and that most valued good, women (Lévi-Strauss 1969:61). Both food and women held special symbolic value in primitive society because of the difficulties which their scarcity or outright lack posed for survival.

It would be almost impossible for an individual by himself to survive, especially at the most primitive levels, where hunting and gardening, as well as collecting and gathering, are made hazardous by the harshness of the geographical environment and the rudimentary nature of techniques. One of the deepest impressions which I retain from my first experiences in the field was the sight, in a central Brazilian native village, of a young man crouching for hours upon end in the corner of a hut, dismal, ill-cared for, fearfully thin, and seemingly in the most complete state of dejection. I observed him for several days. He rarely went out, except to go hunting by himself, and when the family meals began around the fires, he would as often as not have gone without if a female relative had not occasionally set a little food at his side, which he ate in silence. Intrigued by this strange fate, I finally asked who this person was, thinking that he suffered from some serious illness; my suppositions were laughed at and I was told, "He is a bachelor." This was indeed the sole reason for the apparent curse. This example could be multiplied many times. Denied food after bad hunting or fishing expeditions when the fruits of the women's collecting and gathering, and sometimes their gardening, provide the only meal there is, the wretched bachelor is a characteristic sight in native society. But the actual victim is not only the person involved in this scarcely tolerable situation. The relatives or friends on whom he depends in such cases for his subsistence are testy in suffering his mute anxiety, for, from the combined efforts of both husband and wife, a family often barely derives enough to avoid death by starvation. Hence in such societies it is no exaggeration to say that marriage is of vital importance for every individual, being as he is doubly concerned not only to find a wife for himself but also to prevent those two calamities of primitive society from occurring in his group, namely the bachelor and the orphan. (Lévi-Strauss 1969:39)

In Lévi-Strauss's view, any group values what is scarce and essential to its well-being, and the principle of reciprocal exchange is the primary instrument for regulating access to scarce resources. The most elementary experience for man is rooted in survival, and this generates reciprocities of all kinds. The individual life thus is regulated by general rules grounded in shared feelings and backed by a collective will. Society exists to assure survival, and to achieve this end it relies on reciprocal exchange in order that inequities based upon the accidents of distribution can be smoothed out.

> It [society] refuses to sanction the natural inequality of the distribution of the sexes within the family, and on the only possible basis it institutes freedom of access for every individual to the women of the group. This basis is, in short, that neither fraternity nor paternity can be put forward as claims to a wife, but that the sole validity of these claims lies in the fact that all men are in equal competition for all women, their respective relationships being defined in terms of the group, and not the family.
>
> This rule also has advantages for individuals, since, by obliging them to renounce a limited or very restricted share in the women immediately available, it gives everybody a claim to a number of women whose availability, it is true, is checked by the demands of custom, but a number which theoretically is as large as possible and is the same for everyone. (Lévi-Strauss 1969:42)

The access to advantage guaranteed by reciprocal exchange necessarily required renouncement of a similar advantage. Expectably Lévi-Strauss accorded no place for the maximization theory of formalist economics in his structural-functional model. The stress on reciprocity drew him to the substantivist position of Polanyi (1968) and of Dalton (1971a). Nevertheless, the principle of reciprocal exchange did not rule out differentials in access to an economic good. The Nambikwara chief, for example, did have more than one wife. He was accorded this privilege because of his extra-functional contributions to the welfare of the band and its continued existence. His extra wives were a form of compensation as well as a symbol of his power and status.

In making reciprocity central to the organization of society, Lévi-Strauss joined Malinowski—and other moralists—in emphasizing equity as the necessary and integrative bond of society. The principle of reciprocity guaranteed equity in social relations by denying possession in whole and also laid the foundations for uniting society in a bonding of fundamental oppositions. Reciprocity divided people into givers and receivers, and in this perspective primitive society loomed as a network of alliances to effect exchanges in which the exchange of women was central. The division of father's brother's and mother's sister's children and the father's sister's and mother's brother's children into opposing sets—so frequent in primitive society—was critical for the formation of that elementary marital alliance through which social unity was established and maintained. The widespread distinction of parallel and cross cousins, as anthropologists conceptualized these two sets, represented an intuitive understanding by primitive sociologists of those elemental forms upon which culture and society were raised and without which social living could not survive (Lévi-Strauss 1969:101).

Viewed in the perspective of reciprocity, incest definitions were necessary and natural formalizations of the social exclusions that flowed from reciprocity. The fact that parallel and cross cousins were equidistant in biological relationships meant that the incest prohibition was social and not biological in origin (Lévi-Strauss 1969:122). Lévi-Strauss also noted that the importance of the incest definition lay not in the prohibition but in the positive guarantee of social continuity through social alliance. There was little doubt that cross-cousin marriage constituted that elementary social bond, and that this reciprocating relationship was the centrum for other structural arrangements. Exogamic rules, dual organization, and unilineal descent were simply more complex extensions of the elemental reciprocity found in cross-cousin marriage. Even in complex societies, as in France, the critical centrality of cross-cousin marriage was revealed by the fact that the frequency of cross-cousin marriages could be used to project the size of a group of intermarrying people. According to Lévi-Strauss (1963ac:293–294), the size of such intermarrying groups in certain French provinces indicated that the number of people drawn into a network of kin-based relationships was similar in size to what was found among primitive peoples. Equally astounding was the discovery that the smallest intermarrying groups were found not only in isolated regions but also in the large urban centers such as Lyons, Bordeaux, and Paris. One should not explain parallel and cross-cousin distinctions, the marriage of cross-cousins, and the practice of exogamy as a function of unilineal descent—as was commonly attempted—but rather turn the explanation around and trace each of these manifestations to the principle of reciprocity.

Armed with the principle of reciprocity, Lévi-Strauss produced an imaginative and suggestive, if not convincing, analysis of organizational arrangements in primitive society. The strain toward balanced reciprocity provided an affirmative base for the increasing integration of societies as they multiplied their exchange relations and extended them to other peoples. The infrequency of patrilateral cross-cousin exchange in comparison with the matrilateral exchange revealed an intuitive grasp of organizational relationships by primitive sociologists. The direct patrilateral exchange operated as a closed system and thus had limited exchange value. Matrilateral exchanges, on the other hand, permitted a lengthening of the cycle of reciprocity and in this way extended the integrative range of social exchange. Lévi-Strauss concluded that exchanges were of two orders; direct and closed (restricted) and indirect and open (generalized). The extended intertribal Kula ring which united Papuo-Melanesian Islanders in a ceremonial exchange of shell valuables and other items (Malinowski 1961a) stood out as an ideal example of generalized exchange, even though no exchange of women was involved.

Lévi-Strauss's attempt to demonstrate that an understanding of complex social arrangements could be reached by analysis of the mathematical permutations of exchange alliances, modeled on an elementary prototype, represented an extension of French sociological tradition traceable to Durkheim and Mauss. However, he transformed French structural analysis by a pragmatism centered in survival needs and the discharge and calling in of debts. Gone was the metaphysics of religious value and symbolism in the organization of society. In its place Lévi-Strauss offered a dialectic process in which man's thoughts and actions were organized by unconscious processes to effect and extend social solidarity through a union of opposites. His structural analysis of society in accordance with equity—that every man was part giver and part receiver—was reminiscent of Adam Smith's argument. Adam Smith held that equity exchange was intrinsic to the structural-functional requirements of the socioeconomic process, and that no group should take from the whole more than its functional input. The principle of equity constituted a summative explanatory principle for Lévi-Strauss, and in point of method he continued the tradition which accounted for structure as the coordinate of a primary value and the operationalizing of value in social relationships.

An American View of Incest, Exogamy, and Descent: G. P. Murdock

In retrospect, the 1940s was a decade when anthropologists of different theoretical persuasion strove to comprehend the meaning of fundamental social practices in the organization of primitive society. Murdock's *Social Structure* (1949) signaled an American effort to untangle the complex skein of incest, exogamy, and descent and to formulate a comprehensive theory. Murdock was exposed to biofunctionalism under the tutelage of Keller, and Malinowski added later reinforcement. Murdock also became immersed in the cultural-historical tradition of American ethnology, and at Yale took part in the interchange which sought to accommodate behavioral and psychiatric psychology. He was a central participant in setting up cross-cultural files at Yale (now, Human Relations Area Files) with a view to building a complement of data for statistical analysis. He was convinced that social and cultural phenomena were governed by laws, and this became clearer as he worked to quantify the social products of man's life. Social phenomena to Murdock (1949:183) were subject to invariant relationships that rivaled the physical laws governing the combination of atoms or genes. At the same time he was convinced that "causal factors actually operating in any particular situation are always multiple. No single factor or simple hypothesis can account for all observable effects" (Murdock 1949:126).

Nonetheless, through statistical correlations it was possible to show that some factors were of greater importance than others—more notably economic factors, which Murdock (1949:137) considered prime determinants of social structure.

Consonant with his multiple-causal orientation, Murdock drew upon functional, behavioristic, and psychiatric psychology, and the findings of culture history as these converged on a social problem. Psychoanalytic theory was the starting point for understanding the sociopsychological role of incest. A generalized sex drive was frustrated, tamed, and directed into socially advantageous channels through generation of the incest feeling. The family naturally was the locus for the emergence of this incest feeling, since it provided the actors for the primary Oedipal conflict. Awareness of the necessity to control sexual rivalry in the interests of family solidarity, and by extension of the wider society, led to a placement of social value on out marriage, or exogamy.

> No form of conflict is more disruptive than sexual competition and jealousy. The reduction of sexual rivalry between parents and children and between siblings consolidates the family as a cooperative social group, promotes the efficiency of its societal services and thus strengthens the society as a whole. (Murdock 1949:295)

This statement paralleled the explanation for controlling sexual jealousy offered by Malinowski in his biofunctional analysis of family solidarity.

Having united psychoanalytic and social-functional theory, Murdock turned to behavioristic psychology to explain why incest prohibitions were extended so frequently to secondary relatives, and why the kinds of relatives to which incest taboos applied were so diverse. The tendency to extend incest taboos to relatives beyond the nuclear family was elucidated by the psychological mechanism of stimulus generalization (Murdock 1949: 298). However, stimulus generalization failed to explain why such extension took place in certain cases and not in others. Here anthropology furnished data essential to the psychological explanation, notably, the range of diversity in social contexts and modifications traceable in specific cases to cultural-historical change. It was not a range of social types alone that anthropology offered but a set of principles operating in the formation and alteration of social types. In a summative detail of principles Murdock set forth thirteen assumptions, using the twelfth to point up the importance of external factors on social organization.

> Our twelfth assumption is that the forms of social structure are not determined by kinship patterns or terminology, or influenced in any major degree by them, but are created by forces external to social organization, especially by economic factors. It is assumed ... that the available sources of food and the techniques of procuring it affect the sex division of labor and the relative statuses of the sexes, predisposing peoples to particular rules of residence, which can eventuate in the formation of extended families, clans, and sibs. It is further assumed that the prevailing types and distribution of property favor particular rules of inheritance, that wealth or its lack affects marriage

(e.g., encouraging or inhibiting polygyny), and that these and other factors external to social structure can strongly influence rules of residence and marriage and through them the forms of social organization and kinship structure. This assumption is derived from the analysis by Lowie of the origin of sibs, from our own supportive evidence as presented in Chapter 8, and from the various theorists from Marx to Keller who have stressed the importance of economic factors in cultural change. (Murdock 1949:137)

Incest taboos and exogamic rules were not designed to function solely in defense of family solidarity. The muting of sexual rivalry and jealousy was just as important in an adaptive way for kindred, lineage, sib, extended family, clan, or community (Murdock 1949:299).

In any extension of incest rules, what applied to marriage was also overwhelmingly characteristic of premarital and postmarital sexual activity. Throughout these widely reported marriage rules, the preference in initial marriages was for a person of one's own generation. The desire to be with age mates, in conjunction with the intimacies of kin relationships, could be expected to eliminate aunts, nieces, and half-sisters from first considerations of marriage and sexual contact (Murdock 1949:302). These near-universal features of marriage proscriptions meant that significant differences in the ways by which societies extended incest rules would turn up initially in their classifications of first cousins. Four major axes of extension were possible: "symmetrically bilateral, asymmetrically patrilineal, asymmetrically matrilineal, or a combination of some two of these three" (Murdock 1949:302). To provide some measure of distance in extension, Murdock divided his gradations into a four-point scale ranging from nonextension to minimal to normal to maximal extension throughout the kin group. In the perception of social equivalences, only a single social equalizer of primary importance appeared; namely, the person belonged to the same kin group as the tabooed relative (Murdock 1949:303). The keystone of social identification and acceptance thus lay in an individual's participating membership.

Assuming that functionally adaptive incest rules initially centered in the family and then were extended exogamically by psychological generalization to lineage, sib, and moiety, time must be an important factor in the generalization process. Discrepancies in the distance and direction of exogamic extensions in different societies likewise were a function of changes initiated by alterations in the rules of residence and consequent modifications in social structure (Figure 15-1). But once unilineal or bilateral descent groups were formed, they provided the base for perception of social equivalence and hence a logical location for the extension of exogamic rules.

Matrilineal extension of incest taboos follows inevitably after the introduction of matrilineal descent, patrilineal extension after the establishment of patrilineal descent. As time proceeds, exogamy encompasses first the lineage, then the sib, and ultimately the phratry or moiety. In this manner the unilinear kinsmen of Ego's mother and sister are brought under the exogamous taboos

Complex of factors stimulating
male role dominance

Restructured patricentered
complex

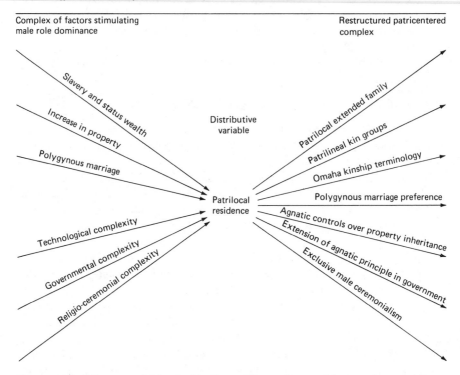

Figure 15-1. Diagram of Murdock's "causal" paradigm with regard to residence.

For Murdock residence acted as a catalytic agent which integrated and filtered a number of factors stimulating, for example, male role dominance. Patrilocal residence, in turn, shaped tendencies toward patrilocal extended families, patrilineal kin groups, and so on. Quite obviously residence cannot explain the trends toward increasing complexity with regard to status, wealth, technology, government, ceremonial, and marriage. That explanation must be sought in antecedent cultural-historical conditions.

in matrilineal societies, and those of Ego's sister and daughter in patrilineal societies. The last phase of unilinear extension consists in generalizing also the father-daughter taboo under matrilineal descent and the mother-son taboo under patrilineal descent. This final step, producing maximal matrilineal or patrilineal extension respectively, is accomplished by applying the rule of exogamy to the father's matrilineal kinsmen under patrilineal descent, in addition to the members of Ego's own unilinear kin group.

Bilateral extension follows the establishment of bilateral kin groups. The mother-son, father-daughter, and brother-sister taboos are extended first throughout the kindred, then ultimately throughout the deme or to all known consanguineal relatives, or even in extreme instances, as among the Quinault, throughout the entire tribe. In the absence of any type of consanguineal kin group, either unilinear or bilateral, there is little tendency to extend primary incest taboos beyond secondary relatives; exogamy in any form is usually completely absent. (Murdock 1949:304–305; compare Radcliffe-Brown 1965i: 66–68 for sociological extension in the interests of "providing a wide-range kinship organization" through accent on the "unity of the sibling group.")

A simple frequency count disclosed the preponderant association of kin groups with a secondary extension of incest rules and the absence of such extensions when consanguineal units were lacking. Murdock (1949:311) concluded that the presence or absence of descent groups, that is, elements of social organization, largely channeled sex behavior and marriage. This finding paralleled what Evans-Pritchard concluded about Nuer lineage solidarity and marriage prescriptions. However, the paths to this common conclusion were not the same. In Evans-Pritchard's view, the extension of marriage rules was an artifact of Nuer strategy to strengthen the range of their social base by using every real and fictive variation of the agnatic theme they could think of. Hence, the extension of marriage rules was a product of social integration, and not vice versa. For Murdock, extension of marriage rules was the product of growth in the complexity of social organization. It was not a product of social strategy, unless one called upon the theory of functional adaptation for survival, which Murdock invoked when attesting to the social advantages of the incest definition. Rather, social complexity was a consequence of a number of factors not very well understood or controlled, but which included economic factors as prime starters. But once an organizational principle, especially descent, was applied to a society, the base existed for extension throughout the whole system following well-known principles of behavioral psychology.

STRUCTURE AND SENTIMENT AND CROSS-COUSIN MARRIAGE

At some point structural explanations settled on a social sentiment as the nuclear element upon which a social order was established and sustained. For Durkheim a social sentiment generated through social interaction created the context for social symbols, which in turn continuously evoked the sentiment and thus perpetuated social action. Radcliffe-Brown offered essentially the same explanation in observing that people ritualized and symbolized critical social needs and relationships. When discussing the role and behavior of the mother's brother in South African tribes, Radcliffe-Brown contrasted the respect accorded the father's kin in a patrilineal society with the relaxed and cooperative relations by which Ego oriented himself to his mother's kin. The warm, tender, and relaxed relations regulating Ego's contacts with his mother's brother and other matrilateral kin suggested to Radcliffe-Brown (1965a:27) that it was a result of the "pattern of behaviour towards the mother, which is developed in the family by reason of the nature of the family group, and its social life."

Radcliffe-Brown's approach to social structure and sentiment accented the role of positive conditioning. In contrast, Homans and Schneider (1955) viewed the sociopsychological states of individuals as conditioned in positive and negative ways according to the nature of social relations. They argued that authority not only engendered respect but also established a measure of social distance between individuals. The absence of authority produced a natural relaxation in relations and invited greater intimacies. Social connections, they argued, followed the line of least emotional distance. Applied to patrilineal and matrilineal orders, one could expect marriage with the mother's brother's daughter to be preferred in the former and marriage with a father's sister's daughter in the latter. In their structuring of positive and negative emotional valences, Homans and Schneider also supported their hypothesis of cross-cousin preference with a Freudian interpretation. In a patrilineal order a male developed an Oedipal syndrome that led him to reject his father and to search for a mother figure, while the daughter rejected the mother in pursuit of a father figure. Out of a selected sample of 33 societies, Homans and Schneider (1955:34) recorded a strong preference for marriage with the mother's brother's daughter in patrilineal societies (22 out of 24), but the results from matrilineal groups were ambiguous in that 5 out of 9 showed a preference for marriage with the father's sister's daughter. In a much larger sample Murdock (1957(59): 687) reported a similar preference, but concluded that the global occurrence of such preference was so minimal that the Homans and Schneider interpretation could not be accepted as final.

The psychological explanation of cross-cousin marriage practices proposed by Homans and Schneider obviously was antithetical to social structural analysis. Needham (1962) criticized them for improper classification, since they had failed to distinguish between mandatory and preferential arrangements. Lévi-Strauss (1969:xxxiii) observed that social structures governed by rules (that is, ideal patterns in culture theory) did not require, nor were they proved or disproved by, frequency counts. Social structures which operated under strict rules were unique as social types and it was sufficient to recognize that the rules were in the foreground of choice. The only proof required was the expectation of a percentage of choices consistent with the ideal specifications that exceeded chance. Such a rule-governed system Lévi-Strauss distinguished as a "mechanical model" or structure. Any grammar could serve as an analogue, but so could the rule-structured social systems described by British social anthropologists.

THE MEANING OF STRUCTURE AND SENTIMENT IN THEORETICAL PERSPECTIVE

The controversy over structure and sentiment, and the variability of processes and contexts used to account for basic features of primitive society, disclosed that ethnologists did not see eye to eye on the reality process. They were still engaged in exploration and were prone to follow and to alternate their choices from a number of theoretical axes that appeared relevant and acceptable to anthropological tradition. The consensus was, as Davenport (1963:198) observed, that Needham's critique had discredited the Homans and Schneider psychological substitute for Lévi-Strauss's structural analysis. However, Needham's analysis did not solve the complexities of the relationship between sentiments and preferred, as against prescriptive, marriage. In the background lurked the long-time bogey of reductionism (Davenport 1963:198). The Homans and Schneider interpretation convinced British social anthropologists that principles of organization were paramount in structuring the social order. They extended their comprehension of structuring by rereading and reprinting French sociological classics which emphasized reciprocities, alliances, and oppositions not normally stressed in their theoretical posture. At the same time they were puzzled by Lévi-Strauss's anchoring of reciprocity to survival needs, as well as his reliance on psychological explanations which they had already cast overboard in rejecting Malinowski's bioculturalism.

Lévi-Strauss's fresh approach to structural explanation through a linguistic and algebraic orientation raised the issue of verification through number. Lévi-Strauss argued that number and sampling could be ignored in a structural context, except possibly to confirm tendencies consistent with structural processes. The conclusion supported the position of American culturalists, who stressed the intrinsic nature of ideal patterns in defining structural regularities, just as British social anthropologists stressed the relation between social principles and structure. There was, however, the issue of factors extrinsic to social structure to which Murdock had referred, more notably the economic. Murdock's analysis clearly recognized factors that induced historical variations and regularities when these factors remained constant. Hence, he concluded that a statistical methodology would discover what historic factors were in constant touch, and what their correlative influence on social structure would be. Murdock thus reintroduced the problem of variation into the reality process. He proposed to solve the problem of structuring by utilizing statistical correlations to uncover the clustering of factors in a random population. Structure could best be viewed as a network of boundary points which set the limits for variation. This set of boundary points would be drawn according to the clustering of occurrences which pointed to regularities beyond chance probability, thereby verifying the relationships postulated according to a principle of reasonable and logical expectations. Lévi-Strauss distinguished two reality processes, the structural and the historical, and opted for the former as basic. Murdock concentrated on the historical and sought to get through to structure by recording regularities in frequencies. In this respect his approach was like that of Boas, despite the emphasis on statistical procedures—a practice Boas avoided with regard to cultural data.

STRUCTURAL RULES, DECISION-MAKING MODELS, AND STATISTICAL MODELS

In their analyses of exogamy, descent, and cross-cousin marriage, Evans-Pritchard, Lévi-Strauss, and Murdock touched on long-standing and unresolved problems: what is the relation between structure and variation, and between evolutionary and historic change? With regard to prescriptive and preferential marriage, Lévi-Strauss (1969:xxxv) offered this opinion:

> Fundamentally, the sole difference between prescriptive marriage and preferential marriage is at the level of the model. It corresponds to the difference which I have since proposed between what I call a "mechanical model" and a "statistical model"; i.e., in one case, a model the elements of which are on the same scale as the things whose relationships it defines: classes, lineages, degrees; while in the other case, the model must be abstracted from significant factors underlying distributions which are apparently regulated in terms of probabilities.

The mechanical model thus converged on structure and the rules by which that structure was established and maintained. The statistical model was a product of variation, or a historic process. In this theoretical perspective Lévi-Strauss (1969:xxxix–xlii) viewed the Crow-Omaha kinship systems as providing a connection between elementary and complex structures. In such transitional systems the element of chance was just as relevant to regularities appearing in marital alliances as in the complex systems of western Europe. Lévi-Strauss implied that structural transitions were initiated by historic variations which became increasingly formalized by circumstances and a limitation of possibilities. However, from his Structuralist posture, Lévi-Strauss, as Murdock and Radcliffe-Brown, was convinced that the laws of social structure had the same tightness of fit as biological laws. Let a "human group . . . proclaim the law of marriage with the mother's brother's daughter . . . [and there follows] a vast cycle of reciprocity between all generations and lineages . . . as harmonious and ineluctable as any physical or biological law, whereas marriage with the father's sister's daughter forces the interruption and reversal of collaborations from generation to generation and from lineage to lineage" (Lévi-Strauss 1969:450).

Traditional African societies generally were showpieces for what Lévi-Strauss called the nonhistorical mechanical, or prescriptive, system. Relations were tied to descent, law, and ritual. The area south of Asia, and eastward into the Pacific islands, offered a different kind of society, where rules of descent did not precisely allocate the individual to a group and assign jural rights and obligations on this basis. To all appearances Ego's placement in an ancestor-based group was a function of factors extrinsic to descent. Such extrinsic factors included land use, inheritance, and the politics of marriage and of prestige. In his study of *Pul Eliya* in Ceylon, Leach (1961:91) concluded that Sinhalese legal rules and their moral order were a function of the pragmatic facts of their ecological environment. In this cultivating economy the one thing that endured the vicissitudes of marriage and inheritance was property. Leach (1961:11) considered that a group of individuals was led to define and maintain a system of consanguine relationships because of their interest in property and its transmission. At any one time any descent system mirrored the marriage patterns strategically entered into with an eye on inheritance, in land and other properties. In the instance of marriage, for example, the decided preference in residence in Pul Eliya was virilocal, but the high proportion of uxorilocal residence (about 40 percent) indicated that land use and inheritance were important considerations. Leach (1961:85) reported that uxorilocal-type marriages involved cases of women who were in line for a land inheritance and males who were not so favored. The steadying force amidst the particulate variation in marriage alliances thus was economic. It produced modalities and structural continuities in descent groups that required no structured system of ideal prescriptions and jural rules for explanation. The preference in marriage for Sinhalese men, nevertheless, was virilocal ("diga" marriage), and where men developed their own land base in newly opened irrigation areas, such marital arrangements accelerated (Leach 1961:84).

His Sinhalese experience demonstrated to Leach (1961:124) that it is a mistake to assume that all social structures are organized by formal rules governing choice. To the contrary, some structures are the product of strategic options exercised by individuals sharing a common interest. Such structuring might be due to the constancy of external forces, as Leach argued, or to the looseness of social structure to which Embree (1950) pointed in the example of Thailand. Here, in contrast with China, Japan, and Vietnam, individualistic behavior was encouraged, and apparently forestalled development of a system of formal rights and duties that structured social action. In ending his work, Leach (1961:306) called upon anthropologists to exhaust all possibilities for explaining culture as a system of pragmatic accommodations to an environmental context before they hauled out metaphysical solutions based on the integrative processes of a normative morality and jural sanctions. Leach thus opted for historical variation which became patterned owing to constancies in the field of forces outside the social structure itself. If he had to choose between the mechanical and statistical models of Lévi-Strauss, Leach preferred the statistical. His position thus was at variance with that of the social Structuralists, but congruent with that of Murdock.

When comparing two rural areas in Ashanti, both commercialized by the cocoa trade, but one more heavily touched by urban influences radiating from Kumasi, Fortes (1963a) found that the life histories of families were not fixated by structural principles alone. Measured by age and sex of family heads and membership, and taken in conjunction with the principle of matrilineal descent, family structure varied according to special circumstances, time, and strains between the formal matrilineal structure and an informal patrilineal structure rooted in custom, not law. Ashanti households headed by males, for example, demonstrated two modalities— one trending toward a perfect patrilocality in residence, the other toward avunculocality. Such modalities appeared to be variants induced by the differential operation of Ashanti principles of organization according to special circumstances. Variations of this order presented serious problems for typing the Ashanti family, both with regard to structure and process.

The futility of blanket terms like "patrilocality" and "matrilocality" in this context is obvious. The use of numerical data has enabled us to see that Ashanti domestic organization is the result of the interaction of a number of fairly precisely defined factors operating both at a given time and over a stretch of time. Granted the dominance of the rule of matrilineal descent and the recognition of paternity in Ashanti law and values, the sex of the household head is the factor of first importance. It determines the main possibilities of the arrangement of kinsfolk in the domestic unit in relation to the polar values of "matricentral" and "patricentral" grouping. The other factors are the tendency to seek a compromise between the opposed ties of marriage and parenthood on the one hand and those of matrilineal kinship on the other; and the ideal that every mature person, especially a man, should have his own household. How these factors interact depends, among other things, on local social conditions and historical circumstances. The domestic arrangements I have described are only possible in long-established, relatively stable capital townships of chiefdoms, where both spouses in every marriage are equally at home. In new villages the ordinary patrilocal household is more common.

This investigation arose out of a consideration of some of Radcliffe-Brown's most recent views on the nature of social structure; that it leads to conclusions not altogether in agreement with his generalizations is a tribute to their significance. Our investigation shows that elementary statistical procedures reduce apparently discrete "types" or "forms" of domestic organization in Ashanti to the differential effects of identical principles in varying local, social contexts. This makes an assessment of the factors underlying the "norms" possible; and it also enables us to relate the "norms" to one another and to the apparent "types" of domestic organization by taking into account the effect of time as an index of growth. "Structure" thus appears as an arrangement of parts brought about by the operation, through a period of time, of principles of social organization which have general validity in a particular society. (Fortes 1963a:83–84)

Fortes' effort had special methodological significance in that he accommodated structural and historical factors when searching for the meaning of the modal structurings of Ashanti households. Female household heads tended to build a membership heavily weighted with matrilineage descendants, and hence correlated closely with the operations of the matrilineal principle. Later maturity was characteristic of household headship, but women had only half the chance of heading households as men. Young brides preferred to live with their own kin, and though wives were inclined during their productive years to live with their husbands, the ties of matrilineal kinship were so strong that almost half of the married women chose to stay with their own kin (Fortes 1963a:78). Thus, it appeared that women in their household affiliations and headships were more sensitive to the operation of structural principles than were men.

The problem of structural and historical processes also was exhibited in efforts to explain participation and group formation by a decision-making model. In the decision model, however, the tendency was to see the action taken and the strategies followed as products flowing out of the application of rules (Goodenough 1961b). Individuals played with kinship rules in Rotuma (Howard 1963) and among the Kwaio (Keesing 1967) to effect strategic marriage arrangements and land transfers. Fluctuations in the population of Kwaio descent groups also affected membership, participation, and the structure of the groups.

> Kwaio descent groups increase in scale and importance, become more thoroughly agnatic in composition and become more localized [with a population increase]. If we observed Kwaio groom's sides under such conditions, they would tend to include mainly members of Ego's descent group. If we observed Kwaio society when population density was low, the groups would more commonly include mainly cognates and often would approach bilateral symmetry. Yet, as the decision model shows, the principles that generate the groups remain the same. (Keesing 1967(6):15)

Thus, Kwaio participation in a descent-group action flowed along rule axes that stressed co-membership in the descent group, childhood associations, local propinquity, and agnation. But then membership in one descent group as against another varied according to personal commitment and frequency of residence changes. Beyond this, individual males used their kin in bilateral extensions to attract clientships and to elevate social reputation through heavy investment in the marriages of kin, near and far.

Like Fortes, Keesing dealt with structural and variational processes within a bounded system and endeavored to assess their respective influences. In the Kwaio situation, Keesing (1967:14) admitted that social structure in the form of "descent groups . . . [is] a sort of epiphenomenon, the statistical outcome of principles about ancestors and property applied under certain circumstances." There was also the sensitive alternation between patrilineal and bilateral structuring as population density varied. In Keesing's observation of Kwaio social structure, individual variation was so great that the rules which governed participation stood out as stabilizers. Hence, a decision model formulated according to the combination and fluctuating influence of the participatory rules was important to the researcher. Yet finally, Keesing (1967:15) admitted that change in the directionality of choice ultimately modified ideology and the rules by which decisions were made. This was tantamount to admitting that people make choices on the basis of historical circumstances. When choices are made consistently on this basis, a tendency is formed. If this tendency persists, a modal variant develops; and when this happens structural alterations follow both in the way people think about their choices and in the way they make them.

The advantage of viewing a social system in a broad historic-structural-ecological context, rather than in the restricted focus of structural principles, was ably presented by Eggan (1950). In treating the western Pueblos, Eggan first endeavored to show how commitment to the lineage principle shaped developments at Hopi, Hano, Zuni, and Acoma. With minor variations, all conformed to a basic type of social structure. The lineage principle succeeded residence as the primary integrater of the kinship structure, following an increase in population which clustered people and aroused interest in passing on the cultural heritage to the succeeding generation (Eggan 1950:133). In the face of modernizing trends that included village schisms, the centrality of the lineage principle still was apparent in the clustering of Hopi matrons and daughters at New Oraibi and the continuation of household tasks on a cooperative basis. However, the presence of married sons or brothers occasionally gave this cluster a bilateral look. Moreover, as men acquired craft skills and entered wage employment, a patrilocal and patrilineal trend in residence and inheritance followed. In the absence of the restrictive ceremonial relationships and obligations that tightened relations among clans and solidified political leadership in traditional villages, the people of New Oraibi broke with tradition and organized themselves under an elected governor and council. In essence, cultural-historical change had introduced ambiguity into the social order, thereby increasing options and accelerating variability.

Eggan's structural analysis of Hopi kinship, which he viewed as the fulcrum of their social order, produced some interesting parallels with Keesing's exposition of the shifting membership of Kwaio groups. Eggan's historic processes were scanned through a patchy record. Yet his study revealed a firmer grasp of the dynamic relations linking structure and variation, and the importance of extrinsic conditions in producing variations leading to an alteration in structure. In the perspective of prehistory, Hopi continuity could be traced to Pueblo IV times, which Eggan (1950:124) dated between 1300 and 1600. During the fourteenth century the size of pueblo villages accelerated, suggesting a relation between a drought in the latter part of the thirteenth century and a retrenchment of dispersed settlements. In Eggan's view, this was an appropriate time for the Hopi to extend the adaptive efficiency and cohesiveness of their matrilocal social order by means of the lineage principle. Such a development paralleled the clustering of agnatic kin, which Keesing noted for the Kwaio as population density increased. Again, as acculturative pressures brought schisms and population dispersal, bilateral and patrilineal groupings competed with the matrilineage. At the time of his description Eggan indicated that the matrilineal principle still dominated in the formation of groups. However, it was evident that the lineage principle alone could not account for variations that appeared in Hopi social structure. While some Hopi variations were viewed as structural variants and elaborations, other structural modifications could be explained only by historic conditions. Similar acculturative modifications had occurred among the Choctaw (Eggan 1937) and Seminole social orders (Spoehr 1947).

The work of Fortes and Eggan indicated an effort by anthropologists to scrutinize specific contexts in the hope of understanding form and variation. They were inclined to grant the importance of factors extrinsic to structure, that is, historic factors, in shaping structure under special circumstances. Lévi-Strauss, who followed a linguistic model, endeavored to freeze relations between structure and variation-as-history in a dialectic process. The dialectic process, in effect, structured history. This is the meaning of the dialectical history charted by historical materialism. Such a process, however, is basically structural and evolutionary in that the relations are between the parts of a structured system. That is, the dialectic model emphasizes immanent processes of change and ignores historic process.

CLASSIFICATION AND THE SOCIAL ORDER

Emic and Etic Orientations to Classification

At any point in the history of a discipline the precision of classification reaches a delicate relation between what is known about a phenomenon and the use of scientific experience to construct an explanatory model. Turning back momentarily to the Developmentalists, it is evident that so long as anthropologists were concerned with identifying social units that described a logical evolution of ideas, there was little practical concern for testing the degree of fit between the investigator's conceptualization and empirical reality. Sensitive regard for the precision of classification came only as anthropologists delved into the social and cultural process in depth and were alerted to the fact that subtle and important differences often were masked by similarities in outer form. This was the argument of culture historicists in challenging the logically constructed archetypal complexes of Developmentalists, for example, totemism.

The purpose and practice of classification did not alter materially with the shift toward culture historicism and social Structuralism. Conceptual types represented a norm which by implication expressed itself as a statistical mode. Concepts such as avunculate, cross-cousin marriage, and matriclan described objective social entities identifiable by a definitive set of behavioral attributes. Such concepts were as real and useful for comparison as concrete objects like arrow points and spear points. Explanations were a different matter. For culture historicist Lowie (1920:177), the surest explanation of elements of social organization was found in the principle that "The history of a people's social organization will vary with its intertribal relations." For social Structuralist Radcliffe-Brown, the reality of his structural principle, the equivalence of siblings, was found, among other things, in symmetrical cross-cousin marriage.

As interest in sociocultural processes deepened, the conviction grew that classifications were of two orders. First, one could classify phenomena and analyze them from the standpoint of an objective observer. Second, one could classify in accordance with the reality principles of the native. The latter was Boas's position with regard to linguistic categories. However, except for linguistics, ethnological and archeological classifications followed a scientific ideal of objectivity which found no real need for the native point of view. With the decline in Structuralism, there was also a tendency to specialize in the varied domains of human behavior (for example, economic anthropology, political anthropology, culture, and personality). Research in depth that accompanied specialization prompted a view that classification based on the subjective processes of the native mind was essential to the collection of valid primary data. This was so for archeologist as well as for ethnologist. Dealing with projectile points and ambiguous ceremonial objects, archeology had long been the proving ground for the niceties of objective classification. There was, however, the problem of coordinating explanation with the historical reality of a people's mental operations.

> In all study of behavior it is essential to distinguish between the traditional or ideal pattern and the actual enactments which result from individual variability in skill, interest, or effectiveness. Variations which never acquire social recognition or meaning beyond their originators are, however, of little historical significance. It is therefore the task of the analyst, working with the variable products of primitive manufacturing techniques, to recover, if possible, the mental patterns which occurred from time to time, and the sources of such changes.
>
> Thus the purpose of a type in archaeology must be to provide an organizational tool which will enable the investigator to group specimens into bodies which have *demonstrable historical meaning in terms of behavior patterns.* Any group which can be labeled a "type" must embrace material which can be shown to consist of individual variations in the execution of a definite constructional idea; likewise, the dividing lines between a series of types must be based upon demonstrable historical factors, not, as is often the case, upon the inclinations of the analyst or the niceties of descriptive orderliness. (Krieger 1944(3):272)

Classifications directed solely to descriptive precision and elegant comparative analysis might give the appearance of being scientific, but might also be useless for historical reconstruction. *Historical meaning* in Krieger's context obviously meant *emic* in Pike's linguistic context. The same issue was raised earlier by Rouse (*Prehistory in Haiti, a Study in Method* 1939) when he emphasized the need for the investigator to so order his analysis within special categories (for example, material, shape, and decoration of pottery) that his resultant types would mirror the directionality of custom.

The emic/etic distinctions enunciated in archeology by contrasting historical and analytical types actually represented separate operations essential to the scientific operation. The emic orientation simply stressed the necessity for proper controls at the particulate level in order that valid primary data could be recovered. The etic orientation was more cross-culturally comparative in approach and sought to employ conceptual constructs useful in developing general propositions. Hence, in archeology Rouse (1970:191) discriminated between historical types which were classified according to their time and geographic occurrence, as against descriptive types which were classified primarily according to their special features. In Rouse's judgment both types were derived from frequency modalities.

In addressing himself to a typology of Latin-American peasantry, Wolf (1955(57):455) also found the concept of history essential to the notion of type. However, Wolf's use of "history" was not quite the same as the archeologists' use of the term "historical" in eliciting the meaning of a classification of artifacts. To be acceptable as types, entities must evidence similarities in the processes of their historic development. This is what Wolf (1955(57):455) meant when he noted,

> The functioning of a particular segment depends on the historical interplay of factors which affect it. This point is especially important where we deal with part-cultures which must adapt their internal organization to changes in the total social field of which they are a part. Integration into a larger sociocultural whole is a historical process. We must be able to place part-cultures on the growth curve of the totality of which they form a part. In building a typology, we must take into account the growth curve of our cultural types.

Insistence that social types were historic products was reminiscent of the culture historicists who believed that acceptance of the identity of forms rested on the comparability of their histories. When comparing closed corporate and open peasant communities in Meso-America and in Central Java, Wolf advanced evidence that proved they were legitimate historic types. Both were historic products of conquest and economic exploitation by a dominant group and illustrated the operation of a principle of socioeconomic polarization.

The taxonomic efforts of archeologists and ethnologists showed that what was emic for one was not necessarily emic for the other. It was understood that the emic varied according to context. Such a situation raised the issue of methodological relativism. One thing taxonomists agreed upon: classification flowed out of the inductive process. If any significance could be attributed to the new emic stress, it would be here.

Variation and Classificatory Ambiguities: Descent, Corporateness, Cognatic Kinship, and Filiation

Whatever can be easily described in concrete terms holds out the possibility of exact control and generalization. This was the case for the study of social groups in anthropology as well as in sociology. Groups had possibilities for precise definitions regarding membership, principles governing assignment and participation, functions, and operant activities measurable in terms of duties and obligations associated with different statuses. Yet, development of a conceptual social inventory in anthropology covering the range of social entities found in primitive societies faced two major problems. The first problem was the limitation of anthropological knowledge at the time a conceptual consolidation was undertaken. As anthropologists successively invaded the different culture regions of the world, their field experience turned up new forms of social organization, or led to new perceptions of the importance of special kinds of social units because of their repeated occurrence. The second problem arose as ethnologists pursued research in depth and tried to uncover the actual workings of social units within particular societies. Confrontation with both problems usually resulted in a proliferation of new terms and challenges to the traditional classification. Thus, structural rules, such as descent, at first appeared to assign and to define relations rigidly. However, introduction of the concepts of cognatic kinship and filiation seriously challenged the validity or usefulness of the descent principle in coping with the problem of groups as corporate entities. In this transmigration from the resolute to the ambiguous, the ethnological experience grew more complex with each added social variation. Under this onslaught of variability, the image of stable and pervasive structure eroded, and the need for an emic or particulate control to effect precise description grew in the ethnological consciousness.

The Ambiguities of Descent. The trend to new insights and classifications began shortly after Murdock's publication of *Social Structure*. This work presented a consolidation and extension of social typologies which drew upon structural interpretations found in cultural historicism and social Structuralism. As Murdock (1949:15) observed, credit for an early determination of structural social principles belonged to Rivers, who defined descent as the assignment of an individual to a group without regard to genealogical relationships. From this vantage point it was possible to determine four rules of descent.

> A rule of descent affiliated an individual at birth with a particular group of relatives with whom he is especially intimate and from whom he can expect certain kinds of services that he cannot demand of non-relatives, or even of other kinsmen. The fundamental rules of descent are only three in number: *patrilineal descent*, which affiliates a person with a group of kinsmen who are related to him through males only; *matrilineal descent*, which assigns him to a group consisting exclusively of relatives through females; and *bilateral descent*, which associates him with a group of very close relatives irrespective of their particular genealogical connection to him. A fourth rule, called *double descent*, combines patrilineal and matrilineal descent by assigning the individual to a group of each type. (Murdock 1949:15)

Murdock's thorough review of social units not only advanced the precision of conventional usages but introduced new discriminations. By combining kinship terminology, descent, residence, social units based on kinship, family types, types of marriage, and extension of exogamic and incest taboos, he demonstrated a clustering of features by which eleven basic types of social organization could be recognized. Some units combined both the principle of descent and of residence. For such localized descent groups (compromise kin group) he proposed the term "clan." This usage differed from current practice in which the term "clan" described a unilineal descent group.

The assignment of type according to a precise structural principle presented a classifier with no serious problem. However, when numbers are introduced to determine whether the basic family of a society is polygynous or monogamous, problems of typing for purposes of comparison arise. Murdock solved the problem by determining that a society must demonstrate 20 percent or more plural marriages if the classification polygynous were to apply. In this case Murdock resorted to an analytic principle to create a classificatory type where a modality seemed appropriate in the interests of comparison.

As to unilineal descent, anthropological experience generally linked the corporate nature of descent groups to exclusive kinship rights and obligations that included access to land and ceremony, as well as legal and marital protections. However, in Polynesia and Micronesia, the clue to understanding the formation of corporate groups was not descent per se but the individual's right to share the land of an ancestor regardless of whether the trace was through the mother's or father's side (Goodenough 1955). The man-land ratio in this Oceanic region was never favorable, and population increases sharpened problems of use inheritance. The Polynesian answer to population-land imbalance was to keep their options open through both paternal and maternal family connections, and to capitalize options through social units according to a pragmatic principle of descent from an original landowning ancestor, or the right of residence. For example, the Gilbertese *oo* included all who had the right to share in land because they were related to a landholding ancestor, either matrilaterally or patrilaterally. As Goodenough (1955(57):80) described the situation:

> Malayo-Polynesian societies characteristically vest land ownership in kin groups. Throughout their history . . . they have had to meet the problem of land distribution in the face of constant fluctuations in kin-group size. One of the simplest possible devices for achieving this end is to keep the land-owning groups nonunilinear. With the *oo* type of group a person has membership in as many *oo* as there are distinct land-owning ancestors of whom he is a lineal descendant. While he can expect little from those *oo* which have become numerically large, he can expect a lot of land from those which have few surviving members. The overlapping memberships inevitable with unrestricted descent groups make them an excellent vehicle for keeping land holding equitably distributed throughout the community.

Goodenough saw the Gilbertese kinship order as basically unstructured by any principle of descent centered in either patrikin or matrikin. Firth (1957), confronting a similar exploitation of land and status advantages within the Maori *hapu*, viewed the capitalization of personal advantage in patrilateral and matrilateral relations as an ambilineal descent arrangement.

At the time the complex bilateralities of Malayo-Polynesian organization came to light, Fortes (1953) uncovered bilateral operations and groupings within African societies formally structured by unilineal descent groups. Fortes saw the relation of parents to children as central to the implicit bilaterality of any kin-organized social order, and he conceptualized this structuring as "filiation." However, in societies possessing unilineal descent, filiation was not expressed in a symmetrical but in a complementary way.

> Since the bilateral family is the focal element in the web of kinship, complementary filiation provides the essential link between a sibling group and the kin of the parent who does not determine descent. So a sibling group is not merely differentiated within a lineage but is further distinguished by reference to its kin ties outside the corporate unit. This structural device allows of degrees of individuation depending on the extent to which filiation on the noncorporate side is elaborated. The [patrilineal] Tiv, for example, recognize five degrees of matrilateral filiation by which a sibling group is linked with lineages other than its own. These and other ties of a similar nature arising out of marriage exchanges result in a complex scheme of individuation for distinguishing both sibling groups and persons within a single lineage. . . . This, of course, is not unique and has long been recognized, as everyone familiar with Australian kinship systems knows. Its more general significance can be brought out however by an example. A Tiv may claim to be living with a particular group of relatives for purely personal reasons of convenience or affection. Investigation shows that he has in fact made a choice of where to live within a strictly limited range of nonlineage kin. What purports to be a voluntary act freely motivated in fact presupposes a structural scheme of individuation. This is one of the instances which show how it is possible and feasible to move from the structural frame of reference to another, here that of the social psychologist, without confusing data and aims. (Fortes 1953(55): 33–34)

Field experience among the patrilineal Tallensi illustrated for Fortes the importance of complementary filiation as a social instrument for accommodating the polarizing effects accompanying assertion of rights over children. This same point had been underscored by Malinowski (1929) in the relation of father to child in matrilineal Trobriand society.

On the surface, the Gilbertese *kainga* illustrated the ambiguities of a descent principle where there were filiative tendencies. The *kainga* resembled a patrilineal descent group in that it comprised all those born and raised within the patrilocal extended family (*wmeenga*), plus those who had moved away in marriage. Unlike the bilateral *oo*, the *kainga* accented affiliation with a set of patrikin who resided together. However, this arrangement was disturbed if a man resided matrilocally. In such instance, neither the man nor a married sister residing patrilocally lost *kainga* membership. However, residence took precedence in the assignment of children to a *kainga*. A married man residing matrilocally had his children assigned to the *kainga* of the mother. Goodenough (1955(57):74–75) argued that the assignment of membership according to residence of parents so weakened the descent principle that at best the *kainga* represented a quasi-patrilineage. This was so in spite of the propensity for patrilocal residence and affiliation with a group of agnates, plus a rule that confined leadership to the male line.

There might be a better explanation of the organization and operations of the *kainga* than through a filiative value principle. Within the Gilbertese social order, as Goodenough (1955(57):74–75) pointed out, there were a number of descent groups—the *oo*, *bwoti*, and *kainga*—whose reason for existence was found in a relation to land and the rights flowing from that relationship. In this circumstance a more reasonable explanation for the complexities by which individuals were plugged into a network of social relations would be that of land inheritance rather than the social principle of parentage.

The distinctions of filiation, ambilineal descent, and nonunilineal kin groups which anthropologists made had one thing in common. Each shifted the outlook on the social order from a structure operating with rigid principles in the assignment of membership, rights, and obligations to an Ego operating within a social system that both offered and denied opportunities to him. This orientation conveyed a more dynamic and flexible quality to primitive social organization. Principles, rights, and duties were there, as Radcliffe-Brown emphasized, but they did not operate like mandatory judicial sentences. Kin were used, deactivated or activated, on demand, and resembled kindreds, that is, an aggregate of individuals sharing a relationship to Ego. Kindreds usually were related by specifying a degree (for example, second, third, or fifth cousins) beyond which the obligations of relationship did not hold. Moreover, they were seldom the same for any two individuals. As Fox (1967:165) observed, "No two people except siblings will have the same kindred, and kindreds will thus endlessly overlap." The ambiguity of kindred membership denied it a corporate quality, yet it was the center for the exercise of rights and obligations. Among the Simboise (Scheffler 1962(1):144), an Ego-based kindred defined the bilateral extension of genealogical relationship within which marriage was forbidden. In Borneo and the Philippines the Iban and Ifugao activated kindreds in headhunting raids, and kindred likewise provided the social axis for determining culpability in the exaction of revenge.

Descent: Role of Intrinsic and Extrinsic Factors. The shift in perspective generated by uncovering cognatic social types in Malaysia and in Polynesia inevitably called for a review of the concept of descent in accounting for the formation of kin groups. The African experience strengthened the interpretation of kin groups as products of a descent principle which assigned the individual to a segment of the society and bound his participation through the exercise of jural rights and obligations. The Oceanic experience suggested that kin relations were exploited to establish groups without the operation of a standardized descent assignment. However, ambiguities surrounding the formation and incorporation of patrilineal groups in the New Guinea highlands indicated that the importance of descent as against economic considerations in the affiliation of kin could not be resolved except through a meticulous analysis of local contexts (see, for example, Barnes 1962; Scheffler 1973:777–780).

In the inevitable debate that followed, three paramount alternatives appeared. First, the concept of descent could be rejected as a point of orientation for understanding the formation of kin groups and their operations in primitive societies. Second, the descent principle could be accepted as operative in forming certain types of kin groups with rigid corporate features. Nondescent, or kinship in a broad way, could be seen as operative with regard to other kinds of kin groups. Third, the principle of descent could be enlarged or generalized to mean nothing more than a way to trace relationship to an ancestor.

The issue of descent underlined the fact that the scientific process is never static, but continually engages in an examination of concepts in order to advance the capacity to define phenomena with precision. In the case of descent, the African experience hardened the anthropological experience, projecting a model of primitive society structured by a kind of constitutional charter. Individuals assumed a position within the structure according to the kinds of status rights and duties conferred upon them through principles intrinsic to the maintenance and operations of the structure. In the interests of structural-functional necessity, rules must be precise and unambiguous. For Radcliffe-Brown a unilineal descent system met the requirements of a precise and efficient social structure. Bilateral organizations, on the other hand, were too ambiguous in their jural assignments; hence Radcliffe-Brown concluded that such must be a rarity in the world ethnographic sample. The African political systems assembled by Fortes and Evans-Pritchard (1962:6) generally were composed of unilineal descent groups which functioned as corporate political units. In contrast, they saw the bilateral family with its ramifying kinship relations as transient and unable to support political integration. The important quality of African lineage systems, as social Structuralists iterated and reiterated, was the legal aspect. The very corporate nature of the lineage meant that all members were legal persons when viewed by the outsider. Thus, any representative of the lineage corporation was considered to speak and act for all (Fortes 1953(55):26). The corporate nature of the lineage, as Fortes (1953(55):27) observed, was found in its continuity through time.

Where the lineage concept is highly developed, the lineage is thought to exist as a perpetual corporation as long as any of its members survive. This . . . means perpetual structural exercise of defined rights, duties, office and social tasks vested in the lineage as a corporate unit. The point is obvious but needs recalling as it throws light on a widespread custom. We often find, in Africa and elsewhere, that a person or descent group is attached to a patrilineal lineage through a female member of the lineage. Then if there is a danger that rights and offices vested in the lineage may lapse through the extinction of the true line of descent, the attached line may by some jural fiction be permitted to assume them. Or again, rather than let property or office go to another lineage by default of proper succession within the owning lineage, a slave may be allowed to succeed. In short, the aim is to preserve the existing scheme of social relations as far as possible.

The uncovering of cognatic organizations, principally in Malaysia and in Polynesia, challenged the view that bilateral orders were rare. Moreover, the shift in perspective accompanying investigation of bilaterality accented factors extrinsic to the social structure. That is, the continuity of corporate groups was not so much a function of immanent principles and processes as it was a product of continuities in external circumstances. Even though individuals sharing in an estate might cluster in a line of descent, pragmatic considerations, usually anchored to a patrimony, were more significant than descent principles in maintaining groups and probably in originating them as well. Such was also the implication of Sahlins' (1961) explanation of the segmentary lineage as an adaptive instrument for territorial expansion.

The intrusion of extrinsic factors into the formation of kin groups and their continuities shifted attention to the nature of groups. The problem of descent inevitably involved a review of the problem of corporateness (see Scheffler 1966). Patrimonies in folk societies commonly involved real estate, and the corporateness of groups usually corresponded with the clustering of members as a residential or localized entity. The corporate perspective thus viewed descent as one of a number of principles upon which stable groups were formed within a kinship context. As noted by Leach (1960:117),

> The notion of a corporation, as derived from Maine, is that an estate comprises a "bundle of rights" over persons and things. At any one time the corporation embraces a number of individuals who share in the assets of the estate according to their particular relative status. Recruitment to such a property-owning corporation may be acquired in a variety of ways, e.g., by purchase, by initiation, or by inheritance. It is the general characteristic of unilineal descent groups that a child automatically inherits corporation membership from one or the other of its recognized parents, but not from both.
>
> Clearly the principle of unilineal descent is a convenient one, but this should not blind us to the fact that several other kinds of "inheritance" are theoretically possible. A system in which all children inherited equal rights from both parents would plainly lead to total confusion, but a system in which children could choose to take particular rights from either the father or the mother (though not from both at once) would not, in principle, lead to a structure any more complex than one of straight unilineal descent. Alternatively, the status might depend not so much upon parentage as on place of residence. Ethnographic examples of both these alternatives have been recorded. The Sinhalese case contains something of both.

If descent were simply one of the principles by which groups were stabilized within a set of kin, it still seemed the natural basis for formalizing the alignment of individuals where kinship was paramount. Indeed, it might be better to consider descent as a pervasive and intrinsic, if latent, principle in all kin-based societies. In addressing himself to the problem of sorting regularities from the variable particulars of kinship entities, Murdock (1960) treated descent as a primary criterion for classification. He also recognized the need for a general term, distinguished from "unilineal," to apply to groups organized by genealogical ties without regard to patrilineal or matrilineal descent and suggested the term "cognatic" (Murdock 1960a:2). The term "cognatic" was best used to designate any type of social system characterized by bilaterality, and on this basis Murdock distinguished bilateral, quasi-unilineal, and ambilineal cognatic subtypes. The bilateral organization relied on kindreds for many of their operations. The quasi-unilineal, through its extended family units, provided a base for lineage-mate organization without formalization of a rule of descent. The ambilineal covered instances where a corporate descent group was functionally important. To designate such an ambilineal descent group, Murdock (1960a:11) suggested Firth's term "ramage." At the same time he eliminated use of "nonunilinear descent groups," recommended by Goodenough (1955), and upgraded Davenport's (1959) term "sept" to describe a bilateral group whose members resided in more than one local community.

> Ramages are the precise functional equivalents of lineages. They are equally consanguineal in composition, and they are equally susceptible to segmentation. Just as the core of a unilocal extended family is called a minimal lineage, so the core of an ambilocal extended family may be termed a minimal ramage. A ramage confined to a ward or similar subdivision of a community may similarly be called a minor ramage, and one co-existent with the community a major ramage. The term "sept" might be retained for a maximal ramage, in parallel to "sib" for a maximal lineage, i.e., for a kin group substantially exceeding the bounds of a single community. Like lineages, ramages occur in both pure or consanguineal and in compromise or localized forms. If the latter are called clans (patrilocal, matrilocal, or avunculocal) in unilineal societies, it would be appropriate in ambilineal societies to designate them as "ambilocal clans." This would, incidentally, return the word clan to its original meaning.

To add substance to his classification Murdock (1960a:13–14) pointed to the clustering of relatively discriminant characteristics associated with each type (see Table 15.1).

The Corporate Nature of Kin Groups. With regard to the aspect of corporateness, Murdock (1960a:5) distinguished three kinds of kin groups in which only small, residentially anchored units qualified as corporate kin groups. Thus, families, lineages, and clans could be declared corporate. Occasional kin groups, such as the Scottish clan, derived their unity from an institutionalized need to assemble and reaffirm commonality in ritual splendor. Circumscriptive kin groups never assembled their members for even occasional get togethers. Rather, they existed solely to establish the extent of the rights and obligations of their members. Sibs in Murdock's definition described a circumscriptive kin group, since they operated simply to define kin boundaries beyond which the rules of exogamy and hospitality did not apply (Murdock 1960a:5).

The restriction of corporateness to a residence criterion, or an assembly

TABLE 15.1 COGNATIC KIN GROUPS AND THEIR DISCRIMINANT FEATURES
(from Murdock 1960a:14)

Structural Feature	Bilateral (Eskimo)	Quasi-unilineal (Carib)	Ambilineal (Polynesian)
Small domestic units	Invariably prominent	Rarely prominent	Rarely prominent
Extended families	Invariably absent	Nearly always present	Usually present
Bilateral kindreds	Usually present	Nearly always absent	Occasionally present
Ambilineal ramages	Usually absent	Invariably absent	Nearly always present
Rule of residence	Always neolocal or ambilocal	Usually unilocal	Nearly always ambilocal
Marriage with first cousins	Often allowed	Allowed with cross cousins	Invariably forbidden
Marriage with second cousins	Usually allowed	Usually allowed	Commonly forbidden
Kinship terms for cousins	Nearly always Eskimo	Nearly always Iroquois	Nearly always Hawaiian
Avuncular terminology	Usually lineal	Usually bifurcate merging	Commonly of generation type

criterion, obviously contradicted the view that corporateness was derived from a constitutional charter. Yet, under common social and legal definition, the idea of corporation stressed the establishment of jural relations among members and the persistence of this legal entity independent of its individual members. It is on the basis of jural rights, derived from a mythological charter, that Hopi justified the predominance of the Bear clan in furnishing chiefs at all major villages and in controlling the Soyal Ceremony (Eggan 1950:64). In the absence of members, a corporation obviously ceases to exist, and at Walpi, where the Bear clan apparently was extinct, the associated Spider clan took over. When Hopi clans took over particular functions of founding clans which had become extinct, they concocted a genealogical mythology to validate their present role. This rationalization of legitimacy testified to common acceptance of the fact that jural-mythological rights are essential to carry out ceremonial and political functions. In West Africa, as Fortes (1953(55):36) observed, the corporate nature of lineages could not be traced solely to their localization in space.

> As I interpret the evidence, local ties are of secondary significance . . . for local ties do not appear to give rise to structural bonds in and of themselves. There must be common political or kinship or economic or ritual interests for structural bonds to emerge. Again spatial dispersion does not immediately put an end to lineage ties or to the ramifying kin ties found in cognatic systems like that of the Lozi. For legal status, property, office and cult act centripetally to hold dispersed lineages together and to bind scattered kindred. This is impor-

tant in the dynamic pattern of lineage organization for it contains within itself the springs of disintegration, at the corporate level of segmentation, at the individual level in the rule of complementary filiation.

Owing to folk mythological charters and assignment of jural rights and obligations in accordance with their provisions, the issue of corporateness could not be resolved solely on the basis of residential unity. There were indeed different kinds of corporateness, with rights that could be exercised on demand, even though members might be dispersed. This was part of Goodenough's message (1961b(63):1343) when he questioned the utility of making unilinearity or its absence central to kin-group theory. With regard to general theory, he thought attention should be directed to the ways natives determined that a person was eligible to participate actively in a social group and held an obligation to participate.

> It is high time ... that we develop a typology that is completely free of statistical and functional considerations, using only structural or formal ones, based on the criteria and principles by which people make membership decisions (as distinct from the kinds of alignments which tend to result from the making of these decisions under a particular set of stable conditions. (Goodenough 1961b(63):1343)

Such a view began with a broad classification comparable to those raised in the distinction of in group and out group, open and closed social systems, and Lévi-Strauss's restricted and generalized exchange. Under an inclusion-exclusion formula, unilinear and nonunilinear descent groups looked alike to Goodenough (1961b(63):1344).

> Personally, I find that unilinear and nonunilinear descent groups which permit active membership in only one at a time and are in this sense mutually exclusive have so many structural and functional possibilities in common as to make it convenient to lump them together as a single type. I would myself extend the terms lineage and sib to cover them all, unilinear or not.

The debate over the question of descent was typical of controversies which plague disciplines when extreme positions are assumed. By the early sixties, when the intellectual duel subsided, anthropologists were readying themselves to approach the study of groups as actional systems. Leach (1961:104) advised the anthropologist not to start out with an abstract concept but rather with a concrete reality, such as a group of people. From there he could proceed to develop an abstract reality, such as a kinship system or a lineage. Scheffler (1966(7):547) recommended that social structures and their operations be viewed in a functional-ecological context before one tried to extract or compare the conceptual principles by which people organized their relationships.

The new empiricism focused on a concern with variation and the histories of such variations. This was exemplified in longitudinal studies of the family and the ways in which families may vary in their formal characteristics according to economic circumstances (see, for example, Smith

1956 on the Guyanese family types). Attention to actional systems challenged the universality of the nuclear family as the functional prerequisite for socialization and continuity. Social units larger than the nuclear family often played a more prominent, if delayed, role in socialization, as the Chinese extended family (Levy and Fallers 1959). According to Adams (1960), the crucial elements of social units, including the nuclear family, were relations, not functions. For the nuclear family, the elemental relations were dyadic: sexual and conjugal, mother and child, and father and child. Recognition of this fact was especially relevant in understanding the matrifocal household types frequent among the Black Caribs of Central America, and of the Caribbean generally.

> If we accept the notion . . . that the basic relational elements of the family are dyadic, and that the nuclear family is a more complex arrangement but one which is probably even less significant temporally than its dyad components, then we are in a position to see women-headed households as alternative or secondary norms rather than forms of disorganization. The assertion that the nuclear family successfully fulfills certain functions is perfectly valid. But the reverse assertion that other social forms can never suitably fulfill these functions is both empirically and theoretically invalid.
>
> The denial of this reverse assertion is also important for our approach to other cultural forms. The search for a fundamental cell or building block of kin organization leads not only to a misplaced emphasis on the nuclear family, but towards a biased approach in the study of the entire family system. (Adams 1960:47)

The new empirical experience thus brought increasing realization that the structure of social units was not captured in an ideal type constructed out of a general theory of need functions. More critical for the organizatonal base was the pattern of interactional relations. Functions varied independently of social networks. In the postwar social experiment of Israel's *kibbutzim*, the nuclear family held neither economic nor educational functions, even though the conjugal relation was legitimatized in ceremony and the genitors of children were identified.

Attention to variation accelerated the search for valid empirical bases for conceptual distinctions, and intensive discourse and reexamination of traditional taxonomies regarding marriage, family, tribe, descent, residence, law, and economics were stimulated. How to relate the particulars of variation to classification was critical, and the issue of constructing a general theory complicated the problem. In the perspective of general theory, there was the temptation to separate structural and variational processes. This was Goodenough's solution in calling for elimination of statistical and need-functional considerations when formulating classificatory terms that would apply in general theory. He viewed the issue of typology as strictly a taxonomic process. However, a typology free of statistical and functional imperatives, as contrasted with one sensitive to such considerations, simply posed the problem of structure and variation in another key. It was the same opposition commonly developed between deductive and inductive operations, and more recently in emic-etic distinctions. Indeed, Goodenough (1970:129) called attention to the problem when discussing the general and the particular with relation to a comparative typology: "So I have come back to etics and emics . . . to the interdependence of the general and the particular . . . [and of] the interdependence of formal and functional considerations in comparative study. . . . In all I have been saying, moreover, I have repeatedly emphasized the importance of our etic concepts for general science." Here Goodenough maintained that the formal aspect of culture (etic) can be used to develop a set of concepts to describe culture objectively without risk of bias or prejudice from the investigator's own cultural experience. He maintained that these formal aspects alone provided the empirical base for cross-cultural comparisons which would eventuate in sound generalizations regarding man and culture universally (Goodenough 1970:129–130).

However, to be truly empirical, the etic or external form must correspond with the emic, or internal design. Given this ideal, the emic base could hardly be attained through a formal analysis of *particular* kinship terminologies, as practiced by Goodenough in order to get at the logic of native mental processes. The whole trend in ethnological thinking since 1940 emphasized a desire to escape the formal analytic straightjacket imposed by the narrow model of social processes under social Structuralist theory. From a methodological standpoint, formal analysis was little different from the social Structuralist positions under attack, since it emphasized the primacy of structural process and relied heavily on deduction. Moreover, at the particulate level, formal analysis did not produce explanations emicized to native clues and mental processes. The very logical elegance of the analysis meant that only a native of exceptional intellectual sophistication would be able to hit upon the same logical construction as the formal analysis. This, of course, was not out of line with the field tactic of relying on a few key or sophisticated informants to produce an ethnographic description. However, this did not seem the best tactic to follow if scientific explanations were to be coordinated with, or emicized to, the modalities and variations of native judgment. There was something about formal analysis which insulated it against the problems of variation and change. Formal analysis projected a rather static conception in which parts moved in a timeless and changeless orbit. Like other theoretical formulations of this order, formal analysis added hypotheses to be tested in the field, rather than final solutions.

A model based on the notion of transformational grammar offered a greater range of choice to the individual and was more sensitive to situational variations. A transformational model had special appeal, since, as in chess, there were ground rules for the production of acceptable events. This prompted Greenberg (1969) to suggest that chess might be the most acceptable model for understanding choice, action, and direction. With such a model, however, there can be no prediction of events from the rules of the game itself, except in a very limited way, and in very special situations. In chess, choices among variational options are linked to factors extrinsic to the rules of the game, including personality dynamics, personal preference in style of play, depth of experience with regard to particular game-shaping openings, knowledge of opponent, and others. One may ask, however, whether scientists who agree on the nature of an effect but disagree on its causal explanation may not be employing different transformational models, or adding or subtracting special rules from the model. Developmentalists, out of their psychological model, emphasized the relation between primitive religious knowledge system and the religious institution as the basic integrater of early society. From his theory of social sentiments and solidarity, Durkheim likewise generated a sacred primitive community. Freud, on the other hand, first generated an Oedipalized community, which then was transformed into a sacra-Oedipal community. From a biopsychic base, Malinowski concluded that social solidarity was a functional requirement of the social order because of the need to exercise control over divisive tendencies in human nature. Beginning with the functional requirements of social living, Radcliffe-Brown likewise focused on solidarity as the ultimate social process. Such differences in starting bases and in explanation, while agreeing on a basic datum, provided examples relevant to formal analysis and to the transformational model of human choice and action.

To achieve the validity and reliability essential to his discipline, the anthropologist must begin with induction. He must not only derive his basic understandings from the experience of his informants but he must also draw them more fully into the process of explaining how things work in native society. If special rules govern the operation of social units, and if principles determine strategies in accommodating social resources to personal ends, the informant is indispensable in their formulation. An informant's perspective would be essential to the operationalizing of research, at least if a decisional and actional model is the key to understanding social and cultural processes. Guemple seemed to capture the anthropological experience in his summary-introduction to the symposium on alliance relationships among the Eskimo. Somehow a full explanation for the flexibility of Eskimo social organization was not reached.

> I think that our inability to explain the system is traceable to the fact that we have not yet taken the native's own implied philosophy sufficiently into account in deciding how his social organization is to be viewed. When that is done, the vast catalogue of minor social strategies under discussion here will be seen to form a coherent plan for social action. (Guemple 1971:8)

The view that the informant be directly involved in the intellectual process of data analysis and in the formulation of principles governing the operations of social units was contrary to the traditional ethnographic approach to fieldwork and the native. The popular view assumed that the native was incapable of grasping the principles guiding social action. The view of informant involvement coincided with a playing down of unconscious processes and the greater emphasis on cognitive processes. Such a position was congenial to an emicized inductive approach. It also was congruent with the view that society and culture existed as a traditional environment which individuals obeyed and manipulated according to their enculturative experiences and personal circumstances. This perspective also coincided with a new emphasis on the direct involvement of those undergoing community development in the processes of planning, organization, and implementation.

SUMMARY

During the thirties social Structuralism became thoroughly entrenched as the theoretical orientation of British social anthropologists. At the same time American cultural anthropologists renewed their interest in social organization, stimulated by the reentry of evolutionary perspective and efforts to synthesize theoretical leads drawn from behavioral psychology, psychoanalysis, functionalism, and culture historicism. French Structuralism also entered a new phase as Lévi-Strauss attempted a synthesis of biopsychic foundations of the processes of classifications, elementary reciprocities necessary to societal relationships, and the dynamics of dialectical oppositions and syncretisms. Concern with reciprocal exchange led to analysis of exchange systems and formulation of a theory of alliance to explain the presence of incest prohibitions and exogamic practices. Analysis of exchange systems also led to distinction of rule-structured contexts (mechanical model) from contexts in which individuals made choices according to a limited number of ranked values, thereby giving rise to a patterning of social relationships and forms (statistical model).

Use of a linguistic model of behavioral processes and of a formal semantic analysis based on the methods of linguists drew French Structuralists and American Culturalists into a common emphasis on psychological processes and their symbolic expressions. French Structuralism and American Culturalism thus converged on a biological and psychological Structuralism, giving attention to universal forms linked to generic response tendencies of human nature. Emphasis on cognitive structure likewise drew French and American Structuralism to mathematical analyses which used statistical procedures and techniques drawn from symbolic logic. The dialectic process and stress on the structuring of exchange systems directed French Structuralism toward use of symbolic logic to understand single systems or a limited number of types, whereas American Culturalism emphasized a statistical approach utilizing cross-cultural comparisons based on a world ethnographic sample.

British social Structuralists maintained a degree of insularity from the French and Americans by emphasizing the primacy of social processes and by attributing any psychological processes embedded in normative behaviors and symbolisms to processes supportive of the social structure. However, British, French, and American theorists shared a common emphasis on a rule-structured or mechanical model of the reality process. They differed on where they put their emphasis. British social anthropologists viewed incest and exogamic rules as instruments for nullifying conflict and intensifying group unity. Individuals used the primary social principles and instruments of their social order to extend their linkages, and in so doing, expanded and intensified solidarity. Murdock's theoretical synthesis relied heavily on the principle of functional necessity to stabilize positive and negative psychological and emotional forces generated by economic and sexual considerations intrinsic to that universal elementary social unit— the nuclear family. By a process of psychological generalization, emotions associated with the elementary structure were extended outward along social axes, giving rise to categories of individuals who could be treated alike because feeling and social distance were coordinate. French Structuralism, on the other hand, located the elementary forms of incest and exogamy in the necessity to exchange food and women, such reciprocity being essential to individual and social survival. Hence, the most elementary form of marital exchange united cross cousins and was based on the elementary division of society into reciprocating givers and receivers.

Each of these Structuralist positions was subject to modification as new evidences challenged structural determinism. The principle of descent and the corporate nature of descent groups commonly accented by social Structuralists were contradicted principally by materials from Polynesia which indicated that economic factors (land use, inheritance rights) induced clusterings of kin which were not true unilineal descent groups. The important element here was the choices individuals made in order to relate themselves advantageously to land and social perquisites, including marriage. Consequently, more attention was given to the way individuals operated within the social order and the importance of bilateral relationships within a social system. This was the meaning of Fortes' attention to complementary filiation and the interest in the kindred and varieties of cognatic kin groups.

Broad issues accompanied these developments in social theory and explanation. A growing awareness that social and cultural systems were not ordered by rules alone opened the door to explanations which involved forces extrinsic to the system—that is, psychological, ecological, and historical processes. At the same time the old issue of structural and variational relations was reopened. The necessity to observe processes and relationships in narrower contexts was more evident, for only then could proper controls be exercised to bring out the relationships of structural-functional, evolutionary, and historic processes.

16

Differentiation
of Economic
Anthropology

INTRODUCTION

Anthropological involvement with economics began with the plotting of economic stages by Developmentalists whose paradigm cited material arts as the prerequisite for releasing the mind to appreciate the finer arts. Material arts were central to the progress of society, since property embodied the fundamental relations that drew men together in a society based on morality, legality, and individuality. Study of the material arts was also useful since it provided a natural yardstick to check the continuity and progress of society.

With the rise of geography, anthropologists learned the utility of plotting culture elements. They noted how pastoralism followed the geography of grasslands, and the presence of cattle in both the classic Asiatic and African areas suggested historic contact. Moreover, natural selection underscored the primacy of adaptation to the geographic environment. Environmentally geared customs assured survival, and, according to the Darwinian social evolutionists Sumner and Keller (1927(1):3–5), "out of the blocks of customs thus evolved and controlled issue all human institutions. Hence the type of society's institutions derives ultimately from the ratio of men to land." However, culture historians were hardly along the way to formulating their own historical determinism when they were forced to engage and refute a geographic determinism. Huntington (1907), Semple (1911), and Taylor (1927) not only explained the uniqueness of cultures according to the challenges and responses induced by variations in environment, but also charted the historic destinies of cultures. To this Kroeber (1939:1) gave the ultimate ethnological reply.

While it is true that cultures are rooted in nature, and can therefore never be completely understood except with reference to that piece of nature in which they occur, they are no more produced by that nature than a plant is produced or caused by the soil in which it is rooted. *The immediate causes of cultural phenomena are other cultural phenomena. At any rate, no anthropologist can assume anything else as his specific working basis.* But this does not prevent the recognition of relations between nature and culture, nor the importance of these relations to the full understanding of culture.

In accenting the historic relations of culture elements, culture historians were handicapped in grasping the significance of economic processes. Their studies of economic processes and ecological relations seemed destined to be submerged by controversy over historic origins. The debate over the origins of Eskimo culture was a classic example, directly generated out of the study of distribution of traits and complexes assembled by Steensby (1916). In the eastern subarctic, man-land relations gave way to the historic problem of aboriginal land tenure. The controversy which began in 1915 (Speck 1915) as to whether land tenure in aboriginal times was communal by band or private by family is still echoing in contemporary ethnological investigation (see Leacock 1954, Hickerson 1967a). Hence, culture-historical contributions to economic and ecological processes were piecemeal, confined to tracing close, but not definitive, correspondences between culture areas and biota (Kroeber 1939). At best they only demonstrated the stimulus value of an adequate habitat in promoting a culture climax (Kroeber 1939). However, Americanists did contribute substance to economics, since their field ethnographies necessarily included an account of habitat, population, settlement pattern, subsistence, seasonal cycle, food preparation, division of labor, craft specialization, property, ownership, and inheritance.

The French Structuralists Mauss and Beuchat (1906), with their studied analysis of Eskimo seasonal ecology and social morphology, entered the ranks of those opposed to geographic determinism. Under the analysis of Mauss and Beuchat the structural-functional adaptation of Eskimo social organization to seasonal exploitation of foods was clear. They noted that geographic influences failed to explain the clustering of Eskimo settlements and implied that seasonal alternations likewise were insufficient to account for the unique qualities of Eskimo organization. On the contrary, only by organizing themselves functionally for an alternating type of exploitation were the Eskimo able to take advantage of seasonal fluctuations in the food supply. However, in citing comparative materials in support of a sociological law, Mauss and Beuchat lamely suggested, as Leacock (1954(56):65) commented, "that all societies show a seasonal variation in their collective activities . . . and that periods of activity and repose alternate in all social life in response to some natural need."

The structural-functional interactional perspective of French and British social anthropologists was better geared to the investigation of economic processes per se than the culture-historical orientation. Yet they too were

diverted from a full consideration of economics by a primary concern with
the structural needs of societies. The French Structuralist Mauss (1954),
in his *Essay on the Gift*, bypassed economic substance in order to prove
the significance of the social principle of reciprocity in primitive societies.
It fell then to Malinowski (1961a), with his stress on culture as an adaptive instrument, to draw attention to the primacy of economic activity and
its functional contribution to the social action of the community. His substantive impact, however, lay in stimulating students to apply his institutional approach to the economic domain, thereby opening up the study of
the economies of primitive societies. The initial involvement of anthropology thus focused on the role of economics as an institution and on the
ways by which economic processes interrelated, implemented, and integrated other institutional processes. Later anthropologists compared the
nature of economic processes in different socioeconomic orders. Much of
the stimulus for such comparison came from the economic historian and
theorist Karl Polanyi. Polanyi offered a basis for comparison in his distinction of reciprocal, redistributional, and market economies, and his work
stirred debate on similarities and differences in the economic behavior of
kin-based and market-oriented societies. Such debate was particularly
relevant to the economic transformation taking place in the developing
nations and stimulated the testing of industrial economic theory with regard
to production, distribution, and consumption. Problems of acculturation
also were involved, as the introduction of the industrial process and market
trade frequently clashed with traditional rhythms of work and incentives
for production. Beyond this, it was apparent that the penetration of Western economic processes set in motion social processes that forecast rapid
and profound alterations in the traditional societies. Recognition of social
and political changes overtaking the emergent nations entering the ecological network of modern industrial economy stirred theoretical speculations about the evolutionary—and revolutionary—transformation of world
societies. The study of economic process expanded to include social and
political processes, their interrelations, causal inputs, and the direction of
structural change, or evolution. Such economic, social, and political developments stimulated a fresh interest in the Marxian interpretation of class
conflict and economic process as the leitmotivs of change in the industrial
world.

As the study of anthropological economics differentiated, it was inevitably drawn into the mainstream of change taking place in the West and
in the world at large, as a consequence of World War II and the decline of
colonialism. The new anthropological experience included participation in
government aid programs designed to enrich the economic base of "traditional" societies and establish a platform for their entrance into the modern
world. Such involvement meant changing the lives of people and raised
moral issues and questions of value. Community development was seen
as an option which native peoples should make and direct. As the older
traditional colonialism faded, the threat of economic colonialism loomed.

Rapid social change, the cry for self-determination, and the political-economic struggles accompanying the jockeying of great powers for supremacy all conspired to make investigation of economic processes a most complex and often frustrating experience in which balance and objectivity were hard to maintain.

THE NATURE AND ROLE OF ECONOMICS
IN PRIMITIVE SOCIETY: MALINOWSKI

Malinowski (1961a) used the Kula exchange of the Trobriands to explode popular conceptions about primitive economic man. However, his primary thrust was to show how the web of economic transactions contributed to Trobriand social solidarity. From a rude instrument of survival the economic institutions had been translated into social instruments. The significance of the Kula exchange lay in its concentration of the "highest and most dramatic expression of the native's conception of value" (Malinowski 1961a:176). To understand the Kula required a grasp of its psychological underpinnings. One thing was certain—the psychology of the Kula would not correlate easily with utilitarian motives. Trobriand life turned around obligations and rights linking lineal, affinal, and collateral kin. The primary principle regulating these and all social relationships was reciprocity, with the exchange of goods and services affirming and reaffirming this primary value. Rather than a crass personal materialism which measured the utility of one exchange against another, Trobriand exchanges measured the value of interpersonal relations; and the web of exchange which had been interwoven in their life revealed the extent to which natives valued the act of giving or receiving for itself alone (Malinowski 1961a:185).

In his analysis of Trobriand reciprocities Malinowski pointed to the nonequivalence of certain exchanges and noted that gifts of equivalent value were characteristic of special relationships, for example, friends. The Kula was a ceremonialized barter in which payment could be deferred, but at all times partners were as bound to receive as to give. Any return made by a partner in the exchange of valuables or food also must be followed by a gift of equal value (Malinowski 1961a:187). There were economic transactions of the order of barter, which Trobrianders distinguished by the term *gimwali*. Here haggling to mutual advantage was the rule and characterized relations between the "industrial communities of the interior, which manufacture on a large scale the wooden dishes, combs, lime pots, armlets and baskets and the agricultural districts of Kiriwina, the fishing communities of the West, and the sailing and trading communities of the South" (Malinowski 1961a:189). Gimwali, however, was denigrated as a form of exchange, and those who hawked their wares were considered inferior. Absent in the gimwali were all ceremony and magic of the Kula.

The tone conveyed by Malinowski throughout his analysis of economics as a social institution was antithetical to any economic determinism (compare White 1959b:240–242). It also questioned Mauss's (1954) view of exchange as dominated by the elementary idea of an indissoluble spiritual affinity between object and person. Wrote Mauss (1954:11–12),

> The pattern of symmetrical and reciprocal rights is not difficult to understand if we realize that it is first and foremost a pattern of spiritual bonds between things which are to some extent parts of persons, and persons and groups that behave in some measure as if they were things.
>
> All these institutions reveal the same kind of social and psychological pattern. Food, women, children, possessions, charms, land, labour, services, religious offices, rank—everything is stuff to be given away and repaid. In perpetual interchange of what we may call spiritual matter, comprising men and things, these elements pass and repass between clans and individuals, ranks, sexes and generations.

Hence, the insistence was on the obligation to receive and to repay. However, like Malinowski, Mauss agreed that exchange in primitive societies was crucial to an understanding of their functioning, in that exchange united a complex of processes—legal, economic, religious, esthetic, and social.

The structural-functional treatment of primitive economics found its most notable and immediate application in followers of Malinowski (for example, Richards 1932, 1939; Firth 1939). In *Land, Labour, and Diet in Northern Rhodesia*, Richards (1939) fashioned a functionally integrated description of Bemba seasonal production, distribution, and consumption within the context of kinship, land tenure, and ritual involving ancestral overlords. Beyond this Richards provided new and informative ethnographic data on Bemba knowledge about soils and their uses, variation in diet according to seasonal productivity, attitudes toward food and food preparation, and family budgeting. Firth (1939:233) offered an exacting description of Tikopian economics, accenting the functional interrelation of Tikopian economic functions.

> It is difficult to conceive what might be the economy of the Tikopia without chiefs. But it is fair to assume that production and consumption of households would be carried on much as at present, that co-operative undertakings such at fish drives, sago extraction, and canoe-building would still take place, as also the elaborate exchanges of goods and initiation, marriage, and mortuary ceremonies. But large-scale assemblies for ritual purposes would be absent, with the recreational facilities they offer; and there would be no ultimate co-ordination of ownership of lands and canoes. There would be no "tribute" to be given to the central authority, but neither would there be any central source of hospitality and economic assistance. Nor would there be any ultimate authority for the adjustment of disputes, no personal rallying point for communal interests, no possibility of checking the emergence of power derived from differential wealth or exploitation by the seizure of the means of production. Moreover the economy would lack the system of co-ordination now provided by the ritual functions of the chiefs, the demarcation of spheres of

interest among them and their precedence. At the present time the chief is a bridge between the kinship structure, the political organization, the ritual, and the economic system; he is the prime human integrating factor in the society. That the co-ordinating value of the chief is a reality to the people is shown by the anxiety which they show when a chief goes off on a voyage.

Ritualization of economic activity in the interests of social and ceremonial purposes was a constant theme of early functional studies of primitive economics. Social anthropological investigation under Radcliffe-Brown had no special economic focus, but in the search for principles of organization, the economy emerged as a suborder integrated by social needs and values (see, for example, Evans-Pritchard 1940 and Wilson (Hunter) 1936, 1963). In viewing economics through the spectrum of value integration, structural-functionalists provided parallels with classic studies of the impact of ideology and value on economic institutions and behavior (for example, Weber 1930; Tawney 1926; Nelson 1969). It also provided linkages with the value-oriented investigations of American culture theorists (for example, Redfield 1941; Kluckhohn, C., and Leighton 1962; Kluckhohn, F., and Strodtbeck 1961). And in their mute grandeur, the monumental architectures of ancient civilizations spoke eloquently for the functional interpretation of economy as the servant, rather than the master, of society.

PRIMITIVE SOCIETY AND SOCIOECONOMIC COMPETITION

In the postwar period, the Oceanic area provided new materials that challenged traditional ethnologic views of descent. The same area again offered data that challenged the kinship and social-value model of economic processes promulgated by Malinowski, Mauss, and Radcliffe-Brown. According to this model, the exchange of goods in primitive societies was so involved in kinship obligations or their extensions (for example, trading partners), that profit was never a serious and dominant motive. Status was seen as an overriding consideration in primitive societies, and control of wealth was a prime instrument in achieving status ends. However, generous distribution of accumulated wealth, not its hoarding, was the key to the wealth-status linkage in primitive societies. Hoarding evoked the accusation of stinginess, a most reprehensible character trait in the simpler societies. The status potlatching of Northwest Coast Indians provided an eloquent example of the fact that possession of wealth was no virtue. Moreover, in economic transactions natives commonly expected individuals of higher status to give more for an item than persons of lesser status. Admittedly, in trade, as in wealth accumulations, items of special value took on the quality of currencies. This was true of the shell monies of northwest California and Melanesia. However, there was a decidedly uneconomic quality to native transactions even with regard to their currencies. For example, on the Micronesian Island of Yap, as Lowie (1947:151) observed,

The natives have shell money but set greater store by limestone wheels from 25 to 75 inches in diameter, the larger ones being made to rest outdoors against house walls of coconut palms. Though used in buying and selling, these curious "banknotes" are mainly for show and social aggrandizement. The islanders are *very* particular about them and do not like to see foreigners so much as touch them. Strangest of all, limestone does not occur in Yap, so the natives are obliged to make a dangerous trip of 240 miles to another island and go to the trouble of loading and unloading the material. All this, however, is cheerfully borne, showing that primitive man is not afraid of work when he is interested.

There was no doubt that natives responded to economic value of sorts, since their kinship services were tied in with economic reciprocities in the form of gifts and services. Moreover, in some wealth-status societies it was evident that the use of wergild for liability in the death of kin also extended to liability for damage to property. Yurok ownership of fishing sites, with rental fees for use by tenants, indicated that productive resources also were defined in terms other than usufruct. It was not hard to find instances where scarcity operated to enhance value. However, natives were so circumscribed by noneconomic prescriptions that transactions based solely on supply and demand were unthinkable. In short, economic transactions based on contract were unknown in primitive societies.

New perspectives on kinship and economics did not penetrate anthropological consciousness until postwar rehabilitation programs drew attention to economic processes. As early as 1930 Mead compared the economic individualism and moral puritanism of the Melanesian Manus with the West. However, her focus on the process of growing up diverted attention from this aspect of Manus life and culture. To the southwest, the Indonesian Alorese likewise were cited as active in market finance, using gongs and drums for extensions of credit and the calling of debts. However, Dubois' (1944) mission was to gather materials useful for a psychoanalytic treatment of culture, and attention to culture-personality linkages left no time for investigating native capitalism. Curiously, in 1888 Benjamin Danks called attention to the paramount importance of shell money in the life of peoples inhabiting New Britain, an island approximately 200 miles southeast of Manus. Less than 200 miles farther south lay the area of the Kula described by Malinowski. Shells were important to the Kula, but they were not used for high finance, as in New Britain. The shell currency of New Britain was loaned at interest, and repayment on time or on demand constituted a powerful incentive, since loss of one's credit rating was as disastrous as in the West. Danks noted how involvement in finance produced a frugal and industrious posture and stimulated a marked sense of proprietary ownership and disposal that extended even to land.

Danks did not report on the influence of kinship on financial transactions of New Britain natives. However, it appears that they conducted their loans and debt recoveries on a contractual basis. This was the point made by Pospisil (1963) regarding the Kapauku of Dutch New Guinea.

Cowrie and shell necklace currencies were used to buy pigs on the hoof in speculative ventures that cycled with expansion of sweet potato gardens for pig feeding and the addition of wives to help in working the gardens and in caring for piglets. While Kapauku transactions were ameliorated in part by kin relationships and custom regulating the timing of debt recovery, kinship did not interfere with high finance. Indeed, the localization of patrilineages meant that sales and loans were more frequent with kin than with strangers. In some ways, the wealth of relations—lineal, collateral, and affinal—was like a bank upon which an individual could draw when expanding economic ventures or when launching a youth's career. When ambition dictated, *tapa*, or fund-raising gatherings, were convoked, with the host providing a feast. At this time debts were called in and loans solicited. *Tapa* also served as public markets, attracting craftsmen who hawked netted work, mats, bowstrings, penis sheaths, rattan, and bamboo water containers, as well as tobacco and meat (Pospisil 1963:332–333).

The mercenary line the Kapauku assumed with regard to property virtually destroyed the notion of a gift. A proprietary right to reclaim on demand what Kapauku classified as "gifts" was never surrendered, even when the recipient was a best friend of the donor. The good taste of custom dictated that the gift should not be demanded until after the death of the recipient; nor could this right be forfeited by the stated wish of the giver. Status was correlated with wealth. Social prestige and an influential command over debtor-followers rose and fell in a cycling of personal gains and losses.

> Because proper investment of credit, especially in pigs, often brings remarkable profit, a marked vertical mobility is assured for many of the Kapauku. Because wealth of an individual, and therefore also his prestige and status, changes with losses and success in pig breeding and trading, the economic as well as political and legal structure of the society is in a constant state of flux. New individuals are elevated to the status of *tonowi* [headman] only to lose their position some years later to younger but always more successful pig breeders and "businessmen." (Pospisil 1963:405)

By dint of a materialistic, manipulative, possessory orientation the Kapauku created an open society in which wealth and status were linked to political influence and power. In this setting individualism was highly prized and set to skills that included sharp bargaining, hoarding of wealth, and speculative investment. Pospisil (1963:401) also reported that embezzlement and theft were quite common. Indeed, the great features of Kapauku society held striking parallels with capitalistic societies, and their *tonowi*, or big men, recalled industrial tycoons whose careers likewise rose and fell according to shrewd investment, key friendships, and luck.

In the African setting of Tanzania, the Turu were much like the Kapauku. Social prestige and personal influence were highly valued, and their achievement was measured by wealth in cattle, women, grain, garden manure, and food. People were paid to help in cultivation and other tasks requiring cooperation. Within the circle of lineage and family kin, the Turu, according to Schneider (1970), were highly competitive and jealous over property rights. Women provided the labor and grain production that could be translated into the most valued currency, cattle. Usufruct in land conveyed to a wife was jealously guarded, and the master of a homestead accommodated his immediate interests to those of his wives when any increase in productivity was at stake. Married sons, whose wives occupied lands given in usufruct by their mother, did not always put the mother's economic needs before their own. In a case witnessed by the ethnographer, a widowed mother was forced to turn some of her stored grain into beer and to pay males from the village to save her crops from damage. Through loans and purchases of cattle and grain, and through marriage, men speculated in a kind of market, rejecting requests for loans from brothers and more distant kin when economic returns were doubtful or when market opportunities beckoned.

Cases like the Kapauku and Turu revealed that primitive kinship was no certain guarantee of a ritualization of economic values in the service of society, or of economic goals limited by kinship reciprocities. Some societies were dominated by kinship reciprocities, but it would be wise to look behind the formal structure and normative specifications. By so doing, Schneider (1970) unmasked the competitiveness of Turu economic practice. It was also evident that wherever a social unit—extended family or lineage—conveyed rights to corporate property, the centrality of economic considerations quieted the insistent demands of kinship. Thus, among the Jie and Turkana (Gulliver 1966) of Uganda and Kenya, respectively, a male formed special bonds with those from whom he could borrow animals when his social needs dictated or when his stock was depleted by epidemics. Starting out in life, a Turkana could expect "Cattle rights . . . in reference to close agnates, close maternal kin (chiefly the mother's brothers), close affines (fathers-, brothers- and sons-in-law) and bond-friends; goat (and sheep) rights exist in reference to other maternal and affinal kin, and to minor bond-friends, and, in Jieland, to clansmen" (Gulliver 1966: 198).

The selective cluster of kinsmen and bond friends with whom a man built up reciprocating animal exchanges constituted an investment in capital upon which he drew when he wished to advance his social career by adding wives and animal wealth. When asked which individuals he valued most, a Turkana listed first cattle-giving associates who enhanced his position by giving him cattle at certain times. While the kin bond provided the axis for requesting economic assistance, the reciprocal use of cattle by kin, according to private need, had the effect of translating kinship into an economic key. Reciprocity was involved—not the soft reciprocity of gift to kin but the hard reciprocity of economic utility. The Turkana followed the practical rule: "If he does not give you stock, you do not give to him. He is not like your mother's brother now" (Gulliver 1966:245).

With such new information men in kinship societies began to look more and more like the prototype of the economic men of the West. The wealth and labor of kin was a mutual fund by which an individual advanced his own career. In such case, reciprocities linking kin were heavily suffused with utilitarian interests, and definitions of kinship obligations would trend toward contract. Behind the façade of kinship lurked a competitive and individualistic economics that hardly sustained the image of primitive communism and social solidarity which Developmentalist and social structural theory had fostered. Primitive communism and social solidarity might hold for simple subsistence societies, but the intrusion of surpluses into kin-based societies seemingly evoked manipulative-competitive tendencies that drove a private utilitarian wedge between the individual and his kin.

Whenever new information surfaces there is danger that the model projected from that data will be taken as ultimate. Considering the careers of Kapauku *tonowi* and their counterparts in Melanesia, it could not be assumed that economic man was everywhere. The Ashanti, Zulu, and Swazi of Africa exemplified societies where private careers were studiously controlled and merged with a corporate destiny. Land and capital essential to productivity and personal-social needs were ceremonialized in the corporate inheritance of ritual powers and symbols regulating fertility, health, prosperity, and protection against outsiders. At every level a hereditary successor, often reinforced by a principle of seniority, exercised a custodial sway over persons and property according to tradition. Such ritualization of authority and function reinforced the corporate nature of the kin group and accented obligations of kinship. For example, the heads of Ashanti matrilineages were charged with the welfare of their members. They had legal authority to settle disputes betweeen lineage members and validated both marriage and divorce. "The heir of a deceased member must be formally approved by the lineage head and his elders, and a widow of any member cannot remarry without their consent" (Fortes 1962a:256). Critical in the *abusua panin*'s lineage function, however, were ritual duties regarding the ancestor shrines, for it was possession of the consecrated stools of his predecessors that validated his status and gave sanction to his decisions.

By the 1960s anthropologists were confronted by two major types of economic systems. One type bore strong resemblances to capitalism in that individuals advanced themselves through speculative investments that required the borrowing and recall of capital. Prices and lending rates were negotiable and fluctuated according to supply and demand. The requirements of high status and social and political influence necessitated capital expenditures in feasts. At the same time, the shrewd striver retained a backlog of material and debt resources that permitted a continuation and expansion of economic ventures. Under such primitive capitalism the assets of kin were paramount, especially of those localized in hamlet or village. Kin provided a first line of economic reliability, but did not constitute a social category entitled to favored economic treatment.

The other system simulated a corporate enterprise. It was commonly chartered under mythological tradition and regulated by decision-making and authority concentrated in the hands of a senior successor who, in turn, was counseled by other senior citizens of the corporation. Basic economic processes were localized under compound heads who served as custodians of corporate wealth and dispensed it to members in accordance with custom. Status, authority, and political influence were fixated by a hereditary succession flowing along a line of descent; hence there was no incentive base for speculative economic ventures. So far as the individual was concerned, the distribution of shares at inheritance provided his basic economic opportunity. Exchange of capital goods characteristically occurred on traditional occasions, and the passage of wealth at the time of marriage was central. The amount and time of payment of traditional items of customary value were negotiated to strike the kind of bargain that reflected the statuses of the families involved. Under such a programmed economic system success did not rest in manipulation of wealth by investment. Rather, success followed investment in social relations. One cultivated key kin so they would honor their obligations to contribute to child, grandchild, or sibling's child on demand.

In their more complex manifestations the corporate organization might possess markets. However, such markets, as in Dahomey (Herskovits 1938b) and West Africa generally, commonly served household needs, and hawking of wares and haggling over price were typical. The important feature of the corporate economy was the way food and other produce surpluses were collected at certain key points in the hierarchical structure, then redistributed except for what was retained for household expenses. This was true both at the level of homestead and at the level of kingship. Ceremonial and ritual occasions commonly mobilized the excess production for redistribution.

Making due allowance for size and added complexity, African states like Dahomey, Ashanti, and Swazi offered striking parallels in their economic organization and processes with other corporate state entities of antiquity (for example, Inca Peru and Babylonia). Controls over surplus and luxury-goods production, along with restrictive controls over trade and market, were characteristic of redistributive economies. In these respects the corporate monarchical states were comparable with corporate socialistic states of the industrial West.

The new perspective regarding primitive economic processes catalyzed debate and research such as what followed the input of new data on kinship. However, the issues joined were not as new as was the novelty of the substance. For example, in accounting for the domain of personal goals and choices operating within the formal structure of Turu society, Schneider (1970) turned to Firth's (1963) distinction of structure and social organization. A discrimination of structure and social organization was analogous to the common recognition of formal and informal organization, ideal and real behavior, unconscious and conscious processes, core and social personality, and evolution and history. In their own way, economic anthropologists took up the fundamental problem of structure and variation. Their immediate experience challenged the traditional kinship model of primitive economics promulgated under Structuralist theory and pointed to the need for in-depth case studies of different kinds of economies within the spectrum of primitive societies. Because of imminent change hanging over the heads of primitive peoples, it was imperative that research be pushed expeditiously. In the meantime, economic anthropologists had before them two contrastive economic models that suggested experience similar to that of students of social organization. The capitalistic and corporate economic systems corresponded to the distinction of open and closed societies, open and closed corporate peasant societies, and restricted and generalized exchange systems. The immediate importance of these common convergences was in a shift in perspective as to the nature of structure and process. Consequently, there was need for new classifications based on a meticulous review of particulars to assure validity in comparisons. The heart of this review of particulars consisted of careful determinations of personal-social networks of interaction.

KINSHIP AND ECONOMIC CHANGE

The winds of change which accompanied European colonial commercialism intensified with industrial expansion during and after World War II. The industrial order encouraged the individual to barter his labor and enterprise for personal success, prestige, and comfort not found in the traditional society. It made no difference whether one looked into Africa, India, Indonesia, or the Americas, the industrial presence moved steadily toward the substitution of private for communal incentives. As early as 1934 Mair (1965:276–277) warned of the rise of economic materialism and individualism among the Baganda.

> What Baganda society has most to fear is not any economic exploitation from without, but the growth among its own members of a spirit of individualistic acquisitiveness in which every man seeks to exploit his neighbour. One can see the signs of it in the younger landlords, who, free from any responsibility towards their tenants, simply regard them as a source of revenue and constantly devise new ways of interpreting the law to their advantage. At present it is only they who are in a position to exploit, and their efforts are kept in check both by government action and by the ample areas of available land. If, indeed, the goal of a land of peasant proprietors was achieved, it might be merely sentimental to regret the passing of the old obligations of mutual aid, and sufficient to look forward to the substitution for them of social services financed by the state.
>
> Yet one cannot help wishing that European teaching did not lay quite so

much emphasis on the advantages to the individual of commercializing his possessions, and that there was more place in it for the growth of a spirit of corporate loyalty. . . . Where the old centre of such loyalty in the chief has gone, the village has ceased to be an entity for any other purpose than that of entry in the land register.

At the outset of new economic opportunities in mines, plantations, and cities of the Congo and of South Africa, the job commonly meant a chance to fulfill kinship obligations with money or exotic products. Bringing money home to ease the hardship of the impecunious life of the village or to add a moment of novelty was expected and frequently honored. Moreover, the depressed social status of Africans in white-dominated centers was more conducive to a shuttling between home base and mine or urban slum than to stable residence. However, once the job was accepted as a way of life, permanent residence in town intensified the separation from kin. City living had its own life-style, and fulfillment of traditional kinship obligations came to be viewed as a burden to be escaped rather than shouldered. Kinship ties were useful when getting located, and modified forms of tribal associations were developed to provide sociability and mutual aid (Little 1957). But the demands of urban-industrial living were counter to kinship, or required new kinds of associations, if products and labor were to be marketed advantageously. In Bamako (Mali) Meillassoux (1968:146) concluded that voluntary associations based on kinship were only superficially connected to basic social problems accompanying urbanization. He forecast that they would lose their members to labor unions, trade associations, and state-dominated parties (Meillassoux 1968:147). Finally, the emergence of an elite oriented to urban principles of organization and educational skills signaled a shift to a class society (Goldthorpe 1955; Mercier 1956; Gutkind 1963; Gluckman 1965; and Lloyd 1966). All this underscored the fact that the city, in concentrating commercial, manufacturing, and administrative operations, constituted a social system in direct contrast with the dispersed rural economy associated with kinship societies.

ECONOMY, ECOLOGY, AND THE PRAGMATICS OF SOCIAL ORGANIZATION

Recognition that kinship obligations were undermined by acculturative economic processes, and discovery of economic competition and contract within kinship groups, suggested that the basic structure of societies was more a pragmatic than a moral order. Such a datum was weighted heavily against those who, like Redfield (1953), charted the subversion of moral folk societies by secular technical orders. The combining of ecological with economic processes seemingly drew the pragmatics of social organization into clear relief. This implied that the determinants of social systems were found in variables external to the system, and which were continuous and constant in their impact. Despite sharing a common cultural ancestry, the

Jie and Turkana offered a good example of tribes divergent in their social arrangements due to differences in ecology. The more inhospitable lands of the Turkana led to a nomadism and dispersal that inhibited formation of stable residential units and larger functional kin groups such as those found among the Jie. At the political and legal level the Jie and Turkana also were contrastive, with these functions among the Turkana dispersed among the agnatic stem familes, the primary subsistence units. Nonetheless, if drought threatened, no Turkana could refuse if a diviner demanded the sacrificial slaughter of an animal according to the will of their high god (Gulliver 1966:263). Indeed, the tribe might force it. The dispersed and individualized cultivation, pig herding, and foraging of the tropical Yaruro also militated against development of a system accenting rank and privilege (Leeds 1969). However, when group interests were involved, the need drew forth a chief comparable to the Roman Cincinnatus. The Turkana and Yaruro demonstrated that dispersed groups do have their corporate moments. However, it was not social sentiments that impelled the renewed dramatization of social togetherness but rather pragmatic considerations linked to economics and ecology.

Other cases indicated that social organization might have had more direct impact on economic and ecological processes than the reverse. In a comparison of two tribal societies side by side within the Kasai River system, Douglas (1971) concluded that the backward economy of the Lele, compared with the Bushong, was due not so much to ecology as to the social order. The Lele habitat betweeen the Loange and Kasai rivers possessed soils that retained less moisture. Vegetation was thinner than in Bushong territory, and the effects of drought were more pronounced. The Bushong cultivated a diversity of plants not found among the Lele, and both in quality and in quantity their diet was more nourishing. The population density of the Bushong also was approximately twice that of the Lele. However, quality of soil and other environmental features were not sufficient to account for Bushong and Lele differences, since in the Congo generally the land could support far greater population density if efficiently utilized. Though disadvantaged, the Lele had not made the best of what they had. Critical to their problem was the way the Lele concentrated the control over economic process in the hands of older men through their institution of polygyny. No provision was made to draw the youth into a continuing and self-fulfilling productivity. In fact, the Lele possessed an unusual proportion of bachelors who "led the good life, of weaving, drinking, and following the manly sports of hunting and warfare, without continuous agricultural responsibilities" (Douglas 1971:79). The polygynous institution had taken away social and economic incentives, and hence the Lele operated at a minimal level of productivity. The perquisites of life came later, usually with inheritance.

Something like a negative feedback appears in the relations of old to young men; the more the old men reserve the girls for themselves, the more the young men are resentful and evasive; the more the young men are refractory, the more the old men insist on their prerogatives. They pick on the most unsatisfactory of the young men, refuse to allot him a wife, refuse him cult membership; the other [sic] note his punishment, and either come to heel or move off to another village. There cannot be an indefinite worsening in their relations because, inevitably, the old men die. Then the young men inherit their widows, and, now not so young, see themselves in sight of polygynous status, to be defended by solidarity of the old.

So we find the Lele, as a result of innumerable personal choices about matters of immediate concern, committed to all the insecurity of feuding villages, and to the frustrations of small-scale political life and ineffective economy. (Douglas 1971:81)

The Lele were not the only historic example of a sociocultural structure directing economic processes to a restricted circulation of wealth, thereby preventing a more diversified and expansive ecological adaptation. The caste-stratified Indian villages, feudalized Latin American communities, and the slave-holding South supplied equally apt illustrations of the restrictive impact on economic diversification and resource exploitation.

That men were not moved solely by utilitarian interest but invested feelings and values in a way of life despite physical and other hardships was a point made by Barth (1961) in a study of nomadic peoples of South Persia. The central fact of Basseri life was the ecologic necessity of migration in order to feed their primary economic stock, sheep and goats. According to the necessities of migration, Basseri social units grew or diminished in size. The migration was also central to their life values. When forced by government policy to settle, they did so. But on the lifting of the ban, they immediately took up their nomadic existence despite the economic burdens involved. However, it was the emotional aspect of the migration that led Barth (1961:153) to suggest that the Basseri were responding in depth to the emotional appeal of the seasonal movement, with its action and related activities, and were not impelled by utilitarian reasons alone. What Barth intuited for the Basseri was well known in the Americas where native people fought desperately to preserve their life ways and their right to be free. In the Plains, the idealized image of the warrior hunter effectively barred easy transition to the life of plough farmer.

In review, economic and ecologic perspectives in the study of society added a pragmatic corrective to the jural-solidarity approach of social Structuralists. The new outlook also added variables that forged a direct link with demography. Inclusion of economic, ecologic, and demographic variables likewise underlined the complexity of sociocultural processes. Moreover, the interactional-adaptive-feedback perspective emphasized a configurated network of interrelations rather than single causal chains. Of interest, too, was the location of vectors important to the social structure outside that structure. Methodologically this meant a convergence with Boas' frequently enunciated position—that the pathway to structure must begin with explanation of variations.

STRUCTURAL-FUNCTIONAL THEORY AND
THE FORMALIST-SUBSTANTIVIST CONTROVERSY

The formalist-substantivist debate which erupted during the sixties represented a clash between structural-functional theorists and those who argued for a more fluid perspective of the economic processes of primitive societies. Curiously, the fluid perspective of substantivists drew a picture of economic process that was just as structured as that of the formalists. In place of a primitive economic man sensitive to kinship reciprocities, formalists substituted an economic man responsive to a maximization of his own ends. The substantivist-formalist controversy simply restated in a new key the old conflict as to whether social considerations predominated in the economic exchanges of the simpler societies or whether men everywhere were alike in a pragmatic pursuit of self-interest by manipulating economic relationships and goods.

Karl Polanyi, an economic historian, supplied the immediate forum for the debate. Applying the structural-functional approach to economic process, Polanyi attempted to formalize differences between market and non-market economies. Wrote Polanyi (1968:307),

> Process and institutions together form the economy. Some students stress the material resources and equipment—the ecology and technology—which make up the process; others, like myself, prefer to point to the institutions through which the economy is organized. Again, in inquiring into the institutions one can choose between values and motives on the one hand and physical operations on the other—either of which can be regarded as linking the social relations with the process. Perhaps because I happen to be more familiar with the institutional and operational aspect of man's livelihood, I prefer to deal with the economy primarily as a matter of organization and to define organization in terms of operations characteristic of the working of the institutions.

Polanyi proposed a classification of economic systems according to their predominant processual principles—reciprocity, redistribution, and market exchange. Reciprocity and redistribution were characteristic of primitive and archaic state economies, respectively, while market exchange was considered a relatively unique and recent economic outgrowth of European industrialization.

The apparent simplicity and generosity-status syndromes of primitive societies early prompted the conviction that primitive economic motives were equally simple and distant from the profit incentives of industrial societies. Moreover, Western concepts should not be applied directly to primitive economic and thought processes (Thurnwald 1932:285). The structural-functional perspective simply solidified the sense of difference commonly attributed to primitive economy by detailing the interrelations of the economic institution with other institutions utilizing economic products and organizing production in uneconomic ways. Yet it was these institutions that wove a pattern of wholeness to which economic processes contributed. This was Firth's message when presenting the *Primitive Eco-*

nomics of the New Zealand Maori (1929). In the Preface Tawney (1929: xv–xvi) commented on the dangers of Western economic fundamentalism and the barriers it created for understanding the complexities of economic behavior in both technologically simple and industrialized societies.

> Civilised peoples are disposed, perhaps, both to underestimate the part played by economic rationalism in primitive society, and to exaggerate that which it plays in their own. Studies such as that contained in the following pages, by correcting the first error, help indirectly to remove the second. Not that Dr. Firth restores to Polynesia the contrary, the whole tendency of his book is to emphasise—it is not only in dealing with the Maori that the emphasis is appropriate—how immensely more complex than is often supposed are the forces that produce the activities commonly described as economic. The life of the Maori, he insists, cannot be explained on the assumption that economic interests and needs have created their social structure. Though modified by them, that structure had biological and social foundations of its own, which fixed the channels along which economic effort should flow and determined the form which it should assume. The economic activities of the Maori were developed, in short, within a framework set by the family, the tribe, the class system, the institution of property, the powers and duties of chiefs. To isolate it from these social institutions is to give a quite abstract and misleading picture even of the economic aspects of Maori society.

The strain in ethnological perspective thus was to discriminate primitive and modern economies as separate types, each supporting a different kind of economic man. At this point in theoretical conceptualization Polanyi came forth with his formulation of economic process and organization, based on structural-functional principles and sensitive to differences disclosed by anthropological materials.

Primitive, Archaic, and Market Economies: Polanyi

Polanyi and associates disclosed their three structural economic types in a series of works that began with *The Great Transformation* (1944; also Polanyi, Arensberg, and Pearson 1957; Polanyi and Rotstein 1966). Exchange in primitive economies was embedded in the reciprocities of kinship. In the economies of archaic states, a centralized government regulated transactions by commanding taxes in services, kind, and archaic money, and then redistributed the collected goods for maintenance of government, temple, social class, and other community functions. At the local level, self-sufficient households prevailed. The market economy was a comparatively recent historic growth and one which was unique to the industrial transformation of Europe during the eighteenth and nineteenth centuries. A market economy, in Polanyi's view, was an integrated system unifying local markets in a vast network of functional exchanges. The rise of a market economy was of great historic importance, since economic processes burst the social and political bonds of the archaic Procrustean bed and achieved an apparent autonomy and self-regulation, which, if not controlled, subordinated all human activity to its own fulfillment.

A market economy is an economic system controlled, regulated, and directed by markets alone; order in the production and distribution of goods is entrusted to this regulating mechanism. An economy of this kind derives from the expectation that human beings behave in such a way as to achieve maximum money gains. It assumes markets in which the supply of goods (including services) available at a definite price will equal the demand at that price. It assumes the presence of money, which functions as purchasing power in the hands of its owners. Production will then be controlled by prices, for the profits of those who direct production will depend upon them; the distribution of the goods also will depend upon prices, for prices form incomes, and it is with the help of these incomes that the goods produced are distributed amongst the members of society. Under these assumptions order in the production and distribution of goods is ensured by prices alone. (Polanyi 1944:68)

There could be no denial of marketing in some primitive and in all archaic-state economies, but these were not part of a self-regulating system. The archaic-state of Dahomey during the height of the slave trade revealed how the crucial indexes of a self-regulating market were not operative.

The role of the exchange pattern in the Dahomean economy reveals a number of unexpected features. While local markets, money, and foreign trade were widely in evidence, exchange as an integrating pattern on an economy-wide scale played scarcely any part in the society. The reason is simple: to play a part, exchange must function through prices that result from market forces; under such conditions production is a function of prices in the markets for consumers' and producers' goods.

In Dahomey none of this applied. Prices were not formed in the market but by agents or bodies external of it. Production was under the control of the monarchy, the sib, and the guild, not of an anonymous competition of individuals or firms directed toward profit made on prices. Thus exchange was barred from developing into an integrating pattern that would structure the economic process. Exchange institutions remained disconnected traits, however vital they might have been within restricted pockets of the economy.

Trade, mainly foreign trade, was institutionally distinct from markets and fell within the state sphere. Neighborhood trade, physically circumscribed by the range of the isolated market, was insignificant in volume and did not grow into middle distance trade. Even less did it merge with the redistributive flow of imports and exports handled by the central power.

The use of money [cowrie shell], while enforced in the local markets, also fell within the control of the state which issued it and where it was vital to the functioning of the redistributive system. Money movements did not add up to "finance" as in the economies where credit played a part in the mobilization of resources. Dahomey was largely an economy "in kind" where even staple finance played a subordinate part.

In the nonstate sphere only a few of the basic requirements of livelihood were tied to the market. In the building of compound walls, the thatching of roofs, the fulfillment of obligations to parents, the cultivation and harvesting of the fields, reciprocal social institutions were at work—the *dokpwe* (labor team), the *so* (craft guild), the *gbe* (mutual aid group), and above all the *sib* (patrilineal lineage society). These allocated the uses of labor and of land, channeled the movements of the economic process, organized production and, mainly acting from outside, set prices in the market. Money and trade were in this way fitted into the redistributive sphere of the state—the taxation system was monetized, the supply of arms and other government imports depended upon a state-organized foreign trade.

While no economy-wide exchange system developed from the markets, cultural creativity found expression in each of the three exchange institutions: In regard to the market, the isolated markets are a singular development. Trade culminated in the port of trade of Whydah, an organ of commercial administration of great elaborateness and efficiency. In the field of money Dahomey produced feats of excellence, rare in the history of currencies. (Polanyi and Rotstein 1966:xxiii–xxv)

The primitive, archaic, and market economies described by Polanyi represented points on a continuum, from a homogeneous (undifferentiated), nonintegrated state to a heterogeneous (differentiated), integrated state (Spencer), or from a mechanical to an organic solidarity or integration, according to Durkheim. The different economies constituted distinct moral orders. As in Redfield's (1941) description of Yucatan, the flow was from a sacralized system of social relationships to a secularized order regulated not by moral imperative but by demands of personal interest. In another sense the primitive and archaic and market-dominated systems presented a contrast of restricted and open societies. Governed by prescriptions that reduced entropy, the primitive and archaic economies approximated Lévi-Strauss's mechanical model while the true market economy had all the earmarks of a statistical model.

It is unfortunate that Polanyi used the terms "primitive" and "archaic" to typify his reciprocating and redistributing systems. He obviously was dealing with ideal types, which, in the attempt to make meaningful discriminations, may be accorded a greater concreteness than they deserve. Emphasizing the discrete nature of each economy type had the disadvantage of rendering their processes incommensurate, whereas it might have been better to apply these transactional modes to all economies in order to discover under what circumstances each might predominate. Thus, in Polanyi's economic analysis there reappeared a flaw not uncommon to the practice of structural-functional analysis—notably, the tendency to arrive at a summative integrative principle or value without due attention to contradictory and even conflictive values and principles of organization.

On the credit side, however, there was a considerable inventory of useful conceptualizations. For one thing, Polanyi's insistence on relating action to context narrowed the definition of what should and should not be included in the meaning of economic. Allocation of scarce means among alternative ends was not called economic unless it was in material and, above all, quantifiable goods. The same held for the economic theory of maximization of wants. As Cancian (1966) pointed out, maximization must be discriminated contextually according to its institutionalization as a norm, or whether such behavior occurred as a common human strategy in the absence of such normative institutionalization. Again, Polanyi's careful attention to the nature and functions of money (payment, standard of value, storage of wealth, means of exchange) clarified the differential exchange circulations found in ancient Babylonia and Dahomey. While a weight of silver served as a standard value in Babylonia, barley was used as the common medium of exchange. For Babylonia as for Dahomey in the eighteenth century, trade was carried on by bartering goods against a standard staple. Under Polanyi's studious analysis the port of trade also was cast in a more comprehensive context, thereby revealing its strategic location and the linkage of two different ecological, economic, and political interactional spheres.

Substantive and Formal Economics

As other structural-functionalists, Polanyi emphasized the empirical basis of his economic analysis. His institutional approach was much like that of Malinowski in that the different kinds of economies operated under distinct charters, personnel, norms, organizations of activities, and ends to be reached.

The heart of the substantivist approach which Polanyi (1968:145) wished to distinguish rested on the empirical investigation of the institutionalized interactions linking man to environment by which a steady flow of material goods for satisfying wants could be assured. Polanyi insisted that economic behavior and process made sense only when placed in proper cultural context. For this reason, as Herskovits (1952:63) observed, anthropologists found economists of an institutional persuasion relevant and congenial partners, since their interests closely paralleled the ethnological position. Formal economics made the mistake of disregarding this institutional context. The error was in narrowing economic functions to a simple allocation of scarce means to alternate ends, thereby reducing all social process to exchanges of a conventional value ultimately determined by the supply-demand operations of an impersonal market. Beyond this, formal economic analysis reduced all men to an economic archetype, the maximizing Everyman.

Behind the facade of the formalist-substantivist controversy were latent problems of the reality process and convergences in thought which have been a part of the anthropological experience (see Cancian 1966; Cook 1968; Dalton 1969). For example, when formalist economic anthropologists formulated general laws regulating the relations among cultural things, their efforts led them to a set of meanings. When they universalized these meanings, their explanations derived from human nature. This was the meaning of the formalist contention that man maximized his ends and means. When determining the elementary forms of social life, Lévi-Strauss turned to human nature to account for their universal distribution. The same strain was evident in the work of cognitive anthropologists. The point about the universality of human nature was made by Malinowski, but he immediately proceeded to locate the organization of this primal biopsychic space in social institutions. All of these positions held one feature in common—they sought the source for their universal culture organizations in universal psychological processes. This was tantamount to resurrecting the ghost of reductionism in relation to social and cultural processes.

In formalist economics culture was a product of man's nature. Human nature accounted not only for the presence of economic activity as a survival phenomenon but also for the way this survival phenomenon was transmuted through the psychological process of maximization. A maximization of ends and means ran like a warp and weft throughout all economic systems, great and small. Maximization was documented daily in the modernization of traditional cultures through technicoeconomic change, as described by Foster 1962, Belshaw 1965, Salisbury 1962, and Nash 1966. Traditional values could not dam the floodtide of maximization released by new economic opportunities. When land was at stake in East Africa, Mair (1957:52) reported that the emotional and religious attitudes regarding land which native tradition fostered consistently gave way in competition with the commercial attitude.

The view of man as a maximizing allocator of ends and means converged on a view growing in the anthropological consciousness—that man was a positive actor in a field of forces that included the social and cultural. This view was congruent with learning theory which accorded a large measure of autonomy to the individual in selecting goals and in mobilizing resources to reach them (Hilgard 1956). It was also in accord with game theory (Von Neumann and Morgenstern 1944), which fostered the view that men universally operate in situations regulated by rules and sanctions, but that these same situations also offer a choice of goals and strategies, as well as a charter of belief that rationalizes the game.

Operating in this intellectual milieu Erasmus (1961) depicted an evolutionary process of change guided by a constant interplay between cognition and motivation. Three basic motivations supplied the impulses for action: "(1) the desire for self-preservation or survival, (2) the desire for sexual gratification, and (3) the desire for prestige, social status, or achievement" (Erasmus 1961:13). However, cognition was the catalytic agent for trial change in that it provided a basis for making decisions and entering into action. The critical domain of cognition lay in predictions of probable outcomes based on frequency interpretations (Erasmus 1961:31). That is, in a population of distributed events, observers noted that action A was related to product B in a large number of instances. People utilizing such knowledge now proceeded on the secure probability that if, say, they used fertilizer A they could expect an increase in yield of the order of B. What held for a fertilizer-yield relationship also would hold in other causal relations.

> The predictive implications of a frequency interpretation give a sense of control to the observer by providing him with a guide to future action. He assumes the existence of a cause and effect relation by which he can act to increase his expectations. A new "control" is a new alternative of action by which people feel that they can increase their expectations of satisfying wants. (Erasmus 1961:32)

Wherever people had the opportunity to test an alternative against a frequency probability, it was Erasmus' (1961:33) experience that they would maximize their expectations, or in economic terms, they would maximize ends and means.

Technology served as a primary testing ground for probable knowledge. Any increase in probable knowledge provided a more secure base for a trial of alternatives as these opened up, either through technical breakthroughs or through introduction from outside. The accumulated probable knowledge constituted a form of capital far more important than the perishable capital of material goods (Erasmus 1961:102). In technically sophisticated societies communication of probable knowledge to the populace was delegated increasingly to experts. Application of technical knowledge to traditional societies to promote change was of a like order, only in this case the expert worked to provide the experience that would allow people to draw their own frequency interpretations. The technicoscientific process of accumulating knowledge evidently served Erasmus as a model. Gradually and progressively man exerted a more secure control over the world he lived in by means of this accumulation of knowledge.

Vital as the accumulation of probable knowledge might be, the way it was used in technical production and in the allocation of surplus was even more critical for the organization of society. Here the social principles of conspicuous consumption, giving, and production were of paramount importance. Economically, simpler primitive societies presented themselves as closed societies where surpluses were accumulated and then distributed as prestige credits through conspicuous giving (Erasmus 1961:113). The ancient stratified Mayan, Mexican, and Peruvian states likewise conformed to the model of a closed society. Ruling elites redistributed some of the surplus products wrung from the enforced labor of commoners, but in large part they operated on the twin principles of conspicuous consumption and ownership (Erasmus 1961:131–134). The redistributive and conspicuous consumption operations of closed societies did not foster specialization which was the hallmark of the open society. Specialization promoted trends toward conspicuous ownership, consumption, and production for exchange effected through conventionalized media, which included money. The contemporary world revealed that specialized-exchange open societies divided themselves into the free or coercive (Erasmus 1961:171). Free open societies accented conspicuous ownership and social advancement through emulation, whereas the coercive open societies (for example, Russia) stressed conspicuous production and applied invidious sanctions to hold individuals in line. Between the closed and open societies lay the underdeveloped countries exhibiting both open and closed features. These were the dual societies. According to Erasmus (1961:177) dual societies

> show great contrasts in wealth and poverty and there is little prosperity in the middle range. The elite is cosmopolitan, educated, specialized in knowledge and skills, and prosperous. Reciprocities with them are more delayed and impersonal and prestige-seeking is more individualistic and acquisitive than among the backward citizens. The latter are illiterate, impoverished in goods and knowledge, and exist primarily by means of unskilled and semiskilled labor. They are only casually or indirectly caught up in the world's industrialization and its infinite expansion of consumption wants and expectations.

In their present situation dual societies made use of the instrument of invidious sanction in order to force an affluent society (for example, the United States) to share more of the benefits of its culture capital.

Erasmus did not consider that a pursuit of prestige and status, both vital to the expansion and evolution of culture capital, meant that men were economic in the classic sense. Indeed, positive controls over the environment effected through specialization increased social interdependency and reciprocity, and negative sanctions developed to contain egoistic self-interest (Erasmus 1961:309). Viewed as exchange systems, the free open society appeared a more adaptive instrument than the coercive society in the creation and accumulation of culture capital. For this reason the coercive open society was doomed to fall behind. Where knowledge is crucial to social advancement, the full potential of the intellectual force of the society must be used and not hampered or misdirected in the interests of special groups (Erasmus 1961:173).

The principle of maximization to which economic materialists, as well as idealists of Erasmus' persuasion, appealed could not account for the specifics of different economics. They were not concerned with the particulars of historic economies. Like the formalist logicians of cognitive anthropology, formalist economists were concerned with general process; that is, with tendencies in the organization of action within the domains of production, distribution, and consumption. This could be elicited only through comparison. One might say that formalists, in contrast with substantivists, were interested in the generic structure of economic process and not the structure of economic species (types of economies). The relation between structure and variation, and the concomitant relation between science and history, thus were a part of the reality staging for the formalist-substantivist debate. Schneider brought this out when criticizing substantivist Dalton for a relativistic and particularist position that was incompatible. with the scientific approach. Schneider (1969(10):91) advised that the "solution to this formalist-substantivist controversy is to stop trying to decide on one or the other approach and recognize that one, the substantive, is essentially historical, and the other, the formalist, is essentially theoretical and scientific. They can exist side by side."

Schneider's recommendation was simply a return to the old-time compartmentalization of the reality problem that had dogged the steps of ethnology from its inception, and which surfaced at every theoretical turn. In point of fact, the trend to a study of human action in context—to get at the emics of behavior—accented a deep concern of anthropologists for understanding the nature of process through particulars. It appeared that formalists ultimately would have to come to grips with the particulars of historic economic types. When this happened, they might find themselves with the unenviable choice of either inserting one psychological trait after another into human nature to account for variable forms of economizing— or of so extending the explanatory range of their principle of maximization that it would be meaningless as explanation. Faculty psychologists tried to account for the specifics of human behavior by coordinating each type of behavior with a specific faculty; but this practice was given up as methodologically unsound. Drawing on the work of ethologists, some were tempted to insert specific drive-product relationships into human behavior. For example, Ardrey (1966:3), in renewing his interest in the human sciences, attributed a territorial specific to man, as to all organisms. He theorized that the pattern of competition between males, commonly believed to be rivalry over females, in reality was an aggressive assertion of control over space and property.

At the start of the century Boas suggested that analysis of the problem of historical variation might be the key to the nature of structure. The virtue of his position lay in the insistence on the induction of generalization from controlled facts. Thus it appeared that the real solution was possible only when the relation of variation to structure, and consequently the relation of historic and evolutionary processes, were admitted as components of a unitary problem (Goldschmidt 1966). The differentiation of specializations revealed a primary concern on the part of anthropologists to deal with on-going process in live contexts. The product of such efforts was intermediate-range theoretical constructs out of which more general theory might be formulated. To these purposes a unitary reality view was more congenial than a compartmentalist view.

THE THIRD WORLD AND ECONOMIC DETERMINISM

The unusually rapid political, social, and economic changes taking place after World War II could not but influence ethnologists in their choice of problems to be researched. Peasant communities, owing to their relations with urban centers of change, came to occupy a special place in the design for economic anthropology. According to Dalton (1971a:32–33; compare Bohannan and Dalton 1962; Nash 1966; Potter, Diaz, and Foster 1967), "Economic anthropology considers the structure and performance of tribal and peasant village economies under pre-colonial, colonial, and post-colonial conditions." The study of traditional and modernizing economies was complementary, providing insights with regard to both structural process and change.

Primitive and peasant economies undergoing transformation offered unparalleled opportunities to test the significance of different institutions for change and stability. Governments, both colonial and postcolonial, stimulated cash cropping and introduced money for exchange and tax services. Thus, economic factors appeared destined to play a leading role in the future of traditional societies. The new relationships offered by cash marketing were conducive to a new sense of personal independence and provided a base for renegotiating traditional service relations. According to Nash (1966:100), static economic systems characterized by religious and hierarchical structures dissolved before the compelling force of money or opportunity for economic gain. Factor analysis of lineality, sex dominance, level of technology, and "norm-sending institutions" (Gouldner and Peterson 1962:59–60) revealed technology to be a better predictor of variance, although norm-sending institutions ran a close second. Moreover, Gouldner and Peterson found that a technological cluster or complex was more tightly integrated functionally than a norm-sending complex. Obviously, a technological cluster is more tightly integrated, since its features are shaped in such a way that they work together and alter their relations as circumstances dictate. If the parts are unable to vary and to accommodate their relations to circumstances, the system doesn't work properly or breaks down. In the case of norm-sending or value institutions, a value principle may be very pervasive, but individual contradictions in human behavior do not produce such a direct or drastic effect as does the malfunctioning of a machine.

A profound sense of self-awareness and a reappraisal of man's place in society were important products of the accelerating changes overtaking peasants and emergent nations. An important effect of this reappraisal was a livening of the search for ways to equalize relations with those who traditionally occupied prominent social positions and controlled economic production and political power. What this new awareness conveyed to the Italian peasants of "*la miseria*" (Friedman 1953), as well as to colonialized Ghana and Nigeria, was a growing sense of their own historicity. They began to see themselves as taking part in shaping their own destinies rather than passively submitting to choices made by others. On the eve of the winds of change in colonial Africa the acculturated elites pressed for modernization. At the root of their demands for greater modernization, according to Robinson (1955:312; Geertz 1963:108), was the compelling urge to achieve for Africans, as individuals and as nationals, a status equal with other peoples and countries of the world.

The deepening and exhilarating sense of emergent involvement exhibited by Third World populations communicated a new perspective with regard to tradition. Classical structural-functional description and interpretation of the ceremonious ritualization of interdependent elements designed to produce social solidarity now seemed anachronistic to some ethnologists. Ethnological moderns were convinced they had arrived in the field at a time when economic forces, in combination with class and nationalistic aspirations, were about to preside over the disintegration of static exploitative social systems. In the vast perspective of the civilizational process, the so-called underdeveloped peoples were seen as a backward backwash of European mercantilism and industrialization. They exhibited the "result of a process of historical incorporation that exploits in order to accelerate the development of other areas" (Ribeiro 1968:108, 1970; see also Wolf 1959; Gibson 1964; Geertz 1966; Worsley 1970). The treadmill of poverty to which the industrial and feudalized agricultural societies had consigned dispossessed minorities evoked a strong moral commitment to intervene with something more than objective description. Scientific advice and action were deemed necessary to influence social policy (Valentine 1968; Frank 1970). Irrepressible and irreversible structural modifications in traditional cultures, resulting from contact with the industrial West, rendered obsolete any theory of cultural continuity with concomitant persistence of indigenous personality features. The modern Ojibwa, for whom persistences in personality characteristics was claimed, were largely the product of their economic marginality, according to James (1970). In such perspective anyone who tried to revitalize Ojibwa culture would be practicing a romantic deception, since there was no Ojibwa culture residue to be revitalized. James's challenge of the theory of cultural persistence raised a common problem in the interpretation of change situations. That is, to what extent is the present form a product of persistence, or to what extent are outwardly similar but intrinsically unlike forms supported by features traceable to changed historical circumstances? There was also the issue as to how tradition could be used to further future developments.

The new economic analysis of poverty groups stressed their marginal participation in a vast interactional system—regional, national, and international—with social and political dominance controlling the means of production. Where the exchange of personal services in the form of productive skills mediated physical survival and social position, economic participation commensurate with a viable life-style required political guarantees. Though seemingly more acute in industrial society, it was equally evident that institutional arrangements in societies organized by kinship or by feudalization (for example, caste in India) likewise regulated access to economic products. In short, economic control and political power were interrelated.

The perspective on change gained from study of the emergent nations did not always confirm the omnipresent determinism of the economic variable. Both economic and noneconomic variables were relevant to the change process, and their relative importance varied according to historical-cultural circumstances. According to Nash (1966:149), there was solid evidence that the variables directing social change, and their relative inputs, varied in accordance with the level of social and economic development.

When summarizing the process of modernization in Southeast Asia, Nash (1966:151–152) listed phases in which the dominance of noneconomic variables was manifest in the restructuring process.

    1. *Metropolitan reaction:* . . . The idiom of politics is anticolonial and pro-socialist, and stresses the rebirth of great cultural traditions. . . . In its extreme form the phase can move into xenophobia; milder manifestations include indigenization of the economy, nationalization, and monument building.

    2. *Politicalization and oligarchic reorganization:* The elite attempts to make political adherents out of the mass, and political allegiances become important marks of belonging to the new nation. Political relations can, in this phase, become the major bases of even local village and town integration. . . . This is a period of political and cultural consolidation, not of economic development. . . .

    3. *The undertaking of educationally and economically feasible tasks:* If the society passes successfully through its period of political and cultural consolidation, it can put less energy into monument building, political control, and symbolic display, and can begin to undertake tasks that it has the skill to execute; agrarian help and reform, technical education, joint ventures between entrepreneurs and government, and limited inflow of foreigners as the nation moves again into international trade.

    4. *Class reformulation and cultural crystallization:* If the tasks undertaken are successfully prosecuted, they lead to cumulative change, greater efforts, and greater social heterogeneity. The class structure and political legitimacy are reworked in favor of the producers and goal attainers. This can be a period of renewed strife. Cultural crystallization includes the emergence of a new set of standards and ideals, often embodied in a political or religious ideology.

    5. *Institutional adaptation:* Since the economy and the polity are the leading sectors in development, the other institutions tend toward adjustment of the pressures generated by behavior in the economic and political spheres. The family, the expressive activities, religion, and education are modified to fit better with the now highly differentiated economy and polity.

What this sequence demonstrated was the necessity to first capture men's minds with ideas and with social pressures. Otherwise, the cooperation necessary for institutional modification was lacking. At Ica in Peru the shifting sinews of political power, in the judgment of Hammel (1969:108–109), owed more to the spread of ideology than to immediate changes in the national economy.

In the last two decades . . . organized and self-conscious foci of power have been developing at . . . subordinate points [in the sociopolitical order]. Many of them are labor unions; others are political parties such as the Communist or APRA, which are popular with the lower and lower middle classes. For the first time, the balance of political power includes not only competing factions of high status (such as *caciques* against Spaniards or creoles against peninsulars in the colonial times) but also groups whose humble position in the overall social scale is recognized even by themselves. The rise of proletarian groups to political eminence is in some ways a result of indigenous economic changes but was directly stimulated by extra-Peruvian developments. The active source of the change is the same intellectual and moral ferment that led to the Russian revolution and to social and labor reform measures in the rest of Europe and the United States, communicated to the Peruvian lower classes by European-oriented liberals such as Gonzalez Prada, Mariategui, and Haya de la Torre.

Lima, of course, was the center of this intellectual diffusion. However, this nationalizing of intellectual culture in Peru was paralleled by centralizing tendencies that spread a national bureaucratic glaze over the land and removed from provincials the power of regulating water rights and of collecting taxes. A similar political centralization was observable in the modernization of Indonesia, India, China, and lesser states in Africa and Asia. Interestingly, it also had characterized the rise of national monarchies in Europe during the later Renaissance.

In the historic circumstances of Tzintzuntzan, described by Foster, ideological change preceded the rise of a secularized status order. According to Foster (1967:314–320), decline in a status ladder of prestigious religious obligation was very perceptible in 1925. It was exacerbated by the struggle for power between Church and state, when priests for three years left their churches and in 1929 refused to say mass. However, the quest for material symbols of status did not become important until 1945 when *braceros* began to form a new socioeconomic group. Despite these extensive changes, the *mayordomia* system still provided passage to meaningful community status, not only for traditionalists but also for new entrepreneurs practicing the manufacture and merchandising of pottery and wood products. If Foster was correct, changes in the social order traceable to altered political and religious belief had preceded any serious input of economic factors by nearly a generation.

Everything in the cultural-historical experience of the emerging countries of Africa and Asia confirmed the erosive modification of traditional-ritualized social orders, with a consequent rise in secular materialism due to economic forces. However, the modernizing of emergent nations was not the product of a simple and gradual expansion of economic process within the institutionalized order. In fact, economic factors shared the causal space of change with a complex of variables that included shifts in knowledge capital and values, as well as in social structure and political authority. Economy, social structure, politics, and an ideology expressive of valued life goals were inextricably joined in an interacting nexus. In this context changes in ideology and political control were critical antecedents for creating the social milieu whereby economic change could take place. Such was the meaning of the independence movements erupting in colonial domains, whether in India or in Africa. The turbulent course of countries freed from colonial control was manifested in coup d'états and the building of monolithic centralized parties. The vital importance of the political process during this period of transition was underscored.

That change could not proceed simply according to a model of rationalized economic process was amply proved in India. The sacred cattle, in the view of secular experts, were far too plentiful for the land to support. Moreover, cattle not used for breeding purposes were neglected, and consequently the land was overrun with ill-fed and aimless beasts. A determination was made that, through slaughter and sale of their hides, the cattle population could be reduced to proper size and the government could realize an export income. However, widespread rioting forced the government to abandon this plan and close down the slaughterhouses. Economic change apparently required a psychic readiness for acceptance, and unless the government was willing to bring the full weight of its repressive forces to bear, no change would take place in the absence of such readiness.

MARX AND CONTEMPORARY ANTHROPOLOGY

The Relevance of Marx for Preindustrial Anthropology

Anthropologists who considered anthropology the science of preindustrial man found Marxism irrelevant to their research for a number of reasons. In point of theory, anthropologists of evolutionary persuasion had their own dialectic, forged of biological, psychological, and social forces, which was in opposition to the metaphysical dialectic of economic contradiction and class conflict proclaimed by Marx and Engels. Later Structuralists were too involved in establishing their own social and cultural determinism to accept a determinism of the social and cultural by economic forces. Anthropological emphasis on structural-functional relationships produced a sense of structured continuity through gradual and cumulative modification, while Marx and Engels marked their evolutionary steps with revolutionary saltations. Moreover, anthropological preoccupation with the structured operations of societies and with documentation of the growth of cultures through historic contact made them regard any theory of social evolutionary stages as unscientific metaphysical doctrine. This empiricism was further supported by the necessity to get scientific descriptions of the cultures of long-neglected societies, which, until their recent discovery by the West, had occupied the quiet eddies of history. There were many cases of rapid change and of occasional destruction of whole cultures which followed European trade, conquest, and settlement. Urgent fieldwork was required to insure that the traditional beliefs and customs of such peoples were recorded and their place in history preserved.

The theoretical orientation and fieldwork involvement of the emergent anthropological discipline provided no points of real contact with a theory of human society based on a dynamic evolution of productive systems and class antagonisms. Classes, let alone class conflicts, were not a fundamental part of the preindustrial world of hunters, fishers, seed gatherers, garden cultivators, and nomadic pastoralists.

Preindustrial societies centered their life ways in social institutions that contrasted with civilized societies and hence were incomparable. Replication of tradition and ritualized reinforcement of social values anchored to kinship relationships characterized preindustrial societies rather than conflict and change. For those governed by tradition, changes were so gradual as to go largely undetected. Marx and Engels themselves admitted that the simpler economic systems, devoid of a real class base, stood outside their dialectic process. The dogma that "The history of all hitherto existing society is the history of class struggles" (Marx and Engels 1848, in 1968:35) struck anthropologists of the day as a metaphysical social doctrine devoid of scientifically proved fact. Moreover, Marx and Engels consistently interspersed their social, economic, and political analyses with calls for political action by the proletariat. Their repetitious assertion that an immanent principle of progressive contradiction accounted for change and ultimate dissolution of social systems, coupled with their predictions of the collapse of capitalism, only added to the skepticism. As delineated by Marx and Engels, historical materialism and its dialectic process appeared more a strategy for change than a measured observation of change processes. Moreover, Marx and Engels compounded the errors of the materialistic dialectic by accepting social evolutionary sequences which scientific anthropologists had discredited. For example, Marx and Engels held to the speculative notion of a primordial promiscuity and supported Bachofen's thesis of a primitive matriarchal stage which was superseded by a more advanced patriarchal organization. The matriarchal-patriarchal sequence was quite congenial to the dialectic process, since men were visualized as ultimately revolting under the matriarchal yoke and seizing the reins of power. In a broad interpretation of process, any supercession of one form by another on functional grounds could be viewed as dialectical. Species evolution, historical conquests of one group of culture bearers by the bearers of a different culture, ecological competitions of plants and animals, as well as the antipathetic relations between interest groups and the sexes—all could be seen as manifestations of a process of basic opposition and transformation.

The anthropological experience did not find relevance in Marxism until the field entered a time of active differentiation of specializations. At this time the discipline was not only infused with fresh perspectives but also the overriding concern for static systemic processes and structural continuities was changing. This reorientation coincided with empirical observations of the internal transformations of colonialized peoples as they attained independence and reorganized their societies politically and socially for the purpose of industrializing their economies. Moreover, postwar communization of East Europe and of China was coupled with active dissemination of Communist ideology and party organization among former colonialized peoples in South and Southeast Asia, Africa, and the economically backward "republics" of Latin America. This provided a datum of social change that could not be ignored.

The Marxist Theory of History and of Process

Basically, Marxism is a philosophy of history which details the purposive development of man as a social being. Like any theory with staying power, the strength of Marxism lies in its comprehensive overview, methodology, and pragmatics or applicability to human ends. Generally speaking, its qualities are shared by all great religious traditions and philosophies, as well as by science. And, like any historically significant theory, Marxism, when viewed in the context of communications theory, is beset with ambiguities which make for variable interpretations. Yet, at the same time, the system possesses a core redundancy which gets the primary message across.

Marxist ambiguities center in the accommodation of structural processes and variational processes. Specifically, Marxism, like Developmentalism, has difficulty in accounting for, or ignores, the relation between evolutionary and historic processes. Such difficulty can be seen in the controversy over the structuring of the historic-social processes by economic conditions (economic determinism). There is some question as to whether Marx and Engels followed a unilineal evolutionary model in describing their succession of socioeconomic and political types. However, like any evolutionary model, Marxism describes a core development or general evolution to which individual variations converge at critical stages. The successive structural reorganizations mark the point of convergence of the historical variations, and hence a unilineal succession is produced.

Sources of Marxism

According to Lenin (1913, in Marx 1932:xxi), Marxism drew upon the best that German philosophy, English political economy, and French socialism were able to muster in the nineteenth century. The basic philosophy of history was that of Hegel, the political economy that of Ricardo and Smith, and the socialist doctrines were derived largely from the revolutionary course of French society as it moved toward industrialization. There was, however, a fourth component—the materialistic orientation. Science advanced on a materialistic view of the world and of process, and Marx and Engels, in combating philosophical idealism, took pride in the fact that their system was scientific. They had discovered not only the scientific way to study society but also how to predict the direction and shapes through which society must proceed according to the scientifically grounded dialectical process. As Engels (1968a:413) noted,

> Nature is the proof of dialectics, and it must be said for modern science that it has furnished this proof with very rich materials increasing daily, and thus has shown that, in the last resort, Nature works dialectically and not metaphysically; that she does not move in the eternal oneness of a perpetually recurring circle, but goes through a real historical evolution. In this connection Darwin must be named before all others. He dealt the metaphysical conception

of Nature the heaviest blow by his proof that all organic things, plants, animals, and man himself, are the products of a process of evolution going on through millions of years.

In the context of their scientific materialism, or historical materialism, as they preferred to call it, Marx and Engels faced a dialectic confrontation with their idealist mentor Hegel. It was Hegel who drew all change processes into one mode—the dialectic. He argued that human thought systematically began with an affirmative, which then generated its opposite negative, and ended by transforming itself into another synthetic affirmative. Then the process began anew. Any system thus could be seen as inevitably generating its opposite number and of being transformed by this negative. For the first time, according to Engels (1968a:413), "the whole world, natural, historical, intellectual, is represented as a process, i.e., as in constant action, change, transformation, development, and the attempt is made to trace out the internal connection that makes a continuous whole of all this movement and development."

The main drawback to taking over Hegel's dialectic of history and nature was his philosophical idealism. Furthermore, Hegel gave first place to God. Man was God's work, and history instructed man through a mental dialectic to reach out to an ultimate human freedom that encompassed both mind and society. But with Hegel's conceptual breakthrough, as Engels (1968a:416) affirmed, socialism assumed the form of a living and inevitable historical reality, for "socialism was no longer an accidental discovery of this or that ingenious brain, but the necessary outcome of the struggle between two historically developed classes—the proletariat and the bourgeoisie."

It is interesting that Marx and Engels arrived at their dialectical confrontation with Hegel by practicing the dialectic. As Engels (1968a:414–415) observed,

The Hegelian system . . . was suffering . . . from an internal and incurable contradiction. Upon the one hand, its essential proposition was the conception that human history is a process of evolution, which, by its very nature, cannot find its intellectual final term in the discovery of any so-called absolute truth. But, on the other hand, it laid claim to being the very essence of this absolute truth [the idea of the always existent spiritualization of God's thought]. A system of natural and historical knowledge, embracing everything and final for all time, is a contradiction to the fundamental law of dialectic reasoning. . . .

The perception of the fundamental contradiction in German idealism led necessarily back to materialism, but, *nota bene*, not to the simply metaphysical, exclusively mechanical materialism of the eighteenth century. Old materialism looked upon all previous history as a crude heap of irrationality and violence; modern materialism sees in it the process of evolution of humanity and aims at discovering the laws thereof. . . . Modern materialism embraces the more recent discoveries of natural science, according to which Nature also has its history in time, the celestial bodies, like the organic species that, under favourable conditions people them, being born and perishing.

From British political economists Marx and Engels absorbed a structural-functional perspective focused on the production, distribution, and consumption of commodities. Adam Smith, and more particularly David Ricardo, inspired an analytic attack on the nature of society from the standpoint of economic operations and systemic relations. Ricardo provided Marx with a hardheaded pragmatism in his approach to economic processes and his basic assumption that the exchange value of any commodity was based on the amount of labor put into its production. Labor, with all its ramifications, stood at the center of the Marxian economic analysis.

The socialistic philosophy accompanying the rise of industrialism in Europe supplied Marx and Engels with their focus on the relations of classes and what they put into and took out of the social economy. The Utopian socialism of Robert Owen, based on humanistic idealism, had no appeal for these pragmatists. Owen's practical successes in Manchester, and more especially in New Lanark, Scotland, were admirable. However, when Owen proposed Socialistic-type solutions to economic issues related to agricultural and factory production, ideas on social reform and criticisms of religion brought him into disfavor with the employers and government. Marx and Engels used the example of Owen to show that scientific socialism required a realistic base of theory as well as method if it were to succeed. They argued that altruistic reforms were not accomplished by working within the system; it was necessary to completely transform the system. It was essential, therefore, to train workers in insurrectional and political strategies, provide inspired and dedicated leaders, and organize workers into fighting battalions for the war against the oppressive bourgeoisie. Only then could the workers attain the political power necessary for the reorganization of productive relationships and the establishment of a society that rewarded individuals according to their needs with work suited to their capabilities. What the workers required was a political manual of field operations. In a letter to the League in 1850, Marx (1932:355–367) outlined the strategy of expedient alliances with enemies whenever necessary to advance their cause. However, workers should never integrate with their enemy allies and should constantly draw upon their own programs to insure their political independence and public visibility. Disruptive tactics aimed at embarrassing their political allies should be used to weaken them and to demonstrate to the workers who their true leaders were. Workers employed by the states were to be organized "in a separate corps or as a part of the proletarian guard with chiefs elected by themselves" (Marx 1932:303). Leaders must be alert to any advantage during conflicts. Victory usually led to complacency, and workers must be kept at a fever pitch of revolutionary excitement. At such times leaders should not restrain the violence of workers directed against the symbols of their oppression. "Far from setting themselves against so-called excesses, examples of popular revenge against hated individuals or public buildings with only hateful memories attached to them, they must not only tolerate these examples but take in hand their very leadership" (Marx 1932:362).

The course of social thought in France, which early dedicated itself to a vigorous change of society, had far more appeal for Marx and Engels than utopian social idealism. They eagerly followed the practical steps taken by local leaders who attempted to extend the economic and political power of the working class, as in the uprising in Lyons (1831) and the first efforts to develop a national working-class movement (Chartists in England, 1842). Worker uprisings and underground conspiratorial activities documented the validity of the dialectic process, since the capitalistic system *was* generating its special contradiction in the form of a growing working class opposed to the owners of production.

The international quality of capitalism necessitated that negative forces within it be organized likewise on an international basis. Hence, Marx and Engels remained in close touch with the working-class movement in all countries and fostered the unification of workers under a Communist League. By 1845 Marx had formulated his materialistic conception of history, and he and Engels joined forces in Brussels to unify the ideologies of the independent working-class movements and give them an international thrust. When the Communist-oriented League of the Just, originally founded in Paris in 1834, gave evidence that it was losing its conspiratorial character and now could serve as an instrument of social change, Marx and Engels decided to join. At the first League Congress in London in 1847, the name was changed to the Communist League; and at the second meeting of the Congress in the same year, Marx expounded his materialistic theory of history and forecast the inevitable overthrow of the bourgeoisie by the proletariat according to the dialectic process. Marx and Engels were immediately commissioned to draw up the Manifesto, which dropped the old motto "All Men Are Brothers" and raised a battle cry, "Working Men of All Countries, Unite."

Historical and Dialectical Materialism

Marx and Engels, as many theorists of the nineteenth century, attempted to bring the forces of the world under one grand summative principle. This was the principle of materialism which expressed itself in two forms: historical materialism and dialectical materialism. Historical materialism provided the rationale for the basic organization of societies and the fundamental operations by which societies moved from one stage of development to another. Dialectical materialism, on the other hand, described the pattern and process by which change took place.

Historical Materialism and the Organization and Evolution of Society. To Marx and Engels, societies were materialistic entities, or instruments, through which basic human needs were fulfilled. According to Engels (1968b:435), Marx "discovered the law of development of human history" paralleling Darwin's great discovery of the "law of development of organic nature." Marx had simply uncovered the fact that men must provide for their survival needs before they could develop political, scientific, artistic, and religious institutions. From this it followed that the "production of the immediate material means of subsistence and consequently the degree of economic development attained by a given people or during a given epoch form the foundation upon which the state institutions, the legal conceptions, art, and even the ideas on religion . . . have been evolved" (Engels 1968b:435). The economic institution thus constituted the foundation upon which other institutions were constructed. Men developed their basic ideas about the world out of their living experience, especially their social relations in the everyday work of living and of producing the wants of life. Hence, the antiidealist conclusion that "It is not the consciousness of men which determines their existence, but on the contrary, it is their social existence which determines their consciousness" (Marx 1932:11).

The economic and sociopolitical analysis of Marx and Engels put labor at the center of the human process. Labor took the raw materials of nature and shaped them into tools that satisfied human needs. Labor, as Engels (1968d:358–368) observed, was the critical factor in the transformation of the apelike ancestor into man. Over thousands of years the hand was tested with new employments until it burst the limitations of the simian hand and attained the capacity to shape and handle tools. The hand was not only the "organ of labour, it had been produced by labor." Labor intensified the social life of these early ancestors by drawing individuals into relations of mutual support. Close association brought greater awareness of the importance of joint cooperation. The intensified social life of these ancestral men also intensified their need and desire to talk to one another (Engels 1968d:360). Such was the origin of language, and Engels went on to describe the crucial interrelationship between the operations of hand and of speech in enlarging the human brain and drawing man ever farther from his ape ancestors as a socially conscious being. In early times human needs were clued largely to survival, but as technology advanced and society grew more complex through a progressive division of labor, human needs were translated into social needs expressed in institutions (political, religious, and so on) according to the level of economic and technological complexity.

The humanizing of the ape ancestor testified to the crucial social role labor played in the advancement of mankind and of human society. In broad perspective, the development of human society gave rise to the concept of private property and was responsible for the perversion of an original natural social relation to land as communal property. In the beginning, individual producers exercised control over their own products, and the future social development of mankind was assigned the task of winning back that ancient barbaric advantage (Engels 1968c:540). The development of human society and of mankind must be followed through the shifting relations of labor regarding both the means of production (raw materials and technical apparatus) and social relations by which production was organized and managed. From such context, it was obvious that the approach must be *materialistic*, for ideas—whether expressed in notions about class, religion, law, government, and even art—existed functionally according to the kinds of social relations regulating society. Certainly, argued Marx and Engels, ideas had no separate or universal existence and could not enter the consciousness of men except through a living experience. Ideas which organized the consciousness of men were related to life conditions largely shaped by the relations of human labor to production. The relativity of human consciousness, in accordance with the nature of production, meant that the study of society must be historical in context. However, for Marx and Engels this historical context was evolutionary rather than historical in the traditional sense. The succession of different economic and sociopolitical types which followed one another along the pathway to civilization described a continuity and a transformation of structural types comparable to the structural types recognized in species evolution.

Marx and Engels sketched five main types of socioeconomic systems exclusive of the final classless form. However, a clear distinction of the types was not their primary objective. Between 1857 and 1858 Marx assembled a manuscript on the "Forms of Pre-Capitalist Production" as a preparation for the *Critique of Political Economy and Capital* (1859). Here Marx distinguished tribal, Asiatic or Oriental, slave (Greco-Roman), feudal, and capitalistic types, with some ambiguous and transitional forms. The reason for the failure to enter into a meticulous documentation of their socioeconomic types and transitions is clear. Marx and Engels were too involved in the working-class movement and in assembling proof that the capitalistic system was sowing the seeds of its own decay to spare the time essential to the research. The *magnum opus*, after all, was *Das Kapital* (Marx 1867–1894, 3 volumes) and not *The Origin of the Family, Private Property and the State, in the Light of the Researches of Lewis H. Morgan* (Engels 1884). Indeed, the task of preparing the second and third volumes of *Capital* for publication fell to Engels. The assignment of tying everything together in some continuity also fell to Engels, for it was he who delved into evolution and the earth sciences to link the dialectic with physical, organic, and social matter (for example, *Dialectics of Nature* (1940), written 1875–1876).

In *The Origin of the Family . . .* , Engels gave a précis of Morgan's (1877) ideas on the origins and evolution of ancient society. At the same time he introduced comments by Marx, supportive data from other sources regarding primeval promiscuity, biological evolution and the family, formation of the state among the ancient Germans, and socioeconomic data to fill out the continuity of class and economy in the transition from the ancient world to capitalism. Engels (1968c:589) described the world societies as arranged productively into the precivilized-collective and the civilized-private. Civilization by definition marked the stage "at which division of labour, the resulting exchange between individuals, and commodity production, which combines the two, reach their complete unfoldment and revolutionise the whole hitherto existing society" (Engels 1968c:589). Economically, civilization was characterized by

> the introduction of 1) metal money and, thus, of money capital, interest and usury; 2) the merchants acting as middlemen between producers; 3) private ownership of land and mortgage; 4) slave labour as the prevailing form of production. The form of the family . . . is monogamy, the supremacy of man over the woman, and the individual family as the economic unit of society. The cohesive form of civilised society is the state, which in all typical periods is exclusively the state of the ruling class, and in all cases essentially a machine for keeping down the oppressed, exploited class. Other marks of civilization are: on the one hand, fixation of the contrast between town and country as the basis of the entire division of social labour; on the other hand, the introduction of wills, by which the property holder is able to dispose of his property even after his death. This institution, which was a direct blow at the old gentile constitution, was unknown in Athens until the time of Solon; in Rome it was introduced very early, but we do not know when. Among the Germans it was introduced by the priests in order that the good honest German might without hindrance bequeath his property to the Church.
>
> With this constitution as its foundation civilisation has accomplished things with which the old gentile society was totally unable to cope. But it accomplished them by playing on the most sordid instincts and passions of man, and by developing them at the expense of all his other faculties. Naked greed has been the moving spirit of civilisation from the first day of its existence to the present time; wealth, more wealth and wealth again; wealth, not of society, but of this shabby individual, was its sole and determining aim. If, in the pursuit of this aim, the increasing development of science and repeated periods of the fullest blooming of art fell into its lap, it was only because without them the ample present-day achievements in the accumulation of wealth would have been impossible.
>
> Since the exploitation of one class by another is the basis of civilisation, its whole development moves in a continuous contradiction. Every advance in production is at the same time a retrogression in the condition of the oppressed class, that is, of the great majority. (Engels 1968c:591–592)

What was was not what it ought to be, and in conclusion Engels (1968c:593) cited Morgan's ending to *Ancient Society*. There Morgan gave credit to the civilizing service which the idea of private property performed. However, presently the human mind was confounded by what it had created—a kind of Frankenstein. The future still beckoned, and Morgan trusted human intelligence, knowledge, and experience to recreate a more advanced society in which the "liberty, equality, and fraternity of the ancient gentes" would be realized.

In retrospect the Marxian formula bore a curious resemblance, but no real identity, to the Christian formula. A "fall" from a near paradise of communal living had occurred when civilized man partook of the fruit of private property in producing commodities for exchange. Since then man has been steering a straight course to corruption. He would ultimately be rescued by the inevitable dialectic which directed the social and economic process for the benefit of the people. The time would come when the working majority recognized that they needed to be saved from capitalistic oppression and that they possessed the instruments and the organized power to attain their salvation.

Dialectical Materialism and Capitalism. The interplay between producers and the owners of production supplied Marx and Engels with the basic antitheses of the materialistic dialectic. The dialectic emphasized process in that it dealt with relationships among categories of individuals united in the productive operation. This emphasis on process and relationships was not new, but Marx and Engels pioneered new ground in drawing attention to the internal arrangements of the productive operations of societies. At the same time they put the internal social arrangements and operations in a dynamic perspective of dialectic-evolutionary change.

Around 1900 sociologists and anthropologists, in shaping their Structuralist perspectives, adopted the term "interaction" to describe the processes linking one part to another in functional and causal ways. However, in emphasizing historical interaction as fundamental to the growth of culture, and of social interaction as basic to the maintenance processes of society, they did not immediately infuse their perspectives with the change dynamic conveyed by the dialectic.

Marx maintained that the social element was the quintessence of productive relationships. In precivilized societies the common ownership of the means of production linked the productive labor of the individual cooperatively with the total community. As Marx (1932:71) phrased it, the precivilized individual "has no more torn himself off from the navel-string of his tribe or community than each bee has freed itself from connexion with the hive." From a productive standpoint, the total value of the products of the community was equal to the social investment of labor power. Such was not the case under private systems of ownership of production.

Marx stressed that capitalism dehumanized the basic social nature of production by turning labor into a mere commodity. The fragmented operations intrinsic to machine manufacture separated the individual's labor from the product, and labor was bought and sold in the marketplace like any other commodity. Without labor no product could be available for exchange; and Marx (1932:32) tried to prove that the amount of social labor put into making a product determined its exchange value. All labor possessed a special value or power, which Marx (1932:36) defined as the time an individual must work to supply basic subsistence needs such as housing, fuel, food, clothing. The worker was required to contribute far more labor time than was actually needed to provide the basic needs of life. The extra labor time spent was, in effect, unpaid and went into the profits of the capitalist producer. This surplus value or profit rightfully belonged to the worker. The producer might argue that some of this profit was ploughed back into machinery for increasing production, lowering costs, and ultimately employing more workers. However, the use of machinery did not free the capitalist from the iron law of labor value, and the productiveness of machines could be measured only by the amount of labor power replaced (Marx 1932:97).

A labor theory of value in commodity exchange contributed a practical ethic to Marx's economic analysis of capitalistic operations. He wished to prove that the proprietor of labor, the working man, was ignored in the commodity production and exchange equation. This was evident in attempts to extend the working day, maintenance of an overabundance of labor through the use of women and children, failure to protect the life of the individual from dangerous working conditions, stifling of the worker's intellectual growth with spiritless technical tasks, payment of starvation wages, and purchase of the worker as a marketable commodity. Marx frequently drew on anecdotal evidence and production figures then available to document the lamentable condition of the worker at the time, and his subjection to the tyrannical demands of the capitalist for more and more surplus labor in the interest of more and more surplus value.

The adverse condition and the progressive alienation of the majority population precluded active participation in the total productive operation and served to document the dialectic contradictions of the capitalist system. There was no automatic regulator of the relations of productivity, labor, price, and surplus value which kept things in a kind of moving equilibrium. The so-called law of supply and demand was really governed by the relative proportion of unemployed to employed (Marx 1932:177). Moreover, the bourgeoisie violated the law by attempting to control supply when demand fell and reduced profits. The more production was increased, the greater the pressure for expanded employment. Increased productivity could never keep up with the demand for employment, and the relative labor reserve (unemployed) progressively got out of phase with job opportunities. The disproportionate number of unemployed simply increased the "accumulation of misery, agony of toil, slavery, ignorance, brutality, [and] moral degradation" of the workers while capital continued to cumulate and concentrate at the opposite social pole (Marx 1932:182). Moreover, beginning with the bourgeoisie subversion of the household craft and guild economy of feudal times, the trend was toward a progressive differentiation of technical and commercial operations. The filling of these jobs by workers inevitably increased the disproportion between the laboring population and the owners of production. The resultant centralization of economic and political power in bourgeoisie hands simply prepared the ground for an easier takeover by the proletariat during a time of crisis.

The dialectic process could be observed in operation everywhere—wherever interest groups opposed each other. The rise of capitalism exploited agricultural production for its own ends and created a new market for its goods by driving peasants into the cities. In so doing, it set town against countryside. Within the bourgeoisie itself, the petty bourgeoisie were driven into the ranks of the proletariat as the big bourgeoisie captured the market. "The lower middle class, the small manufacturer, the shopkeeper, the artisan, the peasant, all these fight against the bourgeoisie to save from extinction their existence as fractions of the middle class" (*Manifesto*, Marx and Engels 1968:44). Of all these classes, however, the proletariat alone was revolutionary and dialectically historical. Capitalism led to a simplification of the class structure in which the bourgeoisie was pitted against the proletariat. The *Manifesto* proclaimed that "The proletarian movement is the self-conscious, independent movement of the immense majority, in the interests of the immense majority" (Marx and Engels 1968:45). Thrown into a state of disequilibrium because of the inability of the bourgeoisie to coordinate production and consumption, the economic crises of capitalism progressively worsen to the point where the time of the "class struggle nears the decisive hour" (Marx and Engels 1968: 44). At such time various of the bourgeoisie, including some of the bourgeois ideologists, would defect and join the proletariat, just as various of the nobility defected to the bourgeoisie at the time of the French Revolution. At this time, the victorious proletariat would enter a period of transition when society, under the dictatorship of the workers, would be renovated in preparation for a truly classless and stateless society. The masses once again would become the owners of production; and at such time Engels believed (cited by Venable 1966:189) humanity would leap "from the realm of necessity into the realm of freedom."

Dialectic Process and Economic Determinism. Marx and Engels used the human necessity of survival to draw the logical conclusion that the economic institution was basic to social life. The economic institution provided the foundational structure upon which ideological and other institutional superstructures were raised. Superstructure and economic structure were in constant interrelationships, each influencing the other in its own way according to circumstances. However, the steadiest, most persistent and directionally aggressive of all these forces was the economic, since it operated out of the bedrock of human needs.

This core structure, centered in the relations of production, provided the continuity between successive economic-social systems. When the ownership of production changed, it usually was accompanied by technical innovations in production. Such changes in the ownership of production always elicited changes in the legal and political system, as well as in social stratification. Social classes were sensitive indicators of the productive system. They were produced by realignments in the means and ownership of production, and they also were the instruments for revolutionary transformations in productive relationships. In renovating economic-social systems, the dialectic process made its initial impact in the technical and social relations of production. In time, however, the major impact of the process transferred to the domain of ideas. This was apparent in the growth of class consciousness and the formation of an ideology consonant with that consciousness of class.

Marx and Engels looked upon the dialectic as a methodological guide to understanding, an operation which allowed them to approach the economics of class struggle historically, thus preserving an empirical base of operations. By concentrating on historical events through which the dialectic presumably operated, they avoided any criticism that they had simply reified a metaphysical conception. Nonetheless, the dialectic is *the* change process. Without the antagonistic interchange between polar units there is no change. Every structure through a process of differentiation provides the basis for internal contradictions necessary for change. The center for these differentiations is in the progressive division of labor which creates working categories and social classes—the active agents of change.

The close association between production and class, and between class action and change, obviously describes a narrow economic basis for the organization of society and how it changes. The dialectic adds directionality and inevitability so characteristic of deterministic systems. Moreover, the fact that the end product of the dialectical interchange is an absolute, the classless society, raises the same contradiction in Marx and Engels' dialectical materialism which turned them against Hegel's absolute ideas. Any absolute is a contradiction in the light of the dialectical process.

Marxism and Anthropology: Economic Theory and the Economic Dialectic

Economic interpretations of social processes do not necessarily mean that the explanations are Marxist. As Marx (cited by Selsam, Goldway, and Martel 1970:30–31) saw his own accomplishments in 1852,

> no credit is due to me for discovering the existence of classes in modern society nor yet the struggle between them. Long before me bourgeois historians had described the historical development of this class struggle and bourgeois economists the economic anatomy of the classes.
>
> What I did that was new was to prove: (1) that the *existence of classes* is only bound up with particular, historic phases in the *development of production*; (2) that the class struggle necessarily leads to the *dictatorship of the proletariat*; (3) that this dictatorship itself only constitutes the transition to the *abolition of all classes* and to a *classless society*.

Explanations of specific social phenomena largely by economic factors were not uncommon before Marx and Engels. Even the Marxist assertion that men first must take care of physical needs before they can produce the leisure time to expand their political, religious, esthetic, moral, and legal consciousness was basic to Developmentalist thinking. All such economic interpretations, however, were not presented as an orderly thesis, since the advancement of human society by critical ideas and the search for the sources of these ideas in universal human experiences seemed more important.

The Marxian accomplishment rested on exposition of a position in which all social, political, legal, and ideological arrangements and meanings derived directly from economic processes. To this they added a purposive evolutionary advance of society, linked to the forces of production through the dialectic of differentiation and of polar opposition. Neither the idea of differentiation, nor of opposition, was foreign to the Developmentalist position, especially in the nineteenth century. The same held with regard to the transformation of structured forms through an adaptive process of opposition and selection.

The Marxian breakthrough did not consist, as the two collaborators liked to think, of discovering the verities of life and process by standing Hegel and philosophical idealism on its head. Marx and Engels admitted that the important datum in human experience was that quality known as consciousness—consciousness of self, admittedly a social self, and of self in relation to others. The proletariat had to be brought to his potential consciousness by inspiring him with the Communist social ideology and sense of purpose. In the long perspective of time, the evolution of society was seen as an emerging drama of the social consciousness and the humanizing of the oppressed. The stage setting changed from one historic-economic epoch to the next, and so did the leading actors. On the eve of the final act to this human drama, the lead role was played by an industrial proletariat consciously aware of his place in society and in history. This is but another way of saying that ideas are the instigators of human action.

The differentiation of anthropology from 1935 to the present witnessed the emergence of economic anthropology as a specialization. Consequently, more attention has been directed to economic organization and processes. In 1936 Childe ascribed the rise of civilization in the Near East to great technical and economic revolutions which reorganized society and transformed knowledge systems. Thompson (1954) suggested that the decline of Mayan civilization was hastened by a revolt of Mayan householders who objected to the oppressive burdens entailed in maintaining the religious buildings, priesthood, and ritual.

The economic emphasis is strengthened by the ecological perspective. In his ecocultural approach, Steward (1949, 1955) focused on a constellation of core institutions integrated conceptually and organizationally by subsistence and production needs. Application of an economic perspective to the study of kinship revealed economic motives and manipulations within descent groups which were formerly obscured by failure to probe the relations of kin in depth.

Developments in the postwar world brought home to anthropologists the importance of the interrelations of social, economic, and political factors in stimulating change. Industrialization of emergent nations was accompanied by a differentiation of social categories and classes, as well as forms of social and political organization functionally adaptive to the changing social and economic scene. Traditional socioeconomic and political arrangements, already eroded by colonial occupation, now were toppled or seriously modified by professional elites and petty bourgeoisie who wished to modernize their political economies and extend their own social and political advantage.

The modification of traditional relations among kings, chiefs, and commoner kin by pressures emanating from changes in the means of production and the owners of production could not be ignored. In Africa, with the withdrawal of colonial control, as in the Congo and Mali, the political vacuum was filled by a struggle for power which intermingled tribal enmities with democratic and Marxist doctrine. In the context of postwar change, the basic datum of the Marxist interpretation, that a hierarchical social order generates oppositions between higher and lower segments and which is focused on a redistribution of social, economic, and political rights and accesses, took on new relevance. This point was underscored by those who concentrated on issues of change rather than a static description of the interrelations of parts.

The Marxist thesis reinforced for anthropologists the necessity for abandoning a static definition of problems for a dynamic one. Changing configurations in the relationships of groups, both within a societal context and within a broader interactional universe, appeared more relevant in developing a research basis for understanding change processes in the industrializing world. Societies were drawn increasingly into complex networks of social, political, and economic relationships that were world-wide.

Vast changes overtaking the anthropological domain of research forged a new anthropological consciousness. This is illustrated in the growing concern for explanations which relate the habits, values, and ideology of the impoverished to the oppressive social, economic, educational, and political restraints imposed upon them by the dominant social group (see, for example, Valentine 1968; compare Lewis 1961; Foster 1965). At the same time anthropologists are called upon to become politically involved in order to alleviate the narrow confines of life of the oppressed and permit them access to the benefits which the powerful enjoy and monopolize (see Diamond 1964; Gjessing 1968; Gough 1968; Ribeiro 1970).

Social, economic, political, ideological, religious, and other changes accompanying the industrialization of the non-Western world makes study of the Marxist interpretation of change both timely and essential. Within anthropology itself the dialectic process can be seen operating in a division of the discipline into those who wish to use the field for political ends and those who wish to preserve the tradition of objective research as a scientific task devoted to the building of knowledge.

The search for knowledge belongs to no creed. Preserving the quality of this search requires alert and bold vigilance, as the history of science in the West discloses. The scientific tradition should draw from any theory and methodology whatever is useful for its goal of expanding knowledge. Certainly the materialistic orientation and the dialectic are not the peculiar property of Marxism. However, there is a Marxist theoretical packet and causal explanation. The best use which anthropologists can make of the Marxist thesis is to test it, along with other theories of change, in the observable historical contexts of the day (see, for example, Firth 1965; Sahlins 1958, 1968; Foster 1942).

By maintaining an objective posture, science can retain the flexibility necessary to advance general knowledge and apply it in the service of man. To align science with a religious or political creed means that truth becomes a matter of doctrine, a thing of relativity according to belief and objectives. To this the cynic may reply that historical circumstance determines the consciousness of men and of science. However, the Marxist limits the historical context to class, so that all science by definition reflects the interests of the ruling class. From this viewpoint, there is a scientific truth for the proletariat, for the middle class, for the upper class, and any other group. If truth is relativized and distributed among social classes, where does truth for man rest? To gain truth in a relativized context, one relies on faith. As Hook (1953:712) points out in his survey of dialectic in history and society,

> The intent of the dialectic method is not to investigate the relationships between the specific empirical valuings of men in concrete interaction with the world and each other, but to discover how one great objective Value or Good [march toward classless society] is being realized in the social and historical process. It is a means of getting by faith what cannot be reached by evidence, obscured by the . . . illusion that what has been begged by faith can be demonstrated as a scientific conclusion.

SUMMARY

Anthropological interest in the economies of primitive societies began with Developmentalist efforts to coordinate types of economies with the evolutionary stages of savagery, barbarism, and civilization. The rise of Structuralism at the turn of the century did not immediately stimulate a concern with preindustrial economies and economic processes per se. Cultural historicists were preoccupied with distributions of cultural features and with disproving the claims of geographic determinists, while social Structuralists were involved in demonstrating the social processes by which communities were integrated positively and functioned as systemic wholes. Consequently, investigation of economies and economic processes was never central to the Structuralist perspective and was only routinely included in their ethnographic reports. Although French Structuralists Mauss and Beuchat (1906) were early concerned with the seasonal variation of Eskimo life, their theoretical interest lay in the impact of social organization on economic and ecological relations rather than the reverse. Distributional studies of the circumpolar region by Scandinavian geographer-ethnologists Hatt (1914) and Steensby (1916) revealed that cultural variations were sensitive to climatic, faunal, and floral distributions. In developing their culture areas, American culture historicists were content to admit an approximation between cultural and ecological boundaries. Radcliffe-

Brown's (1922) description of Andaman life and society paid special attention to the food quest. However, his primary concern was with the ritualization of sentiments associated with economic cooperation and food sharing, and the symbolic value of food which Andamanese built into their social relationships through its use in socialization.

The works of Marcel Mauss (1925) and Bronislaw Malinowski (1922) signaled a new start on the study of economics in the preindustrial world. Mauss's *Essay on the Gift* extended the French Structuralist search for elementary social forms and processes to the social implications of exchange. Reciprocity in gift exchange was seen as fundamental to the relationships of individuals and groups linked by kinship ties and obligations. The unity of preindustrial societies was achieved through elaboration of reciprocating exchanges in a grand cycling of foods, women, songs, dances, heirlooms, and the like, which bound groups together and raised the level of social solidarity. For Mauss, however, reciprocity as a principle and as a process emerged not from economic considerations· but from a mystical sentiment which linked individuals to their possessions and gifts and which compelled a return. Lévi-Strauss later drew upon this principle of reciprocity—divesting it of its mystical components by deriving it from survival needs—to determine cross-cousin marriage as the elementary base for developing social alliances and enlargement of the community.

Malinowski's focus on the institution as a group of people mobilized to satisfy a human need conveyed a pragmatic tone to his social analysis. In *Argonauts of the Western Pacific* (1922) he described a network of exchange whose rules prohibited entrepreneurial adventures and bound trading partners to reciprocities.

Ethnological focus on exchange as an instituted social process accented differences between the kin obligations and reciprocities of preindustrial economics and the impersonal profit-oriented economics of commercial and industrial systems. This distinction received support from the economic historian Karl Polanyi, whose view of economics as an instituted process stressed structural-functional differences between reciprocal, redistributional, and market types of exchange.

The position that primitive economics and economic processes were worlds apart from commercial and industrial systems was intrinsic to Structuralist thinking and prevailed without serious challenge until the postwar period. Participation in government aid programs and the vigorous transformation of former colonial peoples through economic, social, and political forces facilitated the emergence of economic specialization in anthropology and convinced some anthropologists that economic incentives were more important to individuals in kin-based societies than had been previously recognized. Information that supported a measure of "economic man" despite kinship obligations led to spirited debate between exponents of a theory of economic maximization and those who maintained the relative uniqueness of economic ends and means subject to the institution of kinship. Such was the formalist-substantivist controversy which climaxed during the sixties. No clear victory was claimed for either side, since both restrictive-corporate and open-individualized economies existed in practice within kinship organizations. However, the debate broadened perspective regarding economic processes in kin-based societies, and it became evident that there was greater variability in the world of primitive economics than had formerly been granted, and that more precise studies of these variations were essential.

The changing world of the sixties provoked conflicting interpretations as to the place of ethnic minorities and the underprivileged in socioeconomic systems. Were the behavioral patterns of the poor and socially underprivileged due to their socioeconomic marginality, or was their condition a result of the persistence of a cultural tradition, or a combination of both? This issue was readily transformed into consideration of the significance of political and ideological factors versus economic factors in altering stratified socioeconomic orders. Evidence drawn from postwar economic developments suggested that ideological change in developing countries frequently preceded a political shift which, in turn, allowed the implementation of economic programs and a consequent alteration of traditional socioeconomic arrangements. This preliminary finding is relevant to Marx's thesis that a groundwork for change must take place first in the minds of men. It also gave support to those who stressed the importance of shared values, meanings, and expectations as intrinsic to the nature of cultural processes.

17

Differentiation of
Cultural Ecology

CULTURE AND THE FOCUS ON ECOLOGICAL PROCESSES

Ecological influences and their effect on the sociocultural order were given close attention in the United States during the thirties. The study of economic process per se fell to Continental anthropologists largely because their structural-functional posture focused on social interaction. American anthropologists, owing to their emphasis on culture process as an historic interchange or interaction, led off in the direction of ecological study.

Kroeber (1939) first stimulated a renewal of cultural-ecological interest on a broad scale in a work entitled *Cultural and Natural Areas of Native North America.* However, he did not confine his study to ecocultural relations alone; the investigation also considered the historic relations within and between culture areas (Kroeber 1939:1). Culture areas were most congenial for both objectives. The fact that culture areas regionalized cultural manifestations (for example, Plains culture) required attention to habitat, climate, and resources. In the development of uniformities, culture areas were implicated in a common cultural-historical growth. For Kroeber it was a point of great interest to delineate the efflorescence or cultural climax within an area and to relate it to culture growth and decline. The essence of any culture climax was the strain toward integration—toward an "organization in part into a conscious system of ideas, but especially into an integrated nexus of styles, standards, and values" (Kroeber 1939:225). As seen by Kroeber, the trend toward integration was accompanied by a greater facility for assimilation and invention, and it was this organization and flexibility that made a culture dominant over environmental pressures.

For example, in the Northeast the prevalence of internecine warfare and its malign effects upon population growth restricted realization of the economic potential of cultivation on which other cultures capitalized in their rise to civilization (Kroeber 1939:148). Yet, expectably, where summer rains were lacking, or where the growing season of frost-free days was less than 100, the maize-subsisting Pueblo culture was unable to penetrate, except marginally, to the west and north. Dry summers forestalled maize cultivation under aboriginal conditions in California and continued to restrict production even under modern conditions (Kroeber 1939:211).

The evidence of ecocultural relations in culture growth presented by Kroeber demonstrated some striking correspondences with vegetation areas, which again were sensitive to climate and precipitation. In the instance of the California climax among the Pomo, Patwin, Valley Maidu and Nisenan, it was not so much historic culture contact as a favorable ecological situation which promoted a cultural efflorescence (Kroeber 1939: 55). An ecocultural orientation thus permitted the student to appreciate refinements of cultural variants within a broader region, usually traceable to environmental variations. What emerged from Kroeber's population figures was the astounding fact that hunters and acorn gatherers of California were more densely packed per 100 kilometers than Eastern horticulturalists (43.30 and 6.95, respectively). Coastal fishermen and hunters of the Pacific Northwest (28.30 per 100 kilometers) also exhibited heavier population concentrations than interior areas where hunting and/or cultivation were present. From such data it was evident that cultivation did not lead automatically to higher population density. It was also apparent that many primitive peoples were not maximizing their economic operations. They had either been content to remain at ease after fulfilling modest needs, or some noneconomic factors diverted or prevented them from expanding the efficiency of their economies.

ECOLOGY AND SOCIAL ADAPTATION

Steward's Ecosociology and Multilinear Evolution

Whereas Kroeber addressed himself to correspondences between culture areas and environment, Julian Steward investigated the effects of environment on the nature of social units as exploitative adaptations. He thus pioneered in the area of ecosocial processes, emphasizing different levels of sociocultural complexity as a function of technicoecological relations. His theoretical system combined four interrelated ideas: (1) an ecologically determined culture core, (2) levels of sociocultural integration, (3) culture type, and (4) multilinear evolution.

The culture core consisted of features clustered around subsistence and economic activities generally (Steward 1955i:37). Levels of sociocultural integration emphasized the fact that societies were organized differentially according to the complexities of their ecocultural adaptations. This ranged all the way from a familistic level to the level of a national culture. The culture type was the combined product of the culture core and the level of sociocultural integration (Steward 1955g:89). To Steward, Redfield's effort to conceptualize the folk society as an ideal type illustrated his own idea of a level of sociocultural integration. The multifamily integration of the folk contrasted with the simple family integration he found among the western Shoshoni.

The concept of multilinear evolution meant more to Steward as a methodology than as a theory. He saw the taxonomy of culture types as central to multilinear concerns. Multilinear evolution conveyed a temporal dynamism to the ecocultural perspective. Through investigation of forces which shaped his culture types in their day-to-day operations, Steward saw himself as fulfilling the requirements of a typical synchronic structural-functional analysis. Parallels in the way culture types were converted into other types constituted the heart of his evolutionary process. Steward was well ahead of the field in seeing the need for combining both synchronic and diachronic processes in his research model.

Since cultural-historical and cultural-ecological factors induced a multiplicity of culture types within an economic category (for example, hunting and gathering), the evolutionary process in Steward's judgment had to be multilinear. The evolution of society and culture did not start from a unitary base as unilinear theory implied. Neither was it conformant with the general trends emphasized by present-day evolutionists such as White in their views of cultural evolution. Starting from different technicoecological adaptations, cultural evolution proceeded along a number of lines. Steward was more interested in finding parallels of limited occurrence than in universals and considered that the problem of cultural evolution could best be taken up on an intermediate ground—what some today call microevolution (Steward 1955h:15). His approach also involved the use of particular societies and ecocultural traditions whose histories would provide the substance for comparisons of form and process. Multilineal evolution in its methodology thus accented the empirical-inductive rather than the deductive-empirical approach.

Steward (1936, modified in 1955b) began his search for the relations between vital economic processes and social organization with a comparison of patrilineal bands as an ecosocial type. He pointed out that the patrilineal band as a sociocultural type could not be accounted for by the usual cultural-historical explanations of borrowing or as a holdover from an archaic past. However, the essential features of the patrilineal band as it appeared in semiarid, tropical forest, and humid coastal environments could be accounted for by following the exploitative patterns of South African Bushmen, Congo Negritos, Australians, Tasmanians, patrilineal Shoshonean-speaking groups of southern California, and the Ona of Tierra del Fuego.

In its ideal form the patrilineal band was a local group of genealologically related people who worked together because of subsistence needs. The males were integral to the organization of the group since they furnished the primary food. The fact that the technology of the group was simple and confined to human carriers kept the groups localized and reaffirmed the need for males to cluster in order to make the most of their knowledge of land and game habits. Such emphases made patrilocal residence a natural practice, with consequent extension and concentration of relations through the medium of the patrilineage in association with the patrilocal extended family. Incest definitions, rooted in cultural-psychological adaptations integral to the biological family, flowed outward along the patrilineal axis (Steward 1956b:135). The patrilineal band thus was exogamous.

Cultural features associated with the patrilineal band type of organization varied in part according to the geographic location. Geographic contiguities helped explain the presence or absence of particular features that had diffused historically throughout an area—for example, bows and arrows, nets for hunting, traps, myths, games, ceremonies, and special kinship extensions. However, Steward (1955b:134) emphasized that cultural inventories might be alike but the social organization would vary depending on whether the game hunted were scattered and nonmigratory or migratory and in herds.

The small, relatively homogeneous patrilineal band contrasted with the larger composite band. Steward (1955a) saw the composite band as an ecosocial adjustment or adaptation to the hunting and gathering of foods that were seasonally clustered in good quantity. The composite band comprised unrelated nuclear families and was found principally among hunters, fishers, gatherers, and simple cultivators. Abundant clustering of food supplies permitted the clustering of groups numbering several hundred. Sometimes they were in bands, as hunters and gatherers; at other times they formed villages, as fishers and cultivators. In Canada subarctic hunters illustrated the tendency to form composite units in the presence of migratory herd animals. Though preferring patrilocal and patrilineal arrangements, a plentiful supply of food on the hoof permitted special arrangements that affiliated other families with the patrilocal base and brought about a composite social grouping. The reasons for this modification in the nature of the patrilineal band base were largely demographic or social. For example, if a woman or a man had no brothers, a matrilocal arrangement might be made. Or, if a woman's kin had no sister to give in exchange, matrilocal residence might be elected. A general mixture of families of lineal, collateral, and affinal relations was formed which did not rely on exogamic lineages for their basic membership. Rather, the lack of stress on unilineal descent and on ancestral genealogical ties opened the way for the practice of band endogamy. The flexible approach to residence, shifting bases for membership, limited extension of incest taboos, and band endogamy were largely products of the pragmatics of ecological adaptation.

In the Great Basin between the Wasatch and the Sierra Nevada mountains, together with adjacent portions of the semi-arid Columbia River and Colorado Plateaus, Steward (1938) found peoples ecologically adapted at the level of the nuclear family. Finding themselves in a steppelike environment, with unpredictable quantities of rain and food, the western Shoshoni learned that the individual family was the most efficient unit for survival. In its more fertile and watered stretches, the Great Basin supported one Shoshoni for every five square miles. Where water was virtually lacking, the ratio jumped to one to fifty or even one hundred square miles. The mean, according to Steward (1955d:103) was one to twenty or thirty square miles. Piñon nuts, rabbits, antelope, deer, insects, rodents, and larvae were eagerly sought when available. However, Shoshoni technology was not efficient and large game played little part in their diet. Lacking ways of preserving food, the Shoshoni consumed on the spot what was available. Their search for food was incessant, and very often they traveled as single families or as temporary units of one or two related families. The very operations of digging roots, picking berries, and collecting seeds stimulated family separatism rather than collective enterprise. Families constantly alerted each other as to the presence of food in larger quantities. This worked best at the pine nut harvest. By late October or early November, frost forced the cones open and families would congregate. However, the individual families worked alone. Each family restricted itself to an agreed area selected at the time of arrival and stored their seeds in an earth cache for their individual use (Steward 1955d:105).

A kind of winter encampment in the mountains was formed within the pine nut harvest area. Usually it consisted of twenty to thirty families clustered within easy walking and visiting. However, food ran out by spring, and families were forced to split up to make it on their own. The general failure of collective action to produce more group unity and enterprise was attributed to the fact that collective ventures like the rabbit hunt and antelope drive did not materially increase per capita food availability (Steward 1955d:107). Flexibility described the Shoshoni ecosocial adaptation, which permitted separation or cooperation as the pragmatics of circumstances recommended. Food resources were available to all on a first-come, first-served basis, and the first to come to the pine nut harvest selected the choicest spots.

Steward estimated that Shoshoni families were independent for nine-tenths of the year, and thus illustrated a family level of sociocultural integration. Families sometimes preferred to form alliances through a number of marriages with specific families, usually arranged on an exchange of sister for sister. Temporary polyandry and the levirate also reinforced a kind of localism. However, the trend in family relations through marriage was not restrictive in range but extensive, which meant that a person frequently could find relatives within his own local group and also among families in other groups.

In evolutionary perspective Shoshoni ecosociology did not strike Steward as typical or as the base from which social evolution had taken off. There were other basic units, for example, the patrilineal and composite band, which could serve as a basis for multilinear evolution. The Shoshoni ecosocial adaptation seemed unique, though Central Eskimo had made a similar adaptation.

Steward's ecosocial approach forged new lines of communication between technicoenvironmental relations, economics, social organization, settlement patterns, demography, and historic and evolutionary processes. Population density and settlement patterns formed an integral part of his ecoevolutionary interpretation of Pueblo society. Steward (1955c) contended that an increase in population density attributable to growing ethnoecological pressures had promoted the rise of clan organization in the Pueblo region. In his demonstration he drew upon archeological materials that revealed an increase in the ratio of dwelling units to ceremonial *kivas*. The population-productivity ratio also was central to his interpretation of the rise and disintegration of ancient states and empires.

The Ecosociology of Northern Hunters: Hallowell

What now emerged from the new thrust into cultural-environmental relations was an alert appreciation of the way some forms of social organization were sensitive adaptations to an ecological context. Figures compiled by Hallowell (1949) comparing the size of hunting grounds, hunting groups, and population density of the Berens River Saulteaux (Manitoba) and the Grand Lake Victoria Indians (Quebec) disclosed great variability betweeen these two groups of northern hunters. Nonetheless, the ratio of active hunters to nonhunters (both sexes) was approximately one to three in each group, suggesting a "basic fact in the ecological adjustment of . . . northern hunters" and pointing to a "small family consisting of a hunter, his wife, and two children" as the primary economic unit (Hallowell 1949(51):41). Size of hunting territories, and hence population concentration, were related more to animal population than to any cultural variable.

The Ecosociology of Polynesia: Sahlins

The scattering, clustering, and scarcity of natural resources found on volcanic and atoll islands were used by Sahlins (1958) to account for the adaptive radiation of social organization in Polynesia. Ramage and descent-line organization occurred, respectively, in the presence of distributed and clustered resources, situations commonly found on volcanic islands. However, each thrived in a special ecology. Ramage social systems (Tonga, Marquesas, Mangaia, Hawaii, Society Islands, Mangareva, Tikopia, New Zealand, and Easter Island) were associated with scattered food resources which usually were cultivated or harvested by dispersed hamlet populations. For example, in Tahiti (Society Islands) a lowland banana, breadfruit, and taro were cultivated in a variable coastal plain not more than four miles wide. In upland valleys special varieties of yams, taro, and bananas were grown, with occasional irrigation of taro (Sahlins 1958:206–

207). Lagoons, lakes, and rivers were sources for fish. Each of the climatic zones also provided wild plants for harvesting. Exploitation of each of the ecological zones was unified through a ramage system that drew the segmentary unilineal kin groups into ascending levels of political integration. In this way scattered hamlets occupying different ecological zones were consolidated productively through a political organization that conveyed the right of redistributing zonal surpluses to titular chiefs. Political succession generally followed the rule of primogeniture. The political unity effected through the ramage organization also facilitated trade exchanges.

Descent lines were characteristic of Futuna, Samoa, and Uvea. On these volcanic islands there was little ecological diversity, and this was confined spatially to a narrow strip of coast and adjacent upland. This meant that populations concentrated locally in villages, with householders exploiting segments of the ecological niches for their own use. Surpluses for exchange were minimal, with householders usually consuming what they produced.

Atoll organization, exemplified by Tongareva, Tokelau, and Pukapuka, exhibited a social organization that was less stratified in comparison with the volcanic islands but more complex in lateral interlocking relationships. Sahlins attributed the lack of complex stratification to the paucity of atoll resources and the tendency for food to be unevenly distributed due to accidents of drought and storm damage. The limited social stratification and elements of ramage and descent-line systems found on the atolls were part of the cultural equipment carried by migrants from volcanic islands (Sahlins 1958:218). This basic organization had not been expanded, but interlocking groups for the exploitation of locally available resources had been formed. For example, the patri-ramages of Pukapuka controlled strips of land on different islets associated largely with coconut production. Taro lands were in the hands of matrilineages, with women planting and harvesting the taro. There were also age grades of young men organized as communal deep-sea fishing groups. Villages constituted the basic political and productive units. They maintained guards also over communal lands utilized for cultivation and the harvesting of wild plants (Sahlins 1958: 244). Food scarcities thus induced atoll islanders to increase the complexity of their exploitative organization rather than their status system. Differentials in the complexity of atoll socioeconomic adaptations (for example, Pukapuka and Ontong Java versus Tongareva, Manihiki-Rakahanga, and Tokelau) could be explained by earlier settlement of Pukapuka and Ontong Java.

ECOLOGICAL NICHES AND DISTRIBUTIONS

In northern Pakistan Barth (1956) again confirmed how commitment to an ecological niche may so condition a group's adaptation that extension into a less congenial ecology is restricted. Such was the case in the advance of Pathans up the Indus and Swat rivers, for the Pathans halted at the ecological line that barred the taking of two crops, so essential to maintenance of their complex social system. Displaced Kohistanis retreated northward and to higher altitudes, combining one-crop agriculture with the transhumant herding of sheep, goats, cattle, and water buffalo. A third group, the Gujars, occupied the grazing lands and practiced no agriculture. In the territory of the Pathans, the Gujars were able to carry out transhumant herding. However, among the Kohistanis, Gujars were reduced to nomadic herding, since this was the only ecological niche available to them. Barth (1956(58):1088; compare Flannery 1965) concluded that the distribution of ethnic groups was not controlled by natural geographic areas. The important consideration was the distribution of an ecological configuration that articulated or did not articulate with elements of a subsistence pattern. At least so it appeared for the western zone of the Old World. Similarly, the earliest maize sites in the Southwest of the United States turned out to be caves situated at elevations of 6000 feet in New Mexico and Arizona. The date for this elemental pod corn was estimated at 3000 B.C. Since evidence pointed to the diffusion of maize cultivation and other important cultural features from Mexico, the spread of maize cultivation into the Southwest is assumed to have followed the natural habitat of the Sierra Madre (Mangelsdorf and Lister 1956; Haury 1962).

The full potentials of cultivation came only as functional linkages were established between peoples occupying specialized ecological niches. Until such ecofunctional relations were established, population growth did not accelerate and lead to the concentration of populations. Productive richness languished owing to lack of a complex division of technical, practical, priestly, and administrative functions. Social classes did not materialize to organize production, trade, and consumption. Political organization remained dispersed, and hence no central administration served to integrate activities at all levels and to organize labor and surplus in the production of public services.

ECOLOGICAL DIVERSITY: THE STIMULUS TO CIVILIZATION

In the views of Braidwood and Willey (1962:334–338), uniformities in environment (plains, forested areas in tropical and temperate zones) limited urban growth largely because there was no opportunity for regional specialization and interstimulation through trade. Trade was not simply an exchange of products but a catalyst for drawing societies into an expanding and diverse ecological network. Aided by the diffusion of a common technical and ideological base, the regionalizing of interrelations stimulated culture growth and provoked interregional configurations that were later consolidated by imperial conquest.

Where considerable similarity could be found between distant urban developments, the archeologist commonly sought an explanation in the comparative similarity of the cultural-ecological configurations (see Flannery 1961; Sanders 1962). In contrast, no better example of the restrictive nature of a sparse and relatively static environment could be found than in the Great Basin, which, as Haury (1962:112) observed, presented an extraordinary example of a mode of life that had changed little over the past 10,000 years.

The cultural-ecological interpretation of culture growth put forward by Braidwood and Willey joined ethnological views in a common stress on an optimum of unit dispersal, interactions, and developing organization (see, for example, Ezell 1961; Leeds 1961; Hudson 1970; Hickerson 1962). This interpretation was congenial to the efforts of ethnologists who charted the course of political integration whether as an evolutionary or acculturative process (Service 1962; Fried 1967; Cohen and Middleton 1970; Steward 1956; Spicer 1962).

ECOLOGY AND ACCULTURATION

The comparative investigations of ecocultural processes need not be confined to a comparison of socioeconomic arrangements within similar environments. Although environments and resources might be different, the kinds of exploitative relations could be similar and produce similar effects on culture and social organization. Such was the conclusion of Murphy and Steward (1956) after comparing the socioeconomic acculturation of Mundurucu rubber tappers of Brazil with that of Montaignais fur trappers of Quebec and Labrador. Both groups were nonstratified and became increasingly involved in the cropping of wild products for cash sales and exchanges. The greater their dependence on outside goods, the more rapidly their local crafts and skills declined. The increased reliance on purchasing power to supply wants and needs also created pressures toward individualization, with a consequent decline in group solidarity beyond the nuclear family. A network of cooperating kin charged with mutual obligations became more of a liability than an asset.

> The process of gradual shift from a subsistence economy to dependence upon trade is evidently irreversible, provided access to trade goods is maintained. It can be said, therefore, that the aboriginal culture is destined to be replaced by a new type which reaches its culmination when the responsible processes have run their course. The culmination point may have been reached when the amount of activity devoted to production for trade grows to such an extent that it interferes with the aboriginal subsistence cycle and associated social organization and makes their continuance impossible. (Murphy and Steward 1956(4):336)

In this statement Murphy and Steward underscored the development of a critical point in the operations of the aboriginal ecological configuration which signaled an important restructuring of relationships. This critical index emerged when the Indians turned from an accommodative relationship to a reciprocal-complementary one—that is, when tapping and trapping became as central to the livelihood of the Indians as to those who purchased these specialized products. Once this happened the Indians were caught up in an evolutionary process that drew them into ever-expanding trade relations and production for trade. When external demand declined, production in turn fell off, and the directionality of evolutionary change was altered. At the same time individual aspirations, kin obligations, and views on property rights would never be the same again.

ECOLOGY AND THE ECOCULTURAL BIOME

The importance of a regard for ecology was twofold, as Kroeber remarked when reviewing Steensby's (1916) analytical description of the cultural ecology of the Eskimo. First, focus on the noncultural environmental features brought new understandings to the life adaptations of the Eskimo and to the basis for variations in their culture. Second, a more integrated view of Eskimo culture was conveyed.

> He has for the first time outlined, for the whole of Eskimo territory, the importance of shore line, seasonal open water, drift and shore ice, driftwood or timber, and other natural features as they determined the presence or accessibility of various animal species and the habitual movements, occupations, and implement types of the Eskimo. What emerges from the total array of this succinctly analyzed data is not the primacy or priority of one particular economic adaptation, but a picture of the totality of Eskimo culture as a unit, modified by emphasis or reduction of its traits in direct response to local exigencies. Here seals are the important food, there whales, or walrus, or caribou, or birds, or salmon, while others are as good as unavailable. According to ice and water and season, seals are taken by maupok or waiting at the blowhole, utok or creeping, at cracks or the edge of the ice, from the kayak, or by nets. Even this last method, which is so specially developed in Alaska as to look at first as if its spread were determined culturally instead of ecologically, was known in Greenland, Labrador, and the Central regions. . . . Where, as on Coronation Gulf and in parts of Baffinland, seals far from shore are the only dependable subsistence available during a considerable part of the year, and the Eskimo have therefore to live on the ice, the snow house may wholly displace that of stone or sod. In southern Greenland and on the Mackenzie, on the contrary, driftwood is abundant, good-sized timbered houses are built, and the snow house is lacking except as a travel shelter. . . . If whale hunting is productive, the umiak is well equipped and paddled; elsewhere, it is a freight boat, rowed by woman; or where there are no whales and the short season of open sea is spent inland to get caribou, as on the shores of Coronation Gulf and on Boothia Peninsula, the umiak is absent. (Kroeber 1939:22–23)

The integrated overview of cultural-ecological relations to which Kroeber referred was translated into the model of the ecocultural community as a self-regulating biome. Turning to the Fijian island group of

Lau, Thompson (1949(51):265; compare McGee 1895) drew attention to the way in which plants, animals, and men moved inevitably to the formation of a natural community.

It is well known that isolated natural communities tend in time, by processes of symbiosis, accommodation and competition, to develop a delicately balanced, ecological organization wherein the various species of flora and fauna attain a mutually advantageous adjustment within the total environment. Ordinarily we think of the process mainly in terms of plants and animals in relation to the geological structure, climate, soil, water supply and other features of the physical environment. However, a broad-gauged analysis of the available data from this remote, relatively isolated community (where geological and ecological processes have proceeded for millennia relatively undisturbed and where cultural processes have operated for centuries with little interference from without) suggests that all of life is involved in a self-regulating web of relationships, human groups as well as so-called lower animals and plants. Seen as a whole, a natural community actually consists of its total population —plants, animals and human beings—in a complex, mutually interdependent relationship in environmental context.

The structural-functional orientation implicit in tracing ecological relations produced a homeostatic model in which cultural conventions affecting redistributions of products were interpreted as instruments of survival. New interpretations of institutionalized practices followed, stressing the adaptive regulation of access to unevenly distributed necessities. Thus, southern Kwakiutl chiefs of the Northwest Coast, though motivated by status-prestige and the social requirement of validating their status on prescribed occasions (for example, accession to a titled rank, change of title name, signaling maturation of chief's sons and daughters at puberty, marriage), actually triggered exchanges of food and wealth that made up for periodic deficiencies in the productivity and subsistence of the localized numayms and tribes invited to the potlatch (Piddocke 1965). According to Sweet (1965), camel raiding in North Arabia could be viewed as a cultural convention for redistributing camel resources among those suffering losses due to localized drought and disease. Regulation of such raids was in the hands of certain noble tribes who recouped their temporary losses according to ecologized rules of warfare. Reciprocal raiding among these noble tribes was confined to mature camels and horses. It also assured the safety of kinsmen, blacksmiths, and visiting friends of the raiders and made certain that a sufficient supply of camels for women and children to ride were left behind.

If we consider the institution of reciprocal camel raiding as an example, it adds its weight to previous studies which suggest that some predatory activities of human societies may be more fully understood as ecological adaptations supporting particular subsistence patterns at their widest range, and at the maximum advantage for the human societies dependent upon them.... While other factors in North Arabia play reinforcing and elaborating roles— the preservation of dominance over neighboring but distinct ecological types, for example—fundamental service of the reciprocal raid is to sustain a general balance of camel pastoral economies spatially through an extended region which is relatively uniform in geographical imperative. But the economic aspect is not alone supported; the whole network of social and ideological relations of Bedouin life is supported. Raiding emerges therefore as an integral mechanism of Bedouin culture. It is generalized in its multifunctional advantages to a kinship based society; it probably developed as the Bedouin pastoral economy acquired more culturally instigated needs for the basic resource animal. And it effectively met both external pressures and the localized habitat hazards without conflicting with the internal kin-based social relations of Bedouin society. The two or three thousand year time span which we can allot to Bedouin occupation of the North Arabian desert as camel breeding specialists seems to demonstrate quite adequately the success of this system. (Sweet 1965(67):1147–1148)

What held for the redistribution of camels among North Arabian Bedouins seemingly held for pig reduction and sacrifices to ancestors among the Tsembaga of the Central Highlands of New Guinea. Taking a broad ecosystems approach to Tsembaga ethnoecological and ecocultural operations, Rappaport (1968) determined that the ritual sacrifice of pigs served as a homeostat governing the relations of men to men, of men to pigs, and of men to garden and forest crops. The ritual which concentrated this self-regulation was the *kaiko*. This ceremony usually was held when the pig population had grown to such proportions that their feeding reached the limit of economic utility measured in terms of extra work in fencing, utilization of food stuffs normally consigned to human use, and interpersonal conflicts when pigs overran neighboring gardens. Viewing Tsembaga participation in both a local and a regional ecosystem, Rappaport (1967(6):28–29) observed:

The timing of the ritual cycle is largely dependent upon changes in the states of the components of the local subsystem. But the *kaiko*, which is the culmination of the ritual cycle, does more than reverse changes which have taken place within the local subsystem. Its occurrence also affects relations among the components of the regional subsystem. During its performance, obligations to other local populations are fulfilled, support for future military enterprises is rallied, and land from which enemies have earlier been driven is occupied. Its completion, furthermore, permits the local population to initiate warfare again. Conversely, warfare is terminated by rituals which preclude the reinitiation of warfare until the state of the local subsystem is again such that a *kaiko* may be staged and completed. Ritual among the Tsembaga and other Maring, in short, operates as both transducer, "translating" changes in the stage of one subsystem into information which can effect changes in a second subsystem, and homeostat, maintaining a number of variables which in sum comprise the total system within ranges of viability. . . . The operation of ritual among the Tsembaga and other Maring helps to maintain an integrated environment, limits fighting to frequencies which do not endanger the existence of the regional population, adjusts man-land ratios, facilitates trade, distributes local surpluses of pig throughout the regional population in the form of pork, and assures people of high quality protein when they are most in need of it [biochemical alterations due to tension states].

Religious rituals and the supernatural orders toward which they are directed cannot be assumed *a priori* to be mere epiphenomena. Ritual may, and doubtless frequently does, do nothing more than validate and intensify the relationships which integrate the social unit, or symbolize the relationships which bind the social unit to its environment. But the interpretation of such presumably *sapiens*-specific phenomena as religious ritual within a framework which will also accommodate the behavior of other species shows, I think, that religious ritual may do much more than symbolize, validate, and intensify relationships. Indeed, it would not be improper to refer to the Tsembaga and the other entities with which they share their territory as a "ritually regulated ecosystem," and to the Tsembaga and their human neighbors as a "ritually regulated population!"

One might question, however, whether war rather than ritual sacrifice was the key to Tsembaga ecocultural balance. The *koraiko* ritual appears to convey a license for war with the express sanction of ancestors, and the sharing of food with related groups at this time strengthened alliances. In the opinion of the Tsembaga, they may well have performed their last *koraiko*, since, under Australian mandate, they have been forbidden to wage war.

ECOLOGY AND ECOCULTURAL EFFICIENCY

Cybernetics, with its emphasis on self-regulatory processes, proved a fertile model for investigation of relations uniting man, animals, plants, and physical environment in a natural biome. The fate of the biome was equally the destiny of its interdependent participants. By viewing the economic activities of man-in-environment as part of a vast calorimetric system, the energy inputs and takeouts of hunters and swidden cultivators could be measured for specific effects and efficiency. Though figures were crude, Lee (1969) drew an analysis of !Kung Bushmen disclosing a daily food output per person exceeding their body requirements by about 165 calories. New insights were obtained by paying close attention to the diversity of foods and percentages each contributed to the diet. Lee concluded that the !Kung were not on a deficient diet, and moreover, time allotted to subsistence activities usually left them with a four-day leisure week.

Quantification of data on Tsembaga gardens (producing and fallowing), pigs, food intake, labor, and product allowed Rappaport (1968; compare Carneiro 1960) to estimate that their land base could support between 270 and 320 people. In 1963 their enumerated population was 204, and hence the Tsembaga were not living up to their ecological potential. When computing energy input-output ratios, Tsembaga return on their taro-yam and sugar-sweet potato gardens was seventeenfold and sixteenfold, respectively. Quantification of ecoeconomic relations also revealed that the Hanunóo of Mindoro did not fit the common stereotype of the swidden cultivator as a wastrel of tropical environment (Conklin 1954). The cattle complex of India was reviewed by Harris (1966) and calculated to have an important ecoeconomic input expressed in milk production, traction, fertilizer, fuel, and meat and hide products that had been overlooked in attacks on the sacred status of cattle and their extraordinary numbers. According to Harris (1966(7):51), far too much had been made of the impracticality of the Hindu cattle complex and too little of basic relationships of the cattle to the overall economy and maintenance of an ecological balance.

Numerical ratios and inputs and outputs operationalized the economic process and related it to an ecological context. There was, however, another context that could not be ignored—the social and cultural. This area was opened up by students of Malinowski who collected household budgets and data from which quantified statements on production, distribution, and consumption were made (Firth, Raymond 1929, 1946; Firth, Rosemary 1943; Hogbin 1938–1939; Fortes and Fortes 1936; Richards 1939; Richards and Widdowson 1936).

ECOLOGY AND THE ECOSOCIOLOGY OF INFILTRATION

The ecology of swidden cultivation likewise prompted a new look at the economics of primitive warfare. Bohannan's (1954) description of Tiv expansion, despite a loose segmentary organization, led Sahlins (1961) to reexamine the interrelations of their economy and sociopolitical organization. The unique feature of Tiv social organization lay in the mechanism for uniting individual lineages into paired sections at ever-higher levels of organization when challenged by an enemy group. Social organization of this type was ecofunctional in a situation where a tribe infiltrated into an occupied zone. Sahlins (1961(63):342) noted that

> Expansion in an open environment may be accompanied by segmentation, the normal process of tribal growth and spread. But in the absence of competition small segments tend to become discrete and autonomous, linked together primarily through mechanical solidarity. These circumstances . . . favor fission but select against complementary opposition or fusion, and long-term occupation will eventually fix this structure, make it comparatively inflexible. By contrast, growth in the face of opposition selects for complementary opposition as a social means of predation. Thus the *first* tribe in an area is unlikely to develop a segmentary lineage system, but the *second* tribe in that area is more likely to.

Sahlins drew the segmentary organization into an evolutionary schema at the level of the tribe, intermediate between the less evolved bands and the more advanced chiefdoms. The segmentary organization, however, had a limited ecoevolutionary role. It arose and persisted only so long as the competition for land between tribes governed their ecological relations. Segmentary organization had advantages in intertribal competition, but once victory was achieved it no longer had a function and diverse forces reasserted themselves in the political organization of the tribe. In Sahlins' (1961(63):342; compare Vayda 1960, 1961) judgment neolithic economies fostered schisms and fissions of local groups.

ECOLOGY AND ECOCULTURAL LEVELS

In its swidden form the neolithic economy demonstrated unusual potential for supporting large politically organized populations despite tendencies for groups to segment and disperse, as illustrated in the segmentary organization of Tiv and Nuer. There was, for instance, the distinguished Mayan civilization, with its social classes, craft specialists, and monumental religious structures, which thrived for centuries in the lowlands of Yucatan, Honduras, and Chiapas. Apparently gradual increments finally produced a culture platform throughout Mesoamerica that assured accelerated growth after 1000 B.C. The first expression of the new-found cultural potential was centered in the Tabasco Lowlands at La Venta, characterized by a ceremonial pyramid complex and the special Olmec art style whose influences reached into the Mexican highlands (Willey 1966). Using this broad Mesoamerican base, the Maya gradually penetrated the Yucatecan lowlands. With the rise of religious-administrative centers the Maya integrated their ecocultural system by linking rural areas to centers. After a time of efflorescence, the Classic Period (ca. A.D 300–900), the southern portions of these tropical lowlands (Peten) were gradually abandoned over a period of a hundred years. According to Thompson (1954:267),

> The lack of stability and the submergence of old values in the centuries after the close of the Classic Period are reflected in the decadence of the arts. Sculpture, architecture, and ceramics degenerated, sinking with each change for the worse in political and religious life to the pitiable level which the Spaniards encountered.

Cultural decline in a tropical forest setting was documented by Meggers and Evans (1957) in the culture sequence of Marajo Islands at the mouth of the Amazon. Early phases were characterized by a simplicity in technology and in ceremonial which is now reflected in contemporary tropical tribes. None of these early phases represented a continuous growth in a culture tradition; all appeared to be intrusive to the island. Around A.D. 1250 a more complex and technologically sophisticated culture, the Marajoara phase, apparently adapted to a more diverse circum-Caribbean and sub-Andean environment, intruded. Within 175 years the Marajoara culture had phased out, and its passing demonstrated that cultures adapted to varied and expressive environments may not survive when transplanted to a less promising habitat. The real limitations on culture growth seemingly resided in ecocultural relations, and Meggers (1954; compare White 1943, 1959b) considered the subsistence potential of the environment the crucial index of the ecocultural relationship. Therefore, in order to tap this crucial environment relation in culture growth, environments needed to be classified according to their agricultural potentials. Generally speaking, a law of culture growth could be stated as follows: *"the level to which a culture can develop is dependent upon the agricultural potentiality of the environment it occupies.* As this potentiality is improved, culture will advance. If it cannot be improved, the culture will become stabilized at a level compatible with the food resources" (Meggers 1954(56):815).

Megger's classification of evironments according to their potentials for culture growth pointed to the crucial relation between taxonomy and an increase in control over process. However, the independent variable selected by Meggers—the potential for agricultural productivity—proved unstable. This was true of her "Type 3" environment, which she defined as open to improvement through technological advancement, whether by invention or diffusion. An important datum also for the measurement and coordination of cultural achievement and ecological potential was the decline of the level of economic productivity and of cultural complexity. Cradles of civilization spawned by environments of unlimited agricultural potential (Type 4) were swept away by conquests and reduced to a shadow of their former greatness, testifying to the importance of technicosocial organization. This was surely an important consideration in the Maya case (Dumond 1961). In the wake of invasions from the Mexican area, the overcapitalization of religious ceremony and the militarization of society may have contributed to the weakening and fall of the theocratic integration achieved by the Classic Maya (Thompson 1954; Willey 1966). In the context of ecocultural processes, Thompson was struck by the superior achievements of the lowland Maya as compared with Maya in the Guatemalan highlands. "The important point is that the lowland Maya in their harsh setting of tropical rain forest outstripped their neighbors dwelling in highland and plateau country where conditions were so much more favorable" (Thompson 1954:269). Moreover, there was the singular fact that the first great art style of Mesoamerica, the Olmec, had been conceived in a tropical forest zone.

ECOLOGICAL INPUT TO ETHNOLOGICAL THEORY

The structural-functional-interactional posture in ethnological theory was strengthened and extended by the conception of an ecocultural system which operated according to the model of a biotic community. The ecological perspective reaffirmed the stress on systemic integration and the organic interdependence of parts and activities emphasized in structuralist theory. The self-regulating cybernetic model projected for the ecocultural system reaffirmed the concept of functional equilibrium. Moreover, the view of the ecocultural system as a self-regulating biome threatened to reify an internal mechanism (self-regulator or homeostat) that not only automatically adjusted the relations among participating units but also gave directional purpose to the system. Thus, in the instance of Lau (Fiji), Thompson (1949(51):263–264) observed:

> Before concluding we should note one more point . . . vital to an understanding of the Lauan system of production and distribution. . . . Despite its fine adjustment to the ecological setting and its basically self-perpetuating nature, this system could not operate effectively unless it were counterbalanced by a psychocultural arrangement which functioned to regulate and limit the size of the human population in relation to the resources of the community made available by the indigenous technology. Analyzing Lauan culture from this viewpoint, we find a complementary set of institutions which do actually tend to function toward just this end.
>
> For example, after the birth of a child the father moves out of the family dwelling and sleeps in the men's house of the clan. He is not allowed to have sexual intercourse with his wife until the baby is weaned, a period of from nine months to two years. The strict observance of this custom is attested by the fact that siblings in Lau are almost without exception at least eighteen months apart. Thus the men's house complex, correlated with certain tabus, functions as a means of birth spacing and population control and of protecting maternal and infant health. Ritual continence was practiced in Lau on many occasions. Several methods of abortion were used, mainly by unmarried mothers. In Fulanga old people who had outlived their usefulness, according to native standards, were formerly abandoned on a small island in the lagoon. Where chieftainship was highly developed, those who broke tabus concerning the nobility were clubbed to death. Raiding between villages, in the course of which men, women and children were killed, was not infrequent in the group, and those who were captured, regardless of age or sex, were consumed by the victors at cannibalistic feasts. These are some of the Lauan practices which, together with accidents, hurricanes, disease, and a rate of infant and maternal mortality which was probably rather high, tended to limit the size of the population in relation to the available resources within the natural and cultural setting. Although in historic times Fijian population totals were greatly reduced, especially by the ravages of white man's diseases, the low point was reached at about 1911. Thereafter the trend has been slowly upward. The population of southern Lau gained 155 per 1,000 between 1921 and 1935. At the time of the present field work, the population of the community was about 1,500.

In discoursing on the cultural and natural checks on population, Stott (1962) cited evidence showing how both animals and men experienced comparable effects mediated by genetic processes. When food is scarce or tension high, malformations that militate against survival increase among the newborn. Moreover, those who inherit a major defect, such as mental retardation, tend to exhibit a complex of handicaps. During the years 1940–1942, when war-survival tensions were high in England, female infants dying within four weeks of birth owing to malformations were almost twice the number of male infants! With regard to world population, Stott's view was that man could expect certain natural regulators of physiological processes to take control unless man employed his conscious skills in maintaining the ecodemographic balance.

By focusing on the internal mechanism, the homeostat, a view of eco-cultural processes reminiscent of the reign of natural law in biological evolution during the nineteenth century, was projected. Man once again seemed a product of bioadaptive processes. It was apparent, however, that the ecological interpretation frequently reversed explanation, naively substituting bioenvironmental for social or cultural cause. When the calorimetrics of yams and pigs moved to the center of discourse, the social and cultural was shunted aside. As Vayda (1966(7):63) commented on Harris' (1966) analysis of the cultural ecology of India's sacred cattle, use of the adjective "cultural" in Harris' title was superfluous.

> His paper discusses organisms (human, bovine, etc.) in interaction with one another and with their non-living environments. This is just plain ecology, and the general concepts and principles to which Harris has recourse are for the most part as applicable to other species as they are to culture-bearing man.

In point of method, the ecological orientation duplicated communication models rooted in cybernetics and thus presented a convergence with model-building preferences in ethnology. A more critical contribution can be found in the teasing out of interdependencies, uniting environment, demography, human physiology, social psychology, economic activities, social organization, custom, and the institutionalization of values in an interactional universe or configuration.

The ramifications of ecological investigation freshened linkages with physical anthropology (Coon, Garn, and Birdsell 1950) and primatology, where the ecological adaptations of monkeys, apes, and baboons were sifted for leads in the nature and evolution of human expressive behavior, sociality, communication, and superordinate-subordinate relations (see, for example, Washburn 1961; Howell and Bourlière 1963; Jay 1968). In the context of primate ecology, capacities to communicate and to learn took on a special survival aspect, suggesting that these adaptations must be taken in the perspective of evolution if their full significance were to be realized. Thus, following the lead of ethologists (for example, Lorenz, Tinbergen, and Eibl-Eibesfeldt), Washburn and Hamburg (1968:463–464) observed:

> The result of evolution is that behaviors that have been adaptive in the past history of the species, which led to reproductive success, are easy to learn and hard to extinguish. As Hinde and Tinbergen have put it: "This exemplifies a principle of great importance; many of the differences between species do not lie in the first instance in stereotyped behavior sequences but consist in the possession of a propensity to learn."

In the man-environment relation, the exchange of parasites and epidemic and endemic syndromes which correlated with human use of land must be viewed in the perspective of evolutionary selection. For example, cultivation of the tropical rain forest zone in Africa apparently fostered the spread of malaria-bearing mosquitoes by providing areas for their breeding. The human response to this parasite was the genetic formation of sickle cells in the blood, inducing a level of immunity (Livingstone 1958; compare Wiesenfeld 1967). The survival value of genetic adaptation thus permitted continuation of the economic adaptation. However, the lesson was clear—environmental modifications which accompanied the building of culture created a special ecology for microorganisms holding a peculiar affinity for man. Social evolution from hunting band to agricultural village and town, according to Hudson (1965), provided the milieu favorable to the differentiation of *Treponema pallidum* from its original form of yaws into the variety that caused venereal syphilis. *Treponemas* thus were the active agents for syphilis, and the different forms of syphilis were products of variation in the ecology of the parasite. Early hunters and gatherers of the Lower Paleolithic probably experienced yaws as a florid skin eruption so long as they confined themselves to a rain-forest habitat. Once populations entered a drier climate the treponemes concentrated around the moist areas of the body, with lesions forming about the mouth, crotch, and underarms. The later manifestation was found among village cultivators and pastoralists of field and plain. Endemic syphilis or yaws was largely a childhood disease, but with the change to town life the parasite experienced a change in environment. Sanitation and clothing practices inhibited the usual transmission through direct body contact, and the venereal strain apparently differentiated.

> Thus, as towns and cities evolved in ancient times, more and more people grew to maturity without having fallen victim to endemic syphilis. At the same time in the urban milieu promiscuity and prostitution increased to a degree unknown in the village environment; members of the adult population, now vulnerable to the sporadic infection, gradually acquired and transmitted syphilis venereally. This transformation of syphilis from an innocent infection of children to a venereal disease of adults probably took place first in Southwest Asia, but the same thing must have happened everywhere that parallel and comparable events occurred, when village-centered society yielded to urban civilization. What happened in "Western society" eventually had its counterpart in the social evolution of man in India, China, Indonesia, Mexico, Peru and elsewhere. (Hudson 1965(67):895; compare Zinsser 1934)

The strength of the ecological orientation, in final analysis, rested on a broad comprehension of variables operating in combination to produce an effect. It was this holistic emphasis that stimulated lively relations between ethnology and physical anthropology, including ethology, primatology, and epidemiology. The theoretical thrust was not toward simple cause-effect, but rather toward a conception of variables reciprocating in their adjustive interactions and converging in their effects to produce an event. An ecological perspective also accommodated structural-evolutionary change through the conception of ecological succession. At the same time, the problem of variation was taken up by noting how local diversity in environment could produce cultural variants within a broad region. In tracing the movement of peoples from localized ecological niches into broader eco-cultural configurations that expanded and contracted according to circum-stances, the ecological approach likewise supplied a basis for unifying his-toric and evolutionary processes.

SUMMARY

A renewed interest in the relations between society and culture on the one hand and environment on the other was a natural extension of the interest in systemic processes that accompanied the rise of Structuralism. Owing to their institutional bias, social Structuralists and Bioculturalists investigated economic processes, while American culture theorists con-sidered the fit between cultures and environments because of their concern with culture areas and the geographic distribution of culture. Kroeber's (1939) publication of *Cultural and Natural Areas of Native North America* signaled the beginning of new interest in ecological-cultural relations which, however, did not develop in strength until after World War II. At the same time Steward (1936, 1938) began investigating the influence ecological relationships exerted on the size, stability, and organization of social units and cultural systems. Steward's persistent attempts to systematize eco-logical theory and method were largely responsible for the increased atten-tion to ecology and social systems that took hold in the fifties.

The ecological perspective accented the dynamic interdependence of sociocultural and ecological biomes. However, the ecological focus shifted observation from the sociocultural system to a complex of relations that linked men, plants, animals, waterways, erosion processes, soil fertility, temperature, and other environmental features in a commmon destiny. Under ecological analysis, sociocultural systems revealed sensitive adapta-tions to environmental pressures and rhythms that accounted for special elements of social organization. It was tempting to measure the ecological efficiency of sociocultural systems and to see their potential for expansion, and the manner of their expansion, as a function of ecological circum-stances.

Emphasis on a reciprocating network of relationships supported con-ceptions commonly found in Structuralism. The idea of balance or homeo-stasis in particular was stressed. However, as a system, an ecocultural configuration stimulated an analysis that emphasized the production, dis-tribution, and consumption of energy rather than the flow of activity between statuses. At the same time the idea of a succession of ecological systems or biomes favored an evolutionary view of ecocultural relation-ships.

Steward (1955) saw cultures starting from different ecological bases and traversing separate paths. However, because of a common core of institutions derived from economic and ecological necessities, the separate cultures went through similar stages in their evolution. Steward thus translated the theory of parallel evolution held by Developmentalists into an eco-institutional key ("multilineal" evolution). In prehistoric perspective, the critical factor in the advance of civilization was the unification of diverse ecocultural systems into a multifunctional ecocultural configuration through trade networks, ideological and ceremonial diffusions, and conquest (Braidwood and Willey 1962).

Generally speaking, the ecological approach continued the holistic perspective in anthropology, and, in its special concern for bioenvironmental relationships, stimulated fresh linkages between ethnology and demography, physical anthropology, ethology, primatology, and epidemiology. In a world of finite resources and burgeoning populations, ecological considerations became especially relevant for human survival and the nature of society. As Anderson (1973:213) observed, "The collective welfare and ultimately the survival of mankind with any reasonable quality of life will demand a reordering of every modern socioeconomic system." If a reordering of priorities essential to these goals were to be achieved, a humanistic ecological perspective was both necessary and inevitable.

18

Differentiation of Ethnojurisprudence and Ethnopolitics

INTRODUCTION

The differentiation of ethnojurisprudence and of ethnopolitics can be treated together, since in the thinking of scholars, the judicial process often is merged with the political process. That is, the state not only serves as the locus for power but also wields that power in the enforcement of regulations that minimize conflict within the society. Moreover, the theoretical course of these specializations has followed the intellectual succession manifest in Developmentalism, Structuralism, and Differentiative Specialization. In reaching for new understandings, judicial and political anthropologists have reacted to entrenched theory, and at the same time have responded sensitively to changes in the legal and political process taking place in the wider society.

Developmentalists viewed the advancement of law in three modes. First, the moral progress of law could be traced from private retaliation to public law, wherein the rights of both plaintiff and accused were protected by procedural rules. Second, law was gradually disengaged from its association with religious belief and practice, and through secularization, attained its own independence as a social process. Third, law moved progressively from a collective to an individualized process. That is, the rights of individuals, and the protections of individuals, gradually were extended through advancement of the civilized state, sparked by the guarantee of individual property rights.

With regard to the political institution, Developmentalists began by charting the gradual differentiation of responsible authority and its role in stabilizing organized society. By the end of the nineteenth century, they began to place the state center stage in the future advancement of mankind. Concern for the primary role of the state was fed by inputs from three political-philosophic sources:

1. The identification of the individual's destiny and realization of self through his national bloodline, or the state.
2. The view of the state as the critical setting for the mobilization of social forces in the attainment of social reform and social utopias.
3. The view of the state as a repressive order which ultimately must be curbed to allow the natural instincts of men full play in the formation of voluntary corporate associations.

In the rise of the state, progressivists accorded a preeminent role to war (Millar 1806), tracing a continuity from the centralization of power in the hands of war leader to monarch. In the view of evolutionists, the social process of conflict was transformed into an organic law of natural selection, with the state exercising the integrative control that assured societal continuities (Spencer 1900; Gumplowicz 1883). Under the dialectical materialism of Marx, the state was the stage for a power struggle and for the mobilization of forces, human and technical, to establish an egalitarian utopia.

With the rise of Structuralism, the roles of the judicial and political processes in organizing and stabilizing society were merged in a consideration of the structured linkages of statuses. Status was defined as a cluster of legal rights and duties. That is, any status related to another status in a normative demand-right or liability relationship. Such appeared to be the intent of social structural analysis initiated by Radcliffe-Brown and followed by British social anthropologists. A centralized authority, whether chief or monarch, constituted the necessary concentration of force for maintaining a smoothly operating system of demand rights and liabilities. Law and government thus moved to the forefront in this British legalist view of the structural-functional needs of society. However, religious and moral imperatives also were operative in sanctioning social action.

Culture historians, owing to their goal of tracing culture traits and of reconstructing the growth of cultures, did not make any special contribution to the study of law and government. In 1927 Lowie (1962), in *The Origin of the State*, did argue that primitive societies, in their territorial arrangements, possessed the potential for developing political organization. French Structuralists likewise showed little interest in law and politics in their quest for the ultimate symbols of social solidarity in a religious value sentiment. By implication, however, French Structuralists seated the rights and obligations of primitive citizenship in a civil right to participate in the sacred rites of solidarity. This view perpetuated the postion of Fustel de Coulanges, and affirmed a time-honored position that sacred sanctions were at the root of law and order.

Reintroduction of an evolutionary perspective in American ethnology spurred a rash of efforts to classify and arrange political systems in a graded succession, moving from simplicity to complexity. This political-evolutionary perspective was stimulated in part by the parallel interest of prehistorians in the rise of the ancient urban civilizations, by ecological inputs, and by Marxian theory which linked the rise of stratified states to economic processes which controlled the forces of production.

The differentiative thrust toward specialization introduced greater factual depth which tempered the ultralegalistic approach of social Structuralism and drew attention to the dynamic accommodation of legal-political norms and procedures in the social process. New perceptions of legal processes suggested that the extralegal or unintended functions of law constituted a vital domain which had been neglected in the interest of analyses of the formal aspects of legal systems (Nader and Yngvesson 1973: 909).

THE SOCIAL FUNCTIONS OF LAW

The differentiation of juridical anthropology owed much to Malinowski's efforts to correct views of primitive man and primitive law fostered by the faulty evolutionary perspective and method. In *Crime and Custom in Savage Society*, Malinowski (1926) criticized the evolutionists on the following counts:

1. Use of statements stressing ideal or normative practice as the empirical reality.
2. Definition of primitive law as a body of negative prohibitions or taboos sanctioned by the punishing intervention of supernatural forces and spiritual beings.
3. View of primitive social process as bonded by a communal sentiment spontaneously exhibited in savage devotion to custom, and steadied by dread of supernatural punishment.
4. Definition of primitive law as criminal law only, a consequence of their faulty view of primitive man and society.

The heart of Malinowski's counterarguments rested in his view of law as a social process. This being the case, "There must be in all societies a class of rules too practical to be backed up by religious sanctions, too burdensome to be left to mere goodwill, too personally vital to individuals to be enforced by any abstract agency" (Malinowski 1926:67–68). Here was the domain of legal rules, and Malinowski set out to show that wherever economic, kinship, and religious activities involved the mutual adjustment of obligation, there would be legal practice of a binding order, the realm of civil law. The legal rules found in the civil law of the Trobriands were supported by personal interest and social convention that inspired a desire to conform because of the psychological and material rewards accompanying conventional practice:

the binding forces of Melanesian civil law are to be found in the concatenation of the obligations, in the fact that they are arranged into chains of mutual services, a give and take extending over long periods of time and covering wide aspects of interest and activity. To this there is added the conspicuous and ceremonial manner in which most of the legal obligations have to be discharged. This binds people by an appeal to their vanity and self-regard, to their love of self-enhancement by display. Thus the binding force of these rules is due to the natural mental trend of self-interest, ambition and vanity, set into play by a special social mechanism into which the obligatory actions are found. (Malinowski 1926:67)

Yet, in view of a human propensity to evade obligation, often aided by a traditionalizing of certain kinds of evasions, the fundamental function of law was to restrain natural human desires at variance with the common good. As a social process law compelled individuals to surrender some of their private ends and to cooperate to ensure social life. Hence, the importance of a pragmatic reciprocity and appeal to personal interest in the sociolegal process.

In focusing on the social function of law, Malinowski concluded that law emerges from those relations where individuals and groups expect and assert the discharge of a duty.

"Civil law," the positive law governing all the phases of tribal life, consists then of a body of binding obligations, regarded as a right by one party and acknowledged as a duty by the other, kept in force by a specific mechanism of reciprocity and publicity inherent in the structure of their society. These rules of civil law are elastic and possess a certain latitude. They offer not only penalties for failure, but also premiums for an overdose of fulfillment. Their stringency is ensured through the rational appreciation of cause and effect by the natives, combined with a number of social and personal sentiments such as ambition, vanity, pride, desire of self-enhancement by display, and also attachment, friendship, devotion and loyalty to the kin.

It scarcely needs to be added that "law" and "legal phenomena" as we have discovered, described and defined them in a part of Melanesia, do not consist in any independent institutions. Law represents rather an aspect of their tribal life, one side of their structure, than any independent, self-contained social arrangements. Law dwells not in a special system of decrees, which foresee and define possible forms of non-fulfillment and provide appropriate barriers and remedies. Law is the specific result of the configuration of obligations, which makes it impossible for the native to shirk his responsibility without suffering for it in the future. (Malinowski 1926:58–59; compare Seagle 1937)

Law, in Malinowski's judgment, rested on a positive accommodation of the requirements for social living, and hence was something more than a bundle of negative and fearsome prohibitions. Equally important, he asserted that it was not the object that was the focus of attention in understanding concepts about property, but the function of the object in a network of obligatory rights and privileges by which individuals and joint owners were bound to an object as well as to each other. In the example of a canoe, as found in the Trobriands,

> every joint owner has a right to a certain place in it and to certain duties, privileges, and benefits associated with it. He has his post in the canoe, he has his task to perform, and enjoys the corresponding title, either of "master" or "steerman" or "keeper of the nets," or "watcher for fish." His position and title are determined by the combined action of rank, age, and personal ability. Each canoe also has its place in the fleet, and its part to play in the manoeuvres of joint fishing. Thus on a close inquiry we discover in this pursuit a definite system of division of functions and a rigid system of mutual obligations, into which a sense of duty and the recognition of the need of co-operation enter side by side with a realization of self-interest, privileges, and benefits. Ownership, therefore, can be defined neither by such words as "communism" nor "individualism," nor by reference to "joint-stock company" system or "personal enterprise," but by concrete facts and conditions of use. (Malinowski 1926:20–21)

The essence of ownership was not static possession but rather a dynamic affirmation of a right of use, with and in opposition to others.

LAW AND THE FUNCTIONAL PREREQUISITES OF SOCIETY

Any effort to determine the functional prerequisites of society must accord a prominent place to law in supporting the exercise of rights, and in enjoining performance of duties essential to the needs of society. This was Radcliffe-Brown's approach to law as social process. Together with religion and morality, law formed a triad by which human conduct was controlled in the interests of social solidarity and continuity (Radcliffe-Brown 1965h:172). Radcliffe-Brown found the idea of corporateness exceedingly useful for understanding the nature of society and its functional prerequisites. Legal rights exercised with relation to an estate were characteristic of corporations, and the life of these rights, as the powers and liabilities of the corporation, held an existence independent of its members. Essential to the life of the corporation, as to society, was the exercise of three sets of rights:

(a) Rights over a person imposing some duty or duties upon that person. This is the *jus in personam* of Roman law. A father may exercise such rights over his son, or a nation over its citizens.
(b) Rights over a person "as against the world," i.e., imposing duties on all other persons in respect of that particular person. This is the *jus in rem* of Roman law in relation to persons.
(c) Rights over a thing, i.e., some object other than a person, as against the world, imposing duties on other persons in relation to the thing. (Radcliffe-Brown 1965d:32–33)

These demand-rights not only exacted duties from members of the corporation (a) but also rendered the possessory rights of the corporation (b and c) inviolate. The exercise of any of these rights was a function of legal status, and for Radcliffe-Brown (1965d:37), any individual, speaking socially, was a legal person holding status "defined as the totality of all his rights and duties as recognized in the social usages (laws and customs) of the society to which he belongs."

Applied to families, lineages, and clans in primitive society, the corporate analog described an organized set of legal statuses held by persons who carried out special obligatory activities and exacted duties from others. The transfer of these legal statuses from one generation to the next guaranteed the stability and continuity of the social structure. In Radcliffe-Brown's judgment, matrilineal and patrilineal descent was the logical functional adaptation to the need for a clear definition of rights over persons in relation to others—that is, rights *in rem*. What led to this conclusion, apparently, was the nature of the possessory rights maintained by joint families or descent groups over their members in the practice of exogamy, levirate, and sororate. In the context of law, each could be viewed as the transfer, acquisition, or reassertion of rights *in rem*.

Law provided the sinews for the normative specifications of society and drew attention to the formal requirements and the structure of social systems. Law was especially relevant to the political process, and Radcliffe-Brown (1962b:xviii), in seeking to define political structure in a simple society, stressed its unity as a territorial community regulated by the law. Law was recognized in public acceptance of penal sanctions applied to offenders and of traditional means of settling disputes and assessing claims for injury. The role of political authority was to establish and guarantee "social order, within a territorial framework, by the organized exercise of coercive authority, through the use, or the possibility of use, of physical force" (Radcliffe-Brown 1962b:xiv). With law and authority combining to support a normative social order, both must concentrate the symbols and the sentiments which hold great public value.

More so than other aspects of the social structure, the political institution arrogated and rationalized the mystical symbols by which peoples unconsciously experienced their affiliations. Hence, the political institution dominated all other aspects of the social order (Fortes and Evans-Pritchard 1962; compare Gluckman 1955; Gulliver 1963). Social, economic, judicial, religious, and political symbols clustered around African kingship and were drawn into focus by the ritualization of functions relating to accession and public welfare. In this ritualization of the political function, it appeared that the utilitarian interests which united individuals were secondary to the sense of unity experienced in the dramatization of mystical symbols (Fortes and Evans-Pritchard 1962:23). Ultimate values derived from the fabric of social relations thus reigned over pragmatic considerations. The strength of these transcendent social values was detected in ceremonialized role inversions and in licensed expressions of hatred and covetousness directed at chief and king, the prime symbols of group unity and authority (Gluckman 1954, 1955; compare Bohannan 1958). When testing joking relationships, Radcliffe-Brown (1965f) attempted to demonstrate that ceremonialism was the social plaster which prevented the tensions of social living from widening into chasms. In the interests of preserving a friendly unity among local groups, the ceremonialized blood-lettings of Australian hordes seemed to be classic designs for a catharsis of aggression (Howitt 1904; Warner 1958).

In the context of culture, Hoebel (1954) also found law an intrinsic aspect of the social process. Social needs dictated the presence of law in society. In the long perspective of sociocultural growth, the need for law increased with each advance in complexity. The importance of law as a social process was found in the discrimination of the kinds of relations by which individuals and groups were linked. Following Hoebel (1954:48), one could arrange legal relations in four modalities:

Person A	Person B
I. Demand-right	Duty
II. Privilege-right	No demand-right
III. Power	Liability
IV. Immunity	

Of these four modalities linking demand to duty, I and III carried the primary legal process. Under demand-right, the respondent must discharge an obligation. A similar situation followed when A voluntarily initiated action, as in acceptance of a proferred contract, which brought B into hard liability. The essence of law, however, rested on sanctions, implied or explicit, that bonded the relationship. In turn public sentiment guaranteed the application of sanctions; for the real test of law in primitive or civilized society was the legitimate use of coercive force by a socially empowered authority (Hoebel 1954:26). In substance, laws were statements of relationships that should prevail, but they differed from other cultural norms in the thrust and application of socially approved force. That is, *"a social norm is legal if its neglect or infraction is regularly met, in threat or in fact, by the application of physical force by an individual or group possessing the social recognized privilege of so acting"* (Hoebel 1954:28).

The course of legal growth followed a differentiation related to a measure of socioeconomic and cultural complexity. Law began with wrongs in the private sector and moved to the public domain. When law became a public concern, legal process was transformed into judicial process. For example, in simple collecting and hunting societies, the law of persons prevailed, and procedural law was delicately poised between public consensus and the intentions of the parties to the conflict. The more sedentary life of cultivators promoted the accumulation of properties, and the law of goods began to rival in importance the law of persons. Descent groups emerged as the focus for citizenship expressed in economic, legal, and political rights and obligations (Hoebel 1954:316). Hoebel thus affirmed Radcliffe-Brown's perception of descent groups as focal to the emergence of individuals as legal persons.

The differentiation of law proceeded not only in diversification in types of wrongs but also in the increasing importance of civil delicts. New procedural rules developed with chiefs and councils adjudicating private disputes and criminal offenses. The shift from individual and family to corporate descent groups as the primary legal entity likewise strengthened the influence of normative definitions based on public consensus. However, under a corporate descent-group organization, the legal process maintained only a precarious balance between competing interests and loyalties of kin groups and the larger community. In evolutionary perspective, the conflict of interest existing in private, corporate, and public law was decided in favor of public law. Public law first appeared with the institutionalization of chieftainship and a council of advisers and grew with the extension of political power. With the transfer of procedure into the hands of public officials, law entered the stage of judicial process. Hence, the assumption reported by Nader (1965(67):10) that judicial behavior was an aspect of political behavior (see, for example, Hoebel 1940; Nadel 1947; Busia 1951; Bohannan 1957; Richardson 1940).

A functional interpretation of law converged naturally on legal process as the servant of the normative aspirations and operations of society. Following the model of Malinowski, the legal institution included a basic charter of assumptions, value or normative definitions, personnel, organized activities, and goals. Charter and norms articulated basic world views and values, and in his analysis of Eskimo, Ifugao, Comanche-Kiowa-Cheyenne, Trobriand, and Ashanti legal processes, Hoebel (1954) tested disputes and their settlement against value postulates and corollaries to demonstrate their coordinate consistencies. Ifugao assumptions relevant to the legal process could be collapsed into six postulates, fourteen primary and four secondary corollaries.

Postulates and corollaries constituted the grammar by which legal relations to persons and things were produced and defined situations where claims could be entered for breach. Emphasis on the right to an enforceable claim for injury was important in discriminating social from legal custom. Despite the binding obligation of social reciprocity reported by Malinowski, not all reciprocating custom was law. The important property of law vis-à-vis custom, in Bohannan's (1965(67):36) estimation, was the reinstitution-alization of a right-duty relationship in order to give society a set of rules whereby it could maintain its basic functions and operate with orderly procedures. Law as a formal restatement of values and procedures regulating claims of individuals and groups against each other was an essential social process, serving to mute disruptive conflict. In the adjudication of competing and conflicting interests, law was the balance wheel of society, embedding itself pervasively in morality, religion, governance, and economy. But the legal process also provided a source for innovation in that primary institutions were tested against the formal measure of the reinstitution-alized norms. In Bohannan's view, law and established society never were quite in phase, and this absence of fit was a functional requirement for social repair and change (see Fallers 1969).

The relative homogeneity or heterogeneity of sociocultural space exerted a considerable effect on the role of law in accommodating conflicts of interest and in generating new principles of interpretation through disputatious precedent. In a kin-based society operating according to traditional law-ways, fundamental cultural values steadied the legal process and produced settlements congruent with the legal values. This was detected even in colonialized areas where native courts were permitted to function with minimal interference as in the case of Tiv moots assembled to deal with intralineage disputes allegedly involving supernatural powers directed, consciously or unconsciously, against a relative (Bohannan 1957; see Llewellyn and Hoebel 1941; Oberg 1934; Gibbs 1962; Gluckman 1955). However, where cultural differences intruded in conflicts of interest, the legal process reflected political rather than legal values. For example, Tiv youth, emphasizing what Bohannan (1957:209–210) called alien "prestigious cultural values," utilized the colonial judicial system to bring an end to traditional exchange marriage. Cultural pluralism, rigid stratification, and divisive political-economic struggles invited the intrusion of political considerations in legal settlements (for example, Epstein 1951; Schapera 1938; Dundas 1921; Barnes 1961; Tanner 1970; Srinivas 1954; Friedrich 1958). Whether law should be viewed as a "rationalization of conflict" (Tanner 1970; see Pospisil 1958) or as a reinstitutionalization of norms thus depended on context—that is, whether a sociocultural structure was relatively stable and composed of uniform parts, or dynamically accommodative by virtue of competing unlike parts.

The study of law as social process revealed that legal process was as sensitive to the nature of the interactional field as other sociocultural domains. A homogeneous context permitted continuities in process that sensitively reaffirmed values traditional in the regulation of interpersonal and intergroup relations. A heterogeneous context, on the other hand, was more likely marked by conflicts of interest that could be resolved only through compromise or appeal to extralegal processes. Behind these processual distinctions lay the ultimate issues of structural process and historic process. A homogeneous state could be readily translated into a "mechanical model" and the heterogeneous into a "statistical model" after the fashion of Lévi-Strauss. From their data investigators of law shared experiences which crossed those of economic and social anthropologists.

POLITICAL EVOLUTION AND POLITICAL INTEGRATION

Evolutionary Process and Cause

An evolutionary perspective commonly focuses on continuities and differentiations of institutions. At the same time it is difficult to describe the unfolding of an institution, say the political, without making reference to coordinate modifications in other institutions. It is not unusual, then, to find the archeologist Childe (1936) and ethnologists White (1943, 1959b) and Steward (1937, 1949, 1955)—all of whom pioneered in reintroduction of the evolutionary perspective—describing a coordinated process of change that involved social, economic, legal, military, religious, and political institutions. Whether the investigator places causal confidence in one or more variables and factors makes a difference in the type of descriptive analysis produced. Explanations based on single variables lead to evolutionary models that show coordinate divergence stemming from the input of the preferred variable. Introduction of two or more variables produces a more complex network of reciprocal inputs and differentiations. Even in the case of the unitary-cause model, it is not easy to maintain the pervasive continuity of the causal variable. The test for this is simple, as White (1959b:293–296) discovered when seeking to explain the differentiation of two different political economies from a common economic base—that is, the Agricultural Revolution. These two political economies were the commercial and the socialistic, the former stimulating private enterprise and the latter organizing state-controlled enterprise. To explain the divergence, White introduced an intervening variable, degree of integrative continuity, or homogeneity-heterogeneity.

Energy and the Economic-Political Process: White

Taking his cue from a per capita energy-use formula, White (1959b) traced a sequence of political change that followed social-functional adaptations to needs generated by the addition of new forms of energy. Thus the advent of cultivation increased density clustering; and, in consequence, the kinship organization of primitive societies experienced severe pressures to modify the means of production. This adaptive maneuver produced specialists who relied on others for food production; and as trade and monetary exchange improved, society was divided into the debtors and creditors, and ultimately into the rich and the poor (White 1959b:300). The whole structure of kin-based institutions eroded and new institutions were formulated to accommodate private ownership, wealth differentials, occupational specialization, social class, property inheritance, and public institutions centered in law, religion, defense, finance, and political authority. Change moved toward satisfying the functional requirements of the system, and White credited warfare with a special role in centralizing the political power essential to coordination.

> Maintenance of integrity is essential to any system, sociocultural or otherwise. If the new type of civil society that was being produced by the developing technologies of agriculture and animal husbandry were to be able to maintain and perpetuate itself, it would have to achieve and maintain integrity, and this would mean doing three things: (1) coordinating, correlating, and integrating the various parts and functions of which the new sociocultural system was composed, namely, the various public works and community enterprises such as irrigation, communal offices, temples, transportation, public markets, systems of currency, and so on; coordinating and integrating the various social

structures that comprise the system as a whole, namely, the occupational groups—industrial, ecclesiastical, and military. (2) It would have to reconcile the two basic classes of society, the dominant, ruling class and the subordinate class, whose interests were not only different but opposite and conflicting at many points, and prevent the subordinate class from disrupting society and reducing it to anarchy and chaos through insurrection and civil war. And finally (3) it must maintain its autonomy and independence by successful military operations of offense and defense with reference to its neighbors. To accomplish all this, the new society would have to have a special mechanism, a special political device, for coordination, integration, regulation, and control. Such a special mechanism was developed. We shall call it the *state-church.* (White 1959b:300–301)

Measured against the criterion of functional adequacy, kinship institutions proved maladaptive to technological change and hence broke down. In locating the essence of cultural evolution in functional adaptation, White (1959b:302) simply applied a deterministic cause and effect relationship to sociocultural phenomena; that is, when a certain set of conditions developed, a special kind of effect was produced.

Functional Necessity and Integration

As a deterministic cause of evolutionary developments, functional necessity is a logical explanation for adaptive modifications in structure which bear on survival. It is simply the application of the principle of natural selection to social and cultural phenomena. Whether one derives his concept of functional necessity from a machine or an organism makes little difference. A concept of functional necessity patterned after nineteenth-century social evolutionists is the touchstone for those who offer an evolutionary prospectus to uncover social and political process. The problem, as Service (1962:179) observes, involves an ordering of relations with respect to functional necessity and priority of development, which allows the assignment of cause and effect relationships. In tracing the evolution of society, the primary focus might be on those principles and processes that diffuse and coordinate integration. In Service's (1962:181) view, the classificatory possibilities in terms of types and levels of integration are five in number:

(1) familistic bonds of kinship and marriage which by their nature can integrate only the relatively small and simple societies that we call bands; (2) pantribal socialities which can integrate several bandlike societies into one; (3) specialization, redistribution, and the related centralization of authority which can integrate still more complex societies; (4) the state, further integrated by a bureaucracy employing legal force; (5) an industrial society integrated not only by a state apparatus but also by a complex network of specialized, interdependent occupations.

Applying these typologic criteria to the world of primitive man, Service distinguished three sociopolitical arrangements—bands, tribes, and chiefdoms. This typological continuum disclosed a movement from egalitarian status to ranked status, that is, a trend from a homogeneous state to a heterogeneous one. Increments in heterogeneity brought structural change and increased political authority, a functional requisite for coordinating the social system. The Spencerian echo was clear in Service's analysis and obviously crossed Durkheim's distinction of mechanical and organic solidarity. However, an advance in technological complexity apparently did not account for increased productivity and population density found in chiefdoms. Rather, the chiefdom reflected a managerial innovation that accelerated productive specialization and redistribution. "The resulting organic basis of social integration made possible a more integrated society, and the increased efficiency in production and distribution made possible a denser society" (Service 1962:144). The mark of chiefdoms was a coordinating redistributive organization.

In the context of functional necessity, the rise of city states was connected to the increasing organicness of economic relations and interests throughout a broad area (see, for example, Adams 1966; Braidwood and Willey 1962; compare Sjöberg 1955 and Redfield 1953). All ancient civilizations, according to Wittfogel (1957), had water problems. This critical domain served as the catalyst for a bureaucratic managerial process that shaped the ancient states. Faced with the twin problems of periodic flooding and unequal flow to fields, the masses were forced to deliver themselves into the hands of a managerial elite wielding monopolistic powers. Labor and management, that complementary dichotomy of the industrial work world, thus got its start with the need for large water works. The functional need for hydraulic control fed easily into other functional necessities. Government regulation of water meant control over food production. Since labor was paid in kind, government was compelled to regulate the price of food products in the market place and the amount a worker received for his labor. With a firm monopoly over labor and food surplus, government commonly embarked on monumental public construction (tombs, temples, palaces, fortresses), all of which are strikingly absent in the nonhydraulic civilizations. In response to bookkeeping necessities of their operations, each of the "hydraulic agromanagerial" civilizations (for example, Babylonia, Egypt, India, Peru) pioneered in record keeping, census enumeration, calendrics, and arithmetic and geometry. Control over hydraulic works was so critical to other operations in these agricultural civilizations that centralization of power was easily established and maintained. The monolithic institutionalization which followed the course of hydraulic management prevented formation of institutions and groups that could effectively challenge the central authority. There was no counterbalance then to the bureaucratic machine.

Legitimating Political Power: Religion and War

It is characteristic of human society that despotic power cannot reign for long without the element of legitimacy. The principle function of political legitimacy, as Fried (1967:26) observed, is to give explanations that justify the concentration of power in special social groups or agents. In the early agricultural states religion commonly played a prominent role in supplying legitimacy for the social and political order, as Steward (1949 (51):19–20) noted:

> The particular religious patterns of each center arose from complex factors of local development and diffusion, and they gave local distinctiveness to the cultures. In terms of the present formulation, however, these differences are secondary in importance to the fact that in all cases a national religion and a priestly class developed because increasing populations, larger irrigation works, and greater need for social coordination called upon religion to supply the integrative factor. The very great importance of religion at the end of the Formative Era is proved by the effort devoted to the construction of temple mounds, temples, palaces, and tombs, and to the special production of religious ornaments, sculpture, and various material appurtenances of the priesthood and temples. It was the priesthood which, devoting full time to religious matters, now laid the foundations of astronomy, writing, and mathematics in all centers.

Application of functional necessity to the rise of the state stressed internal differentiation within a network of ecocultural relations. This contrasted with the conquest theory of the state which emphasized ethnoecological relations. While the initial differentiation and stratification of early society might accompany the rise of an agro-hydraulic bureaucracy, it was apparent that warfare soon intruded to stimulate a centralized authority. Ancient Mesopotamia, as later Greece and Rome and the valley of Mexico, disclosed a history of warring states and alliances.

> By Early Dynastic times (3000–2425 B.C.) [in Mesopotamia], the war leaders of earlier days appear to have become kings. These kings had large landed estates and at first appear to have been concerned mainly with maintaining the city's defenses and raising and outfitting armies. Although local institutions, and the power of secular and temple officials, varied from city to city, there was a tendency for secular power to increase, as wars became more common in the Early Dynastic period. The needs of the city states, in turn, stimulated increasing occupational specialization to supply armaments, luxury goods, and mass produced necessities. As a result of these developments, the class structure became increasingly differentiated.
>
> Mesopotamian civilization thus arose in a context of warring city states. The development of occupational specializations, of social stratification, and of economic and political institutions appears to have gone on more or less apace, with developments in one sector of regional life closely linked to those in others. Despite a more or less constant struggle for hegemony among the various city states, no monopoly of power was achieved by any one of them until the Akkadian period (c. 2350 B.C.). Likewise, there was a polycentric distribution of power within each state, and the representatives of various interest groups were sometimes in open conflict with one another. It appears that the city, the various city states, and Mesopotamian civilization as a whole, arose more or less simultaneously and as parts of a single process. (Trigger 1968:57)

For Sumer, the significance of political rule varied according to the press of internal and external forces acting and reacting upon each other. At Lagash the descendants of Ur-Nanshe after 2500 B.C. embarked on territorial ambitions that led to excessive taxation and corruption. At a critical point, a servant of the people, Urukagain, stepped forward to overturn the oppressive *ishakku* and to reestablish the freedom of the people (Kramer 1959). As pharaoh in Egypt, the *ishakku* of Sumer symbolized the protective rule of justice (Breasted 1935). Indeed, the ultimate symbolism of a ruler's relations to tutelary gods, to military defense, and to taxation and justice centered in the idea of a holy and righteous protector. For Sumer, the first codification of laws was instituted by Ur-Nammu, who ruled over Ur about 2050 B.C.

The Political Integration of Society

Efforts in ancient empires to join legal, ritual, military, taxation, and political authority under one head were duplicated in African states such as Ashanti, Bunyoro, and Ankole. As Radcliffe-Brown (1962b:xxi) reported,

> in some African societies it may be said that the king is the executive head, the legislator, the supreme judge, the commander-in-chief of the army, the chief priest or supreme ritual head, and even perhaps the principal capitalist of the whole community. But it is erroneous to think of him as combining in himself a number of separate and distinct offices. There is a single office, that of king, and its various duties and activities, and its rights, prerogatives, and privileges, make up a single unified whole.

In capitalistic fashion, African rulers, like their Aztec, Incan, and Mesopotamian counterparts, surrounded themselves with excellent craftsmen. Oberg (1962:147) reported of the Mugabe of Ankole that whenever he fancied a particular brew, he drafted its maker into his private employ. Control over taxation and trade provided other ways for centralizing the economy in the interests of administration. Maintenance of court functions and the reward of loyal functionaries required the levying of taxes in kind and in labor. However, as the symbol of collective life and the collective welfare, the king ideally, as Schapera (1962:76–77) noted regarding the Ngwato of Bechuanaland, should use the collected wealth liberally in behalf of the people.

> The chief's power is further dependent upon the uses to which he puts his wealth. As head of the tribe, he formerly received tribute from his subjects in corn, cattle, wild animal skins, ivory and ostrich feathers, retained most of the cattle looted in war, and kept all unclaimed stray cattle and part of the fines imposed in his court, especially for cases of assault. He could also confiscate the entire property of tribesmen conspiring against him or banished for any other serious offence. In addition, he could through the regimental system command the services of his people for personal as well as tribal purposes. He further had a large number of servants directly attached to him and doing most of his domestic work. Foremost among them were the *batlhanka* (com-

mon headmen) whom . . . he put in charge of his cattle and other servants. The latter were drawn mainly from the ranks of the Kgalagadi and especially the Sarwa, who occupied the position of serfs. At first they merely hunted for him, the skins and other spoils they gave him forming an important part of his income; but under Kgama they were gradually taught to herd cattle also and to carry out menial household tasks.

Owing to the wealth he thus accumulated, the chief was always the richest man in the tribe. He was, however, expected to use his property, not only for his own benefit, but also for the tribe as a whole. He had to provide beer and meat for people visiting him, assisting at his kgotla [council], or summoned to work for him; reward with gifts of cattle and other valuables the services of his advisers, headmen, warriors and retainers; and in times of famine, supply the tribe with food. "Kgosi ke mosadi wa morafe," it was said ("The chief is the wife of the tribe," i.e. he provided the people with sustenance). One quality always required of him was generosity, and much of his popularity depended upon the manner in which he displayed it. Kgama is still gratefully remembered as an extremely liberal chief, who not only imported corn for his people in times of scarcity . . . but also bought many wagons, ploughs, guns, and horses, which he distributed among them, while in several instances he paid large sums of money to free some of them from debt.

Standing at the apex of a human society integrated by religious, legal, and political institutions, African monarchs like those of Ashanti and of Bechuanaland symbolized the moral order which guaranteed the ultimate protections of life and possessions. In guaranteeing life, security of person, and freedom from sickness and want, government necessarily occupied a unique place in projecting the idealism that should reign in human relations. Hence it followed that government was a chief guarantor of morality, though sharing this responsibility with a priesthood, as among the Tallensi (Fortes 1962). Under the Tallensi system, those who worshipped common ancestors were united in a network of reciprocal obligations and rights backed by the authority of ancestors easily offended by dereliction and internal strife. Beyond the morality entrenched in the relations of descent lines lay the domain of public morality. Under their dispersed political system, the Tallensi vested jurisdiction over the public welfare in priests (*tendaanas*) who guarded earth from the sacrileges of violence and bloodshed by interceding and halting conflict. Without the blessing of the *tendaanas* a chief was not properly invested, since he was unable to assure the bounties which only earth provided. Chiefs and priests thus carried out complementary functions in maintaining the legal and moral basis of Tallensi life, to which religious ideology and ritual conveyed a greater sense of national affiliation than the political institution.

Intrinsic and Extrinsic Factors in the Rise of States

The rise of conquest states apparently was preceded, within an eco-cultural zone, by a natural internal differentiation in which one miniature state appeared after another. Fried (1967:111) distinguished pristine situations in which localized states developed exclusively in accordance with local conditions and resources. In secondary situations, more complex states were produced by pressures from contact with societies more advanced in technology, economic organization, social stratification, and government (Fried 1967:198). Preconditions for the emergence of the state cited by Fried (1967:196) included "Population pressure; shifts in customary post-marital patterns; contraction or sharp natural alteration of basic resources; shifts in subsistence patterns arising from ... technological change or the impingement of a market system; development of managerial roles as an aspect of maturation of a social and ceremonial system." By defining stratification as status guaranteed by differential rights of access to material goods and resources, Fried (1967:53, 235) was led to describe the state as a collection of formal and informal institutions, the specialized function of which was to maintain a stratified order.

The essential features of technico-social-political growth described by Fried were sketched earlier by Steward (1949). The Formative Era, which witnessed the centralization of societies under theocratic auspices, was not a time of extensive warfare. In the subsequent Era of Regional Florescence, multicommunity states appeared, and irrigation works were extended to expand production. Warfare now played a more important—but not a clearly dominant—role in state formation. What provoked intensified warfare and imperialistic ambitions, in Steward's (1949(51):23) judgment, was an increase in population coupled with the reaching of a plateau in production.

> When the limits of agricultural productivity under a given system of irrigation were reached, population pressures developed and interstate competition for land and for produce of all kinds began. The resulting warfare led to the creation of empires, warrior classes, and military leaders. It also led to enlargement of irrigation works and to a further increase of population. But the powerful military empires regimented all aspects of culture, and few new inventions were made. Consequently, each culture entered an era of rising and falling empires, each empire achieving a peak of irrigation, population, and political organization and a temporary florescence, but giving way to a subsequent period of dark ages.

From their survey of courses toward urbanization, Braidwood and Willey (1962:355) reached conclusions similar to those of Steward. In the New World, for example, the linking of various ecoregions led to the formation of a broad technicocultural foundation upon which urban living and administrative specialization could be raised. Once this threshold was attained, warfare intensified and regional configurations were broken up and shared by different conquest states.

Redistribution, Stratification, War, and Political Integration

Use of surplus food and other material possessions to promote prestige and status is one of the most striking features of primitive societies. A thorough consideration of the variable uses of surpluses should do much to elucidate the problem of social stratification and the differentiation of political power in conjunction with ritual authority. The manipulation of wealth in generous distribution and for credit by Kapauku *tonowi* (Pospisil 1963(67):45–48) supplied a base for personal leadership and legal arbitration; and, when joined with a courageous front and logical rhetoric, a man could collect lineage followers and take first place among his equals. Utilizing ties of kinship, chiefs on the Northwest Coast were expected to organize wealth distributions to validate their hereditary status (Barnett 1968). In Polynesia the collection and distribution of wealth was a function of people with status. Sahlins (1958:5) hypothecated that whatever increased surplus production also increased the social and political distance between producers and distributors, inasmuch as the latter accrued greater prestige through more lavish and frequent distributions. Hence the conclusion that stratification varied with surplus production.

Control over production admittedly was crucial to class differentiation, but in kin-based societies economic controls frequently were tempered by the concept of stewardship. How could this stewardship be translated into outright ownership, with people considered subjects of the ruler? In Polynesia, Goldman (1955(57):683) pictured traditional ranked societies transformed by status rivalry into fluid competitive structures in which aristocracies and their leaders were constantly challenged by endemic guerrilla warfare. In a situation of chronic insecurity and rapid mobility, kinship ties suffered and family rivalries led to reliance on loyal followers rather than on kin. The shifting balance of power fed by interfamily war made possible the reward of trusted followers with the lands of dispossessed rivals. In this way the struggle for power drove a wedge between chief and kin and paved the way for control over land and resources. As stratification proceeded, the kin protections of the commoner fell away to disclose a landless tribute-bearing laborer who existed at the will of his chief. The balance sheet to this social ledger was a growth in agriculture, craft skills, architecture, poetry, and political administration.

The Polynesian venture in sociocultural evolution portrayed by Goldman (1955(57):695) was an internal growth arrived at by a reshuffling of, and an intensifying of, traditional Polynesian practices. The traditional ranked social system accented the processes that produced new forms of society. Social structure, in Goldman's argument, generated its own momentum for change. In an ecosocial perspective, Sahlins (1958) attempted to show that the dispersion, diversity, clustering, and scarcity of resources induced different degrees of statification. Specifically, any increase in the diversity and dispersion of resources could be expected to evoke a measurable increase in stratification. Critical to the emergence of stratification, however, was the presence of a redistributive process. In Sahlins' (1958:250) view, the redistributive economic organization which prevailed throughout Polynesia facilitated understanding of the close relationship between productivity and stratification in Polynesian societies. Indeed, without socioeconomic techniques for achieving prestige and for magnifying social distance by consuming luxury goods and displaying the symbols of privilege, it would be hard to account for stratification.

Sahlins (1958:19) used the ecosocial perspective to correlate levels of sociopolitical regulation with a hierarchical regulation of economic processes. That is, the socioeconomic organization preceded and accounted for the sociopolitical organization both in type and degree of complexity. Making due allowance for ecoeconomic variation, Polynesian social and political processes were consolidated in the redistributive process. It was not unusual, then, to find that in Hawaii the majority of tabus exercised by chiefs over land use and resources were in the interests of the redistributive process. However, the functions of redistribution in Hawaii, as in Polynesia generally, focused on a sacraceremonial feasting of gods in the public welfare, with the paramount chief a demigod wielding extraordinary supernatural power, or *mana*. Despite the sacrosanct quality of the rulers, the political process in Polynesia disclosed frequent occurrences of rebellion, assassination, and migration. At this point the politically stratified redistributive model of Sahlins seems to be modified and shaped by historical processes of the status-rivalry order described by Goldman.

Turning to Africa, one sees that much of African history since A.D. 1000 has been carried by the restless movement of tribal populations. Conflicts that led to dispossession from traditional lands, or possession at best on sufferance of an overlord, were not unusual. The militarized and stratified societies, organized on a territorial administrative basis and age-graded military regiments, tended to erode kinship ties and protections. Without the umbrella of a strong kinship organization, the protection of a territorial lord or patron was essential. To be without ties to a chief was to be an alien, and among the Watutsi of Ruanda, for example, a stranger could be plundered without redress. Clientship therefore thrived at all levels of Watutsi administration. In South Africa during the nineteenth century the displacement of peoples by war produced states with numerous refugee client groups. Such were the Zulu (Gluckman 1962a), Swazi (Kuper 1947), Lozi (Gluckman 1951), Ngwato (Schapera 1962), and Ngoni (Read 1956) states. Indeed, the widespread principle of clientship in Africa underlined the importance of conquest in creating stratified orders and feudalized political systems (see, for example, R. Cohen 1967; M. G. Smith 1960; Rattray 1929).

European colonization and conquest after 1500 provide unparalleled examples of restless expansion and conquest fed by commercial and later industrial energies. The new economic opportunities were of such magnitude that the very social order sustaining a feudal landed aristocracy was threatened. Land was no longer the *sine qua non* for the possession of wealth, and men of fortune emerged to take their places in history and society—merchants, financiers, slave traders, freebooters, colonizers, explorers, and conquerors of new lands. Europe was on the eve of an individualizing thrust that would lead to the open society.

With the possible exception of the Northwest Coast tribes and the Natchez of Louisiana, no American society north of Mexico at the time of contact developed a stratified social order based on redistributive economy. That redistributive stratified societies were more widespread in the middle Mississippi River drainage system south and throughout the Southeast generally can be presumed from the prehistoric temple-mound complexes associated with Cahokia and Etowah. A population of some 40,000 is estimated to have lived in the vicinity of Cahokia and in outlying hamlets and villages a few miles distant. Curiously, the Natchez did not possess a large population, perhaps 3,500. Their military grades and the importance of the war leader, the Tattooed Serpent, suggest that war was an important trade for the Natchez, though the infiltration of the French may have stimulated their efforts to control and absorb weaker neighbors. On the Northwest Coast the political order did not involve large populations, but was localized at the village level under titled hereditary chiefs. As in Polynesia, lineal, collateral, and affinal kin played prime supportive roles in maintaining the status and socioeconomic powers of Northwest Coast chiefs. Among the Iroquois, titled hereditary civil chiefs counseled on tribal and league affairs, but they had no control over a redistributive socioeconomic process.

The relative effectiveness of the League of the Iroquois in coping with shifting demands of external threats attests to the viability of a federative political system provided challenges are persistent and can be countered. The Iroquois example also reveals that political-military efficiency can be achieved in the absence of a socially stratified redistributive system. The League of the Iroquois presented one solution to the problem of political integration, where localization of economic and political activities, owing to technico-ecological realities, were centered on a day-to-day basis in a lineally based residential unit. Another solution was provided by the federative integration of paired lineages and clans at ascending levels, with each level uniting twin segments into a unit opposed to a comparable entity, as among the Nuer and the Tiv.

The restless flow of European colonists, traders, and soldiers of fortune into North America generated displacements of tribal populations, trade rivalries, and intertribal conflicts that either decimated native populations or led to a successful tightening of tribal political integration. War leaders, diplomats, and orators emerged as the first historic figures of American Indian societies. While the frontier situation remained fluid, favored groups, such as the Iroquois, were able to centralize their hold over water and land trade routes by decimating the Huron middlemen, and by displacement and clientship over lesser tribes (Hunt 1940; Trigger 1960). Facing into the frontier, political-military figures like Pontiac and Tecumseh aspired to unite tribes in a common alliance against the intruders. In the shadow of the frontier tidal wave, and in its wake, religio-political leaders united disaffected segments of tribal populations behind doctrines of world renewal, willed by the creator. Failure of these religious efforts to restore the past was underscored by the fact that a military victory was beyond their resources. At this point, the momentum for political reintegration of tribal societies drained away and transitional forms largely under the direction of the dominant society were put into practice. When the frontier passed, reserved lands for Indians remained, but Indians had become clients of a conquest state. In the historic process, the government of the United States had been created through the instrumentality of war.

SUMMARY

In charting the pathways to political integration, it appeared that war at first was not central to the controls exercised by an elite managing the production and consumption of a redistributive system. A producible surplus that could be manipulated for attainment of preeminent status, as exemplified in the careers of Melanesian Big Men (Barnett 1959), indicated how the simpler socioeconomic systems strained toward a redistributive process. However, the manipulation of wealth and feasting of people by Kapauku *tonowi* did not convey the prestige essential to political persuasion and the attraction of followers (Pospisil 1963). The prestige required for political influence followed only when *tonowi* demonstrated that they possessed oratorical and war skills and were capable of wise and decisive counsel. Apparently, the right to command loyalties and services was consolidated by factors other than wealth distribution.

The Cheyenne Indians offer another instructive example regarding the political process (Grinnell 1923; Llewellyn and Hoebel 1941). Their civil leaders first qualified themselves as warriors, then retired to manage tribal affairs with the wisdom that accrues with experience and age. Their prime task, however, was to serve as guardians of the sacred bundles and ceremonial protocol that secured the public welfare and protected the Cheyenne from disaster. Fittingly then, the head of their "Council of Forty-Four" was the custodian of the Sacred Arrows committed to the Cheyenne by a former chief, Sweet Medicine. More so than others, the five chiefs associated with the sacred bundles and the "four winds" walked a path of ritual prescriptions. Yet when war controlled the minds of those heading the military fraternities, the protective ceremonies of the arrow bundle might be delayed if the timing were not congenial to the military raid. Nor did the wise counsel of the civil chiefs bypass the war leaders in questions of war and peace.

The Cheyenne political process demonstrates how a sacra-political organization may complement a secular-military organization, with neither segment being able to rule independent of the other. Relations between civil-religious and secular-military segments commonly were mediated by the historic challenge. Thus, about 1750, the Cherokee, who divided their political process between sacra-civil and war chiefs, found themselves in a worsening situation with the colonists. War leaders moved to the forefront of the political process, and sacra-civil leaders symbolically subordinated themselves to the former: "the civil priests and the war priests filed past the new war chief and called him "mother's brother." The mother's brother was the disciplinarian of the Cherokee family" (Gearing 1962:51).

African kingdoms in the east and south of the continent likewise exhibited the complementary relation between religious and political functions. Among the Lovedu and the Swazi, either the ruler or the titular queen mother possessed the vital ritual for controlling rain so essential to the growth of crops and fodder. The influence of religion was further entrenched by the mediative role performed by all leaders regarding ancestors and the living community. The process of centralization also incorporated law and war into governmental functions. A striking characteristic of African kingdoms, however, was the system of checks and balances regulating relations between lineal, collateral, and affinal kin, of which the institutions of "queen mother" and a cabinet of "kingmakers" for regulating succession were illustrative (Schapera 1967).

Centralization of civil processes in administrative officers responsible to the crown inevitably strained the kinship organization and promoted the image of a chief's or king's man. The rise of national monarchies in Europe illustrated the success of aggressive monarchs in separating law and taxation from local feudal control. With the assistance of economic processes that forced freemen and serfs to seek new opportunities in market towns, kings ultimately broke up feudal loyalties and built a national military force, that is, the king's army. Among Zulu conquerors, the age-graded military units organized by Chaka cut across kin groups and promoted loyalty to military regiments and to king. The present transition to more modern political systems, with party-type and regional or intertribal organizations, is simply duplicating the feudal-king process in Africa in a new key.

In the process of centralizing political power, religion at first exerted a predominant influence as the most viable institution for transcending localisms and creating a sense of service in the fulfillment of common needs. Religion assisted the formation of stratified orders and promoted transcendant sacralized rulers largely because religious knowledge and practice were linked to fulfillment of basic human needs—food, health, rain, personal protections against extraordinary damages, and the adjudication of disputes. Organized warfare, however, consolidated stratification and political authority by building a military arm to enforce administrative authority and by creating a basis for stratified national societies. In its advanced forms war was as effective in creating an internal proletariat without support of kin as were the capitalistic economic processes which separated serf from land. In its less advanced forms, where competition for ecological space was less keen, warfare nonetheless added a special character to the stratification process. This was seen in the intrusion of pastoralists into the ecological space of horticulturists in East Africa. Yet intense warfare between horticulturist and pastoralist did not result, since both made use of different space without disrupting the economy of the other. The legendary empire of Kitara that united Ankole, Toro, and Nyoro evidently involved a struggle between pastoralists in the wake of successive intrusions. However, conquest, differences in economic bases, and ethnic visibility resulted in establishment of a subject caste of gardeners and craftsmen, who produced for the dominant pastoralists. A similar complex of features quite likely facilitated the development of a caste-stratified society in India.

A productive surplus is a necessary precondition for stratification and the emergence of political power. However, the primary instruments for achieving stratification are status rivalries, religious-community functions, and war. The nature of political systems appears as sensitive to these instrumental variables as it may be responsive to the pragmatic organization of production. The production variable exerts its profound influence at those evolutionary moments when a technico-ecological revolution has taken place, as in the beginnings of cultivation, commercialized crafts, and industry. At such time, the production revolution broadens the interactional configuration by introducing fresh alternatives to which instrumental variables are applied. The selective input of these instrumental variables produce the "historic types" or modalities that distinguish the different kinds of sociopolitical organization (see, for example, Ribeiro 1970). However, the timely input of variables differs according to context and circumstances. Religion apparently proved more influential in supporting the political process where the vagaries of rainfall and other factors created irregularities in production. As technical knowledge expanded control over nature, the link between religion and government was severed, and the connections between technical production, war, and government were strengthened. Such considerations suggest that political integration and the political process are a dynamic configuration in which the selective inputs of variables, according to circumstances, influence the integrity of the political domain and modify its form.

The nature of law and the course of its development are intrinsically linked to the political institution. With the growth of a state organization, the adjudication of disputes was transferred from private and kin-based groups to the organized political community. Religion facilitated subjection of private redress, just as it served to involve individuals and kin groups in ceremonial focused on the public welfare. The ten medicine bundle owners among the Kiowa not only provided sanctuary for offenders but also restrained unbridled revenge by threat of supernatural punishment (Richardson 1940). Supernatural powers wielded by medicine bundle owners invested them with authority and protection which compelled serious attention to their counsel and negotiations. The archaic states of Mesopotamia, Egypt, Mexico, and Peru, as well as African kingdoms such as Dahomey and Ashanti, exhibited the penetration of religious considerations into the substance and procedure of law and politics. Supernatural sanctions validated early law codes just as rulers were protected in their persons and decisions by threat of supernatural punishment.

However, as Malinowski pointed out, the substance of law is drawn from conflicts which grow out of social relationships. The legal character of those social relationships is found in the exercise of rights and the discharge of obligations regarding persons and things. Consequently, the common interests of people prompt them to respect the normative demands of their social order and to establish workable mechanisms to mediate disputes. Trobriand law impressed Malinowski not with its institutionalized forms but with the way individuals generally respected rights and obligations because they recognized that reciprocity was essential to social life.

On the other hand, more complex social and cultural systems possessed mechanisms which institutionalized law as a social process. Of such order were the courts presided over by headmen and chiefs occupying different levels of the sociopolitical system. At the head of the judicial process, as among the Zulu and Kgatla, stood the king's court. Such complex systems usually combined private and judicial process in that informal arbitration usually was attempted by lineage heads and village headmen, with appeal to higher courts available. Within corporate lineage structures, as Radcliffe-Brown pointed out, the roles individuals performed depended on their location (status) in the social structure. Status was institutionalized by legal definitions of rights, obligations, and privileges. Law in his view constituted the institutional process by which a social order operated with legitimacy and maintained its equilibrium. In exercising the judicial authority, the state consolidated integrative processes and brought stability and continuity to the social order. Functional relations between legal and political processes described by Radcliffe-Brown were congruent with those of Marx, who asserted that law functioned to support the stratified social and political order of capitalism. However, as an instituted process, it is hard to see how law could function in any other way—no matter what the socioeconomic and political system.

It would be a mistake to see the legal process solely as a prejudiced supporter of the established order. As other institutions, law is subject to internal and external change processes that bring it into contradiction with traditional practice. There are positive forces within the legal process, as Malinowski observed, which emphasize a moral principle of equity based on reciprocity. This was seen in the blood feud as well as in the formalized dueling of central Australians in which a plaintiff secured retribution by a public wounding of the offender. Though devoid of intellectual and moral sophistication, the principle of retaliation nevertheless expressed a principle of equity in social relations. Negotiations which accompanied inter-lineage offenses opened the door to equitable compromise. Kinship was an integral part of the "judicial" process in kin-based societies; and even in the case of complex rural societies, such as the Kanuri (Cohen 1967), the number of kin a litigant could muster influenced the disposition of a case.

Rapid changes accompanying industrialization of the Third World and the attainment of political independence drew the legal process into close association with political process. The rise of trade unions in Africa and the intensifying of race relations supplied a whole new area of substantive law—that is, the definition of rights and obligations. South African Pass laws accented law as an institutionalized process congenial to Structuralist interpretation in that these laws defined the place of Africans in white society as legal-status persons. At the same time pressure of change building within kin-based societies owing to the participation of youth and women in the work world forced redefinition of rights and obligations. In changing situations the relationship between procedural law and the goal of equity is critical in altering rights and obligations. Although law formally institutionalizes right-duty relationships, such definitions under law are subject to change by a constant testing of the institutionalized norms against the realities of life as it is lived, and this testing is accelerated during periods of transition when discrepancies in rights and obligations frustrate social expectations (Bohannan 1965).

19

Social and Cultural Change: Acculturation and Applied Anthropology

INTRODUCTION

During the thirties factors internal and external to anthropology aroused an interest in change processes stemming from the contact of peoples. In both Africa and the Americas anthropologists increasingly confronted societies whose traditional organization and customs were altering and slipping away. At the same time, governments with subject peoples had run through a cycle of administration and were ready for a review and application of new policies. The Meriam Report of 1928, by the Brookings Institute of Washington, detailed the gross failure of the repressive assimilationist policy applied to American Indians and recommended sweeping changes that would minimize the bureaucratic process in Indian Affairs and give Indians a greater role in formulating programs affecting their lives and future.

In Africa, in contrast with Indians in the United States, large tribal populations, centralized political structures, and inhospitable environments insulated Africans from mass penetration by Europeans. This circumstance facilitated a greater continuity in family, religion, political organization, and economy than was possible for American Indians, who were overrun by the advance of the frontier and confined to reservations. Whether assimilationist or not in their colonial policy, European states out of practical considerations at first followed federative rather than integrative procedures in their administration of African subjects. British indirect rule was the most explicit statement of the federative principle.

However, the spread of industrialization early in the twentieth century not only transformed the African landscape but also stimulated widespread changes in traditional African society and culture. Moreover, the process of contact was characterized more often by contradiction, conflict, and divisiveness than by mutual reciprocities and stimuli to a common growth. In the eyes of Monica Hunter Wilson (1936:10), who viewed the contact process among the Pondo of South Africa,

> The clash is primarily economic. A society poorly developed economically, and laying emphasis on the importance of common rather than of individual wealth, meets a highly developed, industrialized, and economically individualistic society. There is a struggle for land and a conflict of interests over labour. The restriction of land and the introduction of money and of new goods which are wanted alters the internal economy of the reserves, and large numbers go out to work for Europeans in labour centres. For the Bantu agricultural and industrial revolutions are telescoped—the necessity and possibility of developing agriculture, and the growth of a large population employed in industry, and entirely dependent upon wages, come at once, and radical changes follow one another with even greater speed than they did in Europe. All through three forces of change may be traced. First the economic, which alters the internal economy and drives many out to work; second the political, which even non-Marxists may argue was historically but an offshoot of the economic, since the extension of political control in Africa was engendered by the desire to secure, or to prevent other nations from securing, economic control, but which may be distinguished in working from the economic; and thirdly the religious, which includes evangelistic, medical, and educational work.

The African situation was aggravated by an implicit or explicit racism, especially in South Africa. Conflict in British domains appeared more imminent and explicit than in areas controlled by France, Belgium, and Portugal, where, in theory, nonracist assimilative processes were underway. An assessment of administrative needs by General Smuts in 1929 led to a survey by Lord Hailey (1957) of available materials related to colonial administration and policy making. At the same time the British government expanded the efficiency of its native administration by transferring authority from traditional rulers to a trained native personnel answerable to British management. Such bureaucratization threatened to alter drastically the practice of indirect rule and to bring rapid erosion of traditional social, political, and economic organization. From her study of the Baganda experiences Mair (1965) determined that indirect rule was preferable, since the native society was protected from unnecessary change and was preserved as a base for future change. In Mair's opinion disruptions of Baganda life resulted from the introduction of things that added trouble and confusion to Baganda efforts to adapt pragmatically to changing circumstances in accordance with their own needs.

Looking into the future, perceptive anthropologists were convinced that ethnic relations throughout the world were becoming more complicated and tense. As Linton (1940:vii) judged the situation, the dominance of whites in the world had peaked and would begin to decline. As European control weakened, the direct management they exercised over native peoples, backed by threat or use of force, would become ineffective, and in the long run dangerous. There was a clear need for "new techniques and for exact knowledge upon which the development of these techniques can be based" (Linton 1940:vii). If, as Mair (1965:xi–xii) saw the situation, governments altered course and programmed their control of native races scientifically, it would be necessary to monitor the controlled experiment to see what effects followed. There was urgent need to apply scientific know-how to the formulation of policies and programs so as to diminish conflict and ease the strain of changing from one mode of life to another. Science could bring a much-needed objectivity and a perspective in depth to problems of culture contact. In its neutrality science would avoid emotional commitment to one's own cultural values and the negative judgment of alien customs commonly present in the administration of subject peoples.

Despite differences in their theoretical interests and experience with change situations, British social Structuralists and American culture historicists agreed that native societies should be protected from disruptive change. Worthy in their own right, the integrity of native social and cultural systems must be maintained so people could adapt themselves to the modern world according to their perception of their needs.

The International Institute of African Languages and Cultures, funded by the Rockefeller Foundation, produced a research statement emphasizing an urgent need for administration to study a runaway change situation.

> The fundamental problem arising from the interpenetration of African life by the ideas and economic forces of European civilization is that of the cohesion of African society. African society is being subjected to a severe strain, and there is a danger lest the powerful forces that are entering the continent may bring about its complete disintegration, the results of which must be calamitous for the individuals who compose it and at the same time render impossible an orderly evolution of the community. It is proposed, therefore, that the inquiries fostered by the Institute should be directed towards bringing about a better understanding of the factors of social cohesion in original African society, the ways in which these are being affected by the new influences, tendencies towards new groupings and the formation of new social bonds, and forms of co-operation between African societies and western civilization. (*Africa* 1932(5):1)

Modern industry and commerce, government, education, Christianity, and Islam were cited as prime agencies of change. Economic change deserved special attention since its effects ramified throughout the social structure. Land holding, labor, crafts, family, social and political organization, religion, and language were all transformed by the new economics. The trend toward urbanization and the seasonal outflow of young men from the reserves to work in agriculture or in mines indicated that Africans accepted, at least temporarily, the heavy price racist policies exacted in return for economic opportunities. The types of situations the Institute projected for research largely reflected variations in economic contexts: whether or not tribal areas included European settlers or planters; whether or not labor migration was extensive; whether the employment of African labor occurred in urban centers, mining areas, or took the form of native settlements on plantations. The guiding idea behind these projected researches, as Wilson and Wilson (1968:167) later observed, was that "Disequilibrium is not inevitable in the change from primitive to civilized—a moving equilibrium is possible—but a degree of disequilibrium is unavoidable if the change from primitive to civilized be very rapid."

In the United States, Redfield, Linton, and Herskovits constituted a committee established by the Social Science Research Council for the study of acculturation. Their memorandum defined acculturation as comprehending "those phenomena which result when groups of individuals having different cultures come into continuous first-hand contact, with subsequent changes in the original cultural patterns of either or both groups" (Redfield, Linton, and Herskovits 1936(38):149). Acculturation was one type of cultural change. Acculturation and assimilation were not equivalent, although assimilation could be an aspect of the acculturative process. Diffusion was present at all times in acculturation, but diffusion was more relevant to situations where continuous and firsthand contacts were not involved. The memorandum drew attention to psychological processes involved in the acceptance, modification, or rejection of culture traits. Both Herskovits (1938a) and Linton (1940) produced studies in acculturation which accented the close relation between changes in cultural habits and psychological processes. By 1941 Redfield described the process by which the sacralized customs of the folk and the peasant were eroded and secularized through penetration of urban influences.

Critical times often generate bold and forceful strategies, and one such period was the Great Depression. While government turned traditional policies around in order to revitalize the U.S. economy, John Collier gained consent to renovate policy regarding Indians. Convinced that the basics of cultures rested on world views and values relating individuals to each other, Collier launched the Indian Reorganization Act in 1933. He hoped this act would strengthen the human values which he considered integral to the traditional Indian community. The cooperative and humanistic life achieved in aboriginal society contrasted sharply with the competitive and impersonal profit values of industrialized society. It was a case of the spurious driving out the genuine, and Collier hoped to turn this process around. Under the IRA he foresaw tribes organized as corporate entities carrying forward social and economic programs with the financial aid, advice, and limited supervision of government. By 1941, in conjunction with Willard Beatty, Director of Indian Education, he committed the government to research. An Indian Personality and Administration Research program was initiated with the assistance of the Committee on Human Development, University of Chicago, later succeeded by The Society for Applied Anthropology. The program concentrated on Indian communities in the Southwest where there was a high degree of insulation of Indians from white contact and a greater degree of continuity in economy, social organization, political leadership, and religion. Collier (1950:Foreword to Thompson, xiii) was convinced that the integration achieved in this social science research effort could be "swiftly and profoundly creative within the institution of government—within human affairs." In her own case, Thompson (1950:Preface, xvii) pointed to the development of a "field theory of culture and a cross-disciplinary methodology for the multi-dimensional study of the acculturation process, not only in its technological and sociological manifestations but also at the psychological and symbolic levels."

Unfortunately, the euphoria generated by Collier's enthusiasm for rein-vigorating Indian societies by strengthening their traditional values and by sensitizing policy to community needs did not last. By the end of the war the IRA had been in operation for ten years, and approximately 25 percent of the tribes had rejected incorporation and the elective council system. The lack of unity within Indian ranks fed a growing congressional desire to set Indians free. The Bureau of Indian Affairs responded to the new mood in Congress by drawing up an acculturative index of tribes that would give some indication of their individual readiness for termination. At the same time a program to relocate Indians voluntarily in urban areas was initiated. Satisfaction of Indian claims against government admitted through the Indian Claims Commission provided direction as to how judgmental monies should be expended and termination expedited. House Concurrent Resolution 108 legislated in 1954 emphasized the assumption by Indians of their "full responsibilities as American citizens." The resolu-tion also moved for rapid termination of tribes and individual members within the states of California, Florida, New York, and Texas and singled out the Flathead (Montana), Klamath (Oregon), Menominee (Wisconsin), and Potawatomi (Kansas and Nebraska) as ready for independence.

For American Indians the postwar period was one of developing con-sciousness and of a growing determination to determine their own destinies. Similar changes took place in colonial areas. In Africa government policies regarding administration, economic development, education, religion, and gradualized self-government were swallowed up in a wave of nationalism that brought the colonial era to an end. In the United States a growing militancy generated political pressure to turn over the administration of Indian Affairs to Indians and to staff the BIA with qualified Indians. At the same time government withdrew its policy of termination and returned the Menominee to their previous tribal status.

MALINOWSKI'S THREE-CULTURES THEORY

The initial troupe of fieldworkers of the African Institute were assigned to the University of London for a year's training under Malinowski. Malinowski determined, after a short survey, that contemporary Africa, East and South, could be divided into three cultures—"old Africa, imported

Europe, and the new composite culture" (Malinowski 1961b:10). He was convinced that the anthropologist who applied his scientific training to the study of change in Africa had to be a pragmatist. He must be vitally concerned with what was happening to the natives undergoing change, but at the same time he must not evade the practical problems inevitably linked to "constructive colonial statesmanship" (Malinowski 1961b:6). Considering the needs of Africans under administration, there was little value in historic reconstructions of a past which no longer functioned for those now laboring in mines or producing crops for export. Indirect rule was better policy, and Malinowski (1961b:151) saw the anthropologist convincing administrator, missionary, and educator of their obligation to be informed of scientifically established facts before making decisions.

Regarding his three cultures, Malinowski saw them as three separate interacting units, operating according to their own charters and interests and following their own determinisms. While these cultures were in contact, they did not form an integrated functional structure because of the color bar. To capture the change processes descriptively, Malinowski proposed use of a topical chart in which each of the three cultures was related by juxtaposition of similar institutions. The institution was the basic unit of observation, for

> all sociologically relevant impact and interaction is organized, that is, it occurs as between institutions. The real agencies of contact are organized bodies of human beings working for a definite purpose; handling appropriate apparatus of material culture; and subject to a charter of laws, rules, and principles. The chartered company of early days, the European colonial government, the missionary body or the industrial enterprise, a community of planters or settlers—these have been and are the effective influences of the Western world, and 'each has to direct its impact primarily upon its indigenous counterpart: chieftainship, African religion, African systems of agriculture, hunting, fishing, or industry. The missionary [for example] has to supplant the Native forms of belief and worship, to supplement them or to develop an organized system of African dogma and ritual. The entrepreneur or settler has to appropriate a portion of the natural resources of Africa, exploit them by means of European capital, and use African labor in conjunction with Western techniques and methods of working. In Indirect Rule, European administration with its established force and treasury, with its European-bred tradition of Civil Service, with its bases in the European home country, has to coöperate with an equally strongly welded and traditionally founded Native chieftainship.
>
> Whenever effective coöperation occurs, a new form of social organization is engendered: a Native Christian congregation under the supervision and guidance of a White clergy; a mine or a factory where African labor works under the direction of a White staff; a bush school where African children are taught by European teachers; an organized system of Native administration under European control. Thus what results from impact is not a higgledy-piggledy assortment of traits, but new institutions, organized on a definite charter, run by a mixed personnel, related to European plans, ideas, and needs,

and at times satisfying certain African interests. We find, therefore, that to marshal evidence in any other form than by stating the interaction of two institutions, and the resulting creation of a third composite one, leads theoretically to confusion, and practically to blundering. (Malinowski 1961b:65–66)

The way parties in contact perceived that their mutual concerns and respective interests could be served by interchange was crucial to the nature of change and contact processes. For intermediate or adaptive institutions to emerge, both parties must be willing to cooperate, and this was possible only when they shared a measure of interest and intention. In the fact of cultural diversity, and even where one of the parties to the contact was dominant, recognition of common factors promoted cooperative enterprise, thereby producing a composite culture. Such was the virtue of indirect rule, which made use of the best of the European and African political worlds and created a new institution adaptively fitted to the changed scene.

Indirect Rule represents a new development and cannot be regarded as an agglomerate of elements. Its charter is the re-shaping of sovereignty, of the sources of executive power, and of finance and revenue. As a complex experiment, it has nothing at all in it which has been directly taken over from the older cultures. It represents the gradual growth of collaboration; it is the reality which is flanked, as it were, by two cultural responses; it depends on both, but develops by its own laws of growth and has its own determinism [by virtue of its special charter, procedures, and principles of organization]. (Malinowski 1961b:139–141)

In the absence of a common factor making for collaboration, the process of culture contact was etched with the anguish of moral ambiguities. There were clandestine violations of imposed rules and open strife as the dominant party nourished its own interests to the exclusion of the subordinate group. Malinowski recognized that European dominance conveyed a special press that shaped the content and determined the future of composite cultures in Africa. However, the emergence of a composite contact culture was assured by the omnipresence of human needs which aroused establishment of corresponding institutions. The basic requirements of human living thus provided the axes of institutional contact, whether familial, legal, or political. The problem lay in differences in standardized values, loyalties, emotions, and techniques associated with the respective cultural institutions. The deeply rooted nature of human institutions necessitated that change be gradual and collaborative. For example, in the case of ancestor worship, a composite culture could be derived which would satisfy basic Christian principles.

Ancestor worship seems to me in many ways the crucial problem and the touchstone of missionary work. . . . One of the wrong attitudes to adopt toward ancestor worship is to regard it as entirely reprehensible, simply because it is the core of African paganism and because it involves sacrifice, divination, and communion with ancestors, which seem essentially un-Christian. But a fuller knowledge of ancestor worship in Africa and of religious principles would dictate a different course, one not too late to be adopted in some parts at least. For the principle of ancestor worship itself is as sound a theoretical principle as the Fourth Commandment. To work it gradually into a subordinate position, to make it an outcome of monotheism—in short, to harmonize it completely with the Christian attitude of filial piety and reverence to ancestors —would achieve the same end in a slow and much more effective way. In such a compromise may be found the common factor between Christianity and ancestor worship.

As it is, ancestor worship driven underground survives often in forms of fear and dread, reverted to even by ministers of the Christian religion and always there as a stepping stone to religious separation. In general, the principle of an open and honest expression of mental attitudes is preferable to their violent puritanical suppression. But the most important point about ancestor worship is the fact that it is connected with a type of social organization —the family and the clan; the whole legal system is intimately bound up with it. The complete destruction of the dogma is thus sociologically deleterious. The relegation of the dogma to its proper place, while retaining its social, economic, and legal influences would produce the same dogmatic results and satisfy the puritanism of the missionary without producing nefarious results. (Malinowski 1961b:69)

Malinowski expected to pour the new wine of Christian meaning into the bottle of African tradition. Such renovation was necessary if African institutions like ancestor worship were to be adapted to the needs of a composite cultural configuration. He must have considered that ancestor shrines, divining, libations, and sacrifices ultimately would be dropped as the functions of the aboriginal institutions accommodated new meanings. Indeed, the conception of a relatively stable composite culture emerging from the reasoned collaboration of European and native proved to be an ideal rather than a fact in Africa, as in the Americas. The idea of a common factor, or mutual interests of people, as integral to the formation of relatively stable exchanges was a basic datum. However, Malinowski overlooked the practical consequences of contact in three important areas: first, he did not fully appreciate the critical role played by the economic factor in establishing and continuing relationships between groups with different cultures. Second, he overlooked the consequences of the cumulative spread and uneven integration of changes in all institutional sectors. Third, he did not give due consideration to the possibility that contact would generate internal pressures by Africans themselves to drastically alter the rate of change and the institutional arrangements.

With regard to the economic factor, Malinowski's students, like others, learned that the common factor which united two cultural groups in a cooperative enterprise flowed along an axis of material, social, psychological and political wants. Secure employment alone could bring satisfaction of these wants. Prodded at the start by head and other taxes, Africans moved from unstable to stable employment profiles even where racist policies prevailed. The lure of wage employment increased migration to cities, with a consequent mushrooming of black urban areas, altered relations with kin, lessening of traditional religious commitments, weakening of political loyalties, and erosion of customs. The functional requirements of urban life and social organization, including labor unions, began to prevail over tribal commitments.

The job with its convertible good established a complementary relationship that permitted a measure of individual capitalization even when the African had nothing more than his labor to sell. Once in motion there was little desire to turn back from the promises of personal satisfaction, relative autonomy, and individualization.

In the initial press of contact, African and European institutionalized patterns remained anchored to their respective functional, procedural, and ideological bases. The grudging functional accommodations proved insufficient and their inadequacies became more apparent as changes accumulated. The structural-functional interrelations of institutions lost their timing and coherence at crucial moments when solid articulation was essential. In East Africa the disequilibrium (compare cultural lag of Ogburn 1923) and threat of disintegration of African life ways described by Hunter, Mair, and Schapera in the thirties was restated by Wilson and Wilson (1945) in the forties. By the fifties economic and political forces at work transforming East African kingdoms, such as Busoga and Buganda, created a sea of conflicting interest groups which challenged the traditional economic and authority system. According to Fallers (1955(57):294–295),

> In many areas the chief lives in a disordered and conflict-ridden social world, and it is important, if we are to reach some understanding of this chief's position, that we be able to talk about this conflict and disorder . . . in an ordered way. In many regions of Africa today . . . the situation is not simply one of two radically different social systems colliding head on and . . . holding each other at bay. . . . More commonly, African and European social systems have interpenetrated with the result that new social systems embodying diverse and conflicting elements have come into being. We must therefore be prepared to analyze systematically situations in which incompatible values and beliefs are widely held by members of the same social system, where individuals are regularly motivated to behavior which in the eyes of others is deviant and where other individuals have conflicting motivations corresponding with discontinuities among the values of the social system. We must be able to think analytically about these elements of relative disharmony and to determine their consequences for the functioning of such systems as wholes.

Events in Africa moved so rapidly that there was little time to talk about conflict and disorder in an orderly way. The nationalistic ferment drew attention to the political institution as the critical instrument for implementing change of all kinds. Africa seemed to follow a pattern, with regional variations, of social and economic change through a reorganization of political power which could be seen in any moment of striking cultural transformation. In Ghana, where monarchy retained an aloof and conservative role under indirect rule, the forces of change led by Nkrumah swirled around and bypassed traditional rulers. None of these political changes, however, was independent of sweeping modifications taking place in the world at large along a wide front, affecting the ideological, social, political, and economic foundations of societies. The nationalistic strivings of Africans fell in line with the aspirations of Indians and Indonesians to free themselves from colonial rule as World War II ended. According to Richard Wright after a visit to emergent Ghana, the hope of Africa lay in immediate transition into the twentieth century. The step into the present must be accomplished quickly—and by any means—even if it meant militarization of the society.

> The basis, concrete and traditional, for the militarization of African life is there already in the truncated tribal structure. The ideological justification for such measures is simple survival; the military is but another name for fraternalization, for cohesiveness. And a military structure of African society can be used eventually for defense. Most important of all, a military form of African society will atomize the fetish-ridden past, abolish the mystical and nonsensical family relations that freeze the African in his static degradation; it will render impossible the continued existence of those parasitic chiefs who have too long bled and misled a naïve people; it is the one and only stroke that can project the African immediately into the twentieth century.
>
> Over and above being a means of production, a militarized social structure can replace, for a time, the political; and it contains its own form of idealistic and emotional sustenance. A military form of life, of social relations, used as a deliberate bridge to span the tribal and the industrial ways of life, will free you, to a large extent, from begging for money from the West, and the degrading conditions attached to such money. A military form of life will enable you to use *people* instead of money for many things and on many occasions! And if your people knew that this military regime was for their freedom, for their safety, for the sake of their children escaping the domination of foreigners, they will make all the sacrifices called for.
>
> Again I say: Would that Western understanding and generosity make these recommendations futile. . . . But if the choice is between traditional Western domination and this hard path, take the hard path!
>
> Beware of a Volta Project built by foreign money. Build your own Volta, and build it out of the sheer lives and bodies of your people! With but limited outside aid, your people can rebuild your society with their bare hands. . . . Africa needs this hardness, *but only from Africans.* . . .
>
> There will be those who will try to frighten you by telling you that the organization you are forging looks like Communism, Fascism, Nazism; but, Kwame, the form of organization that you need will be dictated by the needs, emotional and material, of your people. The content determines the the form. Never again must the outside world decide what is good for you. (Wright 1954:348–349)

This impassioned advice from a "cultureless" black of the New World to sever themselves from their past was not taken up by African nationalistic leaders. Like others who had stood at a watershed of change,

Africans stepped into the future by retaining something of their past. The very names of Mali and Ghana strengthened identity with the past by conjuring up glories of past empires. However, in dealing with the enervating conflicts of internal politics, they allowed a militarizing of their countries so as to gain the stability which the transition to modernity demanded.

INTERACTIONAL FIELDS AND LEVELS OF INTEGRATION: THE WILSONS

Changes overtaking Africa in the twentieth century underlined the importance of external stimuli in generating the timely foundations for social and cultural modifications. As Dr. Ampofo commented to Wright (1954:199), "The men who went to America and to England [to be educated] came back and injected, and rightly so, the concept of our subjection and the concept of race consciousness into our lives. It came from without."

This point was grasped by Wilson and Wilson (1968), who alone attempted to develop a comprehensive theory of change after the manner of Malinowski. The Wilsons saw each society as integrated into a series of structured interactional fields, beginning locally and extending outward to encompass region, nation, and the world. It had become apparent that the economic, religious, political, and knowledge systems of both East and West were increasingly interpenetrative and that the resultant universalization of certain features of these institutionalizations created a basis for a continued expansion of relationships. Everywhere localized social fields, in which social groups, classes, and national states cycled, were increasingly sensitive to external circumstances and relationships. Moreover, the frequency of contact relations within a local field, and the control which local relations exerted over the individual, diminished as frequency contacts increased externally (Wilson and Wilson 1968:40). Locally the individual enjoyed a considerable degree of autonomy. When the individual's local activities were integrated with another level of interaction, however, he found himself subordinate and functionally dependent on the operations of this external interactional universe. The vicissitudes of African employment in the copper mines offered a prime example.

> Like most of the rest of the world Central Africa suffered, between the wars, from violent fluctuations in the world market, and a period of "over-production" and unemployment. As a result of the curtailment of world copper production ... Africans employed by mines in Northern Rhodesia fell from 16,726 in 1930 to 6,664 in 1932; Europeans from 1,903 to 1,066. The total paid African labour force fell from about 70,000 to about 54,000.
>
> To ensure a market for their goods producers seek to limit production, and to keep down costs, by paying low wages. The Northern Rhodesian copper-producing companies were members of an international copper cartel, and until the outbreak of war had their quota which they might not exceed. Sim-

ilarly, the production of tea and coffee in Central Africa was limited by international agreements, and the production of maize in Northern Rhodesia by a maize control board. The economic colour bar is . . . a further form of restriction of production, for it limits the acquisition of skill, giving the monopoly in certain occupations to a small minority of the community. (Wilson and Wilson, 1968:140)

On the other hand, a siphoning of young males from the tribal reserves to towns lowered agricultural production on the home front, compounding the problem of hunger and malnutrition. Food production in Northern Rhodesia required able-bodied men to work the hard soil and to clear the brush. Women, aside from differences in strength, were thoroughly occupied with day-long tasks of grinding meal, cooking, taking care of children, and drawing branches used in fencing. The Wilsons estimated during the war years that only 20 percent of men under 35 years were available for cultivation, and as a result the other 80 percent of the reserve populations had poorer nutrition than before the labor migrations. Caught up in the labor cycling, many men lost contact with traditional training in agricultural work. The Bantu of Northern Rhodesia needed an agricultural revolution, but this was possible only through special capitalization, which required a market-type production in order to provide incentive for investment (Wilson and Wilson 1968:142–143).

Scale served the Wilsons as a key concept for understanding the interactional relations of a society, both internally and externally. Scale was the combined product of the number of people interacting and the frequency and types of relations. The intensity of relations within any interacting group was measured "by observing the proportion of economic co-operation, of communication of ideas and of feelings within and without the group; together with the relative inclusiveness of value, of dogma and of symbolism within and without the group, and the degree of social pressure exerted within and without the group" (Wilson and Wilson 1968:29). In the Central African situation, Europeans, by virtue of their economic enterprise, literacy, and other qualifications, participated in much broader relations than Africans on tribal reserves. Africans on reserves were handicapped in articulating with the expansive industrial-urban field because of limited literacy, skills, and capital. Africans holding jobs in town operated in a field of interrelations sharply contrastive with the reserve. Increasingly urban Africans were not so much circulating between city and reserve as paying visits to the latter.

Specialization and variety were critical for expanding contacts and increasing the degree of scale. Much of this differentiation essential to increasing the level of scale expanded control over the material environment. Differentiation and variation brought opportunities for intensifying connections between contrastive groups establishing complementary relations in which their diverse and respective interests were served by an exchange relation. Any advance in scale was marked by a corresponding change in differentiative "complexity, control of the material environment, non-magicality, impersonality and mobility" (Wilson and Wilson 1968: 108). The increase in scale brought centralizing processes that generated more uniformity and subordination of the person to the demands of the externally oriented field of forces. At the same time individuals exerted more freedom in their personal relations at the local level.

> The freedom of a primitive man is limited at every point by the pressure of neighbours and kinsmen, living and dead, from whom he cannot escape. He has little privacy. His position in society is largely fixed by sex, age, and blood. The freedom of the civilized man from neighbours and kinsmen, and from the immediate past, is much greater than that of a primitive; not only does he live relatively aloof in his house, but he can escape . . . by moving, and he does not cut himself off from his ancestors by changing his habits. On the other hand, he is dependent upon distant groups—upon banks and cartels, upon his heritage from ancient Greece and Rome, Palestine and China—in a way in which a primitive man is not dependent. (Wilson and Wilson 1968:115)

The movement from the primitive to the civilized world thus must be marked by an acceleration in scale with its concomitant correlates. This was happening in Central Africa, and the Wilsons observed that the conservative nature of Africans described by Europeans faded fast as the element of scale increased (Wilson and Wilson 1968:163). In this change, however, Central Africa developed serious oppositions and conflicts because material change proceeded too rapidly to permit coordination of change in the religious element. It was unwise to allow this disequilibrium to continue indefinitely. The choice was between racialism or nonracialism, since each contradicted the other and frustrated a practical and coherent program of change. The former policy meant more disequilibrium and conflict, with a consequent retraction in scale for African societies; the latter would move Africans forward in scale and was consistent with ultimate values of Western society.

INTERACTIONAL FIELDS AND LEVELS OF SOCIOCULTURAL INTEGRATION: STEWARD

From his research in Puerto Rico after World War II, the Americanist Julian Steward (1955a; also 1956) likewise developed a structural-functional-interactional analysis. Steward accented the bounded quality of interactional relations that accompanied social classes and specialization by occupation. National institutions and sociocultural segments represented two interrelated yet distinct levels of social and cultural integration. The sociocultural segments were of two orders: (1) "vertical or localized groups" such as ethnocultural minorities or groups distinguishable by a subculture traceable to a specialization in production; and (2) "horizontal groups, such as castes, classes, occupational divisions" hierarchically arranged and not localized (Steward 1955e:47–48). Steward noted the way in which these differing sociocultural segments and the national institutions developed a bounded set of interactions. In effect, they were relatively closed systems. In the instance of money, banking, and credit, here a national and international system was operating under a uniform set of rules, regulations, and principles essential to the functioning of the financial structure. The financial structure, as a form fulfilling a special function, embodied a number of key elements or core features sensitively articulated with the state of world trade, industrial development, marketing and legal procedures, as well as many other factors. To Steward, national-international institutionalizations were perfect representatives of the supraindividual segments of culture. They could best be studied without regard to individual behavior and indeed could be understood only by studying their life processes apart from the individuals who daily carried out the operations of these institutions (Steward 1955e:46–47). Heterogeneity and a relatively segregated interdependence of interacting groups apparently were characteristic of complex organizations. In most cases, "the upper class far more than any other social segment . . . understands and controls the national institutions . . . makes use of higher education, technological inventions, advanced medicine, and . . . incorporates the best achievements of national literature, art, music, and the theater into its daily living" (Steward 1955j:71).

In *The People of Puerto Rico* Steward (1956) applied a theory of change which combined ecocultural processes with the sociocultural processes making for different levels of integration. Ecology was the independent variable for checking regularities in shaping social arrangements to local conditions viewed both in a contemporary and historical perspective (Steward 1955i:36–39). In Puerto Rico the constancy of ecocultural variation could be traced in the subculture of the independent tobacco farmers of the mountainous interior and of the coffee hacienda and sugar plantation. All, however, were responsive to the organizational demands of the industrial system. Indeed, the lure of a cash crop turned the subsistence cropper into a farmer-entrepreneur. The capital required for coffee and sugar operations eliminated the small producer and prompted a competitive consolidation of holdings. Wage labor prevailed in the production of coffee and sugar, but greater competition in the open market eliminated the sugar hacienda. The subculture of the coffee hacienda provided a more direct reflection of traditional arrangements under Spanish control: paternalism, stable family labor organized by a patriarchal head, subsistence plots, labor exchange, establishment of compadrazgo relations with hacienda owners, family and community worship of saints, and little political involvement except under the guidance of the hacienda head. In contrast, wage workers of the American-run corporation and government-owned (profit-sharing) sugar plantations were unionized and active in the Popular Democratic Party. Many workers were of heavy negroid admixture, and families, generally plagued by a high rate of divorce, were stabilized by women. Above all, Steward and associates demonstrated that the integrative effect of the national-international industrial system was the major impetus for change and was channeled by close ties with the United States. The upper class, which operated within this national-international nexus, largely mediated the change taking place. Equally evident, the spread of national institutions to the lower sociocultural elements through education, mass means of communication, political parties, and trade unions brought new challenges to the traditional role of the upper class as political, social, intellectual, and economic leaders and innovators.

What Steward and associates described for Puerto Rico had its counterparts in the industrialization of Africa, India, and Indonesia, making due allowance for ecocultural variation and historic circumstances. In the Special Region of Jogjakarta industrialization produced core features that included social, political, and religious patterns congruent with the industrial system. Speaking to the community development of rural Jogjakarta, Selosoemardjan (1962:335–336) noted how

> Many of the socially depressing factors of the colonial period have disappeared or are ... disappearing. Many of the obstacles which ... stood in the way of economic development have ceased to exist or have lost ... their influence. There is now no longer an alien colonial regime which discriminates against Indonesians and in favor of other groups in the population. The foreign tobacco and sugar industries have left the scene, and no alien competition for land, water, or human labor is now hampering the growth of peasant agriculture. The economically unproductive class of the nobility has lost its place as the upper class of society to the new elite of the intelligentsia, which carries the ideals of political, social, and economic progress on its banners. This has given rise to an enormous drive for more and higher education in all classes of society. Knowledge and skill have been accepted instead of social origin as criteria for social mobility; the society has become less resistant to technological and organizational innovations in production and distribution. The atmosphere favorable to an acceleration of the process of change is enhanced by the real autonomy granted to the villages; this has provided the village administration and the community itself with greater self-confidence, which in turn has sparked the development of initiative to seek ways leading to a better social and economic life. The tradition-oriented and self-contained village communities have now started to turn their eyes to the future, while the members of the younger generation are no longer satisfied to live their lives at the same low social and economic levels as their parents. The inferiority attitudes which marked the prewar villagers in their relations with urban dwellers are rapidly disappearing. This is partly because the penetration of formal education into the villages has brought the rural youth to the same educational levels as the urban youth. In addition, the democratic structure of the administration, which has replaced the quasi-feudal government of the prerevolutionary period, has opened the way for both urban and rural dwellers to rise to the highest positions in the administration. Inflation has to a large extent removed the great gap which previously existed in real income—and consequently in social status—between the farmer and the white-collar worker in the administration and in the city. (Compare Okigbo 1956; Epstein 1958; Southall and Gutkind 1957; Powdermaker 1962)

CHANGE AS SOCIAL ADJUSTMENT: BICULTURALISM AND REFERENCE GROUPS

When Steward accented the way national institutions directed change, his ecocultural and structural-functional orientation approached Malinowski's (1961b) view of the institution (organized by charter, material apparatus, personnel, and operational principles) as the primary medium for change. Malinowski's judgment as to the relative insulation of institutional contacts from one another (for example, economic and religious) was also echoed by Steward (1955j). Moreover, as the study of social change in Africa progressed to a more sensitive regard for the nature and kinds of interactional relations, Malinowski's basic position received inadvertent support from one of his most vigorous critics, Max Gluckman (for criticism of Malinowski, see Gluckman 1949). Gluckman opposed the approach to change in Africa which focused on the adaptive nature of the process by which tribesmen became townsmen (Gluckman 1965:348). There was no real problem of detribalization or adaptive change. When in town the African worked and behaved as a townsman, and on returning to his village he acted out the role of the tribal native. Gluckman argued that the tribal village and the town constituted two different interactional fields which did not meet in confrontation, and were not in contact in any significant way. True, no African townsman could avoid some influences from the village, and in the village he did not wholly escape the influence of the town (Gluckman 1965:349). However, the African accommodated himself to the situation, and those who oscillated between town and country provided apt illustration. Much of this oscillation between village and town in Central Africa was linked to African dependence on land rights for security. Rights to land were assigned by virtue of kinship ties and membership in village and tribe. In cases where kindred worked land in cooperation, or in cases of kin organizing and aiding those setting out for town, land was an important element of personal security. The exercise of a right to kin-worked land necessarily meant acceptance of kinship obligations (Gluckman 1965:359). This African adjustment found a parallel among American Indians, who also were linked to reservation land for ultimate security, and who frequently returned to the reserve after varying periods of time in the work world (See Freilich 1958; Voget 1961–1962).

Gluckman's scoring of situational determinants in culture contact can be related easily to reference-group theory (see, for example, Merton 1957; French 1961). The switching of behavior according to sociocultural context described by Gluckman also is related to Dozier's (1961:179) process of compartmentalization among Rio Grande Indians. In this case of Indian villagers, compartmentalization was a contra-acculturative practice that effectively separated Spanish and Pueblo ceremonial while concealing what was offensive to the former behind a facade of Spanish-Catholic form and ritual. The effect once again was to stabilize two interactional arrangements that included a traditional extended family and kinship obligations, continued use of the native language, and a socialization that kept alive the native world view and ethical concepts. However, until the present, a relative isolation insulated the Pueblos from the vigorous economic forces now threatening to erode their subsistence economy and the sacracivil fabric of their lives. The persistence of cultural features was not due to any inherent stability of the features themselves but stemmed from the type of relations established between Spanish and Indians, and the native social structure.

The compartmentalization of the tribal and industrial modes of life by which Gluckman characterized the acculturative processes in Central Africa did not leave room for intermediate institutionalizations which Malinowski advocated and which he saw as the basis for an emergent third culture.

> The nature of culture change is determined by factors and circumstances which cannot be assessed by the study of either culture alone, or of both of them as lumber rooms of elements. The clash and interplay of the two cultures produce new things. Even a material object, a tool or an instrument like money, changes in the very process of culture contact. The anthropologist has to correlate European good intentions with the necessities of the situation; the inspired liberalism and good-will of the missionary with the more materialistic designs of the financier, entrepreneur, and settler. The whole concept of European culture as a cornucopia from which things are freely given is misleading. The European takes as much, in fact a great deal more, than he gives. But what he takes away are not cultural traits but land, wealth, and labor. This is not an indictment nor a piece of pro-Native ranting. It is simply a strong *caveat* that an approach which eliminates from the study of change the real driving forces is insufficient.
>
> It is necessary, I think, to make plain once and for all that to treat the process of culture change as a static product, in which Europeans and Africans have arrived at a system of temporary integration or of harmonized unity, is unprofitable. Equally unprofitable is it to treat the process as a mechanical mixture where the main problem consists in the sorting out and invoicing back of elements. The phenomena of change are new cultural realities, which have to be studied directly with the full consciousness that we have to deal here with at least three phases; that these three phases interact; but that their interaction cannot be anticipated by an assessment of the original ingredients.
>
> The study of culture change must take into account three orders of reality: the impact of the higher culture; the substance of Native life on which it is directed; and the phenomenon of autonomous change resulting from the reaction between the two cultures. . . . Far from being a mere mechanical joining of the two original influences, European and African, the two impinge on each other. The impact produces conflict, cooperation, or leads to compromise. (Malinowski 1961b:25–26)

Differences between Malinowski and Gluckman illustrated the importance of situation in determining what the observer experienced and how he interpreted this experience. Malinowski's field observations came at a time when the relations between African and European were in a formative stage and when government was experimenting with accommodative solutions to African administration. The full impact of the transformation of African politics and government in the interests of efficient management had yet to come, and the same could be said for the processes of industrialization and urbanization of East Africans. Relative to his experience, Malinowski was not wrong in viewing the acculturative processes as cooperative and accommodative, and thus productive of a *tertium quid*. Even when conflict emerged, as among Africans in the copper belt of Northern Rhodesia, accommodative solutions resulted in a type of arrangement not found in usual mine management. Nor could the Africanized social unit developed to aid management be found on a reserve. As Epstein (1958), a student of Gluckman, described the mining center of Luanshya, Northern Rhodesia, the administrative structure was exanded to include management, tribal elders, and government because of an increase in disruption and violence. This unit functioned between 1930 and 1940. The elders, largely drawn from tribal royalty, were appointed by chiefs and kings whose tribal members were on location at the mines. The tribal representatives were given special housing and rations to help newcomers get settled, and for a time, according to Epstein (1958:37), people favored elders as mediators between management and labor, counselors, and *de facto* magistrates for maintaining peace and order in the work compounds. Their activities ranged over the whole of personal-social adjustment to life at the mine.

> Complaints, whether about social or working conditions, were dealt with through the Elders. When distinguished visitors came to Roan [Antelope Mine], it was the Elders with whom they would talk. When news was received of the death of a chief, his tribesmen looked to their Elder to make arrangements for carrying out the traditional mourning ceremonies. But perhaps the most important aspect of their work lay in the settling of disputes between Africans. The Elders had no legal powers in this respect, and their jurisdiction rested mainly on the litigants' willingness to submit to their judgment. Every case was reported to the Compound Manager, who decided whether it was serious enough to warrant reference to an Administrative Officer. (Epstein 1958:37–38)

An Advisory Committee (later Urban Advisory Council), whose eight members also were elders, was devised to assist the district commissioner. Minutes of this advisory body revealed efforts to cope with marriages taking place within the town without customary tribal arrangements. In instances of adultery it was proposed that the husband be compensated at a fixed rate. There was also the problem of custody of children when parties to an intertribal marriage were divorced. Practical matters like washing facilities, transportation, and the expenditure of beer hall funds also were taken up.

The administration of law in the urban setting raised serious and delicate issues for the courts. In the first instance, native legal understandings and procedures were geared to kin-based social orders, and magistrates could not operate with concepts drawn from Western legal practice in the assignment of rights and responsibilities. Second, the intermingling of different tribes in the urban work world introduced a multiplicity of fine distinctions in legal theory and practice that forestalled an easy application of a uniform code. In consequence, a kind of urban customary law emerged to accommodate litigation involving members of different tribes (Epstein 1958:221). To find a basis for judicial decision in the midst of tribal diversity in custom and legal procedure, magistrates were guided by the common core of understandings regulating social relationships, since social relationships were the focus of tribal custom and law. For example, no matter what the tribe, marital relations stressed mutual respect, aid, and cooperation, and it was concern for the quality of social relations under African definition that enabled the courts to establish custom precedents for Africans in the urban area.

The problem of finding a meeting ground for the ethnocultural heterogeneity of Luanshya life is reminiscent of the Roman solution to legal problems when confronted with litigants coming from different cultural regions within the empire—namely the *jus gentium* or law of peoples. The wide variety of voluntary associations which accompanied African urbanization also provided documentation for composite institutionalizations responsive to personal-social and ethnocultural needs in the urban setting. A classification of voluntary associations in West Africa by Little (1957; compare Mitchell 1956; Doughty 1970; Butterworth 1962) revealed some that were rooted in traditional organization and purposes. Others were more composite, integrating traditional and modern features, and some were organized and operated according to principles and functions that were wholly modern. Some of these associations functioned largely as credit unions, others as general mutual aid societies, and some (for example, Ibo State Union) were analogous to the social, mutual aid, and cultural groups formed by immigrants to the United States.

Reference-group and situational theory underlined the relative insulation of the urban and tribal social fields and pictured the individual as a flexible agent alternating his roles according to context. The press in each social field was toward establishment of congruences, following what Epstein (1958:240) called the principle of situational selection. For instance, by 1950 in Northern Rhodesia, the irritation and resentment of young married men in the city provoked a motion in the Western Province Provincial Council to abolish the legal controls which matrilineal kin held over their married daughters. The motion failed, but was a signal of things to come. The emergence of an educated administrative elite also eroded the cohesion of kin and fulfillment of traditional obligations. The trend among Ganda in Kampala, according to Goldthorpe (1955(6):31–47) was to reduce wider clan obligations to lineage kin, and he found that compliance to kin obligations frequently was carried out unwillingly. The professional who wished to get ahead often found himself the target for a "merciless influx of money collectors'" (Goldthorpe 1955(6):39). This is the way kinfolk with their personal demands looked to one educated Ganda. Temporary labor migration produced an impact on the tribal homeland as returnees introduced new wants, aspirations, and voluntary associations sometimes not congenial to those found in the traditional order. For example, Lugbara young men set out for an urban or a plantation settlement with financial backing from family elders. In location they formed fraternities based upon common interests and experience (associations of migrants for a particular year, veterans, school, and church associations). On return to the homeland members maintained their contacts, and these new units found their way into the loosely organized Lugbara system. The new loyalties engendered and the fresh basis for leadership were not viewed with favor by senior heads of the patrilineages. According to Middleton (in Cohen and Middleton 1970:66),

> The older Lugbara, who, as heads of families and lineages, to a large extent control the migration since they control the allocation of land, see their junior kin in the south as comprising extensions of their lineages and subclans, with authority in the hands of their deputies, the senior migrants; for these older men, the associations of migrants are ephemeral and unimportant.

In the dynamic climate of an urbanizing East Africa, where farming itself had become capitalized by African entrepreneurs (Richards 1952), the weight of change fell to the city. Gluckman (1965:359) reported that tribal ties and interests consistently yielded to the interests and loyalties of industrial and urban associations. However, considering the variety and pace of industrial-urban change in the different regions of Africa, history would record to what extent distinctive African-European syncretizations would emerge. The initial contacts of Africans with the industrial work world were fraught with too many day-to-day adjustments to personal needs and job requirements to permit much opportunity for systematic syntheses. Sociocultural synthesis was a slower process, surfacing as a pattern only after a period of time had elapsed and reaction had set in. In the broad area of the Americas under Spanish colonial rule one found cultural traditions notable for their integration of Spanish and native beliefs, organization, and life ways. Such were the folk cultures described by Redfield (1941; also Redfield and Villa 1944) at Tusik and Chan Kom in Yucatan, of Mitla (Parsons 1936), of Yaqui Potam (Spicer 1954), of Chichicastenango (Bunzel 1952), and of the Colombian mestizos of Aritama (pseudonym) described by the Reichel-Dolmatoffs (1961). Extended over centuries the quasi-feudal relation of the hacienda system promoted an intermingling of the local Indian and Spanish heritages.

There were cases in Africa where the rural basis of the individual's experience consistently influenced and introduced a mixture of elements into the urban behavioral pattern, and vice versa. Generally a strain toward individuality and independence with a consequent weakening of the authority of sacred chiefs and of heads of extended families appeared to be a natural product of wage labor and cash cropping. However, among the

Ba-Kongo, the town-dwelling young men remained under the control of lineage heads and contributed to the lineage economy. Balandier (1963: 369) concluded that

> The close tie between the urban and rural milieu does not fail to impose a specific character on the socio-cultural innovations. The latter must have meaning and efficacy for the Ba-kongo villager as well as towndweller; they acquire a kind of ambivalence and take a form which facilitates their insertion into the customary sociological environment. (Compare Marris 1960; also Miner 1953; Bascom 1955)

Those without inherited status but in possession of new wealth looked to traditional institutions as vehicles for added prestige and power. They found one in the Ba-Kongo *malaki,* at which goods accumulated for the year under the lineage head were consumed in honor of the ancestors. The social effect was to reinforce lineage and affinal unity and to enhance the power and prestige of the lineage head (Balandier 1965).

The urban and rural social fields thus need not be segregated, with only artificial and conflictive relations. In the community of Vasilika in Greece, the bonds linking rural and urban kin were strengthened by frequent visiting and mutual respect. According to Friedl (1959(61):35),

> The line of urban cultural influence . . . runs something like this: New ideas and attitudes, and changes in style of life, are brought to the notice of a village family by its urban relatives. However, if a village household adopts at least some of the new traits, it is only partly because of the respect which it pays to its urban kin. A more powerful influence is often the strong sense of competition which the rural household feels toward other village families, on which it hopes to score a point by showing superior sophistication. Those village families which have no urban relatives gradually try to copy the behavior of those which do. Some degree of urban influence stemming from urban relatives of villagers therefore penetrates the entire village community. (Compare Moss and Cappannari 1962; also, Bruner 1961)

Moreover, in certain circumstances, as in Tanganyika and Northern Rhodesia, differentiation of rural and urban migrants according to choice or other circumstances revealed an acculturation process more complicated than a simple alternation of urban and rural roles. Seasonal migrants to the low-wage sisal and tobacco plantations affected little change on the home front.

> He has learned little or nothing which he can or wishes to practice at home; he is glad to be at home free of the authority of employers and the alien routine of estate and labor camps. Because of the low pay he has not been able to develop a taste and demand for the material benefits of the outside world—or at least he has not developed them to a point where they cannot easily be disregarded. . . . Migration is . . . only attractive to the younger men who have relatively few ties at home and relatively few opportunities for earning a little extra with which to dress rather better, to assist towards obtaining a wife, and to establish a home and family. (Gulliver 1960(19):160)

The same complication was observed by Mayer (1961) among Xhosa townsmen in East London. Besides the real townsmen who lived almost exclusively as urban dwellers, there were the rural traditionalists ("Red blanket wearers") and the school (mission-educated and oriented) people. Each of these groups remained relatively insulated from the others and in effect constituted a subgroup with its own "culture" within the total interactional field. The nature and quality of the changes registered by migrants in large part depended on their subcultural orientation.

> It can be said that in East London a migrant's propensity to change culturally (or to resist change) is ultimately bound up with the fate of his extra-town ties. More than anything else, what keeps the conservative Red type of man faithfully Red during all his years in town in his continuing to be bound to one specific Red family, lineage, and community "at home" in the country. It is from here that the critical moral pressures emanate: the wish to go on fitting in here can be called the underlying drive. Two mechanisms keep up the force of these extra-town ties (and thus the continued acceptance of the original home culture).... (a) home-visiting, and (b) organization of relations between amakhaya ["home friends"] while in town. (Mayer 1962(64):590)

The transformation of African societies in the formation of new elites and "classes" added complexity to the interactional configuration. How these emergent elites would react to the rising tide of nationalism and whether they maintained continuous and meaningful relations with other constituents of their societies would affect the extent to which African-European integrations would crystallize. A rise in nationalistic feeling focused attention on the leadership role of native elites, and in Henry's (in Haines 1955:138) observation, the educated African was not prepared to accept Westernization.

> there is a growing conviction among the African elite that not only is there nothing about it to be ashamed of but that Africa's survival depends on a reasonable and limited use of Western technology rather than on total Westernization. The former would serve as an instrument which could be used or not, but which should not be regarded as a means of transforming the existing civilization and philosophy of life.

STRUCTURAL CHANGE AND POLITICAL EVOLUTION

A structural analysis of social change is congenial to conceptualizing the idea of an interactional social field to which the Wilsons directed attention in 1945. As urbanization proceeded, researchers became cognizant of the importance of the degree of homogeneity-heterogeneity exhibited by a social universe. Role playing in two culturally distinct orders became compartmentalized in accordance with the functional demands of situational contexts. A pluralistic social and cultural milieu was characteristic of urbanization in colonialized areas, since there was little intermingling and integration. At the same time the technicoindustrial, administrative, and educational institutionalizations coordinated under Westernization focused the direction of change. The trend in research shifted from the tribe to the city, and to the transformation of Africans as urban dwellers. Historic evidence was useful in charting modifications in political, economic, and juridical institutions, and it was in assembling the descriptive documentation and variability of change in Africa that the major contribution of this research emphasis can be found. By the 1960s, when nationalization of the former colonial territories got underway, similarities in the processes of modernization drew attention to the "structural determinism inherent in the distribution of power, the organization of bureaucracy, the modes of production, the imperatives of urbanization and other related phenomena" (Van den Berghe 1965a:10). This new awareness reopened theoretical issues relevant to the Marxian dialectic, especially with regard to the color bar and the possibility of evolutionary stages through which African societies had passed and the stages they faced in the future.

In this context of emergent national states, it was a political scientist who grounded a theory of African political evolution in the continuity of African culture. Apter (1955, 1961; compare Padmore 1953) saw the passing of colonialism as an opportunity for indigenous values to be reasserted. African development, according to Apter (1961:3), could

no longer be viewed as a consequence of European institutions planted in exotic soil. In the history of Africa the colonial period is but a short moment in time. The changes presently under way represent a process which has a much longer history than European intervention and which, indeed, was interrupted by the colonial experience. African institutional life has a vitality which transcends the specific structural innovations of European origin.

Ashanti in West Africa and Buganda in the East provided two fundamental contrasts in their value bases and in political organization. Where means and ends were approached instrumentally, and joined to a centralized hierarchy as in Buganda, the posture toward change could be more flexible.

Fortified by those institutions she considers appropriate and necessary for continuing her adjustment to the modern world, Buganda has been successful in manipulating external forces which elsewhere have played havoc with age-old institutions. Against both colonialism and Pan-Africanism, she has raised her porcupine quills in the face of political forms and economic patterns which seems to her injudicious and out of keeping with her resolve to bite off those pieces of innovation which she can digest, and which can nourish her. Against the turmoil and distress of a mighty continent in motion, Buganda is a tiny figure of continuity and tradition. (Apter 1961:475–476)

For the Ashanti in Ghana, however, the problem was not so easy. There, ends and means were not so readily separated because of the ritualized context ("consummatory value") to which they were bound. Moreover, the pyramidal-type political organization conveyed a federative quality to the power structure. The Ghanese case demonstrated how drastic reorganization measures were used to effectively transform organizational and instrumental values to achieve a new social system (Apter 1961:475). The ritualized hierarchical system of Ghana, with its emphasis on a consummatory value, required a forceful mobilization of new energies and relationships to facilitate a breakthrough to modernity. The structural-functional order of Ghana was bound to a kind of autistic self-fulfillment. Hence, Ghana experienced revolution, whereas Ganda, possessing a more flexible and instrumental approach to life situations, was able to evolve. Apter's structural analysis emphasized the way in which sociocultural systems became so impregnated with a primary value that this value regulated the intent and direction of group activity. His value analysis produced findings that could be linked to the concept of open and closed societies and related ideas.

The easing of colonial restraints marked a renewal of autonomy and of choice which proved an important factor for future change in Africa. Wherever a degree of autonomy was possible, whether out of benign neglect or discriminatory practices that segregated and threw people on their own resources, indigenous institutional changes demonstrated variability and synthetic qualities. In racially organized South Africa independent African churches frequently incorporated native and Christian beliefs and practices. Some Zulu prophets, according to Sundkler (1948: 104), perceived themselves in a kingly role and often gave identity to their following by attaching their own or their clan's name (for example, "Bantu National Church of Christ (Lamula's)"). The discriminatory Land Act of 1913 opened the door to church-held lands, and consequently prophets were able to assemble a church tribe, as it were, and provide it with lands for settlement and modest subsistence cultivation. In emulation of Zulu chiefs, the church chief also mediated disputes. The heterogeneity of Bantu churches ranging from traditional to Christian, uncovered by Sundkler, was acculturatively analogous to the distinction of rural "traditionalists" and "school people" and "real" urbanized Xhosa described by Mayer. Among the Mende of Sierra Leone, Little (1951:267) described an acculturative continuum of " 'European,' 'Creole,' 'Literate native,' and 'Nonliterate native' . . . marked off from each other by various [culture] forms and degrees of social distance." In this differentiated and complex sociocultural field of the Mende, European status symbols, including material goods, dress, monogamous marriage, Christian religion, literacy, and social relations, provided the magnetic attraction for acculturative change (cf. Powdermaker 1968:60–63). Differentiation of sociocultural groupings, which under certain circumstances took the form of social classes, underscored the fact that changes in life-styles meant that individuals altered their knowledge systems in conjunction with their basic attitudes and habits (Linton 1940:468). The Americanist focus on culture as an interdependent system of socially learned and socially performed behaviors lent itself to a view of change that was sensitive to psychological processes by which habits, attitudes, motives, and values were learned and unlearned. The same issues confronted British social anthropologists when they turned their attention to the process of urbanization. Africans moving in urban life experienced a wide variety of value conflicts as they adapted to the demands of wage work, mutual aid associations, labor unions, and political parties while maintaining their traditional obligations at the kin and village levels.

AMERICANIST THEORIES OF CULTURAL CHANGE

The memorandum for the study of acculturation promulgated by Redfield, Linton, and Herskovits in 1936 continued and expanded the cultural-psychological framework erected by culture historians for the study of cultural diffusion. Five factors appeared important to any analysis of acculturation: (1) the nature of the contact, (2) the type of contact situation, (3) the processes by which cultural exchange took place, (4) the psychological mechanisms by which traits were selectively accepted and integrated into the native culture, and (5) the general impact of the acculturative experience in generating acceptance, adaptive, or reactive attitudes.

Culture historicists contended that the fate of traits introduced to a people was determined largely by the compatibility of the trait with existing culture forms. Whether new traits were perceived as advantageous or as elements to be ignored was largely a function of the unconscious habituations and motivations structured by cultural experience. To reach this cultural-psychological matrix-guiding popular response required a theory of culture coordinated with a theory of human nature and of patterning in personality development.

The theory of culture which took shape under Kroeber, Benedict, Linton, Herskovits, and Kluckhohn stressed an inner core as the foundation or structure of the culture. Here one could locate the value orientations or "unconscious canons of choice" (Benedict) which brought consistency and a distinctive integration or style of life. External forms, like phenotypical features, were subject to variation, but like a suntan, the external forms and their variations were only skin deep. They readily altered or faded, whereas the inner core changed but slowly. Speaking for this conception of the duality of culture, Linton (1936:357–360) related its significance for integration and change:

> No culture . . . will ever . . . have all its elements in a condition of complete mutual adjustment, as long as change of any sort is under way. Since change of some sort, whether due to invention or diffusion, is always going on, this means that no culture is ever perfectly integrated at any point in its history. Integration thus becomes a matter of degree and presumably there is a point below which it cannot sink without the paralysis of the culture and the consequent destruction of the society as a functioning entity. However, this point is rarely if ever reached. All cultures possess an amazing capacity for change and adaptation. It seems that they are able eventually to integrate any new culture element or series of elements which are not in such direct and com-

plete opposition to basic elements in the existing configuration that the society rejects them from the first.

In this the fact that culture is a socio-psychological and not a physical phenomenon once more comes to the fore. The degree of integration which is required for its successful functioning is in no way comparable to that necessary to the successful functioning of an organism. Cultures, like personalities, are perfectly capable of including conflicting elements and logical inconsistencies. There are only two points in the entire culture configuration where such inconsistencies and lack of mutual adjustments can have a paralyzing effect. One of these is in the core of the culture, that mass of largely subconscious values, associations, and conditioned emotional responses which provide the culture with its vitality and the individual with motivations for exercising and adhering to its patterns. The other is in the most superficial zone of culture, that of the habitual patterns for overt behavior. Maladjustments in the first of these leads to constant emotional conflicts within the individual, conflicts between individuals who have made a different choice of values, and a loss of the group's esprit de corps. Maladjustments in the second result in constant interference and lost motion, not to mention a chronic state of irritation.

The elements which compose the core of any culture need not necessarily be consistent in all respects. In fact there are plenty of instances in which a particular society holds values which seem to be quite incompatible. . . .

The content of the culture core is subject to change, like all other parts of culture, but the changes are normally much more gradual than those which take place in the culture's more superficial elements. Certain basic elements may be abandoned if some transformation in the outward aspects of the group's life persistently interferes with their expression in overt behavior. Thus the high value attached to war and personal courage in the cultures of all our Plains tribes can hardly fail to wane when war has been eliminated for several generations. However, this loss is rarely followed by the adoption of new elements which have been developed in other cultures. Thus the loss of the war value in the Plains has not been compensated for by an adoption of the work value of the whites. These tribes are still unconvinced regarding the honorable nature of labor or its desirability for its own sake. Changes in the basic values of a group seem to come almost entirely from within and to be less the result of competition between new and established elements than of conflicts between established elements and an external situation which the society and culture are powerless to modify. Any one who has worked with non-Europeans in process of acculturation can testify how few of the European values win genuine emotional acceptance. Even when the members of such a group have assumed all the trappings of white civilization, some unexpected happening will reveal that the core of the old culture is still alive and vigorous.

Benedict's (1959) approach to cultural integration through psychocultural definitions of ideal-status personality types made no direct connection with Linton's concept of a culture core. Linton saw cultural integration in value orientations as linked to preferred activities. Yet both Linton's institutionalized preferences and Benedict's ideal personality types could only be realized as status personality types through enculturative learnings tied to basic institutionalized patterns, such as warfare in the Plains and the Potlatch on the Northwest Coast. Moreover, both Linton and Benedict agreed that the integral components of the culture core and of culturally selected personality types were sustained by unconscious conditioning. Benedict contended that any well-integrated culture and personality type was capable of picking up a most varied assortment of elements and transforming them into a complex congenial to the values and purposes of the culture and personality type (Benedict 1959:48). Through the Apollonian configuration of the southwestern Pueblos it was possible to understand why they resisted new religious cults, like peyote, which rested on an individualized hallucinatory experience. Pueblo ethos also accounted for their rejection of alcohol, to which their Dionysian neighbors were addicted (Benedict 1959:89–90). The failure of government programs among the Navaho and of Indian administration generally, according to Kluckhohn (1943:(45):218), could be traced to ignorance of the unstated and unconscious assumptions regulating their own behavior and that of their wards. The failure of administration, in Kluckhohn's opinion, must be shared in part by anthropologists, who were more concerned with overt culture and who until recently failed to develop techniques to measure the nature and significance of covert culture.

Linton coined the terms "covert culture" and "overt culture" as well as the distinction between the cultural core and peripheral features. His schema for the analysis of culture and its relevance for change is diagrammed in Table 19-1. The tendency to form dichotomies based on an inner structure in contrast with a superficial outer form fell in line with the contrast between ideal and behavioral patterns and formal and informal organization. The utility of Linton's terminology lay in the handy conceptualization of distinctions toward which others had been groping. At the same time his conceptualization redirected attention to unconscious motivations as the heartland of culture processes and encouraged the study of basic values and personality as the proper foci for the study of change. If change at base were a transformation in the knowledge, attitudes, and habitual behaviors of individuals composing a society, then shifts in values and in personal character would provide the primary signals indicating that such an alteration was underway (Linton 1940:468).

TABLE 19-1. CULTURE: FORM AND VARIATION

	Form	Psychological Processes	Change Rates	Extrapolated Change Processes
Structure	a. Core	Unconscious conditioning of motivations	Gradual (conflict)	Structural (Evolution)
	1. Covert			
Variation	b. Periphery	Habituations subject to conscious control	Rapid (no deep-seated conflicts)	Variation (History)
	1. Overt			

WORLD VIEW AND CHANGING FOLK AND PEASANT SOCIETIES

In *The Folk Culture of Yucatan* Redfield (1941) charted the disintegration of the folk "world view" and the concomitant breakdown of the social
relations and career orientations that bonded and integrated the folk
society. In Yucatan the villager's view of life came to rest in the image of
the pious man ("Taman"). The immanent principles of world order were
epitomized in man's relations to the gods. The forest bush, garden plot,
cenote, and village concentrated and ritualized the relations by which
order existed for man. There was no alternative to piety if the villagers
were to exist in a relatively secure and stable world. Man's relations to
the gods provided the model for organizing society according to the principles of respect, authority, and responsibility (Redfield 1941:123).

In the perspective of historic time, the static world and views of folk
and peasant peoples were revolutionized by changes which accompanied
urbanization. The important events and processes in the histories of the
folk and peasant societies were not found in the conquests and subjections
which they experienced at the hands of technically advanced and organized
peoples. The processes of change affecting the folk societies were more
fundamental than the substitution of technologies, social hierarchies, and
religious practice. Change struck at the core of their social and cultural
order as scientific knowledge redefined human relations to the world of
nature and the bases for moral action with regard to others (Redfield
1953:108–110). The primitive trinity of spirit-morality-cooperation was
succeeded by separation of god from nature, by the notion of a physical
world indifferent to man, and by heterogeneous social relations which
stressed individuality in place of cooperation. Chan Kom, as Redfield knew
it in the early thirties, already was a folk society in transition. On a revisit
in 1948 he was struck by the way these villagers had united their common
energies "To set a goal, to make a program of self-advancement, to define
that progress in terms of more material wealth, power, comfort, and health,
to strive for political and economic power in competition with one's neighbor" (Redfield 1964:24). Like Apter when describing Ganda modernization, Redfield found the folk people of Chan Kom had successfully adapted
to changing circumstances by harmonizing tradition with change. There
had been conflicts, but the intellectual and emotional unity of the people
was maintained by leaders operating according to the traditional world
view and morality. Part of the success of the folk rested on their practical
and prudent approach to life. They had no time for idleness, but esteemed
those who practiced a frugal, industrious, and productive life (Redfield
1964:157). Whatever its source, Chan Kom had the ideological and moral
foundations for the economic and characterological takeoff which modernization required.

Redfield's stress on the importance of ideology and world view in the study of folk and peasant societies was compatible with the cognitive orientation Sapir and Whorf brought to linguistics. His focus on value orientations as basic to cultural integration accorded with theory at the time. However, Redfield's position contrasted sharply with the traditional anthropological view that people were but dimly aware of the cultural and psychological background of their behavior. Redfield traced the products of human activity to the organized mental life which members of a society more or less shared and consciously applied to their common purposes and problems (Redfield 1941:16). Foster (1965), on the other hand, viewed the cognitive orientation of the peasants as an unverbalized and implicit expression of how they accommodated their actions to the necessities of their social and economic situations, as well as to land, climate, and supernatural beings. Foster's peasant was not bound to others and to life by positive feelings. Consequently he was not ruled by the positive affect of custom but rather by an anxious competition with others for the necessities that kept body alive.

> If, in fact peasants see their universe as one in which the good things in life are in limited and unexpandable quantities, and hence personal gain must be at the expense of others, we must assume that social institutions, personal behavior, values, and personality will all display patterns that can be viewed as functions of this cognitive orientation. Preferred behavior . . . will be that which is seen by the peasant as maximizing his security, by preserving his relative position in the traditional order of things. People who see themselves in "threatened" circumstances, which the Image of the Limited Good implies, react normally in one of two ways: maximum cooperation and sometimes communism, burying individual differences and placing sanctions against individualism; or extreme individualism. (Foster 1965(67):301)

Peasants, in Foster's judgment, were extreme individualists. Strong leadership was not found in peasant communities, except sporadically. Structurally speaking, the power base lay outside the rural communities, and local leaders were strong or weak by tolerance of this external force. Peasant families did not require the cooperation of others to survive. Their individualistic tendencies, joined to the principle of limited good, drove them into a highly competitive, relentless, and never-ending struggle with their fellows for a fair share of the scarce resources. Faced with this perpetual struggle for survival, peasants assumed a suspicious and cautious stance. Their reserve masked the true strength or weakness of their position, but in order to forestall the aggression which a weak front invites, peasants cultivated a bold image.

There were a number of ethnologists who produced descriptions and interpretations of the peasant world view similar to that of Foster (see, for example, Lewis 1951; Banfield 1958; Simmons 1959; Carstairs 1958; Dube 1958; Blackman 1927; Wiser and Wiser 1963). However, the comments and criticisms generated by Foster's statement revealed that ethnologists were not in agreement as to the nature of peasant world views and life-styles. Whether a generic peasant type could be defined, or whether several kinds of peasantry needed to be distinguished, were serious considerations (see, for example, Bennett 1966; Kaplan and Saler 1966; Piker 1966; Kennedy 1966).

SOCIOECONOMIC DEPRESSION AND THE "CULTURE OF POVERTY"

The covert patterning of peasant personality by insecurity anxieties, described by Foster, held special relevance for programs aimed at modernization. To overcome the alleged traditional conservatism of the peasant, one first had to eliminate the basis for his defensive negativism—notably his insecure economic station. Foster's peasant had no solid tradition to steady him, nor wise leadership to guide him. Rather, he trusted luck to raise him out of his misery.

Under Foster's analysis the hungry, suspicious, anxious, and defensively aggressive peasant was the inevitable product of his ecocultural station. The poor and largely illiterate workers of Mexico City were the urban counterpart to the impoverished peasants. Using family biographies in conjunction with comparative data on families within two slum areas of Mexico City, Lewis (*Five Families* 1959), developed the theory that social and economic deprivation tends to produce a subculture of uniform properties—the culture of poverty.

> The culture or subculture of poverty comes into being in a variety of historical contexts. Most commonly it develops when a stratified social and economic system is breaking down or is being replaced by another, as in the case of the transition from feudalism to capitalism or during the industrial revolution. Sometimes it results from imperial conquest in which the conquered are maintained in a servile status which may continue for many generations. It can also occur in the process of detribalization such as is now going on in Africa where, for example, the tribal migrants to the cities are developing "courtyard cultures" remarkably similar to the Mexico City *vecindades*. We are prone to view such slum conditions as transitional or temporary phases of drastic culture change. But this is not necessarily the case, for the culture of poverty is often a persisting condition even in stable social systems. Certainly in Mexico it has been a more or less permanent phenomenon since the Spanish conquest of 1519, when the process of detribalization and the movement of peasants to the cities began. Only the size, location, and composition of the slums have been in flux. I suspect that similar processes have been going on in many other countries of the world . . . [developing] some universal characteristics which transcend regional, rural-urban, and even national differences. (Lewis 1961: xxv; see also 1966a,b;1968)

By using the term "culture of poverty," Lewis (1961:xxiv) made the point that living in poverty was not just a condition of economic deprivation and personal and social disorganization. As a way of life, the culture of poverty possessed strategies and defense mechanisms by which the poor rationalized their existence. The culture of poverty exhibited considerable stability and was passed down through family lines from one generation to the next. A catalog of the economic, social, and psychological features of the culture of poverty, as Lewis found it in Mexico City, ran as follows:

> The economic traits which are most characteristic of the culture of poverty include the constant struggle for survival, unemployment and underemployment, low wages, a miscellany of unskilled occupations, child labor, the absence of savings, a chronic shortage of cash, the absence of food reserves in the home, the pattern of frequent buying of small quantities of food many times a day as the need arises, the pawning of personal goods, borrowing from local money lenders at usurious rates of interest, spontaneous informal credit devices (*tandas*) organized by neighbors, and the use of second-hand clothing and furniture.
>
> Some of the social and psychological characteristics include living in crowded quarters, a lack of privacy, gregariousness, a high incidence of alcoholism, frequent resort to violence in the settlement of quarrels, frequent use of physical violence in the training of children, wife beating, early initiation into sex, free unions or consensual marriages, a relatively high incidence of the abandonment of mothers and children, a trend toward mother-centered families and a much greater knowledge of maternal relatives, the predominance of the nuclear family, a strong predisposition to authoritarianism, and a great emphasis upon family solidarity—an ideal only rarely achieved. Other traits include a strong present time orientation with relatively little ability to defer gratification and plan for the future, a sense of resignation and fatalism based upon the realities of their difficult life situation, a belief in male superiority which reaches its crystallization in *machismo* or the cult of masculinity, a corresponding martyr complex among women, and finally, a high tolerance for psychological pathology of all sorts. (Lewis 1961:xxvi–xxvii)

Conceptualizations of the folk and peasant societies and the culture of poverty strove for typological models differentiating distinct designs for living. Like most types, their utility rested on their stimulus value for focused research and controversy (see, for example, Lewis 1951, *Life in a Mexican Village: Tepoztlán Restudied;* Foster 1953 (*American Anthropologist* 55):159–173; Odum 1953 (*Social Forces* 31):193–223; Boskoff 1949 (*American Sociological Review* 14):749–758; Sjöberg 1952 (*American Journal of Sociology*) 58:231–239; for the "culture of poverty" see Valentine 1968 and *"Book Review of Culture and Poverty: Critique and Counterproposals* by Charles A. Valentine" 1969 (*Current Anthropology* (10):181–201).

Redfield described Tepoztlán as the meeting ground for the rural folk and city cultures and stressed the role of the wealthy and literate (*los correctos*) in setting the kind and pace of change. Leaving the plaza area where *los correctos* passed their lives, each step to the periphery seemed like a step into the past, for the small tradesmen-milperos were the conservers of tradition (Redfield 1930:217–223). Twenty years later, Lewis (1951), concentrating on family and interpersonal relations and the distribution of wealth and political power, reported that the ritualized forms of respect, obligation, and cooperation were just a facade. The hidden dimension of Tepoztecan personality disclosed by Rorschach protocols was filled with suspicion, anxiety, conflict, and repressed feelings. Here lurked a problem in methodological validity, or else a stressing of opposite sides of the coin; for both Redfield and Lewis described inner cores, or ethoses of high contrast. Redfield drew attention to the positive conditioning of attitude and idea and the formation of a collective sentiment accompanying a cooperative sharing of ends and means. Lewis, on the other hand, derived his ethos from reactive mechanisms stemming from the Freudian interpretation of the unconscious. Controversy feeds naturally on a dichotomy of issues. Valentine (1968) challenged the idea of a self-perpetuating subculture of poverty by the lower class. In so doing he implicitly denied the possibility of middle-class or upper-class subcultures. Valentine's theory described poverty as a condition resulting from the inequities of the social system. The characteristics and habits of the impoverished were a function of their condition and the consequent restraints on their full participation in the society. Hence, he concluded that the problem rested not with changing the habits of the deprived and dispossessed as the culture of poverty implied, but with changing the system by reducing inequalities, beginning with unrestricted access to wealth, jobs, and education.

Valentine's theory of situational disorganization implied that the habits and conditionings which people exhibited were expediential adaptations to their circumstances. As circumstances changed, they would readily readapt their behavior to the requirements of social living. There was no clear place in Valentine's perspective for any theory of culture which relied on the habituative and integrative processes of enculturation to shape individual purposes and character. Such a view ran counter to earlier studies in acculturation which stressed the close relation between the capacity of the individual to achieve a viable personality and the stability of experience available through his culture. The more acculturated Hopis of Oraibi, child and adult alike, according to Thompson and Joseph (1947(53):19–20), possessed a vague anxiety and a high degree of sensitivity that contrasted with the more balanced, spontaneous, and outgoing personality structure of those attached to the traditional Hopi community. A high level of anxiety coupled with emotional constraint, a pervasive insecurity, and a tendency to lapse into escapist fantasies characterized responses of Dakota children who experienced an identity crisis as traditional Dakota culture eroded and left a vacuum in their lives: "The type of behavior now exhibited by the majority of Pine Ridge children must be regarded primarily as the result of psychological reactions to disorganized cultural conditions. The behavior is only symptomatic and not the basic problem" (Macgregor 1946:186).

LEVELS OF ACCULTURATION AND SOCIAL AND PERSONALITY CORRELATES

It is difficult to find an acculturative situation where one segment within a society, or one society in relation to another, is not dominant. This has important consequences in that the dominant party usually is in a more favorable position to innovate and to regulate the kind and pace of change. As at Tepoztlán, *los correctos* largely funneled change, so the Puerto Rican elite described by Steward were the mediators of change because they exercised control at the national level.

In a class society characterized by upward mobility, the status movement of individuals from one class to another involves acculturation in that new arrivals strive to increase their acceptance by adding features which identify them with their new station. Acceptance may take several generations as newcomers are derogated as the nouveau riche. The situation is considerably different, however, where the society is feudalized by estates or castes which restrict mobility.

An open class society presents a segmented continuum of acculturating individuals and groups. The acculturation process to which American Indian reservation communities are subject frequently results in a segmented continuum of acculturating individuals and groups. The best examples are those communities with a history of long and persistent acculturation. More remote communities, where some continuation of aboriginal economic activity remains, may show little in the way of segmented acculturation. In time, however, the differential acculturation of individuals and of families produces an increasing degree of heterogeneity. Differential acculturation also induces the formation of different value orientations, skills, experiences, and identifications which individuals share according to their acculturative experience. A segmented continuum of sociocultural groups gradually emerges, stretching from the least to the most acculturated when measured from the perspective of the dominant society. Such was the case of the Menomini Indians of Wisconsin described by Spindler and Goldschmidt (1952) in their "Experimental Design in the Study of Culture Change." Using twenty-three statistically controlled schedule items on a selective sample of sixty-eight males, the authors discriminated five relatively discrete categories (see Figure 19-1). Four of the categories flowed progressively along an acculturative continuum. The other was distinguishable on socioeconomic grounds. Religious affiliation proved a critical index of membership in the acculturative categories or sociocultural groups. For example,

> The Medicine Lodge-Dream Dance group . . . are not only participants in these religious observances, but for the most part its members live scattered in the forest at one end of the reservation in rough shacks, intermittently work for wages, at harvesting or logging, and depend upon subsistence hunting and fishing to supplement their larders. They identify deeply with what remains

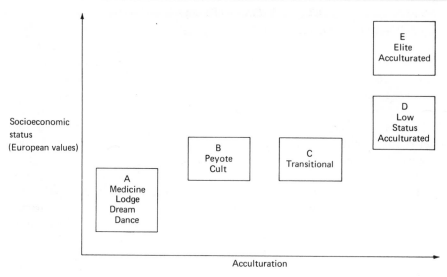

Figure 19-1. Menomini acculturative sociocultural "groups," according to Spindler and Goldschmidt (1952(8):73).

of the old culture: carry on ancient funeral rites, observe "ghost" feasts for the dead and some menstrual taboos, live under constant threat of witchcraft, repeat the Mana'pus tales, and speak Menomini in most social gatherings.

At the other extreme of the continuum are the elite acculturated; men who occupy supervisory or white-collar positions in the mill or agency offices, who have incomes between three and six thousand dollars per year, who have high school educations (or better), who live in excellent, modern frame houses furnished in middle-class style, and who are, almost without exception, members of the Holy Name Society of the Catholic Church. This group provides the effective leader-ship of the tribe today; nearly all of them have served as members of the advisory council. . . .

Between the Peyote Cult and transitional category there are no reliable socio-economic distinctions. It would appear that the membership of the Peyote Cult is actually drawn from personnel in "transition" for whom the stress of this adjustment was especially acute, and if this is the case such similarity would be expected. The distinction here consists of membership definition (the cult is set apart in the reservation community), and in the cultural patterns of Peyotism itself.

Considering the total configuration of differentiations between all five of these categories, it is clear that there is a complex continuum of socio-cultural and economic distinctions running from the Medicine Lodge-Dream Dance to the elite Catholic acculturated group. The divisions of our sample represent distinguishable segments of this continuum with overlap of attributes in the intermediate levels. (Spindler and Goldschmidt 1952(8):74–75)

In a supportive monograph Spindler (1955) presented evidence showing how the segmented acculturative continuum correlated with different degrees of personality organization and perception. The native-oriented male personality exhibited a high degree of integration, whereas intermediate transitionals disclosed a more disoriented and maladjusted personality. The elite, confident of their goals and more involved with the American culture context, demonstrated a more flexible and organized personality structure. Similar findings were reported by Louise Spindler (1962:98) for Menomini women while noting that "women of all acculturative levels retain more values and beliefs of Menomini culture than do the males." Of equal interest was the finding that the intensity and variety of interaction increased from the native-oriented to the elite, reflecting the interrelations of role-playing value orientations, and perceptual structure.

Projective tests used to tap the psychological processes of acculturation elicited generalized emotional orientations at the level of the unconscious. To overcome this deficiency, which gave no place to conscious processes, Goldschmidt and Edgerton (1961) constructed a special picture test and applied it to a Menomini sample to see if they could correlate a conscious selection of values with the five acculturative categories discriminated by the Spindlers. Their instrument gave acceptable correlations on five of the pictures, but required refinement in order to achieve a precise categorization of Menomini subjects according to degree of acculturation. With similar purpose the Spindlers (1965(1):5) developed an instrumental activities inventory to uncover "information on the cognitive orientations pervasively influencing the individual's perception of and response to social reality. At a more discrete level the I.A.I. gives us specific, operational perceptions of social reality organized normatively in means-end relationships."

Applied to the Blood Indians of Alberta, essentially traditional and conservative, with but a small group of progressive ranchers, the Spindlers found that the instrumental choices made by the male sample varied according to the kinds of roles and the goal aspirations of which these were a part. For example, the elite ranchers shared a common cultural concern for a life spent outdoors rather than behind a desk, and they were equally concerned with good health and vigorous activity. Independence was also a common ideal, but the elite thought of it as a "state to be gained by hard work and planning ahead, by acquiring goods and economic security" (Spindler and Spindler 1965(1):15).

The work of the Spindlers was an important contribution to the investigation of the heterogeneity of reservation culture and society. It called attention again to the way religious affiliation initially polarized ideological and political commitment, separating the society into Christians for progress and pagans for tradition. In *The Code of Handsome Lake, The Seneca Prophet*, Parker (1913:13) described the process of religious polarization which followed introduction of the new teaching about 1800.

> Handsome Lake lived to see his people divided into factions, one that clung to the old order and one that followed him. After his death the old order gradually faded out of existence, either coming over to the New Religion or embracing Christianity. Thus by the time of the Civil War in 1861 there were only the two elements, the Christians and the followers of Handsome Lake.

They stand so arrayed today but with the "new religionists" gradually diminishing in number.

Continuing, (Parker 1913:14) reported how the conservative Indian saw his Christian brother as an apostate who betrayed his race by condoning the wrongs which whites had heaped upon the Indians. Ashamed of his own ancestors, the Christian Indian was a poor imitation of the white man. In the eyes of the Christian, those who wore feathers in imitation of the past were like blind people wandering in the wilderness. They were heathens who stood in the way of progress and who resisted change that was inevitable.

NATIVISMS AND POLITICAL MOVEMENTS

With its ceremony, congregation, and meeting house, religion affords high visibility for social identification and commitment. By the 1930s anthropologists became alerted to the power of religion as an instrument for catalyzing the discontent of peoples undergoing heavy acculturation in a dominant-subordinate relationship. Religious movements among American Indians, Africans, and Oceanic peoples organized the intense and varied feelings of peoples straining to escape from social inferiority, political domination, and economic deprivation and who aspired for an ethnocultural identity that was both legitimate and equal to that of their conquerors or superiors. Balandier (1965; compare Linton 1943; Lommel 1953; Voget 1956; Wallace 1956) observed that in Africa religious movements quickly took on a political character. Religious movements stimulated nationalistic feelings which, although unsophisticated, sounded a clear political message. It was also evident that religio-political movements among colonialized peoples coordinated with a worsening of economic conditions (Balandier 1965; Aberle 1966; Nash 1937; Worsley 1968; Krader 1956). The perspective on religious movements among anthropologists converged on a view already drawn by some sociologists, economic historians, and historians (for example, Max Weber 1930; Tawney 1926; Marti 1929). It was equally apparent that religious movements among subordinated native peoples, as Wallace (1956(58):265) pointed out, often sought to revitalize a large segment of the traditional design. Revitalization of the life ways usually came when people were convinced that their culture was so disordered that it could no longer satisfy their needs. Indeed, Wallace (1956 (58):268) argued that "all organized religions are relics of old revitalization movements, surviving in routinized form in stabilized cultures, and that religious phenomena per se originated ... in the revitalization process —that is, in visions of a new way of life by individuals under extreme stress." Revitalization movements might be more or less secular, or religious, but their basic structure and psychodynamics appeared very much alike. For example, the Communist Revolution of 1917 shared a structure commonly observed in religious movements of a revitalistic type. These elements consisted of the following: (1) a disorganized and depressed society, (2) prophetic political leaders who appealed to a revered and infallible authority (Marx), (3) leaders imbued with the zeal of missionaries, and (4) a message which predicted apocalyptically the destruction of a corrupt and oppressive society which would be followed by a social millennium.

Revitalization achieved its primary aims initially when renovations were tackled with energy and enthusiasm. The natural course of such movements then led into structural reorganization which solidified and became the basis for routinization. A clash of views and divided loyalties which split communities along religio-political lines was usual. The spread of Peyotism and Shakerism produced sharp divisions within American Indian reservation communities (see, for example, Barnett 1957; La Barre 1938; Aberle 1966; Petrullo 1934; M. K. Opler 1940; Mead 1932; Radin 1923). The rise of Christianity in Roman times and of Protestantism facilitated the crystallization of political differences and conflicts. Furthermore, the clash between Protestantism and Catholicism was exported overseas in missionary rivalries (see, for example, Redfield 1964; Thompson and Joseph 1947; Rapoport 1954). The struggle for the souls and morals of local peoples, by dividing them and creating factions, inadvertently laid the foundations for later political action. Among the Ba-Kongo, evangelical Protestantism, with its insistence on loyalty to God, the highest authority, inadvertently strengthened religio-political movements such as Kimbangism and its offshoots (Balandier 1963:447). Once underway, however, Protestant missions in the Congo, as well as Catholic, became political targets. In the American Southwest, factionalism was pervasive in traditional village life. However, the Spanish intrusion and subsequent Pueblo acculturative experience under the Americans exacerbated division by providing focal points for conflict in policy and political loyalties (see, for example, Dozier 1966; Fenton 1957; French 1948; Fox 1961; Siegel 1949; Siegel and Beals 1960; Whitman, in Linton 1940; Titiev 1944; compare Walker 1968; Berkhofer 1965; Adair and Vogt 1949).

THE STRUCTURING OF INTERACTION AND CHANGE

Schisms divide and polarize interactional fields by raising walls around units. The restriction on interaction prohibits community-wide projects and inhibits change. American Indian reservations frequently exhibit such polarization of their interactional universes. For example, toward the end of the nineteenth century, progressive and conservative divisions crystallized at Santa Ana Pueblo. The conservatives maintained themselves in power from 1894 to 1935, and during this time they strove to homogenize the interacting community by driving many of their opponents from the Pueblo.

> A nonconformist may be subjected first to damaging gossip and harassment, but if his unbecoming behavior continues the pueblo officials take over. During the Spanish and Mexican periods such a person was often whipped publicly and, where "evidence" of witchcraft was demonstrated, executed. Commonly the indigenous officials have evicted nonconformists from the pueblo and have confiscated their houses, land, and other property. Prior to 1900 those who violated the Pueblo mores joined neighboring Spanish-American communities or else went to live with the Apache or Navaho; today they usually move to urban areas in the Southwest. Since Pueblo communities enjoy sovereignty under United States law, an Indian has no recourse to state or federal courts for the redress of wrongs suffered within the pueblo except in a few cases which come under the jurisdiction of the federal courts. The absolute authority of the pueblo officials has resulted in the elimination of controversial elements within their communities and has served to perpetuate a conservative population dedicated to the continuance of indigenous values and traditional Pueblo patterns of ceremonial organization. (Dozier 1966(5):175)

The result was a conservative homogenizing of the interactional field, but in the instance of Santa Clara Pueblo, the divisiveness reached into the heart of the ceremonial organization and disrupted the normal presentation of ritual drama and dance for the welfare of the community.

Any limitation of contact across social and cultural boundaries necessarily restrains the flow of ideas, goods, and services and limits opportunities for change, both in a quantitative and qualitative way. When restriction is by design, as in the formation of ethnocultural enclaves within urban or rural areas by migrants or religious colonists, various social pressures and ethnocultural pride are used to maintain a degree of insularity (Klass 1961; Mayer 1961; Spicer 1940; compare Kollmorgen 1943; Thomas and Zaniecki 1927). Basing her data on a probability sample of Mexican-Americans in Los Angeles and San Antonio, Joan Moore (1968:25) reported that differences in acculturation were not correlated so much with income as with the kinds of people available for contact. Mexican-Americans living in association with Anglos were more acculturated than Mexican-Americans of equivalent income residing in ethnic neighborhoods. The caste relationship of Indians and Spanish in Latin America illustrated the kinds of restraints on contact and change commonly found in agrarian societies where the consummatory values of a landed aristocracy required a functional-complementary relationship between producer and consumer. The bounded quality of relations among socioeconomic groups and communities in Peru led Holmberg (1960:67) to describe Peru as a "nation of relatively unintegrated plural societies."

Yaqui acculturation described by Spicer (1961a) illustrated a situation where the interactive field linking Spanish, Mexicans, and Indians went through a number of organizational or evolutionary changes. Initially the Yaqui cooperated with their priest-mentors. During this period a new technical, social, and ideological base was established for Yaqui communities. Later, when contacts were interrupted and interactions slackened in rate, kind, and intensity, the Yaqui drew heavily upon these additions to reformulate their own culture, fusing Spanish and Christian elements with Yaqui features. The product was such an intricate blend and synthesis that an objective observer was unable to say that it was more or less Spanish or Yaqui. Among the Gila River Pimas the contact situation was much different from the Yaqui; consequently, the amount and nature of the cultural interchange varied. Spanish contacts with the Pimas were irregular and without intensity, and Spanish influence was confined to a formalization of political-administrative offices, functions, and procedures (Ezell 1961:126). However, the Pima headman and village council organization among the Gila River groups was neither modified nor supplanted, which did occur among southern groups where intense and persistent contact with the Spanish prevailed. Moreover, the Gila River Pimas did not take over the ideology and ceremony associated with the fiesta organization characteristic of the Yaqui and other groups within the orbit of strong Spanish contact. Unable to get the Pimas to move into concentrated settlements, the Spanish were not in position to control the contact processes advantageously, and the Pimas selected Spanish elements which were compatible with their own desires and needs. According to Ezell (1961:126–138), "The form of this acceptance—i.e., whether . . . of form, meaning, and use, or any combination thereof, whether . . . a case of simple addition, or of replacement, or of fusion—depended upon the nature of the element and its compatibility in form, meaning, and use with Pima culture."

A conceptualization of change as a function of regularized interrelations within an interactional field is congenial to an ecological orientation. In tracing contacts in the diffusion of culture elements in prehistoric times, the archeologist likewise deals with interactional networks. Ethnological students of acculturation presently are finding the concept of interactional fields useful in understanding the flow of acceptance and rejection of cultural elements and complexes (Thompson 1961; Netting 1968; Clark 1960; Sanders 1962). As a meeting ground for representatives of diverse ecocultural zones, the port-of-trade can be seen as a unique ecocultural adaptation (Leeds 1961:40). Existing through exchange, the port-of-trade either developed sea power and assumed control over adjacent ecocultural zones and societies, or it was absorbed by one of the larger partners to the trade. Ecologic diversity thus provided a basis for functional differentiation, expansion, and the unification of differing ecocultural areas. According to Leeds (1961:42), the driving force and success of empire lay in welding together areas characterized by considerable technological diversity. Ethnoecologic diversity also was essential to the unification of a segmentary type of organization (Sahlins 1961). From descriptions of the Nuer (Evans-Pritchard 1940) and of the Tiv (Bohannan 1954), Sahlins (1961 (63):337) observed how the "segmentary lineage system consistently channels expansion outward, releasing internal pressure in an explosive blast against other peoples." The internal oppositions which normally took up the time and energy of two segmentary lineages were submerged by a common opposition to an alien people, or by conflict with other segmentalized units which likewise presented a common front against outsiders. Hence, Sahlins hypothecated that the segmentary lineage structurally was better adapted to expand into a contested area than into an unpopulated area where lineages were free to disperse (compare Vayda 1960, 1961). In an evolutionary perspective, peoples at the level of tribal organization faced two options as they expanded in space: (1) by intruding into virgin territory groups they could split and become localized, and (2) by infiltrating or leapfrogging into occupied zones they could form a segmentary lineage system. However, as an evolutionary type, a system of segmentary lineages possessed but limited adaptability; for, once the condition of intertribal competition was removed, unity tended to dissolve in divisive intratribal conflicts (Sahlins 1961). (See Figure 19-2 for evolutionary stages.)

Sahlins' model of segmentary lineague formation and its maintenance rests on a statement of structural relations and necessary consequences. In this respect it bears a striking relationship to the mechanical model of Lévi-Strauss. Since an evolutionary perspective strains at the statement of structural successions, a deterministic formal model appears congenial to the theory. In this respect it contrasts with the view that sees an individual or a group acting under the guidance, but not determinisms, of instrumental rules which state priorities among alternatives (for example, Frake 1962; Howard 1963; Keesing 1967).

ACCULTURATIVE SEQUENCES

Initial efforts at defining acculturative sequences leaned heavily on attitudes people assumed in adapting and reacting to an alien culture, the relative equilibrium-disequilibrium states of the culture-and-personality systems, and the increasing degree to which the borrowed value orientations were internalized (for example, Elkin 1951; Keesing 1941, 1962; Thurnwald and Thurnwald 1935; Vogt 1951; Wallace 1956). However, more recently Foster (1962), making use of Elkin (1936–1937) and Read (1955), developed an attitudinal sequence that ran from antagonistic fear of the new to unrestrained desire to adopt alien ways so as to share the same economic advantages as the outsider. This desire was strengthened by a scorn for traditional custom and came at a time of disillusionment. This also was a time when foreign domination, population losses, and feelings of failure and rejection led to nativistic movements in order to gain release from insecurity. Following the time of troubles, the elite reevaluated the traditional ways and a new identification was made with a modified culture which drew upon traditional values and which could be claimed as one's unique possession. For Foster, nationalistic movements represented a phase which facilitated or restrained development if the traditional was valued solely because it was time honored and unique to the group. (See Table 19-2 for acculturative stages.)

Spicer (1961:521–542), after analyzing American Indian culture con-

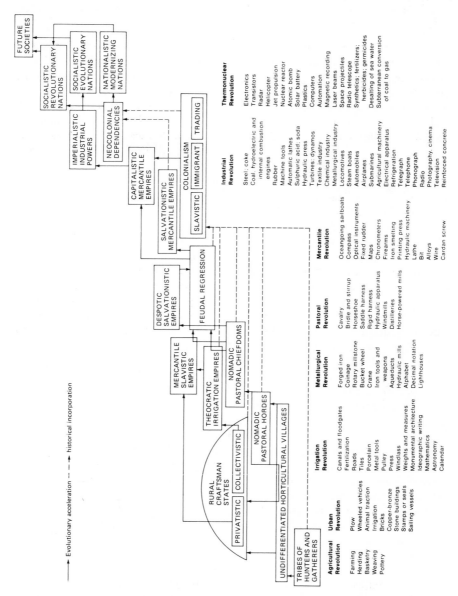

Figure 19-2. Stages of sociocultural evolution and their technological correlates, according to Ribeiro (1970(11):429).

TABLE 19-2. STAGES IN THE ACCULTURATION OF AMAZONIAN INDIAN RUBBER TAPPERS AND LABRADOR INDIAN TRAPPERS[a]

Mundurucu Tappers	*Montagnais Trappers*
1. *Prerubber*	1. *Prefur*
Village consists of men's house, matrilocal extended family households; population divided into patrilineal clans and moieties.	Nomadic composite band hunts large migratory game animals.
Village males form collective hunting and garden-clearing group.	Frequent band breakup during winter scarcity.
Household females form the horticultural unit.	Amalgamation of several winter groups for summer hunting and fishing.
Intensive warfare for headhunting and as mercenaries allied to whites; partial dispersal of villagers in dry season for fishing and war.	Chieftainship weak and shifting—leader of winter group; no summer band chief.
Chief the war leader and representative of village in trade of manioc flour.	Residence bilocal, frequent shifts of winter group membership.
2. *Marginal involvement*	2. *Marginal involvement*
Chief continues as mediator with trader, but is now often trader-appointed—trader gains influence.	Trade by family heads—leaders do not trade for followers.
Dry season population dispersal for rubber production rather than fishing and war—war continues, but lessened in importance.	Trapping secondary to subsistence hunting—subsistence still gotten traditionally, basic social patterns persist.
Basic prerubber economy and settlement pattern unchanged.	No trapping territory.
Continuing displacement of aboriginal crafts.	Linkage to trading posts.
3. *Transitional*	3. *Transitional*
Further displacement of native crafts, increased need of trade goods, increased dependence on trader.	Further displacement of native crafts, increased need of trade goods, increased dependence on trader.
Chieftainship undermined due to new-type chiefs who now represent the trader.	Increased fur production interferes with subsistence hunting.
Agricultural cycle and village life inhibit larger rubber production.	Individual trade conflicts with group solidarity.
Trend toward individual trade.	
4. *Convergence and culmination*	4. *Convergence and culmination*
A. Intermediate	Fur trapping now predominant; winter provisions purchased.
Move to new villages in rubber regions.	Winter groups not necessary with end of collective hunt—family or individual hunting gives greater efficiency, allows conservation.
Chief now intermediary with Indian agent and missionaries.	Shift of economic interdependencies
Individual trade, individualized subsistence economy—end of men's	

house and traditional house and traditional village—village held together only by weakening kin ties and sociability.

Centripetal factors (e.g., sorcery, sexual rivalry) cause fission of these villages and results in B, below.

B. Dispersal (follows upon 3 or 4A)

Leadership no longer integrative.

Individual trade undercuts kin obligations.

Conflict with agricultural cycle resolved by moving to rubber avenue—family now in isolation except for trade bonds.

from group to trader.

Emergence of a chief who serves as intermediary with Indian agents and missionaries.

Nuclear family basic unit at all times of year.

Trapper maintains and transmits right to a delimited hunting territory exploited only by his family.

---

[a] Each stage represents alignment of variables in an interactional field. The Murphy and Steward article underscores the importance of the interactional configuration in producing similarities in tribal histories despite the fact that physical resources may be different. The possession of a natural resource that could be marketed was intrinsic to the formation of the successive interactional configurations.

SOURCE: Murphy and Steward (1956(4):348–349).

tact in six societies, suggested a number of successive phases based largely on the nature of contact. The first phase was characterized by an unhesitating trial of the new, "regardless of the specific forms of contact." At first innovations were taken up as alternatives and did not disturb the aboriginal system. During a succeeding phase the acculturative process shifted according to whether contact was nondirected or directed. If nondirected, a process of incorporative integration prevailed. Spicer defined incorporative integration as "the transfer of elements from one culture system and their integration into another system in such a way that they conform to the meaningful and functional relations within the latter." Directed change produced a shift from incorporation to fusion. Moreover, in the directed type of contact, the type of change was "not set *exclusively* by either one of the cultural systems involved," but depended on the kinds of relations which linked the interests and integrative principles and institutions of the two systems. An assimilative, or replacive, type of integration also was reported as a common process of directed contact under special conditions.

Spicer and his seminar colleagues admitted that North American Indian societies generally passed through a series of stages in cultural adjustment. The sequence began with incorporation and ended with assimilation. However, they observed that presently the great majority of Indians in the United States exhibit neither incorporation nor assimilation as predominant tendencies. Present-day Yaqui demonstrate assimilative tendencies with relation to Mexican industrial culture, adjusting "the core of the old folk culture—the religious observances and beliefs—to the dominant culture, rather than the reverse." However, Spicer and associates hesitated to commit themselves to any invariant sequences that might attend native European contacts, since these varied according to the nature of contact and the types of cultures involved, despite the fact that technological acculturation was visibly heavy for all six societies.

In taking note of the attitudes people assumed toward change, to innovators or contact agents, and to the ecological context, acculturationists implied that the structuring of relations in an interactional field was crucial. The terms, "directed" and "nondirected," described the nature of the interactions involved and the way initiative flowed from one system to another. The distinction in types of contact communities, and the correlation of historical-cultural periods with shifts in the type of community, meant that basic alterations in the interactive field determined decisive moments in contact. The history and evolution of interactional fields thus provided the basis for comparing the development of structures and their growth processes.

As ethnologists developed ethnohistoric interests, their concern for distinguishing historic periods in terms of differences in the nature of contact and exchange situations paralleled objectives and methodological procedures already followed by historians. For example, in the history of the Southwest, both anthropologists and historians agreed that a Spanish and an Anglo-American period must be discriminated. An interest in periodization, however, was not the major focus of anthropological concern (see, for example, Hickerson 1962), but rather a greater attention to process, especially complex relations affecting the economic, social, and political structure of a tribe. In his ethnohistoric account of Cherokee relations Gearing (1962) described the trend toward an integration of policy decisions (diplomacy) in the hands of a tribal representative (about 1755) as the localized and rivalrous village leadership failed to accommodate to the realities of trade competition, politics, and war along the Carolina frontier. The Charles Town government's demand that the Cherokee empower their representatives to treat for the whole and bind them firmly to a contract, in conjunction with internal rivalry, created new functions which strained traditional organization at the time. At this critical turn, the Cherokee relied not on the counsel of warriors but on astute old men whose reputations were based on the logic of their persuasive arguments and the wisdom of their choices. In a process Gearing (1962:110) saw as parallel to steps taken toward an integrated polity in ancient Mesopotamia, the "first Cherokee moves toward statehood were coordinated by religious officials." Investigations of the nature of tribal factionalism and of contra-acculturative religio-political movements without a special regard for acculturative sequences illustrated the anthropological concern with process (see, for example, French 1948; Dozier 1966; Walker 1968; Chance 1962; Aberle and Stewart 1957; Aberle 1966; Stern 1965). In effect, the engagement of ethnologists with ethnohistory was producing the kind of social history which Evans-Pritchard (page 565) considered the proper task of social anthropology for the present and in the future.

CULTURE CHANGE AND PSYCHOLOGICAL PROCESSES

Linton (1940:468) perceived culture change as an alteration in the knowledge, attitude, and behavior of individuals. This perspective continued the interest of American culture theorists with psychological processes through which culture was internalized, maintained, and altered. To follow Linton (1940:481) once more: "The basic processes of culture change are the individual psychological ones of learning and forgetting."

This posture led to an immediate consideration of the nature of motivations which had a part in altering cultural habits and goals. Widespread dissatisfactions with the discrepancies between culturally projected anticipations and rewards provided an important basis for change, as did the lure of personal prestige and the novelty of new experiences (Linton 1940: 474). How a group perceived donors in a system of prestige ranking was important, for the common tendency was to borrow in imitation of admired social superiors (Linton 1940:491–492). However, in a situation of directed change, complex attitudes often intruded, modifying the normal processes of interchange. "All attempts to direct culture change," observed Linton (1940:504), "are really efforts on the part of the dominant group to modify and control its own environment." Forced acculturation evoked a common human and noncultural response of resentment that not only inhibited the transfer of culture but also frequently aroused reactions in nativistic or contra-acculturative movements, to borrow Herskovits' (1938a: 97) term.

To gain some understanding of the psychological processes operating in the acceptance or rejection of alien culture elements, Linton (1936:403–404) analyzed them according to form, meaning, use, and function.

> The *form* of a trait complex will be taken to mean the sum and arrangement of its component behavior patterns; in other words that aspect of the complex whose expressions can be observed directly and which can, therefore, be transmitted from one society to another . . . [as in] the *form* of a ceremony or technique. . . . The *meaning* of a trait complex consists of the associations which any society attaches to it. Such associations are subjective and frequently unconscious. They find only indirect expression in behavior and therefore cannot be established by purely objective methods. . . .
>
> The use of any culture element is an expression of its relation to things external to the social-cultural configuration; its function is an expression of its relation to things within that configuration. Thus the axe has a use or uses with respect to the natural environment of the group, i.e., to chop wood. It has functions with respect both to the needs of the group and the operation of other elements within the cultural configuration. It helps to satisfy the need for wood and makes possible a whole series of woodworking patterns. . . .

The function of a trait complex is the sum total of its contribution toward the perpetuation of the social-cultural configuration. This function is normally a composite which can be analyzed into a number of functions each of which is related to the satisfaction of a particular need.

Continuing, he noted that

The relation between form, use, and meaning is . . . a rather tenuous one. Use and meaning are probably more closely related to each other than either one is to form, but even so their mutual adaptations are loose enough to permit of a wide range of variation. When we try to ascertain the relation of these three elements to function, the situation becomes vastly more complex. Function seems to derive least from form, somewhat more from use, but most from meaning. Any attempt to analyze these relationships in a particular case reveals still another disturbing factor. Many elements of culture have multiple uses, but nearly all of them have multiple meanings [linked to specific needs]. (Linton 1936:410)

Form took precedence over other analytic components in the perception of those confronted with novel features for adoption. "The culture of an alien group presents itself to the potential borrowers as an aggregation of forms stripped of most of their meaning and of all but the most obvious and elementary of their functional relationships" (Linton 1936:487).

Following an analytic pattern like that of Linton, Barnett (1942(44):15) added the concept of principle to the analytic schema. Barnett defined principle as "the dynamic aspect of form; that quality or property which manifests itself only when the form is in action."

When analyzing change within the cultures of the Yurok, Hupa, and Karok of northwestern California, Barnett (1940(42):47) found that the best units for comparison were not generalized categories, such as dress or decoration, but a culture complex centered in a specific activity. Hence he defined his analytic unit "as any configuration of form and meaning which satisfies the social, biological, or psychic requirements of a specific demand" or social situation. In their acceptances and rejections, the northwest California tribes were apt to respond to the context of an actional pattern. For example, the Yurok rejected the Christmas tree as a part of the Christmas complex because it evoked a parallel with the practice of setting up fir shrubs to screen those who handled corpses (Barnett 1940 (42):37). A cultural response thus was total within a relevant context of form and meaning.

In any given culture configuration form becomes linked with a certain set of associations, values, emotional responses (meanings), and functions which are recalled upon the reappearance of that specific form. When it comes as a new trait, that form, if familiar, is incorporated into the culture upon the basis of the familiar meanings attached to it. If it stimulates unpleasant associations, it is resisted or rejected; but whether accepted or rejected this process of reinterpretation tends to break down an introduced complex through the reassociation of the familiar forms of its component elements. (Barnett 1940(42):37)

The critical factor in response turned on the deep-seated meaning anchored to feeling (Barnett 1940(42):42), for it was here that the full registry of the incompatibility of alien traits was found. However, unlike Linton, Barnett stressed the transfer of meaning, along with form-function-principle, in the acceptance of novel complexes. In *Innovation: The Basis of Cultural Change* (1953) Barnett relied heavily on Gestalt theory to explain the tendency to maintain the integrity of the culture complex—that is, to respond within the relevant context.

Both Linton and Barnett continued the common cultural-historical emphasis on the context of form and meaning as critical and determinative in what happened to any proferred trait complex, especially in a nondirected situation. Barnett especially extended comprehension of the nature of the cultural-psychological context (configuration or complex) through which cultural interchange took place. Configurations were integrated into broader institutionalized patterns, but Barnett stressed the situational activity, as did Fortes (1949), in the accommodation of principles to social context. Barnett identified the basic processes of cultural change as follows: incorporation of new elements into an existing complex either as additions or as alternatives, substitution, reinterpretation, and assimilation (compare Spicer 1961b). In the discrimination of similarities and differences, and in the synthesis, assimilation, or recombination of forms and meanings that might occur, Barnett (1940(42):39) noted that the "incorporation of new complexes . . . on the basis of functional equivalences" regarding native culture had been rare in northwest California.

INNOVATORS AND MARGINALITY

A focus on the cultural-psychological processes involved in cultural interchange could not avoid coming to grips with the psychology of innovators. Any new culture element, according to Linton (1940:470) began with "(1) . . . initial acceptance by innovators, (2) . . . dissemination to other members of the society, and (3) the modifications by which it is finally adjusted to the preexisting culture matrix."

Although not unaware of the personal ambiguity of a life between two culture worlds, anthropologists never found the concept of the marginal man (Park 1928; Stonequist 1937) congenial to their observed facts. Park (1928(33):892) defined the marginal man as a cultural hybrid marked by the scars of his conflict experience—a recognizable personality type possessing a "spiritual instability, intensified self-consciousness, restlessness, and malaise."

Park considered that the frustration and restlessness which derived from an ambiguous transitional location between two ways of life aroused an energetic and creative impulse that turned marginal persons into leaders. Where genetic intermixture produced a transitional physical type in combination with cultural hybridity, Park argued that the marginality of the person's status and self-image was marked by heightened tension. Hence, the mixed blood offered the best evidence for defining the marginal man as a type and for measuring the relation between marginality and innovation. "It is in the mind of the marginal man—where the changes and fusions of culture are going on—that we can best study the processes of civilization and progress" (Park 1928(33):893).

The relation of marginality to innovation, individual or social, received little formal treatment by anthropologists, although certain evidences produced in the wake of ecological and culture-personality interests suggest that the stimulus value of marginality may be an important factor in innovation. When criticizing Wissler's view of a culture center as the continuous source for innovation in a culture area, Dixon (1928) cited the stimulus of differing ecologies in producing adaptive innovations at the margins of such areas. The port-of-trade, the trading post (see, for example, Adams 1963), and societies playing the role of middlemen in trade are drawn into or exploit a marginal status. The ambiguous role of participant-observer valued by anthropologists involves impression management and, as Berreman (1962:12) reports, this is "often an exhausting, nerve-wracking effort on both sides, especially in the early phases of contact." In his study of the spread of peyote LaBarre (1938:153; see also Speck 1933; Petrullo 1934) took note of the way in which John Wilson, the Caddo-Delaware leader, adopted features from several cultures and synthesized them within his own personality. In northwest California Barnett (1940; 1941–1942 (20):161) found that mixed bloods were less inclined to uphold traditional practices than full bloods.

> To concern ourselves for the present only with the consequences of the [biracial] union, there is the further important consideration of a mixed heritage, cultural as well as racial, converged in the child. . . . For such a person there is no recognized place in either sphere. He is miscast for both fittings. This cannot fail to produce unease and dissatisfaction, and this . . . would make him a likely subscriber to the new order. Certainly the old one offered him nothing and with its renouncement there was at least the chance to break its bonds. This is what the Yurok half-breed did and . . . the majority of his kind still seek the releases but evade the checks and balances of the white man's living pattern. Whether he is to blame or not, he is still neither Indian nor white, still malcontented, still desocialized. (Compare Jenks 1917:101–107; Kluckhohn and Leighton 1962:112–113; Reed 1942:258–265; Barnouw 1950: 89; Thurnwald and Thurnwald 1935:389–390; Stewart 1944; Walker 1968; Tumin 1945)

In his search for other social elements predisposed to change, Barnett (1941–1942(20):163) developed the thesis "that the misfits, the maladjusted, and the underdogs are in the vanguard of cultural innovation." Even those of high status found that changing conditions involved difficult adjustments, and, unable to meet aboriginal specifications, they often accepted the new to ease personal stress and to end dissatisfaction (Barnett 1941–1942(20):167).

SOCIAL AND CULTURAL CHANGE: CONVERGENCES IN SOCIAL AND CULTURAL THEORY

When introducing a collection of essays under the title *Anthropology and Social Change*, Dr. Lucy Mair (1969:5) noted that British anthropologists found no profit in studying social change as a "process ... of ... acceptance or rejection of cultural traits, nor ... of the differential adaptation of different social systems." Rather, they preferred to view social change as a modification in social structure. Social change then involved "changes in the rules that govern social relationships—rules about the ownership and transmission of property, the right to exercise authority, the duty to co-operate with particular people in particular circumstances" (Mair 1969:121). Any change in rules affected traditional prescriptions regarding status and role, and a good way to define structure was as a configuration of role relationships (Mair 1969:122). When statuses and roles are altered Mair (1969:4) noted that it was the individual who brought changes in statuses and roles by taking advantage of new opportunities. Individual choice was a matter of personal circumstances and not the state of society or culture. Within any society, even those of small scale, individuals have some opportunities for maneuvering because of alternatives. With respect to African societies, important opportunities had come from outside with the imposition of European colonialism. Under this set of altered relations Africans were able to take up new roles as cash farmers, wage earners, civil servants, politicians, and nationalist leaders (Mair 1969: 131). However, prescriptions for a status role under colonialism often were as restrictive as rules regulating participation in the traditional social order. This was especially true in the political arena, but with a return to independence, ambitious and aggressive men were lured by competition for power. In this competitive, interactive structure, there was no dominance of forces to conserve tradition, nor a drive to imitate foreign cultures nor efforts to apply traditional ways to changing situations. There were some who sought to maintain tradition, as there were those who imitated the model of the new. But the dynamics of change rather was found in the altered relations between the new rulers and the people. The new rulers were free of traditional restraints and consequently were able to exploit the potential of an unstructured field of relations. Hence, in following new interactional leads, individuals altered the configuration of statuses and roles and consequently altered the social structure.

Despite differences between British social change and American culture change theory, both are much alike in their orientations regarding a structural-interactional interpretation and related assumptions. If these implicit assumptions were compiled in one piece, they would make a list somewhat as follows (compare Parsons and Shils 1951; Parsons and Smelser 1956):

1. The human reality is made up of interrelated variables—the individual somatic, sociopsychological, social, cultural, technicoecological, and

demographic. These variables are so related within a system that significant alterations in one will lead to alterations in the others.

2. A sociocultural system is organized organically and integrated by style or configuration. This means that a system has maintenance requirements that relate to biopsychic needs *and* normative goals and values expressed in status-personality definitions. A relative state of equilibrium and integration must be sustained if individuals operating within the system are to remain flexible, adaptive, and satisfied.

3. Although a sociocultural system is greater than the sum of its parts, it is not a wholly consistent or tightly integrated structure but contains contradictory trends or acceptable alternatives. Tendencies running counter to the basic integration develop out of tensions created by pressures to conform. However, the variations act to release the tensions engendered and thus maintain system stability, consistency, and continuity.

4. Since variation is a necessary part of any system, an understanding and scientific explanation of the human reality must consider variation as well as structural congruence. In short, as anthropologists noted the diversity of custom and directed their energies to explanations of cross-cultural variations, they realized that internal diversities must also be explained.

5. Common sources of variation in the human situation may be found in any one of the important or generic variables. However, individuals, acting as independent, goal-oriented persons, or as members of a group, are the source of variation in any sociocultural system, and consequently the basic agents of change.

6. Any continuous alteration in structuring constitutes sociocultural change. A change of this order is possible only as the interrelations linking the several dimensions of the structure are modified. Therefore, change begins with alterations in the kind, rate, and intensity of interactions (roles) linking individuals to the significant institutionalized patterns of the system.

7. Since the sociocultural system inclines to the establishment of a dynamic equilibrium, the structuring of the system in terms of its hierarchy of institutions and value orientations tends to inhibit or to facilitate particular kinds of changes. The crucial variable is the compatibility or congruence of the innovation with respect to the total system or relevant parts. In final analysis, compatibility is measured by the needs of individuals, whether latent or consciously expressed as goal aspirations. A proper tension state is required for people to change their interactive patterns and reach for new objects and statuses. However, natural variability within a system usually is not geared to produce a threshold of tension necessary to induce actional reorientations. For this to occur it is necessary for deprivation-desire to reach a point where people are impelled to attempt a new adjustment. Or contact must be made with a new order that attracts people by offering fresh opportunities anchored to different value orientations and motivations. A tension state leading to change usually arises historically through alterations in the interactive field induced by immigration,

emigration, conquest reorganization, technological diffusions, and the like.

8. At any one moment the limits of change for any sociocultural system are bounded by the scale of its structure and the corresponding interactional field. The historical-evolutionary development of any society moves in the direction of the most diverse structure within the limits of its effective interactions. The rate of this movement depends on the frequency, intensity, and kinds of interactions linking the society to the more complex structure and to other units within the field.

Conversely, when a complex structure develops in any area, it organizes adjacent units within an interactive network to sustain its present and latent functional requirements. Therefore, the flow of initiative is from the more differentiated to the less differentiated structure, and the latter will evolve in the direction of the former. The course of this evolutionary development is channeled by the institutionalized patterns that express the core values of the complex structure and by the functional-ecological relations of the less complex to the complex structure. An evolving structure may not attain the exact level of quantitative and qualitative development achieved in the more differentiated system. In time, however, it replicates the majority of the forms, beliefs, and practices in accordance with minimal requirements in scale and in general compatibility that permit articulation with the more complex society. In comparison with other units in a like functional relationship, an evolving unit develops resemblances according to its functional-ecological situation. There is a flow of the admired and desired from the complex structure to the simpler which evokes new wants and arouses activity that leads to a transformation of wants into needs. The basic processes of change include differentiation, replacement, incorporation, and fusion, with strong tendencies to assimilate to the more complex and dominant system. Units occupying different functional-ecological niches within an interactional arrangement provide a basis for a pluralistic order.

9. For a continuous historical-evolutionary movement to take place, a sociocultural system must extend and diversify its interactions (roles) within a universe that is in turn expanding and differentiating. Any serious interruption or slowing down in the effectiveness of contacts brings a leveling off and a functional-interactional retrenchment.

10. Any structuring that inhibits contacts or introduces discontinuities into an interactive field influences the frequency, intensity, and kinds of interactions, which in turn affects the rate of interchange and the type of change. The establishment of two interactive fields joined by an imperfect communication commonly reduces the opportunities for sociocultural exchange. Some factors, usually in combination, which stimulate the maintenance of distance within a potential interactional arrangement are: perceptual incompatibilities, language differences, ethnic separatism and nationalism, socioeconomic exclusiveness, political-legal subordination, ideological separatism, spatial dispersion, geographic barriers, and scale. In reverse, any structuring that facilitates congruent interactions increases

the rate of change through a higher frequency, intensity, and quality of contacts.

11. Imperfections in the frequency, intensity, and kinds of interactions linking two systems result in historical variations in the selective acceptance and alterations of forms, concepts, and activities that may be accessible. Adaptive changes may occur in form-meaning-use-principle-function or in a partial combination of these. The basic processes here are incorporation and reinterpretation, in which acceptors either find items that are realistically attainable or turn innovations into something congruent with their own needs.

12. Since significant alterations in structuring follow changes in the interactive (role) pattern, the definition of acculturative sequences are best established at those historical moments when reorientations in the interactive field are stabilized and appear to be reaching a new equilibrium.

APPLIED ANTHROPOLOGY

Despite an ostensible commitment to make anthropology serve the interests of human welfare, concern for applied anthropology has remained quite secondary. The image of science projected for anthropology directed investigators to a choice of problems that increased the store of knowledge through objective observation and impartial analysis. Application of scientific knowledge was left to the administrator enlightened enough to grasp the insights which anthropological evidence and research methods brought to social problems. Hence, in the two centuries of its unfolding, the anthropological purpose was clued primarily to the pursuit of knowledge. Humanistic expressions of concern for the fate of subjugated peoples were not lacking. However, participation in organized efforts to alleviate the conditions of subject peoples was largely casual and private. The same can be said for *ad hoc* involvement of anthropologists in critical policy decisions and programs which government sought to implement. Anthropologists were the interpreters of primitive man and his society, and it was expected that in time government would ask anthropologists for assistance in understanding Zulu and Navaho and invite their counsel in alleviating pressing problems stemming from unregulated culture contacts. However, government showed little readiness to utilize anthropologists until social scientists demonstrated successfully to industry that the human factor was just as vital to productivity as efficient management and technology. Even then, government was not ready to turn to anthropologists until an impressive array of empirical data was assembled and the anthropologist as fieldworker established his reputation as an expert on the native point of view. Governments holding ethnocultural minorities in colonial or quasi-colonial status also had to develop an awareness of the complexities of culture contact and a recognition of ever-deepening conflicts and failures if their efforts to guide change were confined to administrative decrees. In the United States the Brookings Institution of Washington in 1928 (Lewis Meriam and associates, *The Problem of Indian Administration*) called for a drastic revision of Indian administration and the policy of assimilation. Studies of this order helped arouse public and scientific concern and prod government leadership to examine the moral basis for policy decisions.

During the thirties, both in the United States and on the Continent, government interest in the utilization of anthropological data and personnel as an aid to native administration grew in strength. As Forde (in Kroeber ed., 1953:845) observed regarding the British in Africa, systematic investigation of tribal groups and their social and economic conditions was not undertaken by government until their efforts to modernize Nigeria with a system of taxation aroused physical resistance in the eastern provinces. However, the problem of adjusting role expectations did not permit an immediate and close collaboration between professional administrators and anthropologists (Barnett 1956). Anthropologists usually tried to maintain scientific neutrality and to restrict their role to that of a technical officer providing data analysis. Nonetheless, they could not divorce themselves from administration policies and from actions which ignored the implications of their study. A similar issue was raised when anthropologists participated in government programs directed to American Indians.

From the anthropologists' insistence that functioning Indian life be recognized as a real force to be reckoned with, there arose a curious opposition on the part of administrators to anthropologists themselves. The administrators, failing to understand the significance of expressions of traditional ways of behavior by Indian groups, assumed that anthropologists, in insisting on recognizing these, were arguing for preservation of aboriginal Indian life. Many administrators and missionaries have believed for years that customs and symbols of Indian life that were in opposition to assimilation should at least be ignored, if not actively suppressed by education, regulation, and sometimes force. This stems from one of the major tenets of the American people which underlies the idea of the American "melting pot," namely, that distinct behavioral differences cannot be tolerated. Every effort has been brought to bear upon every group coming into this country to conform to the theoretical American pattern. The value of conformity was bound to produce in American administrators a strong emphasis upon assimilation of the American Indian. The failure of the anthropologists in not fully appreciating the role of conformity in the American value system, which most administrators shared, and the lack of basic indoctrination of administrators in the pertinent concepts of the discipline of anthropology have led to a long and continuing misunderstanding between the two groups. (Kennard and Macgregor 1953:834)

Whether administrator or anthropologist could combine multiple roles in productive activity was an unknown and crucial factor. At the outset, as in Tanganyika (Brown and Hutt 1935), an accommodation which respected the integrity of administration and of anthropology was struck. It was agreed that the anthropologist should produce data bearing on the history and present condition of the tribal community and respond to questions posed by the administrator with technical advice. However, he would avoid "expressing agreement or disagreement with the actions of the administrator, but not from describing their effects; he would not advocate or condemn particular courses, though he would describe their advantages or faults; his principal concern would be to answer to the best of his ability the questions put to him" (Brown and Hutt 1935:xvii). Ambiguities followed efforts to combine executive and research roles, and the role conflicts engendered prevented anthropologists from doing their best work. Successful combinations of executive and research roles were the exception. For the anthropologist, "His neutrality is an essential factor in his effectiveness as a scientist and as an aid to informed government" (Barnett 1956:177).

If the anthropologist were to fulfill a responsible role as liaison agent for two interacting societies, he would be carrying out his traditional role of interpreter or cultural broker. The liaison role implied that administrators and the administered constituted a unified interactional field. To act as a go-between the anthropologist had to be knowledgeable in the theory, practice, and folk ways of both cultures (Leighton 1945; Useem 1946). At Vicos in Peru, Holmberg (1960:63–107) set out to prove that the anthropologist could carry off the dual roles of director and researcher. At the outset, Holmberg realized he had to move gradually to a reorganization of interactional relationships in order that a free interchange of experience would bring a sense of direction to the community. In this respect he achieved notable success; but, at the same time Holmberg had to act as liaison and persuade the Peruvian government to entertain and even assist his experiment in community development.

Holmberg's basic design was to build a technical and ideological floor for change in Vicos by gradually producing a knowledgeable leadership which the community could recognize. This meant the community must be encouraged to formulate its own goals and to organize human and technical resources for the attainment of community objectives. Sol Tax advocated a slightly different action anthropology to cope with the situation of the Fox Indians on a small reserve in Iowa. In their perception of the situation, Tax and associates saw the Fox as trapped in a vicious circle of pressures—political-economic and characteral—that prevented them from acting with confidence in their own self-interest. The Fox were defensively on dead center, and their condition required that they be shown that they could act positively in their own behalf. Like Vicos, the problem rested with self-determination. However, in the Fox instance, the action anthropologists did not forecast the ends for the community and then inch them ahead. Rather, through suggesting and providing opportunities (for example, crafts, scholarships) the Fox were presented with alternatives for decision and left free to formulate and implement their own goals. In the Vicos case Holmberg saw the problem as one of integrating the community into the network of national life in a way that allowed them to attain a new self-respect and to position themselves, as individuals, for acceptance of new opportunities. Under action anthropology, the opportunity for a more pluralistic solution to ethnocultural difference was possible.

These three models for action (technical adviser, humanistic intervener, catalytic discussant) describe the anthropological experience in the application of the discipline to human problems. Obviously, what anthropoligists brought to planned change was not a methodological *schema* that could be applied with predictive confidence, but a perspective. This perspective was people-oriented, enunciating a principle of respect for ethnocultural differences and the right of minorities by self-choice to achieve their own life-style. This is what Tax and associates (Gearing, Netting, and Peattie 1960) meant when they concluded that whatever the Fox wished would prevail and not what the actional anthropologists themselves might consider a better choice. The important value was a gain in self-confidence based on a freedom to act, and a gain in experience based on the opportunity to make choices and to make mistakes. Value choices did prescribe the action to be taken by the counselor-interveners, but these were generic human values and not the values specific to a culture. At the crucial juncture of contradiction between two life-styles, the issue of cultural relativism was bypassed for universal values deemed essential to the development of a viable personality and identity. Yet, in providing new alternatives, the situation in which peoples found themselves would go far in structuring the sources for their opportunities and the limitations of their choices.

An African national state newly emancipated from colonial rule, with a large population and viable traditional culture, had access to a greater range of opportunity than the Fox of Iowa. At the same time, both were restricted by the determinative structuring of national and international interrelations. To participate in the superorder of the industrialized economy gripping the world, the operational specifications for participation had to be met at all levels if an expanding field of interactional opportunities were to be realized. A complex set of factors, both human and physical, determine the extent to which an operational base may be reached and the special functional-ecological niche that may be occupied. However, it is doubtful whether the nation states of African can avoid the choice of modernization.

The application of anthropological theory, method, and perspective to community development, overseas development programs, and to urban and medical domains is governed by the principle that a subject's life-style possesses an intrinsic worth and is directly relevant to a solution of his disturbance. The only exceptions are wartime studies designed to uncover the characteral strengths and weaknesses of the enemy. The most striking evidence for the penetration of an anthropological perspective was the daring renovation of Indian policy under Commissioner John Collier. During his stay Indian tribes were encouraged to participate in decisions and to build on the traditional strengths of their cultures. Thus, in the matter of education, Indian service teachers were to include in their teaching "an understanding and appreciation of their [Indian] own tribal lore, art, music, and community organization" (cited by Peterson 1948:9).

The government of the United States, in its initial efforts to learn from social scientists, allowed considerable latitude in formulation of the research problem to the scientific team. However, the attitude of government altered considerably during the postwar period. As the governments of the United States and of Russia jockeyed for strategic political, military, and economic advantages during the era of the cold war, the overseas development programs took on a more narrowed set of political objectives. As Adams (1964(23):4) remarked when evaluating "Politics and Social Anthropology in Spanish America": "North Americans would do well to remember that the relative freedom of their own research is dependent on large-scale financial support from nongovernmental sources. If and when such sources become more available in Latin America, so research will be freer of governmental control."

The legacy of these government interventions is an abundance of monographs largely relating to experiments in' medical and technical-economic improvements, summaries, reports, and critical evaluations of development programs (see, for example, Paul 1955; Saunders 1954; Opler 1959; Caudill, in Kroeber, ed., 1953, 1958; Polgar 1962; Mead 1953; Kennard and Macgregor, in Kroeber 1953:832–840; Adams *et al.* 1960; Erasmus 1961; Arensberg and Niehoff 1964; Foster 1962; Spicer 1952). The anthropological reviews and evaluations of projects uniformly uncovered the lack of success in coming to grips with the complexities of the local social and cultural context at some phase in the program. At Hualcan in the Andes, Stein (1956) observed how suckling calves were so deprived of milk that they suffered from malnutrition and often died, and grown cattle appeared to exhibit the malign effects of this early nutritional deficiency. He proposed to the householder that more milk be given to the hungry calves and that he would pay for it. The apparent experiment was begun, only to be cut short within a week. This was Stein's initial stint of fieldwork and he soon learned that to divert the milk as proposed raised considerable problems. For one thing, there were the respective rights of husband and wife to the cows and their products, the milk tip usually taken by children serving as herders, the traditional "stealing" of milk from the grazing cows by hungry children, and a value principle of rapid self-sufficiency that applied to animals as to humans. In a Cherokee classroom Dumont and Wax (1969) observed the clash of cultures as Cherokee students lived out their value commitments and pragmatic traditional interpretations of experience in structuring relations among themselves and between the group and the teacher.

> The Cherokee School Society [that is, the informal pupil entity] maintains a rigid law of balance that says, in effect, we will change when the teacher changes. If the teacher becomes involved in appreciating the ways of his students, then they will respond with an interest in his ways. Needless to say, the older the students become, the higher their grade-level, the less is the like-

lihood that this reciprocity will be initiated by their educators. There is thus a deep tragedy, for it is the students who lose and suffer the most. Yet the School Society is their technique for protecting themselves in order to endure the alien intrusiveness of the teacher and the discourtesy and barbarity of the school. Occasionally, observer and students experience a happier interlude, for some teachers are able to enter into a real intercultural exchange. Unfortunately, they are as rare as they are remarkable. And they are sometimes unaware of their truly prodigious achievements in establishing what we term the Intercultural Classroom. (Dumont and Wax 1969 HO(28): 223)

Planned or controlled change obviously requires a sound set of theoretical and practical instruments if success is to be achieved. Yet, as Arensberg and Niehoff (1964:67) observed in their manual designed for Americans in overseas development programs:

There are no set rules that can give pat answers; but there is now a considerable body of helpful information that has been gathered by social scientists and development specialists.

The cultural factors which influence the acceptance or rejection of a new idea can be considered either as obstacles or as stimulants, according to the attitude of the change agents.

The sensitivity clues which social science could bring to planned change include the following: awareness of local needs; limitations of the local ecology; complex interrelations affecting any innovation; problems of unanticipated consequences; utilization of tradition in the interests of modernization and avoidance of a conflictive opposition of old and new; importance of demonstrating pragmatically the advantages of an innovation; getting local people involved by translating their need motivations into action; knowing the social order and the locus for decisions and the mobilization of action; importance of prestige and personal satisfaction, communication and the timing of innovation; and the guarantee of success in the assurance that when responsibility for an operation is transferred to the local people, they will have a shared experience that will impel them to maintain it (Arensberg and Niehoff 1964:66–125; compare Foster 1962; Brokensha and Hodge 1969).

MEDICAL ANTHROPOLOGY

Individual health is as necessary to the stability and continuity of communities as are subsistence activities which assure personal and group survival. Traditional classifications of disease, interpretations of the causes of disease, and practices for restoring health are found in every society. No society is without its specialists to diagnose and treat disease. Preindustrial societies lacked the specialization, controlled experimentation, and diversified techniques of diagnosis and therapy possessed by scientifically oriented societies. Consequently, specialists in preindustrial societies operated according to traditional interpretations and practices, and their innovations elaborated popular belief rather than breaking new ground.

Medical interests of ethnologists at first were byproducts of their ethnographic descriptions. Ideas as to causes of disease and curative practices were important in showing the spread of disease concepts and intercontinental connections, as in the distribution of the soul-loss theory along the north Pacific rim of Asia and North America. They also recorded the malign effects of smallpox and measles on American Indian populations and inferred that racial immunologies accounted for differences in death rates between Indians and Europeans (Dobyns 1966). The susceptibility of native Americans in the Plains to tuberculosis also was described in figures compiled by Wissler (1936). Intensification of intertribal contacts and alterations in ecological relations accompanying European exploitation of Africa also contributed to the spread of sleeping sickness to East Africa which caused an estimated 200,000 deaths between 1901 and 1906 in Uganda. Practical therapy in the use of infusions and in the setting of bones received perfunctory treatment until Ackerknecht (1942, 1947) called attention to respectable achievements of primitive therapy in the use of poultices, laxatives, enemas, baths, trephining, cupping, cautery, bonesetting, and even Caesarian section. At the same time he stressed that medicine did not pursue an independent path, but owed its character and dynamism to its role in a culture pattern. Structural-functional and psychoanalytic theory also encouraged the investigation of the social function of sorcery in controlling in-group aggression by threat of disease and death (Hallowell 1967b). In other cases witchcraft and its specialized diseases appeared to result from conflicts in interpersonal relations embedded within the social order (Kluckhohn 1967; Lieban 1960). Frake's (1961) investigation of Subanum disease categories brought out the relevance of social factors, since Subanum made fine distinctions in those diseases which were important to social acceptance (for example, skin disease) and marital negotiations (communicable disease).

A rise in governmental concern for public health following World War II facilitated the emergence of medical anthropology as a specialization and gave it an applied orientation (see Caudill 1953; Scotch 1963; Polgar 1962; Fabrega 1971). The focus of medical anthropology, as Lieban (1973:1034) noted, is on the mutual interdependencies of influences between medical phenomena and social and cultural knowledge and practice. These mutual influences are distributed over a wide range of relationships linking epidemiologies to ecological conditions, age, sex, occupation, social classes, minority status, nutrition, change processes (urbanization and acculturation), as well as organic elements. The influence of social and cultural factors on personality disorders is also a primary concern of medical anthropology.

The anthropological approach to the incidence of disease generally stressed a complex of interdependent relationships. This holistic approach is shown by Miner's (1960) discussion of the increase of sleeping sickness among the Hausa of northern Nigeria. British pacification changed ethno-ecological relations by permitting people formerly confined to town areas (owing to the prevalent raiding type of warfare) to move out into the countryside and take up farming. In so doing they facilitated the spread of disease by increasing contacts with the breeding areas of the tsetse fly. When government sought to eliminate the breeding areas by cutting brush around water areas, they confronted widespread fear of spirits which were thought to inhabit these localities. So in order to clear away areas of heavy infestation, it was necessary to import laborers from other places. Continued threat of punishment was necessary in order to force local Hausa to continue cutting back the thickets as they were unconvinced of any relationship between this activity and control of the disease.

Miner's descriptive analysis linked ethnoecological relations (warfare or its absence) to popular beliefs about illness, ecosystem of the Trypanosome parasite, local and high level government relationships, and acculturative processes in an interdependent network of cause and effect. In searching for explanations of postpartum sexual taboos and late weaning, Whiting (1964) sought to correlate this cultural practice with climate, diet, ecology, and a widespread tropical disease, Kwashiorkor. Kwashiorkor, a disease of malnutrition, was prevalent where high humidity and high temperatures forced reliance on low protein root crops. The prolonged lactation and coordinate abstinence from sexual relations were seen as adaptive mechanisms to protect the infant from nutritional deficiency.

The subtlety of ecological and epidemiological relations was revealed by May's (1960) discovery that hookworm among Chinese villagers was linked to handling of mud mixed with human excrement when planting rice. Silkworm cultivators in the same village were free of hookworm. The subtleties of adaptations to disease were also revealed in genetic processes. While the sickle-cell gene was adaptive in part to the malarial parasite, individuals survived or suffered early death from sickle-cell anemia according to whether they were heterozygous or homozygous to the gene. Wiesenfeld's (1967) study indicated that the spread of cultivation stimulated a rise of the sickle-cell gene in populations because of increased exposure to the malarial parasite. Equally interesting was the observation by Tooth (cited by Kennedy 1973:1147) that some 8 percent of those treated for sleeping sickness in Ghana showed schizophrenic symptoms.

Culture contact situations or transitions from rural to urban life styles disclosed physiological and psychological disturbances traceable to anxiety and conflict states. Scotch (1963) recorded a greater frequency of hypertension among urban Zulus than in rural areas. However, the important factor contributing to hypertension was not urban life itself, but the introduction of traditional elements into the urban setting (that is, extended family arrangements, traditional religious beliefs and disease practices) which were incompatible with urban living, and thus generated tensions. Native societies also generated special kinds of hysterias, such as pibloktoq among Eskimo (Parker 1962; Wallace 1961), amok and latah described in

Southeast Asia, and the cannabalistic windigo among Ojibwa and Cree Indians (Teicher 1960). Unfortunately common agreement as to the nature and typology of these syndromes (that is, whether neuroses or psychoses, whether of social and cultural or organic origin) was difficult to achieve and indicated the need for more precise evidence.

After World War II, heredity and other noncultural factors received increased attention in explaining unique mental disorders such as windigo, as well as ostensible differences in the kinds of mental disorders prevalent among racial groups. Wallace (1961:266–268) suggested that low concentrations of ionized calcium in the blood may account for the pibloktoq syndrome rather than cultural factors. Muscular spasms affecting the limbs and face, as well as convulsive seizures, were part of the hypocalcemia syndrome; and in the Arctic diet lack of vitamin D3 (due to insufficient sunlight) produced calcium deficiency. The nutritional-organic etiology for pibloktoq was substantiated in Wallace's (1961b:263–264) view by its occurrence in all seasons, its epidemic manifestation (eight of seventeen women with Peary's expedition in 1908), and its appearance among European sailors wintering north of Thule. The apparent confinement of pibloktoq to the northern reaches of Greenland also supported the local dietary deficiency hypothesis. However, since rickets was not prevalent, the situation was confused and required introduction of secondary hypotheses. Lesser activity of the thyroid yielded an "hormonal balance which retains calcium in the bones even if calcium levels in serum fall occasionally" (Wallace 1961b:289). Natural selection had induced this adaptive response in order to forestall the crippling effects of rickets so damaging to survival in the Arctic. Generally speaking, studies in the ethnoepidemiology of mental disorders have provided suggestive distributions, but as yet none supplies a clear set of categories and methods for cross-cultural comparisons (Leighton *et al.* 1963; M.K. Opler 1963).

The ethnography of ethnomedical theory and practice is of special importance for public health programs (see, for example, Saunders 1954; Adair and Deutschle 1958; Weaver 1972). Popular etiologies of diseases and therapies regulate when and from whom to seek assistance. Endemic syndromes may be considered so normal that only extreme symptoms impel the need for medical assistance. Modern and traditional therapies frequently involve different kinds of "psychosomatic" mechanisms supportive of patient recovery and may draw upon a different clientele. The Nubian Zar ceremies described by Kennedy (1967) served to relieve women with severe anxieties, hysterical neuroses, and depression states, and helped restore their participation in the society. Ostensibly the ceremony was designed to accommodate a demonic spirit and the person in whom it resided. The occurrence of mental aberrations indicating such possession is frequent enough to make it a distinctive but not abnormal phenomenon. Males may serve as leaders of the Zar, but the audience is largely women who "have been cured and who are obligated to attend in order to placate their spirits" (Kennedy 1967(26):187).

Symbolic communication is an important part of folk therapy, as illustrated by the drama of shamanistic performances. A group context for therapy (as in the Zar) is important. The symbolic and social elements of folk therapy may account for the way Guatemalans turned to folk practitioners to cure the basic causes of their diseases while resorting to physicians to alleviate disease symptoms (Gonzalez 1966).

Recognition of "traditional" and "modern" diseases and therapies is not unusual after introduction of scientific medicine (Foster 1962; compare Lieban 1967). Acceptance of modern treatment seems related to the degree of contrast between modern and folk therapy in conjunction with experience regarding special diseases. In the treatment of tuberculosis, Navajo did not consider bed rest and seclusion as any improvement over traditonal therapy, but chemotherapy and surgery were recognized as superior (Adair 1963).

The modernizing of public health introduces a wide variety of considerations, including economic, social, ideological, educational, and ecological. As Lieban (1973:1063) observes,

> Health can be an aspiration of people as well as a consequence of social process. Increased awareness of ways to improve it can contribute constructively to social action.

ANTHROPOLOGY AND EDUCATION

The anthropological view of culture as a learned phenomenon drew attention to education as a social process. However, it was not until interests in culture and personality and in processes of change induced by the clash of cultures converged that the role of education in the transmission of culture received much attention. The anthropological view did not restrict education to formal schooling but placed it within the perspective of learning a traditional style of life. The preferred anthropological term for this process was enculturation (Herskovits 1948), complementing and overlapping the sociological term, socialization.

Childhood training for citizenship provided the initial stimulus for anthropological analyses of the educational process and was usually incidental to broader ethnographic investigations (Firth 1936; Fortes 1963a; Hogbin 1931; Raum 1940; M.E. Opler 1941). Initiation rites called attention to formal instruction, marking transitions from pre- to postpubertal status and was a basis for studying the enculturative process in a life-cycle context (Mead 1928, 1930; Whiting 1941; Middleton 1970). Benedict (1938) pointed to discontinuities in the type and content of learning as the individual passed from early to late childhood and adolescence. George Pettit (1946) produced the only survey of native education north of Mexico, disclosing general tendencies to rely on ridicule, praise, supernatural sanction, identification through heroic example and personal names, and self-confidence linked to the protection of a supernatural guardian.

Introduction of psychoanalytic theory during the thirties refocussed the enculturative process on culture-personality relations. In its narrower applications the psychoanalytic perspective confined observation to infancy and early childhood. At the same time it broadened perspective by relating special experiences of the enculturative process to modalities in the behavior and character of adults. Attention was drawn to the balance between frustration and reward levels in interpersonal relations during infancy and childhood (Kardiner 1939). The psychoanalytic approach also reinforced the anthropological tendency to locate basic learnings in feeling states and coordinate unconscious processes. Dorothy Eggan (1956; compare Goldfrank 1945) hypothesized that Hopi inculcation of affect in relation to world view, as well as to specific behaviors, was so successful that it acted to recondition the individual throughout his life. Moreover, the association of emotion with teaching and learning induced such acceptance and conformity that the continuity of individual personality and society was possible without coercive force.

Studies initiated under Commissioner Collier to relate personality, culture, and acculturative processes included data on classroom experience and Indian reactions to assimilative pressures. These works stressed the incompatibility of American and Indian cultural values both regarding the goals of education and principles of instruction (Thompson 1950; Macgregor 1946). Later studies emphasized subtle and overt resistance of Indians to classroom instruction (King 1967; Wolcott 1967). Psychoanalytic autobiographies provided insights into the problems of culture conflict and identity posed by formal education and assimilation (Simmons 1942; Ford 1941). Parsons' (1965) study of Chicano-Anglo relations in the classroom duplicated the experience of Indians in that the teacher usually conveyed, consciously or unconsciously, the values and institutionalized processes of the wider society which in effect defined and maintained the lower status of Chicanos.

Culture and personality relations and the effects of culture contact on indigeneous cultures and personalities provided sound bases for extending anthropological interest to formal teaching in the classroom. Anthropological perspective was linked to the kinds of awareness that arise when people are forced to see themselves through the contrastive behavior of others. That people can better understand what they are through a process of cultural comparison and can thereby act more knowledgeably in defining and implementing desirable goals was a view of progressive educators who viewed education as a dynamically creative and socially innovative process. Brameld (1957) drew these broad philosophic strands linking anthropology and education together in his *Cultural Foundations of Education: An Interdisciplinary Exploration*. At the same time special integrative programs were developed at New York University, Hunter College, and Stanford (Spindler 1963:63–66). An increasing emphasis upon the relevance of anthropology and a desire to achieve a greater anthropological input at the secondary and elementary level led to publication of two volumes on *The Teaching of Anthropology* and *Resources for the Teaching of Anthropology* (Mandelbaum, Lasker, and Albert 1963a, 1963b) by the American Anthropological Association. The Association maintained its interest by establishing a Council on Anthropology and Education in 1968 and in sponsoring, with support from the National Science Foundation, the Anthropology Curriculum Study Project (Gearing 1973). Such programs offered specially prepared materials for use in secondary and elementary schools, designed, according to Collier and Dethlefsen (1968(27): 12) to "democratize a social scientific comprehension of man." This operation involved selection of relevant materials, linking materials related to the student's own experience with methodological practices for eliciting the essentials of a topic and easy grasp of the material. In Georgia, Bailey (Bailey and Clune 1968) assembled an anthropological curriculum which was to be tested on school children in 13 states. Beginning with the concept of culture, the student was introduced to archeology and the culture of the Hopi Indians. Plans called for grades three to six to study "cultural dynamics," while grade seven was presented with a "cross-cultural view of the life cycle."

Despite the potential for mutual enrichment, the strengthening of relations betweeen anthropology and education has lagged. This ideal working relationship may be achieved as anthropologists fulfill requirements for a cross-cultural study of education (Henry 1960) and as educators are drawn increasingly into situations of cultural pluralism.

SUMMARY

The increased attention anthropologists gave in the thirties to the processes of culture contact and the application of anthropological knowledge to community development was a product of theoretical extensions in the discipline and of widespread changes affecting preindustrial and European societies. By the thirties an adequate typology of world ethnographic areas had been achieved, and study of historical relationships derived from geographical distributions disclosed the strengths, weaknesses, and possibilities of this methodology. After two to four or so generations of contact with European commercialism and industrialization, preindustrial societies exhibited serious alterations in their traditional cultures which foreshadowed their breakdown as functioning systems. At the same time, Europeans found that administrative reorganization of their colonial domains along modern lines was necessary in order to permit economic development. Similar attempts were made by the U.S. government to promote a variable economic development for Indian populations west of the Mississippi which were subjugated between 1820 and 1890. Several generations of acculturation, however, forced anthropologists to rely on the memories of the old people in reconstructing aboriginal life descriptions.

The important action was in labor migration, trade unionism, urbanization, ideological conflicts between traditional religion and Christianity, racism, and the challenge of traditional authority by elites who owed their status to special administrative skills and literacy obtained in Western schooling. Government was ready to accept anthropological counsel and to underwrite research which might assist in easing cultural assimilation.

Engagement with change processes forced a realignment of anthropological perspectives and goals. In place of researching the positive factors which integrated social and cultural systems and which were replicated from one generation to the next, anthropologists directed their attention to the contradictions and pressures making for change. Such an orientation altered the Structuralist position and reintroduced evolutionary and historical change processes. At the same time attention to the importance of economic forces, political power, education, social stratification, social personality, ideology, religion, and technicological relations facilitated the differentation of specializations within anthropology.

Culture theorists led in the study of acculturation. Malinowski applied his institutional approach to the study of culture contact in Africa. He noted the institutional differences of native and European societies and emphasized the necessity of finding a compatible basis for contact and mutual benefit. Europeans dominated the contact process and systematically deprived Africans of their land base and their rationale for life by thoughtless destruction of their beliefs, values, and institutions. Malinowski opted for transitional forms, mutual accommodations which permitted Africans to adjust to the demands of modernization by developing modified versions of their traditional institutions and belief systems. The development of mining facilities, factories, trade unions, and urban and rural migration permitted a continuing investigation of special institutions accompanying industrialization. The relative insulation of urban and village life was stressed by Gluckman as central to the change process in Africa. He rejected the possibility of developing intermediate institutions, as Malinowski had advocated, noting that Africans kept their traditional village and urbanized cultures separate since what was suitable to one was unsuitable to the other. Hence, Africans tended to be bicultural as well as bilingual.

American culture theorists stressed the learning and forgetting of culture as an important factor in change. This psychological approach was pioneered by Linton (1936, 1940) through analysis of modifications in form, meaning, use, and function. From their cultural perspective Americans investigated the importance of value orientations (Kluckhohn 1943) and personality factors regarding change (Hallowell 1955). In the perspective of change from simple to complex societies, Redfield (1953) described the process as a growth toward technological and secular values.

In their theoretical orientations American culture theorists and British social anthropologists converged on the concept of interaction as basic to the change process. The institutional approach, in conjunction with the definition of discrete interactional communities (that is, reserve and urban communities) led to the concept of interactional social fields. This construct of the Wilsons (1945) was useful to Spicer and associates (1961) in defining change communities of American Indians. Change studies also indicated that acculturative processes involving dominant and subordinate groups induced a differentiation of sociocultural groups with different goals, kinds, and degrees of acculturation (Little 1961; Spindler 1955). The projection of different goals based on acculturative experience was the basis for internal factionalism as well as for religious and political movements which expressed the distinctiveness and autonomy of native tradition and society. Nationalistic aspirations of colonial peoples, and the rise of ethnic and social consciousness by minorities and the economically depressed accented the importance of cultural identity in the integration of social personality and community.

Anthropological response to applied research and practice was not developed during the Developmentalist and Structuralist epochs, despite the implication that anthropology could assist in the solution of social problems. Government programs after the war facilitated the growth of applied anthropology and the extension of applied interests in medical and education areas. The current emphasis on research that contributes to the quality of life is an incentive for anthropologists to apply their skills to the study of the many subcultures present in complex societies (ethnic, drug, and other small-group "cultures").

20

Cultural Anthropology: Retrospect and Prospects

ANTHROPOLOGY AS AN INSTITUTION

The intellectual experience of cultural anthropology has been sketched in three historic-evolutionary stages: Developmentalism, Structuralism, and Differentiative Specialization. This intellectual adventure does not stand alone, but is part of cultural and social changes in Western civilization reaching back to the Greeks and Romans. Cultural anthropology in effect is an institutional development of the Western cultural tradition. Consolidation of the scientific tradition in the eighteenth century was especially important, since it allowed the projection of a general social science out of which anthropology later differentiated.

Malinowski's conception of an institution is applicable to anthropology. Anthropology is chartered under science and its personnel is guided by rules governing the scientific acquisition of knowledge. Anthropologists are trained to carry out research with the aid of special apparatus. The end or function of cultural anthropology is to produce reliable materials and valid generalizations relevant to its subject—the historical-evolutionary development of preindustrial man in relation to nature, society, and culture.

The institutional nature of anthropology has influenced the character of its development. Four relationships are fundamental: (1) the intellectual currents and societal transformations of Western societies since the eighteenth century, (2) the state of scientific knowledge regarding the physical structure and processes of the world and the universe, (3) the degree of integration of anthropology with other social institutions, and (4) anthropological exploration of its own subject matter, and the relation of its findings to those of the natural sciences as well as to related social science disciplines. These four relationships have mediated the anthropological role and exercised a profound influence on the objectives, means, and processes by which an anthropological consciousness has been achieved. In turn, anthropology has supplied an informational and interpretational feedback which has penetrated the social consciousness and contributed useful concepts, data, and explanations to related disciplines and to the society at large.

ETHNOLOGICAL CORRELATES TO WESTERN INTELLECTUAL AND INSTITUTIONAL EXPERIENCES

As major theoretical turns, Developmentalism, Structuralism, and Differentiative Specialization correspond in a general way with important transformations in Western civilization. The enthusiastic attempt of developmentalists to trace the rise of civilization was correlated with the vigorous thrust of industrialization and spanned a time during which Western domination spread to all corners of the world. The Structuralist epoch witnessed the conceptual distinction of the social and cultural as substantive domains and their exclusive linkage with social and cultural anthropology. While anthropologists explored the structured quality and processes of their unique domain, industralism entered a new period in which the assembly line was introduced to rationalize job operations. In this connection managerial roles proliferated in efforts to analyze and expedite structural-functional linkages and to draw the systemic functions of parts into efficient unison and continuous harmony. The emphasis on formal structure moved to a functional distinction of management, line supervisors, efficiency experts, and workers. Parallel concerns for systemic structure and function also appeared in biology, psychology, economics, political science, and sociology and facilitated the rise of ecology. Understanding structure and structural processes thus gripped not only the managerial but the scientific imagination as well.

Regarding the colonial situation, the pervasive structural orientation led governments to define their relations with subject peoples largely in terms of management. Government needs supplied the goals, and the administrator applied management skills to organize resource production, implement policies, and utilize traditional native authority in the achievement of governmental objectives. From a structural-management vantage point, all an administrator needed to know were those aspects of the native decision-making and executive structure which could be readily articulated with the colonial administrative counterpart. If the native structure lacked such elements, it then became necessary to create them formally. Hence, during this structural-functional period, the major effort of colonial governments was directed to the establishment of workable administrative structures and the training of native personnel to carry out less significant operations. Efforts to draw anthropologists into the management operation underscored the fact that their scientific objectives were incompatible with those of colonial administration, and that anthropologists would require retraining if they were to function satisfactorily in the bureaucratic operation.

Beginning with World War I Western civilization experienced a succession of crises which accelerated social, economic, political, ideological, and esthetic change. The economic depression of the thirties was especially critical in drawing attention to systemic contradictions, conflicts, and disorganization. The Depression and the World War II that followed were profound events which shook the faith of the social scientist in the reality of functional and systemic integration which governed their views and research of society and culture. Systems actually never were in a near state of equilibrium, but appeared constantly out of phase and changing. Soon the economic model of formal-functional management, acting in accordance with the equilibrium laws of supply and demand, was superseded by the out-of-phase deficit spending of the Keynesian model. Work studies, as at the General Electric Hawthorne plant, disclosed human factors affecting production that had no place in a formal-functional managerial system. Communication of meaning now loomed as an integral component in ordering and implementing action, and the formal command-model of management was replaced by the cybernetic mechanics of communication feedback and adjustment to altered circumstances. Cybernetics drew attention to a psychological variable, or human factor, which had been omitted from the structural-functional managerial model.

The new run of crises affecting Western civilization during the thirties marked the beginning of a vast process of differentiation within anthropology. This was a time when the emphasis on static structural-functional relationships began to falter as anthropologists increasingly took note of the accelerated rate of change which the industrial and preindustrial worlds experienced in the wake of their mechanization.

Science and Anthropology: The Lure of the Natural Science Image

The natural sciences expectably exerted a profound influence on the image of anthropology as a science. The control which hard sciences gained over their physical subject matter by special technical and mathematical instruments stimulated the ideal of what science was and should be. The very beginnings of social science in the eighteenth century were inspired by the laws of nature which the physical sciences were in process of uncovering. Why should not similar laws hold for man and his social life? The recurrent theme of all who conveyed their influence in theory and method during those epoch-making reorientations expressed a judgment that social and cultural phenomena were as tightly structured and constant in their operations as physical and organic matter. The application of principles such as geological uniformitarianism, biological evolution, organicism, and the thermodynamics of physics disclosed the reliance of anthropology on natural science. Such borrowing also revealed a desire to effect scientific closure between physical and sociocultural processes by demonstrating that the uniformities found in nature, man, and society were of the same order. The laws of nature thus were used to legitimize the laws of sociocultural matter whether firmly stated or not.

As other social sciences, anthropology has been sensitive to the shifting views of natural scientists with regard to the nature of the world. As natural scientists acknowledged variational processes in matter which did not conform to strict cause-and-effect laws, the anthropologist was quick to justify his own inability to predict behavior. Moreover, he shifted his objective from deterministic predictions to statements of the conditions and rules which operate to produce speech and behaviors which are socially acceptable. Declarations of ironclad cause-and-effect connections gave way to probability statements.

The principle of relativity exerted an important but methodologically ambiguous influence. Applied to the life styles of various historical traditions, the principle of relativity led anthropologists to defend value orientations which differed from the West, and to challenge the objectives and values of industrial culture. The plea for cultural and individual pluralism, and its gradual popular acceptance, had a profound effect in creating more flexible attitudes toward value differences and life-styles. At the same time, the principle of relativity confused methodological issues by insisting that each cultural tradition was so unique that there was no real basis for comparisons, and hence meaningful generalizations about form and process were at best limited, if not impossible. Full utility of methodological relativity in the statement of problems and their methodological solutions is yet to be realized. Failure to apply methodological relativity accounts for many ambiguous conceptual distinctions which separate protagonists into camps, as well as for differences stemming from semantic confusion. This is demonstrated by proclivities to generate polar concepts, such as historical and evolutionary, diachronic and synchronic, emic and etic, structure and variation, mechanical and statistical models, history and science, core and social personality, and so on. A basic requirement of methodological relativism is that the investigator state the level of structure and its relation to other structures within the system when defining the parameters of his problem and the relevance of his generalizations. Only in this way can the application of concepts to process be clarified and relieved of ambiguities.

In future the natural sciences may be expected to recommend general theoretical models useful to anthropology. However, it is doubtful that great summative principles, such as evolution, will be forthcoming to stimulate a new transformation of anthropological theory. The differentiative phase through which anthropology now is passing is strengthening its ties with specialized disciplines (for example, paleontology, psychology) as well as related social sciences; and it is these fresh linkages that will provide the most immediate theoretical and methodological stimuli.

The image and role of science in society will aways remain vital to the future of anthropology. The scientific role is tied to a common human desire to find order in existence. Human beings require assurance that life is not pure anarchy and without purpose, but rather is subject at some points to human control, and that human needs and objectives can and should be served. Magic, religious creeds, sociopolitical doctrines, and science have all served mankind as systems of thought and as procedures for projecting and finding a desirable order and purpose in the world. Whether one calls it faith, commitment, or sentiment, an emotional component appears to be as vital to human behavior as its logical organization by reason. Western culture and philosophic thought is filled with historic moments when an intuitive grasp of truth was advocated against the logical practices of reason. A stand on faith, or intuition, necessarily stresses the uniqueness of man and rejects the suggestion that his experience and his very being are bounded by the objective relations of the world as it exists. The present emphasis on the validity and necessity of the subjective experience poses a serious challenge to science as the ideal of the orderly processes of reason.

The new subjectivism is linked to a rising tide of protest against the failure of the complex institutional arrangements of contemporary society to guarantee individual rights and participation on both legal and moral grounds. Pure and applied natural science have always established close working relations with society in technological improvements affecting medical care, economic productivity, comforts of life, and hot and cold war. The institutional integration of the natural sciences thus has always beeen tighter than that of the social sciences, and of anthropology in particular.

Threat of a nuclear holocaust prompted natural scientists to protest the concentration of such devastating power in political hands without adequate political, technical, and moral safeguards. Nuclear weaponry should and must not become the simple instrument of government policy as had too often been the case in the past. Moreover, the perfected technology of science placed instruments in the hands of government which permitted covert invasions of privacy and sinister controls over citizens. At the same time, disclosures of irresponsible research in which scientists experimented with the lives of their subjects, or used them for ulterior motives, revealed the dangers inherent in an untempered objectivity. An unrestrained, objective, and amoral science could do irreparable damage to research subjects by manipulating them in control and experimental groups. All of this demonstrated that science must be devoted to the ultimate objective of knowledge and must remain responsive to moral considerations which necessarily govern the relations of individuals in society. Without a humanistic morality, scientists could play the same "guilt free" role as religious and political zealots who consigned their heterodox opponents to death at the stake or firing squad.

Forces within and outside science, motivated by humanistic considerations as to the destiny of mankind and the relations linking individuals to society, forced scientists to reconsider their knowledge-seeking objective as well as their own roles in society. Anthropologists and other social scientists have participated in this development.

The increasing integration of anthropology with national institutions and the changing world culture is an important datum in the institutional experience of the discipline. This integration has proceeded along two major axes: (1) ideological and (2) functional.

Ideological Integration: Cultural Relativity and Liberated Consciousness

Leaving aside the substantive contributions of anthropologists to world ethnography, linguistics, prehistory, and human evolution, the clearest evidence of the intellectual impact of ethnology can be found in the widespread acceptance of cultural relativism. This idea has played no small part in undermining adherence to traditional culture norms and in promoting an egocentric measure of things. Cultural relativity thus has played a paramount role in liberating the individual consciousness. The formal statement of this liberation is entrenched in the philosophy of Existentialism. Here the subjective experience is paramount, and in his inner realizations of self, the individual reaches out to the world and actively contributes to the liberation of world consciousness.

For nearly a century serious doubts had been gathering in the West about the kind of person turned out by the industrial culture (Remmling 1967). In 1899 Veblen (1934) punctured the image of the industrial elite by pointing cynically to their conspicuous consumption of wealth and of leisure in a selfish pursuit of social status. Social novelists like Sinclair Lewis looked behind the façade of clergy and businessmen to disclose personal corruption. The new realism expressed in literature was paralleled by the critical realism exhibited in social research. Studies of bureaucracy exposed treadmill pressures exerted by the system upon personnel, forcing conformity to rules and diverting responsibility from public needs to the maintenance functions of the institution (Merton 1940). Lasswell (1936) and Mills (1956) described the concentration of economic and political power in the United States in a sparse elite continuously circulating through these systems. In the formation of human personality, Freud found the social order too repressive, forcing the individual to construct unconscious defenses and impulses that drove him to strain constantly against real or imagined social barriers. In such cases, ego (reason) was unable to mediate the struggle between frustrated id and the demanding social superego. Clinical analysis revealed men to be bundles of unconscious frustrations and impulses that testified to the way their natural dispositions were distorted and brutalized by unnatural civilization. As Frank (1948) observed, society, not man, was the patient. All this created a neo-Rousseauistic mood in which culture stood against man (see, for example, Henry 1963). The bloodletting of World War II and its atomic aftermath simply catalyzed these subjective trends.

Ideological Integration: Subjectivity and Scientific Objectivity in Ethnology

The rise of faith in the subjective reality and the emphasis on involvement inevitably fed back into anthropology. Castaneda's (1972) *The Teachings of Don Juan* provided special anthropological substance to the outreach for self-realization. However, the impact of the cultivation of subjectivity lay much deeper, since it challenged the very nature of the scientific process. Commitment—not objective neutrality in the collection, analysis, and evaluation of factual evidence—flowed from the demand for involvement. Objectivity, indeed, was a scientific myth, the shibboleth of those who served the ethnology of the Establishment. Such, at least, was the argument of those who would rout the would-be scientists from their ethnological ivory tower and pipe them along the pathway to a liberated conscience and consciousness (see, for example, Berreman 1968, with commentaries; also, compare Nash and Wintrob 1972).

The call for a relevant anthropology took on special significance in the context of changing attitudes and aspirations among those whom anthropologists researched. Self-identity, national identity, and the legitimacy of custom and of life-style are too important at this time to permit continuation of scientific research from the point of view of science and the researcher alone. Emergent nations and the underprivileged are too involved in changing their circumstances to accept research which, in their eyes, treats them as an old curiosity shop of custom, belief, and ritual. As Poesy Whiteman, a Crow Indian, stated to the author as early as 1956, "The Indian is no longer a museum piece." The rapidly changing preindustrial world possesses needs which can be aided through research, but these are not necessarily coordinate with the aims of the traditional Ph.D. candidate. The needs of the developing nations, ethnic groups, and classes have a moral imperative with which future research must deal.

However, the shaping of research in response to human needs does not mean that scientific methods are abandoned. The transfer to anthropology of the natural science perspective of objective measurable entities is still indispensable in elucidating the nature of form and process. Indeed, the treating of persons, relationships, and things as objects is implicit in any categorization. This is the meaning of concepts such as social, cultural, class, caste, means of production, relationships of production, bourgeoisie, proletariat, verb, noun, motive, desire, personality, and tree. Treating persons and things as objects is just as important to the mental and actional behavior of laymen as it is to scientists. An objective collection and evaluation of facts by logical controls cannot be rejected by science and ethnology any more than Freudians could throw overboard the image of a strong ego, that is, reason as the central base of a balanced personality. For ethnology, therefore, commitment must remain a scientifically controlled intervention rather than a political intervention.

Formal-Functional Integration of the Ethnologic Institution

The formal institutional linkages of ethnology to the wider society are channeled largely through its teaching and research functions. A steady expansion of undergraduate and graduate training programs in higher education attests to the generalization of the anthropological point of view and a continuing integration within the educational process. In addition, anthropological instructional materials have been integrated into secondary, and even elementary, schools in the United States. Professional organizations maintain the steady connections essential to participation in research operations and exchanges with sister disciplines.

In the wider society, however, momentum is building for pragmatic consolidations. Pressures to shape scientific action to the measure of relevance and improvements in the quality of life are spreading throughout higher education and affecting the kinds of research favored by foundations and government. Quite likely that somewhat neglected specialization, applied anthropology, will play a more dynamic role in shaping the anthropology of tomorrow. If world societies are on the eve of far-reaching planning to assure a kind of sustained yield operation in all domains of social living—owing to technico-demographic-ecological necessities—quite obviously ethnology must orient to such futuristic planning. The role of scientists in China, directly involved in the labor of community improvement, may foreshadow a demand in the industrial societies of the West for scientific technocrats rather than scientists. In any case, the ethical issues now faced by anthropologists should be less traumatic than when they were invited to produce research to assist bureaucratic management of colonial peoples.

No doubt pragmatic application provides the ultimate test of theory and of method. Direct involvement in actional community research which permits controlled observation of individual and collective behavior according to a set of definable conditions cannot help but convey an experiential advantage, provided the researcher can circulate in all levels of decision-making and of execution. This was not the case in the past; and hence the applied anthropologist did not have the depth of experience and control over his study that an ethnographer in the field normally possesses. However, a tightening of institutional relations between ethnology and the wider society, selectively tuned to pragmatic needs, could prove as hazardous to the integrity of the discipline as service in the interests of national cold war aims. Like their counterparts in China and in Russia, who walk a tight line of social significance and are expected to demonstrate the reality and necessity of political dogma, the tightening of the institutional screw in the West seems to be drawing the natural scientist, and the ethnologist, closer to a scientific 1984. The searching question, of course, is, Can science survice as technocracy?

The future of ethnology, and of science generally, will be hazardous unless a degree of detachment can be maintained. In the face of institutional pressures to integrate, none can avoid the same questions confronted when the issue of an applied anthropology was first raised. How can the research needs of scientific ethnology be accomplished if research must be accommodated to pragmatic social needs? The critical issue for one and all is the maintenance of a sufficient measure of autonomy to guarantee self-realization. For ethnology, scientific objectivity is the *sine qua non* for that measure of autonomy essential to its future development (see Kaplan 1974). The involvement of ethnologists with society thus must take the form of linkages rather than full-bodied integration. This has always been the rationale of advocates of "pure" science. By asserting a measure of independence and by maintaining a degree of social distance, science in the past has fulfilled a role in which fallacious traditional ideas and interpretations have been challenged and eliminated. This is the role which knowledge must continue to play.

The importance of a distinctive autonomy was recognized by Marx (1932:360–361) when he recommended political alliances rather than a fusion with any party. It is essential to the future of ethnology that its scientific character be preserved and that ethnologists do not become social technocrats.

HISTORIC-EVOLUTIONARY PROCESSES AND THE ETHNOLOGIC INSTITUTION

An institutional approach to ethnology accents the fact that the discipline has grown and altered according to processes that commonly generate change in social institutions. Two major processes have been at work: differentiation and convergence. Differentiation follows novel variations, or historic branchings in pursuit of new facts, which, on inspection, do not appear to be explained satisfactorily under existing theory. Convergence, on the other hand, produces commonalities that eventuate in the firming up of theoretical structure.

In its own way ethnology has grown by incorporating intellectual traits and methodological complexes from other disciplines, for example, in the application of Western legal concepts in the classification and descriptive analysis of customary law. When taking up concepts from other disciplines ethnologists have reinterpreted terms by extending their coverage to fit the range of variation displayed by ethnographic data (for example, Hoebel's (1954) effort to define a legal norm). Again, without accepting the universality of the symbolisms developed by psychoanalysts, ethnologists used the theory of unconscious processes as reactive syndromes and the theory of early fixation of character to help account for a persistence of behavioral patterns in the face of altering conditions. Through a process of stimulus diffusion (Kroeber 1940), broad theoretical orientations, such as the organic analogy drawn from biology and the biotic community derived from ecology, have been absorbed, yielding new ways of looking at the organization and processes of sociocultural systems. As in other institutions, key personalities at critical moments of transition have left their marks on the formulation of theory and method and the kinds of problems considered vital to ethnological research.

Controversial challenge of entrenched theory usually signals a time of transition. Fundamental disagreements over interpretation go directly to the heart of the reality process. One danger of controversy, however, is the possibility that the heralded advance may be nothing more than a shift from one paradigm to another engineered by a noisy scientific clique. Any alleged breakthrough must be measured against the realities of process and the stimulus it brings to the differentiation of specializations. Thus, from his own view of the reality process, White (1966:54; compare Kuhn 1962) criticized the so-called historical and functional schools for overstructuring the field of inquiry and restricting creativity.

> Schools are as mortal as the individuals who compose them. Eventually the leader must pass from the scene, and one by one the disciples follow in death as they did in life. Then science is released and a free play of concepts, goals, and values again becomes possible. . . . Schools in cultural anthropology have been means of mobilizing human effort and of providing it with inspiration and incentive. But their effect upon this science—its premises, goals, and the evaluation of its achievements—has been on the whole unfortunate. Perhaps with increased maturation our science may provide its own incentives and loyalties, determine its own goals, and establish its own criteria of values.

White correctly observed that these two theoretical positions repressed the investigation of structural change in an evolutionary perspective. On balance, however, each gave rise to specialized differentiations that added new problems and facts directly relevant to the reality process.

ADVANCEMENT OF PERSPECTIVE IN ETHNOLOGY

The Processes of Scientific Growth

The intellectual adventure of cultural anthropology, extending from Developmentalism and Structuralism to the present time of Differentiative Specialization, has exhibited a continuous historic-evolutionary advance in perspective. In holding that cultural anthropology has progressed in its grasp of essentials, no claim is made that the process was managed with precise control over each step. The same can be said for the natural sciences. Admittedly the hard sciences have advanced far beyond the soft sciences in forcing nature to give up her secrets and in applying them to man's advantage. However, since both the natural and social sciences aspire to reality control, it is unlikely that the logic of the process will be different.

Kuhn (1962) reported that the natural sciences advance through a process of substitution or replacement. Diverse explanations found at the start are winnowed and selectively replaced by a dominant paradigm in which older theory has no place. It is important of course that the "new paradigm . . . preserve a relatively large part of the concrete problem-solving ability that has accrued to science through its predecessors" (Kuhn 1962:169). Indeed, without this continuing extension of capacity to solve the outstanding problems about the organization, substance, and operations of nature, no advance would be visible. Extension of operational controls over matter thus constitutes the heart of the replacive process in natural science, even though the pathway to achievement may exhibit considerable trial-and-error learning. This advancement in operational controls was paralleled by the projection of increasingly complex models of reality processes as unanticipated results induced a more sensitive regard for variation and the causes of variation. When Kuhn sees the natural sciences as leaping forward through a process of substitution, he is describing, of course, an evolutionary process.

The developmental process in cultural anthropology likewise demonstrates a succession of differentiative specializations followed by a theoretical convergence in which a dominant paradigm takes over. The rise of successive theoretical orientations is evolutionary, since a previous theoretical position is denigrated and falls out of fashion. Once entrenched, dominant paradigms release fresh differentiations that bring new facts and variables to surface and which often contradict reigning theory. For cultural anthropology, therefore, things have not grown simpler but more complicated, as one variable after another has been admitted to the causal table. Moreover, like natural scientists, cultural anthropologists find themselves edging closer to the issue of variability, and in the process give more attention to particulate situations and subsystems.

Anthropological Exploration of Reality Processes

Basically, the critical measure of any discipline rests on its theory of the reality processes governing its subject matter and the extent to which it can marshal methodological operations to produce factual evidence to support that theory. In his recent Huxley Memorial Lecture, Murdock (1971: 18) expressed the view that anthropology possessed no body of scientifically verified and verifiable theory. Rather, it exhibited a multiplicity of theoretical perspectives which bore a great resemblance to "unverified, and often unverifiable, systems outside the realm of science which we know as mythology, or perhaps as philosophy or even theology." Though commanding a rich and irreplaceable collection of ethnographic fact, anthropologists revealed a singular incapacity to transform these facts into principles which order and explain the diversities of historical social traditions and behaviors. In this regard, their lamentable failure contrasts with the achievements of physical scientists.

Much of the difficulty with anthropology, in Murdock's view, lay in the reification of conceptual abstractions, particularly the concepts of social structure and of culture. Anthropologists should have been concentrating on individual behavior, not social structure and culture. They needed to find out how individual behavior was organized, the conditions to which it was sensitive, and how individuals decided on a course of action. In this context Murdock recommended a closer linkage with psychology, since in psychology the individual was the empirical unit of observation from whom general laws were inducted. The anthropological contribution to the study of human behavior would rest on a definition of the generality and variability of human behavior under specified conditions. Here the rich ethnographic record was indispensable, inasmuch as it provided variabilities with regard to economies, ideologies, values, population distributions and densities, and the "transmitted and partially shared habitual response tendencies that are commonly designated as culture, and the patterned network of interpersonal relationships . . . termed the social structure" (Murdock 1971:21).

The issues Murdock reviewed are of long standing in anthropology and relate directly to fundamental concerns regarding the character and intentions of the discipline. They involve anthropological objectives relative to subject matter, how this subject matter is ordered, and how it operates. This is the basic problem for anthropology. From Murdock's focus on the behavioral action of individuals, in contrast with what he calls the mythology of social structure and culture, it is clear that fundamental differences separate anthropologists regarding the reality they must explain. Murdock's criticism of the misplaced concreteness of the social and cultural denies the very existence of what in the past was taken to be the proper domain of anthropological investigation.

A disenchantment with the scientific quality of anthropological accomplishments, and the necessity to strike out in a new direction, is readily duplicated in the remarks of various anthropologists. Indeed, the intellectual and methodological renovation of anthropology which Murdock called for has been going on ever since the 1930s when the field entered a time of differentiation of specializations. Four developments during this time especially augur for the continuing enlargement of anthropological perspective with regard to reality processes. Moreover, a close consideration of these key developments gives a firm basis for optimism as to the future growth of anthropology. The first of these new perceptions is growing recognition that the social and cultural, though conceptually distinguishable from the psychological and the organic, do not represent distinctive levels of reality and are not self-contained causal systems. Second, the present differentiation has resulted in a broadened conception of reality processes and the complex connections among variables, both of which must be faced if controlled generalizations about process are to be made. Third, there is implicit, if not explicit, recognition that the interrelation of structure and variation is a central conceptual and epistemological problem for anthropology. Anthropologists are no longer willing to solve critical epistemological issues by making conceptual distinctions which have a direct expediency but which ignore serious contradictions. Fourth, anthropologists presently perceive reality processes as a dynamic interchange through time of a configurated field of relationships. Field theory, as this perspective has been called, shifts attention from structure, as a formal arrangement of parts linked by maintenance (functional) relations, to the actional relations themselves. By concentrating on the actional aspects of systems, anthropologists in effect are operationalizing their basic concern with process. None of the above developments is self-standing but each articulates with, and significantly affects, the other perspectives. It is obvious that Murdock's call for attention to the behaving unit is congruent with the emphasis on actional relations within an interactional field.

Abandonment of the Social and Cultural as Autonomous Domains: Some Implications. Scientific anthropology was raised on the assumption that the sociocultural constituted the special substantive domain of the discipline. Obviously, abandonment of the social and cultural as the special province of anthropology poses critical questions for the future of the discipline and its place in an integrated social science. As integrative variables, the social and cultural are useful in providing perspective on a distinctive dimension of the human environment. However, the significance of the social and cultural can be measured only by determining their key components and entering them as variables in an interactional field where noncultural variables also are operating.

British social anthropologists early recognized that they shared the social domain with their sociological colleagues. In a sociological division of labor, their objective was to describe and explain the institutional structures of non-Western societies, with the further hope of formulating general laws governing all social systems. The same objective holds with regard to culture. Throughout its history anthropology sought to describe and explain the preindustrial world and its transformations. If any substantive distinction can be drawn between cultural anthropology and sister disciplines, it must be here. This is a far more meaningful distinction than one raised on the alleged distinctiveness of a methodology, such as participant observation which some claim exclusively for anthropology. Preferences for special methods and techniques are exhibited by all disciplines, but it is not these preferences for scientific instruments that distinguishes the disciplines but what it is they are researching. This does not rule out anthropological interests in the processes of complex societies as developed in urban, medical, and educational specializations. There is some validity to the argument that anthropologists—owing to their holistic perspective, small-group focus, and participant observation technique—

can make special contributions to the study of groups holding interstitial positions in the sociocultural fabric. Similar domains are available for research among preindustrial peoples as they industrialize and urbanize in order to accommodate themselves to altering world conditions.

Presently anthropology is in a favorable position to realize its goal of an integrated science by continued dedication to its traditional subject matter. Ethnology has attained a dynamic and holistic perspective, which, in conjunction with differentative specializations linked to prime variables, now permits the formulation and implementation of integrated studies of non-Western societies. The importance of sociology, political science, and economics does not rest with their existence as disciplines but with the fact that each has particularized itself around a variable intrinsic to the workings of the human reality. The singular advantage of ethnology consists in the fact that it now is in a better position to unify these variables in a study of the preindustrial world.

A first important consequence of the abandonment of the social and cultural as a unique and self-contained causal domain thus is a clarification of anthropological objectives and establishment of a realistic role for the discipline with relation to other social sciences. A second implication concerns the connection between individuals and their sociocultural milieu. The social and cultural cannot be perceived as an entity floating superorganically above the individual and determining his every act and being. Rather, the social and cultural are an environment within which the individual operates privately and collectively according to the historic accidents of birth, time, and place. The individual in relation to his group affiliations thus emerges as the basic actional unit of anthropological investigation rather than interrelations of social and cultural objects. Recent focus on decision-making processes, on logical processes involved in classification, on the individual as strategically manipulating his milieu, and on the superiority of the emic over the etic orientation, collectively accent the growing acceptance of the individual as the actional unit of observation. While individual actions supply the particulars, the ultimate objective is to use these individualized facts for the induction of general psychological processes exhibited by individuals according to type situations.

A focus on individuals interacting according to specified conditions evokes a model in which persons operate in a field of forces both internal and external to their organized egos. The internal and external forces of this actional field must be conceptualized as operational variables in order that they may be observed and their respective effects measured. Human nature, or psychological processes in Murdock's usage, constitutes one such variable. The social and cultural are variables external to the human nature shared by individuals. Nevertheless, the significance of the social and cultural, as well as human nature, is registered in an internal organization of motives, feeling states, goals, and strategies giving a degree of directionality, consistency, coherence, and persistence to the behavior of individuals. Motives, feeling states, and value premises are expressed objectively in the way people selectively relate to other people, use them for private needs, strive to accumulate social and cultural products, and manipulate these products for some valued advantage. However, individuals are never entirely free to make choices according to an internal organization of perceptions, needs, and desires. The sociocultural and physical environments possess an organization of processes which frequently limit and divert choice to an alternative and at times leave no choice. Therefore, the social and cultural, as well as the physical environment, may not be as mythological as Murdock has asserted. Since the social and cultural exist as an organized environment to which the individual is sensitized in order to realize himself as an individual and as a social person, the social and cultural do play a role in accounting for both the covert and overt behavior of the individual.

The process of internalization, as well as the resulting configuration of behavioral motive and action, are crucial to understanding the human process. The problem is doubly complex because the individual, both in relation to self and to the external world of groups and cultural objects, is simultaneously inside and outside an interactional field. Freud, viewing man as intrinsically a compound of biopsychic impulses, saw the social and cultural as external to man—an *agent provocateur* which blocked human nature and aroused frustrative reactions. On the other hand, those who constructed the mythology of the social and cultural perceived the individual as a template of an external traditional heritage. Both were statements of extremes, but Freud's is more acceptable in recognizing the dynamics of internal and external processes.

That the individual actor, like the participant observer, is both inside and outside a field of activity constitutes a critical and omnipresent methodological issue for anthropologists and social scientists generally. The ambiguity of man-as-participant is reinforced by the view of man as intrinsically irrational and rational, and exclusively neither. Ambiguities contained within its subject matter inevitably are communicated to the discipline. A common anthropological solution is to dichotomize by locating the reality process in the internal organization of psychological processes, or in the external world of society and culture. A prime illustration of such theoretical dichotomizing is found in the Structuralist approach to unconscious and conscious psychological processes. In underwriting structural processes and continuities with unconscious processes, Structuralists assigned these processes to anthropology and left the investigation of conscious processes to historians and philosophers. In recognizing the importance of both unconscious and conscious processes in the production of human events, the present orientation restores the whole man to the anthropological perspective. A unitary view of process in which man is considered a partially free and a partially determined agent, according to circumstances, is more realistic than a monolithic view which describes man as a determined component of structural processes. This unitary position was forcefully stated by Geertz (1965, reprinted in Hammel and Simmons 1970):

> we need to look for systematic relationships among diverse phenomena, not for substantive identities among similar ones. And to do that with any effectiveness, we need to replace the "stratigraphic" conceptions of the relations between the various aspects of human existence with a synthetic one; that is, one in which biological, psychological, sociological, and cultural fators can be treated as variables within unitary systems of analysis.

Structure, Variation, and Reality Processes. A focus on structure and structural processes was a necessary part of anthropological development with relation to reality processes. The systematic operations of structures consolidate the activities of particular units and convey a stability of form through a steady persistence of function. Replication is the essence of systemic processes, and hence the constant desire of scientifically-based anthropologists to state the "laws" of social and cultural systems according to their structural organizations. The objective of system analysis was to formulate a general theory of society and culture which would account for universal features and operations. The task of uncovering the universal and consolidative features of societies and cultures complemented dynamic attempts of Developmentalists to pin down the laws governing structural growth. Both objectives were essential to a full comprehension of structural process. Unfortunately, the new structural-functional orientation was considered antithetical to evolutionary theory and method. Cultural-historical theorists likewise opposed the speculative findings of evolutionists. Consequently, a more comprehensive perspective which combined synchronic and diachronic processes was postponed until anthropology entered a time of differentiation around 1940.

An emphasis on structural process appropriately has been carried forward in the theoretical orientations of anthropological specializations. Lévi-Strauss's psycholinguistic Structuralism is the most explicit statement of the continuance of a structural determinism based on unconscious processes. However, within social Structuralism there is increasing attention to the way in which special conditions produce variability in social forms by compromising of social forms according to conditions which induce accommodations to a rigid application of structural principles (for example, Fortes 1963a; M. G. Smith 1962). Interest in the quality of pluralism in societies and cultures represents another facet of a growing preoccupation with systemic variability (see Van den Berghe 1973).

The relation between structural processes and variational processes has emerged as fundamental to the anthropological perception and grasp of reality processes. This perception is linked to the decline of the Structuralist view of social and cultural systems. Viewed in the context of change, social systems lost the static homogeneity, equilibrium, and integrative qualities which Structuralists stressed. This shift in perspective drew the individual into focus and questioned the view that he was a conditioned automation whose behavior was devoted to maintenance of the needs of the social and cultural order. The view of man as both an unconsciously adapting and consciously coping being undermined the interpretation that man's conscious life was devoted largely to a dramatic rationalization in symbolic form of basic unconscious processes. The shift in perspective also meant that the dialectic process could no longer be confined to the unconscious. The primary dialectic was between the unconscious and the conscious.

Structure is no longer perceived as a fixed entity in time and space but as a product of a flow of activities. Any modification in the flow of activities necessarily alters the structuring (see for example, Belshaw 1967 and Barth 1967). For example, in the face of changing conditions in rural Africa, the tribe loses its corporate character to intersecting interactional domains, such as trade unions and political parties. Consequently, the tribe no longer can serve as the unit of observation and of analysis (Vincent 1971).

A view of structure as a structuring of relationships resulting from a flow of action converges on other models of reality processes (for example, cybernetics, decision-making, resource allocation). It implies that cause is distributed within an interactional field according to circumstances, and hence there is no monistic cause which can deterministically account for the nature of human things and processes. Attention to changes in the flow of action, with consequent modifications in the structuring of units and their interrelations, permits the observation of variational process in relation to structural process. In short, the present outlook holds the promise of unifying historical and evolutionary processes. At long last, anthropology appears at the point of freeing itself from the treadmill of oscillation between extremes of polar theoretical distinctions which have dogged its steps.

SUMMARY

In retrospect the Developmentalist, Structuralist, and present Differentiative stages through which anthropology has passed can be seen as essential to the intellectual and methodological growth of the discipline. Each stage added new facts and interpretational experience and advanced anthropological comprehension of the human reality and process. Developed in the context of Western civilization, the anthropological institution reveals a timely sensitivity to the main currents of European thought as well as to the historical state of social, economic, and political conditions. The linkage of anthropology with other institutions promotes a trend toward greater integration which brings with it a threat to the viability of the discipline as a science. Pressure to make anthropology accountable through pragmatic application increases anthropological responsibility, at the same time offering the advantage of practical experience and moral involvement. Despite the apparent advantage which pragmatic tests of the vitality of theory and method may bring, there is a real danger that the delicate autonomy achieved in association with the sciences will erode and that the anthropologist will be transformed into a social technocrat.

Like other institutions, anthropology has altered historically and in an evolutionary way through the processes of differentiation, convergence, and elaboration. Its growth has not been without error. During moments of transition biographical figures have appeared who reordered objectives and methods and succeeded in casting a broad shadow of influence. However, the intellectual exchange between the old theorists and the new theorists usually took the form of a dialectical opposition which did little to encourage efforts to synthesize the partial truths of the opposing positions. Anthropological growth, as a consequence, has been carried forward by a process of replacement. Theoretical substitution, however, has never been complete because differentiative trends uncovered new facts which not only challenged present interpretation but reinforced selected aspects of older theory—for example, the reintroduction of a structural-evolutionary perspective and new emphases on the energy and ecological aspects of sociocultural systems. The selective recovery of older theory, or its rediscovery during a time of differentiation, has added a cumulative character to the anthropological advance in understanding the nature of reality processes. What anthropologists considered they had to know in order to explain human behavior has grown more complex rather than simpler. The key to an infinite extension of factors would seem to lie in the determination of entities which are comparable because of the unitary nature of their organizational principles, processes, and contexts rather than according to formal resemblances (for example, Fortes 1963a).

Without minimizing the seriousness of the theoretical and methodological problems faced by anthropology in its future development, there are a number of striking advances which encourage an optimistic outlook.

1. The investigation of the preindustrial world and its transformations is the appropriate objective of anthropology, and not the investigation of the social or the cultural as self-contained causal systems.
2. There is increasing recognition that the human reality cannot be dichotomized, but must be treated as a unitary process. This is demonstrated by the following:
   a. An increasing effort to investigate the interrelations of structural and variational processes both synchronically and diachronically. This permits a unification of historical and evolutionary processes.
   b. The view that the social and cultural domains do not constitute closed causal systems but that the social and cultural exist as variables in an interactional field of forces which include noncultural variables.
   c. A perspective of man as subject to unconscious processes which are determinative of his behavior but also as capable of conscious

determinations in his own right. The new focus on man as an irrational-rational being allows anthropology to pursue its scientific objective clued to invariant relations and processes, and also to investigate man humanistically according to his conscious selection of values and life-styles.

d. A focus on individual behavior as the proper unit of investigation. Perception of the individual as unconsciously adapting to, as well as consciously manipulating, his environment (biopsychic, socio-cultural, and physical) infuses anthropological investigation with a dynamic outlook essential to understanding the nature of structure and process. Though structure may be embedded in a traditional social and cultural heritage or "constitution," the flow of individual action organizes the flow of structure, either stabilizing it over a period of time or moving it unobstrusively or hastily toward a restructuring. Attention to the behaving individual also satisfies the inductive requirements of scientific investigation and permits conceptualizations of behavioral form and process which are useful and valid in cross-cultural comparison. In short, emic and etic processes can be joined.

3. The present differentiation of cultural anthropology is establishing closer linkages with related disciplines. The resultant conceptual and methodological borrowing is broadening the base upon which a thoroughgoing investigation of preindustrial societies can be carried forward.

4. In accordance with its historical-evolutionary development, the differentiative process is producing intellectual convergences which are leading to a more comprehensive perspective and theoretical consolidation.

No discipline is an island, and the future development of anthropology will proceed in step with advancements in the social sciences generally. The objective of a unified social science lies in the future, and cultural anthropology, by maintaining a broad range of substantive interest, should contribute materially to such an integrative effort. A commitment to fulfillment of an integrated social science would not only permit anthropology to pursue the advancement of knowledge more advantageously but also strengthen application of anthropological capabilities in the interest of human welfare.

From its inception anthropology was guided by the vision of man as an emergent personality. Through the medium of his own social and cultural world man was viewed as advancing himself through control over nature and self. The human drama thus was a movement toward realization of the deep-seated human potential. Anthropology participated in this process of humanization by recording its progress and by formulating, through considered analysis, the principles by which the humanizing process was carried forward, as well as subverted. Achievement of this scientific objective produced facts, knowledgeable experience, and methods which could be applied to assure the continuous improvement of man and society. A moral as well as a scientific commitment have always been a part of the anthropological world view and self-conception.

Despite the pressures of scientism and the historic and national prejudices to which the discipline was subjected, anthropology steadily maintained the humanistic base of its existence. In the past this commitment was largely intellectual and moral. Education, both public and formal, served as the arena and as the instrument for the anthropological message. The anthropological input into the social consciousness of the West has been substantial. At the same time, participation in the emerging social consciousness of Western civilization has compelled anthropologists to continuously reorient themselves. The gradual increase in stress on a moral-political involvement in society at large has become a part of the anthropological experience, and one essential to realization of the intrinsic character of anthropology. However, future development of the discipline will necessitate delicate accommodations rather than partisan loyalties. Anthropology needs no "reinventing," and there is no reinvention of any discipline except in metaphor (see, for example, Hymes 1974a; compare Appel 1974; Kaplan 1974). The problem is one of growth regarding both scientific capabilities and social consciousness. Through a continued dedication to the process of accommodating and synthesizing the traditional scientific and humanistic goals of the discipline, anthropology can press forward; and, in realizing its own self, anthropology can serve the fundamental needs of mankind.

References

ABERLE, D. F.
1957   "The Influence of Linguistics on Early Culture and Personality Theory." G. Dole and R. Carneiro, eds., *Essays in the Science of Culture.* New York: Crowell, 1–29.
1966   *The Peyote Religion Among the Navaho.* Chicago: Aldine.

ABERLE, D. and O. STEWART
1957   "Navaho and Ute Peyotism: A Chronological and Distributional Study." University of Colorado Studies, Series in Anthropology, No. 6. Boulder: University of Colorado Press.

ACKERKNECHT, E. H.
1942   "Problems of Primitive Medicine." *Bulletin of the History of Medicine* 11:503–521.
1947   "Primitive Surgery." *American Anthropologist* 49:25–45.

ACOSTA, J. DE
n.d.   (orig. 1588–1589) *The Natural and Moral History of the Indians.* (Reprinted from the 1604 English trans. ed. of Edward Grimston). Ed. with notes and Introduction by Clements R. Markham. (2 vols.) New York: B. Franklin.

ADAIR, JAMES
1930   (orig. 1775) *Adair's History of the American Indians,* S. C. Williams, ed. Johnson City, Tenn.: Watauga Press.

ADAIR, JOHN
1963   "Physicians, Medicine Men, and Their Navaho Patients." I. Galdston, ed., *Man's Image in Medicine and Anthropology.* New York: International Universities Press, 1963, 237–257.

ADAIR, JOHN and K. DEUTSCHLE
1958   "Some Problems of the Physician on the Navaho Reservation." *Human Organization* 16:19–23.

ADAIR, JOHN and E. VOGT
1949   "Navaho and Zuni Veterans: A Study of Contrasting Modes of Culture Change." *American Anthropologist* 51:547–561.

ADAMS, R. M.
1960   "The Evolutionary Process in Early Civilizations." S. Tax, ed., *Evolution After Darwin* (3 vols.). Chicago: University of Chicago Press, 2:153–168.
1966   *The Evolution of Urban Society.* Chicago: Aldine.

ADAMS, R. N.
1960   "An Inquiry into the Nature of the Family." G. E. Dole and R. L. Carneiro, eds., *Essays in the Science of Culture.* New York: Crowell, 30–49.
1964   "Politics and Social Anthropology in Spanish America." *Human Organization* 23:1–4.

ADAMS, R. N. et al.
1960   *Social Change in Latin America Today: Its Implications for United States Policy.* New York: Random House.

ADAMS, W. Y.
1963   "Shonto: A Study of the Trader in a Modern Navaho Community." Smithso-

nian Institution, Bureau of American Ethnology, Bulletin 188. Washington: Government Printing Office.

AGASSIZ, L.
1840   "On Glaciers and the Evidence of Their Having Once Existed in Scotland, Ireland and England. *Proceedings of the Geological Society of London* 3:327–332 (1838–1842).
1842   "The Glacial Theory and Its Recent Progress." *Edinburgh New Philosophical Journal* 33:217–283.

AMMON, O.
1890   *Anthropologische Untersuchungen der Wehrpflichtigen in Baden.* Hamburg: Verlaganstalt und Druckerei A,–G.
1895   *Die Gesellschaftsordnung und ihre natürlichen Grundlagen.* Jena: G. Fischer.

ANDERSON, J. N.
1973   "Ecological Anthropology and Anthropological Ecology." Honigmann 1973: 179–239.

ANKERMANN, B.
1905   "Kulturkreise und Kulturschichten in Afrika." *Zeitschrift für Ethnologie* 37:54–91.

APPEL, G. N.
1974   *Basic Issues in the Dilemmas and Ethical Conflicts in Anthropological Inquiry.* New York: MSS Modular Publications, Inc., Module 19.

APTER, D. E.
1955   *The Gold Coast in Transition.* Princeton, N.J.: Princeton University Press.
1961   *The Political Kingdom in Uganda.* Princeton, N.J.: Princeton University Press.

ARBER, E. (ed.)
1885   *The First Three English Books on America.* Birmingham, England: Turnbull & Spears.

ARDREY, R.
1966   *The Territorial Imperative.* New York: Atheneum.

ARENSBERG, C. M.
1955   "American Communities." *American Anthropologist* 57:1143–1162.

ARENSBERG, C. M. and A. H. NIEHOFF
1964   *Introducing Social Change. A Manual for Americans Overseas.* Chicago: Aldine.

ARISTOTLE
1943   *Aristotle. On Man in the Universe,* L. R. Loomis, ed. Roslyn, N.Y.: Black.
1964   *The Politics.* Trans. with Introduction by J. A. Sinclair. Bungay, Suffolk, England: Richard Clay and Co.

ATKINSON, J. J.
1908   *Primal Law.* London: Longmans.

AVEBURY, J.
1870   *The Origin of Civilisation and the Primitive Condition of Man. Mental and Social Condition of Savages.* New York: Appleton.
1913   (orig. 1865) *Prehistoric Times,* 7th ed. rev. London: Williams and Norgate.

BACHOFEN, J. J.
1931   (orig. 1861) *Das Mutterrecht.* Introduction trans. by F. Ilmer. V. F. Calverton, ed., *The Making of Man.* New York: Modern Library, 157–167.

BAGEHOT, W.
1875   (orig. 1872) *Physics and Politics, or, Thoughts on the Application of the Principles of "Natural Selection" and "Inheritance" to Political Society.* New York: Appleton.

BAILEY, W. C. and F. J. CLUNE, JR.
1968   Preparation of Elementary School Units on the Concept of Culture." *Human Organization* 27:6–10.

BALANDIER, G.
1960   "Traditional Social Structures and Economic Changes." Van den Berghe 1965: 385–395.
1963   (orig. 1955) *Sociologie Actuelle de l'Afrique Noire.* Paris: Presses Universitaires de France.
1965   "Messianism and Nationalism in Black Africa." Van den Berghe 1965: 443–460.

BALFOUR, H. (ed.)

1907   *Anthropological Essays Presented to Edward Burnett Tylor in Honour of His 75th Birthday.* Oxford: Clarendon Press.

BANFIELD, E.

1958   *The Moral Basis of a Backward Society.* New York: Free Press.

BARNES, J. A.

1961   "Law as Politically Active: An Anthropological View." G. Sauer, ed., *Studies in the Sociology of Law.* Canberra: Australian National University, 167–196.

1962   "African Models in the New Guinea Highlands." *Man* 62:5–9.

BARNETT, H. G.

1940   "Culture Processes." *American Anthropologist* 42:21–48.

1941–1942   "Personal Conflicts and Cultural Change." *Social Forces* 20:160–171.

1942   "Invention and Cultural Change." *American Anthropologist* 44:14–30.

1953   *Innovation: The Basis of Cultural Change.* New York: McGraw-Hill.

1956   *Anthropology in Administration.* New York: Harper & Row.

1957   *Indian Shakers; A Messianic Cult of the Pacific Northwest.* Carbondale: Southern Illinois University Press.

1959   "Peace and Progress in New Guinea." *American Anthropologist* 61:1013–1019.

1968   "The Nature and Function of the Potlatch." Eugene: University of Oregon, Department of Anthropology (mimeographed).

BARNOUW, V.

1950   "Acculturation and Personality Among the Wisconsin Chippewa." American Anthropological Association, Memoir 72.

1961   "Chippewa Social Atomism." *American Anthropologist* 63:1006–1013.

BARTH, F.

1956   "Ecologic Relationships of Ethnic Groups in Swat, North Pakistan." *American Anthropologist* 58:1079–1089.

1961   *Nomads of South Persia. The Basseri Tribe of the Khamseh Confederacy.* Boston: Little, Brown.

1967a   "Economic Spheres in Darfur." R. Firth, ed., *Themes in Economic Anthropology.* London: Tavistock, 149–174.

1967b   "On the Study of Social Change." *American Anthropologist* 69:661–669.

BASCOM, W.

1955   Urbanization Among the Yoruba." *American Journal of Sociology* 60:446–454.

BASTIAN, A.

1860   *Der Mensch in der Geschichte zur Begründung einer psychologischen Weltanschauung.* (3 vols.) Leipzig: O. Wigand.

1866–1871   *Die Völker des östlichen Asien.* (6 vols.) Leipzig: O. Wigand.

1878–1899   *Die Culturländer des alten Amerika.* (3 vols. in 4.) Berlin: Weidmannsche Buchhandlung.

1881   *Der Völkergedanke im Aufbau einer Wissenschaft vom Menschen und seine Begründung auf ethnologische Sammlungen.* Berlin: Dummler.

1886   *Zur Lehre von den geographischen Provinzen.* Berlin: Ernst Siegfried Mittler.

1895   *Ethnische Elementargedanken in der Lehre vom Menschen.* Berlin: Weidmannsche Buchhandlung.

BATESON, G.

1949   "Bali: The Value System of a Steady State." Fortes 1963:35–53.

BEAGLEHOLE, E. and P.

1946   *Some Modern Maoris.* Wellington: New Zealand Council for Educational Research.

BEATTIE, J.

1960   *Bunyoro: An African Kingdom.* New York: Holt, Rinehart and Winston, Inc.

BECKER, C.

1932   *The Heavenly City of the Eighteenth Century Philosophers.* New Haven, Conn.: Yale University Press.

BEDDOE, J.

1885   *The Races of Britain: A Contribution to the Anthropology of Western Europe.* Bristol, England: J. W. Arrowsmith.

BELSHAW, C. S.

1965   *Traditional Exchange and Modern Markets.* Englewood Cliffs, N.J.: Prentice-Hall.

1967 "Theoretical Problems in Economic Anthropology." M. Freedman, ed., *Social Organization: Essays Presented to Raymond Firth*. London: Cass, 25–42.

BENEDICT, R.

1923 "The Concept of the Guardian Spirit in North America." American Anthropological Association, Memoir 29.

1930 "Psychological Types in the Cultures of the Southwest." *Proceedings of the Twenty-third International Congress of Americanists* 1928:572–581.

1932 "Configurations of Culture in North America." *American Anthropologist* 34: 1–27.

1938 "Continuities and Discontinuities in Cultural Conditioning." *Psychiatry* 1:161–167.

1946 *The Chrysanthemum and the Sword: Patterns of Japanese Culture*. Boston: Houghton Mifflin.

1948 "Anthropology and the Humanities." *American Anthropologist* 51:585–593.

1959 (orig. 1934) *Patterns of Culture*. Boston: Houghton Mifflin.

BENNETT, J. W.

1954 Interdisciplinary Research and the Concept of Culture." *American Anthropologist* 56:169–179.

1966 "Further Remarks on Foster's 'Image of Limited Good.'" *American Anthropologist* 68:206–210.

BENNETT, J. W. and M. NAGAI

1953 "The Japanese Critique of the Methodology of Benedict's 'Chrysanthemum and the Sword.'" *American Anthropologist* 55:404–411.

BENNETT, W. C.

1948 (ed.) "A Reappraisal of Peruvian Archaeology." Society for American Archaeology, Memoir 4.

1948a "The Peruvian Co-Tradition." Bennett 1948:1–7.

BERKHOFER, R.

1965 *Salvation and the Savage: An Analysis of Protestant Missions and American Indian Response, 1787–1862*. Lexington: University of Kentucky Press.

BERLIN, B.

1970 "A Universalist-Evolutionary Approach in Ethnographic Semantics." A. Fischer, ed., *Current Directions in Anthropology, A Special Issue*. Bulletins of the American Anthropological Association 3:3–18.

BERLIN, B. and P. KAY

1969 *Basic Color Terms: Their Universality and Evolution*. Berkeley: University of California Press.

BERREMAN, G. D.

1962 "Behind Many Masks: Ethnography and Impression Management in a Himalayan Village." Society for Applied Anthropology, Monograph 4.

1968 "Is Anthropology Alive? Social Responsibility in Social Anthropology." *Current Anthropology* 9:391–396, with commentaries 407–435.

BERRY, W. B.

1968 *Growth of a Prehistoric Time Scale Based on Organic Evolution*. San Francisco and London: W. H. Freeman and Co.

BIDNEY, D.

1953 "The Concept of Value in Modern Anthropology." Kroeber 1953, 182–199.

1967 (orig. 1953) *Theoretical Anthropology*, 2d, augmented ed. New York: Schocken Books.

BIONDO, F.

1471 *Rome Restored* (in Latin).

1473 *Rome Triumphant* (in Latin).

1474 *Italy Illustrated* (in Latin).

1483 *History from the Decline of the Roman Empire* (in Latin).

BIRKET-SMITH, K.

1929 *The Caribou Eskimo: Material and Social Life and Their Cultural Position*. Copenhagen: Gyldendal.

1930 "The Question of the Origin of Eskimo Culture." *American Anthropologist* 32:608–624.

BLACKMAN, W.

1927 *The Fèllāhīn of Upper Egypt*. London: G. G. Harrap & Co., Ltd.

BLUMENBACH, J.
1865   (orig. 1775) "De Generis Humani Veritate Nativa," T. Bendyshe, trans. *The Anthropological Treatises of Blumenbach and Hunter*. London: Anthropological Society, 145–276.

BOAS, F.
1904a   "The History of Anthropology." *Science*, n.s. 20:513–524.
1904b   "Some Traits of Primitive Culture." *Journal of American Folk-Lore* 17:243–254.
1908   "Anthropology." Lecture delivered at Columbia University, Dec. 18, 1907. New York: Columbia University Press, 5–28.
1910   "Changes in Bodily Form of Descendants of Immigrants." Partial report on the results of an anthropological investigation for the U.S. Immigration Commission. Washington: Government Printing Office. (Senate Document No. 208; 1st Congress, 2d session.)
1911   (ed.) Introduction to the *Handbook of American Indian Languages*. Smithsonian Institution, Bureau of American Ethnology, Bulletin 40. Washington: Government Printing Office, Part 1:1–83.
1911–1938   (ed.) *Handbook of American Indian Languages*. (3 Parts.) Smithsonian Institution, Bureau of American Ethnology, Bulletin 40 (Parts 1 and 2). Washington: Government Printing Office. New York: Columbia University Press (Part 3).
1916   *Tsimshian Mythology*. Thirty-first Annual Report, 1909–1910, Smithsonian Institution, Bureau of American Ethnology. Washington: Government Printing Office.
1928a   Foreword to Margaret Mead, *Coming of Age in Samoa*. New York: Morrow.
1928b   *Materials for the Study of Inheritance in Man*. New York: Columbia University Press.
1936   "Effects of American Environment on Immigrants and Their Descendants." *Science*, n.s. 84 (2189):522–525.
1940   *Race, Language and Culture*. New York: Macmillan.
1940a   (orig. 1888) "The Aims of Ethnology." Boas 1940:626–638.
1940b   (orig. 1891) "The Dissemination of Tales Among the Natives of North America." Boas 1940: 437–445.
1940c   (orig. 1896) "The Limitations of the Comparative Method of Anthropology." Boas 1940:270–280.
1940d   (orig. 1896) "The Growth of Indian Mythologies." Boas 1940:425–436.
1940e   (orig. 1899) "Some Recent Criticisms of Physical Anthropology." Boas 1940: 165–171.
1940f   (orig. 1903) "The Decorative Art of the North American Indians." Boas 1940: 546–563.
1940g   (orig. 1908) "Decorative Designs of Alaskan Needle-cases: A Study in the History of Conventional Design, Based on Materials in the U.S. National Museum." Boas 1940:564–592.
1940h   (orig. 1914) "Mythology and Folk-Tales of the North American Indians." Boas 1940:451–490.
1940i   (orig. 1920) "The Methods of Ethnology." Boas 1940:281–289.
1940j   (orig. 1892–1939, rev. and condensed) "Growth." Boas 1940:103–130.
1940k   (orig. 1930) "Some Problems of Methodology in the Social Sciences." Boas 1940: 260–269.
1940l   (orig. 1932) "The Aims of Anthropological Research." Boas 1940:243–259.
1940m   (orig. 1933) "Relationships Between North-West America and North-East Asia." Boas 1940:344–355.
1940n   (orig. 1933) Review of G. W. Locher, *The Serpent in Kwakiutl Religion: A Study in Primitive Culture*. Boas 1940:446–450.
1940o   (orig. 1936) "History and Science in Anthropology: A Reply." Boas 1940: 305–311.
1963   (orig. 1911) *The Mind of Primitive Man*. New York: Free Press.

BODIN, J.
1966   (orig. 1566) *Method for an Easy Comprehension of History*, B. Reynolds, trans. New York: Octagon Books.

BOHANNAN, P. J.
1954 "Tiv Farm and Settlement." Colonial Research Studies No. 15. London: Her Majesty's Stationery Office.
1957 *Justice and Judgment Among the Tiv.* London: Oxford University Press for the International African Institute.
1958 "Extra-Processual Events in Tiv Political Institutions." *American Anthropologist* 60:1–12.
1965 "The Differing Realms of Law." L. Nader, ed., *The Ethnography of Law. American Anthropologist*, special publication 67:33–42.
BOHANNAN, P. and G. DALTON (eds.)
1962 *Markets in Africa.* Northwestern University African Studies, No. 9. Evanston, Ill.: Northwestern University Press.

BOPP, F.
1816 *Über das Conjugationssystem der Sanskritsprache in Vergleichung mit jenem der griechischen lateinischen, persischen und germanischen Sprache.* Frankfurt.

BOSKOFF, A.
1949 "Structure, Function, and Folk Society." *American Sociological Review* 14:749–758.

BOUCHER DE CRÈVECOEUR DE PERTHES, J.
1838–1841 *De la Création. Essai sur l'origine et la progression des êtres.* (5 vols.) Paris: Treuttel et Wurtz.

BOULE, M. and H. VALLOIS
1957 *Fossil Men,* M. Bullock, trans. New York: Holt, Rinehart and Winston, Inc.

BOURDIER, F.
1969 "Geoffroy Saint-Hilaire versus Cuvier: The Campaign for Paleontological Evolution (1825–1838)." C. J. Schneer, ed., *Toward a History of Geology.* Cambridge, Mass.: M.I.T. Press, 36–61.

BRAIDWOOD, R. and G. WILLEY (eds.)
1962 *Courses Toward Urban Life. Archeological Considerations of Some Cultural Alternatives.* Viking Fund Publications in Anthropology, No. 32. New York: Wenner-Gren Foundation for Anthropological Research, Inc.

BRAMELD, T.
1957 *Cultural Foundations of Education: An Interdisciplinary Exploration.* New York: Harper & Row.

BREASTED, J. H.
1935 *The Dawn of Conscience.* New York: Scribner.

BRIFFAULT, R.
1927 *The Mothers. A Study of the Origins of Sentiments and Institutions.* (3 vols.) New York: Macmillan.

BRISTOL, L. M.
1915 *Social Adaptation. A Study in the Development of Adaptation as a Theory of Social Progress.* Cambridge, Mass.: Harvard University Press.

BROKENSHA, D. and P. HODGE
1969 *Community Development: An Interpretation.* San Francisco: Chandler Publishing Company.

BROWN, G. G. and A. HUTT
1935 *Anthropology in Action.* London: Oxford University Press.

BROWN, J. A.
1971 "The Dimensions of Status in the Burials at Spiro." *American Antiquity,* Memoir 25, 92–112.

BRUNER, E.
1961 "Urbanization and Ethnic Identity in North Sumatra." *American Anthropologist* 63: 508–521.

BRYSON, G.
1945 *Man and Society: The Scottish Inquiry of the Eighteenth Century.* Princeton, N.J.: Princeton University Press.

BUCKLAND, W.
1823 *Reliquae Diluvianae; or Observations on the Organic Remains Contained in Caves, Fissures, and Diluvial Gravel and on Other Geological Phenomena Attesting the Action of an Universal Deluge.* London: J. Murray.

BUCKLE, H. T.
1930 (orig. 1857) *History of Civilization in England,* abridged. London: Watts.

BUFFON, G. L. L.
1812   (orig. 1749) *Natural History, General and Particular . . . . The History of Man and Quadrupeds*, W. Smellie, trans.; W. Wood, ed. (20 vols.) London: T. Cadell and W. Davies.

BUNZEL, R.
1952   *Chichicastenango: A Guatemalan Village.* American Ethnological Society, Vol. 22. Locust Valley, N.Y.: J. J. Augustin.

BUNZEL, R. and A. PARSONS
1964   "Report on Regional Conferences" (with comment by M. Mead and R. Metraux). *Current Anthropology* 5:437–442.

BURLING, R.
1964   "Cognition and Componential Analysis: God's Truth or Hocus Pocus?" *American Anthropologist* 66:20–28.
1969   "Linguistics and Ethnographic Description." *American Anthropologist* 71:817–827.
1970   *Man's Many Voices: Language in Its Cultural Context.* New York: Holt, Rinehart and Winston, Inc.

BURY, J. B.
1920   *The Idea of Progress.* London: Macmillan.

BUSIA, K. A.
1951   *The Position of the Chief in the Modern Political System of the Ashanti.* London: Oxford University Press for the International African Institute.

BUTTERWORTH, D. S.
1962   "A Study of the Urbanization Process Among Mixtec Migrants from Tilantongo in Mexico City." *America Indigena* 22:257–274.

CALDWELL, J. R.
1958   "Trend and Tradition in the Prehistory of the Eastern United States." American Anthropological Association, Memoir 88.

CANCIAN, F.
1966   "Maximization as Norm, Strategy, and Theory: A Comment on Programmatic Statements in Economic Anthropology." *American Anthropologist* 68: 465–470.

CARINI, L.
1971   On Evolution and the Origin of Language." *Current Anthropology* 12:385–386.

CARNEIRO, R. L.
1960   "Slash-and-Burn Agriculture: A Closer Look at Its Implications for Settlement Patterns." Wallace 1960:229–234.
1962   "Scale Analysis for the Study of Cultural Evolution." *Southwestern Journal of Anthropology* 18:149–169.
1967   "On the Relationship Between Size of Population and Complexity of Social Organization." *Southwestern Journal of Anthropology* 33:234–243.
1968   "Ascertaining, Testing, and Interpreting Sequences of Cultural Development." *Southwestern Journal of Anthropology* 24:354–374.

CARSTAIRS, G. M.
1958   *The Twice-Born: A Study of a Community of High-Caste Hindus.* Bloomington: University of Indiana Press.

CASSIRER, E. (ed.)
1948   *The Renaissance Philosophy of Man.* Chicago: University of Chicago Press.

CASTANEDA, C.
1968   *The Teachings of Don Juan. A Yaqui Way of Knowledge.* New York: Ballantine.

CAUDILL, W.
1949   "Psychological Characteristics of Acculturated Wisconsin Ojibwa Children." *American Anthropologist* 51:409–427.
1953   "Applied Anthropology in Medicine." Kroeber 1953:771–806.
1958   *The Psychiatric Hospital as a Small Society.* Cambridge, Mass.: Harvard University Press.

CHAMBERLAIN, H. S.
1912   (orig. 1899) *Foundations of the Nineteenth Century*, J. Lees, trans. (2 vols.) London: John Lamp, Ltd.

CHAMBLISS, R.
1954   *Social Thought from Hammurabi to Comte.* New York: Holt, Rinehart and Winston, Inc.

CHANCE, N.
1962 Factionalism as a Process of Social and Cultural Change." M. Sherif, ed., *Intergroup Relations and Leadership; Approaches and Research in Industrial, Ethnic, Cultural, and Political Areas.* New York: Wiley, 267–273.

CHARDIN, P. T. DE
1961 (orig. 1955) *The Phenomenon of Man*, B. Wall, trans. New York: Harper & Row.

CHILDE, V. G.
1951 (orig. 1936) *Man Makes Himself.* New York: New American Library.

CHOMSKY, N.
1957 *Syntactic Structures.* The Hague: Mouton.
1959 Review of *Verbal Behavior* by B. F. Skinner. *Language* 35:26–58.

CHRÉTIEN, C. D.
1966 "Comment on Geographical-Historical versus Psycho-Functional Explanations of Kin Avoidances,' by H. E. Driver." *Current Anthropology* 7:148–149.

CICERO
1911 *M. Tullius Cicero, On the Nature of the Gods; On Divination; On Fate; On the Republic; On the Laws;* and *On Standing for the Consulship*, C. D. Yonge, trans. London: G. Bell.

CLARK, J. D.
1960 "Human Ecology During the Pleistocene and Later Times in Africa South of the Sahara." *Current Anthropology* 1:307–324, with commentaries.

CLARK, R. T.
1955 *Herder: His Life and Thought.* Berkeley: University of California Press.

CODRINGTON, R. H.
1891 *The Melanesians: Studies in Their Anthropology and Folklore.* Oxford: Clarendon Press.

COHEN, F. S.
1942 *Handbook of Federal Indian Law.* Washington: Government Printing Office.

COHEN, RONALD
1967 *The Kanuri of Bornu.* New York: Holt, Rinehart and Winston, Inc.
1968 "Comment on Article by Leo A. Despres." *Current Anthropology* 9:17–18.

COHEN, R. and J. MIDDLETON (eds.)
1967 *Comparative Political Systems. Studies in the Politics of Pre-Industrial Societies.* American Museum Sourcebooks in Anthropology. Garden City, N.Y.: The Natural History Press.
1970 *From Tribe to Nation in Africa. Studies in Incorporation Processes.* San Francisco: Chandler Publishing Company.

COHEN, ROSALIE
1969 "Conceptual Styles, Culture Conflict, and Nonverbal Tests of Intelligence." *American Anthropologist* 71:828–856.

COLBY, B. N.
1973 "A Partial Grammar of Eskimo Folktales." *American Anthropologist* 75:645–662.

COLE, M., et al.
1971 *The Cultural Context of Learning and Thinking: An Exploration in Experimental Anthropology.* New York: Basic Books.

COLLIER, J.
1950 Foreword, L. Thompson, *Culture in Crisis: A Study of the Hopi Indians.* New York: Harper & Row.

COLLIER, M. and E. S. DETHLEFSEN
1968 "Anthropology and the Pre-Collegiate Curriculum." *Human Organization* 27: 11–16.

COMTE, A.
1893 (orig. 1830–1842) *The Positive Philosophy of Auguste Comte.* (2 vols.) Translated and condensed by H. Martineau. London: Kegan Paul, Trench, Trubner.
1968 (orig. 1806) *System of Positive Polity.* (4 vols.) New York: B. Franklin.

CONDILLAC, E. B. DE
1746 *Essai sur l'origine des connaissances humaines.* Amsterdam: Pierre Mortier.
1930 (orig. 1754) *Condillac's Treatise on the Sensations*, G. Carr, trans. Los Angeles: University of Southern California Press.

CONDORCET, MARQUIS DE
1955   (orig. 1795) *Sketch for a Historical Picture of the Progress of the Human Mind*, J. Barraclough, trans. New York: Noonday.

CONKLIN, H. C.
1954   "An Ethnoecological Approach to Shifting Agriculture." *Transactions of the New York Academy of Sciences* 17:133–142.

COOK, S.
1968   "The Obsolete 'Anti-Market' Mentality: A Critique of the Substantive Approach to Economic Anthropology." Le Clair and Schneider 1968:208–233.

COON, C., S. GARN, and J. BIRDSELL
1950   *Races . . . A Study of the Problems of Race Formation in Man.* Springfield, Ill.: Charles C Thomas.

COUNT, E. (ed.)
1950   *This Is Race.* New York: Abelard-Schuman.

CRAWLEY, E.
1960   (orig. 1902) *The Mystic Rose: A Study of Primitive Marriage and of Primitive Thought in Its Bearing on Marriage.* Revised and enlarged by Theodore Besterman. New York: Meridian.

CUNNINGHAM, D. J.
1908   "Anthropology in the Eighteenth Century." *Journal of the Royal Anthropological Institute* 38:10–35.

CUVIER, G.
1834–1836   (orig. 1812) *Recherches sur les ossements fossiles, ou l'on rétablit les caractères de plusieurs animaux dont les revolutions du globe ont détruit les espèces.* Paris: E. d'Ocagne.

CUVIER, G. and A. BRONGNIART
1808   "Essai sur la géographie minéralogique des environs de Paris avec une carte geonostique et des coupes de terrain." *Annales du Muséum d'Histoire Naturelle de Paris* 11:293–326.

CZEKANOWSKI, J.
1911   "Objective Kriterien in der Ethnologie." *Korrespondenzblatt der Deutschen Gesellschaft für Anthropologie und Urgeschichte* 42:71–75.

CZAPICKA, M.
1914   *Aboriginal Siberia: A Study in Social Anthropology.* Oxford: Clarendon Press.

DALTON, G.
1968   *Primitive, Archaic and Modern Economies: Essays of Karl Polanyi.* Garden City, N.Y.: Doubleday.
1969   "Theoretical Issues in Economic Anthropology." *Current Anthropology* 10:63–102.
1971   (ed.) *Economic Development and Social Change: The Modernization of Village Communities.* Garden City, N.Y.: Natural History Press.
1971a   Introduction. Dalton 1971:1–35.

DANIEL, G. E.
1950   *A Hundred Years of Archaeology.* London: Duckworth.

DARWIN, C.
1936   (orig. 1859, 1871) *The Origin of Species by Means of Natural Selection or the Preservation of Favored Races in the Struggle for Life* and *The Descent of Man and Selection in Relation to Sex.* New York: Modern Library.

DAVENPORT, W.
1959   "Nonunilinear Descent and Descent Groups." *American Anthropologist* 61:557–572.
1963   "Social Organization." Siegel 1963:178–227.

DAVIS, A. and J. DOLLARD
1940   *Children of Bondage.* Washington, D.C.: American Council on Education.

DE BROSSES, C.
1760   *Du culte des dieux fétiches, on parallèle de l'ancienne religion de l'Egypte avec la religion actuelle de Nigritie.* Paris.

DE LAGUNA, G.
1949   "Culture and Rationality." *American Anthropologist* 51:379–391.

DEGÉRANDO, J.-M.
1969 (orig. 1800) *The Observation of Savage Peoples*, F. C. T. Moore, trans. London: Routledge.

DENNIS, W.
1965 (orig. 1940) *The Hopi Child*. New York: Wiley.

DESMOULINS, A.
1826 *Histoire naturelle des races humaines du nord-est de l'Europe, de l'Asie boréale et orientale, et de l'Afrique austral, d'après des recherches spéciales d'antiquités, de physiologie, d'anatomie et de zoologie, appliquée à la recherche des origines des anciens peuples, à la science étymologique, à la critique de l'histoire . . .* (2 vols.) Paris: Méquignon-Marvis.

DEVEREUX, G.
1951 *Reality and Dream: Psychotherapy of a Plains Indian*. New York: International Universities.

DIAMOND, S.
1964 "Anthropology and World Affairs as seen by U.S.A. Associates: A Revolutionary Discipline." *Current Anthropology* 5:432–441.

DIAZ DEL CASTILLO, B.
1908–1916 (orig. 1562) *The True History of the Conquest of New Spain*, A. P. Maudslay, trans. London: Hakluyt Society.

DIXON, R. B.
1923 *The Racial History of Man*. New York: Scribner.
1928 *The Building of Cultures*. New York: Scribner.

DOBYNS, H. F.
1966 "Estimating Aboriginal American Population: An Appraisal of Techniques with a New Hemispheric Estimate." *Current Anthropology* 7:395–449.

DOLLARD, J.
1935 *Criteria for the Life History*. New Haven, Conn.: Yale University Press.
1938 "The Life History in Community Studies." *American Journal of Sociology* 3:724–737.

DOLLARD, J. and N. MILLER
1950 *Personality and Psychotherapy: An Analysis in Terms of Learning, Thinking, and Culture*. New York: McGraw-Hill.

DOLLARD, J., N. MILLER, L. DOOB, O. H. MOWRER, and R. SEARS
1939 *Frustration and Aggression*. New Haven, Conn.: Yale University Press.

DOUGLAS, M.
1971 "Lele Economy Compared with the Bushong: A Study of Economic Backwardness." Dalton 1971:62–87.

DOUSHTY, P.
1970 "Behind the Back of the City: 'Provincial' Life in Lima, Peru." Mangin 1970:30–46.

DOZIER, E. P.
1961 "The Rio Grande Pueblos." Spicer 1961:94–186.
1966 "Factionalism at Santa Clara Pueblo." *Ethnology* 5:172–185.

DRIVER, H. E.
1953 "Statistics in Anthropology." *American Anthropologist* 55:42–59.
1956 "An Integration of Functional, Evolutionary, and Historical Theory by Means of Correlations." Indiana University Publications in Anthropology and Linguistics, Memoir 12.
1966 "Geographical versus Psycho-functional Explanations of Kin Avoidances." *Current Anthropology* 7:132–182.
1970 "Statistical Refutation of Comparative Functional-Causal Models." *Southwestern Journal of Anthropology* 26:25–31.

DRIVER, H. E. and W. C. MASSEY
1957 "Comparative Studies of North American Indians." *Transactions of the American Philosophical Society* 47, Part 2.

DUBE, S. C.
1958 *India's Changing Villages: Human Factors in Community Development*. London: Routledge.

DUBOIS, C.
1961   (orig. 1944) *The People of Alor: A Socio-Psychological Study of an East Indian Island.* New York: Harper & Row.

DUMOND, D. E.
1961   "Swidden Agriculture and the Rise of Maya Civilization." *Southwestern Journal of Anthropology* 17:301–316.

DUMONT, R. V. JR., and M. WAX
1969   "Cherokee School Society and the Intercultural Classroom." *Human Organization* 28:217–226.

DUNBAR, J.
1780   *Essays on the History of Mankind in Rude and Cultivated Ages.* London: W. Strahan.

DUNDAS, C.
1921   "Native Laws of Some Bantu Tribes of East Africa." *Journal of the Royal Anthropological Institute* 51:217–278.

DURKHEIM, E.
1938   (orig. 1895) *The Rules of Sociological Method,* S. Solvay and J. Mueller, trans.; G. E. G. Catlin, ed. Chicago: University of Chicago Press.
1947   (orig. 1912) *The Elementary Forms of the Religious Life: A Study in Religious Sociology,* J. W. Swain, trans. New York: Free Press.
1949   (orig. 1893) *The Division of Labor in Society,* G. Simpson, trans. New York: Free Press.
1951   (orig. 1887) *Suicide,* J. Spaulding and G. Simpson, trans. New York: Free Press.
1960   (orig. 1892) *Montesquieu and Rousseau: Forerunners of Sociology,* R. Manheim, trans. Ann Arbor: University of Michigan Press.
1963   (orig.1897) *Incest: The Nature and Origin of the Taboo,* E. Sagarin, trans. New York: Lyle Stuart.

DURKHEIM, E. and M. MAUSS
1963   (orig. 1903) *Primitive Classification,* R. Needham, trans. Chicago: University of Chicago Press.

DYK, M., (ed.)
1938   *Son of Old Man Hat: A Navaho Autobiography.* New York: Harcourt.

EGGAN, D.
1956   "Instruction and Affect in Hopi Cultural Continuity." *Southwestern Journal of Anthropology* 12:347–370.

EGGAN, F.
1937   "Historical Changes in the Choctaw Kinship System." *American Anthropologist* 39:34–52.
1950   *Social Organization of the Western Pueblos.* Chicago: University of Chicago Press.

EISELY, L.
1961   *Darwin's Century: Evolution and the Men Who Discovered It.* New York: Doubleday.

ELKIN, A. P.
1936–1937   "The Reaction of Primitive Races to the White Man's Culture." *The Hibbert Journal* 35:537–545.
1951   "Reaction and Interaction: A Food Gathering People and European Settlement in Australia." *American Anthropologist* 53:164–186.

ELLIS, H.
1926   (orig. 1904) *A Study of British Genius.* Boston: Houghton Mifflin.

ELWIN, V.
1947   *The Muria and Their Ghotul.* Bombay: Oxford University Press.

EMBREE, J. F.
1950   "Thailand: A Loosely Structured Social System." *American Anthropologist* 52:181–193.

ENCYCLOPÉDIE, OU DICTIONNAIRE RAISONNÉ DES SCIENCES, DES ARTS ET DES MÉTIERS
1967   (orig. 1765) Stuttgart-Bad Canstatt: Friedrich Frommann Verlag (Günther Holzboog). Vol. 14, articles on religion and natural religion, pp. 78–88.

ENGELS, F.
1940   (orig. 1876) *Dialectics of Nature,* C. Dutt, trans. and ed. New York: International Publishers.

1968a (orig. 1880) *Socialism: Utopian and Scientific.* Marx and Engels 1968: 399–434.

1968b (orig. 1883) *Speech at the Graveside of Karl Marx.* Marx and Engels 1968: 435–436.

1968c (orig. 1884) *The Origin of the Family, Private Property and the State.* Marx and Engels 1968:455–593.

1968d (orig. 1876) *The Part Played by Labour in the Transition from Ape to Man.* Marx and Engels 1968:358–368.

EPSTEIN, A. L.

1951 "Some Aspects of the Conflict of Law and Urban Courts in Northern Rhodesia." *Rhodes-Livingstone Journal* 12:28–40.

1958 *Politics in an Urban African Community.* Manchester, England: Manchester University Press for the Rhodes-Livingstone Institute.

EPSTEIN, S.

1967 (orig. 1959) "A Sociological Analysis of Witch Beliefs in a Mysore Village." Middleton 1967:135–154.

ERASMUS, C.

1961 *Man Takes Control: Cultural Development and American Aid.* Minneapolis: University of Minnesota Press.

ERIKSON, E. H.

1943 *Observation on the Yurok: Childhood and World Image.* Berkeley: University of California Press.

1948 (orig. 1945) "Childhood and Tradition in Two American Indian Tribes: A Comparative Abstract with Conclusions." Haring 1948:172–203.

EVANS-PRITCHARD, E. E.

1934 "Social Character of Bride-Wealth, with Special Reference to the Azande." *Man* 34, no. 194.

1937 *Witchcraft, Oracles and Magic Among the Azande.* Oxford: Clarendon Press.

1940 *The Nuer.* Oxford: Clarendon Press.

1949 *The Sanusi Cyrenaica.* Oxford: Clarendon Press.

1951 *Kinship and Marriage Among the Nuer.* Oxford: Clarendon Press.

1964 (orig. 1950) "Social Anthropology: Past and Present." E. E. Evans-Pritchard, *Social Anthropology and Other Essays.* New York: Tree Press, 139–154.

EZELL, P. H.

1961 "The Hispanic Acculturation of the Gila River Pimas." American Anthropological Association, Memoir 90.

FABREGA, H. JR.

1972 "Medical Anthropology." Siegel 1971:167–229.

FAGAN, B. M. (ed.)

1970 *Introductory Readings in Archaeology.* Boston: Little, Brown.

FALCON, W.

1781 *Remarks on the Influence of Climate, Situation, Nature of Country, Population, Nature of Food, and Way of Life, on the Disposition and Temper, Manners and Behaviour, Intellects, Laws and Customs, Form of Government, and Religion, of Mankind.* London: C. Dilly.

FALLERS, L.

1955 "The Predicament of the Modern African Chief: An Instance from Uganda." *American Anthropologist* 57:290–305.

1969 *Law without Precedent.* Chicago: University of Chicago Press.

FENTON, W. N.

1957 "Factionalism at Taos Pueblo, New Mexico." Bureau of American Ethnology, Bulletin 164.

FERGUSON, A.

1789 (orig. 1767) *An Essay on the History of Civil Society.* Basil: J. J. Tourneisen.

1792 *Principles of Moral and Political Science.* (2 vols.) Edinburgh: A. Kincaid and J. Bell.

FIRTH, J. R.

1964 "Ethnographic Analysis and Language with Reference to Malinowski's Views." Firth 1964:93–118.

FIRTH, RAYMOND

1929 *Primitive Economics of the New Zealand Maori.* London: Routledge.

1957 (orig. 1936) *We, the Tikopia: A Sociological Study of Kinship in Primitive Polynesia.* London: G. Allen.
1963 (orig. 1951) *Elements of Social Organization.* Boston: Beacon.
1964 (ed.) *Man and Culture: An Evaluation of the Work of Bronislov Malinovski.* New York: Harper & Row.
1964a "Introduction: Malinowski as Scientist and as Man." Firth 1964: 1–14.
1965 (orig. 1939) *Primitive Polynesian Economy,* 2d ed. London: Routledge.

FIRTH, ROSEMARY
1943 *Housekeeping Among Malay Peasants.* London: P. Lund, Humphries and Co. for the London School of Economics and Political Science.

FLANNERY, K. V.
1961 *Early Village Farming in Southwestern Asia.* American Ethnological Society, Symposium on Patterns of Land Utilization and Other Papers. Seattle: University of Washington Press.
1965 "The Ecology of Early Food Production in Mesopotamia." *Science* 147:1247–1256.

FORD, C. S.
1941 *Smoke from Their Fires. The Life of a Kwakiutl Chief.* New Haven, Conn.: Yale University Press.

FORDE, C. D.
1927 *Ancient Mariners. The Story of Ships and Sea Routes.* London: G. Howe.
1941 "Marriage and the Family Among the Yakö in Southeast Nigeria." London School of Economics, Monographs in Social Anthropology, No. 5.
1953 "Applied Anthropology in Government: British Africa." Kroeber 1953:841–865.
1957 (orig. 1934) *Habit, Economy and Society: A Geographical Introduction to Ethnology.* New York: Dutton.

FORTES, M.
1938 "Social and Psychological Aspects of Education in Tabelaud." *Africa* 11(4): supplement.
1945 *The Dynamics of Clanship Among the Tallensi, Being the First Part of an Analysis of the Social Structure of a Trans-Volta Tribe.* London: Oxford University Press for the International African Institute.
1949 *The Web of Kinship Among the Tallensi.* London: Oxford University Press for the International African Institute.
1953 "The Structure of Unilineal Descent Groups." *American Anthropologist* 55: 17–41.
1962a "Kinship and Marriage Among the Ashanti." Radcliffe-Brown and Forde 1962:252–284.
1962b (orig. 1940) "The Political System of the Tallensi of the Northern Territories of the Gold Coast." Fortes and Evans-Pritchard 1962:239–271.
1963 (ed.) (orig. 1949) *Social Structure, Studies Presented to A. R. Radcliffe-Brown.* New York: Russell and Russell.
1963a (orig. 1949) "Time and Social Structure: An Ashanti Case Study." Fortes 1963: 54–84.
1964 "Malinowski and the Study of Kinship." Firth 1964:157–189.

FORTES, M. and S. L. FORTES.
1936 "Food in the Domestic Economy of the Tallensi." *Africa* 9:237–276.

FORTES, M. and E. E. EVANS-PRITCHARD
1962 (orig. 1940) *African Political Systems.* London: Oxford University Press for the International African Institute.

FOSTER, G.
1942 "A Primitive Mexican Economy." American Ethnological Society Monograph No. 5. Seattle: University of Washington Press.
1953 "What Is Folk Culture?" *American Anthropologist* 55:159–173.
1962 *Traditional Cultures and the Impact of Technological Change.* New York: Harper & Row.
1965 "Peasant Society and the Image of Limited Good." *American Anthropologist* 67:293–315.
1967 *Tzintzuntzan: Mexican Peasants in a Changing World.* Boston: Little, Brown.

FOULKS, E. F.

1972 "The Arctic Hysterias of the North Alaskan Eskimos." American Anthropological Association, Study 10.

FOX, C. E.

1924 *The Threshold of the Pacific: An Account of the Social Organization, Magic and Religion of the People of San Cristoval in the Solomon Islands.* New York: Knopf.

FOX, J. R.

1961 "Veterans and Factions in Pueblo Society." *Man* 61:173–176.

FOX, R.

1967 *Kinship and Marriage: An Anthropological Perspective.* Baltimore: Penguin Books.

FRAKE, C. O.

1962 "Cultural Ecology and Ethnography." *American Anthropologist* 64:53–59.

1964a "Further Discussion of Burling." *American Anthropologist* 66:119.

1964b "Notes on Queries in Ethnography." A. K. Romney and R. G. D'Andrade, eds., *Transcultural Studies in Cognition. American Anthropologists, Special Publication* 66:132–145.

FRANK, A. G.

1970 "On Dalton's 'Theoretical Issues in Economic Anthropology.'" *Current Anthropology* 11:67–71.

FRANK, L. K.

1948 *Society as the Patient.* New Brunswick, N.J.: Rutgers University Press.

FRAZER, J. G.

1900 (orig. 1890) *The Golden Bough.* (3 vols.) London: Macmillan.

1913 *Psyche's Task: A Discourse Concerning the Influence of Superstition on the Growth of Institutions.* London: Macmillan.

1918 *Folk-lore in the Old Testament: Studies in Comparative Religion, Legend and Law.* (3 vols.) London: Macmillan.

1922 *The Golden Bough* (abridged in 1 vol.). New York: Macmillan.

1925–1930 *The Golden Bough.* (12 vols.) London: Macmillan.

1935 (orig. 1910) *Totemism and Exogamy. A Treatise on Certain Early Forms of Superstition and Society.* (4 vols.) London: Macmillan.

1939 *Anthologia Anthropologica,* annotated by Robert A. Downie. London: P. Lund, Humphries & Co.

FREILICH, M.

1958 "Culture Persistence Among the Modern Iroquois." *Anthropos* 53:473–483.

FRENCH, D.

1948 "Factionalism in Isleta Pueblo." American Ethnological Society, Monograph 14, 1–48.

1961 "Wasco-Wishram." Spicer 1961:337–430.

FRERE, J.

1800 (orig. 1797) "Account of Flint Weapons Discovered at Hoxne in Suffolk." *Archaeologia* 13:204–205. (Reprinted in Heizer 1962:70–71.)

FREUD, S.

1918 (orig. 1913) *Totem and Taboo; Resemblances Between the Psychic Lives of Savages and Neurotics,* A. Brill, trans. New York: Moffat, Yard and Co.

1939 *Moses and Monotheism,* K. Jones, trans. London: Hogarth Press and the Institute of Psycho-Analysis.

1958 (orig. 1930) *Civilization and Its Discontents,* J. Riviere, trans. Garden City, N.Y.: Doubleday.

FRIED, M. H.

1967 *The Evolution of Political Society, An Essay in Political Anthropology.* New York: Random House.

FRIEDERICI, G.

1907 *Die Schiffahrt der Indianer.* Stuttgart: Strecke and Schröder.

1926 *Die Heimat der Kokospalme und die vorkolombische Entdeckung Amerikas durch die Malaio-Polynesier.* Berlin: Der Erdball, Jahrgang I.

FRIEDL, E.

1956 "Persistence in Chippewa Culture and Personality." *Aemrican Anthropologist* 58:814–825.

1959 "The Role of Kinship in the Transmission of National Culture to Rural Villages in Mainland Greece." *American Anthropologist* 61:30–38.

FRIEDMAN, F.
1953 "The World of 'La Miseria.'" *Partisan Review* 20:218–231.

FRIEDRICH, P.
1958 "A Tarascan Cacicazgo: Structure and Function." V. F. Ray, ed., *Systems of Political Control and Bureaucracy; Proceedings of the American Ethnological Society,* 23–29.

FROBENIUS, L.
1897 "Der Westafrikanische Kulterkreis." *Petermann's Geographische Mitteilungen* 43:225.
1898 *Der Ursprung der afrikanischen Kulturen.* Berlin: Verlag gebrüder Borntraeger.

FROMM, E.
1955 *The Sane Society.* New York: Holt, Rinehart and Winston, Inc.

FUSTEL DE COULANGES
1956 (orig. 1864) *The Ancient City. A Study on the Religion, Laws, and Institutions of Greece and Rome.* Garden City, N.Y.: Doubleday.

GALTON, F.
1962 (orig. 1869) *Hereditary Genius: An Inquiry into Its Laws and Consequences.* New York: Meridian.

GEARING, F. O.
1962 "Priests and Warriors: Social Structures for Cherokee Politics in the 18th Century." American Anthropological Association, Memoir 93.
1973 "Anthropology and Education." Honigmann 1973:1223–1249.

GEARING, F., R. MC C. NETTING, and L. PEATTIE (eds.)
1960 *Documentary History of the Fox Project, 1948–1959: A Program in Action Anthropology,* S. Tax, dir. Chicago: University of Chicago Press.

GEERTZ, C.
1959 "Form and Variation in Balinese Village Structure." *American Anthropologist* 61:991–1012.
1963 (ed.) *Old Societies and New States.* London: Collier Macmillan, Ltd.
1963a "The Integrative Revolution: Primordial Sentiments and Civil Politics in New States." Geertz 1963:105–157.
1966 *Agricultural Involution: The Process of Ecological Change in Indonesia.* Berkeley: University of California Press.
1970 (orig. 1965) "The Impact of the Concept of Culture on the Concept of Man." E. Hammel and W. Simmons, eds., *Man Makes Sense. A Reader in Modern Cultural Anthropology.* Boston: Little, Brown, 47–65.

GENNEP, A. VAN
1920 *L'état actuel du problème totémique.* Paris: E. Leroux.
1960 (orig. 1908) *The Rites of Passage,* M. B. Vizedom and G. Caffee, trans. London: Routledge.

GEOFFROY SAINT-HILAIRÉ, E.
1829 "Fragment sur la nature: ou, Quelques idées générales sur les existences du monde physique considérées d'ensemble et dans l'unité." *Encyclopédie moderne,* Vol. XVII.

GIBBON, E.
1776–1788 *The Decline and Fall of the Roman Empire.* (6 vols.) London.

GIBBS, J.
1962 "Poro Values and Courtroom Procedures in a Kpelle Chiefdom." *Southwestern Journal of Anthropology* 18:341–349.

GIBSON, C.
1964 *The Aztecs Under Spanish Rule: A History of the Indians of the Valley of Mexico.* Stanford, Calif.: Stanford University Press.

GINSBERG, M.
1965 Introduction. L. Hobhouse, G. Wheeler, and M. Ginsberg, *The Material Culture and Social Institutions of the Simpler Peoples. An Essay in Correlation.* London: Routledge, i-xiv.

GILLIN, J.
1954 *For a Science of Social Man. Convergences in Anthropology, Psychology, and Sociology.* New York: Macmillan.

GIRAUD-SOULAVIE, A.
1780–1784 *Histoire Naturelle de la France Meridionale.* (7 vols.) Paris.

GJESSING, G.
1968 "The Social Responsibility of the Social Scientist." *Current Anthropology* 9:397–402, with commentaries, 407–435.

GLADWIN, T. and S. SARASON
1953 *Truk: Man in Paradise.* Viking Fund Publications in Anthropology, No. 20. New York: Wenner-Gren Foundation for Anthropological Research.

GLUCKMAN, M.
1949 *An Analysis of the Sociological Theories of Bronislaw Malinowski.* New York and London: Oxford University Press for the Rhodes-Livingstone Institute.
1951 "The Lozi of Barotse-land in Northwestern Rhodesia." E. Colson and M. Gluckman, eds., *Seven Tribes of British Central Africa.* London: Oxford University Press for the Rhodes-Livingstone Institute, 1–93.
1954 *Custom and Conflict in Africa.* New York: Free Press.
1955 *The Judicial Process Among the Barotse of Northern Rhodesia.* Manchester, England: Manchester University Press for the Rhodes-Livingstone Institute.
1962a (orig. 1940) "The Kingdom of the Zulu of South Africa." Fortes and Evans-Pritchard 1962:25–55.
1962b (orig. 1950) "Kinship and Marriage Among the Lozi of Northern Rhodesia and the Zulu of Natal." Radcliffe-Brown and Forde 1962:166–206.
1965 (orig. 1960) "Tribalism in Modern Central Africa." Van den Berghe 1965:346–360.

GOBINEAU, J. A.
1915 (orig. 1853–1855) *The Inequality of Human Races,* Vol. 1 (of 4). Collins, trans. New York: Putnam.

GOGGIN, J.
1949 "Cultural Traditions in Florida Prehistory." J. W. Griffin, ed., *The Florida Indian and His Neighbors.* Winter Park, Fla.: Rollins College, 13–44.
1968 *Spanish Majolica in the New World. Types of the Sixteenth to Eighteenth Centuries.* New Haven, Conn.: Yale University Publications in Anthropology, No. 72.

GOGUET, A. Y. and A. C. FUGERE
1775 (orig. 1758) *The Origin of Laws, Arts and Sciences, and Their Progress Among the Most Ancient Nations.* (3 vols.) R. Henry, D. Dunn, and A. Spearman, trans. Edinburgh: G. Robinson.

GOLDENWEISER, A. A.
1917 "The Autonomy of the Social." *American Anthropologist* 19:447–449.
1922 *Early Civilization; An Introduction to Anthropology.* New York: Knopf.
1933 *History, Psychology, and Culture.* New York: Knopf.
1933a (orig. 1910) "Totemism, An Analytical Study." Goldenweiser 1933:213–332.
1936 "Loose Ends of Theory on the Individual, Pattern, and Involution in Primitive Society." *Essays in Anthropology in Honor of Alfred Louis Kroeber,* R. Lowie, ed. Berkeley: University of California Press, 99–104.
1937 *Anthropology: An Introduction to Primitive Culture.* New York: Appleton.

GOLDFRANK, E.
1945 Socialization, Personality, and the Structure of Pueblo Society." *American Anthropologist* 47:516–539.

GOLDMAN, I.
1955 "Status Rivalry and Cultural Evolution in Polynesia." *American Anthropologist* 57:680–697.

GOLDSCHMIDT, W.
1959a (ed.) "The Anthropology of Franz Boas: Essays on the Centennial of His Birth." American Anthropological Association, Memoir 89.
1959b *Man's Way: A Preface to the Understanding of Human Society.* New York: Holt, Rinehart and Winston, Inc.

1966   *Comparative Functionalism.* Berkeley: University of California Press.

GOLDSCHMIDT, W. and R. EDGERTON

1961   "A Picture Technique for the Study of Values." *American Anthropologist* 63: 26–47.

GOLDTHORPE, J. E.

1955   "An African Élite: A Sample Survey of Fifty-Two Former Students of Makerere College in East Africa. *British Journal of Sociology* 6:31–47.

GOMME, G. L.

1908   *Folklore as an Historical Science.* London: Methuen.

GONZALEZ, N. S.

1966   "Health Behavior in Cross-Cultural Perspective: A Guatemalan Example." *Human Organization:* 25:122–125.

GOODENOUGH, W. H.

1955   "A Problem in Malayo-Polynesian Social Organization." *American Anthropologist* 57:71–83.

1961a   "Comment on Cultural Evolution." *Daedalus* 90:521–528.

1961b   Review of George P. Murdock, ed., *Social Structure in Southeast Asia. American Anthropologist* 63:1341–1347.

1963   "Some Applications of Guttman Scale Analysis to Ethnography and Culture Theory." *Southwestern Journal of Anthropology* 19:235–250.

1964   (ed.) *Explorations in Cultural Anthropology.* New York: McGraw-Hill.

1967   "Componential Analysis." *Science* 156:1203–1209.

1970   *Description and Comparison in Cultural Anthropology.* Chicago: Aldine.

GOODY, J. (ed.)

1958   *The Development Cycle in Domestic Groups.* Cambridge: Cambridge University Press.

GORER, G.

1938   *Himalayan Village.* London: Michael Joseph.

1948a   *The American People.* New York: Norton.

1948b   (orig. 1942) "Themes in Japanese Culture." Haring 1948:237–255.

GORER, G. and J. RICKMAN

1950   *The People of Great Russia.* New York: Chanticleer.

GOUGH, K.

1968   "New Proposals for Anthropologists." *Current Anthropology* 9:403–407.

GOULDNER, A. W. and R. A. PETERSON

1962   *Notes on Technology and the Moral-Order.* Indianapolis, Ind.: Bobbs-Merrill.

GRAEBNER, F.

1905   "Kulturkreise und Kulturschichten in Ozeanien." *Zeitschrift für Ethnologie* 37: 28–53.

1909   "Die melanesische Bogenkultur und ihre Verwandten." *Anthropos* 4:726–780, 998–1032.

1911   *Methode der Ethnologie.* Heidelberg: Winter.

1931   "Causality and Culture," trans. of *Methode der Ethnologie* by F. Illmer. V. F. Calverton, ed., *The Making of Man.* New York: Modern Library, 421–428.

GRAVES, T., N. KOBRIN, and M. KOBRIN

1969   "Historical Inferences from Guttman Scales: The Return of Age-Area Magic?" *Current Anthropology* 10:317–338.

GREENBERG, J. H,

1971   "Is Language Like a Chess Game?" American Anthropological Association Bulletin 4, 53–67.

GREENBAUM, L.

1970   "Evaluation of a Stratified versus an Unstratified Universe of Cultures in Comparative Research." *Behavior Science Notes* 5:251–281.

GREENE, J. C.

1959   *The Death of Adam: Evolution and Its Impact on Western Thought.* Ames, Iowa: Iowa State University Press.

GRIFFIN, J. W. (ed.)

1949   *The Florida Indian and His Neighbors.* Winter Park, Fla.: Rollins College.

GRIMM, J.
1822–1837 (orig. 1819) *Deutsche Grammatik* (4 vols.) Göttingen: Dietrichsche Buchhandlung.
1875–1878 (orig. 1835) *Deutsche Mythologie*. Berlin: F. Dümmler.
GRINNELL, G. B.
1923 *The Cheyenne Indians, Their History and Ways of Life.* (2 vols.) New Haven, Conn.: Yale University Press.
GRUBER, J.
1965 "Brixham Cave and the Antiquity of Man." M. Spiro, ed., *Context and Meaning in Cultural Anthropology.* New York: Free Press, 373–402.
1967 "Horatio Hale and the Development of American Anthropology." *Proceedings of the American Association for the Advancement of Science* 3:5–37.
GUEMPLE, L.
1971 (ed.) *Alliance in Eskimo Society.* Seattle: University of Washington Press.
1971a Introduction. Guemple 1971:1–8.
GULLIVER, P. H.
1966 (orig. 1955) *The Family Herds: A Study of Two Pastoral Tribes in East Africa, the Jie and Turkana.* London: Routledge.
1960 "Incentives in Labor Migration." *Human Organization* 19:159–163.
1963 *Social Control in an African Society: A Study of the Arusha, Agricultural Masai of Northern Tanganyika.* Boston: Boston University Press.
GUMPLOWICZ, L.
1883 *Der Rassenkampf.* Innsbruck: Washer'oche Univ. Buchhandlung.
1963 (orig. 1885) I. Horowitz, ed., *Outlines of Sociology.* New York: Paine-Whitman.
GURVITCH, G. and W. E. MOORE (eds.)
1945 *Twentieth Century Sociology.* New York: Philosophical Library.
GUSINDE, M.
1931–1939 *Die Feuerland-Indianer.* (3 vols.) Mödling bei Wien. "Anthropos"-Bibliotek.
GUTKIND, P. C. W.
1963 *The African Administration of the Kibuga of Buganda.* The Hague: Mouton.
HAHN, E.
1896 *Die Haustiere und ihre Beziehungen zur Wirtschaft des Menschen: Eine geographische Studie.* Leipzig: Duncker und Humboldt.
1904 *Die Entstehung der Pflugkultur (unseres Ackerbaus).* Heidelberg: Winter.
1905 *Das Alter der wirtschaftlichen Kultur der Menschheit; ein Rückblick und ein Ausblick.* Heidelberg: Winter.
1919 (orig. 1914) *Von der Hacke zum Pflug: Garten und Feld, Bauen Hirten in unserer Wirtschaft und Geschichte.* Leipzig: Quelle und Meyer.
HAILEY, W. M.
1957 (orig. 1938) *An African Survey: A Study of Problems Arising in Africa South of the Sahara.* London: Oxford University Press.
HAINES, C. G. (ed.)
1955 *Africa Today.* Baltimore: The Johns Hopkins Press.
HALL, E. T.
1961 (orig. 1959) *The Silent Language.* New York: Fawcett.
1966 *The Hidden Dimension.* Garden City, N.Y.: Doubleday.
1968 "Proxemics." *Current Anthropology* 9:83–95.
HALLOWELL, A. I.
1946 "Some Psychological Characteristics of the Northeastern Indians." F. Johnson, ed., *Man in Northeastern North America.* Papers of the R. S. Peabody Foundation for Archaeology, 3, 195–225.
1949 "The Size of Algonkian Hunting Territories: A Function of Ecological Adjustment." *American Anthropologist* 51:35–45.
1950 "Personality Structure and the Evolution of Man." *American Anthropologist* 52:159–173.
1954 "Psychology and Anthropology." J. Gillin et al., eds., *For a Science of Social Man: Convergences in Anthropology, Psychology, and Sociology.* New York: Macmillan, 160–226.
1959 "Behavioral Evolution and the Emergence of the Self." B. J. Meggers, ed.,

Evolution and Anthropology: A Centennial Appraisal. Washington, D.C.: Anthropological Society of Washington, 36–60.

1960   "Self, Society, and Culture in Phylogenetic Perspective." S. Tax, ed., *The Evolution of Man.* Chicago: University of Chicago Press, 2:309–372.

1961   "The Protocultural Foundations of Human Adaptation." Washburn 1961:236–255.

1967   (orig. 1955) *Culture and Experience.* New York: Schocken.

1967a   (orig. 1940) "Aggression in Saulteaux Society." Hallowell 1967: 277–290.

1967b   (orig. 1941) "The Social Function of Anxiety in a Primitive Society." Hallowell 1967: 266–276.

1967c   (orig. 1950) "Values, Acculturation, and Mental Health." Hallowell 1967:358–366.

1967d   (orig. 1951) "Acculturation and the Personality of the Ojibwa." Hallowell 1967:345–357.

HAMMEL, E. A.

1969   *Power in Ica: The Structural History of a Peruvian Community.* Boston: Little, Brown.

HAMMEL, E. and W. SIMMONS (eds.)

1970   *Man Makes Sense: A Reader in Modern Cultural Anthropology.* Boston: Little, Brown.

HAMMER, M.

1966   "Some Comments on Formal Analysis of Grammatical and Semantic Systems." *American Anthropologist* 68:362–373.

HARDING, T. G.

1964   "Morgan and Materialism: A Reply to Professor Opler." *Current Anthropology* 5:109.

HARING, D. (ed.)

1948   *Personal Character and Cultural Milieu.* Ann Arbor, Mich.: Edwards Brothers, Inc.

HARRIS, M.

1966   "The Cultural Ecology of India's Sacred Cattle." *Current Anthropology* 7:51–66.

1968   *The Rise of Anthropological Theory, A History of Theories of Culture.* New York: Crowell.

HARRISON, H. S.

1930   "Opportunism and the Factors of Invention." *American Anthropologist* 32:106–125.

HARTLAND, E. S.

1909–1910   *Primitive Paternity. The Myth of Supernatural Birth in Relation to the History of the Family.* (2 vols.) Publications of the Folk-Lore Society, Vols. 65 and 67. London: David Nutt.

HATT, G.

1914   "Moccasins and Their Relation to Arctic Footwear." American Anthropological Association, Vol. 3, No. 2.

1916   "Moccasins and Their Relation to Arctic Footwear." American Anthropological Association, Memoir 3, 149–250.

1934   "North American and Eurasian Culture Connections." *Fifth Pacific Science Congress* 4:2755–2765. Toronto: University of Toronto Press.

HAURY, E. W.

1962   "The Greater American Southwest." Braidwood and Willey 1962:106–131.

HEINE-GELDERN, R.

1959   "Representation of the Asiatic Tiger in the Art of the Chavin Culture: A Proof of Early Contacts Between China and Peru." *Actas del 33rd Congreso International de Americanistas,* San José, Costa Rica, 1958, 321–326.

1964   "One Hundred Years of Ethnological Theory in the German-Speaking Countries: Some Milestones." *Current Anthropology* 5:407–418, with commentary by Paul Leser, 416–417.

HEINE-GELDERN, R. and G. ECKHOLM

1951   "Significant Parallels in the Symbolic Arts of Southern Asia and Middle America." S. Tax, ed., *Selected Papers of the XXIXth International Congress of Ameri-*

canists, The Civilizations of Ancient America. Chicago: University of Chicago Press, 299–309.

HEIZER, R. F. (ed.)

1962 *Man's Discovery of His Past: Literary Landmarks in Archaeology.* Englewood Cliffs, N.J.: Prentice-Hall.

HELM, J. (ed.)

1966 *Pioneers of American Anthropology.* American Ethnological Society, Monograph 43. Seattle: University of Washington Press.

HENRY, J.

1959 "Culture, Personality and Evolution." *American Anthropologist* 61:221–226.

1960 "A Cross-Cultural Outline of Education." *Current Anthropology* 1:267–305.

1963 *Culture Against Man.* New York: Random House.

HENRY, J. and z.

1944 "Doll Play of Pilagá Indian Children." American Orthopsychiatric Association Research Monographs No. 4. (Abridged in Kluckhohn, Murray, and Schneider 1953: 292–307.)

HENRY, P.

1955 "The European Heritage: Approaches to African Development." Haines 1955: 119–141.

HENRY, W. E.

1947 "The Thematic Apperception Technique in the Study of Culture-Personality Relations." *Genetic Psychology Monographs* 35:3–135.

HERDER, J.

1772 *Abhandlung über den Ursprung der Sprache.* Berlin: Voss.

1952 (orig. 1784–1791) *Zur Philosophie der Geschichte: Eine Auswahl in Zwei Bänden.* (Selection, 2 vols.) Berlin: Aufbau-Verlag.

HERODOTUS

1921–1938 *Herodotus, with an English Translation by A. D. Godley.* (4 vols.) Cambridge, Mass.: Harvard University Press.

1942 *The Persian Wars,* G. Rawlinson, trans. New York: Random House.

HERSKOVITS, M. J.

1934 *Rebel Destiny: Among the Bush Negroes of Dutch Guiana.* New York: Whittlesey.

1938a *Acculturation. The Study of Culture Contact.* Locust Valley, N.Y.: J. J. Augustin, Inc.

1938b *Dahomey, an Ancient West African Kingdom.* (2 vols.) Locust Valley, N.Y.: J. J. Augustin, Inc.

1940 *The Economic Life of Primitive Peoples.* New York: Knopf.

1941 *The Myth of the Negro Past.* New York: Harper & Row.

1948 *Man and His Works: The Science of Cultural Anthropology.* New York: Knopf.

1952 *Economic Anthropology.* New York: Knopf.

1953 *Franz Boas: The Science of Man in the Making.* New York: Scribner.

HEYERDAHL, T.

1953 *American Indians in the Pacific: The Theory Behind the Kon Tiki Expedition.* Skokie, Ill.: Rand McNally.

HICKERSON, H.

1962 "The Southwestern Chippewa: An Ethnohistorical Study." American Anthropological Association, Memoir 92.

1967a "Land Tenure of the Rainy Lake Chippewa at the Beginning of the 19th Century." *Smithsonian Contributions to Anthropology,* 2:41–63.

1967b Some Implications of the Theory of the Particularity, or 'Atomism' of Northern Algonkians. *Current Anthropology* 8:313–328, with commentary and reply, 328–343.

HILGARD, E. R.

1956 *Theories of Learning.* New York: Appleton.

HIPPOCRATES

1962 *Hippocrates,* W. H. S. Jones, trans. (4 vols.) Cambridge, Mass.: Harvard University Press.

HOARE, SIR R. C.
1812–1821 (orig. 1810) *The Ancient History of . . . Wiltshire.* (2 vols.) London: W. Miller.

HOBBES, T.
1958 (orig. 1651) *Leviathan.* New York: Liberal Arts Press.

HOBHOUSE, L. T.
1925 (orig. 1906) *Morals in Evolution: A Study in Comparative Ethics.* New York: Holt, Rinehart and Winston, Inc.

HOBHOUSE, L. T., G. D. WHEELER, and M. GINSBERG
1965 (orig. 1915) *The Material Culture and Social Institutions of the Simpler Peoples: An Essay in Correlation.* New York: Humanities Press.

HODGEN, M. T.
1950 "Similarities and Dated Distributions." *American Anthropologist* 52:445–467.
1964 *Early Anthropology in the Sixteenth and Seventeenth Centuries.* Chicago: University of Chicago Press.

HOEBEL, E. A.
1940 "The Political Organization and Law-Ways of the Comanche Indians." American Anthropological Association, Memoir 54.
1954 *The Law of Primitive Man: A Study in Comparative Legal Dynamics.* Cambridge, Mass.: Harvard University Press.

HOFSTADTER, R.
1964 (orig. 1944) *Social Darwinism in American Thought.* Boston: Beacon Press.

HOGBIN, H. I.
1931 "Education at Ontong-Java." *American Anthropologist* 33:601–614.
1934 *Law and Order in Polynesia: A Study of Primitive Legal Institutions.* London: Christophers.
1938–1939 "Tillage and Collection: A New Guinea Economy." *Oceania* 9:127–151, 286–325.

HOIJER, H.
1954 (ed.) "Language in Culture." American Anthropological Association, Memoir 79.
1954a "The Sapir-Whorf Hypothesis." Hoijer 1954:92–105.

HOLBACH, BARON D'
1853 (orig. 1770) *The System of Nature,* H. Robinson, trans. Boston: J. P. Mendum.

HOLMBERG, A. R. et al.
1960 "Changing Community Attitudes and Values in Peru: A Case Study in Change." R. N. Adams et al., eds., *Social Change in Latin America Today: Its Implications for United States Policy.* New York: Random House, 63–107.

HOLMES, W. H.
1915 "Areas of American Culture Characterization Tentatively Outlined as an Aid to the Study of Antiquities." *Anthropology in North America,* with F. Boas and others. New York: G. E. Stechert, 42–75.

HOMANS, G. C.
1941 "Anxiety and Ritual: The Theories of Malinowski and Radcliffe-Brown." *American Anthropologist* 43:164–172.

HOMANS, G. C., and D. M. SCHNEIDER
1955 *Marriage, Authority, and Final Causes: A Study of Unilateral Cross-Cousin Marriage.* New York: Free Press.

HONIGMANN, J. J.
1949 *Culture and Ethos of Kaska Society.* New Haven, Conn.: Yale University Press.
1954 *The Kaska Indians: An Ethnographic Reconstruction.* New Haven, Conn.: Yale University Press.
1973 (ed.) *Handbook of Social and Cultural Anthropology.* Skokie, Ill.: Rand McNally.

HOOK, S.
1953 "Dialectic in Society and History." H. Feigl and M. Brodbeck, eds., *Readings in the Philosophy of Science.* New York: Appleton, 701–713.

HORR, D. A. (ed.)
1973–1974 *American Indian Ethnohistory.* New York: Garland Publishing, Inc.

HOSE, C., and W. MC DOUGALL
1912 *The Pagan Tribes of Borneo: A Description of Their Physical, Moral and Intellectual Condition with Some Discussion of Their Ethnic Relations.* (2 vols.) London: Macmillan.

HOWARD, A.
1963 "Land, Activity Systems, and Decision-Making Models in Rotuma." *Ethnology* 2:407–440.

HOWELL, F. C. and F. BOURLIÈRE (eds.)
1963 *African Ecology and Human Evolution.* Viking Fund Publications in Anthropology, No. 36. New York: Wenner-Gren Foundation for Anthropological Research.

HOWITT, A. W. and L. FISON
1904 *Native Tribes of Southeast Australia.* London: Macmillan.

HRDLIČKA, A.
1930 *The Skeletal Remains of Early Man.* Washington, D.C.: Lord Baltimore Press for the Smithsonian Institution.

HSU, F.
1959 "Structure, Function, Content, and Process." *American Anthropologist* 61:790–805.
1961 (ed.) *Psychological Anthropology: Approaches to Culture and Personality.* Homewood, Ill.: The Dorsey Press.

HUBERT, H. and M. MAUSS
1964 (orig. 1899) *Sacrifice: Its Nature and Function,* W. D. Halls, trans. Chicago: University of Chicago Press.

HUDSON, C. M.
1970 *The Catawba Nation.* Athens: University of Georgia Press.

HUDSON, E. H.
1965 "Treponematosis and Man's Social Evolution." *American Anthropologist* 67: 885–901.

HUEBNER, R.
1891–1893 *Historical Sources of the Frankish Period.* (2 vols.) Weimar: H. Bohlau.
1918 *A History of German Private Law.* Boston: Little, Brown.

HULTKRANTZ, A.
1968 "The Aims of Anthropology: A Scandinavian Point of View." *Current Anthropology* 9: 289–310.

HUMBOLDT, A. F. VON
1814–1829 *Personal Narrative of Travels to the Equinoctial Regions of the New Continent During the Years 1799–1804,* H. M. Williams, trans. (9 vols.) London: Longman, Hurst, Rees, Orme, and Brown.

HUME, D.
1854 *The Philosophical Works of David Hume.* (4 vols.) Boston: Little, Brown.

HUNT, G. T.
1940 *The Wars of the Iroquois: A Study in Intertribal Trade Relations.* Madison: University of Wisconsin Press.

HUNTINGTON, E.
1907 *The Pulse of Asia: A Journey in Central Asia Illustrating the Geographic Basis of History.* Boston: Houghton Mifflin.

HUTTON, J.
1788 (orig. 1785) Theory of the Earth, or an Investigation of the Laws Observable in the Composition, Dissolution, and Restoration of Land Upon the Globe." *Transactions of the Royal Society of Edinburgh* 1 (Part 2): 209–304.

HUXLEY, T. H.
1896 *Evolution and Ethics and Other Essays.* New York: Appleton.
1899 (orig. 1863) *Man's Place in Nature and Other Anthropological Essays.* New York: Appleton.

HYMES, D.
1974 (ed.) *Reinventing Anthropology.* New York: Random House.
1974a "Introduction: The Use of Anthropology: Critical, Political, Personal." Hymes 1974:3–79.

INTERNATIONAL INSTITUTE OF AFRICAN LANGUAGES AND CULTURES
1932 "A Five-Year Plan of Research." *Africa* 5:1–14.

IZIKOWITZ, K. G., C.-A. MOBERG, and A. ESKERÖD
1959   "Anthropology in Sweden." *American Anthropologist* 61:669–676.

JAMES, B.
1954   "Some Critical Observations Concerning Analyses of Chippewa 'Atomism' and Chippewa Personality." *American Anthropologist* 56:283–286.
1961   "Socio-Psychological Dimensions of Ojibwa Acculturation." *American Anthropologist* 63:721–746.
1970   "Continuity and Emergence in Indian Poverty Culture." *Current Anthropology* 11:435–452.

JANOWITZ, M.
1963   "Anthropology Among the Disciplines: Anthropology and the Social Sciences." *Current Anthropology* 4:149–154.

JAY, P. C. (ed.)
1968   *Primates: Studies in Adaptation and Variability.* New York: Holt, Rinehart and Winston, Inc.

JENKS, A.
1917   "The 'Half-Breed' Ascendant." American Sociological Society, Publication 12, 101–107.

JENNESS, D.
1936   "The Ojibwa Indians of Parry Island, Their Social and Religious Life." National Museum of Canada, Ottawa, Bulletin 78.

JENSEN, A. E.
1963   (orig. 1951) *Myth and Cult Among Primitive Peoples,* M. T. Choldin and W. Weissleder, trans. Chicago: University of Chicago Press.

JESPERSEN, O.
1928   (orig. 1922) *Language: Its Nature, Development, and Origin.* New York: Holt, Rinehart and Winston, Inc.

JEVONS, F. B.
1927   (orig. 1890) *An Introduction to the History of Religion.* London: Methuen.

JONES, P.
1861   *History of the Ojibway Indians.* London: A. W. Bennett.

JOSEPH, A., R. SPICER, and J. CHESKY
1949   *The Desert People. Chicago:* University of Chicago Press.

JUNG, C. G.
1916   *The Psychology of the Unconscious,* B. M. Hinkle, trans. New York: Moffat, Yard.

KAMES, LORD (H. HOME)
1761   (orig. 1757) *Historical Law Tracts.* Edinburgh: A Kincaid and J. Bell.
1778   (orig. 1774) *Sketches of the History of Man.* (4 vols.) London: W. Strahan and T. Cadell.
1779   (orig. 1774) *Sketches of the History of Man.* (2 vols.) Dublin: J. Williams.

KANT, I.
1939   *Perpetual Peace.* Ed. with Introduction by N. M. Butler. New York: Columbia University Press.

KAPLAN, B.
1954   *A Study of Rorschach Responses in Four Cultures.* Cambridge, Mass.: Harvard University Press.
1961   "Cross-Cultural Use of Projective Techniques." Hsu 1961:235–254.

KAPLAN, D.
1974   "The Anthropology of 'Authenticity'; Everyman His Own Anthropologist: An Essay-Review." *American Anthropologist* 76: 824–839.

KAPLAN, D. and B. SALER
1966   "Foster's Image of Limited Good: An Example of Anthropological Explanation." *American Anthropologist* 68:202–206.

KAPPLER, C. J.
1904   *Indian Affairs: Laws and Treaties.* (2 vols.) Washington: Government Printing Office.

KARDINER, A.
1939   *The Individual and His Society.* New York: Columbia University Press.

KARDINER, A. and L. OVESEY.
1951   *The Mark of Oppression.* New York: Norton.
KAY, P.
1970   "Some Theoretical Implications of Ethnographic Semantics." A. Fischer, ed., *Current Directions in Anthropology, A Special Issue.* American Anthropological Association, Bulletin 3, 19–31.
KEESING, F. M.
1941   *The South Seas in the Modern World.* New York: John Day.
1962   "Aftermath of Renaissance: Re-Study of a Maori Tribe." *Human Organization* 21:3–9.
KEESING, R. M.
1967   "Statistical Models and Decision Models of Social Structure: A Kwaio Case." *Ethnology* 6:1–16.
KELLER, A. G.
1931   (orig. 1915) *Societal Evolution: A Study of the Evolutionary Basis of the Science of Society.* New York: Macmillan.
KENNARD, E. and G. MACGREGOR
1953   *Applied Anthropology in Government: United States.* Kroeber 1953:832–840.
KENNEDY, J. G.
1966   " 'Peasant Society and the Image of Limited Good': A Critique." *American Anthropologist* 68:1212–1225.
1967   "Nubian Zar Ceremonies as Psychotherapy." *Human Organization* 26:185–194.
1973   *Cultural Psychiatry.* Honigmann 1973:1119–1198.
KHALDŪN, I.
1950   *An Arab Philosophy of History: Selections from the Prolegomena of Ibn Khaldūn of Tunis,* C. Issawi, trans. London: J. Murray.
1958   *The Muqaddimah; An Introduction to History,* F. Rosenthal, trans. New York: Pantheon.
KIDD, B.
1920   (orig. 1894) *Social Evolution.* New York: Putnam.
KIMBALL, S. T.
1955   "Problems of Studying American Culture." *American Anthropologist* 57:1131–1142.
KING, A. R.
1967   *The School at Mopass: A Problem of Identity.* New York: Holt, Rinehart and Winston, Inc.
KLASS, M.
1961   *East Indians in Trinidad: A Study of Cultural Persistence.* New York: Columbia University Press.
KLEMM, G.
1843–1851   *Allgemein Kultur-Geschichte der Menschheit.* (7 vols.) Leipzig: Teuber.
1854–1855   *Allgemeine Kulturwissenschaft. Die Materiellen Grundlagen menschlicher Cultur.* (2 vols.) Leipzig: Romberg.
KLUCKHOHN, C.
1941   "Patterning as Exemplified in Navaho Culture." L. Spier, ed., *Language, Culture, and Personality.* Menasha, Wisc.: Sapir Memorial Publication Fund.
1943   "Covert Culture and Administrative Problems." *American Anthropologist* 45:213–227.
1945   "Commentary" to papers in L. Bryson, L. Finkelstein, and R. MacIver, eds., *Approaches to National Unity.* New York: Harper & Row, 628–634.
1949a   *Mirror for Man: The Relation of Anthropology to Modern Life.* New York: McGraw-Hill.
1949b   "The Philosophy of the Navaho Indians." Northrop 1949:353–383.
1951   Introduction. Vogt 1951.
1952   "Values and Value Orientations in the Theory of Action." Parsons and Shils 1952:388–433.
1953   "Universal Categories of Culture." Kroeber 1953:507–523.
1954   Foreword. Kaplan 1954:v.
1962a   (orig. 1946) "Personality Formation Among the Navaho Indians." R. Kluckhohn,

ed., *Culture and Behavior: The Collected Essays of Clyde Kluckhohn.* New York: Free Press, 177–181.

1962b   (orig. 1951) "Some Notes on Navaho Dreams." R. Kluckhohn, ed., *Culture and Behavior. The Collected Essays of Clyde Kluckhohn.* New York: Free Press, 350–363.

1967   (orig. 1944) *Navaho Witchcraft.* Boston: Beacon Press.

KLUCKHOHN, C. and W. H. KELLY
1945   "The Concept of Culture." Linton 1945b: 78–106.

KLUCKHOHN, C. and D. LEIGHTON
1962   (orig. 1946) *The Navaho.* Garden City, N.Y.: Doubleday.

KLUCKHOHN, C. and O. H. MOWRER
1944   "Culture and Personality. A Conceptual Scheme." *American Anthropologist* 46: 1–29.

KLUCKHOHN, C. and H. MURRAY
1948   *Personality in Nature, Society, and Culture.* New York: Knopf.

KLUCKHOHN, C., H. MURRAY and D. SCHNEIDER (eds.)
1953   *Personality in Nature, Society, and Culture.* New York: Knopf.

KLUCKHOHN, F. R. and F. STRODTBECK (eds.)
1961   *Variations in Value Orientations.* New York: Harper & Row.

KÖBBEN, A. J. F.
1967   "Why Exceptions? The Logic of Cross-Cultural Analysis." *Current Anthropology* 8:3–34.

KOFFKA, K.
1931   "Gestalt." *Encyclopedia of the Social Sciences.* New York: Macmillan, 6:642–646.

KOHLER, J.
1918   *Grundlagen des Völkerrechts: Vergangenheit, Gegenwart, Zukunft.* Stuttgart: F. Enke.

KOHLER, W.
1959   (orig. 1947) *Gestalt Psychology: An Introduction to New Concepts in Modern Psychology.* New York: New American Library.

KOLLMORGEN, W. M.
1943   "The Agricultural Stability of the Old-Order Amish and the Old-Order Mennonites of Lancaster County, Pa." *American Journal of Sociology* 49:233–242.

KOPPERS, W.
1924   *Unter Feuerland—Indianern.* Stuttgart: Strecker und Schröder.

1959   "Grundsätzliches und Geschichtliches zur ethnologischen Kulturkreislehre." *Beiträge Österreichs zur Erforschung der Vergangenheit und Kulturgeschichte der Menschheit.* Horn, Austria: F. Berger, 110–126.

KORTMULDER, K.
1968   "An Ethological Theory of the Incest Taboo and Exogamy with Special Reference to the Views of Claude Lévi-Strauss." *Current Anthropology* 9:437–449.

KOVALEVSKI, M.
1890   *Tableau des origines et de l'évolution de la famille et de la propriété.* Stockholm.

1891   *Modern Customs and Ancient Laws of Russia.* London: D. Nutt.

KRADER, L.
1956   "A Nativistic Movement in Western Siberia." *American Anthropologist* 58:282–292.

1966   (ed.) *Anthropology and Early Law.* London: Basic Books.

KRAMER, S. N.
1959   *History Begins at Sumer.* Garden City, N.Y.: Doubleday.

KRIEGER, A. D.
1944   The Typological Concept." *American Antiquity* 9:271–288.

KROEBER, A. L.
1915   "Eighteen Professions." *American Anthropologist* 17:283–288.

1920   Review of R. H. Lowie, *Primitive Society. American Anthropologist* 22:377–381.

1923   *Anthropology.* New York: Harcourt.

1925   *Handbook of the Indians of California.* Bureau of American Ethnology, Bulletin 78. Washington: Government Printing Office.

1935 Review of R. Benedict, *Patterns of Culture. American Anthropologist* 37:689–690.
1939 *Cultural and Natural Areas of Native North America.* Berkeley: University of California Press.
1940 "Stimulus Diffusion." *American Anthropologist* 42:1–20.
1948a *Anthropology.* New York: Harcourt.
1948b "White's View of Culture." *American Anthropologist* 50:405–415.
1952 *The Nature of Culture.* Chicago: University of Chicago Press.
1952a (orig. 1909) "Classificatory Systems of Relationship." Kroeber 1952:175–181.
1952b (orig. 1917) "The Superorganic." Kroeber 1952:22–51.
1952c (orig. 1935) "History and Science in Anthropology." Kroeber 1952:63–65.
1952d (orig. 1936) "So-called Social Science." Kroeber 1952:66–78.
1952e (orig. 1949) "The Concept of Culture in Science." Kroeber 1952:118–135.
1952f (orig. 1950) "Reality Culture and Value Culture." Kroeber 1952:152–166.
1953 (ed.) *Anthropology Today: An Encyclopedic Inventory.* Chicago: University of Chicago Press.
1956 "The Place of Boas in Anthropology." *American Anthropologist* 58:151–159.
1963 (orig. 1944) *Configurations of Culture Growth.* Berkeley: University of California Press.
KROEBER, A. L. and C. KLUCKHOHN
1963 (orig. 1952) *Culture: A Critical Review of Concepts and Definitions.* New York: Vintage Books.
KROEBER, A. L. et al.
1943 "Franz Boas, 1858–1942." American Anthropological Association, Memoir 61.
KROPOTKIN, P.
1902 *Mutual Aid.* London: Heinemann.
KUHN, T. S.
1962 *The Structure of Scientific Revolutions.* Chicago: University of Chicago Press.
KUPER, H.
1947 *An African Aristocracy.* London: Oxford University Press.
LA BARRE, W.
1938 "The Peyote Cult." Yale University Publications in Anthropology, No. 19.
1954 *The Human Animal.* Chicago: University of Chicago Press.
LAFITAU, J.
1774 (orig. 1724) *Moeurs des sauvages amériquains comparées aux moeurs des premiers temps.* (4 vols.) Paris: Saugrain l'Aine.
LAMARCK, J. B.
1914 (orig. 1809) *Zoological Philosophy: An Exposition with Regard to the Natural History of Animals.* Trans. with Introduction by Hugh Elliot. London: Macmillan.
1801 *Système des Animaux sans Vertèbres.* Paris: Deterville.
LANDA, D. DE
1941 (orig. 1565) *Landa's Relación de las Cosas de Yucatan,"* A. M. Tozzer, ed. Cambridge, Mass.: Harvard University Press.
LANDES, R.
1937 *Ojibwa Sociology.* New York: Columbia University Press.
1938 *The Ojibwa Woman.* New York: Columbia University Press.
LANDGRAF, J.
1954 *Land Use in the Ramah Area of New Mexico: An Anthropological Approach to Areal Study.* Cambridge, Mass.: Harvard University Press.
LANG, A.
1887 *Myth, Ritual, and Religion.* (2 vols.) London: Longmans.
1898 *The Making of Religion.* London: Longmans.
1901 *Magic and Religion.* New York: McKay.
1903 *Social Origins.* London: Longmans.
1904 (orig. 1884) *Custom and Myth.* London: Longmans.
1905 *Secret of the Totem.* New York: McKay.
1907 "Edward Burnett Tylor." Balfour 1907:1–15.
1908 *The Origins of Religion and Other Essays.* London: Watts.
LANTIS, M.
1960 "Vernacular Culture." *American Anthropologist* 62:202–216.

LARTÉT, E. and H. CHRISTY
1865–1875   *Reliquiae aquitanicae; Being Contributions to the Archaeology and Palaeontology of Périgord and the Adjoining Provinces of Southern France*, T. R. Jones, ed. London: Williams and Norgate.

LASSWELL, H. D.
1936   *Politics: Who Gets What, When, How*. New York: McGraw-Hill.

LAUFER, B.
1938   (orig. 1929) *The American Plant Migration*. Chicago: Field Muesum of Natural History, Publication 418.

LAW, E.
1774   (orig. 1745) *Considerations on the Theory of Religion*. Cambridge: J. Archdeacon.

LAWRENCE, SIR W.
1819   (orig. 1816) *Lectures on Physiology, Zoology, and the Natural History of Man*. London: J. Callow.

LEACH, E. R.
1958   "Concerning Trobriand Clans and the Kinship Category 'Tabu.'" J. Goody, ed., *The Developmental Cycle in Domestic Groups*. Cambridge: Cambridge University Press.
1960   "The Sinhalese of the Dry Zone of Northern Ceylon." Murdock 1960:116–126.
1961   *Pul Eliya. A Village in Ceylon*. Cambridge: Cambridge University Press.

LEACOCK, E.
1954   "The Montagnais 'Hunting Territory' and the Fur Trade." American Anthropological Association, Memoir 78.
1964   "Morgan and Materialism: A Reply to Professor Opler." *Current Anthropology* 5:109–110.

LEACOCK, S.
1954   "The Ethnological Theory of Marcel Mauss." *American Anthropologist* 56:58–73.

LECLAIR, E. JR. and H. K. SCHNEIDER (eds.)
1968   *Economic Anthropology: Readings in Theory and Analysis*. New York: Holt, Rinehart and Winston, Inc.

LEE, R.
1969   "!Kung Bushman Subsistence: An Input-Output Analysis." Vayda 1969:47–79.

LEEDS, A.
1961   "The Port-of-Trade in Pre-European India as an Ecological Evolutionary Type." V. Garfield, ed., *Symposium on Patterns of Land Utilization and Other Papers, Proceedings of the American Ethnological Society*. Seattle: University of Washington Press, 26–48.
1969   "Ecological Determinants of Chieftainship Among the Yaruro Indians of Venezuela." Vayda 1969:377–394.

LEHMANN, W. C.
1930   *Adam Ferguson and the Beginnings of Modern Sociology*. New York: Columbia University Press.

LEIGHTON, A.
1945   *The Governing of Men*. Princeton, N.J.: Princeton University Press.

LEIGHTON, A. and D.
1949   *Gregorio, The Hand-Trembler: A Psychobiological Personality Study of a Navaho Indian*. Cambridge, Mass.: Harvard University Press.

LEIGHTON, A. et al.
1963   *Psychiatric Disorder Among the Yoruba*. Ithaca, N.Y.: Cornell University Press.

LEIGHTON, D. and J. ADAIR
1966   *People of the Middle Place*. New Haven, Conn.: Human Relations Area Files.

LEIGHTON, D. and C. KLUCKHOHN
1962   (orig. 1947) *Children of the People*. Garden City, N.Y.: Doubleday.

LEITH-ROSS, S.
1956   "The Rise of a New Elite Amongst the Women of Nigeria." *International Social Science Bulletin* 8:481–488.

LENIN, V. I.
1913   "The Three Sources and Three Constituent Parts of Marxism." M. Eastman, ed.,

1932, *Capital, The Communist Manifesto, and Other Writings by Karl Marx*. New York: Modern Library, xxi–xxvi.

LESER, P.
1964 "Commentary" on article by R. Heine-Geldern. *Current Anthropology* 5:416–417.

LESSER, A.
1961 "Social Fields and the Evolution of Society." *Southwestern Journal of Anthropology* 17:40–48.

LETOURNEAU, C.
1881 *Sociology Based Upon Ethnography*, H. M. Trollope, trans. London: Chapman and Hall.

LÉVI-STRAUSS, C.
1945 "French Sociology." G. Gurvitch and W. E. Moore, eds., *Twentieth Century Sociology*. New York: Philosophical Library 503–537.
1963a (orig. 1958) *Structural Anthropology*, C. Jacobson and B. Schoepf, trans. New York: Basic Books.
1963aa (orig. 1945) "Structural Analysis in Linguistics and in Anthropology." Lévi-Strauss 1963a:31–54.
1963ab (orig. 1949) "Introduction: History and Ethnology." Lévi-Strauss 1963a:1–27.
1963ac (orig. 1953) "Social Structure." Lévi-Strauss 1963a:277–323.
1963ad (orig. 1953) Linguistics and Anthropology." Lévi-Strauss 1963a:67–80.
1963ae (orig. 1955) "The Structural Study of Myth." Lévi-Strauss 1963a:206–231.
1963af (orig. 1956) "Do Dual Organizations Exist?" Lévi-Strauss 1963a:132–163.
1963ag (orig. 1956) "Structure and Dialectics." Lévi-Strauss 1963a:232–241.
1963b *Totemism*, R. Needham, trans. Boston: Beacon Press.
1969 (orig. 1949) *The Elementary Structures of Kinship*. London: Eyre & Spottiswoode.

LEVY, D.
1939 "Sibling Rivalry Studies in Children of Primitive Groups." *American Journal of Orthopsychiatry* 9:205–214.

LEVY, M. J. JR. and L. FALLERS
1959 "The Family: Some Comparative Considerations.." *American Anthropologist* 61:647–651.

LÉVY-BRUHL, L.
1903 (orig. 1900) *The Philosophy of Auguste Comte*, F. Harrison, trans. New York: Putnam.
1910 *Les Fonctions mentales dans les sociétés inférieures*. Paris: F. Alcan.
1922 *Primitive Mythology: The Mythic World of the Australians and Papuans*. Paris: F. Alcan.
1931 *The Supernatural and Nature in Primitive Mentality*. Paris: F. Alcan.
1938 *The Mystic Experience and Symbolization Among Primitives*. Paris: F. Alcan.
1965 (orig. 1927) *The "Soul" of the Primitive*, L. A. Clare, trans. London: G. Allen.
1966 (orig. 1923) *Primitive Mentality*, L. A. Clare, trans. Boston: Beacon Press.

LEWIS, O.
1951 *Life in a Mexican Village: Tepoztlán Restudied*. Urbana: University of Illinois Press.
1959 *Five Families*. New York: Basic Books.
1961 *The Children of Sánchez: Autobiography of a Mexican Family*. New York: Random House.
1966a "The Culture of Poverty." *Scientific American* 215(4):19–25.
1966b *La Vida*. New York: Random House.
1968 *A Study of Slum Culture: Backgrounds for La Vida*. New York: Random House.

LEY, W.
1968 *Dawn of Zoology*. Englewood Cliffs, N.J.: Prentice-Hall.

LIEBAN, R. W.
1960 "Sorcery, Illness and Social Control in a Philippine Municipality." *Southwestern Journal of Anthropology* 16:127–143.
1973 "Medical Anthropology." Honigmann 1973:1031–1072.

LINNAEUS (C. VON LINNÉ)
1735 *Systema naturae, sive Regna tria naturae systematice proposita per classes, ordines, genera & species.* Lugduni Batarorum, apud T. Haak.

LINTON, R.
1936 *The Study of Man.* New York: Appleton.
1939 Foreword. Kardiner 1939:v–xviii.
1940 (ed.) *Acculturation in Seven American Indian Tribes.* New York: Appleton.
1943 "Nativistic Movements." *American Anthropologist* 45: 230–240.
1945a *The Cultural Background of Personality.* New York: Appleton.
1945b (ed.) *The Science of Man in the World Crisis.* New York: Columbia University Press.

LIPPERT, J.
1886–1887 *Kulturgeschichte der Menschheit in ihrem organischen Aufbau.* Stuttgart: F. Enke.
1931 (orig. 1886–1887) *The Evolution of Culture,* G. P. Murdock, trans. New York: Macmillan.

LITTLE, K.
1951 *The Mende of Sierra Léone.* London: Routledge.
1957 "The Role of Voluntary Associations in West African Urbanization." *American Anthropologist* 59:579–596.
1962 "Some Traditionally Based Forms of Mutual Aid in West African Urbanization." *Ethnology* 1:197–211.

LIVINGSTONE, F. B.
1958 "Anthropological Implications of Sickle Cell Gene Distribution in West Africa." *American Anthropologist* 60:533–562.
1969 "Genetics, Ecology and the Origins of Incest and Exogamy." *Current Anthropology* 10:45–49.

LLEWELYN, K. N. and E. A. HOEBEL
1941 *The Cheyenne Way: Conflict and Case Law in Primitive Jurisprudence.* Norman: University of Oklahoma Press.

LLOYD, P. C.
1966 The *New Elites of Tropical Africa.* London: Oxford University Press.

LOCKE, J.
1947 (orig. 1690) *Two Treatises of Government.* New York: Hafner.

LOMMEL, A.
1953 *Der "Cargo-Kult" in Melanesien. Ein Beitrag zum Problem der "Europaisierung" der Primitiven.* Zeitschrift für Ethnologie 78:17–63.

LOUNSBURY, F.
1964 "A Formal Account of Crow- and Omaha-type Kinship Terminologies." Goodenough 1964:351–387.

LOVEJOY, A. O.
1923 "The Supposed Primitivism of Rousseau's Discourse on Inequality." *Modern Philology* 21:165–186.
1933 "Monboddo and Rousseau." *Modern Philology* 30:275–296.
1942 *The Great Chain of Being. A Study of the History of an Idea.* Cambridge, Mass.: Harvard University Press.

LOWIE, R. H.
1920 *Primitive Society.* New York: Boni and Liveright.
1924 *Primitive Religion.* New York: Boni and Liveright.
1929 (orig. 1917) *Culture and Ethnology.* New York: Peter Smith.
1936 "Cultural Anthropology: A Science." *American Journal of Sociology* 52:301–320.
1937 *The History of Ethnological Theory.* New York: Holt, Rinehart, and Winston, Inc.
1946 "Evolution in Cultural Anthropology: A Reply to Leslie White." *American Anthropologist* 48:223–233.
1947 *An Introduction to Cultural Anthropology.* New York: Holt, Rinehart and Winston, Inc.
1962 (orig. 1927) *The Origin of the State.* New York: Russell and Russell.

LUCRETIUS
1956 A. D. Winspear, *The Roman Poet of Science. Lucretius: De Rerum Natura.* New York: S. A. Russell.

LYELL, SIR C.

1830–1832 *The Principles of Geology. An Attempt To Explain the Former Changes of the Earth's Surface by Reference to Causes Now in Operation.* (2 vols.) London: J. Murray.

1863 *The Geological Evidences of the Antiquity of Man with Remarks on the Origin of Species by Variation.* London: J. Murray.

1877 *Principles of Geology or the Modern Changes of the Earth and Its Inhabitants Considered as Illustrative of Geology,* 11th ed. (2 vols.) New York: Appleton.

MACGREGOR, G.

1946 *Warriors without Weapons. A Study of the Society and Personality of the Pine Ridge Sioux.* Chicago: University of Chicago Press.

MACHIAVELLI, N.

1935 (orig. 1532) *The Prince,* L. Ricci, trans. London: Oxford University Press.

MAINE, SIR H.

1875 *Lectures on the Early History of Institutions.* New York: Henry Holt and Co.

1880 (orig. 1871) *Village-Communities in the East and West.* New York: Henry Holt and Co.

1883 *Dissertations on Early Law and Custom, Chiefly Selected from Lectures Delivered at Oxford.* New York: Henry Holt and Co.

1887 (orig. 1861) *Ancient Law: Its Connection with the Early History of Society and Its Relation to Modern Ideas.* London: J. Murray.

MAIR, L. P.

1957 *Studies in Applied Anthropology.* London School of Economics Monographs in Social Anthropology, No. 16. London: Athlone Press.

1965 (orig. 1934) *An African People in the Twentieth Century.* London: Routledge.

1969 *Anthropology and Social Change.* London School of Economics Monographs in Social Anthropology, No. 38. London: Athlone Press.

MALINOWSKI, B.

1923 "The Problem of Meaning in Primitive Languages." Ogden and Richards 1923: 451–510.

1926 *Crime and Custom in Savage Society.* London: Routledge.

1927a *The Father in Primitive Psychology.* New York: Norton.

1927b *Sex and Repression in Savage Society.* New York: Humanities Press.

1929 *The Sexual Life of Savages in North-Western Melanesia. An Ethnographic Account of Courtship, Marriage and Family Life Among the Natives of the Trobriand Islands, British New Guinea.* New York: Harcourt.

1931 "Culture." *Encyclopaedia of the Social Sciences.* New York: Macmillan, 4:621–645.

1935 *Coral Gardens and Their Magic. A Study of the Methods of Tilling the Soil and of Agricultural Rites in the Trobriand Islands.* (2 vols.) London: G. Allen.

1939 "The Group and the Individual in Functional Analysis. *American Journal of Sociology* 44: 938–964.

1944 *Freedom and Civilization.* New York: Roy Publisher.

1954 (orig. 1948) *Magic, Science and Religion.* Garden City, N.Y.: Doubleday.

1954a "Baloma: The Spirits of the Dead in the Trobriand Islands." Malinowski 1954: 149–274.

1954b "Magic, Science and Religion." Malinowski 1954: 17–148.

1960 (orig. 1944) *A Scientific Theory of Culture and Other Essays.* New York: Oxford University Press.

1961a (orig. 1922) *Argonauts of the Western Pacific. An Account of Native Enterprise and Adventure in the Archipelagoes of Melanesian New Guinea.* New York: Dutton.

1961b (orig. 1945) *The Dynamics of Culture Change: An Inquiry into Race Relations in Africa.* New Haven, Conn.: Yale University Press.

1963 (orig. 1913) *The Family Among the Australian Aborigines: A Sociological Study.* New York: Schocken Books.

1967 *A Diary in the Strict Sense of the Term,* N. Guterman, trans. New York: Harcourt.

MALTHUS, T.

1965 (orig. 1798) *First Essay on Population, 1798,* notes by J. Bonan. New York: A. M. Kelley.

MANDELBAUM, D. G. (ed.)

1949   *Selected Writings of Edward Sapir in Language, Culture and Personality.* Berkeley: University of California Press.

MANDELBAUM, D., G. LASKER, and E. ALBERT (eds.)

1963a   "The Teaching of Anthropology." American Anthropological Association, Memoir 94.

1963b   "Resources for the Teaching of Anthropology." American Anthropological Association, Memoir 95.

MANGELSDORF, P. C. and R. H. LISTER

1956   "Archaeological Evidence on the Evolution of Maize in Northwestern Mexico." *Botanical Museum Leaflets*, Harvard University, 17:151–178.

MANGIN, WILLIAM (ed.)

1970   *Peasants in Cities: Readings in the Anthropology of Urbanization.* Boston: Houghton Mifflin.

MAQUET, J. J.

1964   "Objectivity in Anthropology." *Current Anthropology* 5:47–55.

MARETT, R. R.

1909   (orig. 1900) *The Threshold of Religion.* London: Methuen.

1912   *Anthropology.* New York: Holt, Rinehart and Winston, Inc.

1920   *Psychology and Folklore.* London: Methuen.

1932   *Faith, Hope and Charity in Primitive Religion.* New York: Macmillan.

1933   *Sacraments of Simple Folk.* Oxford: Clarendon Press.

1935   *Head, Heart and Hands in Human Evolution.* London: Hutchinson.

MARRIS, P.

1960   "Slum Clearance and Family Life in Lagos." *Human Organization* 19:123–128.

MARSHALL, D. S.

1967   "General Anthropology: Strategy for a Human Science." *Current Anthropology* 8:61–66.

MARTI, O. A.

1929   *The Economic Causes of the Reformation in England.* New York: Macmillan.

MARX, K.

1904   (orig. 1859) *A Contribution to the Critique of Political Economy*, N. I. Stone, trans. New York: International Library Publishing Co.

1932   *Capital, The Communist Manifesto, and Other Writings by Karl Marx*, M. Eastman, ed. New York: Modern Library.

1934   (orig. 1867–1894) *Capital (A Critique of Political Economy).* E. and C. Paul, trans. (2 vols.) New York: Dutton.

1965   (orig. 1857–1858) *Pre-Capitalist Economic Formations*, J. Cohen, trans.; E. J. Hobsbawm, ed. New York: International Publishers.

1970   (orig. 1852) Letter to Weydemeyer. Selsam, D. Goldway, and Martel 1970:30–31.

MARX, K. and F. ENGELS

1968   *Selected Works.* London: Lawrence and Wishart.

1968a   (orig. 1848) *Manifesto of the Communist Party.* Marx and Engels 1968: 35–63.

MASON, O. T.

1884   *Basket-Work of the North American Aborigines.* Report of the U.S. National Museum. Washington: Government Printing Office, Part 2, 291–306.

1887   *Cradles of the American Aborigines.* Report of the U.S. National Museum. Washington: Government Printing Office, Part 3, 161–212.

1894a   *Primitive Travel and Transportation.* Report of the U.S. National Museum. Washington: Government Printing Office, Part 2, 237–593.

1894b   *Woman's Share in Primitive Culture.* New York: Appleton.

1895   *The Origins of Invention: The Study of Industry Among Primitive Peoples.* London: W. Scott.

1900   *Aboriginal American Harpoons.* Report of the U.S. National Museum. Washington: Government Printing Office, Part 2, 193–304.

MATHIASSEN, T.

1924   "Preliminary Report of the Fifth Thule Expedition." *Proceedings of the Twenty-First International Congress of Americanists*, Paris. 2:206–215.

1930   "The Question of the Origin of Eskimo Culture." *American Anthropologist* 32: 597–601.

MAUSS, M.
1954 (orig. 1925) *The Gift: Forms and Functions of Exchange in Archaic Society*, I. Cunnison, trans. London: Cohen and West.

MAUSS, M. and H. BEUCHAT
1906 "Essai sur les variations saisonnières des sociétés eskimos. Étude de mor- phologie sociale." *L'Année sociologique*, Paris, 9:39–132.

MAY, J. M.
1960 "The Ecology of Human Disease." *Annals of the New York Academy of Sci- ences* 84 (17):789–794.

MAYER, P.
1961 *Townsmen or Tribesmen: Conservatism and the Process of Urbanization in a South African City*. Cape Town: Oxford University Press.
1962 "Migrancy and the Study of Africans in Towns." *American Anthropologist* 64: 576–592.

MAYR, E.
1959 "Darwin and the Evolutionary Theory in Biology." B. Meggers, ed., *Evolution and Anthropology: A Centennial Appraisal*. Brooklyn, N.Y.: Theodore Gaus' Sons for the Anthropological Society of Washington, 1–10.

MC DOUGALL, W.
1914 *An Introduction to Social Psychology*. Boston: John W. Luce and Co.

MC GEE, W. J.
1895 "The Beginnings of Agriculture." *American Anthropologist* (old series) 8:350– 375.
1897 "The Beginning of Zooculture." *American Anthropologist* (old series) 10:215– 230.

MC KERN, W. C.
1939 "The Midwestern Taxonomic Method as an Aid to Archaeological Culture Study." *American Antiquity* 4:301–313.
1940 "Application of the Midwestern Taxonomic Method." *Archaeological Society of Delaware, Bulletin* (3):18–21.

MC LENNAN, J. F.
1865 *Primitive Marriage: An Inquiry into the Origin of the Form of Capture in Marriage Ceremonies*. Edinburgh: Black.
1869 "The Worship of Animals and Plants." *The Fortnightly Review* 6:407–427, 562– 582.
1870 "The Worship of Animals and Plants." *The Fortnightly Review* 7:194–216.
1885 *The Patriarchal Theory*, D. McLennan, ed. London: Macmillan.
1886 *Studies in Ancient History*, new ed. New York: Macmillan.
1896 *Studies in Ancient History*, D. McLennan and A. Platt, eds. New York: Macmillan.

MEAD, M.
1928 *Coming of Age in Samoa*. New York: Morrow.
1930 *Growing Up in New Guinea*. New York: Morrow.
1932 *The Changing Culture of an Indian Tribe*. New York: Columbia University Press.
1937a (ed.) *Cooperation and Competition Among Primitive Peoples*. New York: McGraw-Hill.
1937b "A Reply to a Review of 'Sex and Temperament in Three Primitive Societies.' " *American Anthropologist* 39:558–561.
1947 "On the Implications for Anthropology of the Gesell-Ilg Approach to Matura- tion." *American Anthropologist*, 49:69–77.
1950 (orig. 1935) *Sex and Temperament in Three Primitive Societies*. New York: New American Library.
1952 *Male and Female. A Study of the Sexes in a Changing World*. New York: Morrow.
1953 "National Character." Kroeber 1953:642–667.
1959 *An Anthropologist at Work. Writings of Ruth Benedict*. Boston: Houghton Mifflin.
1961 (orig. 1956) *New Lives for Old: Cultural Transformation—Manus*. New York: New American Library.

1970 *Culture and Commitment: A Study of the Generation Gap.* Garden City, N.Y.: Natural History Press.

MEEK, C. K.
1946 *Land Law and Custom in the Colonies.* New York: Oxford University Press.
1957 *Land Tenure and Land Administration in Nigeria and the Cameroons.* London: Her Majesty's Stationery Office.

MEGGERS, B.
1954 "Environmental Limitation on the Development of Culture." *American Anthropologist,* 56:801–824.

MEGGERS, B. J. and C. EVANS
1957 "Archeological Investigations at the Mouth of the Amazon." Smithsonian Institution, Bureau of American Ethnology, Bulletin, 167. Washington: Government Printing Office.

MEGGERS, B., C. EVANS, and E. ESTRADA
1965 "Early Formative Period of Coastal Ecuador. The Valdivia and Machalilla Phases." Smithsonian Institution, Smithsonian Contributions to Anthropology, Vol. 1. Washington: Government Printing Office.

MEIGS, J. A.
1950 (orig. 1857) "On the Cranial Characteristics of Man." E. Count, ed., *This Is Race.* New York: Henry Schuman, 90–92.

MEILLASSOUX, C.
1968 "Urbanization of an African Community: Voluntary Associations in Bamako." American Ethnological Society, Monograph 45. Seattle: University of Washington Press.

MEINERS, C.
1785 *Grundriss der Geschichte der Menschheit.* Lemgo: Im Verlage der Meyerschen Buchhandlung.

MENGHIN, O.
1931 *Die Weltgeschichte der Steinzeit.* Wien: A Schroll.

MERCIER, P.
1956 "Evolution of Senegalese Elites." *International Social Science Bulletin* 8:441–451.

MERIAM, L. *et al.*
1928 *The Problem of Indian Administration.* Baltimore: The John Hopkins Press.

MERTON, R. K.
1940 "Bureaucratic Structure and Personality." *Social Forces* 18:560–568.
1957 *Social Theory and Social Structure.* New York: Free Press.

MIDDLETON, J. (ed.)
1967 *Magic, Witchcraft, and Curing.* Garden City, N.Y.: Natural History Press.
1970 *From Child to Adult: Studies in the Anthropology of Education.* Garden City, N.Y.: Natural History Press.

MIDDLETON, J. and D. TAIT
1970 "The Lineage and the Lineage System." P. Bohannan and J. Middleton, eds., *Kinship and Social Organization.* Garden City, N.Y.: Natural History Press, 155–160.

MILLAR, J.
1806 (orig. 1771) *The Origin of the Distinction of Ranks: or, an Inquiry into the Circumstances Which Give Rise to Influence and Authority in the Different Members of Society.* Edinburgh: G. Caw for W. Blackwood.

MILLER, N. and J. DOLLARD
1941 *Social Learning and Imitation.* New Haven, Conn.: Yale University Press.

MILLS, C. W.
1956 *The Power Elite.* New York: Oxford University Press.

MINER, H.
1953 "The Primitive City of Timbuctoo." Memoirs of the American Philosophical Society, No. 32. Princeton, N.J., and Philadelphia.
1960 "Culture Change Under Pressure: A Hausa Case." *Human Organization* 19:164–167.

MINTURN, L. and J. HITCHCOCK
1963 "The Rājpūts of Khalapur, India." B. Whiting, ed., *Six Cultures, Studies of Child Rearing.* New York: Wiley, 207–361.

MITCHELL, J. C.
1956 "The Kalela Dance." Rhodes-Livingstone Paper 27. Manchester: Manchester University Press for the Rhodes-Livingstone Institute.
MOIR, J. R.
1919 *Pre-Paleolithic Man.* London: Simpkin, Marshall, Hamilton, Kent & Co.
MONBODDO, J. B.
1773 *Of the Origin and Progress of Language,* Vol. 1. Edinburgh: J. Balfour.
1774–1792 *Of the Origin and Progress of Language.* (6 vols.) Edinburgh: J. Balfour.
1779–1799 *Ancient Metaphysics: or, the Science of Universals.* (6 vols.; Vols. 4 and 5, *The History of Man.*) Edinburgh: J. Balfour.
MONTAGU, A. (M. F. ASHLEY-MONTAGU)
1950 *On Being Human.* New York: Henry Schuman.
MONTAIGNE
1946 (orig. 1580) *The Essays of Montaigne.* E. J. Trechmann, trans. New York: Modern Library.
MONTESQUIEU, C.
1900 (orig. 1748) *The Spirit of Laws.* T. Nugent, trans. (2 vols.) New York: The Colonial Press.
MOORE, J. W.
1968 "Social Class, Assimilation and Acculturation." American Ethnological Society, *Proceedings of the 1968 Annual Spring Meeting* 19–33.
MORGAN, J.
1909 *Les premières civilisations.* Paris: E. Leroux.
MORGAN, L. H.
1871 *Systems of Consanguinity and Affinity of the Human Family.* Smithsonian Instituition, Contributions to Knowledge, Vol. 17, article 2. Washington, D.C.: Government Printing Office.
1881 *Houses and House-Life of the American Aborigines.* Washington, D.C.: Government Printing Office.
1954 (orig. 1851) *League of the Ho-De-No-Sau-Nee or Iroquois.* (2 vols.) New Haven, Conn.: Human Relations Area Files.
1963 (orig. 1877) *Ancient Society,* E. Leacock, ed. New York: World Publishing Co.
1877 *Ancient Society.* New York: Henry Holt.
1964 *Ancient Society,* L. White, ed. Cambridge, Mass.: Harvard University Press.
MORRIS, C.
1900 *Man and His Ancestors: A Study in Evolution.* New York: Macmillan.
MORTILLET, G. DE
1839 *Crania Americana; or, A Comparative View of the Skulls of Various Aboriginal* ogie 1:432–442.
1900 (orig. 1883) *Le préhistorique; origine et antiquité de l'homme.* Paris: C. Reinwald.
MORTON, S.
1839 *Crania Americana; or, A Comparative View of the Skulls of Various Aboriginal Nations.* Philadelphia: J. Dobson.
MOSS, L. W. and S. CAPPANNARI
1962 "Estate and Class in a South Italian Hill Village." *American Anthropologist* 64:287–300.
MÜLLER, F. M.
1873 *Introduction to the Science of Religion.* London: Longmans.
MURDOCK, G. P.
1940 "The Cross-Cultural Survey." *American Sociological Review* 5:361–370.
1945 "The Common Denominator of Cultures. Lineton 1945b:123–142.
1947 "Bifurcate Merging, a Test of Five Theories." *American Anthropologist* 49: 56–68.
1949 *Social Structure.* New York: Macmillan.
1951 "British Social Anthropology." *American Anthropologist* 53: 465–473.
1954 "Sociology and Anthropology." J. Gillin, ed., *For a Science of Social Man. Convergences in Anthropology, Psychology, and Sociology.* New York: Macmillan, 14–31.
1957 "World Ethnographic Sample." *American Anthropologist* 59:664–687.

1959   *Africa, Its Peoples and Their Culture History.* New York: McGraw-Hill.
1960   (ed.) *Social Structure in Southeast Asia.* Viking Fund Publications in Anthropology, No. 29. New York: Wenner-Gren Foundation for Anthropological Research.
1960a   "Cognatic Forms of Social Organization." Murdock 1960:1–14.
1967   "Ethnographic Atlas: A Summary." *Ethnology* 6:109–236.
1971   "Anthropology's Mythology." The Huxley Memorial Lecture, 1971. *Proceedings of the Royal Anthropological Institute of Great Britain and Ireland for 1971* 17–24.
MURDOCK, G. P. and D. R. WHITE
1969   "Standard Cross-Cultural Sample." *Ethnology* 7:329–369.
MURRAY, H. A. and C. KLUCKHOHN
1953   "Outline of a Conception of Personality." Kluckhohn, Murray, and Schneider 1953:3–49.
MURPHY, R. F. and J. H. STEWARD
1956   "Tappers and Trappers: Parallel Process in Acculturation." *Journal of Economic Development and Cultural Change* 4:335–355.
NADEL, S. F.
1947   *The Nuba: An Anthropological Study of the Hill Tribes in Kordofan.* London: Oxford University Press.
1951   *The Foundations of Social Anthropology.* London: Cohen and West.
NADER, L., ed.
1965   "The Ethnography of Law." *American Anthropologist,* Special Publication, Vol. 67, No. 6, Pt. 2.
NADER, L. and B. YNGVESSON
1973   "On Studying the Ethnography of Law and Its Consequences." Honigmann 1973:883–921.
NAROLL, R.
1961   "Two Solutions to Galton's Problem." *Philosophy of Science* 28:15–39.
NAROLL, R. and R. G. D'ANDRADE
1963   "Two Further Solutions to Galton's Problem." *American Anthropologist* 65:1053–1067.
NASH, D. and R. WINTROB
1972   "The Emergence of Self-Consciousness in Ethnography." *Current Anthropology* 13:527–542.
NASH, M.
1966   *Primitive and Peasant Economic Systems.* San Francisco: Chandler Publishing Co.
NASH, P.
1955   (orig. 1937) "The Place of Religious Revivalism in the Formation of the Intercultural Community on Klamath Reservation." F. Eggan, ed., *Social Anthropology of North American Tribes.* Chicago: University of Chicago Press, 377–444.
NEEDHAM, R.
1962   *Structure and Sentiment: A Test Case in Social Anthropology.* Chicago: University of Chicago Press.
1963   *Introduction to Emile Durkheim and Marcel Mauss, On Some Forms of Primitive Classification: Contribution to the Study of Collective Representations,* R. Needham, trans. under title *Primitive Classification.* Chicago: University of Chicago Press, vii–xviii.
NELSON, B.
1969   *The Idea of Usury.* Chicago: University of Chicago Press.
NETTINS, R. MC G.
1968   "Hill Farmers of Nigeria. Cultural Ecology of the Kofyar of the Jos Plateau." American Ethnological Society, Monograph 46.
NEWELL, H. P. and A. D. KRIEGER
1949   "The George C. Davis Site, Cherokee County, Texas." Society for American Archaeology, Memoir 5.
NIETZSCHE, F. W.
1910   *The Will to Power.* A. M. Ludovici, trans. (2 vols.) Edinburgh: T. N. Foulis.
NILSSON, S.
1868   (orig. 1838) *The Primitive Inhabitants of Scandinavia. An Essay on Compara-*

tive Ethnography and a Contribution to the History of the Development of Mankind . . ., J. Lubbock, ed. London: Longmans.

NOON, J. A.
1949 *Law and Government of the Grand River Iroquois.* Viking Fund Publications in Anthropology, No. 3. New York: Wenner-Gren Foundation for Anthropological Research.

NORDENSKIÖLD, BARON, E.
1919 *An Ethno-geographical Analysis of the Material Culture of Two Indian Tribes in the Gran Chaco.* Göteborg: Elanders Boktryckeri Aktiebolag.
1919–1931 *Comparative Ethnographical Studies.* (9 vols.) Göteborg: Elanders Boktryckeri Aktiebolag.

NORTHROP, F. S. C. (ed.)
1949 *Ideological Differences and World Order.* New Haven, Conn.: Yale University Press.

NOTT, J. C. and G. R. GLIDDON
1855 *Types of Mankind; or, Ethnological Researches, Based Upon the Ancient Monuments, Paintings, Sculptures, and Crania of Races, and Upon Their Natural, Geographical, Philological and Biblical History.* Philadelphia: Lippincott.
1857 *The Indigenous Races of the Earth.* Philadelphia: Lippincott.

NUTINI, H. G.
1965 Some Considerations on the Nature of Social Structure and Model Building: A critique of Claude Lévi-Strauss and Edmund Leach." *American Anthropologist* 67: 707–731.

OAKLEY, K. P.
1954 "Skill as a Human Possession." C. Singer, E. J. Holmyard, and A. R. Hall, eds., *A History of Technology.* (5 vols.), Oxford: Clarendon Press, 1:1–37.

OBERG, K.
1934 "Crime and Punishment in Tlingit Society." *American Anthropologist* 36:145–148.
1962 "The Kingdom of Ankole in Uganda." *African Political Systems.* Fortes and Evans-Pritchard 1962:121–164.

ODUM, H. W.
1953 "Folk Sociology as a Subject Field for the Historical Study of Total Human Society and the Empirical Study of Group Behavior." *Social Forces* 31:193–223.

OGBURN, W. F.
1923 *Social Change.* New York: B. W. Huebsch.

OGDEN, C. K. and I. A. RICHARDS
1923 *The Meaning of Meaning: A Study of the Influence of Language upon Thought and all the Science of Symbolism.* New York: Harcourt.

OKIGBO, P.
1956 "Social Consequences of Economic Development in West Africa." *Annals of the American Academy of Political and Social Science* 305:125–133.

OLSCHKI, L.
1954 *The Genius of Italy.* Ithaca, N.Y.: Cornell University Press.

OPLER, M. E.
1941 *An Apache Life-Way.* Chicago: University of Chicago Press.
1945 "Themes as Dynamic Forces in Culture." *American Journal of Sociology* 51: 198–206.
1948 "Some Recently Developed Concepts Relating to Culture." *Southwestern Journal of Anthropology* 4:107–122.
1949 "The Context of Themes." *American Anthropologist* 51: 323–325.
1959 "Component, Assemblage, and Theme in Cultural Integration and Differentiation." *American Anthropologist,* 61:955–964.
1964 "Morgan and Materialism: A Reply to Thomas G. Harding and Eleanor Leacock." *Current Anthropology* 5:110–114.
1968 "Tylor's Application of Evolutionary Theory to Public Issues of His Day." *Anthropological Quarterly* 41:1–8.

OPLER, M. K.
1940 "The Southern Ute of Colorado." Linton 1940:119–203.

1959   *Culture and Mental Health; Cross-Cultural Studies.* New York: Macmillan.
1963   "The Need for New Diagnostic Categories in Psychiatry." *Journal of the National Medical Association* 55:133–137.

ORLANSKY, H.
1949   "Infant Care and Personality." *Psychological Bulletin* 46:1–48.

OVIEDO Y VALDES, G. F. DE
1885   (orig. 1526) "The Natural History of the West Indies." E. Arber, ed., *The First Three Books on America.* Birmingham: Turnbull and Spears, 205–242.

PADMORE, G.
1953   *The Gold Coast Revolution.* London: Dennis Dobson.

PAGE, L. E.
1969   "Diluvialism and Its Critics in Great Britain in the Early Nineteenth Century." C. J. Schneer, ed., *Toward a History of Geology.* Cambridge, Mass.: M.I.T. Press, 257–271.

PARK, R. E.
1928   "Human Migration and the Marginal Man." *American Journal of Sociology* 33: 881–893.

PARKER, A. C.
1913   "The Code of Handsome Lake, The Seneca Prophet." Albany: New York State Museum Bulletin 163.

PARKER, S.
1962   "Eskimo Psychopathology in the Context of Eskimo Personality and Culture." *American Anthropologist* 64:76–96.

PARSONS, E. C.
1936   *Mitla: Town of the Souls.* Chicago: University of Chicago Press.

PARSONS, T. and E. SHILS (eds.)
1952   *Toward a General Theory of Action.* Cambridge, Mass.: Harvard University Press.

PARSONS, T. and N. SMELSER
1956   *Economy and Society: A Study in the Integration of Economic and Social Theory.* London: Routledge.

PARSONS, T. W.
1965   "Ethnic Cleavage in a California School." Ph.D. dissertation, Stanford University, Stanford, Calif.

DALTON, G. (ed.)
1968   *Primitive, Archaic and Modern Economies: Essays of Karl Polanyi.* Garden City, N.Y.: Doubleday.

PAUL, B. D.
1950   "Symbolic Sibling Rivalry in a Guatemalan Indian Village." *American Anthropologist* 52:205–218.
1953   "Sibling Rivalry in San Pedro" (abridgment of Paul 1952). Kluckhohn, Murray, and Schneider 1953:321–341.
1955   (ed.) *Health, Culture, and Community; Case Studies of Public Reactions to Health Programs.* New York: Russell Sage.

PAUSANIAS
1959–1961   (orig. 1918–1935) *Description of Greece,* W. H. S. Jones, trans. (5 vols.) London: Heinemann.

PENNIMAN, T. K.
1965   (orig. 1935) *A Hundred Years of Anthropology.* London: Duckworth.

PERRY, W. J.
1927   (orig. 1923) *The Children of the Sun: A Study in the Early History of Civilization.* London: Methuen.

PETERSON, S.
1948   *How Well Are Indian Children Educated?* Chicago: University of Chicago.

PETRULLO, V.
1934   *The Diabolic Root.* Philadelphia: University of Pennsylvania Press.

PETTIT, G. A.
1946   *Primitive Education in North America.* Berkeley: University of California Press.

PEYRÈRE, I. DE LA
1655   *Prae-adamitae.*

PICO, DELLA MIRANDOLA, G.
1948 (orig. 1486) "Oration on the Dignity of Man." Cassirer 1948:223–225.

PIDDOCKE, S.
1965 "The Potlatch System of the Southern Kwakiutl: A New Perspective." *Southwestern Journal of Anthropology* 21: 244–264.

PIGGOTT, S.
1965 *Ancient Europe: From the Beginnings of Agriculture to Classical Antiquity.* Chicago: Aldine.

PIKE, K.
1966 (orig. 1954) "Etic and Emic Standpoints for the Description of Behavior." Smith 1966:152–163.

PIKER, S.
1966 "The 'Image of Limited Good': Comments on an Exercise in Description and Interpretation." *American Anthropologist* 68: 1202–1211.

PITT-RIVERS, A. L.-F.
1906 *The Evolution of Culture and Other Essays.* Oxford: Clarendon Press.

PITT-RIVERS, G. H. LANE-FOX
1927 *The Clash of Culture and the Contact of Race: An Anthropological and Psychological Study of the Laws of Racial Adaptability, with Special Reference to the Depopulation of the Pacific and the Government of Subject Races.* London: Routledge.

PLATO
1958 (orig. 1941) *The Republic of Plato,* F. M. Cornford, trans. New York: Oxford University Press.

PLINY
1952 *Natural History,* H. Rackham, trans. (10 vols.) Cambridge, Mass.: Harvard University Press.

POLANYI, K.
1944 *The Great Transformation.* New York: Holt, Rinehart and Winston, Inc.
1947 "Our Obsolete Market Mentality." *Commentary* 13:109–117.
1960 "On the Comparative Treatment of Economic Institutions in Antiquity: With Illustrations from Athens, Mycenae, and Alalakh." Dalton 1968: 306–334.

POLANYI, K., C. W. ARENSBERG, and H. W. PEARSON. (eds.)
1957 *Trade and Market in the Early Empires.* New York: Free Press.

POLANYI, K. and A. ROTSTEIN
1966 *Dahomey and the Slave Trade.* Seattle: University of Washington Press.

POLGAR, S.
1962 "Health and Human Behavior: Areas of Interest Common to the Social and Medical Sciences." *Current Anthropology* 3:159–205.

POLLOCK, F.
1883 *The Land Laws.* London: Macmillan.

POLLOCK, F. and F. W. MAITLAND
1899 (orig. 1889) *The History of English Law Before the Time of Edward I.* (2 vols.) Boston: Little, Brown.

POLYBIUS
1960 (orig. 1922) *The Histories,* W. R. Paton, trans. (6 vols.) Cambridge, Mass.: Harvard University Press.

POSPISIL, L.
1958 *Kapauku Papuans and Their Law.* New Haven, Conn.: Yale University Press.
1963 *Kapauku Papuan Economy.* New Haven, Conn.: Yale University Press.
1965 "A Formal Analysis of Substantive Law: Kapauku Papuan Laws of Inheritance." *American Anthropologist, Special Publication* 67:166–185.

POST, A. H.
1880–1881 *Bausteine für eine allgemeine Rechtswissenschaft auf vergleichend-ethnologischer Basis.* Oldenburg: Schulze.
1894–1895 *Grundriss der ethnologischen Jurisprudenz.* (2 vols.) Oldenburg: Schulze.

POTTER, J. M., M. N. DIAZ, and G. M. FOSTER (eds.)
1967 *Peasant Society: A Reader.* Boston: Little, Brown.

POWDERMAKER, H.
1962 *Copper Town: Changing Africa.* New York: Harper & Row.

1968   (orig. 1939) *After Freedom: A Cultural Study in the Deep South*. New York: Atheneum.

POWELL, J. W.

1888a   "Competition as a Factor in Human Evolution." *American Anthropologist* (old series) 1:297–324.

1888b   "From Barbarism to Civilization." *American Anthropologist* (old series) 1:97–124.

PRESTWICH, SIR J.

1965   (orig. 1889) "On the Occurrence of Paleolithic Flint Implements in the Neighborhood of Ightham." Penniman 1965:175.

PRICHARD, J. C.

1855   (orig. 1813) *The Natural History of Man. Comprising Inquiries into the Modifying Influence of Physical and Moral Agencies on the Different Tribes of the Human Family*, E. Norris, ed. (2 vols.) London: Baillière.

PRIESTLY, J.

1771   *An Essay on the First Principles of Government; and on the Nature of Political, Civil, and Religious Liberty.* London: J. Johnson.

QUATREFAGES, A. DE

1879   *The Human Species.* New York: Appleton.

RADCLIFFE-BROWN, A. R.

1913   "Three Tribes of Western Australia." *Journal of the Royal Anthropological Institute* 43:143–194.

1930–1931   "The Social Organization of Australian Tribes." *Oceania Monographs* No. 1:371.

1935   "On the Concept of Function in Social Science." *American Anthropologist* 37:394–402.

1948   (orig. 1922) *The Andaman Islanders.* New York: Free Press.

1957   *A Natural Science of Society.* New York: Free Press.

1958   *Method in Social Anthropology. Selected Essays by A. R. Radcliffe-Brown*, M. N. Srinivas, ed. Chicago: University of Chicago Press.

1958a   (orig. 1923) "The Methods of Ethnology and Social Anthropology." Radcliffe-Brown 1958:3–38.

1958b   (orig. 1931) "The Present Position of Anthropological Studies." Radcliffe-Brown 1958:42–95.

1958c   (orig. 1944) "Meaning and Scope of Social Anthropology." Radcliffe-Brown 1958:96–107.

1958d   (orig. 1951) "The Comparative Method in Social Anthropology." Radcliffe-Brown 1958:108–129.

1962a   (orig. 1950) Introduction. Radcliffe-Brown and Forde 1962:1–87.

1962b   (orig. 1940) Preface. Fortes and Evans-Pritchard 1962:xi–xxiii.

1965   (orig. 1952) *Structure and Function in Primitive Society.* New York: Free Press.

1965a   (orig. 1924) "The Mother's Brother in South Africa." Radcliffe-Brown 1965:15–31.

1965b   (orig. 1929) "The Sociological Theory of Totemism." Radcliffe-Brown 1965:117–132.

1965c   (orig. 1933) "Social Sanctions." Radcliffe-Brown 1965:205–211.

1965d   (orig. 1935) "Patrilineal and Matrilineal Succession." Radcliffe-Brown 1965:32–48.

1965e   (orig. 1939) "Taboo." Radcliffe-Brown 1965:133–152.

1965f   (orig. 1940) "On Joking Relationships." Radcliffe-Brown 1965:90–104.

1965g   (orig. 1940) "On Social Structure." Radcliffe-Brown 1965:188–204.

1965h   (orig. 1945) "Religion and Society." Radcliffe-Brown 1965: 153–177.

1965i   (orig. 1941) "The Study of Kinship Systems." Radcliffe-Brown 1965:49–89.

RADCLIFFE-BROWN, A. R. and D. FORDE (eds.)

1962   (orig. 1950) *African Systems of Kinship and Marriage.* London: Oxford University Press.

RADIN, P.

1920   "The Autobiography of a Winnebago Indian." *University of California, Publications in American Archaeology and Ethnology* 16:381–473.

1928   *The Winnebago Tribe.* Washington: Government Printing Office.

1933 *The Method and Theory of Ethnology: An Essay in Criticism.* New York: McGraw-Hill.
1957a (orig. 1927) *Primitive Man as Philosopher.* New York: Dover.
1957b (orig. 1937) *Primitive Religion: Its Nature and Origin.* New York: Dover.

RAPOPORT, R.
1954 "Changing Navaho Religious Values: A Study of Christian Missions to the Rimrock Navahos." *Papers of the Peabody Museum of American Archaeology and Ethnology* 41(2).

RAPPAPORT, R. A.
1967 "Ritual Regulation of Environmental Relations Among a New Guinea People." *Ethnology* 6:17–30.
1968 *Pigs for the Ancestors: Ritual in the Ecology of a New Guinea People.* New Haven, Conn.: Yale University Press.

RASK, R.
1818 *Undersögelse om det gamle Nordiske eller Islandske sprogs oprindelse.* Kjöbenhavn: Gyldendal.

RATTRAY, R. S.
1929 *Ashanti Law and Constitution.* Oxford: Oxford University Press for the International African Institute.

RATZEL, F.
1878–1880 *Die Vereinigten Staaten von Nord-Amerika.* (2 vols.) München: R. Oldenbourg.
1896–1898 (orig. 1885–1888) *The History of Mankind,* A. J. Butler, trans. (3 vols.) New York: Macmillan.

RATZENHOFER, G.
1893 *Wesen und Zweck der Politik, als Theil der Sociologie und Grundlage der Staatswissenschaften.* (3 vols.) Leipzig: F. A. Brockhaus.

RAUM, O. F.
1940 *Chagga Childhood.* Oxford: Oxford University Press.

READ, C.
1925 (orig. 1920) *The Origin of Man.* Cambridge: Cambridge University Press.

READ, M.
1955 *Education and Social Change in Tropical Areas.* Toronto: Nelson.
1956 *The Ngoni of Nyasaland.* London: Oxford University Press for the International African Institute.

RECLUS, E.
1891 *Primitive Folk: Studies in Comparative Ethnology.* London: W. Scott.

REDFIELD, R.
1930 *Tepoztlán, a Mexican Villlage: A Study of Folk Life.* Chicago: University of Chicago Press.
1941 *The Folk Culture of Yucatan.* Chicago: University of Chicago Press.
1947 "The Folk Society." *American Journal of Sociology* 52:292–308.
1953 *The Primitive World and Its Transformation.* Ithaca, N.Y.: Cornell University Press.
1964 (orig. 1950) *A Village that Chose Progress: Chan Kom Revisited.* Chicago: University of Chicago Press.

REDFIELD, R., R. LINTON, and M. J. HERSKOVITS
1936 "Memorandum for the Study of Acculturation." *American Anthropologist* 38: 149–152.

REDFIELD, R. and A. VILLA
1944 *Chan Kom: A Maya Village.* Washington, D.C.: Carnegie Institution of Washington.

REED, S. W.
1942 *The Making of Modern New Guinea, with Special Reference to Culture Contact in the Mandated Territory.* Philadelphia: American Philosophical Society.

REICHEL-DOLMATOFF, G. and A. REICHEL-DOLMATOFF
1961 *The People of Aritama: The Cultural Personality of a Colombian Mestizo Village.* Chicago: University of Chicago Press.

REID-MOIR, J.
1950 (orig. 1919) "Pre-Paleolithic Man." Daniel 1950:333.

REMMLING, G. W.
1967   Road to Suspicion: A Study of Modern Mentality and the Sociology of Knowledge. New York: Appleton.

RESEK, E.
1960   Lewis Henry Morgan: American Scholar. Chicago: University of Chicago Press.

RETZIUS, A.
1950   (orig. 1856) "A Glance at the Present State of Ethnology, with Reference to the Form of the Skull." E. Count, ed., This Is Race. New York: Abelard-Schuman, 75–89.

RIBEIRO, D.
1968   The Civilizational Process: Stages of Sociocultural Evolution. Washington, D.C.: Smithsonian Institution.
1970   "The Culture-Historical Configurations of the American Peoples." Current Anthropology 11:403–435.

RICHARDS, A. I.
1932   Hunger and Work in a Savage Tribe: A Functional Study of Nutrition Among the Southern Bantu. London: Routledge.
1939   Land, Labour and Diet in Northern Rhodesia: An Economic Study of the Bemba Tribe. London: Oxford University Press.
1952   (ed.) Economic Development and Tribal Change: A Study of Immigrant Labour in Buganda. Cambridge: Heffer.

RICHARDS, A. I. and E. M. WIDDOWSON
1936   "A Dietary Study in North-eastern Rhodesia." Africa 9:166–196.

RICHARDSON, J.
1940   Law and Status Among the Kiowa Indians. New York: J. J. Augustin.

RICHARDSON, J. and A. L. KROEBER
1952   "Three Centuries of Women's Dress Fashions: A Quantitative Analysis." Kroeber 1952: 358–372.

RINK, H. J.
1875   Tales and Traditions of the Eskimo, with a Sketch of Their Habits, Religion, Language and Other Peculiarities, H. J. Rink, trans. Edinburgh: Blackwood.

RIVERS, W. H. R.
1907   "On the Origins of the Classificatory System of Relationships." Balfour 1907: 309–323.
1910   "The Genealogical Method of Anthropological Inquiry." Sociological Review 3:1–10.
1914a   The History of Melanesian Society. (2 vols.) Cambridge: Cambridge University Press.
1914b   Kinship and Social Organization. London: Constable.
1922   (orig. 1920) Instinct and the Unconscious: A Contribution to a Biological Theory of the Psycho-Neuroses. Cambridge: Cambridge University Press.
1924   Social Organization. New York: Knopf.
1926   Psychology and Ethnology. London: Routledge.

ROBERTS, J. M.
1951   "Three Navaho Households: A Comparative Study in Small Group Culture." Papers of the Peabody Museum of American Archaeology and Ethnology 40(3). Cambridge, Mass.: Harvard University Press.

ROBERTSON, W.
1822   (orig. 1777) The History of America. (2 vols.) Philadelphia: Robert and Thomas Desilver.

ROBINSON, K.
1955   "French Africa and the French Union." Haines 1955:311–331.

RÓHEIM, G.
1925   Australian Totemism; a Psycho-analytic Study in Anthropology. London: G. Allen.
1934   The Riddle of the Sphinx. London: Hogarth.
1945   The Eternal Ones of the Dream. A Psychoanalytic Interpretation of Australian Myth and Ritual. New York: International Universities Press.
1948   "Psychoanalysis and Anthropology." Haring 1948:472–496.
1950   Psychoanalysis and Anthropology. New York: International Universities Press.

ROHNER, R.
1966   "Franz Boas: Ethnographer on the Northwest Coast." Helm 1966:149–122.

1969 (ed.) *The Ethnography of Franz Boas*, H. Parker, trans. Chicago: University of Chicago Press.

ROHNER, R. and E. ROHNER
1969 "Franz Boas and the Developemnt of North American Ethnology and Ethnography." Rohner 1969:xiii–xxx.

ROUSE, I.
1939 "Prehistory in Haiti, a Study in Method." Yale University Publications in Anthropology, No. 21.
1955 "On the Correlation of Phases of Culture." *American Anthropologist* 57:713–722.
1970 (orig. 1960) "Classification of Artifacts." Fagan 1970:185–200.

ROUSSEAU, J. J.
1950 *The Social Contract and Discourses*, G. D. H. Cole, trans. New York: Dutton.
1962 (orig. 1755) *The Political Writings of Jean Jacques Rousseau*, C. Vaughan, ed. (2 vols.) New York: Wiley.
1969 (orig. 1782) "Essay on the Origin of Languages." Salus 1969:138–149.

ROWE, J.
1965 "The Renaissance Foundations of Anthropology." *American Anthropologist* 67: 1–20.

RUDWICK, M. J. S.
1969 "Lyell on Etna, and the Antiquity of the Earth." C. J. Schneer, ed., *Toward a History of Geology*. Cambridge, Mass.: M.I.T. Press, 288–304.

SACHS, W.
1947 (orig. 1937) *Black Hamlet*. Boston: Little, Brown.

SADE, D. S.
1968 "Inhibition of Son-Mother Mating Among Free-Ranging Rhesus Monkeys." J. H. Masserman, ed., *Animal and Human Scientific Proceedings of the American Academy of Psychoanalysis* 7:18–38.

SAHAGÚN, B. DE
1950–1970 *General History of the Things of New Spain; Florentine Codex*, A. J. O. Anderson and C. E. Dibble, trans. Santa Fe, N. M.: School of American Research.

SAHLINS, M. D.
1958 *Social Stratification in Polynesia*. Seattle: University of Washington Press.
1961 "The Segmentary Lineage: An Organization of Predatory Expansion." *American Anthropologist* 63:322–345.
1968 *Tribesmen*. Englewood Cliffs, N.J.: Prentice-Hall.

SALISBURY, R. F.
1962 *From Stone to Steel*. Melbourne: University of Melbourne Press.

SALUS, P. H. (ed.)
1969 *On Language: Plato to von Humboldt*. New York: Holt, Rinehart and Winston, Inc.

SANDERS, W. T.
1962 "Cultural Ecology of Nuclear America." *American Anthropologist* 64: 34–43.

SANDERS, W. and B. PRICE
1968 *Mesoamerica: The Evolution of a Civilization*. New York: Random House.

SAPIR, E.
1907 "Herder's 'Ursprung der Sprache.'" *Modern Philology* 5:109–142.
1917 "Do We Need a 'Superorganic'?" *American Anthropologist* 19:441–447.
1921 *Language: An Introduction to the Study of Speech*. New York: Harcourt.
1949 Selected Writings of Edward Sapir in *Language, Culture and Personality*, D. G. Mandelbaum, ed. Berkeley: University of California Press.
1949a (orig. 1916) "Time Perspective in Aboriginal American Culture: A Study in Method." Sapir 1949:389–462.
1949b (orig. 1924) "Culture, Genuine and Spurious." Sapir 1949:308–331.
1949c (orig. 1927) "The Unconscious Patterning of Behavior in Society." Sapir 1949: 544–559.
1949d (orig. 1929) The Status of Linguistics as a Science." Sapir 1949:160–166.
1949e (orig. 1934) "Personality." Sapir 1949:560–563.
1949f (orig. 1934) "The Emergence of the Concept of Personality in a Study of Cultures." Sapir 1949:590–597.

1949g (orig. 1938) "Why Cultural Anthropology Needs the Psychiatrist." Sapir 1949:569–577.

SAUNDERS, L.
1954 *Cultural Differences and Medical Care.* New York: Russell Sage.

SAYCE, R. U.
1963 (orig. 1933) *Primitive Arts and Crafts: An Introduction to the Study of Material Culture.* New York: Biblo and Tannen.

SCHAPERA, I.
1938 *Handbook of Tswana Law and Custom.* Oxford: Oxford University Press.
1941 *Married Life in an African Tribe.* New York: Sheridan House.
1962 "The Political Organization of the Ngwato of Bechuanaland Protectorate." Fortes and Evans-Pritchard 1962:56–82.
1964 "Malinowski's Theories of Law." Firth 1964:139–155.
1967 (orig. 1956) *Government and Politics in Tribal Societies.* New York: Schocken Books.

SCHEBESTA, P.
1929 *Among the Forest Dwarfs of Malaya* A. Chambers, trans. London: Hutchinson.
1938–1950 *Die Bambuti—Pygmäen vom Ituri.* Memoirs of the Moral and Political Sciences, Vols. 1, 2, and 4. Brussels: Belgian Royal Colonial Institute.

SCHEFFLER, H. W.
1962 "Kindred and Kin Groups in Simbo Island Social Structure." *Ethnology* 1:135–157.
1966 "Ancestor Worship in Anthropology: Or, Observations on Descent and Descent Groups." *Current Anthropology* 7:541–548; reply to commentaries, 549–551.
1973 "Kinship, Descent, and Alliance." Honigmann 1973:747–793.

SCHMERLING, P. C.
1833–1834. *Recherches sur les Ossemens Fossile découverts dans les Cavernes de la Province de Liège.* (2 vols.) Liège: Collardin.

SCHMIDT, W.
1931 *The Origin and Growth of Religion. Facts and Theories,* H. J. Rose, trans. London: Methuen.
1939 *The Culture Historical Method of Ethnology. The Scientific Approach to the Racial Question,* S. A. Sieber, trans. New York: Fortuny's Publishers.

SCHNEIDER, G. C. and D. M. SCHNEIDER
1955 *Marriage, Authority and Final Causes. A Study of Unilateral Cross-Cousin Marriage.* New York: Free Press.

SCHNEIDER, H. K.
1969 "Comment on George Dalton's 'Theoretical Issues in Economic Anthropology.'" *Current Anthropology* 10:89–91.
1970 "The Wahi Wanyaturu. Economics in an African Society." Chicago: Aldine.

SCHNEIDER, L. (ed.)
1967 *The Scottish Moralists on Human Nature and Society.* Chicago: University of Chicago Press.

SCHOOLCRAFT, H. R.
1839 *Algic Researches, Comprising Inquiries Respecting the Mental Characteristics of North American Indians.* (2 vols.) New York: Harper and Brothers.
1852–1857 *Information Respecting the History, Condition and Prospects of the Indian Tribes of the United States.* (6 vols.) Philadelphia: Lippincott.

SCHULTZ, A. H.
1961 "Some Factors Influencing the Social Life of Primates in General and of Early Man in Particular." Washburn 1961:58–90.

SCHURTZ, H.
1900 *Urgeschichte der Kultur.* Leipzig: Bibliographische Institute.
1902 *Altersklassen und Männerbünde, Eine Darstellung der Grundformen der Gesellschaft.* Berlin: G. Reimer.

SCHUSKY, E.
1965 *The Right To Be Indian.* Vermilion, S. D.: Institute of Indian Studies.

SCHWARTZ, T.
1962 "The Palian Movement in the Admiralty Islands, 1946–1954." American Museum of Natural History, Anthropological Papers, 49(2).

SCOTCH, N. A.
1963a "Medical Anthropology." Siegel 1963:30–68.
1963b "Sociocultural Factors in the Epidemiology of Zulu Hypertension." *American Journal of Public Health* 53(8):1205–1213.

SEAGLE, W.
1937 "Primitive Law and Professor Malinowski." *American Anthropologist* 39:275–290.

SEARS, R. R.
1943 *Survey of Objective Studies of Psychoanalytic Concepts.* New York: Social Science Research Council.

SEEBOHM, F.
1883 *The English Village Community Examined in Its Relations to the Manorial and Tribal Systems and to the Common or Open Field System of Husbandry. An Essay in Economic History.* London: Longmans.
1895 *The Tribal System in Wales; Being Part of an Inquiry into the Structure and Methods of Tribal Society.* London: Longmans.
1902 *Tribal Custom in Anglo-Saxon Law.* London: Longmans.

SELOSOEMARDJAN
1962 *Social Changes in Jogjakarta.* Ithaca, N.Y.: Cornell University Press.

SELSAM, H., D. GOLDWAY, and H. MARTEL (eds.)
1970 *Dynamics of Social Change. A Reader in Marxist Social Science from the Writings of Marx, Engels and Lenin.* New York: International Publishers.

SEMPLE, E. C.
1911 *Influences of Geographic Environment, on the Basis of Ratzel's System of Anthropo-Geography.* New York: Holt, Rinehart and Winston, Inc.

SERVICE, E. R.
1962 *Primitive Social Organization. An Evolutionary Perspective.* New York: Random House.

SHAPIRO, H. L.
1957 "The Population Unit and Culture." *Cold Spring Harbor Symposia on Quantitative Biology* 22:409–414.

SHERIF, M., ed.
1962 *Intergroup Relations and Leadership; Approaches and Research in Industrial, Ethnic, Cultural, and Political Areas.* New York: Wiley.

SIEGEL, B. J.
1949 "Some Observations on the Pueblo Pattern at Taos." *American Anthropologist* 51:562–577.
1963 (ed.) *Biennial Review of Anthropology.* Stanford, Calif.: Stanford University Press.

SIEGEL, B. J. and A. R. BEALS
1960 "Pervasive Factionalism." *American Anthropologist* 62:394–417.

SIKKEMA, M.
1947 "Observations on Japanese Early Childhood Training." *Psychiatry* 10:423–432.

SIMMONS, L. W. (ed.)
1942 *Sun Chief: The Autobiography of a Hopi Indian.* New Haven, Conn.: Yale University Press.

SIMMONS, O. G.
1959 "Drinking Patterns and Interpersonal Performance in a Peruvian Mestizo Community." *Quarterly Journal of Studies on Alcohol* 20:103–111.

SJÖBERG, G.
1952 "Folk and 'Feudal' Societies." *American Journal of Sociology* 58:231–239.
1955 "The Preindustrial City." *American Journal of Sociology* 60:438–445.

SLOTKIN, J. S. (ed.)
1965 *Readings in Early Anthropology.* Viking Fund Publications in Anthropology, No. 40. New York: Wenner-Gren Foundation.

SMITH, A.
1937 (orig. 1776) *An Inquiry into the Nature and Causes of the Wealth of Nations,* E. Cannan, ed. New York: Modern Library.
1892 (orig. 1759) *The Theory of Moral Sentiments; to Which Is Added, A Dissertation on the Origin of Languages.* London: G. Bell.

SMITH, A. G. (ed.)
1966 *Communication and Culture: Readings in the Codes of Human Interaction.*
New York: Holt, Rinehart and Winston.

SMITH, C. T.
1970 "Depopulation of the Central Andes in the 16th Century." *Current Anthropology* 11:453–464.

SMITH, SIR G. E.
1924 *Elephants and Ethnologists.* New York: Dutton.
1929 *Human History.* New York: Norton.
1933 *The Diffusion of Culture.* London: Watts.

SMITH, SIR G. E. et al.
1928 (orig. 1927) "The Diffusion of Culture." G. E. Smith and others, eds., *Culture: The Diffusion Controversy.* London: Routledge, 7–22.

SMITH, M. G.
1960 *Government in Zazzau, 1800–1950.* London: Oxford University Press.
1962 *West Indian Family Structure.* Seattle: University of Washington Press.
1965 *The Plural Society in the British West Indies.* Berkeley: University of California Press.

SMITH, R. T.
1956 *The Negro Family in British Guiana.* London: Routledge.

SMITH, W.
1815 (orig. 1794) *A Memoir to the Map and Delineation of the Strata of England and Wales, with Part of Scotland.* London: J. Cary.

SMITH, W. and ROBERTS, J. M.
1954 *Zuni Law. A Field of Values.* Cambridge, Mass.: Harvard University Press.

SMITH, W. R.
1903 (orig. 1885) *Kinship and Marriage in Early Arabia,* S. A. Cook, ed. London: A. & C. Black.
1957 (orig. 1889) *The Religion of the Semites. The Fundamental Institutions.* New York: Meridian Books.

SOROKIN, P. A.
1937–1941 *Social and Cultural Dynamics.* (4 vols.) New York: American Book Company.
1941 *The Crisis of Our Age: The Social and Cultural Outlook.* New York: Dutton.

SOROKIN, P. A., C. C. ZIMMERMAN, and C. J. GALPIN (eds.)
1930–1932 *A Systematic Sourcebook in Rural Sociology.* (3 vols.) Minneapolis: University of Minnesota Press.

SOUTHALL, A. W., and P. C. GUTKIND
1957 *Townsmen in the Making.* Kampala, East African Studies No. 9.

SPECK, F. G.
1915 "The Family Hunting Band as a Basis of Algonkian Social Organization." *American Anthropologist* 17:289–305.
1933 "Notes on the Life of John Wilson, the Revealer of Peyote, as Recalled by His Nephew, George Anderson." *General Magazine and Historical Chronicle* 35:539–556.

SPENCER, H.
1857 "Progress: Its Laws and Causes." *Westminster Review* 67:445–485.
1864–1867 *The Principles of Biology.* (2 vols.) London: Williams & Norgate.
1870–1872 (orig. 1855) *Principles of Psychology.* (2 vols.) London: Williams & Norgate.
1874 *The Study of Sociology.* New York: Appleton.
1880 (orig. 1862) *First Principles.* (Reprinted from the fifth London edition.) New York: A. L. Burt.
1880–1896 (orig. 1876–1896) *The Principles of Sociology.* (3 vols. in 5.) New York: Appleton.
1895–1897 (orig. 1876–1896) *The Principles of Sociology.* New York: Appleton.
1897a (orig. 1879) *The Principles of Ethics.* (2 vols.) New York: Appleton.
1897b (orig. 1850) *Social Statics* (abridged and revised). New York: Appleton.
1900–1901 (orig. 1876–1896) *The Principles of Sociology.* (3 vols.) New York: Appleton.
1910 *Essays, Scientific, Political, and Speculative.* (3 vols.) New York: Appleton.

1910a (orig. 1870) "The Origin of Animal Worship." Spencer 1910(1):308–330.

SPENCER, R.
1958 "Culture Process and Intellectual Current: Durkheim and Ataturk." *American Anthropologist* 60:640–657.

SPICER, E. H.
1940 *Pascua. A Yaqui Village in Arizona.* Chicago: University of Chicago Press.
1952 (ed.) *Human Problems in Technological Change. A Casebook.* New York: Russell Sage.
1954 "Potam, a Yaqui Village in Sonora." American Anthropological Association, Memoir 77.
1961 (ed.) *Perspectives in American Indian Culture Change.* Chicago: University of Chicago Press.
1961a "Yaqui." Spicer 1961:7–93.
1962 *Cycles of Conquest. The Impact of Spain, Mexico, and the United States on the Indians of the Southwest, 1533–1960.* Tucson: University of Arizona Press.

SPIER, L.
1935 *The Prophet Dance of the Northwest and Its Derivatives: The Source of the Ghost Dance.* General Series in Anthropology, No. 1. Menasha, Wisc.: Banta.

SPINDLER, G. D.
1955 *Sociocultural and Psychological Processes in Menomini Acculturation.* Berkeley: University of California Press.
1963 (ed.) *Education and Culture—Anthropological Approaches.* New York: Holt, Rinehart and Winston, Inc.

SPINDLER, G. and W. GOLDSCHMIDT
1952 "Experimental Design in the Study of Culture Change. *Southwestern Journal of Anthropology* 8:68–83.

SPINDLER, G. and L. SPINDLER
1965 "The Instrumental Activities Inventory: A Technique for the Study of the Psychology of Acculturation." *Southwestern Journal of Anthropology* 21:1–23.

SPINDLER, L.
1962 "Menomini Women and Culture Change." American Anthropological Association, Memoir 91.

SPIRO, M. E.
1954 "Human Nature in Its Psychological Dimensions." *American Anthropologist* 56:19–30.

SPOEHR, A.
1947 "Changing Kinship Systems." Anthropological Series, Field Museum of Natural History, Chicago 33(4).

SRINIVAS, M. N.
1954 "A Caste Dispute Among Washermen of Mysore." *Eastern Anthropologist* 7:149–168.

STARCKE, C. N.
1889 *The Primitive Family in Its Origin and Development.* New York: Appleton.

STEENSBY, H. P.
1916 "An Anthropogeographical Study of the Origin of Eskimo Culture." *Meddelelser om Grönland, Copenhagen* 53:39–228.

STEINMETZ, S. R.
1928 (orig. 1894) *Ethnologische Studien zur Ersten Entwicklung der Strafe, nebst einer psychologischen abhandlung über grausamkeit und rachsucht.* (2 vols.) Groningen: P. Noordhoff.

STEIN, W.
1956 "The Case of the Hungry Calves." *Human Organization* 15:15–21.

STERN, T.
1965 "The Klamath Tribe. A People and Their Reservation." American Ethnological Society, Monograph 41. Seattle: University of Washington Press.

STEWARD, J. H.
1936 "The Economic Basis of Primitive Bands." *Essays in Honor of Alfred Louis Kroeber,* R. H. Lowie, ed. Berkeley: University of California Press, 311–350.
1937 "Ecological Aspects of Southwestern Society." *Anthropos* 32:87–104.

1938   "Basin-Plateau Aboriginal Socio-political Groups." Bulletin 120, Bureau of American Ethnology. Washington: Government Printing Office.

1949.   "Cultural Causality and Law: A Trial Formulation of the Development of Early Civilization." *American Anthropologist* 51:1–27.

1955   *Theory of Culture Change. The Methodology of Multilinear Evolution.* Urbana: University of Illinois Press.

1955a   (orig. 1936) "The Composite Band." Steward 1955:143–150.

1955b   (orig. 1936) "The Patrilineal Band." Steward 1955:122–150.

1955c   (orig. 1937) "Lineage to Clan: Ecological Aspects of Southwestern Society." Steward 1955:151–172.

1955d   (orig. 1938) The Great Basin Shoshonean Indians: An Example of a Family of Sociocultural Integration." Steward 1955:101–121.

1955e   (orig. 1951) "Levels of Sociocultural Integration: An Operational Concept." Steward 1955:43–63.

1955f   (orig. 1953) "Analysis of Complex Contemporary Societies: Culture Patterns of Puerto Rico." Steward 1955:210–222.

1955g   (orig. 1953) "Culture Area and Culture Type in Aboriginal America: Methodological Considerations." Steward 1955:78–97.

1955h   (orig. 1953) "Multilinear Evolution: Evolution and Process." Steward 1955: 11–29.

1955i   (orig. 1950) "The Concept and Method of Cultural Ecology." Steward 1955: 30–42.

1955j   "National Sociocultural Systems." Steward 1955:64–77.

STEWARD, J. et al.

1956   *The People of Puerto Rico.* Urbana: University of Illinois Press.

STEWART, D.

1892   "Account of the Life and Writings of Adam Smith, LL.D." Smith 1892:xi–lxix.

STEWART, J. H.

1963   *The Moral and Political Philosophy of David Hume.* New York: Columbia University Press.

STEWART, O. C.

1944   *Washo-Northern Paiute Peyotism: A Study in Acculturation.* Berkeley: University of California Press.

STOCKING, G. W., JR.

1960   "Franz Boas and the Founding of the American Anthropological Association." *American Anthropologist* 62:1–17.

1963   "Matthew Arnold, E. B. Tylor, and the Uses of Invention." *American Anthropologist* 65:783–799.

1966   "Franz Boas and the Culture Concept in Historic Perspective." *American Anthropologist* 68:867–882.

1964   "French Anthropology in 1800." *Isis* 55:135–150.

STONEQUIST, E. V.

1937   *The Marginal Man: A Study in the Subjective Aspects of Cultural Conflict.* New York: Scribner.

STOTT, D. H.

1962   "Cultural and Natural Checks on Population Growth." M. F. Ashley-Montagu, ed., *Culture and the Evolution of Man.* New York: Oxford University Press 355–376.

SUMNER, W. G.

1960   (orig. 1906) *Folkways. A Study of the Sociological Importance of Usages, Manners, Customs, Mores, and Morals.* New York: New American Library.

SUMNER, W. G. and A. G. KELLER

1927   *The Science of Society.* (4 vols.) New Haven, Conn.: Yale University Press.

SUNDKLER, B.

1948   *Bantu Prophets in South Africa.* London: Lutterworth Press.

SWANTON, J. R.

1942   "Source Material on the History and Ethnology of the Caddo Indians." Smithsonian Institution, Bureau of American Ethnology, Bulletin 132. Washington: Government Printing Office.

1946 "The Indians of the Southeastern United States." Smithsonian Institution, Bureau of American Ethnology, Bulletin 137. Washington: Government Printing Office.

SWEET, L. E.
1965 "Camel Raiding of North Arabian Bedouin: A Mechanism of Ecological Adaptation." *American Anthropologist* 67:1132–1150.

SWIFT, J.
1965 *Jonathan Swift: A Selection of His Works*, P. Pinkus, ed. Toronto: Macmillan.

TACITUS
1942 *The Complete Works of Tacitus*, M. Hadas, ed.; A. J. Church and W. J. Brodribb, trans. New York: Random House.

TANNER, N.
1970 "Disputing and the Genesis of Legal Principles: Example from Minangkabau." *Southwestern Journal of Anthropology* 26:375–401.

TAWNEY, R. H.
1926 *Religion and the Rise of Capitalism. A Historical Study.* New York: Harcourt.
1929 Preface. Firth 1929.

TAX, S.
1955 "The Integration of Anthropology." *Yearbook of Anthropology,* W. Thomas, Jr., ed. New York: Wenner-Gren Foundation, 313–328.
1960 (ed.) *Evolution after Darwin.* (3 vols.) Chicago: University of Chicago Press.

TAYLOR, T. G.
1927 *Environment and Race: A Study of the Evolution, Migration, Settlement and Status of the Races of Man.* London: Oxford University Press.

TAYLOR, W.
1948 "A Study of Archeology." American Anthropological Association, Memoir 69.

TEICHER, M.
1960 "Windigo Psychosis. A Study of a Relationship Between Belief and Behavior Among the Indians of Northeastern Canada." *Proceedings of the 1960 Annual Spring Meeting of the American Ethnological Society.*

THOMAS, W. I. and F. ZANIECKI
1927 *The Polish Peasant in Europe and America.* (2 vols.) New York: Knopf.

THOMPSON, J. E.
1954 *The Rise and Fall of Maya Civilization.* Norman: University of Oklahoma Press.

THOMPSON, L.
1949 "Relations of Men, Animals, and Plants in an Island Community (Fiji)." *American Anthropologist* 51:253–267.
1950 *Culture in Crisis, a Study of the Hopi Indians.* New York: Harper & Row.
1961 *Toward a Science of Mankind.* New York: McGraw-Hill.
1967 "Steps Toward a Unified Anthropology." *Current Anthropology* 8:67–91.

THOMPSON, L. and A. JOSEPH
1944 *The Hopi Way.* Chicago: University of Chicago Press.
1947 "White Pressures on Indian Personality and Culture." *American Journal of Sociology* 53:17–22.

THOMSEN, C.
1837 *Leitfaden zur Nordischen AlterthumsKunde.* Kopenhagen: Königliche Gesellschaft für Nordische Altherthums-Kunde.

THUCYDIDES
1934 *The Complete Writings of Thucydides, the Peloponnesian War,* R. Crawley, trans. New York: Modern Library.

THURNWALD, R.
1932 *Economics in Primitive Communities.* London: Oxford University Press.

THURNWALD, R. and H. THURNWALD
1935 *Black and White in East Africa.* London: Routledge.

THWAITES, R. G. (ed.)
1896–1901 *The Jesuit Relations and Allied Documents.* (73 vols.) Cleveland: Clark.

TIGER, L.
1970 *Men in Groups.* New York: Vintage Books.

TITIEV, M.
1944   "Old Oraibi." Papers of the Peabody Museum of American Archaeology and Ethnology, 22:1–277. Cambridge, Mass.: Harvard University Press.

TOPINARD, P.
1950   (orig. 1892) "On 'Race' in Anthropology." Count 1950:171–177.

TOYNBEE, A. J.
1935–1961   *A Study of History.* (12 vols.) New York: Oxford University Press.
1947–1957   *A Study of History.* Vols. 1–6 abridged by D. C. Somervell. New York: Oxford University Press.

TREITSCHKE, H. VON
1916   *Politics,* B. Dugdale and T. de Bille, trans. (2 vols.) New York: Macmillan.

TRIGGER, B.
1960   "The Destruction of Huronia: A Study in Economic and Cultural Change, 1609–1650." *Transactions of the Royal Canadian Institute* 33:14–45.
1968   *Beyond History: The Methods of Prehistory.* New York: Holt, Rinehart and Winston, Inc.

TUMIN, M.
1945   "Some Fragments from the Life History of a Marginal Man." *Character and Personality* 13:261–296.

TURGOT, A. R., BARON DE LAUNE
1749   *On the Benefits Which the Christian Religion Has Conferred on Mankind.* (In Latin)
1750   *On the Historical Progress of the Human Mind.* (In Latin)

TUVESON, E.
1964   (orig. 1949)   *Millennium and Utopia: A Study in the Background of the Idea of Progress.* New York: Harper & Row.

TYLER, S. A. (ed.)
1969   *Cognitive Anthropology.* New York: Holt, Rinehart and Winston, Inc.

TYLOR, SIR E. B.
1861   *Anahuac or Mexico and the Mexicans, Ancient and Modern.* London: Longmans.
1873   "Primitive Society." *Contemporary Review* 21:701–718; 22:53–72.
1874   (orig. 1871) *Primitive Culture. Researches into the Development of Mythology, Religion, Language, Art and Custom.* (2 vols.) Boston: Estes & Lauriat.
1889   "On a Method of Investigating the Development of Institutions; Applied to Laws of Marriage and Descent." *Journal of the Royal Anthropological Institute of Great Britain and Ireland* 18:245–269.
1899   "Remarks on Totemism with Especial Reference to Some Modern Theories Respecting It." *Journal of the Royal Anthropological Institute* 50:138–148.
1911   "Anthropology." *Encyclopaedia Britannica* 2:108–119. New York: Macmillan.
1937   (orig. 1881) *Anthropology.* (2 vols.) London: Watts.
1964   (orig. 1865) *Researches into the Early History of Mankind and the Development of Civilization,* P. Bohannan, ed. Chicago: University of Chicago Press.

USEEM, J.
1946   "Americans as Governors of Natives in the Pacific." *Journal of Social Issues* 2:39–49.

VALENTINE, C. A.
1968   *Culture and Poverty: Critique and Counter-Proposals.* Chicago: University of Chicago Press.

VAN DEN BERGHE, P. L.
1965   (ed). *Africa: Social Problems of Change and Conflict.* San Francisco: Chandler Publishing Co.
1965a   Introduction. Van den Berghe 1965:1–11.
1973   "Pluralism." Honigmann 1973:959–977.

VATTEL, E. DE
1916   *The Law of Nations or the Principles of Natural Law. Applied to the Conduct and to the Affairs of Nations and of Sovereigns,* C. G. Fenwick, trans. (3 vols.) Washington: Carnegie Institution.

VAYDA, A. P.
1960 "Maori Warfare." Maori Monograph No. 2. Wellington, N. Z.: Polynesian Society.
1961 "Expansion and Warfare Among Swidden Agriculturalists." *American Anthropologist* 63:346–358.
1966 "Comment on Harris re India's Sacred Cattle." *Current Anthropology* 7:63.
1969 (ed.) *Environment and Cultural Behavior. Ecological Studies in Cultural Anthropology.* Garden City, N.Y.: Natural History Press.

VEBLEN, T.
1934 (orig. 1899) *The Theory of the Leisure Class. An Economic Study of Institutions.* New York: Modern Library.

VENABLE, V.
1966 (orig. 1945) *Human Nature: The Marxian View.* New York: World Publishing.

VICO, G.
1948 (orig. 1725) *The New Science.* M. H. Fisch and T. G. Bergin, trans. Ithaca, N.Y.: Cornell University Press.

VINCENT, J.
1971 *African Elite: The Big Men of a Small Town.* New York: Columbia University Press.

VINOGRADOFF, P.
1905 *The Growth of the Manor.* New York: Macmillan.
1920 *Outlines of Historical Jurisprudence.* (2 vols.) London: Oxford University Press.

VIRCHOW, R.
1950 (orig. 1896) "Heredity and the Formation of Races." Count 1950:178–193.

VITRUVIUS
1926 *The Ten Books on Architecture,* M. H. Morgan, trans. Cambridge, Mass.: Harvard University Press.

VOGET, F. W.
1956 "The American Indian in Transition: Reformation and Accommodation." *American Anthropologist* 58:249–263.
1961–1962 (ed.) *American Indians and Their Economic Development.* Society for Applied Anthropology, Special Issue, *Human Organization* 20(4).
1964 "Warfare and the Integration of Crow Indian Culture." Goodenough 1964: 483–509.
1967 "Progress, Science, History and Evolution in Eighteenth- and Nineteenth-Century Anthropology." *Journal of the History of the Behavioral Sciences* 3:132–155.
1968 "Anthropology in the Age of Enlightenment: Progress and Utopian Functionalism." *Southwestern Journal of Anthropology* 24:321–345.

VOGT, E. Z.
1951 "Navaho Veterans: A Study of Changing Values." Papers of the Peabody Museum of American Archaeology and Ethnology, 41(1).́ Cambridge Mass.: Harvard University Press.
1965 "Structural and Conceptual Replication in Zinacantan Culture." *American Anthropologist* 67:342–353.
1969 *Zinacantan: A Maya Community in the Highlands of Chiapas.* Cambridge, Mass.: Harvard University Press.

VON NEUMANN, J. and O. MORGENSTERN
1944 *Theory of Games and Economic Behavior.* Princeton, N.J.: Princeton University Press.

WAITZ, T.
1859 *Anthropologie der Naturvölker.* (3 vols.) Leipzig: F. Fleischer.
1863 (orig. 1859) *Introduction to Anthropology* (trans. of Vol. 1 of *Anthropologie der Naturvölker,* with additions by J. Collingwood). London: Longmans.

WAKE, C. S.
1967 (orig. 1889) *The Development of Marriage and Kinship,* R. Needham, ed. Chicago: University of Chicago Press.

WALKER, D. E. JR.
1968   Conflict and Schism in Nez Percé Acculturation: A Study of Religion and Politics. Pullmann: Washington State University Press.

WALLACE, A.
1952   "The Modal Personality Structure of the Tuscarora Indians, as Revealed by the Rorschach Test." Smithsonian Institution, Bureau of American Ethnology, Bulletin 150. Washington: Government Printing Office.
1956   "Revitalization Movements." American Anthropologist 58:264–281.
1960   (ed.) Men and Cultures. Selected Papers of the Fifth International Congress of Anthropological and Ethnological Sciences. Philadelphia: University of Pennsylvania Press.
1961a   Culture and Personality. New York: Random House.
1961b   "Mental Illness, Biology, and Culture." Hsu 1961:255–295.
1965   "The Problem of the Psychological Validity of Componential Analyses." Special Publication, American Anthropologist 67:229–248.

WALSH, W. H.
1951   An Introduction to Philosophy of History. London: Hutchinson House.

WARD, L.
1883   Dynamic Sociology; or Applied Social Science as Based Upon Statical Sociology and the Less Complex Sciences. New York: Appleton.
1895   "Relation of Sociology to Anthropology." American Anthropologist (old series) 8:241–256.

WARNER, W. L.
1958   (orig. 1937) A Black Civilization: A Social Study of an Australian Tribe. New York: Harper & Row.

WASHBURN, S. L. (ed.)
1961   Social Life of Early Man. New York: Wenner-Gren Foundation.

WASHBURN, S. L. and D. A. HAMBURG
1968   "Aggressive Behavior in Old World Monkeys and Apes." Jay 1968:458–478.

WASHBURN, S. L. and J. B. LANCASTER
1971   "On Evolution and the Origin of Language." Current Anthropology 12:384–385.

WATSON, J. B.
1913   "Psychology as the Behaviorist Views It." Psychological Review 20:158–177.

WEAVER, S. M.
1972   "Medicine and Politics Among the Grand River Iroquois: A Study of the Non-Conservatives." Publications in Ethnology, No. 4. Ottawa: National Museums of Canada.

WEBER, M.
1930   (orig. 1904) The Protestant Ethic and the Spirit of Capitalism, T. Parsons, trans. New York: Scribner.

WEBSTER, H.
1968   (orig. 1908) Primitive Secret Societies: A Study in Early Politics and Religion. New York: Octagon Books.

WEDEL, W. R.
1959   "An Introduction to Kansas Archeology." Smithsonian Institution, Bureau of American Ethnology, Bulletin 174. Washington: Government Printing Office.

WENDT, H.
1956   In Search of Adam. The Story of Man's Quest for the Truth About His Early Ancestors, J. Cleugh, trans. Boston: Houghton Mifflin.

WESTERMARCK, E. A.
1914   Marriage Ceremonies in Morocco. New York: Macmillan.
1922   (orig. 1889) The History of Human Marriage. (3 vols.) New York: Allerton.
1924   (orig. 1906–1908) The Origin and Development of Moral Ideas. (2 vols). London: Macmillan.
1926   (orig. 1906–1908) Ritual and Belief in Morocco. (2 vols.) London: Macmillan.

WHATELY, R.
1861   "On the Origin of Civilization." Miscellaneous Lectures and Reviews. London.

WHITE, L.
1943   "Energy and the Evolution of Culture." American Anthropologist 45:335–356.

1945a "Diffusion vs. Evolution: An Anti-Evolutionist Fallacy." *American Anthropologist* 47:339–356.
1945b "History, Evolutionism, and Functionalism: Three Types of Interpretation of Culture." *Southwestern Journal of Anthropology* 1:221–248.
1949 *The Science of Culture.* New York: Grove Press.
1949a (orig. 1938) "Science Is Sciencing." White 1949:3–21.
1949b (orig. 1940) "The Symbol: The Origin and Basis of Human Behavior." White 1949:22–39.
1949c (orig. 1947) "The Expansion of the Scope of Science." White 1949:55–117.
1954 *Double review:* A. L. Kroeber, *The Nature of Culture;* A. L. Kroeber, and C. Kluckhohn, *Culture: A Critical Review of Concepts and Definitions. American Anthropologist* 56:461–468.
1959a "The Concept of Culture." *American Anthropologist* 61:227–251.
1959b *The Evolution of Culture.* New York: McGraw-Hill.
1966 "The Social Organization of Ethnological Theory." Rice University Studies, Monographs in Cultural Anthropology 52(4).
WHITING, B.
1950 *Paiute Sorcery.* New York: Wenner-Gren Foundation.
1963 (ed.) *Six Cultures, Studies of Child Rearing.* New York: Wiley.
WHITING, J.
1941 *Becoming a Kwoma.* New Haven, Conn.: Yale University Press.
1961 "Socialization Process and Personality." Hsu 1961:355–380.
1964 "Effects of Climate on Certain Cultural Practices." Goodenough 1964:511–544.
WHITING, J. W. and L. CHILD
1962 (orig. 1953) *Child Training and Personality: A Cross-Cultural Study.* New Haven, Conn.: Yale University Press.
WHITMAN, W.
1940 "The San Ildefonso of New Mexico." Linton 1940:390–462.
WIESENFELD, S.
1967 "Sickle-Cell Trait in Human Biological and Cultural Evolution." *Science* 157: 1134–1140.
WILLEY, G. R.
1962 "The Early Great Styles and the Rise of Pre-Columbian Civilization." *American Anthropologist* 64:1–14.
1966 *An Introduction to American Archaeology.* Vol. 1: *North and Middle America.* Englewood Cliffs, N.J.: Prentice-Hall.
WILLEY, G. R. and P. PHILLIPS
1965 (orig. 1958) *Method and Theory in American Archaeology.* Chicago: University of Chicago Press.
WILSON, G. and M. WILSON
1968 (orig. 1945) *The Analysis of Social Change Based on Observations in Central Africa.* Cambridge: Cambridge University Press.
WILSON, L. G.
1972 *Charles Lyell. The Years to 1841: The Revolution in Geology.* New Haven, Conn.: Yale University Press.
WILSON, M. H.
1936 *Reaction to Conquest: Effects of Contact with Europeans on the Pondo of South Africa.* London: Oxford University Press.
1963 (orig. 1951) *Good Company: A Study of Nyakyusa Age-Villages.* Boston: Beacon Press.
WISER, W. H. and C. WISER
1963 *Behind Mud Walls, 1930–1960.* Berkeley: University of California Press.
WINSPEAR, A. D.
1956 *The Roman Poet of Science. Lucretius: De Rerum Natura.* New York: S. A. Russell.
WISSLER, C.
1915 "Material Cultures of the North American Indians." *Anthropology in North America,* with Franz Boas and others. New York: Stechert, 76–134.
1922 (orig. 1917) *The American Indian.* New York: Oxford University Press.
1923 *Man and Culture.* New York: Crowell.

1936   "Changes in Population Profiles Among the Northern Plains Indians." Anthropological Papers, American Museum of Natural History, 36:1–67.

WITTFOGEL, K. A.
1957   *Oriental Despotism*. New Haven, Conn.: Yale University Press.

WOLCOTT, H. F.
1967   *A Kwakiutl Village and School*. New York: Holt, Rinehart and Winston.

WOLF, A. P.
1966   "Childhood Association, Sexual Attraction, and the Incest Taboo." *American Anthropologist* 68:883–898.

WOLF, E. R.
1955   "Types of Latin American Peasantry." *American Anthropologist* 57:452–459.
1959   *Sons of the Shaking Earth*. Chicago: University of Chicago Press.

WOODWARD, W. H.
1897   *Vittorino da Feltre and Other Humanist Educators: Essay and Versions. An Introduction to the History of Classical Education*. Cambridge: Cambridge University Press.

WORSLEY, P.
1968   *The Trumpet Shall Sound: A Study of "Cargo" Cults in Melanesia*, 2d ed. New York: Schocken Books.
1970   *The Third World*. Chicago: University of Chicago Press.

WRIGHT, R.
1954   *Black Power*. New York: Harper & Row.

WUNDT, W.
1897   *Outlines of Psychology*, H. Judd, trans. New York: Stechert.
1928   (orig. 1912) *Elements of Folk Psychology. Outlines of a Psychological History of the Development of Mankind*, E. L. Schaub, trans. New York: Macmillan.
1900–1920   *Völkerpsychologie; eine Untersuchung der Entwicklungsgesetze von Sprache, Mythus und Sitten* (10 vols.) Leipzig: W. Engelmann.

YOUMANS, E. L.
1874   Preface to the American edition of H. Spencer, *The Study of Sociology*. New York: Appleton, iii–vii.

ZINSSER, H.
1934   *Rats, Lice and History*. Boston: Little, Brown.

Glossary

Acculturation: the process of intercultural exchange between two societies, involving persistent and interpenetrative change and accommodation over a prolonged period of time. The term usually is applied to contact situations where one society possesses a more complex culture and dominates the intercultural process.

Anthropometry: the anthropological specialization which measures body and skeletal relationships between conventionalized points and develops indices which express these relationships to effect intergroup comparisons.

Behavioral (real) **pattern** (culture): A term applied to behaviors which contrast with traditional social expectations (*see* Ideal pattern).

Componential analysis: an analytic method designed to elicit the patterned meanings of culture forms and cognitive principles of categorization by a particularized analysis of their attributes segregated by levels of contrast.

Configuration: a term borrowed from Gestalt psychology to emphasize the integrated nature of psychological processes as they are conventionalized by cultural tradition. However, the term may also be applied to any complex network of systemic interrelations.

Degradation theory: biologically speaking, the theory of an original or archetypal form from which subsequent forms have derived through variation. Theologically speaking, the view that mankind began in a state of innocence and purity and "fell" from a pristine state of grace through disobedience of divine injunctions. In Christian theology, Adam's fall initiated an inevitable process of corruption which could be arrested only through divine intervention.

Dialectic: a structural-evolutionary and deterministic theory of change processes devised by Georg Hegel. The dialectic process involves the generation within a structured system of a central tendency, or thesis, and its opposite, or antithesis. The opposition between thesis and antithesis leads to a synthesis, which then is followed by the generation of a contradiction to the thesis, and so on, *ad infinitum.*

Emic: a term coined by the linguist, Kenneth Pike, to describe the subjective meanings shared by speakers of a language. The term has been extended to apply to the subjective experience of conventionalized behavior generally. Pike stressed the need to get at the subjective categorizations and meanings in researching the nature of human behavior (*see* Etic).

Ethnocentrism: the tendency for individuals and groups, by virtue of the enculturative process, to distinguish self from others and to measure the behavior of outgroups by the conventionalized values, ends, means, and customs of their own group.

Ethos: a term used to describe the unconscious organization of feeling around conventionalized goals, values, and means.

Etic: a term employed by the linguist, Kenneth Pike, to describe the practice of formal analysis and categorization commonly employed by scientists in developing their units of comparison (*see* Emic).

Evolution: the process by which structural reorganization is affected through time, eventually producing a form or structure which is qualitatively different from the ancestral form. Evolution can be applied to organisms and matter, as well as to society and culture, in the sense that a succession of structurally distinctive but "genetically" related forms are involved. The evolutionary process stresses adaptation for survival, commonly expressed in the principle, "survival of the fittest."

Evolutionist: in the anthropological context, an exponent of human and/or social and cultural evolution based on the process of natural selection. Application of the principle of natural selection solely to the social gave rise to "Social Darwinism" in the last quarter of the nineteenth century. Anyone who accepts the view that structural continuities and transformations express the basic processes of change.

Functionalism: a term originally applied to Malinowski's biopsychic approach to the institutional organization of culture. Cultural institutions were viewed as developed in response to common human biological and psychological needs.

Functionalist: a term usually applied to anyone who stresses an adaptive relationship between basic needs and corresponding structures, institutions, or behaviors.

Holistic: the anthropological perspective which emphasizes the unitary and interrelated nature of social and cultural phenomena. Holism is the anthropological counterpart to Gestalt configurationalism. The holistic perspective is in opposition to a simple behavioralist and particularizing analysis of social and cultural phenomena.

Ideal pattern (culture): the conventional behavior which should be followed in a social situation. The ideal pattern is clued to values and normative behaviors which the society considers to be essential to the relations of individuals and between individuals and groups and society-at-large (*see* Behavioral pattern).

Mechanical model: a term used by Lévi-Strauss to describe a situation in which rules rigidly prescribe the action to be taken (compare with ideal pattern). Mechanical models focus on structural regularities and their conventionalized products.

Ontogeny–Phylogeny: the development and life history of individual organisms in contrast with the development or evolution of a species (phylogeny).

Organic analogy: the use of organic structure and processes to elucidate the nature and processes of society and culture.

Phylogeny: *see* Ontogeny.

Progressivist: a humanistic exponent of the advancement of mankind through intellectual and moral improvement linked to new social opportunities which promote individuality and realization of the human potential. Progressivists emphasize the importance of property in providing the basis for the emergence of individuality and the legal and moral guarantees which should reign in society.

Projection: a psychological process in which the individual constructs his outer world in accordance with his own inner awareness.

Reality problem: the nature and processes of what is to be explained. Every discipline selects a subject matter (reality problem) which it seeks to describe and explain in terms of its structure, processes, continuities, and changes. For its subject matter anthropology focuses on the early history of mankind, emphasizing the origin and evolution of the human species, the general evolution of human society and culture, and the nature, order, and processes of non-Western societies and cultures.

Reality processes: processes associated with the order, continuity, and change in whatever is to be explained. Usually these processes, like the faces of a coin, describe two interrelated processes (for example, stability and change; structural evolution and historical variation). The scientific problem is to interrelate the processes rather than to study them separately.

Statistical model: a term coined by Lévi-Strauss to describe situations where a number of factors influence choices and behavioral outcomes. The statistical model describes situations sensitive to variability in circumstances, and hence relates to historical processes in contrast with the mechanical model.

Structuralist: a theorist who emphasizes the formal ordering of parts and their functional interrelations according to the maintenance needs of the structured system. Structuralists may be interested solely in describing the functional arrangements and activities of the parts making up the structure. However, when translated into change continuities, structural processes relate to evolutionary sequences.

Social structuralist: a theorist who emphasizes the formal arrangement of statuses and roles as constituting the social structure, and who views the operations of society as supportive of this structure. Social structuralists justified their focus on the formal order by linking it to a general theory of needs and functions essential to the maintenance of the social organism.

Teleology: the theory that the activities and evolution of biological, social, and cultural forms are clued to their structural-functional designs.

Index

A

Acculturation, 548–549; and applied anthropology, 721–785; and ecology, 684–685; and ethnopsychoanalysis, 463–467; factors of, 745; levels of, and personality, 753–756; and religion, 756–757; sequences in, 760–765

Acosta, J. de, 23

Acquired instincts, 158; evolutionary view of, 251–255

Action anthropology, 773–775

Actional systems, 558–560

Adams, R.N., 625

Adaptation, and evolution, 193

Administration of policy, 586–587; and anthropology, 747, 772–777

Africa, interaction and integration, 731–733; three cultures of, 725–731

Age classes, 239–240

Age-area principle (Wissler), *338*

Aggression, 278

Alimentary metaphysics, 454–455

Alliance theory, 592–593

American Indian, 402; acculturation of, 753–756; administrative policy, 467–468, 773

Ammon, O. H., 157

Analogical introspection, 62; Boas on, 329

Analogy, principle of, 202, 207; organic, 507–509

The Ancient City (Fustel de Coulanges), 234–235

Ancient Society (Morgan), 189, 292

Animal worship, 222; *see also* Totemism

Animation of nature, 208–209

Animism, 150, 211; and supernaturalism, 214–215

Anthropological societies, 132–136

Anthropologists, as liaison agent, 774

Anthropology, and administration, 586–587; and ancient classical world, 4–5; applied, 772–777; cultural, 786–805; cultural-historical antecedents, 1–40; differentiation of, 114–164, 541–590 (*see also* Differentiation; Specialization); dif-

(Anthropology (*cont.*)
ferentiation of, 1890–1935, *315*; differentiation of, after 1935, *543*; distinguished from sociology, 142–144; and education, 781–783; epistemological, 576–578, 594; foundations of, 304–308; goals of, 134–135, 564–568; as institution, 786–787; interdisciplinary approach, 415–416; and Marxism, 658–673; medical, 777–781; and natural science image, 788–791; nineteenth-century founders, 144–162; philosophic diversity, 583–588; physical, 125–128; professionalization of, 135–136, 336–367; and psychiatry, 440–441; and reality processes, 796–802; Renaissance antecedents, 20–24; social, 143; social, in Great Britain, 501–513, 533–535; statistics in, 580–581; teaching and research functions, 793

Anthropometry, 126–128

Anxiety, and custom, 507; and ritual, 506–507

Apache culture themes, 422–423

Applied anthropology, 772–777

Apollonian temperament, 406

Apter, D. E., 743–744

Arab culture, 29–38

Archaic economy, 646–649

Archeology, and cultural historicism, 389–396; emergence of, 102–104; Paleolithic chronology, 120–122; phase, as unit of study, 390; rise of, 117–120; theory of process, 392

Arensberg, C. M., 777

Aretino, L. B., 27

Aristotle, on principle of natural dominance, 12–13

Association of opposites, 246

Atkinson, J. J., 264–265

Atoll social organization, 682

B

Bachofen, J. J., 149; on male-female qualities, 167; on religion, 152–153, 233–234

Baer, K. E. von, 171

Schmerling, P. C., 101–102
Schmidt, W., 353–355
Schneider, D. M., 605–607
Schneider, H. K., 652–653
Schurtz, H., 149; on totemism, 239–240; on war, 277
Science, and natural religion, 69–70; pure and applied, 91–92
Scientific discipline, criteria of, 3–4
Scientific growth, 795–796
Secret societies, 239–240
Selection, anthroposocial and social, 156–158
Self, evolution of, 474–477
Self-awareness, 555–556; in Third World, 654
Self-esteem, 443
Semitic religion, 237–238
Service, E. R., 707–708
Sex differences, in society, 167
Sex roles, 408–411; in Japan, 449–450; Mead on, 453–454
Sexual jealousy, 264–267, 268
Sexual reform, and exogamy, 263–264
Sibling hostility, 419, 458–459
Situational selection, principle of, 739
Slavery, 106
Smith, A., 19, 20, 75, 76, 601; on division of labor, 78–79; on language origins, 200
Smith, G. E., 343–345
Smith, W. R., 93, 153, 237–238
Social, the, autonomy of, 481–491, 798–801; as cause, 157; versus the cultural, 360–361, 386–389
Social anthropology, 311, 549–550, 591–629
Social Darwinism, 168–169, 223–224
Social equilibrium, 274–278
Social facts, 483–485; generation of, *485*
Social instincts, 251–255; and promiscuity, 265–266
Social norms, 704
Social organization, and religion, 233–246
Social phylogeny, 158
Social process, and psychoanalysis, 460–462
Social progress, and biology, 168–174
Social science, 138–144, 166–168, 304–308
Social sentiment, 605–607; sacred and profane, 485–487; symbolizing of, 487–491
Social structure, and organic analogy, 507–509; pragmatics of, 642–644; and sentiment, 605–607
Socialization, 472–473; in Japan, 450–451
Society, and law, 154–156; moral basis of, 75–76; open, closed, and dual, 651–652; political integration of, 710–711; primitive versus industrialized, 493; structural principles of, 511–513

Sociology, 139–142; comparative (France), 491–495; Comte's, 109–111; converging approaches, 500–501; distinguished from anthropology, 91, 142–144; foundations of, 304–308; psychological deviationism (France), 495–500; static and dynamic, 141–142
Sorokin, P., 428–429
Soul concept, 488–489
Specialization, 548–583
Spencer, H., 139–142, 156, 158, 168–169; on differentiation and retrogression, 192–194; divergence and convergence, *197*; on duality, 209–210; equilibrium theory, 166–167; on governance, 275–276; on morality and evolution, 230–232; as pioneer, 145–147; on primitive technology, 289; on religion, 218–223; on savage, 183; on social capabilities, 252–253; on social complexity, 198–199; on survival and energy, 176; as synthesizer, 170–174; and unilinear progress, 195–196
Spengler, O., 425
Spicer, E. H., 760–764
Spindler, G., 753–755
Spindler, L., 755
Spiro, M. E., 474, 476
State, city-, rise of, 708, 711–712; Comte and Spencer on, 141; control by, and social equilibrium, 274–278; evolutionist view, 279–285; natural and artificial, 82–83
Statistical model, 570–573
Statistics, 512, 578–580
Stereotypes, 26
Steward, J., 552–553, 582, 684–685; ecosociology of, 677–681; on interaction and integration, 733–735; on political power, 709; on warfare, 712
Stewart, D., 85
Stott, D. H., 692–693
Stratification, 712–716; in North America, 715–716
Strodtbeck, F., 415
Structural-functionalism, 480–538; formalist-substantivist controversy, 645–653; methodology, 512; of Radcliffe-Brown, 501–513
Structuralism, 311–359; biocultural into social, 531–535; common factors in types of, 312–314; on descent and incest, 595–597; key figures in, 314–316; theoretical differentiation, 316; types of, 311–312
Structure, 801–802
A Study of History (Toynbee), 428
Subjective idealism, 385–386
Subsistence stages, 290–291
Suicide, patterns of, 482
Sumner, J., 94